Educational Foundations

Educational Foundations

SECOND EDITION

Leslie S. Kaplan
Administrator, Newport News Public Schools (Retired)

William A. Owings
Old Dominion University

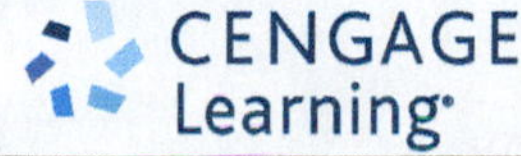

Australia • Brazil • Japan • Korea • Mexico • Singapore • Spain • United Kingdom • United States

***Educational Foundations*, Second Edition**
Leslie S. Kaplan and William A. Owings

Senior Product Manager: Mark Kerr
Content Developer: Kate Scheinman
Content Coordinator: Paige Leeds
Product Assistant: Coco Bator
Media Developer: Renee Schaaf
Senior Marketing Manager: Kara Kindstrom
Content Project Manager: Samen Iqbal
Senior Art Director: Jennifer Wahi
Manufacturing Planner: Doug Bertke
Rights Acquisitions Specialist: Dean Dauphinais
Production Service: Jill Traut, MPS Limited
Photo Researcher: PreMedia Global
Text Researcher: Karyn Morrison
Copy Editor: Araceli Popen
Text Designer: Diane Beasley
Cover Designer: CMB Design Partners
Compositor: MPS, Limited

Library of Congress Control Number: 2013944146

ISBN-13: 978-1-133-60309-2

ISBN-10: 1-133-60309-2

Cengage Learning
200 First Stamford Place, 4th Floor
Stamford, CT 06902
USA

Cengage Learning is a leading provider of customized learning solutions with office locations around the globe, including Singapore, the United Kingdom, Australia, Mexico, Brazil, and Japan. Locate your local office at: **www.cengage.com/global**

Cengage Learning products are represented in Canada by Nelson Education, Ltd.

To learn more about Cengage Learning Solutions, visit **www.cengage.com**

Purchase any of our products at your local college store or at our preferred online store **www.cengagebrain.com**

Printed in the United States of America
2 3 4 5 6 7 19 18 17 16 15

Brief Contents

Contents

CHAPTER 3 Philosophy of Education 65

PART 2 Historical Foundations

CHAPTER 4 The History of American Public Education 99

PART 3 Social Foundations

CHAPTER 6 Competing Goals of Public Education 175

CHAPTER 7 Cultural, Social, and Educational Causes of the Achievement Gap and How to Fix It 207

PART 5 Curricular and Instructional Foundations

CHAPTER 12 Curriculum 395

CHAPTER 13 Instruction 431

CHAPTER 14 Standards, Assessment, and Accountability 461

CHAPTER 15 Best Practices for Effective Schools 493

Preface

This second edition of *Educational Foundations* is written to help those considering a career in education make sense of today's schools. We do this by making educational foundations' topics relevant and personally meaningful to young and mature adult learners while offering the comprehensive scope, the scholarly depth, and the conceptual analysis of contemporary issues that demanding professors expect.

College students taking their first education course often do not see how foundations topics connect to their future careers. While preparing to write the first edition of this text, the authors saw why. Many foundations textbooks read like encyclopedias. They seemed to have been written for fellow professors or for doctoral students. In contrast, less encyclopedic textbooks had attention-grabbing photos and less dense text but little in-depth discussion or debate of provocative education concepts that college-age students or future educators need to understand so they can make successful transitions into their own classrooms.

So rather than over- or underwhelm readers, the authors decided to create an educational foundations textbook that met both students' needs for relevance and meaning and professors' needs for respected foundations' content and conceptual challenge.

The text's authors and instructors teaching an introductory course in education share many common goals for their students:

- To use a textbook that college and adult students will find readable, interesting, balanced, and relevant.
- To address what future educators need to know and understand to help them smoothly transition into the education profession.
- To respect the traditional educational foundations' content.
- To give immediacy and relevance by continually linking foundation issues to "hot-button" contemporary educational concerns.
- To provide scholarly support for important concepts with current research findings.
- To *educate*, not *inculcate*[1] by introducing students to varied perspectives on American public education and the larger social and political contexts so they can assess the information and draw their own conclusions.
- To infuse teaching's and learning's "best practices" by continuously engaging students and professors in reading a limited chunk of narrative, applying the content in a relevant context, and reflecting on its meaning.
- To generate socially mediated learning experiences where students can foster deeper understanding of ideas and issues by discussing them with peers and professors.
- To develop culturally responsive teachers who respect and understand diverse students and recognize (and use) the cultural assets these students bring to school.

[1] Liston, D., Whitcomb, J., and Borko, H. (2009). The end of education in teacher education. Thoughts on reclaiming the role of social foundations in teacher education. *Journal of Teacher Education 60*(2), 107–111.

- To cultivate reflective practitioners by providing ongoing occasions for students to think about what they are reading, interact with fellow students and their professors to create fuller meaning, and develop a philosophy of education.
- To energetically involve more students by including visual, auditory, graphic, and interpersonal learning and technology activities as part of the instruction.

Features of Educational Foundations

This text offers special features to help educational foundations students learn the content of each chapter.

- *Learning objectives* correlated to the main sections in each chapter show students what they need to know to understand the information presented. After completing the chapter, students should be able to demonstrate how they can understand and apply their new knowledge and skills.
- *Standards:* The text has been thoroughly revised to reflect current standards, including InTASC and Common Core State Standards. A list of InTASC Standards addressed appears at the start of each chapter, and specific page references to each standard appear inside the covers.
- *Did You Get It? quizzes* allow students to measure their performance against the learning objectives in each chapter. One question for each learning objective is featured in the textbook to encourage students to go to CengageBrain.com, take the full quiz, and check their understanding.
- *TeachSource Videos* feature footage from the classroom to help students relate key chapter content to real-life scenarios. Critical-thinking questions, artifacts, and bonus video help the student reflect on the content.
- *American Educational Spotlight:* Each chapter contains personal and professional portraits of notable individuals from diverse backgrounds who have contributed in a major way to the topic under study. *Spotlights* profiles include: Nel Noddings (Chapter 1); Albert Shanker (Chapter 2); Diane Ravitch (Chapter 3); Horace Mann (Chapter 4); Ruby Bridges (Chapter 5); Richard Rothstein (Chapter 6); Sonia Nieto (Chapter 7); John U. Ogbu (Chapter 8); Amy June Rowley (Chapter 9); Arne Duncan (Chapter 10); Michael Rebell (Chapter 11); Lisa Delpit (Chapter 12); Linda Darling-Hammond (Chapter 13); W. James Popham (Chapter 14); and Ronald R. Edmonds (Chapter 15).
- *Flip Sides:* In every generation, education debates roil the profession. *Flip Sides* presents readers with a range of philosophical and practical education dilemmas, garners arguments for each position, and invites readers to decide for themselves. Attention-grabbing *Flip Sides* issues include: "Are Today's Teachers Less Intelligent Than Those a Generation Ago?" (Chapter 1); "Should Effective Teachers Receive Merit Pay?" (Chapter 2); "Essentialist or Critical Theory? Which Philosophy of Education Should Guide Today's Schools?" (Chapter 3); "Child-Centered versus Subject-Centered Education" (Chapter 5); "Should American Schools Stress Reading and Math Proficiency or More Comprehensive Educational Goals?" (Chapter 6); "Should Ability Grouping or Open Access Be the Way to Place Students into High-Status Courses?" (Chapter 7); "Traditional Teaching vs. Cultural Competence Teaching. Which Approach Will Help Today's Diverse Students Learn to High Levels?" (Chapter 8); "Can

a School Discipline a Student for Internet Behavior Conducted from a Home Computer?" (Chapter 9); "Do School Boards Matter?" (Chapter 10); "Does Money Matter in Student Achievement?" (Chapter 11); "Should Curricula Provide *Schooling or Educating*?" (Chapter 12); "Teaching: Art or Science?" (Chapter 13); "The Case for and against Standardized Testing" (Chapter 14); and "Which Matters Most in Student Achievement—Families or Schools?" (Chapter 15). In short, *Flip Sides* helps professors bring more relevance, conceptual challenge, and intellectual excitement to the foundations classroom.

- *Diverse Voices:* Disability, Race, Sexual Identity, Poverty, Academic Capacity. How do these dynamics affect teaching and learning? Just as a picture can be worth 1,000 words, getting a first-hand experience can make an abstraction real—and memorable. Several chapters include personal essays from individuals who have lived the issues discussed and suggest ways teachers can help students like them. For example: How can teachers keep academic expectations high for students who are not "academic stars"? (See "A Teacher Finds His Niche," Chapter 1.) What is it like to have a disability while learning and becoming part of a school community? (See "Scott's Journey," Chapter 5.) Why can receiving a high-quality education mean so much to African American students? (See "One Teacher Explains How Her African Ancestry Influenced Her Love of Education and Learning," Chapter 8.) How can teachers make schools more welcoming and supportive to students who feel isolated by their gender identities? (See "LGBT Students to Teachers: Please Speak Up for Us," Chapter 9.) Why closing schools as an education reform strategy may neither save money nor raise students' academic achievement? (See "Closing Schools? Proceed with Caution," Chapter 10.) And what is it like to desire a quality education when one grows up bright, ambitious, and poor? (See "Looking to Low-Income Students' Strengths," Chapter 15.)
- *Reflect & Discuss Activities:* Successful teachers are skilled at being reflective practitioners. We help future educators begin to develop this essential professional habit. Located immediately following major concepts in each chapter, these minds-on, small group, and class exercises help students make the information they just read relevant and personally meaningful. Professors can adapt and revise these socially mediated or individual activities as they desire to accomplish their instructional goals.
- *Icons:* Are you especially interested in exploring issues of Diversity, Common Core State Standards, Twenty-First-Century Skills, Technology, and InTASC Standards? Unique icons visibly incorporated throughout each chapter flag these topics in the text. In addition, each chapter begins by identifying the InTASC standards discussed within it.

Organization of the Second Edition

The text is organized into five parts.

Part 1 Professional and Philosophical Foundations

Chapter 1, So You Want to Be a Teacher? describes teaching as an inspiring, satisfying, and important profession. It discusses the qualities of effective teachers as persons and educators and gives readers the opportunity to rank their favorite and "worst" teachers—and themselves—on these characteristics. The chapter also introduces education's moral purposes and considers trends affecting education in a global environment and the importance of teaching the twenty-first-century skills our students need to know. *Diverse Voices*, "A Teacher Finds His Niche," relates how a secondary teacher learned how to work effectively with a wide variety of students. *Flip Sides* asks, "Are today's teachers less intelligent than those a generation ago?" Students can consider the competing data and make up their own minds. To conclude, the Interstate Core Standards for New Teachers (InTASC) that prepare teachers to work effectively in today's challenging classrooms are presented.

Chapter 2, Teaching as a Profession, considers who becomes a teacher, the factors that make teaching a profession (including its prestige and economic standing), and the profession's cultural shifts over time. The chapter describes how teachers are best prepared for classroom success, discusses state and national board certification and licensure, and presents the research findings on teacher preparation, teaching effectiveness, retention in the profession, and student achievement. *Flip Sides* asks, "Should effective teachers receive merit pay?" The chapter also considers teachers' unions' role in advancing teachers' interests and education reform (one section asks, "Should teachers strike?") and the organizations and agencies that improve teaching as a profession. The *American Education Spotlight* shines on the late Albert Shanker, former head of the American Federation of Teachers and his influence on teachers' salaries, working conditions, and national education reform. To conclude, the chapter discusses how schools' professional culture can ease the transition into successful teaching. Understanding these issues can help future teachers move more smoothly into the profession.

Chapter 3, Philosophy of Education, looks at four major educational philosophies that actively influence American public education—traditional, progressive, existential, and critical theory. Varying beliefs about the purposes of school, the criteria for excellence, the practice of democratic citizenship, the knowledge most essential for students to learn, and other value-laden questions play essential roles in how teachers translate their knowledge and skills into classroom practice. Readers will consider each philosophy's contributions and begin developing a personal philosophy of education. *Flip Sides* asks students to debate and decide, "Essentialist or critical theory? Which philosophy of education should guide today's schools?" Diane Ravitch, former U.S. Secretary of Education and educational historian who has undergone significant changes in her own philosophy of education, receives the *American Education Spotlight*.

Part 2 Historical Foundations

In **Chapter 4, The History of American Public Education**, and **Chapter 5, Education Reform, 1900 to Today**, we look at public education from the earliest colonial days through the current Race to the Top, the Common Core State Standards, and virtual education. **Chapter 4** examines what teaching and learning looked like in the emerging public school in early American colonial and national periods through Horace Mann (the focus of this chapter's *American Education Spotlight*) and the movement toward universal public schooling. Education of women, African Americans, Native Americans, and students with special needs receives attention.

Chapter 5 considers educational changes in the twentieth and twenty-first centuries. Topics include the societal and political influences on public school curriculum and the swings between subject-centered and student-centered pedagogy. *Flip Sides* poses the question, "Should teaching be child-centered or subject-centered?" for readers to discuss and decide. An in-depth focus examines how underserved student populations have gained access to public schools through African American leaders and the 1954 *Brown v. Board of Education* decision. In *American Education Spotlight*, Ruby Bridges discusses her girlhood experiences as the first African American child to integrate a formerly all-white elementary school and her life since. In *Diverse Voices*, "Scott's Journey" tells about how a young man with disabilities successfully met his academic and social challenges with supportive teachers and classmates in a regular public school. Additional topics range from the educational impacts of World War I and II, the Great Depression, vocational education, technology, the Coleman Report; *A Nation at Risk*; the Individuals with Disabilities Education Act (IDEA); to the twenty-first-century's No Child Left Behind Act, Race to the Top, Common Core State Standards, charter schools, and virtual education.

Part 3 Social Foundations

Chapter 6, Competing Goals of Public Education, reviews public education's intellectual, social, political, economic, and personal purposes that have changed over the past 250 years and that sometimes work at cross purposes. *Flip Sides* asks students to debate and decide, "Should American education focus on reading and math skills or on a more comprehensive set of educational goals?" Richard Rothstein, an education policy researcher and writer who recognizes the many influences (in addition to teachers) on students' learning, receives the *American Education Spotlight*. The chapter also considers how conservative, liberal, and critical theory advocates view and contribute to educational goals. Lastly, it explains how education is an investment in human capital.

Chapter 7, Cultural, Social, and Educational Causes of the Achievement Gap and How to Fix It, describes how society and schools present obstacles that limit minority and low-income students' educational opportunities. The chapter reviews the ethnic and racial makeup of today's and tomorrow's students, describes how social class practices and opportunities affect the achievement gap, shows how teachers' expectations influence student achievement, and identifies school practices (segregation, tracking/ability grouping, discipline policies, school climate) that reduce students' opportunities to learn and achieve. Sonia Nieto, a highly regarded teacher educator with practical advice for effectively teaching diverse students, holds the *American Education Spotlight*. *Flip Sides* asks students to discuss and decide, "Ability grouping or open access to high-status curriculum? Which is the best approach for instructing students?" And in *Diverse Voices*, a retired English teacher explains how her African American ancestry influenced her love of learning and teaching. The chapter also highlights institutional perspectives that foster inequity and explains multicultural education's academic and social benefits.

Chapter 8, Diversity and Cultural Assets in Education, reviews current student achievement data for traditionally underserved student groups. It explores how persons develop their racial and cultural identities and how these impact their school achievement. Topics include stereotype threat, cultural opposition theory, and minority group coping strategies. The late anthropology professor John U. Ogbu, who coined the term "acting white" as a theory of minority underachievement, takes the *American Education Spotlight* profile. Next, the chapter explains how teachers can use African Americans', Latinos', low-income students', and students with disabilities' cultural assets—especially for relationships, compatible learning goals, and cultural/family influences—to increase their learning and school success; and it provides the research supporting this cultural asset approach. The chapter then discusses why teachers should discard the "deficit" mental model for students who have characteristics outside the mainstream and offers teachers culturally responsive strategies for fostering diverse students' resilience and increasing their achievement. Finally, *Flip Sides* asks students to consider the arguments and decide, "Which teaching approach is most effective for working with low-income and minority students: the traditional or cultural competence approach?"

Part 4 Legal, Political, and Fiscal Foundations

Chapter 9, Teachers, Ethics, and the Law, provides the basic essentials of what every new teacher needs to know about professional ethics and school law. In down-to-earth language, the chapter discusses and answers the following questions: What are the limits of teachers' academic freedom in public schools? How does working in schools affect teachers' constitutional freedoms of speech, religion, and protection from unreasonable search and seizure? What privacy rights do teachers and students have in schools? What are teachers' roles concerning sexual harassment? In addition, the chapter addresses professional concerns about using social networking sites, teacher employment contracts, tenure, negligence, freedom of expression, students' rights, and other professional and classroom issues. In *American Education Spotlight,* Amy June Rowley, the child with a hearing disability in the center of the 1982 landmark U.S. Supreme Court Case that helped shape education law for students with disabilities, talks as an adult (and now a college teacher) about her early school experiences and what key lessons she learned inside—and outside—the classroom. In *Diverse Voices,* LGBT students ask teachers to speak for them in school to help them socially and academically. And *Flip Sides* asks students to consider the arguments and decide, "Should schools discipline a student for Internet behavior conducted from a home computer?"

In **Chapter 10, School Governance and Structure**, we look at the federal role in education, state boards of education, local school boards, the consolidation of schools and school districts, and the roles of superintendents, school board personnel, and principals. Here, the *American Education Spotlight* turns to Arne Duncan, the U.S. Secretary of Education who calls education "the civil rights issue of our generation" and sees high-quality teachers as essential to ensuring America's long-term economic prosperity. Also discussed are education professionals who work with teachers (namely, school counselors, school nurses, special education teachers) and how they contribute to student learning and achievement. *Flip Sides* asks students to consider the pros and cons and decide, "Do school boards matter?" The chapter concludes with a discussion about how school structure and school and class size affect student learning and achievement.

Chapter 11, School Finance, reviews federal, state, and local responsibilities for funding education, explains the reasons for increased education spending, and describes how school districts spend education dollars. Contemporary issues of equality and equity in school funding, educational adequacy, and "taxpayer revolts" and their impacts on student learning and achievement receive attention. *American Education Spotlight* shines on Michael Rebell, a fiscal equity legal and policy advocate who seeks funding adequacy to advance high-quality education for all students. *Flip Sides* asks, "Does money matter in student achievement?" Closing the chapter, data about education as an investment in human capital support the idea that education improves a community's quality of life.

Part 5 Curricular and Instructional Foundations

Chapter 12, Curriculum, explains how curriculum responds to a society's intellectual, social, and political beliefs about schools' major goals and looks at essential ideas about curriculum. *Flips Sides* asks readers to debate and decide whether they would prefer a curriculum that provides *schooling* or *educating* practices. *American Education Spotlight* profiles Lisa Delpit, an educator and author who advises teachers to help low-income and minority students' access, learn,—and then move beyond—the curriculum. The chapter also considers the Common Core State Standards—what their advocates and their critics say—and how they plan to address current weaknesses in teaching, learning, and achievement in English language arts, mathematics, science, and social studies. Ralph Tyler, Hilda Taba, Benjamin Bloom, and Grant Wiggins and Jay McTighe and their major contributions to curriculum ideas also appear. Finally, the chapter investigates the relationship between the arts and student achievement and cites the research supporting their inclusion for educating the whole child.

Chapter 13, Instruction, considers the research on teaching effectiveness and student achievement and the research on teacher preparation and student achievement. It describes how teachers use the behaviorist, cognitive, and constructivist instructional models to generate student learning and describes each approach's strengths and weaknesses. *Flip Sides* asks students to debate and decide whether effective teaching is an art or a science. Linda Darling-Hammond, the national authority on equity, educational reform, and teacher effectiveness who propelled the issue of teacher quality into a national focus, takes the *American Education Spotlight*. The chapter also relates research-affirmed best teaching practices to help teachers become more effective educators.

Chapter 14, Standards, Assessment, and Accountability, discusses how assessment is an integral part of everyday teaching and learning and is essential to increasing student achievement. This chapter considers the role of standards in driving accountability—including the Common Core State Standards, opportunity to learn standards, and professional education standards—as well as criticism of standards, and the variable nature of "proficiency." W. James Popham, an advocate of common sense assessment, stands in the *American Education Spotlight*. In addition, the chapter discusses key principles of school assessment and teachers' practices as well as the characteristics of high-quality assessments. The case for and against standardized testing appears in *Flip Sides* and gives readers the chance to review arguments on each side and then make up their own minds. The chapter concludes with discussions of equity and ethical issues in testing and accountability, identifies the goals for education and accountability, and offers reasons for developing a holistic accountability system.

In **Chapter 15, Best Practices for Effective Schools**, considers how today's schools can increase all students'—especially minority and low-income students'—achievement. The chapter reviews the Effective Schools Movement's emergence and its research-affirmed correlates for increasing student achievement: safe and orderly climate; clear focused mission; instructional leadership; climate of high expectation for success; opportunity to learn and student time-on-task; frequent monitoring of student progress; and cooperative home-school relations. *American Education Spotlight* focuses on the late Ron Edmonds, who helped advance the idea that whether or not we effectively teach low-income and minority students depends more on politics than on social science. In *Flip Sides*, students consider which matters most in student achievement—families or schools. In *Diverse Voices*, a college professor who grew up bright, ambitious, and poor speaks about teachers' need to have high expectations for every child, regardless of background. Finally, the chapter shows what these achievement-producing factors look like in today's schools.

Ancillaries

Student Ancillaries

Education CourseMate

Cengage Learning's Education CourseMate brings course concepts to life with interactive learning, study, and exam preparation tools that support the printed textbook. Access the eBook, Did You Get It? quizzes, TeachSource Video Cases, flashcards, and more in your Education CourseMate. Go to CengageBrain.com to register or purchase access.

TeachSource Videos

The TeachSource videos feature footage from the classroom to help students relate key chapter content to real-life scenarios. Critical-thinking questions provide opportunities for in-class or online discussion and reflection.

Instructor Ancillaries

Education CourseMate

Cengage Learning's Education CourseMate brings course concepts to life with interactive learning, study, and exam preparation tools that support the printed textbook. CourseMate includes the eBook, quizzes, TeachSource Video Cases, flashcards, and more—as well as EngagementTracker, a first-of-its-kind tool that monitors student engagement in the course. The accompanying instructor website, available through login.cengage.com, offers access to password-protected resources such as PowerPoint® lecture slides and the online Instructor's Manual with Test Bank. CourseMate can be bundled with the student text. Contact your Cengage sales representative for information on getting access to CourseMate.

Online Instructors Manual with Test Bank

An online Instructor's Manual accompanies this book. It contains information to assist the instructor in designing the course, including sample syllabi, discussion questions, teaching and learning activities, field experiences, learning objectives, and additional online resources. For assessment support, the updated test bank includes true/false, multiple-choice, matching, short-answer, and essay questions for each chapter.

Online PowerPoint Slides

These vibrant, Microsoft PowerPoint lecture slides for each chapter assist you with your lecture by providing concept coverage using images, figures, and tables directly from the textbook!

Cengage Learning Testing Powered by Cognero

- author, edit, and manage test bank content from multiple Cengage Learning solutions
- create multiple test versions in an instant
- deliver tests from your LMS, your classroom, or wherever you want

Acknowledgments

Writing this book has been a genuinely interesting, enjoyable, and collaborative experience. Our sincere thanks and appreciation to:

Dan Alpert, our most talented development editor for *American Public School Finance* (1st edition, Cengage, 2006), *Educational Foundations* (1st edition, Cengage, 2011), and our *Culture Re-Boot* (Corwin, 2013), who always gives us invaluable suggestions about creating a winning content with an engaging voice. Dan has become a dear and trusted friend.

Mark Kerr, our Cengage project manager, and Kate Scheinman, our highly skilled and always conscientious Cengage content developer, gave us invaluable support. Kate knowledgeably guided us through the redevelopment and revision processes with always-excellent suggestions, new challenges, consistent encouragement, sunny good humor, and a capable eye for making text more reader friendly.

Jill Traut and Christina Ciaramella were trustworthy resources during the production phase. Jill's ideas, flexibility, and organizational skills were truly helpful while Christina's keen eye secured beautiful and insightful artwork to illustrate the text.

Additional thanks go to other members of the Cengage team who made meaningful contributions to this second edition, namely, Araceli Popen, Samen Iqbal, Paige Leeds, Renee Schaaf, Jennifer Wahi, Coco Bator, Dean Dauphinals, Diane Beasley, and the always helpful Kara Kindstrom.

Our peer reviewers provided extremely valuable and useful feedback. They told us when we were on the right track, when we needed to rethink and revise, and which key topics their students really wanted to understand. These reviewers became welcome and virtual collaborators as we developed and refined this text:

Reviewers

Kathy Allen, *Blue Ridge Community College*
LaShundia Carson, *Alcorn State University*
Patricia Walsh Coates, *Kutztown University*
Kathleen Davenport, *Mesa Community College*
Sherri Davis, *Polk State College*
Elizabeth Dorman, *Regis University*
Brian Dotts, *The University of Georgia*
Joshua Francis, *Defiance College*
Rebecca Fredrickson, *Texas Woman's University*
Virginia Garland, *University of New Hampshire*
Richard Gibson, *Friends University*
Richard Gordon, *California State University–Dominguez Hills*
Cheresa Greene-Clemons, *North Carolina Central University*
Bridget Ingram, *Clark State Community College*
Kathleen King, *North Central College*
Leanna Manna, *Villa Maria College*
Neil F. Mathews, *Louisiana State University*
Sarah McMahan, *Texas Woman's University*
Lori Nanney, *Cleveland Community College*
Chuck Okezie, *Marygrove College*
Anthony Pellegrino, *George Mason University*
Denise Rattigan, *Carthage College*
Denise Simard, *SUNY Plattsburgh*
Ludovic A. Sourdot, *Texas Woman's University*
Patricia Spradley, *Queens College*
Maria Carmen Tejeda-Delgado, *Texas A&M University–Corpus Christi*
Robin Voetterl, *Siena College*
Mary Ware, *SUNY Cortland*
Amy Williamson, *Angelo State University*
D. R. Wilson, *Houston Baptist University*
Lynda Wolverton, *Polk State College*
Bettye Wright, *University of Arkansas Pine Bluff*
Julia Zoino-Jeannetti, *Framingham State University*

About the Authors

Leslie S. Kaplan, a retired school administrator in Newport News, Virginia, is a full-time education writer and an adjunct research professor at Old Dominion University. She has provided middle school and high school instructional leadership as well as central office leadership as a director of program development. Before becoming a school administrator, she worked as a middle school and high school English teacher and as a school counselor with articles frequently published in *The School Counselor*. Kaplan's scholarly publications, co-authored with William A. Owings, appear in numerous professional journals. She also has co-authored several books and monographs with Owings, including *Culture Re-Boot: Reinvigorating School Culture to Improve Student Outcomes; Leadership and Organizational Behavior in Education, American Education: Building a Common Foundation; American Public School Finance* (2nd ed.); *Teacher Quality, Teaching Quality, and School Improvement; Best Practices, Best Thinking, and Emerging Issues in School Leadership*; and *Enhancing Teacher and Teaching Quality*. Kaplan is co-editor of the *Journal for Effective Schools* and also serves on the NASSP Bulletin Editorial Board. As a person with experiences in a variety of education roles, she has the unique distinction of being honored as both Virginia's Counselor of the Year and Assistant Principal of the Year. She is a past president of the Virginia Counselors' Association and the Virginia Association for Supervision and Curriculum Development and she is currently a board member of Voices for Virginia's Children.

William A. Owings is a professor of educational leadership at Old Dominion University in Norfolk, Virginia. Owings has worked as a public school teacher, an elementary school and high school principal, assistant superintendent, and superintendent of schools. His scholarly publications, co-authored with Leslie S. Kaplan, include books on educational leadership and school finance as well as articles in *National Association of Secondary School Principals (NASSP) Bulletin, Journal of School Leadership, Journal of Effective Schools, Phi Delta Kappan, Teachers College Record*, the *Journal of Education Finance*, and the *Eurasian Journal of Business and Economics*. Owings has served on the state and international board of the Association for Supervision and Curriculum Development (ASCD), is currently the editor of the *Journal for Effective Schools*, and is on the *Journal of Education* Finance Editorial Advisory Board. He is a frequent presenter at state and national conferences and a consultant on educational leadership, school finance, and instructional improvement. Owings and Kaplan share the 2008 Virginia Educational Research Association Charles Edgar Clear Research Award for Consistent and Substantial Contributions to Educational Research and Scholarship.

Educational Foundations

Students want to work hard and learn for teachers they think like them and who believe in their ability to learn.

David Young-Wolff/PhotoEdit

CHAPTER 1

So You Want to Be a Teacher?

InTASC Standards Addressed: 1, 2, 3, 4, 5, 6, 7, 8, 9, and 10

LEARNING OBJECTIVES

After you read this chapter, you should be able to:

1-1 Explain why teaching is an inspiring, satisfying, and important profession.

1-2 Identify the personal qualities of effective teachers.

1-3 Describe education's moral purposes.

1-4 Summarize the trends affecting education in a global environment.

1-5 Identify and explain the twenty-first-century skills today's students need to learn.

1-6 List and describe the InTASC core standards for new teachers.

Most U.S. students attend public schools. Public schools educate nearly 9 out of every 10 K–12 students in this country. Over 49 million students attend 66,458 elementary schools and 23,900 secondary schools in the United States. More than 3.2 million teachers teach them. Another 5.9 million students attend private/independent schools, and approximately 1.5 million are homeschooled.[1] It is not through the "school" that real learning occurs, however, but rather through the caring, one-to-one teacher–student relationships.

Being a teacher is important and challenging work. "It takes a great deal of dedication to walk into school every day with enthusiasm, energy, and love, often in spite of conditions that make doing so a constant struggle. Yet some teachers do it all the time, and many remain in the classroom for years with a commitment that is nothing short of inspirational."[2]

Noted education professor Sonia Nieto observes that teachers' values, beliefs, and dispositions energize them to stay in the profession. Their love for children, desire to engage with intellectual work, hope of changing students' lives, strong belief in public education's democratic potential, and anger at public education's shortcomings all lie at the heart of what makes for excellent and caring teachers.[3] Having a sense of mission, solidarity, and empathy for students, the desire to be lifelong learners, the courage to challenge conventional thinking, improvisational abilities, and a passion for social justice motivate and keep teachers in the profession.[4] Comfort with uncertainty, endless patience, and a sense of humor also help.

And students know the difference when they have teachers who care about them and want to help them learn. When asked how they make this determination, they answer: The teacher *teaches well* (makes the class interesting, stays on task, stops to explain), and the teacher *treats them well* (is respectful, kind, and fair).[5] In these ways, a "caring teacher" models how children can become both smart and good.

The need for excellent public school teachers has never been greater. More students and increasingly diverse students are sitting in today's classrooms. Becoming educated and employable in the twenty-first century requires knowledge and skills beyond those needed even one generation ago. Our communities and our country's well-being depend on educating all students for full participation in our economy and democracy. Teaching is a critically important career where the challenges—and the satisfactions—are many.

This chapter discusses the crucial importance of education for today's world and describes the social and economic contexts in which we work. We will look at how teaching inspires its best practitioners; effective teachers' personal qualities; education's moral purposes; education's role in an interconnected, global environment; teaching twenty-first-century knowledge and skills; and core standards for new teachers.

As you begin your induction into our profession, these perspectives will help you better understand your role and determine how you can create the conditions for high levels of student learning and your own professional satisfaction. ●

1-1 Teaching as an Inspiring, Satisfying, and Important Profession

Since 1952, the National Teacher of the Year program has focused public attention on excellence in teaching. As part of its 50th anniversary celebration, each National Teacher of the Year winner from past years was invited to submit a letter "for the future." One of the teachers' options was to write to an elementary or secondary student whom they knew would make a wonderful teacher or a newly trained teacher getting ready to begin a classroom career. Their letters would offer insights to what motivates successful teachers.[6]

The 1997 National Teacher of the Year, Sharon M. Draper, chose this option. In her "Letter to a Prospective Teacher," she writes:

> Dear Friend:
>
> . . . I was probably born to be a teacher. I never wavered in my desires and determination to become not just a teacher, but a really good teacher who made memories in the minds of children. From my early days of student teaching when I learned that acting out history made it memorable for me as well as my students, to my first teaching assignment where I broke down and cried in front of the class because thirty-five disruptive students in a makeshift, renovated classroom did not fit my glossy vision of educational excellence, to today where my seniors wear T-shirts, proudly proclaiming, "I Survived the Draper Paper," I continued to try to make a difference—one child at a time. For our greatest accomplishments in education are not the

plaques and awards, but the smiles and hugs and memories of children touched today and somehow influenced tomorrow.

They ask me about the lack of respect for the profession. I respond with, "Raise your hand if you don't respect me!" They grin and see my point. They want to know about the lack of financial rewards. I tell them honestly, "I'll never make what a basketball player makes, but then neither will most of you. It's not fair that our society pays its entertainers more than its educators, but I make a good living, can support a family, and send my children to college. And I get extra benefits—smiles, hugs, and the knowledge that what I do really matters."

I once asked a class of fourth graders to give me their definition of a good teacher. These are their responses:

- A good teacher is soft enough to hug, but too hard to punch. . . .
- A good teacher is not scared of thunder and lightning and knows what to do when the lights go out.
- A good teacher never makes fun of you when you do dumb stuff like throw up or forget the answer. . . .
- A good teacher makes you have so much fun you don't know you're learning, and then when you've learned it, you realize it wasn't hard at all.
- A good teacher never has bad breath.
- A good teacher loves you and you know it.

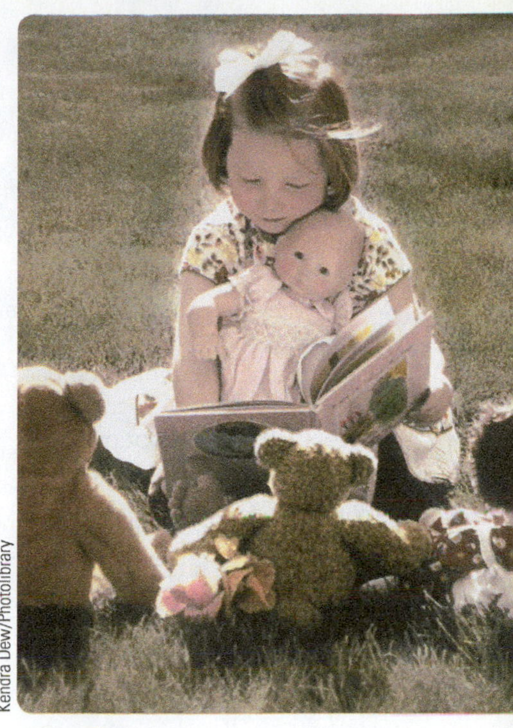

Kendra Dew/Photolibrary

"I was probably born to be a teacher."

If we could all live up to this simple list, we'd be successful teachers. The children are waiting.[7] (Excerpts from "A Letter to Prospective Teachers" by Sharon M. Draper in *Teaching from the Heart: Reflections, Encouragement, and Inspiration*. Copyright © 2000 by Sharon M. Draper. Published by Heinemann, Portsmouth, NH. Reprinted by permission of the publisher. All rights reserved.)

Similarly, John A. Ensworth, 1973 National Teacher of the Year, recalls:

Dear New Teacher:

. . . It all started with the death of a banty hen on my forty-acre ranch. I brought the dead hen to the fifth-grade classroom where we removed the skin and feathers and cooked the chicken until the meat fell off the bones. Several students who were interested reconstructed the skeleton. One of the students was Karen Gunson. She was just named Oregon's first female State Medical Examiner. In the state-wide article "Bend Doctor Owes Much to Grade School Teacher" (Monday, September 27, 1999, *Bend Bulletin*), [the reporter wrote of Gunson]: "But a small portion of the credit for her success goes to the teachers she studied with along the way, in particular Mr. Ensworth, whose talent made her fifth grade year so pivotal in her life. . . ."

Glen Burleigh, a former student, and I were fishing one day. He started talking about the time he spent in my classroom. Glen said, "Mr. Ensworth, the one thing I remember about our class was that you were having as much fun as we were. . . ."

Our class motto was as follows: "Do your best even if it falls short of what the experts think is excellent. The forest would be far too quiet if only the most beautiful birds sang."[8] (Reprinted by permission of John Ensworth.)

Looking at teaching from a career-switcher's perspective, Michael Geisen, 2008 National Teacher of the Year, reminds future teachers that ours is a profession rich in opportunities to give our lives deeper meaning.

. . . I was on the edge of a chasm; a deep chasm of darkness and depression. . . . Earlier in my forestry career, I had spent several months as a teaching

Reflect & Discuss

Discuss in pairs and then as a class:

A. What satisfactions and cautions do these four excellent teachers offer prospective educators?
B. What motivates you to consider a teaching career?
C. Describe an experience you had as an elementary or secondary student with an exceptional teacher who had a meaningful impact on who you are as a person, or describe who influenced you to become a teacher.

assistant at the University of Washington's experimental forest. For 12–14 hours a day, I designed and implemented exercises to teach Forestry majors the field skills they needed to succeed, and spent hours in the forest helping them, guiding them and getting to know them. . . . That day on the rainy hillside, I realized why I was barely able to get up every morning: I needed to give. My vocation needed to have deeper meaning, to have relationship, to have heart. I needed to teach! . . . . I kept on as a forester and went back to school to work towards a Masters in Teaching. But when I was hired in a rural district in Central Oregon to teach middle school, I knew the real work was just beginning. . . . Welcome to my new life. I love it. . . .

If we are going to unite students together into a community of learners, each classroom needs to be warm, welcoming and inviting to everyone. I make it a goal to greet students each day as they enter, call them by name as often as possible, and to use humor to break down barriers of class, race, age and ability. I want to have a unique and meaningful relationship with each of my students. This is really the heart of teaching. . . . I love and enjoy them for who they are right now. I encourage them by example to do the same. . . . In a decade or two, when some of the scientific details have faded, students will remember their 7th grade science classroom as a fun and engaging place to be, a safe place where they could take risks and learn from their mistakes, and a place where they were treated with the dignity and respect that all people deserve. We are not merely teachers and students. We are human beings. . . .

The rewards of all this extra work are enormous. Mostly it's the ridiculously large salary. . ., but there are a few other less tangible fringe benefits, too—the frequent smiles of children, adolescents helping each other, a visit from a former student. Although I definitely made more money in my previous vocation, there were no benefits this deeply satisfying. I'm making a difference in the lives of children. I think I've made the right career choice.[9] (Reprinted by permission of Michael Geisen.)

TeachSource Video 1.1

Voices and Advice from the Field

Practicing teachers have a lot of insight into their profession. Being a teacher is a complex undertaking that challenges one as a person and as a professional. Watch the video clips, study the artifacts in the case, and reflect on the following questions:

1. What are the similarities and differences in how these teachers came to choose teaching as a profession?
2. What do teachers view as the most important prior experiences and personal attributes that help individuals become effective teachers?
3. What advice that the teachers in this video give do you think will be the easiest for you to take? What advice do you think will be the most difficult for you to take?

Watch on CourseMate.

For a final look at how teaching inspires its best practitioners, Jennifer Wellborn, a middle-school science teacher, writes about why she teaches[10]:

I may be naive, but I believe that what I do day in and day out *does* make a difference. Teachers *do* change lives forever. And I teach in public school because I still believe in public school. I believe the purpose of public school, whether it delivers or not, is to give quality education to all kids who come through the doors. I want to be part of that lofty mission. The future of our country depends on the ability of public schools to do that.[11] (Reprinted by permission of the Publisher. From Sonia Nieto, Editor, *Why We Teach*, New York: Teachers College Press. Copyright © 2005 by Teachers College, Columbia University. All rights reserved.)

These teachers, and countless thousand others, give clear voice to the belief that teaching is an inspiring, satisfying, highly demanding, and vitally important profession.

Did You Get It?

Decide, if you haven't already, why you want to be a teacher. Very high up among your reasons for wanting to teach will probably be a

- **a.** Genuine pleasure in learning and sharing that learning with children.
- **b.** Desire for the traditional trappings of success.
- **c.** Desire for respect, tangibly manifested in a good salary.
- **d.** Strong desire to tell other people what to do.

Take the full quiz on CourseMate.

1-2 Personal Qualities of Effective Teachers

In their letters to the future, these Teachers of the Year's most vivid memories were about their students. The reverse is true for students, too. Although we may not always remember specific facts learned in a particular class, most of us can easily recall volumes about the teacher's personality.

Before any individual becomes a professional, he or she is first a unique person of distinct appearance, personality, interests, abilities, talents, and ways of interacting with others. A teacher's personality is one of the first characteristics that students, parents, and administrators notice. Who the teacher is as a person has a tremendous influence on the classroom climate and students' learning experiences. Even more impressive, teachers' psychological influence on students has been linked to student achievement in various studies of educational effectiveness.[12] Although many aspects of effective teaching can be taught and developed, changing an individual's personality is difficult.

David Shwatal/Alamy

Teachers show interest in students inside and outside the classroom.

Reflect & Discuss

A. Describe your favorite teacher—the one who was most influential in motivating you to become a teacher. Use the information in the list to describe this teacher's characteristics. Using Figure 1.1, respond in the box or on a separate paper in a word, picture, or cartoon to the questions about your favorite teacher: How did that teacher become so influential to you? Which behaviors and attitudes did the teacher regularly use in class?

B. Describe the worst teacher you had in school, and fill in a second column in the chart by answering the same questions for that teacher.

Here are some of the research-based findings about effective teachers' personal qualities.[13] See if you can identify some of your own favorite teachers here:

- *Effective teachers care about their students.* They show their caring in ways that students understand, see, and feel. These teachers bring out the best in students by affirming and encouraging them with patience, trust, honesty, courage, listening, understanding, and knowing their students as people and as learners.
- *Effective teachers show all students (and colleagues) fairness and respect.* They establish rapport and credibility by emphasizing, modeling, and practicing evenhandedness and showing esteem. For instance, they respond to student misbehavior on an individual level—rather than by punishing the entire class. They tell students what they need to do right—and get all the facts before speaking with students about what they did wrong. And they treat students equitably and do not show favoritism.
- *Effective teachers show interest in their students both inside and outside the classroom.* When students are having difficulties, these teachers work with them—rather than scold or ignore them. Attending football games, plays, and choral concerts in which their students participate also shows students that their teachers genuinely care about them, and it increases students' feelings of belonging in their classrooms. At the same time, teachers maintain the appropriate professional role with students. The ability to relate in these positive ways creates a learning environment that promotes student achievement.
- *Effective teachers promote enthusiasm and motivation for learning.* Teacher enthusiasm has been shown to increase both positive relations with students and student achievement. Effective teachers know how to inspire all students—by understanding their individual interests and making connections whenever possible to familiar and valued prior knowledge. These teachers also give students choices about what and how they will study, thereby creating intrinsic motivation for students to learn. Students want to work hard and learn

FIGURE 1.1 Characteristics of My Most Influential Teachers

Teacher Characteristics	Favorite Teacher	"Worst" Teacher
What influenced me the most		
How the teacher made me feel in class		
Teacher's excitement about the subject taught		
Made learning personally meaningful		
Presented challenging work I wanted to learn		
Delivered work of an appropriate difficulty for my experience and age		
Gave me some control and choice over my learning		
Used my prior knowledge		
Provided opportunities for interaction		
Gave helpful feedback		
Taught me new ways to learn better		
Created a positive emotional climate		
Created a positive class environment		

for teachers they think like them and who believe in their ability to learn.

- *Effective teachers have a positive attitude toward their own learning and to the teaching profession.* They have a dual commitment to student learning and to personal learning. They believe that all students can learn the school's essential curriculum—and this is not just a slogan to them. Furthermore, effective teachers see themselves as responsible, capable, and willing to deliver for their students' success. They also work collaboratively with other teachers and staff, sharing ideas and assisting to resolve difficulties.
- *Effective teachers are reflective practitioners.* They continuously and thoughtfully review their teaching practice daily, class by class. Research consistently affirms the value of reflection in developing effective teaching.[14] Self-evaluation and self-critiquing are essential learning tools. Effective teachers seek greater understanding of teaching through experience, scholarly study, professional reading, and observing master teachers. Likewise, they desire feedback to improve their performance. As they become better, their sense of **efficacy**—their belief in their own ability to make a difference—increases. They gain confidence both in their skills and in their results. Their students and colleagues see this transformation in action.

Teaching is more than what you know and can do in the classroom. Who you are as a person greatly affects how effective you are as a teacher.

Reflect & Discuss

Getting to know a teacher's personality is one of students', parents', and administrators' first priorities. Working individually for three minutes, complete the "Positive Teacher Qualities" chart in Figure 1.2 by filling in qualities *that you see in yourself.* Then, working in pairs, discuss the five characteristics you see as your strengths now and the five characteristics that you want to develop more fully.

Report both sets of characteristics to the large group, and have a person tally them for the class as a whole. Discuss where and how in your teacher preparation program you can find resources, people, or environments where you can more fully develop those qualities that still need strengthening or refinement.

efficacy The belief in one's own ability to make a difference.

FIGURE 1.2 Personal Assessment of Positive Teacher Qualities

Positive Teacher Qualities	Personal Assessment: The Degree to Which I Have the Quality		
	Less Developed	Moderately Developed	Highly Developed
1. I have personal experiences working with students as a tutor, teacher, counselor, or mentor.			
2. I assume responsibility for my students' success.			
3. I understand students' feelings.			
4. I am a good listener.			
5. I communicate clearly.			
6. I admit my mistakes and quickly correct them.			
7. I think about and reflect on my behavior so I can improve.			
8. I have a sense of humor.			
9. I dress appropriately for the teaching position.			
10. I am structured but also flexible and spontaneous.			
11. I expect to enjoy teaching and expect students to enjoy learning.			
12. I look for a win-win resolution in conflict situations.			
13. I listen carefully to students' questions and comments.			
14. I respond to students with respect, even in difficult situations.			
15. I consistently express high expectations and high confidence.			
16. I treat students equally and fairly.			
17. I have positive dialog with students outside the classroom.			
18. I maintain a professional manner at all times.			

TeachSource Video 1.2

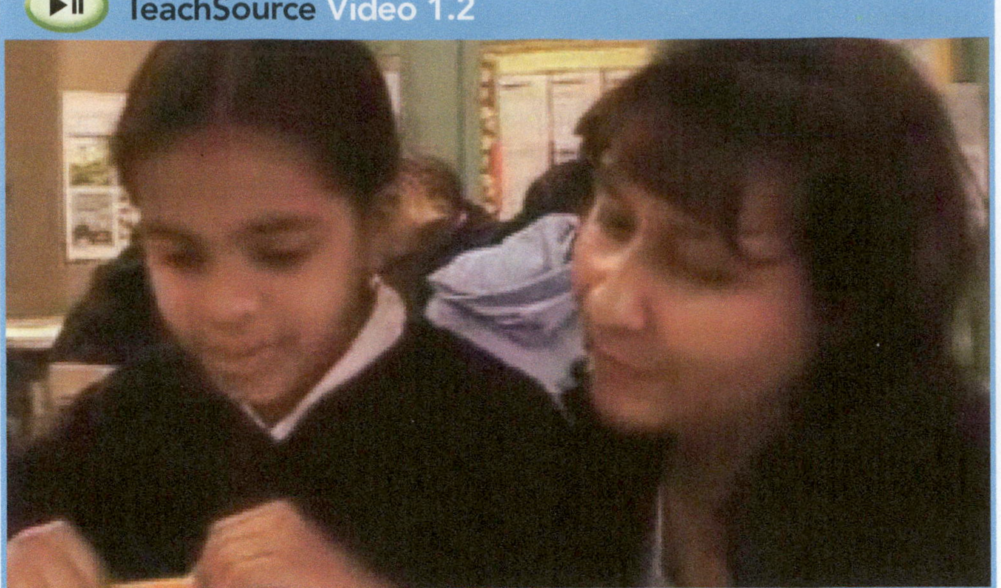

Teaching as a Profession: What Defines Effective Teaching?

There are many aspects to being an effective teacher. Competence as a teacher requires having strong content knowledge and an array of pedagogical and "people" skills. Watch the video clips, study the artifacts in the case, and reflect on the following:

1. Identify four personal/professional characteristics discussed in the video that are very important to becoming an effective and caring teacher, and explain why these qualities are so essential.
2. Why is it essential to have strong content knowledge, a deep understanding of your students, and an array of pedagogical skills to teach it?
3. What are the benefits gained by watching an experienced and effective teacher teach—both in your subject and in a different subject?

Watch on CourseMate.

Did You Get It?

Choose the false statement about effective teachers.

a. Many aspects of teaching can be taught but changing a teacher's personality is difficult.
b. Who you are as a human being greatly affects your ability to teach.
c. Personality is one of the first things everyone notices about a teacher.
d. Teaching is about what you can do in the classroom.

Take the full quiz on CourseMate.

1-3 The Moral Purposes of Education

Teaching affects both the local community and the larger society. Michael Fullan, professor emeritus at the University of Toronto and an international leader in teacher education, explains that schools have a moral purpose. Schools are charged with improving their students' lives, regardless of those individuals' backgrounds, and developing citizens who can live and work productively in increasingly dynamic and complex societies.[15] The individual teacher is the building block of this educational endeavor, linking caring and competence through professional practice. In this view, teachers' personal purpose has a social dimension: They are the agents of educational change and societal improvement.

Likewise, John Goodlad, an influential author and researcher on teacher education, believes that schools have four moral imperatives: preparing students for responsible citizenship, providing essential knowledge and skills, building effective relationships, and practicing sound stewardship.[16]

1-3a Preparing Students for Responsible Citizenship

First, a public school is the only national institution specifically assigned to prepare students to live responsibly in a democratic republic. Our federal government, state, and local communities have charged public schools as the agents of societal well-being. Children need to develop the information, skills, and habits of mind that make them informed citizens who can effectively participate in our representative government and can constructively fulfill their obligations as voters, law abiders, and taxpayers. Through school, students acquire the knowledge and reasoning skills that allow them to become self-supporting and productive contributors to our society.

Living in the U.S. democracy requires getting along with other people who hold different viewpoints. Students tend to live in neighborhoods with others like themselves. Schools, by contrast, gather several neighborhoods together into a larger and more diverse educational community. In schools, students develop the interpersonal skills they need to understand and appreciate the common ties they share with classmates from different families, genders, races, and economic backgrounds. Schools help both native-born individuals and immigrants, as well as people from different regions of the same state and the country, to identify and celebrate their unifying American traditions and beliefs and to build a common civic purpose. Students also get to know unfamiliar peers with different backgrounds as pleasant individuals much like themselves and learn how to show respect and appreciation for their individual traditions.

1-3b Providing Essential Knowledge and Skills

U.S. schools also offer students access to knowledge. Schools help students learn about the Earth as a series of physical and biological systems and develop communication skills through verbal and numerical fluency. They help students learn the historical, political, social, economic, and cultural realities in which they live. In addition, schools provide students with instruction on how to gather, assess, and judge information and to express well-reasoned, informed opinions. They also ensure that no belief, attitude, or practice keeps students from getting the necessary knowledge.

1-3c Building Effective Relationships

Although teaching is a professional activity, it is also an acutely personal one. Teaching entails much more than just the mechanics of delivering content: It involves caring about and interacting with individual students in a group setting. The teacher–student relationship can either help or hurt learning. Effective teachers create and sustain a safe, caring, and intellectually challenging environment. If students feel frightened, humiliated, or discounted by their teacher, they won't learn. Students know when teachers respect and like them. They know when teachers hold high expectations for students' achievement—and when they don't. And students respond accordingly—by engaging in the material or by withdrawing from it. Although important interpersonal and professional boundaries exist,

David Young-Wolff / PhotoEdit

Classrooms create diverse communities.

good teachers combine teaching's generalizable principles and subject-specific instruction with a genuine sensitivity to their students' uniqueness and humanness as learners.

1-3d Practicing Good Stewardship

Goodlad affirms that schools and teachers must practice good **stewardship**.[17] A steward is a caretaker who looks out for and manages an estate's or organization's affairs. Similarly, teaching involves more than working with students behind the classroom door. By virtue of their faculty membership and school district employment, teachers have ethical duties and obligations that go beyond the classroom. As good stewards, they attend to the school's mission and protect the school's reputation in the community. Similarly, teachers have an ethical obligation to protect the reputation of the teaching profession as a whole.

stewardship The act of being a caretaker who looks out for, protects, and manages an estate's or organization's affairs.

As stewards, teachers ensure that their school is committed to students' advancement and to society's well-being. To do so, they assure the highest-quality teaching and learning for all students in the school (not just those inside their own classrooms). Meeting this goal means that teachers must be constructive and helpful colleagues who share the mutual goal of making the school an increasingly effective and satisfying place for everyone to learn and work. Stewardship also means keeping the community informed about the school's accomplishments and activities and enlisting local support to make school even better. It means practicing responsible citizenship, thinking critically, and acting deliberately in a pluralistic world—and educating students to do the same.

Finally, fulfilling the demands of teacher stewardship means becoming a transformational learner. Changing the world begins with changing oneself. Teachers must be enthusiastically engaged with their own learning, continue to learn, and show students how to learn. Students are more likely to find learning a specific subject fascinating and motivating when they see that their teacher finds it fascinating as well. Put simply, teachers encourage student learning by being enthusiastic learners themselves.

Enacting these four moral imperatives—acculturating students, providing essential knowledge and skills, developing effective relationships with students, and providing stewardship—are more than a matter of teachers' personal preferences. Fullan and Goodlad believe teachers are morally obligated to take on these roles. Teaching is clearly more than a job or career. As teachers, we touch our entire community and nation through the students we educate.

1-3e Enacting Schools' Moral Purpose through Caring

Nel Noddings, a Teachers College, Columbia University and a Stanford University education professor, has focused on the relationship aspect of teachers' moral purpose, reflecting the belief that teaching has a human outcome. Contemporary teachers enact schools' moral purpose through *caring*[18], and our schools should produce competent, considerate, loving, and lovable people.[19] In addition to developing academic adequacy, all children must learn to care for other human beings as well as for animals, plants, the physical and global environments, objects, instruments, and ideas. By furthering students' development in this way, schools produce people who can care competently for their own families and contribute effectively to their communities, both local and international.

In Noddings's view, American schools have traditionally promoted the belief that students develop character through academic skills and intellectual pursuits.[20] Historically, educators assumed that knowledge of "the basics" (whether classical studies or fundamental reading and math) along with self-sacrifice, success, determination, ambition, and competition would enable students to build the attitudes and skills appropriate to life in a capitalist society. The school was not expected to cure social ills; instead, it was expected to vigorously teach the values that society deemed important. In this way, teaching academic skills reinforced the society's desired moral and economic ends.[21] Noddings objected to this approach; to her, schools should address human values and concerns, not merely cognitive ones.

Ethical caring and relationships Caring relationships involve moral and ethical behaviors. Ethics and morals are theory and practice, respectively. That is, **ethics** denotes the theory of right and wrong actions, whereas **morals** indicate those actions' practice within guidelines. Relationships connect individuals with an emotion. According to Noddings, a person who behaves ethically seeks to preserve or transform the relationship into a caring one. This ethical caring is more highly abstract than mother–child caring, also known as natural caring. **Ethical caring** is neither as intense nor as intimate as natural caring. With an ethic of caring, one acts out of affection or inclination rather than simply from duty and principle. For teachers and students, these caring relationships occur within the school and classroom settings during the teaching and learning process.

ethics The theory of right and wrong actions; sometimes used interchangeably with "morals."

morals The practice of enacting right or wrong behaviors within guidelines; sometimes used interchangeably with "ethics."

ethical caring Acting out of affection or inclination rather than simply from duty and principle.

Ethically caring teachers enjoy working with students. To them, teaching encompasses more than just doing their job and earning a paycheck. With caring, the relationship itself is important—how the other person feels and responds. Thoughtful teachers respond to their students' needs, wants, and requests. Ideally, the students recognize and respond to teachers' caring by thoughtfully completing assigned work. The ethic of caring, therefore, is often characterized as responsibility and response. Students learn and develop this caring outlook and behaviors through their relationships with their teachers.

Caring teachers extend their goals for students beyond simply learning the content and performing well on tests. They want to help their students grow into likeable and ethical people: "persons who will support worthy institutions, live compassionately, work productively but not obsessively, care for older and younger generations, be admired, trusted, and respected."[22] For this type of development to happen, teachers need to know both their subjects and their students very well.

Caring relationships place cognitive and emotional demands on both teacher and student. Both parties allow themselves to be known as people within their different roles and responsibilities. Every interaction then brings with it the possibility of deeper caring. In turn, each party must decide how to respond to the other while maintaining the appropriate role

Ethically caring teachers enjoy working with students.

kali9/iStockphoto

boundaries. Teachers do not strive to be students' pals, but rather to be their caring adult educators.

How teachers model caring For Noddings, teachers claiming to care about their students is not enough. Students may recognize and respect a "tough" teacher who makes them work hard. Although they have no real interest in what is being taught, students do what they are told. They come to link caring with coercion and good teaching with hard work and control. They may recognize a teacher as "caring," but they do not themselves feel cared for. Rather, teacher caring—that students feel as caring—involves teachers recognizing students' feelings and desires and responding as positively as the teachers' values and abilities allow. Receptive teachers can see that their caring has been received by watching the students' responses. Do students smile at or thank the teacher or more confidently engage in their own project? In Noddings' view, without a positive response from a student, teachers cannot call an encounter or relation caring.

Teachers model caring for students in many ways. First and foremost, they consistently treat students with respect and consideration, and expect them to treat other students in the same way. Teachers show students how intellectual activity is useful, fun, and important. They limit lectures to the presentation of essential information and then use class time for students to interact and explore how the information addresses issues that are real and relevant to them. Teachers work with students to develop learning objectives that meet both the school's and the students' needs; when they use discussion to elicit and respond thoughtfully to students' ideas; and when they give students timely, specific written feedback on their work. They try to understand and address the motives that underlie students' sometimes annoying behaviors rather than responding quickly and punitively to the behavior itself.

Fostering caring relationships requires open dialog. In this type of exchange, neither the teacher nor the student draws conclusions before beginning the discussion. This does not mean that all viewpoints and choices are equally acceptable or that one party in the relationship must give in to the other's views or wishes. It does mean, however, that teachers and students must trust and respect one another well enough to express differing viewpoints or decisions and thoughtfully consider the reasons given that oppose their original stand.

In addition, caring teachers encourage students to practice caring and support for one another. They offer opportunities for students to interact as peers working collaboratively on projects of shared interest. The quality of their interactions reflects the respect and appreciation required to build their classroom community. Teachers encourage students to care for animals, plants, and the environment in ways consistent with caring for humans. Likewise, teachers help students feel at home in and appreciate the technical, natural, and cultural worlds.

Further, teachers help students understand that caring in every domain implies competence. When we care, we accept the responsibility to work continuously on our competence so that the recipient of our attention—whether a person, animal, object, or idea—is enhanced. Caring is the strong, resilient backbone of human life.

Finally, caring teachers support students by responding to their actions in ways that reinforce the type of individual we want them to be. Caring teachers assume that students are well intentioned and act from worthy motives. When teachers respond to students with respect for the quality person that student either is now or can become, the student feels confirmed, validated as commendable and competent. What teachers reveal to students about themselves as ethical and intellectual beings has the power to either nurture that ideal or destroy it. Through their interactions, tea[illegible]nd students become partners in fostering the students' growth.

Diverse Voices

A Teacher Finds His Niche

By Robert Meade, Retired English teacher, Dumont High School, Dumont, New Jersey.

As I look back on my 80 years and the almost four decades of my teaching career, I am awed by the incredible diversity of population here in northeastern New Jersey, with a variety of peoples, races, and cultures that were not here a few years ago. When I grew up, the population was overwhelmingly white, middle-class, and Christian. Actually, in high school, I was the one providing diversity, as the only Jew in a class of 150 students.

It wasn't until I entered New York University (NYU) that I came in close contact with anyone nonwhite or an ethnic minority. After graduation, I entered the U.S. Air Force as an officer, having been a member of the Reserved Officers' Training Corps. Military service impressed upon me that the ethnicity, religion, or other differences of superiors or subordinates were irrelevant. Our daily briefings reminded us that succeeding in our mission was all that mattered. We were in the Cold War, and we were each expected to fulfill our duties to the best of our individual abilities.

I left the Air Force and returned to my high school alma mater as an English teacher. From the beginning, I found it difficult and unrewarding to teach a classroom of thirty-five students whose abilities ranged from future valedictorian to a boy who spelled Bob with three b's (Bobb). Within a few years, however, at least three-fifths of my classes were "non–college preparatory"—those students who had no desire for any education beyond high school. Many were in class only because the law required it. To my delight, I realized that I had found my niche.

I liked the nonacademic courses because, although the curriculum set out specific goals, the content and methodology were left entirely to the teacher to determine. All could be altered to fit the various ways the students learned. Because I knew that students learn in different ways—such as orally, visually, and even tactually—I tried to design most units to use more than one methodology. I also graded students so that all could earn credit in one or more ways, depending upon their individual strengths—with test grades, or with written work (homework included), or by class participation.

I remember the most diverse eleventh-grade class I ever taught. By some weird scheduling fluke, it began with only three students. Within a month, one moved out of town. One of the two remaining, Frank, was white, a varsity football player, and although he had some hearing, was officially classified as legally deaf. His speech was not affected. The other student, Hong, was a Vietnamese refugee, in this country less than three years. Hong had not gotten past third grade in Vietnam. His conversational English was acceptable, but his reading ability wasn't that good.

I was determined to try to keep their course content as close as possible to what their friends in my other nonacademic classes were receiving. I wanted to avoid them having any perception that I might not consider them capable of the same work.

For this course, I had developed a unit using Victor Hugo's *Les Miserables*, written for nonacademic eleventh graders, and an audio recording of the Broadway musical production, *Le Miserables*. The students would read a segment of the short narrative, listen to the songs the composers used to advance that part of the story, and discuss the plot, characterizations, and other key aspects.

My "two-man" class worked this way: During the reading, if Hong had a problem understanding the language, Frank helped him. If Frank could not hear part of a song, Hong told what he missed. Then they had the same discussions as any other class, each student contributing what he could. For spelling and vocabulary, I obtained a workbook expressly written for their skill and grade level. Hong and Frank decided to turn the weekly spelling quizzes into a friendly competition. I believe both did well because of it. My contribution was to praise each week's "winner" and encourage the "loser."

Because both Hong and Frank were persuaded to use the skills that they had—including hearing and command of the language—and wanting to learn, they both persisted. They were not afraid to make mistakes and learn from them. They both felt confident in their futures and had positive goals for work and life. I expected them to learn what everyone else was learning, and they did.

After graduation, Hong enrolled in a trade school, but his instructors didn't have the patience or skills for someone with his limited language ability, and he dropped out. Last I saw him, Hong had opened his own nail salon after learning the business by working in his family's salon chain. He is doing well by any measure. I have no idea what happened to Frank, but I'll bet on him being successful somewhere (I should look him up on Facebook or Google).

It has always been a facet of my teaching philosophy that no student be permitted to think that he or she cannot succeed as a result of being different from other students in any way. Each has to be encouraged to use his or her unique individual abilities. Because our student bodies have become so diverse, any teacher that does not adopt that philosophy should, in my opinion, leave the profession.

American Education Spotlight

Courtesy of Richard Balzar

Nel Noddings believes that teaching has a human outcome.

Nel Noddings

Nel Noddings believes that caring relationships should be the foundation for teaching and learning.

A leader in the field of educational philosophy, Nel Noddings is currently professor of philosophy and education at Teachers College, Columbia University and the Lee L. Jacks Professor Emeritus of child education at Stanford University. She is an award-winning teacher—having won the Excellence in Teaching Award at Stanford in 1981, 1982, and 1997—and an accomplished scholar. Through her work, she has demonstrated the importance of caring and relationship as both an educational goal and as a fundamental aspect of education.

Noddings is very familiar with life inside public school classrooms. From 1949 to 1972, she was an elementary and high school teacher and administrator in New Jersey public schools. Equally comfortable at home as at the university, she describes herself as "incurably domestic," having raised ten children, staying married to the same man for forty-eight years (as of 1998), and likes "order in the kitchen, a fresh tablecloth, flowers on the table, and food waiting for guests."[23]

According to Noddings, teachers can take several steps to develop caring relationships with their students. "First, as we listen to our students, we gain their trust and, in an ongoing relation of care and trust, it is more likely that students will accept what we try to teach. They will not see our efforts as 'interference' but, rather, as cooperative work proceeding from the integrity of the relation. Second, as we engage our students in dialogue, we learn about their needs, working habits, interests, and talents. We gain important ideas from them about how to build our lessons and plan for their individual progress. Finally, as we acquire knowledge about our students' needs and realize how much more than the standard curriculum is needed, we are inspired to increase our own competence."[24]

Noddings regrets that we live in an age of high-stakes accountability that relies too narrowly on a constricted curriculum and standardized testing that reduce the time available for developing caring teacher–student relationships.

Critics of Noddings' views include feminists (who see the one caring as carrying out the traditional female role in our culture while receiving little in return), and those favoring more traditional (masculine) approaches to ethics who believe the partiality given to those closest to us is inappropriate. Others view the problematic nature of building an ethical theory upon those in unequal relationships.

Nel Noddings has made a substantial contribution to deepening our appreciation of what education entails. She shows us that caring is a moral attitude informed by the complex skills of interpersonal reasoning. Caring has its own forms of rigor and can be enacted professionally. Her views provide deeper insight into how effective teachers think and act.

Sources: Smith, M. K. (2004). Nel Noddings, the ethics of care and education, The Encyclopaedia of Informal Education. Retrieved from www.infed.org/thinkers/noddings.htm; Noddings, N. (1999). Caring and competence. In G. Griffen (ed.), *The education of teachers* (pp. 205–20). Chicago: National Society of Education; and Noddings, N. (2005). Caring in education, The Encyclopedia of Informal Education. Retrieved from www.infed.org/biblio/noddings_caring_in_education.htm.

Did You Get It?

Decide what the moral purpose of education/good teaching is.

- **a.** It prepares students to live responsibly in a democratic republic.
- **b.** It makes teachers into stewards of the education profession.
- **c.** It provides students with the habits of good attendance and following directions.
- **d.** It helps students learn how to make friends with their classmates.

Take the full quiz on CourseMate.

For the relationship between teachers and students to develop, they need to spend time together. Creating opportunities to greet and interact with students every day through welcoming them into the classroom, talking about students' interests, and providing engaging lessons are positive starting points for forging such connections. Similarly, creating smaller schools, limiting class sizes, and keeping students and teachers working together over multiple years can provide the extra time needed to develop strong teacher–student relationships. In addition, schools can organize their curriculum around themes of care rather than traditional disciplines.[25] Working to create more caring schools would help both teachers and students develop more ethical selves.

Reflect & Discuss

Nel Noddings believes that schools should produce more competent, caring, loving, and likeable people. Teachers enact their moral purpose by developing caring relationships with their students. As a class:

A. Explain the different behaviors that characterize "ethical caring" and "natural caring." How can teachers recognize the "line" between the two? How can crossing this boundary confuse both teacher and student?
B. Identify the behaviors that one might observe in classrooms that are characterized by caring and respectful teachers and students.
C. Discuss how a teacher knowing individual students well can improve the quality of student learning and the relationships in the classroom.

1-4 Trends Affecting Education in a Global Environment

Throughout most of human history, people lived and organized their lives around boundaries structured by local geography and topography, family and kinship, community social organizations, religions, and local worldviews. This is no longer true. Today's world is changing, and so is our understanding of what it means to be "educated." Today, youth grow up linked to economic realities, social media, technologies, and cultural movements that spill over local and national borders.

Just to get a sense of how the world has changed, consider this example: In 1969, an international telephone call from Hong Kong to Chicago cost nearly $10 per minute. In 2011, the same call can cost about 3.9 cents per minute.[26] In the 1960s and 1970s, immigrants working in London relied on the postal system and personal letter carriers to communicate with family back home in India, Malaysia, or China. They waited two months to receive a reply to each letter. Calling by phone was not even possible. By the late 1990s, however, their grandchildren used mobile phones that linked them instantly with their cousins in Calcutta, Singapore, or Shanghai.[27]

Today, helping young people become fully educated is especially critical. Unlike when your parents were in K–12 schools, you will teach in an interconnected, globalized world. "Education's challenge will be to shape the cognitive skills, interpersonal sensibilities, and cultural sophistication of children and youth whose lives will be both engaged in local contexts and response to larger transnational processes."[28]

1-4a Technology, the Workplace, and Globalization

Technology is clearly changing the workplace, by virtue of its ability to connect people together in a virtual environment. Thanks to computer networks, people no longer have to be physically next to one another to work together. Standardized protocols can now connect everyone's machines. Software applications encourage the development of standardized business processes for how certain kinds of commerce or work will be conducted, allowing people in distant locations to work seamlessly together. Companies have access to talent sitting in different parts of the world, and these widely dispersed workers can complete needed tasks in real time.

Naturally, **globalization**—that is, the trend of de-territorializing skills and competencies so that people working anywhere in the world can collaborate with

globalization The trend of de-territorializing skills and competencies so that people working anywhere in the world can collaborate with those working elsewhere.

those working elsewhere—affects what students worldwide need to know. Globalization has major implications for American education and students' eventual careers and lifestyles. Anything that can be digitized[29] can be outsourced to either the smartest producer or the cheapest producer—or the producer that fits both descriptions. Many manufacturing jobs that traditionally provided middle-class salaries for relatively low-skilled workers have already been automated (using fewer workers) or moved offshore. Increasingly, jobs that require a college education are going to well-educated, highly trained, English-fluent workers with a strong service orientation around the world who are willing and able to work for much less money than their U.S. counterparts, yet who still manage to have a relatively high standard of living in their own country. The wages and rents in Bangalore, India, for example, are less than one-fifth what they are in Western capital cities. An investment analyst in Bangalore earns about $15,000 in total compensation, as compared with $80,000 for a person filling the same position in New York or London. Even for jobs remaining in the United States, salaries for highly skilled workers are much higher than those for low-skilled workers.[30] Learning that enables students to develop high levels of knowledge and skills and the ability to use them flexibly to solve real-world problems is a necessary condition for obtaining well-paying employment, but it is not a guarantee that such opportunities will open up when—or where—students are ready to join the workforce.

21ST CENTURY SKILLS

1-4b Competing in a Global Environment

Are American students ready for this international competition for employment? Red flags are up, suggesting a possible international achievement gap with U.S. students faring "average" rather than best. In 2009, of the 70 countries whose 15-year-olds took the PISA (Programme for Student Assessment)—the system of international assessments that focuses on 15-year-olds' capabilities in reading, mathematics, and science, the United States ranked 14 out of 34 Organization for Economic Cooperation and Development (OECD) countries for reading skills, 17th for science, and a below-average 25th for mathematics.[31]

Performance by U.S. students in international math and science assessments are improving. Trends in International Mathematics and Science Study (TIMSS) is an international assessment measuring trends in student achievement in mathematics and science in more than 60 educational systems. TIMSS tests emphasize cognitively demanding questions and tasks that offer better insight into the analytical, problem-solving, and inquiry skills and capabilities of fourth- and eighth-grade students. In the 2011 TIMSS, U.S. fourth- and eighth-grade students did not score among the top 10 achieving countries on math (it ranked 11th). In science, U.S. fourth graders were seventh—whereas U.S. eighth graders were 10th—among the top achieving nations. In both math and science, the United States was identified as an "improving" country.[32] Asian countries had the highest percentage of students reaching the advanced international benchmarks.[33]

When jobs in a globalized world go where the best skills for the lowest wage are, any serious skill gap places many future U.S. workers at a serious disadvantage.

It is almost universally recognized that the effectiveness of a country's educational system is a key factor in establishing a competitive advantage in an increasingly global economy. Education is a fundamental part of a country's economic and social development as well as in its citizens' personal development. Education is a primary means to reduce social and economic inequalities. Keeping U.S. education strong and viable in a globalized world is essential to maintain the U.S. citizens' standard of living and our national security. In this context, effective teachers and effective schools are vital components of our national well-being.

Did You Get It?

Which of the following statements about globalization, the de-territorialization of skills and competencies, is true?

- **a.** It has not affected American education.
- **b.** It has major implications for American education.
- **c.** American students are extremely competitive in the global marketplace.
- **d.** The American classroom is largely unchanged by the impact of globalization.

Take the full quiz on CourseMate.

1-5 Teaching Twenty-First-Century Skills Our Students Need to Learn

We do not know what the world will be like in 5 years, let alone in 60 years when today's kindergartners retire. As part of globalization, our students are facing many emerging issues such as worldwide fiscal crises, retreats from government spending on public services and institutions (including public schools), climate change, poverty, health issues, a growing and educated global middle class, international population increases, and other environmental and social issues. Our economy is generating fewer jobs in which workers engage in repetitive, assembly line–type tasks throughout their day and more information-rich jobs that challenge employees with novel problems that require knowledge, analysis, and teamwork. These realities require that students learn how to skillfully communicate, function, and create change personally, socially, economically, and politically on local, national, and global levels.

To be successful in the twenty-first century, our students will need more than a factory-model education based on the needs of Industrial Age employers. Through the late nineteenth and early twentieth centuries, good preparation for factory employment meant schoolchildren "sat and listened" while teachers "stood and delivered" textbook lessons, and students changed classrooms to ringing bells. Today, companies have altered how they organize and do business. Workers have more responsibility and contribute more to productivity and innovation. Advanced economies, innovative industries and firms, and high-growth jobs require more educated workers with the ability to respond flexibly and knowledgeably to complex problems, communicate effectively, manage information, work in teams, and produce new knowledge. And many of these workers can work in any country with Internet connectivity.

As a result, twenty-first-century students need a broader and deeper array of knowledge and skills, and the capacity to apply their learning to solve real-world problems if they are to move confidently into the economic and social milieu. Figure 1.3 shows these twenty-first-century skills.

These are not habits of mind or skills that students can learn by sitting passively at their desks listening to teacher lectures within their four classroom walls. Increasingly, twenty-first-century students will be assessed on what they can do with what they have learned rather than on what they can memorize or accumulate by seat time. Teachers' expectations for all students' learning will be high. The

FIGURE 1.3 Skills Required to Be an Effective Twenty-First-Century Citizen

- Deep understanding of core subject matter—knowing the facts and how they fit together
- Critical thinking, judgment making, and complex, open-ended problem solving—tied to content
- Collaboration—with peers, teams, and experts across several networks
- Cognitive flexibility and adaptability—to use information and skills in new ways and to adjust oneself to new realities, new roles, and lifelong learning
- Effective oral and written communication—for interacting competently and respectfully with others across cultural and geographic boundaries
- Information access and analysis—to find necessary resources, critique its accuracy and value, make reasoned decisions, and take purposeful action
- Curiosity, imagination, and creativity—thinking "outside the box"
- Initiative and entrepreneurialism—making well-reasoned decisions and taking action

curriculum will be connected to students' interests, experiences, talents, and the real world rather than be irrelevant and meaningless to students. Lessons will include occasions for students to analyze, synthesize, evaluate, and create rather than merely comprehend information or practice context-free skills. Students will be actively involved in making their learning happen and making choices about study topics and projects rather than on receiving teachers' accumulated wisdom.

Likewise, twenty-first-century students will work collaboratively with classmates—on site and around the world—rather than learn at their solitary desks in their classrooms. The curriculum will be thematic, interdisciplinary, and project-based as it is in the real world, rather than artificially fragmented into separate departments. Literacy will expand from the 3 Rs to multiple media that reflect the communication platforms of our globalized world. Student performances, projects, and many forms of media are used for learning and assessment rather than relying primarily on standardized tests and print. In short, the concept and practice of twenty-first-century education will need to be different from the one most college students experienced earlier in their education careers. And teachers' roles will change, from content deliverer to learning facilitator.

Should America's teachers and best students worry? Maybe. This new reality poses a challenge to all industrialized nations. Although Americans and Western Europeans produced many twentieth-century innovations, we have no guarantee that we will permanently lead in technological development. After World War II, the United States had no serious economic or intellectual competition. In recognition of its dominance, the twentieth century was often called the American Century. Some believe that this economic, military, and cultural preeminence "bred a sense of entitlement and cultural complacency" in the United States.[34] Achieving a preeminent place in the twenty-first century will not be as easy for Americans as it has been in the late twentieth century.

Even though education means much more than securing a well-paying job, "learning more to earning more" is still a realistic goal. Americans who want to compete successfully for decent-paying jobs will need the right attitudes, knowledge, and skills to vie for the information-rich careers in new specialties that will likely become available in this country. Individuals with low-knowledge skills, whose jobs can be moved elsewhere, have reason to worry. For example, the "grunt work" in the accounting profession (that is, bookkeeping, preparing payrolls) has been moving overseas. Meanwhile, the job of designing and creating complex tax sheltering strategies with quality-time discussions with clients remains anchored in the United States.

"The 'ovarian lottery' has changed—as has the whole relationship between geography and talent,"[35] argues Bill Gates, Microsoft's founder and now head of the Bill and Melinda Gates Foundation. As the world has become globalized, people can "plug and play" from anywhere, and natural talent has started to become more important than geography. "Now," Gates says, "I would rather be a genius born in China than an average guy born in Poughkeepsie (New York)."[36]

Likewise, Thomas Friedman, the three-time Pulitzer Prize–winning *New York Times* columnist and author, writes that when he was young, his parents used to tell him to finish his dinner because people in China and India would love

In a globalized world, people will need the ability to work well with people different from themselves.

Joshua Hodge Photography/iStockphoto

FlipSides

Are Today's Teachers Less Intelligent Than Those a Generation Ago?

Has teacher quality changed over the past 30 years? The research community has reached consensus that a link exists between teachers' academic ability and student achievement. Nonetheless, some advocates argue that today's teachers are less intelligent than those a generation ago. In contrast, others assert that today's teachers are increasingly intelligent and capable. Consider the differing viewpoints and evidence and decide what you think.

Are Today's Teachers Less Intelligent Than Those a Generation Ago?	
Yes. The intellectual quality of prospective teachers is low.	**No. Dramatic improvements are evident in today's teachers' intellectual quality.**
▪ In the 1950s and 1960s, intelligent women seeking careers became teachers because it fit cultural expectations that limited women in the workplace. ▪ The 1960s' and 1970s' women's movement opened other professions to intelligent women, diverting many from teaching.	• A 1998 federal law requiring teacher education institutions to report their program completers' teacher licensure test passing rates led to more rigorous teacher education admission and completion standards, resulting in an improved academic profile for the entire teacher candidate pool over the last fifteen years.[39]
▪ K-12 teachers have the lowest SAT scores of people in any professional occupation.	• College admissions test scores are incomplete proxy for academic quality, and those who score highly on SATs or ACTs do not automatically make good teachers.
▪ For many years, high school seniors who planned to major in education scored lower, on average, on college admissions tests of verbal and qualitative ability than other college-bound peers.	• Over the past twenty years, SAT scores for teacher candidates in secondary subjects has greatly increased; undergraduate GPAs for teacher candidates taking the Praxis II have increased (about 40 percent had GPAs of 3.5 or higher on a 4-point scale) than those in the mid-1990s; while passing rates on a more rigorous Praxis II have substantially decreased.[40]
▪ Teachers have academic abilities equal to or below those in the general college population.	• Teachers in academic subject areas have academic abilities equal to or higher than those in the general college population.
▪ Children in high-poverty schools were often assigned teachers in core academic subjects who did not have college majors in the subject they were teaching.	• The 2001 No Child Left Behind Act required that all teachers of core subjects to demonstrate competence in the subject matter taught—usually by a college major or passing the state's licensure exam in that subject.
▪ Teacher preparation programs lacked rigorous accountability for their program completers' teaching effectiveness.	• Since 2000, national accrediting boards require teacher education programs to provide evidence that prospective teachers are able to use knowledge of content and pedagogy in their teaching.
▪ The most successful educational systems —such as in Singapore and Finland—recruit teachers from among the top third of their college graduates. By contrast, some studies over the years have found that the United States recruits from the bottom third.[41]	• The U.S. culture does not honor teachers with the compensation, working conditions, and status accorded them in certain other countries, discouraging many top candidates from seeking education careers. Nonetheless, traditional and alternate teacher preparation programs produce more academically strong candidates than in prior decades.

Given the points offered about the differences in intellectual quality between earlier generations of teachers and today's, what do you believe?

to have his food. Now his advice to his daughters is, "Finish your homework. People in China and India would love to have your jobs."[37]

1-5a What the Globalized World Means for Teachers

Preparing students for citizenship, work, and lifestyle in a globalized world has clear implications for teaching and learning:

- Globalization impacts the way employees will work and learn. This has implications for how we think about and conduct education.
- Globalization is changing the nature of life from labor to knowledge, from retaining information to using it for analysis, synthesis, evaluation, and creativity.
- A globalized economy will increase international competition for well-educated and highly skilled workers who can provide the best, user-tailored products for the most reasonable costs, accessing work across a virtual world without moving physically.

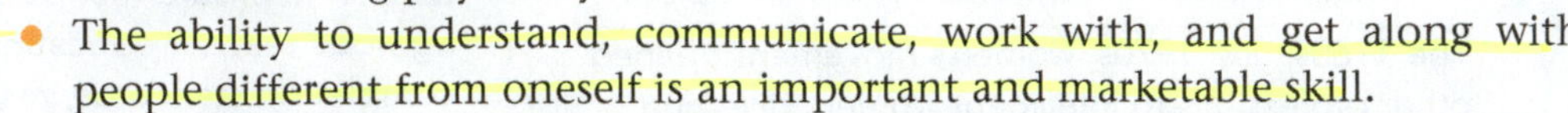

- The ability to understand, communicate, work with, and get along with people different from oneself is an important and marketable skill.
- High-level knowledge and skills and the ability to keep learning are necessary conditions to secure a well-paying career and a satisfying quality of life.
- High-level skills and knowledge and the ability to keep learning do not guarantee that anyone possessing them will secure or keep a well-paying career.
- Education necessary for satisfaction and success in this changing world is broader and deeper than education for employment. It is lifelong and focuses on living an aware, productive, personally and socially responsible, and satisfying life.

In short, effective twenty-first-century teachers may have to teach very differently than they were taught. They will have to help their students learn the attitudes and skills to thrive outside their present communities, states, and nation. They will have to help their students learn to understand, respect, and work well with others who have backgrounds very unlike their own. And they will have to help their students learn to become lifelong learners.

Did You Get It?

When you create or help create your classroom curriculum, it will probably emphasize which following skill as particularly useful in the globalized world?

a. A deep understanding of the subject matter: not only knowing facts, but understanding how they fit together.
b. Repetitive memorization to shape and strengthen students' recall ability.
c. Sitting still and learning in a solitary manner so that students learn how to work and think independently.
d. The "3Rs" as a strong foundation.

Take the full quiz on CourseMate.

1-6 InTASC Model Core Standards for New Teachers

New teachers enter the profession inspired and excited about their new role. They want to be prepared and confident to meet the classroom demands they will face. The profession has built frameworks to support this effort.

In 1992, the Interstate New Teacher Assessment and Support Consortium (InTASC), a program of the Council of Chief State School Officers, developed model standards for licensing new teachers. These represent the common core of teaching knowledge and skills that will help future students learn the twenty-first-century skills appropriate for a knowledge-based economy. These InTASC standards were designed to be compatible with those set by the **National Board for Professional Teaching Standards (NBPTS)**, a national professional organization that certifies teachers who can document meeting advanced standards of

National Board for Professional Teaching Standards (NBPTS) A national professional organization that certifies teachers who can document meeting advanced standards of practice that improve teaching and learning through intensive study, expert evaluation, self-assessment, and peer review.

practice that improve teaching and learning through intensive study, expert evaluation, self-assessment, and peer review. NBPTS certification is the highest level of professional teaching practice now available. InTASC updated its standards in 2011 to be compatible with the newly released Common Core State Standards for mathematics and English language arts, the NBPTS, National Council for Accreditation of Teacher Education (NCATE, now the Council for the Accreditation of Educator Preparation, CAEP), the National Staff Development Council (now called Learning Forward), and the Interstate School Leaders Licensure Consortium (ISLLC) 2008, the Council of Chief State School Officers' (CCSSO's) educational leadership policy standards and performance expectations for education leaders.

InTASC 2011 standards address the performances, essential knowledge, and critical dispositions common to all teachers, regardless of academic discipline or specialty area, who are able to ensure that all their students learn to high levels. These include knowledge of student learning and development, curriculum and teaching, and contexts and purposes that create a set of professional understandings, abilities, and ethical commitments that all teachers share.

The InTASC standards are performance-based.[42] They describe what teachers should know and be able to do. These behaviors are assessable. The InTASC standards also permit states and schools to incorporate more innovation and diversity in their teacher education programs by looking at teacher outcomes rather than inputs, such as lists of courses taken. These standards are based on five propositions:

1. Teachers are committed to students and their learning.
2. Teachers know the subjects they teach and know how to teach those subjects to diverse learners.
3. Teachers are responsible for managing and monitoring student learning.
4. Teachers think systematically about their practice and learn from experience.
5. Teachers are members of learning communities.

Within this context, InTASC has identified 10 principles that guide teacher education and teacher licensing (InTASC Model Core Standards for New Teachers from The Council of Chief State School Officers, Washington, DC.) Teacher education programs following these principles work toward helping their students gain the knowledge, skills, dispositions, and behaviors that lead to greater teaching effectiveness in today's diverse classrooms. Aspiring educators and their professors would do well to consider how effectively candidates are learning and demonstrating these principles in their college and teacher preparation courses.

Standard 1: Learner Development The teacher understands how learners grow and develop, recognizing that patterns of learning and development vary individually within and across the cognitive, linguistic, social, emotional, and physical areas, and designs and implements developmentally appropriate and challenging learning experiences.

Standard 2: Learning Differences The teacher uses understanding of individual differences and diverse cultures and communities to ensure inclusive learning environments that enable each learner to meet high standards.

Standard 3: Learning Environments The teacher works with others to create environments that support individual and collaborative learning, and that encourage positive social interaction, active engagement in learning, and self motivation.

Standard 4: Content Knowledge The teacher understands the central concepts, tools of inquiry, and structures of the discipline(s) he or she teaches and creates learning experiences that make the discipline accessible and meaningful for learners to assure mastery of the content.

TeachSource Video 1.3

The First Year of Teaching: One Colleague's Story

First-year teachers face a range of challenges and rewards. They can use their enthusiasm and energy for teaching, along with the wisdom from experienced colleagues, to learn more about themselves and how to best approach difficult situations. Watch the video clips, study the artifacts in the case, and reflect on the following questions:

1. How can a collegial and supportive staff create a successful environment in which to be a first-year teacher?
2. What are the best ways for a first-year teacher to learn how to effectively manage his or her own classroom—academically and behaviorally?
3. How do you respond to the first-year teacher's advice, "Be prepared to struggle"?

Watch on CourseMate.

Standard 5: Application of Content The teacher understands how to connect concepts and use differing perspectives to engage learners in critical thinking, creativity, and collaborative problem solving related to authentic local and global issues.

Standard 6: Assessment The teacher understands and uses multiple methods of assessment to engage learners in their own growth, to monitor learner progress, and to guide the teacher's and learner's decision making.

Standard 7: Planning for Instruction The teacher plans instruction that supports every student in meeting rigorous learning goals by drawing upon knowledge of content areas, curriculum, cross-disciplinary skills, and pedagogy, as well as knowledge of learners and the community context.

Standard 8: Instructional Strategies The teacher understands and uses a variety of instructional strategies to encourage learners to develop deep understanding of content areas and their connections, and to build skills to apply knowledge in meaningful ways.

Standard 9: Professional Learning and Ethical Practice The teacher engages in ongoing professional learning and uses evidence to continually evaluate his/her practice, particularly the effects of his/her choices and actions on others (learners, families, other professionals, and the community), and adapts practice to meet the needs of each learner.

Standard 10: Leadership and Collaboration The teacher seeks appropriate leadership roles and opportunities to take responsibility for student learning, to collaborate with learners, families, colleagues, other school professionals, and community members to ensure learner growth, and to advance the profession.*

If these 10 standards reflect what newly licensed teachers must know and be able to do, what do mature and effective teachers need to know and be able to do? InTASC debated this question, asking what distinguished the beginning practice of competent, newly licensed teachers from the advanced levels of teaching performance expected of experienced teachers with National Board for Professional Teaching Standards certification. They concluded that the differences between beginning and advanced practice rested more in the degree of sophistication teachers used in applying their knowledge than in the kind of knowledge they needed. All teachers must be able to meet these ten standards, but they will differ in the expertise with which they do so.

For example, advanced practitioners have developed the ability to deal simultaneously with more of the complex facets of teaching. They can more effectively integrate and adapt their understandings and performances to meet students' individual needs. To eventually become an expert practitioner, beginning teachers

*The Interstate New Teacher Assessment and Support Consortium (INTASC) standards were developed by the Council of Chief State School Officers and member states. Copies may be downloaded from the Council's website at http://www.ccsso.org. Council of Chief State School Officers. (1992). model standards for beginning teacher licensing, assessment, and development: A resource for state dialogue. Washington, DC: Author.

must have at least an awareness of the kinds of knowledge and understandings needed—as well as the resources available—to develop these skills, knowledge, dispositions, and behaviors that increase all students' learning. Having a core content of common knowledge gives teachers a professional base from which to learn, grow, and perform.

The InTASC competencies accurately reflect the complex and high-stakes world of today's diverse classrooms. What is more, many content areas have their own additional standards that teachers must meet. Learning to become an effective newly licensed teacher takes time, learning experiences, quality feedback, and increasingly extended doses of practice and reflection.[43] Becoming a teacher blends the individual's personality with the professional attitudes, knowledge, and skills shared by the profession as a whole. Becoming an educator takes a moral and ethical commitment for a lifelong journey.

Did You Get It?

As you progress in the teaching profession, you will have access to professional frameworks that help you develop

a. InTASC standards for new teachers that are different than those for more experienced teachers.

b. The Interstate New Teacher Assessment and Support Consortium (InTASC) that provides model standards for licensing new teachers.

c. InTASC standards that address teaching expectations for the core subjects.

d. InTASC that has identified eight principles to guide teacher education and licensing.

Take the full quiz on CourseMate.

SUMMARY

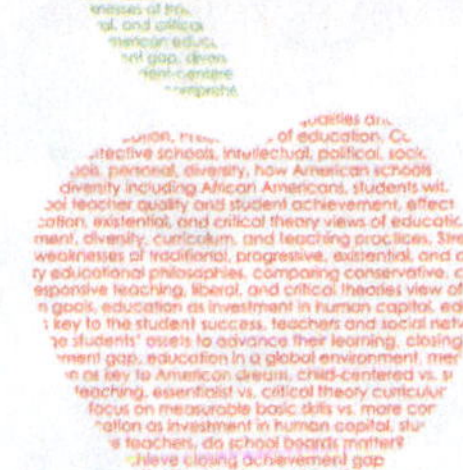

- Future teachers are preparing to enter an inspiring, satisfying, and important profession that can significantly affect the quality of life for their students, themselves, their communities, and our nation.
- Schools and teaching have moral purposes—to support societal well-being by helping students develop the cognitive and interpersonal skills and habits they need to thrive as people, workers, and citizens.
- Effective teachers are people who care about their students inside and outside the classroom, treat all students with care and respect, motivate student learning, have a positive attitude toward their own learning and the profession, are reflective practitioners, and continue to learn throughout their career.
- Globalization links today's youth to economic realities, social media, technology, and cultural movements that cross local and national boundaries, and teachers must help prepare them to live and work within this broader, more competitive arena.
- Teaching students twenty-first-century knowledge and skills means preparing them to respond knowledgeably and flexibly to complex real-world problems, to think creatively, to communicate effectively, to manage information, to work well in teams, and to produce new knowledge.
- InTASC standards represent the common core of professional teaching performance, knowledge, and dispositions that will aid newly licensed teachers in helping their diverse students learn the high-level twenty-first-century skills appropriate for a knowledge-based economy.
- InTASC standards include: Learner Development, Learning Differences, Learning Environments, Content Knowledge, Application of Content, Assessment, Planning for Instruction, Instructional Strategies, Professional Learning and Ethical Practice, and Leadership and Collaboration. The InTASC principles differ only in intensity (but not in type) from those that characterize an advanced professional teacher.

Visit the Education CourseMate for this textbook to access the eBook, Did You Get It? quizzes, TeachSource Video Cases, flashcards, and more. Go to CengageBrain.com to log in, register, or purchase access.

Teachers working together to improve their teaching practices. Teaching is a career that requires lifelong professional learning.

CHAPTER

2

Teaching as a Profession

InTASC Standards Addressed: 1, 2, 3, 4, 5, 6, 7, 8, 9, and 10

LEARNING OBJECTIVES

After you read this chapter, you should be able to:

2-1 Identify and define the factors that make teaching a profession.
2-2 Trace how teaching as a profession has changed over the past decades.
2-3 Summarize how teacher preparation in the United States has evolved.
2-4 Explain the research findings relating teacher preparation to teaching quality, student achievement, and teacher longevity.
2-5 Describe teacher licensure's rationale and state licensure practices.
2-6 Identify the organizations that support teaching professionals and summarize how each benefits the profession.
2-7 Discuss how schools' professional culture can orient, develop, and keep the teachers they hire.

The teaching profession has become the focus of national attention. As one journalist insightfully wrote, "Teacher quality is not just an important issue in addressing the many challenges facing the nation's schools: It is *the* issue."[1]

Teacher and teaching quality (often called teacher attributes and teaching effectiveness, respectively) are related policy challenges from the statehouse to the schoolhouse. Significant research evidence suggests that teacher and teaching quality are the most powerful school-based predictors of student success.[2] Research also describes superlative teachers' characteristics and explains which classroom behaviors result in high student learning.[3] Better teaching is the key to higher student achievement. And better teaching depends, in part, on viewing teaching as a profession.

The perception of teaching as a profession depends, largely, on practitioners receiving adequate and appropriate preparation to learn the knowledge, skills, and high-level thinking that goes into successful teaching. New teachers agree. As one beginning teacher who entered the classroom through a fast-track alternative-route preparation program reflected:

> I knew if I wanted to go on teaching there was no way I could do it without training. I found myself blaming my kids because the class was

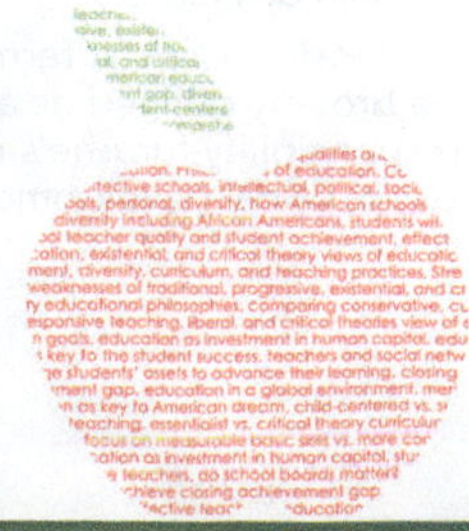

crazy and out of control, blaming the parents as though they didn't care about their kids. Even after only three-fourths of a semester [in a teacher preparation program] I have learned so much that would have helped me then.[4]

Another once-new teacher wrote of her early teaching experience in Philadelphia:

> My impeccably planned morning went smoothly for a grand total of eight minutes . . . then chaos ensued. We entered into negotiations. Would they work for a prize? How about a ten-minute break afterward? . . . I stood in a classroom wearing ugly, rubber-soled shoes, shouting at eleven-year-olds. I felt I had aged twenty years in two months. . . . Who ever thought this could be done by anyone, and without any training?[5]

Teaching as a profession has never been stronger. We know how to prepare effective teachers and how to support them once they enter their own classrooms. We know how to keep teachers developing their expertise and leadership throughout their careers. This chapter will consider the factors that make it so.

2-1 Factors That Make Teaching a Profession

Teachers are professionals with expert knowledge about instruction and curriculum in their particular disciplines. They understand child development and the ways in which learners learn. As a group, teachers are well organized and increasingly participate in making decisions about educational practices and their work conditions.

2-1a Defining a Profession

Sociology professor Andrew Abbott defines a **profession** as an exclusive occupational group that applies abstract knowledge to particular cases and has expertise and influence to practice in a given domain or field.[6] Establishing a profession means that individuals in a certain occupation claim an authority—power, confidence, and right—to practice that livelihood. Because they can demonstrate expertise, these individuals receive the opportunity to do the profession's work.

profession An exclusive occupational group that applies abstract knowledge to particular cases and has expertise and influence to practice in a given domain or field.

professionalism A term that can be broadly defined as accepting responsibility for one's own professional development and growth.

Professionalism can be broadly defined as accepting responsibility for one's own professional development and growth. For teachers, professionalism means incorporating specialized knowledge, self-regulation, special attention to students' unique needs and welfare, autonomous performance, and responsibility into their practice.[7] In addition, teacher professionalism implies a sense of stewardship, of caring and doing everything possible to improve teaching and learning—even beyond their own classroom and school. Accomplishing all this requires values such as honesty, fairness, and integrity in the practitioner.[8]

A profession can keep its authority if the public accepts its claims of expertise and if the profession's internal structure of well-defined and agreed-upon knowledge and skills support it. For instance, people believe that physicians are professionals because they know anatomy, physiology, biochemistry, and pathology, and have specialized information and abilities gained through their study in an accredited medical school. The medical profession includes organizing groups that provide written and performance tests that enable doctors to become board certified and earn advanced credentials.

"Few would require cardiologists to deliver babies, real-estate lawyers to defend criminal cases, chemical engineers to design bridges, or sociology professors to teach English. The commonly held assumption is that such traditional professions require a great deal of skill and training; hence, specialization is assumed to be necessary."[9]

Characteristics of a profession include the following elements[10]:

- A clearly defined, highly developed, specialized, and theoretical knowledge base beyond that understood by laypersons
- Autonomy in making decisions about selected aspects of work
- Agreed-upon standards of professional practice shaped by practitioners
- A code of ethics to help clarify ambiguous issues related to services rendered
- A lengthy period of specialized training
- Control of licensing and certification standards and entry requirements
- Control over training new entrants
- Self-governing and self-policing authority by members of the profession, especially about professional ethics (acceptance of responsibility for judgments made and acts performed related to service rendered)
- A commitment to public service
- Professional associations and elite groups that provide recognition for individual achievements
- High prestige and economic standing

Let's see how the teaching profession compares with other fields such as law, engineering, and medicine in four key areas: (1) a defined body of knowledge and skills beyond that which laypersons recognize as unique and special; (2) control over licensing standards and/or entry requirements; (3) autonomy in making decisions about certain work areas; and (4) high prestige and economic standing.[11] We will consider professional associations and elite groups later in this chapter and discuss teachers and ethics in Chapter 9.

A defined body of knowledge All professions have a certain knowledge and skills specialty requiring complex reasoning and problem solving with large amounts of information that separates their members from the general public. When members make this clearly defined expertise widely known, they protect the public from untrained amateurs by denying them professional membership.

Until relatively recently, however, "teaching" had no agreed-upon specialized body of knowledge.[12] Traditionally, teaching has not been guided by extensive procedural rules as found in law or by established methods such as those found in the physical sciences and health care. As a result, many people talk about education as if they—the laypersons—were also experts. To them, teaching holds no mystery because they have all had personal experiences as students. Because they cannot see teachers' complex mental planning decisions or moment-by-moment thinking choices made in a dynamic classroom, laypeople assume that teaching does not require any extraordinary knowledge or skills apart from knowing their subject. In fact, Daniel C. Lortie, professor emeritus of education at the University of Chicago, has coined the phrase **"apprenticeship of observation"** to describe the phenomenon where laypersons who have spent thousands of hours as schoolchildren watching and judging teachers

"apprenticeship of observation" The phenomenon where laypersons who have spent thousands of hours as schoolchildren watching and judging teachers in practice develop many false ideas about teaching and mistakenly consider themselves to be "experts."

in practice develop many false ideas about teaching and mistakenly consider themselves to be "experts."[13]

Furthermore, teaching's less well-defined body of knowledge than law or the physical sciences has allowed teacher education course requirements to vary from state to state, and even among teacher training institutions within a given state. While teacher education usually includes three major components—general education, specialized subject education, and professional education—heated discussions would frequently arise over which is more important and by how much. For instance, how many credit hours should a prospective teacher have in professional practice (pedagogy) compared to course hours in a specialized subject field? How much clinical experience in actual school settings should be required? Should students learn the subject discipline in a liberal arts college or within specialized teacher education schools? One might logically ask, if leaders in teacher education cannot clearly agree on the profession's body of knowledge, how can the general public expect to see teachers as true professionals?[14]

Notably, this situation is improving as states increasingly are adopting a common set of high-quality, national professional benchmarks. Since 1954, the **National Council for Accreditation of Teacher Education (NCATE)**, a national teacher education accrediting organization (recently merged with the Teacher Education Accreditation Council to form a new accrediting organization discussed later in this chapter), set high, clear standards that specify the courses to be taken and the faculty qualifications for teaching them. By 2009, 25 states had adopted or adapted the NCATE unit standards as the state unit standards, and 48 states and the District of Columbia and Puerto Rico had teacher preparation programs that reflected NCATE's influence. Increasingly, teacher preparation programs agree that having a nationally recognized, respected, and clearly defined body of knowledge strengthens teaching as a profession.[15]

National Council for Accreditation of Teacher Education (NCATE) A national teacher education accrediting organization that has set high, clear standards that specify the courses to be taken and the faculty qualifications for teaching them.

Controlling requirements for entrance and licensing Typically, entry into a profession requires a license, or certificate, acquired only after the candidate completes an officially approved preparation program and passes specialized examinations. Entry requirements for teaching, however, is an area of disagreement. Some say entry into teaching should be more highly restricted to upgrade teacher and teaching quality, whereas others argue for looser requirements to encourage talented career switchers and candidates from fast-track preparation programs to join the ranks quickly. Unlike other professions, teaching has historically lacked uniform requirements for professional entry and licensing. Certification requirements vary from state to state, and the trend toward testing teachers to assess their basic knowledge and skills remains controversial. Recent reforms, however, have required prospective teachers in most states to pass minimum competency tests. But because states control the "cut scores" that mark the difference between passing and failing, a teacher who receives a certain score may "pass" in one state but "fail" in another.

In short, the teaching field does not control professional entry and licensing with consistent standards across states. For the most part, states make these decisions based on political influences and other local considerations.

Autonomy in deciding work responsibilities Every profession considers all group members qualified to make expert judgments about their work; outsiders are deemed unqualified to make such decisions. In comparison, teachers traditionally have had little input about what they teach or the resources they use. School officials often hired outside "experts" with little teaching experience to help teachers select textbooks, write grant proposals, or resolve local community issues. Likewise, school reform ideas often came from government officials, business leaders, and civic groups—not from teachers. More and more, this situation is changing as federal laws now require all core academic subjects be taught by a "highly qualified" teacher who is fully certified or licensed by his or her state to teach that subject, hold at least a bachelor degree from a four-year institution, and demonstrate competence in each core academic subject area in which he or she teaches. These teachers are deemed fully qualified and ready to take autonomy in deciding many of their work responsibilities. Likewise, educators at all levels are having more input into education policy decisions.

As teachers expand their knowledge about effective teaching and learning practices, become increasingly competent at generating student learning, and actively participate in site-based leadership, they are likely to increase their autonomy in influencing their own work responsibilities.[16]

Prestige and economic standing **Prestige** is the level of social respect or standing, the good reputation and high esteem accorded to an individual or a group because of their position's status. Occupations have high prestige if the public believes the people who fill them make especially valuable contributions to society. In our culture, the most prestigious occupations require a high level of education or skill and little physical or manual labor.

prestige The level of social respect or standing, the good reputation and high esteem accorded to an individual or a group because of their position's status.

In the United States, public opinion polls repeatedly show that elementary and secondary teachers have relatively high occupational esteem. Teaching is less prestigious than law or medicine but more prestigious than most blue- or pink-collar work (such as truck drivers or secretaries, respectively). In an annual Harris Poll (2009), a nationwide sample of adults measuring public perceptions of 23 professions and occupations placed teachers among the "most prestigious occupations," in a tie with military officers for fifth place after firefighters, scientists, doctors, and nurses. Real estate agents, accountants, and stock brokers were viewed as occupations having the "least prestige." In addition, the percentage of those who see teachers as having "very great prestige" has risen 22 points, from 29 percent to 51 percent since 1977. Notably, teachers are the only occupation, among the 11 tracked since 1977, to see a large rise in prestige.[17]

Recently, however, teachers' satisfaction with their profession has taken a big hit. Because work occupies a large part of each employee's day and provides the main source of social standing and income, satisfaction with one's job is an important component in overall well-being. In fact, job satisfaction and general happiness are positively related. But in the face of an extended national economic downturn, K-12 teachers' job satisfaction has fallen to its lowest level since the 1980s. In a MetLife (2012) survey, those expressing that they were "very satisfied" dropped 15 points between 2009 and 2011, from 59 to 44 percent. At the same time, the percentage of teachers who say they "very" or "fairly likely" to leave the profession within the next five years and enter a different occupation has increased by 12 points since 2009, from 17 percent to 29 percent. Teachers with low job

Today's teachers enter the profession from a variety of backgrounds, including prior careers.

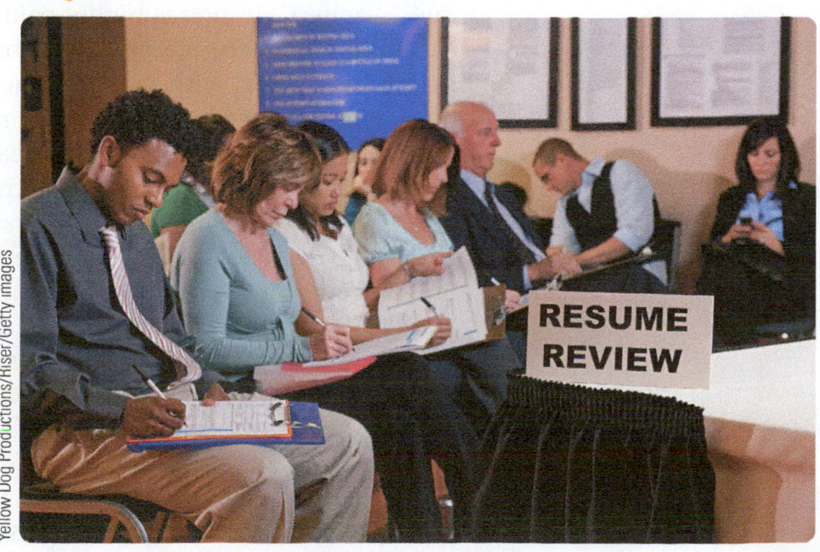

Yellow Dog Productions/Riser/Getty images

satisfaction are more likely to work in schools that have undergone cuts in programs, services, or staffing during the past 12 months. As a result of this lowered morale, many worry that student achievement will suffer.[18]

Many factors contribute to teachers' job dissatisfaction. The national policy debate pointing to "failing schools"; the widespread pressure on teachers to increase students' achievement test scores; the challenging economic conditions that are chopping school budgets, undermining teachers' job security, and reducing educational resources; the increasing number of children living in poverty who come to school worried, hungry, or who move to another school during the year; and the new expectations that tie teacher evaluations with their students' achievement test scores all combine to make teaching more difficult and less satisfying. Clearly, the demands—and the scrutiny—placed on teachers are greater than ever before, and the declines in professional satisfaction are understandable.

Despite the present challenges, teaching as a career has experienced several changes that have improved its status. First, teachers' average education level has increased significantly over the past century. Now, all teachers have bachelor's degrees; many have master's degrees and even doctorates. Second, teaching has become increasingly complex. Effective teachers use high-level thinking in selecting appropriate subject content, planning and targeting instruction to meet diagnosed student learning needs, facilitating student engagement and mastery, and assessing learning outcomes in ways that increase students' knowledge and skills and improve teaching. Likewise, effective teachers have high levels of language proficiencies in reading, writing, and speaking and expertise using a wide array of media to promote learning. Teachers also work successfully with a variety of people— students, colleagues, parents, and administrators. All these factors positively impact teachers' prestige and esteem in their communities.

At the same time, several factors limit teachers' status and public regard. First, the clientele's size and nature play a role in determining a group's occupational prestige. For instance, people accord more respect to occupations in which the individuals deal with one person at a time, especially when that person comes voluntarily. A doctor treats a patient with an illness, and a lawyer litigates on the client's behalf. Teachers, by comparison, tend to work with groups of young persons who are required by law to attend school; students are a captive audience. The result: relatively lower prestige for teachers. Further, because most adults have seen teachers in action, teaching holds no "mystique," whereas less familiar professions do.[19]

Teacher salaries Salary plays a key role in determining an occupation's prestige. Teachers are not as highly paid as physicians, lawyers, engineers, business executives, and college professors because the public believes that these other professionals deal with more abstract and complex material than K-12 teachers do. In addition, these fields require more demanding academic preparation and licensure than does public school teaching.

In addition, the facts that the teaching profession is large and schools run on taxpayers' dollars also limit what teachers can earn. Teacher salaries typically lag behind inflation. From 1997 to 2007, the average salary for public school teachers increased only 1.3 percent after adjusting for inflation.[20] An analysis of U.S. Census data from 1940 to 2000 shows that the annual salary teachers receive has fallen sharply relative to the annual pay of other workers with college degrees.[21] In 2010, public school teachers earned, on average, 20 percent less than workers in other professions that require similar education and skills, including accountants, registered nurses, and computer systems analysts.[22] Economic downturns and political decisions about fiscal policies—like those that occurred in 2007 through 2013—also mean less public money is available for school budgets, teachers' salaries, and benefits increases.

Nevertheless, most teachers (77 percent) say they are treated as professionals, 67 percent say that their health insurance benefits—and 61 percent say their retirement benefits—are fair for the work they do. But two-thirds (65 percent) of teachers report that their salaries are not fair for the work they do.[23]

Perceptions of salary "fairness" are one thing; actual dollars are another. The Bureau of Labor Statistics (BLS) reports the mean annual wages for occupations. For May 2010, teacher salaries are presented in various categories such as kindergarten, elementary, middle, high, special education, career and technical, and literacy teachers. The mean of all 10 teacher categories is $54,780.[24] Comparing teacher mean wages with other occupations requiring a bachelor's degree can be seen in Table 2.1. The average teacher earns $12,940 less than the next closest profession, registered nurse, and almost $14,180 per year less than an accountant—even though entry into each of these fields requires a four-year college degree. Studies have also found that teacher salaries are important in attracting individuals to teaching from the college-educated pool.[25]

One 2008 study found that an individual with similar credentials in another profession could earn roughly $175 more in one week than a teacher.[26] An original analysis by the Editorial Projects in Education (EPE) Research Center found that public school teachers across the United States make 88 cents for every dollar earned in 16 comparable occupations. Only 10 states reach or surpass the pay-parity line, meaning teachers earn at least as much as comparable workers.[27] Yet for all the analyses detailing the comparatively lower pay for schoolteachers as compared with professions requiring similar years of preparation, a variety of issues complicate this research and make the data somewhat misleading.[28]

One confounding issue is the salary variations from state to state. According to National Education Association (NEA) Research, the U.S. average public school teacher salary for 2009–2010 was $55,202. State average public school teacher salaries ranged from those in New York ($71,633), Massachusetts ($69,273), and California ($68,203) at the high end to South Dakota ($38,837), North Dakota ($42,964), and Missouri ($45,317) at the low end.[29] This unevenness makes drawing general conclusions about salary comparisons difficult. A teacher's salary—as well as its buying power—depends on where one is teaching and living.

TABLE 2.1

Trends in Average Salaries across Selected Professions, 2010

Profession	National Average Salary
College graduate	$50,034
Teacher	$54,780
Educational administrator	$89,990
Registered nurse	$67,720
Accountant and auditor	$68,960
Mechanical engineer	$82,480
Computer systems analyst	$81,250
Sociologist	$80,130
Dental hygienist	$68,680

Sources: For all listed occupations: Bureau of Labor Statistics. (2011, May 17). *Occupational employment and wages new release.* Washington, DC: Author, U.S. Department of Labor. Retrieved from http://www.bls.gov/news.release/ocwage.htm; For college graduate: Ellis, B. (2011, February 10). Class of 2011: Your paychecks will be bigger. *CNN Money.* Retrieved from http://money.cnn.com/2011/02/10/pf/college_graduates_salaries/index.htm

Then, too, teacher salary analyses typically look at teachers' average salary levels of particular types of schools and localities. This can be misleading because teacher salary levels are often standardized according to a uniform schedule based on education levels and years of experience. When considering average salaries, therefore, it is difficult to know whether the salary differences are due to a more mature teacher workforce (who are paid higher for their extra years on the salary scale) or actual differences in compensation.

Other factors also confuse the issue of teacher compensation. One is teachers' pension benefits, which usually include regular payments and health care plans to vested employees upon their retirement. Typically, both teachers and employers make annual contributions to a pension trust fund. States and localities often choose to contribute to teacher pension benefits—which promise future advantages—rather than provide present-day increases in teacher salaries, which have immediate economic and political consequences. Pension rights are typically considered part of a contract between the employer and the employee, often the result of collective bargaining agreements. Once approved, these plans have constitutional protections in certain states.

Most states use defined benefit (DB) plans—in which employers guarantee employees a special annual retirement benefit based on a formula, generally considering final average salaries and years of services. Notably, individual benefits are not tied to contributions. Because retirees are guaranteed a certain benefit amount—in addition to features often including cost of living adjustments, young age for normal retirement, early retirement benefits, and retiree health benefits—the government (taxpayers) must make up any shortfalls resulting from less-than-expected actual investment returns. Such features are rare in private sector pensions. Considering teachers' pension benefits as part of their compensation places salary in a different context (although the Great Recession and its fiscal aftermath are likely to press states to restructure educators' retirement benefits to reduce state costs).

Making sense of teachers' salaries also requires an appropriate frame of reference. The BLS estimates that full-time public teachers work an average of 36.5 hours per week during the school year, which usually lasts fewer than 200 days.[30] According to a 2007 Manhattan Institute for Policy Research study of teachers' hourly salaries, public school teachers are paid 11 percent more than the average professional worker.[31] But in reality, few public school teachers only work from morning bell to students' afternoon dismissal. Recognizing this, Stanford University professor Linda Darling-Hammond asserts that teachers actually work 10–12 hours per day.[32] That totals an extra 12.5 weeks of work each year not accounted for in the BLS figures. Making the matter more complicated, these numbers don't account for the benefits that most school districts offer their educators: comprehensive health and life insurance; solid retirement and pension plans; opportunities to earn stipends as club sponsors, department heads, coaches, and summer school instructors; and additional money for earning advanced degrees. Many school districts offer opportunities for continuing education as well.[33] Although teachers can make a comfortable living depending on their subject specialty, their state and school district, and their initiative, recruiting and keeping capable, qualified, and committed teachers is critical. Given our market-driven economy, persons with high-demand skills can find attractive incentives in occupations other than education: the law of supply and demand does not stop at the schoolhouse door.[34]

Lastly, teaching as a profession has always been about more than the money. Teachers have the essential task of ensuring children's intellectual growth and preparing each new generation to competently enter the economic, political, and social realms. It would be reasonable to expect that our society would reward such important work with high status and appropriate compensation. Yet as Table 2.1 shows, the average teacher earns less than his or her colleagues in professions requiring similar educational preparation. Fortunately, as Lortie (1975) has observed, teachers tend to seek the "psychic" rewards—the desire to give children a strong start in life and the pleasure of seeing them learn—rather than material rewards for their efforts.[35] Teachers have the real satisfaction of doing important work in the public good.

Pay for performance Believing that effective teachers are not well paid for the responsibility they hold and the important results they achieve, policy makers have identified new ways to address their compensation. **Pay for performance**, specifically, **merit-based pay**, refers to salary plans that reward individual teachers, groups of teachers, or schools on a variety of items (including student achievement scores) that hinge on student outcomes attributed to a particular teacher or group. Merit pay is considered as a policy tool: a way to recruit and retain highly effective teachers.

Many Americans are willing to pay teachers based on how well they can boost student achievement, and the federal government is supporting this approach. First authorized in 2006, the national Teacher Incentive Fund (TIF) grant program gives states, districts, and schools opportunities to create effective performance-based compensation systems for teachers and principals. More recently, 40 states and the District of Columbia ended legal barriers that prevented schools from tying teacher pay to student test scores to make the states eligible to apply for the $4.35 billion Race to the Top Fund—opening the door to paying teachers more for generating measurably improved student performance. Consider the evidence on both sides of this issue and decide for yourself whether teachers should be paid more money if they measurably increase their students' achievement.

TeachSource Video 2.1

Teacher Incentive Pay: Pay for Performance

Teacher incentive pay—paying teachers cash bonuses if they increase their students' achievement—is a controversial practice. Research about its effectiveness is mixed and it can have negative outcomes. Watch the video clips, study the artifacts in the case, and reflect on the following questions:

1. Advance an argument about how performance incentives for teachers DOES or DOES NOT make a positive difference in student achievement.
2. What impact might replacing the principal and 29 or 43 teachers (60% of the staff) have had on improving student achievement at Sulphur Springs Elementary School—apart from the performance pay?
3. Why is encouraging competition among individual teachers within a school harmful to teachers and students?

Watch on CourseMate.

pay for performance (merit-based pay) Refers to salary plans that reward individual teachers, groups of teachers, or schools on a variety of items (including student achievement scores) that hinge on student outcomes attributed to a particular teacher or group.

Did You Get It?

Why is teaching a profession, rather than a service?

- **a.** Teachers have expert knowledge about instruction and curriculum in their particular disciplines.
- **b.** Teachers are not stewards nor do they apply the principles of stewardship, of conserving resources for another's use.
- **c.** Teachers are well-educated generalists, rather than specialists.
- **d.** It isn't: professions (traditionally, the military, law, engineering and medicine, which was understood not to be nursing) are male.

Take the full quiz on CourseMate.

FlipSides

Should Effective Teachers Receive Merit Pay?

Effective teachers are the most important school contributor to student learning, and every school would like more of them. Accordingly, policy makers are asking whether schools could reward their best performers as well as attract and keep more highly effective teachers if they offered higher salaries or bonuses to those who demonstrate superior capacity to generate student learning. As a future teacher, do you think merit pay for teachers a good idea whose time has come?

Pay Teachers More Based on Their Performance	Don't Pay Teachers More Based on Their Performance
■ The percent of Americans who believe that teachers should be paid based on their effectiveness rather than on a standard salary scale has increased from 61% in 1983 to over 70% in 2010.[36] ■ The idea of merit pay for teachers is becoming a popular market-based way to improve teachers' compensation. ■ Some believe that using merit pay for outstanding performance will attract more highly effective individuals into the teaching profession.	● Research on whether teacher pay for performance improves student outcomes is small and has mixed findings: ▶ Early studies often failed to find a relationship.[40] ▶ Other investigations found some positive effects on student achievement plus unintended, and undesired outcomes (i.e., cheating by students, teachers, administrators).[41] ▶ Studies in 2010 found that teacher pay-for-performance did not raise student achievement.[42, 43] ▶ Links found between teachers' merit pay and increased student learning may not be cause and effect.
■ Many studies confirm that teacher and teaching quality (teacher attributes and effectiveness) are among the strongest school determinants of student achievement.[37] Bonuses for high performance may attract and keep higher-quality teachers.	● Various factors that affect student achievement lie outside the teacher's influence (i.e., students' prior knowledge and experiences, students' health, attendance, family situation, family mobility). This would unfairly advantage certain teachers while unfairly disadvantaging others.
■ Although about 99% of all U.S. teacher pay and salary increases are based on teachers' years of experience and graduate credits and degrees,[38] research shows: ▶ Paying for longevity has little effect on student achievement and is not an efficient way to attract high-quality teachers.[39] ▶ Master's degrees are generally not related to student achievement.[39]	● Money does not necessarily motivate teachers' best efforts in helping students learn. ● Most teachers do not hold back their best instructional practices while waiting for merit pay to incentivize their use. They use the instructional skills they have. ● Working collegially with other teachers to assess and improve their instructional effectiveness and improve student learning – shared learning with accountability from their peers – is a successful way to improve teaching and learning without financial incentives.
■ Salary schedules (in which all teachers with the same years of teaching experience receive the same salary) do not reflect twenty-first-century labor market realities (and cannot effectively recruit or retain highly effective teachers): ▶ More effective professionals should be able to earn more than the least effective professionals.	● Cultural differences between schools (which value collaboration) and businesses (which value competition and profits) make merit pay unworkable in schools: ▶ Merit pay within a department may foster competition rather than collaboration among colleagues, reducing teachers' willingness to share successful methods, experiences, and sources—to students' detriment.

(*continued*)

FlipSides

Should Effective Teachers Receive Merit Pay? (*continued*)

Pay Teachers More Based on Their Performance	Don't Pay Teachers More Based on Their Performance
▶ Individual effort and productivity should be recognized and rewarded. ▶ Salary should distinguish between high- and low-demand fields (such as math and science as compared with social studies). ▶ Salaries should attract—not discourage—high-achieving college graduates into a profession.	● Serious limitations make performance pay for teachers invalid, unreliable, and unethical: ▶ Measurement errors in the data used to identify effective teachers[44, 45, 46] ▶ Cheating, narrowing the curriculum, other opportunistic behaviors may result[47] ▶ Teachers' performance tends to improve during the first three to five years in the classroom but may become less effective over time.[48]
■ Not recognizing and rewarding the organization's highest performers encourages mediocrity rather than excellence.	● Teacher quality and effectiveness show themselves in more than students' reading and mathematics test scores. Reducing teacher and teaching quality to a test score is inaccurate and unethical. ● Monies to award merit pay to teachers with outstanding performance are not always available.

Given the reasoning and data about giving teachers' performance pay, do you think schools should pay teachers more for outstanding performance?

2-2 How Teaching as a Profession Has Changed over the Decades

As an occupation, teaching is highly demanding, exciting, and important. Today's teachers bear society's expectations of higher achievement for all students, regardless of their backgrounds or life circumstances. As a result, teaching and schooling have changed more dramatically in the past few decades than they did in the two centuries before. Teachers today are working by a whole new set of rules.

2-2a Teaching's Career Structure

Although the first American teachers were male "schoolmasters," by 1870 women outnumbered men as teachers across the nation—an imbalance not reversed since it began.[49] As a result, teaching has been a profession largely shaped by a "gendered bureaucracy" in which men, viewed as professionals, supervised and trained women, who actually taught.[50] For the most part, young women teachers did not remain in their classrooms for long. Many married and left to have families. Female teacher turnover was an expected part of the school culture. Because they were seen as a source of cheaper and less aggressive labor than men throughout the nineteenth century and into the twentieth century, women teachers were paid less than their male counterparts.[51]

In the early twentieth century, the U.S. educational system organized teaching and learning in simple and mechanistic ways. Administrators—usually men—maintained their schools' continuity. They hired departing teachers' replacements and tried to get newcomers up to speed as efficiently as possible. To achieve this feat, schools typically took an unsophisticated view of teaching. The hiring protocol addressed basic questions:

- Did teachers know their subjects (at least better than their students)?
- Could teachers keep their classrooms orderly, quiet, and purposeful?
- Could teachers move all students out of the halls by the time the next class's bell rang?
- Could teachers' students score highly on tests (so administrators could infer what they learned)?

Thus, although teachers considered themselves to be professionals, the organizations in which they worked—schools—often did not always treat them as such.

In the two decades following World War II, teaching changed from an occupation requiring relatively little specialized training to a profession that demanded increasing levels of preparation and competence. Yet partially in response to the earlier political and life-choice realities, teaching remained an "unstaged" career, lacking a progression of steps through which one could advance.[52] Unlike most other professions, teaching does not have career ladders that employees climb as they mature, become more productive, and show leadership. Teachers' responsibilities seldom change over the years, from their first to their last workdays.

Analysts offer differing explanations for teaching's traditional lack of career stages.[53] Some say teaching, because it was widely regarded as "woman's work," did not require the same kinds of promotions that signaled advancement in male-dominant careers.

Next, because child rearing has traditionally shaped women's employment patterns, teaching has been a high-turnover field, not easily plotted out into stages. A national survey of first-year teachers in 1956 found that whereas 80 percent of the male respondents expected to remain continuously employed as teachers or administrators, only 25 percent of the female respondents had similar expectations. The vast majority of women who planned to leave education listed raising a family as their reason, even though many of those same women returned to teaching after their children were in school.[54] With women living in a society that expected mothers to stay home with their children, personal and family changes often dictated career changes.

Other analysts point to schools' customary "egg crate" structure, in which teachers work alone rather than as members of an integrated and tiered organization, for the lack of career stages. In this view, hiring teachers to fill vacant classrooms could supposedly occur with relatively little disruption to the rest of the organization. Some blame the lack of career steps on the influence of teaching's conservative milieu, which discourages efforts to distinguish individuals by competence. Finally, certain analysts conclude that teaching's unstaged nature results from teachers' tendency to define their success based on their work inside the classroom rather than their ability to move up to higher-status positions outside it. This may be circular reasoning because teachers may have looked for success markers from those items available to them. Such has traditionally been teaching's professional culture: rationalizing and minimizing the absence of teaching career stages, promotions, and tangible rewards.[55]

2-2b Changing Career Expectations over Past Decades

Not only has the teaching profession changed, but future teachers have changed, too. Those entering teaching today have different expectations for their careers than did the teachers who entered the profession a generation ago.

Until the mid-1960s, teaching was the primary career option for large numbers of well-educated women and people of color to whom other professions were formally or informally closed. This is no longer true. Today, persons considering teaching have many more career options than did the retiring veterans of the current school system. Many of these alternative careers offer higher salaries, greater status, and better working conditions than does teaching. As a result, many of today's prospective teachers are drawn from a narrower population than the one that filled the teaching ranks decades earlier.

In addition, today's new and prospective teachers differ from retiring teachers in other important ways: They enter teaching at different career stages, they take multiple routes to the classroom, and they plan to spend fewer years there.[56]

First, more new teachers already have worked several years in other career fields and are entering teaching at a midcareer point in their lives. In one sample of 50 first- and second-year teachers, 52 percent entered teaching as a first career, on average at age 24, whereas 48 percent entered it at midcareer, on average at age 36.[57] Midcareer new teachers come to teaching believing that it offers more meaningful work than their previous employment.

Second, new teachers are reaching the classroom through a variety of paths. Most new teachers enter the profession using the traditional undergraduate or graduate teacher preparation programs. These programs include at least one academic year of specific coursework, opportunities to practice their skills under an experienced teacher's supervision during 6 to 10 weeks of student teaching, and state certification. By contrast, approximately 36 percent of teachers in one study entered teaching through an alternative route.[58] These teaching newcomers rely more on their innate teaching ability and other work experiences than on professional teacher education to prepare them for successful teaching.

Third, the concept of work and career has evolved over the past century. Traditionally, careers were thought to progress in linear career sequence within the context of one or two firms.[59] Success was defined by the organization and measured in promotions and salary increases.[60] In comparison, by 2000, most Americans changed jobs every four-and-one-half years.[61] Consequently, whereas veteran teachers expected to remain in their classrooms from novice years until retirement, many new teachers approach teaching tentatively, conditionally, or as one of several careers they expect to have over their working lives. Few see themselves remaining in the classroom for the long term. Even first-career teachers do not expect to be full-time teachers until they retire. Although they expect to be excellent teachers, they do not plan to make classroom teaching their life's work.[62]

In summary, new teachers have more career choices available to them and do not expect to make classroom teaching their sole occupation. Many have solid employment experiences in other career fields and arrive at teaching with a maturity born of greater chronological age and life-earned wisdom. Given these factors, it is the teacher's preparation and the school's professional culture that often make the difference between teachers who leave and teachers who stay.

Did You Get It?

Which hypothesis is probably false about teaching?

a. The low socioeconomic status of women, and their low civic and political status relative to men, made them attractive to male administrators: they could be paid less and treated worse, with fewer consequences, than male schoolmasters.

b. Until the mid-1960s, American teachers were so good because so many of them were educated and intelligent women and people of color, who had no other professional outlet.

c. Teaching's conservative milieu, which discourages efforts to distinguish individuals by competence, is probably the result of a lack of tangible rewards and promotions.

d. Their great knowledge and hard work meant that female schoolteachers have traditionally been respected by the generally male school administration—despite societal sexism.

Take the full quiz on CourseMate.

2-3 How Teacher Education in the United States Has Evolved

Quality teacher preparation programs are essential if we are to educate teachers to successfully handle the varied challenges they will face in modern-day schools. In this section, we briefly look at how teacher preparation programs developed and examine the data supporting their effectiveness.

2-3a Early Teacher Training and Normal Schools

In the early 1800s, American society did not require a highly educated workforce. Instead, it needed large numbers of people with basic skills to drive its economy. The public schools met this need.

Beginning in the early 1800s, states saw the need to train teachers to be more effective. Recognizing that educated citizens were essential to protect and preserve our democratic institutions, New York governor DeWitt Clinton advocated for better teacher preparation, noting that "the mind and morals of the rising and perhaps the destinies of all future generations, be not entrusted to the guardianship of incompetence."[63]

By 1810, the Lancastrian higher schools in New York and elsewhere had developed classes for training monitors as teachers. Although they offered an extremely narrow concept of what teaching should be, these schools represented the only teacher training institutions available at the time. In 1827, Governor Clinton recommended the creation of a "central school in each county for the education of teachers," and the New York legislature appropriated the state funds necessary to fulfill this goal.[64] Similarly, in 1834, the New York legislature enacted the country's first law providing for elementary school teachers' professional education in a teacher training institute called a normal school.[65]

normal schools From the French model, *ecole normale;* one- or two-year training institutions for prospective teachers who were expected to uphold and teach society's norms and rules.

Normal schools and academies **Normal schools** were one- or two-year training institutions for prospective teachers. The term "normal school" comes from the French model, *ecole normale*. Literally, as normal school graduates, teachers were expected to uphold and teach society's norms and rules.[66]

The first normal schools were actually secondary schools that prepared teachers for elementary schools; they were not college-level institutions. Most of their students had only an elementary education. Because a high proportion of normal school students needed remediation, the curriculum included an eclectic mix of basic subject matter and pedagogy. Normal schools operated locally and enrolled neighborhood students who would teach for community schools.[67]

Prospective teachers could also receive training in academies. The academy teacher training program was entirely academic because no professional body of teaching knowledge existed at the time. In these institutions, lecturers taught principles of teaching and school management primarily by using personal anecdotes drawn almost entirely from their own school experiences. Future teachers reviewed elementary school subjects and advanced academic studies.[68]

Because education was a state responsibility, each state decided how to prepare teachers for its public schools. By 1860, nine states had established state normal schools. By 1865, the United States had 22 state normal schools. After that time, public and private teacher training schools grew rapidly.

Teachers' colleges In the late nineteenth century, colleges and universities claimed the right to prepare new teachers. To compete with colleges, normal schools transformed themselves by adopting the newly developed accrediting and professional standards. They also raised their admissions standards, requiring all applicants to have a high school diploma, and extended their teacher training programs to two years for elementary school teachers and four years for high school teachers. They added research, liberal arts departments, and professors to their organizations. In short, they become teachers' colleges.[69]

2-3b Teacher Education in the Twentieth Century

In the late nineteenth and early twentieth centuries, American universities began to develop more sophisticated teacher preparation programs. Given that only 4 percent of the college-aged population attended college in 1900, college and universities saw teacher preparation as a possible source of students and income and competed to enroll them.[70]

Until 1900, education studies were largely devoted to history and philosophy of education, teaching methods, and school management. After 1900, because high school teaching depended on mastering a subject or discipline, teacher education began to include more advanced content, including testing and measurement, educational philosophy, school surveys, and educational research. By 1915, a majority of colleges provided teacher education coursework.[71]

In 2006, Arthur Levine, former president of Columbia University Teachers College and current president of the Woodrow Wilson National Fellowship Foundation at Princeton, NJ, surveyed principals and found that 60 percent thought education schools were doing a good job in preparing future teachers in mastery of subjects, understanding of how students learn, ability to use different pedagogies, and capacity to implement state standards.[72] Levine also found that strong teacher preparation programs integrate and balance academic and clinical instruction.

A telling anecdote highlights the importance of connecting teacher preparation theory and practice. As one teacher education alumnus reported, "I could talk about [influential psychiatrist] Carl Jung, scaffolding, cooperative learning groups, [and] the advantages of constructivism," but had no idea what to do "when Johnny goes nuts in the back of the class, or when Lisa comes in abused, or when Sue hasn't eaten in three days."[73]

Today's schools of education are in the business of preparing teachers for a new world in which all students are expected to learn to high levels. Joining teaching theory with real-world application and practice as well as expert supervision and detailed, timely feedback gives future teachers the basic knowledge and skills necessary to ensure their effectiveness in the modern-day classroom.

Did You Get It?

Teaching has developed over the past two centuries. Pick the most accurate statement of the following.

- **a.** The 1800s, an era of tremendous growth in many areas, including scientific knowledge and industrial and mechanical development, required a work force that was extremely well-educated, even if the subjects themselves were fairly basic.
- **b.** Modern American teachers have to understand how to reach each student as a learner who may come from a low-income family, be working well below grade level, speak English as a second language, or have a physical or cognitive disability.
- **c.** Due to Governor Clinton's understanding that public education was of central importance to America's future, the first "normal schools" to train teachers were four-year college-level institutions.
- **d.** In order to attract male students to teaching, by the late 1800s, normal schools transformed themselves into universities granting terminal (Ph. D., usually) degrees.

Take the full quiz on CourseMate.

2-4 Research Studies Relate Teacher Preparation to Teaching Quality, Student Achievement, and Teacher Longevity

In *Doing What Matters Most: Investing in Quality Teaching*, Linda Darling-Hammond concludes that reviews of more than 200 studies contradict the myth that "anyone can teach" and that "teachers are born and not made":

> Teachers who are fully prepared and certified in both their discipline and in education are more highly rated and are more successful with the students than are teachers without preparation, and those with greater training . . . are more effective than those with less.[74]

2-4a Teacher and Teaching Quality, Teacher Preparation, and Student Achievement

Darling-Hammond's research connects effective teacher preparation and teaching behaviors to student achievement. In a national survey, Darling-Hammond found that factors such as student poverty, minority status, and language background appear less important in predicting individual achievement levels than "teacher quality" variables. Fully certified teachers who had a college major in the subject they were teaching had a greater positive impact on student achievement than could be predicted from students' poverty, minority status, or language. Similarly, teacher preparation had a stronger connection with student achievement than class size, overall spending, or teacher salaries, even after taking students' backgrounds into account.[75]

In addition, Darling-Hammond and University of Washington professor John Bransford studied the research on the relationship between student learning and teacher education. They found that the following teachers' personal attributes and teaching effectiveness and teacher preparation factors related to increased student achievement[76]:

- The teacher's verbal ability
- The teacher's knowledge of the content and understanding of how to teach it to a diverse range of students
- Education coursework on teaching methods in the teacher's discipline, the ways in which students learn and develop, and assessment
- The teacher's scores on state licensing exams that measure both basic skills and teaching knowledge
- Teaching behaviors including purposefully, diagnostically, and skillfully using a broad repertoire of approaches that respond to student and curricular needs, and giving student opportunities to learn criterion material
- The teacher's ongoing voluntary professional learning
- The teacher's enthusiasm for learning
- The teacher's flexibility, creativity, and adaptability
- Amount of teaching experience (teachers with fewer than three years of classroom practice are less effective, although there are few gains from experience to effectiveness after this point)
- The teacher asking students higher-order thinking questions and probing their responses
- The teacher's class sizes, planning time, opportunities to work with colleagues, and curricular resources
- The interaction among these variables

Darling-Hammond believes that effective teacher education requires students to integrate and relate knowledge of the learners' characteristics with knowledge of the subject taught, and then to connect both of these factors to the relevant teaching practices. Only when these three dimensions—the learner, the subject, and the pedagogy—overlap and interact in professional practice can effective teaching and learning occur.

2-4b Learning How to Teach Well

In 2003, the Education Commission of the States reviewed the entire body of teacher preparation research to see its findings and determine policy implications. The members of the Commission found that teachers' subject matter knowledge, preparation in how to teach a particular subject, and core teaching skills such as how to manage a classroom, assess student learning, and develop curriculum are all supported by research as making key contributions to effective teaching.[77]

Likewise, in a study on mathematics teaching, Dan Goldhaber and Dominic Brewer concluded that the effects of teacher licensure on student achievement are greater than the effects of having a content major in the field; this finding suggests that what licensed teachers learn about teaching methods, in education coursework and in practice, adds to their actual abilities in the classroom.[78] In another study that gathered data for more than 2,800 students, David Monk determined that courses in methods of teaching math and science shared the same positive relationship to student achievement as actual content preparation in those fields. In mathematics, additional teaching methods courses had "more powerful effects" than additional preparation in the content area.[79]

The results in several other research reports reinforce these findings. For example, the National Research Council's Division of Behavioral and Social Sciences and Education found that effective teaching requires teachers with a deep knowledge of the subject, an understanding of how people learn, and an ability to use principles of learning and teaching to stimulate student learning and achievement.[80]

In another study, an American Educational Research Association Panel of nationally recognized scholars analyzed the empirical evidence related to practices and policies in preservice U.S. teacher education. They found that education programs that produce successful teachers include collaborative arrangements between university programs and local school districts—known as **professional development schools** (PDSs)—that have a positive impact on K-12 students in measurable ways, such as increases in standardized test scores.[81] They also found positive correlations between licensure and student achievement, especially in mathematics education. These results led the Panel to conclude that licensure in the field, gained by university-based teacher preparation, is a predictor of effective teaching and student achievement.[82]

professional development schools (PDSs) Education programs that include collaborative arrangements between university programs and local school districts that produce successful teachers.

Similarly, the Center for the Study of Teaching and Policy analyzed 57 studies published in peer-reviewed journals. Researchers found that a teacher's pedagogical preparation—that is, training in how to teach—had a positive impact on both teaching practice and student achievement. The report concludes, "The solution [to becoming an effective teacher] is more complicated than simply requiring a major or more subject matter courses."[83]

2-4c Preparedness and Teaching Longevity

Teachers' ages and years in their career are major influences on their decisions whether and when to leave the profession.[84] Beginning teachers leave their classrooms at higher rates than do colleagues with more teaching experience. In his seminal 2003 investigation, Richard Ingersoll, a University of Pennsylvania professor, observed that 14 percent of beginning teachers left after one year, and another 10 percent left after the second year; thus a cumulative total of 24 percent of all new teachers had abandoned teaching after only two years in the classroom. After five years, fully 46 percent of the original teaching pool had exited the profession (see Figure 2.1).[85]

Importantly for prospective teachers, research finds that well-prepared graduates who can show competence in the classroom are more likely to remain in teaching and contribute to developing a strong professional learning community in their schools. In findings that reinforce Ingersoll's, Jianping Shen, a professor at Western Michigan University, examined new teacher attrition rates five years after college graduation and found that teachers with no pedagogical training were three times more likely to leave teaching during any given year. By comparison, those who completed student teaching, acquired certification, and participated in a new teacher induction program were four times more likely to stay in teaching than those who had no training. Likewise, Donald Boyd, an economist who studies teacher labor markets and school finance, and his colleagues' investigation of New York City's new

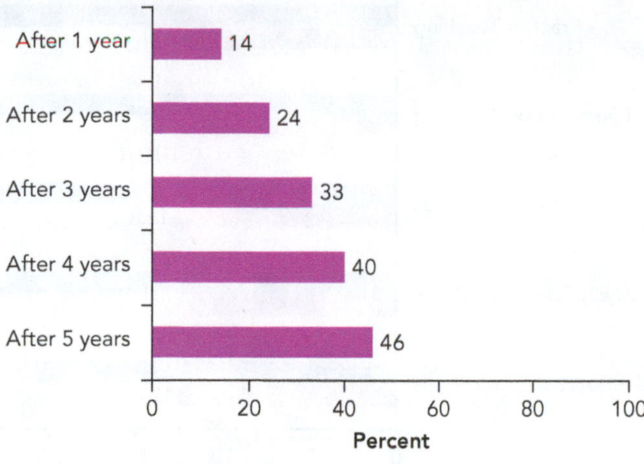

FIGURE 2.1 Cumulative Percentage of Beginning Teachers Leaving the Profession

Source: Ingersoll, R. (2003). Is there really a teacher shortage? Retrieved December 12, 2006, from http://www.ncctq.org/issueforums/atrisk/presentations/keynoteIngersoll.ppt, Beginning Teacher Attrition (Cumulative Percent Teachers Having Left Teaching Occupation, by Years of Experience).

teachers determined that the more effective teachers—regardless of preparation pathway—tended to remain in teaching, whereas those who were less effective were more likely to leave.[86] More specifically, Richard Ingersoll found that when first-year teachers' preparation includes five key elements—training in selection and use of instructional materials, training in child psychology and learning theory, observation of other classes, feedback on teaching, and practice teaching—cut the attrition rate for those teachers in half (see Reflect & Discuss).[87]

Reflect & Discuss

Figure 2.2 compares the percentage of novice teachers leaving the classroom after one year and their various preparation experiences. As the figure shows, 25 percent of new teachers without practice teaching left the profession after the first year, as compared with 11.6 percent of those new teachers who successfully completed practice teaching. Using the figure, answer and discuss the following questions.

A. What teacher preparation areas have the most impact in reducing new teacher attrition?

B. What specific information or insights might novice teachers have gained in each of the five teacher preparation experiences that might have helped them be more successful than their colleagues who lacked those experiences?

C. In which teacher preparation courses will you be receiving these five professional education and related experiences?

What the research shows The research on teacher preparation and teaching effectiveness is clear and consistent. High-quality preservice teacher preparation provides beginning teachers with the knowledge and skills needed for effective teaching in today's diverse classrooms. Effective teachers know their subjects very well, and they know how to teach them so that students learn and increase their measured achievement. Teachers understand and apply knowledge of child and adolescent development to motivate and engage students. They are able to diagnose individual learning needs. They know how to make their classroom a safe and stimulating learning environment. In addition, when prospective teachers have sufficient opportunities to practice their learning in real classroom settings with effective supervision from experienced teachers and mentors who give them accurate, detailed, real-time feedback, both they and their students are more likely to be successful.

In short, although content knowledge is essential, by itself it cannot ensure that the teacher is able to teach or that his or her students will learn.

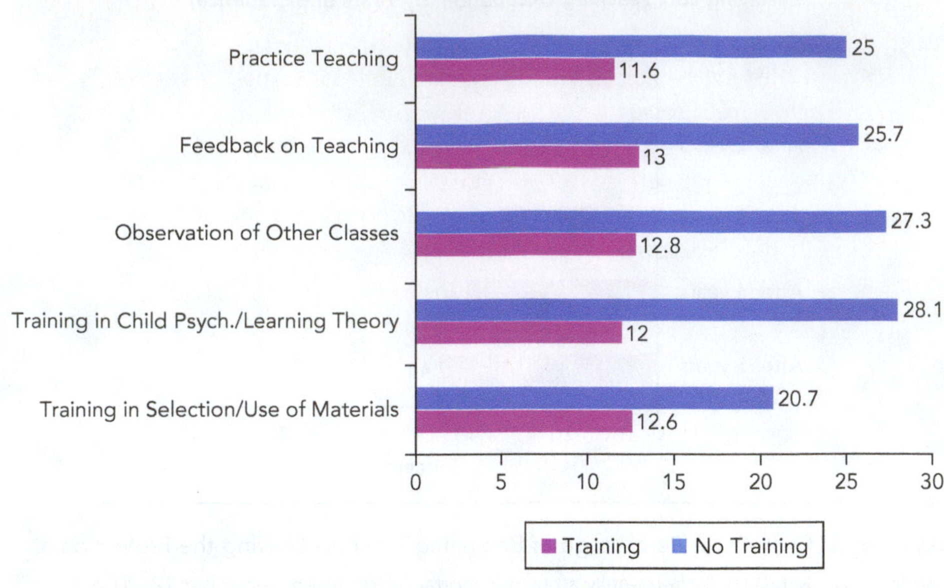

FIGURE 2.2 Teacher Preparation Reduces Attrition of First-Year Teachers

Source: Darling-Hammond, L., & Sykes, G. (2003). Wanted: A national teachers supply policy for the right way to meet the "highly qualified teacher" challenge. Education Policy Analysis Archives, 11 (33), p. 24. Used by permission of the author.

Did You Get It?

There is a myth about teaching: Anyone can teach [because] teachers are born and not made. Your analysis of this myth indicates that

- **a.** Virtually all of us teach at some point or another in our lives, be we parents, employees, supervisors, friends—the skill just needs to be developed.
- **b.** Many of us at some point or another do find ourselves informally teaching, but to do it day in and day out, very well to diverse learners requires specialized education and training.
- **c.** If you don't have the appropriate personality, you can't teach, no matter how committed you are to becoming a teacher.
- **d.** Teaching reflects innate personality traits, and any talk about spending money on improving teacher salaries, class sizes, and school quality is a waste of scarce funding that could be better spent on law enforcement.

Take the full quiz on CourseMate.

2-5 The Rationale for State Licensure of Teachers and State Licensure Practices

licensure and **certification** Indicate the state's formal approval of teaching candidates for professional practice. These two terms are often used interchangeably.

If students are to be held to high standards, their teachers must also be held to high standards. **Licensure** and **certification** indicate the state's formal approval of teaching candidates for professional practice. These two terms are often used interchangeably.

States have a compelling interest in setting meaningful teacher standards. Students and communities cannot afford to work with unqualified teachers. We expect our schools—when successful—to provide benefits to society that go beyond the sum of those conferred upon individual students.

Similarly, states license individual teachers and accredit their teacher preparation programs. Without strong, meaningful, and well-enforced licensure and accreditation requirements, not only will districts lack important information about the teacher candidates, but parents will lack important information about the individuals to whom they entrust their children. Likewise, states will lack the policy tools needed to encourage improvements in teacher training and make quality teachers available to all schools.

2-5a Brief History of Teacher Licensure

Nineteenth-century teachers usually achieved licensure or certification by taking an examination administered by the local employing school system or county board of education. The number of education courses the candidate had taken did not matter. In 1898, only four states had state-centralized licensing.[88]

In the late nineteenth and early twentieth centuries, as the United States evolved from a rural to an industrialized nation, responsibility for teachers' professional qualifications moved from the localities to the states. By 1933, 42 states had centralized their teaching licensing at the state level. At that time, completion of most teacher education and other courses became the key criterion for awarding certification.[89]

Reflect & Discuss

The research on teacher education clearly supports the need for future teachers to learn both content knowledge and pedagogical skills.

A. As a class, divide into two groups. One group will consider those characteristics of the teacher as an individual that research finds contribute to teaching effectiveness. The other group will consider those teaching behaviors and practices that research finds increase student achievement. Each group will take 10 minutes to discuss, list, and describe the characteristics and behaviors in their area of study. It will then report its findings to the entire class.

B. Working as a group, discuss which characteristics or behaviors a person must develop through personal and professional experiences, feedback, and reflection, and which can be taught in a classroom. Which characteristics and behaviors need both personal and classroom learning?

Educational Testing Service's (ETS) Praxis II and National Evaluation Systems (NES) develop most of these licensing tests, which measure basic skills, content knowledge, and knowledge of teaching strategies. States often use licensure tests for several purposes: for admission to teacher education programs, as a condition of graduation, and for initial teacher certification.[90] Thus licensing tests provide the public with assurance that the person meets the minimal qualifications to be a teacher.

2-5b State Variations in Licensing Teachers

Wide state-by-state variations exist in teacher licensure requirements.[91] Forty-six states require teacher candidates to pass a basic skills test in order to receive a license.[92] States differ on how much content and pedagogical knowledge they expect their beginning teachers to have. For example, New York requires new teachers to pass exams in general liberal arts knowledge, teaching pedagogy, and pedagogical content knowledge and general subject knowledge. Meanwhile, neighboring New Jersey assesses only subject matter knowledge.[93]

Research findings show teaching requires knowledge of subject, pedagogy, and learner.

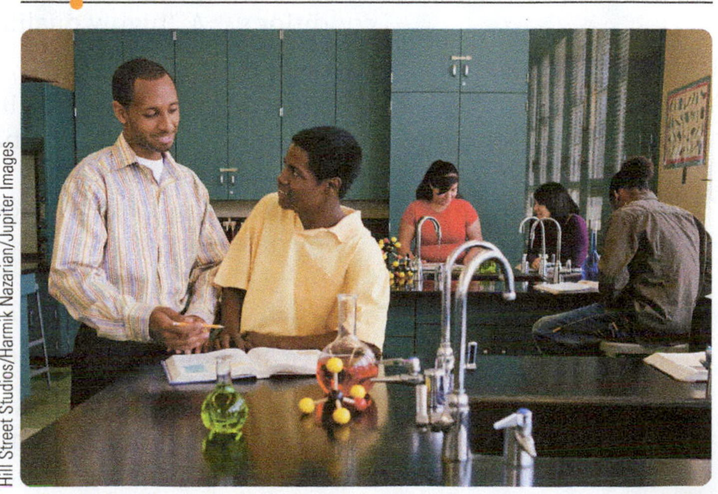

Hill Street Studios/Harmik Nazarian/Jupiter Images

2-5c How Does a New Teacher Become Licensed?

"Are you licensed?" is one of the first questions school district employers will ask candidates applying for teaching positions. Becoming licensed or certified usually means the individual has completed the appropriate academic training and satisfied the requirements specified by state procedures and regulations. Each state has its own specific rules and regulations for teacher certification, but most require a combination of some or all of the following[94]:

- *Formal academic training.* General elementary teachers need a major or minor in education and must have taken college-level courses in math, science, English, and social studies. To become a secondary teacher, one usually is required to major in the subject area to be taught.
- *Completion of an accredited teacher preparation program.* Traditional college and university teacher education programs are designed so that students can work toward the major or minor coursework while also taking teacher preparation courses. These programs include practicum (a required number of hours) and a student-teaching internship, usually a semester in length. Many education programs lead to teacher certification upon graduation. One-year teacher preparation programs after a person has obtained a bachelor's degree are also available.
- *Statewide assessments and testing.* Each state requires teachers to pass a series of tests that evaluate their basic liberal arts knowledge as well as their teaching skills. Many states use ETS's Praxis series or the NES tests. Some states allow candidates to take the test within a year or two of being granted a provisional license.
- *Additional checks.* Many states now require applicants to complete a background check and undergo fingerprinting to ensure that only persons without a criminal record are working with children.

Because each state has different licensure or certification requirements, it is best to contact the education department or licensing office in the state where one plans to teach for more information about its teacher-related requirements.

2-5d "Highly Qualified" Teachers

In the past, many states required a bachelor's degree in a content area for teacher certification,[95] but these standards were not always enforced. In 2002, however, the federal government's No Child Left Behind Act (NCLB) specified new definitions of "highly qualified" teachers and required all teachers of core academic subjects to be "highly qualified."

According to NCLB, teachers are "highly qualified" when they meet three conditions.[96] A "highly qualified" teacher has:

- A college degree.
- Full state certification or licensure, which specifically does not include any certification or licensure that has been "waived on an emergency, temporary, or provisional basis."
- Demonstrable content knowledge in the subject the teacher will be teaching or, for elementary teachers, in at least reading, writing, and mathematical ability and teaching skills. Middle and secondary school teachers do not have to demonstrate teaching skills.

Teachers may demonstrate their content knowledge in several ways:

- New elementary teachers must pass a state test of literacy and numeracy.
- New secondary teachers must either pass a rigorous test in the subject area or have a college major in that subject.

- Veteran teachers may either pass the state test, or have a college major, or demonstrate content knowledge through some other uniformly applied process designed by the state.

Not everyone believes that NCLB's "highly qualified" definition actually ensures teacher quality or teaching effectiveness.[97] For example, by this definition, only elementary school teachers must demonstrate their ability to teach. Ironically, some have called this "highly qualified" teacher requirement "an exercise in meeting the lowest common denominator of quality."[98] Although this mandate does improve the odds that low-income and minority students will have a teacher who has studied the subject he or she is teaching, the law does not guarantee that the 3 million teachers in classrooms nationwide will know *how* to teach. "Highly qualified" teacher does not mean "high quality" teaching.

2-5e Research on Teacher Certification and Student Achievement

Although states try to increase teacher and teaching quality by setting licensure and certification requirements, the literature on the relationship between teacher certification and student achievement has produced mixed and controversial results. On the one hand, Darling-Hammond and colleagues have found that teacher preparation and certification are the strongest correlates of students' math and reading achievement.[99] On the other hand, little research on teacher testing or licensing prior to 2005 meets the standard for scientific evaluation.[100] The research that did meet this standard has yielded tentative and inconclusive results.[101]

Nevertheless, the emerging studies on teacher certification and student achievement are bringing a fuller understanding closer. Overall, the teacher certification evidence suggests that existing credentialing systems do not distinguish very well between effective and ineffective teachers. Wide variation in teacher effectiveness exists within each certification type with effective (and ineffective) teachers coming from both traditional and nontraditional certification routes.[102] Therefore, teacher certification may be a necessary, but not a sufficient, condition for increasing student achievement.

Additionally, research finds that teacher experience, rather than type of certification, tends to make a difference in increasing student achievement. Many studies document improved student achievement with increases in teacher experience during the first three to five years in the classroom with virtually no additional gains for experience beyond the first five years.[103]

Did You Get It?

A state has a compelling interest in licensing teachers. Based upon the concept that teaching is a profession with obligations to society, which reason is most important?

a. Successful schools benefit society in ways that go beyond the sum of the benefits to individual pupils.

b. Parents need to know about the people to whom they are entrusting their children.

c. Children need to be safe with their teachers: not just from harm, but positively, in the sense that teachers will help shape them into their full human potential.

d. The state needs policy tools to improve teacher training.

Take the full quiz on CourseMate.

2-6 Organizations That Support Teaching Professionals

Over the years, the rules governing teachers' behavior and working conditions have evolved. For example, a 1922 Wisconsin teacher's contract forbade a female teacher from dating, marrying, staying out past 8 p.m., smoking, drinking, loitering in ice cream parlors, dyeing her hair, and using lipstick or mascara.[104] More significantly, until the mid-twentieth century, married women teachers were not allowed to earn tenure.[105] Professional organizations for teachers, such as the NEA and the American Federation of Teachers (AFT), have long worked to improve teachers' quality of work life and advance teaching as a profession. National accrediting associations, the Interstate New Teacher Assessment and Support Consortium (InTASC), and the National Board for Professional Teaching Standards (NBPTS) have also increased teacher professionalization.

2-6a Teachers' Unions

With over 4.6 million teachers and paraprofessionals nationwide and providing over $92 million to political candidates in the 1989–2012 election cycles combined,[106] teachers' organizations—the NEA and the AFT—have become one of the most influential special interest groups in national and state politics. Often referred to as unions, these teachers' organizations are considered powerful because of their size, resources, and their statutory authority in certain states to negotiate the contents of collective bargaining agreements with district school boards about teachers' compensation, working conditions, and benefits.

union A group of employees who come together voluntarily with the shared goal of improving their working conditions and having a voice at their place of employment.

collective bargaining A formal process that gives union members a voice in decisions regarding education policy and practices in the school and district workplace.

Broadly defined, a **union** is a group of employees who come together voluntarily with the shared goal of improving their working conditions and having a voice at their place of employment. **Collective bargaining** is a formal process that gives union members a voice in decisions that spell out many facets of education policy and practice in the school and district workplace and the day-to-day interactions among teachers, students, and administrators. Union officials represent their teacher members in legal contract discussions to determine salary, benefits, hours, and working conditions. These may include class schedules, health insurance, layoffs, pay for special duties, seniority, salary schedule, duty-free lunch, hours of work, sick leave, transfers, pupil discipline, parental complaints, and grievance procedures. Collective bargaining negotiations also help protect teachers from receiving unfair treatment. The state controls the legal right to collectively bargain.

The National Education Association (NEA) and the American Federation of Teachers (AFT) Started in 1857, the NEA is the largest professional organization and largest labor union in the United States. In addition to teachers, it represents education support professionals, higher education faculty, school administrators, retired educators, and education students who plan to become teachers. In 2009, the NEA had 3.3 million members, a staff of 555, and an annual budget exceeding $300 million.[107] But an estimated loss of 308,000 full-time members by 2013–2014 as a result of the national economic downturn and young teachers not joining because they do not expect to remain in teaching as a career has reduced its membership.[108]

Founded in 1916, the AFT, an affiliate of the AFL-CIO, represents more than 1.5 million pre-K through 12th-grade teachers and other educators, paraprofessionals, and retirees in more than 3,000 local affiliates nationwide.[109]

At various times during the late twentieth century, the NEA and AFT considered merging their two teacher organizations, but irreconcilable differences at the national level prevented it. Mergers did occur in certain states. Meanwhile, the two unions have established the AFT-NEA Joint Council to develop common positions on issues of mutual interest.

Teacher Unions and Education Reform The NEA and AFT are trying to define their place in today's education reform. Both groups believe that teachers should be held accountable for their students' academic performance, and they want an accountability system that does not limit or distort instruction. For example, an NEA's 2011 policy statement proposed using student achievement test scores as part of teacher evaluation and accountability and to also include a mix of observations and a process for supporting teachers with below-par evaluations.[110] Controversy remains, however, about how to determine teacher accountability and what the outcomes from that assessment should be.[111]

Likewise, the AFT acknowledges that teachers and teaching must change, and instructional effectiveness depends on evidence of adequate student learning. When the teacher's work is inadequate, the AFT asserts, the teacher or the school as a whole is responsible for providing additional, refocused opportunities to learn.[112] Rather than protecting ineffective teachers from accountability, the AFT wants to substantially improve teacher evaluation practices to include rigorous reviews by trained experts, peer evaluators, and principals based on professional teaching standards, best practices, and student achievement.[113] The AFT also asserts that student achievement—including student test scores based on valid and reliable assessment that show students' real growth while in the teacher's classroom—should be an essential component of teacher evaluation.[114] Despite the many complexities involved in making this intention into a reality, willingness to consider teacher accountability for student learning is an important ethical and professional advance in teacher unions' thinking.

With their impact on district policies, unions and teacher contracts have become a flash point in contemporary policy debates. Advocates of teachers' unions argue that unions are necessary to protect teachers from arbitrary and potentially unfair administrator decisions and to help teachers gain the compensation, benefits, and working conditions that their important and challenging work deserves. In contrast, opponents believe that teachers' unions protect ineffective teachers and thereby harm the education system. Antiunion sentiment is growing among the public—largely because they perceive that teachers' unions block school reform and accountability—putting teachers' interests ahead of students.[115]

Additionally, some critics assert that the NEA and AFT have been relying on government protection or regulation to promote their interests instead of providing better services at lower costs and opposing competition in their labor markets by combating vouchers, tuition tax credits, contracting out, home schooling, and lowering the compulsory minimum age for leaving school. Others wonder if the AFT's and the NEA's "good faith" plans for reform actually represent the unions' sincere effort to get in front and lead reform rather than have reform "done" to them. Likewise, certain detractors object to what they view as unions advancing certain "quality of life" objectives, such as allegedly promoting a gay rights agenda. The organizations' internal practices have also been subject to critical scrutiny.[116]

Research on teachers' unions has found mixed evidence regarding the unions' impact on school districts and students. Researchers generally find that union involvement is associated with increased spending, and that the typical student in unionized districts performs better academically.[117] The few studies that find negative effects of unions on student achievement tend to suffer from weak methodology and measurement error.[118] Research also finds that the presence of teachers' unions has an impact on district spending for policies such as higher salaries for teachers and administrators, smaller class sizes, and longer preparation periods—all of which are costly to the district.[119]

Since the 1960s, the NEA and AFT have been major players in public education, and they vigorously act on behalf of the employees they represent. Increasingly, teachers' unions' public statements, publications, and professional development reflect their recognition that teachers are accountable for student learning and accept the use of student achievement test results as part of teacher evaluation data. School leaders should take them at their word. Only by working together—with teachers and their representatives—will public schools be able to drive teacher and teaching quality, advance student learning, and bring about meaningful school improvement.

2-6b Should Teachers Strike?

Teachers face ethical dilemmas when they are expected to behave in ways about which they have conflicted feelings. Participating in a teachers' strike is one example. Acting professionally in problematic situations involves thoughtfully addressing issues of personal, moral, and ethical significance.

strikes Employee work stoppages in support of demands made on their employer, such as higher pay or improved conditions.

Causes of teacher strikes

Between 1918 and 1960, more than 120 teacher **strikes**—that is, employee work stoppages in support of demands made on their employer, such as higher pay or improved conditions—occurred. Usually, teachers were responding to economic hardships, such as lagging or unpaid salaries.[120]

Teachers also strike to express their strong objections to educational policy and practices over which they feel powerless to influence.[121] They want their concerns and ideas heard in their schools' decision making about educational programs and improved educational services for students.

The legality of strikes varies from state to state. Teachers who decide to strike in states where this practice is illegal can be fired from their jobs. Likewise, the public often reacts negatively to striking teachers. They accuse teachers of acting illegally, victimizing children, violating their contracts, disregarding their districts' poor financial circumstances, and following small groups of "malcontents."[122]

What strikes can accomplish

Teachers strike because it produces results. Having the legal right to strike affords teachers greater power to increase the dollar value of their work. Even where strikes are illegal, teachers who strike win better salaries and working conditions. A national 43-state analysis conducted in 1996 found evidence that when teachers go on strike, whether legally or illegally, or have a neutral party arbitrate their dispute, they win salary increases of 3.6 to 11.5 percent and reduce class hours between 37 and 70 minutes per day. In contrast, fact-finding missions and voluntary arbitration have no significant influences on outcomes.[123]

The dilemma for teachers

Considering whether to participate in a strike requires teachers to ponder several dilemmas involving their personal and professional code of ethics, their employment, their colleagues, their students, and their administrators.[124] For professionals, the first ethical principle is "Do no harm." Teachers must consider all of the following as they decide:

- *Personal/professional ethics.* As individuals and as professionals, teachers develop a set of ethical guidelines that influence their thoughts and actions about what is "right and appropriate." Teachers' understanding of

American Education Spotlight

Dennis Brack/Landov

Albert Shanker

Albert Shanker

Albert Shanker transformed American education, arguably as influential in the twentieth century as Horace Mann and John Dewey had been generations earlier.

At a time when organizing public sector employees was considered virtually impossible (because the law forbade most civic employees from striking), Albert Shanker (1928–1997) morphed the 2,500-member New York Teachers Guild into a 70,000-member United Federation of Teachers (UFT) in New York City. The union worked with the city to recruit qualified teachers, improve challenging schools, reduce class sizes, and strengthen the curriculum. Eventually, Shanker became president of the 900,000-plus-member national teachers' union, the American Federation of Teachers (AFT). Under his tenure, the AFT significantly boosted teacher salaries, equalized pay between men and women, ensured minimum standards in schools (such as limiting class sizes), and persuaded the National Educational Association (NEA), the nation's most powerful teachers' union, to support collective bargaining. In addition, Shanker encouraged his membership to embrace necessary reform. He endorsed provisions for ousting incompetent teachers, promoted public school choice, and championed the standards movement.

The son of Russian Jewish immigrants, Shanker was raised in New York City. Because the family primarily spoke Yiddish at home, young Al did not know any English when he began school. He quickly fell behind, lost interest in school, and received failing grades. As a young child, he got into trouble frequently. His mother took him to counseling, and some relatives suggested his parents send him to reform school. Despite this, young Al developed an affectionate relationship with his grandmother who treated him like a prince and told him that he was exceptional and would do great things.

In the 1950s, Shanker began his education career as a substitute mathematics teacher in East Harlem. In 1959, he went to work for the Teachers' Guild as a labor organizer. In 1964, he was elected president of New York City's UFT.

In the late 1960s, when it was illegal for public employees to go on strike, Shanker and his colleagues convinced several thousand NYC teachers to break the law and risk being fired. The series of strikes paralyzed the city's 900 public schools for 55 days. Because the school board could not dismiss all the demonstrating teachers, it retreated and eventually recognized the union's right to bargain on teachers' behalf. Shanker was jailed for his role.

Collective bargaining substantially changed the teaching culture. Accustomed to taking orders, receiving low wages, eating lunch while supervising students, and having to bring a doctor's note if they were out sick, collective bargaining brought teachers higher salaries, dignity, and self-respect. Some called Shanker, "the George Washington of the teaching profession."

Shaker became head of the national union, the AFT, from 1974 to 1997 and became a leading education reformer. He proposed a rigorous national competency exam for new teachers, devised a plan to give teachers with superior performance higher salary, and suggested what would become the National Board for Professional Teaching Standards—all part of an affirmative vision to professionalize teaching. In what some call his greatest impact, Shanker favored a system of education standards, testing, and accountability comparable to that of most leading European and Asian nations. To advance this goal, Shanker joined with governors and business leaders to push for meaningful educational improvement.

Some critics observed that Shanker was much more skillful than NEA leaders in packaging and selling the union interests as the public interest. But despite his rhetoric about higher standards, skeptics found no significant differences between AFT and NEA contracts on so-called reform issues—and that Shanker's reform issues had safely noncontroversial, poll-driven popularity. Nonetheless, critics admit that Shanker deserved credit for gaining the widespread perception that the teachers' unions were not obstacles to education reform and preventing the two teachers' unions from merging (Shanker agreed to merge with the NEA only if the combined organization affiliated with the AFL-CIO—an idea that the NEA membership rejected.)

Shanker's charisma, vision, and talents converted New York City's teachers' union into one of the most powerful trade unions in the nation, and then he used his platform to shape labor and educational policy across the country and worldwide. Today, the life of every teacher in America has been touched by Shanker's own.

Sources: Kahlenberg, R. D. (2007). Tough liberal: *Albert Shanker and the battles over schools, unions, race, and democracy.* New York: Columbia University Press; Lieberman, M. (2000). *The teacher unions: How they sabotage education reform and why?* San Francisco: L Encounter Books. Retrieved from http://eric.ed.gov/PDFS/ED468097.pdf; Mosle, S. (1998, January 4). The lives they lived: Albert Shanker; labor's love lost. New York: *New York Times Magazine.* Retrieved from http://www.nytimes.com/1998/01/04/magazine/the-lives-they-lived-albert-shanker-labor-s-love-lost.html?ref=albertshanker; Mosle, S. (2007, October 1). The man who transformed American education. *Slate.* Retrieved from http://www.slate.com/id/2175023/; Steinberg, J. (1997, March 26). Shanker is eulogized as a towering educator. New York: *The New York Times,* N.Y./Region. Retrieved from http://www.nytimes.com/1997/03/25/nyregion/shanker-is-eulogized-as-a-towering-educator.html?ref=albertshanker.

professional stewardship and their personal values play into how they define the correct behavior in this situation.

- *Employment.* If participating in a strike is not legal, teachers who strike may lose their jobs. An individual teacher must consider whether participating in an illegal walkout is worth the possibility of forfeiting one's employment (and perhaps future positions if the teacher cannot get a letter of recommendation from this employer).
- *Colleagues.* Some teachers interpret "collegiality" as having unquestioned loyalty, group solidarity, and the belief that teachers as professionals should not interfere in other teachers' business or criticize them or their practices, even at the expense of students' well-being. In the face of this "peer pressure," individual teachers may feel coerced into not "breaking ranks" with colleagues, even if they believe that such loyalty compromises students' needs and welfare.[125]
- *Students.* Teachers transmit societal values by providing formal instruction and by becoming role models. They may feel torn between advocating for improved professional benefits and meeting their responsibilities toward their students. Teachers are aware that their respect (or lack of it) toward school rules and commitment to their students' well-being sends them powerful messages about integrity and appropriate behavior.[126]
- *Administrators.* Walking out in a strike may place teachers in an adversarial relationship with their administrators and school boards. Teachers must consider whether participating in a strike is worth jeopardizing the collaborative and trusting relationship they have built with their principal and the school board (the teacher's actual employer).

Applying abstract ethical standards to actual situations is very difficult. When teachers are not sure how to act, they need to be able to rely on their own sense of what is right and appropriate as well as on the expressed and shared professional norms about what constitutes ethical behavior. Prospective educators—in fact, all educators—can develop more mature ethical judgment when they reflect seriously on their own values, expectations, and professional norms as well as consider with colleagues how to act ethically and professionally in given situations.[127]

2-6c National Accreditation Organizations

Students in teacher education programs want to know that they are receiving the best possible preparation to become successful teachers. Completing an accredited teacher education program is one such guarantee.

For almost a century, professional accreditation has played a key role in quality assurance in medicine, and more recently, law, psychology, physical therapy, and other established professions. Its success is due—in large part—to an uncompromising expectation for preparation programs to apply high-quality and rigorous external standards. Receiving a public or private accrediting body's endorsement is one way that teacher education programs show their worth and assure the public that it will receive adequately prepared teachers. Like most other academic fields, **accreditation** in teacher education programs is a means of self-policing and quality control.

accreditation Applying high quality and rigorous external standards as a means of self-policing and quality control.

Formerly, two independent accrediting bodies served teacher education: the National Council for Accreditation of Teacher Education (NCATE) and the Teacher Education Accreditation Council (TEAC). Separately, each organization accredited undergraduate and graduate professional education programs at colleges and universities across the country. In October 2010, the two groups merged into the Council for the Accreditation of Educator Preparation (CAEP). In combining the best attributes of NCATE and TEAC, CAEP leaders believe they will raise the profession's stature.

NCATE, TEAC, and CAEP NCATE, founded in 1954, was an independent organization that had accredited more than half (656) of the United States' 1,200 college and university teacher education programs with more seeking its endorsement. Over two-thirds of the nation's new teacher graduates came from NCATE-accredited institutions. Based in Washington, DC, the group was a coalition of 33 member organizations of teacher education producers, consumers, and regulators, making NCATE the teaching profession's largest collective educational organization.[128]

TEAC, founded in 1997 as a reform-minded accreditor, had membership from a broad range of higher education institutions, from small liberal arts colleges to large research universities, mainly composed of representatives of teacher preparation institutions or their designees. TEAC was based in Washington, DC, and at the University of Delaware. Formed by a group of college presidents who wanted a less intensive teacher accreditation process than NCATE offered, TEAC presented an alternative approach.[129] As of 2008, TEAC had approved 80 teacher education programs with 100 more in the pipeline.[130]

Combined, the two organizations currently accredit almost 900 of the more than 1,400 teacher education institutions in the country. CAEP is designed in a way that education programs seeking or renewing accreditation will still have the opportunity to use the NCATE or TEAC systems with a common set of unified standards. Advancing its agenda, in February 2013, CAEP proposed teacher preparation standards that were fewer, more detailed, and more outcomes oriented than had previously been available in the 60 years of teacher college accreditation. It required programs to consider "value-added" test score growth data plus other measures to examine graduates' ability to increase P-12 students' academic achievement and to keep improving existing quality assurance measures. Notably, CAEP recommends that no teacher preparation program be accredited unless it is determined to have a satisfactory impact on student learning.[131]

Accreditation standards matter to prospective teachers because they define to educators and employing school districts how well prepared and ready the candidates will be to teach effectively in high-accountability environments with diverse students. And, if CAEP can advance teacher professionalization by having education schools review and evaluate their own programs in light of respected, relevant, externally validated professional standards in a flexible, cost-effective, and timely process, future teachers—and their students—stand to gain.

2-6d Interstate New Teacher Assessment and Support Consortium

Created in 1987, InTASC is a group of state education agencies and national educational organizations dedicated to reforming teachers' preparation, licensing, and ongoing professional development. InTASC standards outline what teachers should know and be able to do—the performances, essential knowledge, and critical dispositions—to ensure that every K-12 student will be ready to enter today's college or workforce. One basic premise guides its work: An effective teacher must be able to customize learning for learners with a range of individual differences and integrate content knowledge with students' specific strengths and needs to ensure that *all* students learn and perform at high levels.[132]

Updated in 2011 from the 1992 standards, InTASC aligns itself with the range of newly released standards for curriculum, professional development, and leadership from other professional education associations. By offering consistency among these documents, InTASC ensures that teachers have a coherent continuum of expectations from the first days in the classroom through accomplished practice and the conditions needed to support professional development along this continuum. In InTASC's view, only the degree of sophistication in performances, knowledge, and dispositions distinguishes the beginning from the accomplished teacher.

InTASC's philosophy asserts that teachers need to recognize that all learners come to school with varying experiences, abilities, talents, and prior learning as well as language, culture, and family and community values. These factors are assets that teachers can use to promote learning. To do this effectively, teachers must have a deeper understanding of their own frames of reference (e.g., culture, gender, language, abilities, ways of knowing), and their own potential biases and likely impact on expectations for and relationships with learners and their families. Also, teachers need to provide each student with multiple approaches to learning. Specifically, InTASC has developed a set of model core teaching standards that integrate cross-disciplinary skills (e.g., communication, collaboration, critical thinking, and technology use) and literacy building across the curriculum because of their importance for learners. Additionally, the core teaching standards help learners address interdisciplinary themes and adopt multiple perspectives in exploring ideas and solving problems. Teachers also learn how to develop and balance **formative** and **summative assessments** to make data-informed decisions about a learner's progress, adjust instruction as needed, provide feedback to the learner, and document the learner's progress against standards. Likewise, the standards stress teacher collaboration and new leadership roles to improve student learning and teachers' working conditions. Finally, InTASC provides ongoing technical assistance to states as they implement standards-based licensing systems.

formative assessments Tools that teachers use to promote student learning by collecting continuous and specific classroom feedback about students' areas of mastery and weakness and using this information to adjust instruction to create more learning.

summative assessments Tools that teachers use to assess whether or not students learned the required material or skills to the required level of competence.

2-6e National Board for Professional Teaching Standards

The NBPTS, established in 1987, operates a voluntary system to provide a national advanced teaching credential for most pre–K-12 teachers by assessing and certifying high-quality teaching. NBPTS sets high standards for what highly effective teachers know and do. Its goal is to improve the teaching profession and positively influence student learning. It complements but does not replace a state's teacher license. As of October 2012, nearly 100,000 teachers—about 2.5 percent of the profession—had earned their National Board Certification (NBC) in 25 fields.[133] In 2008, 49 percent of these board-certified teachers taught in high-needs schools where at least 40 percent of students received free or reduced-price lunches.[134]

The voluntary certification process The certification process connects teaching and student learning by having applicants complete 10 assessments that are reviewed by trained teachers in their certificate areas. These assessments give candidates the opportunity to demonstrate knowledge of their subject matter and pedagogy; manage and monitor student learning; systematically think about classroom practice and learn from experience; and participate in learning communities. These assessments include four portfolio entries that feature teaching practice in which candidates videotape and analyze their lessons to diagnose student learning difficulties, evaluate student data, and reflect on how to improve both the lesson and the learning and six constructed response exercises that assess content knowledge. The cutoff for passing is very high. In 2005, fewer than half of those candidates who sat for NBPTS certification for the first time ultimately achieved it.[135]

Notably, more minority teachers are earning national certification. Between 2005 and 2006, the number of African American teachers earning this credential rose by 24 percent, the number of Latino teachers increased by 13 percent, and the number of Native American teachers increased by 50 percent. Because African American, Latino, and Native American teachers are more likely to work in schools with minority populations and low-income families, this means more highly qualified NBC teachers are working in traditionally low-income, low-performing schools.[136]

With widespread national professional support from major education associations, governors, state legislators, and school boards,[137] virtually every state and more than 25 percent of all U.S. school districts have offered financial rewards or incentives for teachers seeking NBC.[138] However, in attempts to control spending during difficult economic times, the number of states providing financial incentives for teachers to earn national board certification—from $2,500 for the application to salary supplements for successful certification—dropped from 39 in 2005 to 24 in 2012.[139]

Research on NBPTS teachers The NBPTS has been under pressure to demonstrate that the millions of state and district dollars spent on bonuses for nationally certified teachers buy the likelihood of greater student learning. As of 2007, the NBPTS noted that 150 research studies had examined its effectiveness, and more than 75 percent have found positive effects on teacher performance and student learning, engagement, and achievement.[140]

Results from studies focusing on the influence of NBC on student achievement are mixed but generally positive. Sample sizes tend to be small, limiting the ability to generalize conclusions. Research is consistently positive about NBC's effect on teachers' instructional practices, professional development, and student achievement.[141] However, two major studies using large student samples found that students of board-certified teachers did not show statistically significant academic gains from working with these teachers.[142]

Gains from NBPTS certification Gains from NBPTS certification extend well beyond students' test scores. NBPTS certification provides a valid, reliable, and highly respected assessment and credentialing system to recognize "accomplished" teachers. It affords the teaching profession with a way to create stages to an otherwise "unstaged" profession, while keeping excellent teachers teaching.

Similarly, schools and school districts frequently use board-certified teachers for instructional leadership. They can model excellent classroom practice that increases students' learning, mentor novice teachers, provide professional development to their colleagues, serve as peer assessors, and work as curriculum coordinators. When used (and appropriately compensated) in these ways, board-certified teachers can help transform schools into high-achieving and professionally rewarding learning communities.

Did You Get It?

Teacher's organizations—such as the National Education Association (NEA) and the American Federation of Teachers (AFT)—are often controversial. A number of reasons for their controversial status are mentioned in your textbook. Which of the following is not mentioned?

- **a.** Teaching is still a gendered profession and as a society, we are still deeply ambivalent about women exercising authority (rather than influence) and asserting their needs, rather than nurturing other people.
- **b.** These organizations are very influential special interest groups in state and local politics.
- **c.** These organizations are seen as unwilling to hold teachers accountable for student learning, at least in so far as a teacher can control student learning.
- **d.** An increase in anti-union sentiment dovetails with a belief that teachers' unions advocate for teachers' interests over students' interests.

Take the full quiz on CourseMate.

2-7 Schools' Professional Culture and Teacher Retention

Teaching is the only profession without a built-in apprenticeship period. Schools expect new teachers to do the same job as 15-year veterans—a tall order. And new teacher initiation is often a trial by fire.[143]

As discussed earlier, teaching has an unusually high attrition rate with as many as 50 percent of new teachers leaving the field within their first five years on the job.[144] If school districts want to keep and develop the teachers they hire, schools need ways to support new teachers as they begin working and throughout their professional tenure.

InTASC

2-7a Induction, Mentoring, and Professional Development

The terms "induction" and "mentoring" are often used interchangeably. In reality, the two terms mean slightly different things.

induction A comprehensive, coherent, and sustained professional development process that the school district organizes to train, support, and retain new teachers.

mentoring A specific type of induction consisting of a collegial, supportive relationship developed between a veteran and a new teacher to ease the transition into the realities of daily classroom teaching.

Induction is a comprehensive, coherent, and sustained professional development process that the school district organizes to train, support, and retain new teachers. Good induction seamlessly moves new teachers into a lifelong learning program. Beginning before the first day of school and continuing through the first two or three years of teaching, induction includes new teacher orientation, support, and guidance programs.

Mentoring is a specific type of induction program. It consists of a collegial, supportive relationship developed between a veteran and a new teacher to ease the transition into the realities of daily classroom teaching. Typically, mentoring includes giving moral support and practical suggestions.

In both induction and mentoring, teachers "who know the ropes" help novices understand and successfully handle events happening in their classrooms and schools. These programs acculturate the new teachers, who use the guidance and practical advice to learn how to prevent and solve problems on their own. With a variety of caring and knowledgeable colleagues to help the novice make sense of the transition to teaching, develop new skills, and gain essential insights, a new teacher can quickly build competence and a feeling of "I can do this!" No wonder that more than half of the deans, faculty, alumni, and principals believe that inadequate induction and mentoring are among the key reasons why so many new teachers leave the profession.[145]

Induction programs provide caring, knowledgeable colleagues who help ease the transition into successful teaching.

Lon C. Diehl/PhotoEdit

Induction Effective induction programs recognize that the art and craft of teaching develops over time. Typically, induction programs focus on learning the district's culture—its philosophy, mission, policies, procedures, and goals—and improving the novice's teaching effectiveness.

No two induction programs are exactly alike. Effective induction programs may include any or all of the following components[146]:

- Offer seminars or classes for beginning teachers
- Provide study groups in which new teachers can network and build support, commitment, and leadership in a learning community
- Furnish a mentor who is a successful teacher in the same subject area as the new teacher and who is willing to put in the time and patience to help the novice
- Supply common planning time with other teachers in their subject area
- Give common planning time with a mentor
- Participate with a network of teachers, such as one organized by the school, an outside agency, within the larger school division, or over the Internet
- Offer regular supportive communication with the principal, other administrators, or department chair
- Present a structure for modeling effective teaching during professional development activities

Strong induction programs understand that new teachers want to become good at what they are doing and experience success. They also want to connect with colleagues and contribute to a group. Therefore, the best induction programs structure new teachers' ties within learning communities that allow new and veteran teachers to interact respectfully and to value one another's contributions. Teachers remain in teaching when they belong to professional learning communities based in high-quality interpersonal relationships founded on trust and respect.[147]

Mentoring Although mentoring has become the most popular teacher induction practice during the past 20 years, the program formats vary widely. They may be a more or less structured coaching relationship. Mentoring may consist of only one hasty meeting during the first week of school, or it may involve regularly scheduled, weekly hour-long meetings during time provided apart from teachers' regular teaching schedules. Some mentoring programs include any teachers new to the schools; others focus solely on teachers new to the profession. Certain school districts prepare the mentors to increase their effectiveness— devoting from 40 to 100 hours of training for each mentor.[148]

Although offered as a stand-alone activity, mentoring does not automatically help novice teachers adjust successfully or persuade them to stay in teaching. In many school districts, mentors are not part of a comprehensive induction program. Instead, they are simply veteran teachers whom principals assign to work with newcomers—like a blind date. Without strong administrative support to visibly endorse its value, mentoring rarely works.[149]

TeachSource Video 2.2

Teaching as a Profession: Collaboration with Colleagues

Collaboration among teachers is a way of working together with a common purpose and a common goal. It is based on the belief that different voices lead to better outcomes—for teachers and students. Five teachers come together to discuss how collaboration makes them better teachers. Watch the video clips, study the artifacts in the case, and reflect on the following questions:

1. In what ways do the teachers say that collaboration makes them better teachers and their students better learners?
2. In what ways is collaboration among teachers an occasionally uncomfortable process that brings positive results for classroom practice?
3. What are the advantages for collaboration of having all participants sit around a table as they share and discuss their common issues?

Watch on CourseMate.

Research on induction and mentoring The quality and effectiveness of local schools' induction and mentoring programs vary. Their success with new teachers depends on the funding availability, the quality and number of mentors, and principals' and superintendents' commitment to make the programs work.[150]

Increasingly, research is showing that well-conceived and implemented teacher induction and mentoring programs successfully increase new teachers' job satisfaction, efficacy, and retention rates.[151] Comprehensive induction programs move beyond the new teachers' initial classroom management concerns to helping them better focus on student learning. Studies find that the more helpful induction or mentoring supports that new teachers received, the lower the likelihood of their leaving teaching or moving to other schools after their first year[152]; and participating in an induction program reduced new teacher attrition rates within the first three years to 15 percent, compared with 26 percent for teachers without any induction support.[153] For example, school districts including Cincinnati, Columbus, and Toledo, Ohio, and Rochester, New York, have reduced beginning teacher attrition rates from more than 30 percent to less than 5 percent by providing an induction program with expert mentors and release time to coach first-year teachers.[154] A 2008 study found that urban teacher residency programs in Boston and Chicago that focused heavily on classroom-based training and on-the-job support for new teachers increased new teacher retention in their districts to 90 percent and 95 percent, respectively, after just three years.[155]

Comprehensive induction programs help young teachers become competent more quickly and stay in the profession at higher rates than those who learn by trial and error. The New Teacher Center, a national resource center on teacher induction, has found that new teachers' productivity in comprehensive induction programs rivals that of their third- and fourth-year colleagues.[156] Thus a well-inducted first-year teacher is likely to produce the same levels of student achievement as a fourth-year teacher. Likewise, research shows that teachers learn more in collaborative teacher networks and study groups than with mentoring. They learn more in professional development programs that are longer, more sustained, and more intensive than they do in shorter ones. Additionally, they learn more when there is collective participation, and when they see teacher learning and development as part of a coherent professional growth program in which all teachers—veterans and newbies alike—participate. Demonstrating that quality teaching is a group responsibility—not just an individual concern—is another hallmark of successful induction programs.[157]

What do these data mean? First, effective teacher induction programs can help teachers successfully adjust to their new careers. The most effective induction programs include a package of supports, especially mentors from the same field, the chance to participate in group or collective planning, and collaborative learning activities. Novice teachers need stronger teacher–teacher relationships that promote trust, motivation, commitment, and collective sense of their own capacities to do their job well.[158] Beginning teachers are more likely to stay in schools where they believe and see that they can succeed.

2-7b Professional Development

For new and veteran teachers alike, lifelong learning is an essential part of becoming a skilled professional. Learning the teaching "basics" is critical before reaching the job setting. Developing the know-how to do the job well once in the field builds new teachers' competence and confidence. Whether called "professional development," "staff development," or "in-service programs," these adult learning activities convey to new teachers the professional culture of continuous improvement, shared responsibility for mutual growth, and increased student—and teacher—achievement.

High-quality professional development that enhances teaching practices and increases student achievement is not one-shot "sit-and-get" or "workshop" activity in which teachers listen to an outside expert explain how to do things. **National professional development standards** define effective teacher learning as a comprehensive system of consistent and sustained job-related activities directly related to teachers' actual classroom responsibilities. This high-quality professional development is driven by data concerning what teachers' own students presently know and can do and what they need to know and be able to do. It involves teachers working and learning together in collegial conversations about their actual students' work and then designing and applying strategies to improve their own classroom practices and student learning. Instead of calendar days set aside for staff development events, professional development involves "just-in-time" learning that occurs during the regular workday. Teacher learning in this manner that makes sense and has immediate relevance benefits both educators and all their students.

national professional development standards Define effective teacher learning as a comprehensive system of consistent and sustained job-related activities directly related to teachers' actual classroom responsibilities.

To be successful, professional development programs must include four components: theory, demonstration, practice, and feedback.[159]

- *Theory.* Teachers need to understand how this new information fits with their professional knowledge and connects to their beliefs about teaching and learning.
- *Demonstration.* Teachers need to watch an expert enact the instructional practice in question. They need to see what it looks and sounds like so they will have a visual and auditory model upon which to draw as they practice the technique themselves.
- *Practice.* Teachers need opportunities to try out the new approach using role play or visualization as well as in their own classrooms.
- *Feedback.* Teachers need clear, accurate, and timely feedback on how well they accomplished their goal. Did they do everything they planned to do? How did the students respond during the activity? What does assessment of student learning show they gained? Collecting feedback from caring and informed colleagues, thinking about how to use it, and making adjustments before the next attempt can bring the new practice slowly into the classroom.

Research on professional development A growing body of research shows that improving teacher knowledge and teaching skills are essential to raising student performance.[160] For example, Eric Hanushek, Senior Fellow with the Hoover Institution at Stanford University, estimates that "the difference between a good teacher and a bad teacher can be a full level of [student] achievement in a single year."[161] The National School Boards Foundation calls investment in teacher learning "the primary policy lever that school boards have to raise student achievement."[162]

In one study, sustained participation in professional development activities tied to a state's elementary school mathematics curriculum successfully improved teachers' knowledge of mathematics and their ability to transfer this knowledge to students.[163] Similarly, 65 percent of teachers who participated in professional development activities centered on standards were much more likely to teach using three or four "mathematics reform" activities that raised students' achievement, as compared with 35 percent of teachers *without* this professional training.[164] Teachers report that professional development improves their teaching behaviors and encourages more learning, influencing them to change their teaching practices, seek more information or education, and alter their views on teaching.[165]

culture The school's norms, values, beliefs, and practices that influence teachers' and administrators' thoughts and actions.

Professional development and school culture A school whose **culture**—that is, the school's unspoken norms or "the way we do things around here"—values professional learning enhances both teachers and students. New teachers can get better, marginal teachers can improve, and successful teachers can keep strengthening their expertise through well-designed programs. In addition, the professional culture that supports all teachers' learning provides the moral and technical support that new teachers desperately need to survive their first classroom days and become competent and confident professionals. This school climate helps reduce teacher turnover and attrition and allows more students to work with effective, maturing teachers.

According to Linda Darling-Hammond, "An occupation becomes a profession when it assumes responsibility for developing a shared knowledge base for all of its members and for transmitting that knowledge through professional education, licensing, and ongoing peer reviews."[166] Today, teachers have clear articulated standards for what they should know and be able to do that are empirically tied to student learning. The alignment of CAEP, InTASC, and NBPTS standards has established a powerful professional model. These principles can guide preservice and practicing teachers along a continuum of professional growth from novice to master teacher. Together, they provide the profession with a defined body of knowledge, influence teacher preparation, entry, and licensing requirements; affect teachers' autonomy in deciding work responsibilities; and provide higher prestige and increased economic benefits for teachers. As a result, teaching, as a profession, has never been better positioned to make a difference to teachers, students, and their communities.

Did You Get It?

What is perhaps the single most important reason schools have an approximately 50% attrition rate within the first five years?

a. It has ridiculously low pay relative to its socioeconomic importance.
b. It is the only profession without an apprenticeship program.
c. Many teachers lack preparation in effective pedagogy.
d. Teachers are held in political contempt.

Take the full quiz on CourseMate.

SUMMARY

- Teaching as a profession has specialized knowledge and skills, practitioner-shaped and agreed upon standards of professional practice, increased autonomy in deciding work responsibilities, a code of ethics, and moderately high prestige but relatively low economic standing.
- Over the past decades, teaching has become a profession requiring increased preparation and competence; collaborative working and learning; a destination for mid-career changers from varying preparation routes; and viewed as one of many careers over a lifetime.
- Beginning in the early 1800s, teachers were prepared in normal schools, which evolved into teachers' colleges. Today, teacher education programs are found in many colleges and universities. Alternative teacher preparation programs are also available.
- Research findings relating teacher quality and preparation to teaching effectiveness, student achievement, and teacher longevity show teachers' verbal abilities, content knowledge, ongoing professional learning, enthusiasm, flexibility, and creativity are all related to student learning and achievement. At least three years of classroom experience, asking students

higher-order thinking questions and probing their responses, class sizes, opportunities to work with colleagues - and the interactions among these - are all related to increased student achievement. Lastly, strong preparation and experiences in learning how to teach a particular subject, understanding how students learn, and an effective induction program help keep new teachers from leaving the profession.

- The data for first-year teachers' attrition show that teachers who had opportunities to do practice teaching, have feedback on their teaching, have occasions to observe other classes, received training in child psychology, learning theory, and the selection and use of curricular materials were significantly *less likely* to leave the profession after the first year than teachers who did not have these preparation experiences.
- States license (or certify) teachers—give their formal approval of teaching candidates for professional practice—to protect the public from unqualified teachers. Most state licensure requirements include: formal academic training, completion of an accredited teacher preparation program, state assessment and testing, and other checks. States vary in their licensure and certification requirements.
- Research finds that teacher certification and licensure does not distinguish very well between effective and ineffective teachers.
- The National Education Association (NEA) and the American Federation of Teachers (AFT), often referred to as teacher unions, are two organizations that support professional teachers, have both worked to improve teachers' salaries and working conditions, publicly support more rigorous teacher evaluations, and have critics who claim they resist educational reform.
- Factors that influence teachers to join a strike include their desire for improved salaries and working conditions, teachers' personal and professional ethics. and potential real world consequences about walking off their jobs.
- Other organizations that support teaching include national teacher accreditation organizations (the Council for the Accreditation of Education Preparation, or CAEP, composed of NCATE and TEAC), the Interstate Teacher Assessment and Support Consortium, and the National Board for Professional Teaching Standards.
- The Interstate New Teacher Assessment and Support Consortium's (InTASC) philosophy affirms that all students are different and come to school with unique experiences that teachers can use as assets to assist their learning; an effective teacher must customize learning for each student; all teachers need to understand their own perspectives and biases and how these affect their relationships with students and parents; and the only differences between novice and veteran teachers are the degree of sophistication in their performances, knowledge, and dispositions in what they know and are able to do.
- The purpose of the National Board for Professional Teaching Standards (NBPTS) is to provide a highly respected, national advanced K-12 teaching certification. This credential sets and assesses high standards for what very effective teachers know and do to positively impact student learning.
- Schools use induction, mentoring, and professional development programs to orient, mature, and keep the teachers they hire.

Visit the Education CourseMate for this textbook to access the eBook, Did You Get It? quizzes, TeachSource Video Cases, flashcards, and more. Go to CengageBrain.com to log in, register, or purchase access.

Schools should prepare young people for an informed life in a democratic society.

Stephanie Maze/Corbis

CHAPTER 3

Philosophy of Education

InTASC Standards Addressed: 1, 2, 3, 4, 5, 7, 8, 9, and 10

LEARNING OBJECTIVES

After you read this chapter, you should be able to:

3-1 Define what an educational philosophy is and explain how it differs from an opinion.

3-2 Explain how traditional education philosophy contributes to our understanding of school's purposes and practices.

3-3 Describe how progressive education philosophy contributes to our understanding of school's purposes and practices.

3-4 Generalize how existential education philosophy contributes to our understanding of school's purposes and practices.

3-5 Identify how critical theory education philosophy contributes to our understanding of school's purposes and practices.

3-6 Summarize the key characteristics of the four educational philosophies that influence today's public schools.

No decision is more important than determining what to teach and toward what ends. The "right thing to do," regardless of context or profession, always relies on values as well as facts. Communities' system of values and beliefs about education—that is, their philosophy of education—influences what, how, and to what purposes schools teach. Different philosophies lead schools in different directions.

Competing views exist about schools' purposes and practices:

- Traditionalist educators believe that schools' purpose is to foster students' intellectual development by teaching the Western European classics and thought to prepare students for further education and work.
- Progressive educators believe that schooling *is* life, not preparation for life, and should be child centered, not subject centered. According to this view, schools should prepare students for an informed life in a democratic society.

- Existentialist educators believe that education's most important goals are to awaken human consciousness to the human condition and to the freedom to choose and create the personal self-awareness that helps make each individual unique.
- Critical theorist educators believe that schools should create the conditions for teachers to act as public intellectuals to challenge the present power structure and create a more democratic society.

Our philosophy shapes us and determines how we approach the world. Our philosophy of education influences our views about what schools are for and how we should educate our students. Deciding what, why, and how to teach is a value-laden enterprise, influenced by plural beliefs available in a multicultural democracy. Understanding the merits and limits of each approach will help prospective teachers develop, articulate, and enact their own views about education's purpose and process.

3-1 What Is an Educational Philosophy?

philosophy The general beliefs, concepts, and attitudes that an individual or group possesses.

educational philosophies Viewpoints that help educators interpret, find meaning, and direct their work.

Philosophy comes from two Greek words: *philos,* meaning "love," and *sophy,* meaning "wisdom." Literally, philosophy means love of wisdom. In everyday usage, this term refers to the general beliefs, concepts, and attitudes that an individual or group possesses. Most people have a set of ideas, values, and attitudes about life and education.

3-1a What Is Philosophy?

Philosophy is difficult to define. Philosophy is "the investigation of causes and laws underlying reality" and "inquiry into the nature of things based on logical reasoning rather than empirical methods." It is also "a system of motivating concepts of principles" and "a basic theory or viewpoint" or "system of values by which one lives" as well as "the critique and analysis of fundamental beliefs as they come to be conceptualized and formulated."[1] In short, analytic questioning and reasoning about a reality's true nature creates a philosophy (a motivating viewpoint and value system), and that philosophy then directs one's beliefs and actions concerning that reality.

Having a philosophy involves more than simply having an opinion. An opinion requires only a point of view; it does not have to be supported by data or rational analysis. A philosophy, by contrast, requires intellectual and rational inquiry, a systematic critical thinking without reference to experiments or religious faith. A philosopher pursues knowledge for its own sake to more fully understand the world and its ideas. Having a philosophy or critically analyzed point of view gives people a frame of reference by which to make sense of their experiences and to chart a course for future ones.

3-1b What Is an Educational Philosophy?

Unlike philosophy as a discipline that stands on its own as a way of making abstract sense of the world, educational philosophy focuses on practice. **Educational philosophies** are viewpoints that help educators interpret, find meaning, and direct their work. Different educational philosophies exist because educators and policy makers hold different ideas and values about education's purposes and practices.

Educational philosophy asks many questions, such as these:

- What is education? What are its goals?
- What is school?
- What is an educated person?
- Which knowledge, attitudes, and skills should be taught?
- Who should decide what is taught?
- How should students be taught?
- What is the teacher's role?
- What is the student's role?

Educational philosophies reflect our society's pluralism. The philosophies considered in this chapter have well-established roots in educational thought and practice. Although science can provide guidance, it cannot yet verify that one educational philosophy is empirically and objectively superior to any other. Nor can science determine the world's "best" culture or the "truest" religious faith. All of these decisions are part of value-driven, affective belief systems. For most humans, our beliefs more powerfully determine our thoughts and actions than do any scientific conclusions—that is, unless scientific rationality as the basis for thought and actions is part of our belief system.

3-1c Influences on Educational Philosophies

As one might expect in a pluralistic society, Americans' sets of beliefs, concepts, and attitudes—their educational philosophies—about what should happen in schools vary greatly. Factors such as the historical era, the geographic location, the local and larger cultures, the ease of communication and travel between those cultures and others, and the specific persons involved all influence the prevailing educational philosophy. For example, an educational philosophy that grows and flourishes during an era of limited communication and transportation between and among different world cultures and limited education among its society's members may not be the same educational philosophy that develops in a more fluent, interconnected world that depends on a highly educated populace to survive economically and politically. Naturally, educational philosophies change over time as events and personalities emerge and affect thinking and living.

3-1d The Values behind Education

Philosophy matters. Americans place great faith in education because it prepares individuals to live as responsible and productive citizens in a democratic republic, and it extends our country's cherished values into the future. At their best, public schools are the "great equalizer," bringing together students of diverse backgrounds and giving them a common American heritage. Indeed, schools have been the agency of Americanization for generations of immigrants. Likewise, a solid education can overcome limitations on students imposed by their background, creating opportunities for social and economic mobility. These beliefs and values underlie American schools.

Clearly, education is not a mechanical or neutral act. Rather, it is a value-laden process that influences the direction, knowledge, and nature of the students' learning experiences. Through a philosophy of education, or logical systematic point of view, a school, district, state, or nation selects which information and skills students will learn and how they will learn them. A philosophy of education provides answers about *why* one does things. Learning *why* to do something is an essential first step before teachers can learn *how* to do it. Educational philosophy offers the frame of reference that guides and makes sense of all other educational decisions. It provides a rationale and justification for making choices about curriculum, instruction, and student–teacher relationships.

InTASC

3-1e Educational Foundations and Future Teachers

Educational foundations coursework has the potential to give prospective teachers the ability to make sense of pedagogy and policy decisions within the larger social context. It helps future teachers understand the ideologies and values that shape and inform their future school districts' actions as well as their own teaching choices. Effective foundations experiences encourage teacher education students to consider their personal values and determine how they want to relate to others and how the educational concepts they choose reflect these perspectives.[2]

As such, educational philosophy offers an essential conceptual base for future teachers. A philosophy of education allows current and future practitioners to apply systematic approaches to making decisions in schools. It also highlights larger issues in the complex relationship between schools and society.

At the same time, understanding their own educational philosophy and being able to better express their beliefs and values can help future educators relate to those who view the world differently. Understanding and thoughtfully speaking about the teacher's educational philosophy can help defuse tensions among those who care about improving schools but who bring different perspectives and value sets to the discussion.

When looking at educational philosophies, it is tempting to oversimplify the arguments and define clear-cut "either–or" categories. The "traditional" educational philosophy versus the "progressive" educational philosophy, for instance, pits one set of views against a different set of views. To draw either–or comparisons between educational philosophies, however, would be imprecise and incorrect. In the real world, differences exist within each category as well as between the various categories. As so often happens with ideas in the real world, the process of drawing distinctions between philosophies is not always neat and orderly.

The following pages discuss four major perspectives on educational philosophy that have influenced—and continue to influence—the way people view and practice American education. The classical and contemporary educational philosophies affect the ways people today think about schools. Understanding these educational philosophies will make prospective teachers be both more knowledgeable educational consumers and more reflective practitioners.

Did You Get It?

The difference between having an opinion about education and a philosophy of education is (select the one that does not apply) that

a. Opinion is another word for philosophy; the only difference is that opinions are held by individuals and philosophies are expressed by institutions and collectives.

b. Opinions are personal beliefs, although some people may hold beliefs organized by underlying philosophy.

c. Educational philosophies are based upon abstract worldviews that help educators direct their work in an organized and meaningful manner.

d. Opinions do not have to be supported in a factual manner but philosophies require systematic critical thinking.

Take the full quiz on CourseMate.

3-2 Traditional Philosophy of Education

The conservative traditionalists adapt educational beliefs and practices extending back to ancient Greece and the Middle Ages.[3] The **liberal arts** vision of education believes that mastering the academic disciplines—mathematics, logic, philosophy, sciences, history, literature, and the arts—characterizes the educated person. Students pursue liberal studies to develop both their intellectual and moral excellence.

Traditional educational philosophies are incorporated into two educational approaches. **Perennialists** focus on teaching what they view as universal truths through the Western civilization's classics. **Essentialists** prefer to select those subjects from the Western tradition that would be most relevant to the current student generation. Box 3.1 compares the key ideas of these two traditional approaches that continue to influence contemporary U.S. education.

liberal arts The education concept that advocates that mastery of the academic disciplines—mathematics, logic, philosophy, sciences, history, literature, and the arts—characterizes the educated person.

perennialist Traditional educational philosophy that focuses on teaching "universal truths" through the Western civilization's classics.

essentialist Traditional educational philosophy that selects subjects from the Western tradition most relevant to current student generations.

3-2a Essentialists

Both conservative in tradition, essentialists and perennialists view the Western classics and Western thought as the canon in which American children should be educated. The two approaches differ, however, in how they use the classics. As pointed out in Box 3.1, perennialists think students should learn the classics as timeless truths that are able to guide contemporary reasoning and life. Essentialists, in contrast, want to select from the Western classics those most suitable to adaptability and usefulness in contemporary life. Because essentialists adapt the classic liberal arts curriculum to meet more contemporary societal demands, they are sometimes called pragmatic traditionalists. The essentialist curriculum largely underlies today's U.S. public schools' curriculum.

Box 3.1 Key Traditional Educational Ideas: Perennialist and Essentialist

Key Ideas	Perennialist	Essentialist
Learning is subject centered. The teacher and the text are the classroom's central focus.	X	X
Western European civilization provides the core curriculum. It carries the accumulated universal and eternal truths and virtues that all students need to develop their minds and live good lives.	X	X
Schools' purpose is to transmit and preserve this common cultural knowledge. Teachers and curriculum socialize students into society's essential dimensions of truth, beauty, values, and wisdom.	X	X
Educators select the knowledge and skills most important to help students function successfully in a particular time and society.		X
Educators work with the community to identify essential knowledge and skills.		X
Schools' purpose is to prepare students for further education and work.		X

3-2b The Essentialist Curriculum

Over time, society has found that certain skills—such as reading, writing, mathematics, and, most recently, computer skills—are essential for people to function effectively in their world. Both perennialists and essentialists share a basic commitment to train the intellect through subject-centered knowledge. Their differences revolve around what they consider to be most worth knowing.

mental discipline A learning doctrine of early American schooling, which suggested that studying certain rigorous academic subjects strengthens the student's mind and character.

Essentialist thinking has its roots in the **mental discipline** learning doctrine of early American schooling, which suggested that studying certain rigorous academic subjects strengthens the student's mind and character. According to the essentialist perspective, schools' focus should be subject centered, academic, and cognitive. Curriculum is a logically organized sequence of separate academic disciplines, such as one would see in a high school or college course handbook. Students experience highly structured study in language and grammar, mathematics, sciences, history, and foreign languages. This subject matter lays the intellectual foundation necessary for students to understand and function successfully within their society's shared culture.

Essentialists believe that every student needs this general education to succeed in life in our democratic society. To deny this course of study to any student, essentialists argue, would be inequitable, regardless of that student's ability, interest, or career direction. The subject matter itself is the important variable, just as it would be for a perennialist.

At the height of essentialism's popularity, essentialist concerns were more nationalistic than democratic. During the Cold War (i.e., the latter half of the twentieth century), essentialists saw their discipline-centered academic education as a shield protecting the United States against Soviet imperialistic intentions. The Soviets' 1957 launch of the Sputnik satellite humiliated the United States, which had fully expected to be first nation into space. Americans blamed the public education system for not producing enough sufficiently talented scientists and engineers to propel the United States into outer space ahead of its then-enemy.

Educators responded by developing a more intellectually demanding curriculum. The math, sciences, and reasoning skills fostered in the essentialist curriculum, proponents claimed, would produce the scientists, engineers, and technology workers who would defend and protect the United States from outside threats. Students' intellectual training became a critical weapon of national defense. To this day, most American high schools continue to rely on an essentialist curriculum.

The essentialist curriculum emphasizes subject-centered learning to build reasoning skills, character, and a shared culture.

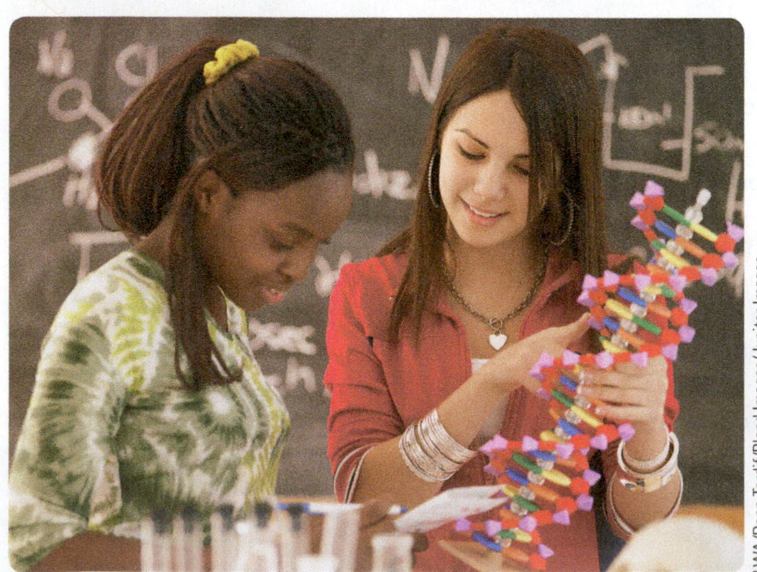
LWA/Dann Tardif/Blend Images/Jupiter Images

3-2c Essentialist Instruction

The national security panic about schools' failings led in two directions. First, students would have to study math, science, and technology in greater depth and with more application to real situations. Instructionally, this meant an increase in inquiry teaching strategies to enhance thinking, reasoning, and problem solving by schools' high achievers.

Meanwhile, critics expressed concern that average and slower-learning American students were not mastering the basics in reading, writing, math, science, and other areas. The controversial report *A Nation at Risk* (1983), for example, suggested that U.S. children lagged behind other nations' achievement level in basic subjects. Public schools needed to improve their teaching and improve students' skills in these areas, the report's authors concluded. Wide support for the "back to basics" curriculum followed.

Instructionally, essentialists support lecture, recitation, discussion, demonstration, question and answer, and competency-based assessments to determine student mastery of subjects. Drill and practice are also commonly employed learning strategies.

Essentialist teachers use a variety of learning materials to make sure that students learn the content. Typically, students learn from listening, talking, and watching rather than from engaging in first-hand exploration of the content. They demonstrate their learning of content and skills on achievement tests. Frequently, these are standardized tests used to make local, regional, statewide, and national comparisons.

Finally, essentialist schools are strictly academic learning centers. Teachers and administrators expect students to leave their emotional or behavioral concerns behind. Nonacademic activities interfere with schools' primary purpose, so schools' aim does not include remedying these types of problems in students' lives.

3-2d The Essentialist Teacher's Role

In the essentialist classroom, teachers transmit cultural and community-valued knowledge and expect students to learn it. To be successful, teachers must know their subjects very well. They organize the curriculum into a series of topics, taught in sequence, progressing from less complex to more complex ideas and skills through successive grade levels. The teacher's role is to engage students in mastering the content and manipulating it with high-level thinking, reasoning, questioning, evaluating, and problem solving. In addition, teachers show students that clear standards and criteria exist for judging art, music, poetry, and literature; and they show students how to evaluate and assess these works.

As intellectually satisfying as the essentialist classroom might be for teachers of high-achieving students, helping more slowly achieving students learn rigorous content can be less exciting. Slower-learning students typically spend more classroom time recognizing and comprehending the basic material through lecture, drill, and practice, while their faster-learning peers devote more time to extending their understanding and competency of the material through analysis, evaluation, synthesis, and creative problem solving.

3-2e A Contemporary Essentialist

Educators in the mid-1950s and 1960s focused on teaching students specific academic disciplines, but by the late 1980s essentialists had returned to the idea of general education as necessary for students to participate responsibly in a democracy.

Spurred to action by what they saw as a lax approach to teaching and learning, essentialists identified two factors that had been neglected in youths' education in the previous decades. First, schools were not effectively training students' minds. Second, students were failing to gain the cultural background knowledge—that is, the shared vocabulary and information—they needed to develop a common national identity and participate fully in their culture. E. D. Hirsch proposed a remedy for this situation: bringing the academic disciplines back to the curriculum's center.

Eric Donald Hirsch, Jr. E. D. Hirsch (born 1928) is an American educator and literary critic. In his 1996 book *The Schools We Need and Why We Don't Have Them,*

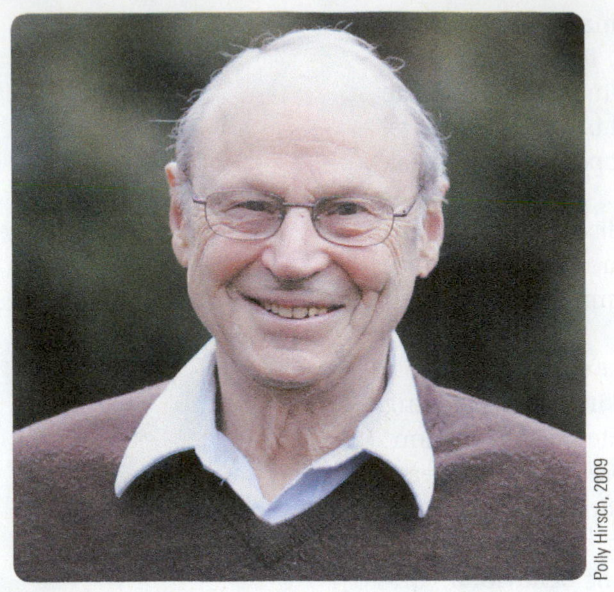

Polly Hirsch, 2009

Eric Donald (E. D.) Hirsch, Jr., advocate of cultural literacy

Hirsch suggests that the progressive and romanticized, anti-knowledge theories of education that prevailed in America for more than 60 years were the cause of America's lackluster educational performance as well as the widening inequalities in class and race that characterize the country. Hirsch believes that schools have placed more importance on self-esteem and freedom of expression than on challenging intellectual work, learning the "basics," and academic achievement.

Further, Hirsch thinks that American students have not been prepared to succeed in a highly competitive, information-based economy. This is especially true for economically disadvantaged children whose families cannot provide the "cultural capital" that more privileged children have available when they enter school. Hirsch views this basic knowledge as a "civil right." A definite correlation exists, he argues, between equality of opportunity and the learning of a core curriculum. To not teach all students the high-status curriculum hurts their chances of economic, social, and cultural advancement—limiting the social mobility that is the touchstone of American public education.

Hirsch proposes a common national core-knowledge curriculum that includes the basic principles of constitutional government; important events of world history; essential elements of math and oral and written expression; masterpieces of art and music; and stories and poems passed down through the generations. He asserts that general factual knowledge is a vital part of learning and suggests that schools should measure this learning with high-stakes standardized tests based on specific nationwide educational standards.

Reflect & Discuss

E. D. Hirsch believes that all school children should have rigorous, demanding academic learning in a core curriculum. He disagrees with Americans who think that children shouldn't be asked to do difficult things with their brains while they are young, rejecting the view, "Let them play now; they'll study at the university."

In groups of four, discuss the following questions:

A. What does Hirsch mean when he writes that American schools have operated on the assumption that challenging children academically is unnatural for them? Do you agree? What examples can you cite to support your opinion?

B. Hirsch believes that giving all students the "cultural capital" necessary to succeed in a highly competitive, information-based economy a "civil right." Do you agree or disagree? If you agree, how can schools provide the "cultural capital" to students whose families cannot provide it? If you disagree, how can our society avoid ending opportunities for meritocracy and social mobility?

C. How would you have responded as a student to a classroom that used Hirsch's educational approach and curriculum?

D. How do you think Hirsch might respond to the widespread adoption of the Common Core State Standards for Reading/Language Arts and mathematics and their assessments by 45 states and the District of Columbia?

Source: Hirsch, E. D., Jr. (1996). *The schools we need and why we don't have them.* New York: Doubleday. Retrieved from http://mwhodges.home.att.net/tracy/tracy-hirsch.htm.

American Education Spotlight

Steve Liss//Time Life Pictures/Getty Images

Diane Ravitch

Diane Ravitch

"I had never imagined that [the No Child Left Behind (NCLB) achievement testing] . . . would someday be turned into a blunt instrument to close schools—or to say whether teachers are good teachers or not—because I always knew children's test scores are far more complicated than the way they're being received today."*

Diane Ravitch (1938–), research professor of education at New York University and senior fellow at the Brookings Institution, has become a champion among public school teachers in what they see as a governmental and business assault on their profession.

A 73-year-old grandmother and education historian, Ravitch is a native of Houston, the third of eight children, and public schools graduate. She received a BA from Wellesley College in 1960. Married soon after college, Ravitch had two children and became a housewife. At 32, she returned to graduate school and earned a PhD in History of American Education from Columbia University. A highly respected voice in the profession, Ravitch has written education histories, champions the need for a strong and balanced curriculum, and promotes the idea of voluntary state and national curriculum standards. She is the author or editor of over 20 books, most recently, *The Death and Life of the Great American School System* (2010).**

Considered an essentialist in her advocacy for a rigorous, coherent national curriculum, Ravitch had been a visible and vocal promoter of standardized testing, accountability, charter schools, voucher programs, and evaluating teachers based on their students' test scores. Ravitch served as an education official for President George H. W. Bush, and President Bill Clinton appointed her to the National Assessment Governing Board, which oversees federal testing. She left government service in 1993.

Over time, Ravitch became disillusioned with the strategies that once seemed so promising. Since 2004, she has renounced her earlier positions and is now looking for solutions that she believes are compatible with schooling for democracy.

Briefly, she currently holds views about:

- *Standardized testing*: Outcomes of high-stakes testing often compromise education by lowering standards, narrowing the curriculum, gaming the system, teaching to tests, and cheating. By emphasizing testing of basic skills, NCLB guarantees that students will have less time for science, history, the arts, or foreign language, those very subjects that encourage creativity, innovation, and imagination.
- *Curriculum*: Teachers should rely less on textbooks as curriculum. Texts have been so highly censored, sanitized, and homogenized by pressure groups that they make students bored and cynical. Students need a curriculum that allows them to engage with controversy, see the bad and good in world events, and gain a broader, richer perspective.
- *Charter schools*: The overwhelming majority of high-quality research studies on charters show that some are excellent, some are awful, and most are no better than public schools. Charters should not be for profit; they should be answerable to students and parents, not stockholders, and public charters should help students with the highest needs.
- *Corporate-driven reforms*: Public schools are not a business. "Venture philanthropy" such as the Broad Foundation or the Bill and Melinda Gates Foundation—which begin with a strategy or reform idea and give schools the money to do it—are using their money to control public policy without accountability.
- *Poverty and education*. Poverty impacts academic achievement, and our society must both improve schools and reduce poverty. We must invest in parental education, prenatal care, and preschool to make sure that children arrive in school well nourished, healthy, and ready to learn.

Critics of Ravitch's ideas say that apart from her calls for better curriculum, child health care, and increased funding for early education, she does not offer clear alternative solutions for education policy makers and she ignores the complexity of school accountability policy. Others attack her for changing her position.

Ravitch concludes that there is no single answer to educational improvement. She argues that our schools need experienced and well-respected

(*continued*)

American Education Spotlight (continued)

teachers and principals. Students need to learn the subjects that prepare them for the duties of citizenship. After all, isn't the primary purpose of public education to sustain our democracy?

* NPR Staff. (2011, April 28). Ravitch: Standardized testing undermines teaching. *National Public Radio.* Retrieved from http://www.npr.org/2011/04/28/135142895/ravitch-standardized-testing-undermines-teaching.

** Ravitch, Diane. (2010). *The death and life of the great American school system. How testing and choice are undermining education.* New York: Basic Books.

Sources: Phillip, A. (2011, August 1). Ravitch rallies teachers vs. 'astroturf.' *Politico.* Retrieved from http://www.politico.com/news/stories/0711/60279.html; Ravitch, D. (2011, July 1). Invitation to a dialogue: Fixing the schools. To the Editor. *The New York Times.* Retrieved from http://www.nytimes.com/2011/07/06/opinion/l06dialogue.html?_r=4; Ravitch, D. (2010, March 9). Why I changed my mind about school reform. *The Wall Street Journal.* Retrieved from http://online.wsj.com/article/SB10001424052748704869304575109443305343962.html; Ravitch, D. (2011, May 31). Waiting for a school miracle. Op-Ed Contributor. The Opinion Pages. *The New York Times.* Retrieved from http://www.nytimes.com/2011/06/01/opinion/01ravitch.html?_r=1; Rizga, LK. (2011, May 16). The education of Diane Ravitch. *Mother Jones.* Retrieved from http://motherjones.com/politics/2011/03/diane-ravitch?page=2; Rotherham, A. J. (2010, March 17). Is education on the wrong track? *The New Republic.* Retrieved from http://www.tnr.com/article/education-the-wrong-track-0; Wattenberg, B. (2003, June 13). The language police/Textbook PC. PBS. *Think tank with Ben Wattenberg.* Retrieved from http://www.pbs.org/thinktank/transcript1116.html.

transmission of meaning Teachers hold knowledge in their heads, and their job is to transmit it in the most efficient way into students' heads.

Criticism of Hirsch's ideas Hirsch's educational ideas have been controversial. He has been attacked as a conservative advocate for a "lily-white" curriculum, a promoter of "drill and kill" pedagogy, and a reactionary force. By emphasizing content, critics claim, Hirsch underestimates the importance of pedagogy—that is, good teaching practices. Critics claim that Hirsch views schooling as simply **transmission of meaning:** Teachers hold knowledge in their heads, and their job is to transmit it in the most efficient way into students' heads. Frequently, critics add, Hirsch's approach leads to whole-class instruction, telling, and rote memorization as the most effective means for accomplishing this transmission.[4]

Although Hirsch's critics agree that targeted ("rote") practice can be a useful learning tool, they observe that students must also actively manipulate the content if they are to understand and learn it. Likewise, critics have challenged Hirsch's theories for not addressing differences in learning styles and for omitting cultural contributions from minorities.

Box 3.2 summarizes the essentialist education philosophy. Each philosophy discussed in this book has its own box, making comparing and contrasting them easier.

Did You Get It?

Traditional educational philosophy (pick the statement that applies)

a. Being based on rote instruction, is hostile to the liberal arts belief that mastering the academic disciplines characterizes the educated.

b. Is deeply hostile to teaching the classics of Western Civilization because those classics foster independent thought.

c. Does not accept a selective approach to the canon of Western Civilization.

d. Adapts educational beliefs and practices dating back to classical Greece to the modern world in ways that influence contemporary U.S. education.

Take the full quiz on CourseMate.

Box 3.2 Essentialist's Conceptual Features Summary

Ideal of learner: a rational mind developed by studying the core academic disciplines of Western thought.

Ideal of subject matter: a strictly academic and discipline-centered curriculum that strengthens students' mental powers and selected for its relevance for today and its respect for yesterday.

Ideal of school: a rational, organized place that transmits important cultural knowledge and skills to students.

Ideal of society: a democracy depends on a common or shared core of academic knowledge.

3-3 The Progressive Philosophy of Education

Just as the conservative traditionalists seek to preserve and transmit a core culture through schools, adherents to the progressive educational philosophy aim to change the society and culture. A relatively contemporary perspective, **progressive** is defined as moving forward, ongoing, advancing; a person who favors or strives for reform in politics, education, or other fields.[5] Likewise, **progressive education** is "a set of reformist educational philosophies and methods that emphasize individual instruction, classroom informality, and the use of group discussions, children's experiences, and laboratories as instructional techniques."[6]

The term "progressive" arose from a period (roughly 1890–1920) during which time many Americans took a careful look at the political and social effects of vast concentrations of corporate power and private wealth. From the inception of their movement, progressives argued that state systems of public schooling have primarily tried to achieve cultural uniformity, not diversity. The schools' goal, they proposed, should be to educate reasoning—not passive—citizens. Progressivism consistently rejected the traditional teacher-centered, curriculum-centered education in favor of a more student-centered approach.

Briefly stated the **progressive philosophy** views students—rather than content—as education's focus. In this perspective, education's purpose is to prepare students to be lifelong learners in an ever-changing society.

As a movement, progressive education incorporated a variety of viewpoints and practices. Educational progressives were pluralistic and often self-contradictory, yet always closely tied to broader currents of social and political progressivism.[7] In this section, we first discuss the general progressive philosophy. Next, we review John Dewey's approach. Later, we will investigate the critical theory, a radical contemporary offshoot of progressive philosophy.

progressive A philosophy that stresses moving forward or a person who favors reform in politics, education, or other fields.

progressive education A set of educational philosophies and methods that emphasize individual instruction, classroom informality, and using group discussions, children's experiences, and laboratories as instructional techniques.

progressive philosophy An approach that views students, not content, as education's focus.

social efficiency An emphasis on classroom control, management, obedience to authority, and a structured curriculum that focused on memorization and rote skills.

3-3a Key Ideas of Progressivism

During most of the twentieth century, progressive educators shared the belief that democracy means active participation by all citizens in social, political, and economic decisions that will affect their lives. This progressive approach contrasted with the U.S. educational model that prevailed in the early 1900s, which used a traditional curriculum with classroom methods based in **social efficiency**—that is, an emphasis on classroom control, management, obedience to authority, and a structured curriculum that focused on memorization and rote skills. (Chapter 5 discusses American education in the early twentieth century in fuller detail.)

The progressive curriculum Progressives believe that because learning is a natural response to students' curiosity and their need to solve problems, students' interests and desire to seek solutions should guide the curriculum. Accordingly, the progressive curriculum focuses on adapting the program of study to students' needs—academic, social, and physical. The formal

Progressive educators focus on both student and curriculum.

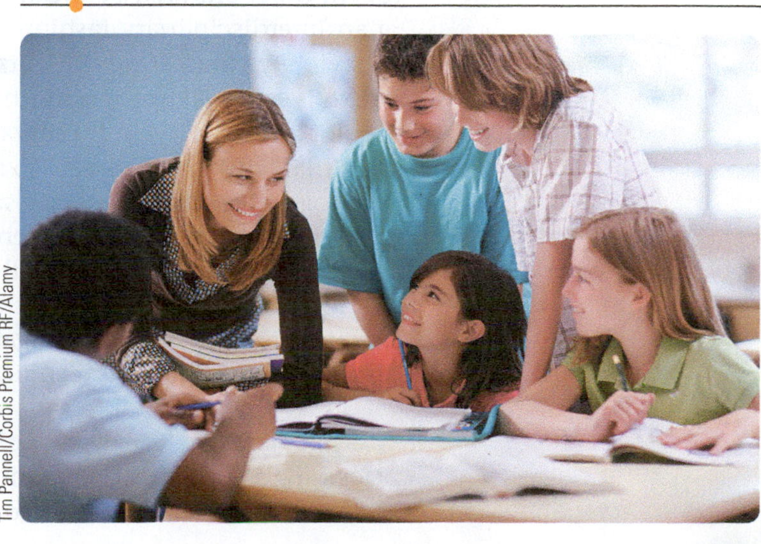

Tim Pannell/Corbis Premium RF/Alamy

Box 3.3 Progressive Educators' Key Ideas

Education should be child centered. Each individual should be free to develop naturally. Students' interests should guide teaching. Some debate exists on the extent to which a school should encourage children to freely develop these potentialities.

Schools are a means of social reform and improvement. A child-centered school is the best guarantee that the larger society will be truly devoted to human worth and excellence.

Education's purpose is to create engaged citizens for a democratic republic. Schools create small communities in which students and teachers show respect for one another and work together in mutually beneficial ways.

Educators should respect diversity. They should recognize each individual for his or her own abilities, interests, ideas, needs, and cultural identity as well as encourage students to be independent thinkers and creative beings.

Students are whole people. Developing the whole student—physically, mentally, socially, and morally—is essential for the student's intellectual growth.

Teachers should motivate learning. In this role, they should serve as guides, not taskmasters.

Schools and homes should cooperate to meet students' needs. Parents are children's first educators and should work with schools to help children learn.

written curriculum is interdisciplinary, reflecting knowledge as it appears in the real world. The teacher, the student, and the curriculum need to work together to find the best fit to promote the most learning.

In addition, progressives believe that although the past produced great ideas and thoughts, knowledge and social environments constantly change.[8] Given this dynamic nature, reliance on a classical Western—or any—tradition of thought would quickly lead to an outdated curriculum. Students' job is to learn how to learn so they can cope successfully with new life challenges and discover relevant truths in the present. Learning how to learn and making learning personally meaningful to students are more important than transmitting a set body of once-valued knowledge to students. Box 3.3 illustrates the progressive education philosophy's key ideas.

Progressive instruction Progressives believe that education's aim is to prepare students for life. For this reason, they suggest, instruction should begin with real-world objects rather than abstractions. Teachers show young children how to observe, describe, classify, assess, and eventually generalize what they see and touch. Older children's education includes the traditional curriculum but taught in an interdisciplinary fashion. Teachers help students learn appropriate moral behavior by connecting students' acts with natural consequences. Because bodily health is essential to cognitive health, teachers also encourage students in physical play and activity. In these ways, teachers provide the range of knowledge and skills that will enable people to adapt more readily to their circumstances.[9]

Progressive teachers engage students in inquiries or investigations that the students develop themselves. Students learn from one another in cooperative learning groups. This approach fosters both intellectual and social learning. In the progressive classroom, the teacher becomes a facilitator, a resource person, and a co-inquirer. Through students' own investigations, they continuously develop new and deeper understandings. Students learn in a hands-on, minds-on, interactive classroom.

The progressive teacher's role From the beginning, progressive approaches placed high demands on teachers' knowledge, time, and ability. Teachers must know their subjects inside and out to integrate them with related disciplines and, at the same time, connect them to students' social, physical, and cultural environments. Teachers must be lifelong learners so they can continually introduce students to new scientific, technological, literary, and artistic developments to illustrate that knowledge is constantly changing. Similarly, teachers need a repertoire of effective instructional skills and an extensive array of teaching materials to accommodate students' preferred learning styles.

In addition, teachers should get to know their students very deeply as individuals and as learners, looking for opportunities to connect students to content through these learner-centered factors. Because students' needs have academic, social, and physical aspects, teachers must design learning activities to have children interact with one another around the content in cognitive, social, hands-on, and minds-on ways.

3-3b Progressive Education Critics

In the hands of first-rate instructors, progressive innovations were highly successful. In the hands of average teachers, however, they led to chaos. Done poorly, progressive education could be worse for children's learning than the formalism it sought to replace.

Some progressive advocates greatly expanded this perspective's child-centered focus. In doing so, they unwittingly turned progressive education into a gross and anti-intellectual caricature, quickly and inaccurately popularized as the child controlling the classroom. As a result, in too many classrooms, "license began to pass for liberty, planlessness for spontaneity, and chaos for education."[10] Phrases such as "whole child" and "creative self-expression" became clichés, too vague to serve as useful guides to constructive educational practice.

Critics claimed that progressive educators were trying to reengineer society along collectivist lines by eliminating competition and independent thought from schools.[11] A few even attacked progressive educators as Communists. For example, pamphlets bearing slogans such as "Progressive education increases juvenile delinquency" and "The commies are after your kids" appeared.[12] By the mid-1950s, the progressive movement had lost its central influence on school practice, and it eventually disintegrated as an identifiable educational movement.

3-3c Enduring Progressive Contributions

Despite the controversy over certain educational practices enacted under the progressive umbrella, by the end of World War II, much progressive philosophy had become conventional wisdom. Education policy discussions routinely included phrases such as "recognizing individual differences," personality development," "the whole child," "social and emotional growth," "the learners' needs," "intrinsic motivation," "bridging the gap between home and school," and "teaching children, not subjects." Many aspects of progressive education simply had become accepted as good education.[13]

In the late twentieth and early twenty-first centuries, various educational groups rediscovered and revised progressive beliefs and practices to address the changing needs of schools, children, and society. Open classrooms, schools without walls, cooperative learning, multiage approaches, whole language, the social curriculum, experiential education, and numerous forms of alternative schools all have important philosophical roots in progressive education. The progressive philosophy offers hopeful alternatives to the one-size-fits-all curriculum and assessments and the mechanized school organization that characterize today's schools. Box 3.4 highlights progressive education philosophy's key features.

Box 3.4 Progressivism's Conceptual Features Summary

Ideal of the learner: the student is a whole person with cognitive, emotional, social, and physical needs central to learning to use his or her mind well and interact effectively with others.

Ideal of the subject matter: interdisciplinary, problem focused, inquiry based in a real-life context and using real-world resources so students learn to use their minds well and see education as relevant to their real world.

Ideal of the school: a small community that teaches the cognitive and interpersonal skills necessary for all students to live an American democratic life.

Ideal of the society: a democratic society made up of caring, responsible, interacting intelligent citizens respecting each other and working for the common good.

3-3d A Notable Progressive Educator

In the 1920s and 1930s, John Dewey (1859–1952), a philosopher and educator, became one of the key figures in the progressive education movement. Considered an American pragmatist (pragmatism was a very influential philosophy during his time), Dewey inspired but did not lead the progressive education movement. In fact, over time he became one of the movement's most vocal critics. Through his writings and laboratory work at the University of Chicago, Dewey tested and refined his ideas about how to best help students learn.

John Dewey's view of education To John Dewey, education's aim was ultimately to make human beings who would live life to the fullest, continually add to the meaning of their experiences, and increase their abilities to direct their lives. Educated students had both personal initiative and adaptability and were able to control (or at least influence) their surroundings, rather than simply adjust to them. Likewise, Dewey saw intelligence as the purposive reorganization, through action, of actual world-based experience.[14]

Dewey believed:

- *Each student is unique,* both genetically and experientially.[15] Children have cognitive, emotional, social, and physical differences and growth rates. Even when teachers present a standard curriculum using established pedagogical methods, each student will respond uniquely to the experience. Thus teaching and curriculum must be designed in ways that allow for such individual differences if all students are to learn effectively.
- *Education must serve a broader social purpose.* Education must help people become more effective members of a democratic society. Democracy, for Dewey, is more than just a form of government; it incorporates all of the associated living and shared experiences. Students practice successful democratic citizenship through their classroom behaviors. Schools that place students in the center of active, meaningful, shared learning become levers of social change.
- *Teaching practices must be democratic.* Dewey argued that authoritarian schools' one-way delivery style, from teachers to students, does not provide a good model for life in democratic society. Instead, students need educational experiences that will enable them to become valued, equal, self-directed, and responsible citizens.
- *Students' experiences affect their learning.* People do not experience one common reality. Instead, each person experiences his or her own reality, depending on

his or her previous experiences; these experiences, in turn, influence the individual's perceptions and actions in the present situation.

- *Curriculum includes real-world experiences.* Each school is an embryonic community, active with the various types of occupations that reflect the larger society. Through interaction, students learn the spirit of service and the capacity for self-direction. Increasing the number of student viewpoints, their number of shared interests, their freer interactions, and mutual adjustments will eventually create a more democratic society.
- *Schooling is life, not preparation for life.* Learning's outcome is behavior. Schooling is a means to improve students' thinking, skills, capacities, democratic interactions, and eventually to improve society.
- *Curriculum integrates culture and vocation.* Curriculum should be both egalitarian and democratic, always stressing use of the mind and applying learning to real-world situations.

Defining a balance Dewey rejected the idea that traditional liberal arts curriculum was the only education students needed. He also challenged the age-old separation between culture and vocation. For centuries, "culture" and higher social standing had meant possessing certain kinds of knowledge associated with wealth, leisure, and theory—as opposed to poverty, labor, and practice. In Dewey's view, the traditional curriculum was thoroughly useful to statesmen, professionals, and intellectuals, but it was largely irrelevant for most other persons. Dewey, therefore, rejected it as both exclusive and inequitable.

Dewey did not simply discard the traditional subject matter but rather sought to balance it with teaching that accounted for the principles of children's growth and development, children's needs and interests, and learning styles at different ages. Schools became "child centered" to the extent that teachers tailored the curriculum and instruction to facilitate the child's learning in concert with the individual student's development. This "child-centered" curriculum considered the child's physical, intellectual, and emotional growth as these forces interacted with the curriculum. In this context, the curriculum's role was seen as developing children's own capacities and intelligence and nurturing children's own thinking rather than simply transmitting knowledge and facts. Dewey's educational vision included was "both–and," not "either–or."

When following Dewey's approach, teachers designed learning experiences for students that would provide data for students' observations, reflections, meaning creation, and learning. The resulting curriculum was both hands-on and minds-on. The younger the students, the more concrete and hands-on the curriculum. As a result, the curriculum was largely interdisciplinary, problem focused, and inquiry based, and it connected students to the real world outside the classroom.

Dewey believed in three types of subject matter:

- The active pursuit of occupations, such as carpentry, sewing, or cooking
- Studies dealing with the background of social life, such as history and geography
- Studies that provided command of the forms and methods of intellectual communication and inquiry, such as reading, grammar, and arithmetic

Generally, this curriculum moved from the concrete, which was immediately knowable by physical experience, to the social, which focused on a more abstract interpersonal knowing, to intellectual abstraction and reasoning.

The importance of teaching and learning The child-centered approach contrasted in key ways with the traditional "teacher-centered" classroom. In teacher-centered classrooms, the teacher transmitted skills, facts, and values largely through lecturing and seatwork. Thus knowledge was transferred from teacher to students; it went in a one-way direction, with teachers determining the subjects, standards, and methods of teaching. Children's participation in deciding on learning processes and purposes was minimal; their task was to receive and retain the information and master the skills.

By comparison, in a "child-centered" classroom, the teacher considered both the individual children's needs and the prescribed curriculum. Therefore, the teacher's role changed from transmitter of the official curriculum to facilitator of student learning. Teachers now designed and enacted ways to connect students to content through activities that made sense and had meaning to the learners. In addition, they encouraged student collaboration in real-world problem solving with learned content to build deeper understanding, analysis, synthesis, evaluation, and application of what they learned in practical and creative ways. At the same time, teachers helped students work collaboratively to increase their interpersonal skills. This knowledge and skill base, Dewey thought, would best prepare students to live responsibly in a democratic society.

Dewey believed that teachers needed thorough knowledge of two arenas: subjects and students. First, teachers needed a deep and wide knowledge of their academic disciplines. They needed to understand how to connect their subject content to the meaningful themes and related disciplines that students studied. Second, teachers needed a strong awareness of those common childhood experiences that they could use to lead children toward understandings that the knowledge represented. Making this connection successfully required teachers to know sufficient detailed information about children's physical, cognitive, psychological, and social growth and development.

Beyond the "Paradigm War" Progressive education accommodated a substantial variety of curricula and teaching approaches. Although many people identify John Dewey with progressive education, throughout the 1920s he became less the progressive education movement's interpreter and synthesizer and more its prime critic.

Dewey saw traditional educational philosophy and progressive education philosophy as representing two extremes in the education paradigm. On one side, the traditional philosophy encouraged a relatively structured, disciplined, ordered, didactic, teacher-directed education; on the other side, the progressive philosophy advanced a relatively unstructured, highly flexible, student-directed education. Although each approach might have some merit, neither approach alone could be successful.

In Dewey's view, the traditional education brought a constructive structure and order to learning, although it lacked a holistic understanding of students. Further, the traditional approach led to design of a curriculum that was too focused on content and not enough on how teachers could help diverse students learn it. Dewey suggested that teachers must consider both the subject and the learners' needs it if they were to make a positive difference in their students' lives.

Similarly, Dewey argued that progressive education misapplied freedom. He disapproved of completely "student-driven" education. He recognized that students often did not know how to structure their own learning experiences for maximum benefit. Many progressive teachers did not sufficiently direct or constrain students. All too often, they provided freedom without really knowing how or why freedom could be most useful to promote student learning. They used the superficial trappings of progressive philosophy while missing its central core. Freedom, without structure and focus, was not the answer.

Dewey proposed that education move beyond this "paradigm war" and seek first to understand the nature of human experience. Learning needed structure *and* awareness of how children learned, both–and, not either–or. Learning should be based on a clear theory of experience, not simply teachers' or students' whims.

Discarding the traditional versus progressive paradigm, Dewey suggested that American education follow a middle ground. According to him, teachers need content knowledge along with strong attention to students' subjective experiences, present and past. Education needs a systematic organization of activities and subject matter for students to become knowing and thinking individuals. Furthermore, education becomes scientific, Dewey observed, only as teachers attempt to be more intelligent about their goals and practices used to achieve these ends.

In Dewey's view, schooling's goal was to develop an educated person, able to reason effectively, act creatively, behave responsibly within a democratic society, adapt when necessary, initiate and control when possible, and continue lifelong learning.

3-3e Reconciling Traditional and Progressive Viewpoints

The pendulum has continued to swing between traditional and progressive educational approaches for more than 100 years. One approach takes hold, influences school programs, and inevitably has some glaring failings in its outlook and implementation. Then, its opponents reject the approach and substitute its opposite. A while later, the cycle repeats itself, exasperating educators, policy makers, and teachers while confusing students, parents, and the general public.

Good intentions are one of the teaching profession's strengths. Both traditionalists and progressives continue to offer educational theories based on sincere positive aims. Both viewpoints have cadres of dedicated and enthusiastic supporters. Yet, no evidence exists that good intentions increase learning beyond a basic level.

Clearly frustrated by the tug of war over American educational philosophy, Stanley Pogrow, Education Professor at San Francisco State University, writes, "Pure traditionalists are brain dead. Pure progressives live in a fairy-tale land. And while good intentions are better than bad intentions, relying primarily on their power is not effective."[16] Likewise, as the late-writer Michael Crichton, author of *State of Fear*, has observed, the combination of good intentions and bad information is "a prescription for disaster."[17]

In reality, both traditional and progressive approaches have strengths and weaknesses. Each philosophy supplies an important piece of the puzzle in our quest to create better schools. Although these two educational philosophies appear at loggerheads, they are, in fact, complementary. As David B. Ackerman, a former school superintendent and curriculum administrator observes, "They are intertwined taproots of our professional outlook, the warp and woof

Reflect & Discuss

John Dewey believed that education's ultimate goal was to make human beings who had initiative, adaptability, and good citizenship continually add to the meaning of their experience and increase their abilities to direct their own lives.

A. Explain to a partner how—if at all—your K-12 experiences have helped you reach any of these outcomes. Describe what might have been present or missing in your schooling or home environment that led to these outcomes.

B. After reading Dewey's beliefs about what education should be, identify which aspects you would want to include in your own teaching practice and why.

C. Explain the value of having a "hands-on" and "minds-on" education. To what extent was your K-12 education hands-on and minds-on? To what extent is your university education hands-on and minds-on? What percentage of each do you think would create your optimal education?

of the fabric of beliefs that guide us when we walk into a classroom."[18] In their extreme versions, however, neither approach works. In their reasonable versions, one approach will not work without the other.

The problem comes when influential groups seeking to establish their philosophical (and political) dominance take their ideas to illogical extremes. Educators and policy makers all too often use exaggerated rhetoric as a means to capture the most followers. As Dewey and others observed, both extremist traditional and progressive positions are mistaken on how teaching and learning occur for most students. The vast majority of students do not function or learn best in a purely structured or purely unstructured approach. Meanwhile, the current research cannot smooth out the pendulums' oscillations. The traditional and progressive educational philosophies' lasting insights appear in Box 3.5.

Here are each view's enduring and valid insights[19]:

Box 3.5 Enduring and Valid Insights from Traditional and Progressive Philosophies

Traditionalists:

- **Teach students what is of deepest value.** Choose texts that will help young people understand and appreciate the best of the world's thoughts and words as they relate to truth, beauty, goodness, meaning, and pleasure. Choose content that will lift students beyond themselves, thereby creating a sensibility and vision of a thoughtful and well-lived life.
- **Teach with rigor.** Tactfully insist that students and teachers engage with challenging materials and express their thoughts clearly to open minds and better express ideas.
- **Uphold standards of excellence.** Hold students' work to high standards to promote real achievement.
- **Use instructional time in meaningful ways.** Lecture is not inherently "bad" and cooperative learning is not inherently "good." In the time available, identify and use the pedagogical pathways most likely to lead all students to the most learning.
- **Acknowledge that discipline-based knowledge is the firm foundation for any transdisciplinary learning.** Subject disciplines provide important essential information about the nature of human beings and the world as well as powerful, indispensable perspectives and tools of inquiry. Content knowledge is a necessary (but not a sufficient) condition for learning.

Progressives:

- **Children are whole people.** Students have intellectual and psychological characteristics that affect how well they learn.
- **One standard does not fit all.** Standards of excellence are absolute, but individual students' performance standards may not reach them at a particular time. We teach individual students, not categories of them.
- **A child's mind is not a receptacle.** Meaning is not inert. Students need to think actively about what they have heard or read and relate it to prior knowledge and experience so they may create sense and meaning from it, comprehend it, and learn it. They need to be minds-on.
- **Children bring their unique beliefs and attitudes into the classroom.** Teachers must consider these existing assets as part of students' learning experiences and use them to facilitating new learning.
- **Students find holistic knowledge more meaningful.** Teachers need to help students make disciplinary knowledge personally germane by connecting information fragments into a coherent, relevant, and harmonious set of lenses for understanding the world.

An educational philosophy that takes the best of both traditional and progressive approaches values both the teacher and the student having an engaged mind during the learning process. It provides a strong disciplinary focus as well as knowledge integration. It understands the values and limitations of both content "depth" and "coverage" and balances the necessary tradeoffs. It uses student ability grouping—and ungrouping—when appropriate to the learning tasks at hand. It evaluates students on their progress toward achieving personal excellence as they grow toward meeting standards of measurable excellence.

In this way, prospective teachers can find the positive aspects in varied educational philosophies. It is not necessary to take each approach as absolute and extreme. Rather, it is important to acknowledge that each can make a positive contribution in the classroom. Although existential and critical theory approaches do not routinely appear in American public schools, they offer perspectives that can give teachers more choices about ways to make learning more attainable and meaningful for our diverse students.

Did You Get It?

Progressive educational philosophy (choose the statement that is false)

a. Aims to change society and culture by educating critical citizens.
b. Is, despite the name, a very old—but minority—philosophical approach toward learning.
c. Is a student-centered approach.
d. Grew out of an era in which Americans were confronting the social effects of vast corporate and personal power and wealth.

Take the full quiz on CourseMate.

3-4 The Existential Philosophy of Education

As a philosophy, existentialism represents both the desperation and the hope inherent in modern living. An **existential educational philosophy** is a viewpoint in which curriculum and instruction encourage deep personal reflection on one's identity, commitments, and choices. Its approach is cognitive, affective, and highly individual.

existential educational philosophy A viewpoint in which curriculum and instruction encourage deep personal reflection on one's identity, commitments, and choices.

existentialist philosophy A viewpoint that celebrates the individual and recoils from the world's chaos.

existentialism A philosophy that focuses on the existence of the individual and individual responsibility.

3-4a Existential Philosophy Beliefs

Existentialism is a relatively modern philosophy that became prominent after World War II. Its roots, however, trace back to the Bible. As a philosophy relevant to today's education, one may date its modern influences to the nineteenth-century European philosopher Soren Kierkegaard (1813–1855). More recently, philosophers advocating this approach include Martin Buber (1878–1965), Karl Jaspers (1883–1969), Jean Paul Sartre (1905–1986), and the contemporary educator, Maxine Greene.

Existentialist philosophy reacts against two factors. First, it rejects the conservative education tradition that respects only the Western classics and shows little regard for the individual. Second, it recoils from the horrors of World War II and the Holocaust as vivid examples of a world gone mad. Instead of the world's chaos, **existentialism** focuses on the existence of the individual and individual responsibility. Existentialists believe that people must create themselves by shaping their own meaning and choices. The key ideas associated with this perspective appear in Box 3.6.

Existentialism rejects any source of allegedly objective, authoritative truth about the world. Instead, existentialists emphasize that people are responsible for defining themselves. The only "truth" is the "truth" that the individual determines is true. Therefore, individuals create their own realities—and themselves—through the choices they make. To exist is to choose. According to existentialists,

Box 3.6 Key Ideas of Existentialism

The world is chaotic, producing anxiety and hurt. People free themselves from this disorder through awareness and choices.

People are responsible for defining themselves through their choices. Although people may not be able to control events, they can control their responses to these events. Accordingly, they create personal meaning and value through the decisions they make and the knowledge they wish to possess.

People's most significant realities are personal and nonscientific. Although people live in a world of physical realities and have developed scientific and useful knowledge about these realities, their subjective experiences are the ones most meaningful to them.

Education's most important goal is to awaken human consciousness to the human condition and to the freedom to choose and create the personal self-awareness that helps make each person authentic, genuine, and unique.

Education should focus on both cognitive and affective dimensions. Both aspects are necessary if an individual is to become a fulfilled whole person.

people have two options. They can either define themselves or have others define them. Humans always face the threat of people, institutions, and agencies imposing an artificial truth on them and restricting their individual freedom. Existentialists believe that individuals are in a constant state of becoming, creating chaos or order, creating good or evil. Each person has the potential for loving, producing, and being an inner-directed, authentic person. An authentic person recognizes this freedom and knows that every choice is an act of personal value creation.[20]

Education, say existentialists, should focus on individuals' cognitive and affective needs, stressing students' individuality. It should include topics about the rational and irrational world and the anxiety that conflict generates. In this way, education can give individuals the cognitive and emotional tools they need to liberate themselves from the world's disorder and absurdity. By studying aspects of literature, history, science, and the arts and learning how to think and communicate about them effectively, young people gain the power to make choices and create meaning in their lives.

3-4b Existential versus Traditional Views

Existentialists and traditionalists view the world and education very differently. Existentialists reject the traditionalists' views about the primacy of Western classics as the source of universal virtue and wisdom. To existentialists, one curriculum does not fit all. Instead, existentialists see each student as a separate individual needing a highly personalized education. Conservatives see the world as stable and able to benefit from unchanging truths. Existentialists, in comparison, see the world as indifferent to human wishes and anarchic. Individuals, however, have the responsibility to impose a meaning and order on the world. Death is the only given.

The existential curriculum Existentialists believe that the great thinkers of the past had their own ways of considering life and the natural world, and they developed their own conclusions. Likewise, today's students need to find their own ways of thinking about these issues and make up their own minds. To this end, the existential curriculum is heavily geared toward the humanities.

The humanities provide students with vicarious experiences that will help them better understand the world and respond to it with their own imagination and self-expression. For example, rather than emphasizing historical events, existentialists focus on historical figures' actions, which serve as possible models for students' own behaviors. In deference to the humanities, the existential curriculum may de-emphasize math and the natural sciences, presumably because their subject matter would be considered "cold," "dry," "objective," and, therefore, less useful to increasing students' self-awareness.

Existential educators regard vocational education as a method of teaching students about themselves and enabling them to recognize their own potential, rather than as a means for earning a livelihood. Similarly, as part of the emphasis on teaching art, existentialism encourages individual creativity and imagination more than copying and imitating established models.

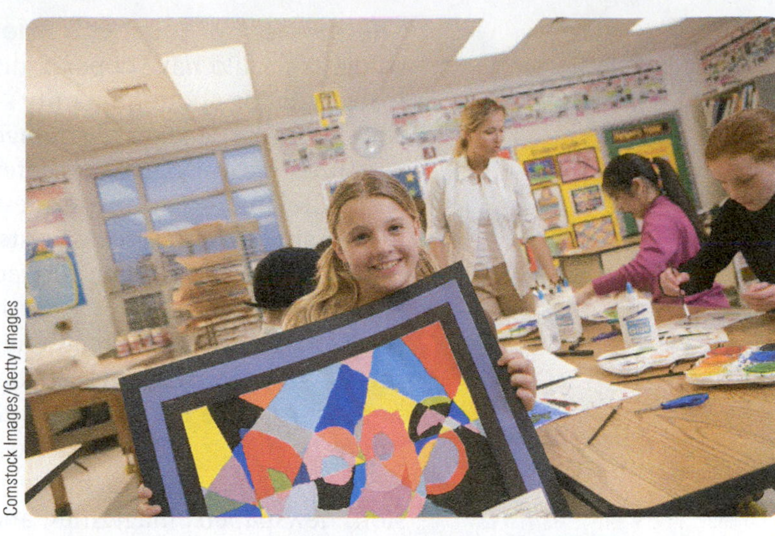

Comstock Images/Getty Images

Art in existentialist classrooms help students learn about meaning, options, and self-expression.

Literature, especially biography, has important meaning in an existential classroom. Drama and films also provide ample material illuminating the human condition. Because these media re-create the author's experiences, thoughts, emotions, and images around profound life issues, they illustrate conditions in which individuals make choices. As such, media can evoke readers' responses that increase their levels of awareness. What is more, art, drama, and music encourage personal interaction with the content. From an early age, children in existential classrooms receive exposure to life's problems and possibilities, humanity's horrors and accomplishments. In such contexts, students can better learn about personal preferences and values.

Likewise, students must create their own means of self-expression. They must be able to freely employ language and artistic media to illustrate and communicate their emotions, feelings, and insights. Educational technology and multimedia enhance students' range of self-expression. In such classrooms, students write plays, create graphic images, produce films, and craft poems to express their own voices.

In the existentialist classroom, subject matter takes second place to helping students understand and appreciate themselves as unique individuals who accept complete responsibility for their thoughts, feelings, and actions. The existential curriculum is a means to an end, not an end in itself, as conservative educators would have it. Instead, teachers and schools offer the topics they consider appropriate for students at each grade level to study. From these subjects, students make personal decisions and select what they need to study. Because every student is different, no single set of learning outcomes is appropriate for all students. Likewise, because feeling is not divorced from reason in decision making, the existentialist expects the school to educate the whole person—mental, emotional, social, and physical.

Although many existentialist educators provide some curricular structure, existentialism—more than other educational philosophies—affords students a wide variety of curricular options from which to pick. As a result, in the existential classroom, students are actively involved in a range of different topics and activities at the same time. For instance, in one classroom, several students may watch a video of Martin Luther King, Jr.'s "I Have a Dream" speech, two or three may listen on headphones to Abraham Lincoln's Gettysburg Address, several students may dissect a frog, others may read books, and a few others may draw pictures of the human skeletal system. The teacher moves from group to group, working to help advance students' understandings, furthering their investigations, asking questions to challenge their conclusions, and prompting them to refine their products.

The existential teacher's role Existentialists believe that both teachers and students should have opportunities to ask questions, suggest answers, and participate in dialog about humanity's important issues—namely, life, love, and death. An existential teacher encourages students to philosophize, question, and discuss life's meaning, using whatever curriculum engages students in that dialog. Since the answers to these questions are personal and subjective, they are not measurable by standardized tests.

As a resourceful guide and facilitator, the teacher's role is to help students define their own essence by exposing them to various paths they may take in life. To do so, teachers create an environment in which students may freely choose their own preferred way. Teachers work with each student to help him or her find appropriate materials and the best study methods to address the student's interests. In this kind of classroom, the teacher is a resource—along with other students, books, classical masterpieces, contemporary works, the Internet, television, newspapers, magazines, and other people.

Obviously, existential educators reject the standards movement, opposing the imposition of one common curriculum and the use of standardized testing as a way to measure academic success. Rather, they see this movement as a trend away from individuality, personal choice, and freedom, and toward conformity and loss of freedom.

Additionally, teachers in an existential classroom face demands on their own affective and cognitive dimensions. When teaching under the existential umbrella, teachers need to understand their personal lives and the values and beliefs they have constructed from their personal experiences. Without this personal experience and introspection, they cannot help their students make sense and reasonable choices in their own lives. Likewise, teachers need to be able to take intellectual and emotional risks to open their thinking and feeling to students, to let students know them as thinking and experiencing individuals. Such intimate sharing helps students become awake to the possibilities within themselves in their own worlds. In this role, teaching is intensely personal and carries significant responsibility because the line between the teachers' personal and professional behaviors is notably more fluid than in a traditional classroom.

Existential instruction Existential classrooms are open learning environments. Instruction is largely self-directed and self-paced and includes a great deal of individual contact with the teacher. Existentialist methods focus on the individual. Because each student has a different learning style and different learning topic, the teacher's primary job is to discover what works for each student and then provide the student with the necessary resources to let learning happen.

In this kind of environment, instruction is frequently informal and highly interpersonal. The teacher relates to each student openly and honestly. In an intense relationship with each one, the teacher helps every pupil understand the world by posing questions, generating activities, and working together. Martin Buber, an existential philosopher, wrote about an "I–thou" approach, in which student and teacher learn cooperatively from each other in a nontraditional, nonthreatening "friendship."[21]

Maxine Greene One influential contemporary existential educator is Maxine Greene, a professor emeritus of philosophy and education at Teachers College, Columbia University. Greene believes in the intersection of the arts with social action. Her philosophy sees education as a process of awakening diverse persons, enabling them to develop their talents, and work with one another. Their common goal is to bring a better and more just social order and more meaningful way of being in the world into existence.

Greene sees education's goals as helping students to realize their deep responsibility for themselves and recognize their connections to other human beings who share this world. Learning's purpose, in her view, is to nurture students' intellectual talents so they can construct a more democratic, just, and caring society. Citizens must be well informed and have the educational abilities and sensitivities needed to critically examine our world.

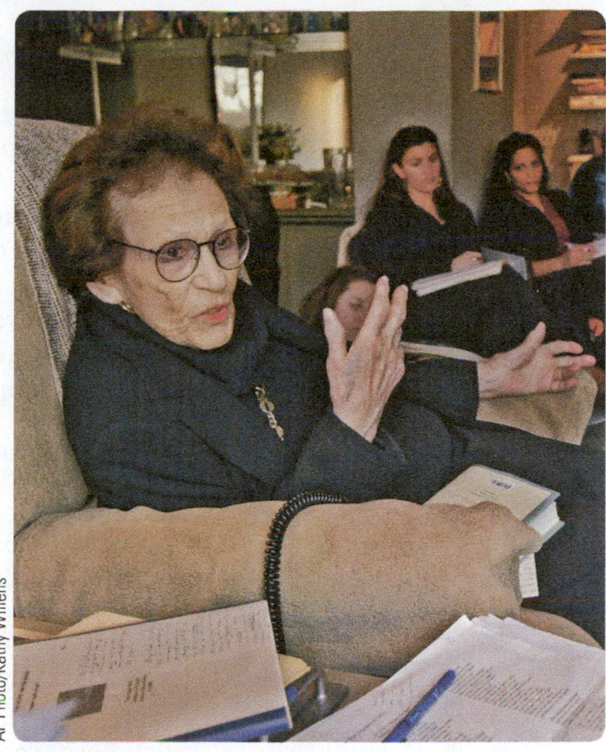
AP Photo/Kathy Willens

Maxine Greene, an advocate for existential education

In today's hyperconnected environment, finding a calm, optimistic, personal space can be difficult. Technology makes everyone's pain and society's violence visible to anyone with a TV, Internet hookup, or smartphone. As a result, the current world is a challenging place to live and to teach children to have a positive outlook. For these reasons, Greene believes in an education that stresses self-defining, choosing, and acting responsibly.

Greene has put her beliefs into action. The Maxine Greene Foundation for Social Imagination, the Arts, and Education awards as much as $10,000 to everyday educators who are capable of inventiveness and who go "beyond the standardized and ordinary."[22] The Foundation also supports artists whose works embody new social visions, and individuals who radically challenge or alter the public's imagination around social policy issues.

Greene writes, "As a teacher and teacher educator, never certain about right and wrong, I am very concerned about how we teach the young at a time when we are surrounded by obvious lies and manipulations. How can children be encouraged to discover some authentic way of being in a world that is so decayed?"[23] She sees the existential classroom as being rich in humanities and the arts and staffed by caring, aware teachers; in these refuges from unsafe external realities, teachers help students find occasions for constructive possibilities.

Greene expects teachers to create communities in their classrooms. Students and teachers listen carefully to one another as they try to make sense of others' and their own experiences, learning how to respect their individual differences. With their teachers' guidance, students integrate their responses to these experiences into their intellectual and emotional growth and their quests for decency

Box 3.7 Existentialism's Conceptual Features Summary

Ideal of learner: a unique individual who discovers his or her identity, makes choices, creates his or her own meaning, and brings order to the world's chaos.

Ideal of subject matter: the humanities bring opportunities for students to explore life's heights and depths and to develop personal insights to inform future choices.

Ideal of school: schools create an environment for individuals to learn how to define self and create meaning for their life choices in a disorderly world.

Ideal of society: the world is chaotic and absurd, and individuals must decide who they are and how they wish to respond to events in their lives. The ideal society would be composed of such unique, authentic, knowledgeable, and responsible individuals.

and social justice.[24] Box 3.7 highlights the essential features of existential education philosophy.

Criticism of existential philosophy in schools Existentialism is a highly individualistic philosophy with educational implications. Although elements of existentialism occasionally appear in public schools, this perspective has found wider acceptance in private schools and in some alternative public schools founded in the late 1960s and early 1970s. To be effective as an educational approach, existential philosophy requires a smaller, more homogeneous school environment where students have family backgrounds rich in learning experiences before they come to school so they do not need to spend much time mastering basic skills or developing the "appropriate" social behaviors in order to succeed in life.

Reflect & Discuss

The existential philosophy of education is highly individualized and rooted in the humanities. Its goal is for students as individuals to develop the thinking and affective skills for self-definition, self-expression, and the capacity to impose a meaning and order on their world. Discuss answers to the following questions with a partner.

A. After reading about the existential curriculum and teaching practices, what do you think you might have gained from being a student in a K-12 existential educational experience? What do you think you might have missed?
B. What aspects of teaching in a school with an existential philosophy do you think you would most enjoy? Which aspects do you think you would find most frustrating?
C. Explain what Maxine Greene means when she says that one educational goal is to help individuals find their calm, optimistic, personal space. Why would this be important to learning? Where do you find yours?

Did You Get It?

Existential educational philosophy (choose the statement that is true)

a. Is a Cold War-era philosophy.
b. Asserts the importance of the individual and of individual responsibility through its cognitive and affective approach.
c. Acknowledges the inconsequentiality of individuals and asserts the importance of social, collective responsibility.
d. Grew out of the horrors of trench warfare on the Western Front during World War I.

Take the full quiz on CourseMate.

3-5 The Critical Theory Philosophy of Education

Critical theory is a social philosophy oriented toward using education to increase human freedom from domination by our society's social, economic, and political elites.

social reconstruction The 1930s progressive education movement's offshoot that advocated for serious social reform and led to critical theory.

The progressive education movement led to the development of a more radical offshoot in the 1930s, known as **social reconstruction**. These progressive educators looked to schools for leadership in creating a new and more equitable society than the one that had given birth to the Great Depression. As a consequence, social reconstructionists advocated for serious societal reform. Critical theory developed from this progressive offshoot.[25]

3-5a Critical Theory

Critical theory is well known within the education mainstream, and its development revitalized the debate about democratic schooling in this country.[26] The late 1970s saw a reaction to the conservative movement of the 1950s and 1960s, which sought to strengthen public schools' liberal arts and sciences curricula. Working independently, a group of American scholars began to critique public schooling. They saw public school as an arena for ideological struggle with a hidden curriculum and socialization for capitalistic needs that neglects issues of class, race, and gender that create large societal inequities.

3-5b Key Ideas of Critical Theory

Critical theorists reject schools' transmission of traditional mainstream culture and values as indoctrination. They see schools' traditional purpose as way for the wealthy and powerful in our culture to convince most people that their privileged interests are also society's interests. As a result, these influential persons shape our schools by making their curriculum our "official knowledge."[27]

critical theorists An educational philosophy that rejects schools' transmission of the status quo and seeks to make schools and society more equal.

Critical theorists believe that students from less privileged socioeconomic backgrounds begin school with unequal opportunities. These limitations, they argue, can be removed only by changing the society's political and economic systems (Box 3.8). Critical theorists would change both schools and the society that makes and keeps people unequal.[28]

Critical theory suggests that schools can sow the seeds of societal transformation. Peter McLaren, Michael W. Apple, and Henry Giroux, for example, see schools' potential as serving as a positive fulcrum for social justice.[29] As presently organized, public schools simply replicate and reinforce the status quo, including its inequities and undemocratic practices. Sounding the call for pedagogical empowerment, these critical theorists see teachers' role as helping students make sense of and engage the world around them. When necessary, teachers should help students change the world for the better. In this way, schools can become the agents that raise children to question and challenge their society's limitations and failings. When students learn how to push against the status quo's "fit," they will be well prepared to improve their communities and the nation as a whole. Thus adoption of the critical theory perspective raises educators' consciousness beyond the classroom and school yard to consider broader social and cultural concerns.

Box 3.8 Critical Theory's Key Ideas

Education is values based. It takes place within a particular culture. Education, rather than pursuing child development or human achievement in a norms-free vacuum, revolves around the particular culture's values.

Education involves types of imposition and indoctrination. Because education has its roots in both culture and values, the real question is not whether imposition and indoctrination of students will take place, but rather from which source it will come.

Education represents a political activity. It involves degrees and types of imposition and indoctrination that follow the ruling groups' and classes' wishes.

Teachers engage in political activity. This action usually occurs without conscious awareness of their work's political nature. Teachers are not teaching an objective "truth," but rather the social elites' values. Teachers need to respond to the genuine interests of people other than the upper-middle-class and upper-class who use schools to keep their power by reproducing the status quo (and reinforcing their places in it).

Teachers should work for social justice. Teachers can help students critique the status quo and unequal power relations and work for social justice in their society. Schools can transform society.

Critical theory curriculum A curriculum based on critical theory is designed around contemporary social life rather than traditional academic disciplines. It includes whatever will help a culture to evolve, change, and solve real problems.

A critical theory curriculum incorporates several organizing ideas. First, it views culture as a product of power relations. Next, it helps students investigate issues of inequality in their own environments and encourages them to take action against those conditions. It conceptualizes culture and identity as complex and dynamic, and it considers all cultures to be integral parts of the curriculum.

In addition, a curriculum based on critical theory organizes studies that incorporate students' backgrounds, learning styles, and experiences. It purposely uses schools as laboratories to prepare students to participate actively in a democratic society and become change agents in their culture. Lastly, such a curriculum creates an environment that celebrates diversity, and it teaches students to build coalitions and develop cooperative learning strategies.[30]

To accomplish these goals, the critical theory curriculum integrates all traditional subjects into single-theme, interdisciplinary units. By interacting with this highly relevant, contemporary, and interdisciplinary curriculum, teachers can help their students understand current social problems' validity and urgency. With teachers' guidance, students decide which problems to study and which educational objectives they want to reach.

For example, a mathematics lesson on "sweatshop accounting" could help students look closely at profit distribution for shoes and clothes in different areas of the world. The class might receive sets of data to extract and analyze what the price of a brand-name shoe represents and determine the relative salaries going to the shoemaking workers, retail store owners, and marketing spokespersons.[31] A social studies class could consider the world's distribution of wealth, where cookies represent wealth and students are assigned to different continents. Some continents would receive more cookies than others, and students can eat what they have been given. When one or two students receive many cookies apiece at the same time as other students must share only a few, the obvious unfairness becomes apparent.[32] Similarly, issues such as terrorism, violence, hunger, poverty, inequality, racism, sexism, homophobia, and homelessness might all become relevant topics for class study.

Working together, the teacher and students explore the issues at hand, suggest alternative viewpoints for fuller understanding, analyze the topic, and form conclusions. Throughout this endeavor, the teacher models the democratic process, listening carefully and respecting diverse viewpoints.

Curriculum materials may come from a variety of sources inside and outside the school. Students can learn through internships, work–study programs, and other cooperative relationships with the community and outside resources.

Critical theory instruction Critical theorists believe that students learn through a cultural context and participation in a democratic process. Key elements of this type of learning include use of a problem-based framework and cooperative investigation. As exemplified by the "sweatshop accounting" case, students learn that history is influenced by past and present cultural and social environments, analyze the data, and use their findings to inform their decision making. Along the way, students acquire skills and knowledge as they continually interact between their school and their community.

Similar to what happens in an existential classroom, students in a critical theory-based classroom engage in many different activities to study the agreed-upon topic. Teachers guide and facilitate them to learn how the scientific method—observe, ask a question, research the topic, experiment or test, gather data, assess, draw conclusions, and report findings—applies not just to physics, chemistry, or biology, but to the whole of life, including students' personal and social lives.

For example, one math lesson grew out of student-raised real-life concerns about how fast the middle school was growing. The school district's lack of space forced the school to occupy the top floor of an older building with a leaky roof. The student body doubled in size, from 100 to 200 students. After the terrorist attacks on September 11, 2001, the students worried about being trapped in a fire and stampeded in an emergency. Their teacher organized them into groups and challenged them to use math to make their case for more school space.

TeachSource Video 3.1

Philosophical Foundations of American Education: Four Philosophies in Action

Scholars classify philosophies underlying American education in various ways. Progressivist, critical theory, perennialism, and essentialism are four such constructs, each with implications for classroom practice. Teachers can use insights from these theories to develop their own ideas about children and learning and as a rationale for making instructional decisions. Watch the video clips, study the artifacts in the case, and reflect on the following questions:

1. Segment 1: Progressivism. What is the progressivist philosophy and what are some ways that it influences teachers' role, curriculum, instruction, learning, assessment, and classroom arrangement?
2. Segment 2: Critical Theory. What is the basic focus of critical theory and what are some ways it influences teachers' role, curriculum, instruction, learning, assessment, and classroom arrangement?
3. Segment 3: Perennialism. What is the basic understanding in perennialism, and what are some ways it influences teachers' role, curriculum, instruction, learning, assessment, and classroom arrangement?
4. Segment 4: Essentialism. What is the basic understanding in essentialism, and what are some ways it influences teachers' role, curriculum, instruction, learning, assessment, and classroom arrangement?
5. How might a teacher use selected aspects from each philosophy in his or her teaching?

Watch on CourseMate.

After taking measurements, comparing their school with one in a more affluent neighborhood, and collecting and analyzing data, the sixth graders compiled their findings and presented their report to the school advisory council, which reported directly to the school board.[33]

Critical theory recommends use of a variety of instructional methods, including simulations, demonstrations, group research, reports, analysis of current issues, reading, guest speakers, small-group discussion, field trips, interviews, internships, and essay writing. In addition, students can conduct Internet research, read case histories, analyze multiple aspects of the topic, formulate predictions, propose and justify revisions and solutions, and act to implement these solutions.

The critical theory teacher's role Critical theory sees teachers as change agents and the classroom as a site for political action. Critical theorists encourage teachers to empower themselves by conducting a challenging review of their school's purpose, its curriculum content and organization, and the teaching profession's role and mission. Critical theorists recommend that teachers take responsibility for shaping their own futures and for helping students shape their own lives and the world in which they will live.

To make this happen, critical theorists believe that teachers need greater self-awareness regarding their political role in maintaining the existing governmental and social power structure. Teachers must understand how a society constructs knowledge from various positions if they are to understand how to create equitable and culturally responsive teaching strategies.

In this regard, many U.S. teachers may be at a significant disadvantage. Critical theorists claim that because most prospective teachers are heterosexual white women from European American, middle-class backgrounds, they may not immediately recognize the unique ways in which their racially privileged, class-dominant, gender (either an advantage or disadvantage), and heterosexually oriented positions influence and transform their teaching. How they teach influences how their students view and experience the world—specifically, it encourages students to adopt the teacher's own perspective.[34]

The task of teacher-preparation programs, critical theorists argue, is to awaken prospective teachers' awareness of the same oppression that they might potentially reinforce in their classrooms.[35] This process can be very difficult, and even threatening, to undergraduates who are still forming their collegiate and young adult identities—and to their professors who espouse a different philosophical orientation. In fact, every individual's identity has multiple aspects that must be considered: a person can be a son or a daughter; male or female; brother or sister; Caucasian, African American, Latino, Asian, or mixed race; thin or stout; marathon runner or couch potato. Each individual has more than one persona; reality is complex. To emphasize only one of these aspects of self, instead of recognizing and accepting them all, critical theorists claim, leads to cognitive dissonance. Likewise, valuing teaching the common beliefs and heritage that all Americans share—and at the same time criticizing how different power groups in our society create persistent inequities among families and children—can lead to cognitive dissonance. Rather than pick one view over the other, a mature mind may be able to accept the reality that both views contain aspects that may be true.

Henry Giroux's critical pedagogy Henry A. Giroux, a professor at McMaster University in Ontario, Canada, offers a clear definition of the public schools as a battleground of political ideas. With a thorough understanding of public school education from life experiences as a teacher and intellectual experiences

Box 3.9 Critical Pedagogy's Main Ideas

Struggling for democracy is both a political and educational task. For a vibrant democratic culture to arise, education must be treated as a public good. More than a place to benefit individual students, schools are a crucial site where students gain a public voice and come to understand their own power as individual and societal agents. Giroux believes that incorporating different groups' experiences and voices into the curriculum and having students reflect on these perspectives help build a democratic community.[36]

Teaching is a political activity. Teaching is not objective and value neutral. Instead, teachers are cultural producers who are deeply implicated in public issues. If public schools' purpose is to indoctrinate students into preserving the society and political power structure as they are,[37] teachers must become transformative intellectuals, helping students identify where their society's power is located and how the power structure communicates its ideology and values. Educators should teach "students how to think in ways that cultivate the capacity for judgment essential for the exercise of power and responsibility by a democratic citizenry," expanding the possibilities of a democratic society and social transformation.[38]

Ethics is a central concern of critical pedagogy. Education is more than just "economic capital" necessary to get a job. Education should be about self-definition, social responsibility, and individuals' capacities to expand the range of freedom, justice, and democratic practices. Knowledge has ethical value. Without an ethical perspective, students cannot see a society's ideology as being deeply implicated in individuals' struggles for identity, culture, power, and history. Nor can knowledge without ethics help teachers and students push against the oppressive boundaries of gender, class, race, and age domination.

The curriculum should include diverse student voices. The curriculum should expand beyond the Western European tradition. In 1940, 70 percent of new U.S. immigrants came from Europe. In 1992, by comparison, only 15 percent came from Europe, 44 percent came from Latin America, and 37 percent came from Asia.[39] The "melting pot" metaphor, in which schools "Americanize" all newcomers to accept traditional Western thought and values, no longer works for such a diverse population with multiple narratives, cultural myths and beliefs, and ready access to worldwide communications media and travel. Schools need to adopt a multicultural curriculum to accommodate their more diverse populations.

Critical pedagogy should be politically transformative. Knowledge is not just to *learn*; it is to *use* to make the world better and more democratic. Students need to understand how the curriculum presents different viewpoints, voices, and identities; how these relate to historical and social forces; and how they can be used as the basis for change. In addition, teachers and students need to critically address issues related to life in a vastly more globalized, high-tech, and racially diverse world than has existed at any other time in history.[40]

An interdisciplinary curriculum permits students to consider important social issues. Although the traditional curriculum does contain some content useful for the critical theory classroom, the curriculum best suited to developing critical reflection among students and the community is interdisciplinary in scope and recognizes that knowledge is partisan and culturally determined. It should examine the hidden examples of power in everyday life.[41] Giroux believes that reading the liberal curriculum as popular culture rather than viewing it as an immutable canon or great narrative could be useful.

as a scholar, Giroux developed a **critical pedagogy**, an instructional perspective whose purpose is to transform teachers, schools, and society into agents for social justice.

critical pedagogy An instructional perspective whose purpose is to transform teachers, schools, and society into agents for social justice.

Giroux clearly articulates his views about critical pedagogy (Box 3.9).

Lastly, Giroux says public schools need to rethink their purpose. Educators should abandon the long-held assumption that school credentials provide the best route to economic security and class mobility. In his view, the U.S. economy has experienced long-term stagnation with real incomes declining for low- and middle-income groups. Instead of training students for specific labor tasks, teachers should facilitate students in thinking differently about the meaning for work and prepare them to demonstrate the skills and attitudes necessary to hold multiple jobs over the course of a career. Achieving this goal will require a curriculum

FlipSides

Essentialist or Critical Theory? Which Philosophy of Education Should Guide Today's Schools?

American public schools should keep essentialist tradition to guide curriculum and instruction.	American public schools should use a critical theory approach to guide curriculum and instruction.
■ The essentialist philosophy underlies the current U.S. public school curriculum. Schools' purposes should continue to transmit and preserve the common Western (European) culture and knowledge.	● The critical theory philosophy is well-known within education mainstream. It asserts that schools should teach children to transform society to reduce its political, social, and economic inequalities.
■ Schools should provide students with the intellectual training required for thinking, reasoning, and problem solving to prepare them for further education and work.	● Schools should provide students with the intellectual and social awareness training, reasoning, and problem-solving skills to prepare them for further education, and work, and to make their society more equal and fair.
■ Learning is a subject-centered, intellectually demanding academic curriculum that builds knowledge and moral character necessary for life in a democratic society.	● Learning is values based, a political activity that occurs within a specific culture; public schools should respond to the genuine interests regarding class, gender, and race—rather than to upper-middle and upper-class interests.
■ The teacher and the text should be the classroom's main focus.	● The teacher should use the curriculum to work for social justice, helping students understand and critique the status quo and challenge unequal power relationships.
■ Teachers' role is to engage students in high-level thinking, reasoning, questioning, evaluating, problem solving, and meeting clear academic standards.	● Teachers' role is to become change agents who engage students by incorporating their backgrounds, learning styles, and experiences; celebrate diversity; teach students to develop coalitions and work cooperatively.
■ Curriculum should strictly emphasize Western European civilization, which is most suitable to adaptability and usefulness to contemporary life.	● Curriculum should include all cultures and diverse students' voices, using highly relevant, contemporary, single-theme interdisciplinary units organized around contemporary social life rather than academic disciplines.
■ Dominant instructional practices should include lecture, discussion, demonstration, question-and-answer recitation, drill and practice, and assessments.	● Dominant instructional practices should include collaborative study, consider and respect alternative viewpoints, analyze topics, make informed conclusions, and conduct informed actions.
■ Modes of student engagement should include listening, talking, watching, and test taking.	● Modes of student engagement should include cooperative investigations of contemporary problems and helping children take informed action against inequalities in their own environment.
■ Educators work with the community to identify essential knowledge and skills to teach students.	● Educators work with the community to provide students with internships, work–study programs with community and outside resources.
■ Criticism of essentialist education concludes that it leaves slower-learning students behind in achievement and its strictly academic approach excludes students' nonacademic needs.	● Criticism of critical theory education is that it undermines the status quo in school, community, nation; it has little empirical research supporting its benefits to student learning; and it has little connection of theory to practice.

Which philosophical approach to curriculum and instruction do you believe is best for twenty-first-century American public school students? How might a teacher incorporate strengths from each approach into the classroom?

Box 3.10 Critical Theory's Conceptual Features Summary

Ideal of learner: a liberated individual seeking genuine meaning and identity in a diverse and complex world

Ideal of subject matter: knowledge understood in relation to its connection to the society's dominant ideology and power structure.

Ideal of school: an agency of societal transformation to provide more economic and political equality in a democratic society.

Ideal of society: individuals and groups finding identity, understanding, and meaning in an unjust society.

characterized by new forms of literacy, vastly expanded understanding of how power works within a culture, and an appreciation for how the mass media play a decisive role in constructing multiple and diverse social identities.[42]

Box 3.10 summarizes critical theory's philosophy of education.

Criticism of critical theory Like other educational viewpoints, critical theory has its opponents. First, according to many of these critics, critical theory education writers use a language that is difficult to understand; this makes it difficult to clearly comprehend what they are saying and use it for changing public schools. Second, critical theories usually avoid using empirical research methods to study schools. As a consequence, they have much to say but little evidence to back it up. Finally, critical theories of education often fail to connect theory to practice in ways that practitioners can find meaningful or useful.

Reflect & Discuss

Critical theorists would change both schools and society that make and keep people unequal. Teachers' role is to help students to challenge, make sense of, and engage constructively with the world around them. Work with a partner to answer the following questions.

A. Describe any aspects of critical theory philosophy that you saw or experienced in your K-12 education.
B. Explain the reasons why a community or national groups might favor a critical theory philosophy of education. What reasons might a community or group have to reject them?
C. What aspects of critical theory do you think you would want to use as a teacher? Which aspects would you not want to use. Explain.

Did You Get It?

The critical theory philosophy of education does not

a. Ask teachers to act as public intellectuals to challenge the present power structure.
b. Use the curriculum to orient students to accept the status quo in a democratic society.
c. Come from the social reconstruction branch of education theory during the Great Depression.
d. Examine issues of race, class, and gender that had not been previously addressed.

Take the full quiz on CourseMate.

3-6 Reflections on the Four Educational Philosophies

Educational philosophies construct a lens through which a teacher filters ideas about education's purpose, teaching, and learning.

Not all educational philosophies have equal respect and standing in today's public schools or policy circles. Yet any philosophy may have some merit. Where educational philosophy seeks to improve a classroom, it must offer insight into the learner, the subject matter, and the society. If taken to illogical extremes, however, no educational philosophy can support all students' learning. In addition, philosophies that seek to overturn the prevailing culture are not well received by those who stand to lose their influence and social, economic, or political power under the new schema. Given this context, four perspectives inform the educational philosophy that governs today's public schools: traditional, progressive, existential, and critical theory.

Traditional views are deeply subject centered, anchored in the psychology of mental discipline and the purpose of transmitting the Western European culture through knowledge of the time-honored academic subjects. Essentialists attempt to build a common set of understandings and loyalty among diverse students to a shared American society.

Progressives—in many varieties—focus less on the strict academic disciplines and mental exercises and rely more on relating the subject content to the learners' needs. They seek to teach the skills, competencies, and attitudes needed to lead an intelligent and economically sustainable life in a pluralistic democratic society. Part of this approach entails applying the scientific method to social thinking.

Existentialists stress the importance of individuals' choices in creating their identity, values, and personal meaning. With this perspective, the humanities and arts form the basic curriculum. Because this approach is so highly individualized, it is not widely used in today's public schools.

Finally, critical theorists see public schooling as a political activity. By using a relevant and varied curriculum and engaging in intellectual inquiry, teachers have the power to challenge the inequitable power bases inherent in schools' curriculum and society's structure; give diverse students a voice; and use problem solving, cognitive growth, and social action to radically improve our society as a whole.

Did You Get It?

When speaking of educational philosophies generally, we can safely say that

a. No philosophy, taken to extremes, can support all students' learning.
b. The merit of a philosophy depends upon the time: some philosophies really are passé.
c. The prevailing culture is often surprisingly open to changes in educational philosophies.
d. There is a growing national consensus that all educational philosophies are necessary and valuable in today's schools.

Take the full quiz on CourseMate.

SUMMARY

- Teaching is a value-laden enterprise influenced by the many beliefs available in a multicultural democracy. Many different viewpoints about education's purposes and practices exist.
- An educational philosophy is a theoretical map that guides viewpoints about schools' purpose, the nature of teaching and learning.
- Prospective educators benefit from developing a philosophy of education because they provide frames of reference to help educators interpret, find meaning, and maker informed choices about how they want to practice teaching and learning. They also help educators relate to those who see the world differently than they do.
- Traditional education philosophy contributes to the preservation and transmission of core Western cultural knowledge and skills believed to be essential to enable society's children function successfully within their environment.
- Progressive education philosophy contributes student-centered practices that combine academic rigor with real world relevance; develops children's intellectual, physical, social, and moral dimensions; prepares children for lifelong learning; creates engaged citizens for a democratic republic; and serves as a vehicle for societal reform and improvement.
- Existential education philosophy contributes a highly individualized largely arts and literature curriculum and instruction that encourages deep reflection to help students understand themselves and their choices in a chaotic world.
- Critical theory education philosophy contributes a belief that schools are places where teachers act as "public intellectuals" who use an interdisciplinary curriculum around contemporary issues in students' lives to help students think critically and act thoughtfully in order to create a more just society.
- Educators can successfully reconcile the traditional and progressive viewpoints by selecting and using each approach's strengths and avoiding each's weaknesses.
- Each philosophy of education discussed in this chapter informs the traditions that guide today's public schools.

Visit the Education CourseMate for this textbook to access the eBook, Did You Get It? quizzes, TeachSource Video Cases, flashcards, and more. Go to CengageBrain.com to log in, register, or purchase access.

We can better understand where U.S. education is today by understanding where we have been.

CHAPTER 4

The History of American Public Education

InTASC Standards Addressed: 1, 2, 3, 5, 8, and 9

LEARNING OBJECTIVES

After you read this chapter, you should be able to:

4-1 Identify the major cultural influences on education in early colonial America.
4-2 Describe the characteristics of education in the early New England colonies.
4-3 Identify the characteristics of education in the middle colonies.
4-4 Summarize the characteristics of education in Virginia and the other Southern colonies.
4-5 Describe early education in other states.
4-6 Compare how the early colonies and early national period educated African Americans and Native Americans with how they educated white children.
4-7 Trace how public schooling changed during the early national period.
4-8 Outline the factors that influenced the U.S. movement toward universal public schooling.
4-9 Discuss the status of schooling in the late nineteenth century.

We can better understand where U.S. education is today by seeing where we have been. To a large extent, today's education reflects its roots.

This chapter looks at American education from the colonies' earliest days through the movement toward universal public schooling. We will consider how the earliest settlers brought European educational ideas and institutions to their new homeland, and how our American environment transformed these Old World beliefs and practices. We will see how the early interaction of three key factors—the economy, religion, and the view of governmental control—led to the types of schools that each community, and then state, developed. In addition, we will discuss how our forebearers' attitude about the type of democracy and the government they wanted affected the educational system. The extension of the right to vote, the rise of manufacturing, and the increasing diversity of the American population all encouraged public schools' expansion to higher grades and its spread across the nation. Many of the educational challenges we face and are overcoming today have their roots in these earlier schools.

4-1 Cultural Influences on Education in Early Colonial America

The North American continent was not empty when the European settlers arrived. Native Americans had been here for centuries, developing their own civilizations. Culture contact, the initial reality of American education, also proved to be its ongoing challenge.

4-1a Settling North America

When the Pilgrims came to America in December 1620, they were a community seeking to preserve their religious and cultural integrity. Although they were only a minority of the Plymouth, Massachusetts, population, their views dominated the colony's character. As in the earlier (but failed) Jamestown settlement in Virginia, family and church initially were responsible for educating the colony's children. A key reason: The settlers included few people with formal learning.[1]

Like the Pilgrims before them, the Puritans who settled Massachusetts in later years arrived as a community linked by family, friendship, and common loyalty. They were attempting to preserve their religious and cultural heritage by creating a Christian commonwealth. Within such a society, education would transmit their intellectual traditions and prepare young people to pursue the Puritans' cultural ideal. Family, church, school, university, and community all provided education dedicated to molding persons.

American settlers also came from other countries. The Spanish founded the first permanent European settlement north of the Gulf of Mexico at St. Augustine, Florida, as early as 1565. The French had permanent colonies in Nova Scotia and Quebec in 1605 and 1608. By 1664, New Amsterdam (later renamed New York) was a prosperous Dutch market town of about 1,500 inhabitants. Englishmen, Swedes, French, Portuguese, and Africans lived in its extensive colonial province. There were scattered settlements of French Huguenots, Spanish and Portuguese Jews, Scottish Presbyterians, and German sectarians. These early immigrants came as individuals, as independent families, and in groups of families looking to share a common life in a new land under unfamiliar but tolerant civil authorities.[2]

From its inception, diversity and cultural competition, accommodation and blending were fundamental facts of American life.[3]

English influence By 1689, English settlements stretched from Maine to the Carolinas and east to the West Indian Islands. Of the 200,000 Europeans on the North American continent, the English represented the largest group. Owing to their greater numbers than the French, Dutch, and Spanish settlers and their technological superiority to the Native Americans and the Africans, the English were uniquely positioned to influence colonial development.

English colonists spread their decisive cultural influence in North America through their educational system. By the 1620s, England saw its colonies as permanent, self-sustaining communities. These communities embraced families, churches, missions, print shops, and schools, which would systematically advance English ideas, customs, language, law, and literature. Although settlers from other countries had families in North America during the seventeenth century, and some had churches, missions, and schools, none of these groups managed to develop an educational system as extensive as the English version. As a result, England achieved intellectual as well as political influence that, although challenged, would not be overthrown.[4]

4-1b Renaissance Influences on Early Colonists' Intellectual Traditions

The Renaissance and its contradictions influenced those who came to America. Colonists were both overly believing and skeptical, idealistic yet pragmatic. Colonists accepted witchcraft and the new sciences. They believed in improving themselves while preserving valued customs. Their books included Christian classics and ancient texts. Renaissance scholarship looked backward toward the past exemplars and focused on contemporary religious works as well as manuals of law, medicine, politics, surveying, agriculture, and conduct. Poetry, drama, history, and fiction offered colonists opportunities to experience refined living once basic survival was ensured. Wanting to safeguard their civilization's continuity in the New World, the colonists used these books to express their shared aspirations and the forms of education they would support.

The early settlers' intellectual tradition included humanistic ideas about education developed by Desiderius Erasmus, Sir Thomas Elyot, and John Locke. Erasmus's *The Education of a Christian Prince* (1516) identified education as necessary to develop a competent ruler who uses his power to advance the people's welfare rather than his own—or his friends'—economic and social gains. To fulfill this essential educational responsibility, a tutor of fine character, high morals, pure life, and affable manner was widely sought and highly valued. The curriculum taught by such a tutor would include the Bible, Greek and Roman literature, and classical historians.[5] Influenced by Erasmus, Sir Thomas Elyot's *The Boke Named the Governour* (1531)[6] extended a good education's value from hereditary monarchy to those who would govern. The key idea was that common-born administrators and professionals needed a proper education if they were to join with traditional aristocracy in government service.

British philosopher John Locke believed in the principle that the people, not their kings, had civil and political rights.[7] As a result of his contractual theory of government, some would consider Locke to be the grandfather of the American Declaration of Independence.[8] Locke believed education had useful purposes—for the business of living (not simply for the university) and for the possibility of advancing progress. In *Some Thoughts Concerning Education* (1693), Locke advised parents on how to raise their children into moral, social persons with the virtue (have a good life based on Christian principles) and the wisdom (able management of one's business affairs) necessary for living in the world. In his view, education helped shape the child's psychological and motivational structure, enabling the child to take rational control over his or her own life.

Reflect & Discuss

A. Discuss the difference between "an education that *confirms* status to an education that *confers* status."

B. How does this idea fit with the American belief in the values of meritocracy and social mobility?

C. If you were living in colonial America in a family of modest means, what would belief in "education that confers status" mean for your own schooling and life opportunities?

D. What current trends threaten to undermine Americans' confidence in a public education that advances a meritocracy and "confers status"?

The Renaissance's religious conflicts also influenced American education. The sixteenth century's Protestant Revolution challenged the Catholic Church's authority, and this revolt did not stop at the Atlantic Coast. Individual responsibility for salvation became more dominant than the church's collective influence. Accordingly, individual responsibility required all people to be educated. Education became viewed as a vital necessity, requiring a new type of school—elementary, for the masses, and in the native tongue. The American colonies would faithfully reflect this belief.[9]

In short, sixteenth-century political and religious thought culminated in a significant humanistic shift in how the English viewed education. The same education that Erasmus, Elyot, and Locke realized would prepare the aristocracy to rule could also prepare common persons to rule and live productive lives. Convinced of education's value, "it is but a short step from an education that *confirms* status to an education that *confers* status."[10] Education, it was realized, could lift men up to a higher station in life. It did not just humanize those who ruled; rather, education could *qualify* men to rule, whatever the circumstances of their birth and the conditions of their early life. Education would make meritocracy possible.

4-1c Schooling in the Early Colonies: Three Key Factors

Available schooling in the early colonies depended on three key factors that influenced people's thoughts and actions about educating their children: the local economy, local religious practices, and the locality's views on government involvement in their schools. Table 4.1 clarifies these relationships and identifies the type of schooling each

TABLE 4.1

Types of Early Colonies and Types of Schools

	Geographic Regions		
Factors Influencing the Type of School Desired	New England*	Middle Colonies (Pennsylvania, New Jersey, New York, Delaware, Maryland)	Virginia and Southern Colonies
Economy	Small farms, trades, lived in small villages, towns, cities.	Small farms, trades, lived in small villages, towns, cities.	Large plantations, highly stratified society of great wealth, servants, slaves.
Religion	Mostly Puritan. Calvinist; wanted a church-based society.	Varied. Did not want religion dominating the others.	Varied. Did not want religion dominating the others.
Community's view of government involvement in its schools	State and local control favored to require, pay for, and maintain public schools.	No government involvement with schools wanted.	No government involvement with schools wanted.
Type of school	Church-run, later becoming public schools for all.	Parochial or charity schools for the few.	Parochial and charity schools for the few.

* New England is generally considered to include Maine, Vermont, New Hampshire, Massachusetts, Connecticut, and Rhode Island.

region developed.[11] Of course, diverse viewpoints existed in every region, but general trends can be described.

Early American public education arose from collaboration between churches and colonial governments. Most of the first colonists arrived from Western Europe and had a range of ideas about what education in the New World should be. Figure 4.1 shows their settlements along the Atlantic Coast.

Outside New England, settlers rejected the idea that church and state should join as partners in running the colonies, including their educational systems. They also rejected the notion of using public monies for public schools. Because these other colonies varied from one another in religious

FIGURE 4.1 Immigrant Groups in the U.S. Colonies

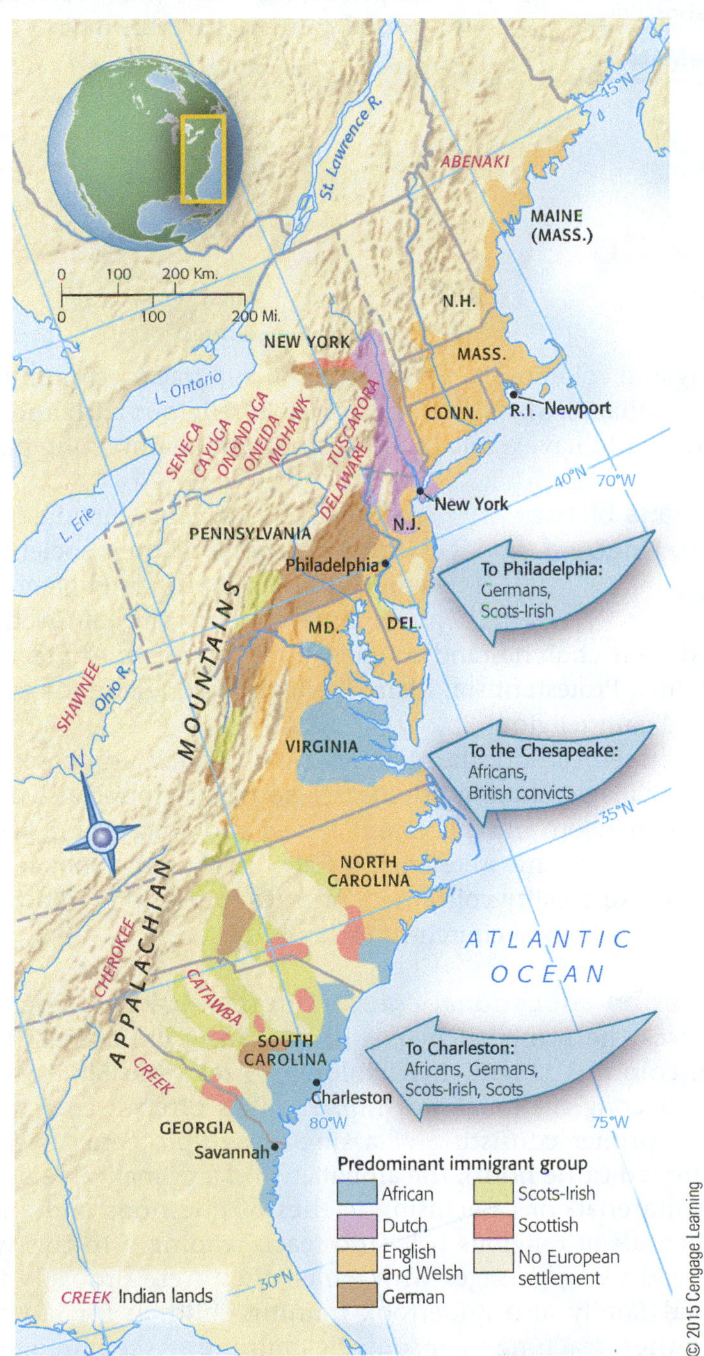

> **Did You Get It?**
>
> **Which statement is false about the influences affecting education in early colonial America?**
>
> **a.** Contact with Native Americans, particularly the Iroquois Confederation, was profoundly influential.
>
> **b.** The Pilgrims and Puritans were attempting to preserve their own cultural heritage by creating a Christian commonwealth.
>
> **c.** Religious and cultural diversity—provided by Spanish and Portuguese Jews, French Huguenots, the Dutch, Scottish Presbyterians, German sectarians—were fundamental facts of American life from very early in our colonial history.
>
> **d.** Early American public education was a product of what we would now call church–state collaboration.
>
> **Take the full quiz on CourseMate.**

backgrounds, social classes, and economies, they did not want one sect's religious leaders controlling all students' learning. Furthermore, the Southern caste system in which wealthy whites ruled over African American slave labor and white indentured servants made the idea of publicly funded education of diverse social and economic classes and races totally unthinkable.[12] Adding to the mix, every colony had private venture schools whose owners, for a price, promised to teach their students whatever they wanted to learn.[13] The push-and-pull between local and state control of public schooling that emerged during this period continues to this day.

4-2 Early Education in New England Colonies

The New England colonies shared a small farm and trades economy. Most people lived in small villages. Many shared a common religious faith and believed that government should have a role in establishing and maintaining public schools.

4-2a Puritans Shape Early New England Education

New England's Puritans valued education as the essential backbone of their society and government. While still living in England, Puritans opposed close church–state connections. Instead, they wanted their churches and congregations to be free to practice their own style of Calvinist Protestantism. Many Puritans fled England for America to save their lives and gain religious liberty.

The Puritans settled along the Atlantic Coast in a small farm-based economy, living together in villages, sharing a similar religious background and the philosophy that education, religion, and the state all served a common good. Because most of the colony's early residents were English Calvinist Puritans, they felt comfortable having the state or locality collect fees or taxes to pay for, build, maintain, and require attendance in local church-run schools.

hornbook An early reading primer consisting of a single page protected by a transparent sheet of flattened cattle horn.

The family as an educational agency In the early New England colonies, the family was the principal means of educating children. Through home instruction, colonists taught their children to read the Bible and participate in family and congregational worship. Families often used a **hornbook** (an early reading primer consisting of a single page protected by a transparent sheet of flattened cattle horn), the alphabet, and a primer (an elementary book of religious material) or catechism (a series of questions and answers giving the fundamentals of religious belief) to teach reading.[14] In this way, children learned to read using passages with which they were probably familiar. The early colonial family also undertook training children for labor or employment with fathers teaching their sons the multiple arts required to manage the household, farm, and workshop, and mothers instructing their daughters in varied domestic skills.

When they wished to follow a vocation not pursued in their own homes, children would apprentice in another household, where a parent-surrogate systematically taught the new trade. Apprentices learned by direct example with immediate participation and appraisal by the parent or master. Young men who wanted to enter a more learned profession might substitute a period of formal schooling for the apprenticeship. The masters of the school stood in *loco parentis* (in place of the parents), and the curriculum of reading, writing, and principles of religion either incorporated or supplemented the trades portion of the education. This educational arrangement did not hold for all New England families, however. The English settlers sharply disrupted the Native Americans' family life and education, and many indigenous people eventually withdrew from the tribal environment and attempted to live as Europeans did. An even sharper rupture of family life and education occurred among the Africans who were brought forcibly to America as servants or slaves and placed as property within colonial households. We know practically nothing about the education provided in such families. These involuntary immigrants likely transmitted African stories to their children, and adapted their tribal lore to their New World circumstances.[15]

New England laws regarding town schools In New England, the Plymouth Colony originally left education to households and churches. Different towns experimented with providing grammar (elementary) schools. By the end of the settlement's first decade, 7 of the 22 Massachusetts towns had taken some public action on behalf of schooling, although not all of these attempts survived.[16]

Because most colonial townships had not provided formal schooling for their residents, the state government felt compelled to act. In 1642, Massachusetts passed ground-breaking legislation that empowered the selectmen of each town to periodically visit local homes where they expected parents or masters to explain how they were providing for their children's education. Children were to learn how to read well enough to understand religion and secular laws.

With this law, education became compulsory for all youths in the Massachusetts Bay Colony—boys and girls alike.[17] To the Puritans, both genders' eternal souls were at stake. Most notably, the responsibility for encouraging and overseeing family education now moved from the clergy to secular officials.

Intended more for parental guidance than as a legal requirement, these laws were not usually enforced. From time to time, Massachusetts towns would crack down on parents and masters whose dependents remained ignorant and illiterate. After five years, the general court realized that the school law was not working as intended.

Early school finance laws Acting more firmly, the court established the law of 1647—the famous "Ye Olde Deluder Satan" law. Because Puritans saw children as depraved—prone to idleness and foolishness—the law assumed that those who could read and understand the Bible could not be lured to follow Satan's temptations (and possibly offend God and neighbors).

The 1647 law required towns that had at least 50 households to appoint and pay for a teacher to instruct all children to read and write. Any town with 100 or more households was required to set up a grammar school and hire a teacher to prepare youth for university. Towns generated school funds by direct taxation of the entire town, by taxing all those with boys of school age (typically 6- to

12-year-olds), by charging tuition, by selling some town land, or by some combination of such measures.[18]

Selectmen were authorized to impose fines on those parents who were not educating their children. Violators might endure public humiliation in the stockades.[19] Despite the legal penalties, most towns responded with a variety of strategies, ranging from outright noncompliance to meeting the letter of the law but compromising on its spirit.[20]

Most importantly, civil authorities—not religious ones—retained functional control over schools. Town funds—not church funds—financed schools. Elected local officials now had the duties that had formerly belonged to ministers—hiring teachers, inspecting schools, supervising curriculum, and encouraging student attendance.

The Puritans had few objections to moving the school into civil government's hands. After all, they saw religious and civic government as one in the same, sharing a common purpose in educating children to prepare them for a righteous religious and civic life. Not until 1789, after the American Revolution, did Massachusetts require community (secular) sponsored schools.

Initially, Massachusetts's approach to state-controlled education had limited impact outside what are now the neighboring states. In Connecticut, the law of 1650 ordered that children and apprentices be taught to read. Like its neighboring colony to the north, Connecticut established Latin grammar schools to prepare male students for the state college, Yale College, where they would study for the ministry.

To the New England Puritans, education's primary goal was not to advance a child's personal interests, but rather to protect and enhance the community and the state. Public schools were not supposed to replace parents' role in teaching and socializing their children. An educated populace was as much a moral issue as a civic necessity. The state, however, was in a better position than parents to enforce this expectation for learning. State oversight and control of schools had begun.

4-2b Four Types of Schools

Most New England colonials saw the family unit as the source for all education—practical, moralistic, and religious. The family controlled its children's future social and economic mobility. Wealthy (and many middle-class) families could afford for their children to get an education rather than to work as laborers or apprentices. They could pay for private tutors, send their children to private tuition-based schools, or send them to Europe to receive a cosmopolitan education. If they wanted their sons to become lawyers, physicians, or ministers, they could send them to college.

Not all families believed that women needed an education to meet their house hold and social responsibilities.[21] Families with means who wanted to educate their daughters could send them to an entrepreneurial school, if one were available.[22] As for children from poor families, unless they lived in a town that required school attendance for a few years, they received no formal instruction at all. Their future economic survival depended on gaining an apprenticeship or undertaking hard, backbreaking manual or household labor.

New England colonists re-created the dual-track system they had seen in England. The dual track included a minimum education for most children (at the English elementary, town, or common school) and preparation for college for affluent young men (at the Latin grammar school). A third type of school, the dame school, became available to prepare young children with the skills to enter elementary (common) school. A fourth type, the academy, was a newer and less well-defined institution for older students not attending college.

4-2c English (Elementary) Town Schools

The New England town (elementary) school was controlled locally and welcomed both boys and girls, ages 6 through 13 or 14. Attendance was irregular, depending on the weather and the need for children to work on their families' farms. The schools' curriculum included reading, writing, arithmetic, catechism, and religious hymns. Children learned the alphabet, syllables, words, and sentences by memorizing the hornbook. Older children read the *New England Primer,* which included the Ten Commandments, the Lord's Prayer, and the Apostles' Creed. Math went as far as counting, adding, and subtracting.

Town school teachers Initially, all teachers in New England town schools were men. Some were earning a living as a teacher while preparing to become ministers or enter another profession. Some became teachers to repay debts owed for their trips from Europe to North America. In the late seventeenth century when a few towns did hire women ("school dames") for teaching, they employed them only as adjuncts to the town schoolmaster, who remained the "revered and accepted instructor of children."[23]

Eventually, the schoolmasters' jobs went to itinerant teachers and college students in the winters and to women teachers in the summers. Girls were usually admitted to the summer school with the female instructors but not to the winter schools.[24] Girls, therefore, learned a small amount of reading, writing, religion, and ciphering (using arithmetic to solve problems).[25] Only toward the end of the colonial period—and then only for girls "from the best families"—did girls receive education beyond domestic training for the home.[26]

Teaching salaries remained modest. Reading and writing masters in smaller rural communities could earn 10 pounds per year. Meanwhile, distinguished grammar schoolmasters could earn a more generous 25 to 50 or 60 pounds per year. Given colonial New England's labor shortages, salaries for competent teachers could sometimes approach 75 to 100 pounds per year.[27] Unfortunately, because parents did not always pay their school fees, teachers were often not paid on time. On the plus side, teachers occasionally received special grants and benefits such as gifts of land, houses, and firewood; a share of tuition fees; and exemptions from taxes and military service.[28]

Teacher turnover was high during this era. In fact, most schoolmasters changed jobs yearly.[29] Only about 3 percent of the graduates remained in teaching permanently because ongoing labor shortages opened attractive alternatives to talented schoolmasters. The result was a chronic scarcity of schoolmasters and the presence of many transient, part-time teachers. The best teachers soon left the classroom for higher-paying careers in medicine, business, public service, and the ministry. Many teachers "doubled up," simultaneously serving as ministerial assistants, practicing law and medicine, acting as justices of the peace and captains of the militia, and working as brewers, tailors, innkeepers, and gravediggers.[30]

As a result, pupils were taught by anyone and everyone, including parents, tutors, clergymen, lay readers, physicians, lawyers, artisans, and shopkeepers. In large towns such as Boston, New York, and Philadelphia, "virtually anyone who could command a clientele could conduct classes." The content and sequence of learning remained fairly well defined, and each student progressed from textbook to textbook at his or her own pace.[31]

School buildings Formal schools started wherever space could be found: a meeting room, a barn, or a spare room in a large home. Without models for schools to copy, townsfolk built utilitarian and practical shelters—one room, with benches and a stove. Multiple grades of students attended the same school, where they were taught by a single teacher.[32]

More often than not, these schools were built cheaply and quickly and deteriorated almost as quickly. In 1681, one Roxbury, Massachusetts, citizen complained that the local schoolhouse was "not fitting for to reside in; the glass broken and thereupon very raw and cold; the floor very much broken and torn up to kindle fires; the hearth spoiled; the seats, some burnt and others out of kilter, so that one had as well nigh as good keep school in a hogsty as in it."[33]

In most cases, school furnishings were threadbare, consisting of a rough floor and planks on barrels or stakes for desks, and benches running around the walls for seats. Paper greased with lard often substituted for windows.[34] In the winters, many schools went unheated. Those that were heated often relied on poorly vented fireplaces or stoves, sometimes making breathing difficult. Heating the school building used much wood, which sometimes led to a wood tax levy on families with children attending school.[35]

If the town did not build schoolhouses, summer school might be held in barns, watch houses, or meeting houses. In winter, however, classes needed warmth as well as space, so schoolmasters rented a room with a fireplace—sometimes a kitchen.[36]

Teaching resources Teachers had an almost complete lack of teaching supplies, books, and effective teaching methods. Desks would not appear for many years, and blackboards did not appear until 1820s. Pencils and steel pens were not available until later still. Paper was expensive and of poor quality, so pupils used it as little as possible. Sometimes students wrote their letters and numbers on birch bark or traced letters in sand. One of the schoolmaster's job requirements was the ability to make and repair goose quill pens. Meanwhile, the ink was homemade and often poor quality.[37]

Instructional methods Instructional methods in the colonial era were relatively unsophisticated. The vast majority of schools were ungraded, and most instruction was individual with pupils approaching the master's desk or lectern and reciting orally or displaying their work for praise or correction.[38] Other students practiced their drills and waited their turns. Memorizing was the norm. The teaching and learning process was so inefficient and ineffective that students could attend school for years and gain only the most minimal reading and writing skills.

Teachers' time was spent on listening to individual students' recitations, assigning students new tasks to learn, preparing copies, making quill pens, dictating math addition problems, and keeping order.[39]

Classroom management Townsfolk considered teachers to be failures if they could not keep their students under tight control. As a consequence, school discipline was severe. Even college men occasionally received whippings. Whipping, standing in the corner, wearing a dunce cap, and other humiliating consequences were commonplace.[40] Some schoolrooms even had their own whipping posts in the classroom—or the post stood in the school yard or street.[41]

Milder punishments included forcing students to sit on air or "standing in the corner, face to the wall; stooping down to hold a nail or peg in the floor, the culprit often getting a stinging slap on his rear to keep him from bending his knees. Another punishment included being forced to sit among the girls, which in time came to be called "*capital* punishment."[42] In colonial schools, students frequently received blistered hands, swollen ears, and throbbing limbs along with their ABCs.

4-2d Dame (Primary) Schools

Town schools made no provisions for beginning learners. Students were supposed to learn how to read at home before they entered the town school at age 8.[43]

Providing something between day care and primary reading instruction, dame schools began to prepare certain students for the town school. These schools were fee-based lower elementary or primary schools typically held in a widowed or unmarried townswoman's home. If young children could "stand up and keep their places," they could attend. For a few pennies a week from parents or the town treasury, the dame took neighbors' children into her home and helped them learn the beginnings of reading and spelling, basic writing, and counting. More often, dames taught what they knew best—and students learned rudimentary sewing and knitting. In time, schoolmasters' daughters were trained to keep a dame school to prepare boys for the town's grammar school.[44]

Unlike today's kindergartens and early primary grades, the dame schools were not pleasant, colorful, child-friendly places. The alphabet and the Bible formed the heart of the curriculum, and the atmosphere was stern and dogmatic.[45]

Knowing the ABCs and basic reading and writing soon became a prerequisite for admission to the town grammar school. Eventually compulsory attendance legislation provided regular public funding for the dame school, and it evolved into the town primary school.

By 1750, most New England towns had elementary or common schools available to children with primary schools available after 1820 to bring education to beginning learners. For most children, however, formal education ended at age 7. Girls left school to attend to their household duties. They were generally excluded from Latin grammar schools and higher education. Similarly, after attendance at a dame school, most boys went on to apprenticeships or farm work. For both girls and boys, the household and workplace continued to be the most frequent sources of education.

Color engraving of a New England dame school, 1713

Bettmann/Corbis

4-2e Latin Grammar Schools

At a time when the more fortunate poor and middle-class students completed their education in the town schools, upper-class sons ages 7 or 8 went to Latin grammar schools, which prepared them to begin college at age 15. America's seventeenth- and eighteenth-century Latin grammar schools were often modest, one-room structures. The "Latin School" at Boston was established in 1635 (and still exists today as the nation's oldest school) with others soon following in Massachusetts towns.

Latin grammar school teachers The towns' best teachers worked in Latin grammar schools, and their pupils called them "Master." These instructors were frequently well-educated men who held college degrees and enjoyed a higher social position than did the elementary teachers. They were strictly religious and capable instructors. Because they served wealthy men's children, their salaries were relatively higher and more consistently paid than the salaries of their town school colleagues.[46]

Curriculum Because Latin was considered the sacred language of religion and advanced learning, students studied works by ancient Roman writers Cicero, Caesar, Virgil, and Horace. More advanced students studied works by Greek authors such as Socrates and Homer. Any given grammar school could include an additional offering that ranged from introductory reading and writing in English to arithmetic, geometry, trigonometry, navigation, surveying, bookkeeping, geography, rhetoric, logic, algebra, and astronomy.[47] Vocational subjects and instruction in fine arts were not available.

After Latin grammar school, upper-class boys often applied for admission to Harvard or Yale College to prepare for the ministry. Middle-class boys and girls did not expect to attend college. Students had to demonstrate competency in Latin and Greek to be admitted to Harvard, where they received an education in grammar, logic, rhetoric, arithmetic, geometry, astronomy, ethics, metaphysics, and natural science, in addition to Hebrew, Greek, and ancient history (useful for Bible study).

The middle and Southern colonies did not share New England's fondness for classical studies, but a few Latin grammar schools were founded in several large towns in those regions. Instead of focusing on classical languages and curriculum, these schools leaned toward more commercial and practical courses and introduced merchants' accounts, navigation, surveying, and higher math as subjects of study. In time, these schools evolved to become English grammar schools.[48] By the mid-eighteenth century, classical Latin grammar schools had declined in popularity, even in Massachusetts.[49]

academy An institution providing "higher schooling," the most flexible and loosely defined of provincial schools.

4-2f The Academy

The **academy**, an institution providing "higher schooling," was the most flexible and loosely defined of provincial schools. Academies were a good educational "fit" with commercial and early industrial economies, which demanded a modest number of people to fill those professions, later called "white-collar" positions, that required higher schooling. The academy was incorporated to ensure financial support beyond that available through tuition alone.[50] The families of small businessmen, merchants, professionals, and large landowners—that is, the "middling classes"—generated enough youths to provide the base population for an academy. In addition, by accommodating part-time and older students, academies fit the varied life cycles pursued by people of the time and maximized their enrollments.[51]

Most academies catered to common school students. At their highest level, academies overlapped with colleges.[52] For the most part, early academies offered as their curriculum what the master was prepared to teach, what the students were prepared to learn, what the academy's sponsors were prepared to pay for, or some combination of the three.[53]

Governance Although open to the public, academies were not free; they were reasonably affordable. Many academies were church-sponsored institutions. Other academies were supported by gifts or estates left by wealthy civic-minded individuals in their wills for the purpose of educating children. Many others were organized by private subscriptions or as private stock companies. They usually retained private management.[54]

In time, towns, counties, or states began to charter and help maintain the academies, and they evolved into semipublic institutions. Many mingled private and public funds to support their activities.[55] Almost all charged students a tuition or fee, and most had dormitories and boarding halls. A few even provided some form of manual labor—an early work–study program to defer school expenses. Additionally, with the creation of boards of trustees to oversee the development of curriculum and assessment, academies became more accountable to the community for the quality of their students' learning.

Curriculum and instruction Academies maintained a degree of curricular choice and flexibility distinct from both the earlier Latin grammar schools and the later public high schools. Unlike the Latin grammar schools, academies were not devoted solely to college preparation; they also sought to prepare students for business life and the rising professions. Teachers taught classes in English. Although students might still have learned Latin and Greek, the curriculum now included English grammar, English literature, oratory, arithmetic, algebra, geometry, geography, botany, chemistry, general history, American history, surveying, rhetoric, and natural and moral philosophy. Courses in navigation, needlework, vocal music, or dance might have been available as well.[56] The curriculum was both traditional and, for its day, contemporary.

Rote memorization and student recitation remained the common practice in schools at all levels through much of the nineteenth century. The system of emulation—a form of competition in which prizes were generally awarded in public—was another popular instructional method. Teachers encouraged students to imitate and surpass their highest-achieving peers.[57]

Women's education The Latin grammar schools had been created exclusively for boys, but the academies rather freely admitted girls.[58] Supply and demand played a role in bringing young women into this "advanced education." In 1800, the United States had only 25 colleges but hundreds of academies. The increased number of academies meant there was more competition for students, which in turn required academies to appeal to a broader constituency. Thus academy education was the only form of higher schooling available to women in the early republic.

The academies soon became teacher training schools, the chief supply source for the best-educated elementary teachers. Although they rarely offered instruction in how to teach, their advanced instruction in subjects related to the common schools' curriculum made their future common school teachers more knowledgeable about the subjects they would be teaching. Normal schools would eventually replace academies as sources of teacher preparation. Likewise, the public high school became the main provider of what became known as "secondary" education. Eventually, academies were converted into high schools, became private, tuition-based "prep" schools, or ceased to exist.[59]

Facilities Academies' special contribution to the U.S. educational system included its good-quality facilities and resources for educating students. A larger school building replaced the resource-poor, one-room schoolhouse that had long served as the town school and Latin grammar school. Academies included a public hall for meetings and rhetorical exercises, and they

Did You Get It?

Pick the true statement.

a. In the early New England Colonies, families were too busy surviving to educate their children, hence their strong desire—and willingness to pay—for public education.

b. The Puritans make public education compulsory for boys but not girls because they believed that learning to read would encourage men to godliness but girls to wantonness.

c. Virtually from the very beginning, civil authorities retained control over public schools because the strong religious beliefs of New Englanders meant that they never trusted even their own church leadership to be sufficiently saved.

d. The strong religious faith of most New Englanders was in no way a hindrance to government establishment and maintenance of public schools.

Take the full quiz on CourseMate.

provided maps, charts, globes, and libraries for students' use. The extra funds available to this kind of semipublic institution brought teachers and students a wider range of educational assets to improve their learning climate and their learning.

Academies took students who had completed the common schools' English education and gave them an advanced education in modern languages, the sciences, mathematics, history, and the more useful subjects of the time. In this way, they built upon the common school courses but marked a transition from the aristocratic and largely exclusive college-preparatory colonial Latin grammar schools to the more democratic public high schools we have today.

Reflect & Discuss

Discuss in pairs and then as a class:

A. Separate into three groups of early colonial New England children: those from poor families, those from middle-class families, and those from well-to-do families. Each group of "children" will prepare and give three-minute reports on the following topics:
Their educational experiences (which schools or training they received)

What they were taught and what they learned
Their teachers and school facilities
Their present life and/or career options
Their parents' reasoning for making these educational decisions for them

B. After the presentations, as a class discuss how children's social strata dramatically affected their educational, work, and life options in the early colonies.

C. As individuals, explain how this system would have personally affected you had you been living at that time.

4-3 Early Education in the Middle Colonies

In the heterogeneous middle colony communities, people believed that responsibility for education belonged to the family, church, charitable organizations, or private efforts. Reflecting the immigrants' many different cultures and religious sects, this region's early colonists did not want the state controlling education. They feared having one group or religion force its views on all students through a state-sponsored curriculum or teachers dedicated to a particular faith. Instead, the state's only responsibility was to maintain pauper schools for the students living in or near poverty. Colonies adhering to this view included Pennsylvania, New Jersey, New York, Delaware, and Maryland.

At the same time, middle colonies' settlers supported church (parochial) or private schools for those who could afford to attend. Each family paid tuition to send its children to the school run by its own religious denomination. Students often received lessons in the dominant community group's native language. Church schools also emphasized the sponsoring church's religious beliefs along with reading, writing, and math.[60] A few of the larger towns opened private, tuition-based schools to educate children from more affluent families.

Impoverished children, if their families allowed, could attend church or philanthropic charity-run schools (if available), where they received a minimal education. Many of the charity-run schools were geared toward sons and daughters of "middling income" who could not afford tuition but whose families were not in need of financial support.[61] These charity schools' curriculum was similar to dame schools, and they focused on teaching the ABCs, basic reading, and counting. Orphans and children in very poor families typically received their education through apprenticeships.

Teachers in the middle colonies' parochial schools were usually clergymen until a regular schoolmaster could be found and hired. The local churches employed school-masters if they were solid believers in their denomination's faith, had a respectable education of their own, and were willing to work hard. For a small extra fee, many parochial school teachers were part-time choir masters, church chorus members, bell-ringers, sextons, and janitors.[62]

Different middle colonies developed some unique educational features. In New York City, which served as a commercial port, several private, for-profit schools charged students fees to study navigation, surveying, bookkeeping, Spanish, French, and geography. In the seventeenth century, these private entrepreneurial schools came to shoulder an increasing share of New York City's formal education burden. During the eighteenth century, they expanded to educate more pupils. These private schools were popular because teachers taught in English and because artisans, tradesmen, and shopkeepers presented a practical curriculum.[63]

Pennsylvania's Quaker settlers took a special interest in their local schools. Active since 1683, Quaker schools displayed a strong social justice bent, educated girls and boys, whites, African Americans, and Native Americans, emphasizing reading, writing, arithmetic, and religion as subjects of study. Quakers also sponsored a network of charity-run schools throughout the colonies to educate African American and Native American children. Reflecting the Quakers' practical-minded view, their curriculum included vocational training, crafts, and agriculture. Pacifists and conscientious objectors by religious principle, Quaker teachers did not use corporal punishment to control their students.

Centrally located between different colonies, New Jersey developed an educational system that reflected influences coming into the colony from varied directions. Each settler group brought its own education traditions. After the English colonized New York in 1664, however, English methods and practices came to influence most of New Jersey. As a consequence, education in New Jersey became limited to families with money or was provided haphazardly through charitable schools for poor children.

Thus the middle colonies depended on a mixture of church-run and private schools for their educational opportunities. Without state involvement, education was very rudimentary, of limited availability, and often nonexistent. Each parochial (church) school did what it wished. Poor and orphaned children, if lucky, attended charity schools or entered apprenticeships. Meanwhile, children from wealthy families still had private tutors or attended private, tuition schools.

Did You Get It?

In the Middle Colonies

a. States typically maintained schools for all but the very wealthiest, who hired private tutors.

b. School diversity reflected the ethnic, religious, and political diversity of the region.

c. It was very common for clergy to run interdenominational schools, de-emphasizing sectarian differences in favor of the common interest in good education.

d. Orphaned students and students from very poor families usually had their fees paid for by local philanthropists.

Take the full quiz on CourseMate.

4-4 Early Education in Virginia and Southern Colonies

Colonized by wealthy, successful European immigrants, Virginia and other Southern colony settlers came to America with—or seeking—their fortunes. Although religion was important to them, it was not the central guiding force in their lives.

Climate, crops, and social class influenced Virginians to develop large plantation-style settlements rather than the compact towns found in New England. The introduction of indentured servants and African slaves—along with well-to-do planters, landholders, and independently wealthy gentlemen—led to a highly stratified class-based society instead of New England's popular democracy. Given these social realities, early Virginians had no motivation, from a public policy standpoint, to provide free and common public schools. What is more, these settlers believed that education was the family's—not the state's—business.

Virginians held traditionally English views about education. High-quality schooling was reserved for the elite. Wealthy students received private tutoring at home, attended small private or church-sponsored select schools, or received their education abroad. Young men learned basic academic skills, social graces and good manners, and management skills related to plantations and slaves. Daughters of wealthy families learned how to be successful hostesses. Children of self-taught, literate poor white farmers often learned from their parents. Students from meager backgrounds learned through apprenticeships, in charity-provided pauper schools (if available), or in church-run schools. At best, impoverished children received a minimal education, lasting only a few years.[64]

With parents under no legal requirement to educate them, most children of penniless Southerners ended up as field laborers without any training in reading, writing, or arithmetic. In 1642, the Virginia legislature passed a law providing compulsory apprenticeship education to children of indentured servants, orphans, and poor children, usually little more than simple vocational training.

Meanwhile, girls' education in Virginia and the South was generally more restricted than it was in the North. Virginians' expectations for women's education were modest. Girls were expected to learn the domestic skills such as cooking and sewing. As far as schooling, girls could learn the basics of reading, writing, and arithmetic. If their parents permitted, girls were able to attend charity schools, private schools, and—for the wealthiest—tutoring, boarding, or finishing schools. Most young women received informal instruction at home to do those things that would make them better wives, mothers, and housekeepers.[65]

Did You Get It?

Regarding education in Virginia and other Southern colonies

a. Religious differences kept settlers from creating common schools.
b. African Americans created their own schools.
c. The lack of quality public education both reflected and created a heavily-stratified society deeply fractured upon lines of race, gender, and wealth.
d. Girls attended schools and learned the basics of reading, writing, mathematics, and domestic skills related to managing a household.

Take the full quiz on CourseMate.

4-5 Early Education in Other States

Given their economies, religions, and views about government control, settlers in Rhode Island, North Carolina, Tennessee, Kentucky, Alabama, and Mississippi resisted the idea of the local or state government having a role in educating children. Among the New England states, only Rhode Island did not adopt the Massachusetts education laws. Desiring religious freedom, Rhode Island residents did not want one religious group dominating thought in schools. Instead, their first public schools did not emerge until the early nineteenth century.

Initially, these states were indifferent to providing a common education for their populace. As in other states, parents with money bought their children an education. If parents did not have the means, if parents did not want their children formally educated, or if no schools were available locally, children went without.

Farther west, Indiana and Illinois settlers held conflicting views about education, depending on their backgrounds before emigrating. Those coming from New England wanted a strong state hand in establishing and regulating schools. Those coming from the South believed the state had no legitimate role in educating children—and even if it did, mixing students from various social classes was unthinkable. In the end, settlers reached a stalemate, substantially limiting education's development in each state.

Although not all of the early states have been mentioned in these discussions, the economy, religion, and local views about government involvement in education contributed to the settlers' varying beliefs and practices regarding public schools.

Did You Get It?

Which following statement is false?

a. Settlers tended to adopt the types of schools they had in their previous states.

b. Settled by poor whites fleeing the Southern colonies, Tennessee and Kentucky were originally early adopters of strong public education.

c. New England settlers were united in wanting a good education for their children.

d. Unlike all other New England states, Rhode Island did not adopt Massachusetts's education laws.

Take the full quiz on CourseMate.

4-6 Early Education of African Americans and Native Americans

> Both schooling for democratic citizenship and schooling for second-class citizenship have been basic traditions in American education. . . . Both were fundamental American conceptions of society and progress, occupied the same time and space, fostered by the same governments, and usually embraced by the same leaders.[66]

Attempts to provide formal schooling for Native Americans or African immigrants and their descendants throughout the early 1700s were limited in scope and local in influence. Some missionary societies continually taught small numbers of free and unfree African Americans and Native Americans, eventually baptizing many of them. The pupils' day-to-day realities, however, often undermined their formal education.

4-6a Educating African American Slaves

The successful campaign to contain and repress literacy among enslaved Americans grew just as efforts to provide popular education for free people began to flourish. Between 1800 and 1835, most of the Southern states enacted laws making it a crime to teach enslaved children to read or write. Wanting to create and maintain a submissive and obedient labor force, slave owners understood that education could undo their economic system by liberating African American slaves' thoughts. Learning to read, write, add, and subtract would give slaves "dangerous" notions about their own abilities and destinies. In addition, many Southern slaveholders believed that Africans were racially inferior to whites and did not have the intellect to learn. Some free Southern African Americans might attend Quaker schools and missionary schools set up by abolitionists. In spite of the dangers and difficulties, thousands of slaves somehow managed to learn to read and write. By 1860, approximately 5 percent of slaves were literate.[67]

Some education occurred as slave owners and their families taught African American children the lessons related to their status and work. Certain lessons taught the skills and manners required to properly complete their tasks, whether as field hands or as skilled and semiskilled craftsmen, house servants, coachmen, midwives, preachers, healers, and parent-surrogates. All lessons were expected to nurture slaves' submissive and obedient attitudes toward the master in particular and toward white people in general. For the most part, "it was the whip and the Bible that served as the two most important pedagogical instruments in instructing . . . [African Americans] in the White version of their place in the world."[68]

Although missionaries hoped that immigrant Africans and Native Americans would welcome conversion to Christianity, masters of African slaves objected. Owners feared that conversion would imply setting slaves free or at least impose certain obligations on owners such as charity, humanity, and keeping slave families together. To quell this concern, missionary societies did their best to convince slaveholders that baptism did not imply earthly freedom.[69] On some plantations, slaves were allowed to attend church services to learn their duties and obligations in Christianity that supported white oppression. At the same time, African Americans learned covert lessons necessary to their survival as a people and as human beings rather than as property through teachings by their slave community, their families, and their clandestine religious congregations.[70]

The pedagogy of the African American family helped their children learn gardening, hunting, fishing, quilting, sewing, cooking, and loyalty to kin that endured in spite of physical separation. Parents also taught their children lessons about personal dignity and pride, family and community solidarity, resistance to white oppression, and aspirations to freedom and salvation. Music and stories transmitted the African American culture from one generation to the next, perpetuating itself, expressing and inspiring an essential educational message. The pedagogy of their secret congregations located in the woods or swamps adjacent to their living areas provided adult slaves with emotional release, a sense of camaraderie and community support, and expression of the belief that they would transcend their daily miseries. The family and the church were the chief institutions that free African Americans relied on for their own education with churches often establishing and maintaining schools for these individuals.[71]

4-6b Educating Native Americans

In New England, the Puritans remained ambivalent about the Native Americans' capacity to be educated or converted to Christianity. In the early years, the colony vigorously promoted Native American schooling. Evidence exists that as early as 1650, Native American children attended Massachusetts common schools alongside white classmates. Harvard's charter even mentions educating "English and Indian youth of this country." Nevertheless, efforts to provide Native American youth with formal schooling had few permanent results because pupils' tribal folkways overwhelmed any white teachings.[72] Then, too, the immense gap between what missionaries said about the brotherhood of man and how whites actually treated Native Americans and African immigrants made skeptical students question any religious teachings. No other region did as well as New England in trying to educate the original inhabitants of America, although missionaries tried to provide schooling for Native Americans in all the colonies.

Budding Scholar, Roseland, Henry Herman (1866-1950)/Private Collection/ Photo ~© Christie's Images/The Bridgeman Art Library

Thousands of African Americans learned how to read and write in spite of the difficulties.

The Native American educational experience was no more successful in the South, although native children had an early history of education there. In 1622, Virginia settlers established a school, called Henrico, to educate native children in reading and knowledge of Christian principles.[73] The purpose was wholly evangelistic: to save these innocents' souls. This endeavor had limited success. Hostile relations frequently arose between the Native American population and the English settlers who wanted the young students to reject their tribal traditions in favor of the Western belief system. In addition, Native American children were highly susceptible to European diseases; as a result, many who attended the settlers' schools got sick and died.[74]

The large variety of Native American tribes and forms of social organization make generalizing about their education difficult, but for the most part, the family carried important teaching responsibilities in these groups. A clear division of labor occurred between the sexes. Women assumed responsibility for planting, cultivating, harvesting, preparing foods, and making clothes. Men engaged in hunting or fishing and making war. Training the young occurred continuously through showing, explaining, and imitating, with young men undergoing instruction in age cohorts. Most tribes relied on praise, reward, and prophesy rather than physical punishment to stimulate knowledge and skill mastery. Competition provided an additional incentive. Likewise, tribes imposed meaning on the world through songs, stories, dances, and ceremonies. This family and community pedagogy was very powerful. Compared to it, any curriculum taught to Native American children by white "outsiders" in "school" appeared weak, disruptive, or meaningless.[75]

Although many Native Americans and African Americans became Christian, only some of them became literate. A few were permitted to pursue respectable careers as free tradesmen. A handful even influenced the thinking of their time, such as the Native American clergyman Samson Occom and the African American scientist Benjamin Banneker. Nevertheless, tribal values continued to dominate Native American thought and action, and most African Americans were constrained by the slave system and the attitudes toward race that supported it.

Did You Get It?

How were African American and Native American children educated in comparison to white children?

- **a.** Generally speaking, they were educated as second-class citizens, if not second-class human beings.
- **b.** If they were so lucky as to receive a formal education, they were typically schooled by masters deeply opposed to the concept of a second-class citizen. (These masters were usually Quakers.)
- **c.** In the ancient Greco-Roman tradition, slave masters usually educated their slaves because it made them more useful and valuable.
- **d.** New England was very successful in educating Native Americans alongside European colonists, a success that led to enduring peace treaties.

Take the full quiz on CourseMate.

Reflect & Discuss

The early colonies took different approaches toward educating their young people. Much depended on how similar the settlers were—in terms of religion, ethnicity, and economic focus—to their town neighbors.

Given the realities of early colonial schooling, suppose that you were growing up as a person of your same racial or ethnic background, socioeconomic class, and gender. Answer the following questions:

A. In which colony would you have *most* preferred to have grown up? Which type of schooling opportunities would have been available to you? How would have your educational opportunities made a difference in your adult lifestyle?

B. In which colony would you have *least* preferred to have grown up? Which type of schooling opportunities would have been available to you? How would have your educational opportunities made a difference in your adult lifestyle?

4-7 Public Schooling during the Early National Period

Schooling had been firmly transplanted to America during the initial decades of this country's settlement, especially in New England, by a population that highly valued education. As the colonies grew economically, the demand for schooling kept pace. People widely perceived and used schooling as a vehicle for personal advancement, such as moving artisans' children into the professions. Schools also increased in number as competing Protestant sects used schools for missionary purposes. Finally, a growing interest in public affairs during the last half of the eighteenth century increased the incentive for schooling. One needed to know how to read to keep up with the newspapers, almanacs, pamphlets, and books dealing with current events, especially after the Stamp Act crisis of the 1760s lit the fuse to the American Revolution.

By the middle of the eighteenth century, secular schooling gained popularity. In New England, secular schools replaced earlier religious schools. In the middle colonies, many of the parochial schools had closed. In the Southern colonies, the highly stratified class-based society, the large distances between communities, and the ongoing presence of African American slavery still made common schools socially and politically unrealistic.

4-7a The Secular Mandate

Colonial leaders, proud of what they had accomplished in their new homeland, worked to gain their political and economic independence from England. The American Revolution, which took place from 1776 to 1781, ultimately ended British rule in the 13 colonies.

The new republic's leaders agreed that a self-governing people needed universal education that would motivate all citizens to choose public over private interest.[76] Although the U.S. Constitution does not mention education, the nation's leaders agreed that public education was essential to maintaining a republican form of government. This meant consciously fashioning schooling based on American art, history, and law, independent thinking, and commitment to the promise of an American culture.[77] Education's task was to erect and maintain the new American nation. The first U.S. president, George Washington, believed in widespread public education. A free people would inevitably have opinions about their government, and Washington preferred that these views be enlightened.[78] John Adams, the second U.S. president, observed that to act as a free person and participate in self-government, "I must judge for myself, but how can I judge, how can any man judge, unless his mind has been opened and enlarged by reading."[79] Continental Congress leaders and future presidents, Thomas Jefferson and James Madison; Continental Congress president and future first U.S. chief justice, John Jay; and revolutionary pamphleteer, Thomas Paine, all advocated for education as a necessary source of general knowledge for citizens in a democracy. By the 1820s, the need of a self-governing people for universal education had become a familiar part of American politics. Although the founding fathers valued educating the nation's children for a few years at state expense, they disagreed about how to do it. Consensus would not arrive until the early nineteenth century. Education for self-government would have three central parts: popular schooling for literacy along with a certain common core of knowledge, morality, and patriotism; a free press to express multiple views on important public issues to inform public opinion; and a variety of voluntary associations to serve the public good. Schooled for literacy and armed with newspapers containing up-to-date information, a free American citizenry would learn how to become self-governing by doing it.

Separating church and state Separating church and state was on the framers' minds when they developed the U.S. Constitution. The new United States was a land of increasing religious and cultural diversity. The Constitution's authors supported the free exercise of religious faith for all by banning any state-sponsored religion. In this new nation, church and state could no longer be partners in public education. In turn, the public school began its transformation from an institution dominated by religious purpose and content into one charged with enlightening a diverse citizenry for civic participation. Its rationale became wholly civic, not religious. This essential idea laid the foundation for our system of free, common, public, tax-supported, nonsectarian schools that endures to this day.

4-7b Social, Political, and Economic Changes

After the Revolutionary War ended and the U.S. formed a national government, significant social, political, and economic movements continued to alter the fledgling nation's character and direction. Three of the most important influences were the rise of cities and manufacturing, extension of voting rights, and the growth of a new social class's demands for schools. All of these forces would change the U.S. system of public education.

Growth of city populations and manufacturing When the U.S. national government was originally formed, almost every American lived on a farm or in a small village. As late as 1820, the country had only 13 cities of 8,000 people or more in 23 states, containing only 4.9 percent of the total national population.[80]

After 1825, an increasing number of little villages evolved into the cities of the future. Some developed near waterfalls where cheap power made large-scale manufacturing possible. For instance, Lowell, Massachusetts, did not exist in 1820. Yet by 1840, more than 20,000 people lived there, largely to work in the mills powered by the Merrimack River. Cincinnati and Detroit grew because their locations made them good trade and commerce centers. Driven by the improving economy after the 1812 War with England, U.S. cities increased rapidly in both size and number.[81]

The emergence of new cities and the rapid growth of older ones appreciably altered education by producing an entirely new set of economic, social, and educational conditions. Cities along the Atlantic Coast—especially in Pennsylvania, New York, and New England—rapidly developed a manufacturing economy. Factory work meant the beginning of the end of the home-and-village industries. Eventually the informal apprenticeship system foundered. Rural populations moved toward the cities and employment in large factories. More people lived and worked in close proximity with others different from themselves.

The factory system altered village and home life as well as education. Living in large, crowded cities of diverse people brought to the fore many social and moral problems that were not evident when people lived in a small, familiar community. The villages' church, private, and charity school systems broke down under the strain of trying to educate many more children than they had the resources to do successfully. As a result, people started demanding that state funds or grants partially support both church and philanthropic society schools. Likewise, several charity organizations arose in various cities to help address poverty, juvenile delinquency, and other urban problems.[82]

These economic and societal changes did not affect everyone. The South's economy and society—which continued to be based on plantation life, African American slavery, indentured servants, and lack of manufacturing—remained largely unaffected by the changing economic and social conditions until well after the Civil War. Similarly, its educational practices changed very little over this period.

Likewise, Native Americans were considered alien members of their respective tribes with which the United States negotiated treaties. Nonetheless, they received few of the traditional benefits given foreign neighbors.

Extending voting rights Women, men who were not citizens or were not wealthy enough to own property, and nonwhites could not vote in the nation's early days. Change in voting rights came slowly. Western states, formed by people who lacked "old money" or large estates, judged persons more on their earned merits than on their inherited family backgrounds, championed the voting rights movement. By 1828, all white men could vote, giving rich and poor, Westerners and members of the Eastern manufacturing classes, employers and laborers greater influence in their government and their own affairs.

During the nation's early years, women could only vote in states where the constitutions did not specifically deny them this right.

Poor and working-class demands for schools Gaining the right to vote made white men of all social classes recognize that general education for knowledge and civic virtue was a basic necessity for their own and society's well-being. Governors began to recommend that their legislatures establish tax-supported schools. The new labor unions formed after 1825 joined in the demands for schools and education because their members saw the free education of their own children as their natural economic and political right.

The nineteenth century's second quarter witnessed the movement for tax-supported, publicly controlled and directed, nonsectarian common schools. Bitter arguments, legislative fights, religious jealousies, and private interests characterized the process of establishing free public schools. By 1850, however, tax-supported, nonsectarian, public schools had become a reality in almost every Northern state. In North Carolina, free taxpayer-supported schools were established, marking the first implementation of this trend in the South.

Two developments—the newly invented steam printing press and the first low-cost modern newspapers—also appeared at this time. These widely read publications strongly influenced popular opinion to support free common public schools. In time, the desirability of common, free, tax-supported, nonsectarian, state-controlled schools—open to all students—became clear to most American citizens as a means to perpetuate a free democracy and to advance public well-being.[83]

Developing a national educational consciousness The post–Revolutionary War period signaled a turning point in American education. The schools' tradition of promoting religious doctrine could no longer hold, although it took time for this practice to fade.[84] Now, people would have to share a common national loyalty and political allegiance with others whom they did not know, who did not live in their towns or states, and who saw and acted upon the world in different ways than they did. Secular purposes would direct schools. A new generation of young people had to be socialized to adopt the attitudes and behaviors needed to responsibly participate in the young constitutional democracy.

Before 1820, outside New England and New York, people had not developed an educational consciousness for a variety of reasons. First, no economic demand for education existed. The era's simple agricultural life—the colonies' largest occupation—did not require formal schooling. A person who could read, write, and cipher was considered educated, and those who could not lost no respect.[85]

Second, after the Revolutionary War, the United States was very poor. The country had few industries and weak foreign trade. Political leaders focused on immediate problems: strengthening the existing government and finding necessary resources to make essential infrastructure improvements. These critical responsibilities demanded their attention at the expense of providing universal education.

Until this time, travel and communication were difficult, and people did not often interact with others holding differing views and values. It was not necessary for everyone to speak the same language or speak a common language in the same way. They did not need formal schools to acculturate them to their shared society. Similarly, the early colonies had few cities that would bring diverse people together and require that they get along with each other if they were to survive and advance. Instead, the colonial villages' isolation and independence allowed them to remain indifferent to providing a common, free education to their children unless, like the Puritans and Quakers, religious and humanity concerns motivated the residents.

In addition, no widespread voting eligibility, behaviors, or institutions existed in which citizens could publicly express their views or agitate for widespread education. The day's politics did not envision popular voting to settle important local or national questions. Political decisions, including those of war, taxes, the military draft, or writing a national Constitution, still remained in the hands of wealthy white men—and these influential individuals could always afford to educate their own children.

By the War of 1812–1814, when Americans finally pushed the defeated British out of the United States, they had built a democratic national consciousness. Confident that the Union would survive as a stable political entity, the citizens of the United States finally had the energy, the self-assurance, the money, and the interest in creating a democratic system of public schools, a common language, and shared traditions. As a consequence, plans for education and national development began to receive serious consideration.

Reflect & Discuss

During the colonial and early national periods in American history, public schools had distinctive philosophical underpinnings. Controversy still rages, however, about whether our public schools were—or should be—religious or secular in purpose and practice.

A. Discuss the extent to which early American colonists practiced religion in public schools. Where did it occur and for what reasons? Where did it not occur and for what reasons?

B. What ended the teaching of religion in U.S. public schools? Which reasons and conditions prompted this secular focus?

C. Why is it still important to keep American public schools secular in outlook and practice?

As the national consciousness began to rise, with it came a democratic awareness. People wanted something more practical and less exclusive than the Latin grammar schools, which had always been a European transplant and was never especially well suited to American needs. They wanted a school better adapted to the frontier, able to provide social mobility, and support democratic environments.

4-7c Schools in the Early National Era

The early national era saw the common school, the Latin Grammar School, and the academy continue while three new types of schools began: the infant school, the public high school, and "supplementary" schools.[86]

Infant (primary) schools Infant schools were an educational innovation that prepared very young children to attend the common school. In nineteenth-century England, children as young as five often worked up to 14 hours a day in factories. One philanthropic factory owner, Robert Owen, offered an education to children between ages three and five, partly to let youngsters have some fun before they entered factory life and partly to provide them with moral and intellectual training. These schools were known as infant schools because their students were virtually babies!

In 1816, infant schools arrived in America as an English import to supplement the common school. Established initially in the eastern cities, they were designed for children between the ages of four and seven. Women were the teachers. Infant schools created a home-like learning environment for young children, resembling a large nursery with the purpose of engaging and amusing the pupils. The innovation flourished for a while but then fell out of favor. Later, in the 1850s, the infant school was revived as the kindergarten.

Infant schools tried to advance a new teaching theory propelled by a psychological view of children. For the first time, American schools considered the learner's needs and interests and the teaching methods needed to help them best learn.[87]

Over time, New England's infant schools evolved into kindergartens. Primary schools took over the dame school and infant school instruction as a public function and added the primary grades to the existing common schools. To this day, we still use the term "primary grades" to describe kindergarten through grade 3 of elementary school.

Public high schools Empowered with new money and new political rights, middle-class and business people clamored for the taxpayer-supported public high school as a cooperative effort to offer something beneficial for their children.

The public high school originated in 1821 in Boston as an alternative to the Latin grammar school. Its practical aim was to prepare young men for a private and public life in a profession (not requiring college) at no fee. English was the only language taught, along with reading, writing, grammar, science, math, history, and logic. This type of school quickly developed into a public institution offering the option of an English or a classical curriculum.

Under public control, the high school largely reproduced the academy's upper academic levels, making available to day students at modest cost or for free the same education that had once been available only to boarding students at a substantial cost.[88] Where high school extended education beyond primary, grammar, or intermediate school, it created an additional step on the American educational ladder, which was clearly evolving into a unitary school system for all the community's children.

Several factors provided the momentum for establishing public high schools. First, colleges required that students receive advanced education between elementary school and college, but no fully free, tax-supported schools yet bridged that gap. As city dwellers became more affluent and could afford to allow their children to attend school (rather than going to work), more students completed the elementary courses and wanted advanced training.

Second, the new manufacturing and commercial activities of the time required job applicants to have more—and different—knowledge and skills to be effective. Workers in these emerging jobs needed learning beyond elementary school but not as much as college.

Supplementary schools Supplementary schools were educational units that filled in the learning gaps for individuals whose school attendance had ended prematurely. Such schools emerged during the early national era under private, quasi-public, and public auspices for groups of students having special educational needs that the community thought best met in separate facilities. These students included children with disabilities, youths alleged to be delinquent, and African American and Native American children judged to be unacceptable in regular classrooms.[89]

Localities in the early 1800s also established several private or semiprivate voluntary alternatives to tax-supported schools. These included the Sunday School Movement, the Public School Society, philanthropic societies for education, and monitorial schools. These innovations, however, remained local institutions rather than serving as national models.

4-7d Teaching and Learning in the Early National Era

Schooling's popularization brought a change in the teaching profession's character and composition. Teaching became an increasingly female-dominated profession, especially in the primary and intermediate grades.

Increase in women teachers During this period, women, as compared to men, were considered more temperamentally and morally suited to work with younger children. Notably, they were also willing to work for half the salary (or sometimes one-third the salary) of men, and schools' male supervisors found women more open to suggestions. At the same time, teaching became more professional, making it a sacred calling second only to the ministry in its importance to society.

Particularly among male high school and academy teachers and state and city education leaders, providing teacher training for higher skills and standards became a priority. Intended or not, professionalism served to create an almost exclusively male-elite control of an increasingly female occupation.[90]

The learning environment The one-room district school with one teacher instructing between 40 and 60 boys and girls of varying ages remained the rule in most parts of the United States during this time. Teachers informally grouped students for different subjects taught at different levels, trying to keep youngsters focused and working. Sometimes, the entire student group would learn through a sing-song drill together, spelling a group of words, reciting a multiplication table, or listing state capitals. At other times, groups of three or four students would recite together. Occasionally, individual students would take turns going through a question-and-answer drill with the teacher. Students occasionally helped one another. It was, however, a relatively inefficient process, especially for inexperienced teachers.[91]

Discipline problems often arose in these large classes. It was often the new teacher's job to test his or her charisma and classroom management skills against the "big boys" before the class could begin its serious work.[92]

Changes in student discipline Successful efforts to limit physical punishment to control wayward student behaviors began in the 1820s and 1830s. By the last quarter of the nineteenth century, some urban schools had banned corporal punishment altogether. Where it was not forbidden, it often fell into disrepute.[93]

After the American Revolution, order and authority no longer rested with the king, the nobility, and their agents, but rather was delegated to families and schoolmasters. The Enlightenment, American republicanism, the market economy, industrialism, and other factors came together to fundamentally alter colonial schooling. Social relationships were changing, and schools needed to reflect these changes.

At this time, two different school discipline innovations occurred that altered the face of the classroom: bureaucratic discipline and affectionate discipline. In bureaucratic discipline, an impersonal institutional authority, other than the teacher, enforced the rules. For example, in Joseph Lancaster's early-nineteenth-century monitorial schools, which catered to the new industrial poor, students worked in a group relationship with **monitors**, more advanced pupils who earned their rank through merit. Surveillance of students was continuous and multiple with each monitor responsible for teaching, assessing, and overseeing a small group of learners' study. In turn, higher-level monitors watched over them and multiple groups.

monitors More advanced pupils who supervised less advanced pupils and who earned their rank through merit.

Instead of motivating students to achieve and behave appropriately through fear, Lancaster offered an elaborate system of rewards, prizes, and promotions. For example, a well-mannered student who mastered the assigned lessons could aspire to become a monitor, signified publicly by wearing a badge and chain around the neck. Students and classes competed against one another for public status. This kind of bureaucratic discipline, reinforced by ever-present surveillance and exams, encouraged students to internalize authority and prepared them for the larger world's "modicum of mobility . . . available to the diligent and fortunate."[94] Failure in the race for position brought students unpleasant consequences: Public humiliation was more unpleasant than physical beatings. Although monitorial schools fell into disfavor because they did not provide a reliable way of controlling costs or imparting instruction, bureaucratic discipline became a common nineteenth-century school practice.[95]

Affectionate discipline, like the bureaucratic approach, sought to instill in students an internalized authority but without external scrutiny. Instead, affectionate discipline depended on forging a deeply personal, warm, individualized relationship between teacher and student. Ideally, these positive emotional ties would trigger students' conscience, self-surveillance, and automatic obedience. In this disciplinary model, the ideal school—like the ideal family—showed love, affection, and intense emotional dependence on the authority figure. Students were self-disciplined by their fear of the teacher's withdrawal of affection and expressions of disappointment. The increasing presence of female teachers facilitated this disciplinary approach.

Both types of discipline were introduced to manage classroom behaviors and motivate learning by creating incentives for students to manage themselves. Other aspects of nineteenth-century school life also advanced these approaches. For instance, where sufficient enrollment permitted, schools moved toward self-contained, graded classrooms, closely regulated school rituals and practices, and systems of promotion, retentions, and demotions. In these more intimate settings, teachers could better supervise students and interact with them more frequently. Forerunners of the modern report card and merit–demerit systems appeared as well. More whole-class teaching and learning-by-doing replaced the practice of memorization and recitation. Throughout the century, both bureaucratic and affectionate discipline approaches coexisted in the same classrooms.[96]

4-7e Varied Opportunities for Varied Students

Schooling was far less available for African Americans and Native Americans than for white children. Many Southern states made it illegal to teach slaves to read and write. Schooling was both less available and less used by first-generation immigrants than by their children and native-born whites. Lastly, comparatively few women attended academies and colleges before the Civil War, and their choices among these institutions were limited.

Freed African Americans expressed their liberty through their struggle for education. After the Civil War, former slaves campaigned for universal schooling. The wealthy planters did not believe in state-enforced public education, however, and other classes of native white Southerners with whom they shared economic, psychological, and social interests did not disagree. Nevertheless, with help from Republican politicians, ex-slaves gained influence in state governments and laid the foundation for public schooling.

Without free schools, now-free African Americans taught themselves to read and write. By 1866, they had created at least 500 "native schools" in which the newly educated would teach other pupils. Ex-slaves also initiated free, church-sponsored "Sabbath" schools that operated mainly in the evening and on the weekend, providing basic literacy instruction. Newly liberated African Americans accepted help from Northern missionary societies, the Freedmen's Bureau, and certain Southern whites, but their own actions were the primary force that brought schools to their children.[97]

The dilemma at the heart of both African American and Native American education was that nineteenth-century whites assumed that neither group could be assimilated into the larger society. The key issue, put simply, was race. To educate African Americans would raise their hopes for a lifestyle and privileges that they could never attain because of their distinctive physiognomy and former-slave status. Native Americans who accepted the invitation to become educated to Western knowledge and skills in an effort to become part of the larger society found that no amount of "civilizing" would make their white neighbors accept them as equals. The prevailing assumption was clear. People could be educated to transcend ethnic and religious barriers to become full-fledged members of the American community, but they could not be educated to overcome the barriers of race.[98]

4-7f Increasing Access to Colleges

The earliest colleges—Harvard, William and Mary, Yale—were initially created with religious and state support to prepare men for ministry professions. Nationhood, however, brought a demand for more higher education opportunities for more citizens beyond those training for a religious vocation.

After nationhood, the nine original colonial colleges[99] reorganized to bring themselves more in line with the new government's ideas. Columbia and Pennsylvania changed for a time into state universities. At Harvard and Yale, divinity as a focus of study declined in importance while history and modern languages became more popular.[100]

The Western migration also influenced college availability. Immediately after the Revolutionary War, settlers began to move to the new western territories along the Ohio River. When "The Ohio Company" (a New England-based company) bought 1.5 million acres in south-central Ohio, the U.S. Congress granted it land for schools and a university. In 1788, upon the sale of 1 million acres near Cincinnati, Congress granted the township land for educational purposes. The former university became Ohio University at Athens, and the latter became Miami University at Oxford. The practice of granting townships land for schools and for state universities continued with the admission of each new Western and Southern state.

After 1820, with the growing national consciousness favoring free public education, interest in founding new colleges increased. The already widespread dissatisfaction with colleges' exclusivity and curricular narrowness grew. Until about 1870, providing higher education was largely a private effort. Most colleges required students to pay tuition. Because most colleges were founded by different religious denominations, people viewed them as representing and advancing their own parochial interests rather than the state's—or general public's—interests.

When some states discovered that they could not legally take over existing denominational colleges, they began to create their own universities. The University of Virginia, the University of North Carolina, and the University of Tennessee were just some of the resulting schools. The period of great state university expansion came after 1850. By 1860, the public educational stepladder spanning from first grade through college had become a reality.

Over time, colleges opened their doors to women. In 1800, no college admitted women. By 1860, 61 colleges admitted women. After the Civil War, during which time many women filled work positions formerly held by men—especially in teaching—regular colleges began welcoming women as students. Every state west of the Mississippi River made its state university coeducational from its first days of admitting students. Many eastern universities followed suit later in the nineteenth century.[101]

The new land-grant colleges Before 1825, eight states had started building future state universities. The national government further encouraged the development of state-sponsored higher educational institutions by granting to each new state, beginning with Ohio in 1802, two entire townships of land to help endow a "seminary of learning" in each. This practice eventually led to the founding of a state university in every new state.

In 1862, the federal government granted funds under the Morrill Act to establish colleges of agriculture and the mechanical arts, thereby encouraging the founding of new institutions and expanding older ones. The Morrill Act granted 30,000 acres for each U.S. senator and U.S. representative that the state had. The result: more than 11 million acres of public land was given to states to endow institutions for teaching these new college subjects, an area half as large as the state of Indiana. The educational return on the land-grant colleges has been very large. Today, all states still receive federal money to carry on this work.

Did You Get It?

During the early national period, it can best be stated that

a. Economic growth fueled a demand for schooling.
b. Economic growth, religious competition, and intense interest in political events all resulted in a population that highly valued education, particularly in New England, based as it was on free labor.
c. Competing Protestant sects increased a public desire for secular schooling.
d. Increasing interest in public affairs increased a personal desire for literacy.

Take the full quiz on CourseMate.

4-8 Movement toward Universal Public Schooling

As public schools expanded in number and variety to meet increased workplace and literacy demands, immigrants from around the world began arriving in the United States. By the 1850s, more than 500,000 immigrants entered the United States each year, representing an increasingly wider range of backgrounds and cultures. Between 1840 and 1870, the country's population doubled; it then doubled again between 1870 and 1900. By 1900, one out of every seven Americans was foreign born.[102] It became clear that a socializing institution was needed to build political communities and help the newcomers adjust to their new homeland. The public school filled that gap, serving as a means to promote a common national experience.

The nineteenth century's second and third quarters saw the rise of local school districts. But by the decade 1840–1850, serious organizational and practice defects had become obvious. State control of school systems would appear as a solution to better and more equitable education for America's increasingly diverse students.

4-8a Creating School Systems

The formal legal movement toward the creation of public school systems was uneven. State constitutions would adopt principles, which their legislatures would then interpret or ignore. For instance, Indiana's 1816 constitution made it the general assembly's duty to make a law for a general education system from township to state university "as soon as circumstances will permit." Circumstances did not "permit" for more than 30 years.[103]

Finding popular support for a state-governed education system was difficult. In the mid-1800s, political control remained firmly lodged at the district, town, or county level. The technology and concept of state control had not yet been fully developed. Local citizens squared off over highly divisive financial and symbol-laden issues, including levying taxes and allocating public monies, selecting curriculum, maintaining discipline, and drawing school districts.[104]

These growing state systems drew in an increasing number of amateurs, semiprofessionals, and professionals advocating for public schooling. Before the Civil War, these "friends of education" appeared in every state, spearheading the public school movement, articulating and publicizing its goals. Horace Mann and Henry Barnard helped to make the public school movement one of the most enduringly successful of all pre-Civil War reforms.

4-8b Horace Mann

In 1837, Massachusetts created the first State Board of Education. Horace Mann was its first appointed secretary of education. In the nineteenth century, no one did more to convince the American people that education should be universal, nonsectarian, and free, and its aim should be social efficiency, civic virtue, and character building. Under Mann's leadership, an unorganized and differing series of community school systems became a unified state school system, both in his state and throughout the Northern states. In recognition of his accomplishments, Mann is sometimes called "The Father of American Education."

Neither the Massachusetts State Board of Education nor its secretary had any powers to enforce their ideas. Their job was to investigate conditions, report facts, expose defects, and make recommendations regarding actions to the legislature. Any influence that they had would entirely depend on the secretary's intellect, energy, and charisma.

As an educational leader, Mann's central purpose was to put Adams' and Jefferson's democratic educational vision into widespread practice. Aware of America's diversity in origins and traditions, he called for a publicly supported, publicly controlled "common school" that would be open to all students regardless of race, class, or gender with the goal of fostering a sense of community by sharing a "public philosophy."[105] This was not a school for the common people, but rather a school common to all the people, rich and poor alike. According to Mann's vision, public schools would become "the great equalizer," helping end poverty and social class distinctions.[106] By bringing children from such diverse backgrounds together, schools would develop friendships and mutual respect that would create societal harmony and reduce adult life conflicts. Mann concluded, "As the child is father to the man, so may the training of the schoolroom expand into the institutions and fortunes of the state."[107]

To Mann, education and freedom were inextricably linked. Education was necessary for all citizens to learn the self-discipline required to live responsibly in a democratic republic. If the common people were wise, the problem of leadership would take care of itself.[108] He observed, "A republican form of government, without intelligence in the people, must be, on a vast scale, what a mad-house, without superintendent or keepers, would be on a small one."[109]

Mann did not believe that the self-regulating district system, which was not accountable to local or state concerns, was an effective way to identify and spread successful teaching practices. Instead, Mann suggested, local schools needed a shared mission under an overseeing agency devoted to maintaining certain standards in all children's education. He advanced the idea of an education system, a functional organization of individual schools and colleges that put them into regular relationship with one another and with the state.

To this end, Mann articulated general principles on which intelligent educational choice could depend. His goal was to ensure educational equity and rationality (not uniformity) to all students in all locations.[110] In his *Fourth Annual Report,* in 1840, he asked small districts to consolidate into larger ones—and sought to bring them under state authority. The societal costs for not educating all students in effective schools, he reasoned, were greater than the cost of doing so.[111]

The fundamental issues underlying the American Revolution spoke to human rights. As an outgrowth of this movement, some advocated that women were the natural equals of men in terms of rights, liberties, and abilities, and pointed out that a proper education (and employment) would make them equals in actuality. Mann asserted that mothers needed an education even more than leaders because of their critical influence on the next generation of citizens. Many disagreed with this view, however, and flatly opposed female education on the grounds that it was harmful and wasteful.[112]

Mann successfully met this challenge, making a difference through his intelligence, presentation of relevant data, personal charisma, excellent writing and speaking skills, and persistence. He held forums at teachers' institutes and public meetings in every county, raising public consciousness about the issues at hand. Besides public speaking, Mann's other instrument of persuasion and influence was his *Annual Report* (of which he wrote 12) that set out his vision of what education should be in a free society.

Arousing critics Overturning the status quo incited critics of Mann's views, actions, and outcomes—asserting that he did not go far enough or that he went too far. In all his writings and commentary, Mann did not raise difficult questions that might have undermined the fragile coalitions he had cobbled together to support public schools. For example, he was unable to reconcile his desire to train students for responsible citizenship and his need to avoid controversial classroom topics.[113] Although Mann served in Congress after 1848 as an uncompromising abolitionist, he did not address providing education for African American children. Nor did he argue for public education exclusively.[114] He did not call for free higher education because his concern was with the greatest general proficiency of average students rather than the exceptional progress of a few.[115] Although he exhorted against parental indifference to schooling, he did not recommend compulsory attendance. Rather, Mann advocated regulations that would require children to attend either regularly or not at all. Eventually, organized labor and reform groups pressed for compulsory school attendance to end youthful idleness and prevent youth exploitation.[116]

From the other side, Mann's contemporary critics viewed his call for school systems, educational consistency, and equity as partisan and political, rather than as common sense. Edward A. Newton and Matthew Hal Smith suggested that no idealistic equity could ever justify a rigid educational uniformity.[117] Likewise, Orestes A. Brownson, a Unitarian minister who later joined the Catholic Church, vigorously criticized Mann's advocacy for children's attendance of state-sponsored secular schools, seeing them as promoting a "civil religion" that was a plot to end Christianity.[118] For the first (but not the last) time in our history, public school opponents cried, "The public schools are Godless schools!"

4-8c Henry Barnard

At the end of the colonial period, Connecticut schools had greatly deteriorated. An 1838 investigation showed that only one-half of 1 percent of the state's children attended school. The available public schools were poor, private tuition-charging schools were increasing, the citizens objected to taxation, and teachers lacked training or professional interest.[119] Henry Barnard's work restored this state's educational effectiveness and its pride in its public schools.

Henry Barnard accomplished important educational improvements in both Connecticut and Rhode Island. A Yale-educated lawyer, he became deeply interested in teaching. He subsequently spent much of his personal fortune to publish journals advocating educational reform. Influenced by European educators who respected children as learners, Barnard helped pass the Connecticut state law setting up the State Board of Education with a secretary, like the Massachusetts plan. Barnard was then elected the first secretary—at the grand salary of $3 per day plus expenses.[120]

As Connecticut's secretary of the Board of Commissioners of the Common Schools, Barnard visited many schools, made numerous speeches championing public education, and issued a series of reports identifying and detailing the problems he hoped to solve.[121] Barnard invoked the state government's authority to force each district to meet certain standards for buildings, teachers, attendance, and textbooks. In 1839, he organized the first teachers' institute in America, which met for more than a few days—long enough for teachers to learn new instructional techniques. Barnard professionalized teaching by awakening teachers to learn and use appropriate pedagogical behaviors. Likewise, he worked to improve the physical

Henry Barnard, American education scholar

Hulton Archive/Stringer/Hulton Archive/Getty Images

American Education Spotlight

The Art Archive/Culver Pictures

Horace Mann, the "Father of American Education"

Horace Mann

Through force of personality, Horace Mann convinced the American people that education should be universal, nonsectarian, and free; and he educated public opinion to support schools' value to the community.

Born in a small Massachusetts town in 1796, young Horace was educated in the local one-room schoolhouse. Reading extensively at the town library, he learned enough to be admitted to Brown University. As a lawyer elected to the Massachusetts State Senate, and then as the Senate president, he helped pass the bill creating the Massachusetts State Board of Education. In 1837, Mann shocked family and friends by taking the job as the board's first secretary. He now worked for an agency with no money or control over local schools—and which paid him a meager $1,500 salary, no provision for rent, clerical help, or supplies, and a title without honor.

Mann's was a time of tremendous social change: immigrants were pouring into the Northeastern states, farmers were leaving rural areas to work in factories, and cities were growing rapidly with rising crime and poverty. In response, Mann and other reformers promoted state-regulated public education as a way to bring order and discipline to the working class in this rapidly changing society. They believed that educating youths would reduce crime and moral vices such as violence and fraud. This perspective supplemented their ideals about preparing an educated public for a representative democracy.

Despite their potential for civic good, public schools of Mann's era were unpleasant and inefficient. Visiting almost 1,000 schools while Massachusetts secretary of education, he found poor facilities lacking adequate heating, lighting, and ventilation. Schools had no blackboards and no common textbooks. Memorization and recitation were the primary pedagogy. Inequality of educational opportunity was everywhere. Wealthy children attended school for longer periods, and the poorest often did not attend because they could not afford the minimal tuition. At one point, Mann commented that Massachusetts took better care of its livestock than its children. He also vigorously opposed the punishment used by schoolmasters, noting that they, "crowd from forty to sixty children into that ill-constructed shell of a building, there to sit in the most uncomfortable seats that could be contrived, expecting that with the occasional application of the birch [a tree branch used to hit uncooperative students] they will then come out educated for manhood or womanhood." *

When it came to teaching and learning, Mann was an innovator who recognized the student as a learner. He observed that children differed from one another in temperament, ability, and interest. Teachers would need to adapt their lessons to accommodate these differences. Rather than have students passively memorize and recite their lessons, Mann wanted classroom interactions that allowed students to ask questions and hold group discussions, arrive at answers for themselves, and receive more humane and caring treatment. Teachers should help children build their own powers of seeing, judging, and reasoning and encourage their initiative. Mann's regard for learners led him to develop a statewide teacher training system that would produce teachers who used instructional practices related to helping students learn.

Because his concern lay with the greatest general proficiency for average students— rather than the remarkable progress of the few—teaching for all students' learning was of critical importance to Mann. The societal costs for not educating all students in effective schools, he reasoned, were greater than the cost of doing so.

During Mann's 12 years as secretary, public education appropriations more than doubled, teachers' salaries greatly increased, and the school term added a full month—increasing the school year's length to six months. He wrote and spoke persuasively to modify the conditions of existing schools and build new ones. Mann's efforts led to providing more free nonreligious public schools for boys and girls, better schoolbooks, improved teaching, higher pay for teachers, better student attendance, and a more educated population.

Mann's influence was significant and permanent. His vision and efforts helped realize the founders' dreams about education of all for a democratic society.

*Sarah Mondale and Sarah B. Patton (Eds.). (2001). *The Story of American Public Education*. Boston: Beacon Press, pp. 27–28.

Sources: Cubberley, E. P. (1947). *Public education in the United States*. Cambridge, MA: Riverside Press; Horace Mann (1796–1859). Only a Teacher. Schoolhouse Pioneers. *PBS Online*. Retrieved from http://www.pbs.org/onlyateacher/horace.html; Mondale, S. and Patton, S. B. (Eds.). (2001). *The Story of American Public Education*. Boston: Beacon Press, pp. 27–28.

conditions of schools by writing extensively about schoolhouse construction. He studied school data and used the statistical returns about school activities and accomplishments to engage public interest in education.[122]

Barnard's educational innovations met with active resistance. When the Connecticut legislature abolished both the board and his position in 1842, Barnard moved to Rhode Island to examine and report on the conditions in that state's schools. He served as Rhode Island's commissioner of public schools from 1845 to 1849. Like Mann, Barnard was a strong campaigner and fearless organizer, holding public meetings across the state to arouse interest in the state's educational system. He organized a series of town libraries throughout the state and developed a traveling model school for his teachers' institutes, demonstrating lessons that showed current and prospective teachers how to teach.

In 1851, Barnard returned to Connecticut as head of the state normal school (teachers' college) and ex-officio secretary of the State Board of Education. In this role, he rewrote school laws, increased taxation for schools, checked the power of local school districts, and laid the foundation for Connecticut's state schools system. In 1855, Barnard also began editing his *American Journal of Education*, a large encyclopedia of educational information, which provided American educators with an understanding of their educational inheritance as well as recent practices in teaching. By some opinions, Barnard became American's first great education scholar.

Mann and Barnard were two highly visible, extremely influential leaders during the formative period of American education. Mann's and Barnard's work to build and strengthen state departments of education and create state-wide school systems inspired educators throughout the Northern states and encouraged friends of education elsewhere.

Did You Get It?

Perhaps the single most important factor behind the rise of universal public schooling was

a. The importance of immigration to America's population growth, requiring a means of providing a common national experience.
b. The fact that increasing industrialization and mechanization required a better-educated workforce.
c. The demand of women to participate in public life, which meant they had best be educated.
d. A lively printing industry that produced everything from great political pamphlets to penny horrors dramatically increased the desire of people to read in order to entertain themselves.

Take the full quiz on CourseMate.

4-9 The Status of Public Schooling in the Late Nineteenth Century

By the last half of the nineteenth century, public schools reflected regional differences. The Northern and Mid-Atlantic states saw substantial growth in their public school systems. Public schools in the Midwest expanded; public schools in the South grew only modestly.

Within the various regions, schools differed in the school term's length and education's availability beyond the primary level. Significant racial, ethnic, gender, and religious differences continued to affect access to schooling. In addition, the sizable differences in teacher qualifications and effectiveness made a year of schooling in one institution or locality significantly different from a year of schooling in another institution or locality.[123]

During this era, school was intended to prepare youngsters for productive work outside the household, where literacy and punctuality, the ability to follow rules and procedures, and cooperation with others would be expected. After receiving an education, American citizens could read and appreciate newspapers. They knew social norms beyond the family. Whatever their limitations, by the late nineteenth century public schools were preparing increasingly more students for adult life in a democracy. As Alexis de Tocqueville, the French political thinker and historian who toured the early-nineteenth-century United States and wrote *Democracy in America* (1835), observed, if the United States had few individuals who could be described as learned, it also had fewer illiterates than anywhere else in the world.[124]

At the same time, the white community's cultural assumptions affirmed that people could be educated to transcend ethnic and religious barriers to become fully functioning American citizens, but they could not be educated to transcend the barriers of race. African Americans, Native Americans, and other peoples of color largely remained outside this American cultural community and its public education system.

Did You Get It?

By the last half of the 19th century, public schools

a. Reflected a growing standardization of access, quality, and scope.

b. Were intended to prepare students for intellectual inquiry.

c. Increasingly prepared students for a life of submission to the industrial elites.

d. Reflected sharp regional differences in access, quality, and scope.

Take the full quiz on CourseMate.

SUMMARY

- Major cultural influences on education in early colonial America included diverse neighbors, English colonists, European Renaissance thinkers, and changing religious beliefs. Renaissance ideas about common people and education led English colonists in America to think that education could confer—as well as confirm—status.
- In the colonial and early national period, three key factors—economy, religion, and local views about government involvement in social matters—interacted to determine the type of education a colony provided its children.
- Education in the early New England colonies included town schools, Dame schools, Latin grammar schools (for boys from wealthy families), and academies. Very poor or orphaned children went into apprenticeships or manual labor.
- Education in the middle colonies was not widely available Colonists of varied religious sects did not want government controlling education. Instead, families relied on church-run, private (for profit), charity-sponsored schools, or state-run pauper schools, where available. Children without resources learned from their parents or through apprenticeships.
- Early education in other states reflected their settlers' indifference to providing a common education for their children. Children's formal education—or its lack—depended wholly on their parents.
- Teachers in early colonial schools were initially all men who earned a living while preparing for another profession or to repay a debt. In general, teaching was ineffective and inefficient and took place in poor facilities with no resources.
- Education opportunities for African American and Native American were limited, sporadic, or banned.

- During the early national period, public schooling changed in response to the rise of cities, manufacturing, and extended voting rights; it became a state as well as family responsibility; and teaching became increasingly female dominated. After 1820, many states established their own colleges.
- In late-nineteenth-century schools, student discipline practices to maintain classroom behaviors and to motivate student learning moved from physical punishment to creating incentives for self-management.
- The founding of free public high schools and state universities created greater access to education, helped to unify the increasingly diverse American population, provided common ideals and a sense of community, created opportunities for learning and occupational and social advancement, and prepared people for civic leadership and service.
- Horace Mann and Henry Barnard, in Massachusetts and Connecticut/Rhode Island, respectively, led the movement toward universal public schools. They worked to broaden educational opportunities for all students, educated public opinion to support public schools, provided training for teachers, and unified community school systems into unified state school systems.
- In the late nineteenth century, the American public school reflected regional differences and great variabilities in the length of the school year, student access, and teacher qualifications. People of color remained outside the American cultural community and its public education system.

Visit the Education CourseMate for this textbook to access the eBook, Did You Get It? quizzes, TeachSource Video Cases, flashcards, and more. Go to CengageBrain.com to log in, register, or purchase access.

Since 1900, American education has focused increasingly on providing access and success of *all* students.

Bob Daemmrich/PhotoEdit

CHAPTER

5

Education Reform, 1900 to Today

InTASC Standards Addressed: 1, 2, 3, 4, 5, 6, 7, 8, and 10

LEARNING OBJECTIVES

After you read this chapter, you should be able to:

5-1 Discuss how G. Stanley Hall's and John Dewey's views of education as human development challenged the traditional, subject-centered views and practices.

5-2 Explain how national reports and Frederick Taylor's scientific management theory influenced the organization and curriculum of public high schools.

5-3 Identify how Booker T. Washington, W. E. B. DuBois, and legal and legislative actions advanced education for African American and other underserved students.

5-4 Summarize how World War I, the Great Depression,and vocational education influenced public education in the twentieth century.

5-5 Evaluate how the 1966 Coleman Report about educating the disadvantaged affected U.S. views about schools' capacity to make a difference with all students.

5-6 Describe the components of providing free and appropriate education to students with disabilities.

5-7 Discuss how *A Nation at Risk* impacted public schools.

5-8 Analyze how No Child Left Behind, Race to the Top, and Common Core Standards have helped or hindered the education of all students.

5-9 Describe how innovations, technology, virtual education, and charter schools have affected American education.

5-10 Assess where the United States stands today regarding the quest to successfully educate all its students.

As a society, we have adopted Horace Mann's vision that public schools are our society's great equalizers. Our early national leaders believed universal education was necessary to ensure the political and social well-being of the United States. They foresaw a country with a unified history, traditions, and common language—all rooted strongly on their own English traditions, religion, language, democratic principles, and school practices.

Ideals about education for all children outran the early national leaders' abilities to put these values into action, however. Societal ignorance and prejudice prevented African Americans, economically disadvantaged students, and students with disabilities from attending—let alone benefiting from—America's public schools. To a large extent, the second part of American public schools' history demonstrates our nation's attempt to extend and address these unmet needs.

In this chapter, we discuss the changing concepts of schooling emerging from the late 1800s through the early twenty-first century. Along the way, we look at educational figures who tried to remove obstacles to all students' learning. We consider the legal, legislative, and financial interventions used to increase access and success of all students, especially the underserved. Finally, we examine the ways American public schools have tried to meet these goals. ●

5-1 Education as Human Development Challenges the Traditional Subject-Centered Concepts of Schooling

Colonial and early national educators believed that certain book knowledge would give students the training necessary for life and citizenship. They assumed that all children learned in the same ways. Memorization and recitation—getting the facts into students' heads through practice and then repeating them back to the teacher—were the most frequently used teaching and learning techniques.

As the twentieth century approached the idea of **pedagogy**—that is, teaching as a profession with certain methods, techniques, and materials to promote student learning—took new scientific and philosophical directions. Fresh ideas challenged traditionalist thinking about curriculum and instruction. Heated debates would soon follow between those favoring a child-centered approach that considered how children learned and those who focused on a subject-centered approach for transmitting important cultural knowledge.

pedagogy Teaching as a profession with certain methods, techniques, and materials to promote student learning.

faculty psychology The nineteenth-century viewpoint that intellect, will, and emotions all had their own "place" in the mind, and the mind could be trained by a uniform procedure of mental discipline and drill.

mental discipline The educational theory that building the "powers of the mind"—through memorization, practice, and recitation developed children's moral character while they learned important information.

5-1a The Subject-Centered Education Approach

Between 1860 and 1890, **faculty psychology** became popular. Those who held this viewpoint believed that intellect, will, and emotions all had their own "place" or compartments in the mind, and the mind could be trained by a uniform procedure of mental discipline and drill. According to **mental discipline** theory, building the "powers of the mind"—attention, will, memory, imagination, feelings, judgment, reasoning, observation, and sense discrimination—through memorization, practice, and recitation developed children's moral character while they learned important information.

If "mental discipline" was the pedagogy, then traditional western European subjects formed the curriculum. Latin, Greek, French, German, mathematics, rhetoric, grammar, history, physics, chemistry, government, biology, and the Great Books were seen as the anchors of a strong education. The rationale was simple and circular: The more difficult the curriculum, the more the students had to exercise their minds.

The more exercise, the more value attributed to the subject. Any academic subjects that could not find a mental discipline rationale remained outside the curriculum.

The mental discipline approach required a very detailed set of courses that precisely spelled out the work that all pupils in each grade in all town or city schools would master. Regardless of students' age, past experiences, future prospects, or physical or mental condition, one course of study was assumed to be appropriate for all. Proponents viewed this system as egalitarian because everyone received the "elite" curriculum. Teachers taught. Intensive drill, practice, and memorization were keys to learning. Students either learned or left school. Many aspects of this traditional approach remain to this day.

5-1b The Child-Centered Education Approach

In the late 1800s, a new academic discipline, psychology, made many educators rethink the processes of teaching and learning. **Psychology** entailed the scientific study of human behavior in general and the mind in particular. Reversing the traditional subject-centered model, psychologists now placed students—not subjects—at teaching's center. The educational focus moved to the learner and the ways the learners learned.[1] In turn, the view that a school's purpose was to assist children to develop their inborn capacities began to gain favor.

psychology The scientific study of human behavior in general and the mind in particular.

child study movement The late nineteenth-century group pioneered by G. Stanley Hall who investigated how children's minds and personalities developed to help educators make practical judgments about how to best educate young people.

Many of the early impulses toward placing students rather than subjects at the center of education efforts came from Europe. Advocates of a "new education" insisted that young children should be educated in kindly and natural ways, and that they learned best not through books but through sensory experience and contact with real objects.[2] These concepts would profoundly influence American thinkers about the most effective ways of educating children.

5-1c G. Stanley Hall

In the 1880s and early 1890s, members of the **child study movement** investigated how children's minds and personalities developed. Their goal was to help educators make practical judgments about how to best educate young people. G. Stanley Hall (1844–1924) and his students at Clark University in Massachusetts formed the leading center of this popular movement.

An American psychologist, Hall pioneered the experimental study of child development. In 1878, he earned Harvard's first doctorate in psychology.[3] Soon thereafter, he began to study children's minds at the age when they entered school. Using questionnaires, Hall and his colleagues systematically observed, questioned, and measured children, tabulating a variety of traits, opinions, and types of information. Hall's scientific approach to observing children brought credibility to the child study movement. As a result, by 1900, the child study movement had become a key part of educational psychology.

Hall believed that a child's psychological life and behaviors develop through a series of stages that correspond more or less to the stages through which the human race has traveled from savagery to civilization. Children's normal mental growth requires living through each of the stages, and each stage provides the building blocks for the next. According to this belief, the task of family and school is to adjust to and foster that development rather than to try to shape or control it. "To a nation about to celebrate 'the century of the child,' his doctrines had enormous appeal."[4]

First at Johns Hopkins University and later at Clark University, Hall and his colleagues concluded that teachers using child study findings

G. Stanley Hall, child-study movement pioneer

Bettmann/Corbis

could be more effective by adapting their instructional practices to meet students' learning needs. For teachers, this meant extending kindergarten's informality upward into the elementary grades and adjusting the curriculum to fit children's natural rhythms of interest and need. Hall introduced art, music, gardening, manual training, domestic science, and physical education into the school program and encouraged development of parks and playgrounds.[5]

Hall's work helped shift teaching's focus from the subject to the student through his assertion that no education could be worthy, much less efficient, if it ignored students' actual nature, needs, and development. His work placed a new emphasis on the scientific study of students' feelings, dispositions, and attitudes as part of the learning process. Most importantly, Hall's approach "subtly shifted the burden of proof in the educational situation, and in so doing, the meaning of equal opportunity as well."[6] This view would later lead to substantial changes in both curriculum and instruction.

Criticism of child-centered methods Hall's child-centered approach risked moving school too close to the student, creating schools dedicated to allowing students to set all the terms and conditions on the learning content and process. Reacting to education's traditional overemphasis on control, order, and disregard for the learners' interests and welfare, the child-centered movement pulled too far in the other direction. Neither approach was fully in the students' best interests. The middle ground between the subject-centered and child-centered extremes would be a more reasonable and effective place for teaching and learning.

progressive An educational movement begun in the late nineteenth century in which children were believed to learn best from real-life experiences with other people; associated with John Dewey.

5-1d John Dewey

John Dewey brought education reform back to the middle. Dewey advanced a pedagogy that included both content and students within their social contexts. In turn, the struggle over school curriculum would become a broader struggle over how the schools would contribute to social progress. With Dewey, educational concerns affecting African Americans, women, the poor, and immigrants became public policy issues connected to social improvements.

John Dewey focused on subjects, students in their social context, and effective teaching.

Hulton Archive/Getty Images

John Dewey did not coin the term **progressive** (that credit goes to an educational movement that began in the late nineteenth century in which children were seen to learn best from real-life experiences with other people), but it ultimately became associated with him.[7] Educated as a psychologist, Dewey completed his doctoral studies at Johns Hopkins University. He eventually set up a laboratory school at the University of Chicago to test his ideas about teaching children. In 1905, he left Chicago for Columbia University, where he worked until his death in 1952.

Dewey's era was characterized by many calls for educational improvement. Businesses and labor unions wanted schools to provide students with apprenticeships to prepare them for work. Settlement workers and municipal reformers wanted schools to provide poor residents and immigrants with instruction in hygiene, domestic science, manual arts, and child care. Patriots wanted schools to teach children how to become better Americans. Agrarians wanted schools to train students to appreciate country life and stop moving to the cities. All of these demands reflected a common message: The family, neighborhood, and workshop were no longer fulfilling their time-honored educational functions. Schools had inherited the educational role from other social institutions that could no longer do what they had always done because the modern world was too complex and too large.[8]

In *School and Society*,[9] Dewey blamed industrialism for education's then-current dilemma. He believed that society educates individuals by providing children with shared, meaningful work. According to Dewey, this close and intimate firsthand experience—doing important tasks with actual tools—built students' knowledge, character, and discipline. Now, schools would have to assume all the educative aspects of what the agrarian society had always provided. Achieving this goal meant both expanding the school curriculum and connecting school to the real world.

In Dewey's view, schools had the mission to advance democratic principles and form common democratic communities. Rather than strictly focusing on child-centered self-expression and self-development, or on the traditional curriculum that left students unconnected to their real world, Dewey believed that the larger society was a vitally important part of education. "Democracy has to be born anew every generation, and education is its midwife," Dewey observed. He emphasized the importance of students developing social insights and a sense of community consciousness. Schools, he thought, could become a miniature democracy where students learned about their differences and commonalities, where vocational studies coexisted with academic ones, and where tolerance and diversity partnered with critical mindedness. To this end, Dewey pressed insistently for the type of common schooling that would bring the children of all classes, creeds, and ethnic backgrounds into little "embryonic communities."[10]

At the same time, Dewey regarded the traditional curriculum as undemocratic: "A democracy cannot flourish where there is a narrowly utilitarian education for one class and broadly liberal education for another. It demands a universal education in the problems of living together, one broadly human in outlook."[11] He recognized that the classical subject-centered curriculum served as a means to preserve social and class status through exclusivity and inequity. Unless students were planning to become statesmen, professionals, or intellectuals, they did not need to learn Latin and Greek languages. Instead, students needed to learn English and other practical knowledge and skills. Dewey believed in a common culture based on individual growth and development linked with social integration.

Effective teaching interested Dewey. Based on his laboratory work, he determined that good teaching must address three factors. First, teachers need to understand the learners' interests, problems, and developmental level. Second, teachers must present knowledge in ways that are relevant and make sense to the learners. Third, classrooms should reflect society's highest democratic values: tolerance, cooperation, critical mindedness, and political awareness.[12]

To connect formal learning and the real world, Dewey's lab school built its curriculum around social occupations such as cooking, carpentry, and sewing. From these occupations, students learned arithmetic, reading, writing, and sciences as each developed from their experiences with their lives outside school. In this context, motivating student learning no longer depended on threats or punishments. Students were genuinely interested in the learning activities that they saw as worthwhile, relevant, and understandable. Likewise, Dewey believed that school should teach students how to be problem solvers by helping them learn how to think rather than simply having them memorize large amounts of information.

Armed with this innovative perspective, Dewey merged ideas about science with those of democracy. He advocated using the scientific method in teaching and learning, believing that intelligent inquiry could transform problems into progress. Students in a healthy democracy needed to know how to think by themselves and act with social responsibility. Good learning, he concluded, originates in genuine life experiences, framed intellectually as problems to be investigated, hypotheses generated and tested to bring new insights on the original problem.

FlipSides

Child-Centered versus Subject-Centered Education

For over 100 years, educators have been arguing the merits of child-centered teaching as compared with subject-centered teaching. As a future teacher, which approach do you think best supports and advances student learning?

Children—not subjects—should be at the center of learning.	Subjects—not children—should be at the center of learning.
■ All children are different and learn in different ways.	● All children learn the same way.
■ Teachers should consider children's actual nature, needs, and development in planning their lessons.	● Teachers should provide students with intensive drill and practice of new learning through memorization and recitation to help them remember what they are learning and build the students' moral character.
■ Educators' job is to adapt their instructional practices to and foster children's development of their inborn capacities.	● Educators' job is to transmit our important cultural knowledge by stressing the subject content.
■ Children learn best through sensory, real-life experiences with other people (rather than by books and lectures).	● Children learn best by mental practice, memorization, and recitation of what they have learned.
■ Theory developed through systematic observations, questioning, and measurement of how actual children learned.	● Theory developed on belief that the human mind can be strengthened through exercise and mental discipline.
■ Every student should include academic subjects as well as art, music, physical education, and vocational subjects that naturally fit children's interests and needs.	● All students should study the same "elite" curriculum, regardless of their past experiences and future goals. This makes education egalitarian.
■ Students need to learn the common culture that all Americans share.	● Students who do not learn the "elite" curriculum can either work harder or leave school.
■ Students need to develop critical thinking skills and learn to be problem solvers.	● Students need to learn the big ideas of Western culture.
■ Students need to develop social insights and a sense of community—learning how to get along with others who may be different than themselves—to prepare them to live in a democratic society.	● Students need to learn the subjects that reflect our cultural heritage.
■ Teaching effectiveness matters: Understand students' needs; present knowledge in ways that are relevant and meaningful to students; classrooms should be tolerant, cooperative, critical minded, and politically aware.	● Teaching effectiveness depends on giving students the "elite" curriculum with sufficient drill and practice to help them learn it.
■ Teachers motivate students by making learning relevant and interesting.	● Teachers motivate students by threats and punishment.
■ Main criticism of the other view: Subject-centered/traditional pedagogy tended to overemphasize control, order, and disregard for learners' interests or well-being.	● Main criticism of the other view: Child-centered pedagogy, when misapplied, lets children (rather than experts) set the terms and conditions and keeps them unconnected from the real world.

What do you see as the strengths and weakness of each approach for educating twenty-first-century children? How might you as a teacher use aspects of each approach to generate student learning?

For Dewey, education did not consist solely of transmitting information to passive learners. Instead, education was an act of reconstruction: adding to experiences' meaning in ways that made sense to students and increased their ability to direct later experiences and control their surroundings. Active learning, Dewey insisted, was essential to education. Intelligence was the purposive reorganization of experience.

Dewey's educational ideas tried to reconcile the seemingly unworkable dualism between the subject-centered and child-centered views. Over time, his work would change teaching and learning in American public schools.

Did You Get It?

Which statement, reflecting a view of education, is correct as a statement, not good educational philosophy as we understand it today?

a. Colonial and early national educators believed that a certain level of book knowledge would give students a good life foundation.

b. Colonial and early national educators relied upon memorization, but they also understood that students were individuals who learned in different ways.

c. The child-centered approach was always understood to be fundamentally compatible with the subject-centered approach.

d. Traditionalists who were complete masters of their subjects but unsatisfied with their ability to reach many of their students developed fresh ideas about curriculum.

Take the full quiz on CourseMate.

5-2 National Reports and Scientific Management Theory Influence Public Schools' Organization and Curriculum

In the late 1800s and early 1900s, as waves of varied and impoverished newcomers arrived to make their homes and futures in America, well-to-do citizens realized that their country's best interests lay in educating the "lower" classes. To tackle this problem, between 1842 and 1918, all states passed compulsory education attendance laws.

At the same time, differences among schools increased. In the North, African American children were attending separate, segregated schools resulting from neighborhood segregation or gerrymandered school districts. Southern law and custom largely closed public education to students of color. Vocational high schools were becoming common in the larger cities, sorting students along class and gender lines, as did the vocational tracks within comprehensive high schools. A fresh look at curriculum was imminent.

5-2a Liberal Arts and the High School Curriculum

In the 1890s, less than 5 percent of the U.S. student-age population attended high school.[13] Almost all of those individuals went on to graduate and then enroll in college. Because each college had its own requirements, a common high-status high school curriculum was just what policy makers thought was needed to make sure that all prospective college students had the appropriate academic background.

Committee of Ten In 1893, the National Education Association (NEA) appointed a Committee of Ten to establish a standard high school curriculum for students planning to attend college.[14] The committee's final report advanced a highly traditional set of liberal arts studies: Latin, English literature, modern languages (such as German or French), algebra, geometry, physics, chemistry, natural history, history, and geography. All students were to take these courses, regardless of their background, educational plans, or career directions.

Committee of Fifteen Next, the NEA formed the Committee of Fifteen to address elementary education. In 1895, the Committee of Fifteen endorsed the traditional subject-centered courses: grammar, literature, arithmetic, geography, and history. Unlike the high school report, however, the elementary curriculum report urged that academic topics be "correlated" with—not taught in isolation from—the arts (vocal music, drawing, physical exercise, and hygiene). For seventh- and eighth-grade boys, it recommended manual training, such as woodwork; for girls, it recommended sewing and cooking.[15]

The Committee of Ten never imagined that secondary school would become universal or that students preparing for the workforce would need such an academically oriented curriculum. Nevertheless, the subject-centered emphasis of its report and its active disregard for differing students' needs would find a strong reaction among future educators.

The *Cardinal Principles Report* of 1918 During the early 1900s, high schools grew in number and popularity as they prepared increasing cohorts of middle-class students for work and college.[16] From 1890 to 1930, public high school enrollments virtually doubled every decade, bringing in more students who were not preparing for college.[17] High schools began to include alternatives to traditional liberal arts, permitting different students to study different subjects within the same school.

Recognizing the trend toward a more diverse student body, the NEA sponsored a new report on high schools. The resulting *Cardinal Principles* report of 1918 became one of the twentieth century's most influential education documents. It called for expanded and differentiated high school programs that would better serve the new, highly dissimilar secondary school student population.

The proponents of the *Cardinal Principles* believed that requiring all students to follow the same traditional academic course of study increased educational inequality. The 1918 report recommended that high schools adopt a more comprehensive approach, placing equal value on traditional liberal arts, vocational development, citizenship education, physical activity, and such personal needs as instruction in personal hygiene, the "worthy use of leisure," and wholesome boy–girl relationships.[18]

To do this, *Cardinal Principles* advocated a common core of knowledge and courses that would be far less academically substantial than the traditional college preparatory curriculum. Reflecting what was actually occurring in public high schools, *Cardinal Principles* established a blueprint for the modern comprehensive high school.[19] Intending to develop the whole student for life and work, high schools dropped the preoccupation with academic and intellectual disciplines and replaced it with a broadened curricular scope and a sorting function related to students' perceived abilities and future vocations.

This new vision of schooling affected high schools in several ways. Schools' differentiated curriculum allowed students to follow their own academic or vocational interests and plans. All students took courses in general education, designed as unifying learning experiences to promote the common knowledge and shared values needed for responsible democratic citizenship. To help students make curricular and career selections, guidance and counseling programs along with intelligence and achievement tests and other educational measurement instruments became integral parts of education.

Criticism of the comprehensive high school If the Committee of Ten's recommendations were weighted too heavily toward a classical academic curriculum, then the *Cardinal Principles* recommendations went too far in the opposite direction, diluting high schools' academic focus.[20] Designed to meet individual differences, the comprehensive high school developed a tracked curriculum and did not do enough to raise all students to high academic standards. The availability of advanced, average, and below-average courses ensured that all students moved through the program at varying levels of intellectual rigor. The common learning intended to provide a shared experience in American ideas and values became a required core curriculum that "tracked" students did not share. Advanced, average, and below-average students might enter the same school building in the morning and never meet in the classrooms. Nevertheless, this commitment to educating all high school students under the same roof with a range of curricular choices has remained a mainstay of the U.S. educational system.

5-2b Scientific Management and Schools

Early twentieth-century business and industry leaders saw education as an important way to promote efficiency and profitability. Highly influenced by industrialization's mechanisms, factory productivity, and good organization, educators and business proposed applying **scientific management**, a process for increasing institutional competence, to ensure quality, standardized school outcomes. This organizational approach fit well with the *Cardinal Principles* report in arranging high schools for maximum cost-effectiveness.

scientific management A process for increasing institutional competence, to ensure quality, standardized outcomes.

5-2c Frederick Taylor

Frederick Taylor (1865–1915), an engineer and the world's first efficiency expert, developed the concept of scientific management to provide businesses and factories with increased production and lower costs. To implement his ideas, Taylor contracted with companies to rearrange their production processes, simplifying each employee's tasks. According to Taylor, the "best practices" were those that gained the highest productivity with the least effort. Instead of doing many different things, workers in "Taylorized" factories executed the same simple tasks over and over. This increased production, reduced an employer's need for skilled labor, and lowered management's costs.

Educators adapted Taylor's views on organizational efficiency to American schooling. For schools, scientific management was not a natural fit, however. Laboring on an assembly line was not the same as educating dissimilar children. In making a factory model work in schools, teachers had to identify actual learning outcomes and take measurements to determine whether students had achieved those outcomes. The adaptation of Taylor's approach to the classroom, therefore, begat the science of school measurement: finding supposedly objective and numerical ways to demonstrate student achievement. Other efficiency reforms required teachers to document their teaching activities to prove that they were minimizing "waste." Because many of Taylor's education disciples were not educators themselves, they seldom tried to tell teachers what or how to teach.

How scientific management worked in schools Scientific management in schools had curricular, instructional, and social implications. Schools developed tracking practices, placing students into unique programs of study, such as college-preparatory or vocational education, based on their demonstrated or assumed intelligence. In this way, high schools sorted and selected society's future leaders and workers.

Educators liked this system because it appeared to reward student merit. Students who learned well received rewards; students who did not learn as readily did not. Likewise, students saw themselves either as intelligent, superior, and worthy of a promising future or as not intelligent and unworthy. As a consequence, self-fulfilling prophesies were set in motion.

Between 1900 and 1930, school administrators began to see themselves as managers, rather than as educators. They used scientific management ideas to help their schools accommodate the large numbers of immigrant children at low cost. Children entered school and moved through the grades with their age-peers, changing classes at predetermined intervals to ringing bells. Today, we know that children grow and develop at different and variable rates, so automatically moving students in tandem with those of their chronological age rewarded students who showed quicker development. Those who developed more slowly fell behind and dropped out.[21]

factory model The type of school strictly based on scientific management ideas, whose popularity reached its peak in 1908.

platoon schools Schools organized like factories that used a bell schedule to organize learning time, provided a varied curriculum, organized academic departments in separate disciplines, and outfitted certain rooms for special uses.

The **factory model** idea reached its peak in 1908 in Gary, Indiana, where **platoon schools** became popular. Organized like factories, these schools used a bell schedule to organize learning time, provided a varied curriculum, organized academic departments to guide instruction in separate disciplines, and outfitted certain rooms for special uses. Hundreds of cities' schools adopted this plan, thinking that it made better use of schools' facilities. Many of these practices persist in schools today.

Criticism of scientific management In the long run, the factory model proved ill suited to both business and schools. Although mass production and its industrial ethos were brilliant innovations in their time, by the late twentieth century, they had become liabilities for companies having to survive in competitive, rapidly evolving world markets. Daily work routines have a powerful impact in shaping an organization's culture. Instead of dividing work into smaller and less meaningful tasks in which quality was someone else's responsibility, organizations in the late twentieth and twenty-first centuries had to educate, empower, and engage all of their employees in a process of continuously improving their product's quality—and their own skills.

Scientific management had a similar effect in schools, which became increasingly bureaucratic, impersonal, departmentalized, and isolated from the larger society. School codes and procedures spelled out exactly how to address every detail of school life. Students moved through the fragmented curriculum, and standardized tests purported to measure the quality of their learning. As learning became less meaningful to students, misbehavior increased, absences and dropouts increased, and academic quality and student achievement declined.[22]

5-2d The Myth of the Common School

John Dewey, like Horace Mann before him, believed in the common school's power to integrate students of varied economic, ethnic, and cultural backgrounds and help them become educated people capable of living in and supporting a democratic republic. How well did this vision become a reality?

The common school was essentially a phenomenon in America's North and West, thriving best where a reasonable homogeneity of race, class, and religion already existed. Common schools were decidedly less common in the South and in America's large cities. Three trends undermined this ideal in those areas.

First, newly freed African Americans in the South were systematically barred from access to common schools. Public elementary schools became available to the majority of southern African American children only during the first third

Reflect & Discuss

The mid- to late nineteenth and early twentieth centuries saw many innovations in thought and practice that would define modern American public schools at all levels (K-12).

A. Complete Table 5.1, using the text and a partner as a resource.

TABLE 5.1

Public School Innovations and Practices, Early Twentieth Century

	Description of Key Ideas and Practices			Where This Aspect Is Seen in Public Schools Today
Rationale/Philosophy	Curriculum	Instructional Practices	Major Proponent/s	
Mental discipline/ subject-centered education				
Child-centered education				
Scientific management and *Cardinal Principles*, 1918				

B. Discuss your findings as a class.

Which rationales and practices make sense to you?
Which strengths and weaknesses does each approach contain?
As a student, under which educational system would you like to learn, and why?
As a teacher, under which educational system would you like to teach, and why?

of the twentieth century, long after common schools became available for other American children.[23] For many southern African American youth, high school education did not become available until later still.

Second, on religious grounds, some parents would not forgo their own sacred doctrine for that of another group or for schools' secular needs. Roman Catholics created Catholic schools for all their children. Several ethnic groups—Pennsylvania Amish, for instance—resisted common schooling on the belief that it would prevent their children from properly appreciating their Old World language and customs.

Third, members of the Eastern upper classes often sent their children to private schools while residential segregation separated students by social class on a geographic basis. Living in neighborhoods reflecting their parents' level of wealth, children of different classes went to different neighborhood schools. One celebrated common school, however, was the single–social class slum schools that brought together immigrant children of different ethnic and religious backgrounds.[24]

Certain parents did not want their children to mix with students from other social classes or ethnic/racial groups. Others expressed genuine concern about the common schools' poor academic quality, preferring to educate their children in private schools rather than upgrade the public educational programs.[25] These arguments remain with us, influencing some of our most difficult educational and political problems.[26]

Did You Get It?

How did the *Cardinal Principles* report of 1918 influence the organization and curriculum of public high schools?

a. The proponents of the *Cardinal Principles* believed that requiring all students to follow the same traditional academic course of study reduced educational inequality.

b. Recognizing that America's increasingly diverse society needed a common bond, the report established an academically rigorous and substantial core curriculum in order to maximize a student's options later in life.

c. The report established a foundation for all students to be taught in intellectually demanding ways to prepare them for either a profession or a trade, while attempting not to "track" students too early in life.

d. The report established a blueprint for the modern comprehensive high school.

Take the full quiz on CourseMate.

5-3 Booker T. Washington, W. E. B. DuBois, Legal and Legislative Actions Advance African American Education

African Americans emerged from slavery with a strong belief in the desirability of learning how to read and write, and they demanded universal schooling. Mostly impoverished, they had to find a new way of life—one that included education to make the other promises possible.[27]

5-3a Seeking Educational Gains

From 1865 to 1872, the Bureau of Refugees, Freedmen, and Abandoned Lands (more simply called the Freedmen Bureau) helped resettle African Americans. It constructed and operated schools for African American children, collecting money from various private aid agencies and philanthropic societies to purchase buildings, provide curriculum materials, and hire teachers. During its first few years, it had no Congressional appropriations.

Without publicly supported Southern schools, many ex-slaves established their own educational collectives and associations and staffed schools entirely with African American teachers. At least 500 of these "native schools" were found throughout the South.[28] By the 1870s, African American Southerners had constructed and maintained a semblance of a common school system using their own scant resources.[29]

In the late nineteenth century, many Southern whites opposed universal schooling. They feared political instability if educated African Americans competed for jobs with white laborers. In addition, they recognized that teaching African Americans to read and write would enable them to read and sign their name to voting ballots. In many Southern states, African Americans accounted for 40 to 60 percent of the total population, giving the principle of "one man, one vote" ominous implications. Therefore, during the Southern education movement of 1901 to 1915, the region resisted educational reforms on African Americans' behalf, opposing public school appropriations, and excluding these students from compulsory school laws.[30]

Despite the Fourteenth Amendment's due process protections, African Americans were neither safe nor equal under the law. The South witnessed 49 racially based lynchings in 1882, and 155 of these murders 10 years later.[31] In the South, "separate but equal" became the dominant social doctrine, officially approved in the 1896 *Plessy v. Ferguson* Supreme Court ruling. (This case is discussed in more detail later in this chapter.) Hate groups like the Ku Klux Klan became popular. It would take compelling African American leaders, later rulings by the U.S. Supreme Court, and federal legislation to make high-quality public education a possibility for African American students—and other students of color.

5-3b Booker T. Washington

Born in Virginia, son of an African American mother and a white father, Booker Taliaferro Washington (1856–1915) grew up as a slave. In 1865, when freedom came, his family moved to a West Virginia mining town, where his stepfather found work. As a young boy, Washington took a job in a salt mine that began at 4 a.m. so he could attend school later in the day. He learned to read and write at the local African American Baptist church. At age 10, he took a servant's job at a wealthy general's home. Washington had permission to use the family library, allowing him to further his self-education. These experiences formed Washington's intelligence and attitudes, likely giving him an early orientation in accommodation and compromise.

At 16, with his parents' permission to quit work and go to school, Washington walked 200 miles to attend the Hampton Institute (now University) in Virginia, arriving with 50 cents in his pocket.[32] He paid his tuition and board by working as the janitor. The head teacher was suspicious of Washington's country ways and ragged clothes, and she admitted him only after he had cleaned a room to her satisfaction.[33]

At Hampton Institute, Washington aspired to become a lawyer but received a vocational education. Hampton's mission was to provide an industrial education as a dignified pursuit and a reasonable first step in assisting African Americans to move out of poverty. Students learned vocational practices as well as attitudinal and moral ones: thrift, abstinence, order, and cleanliness. At Hampton, it was understood that once people of color had job skills, they could assimilate and become part of the larger culture.[34] Washington adopted this practical philosophy for himself.

Strongly believing that education would raise his people to equality in this country, Washington became a teacher. In 1881, he founded the Tuskegee Normal and Industrial Institute in Tuskegee, Alabama, with the goal of training teachers, farmers, and tradesmen. He encouraged graduates to return as educated individuals to their hometowns to raise African American education levels. As the head of Tuskegee Institute, he traveled the country to raise funds from African Americans and whites alike, and through his journeys, became a well-known speaker.

Washington's vision was pragmatic and sometimes controversial. A believer in self-reliance, he asserted that African Americans could secure their constitutional rights through their own economic and moral advancement rather than through legal and political changes. For instance, to prevent racial strife, Washington discouraged African Americans from voting, running for political office, and pursuing civil equality.[35]

A practical realist, Washington saw African Americans' social and economic improvement as a long struggle to be won one step at a time. Education for people of color meant developing practical wage-earning skills and diligent work habits that set the foundation for self-sustaining, segregated communities. Only later could African American communities demand and expect increased political, educational, and economic opportunities.[36] Washington encouraged a peaceful apartheid between African Americans and whites and worked to develop educational and economic opportunities for his people.

In Washington's perspective, racial segregation had its advantages—specifically, it provided a business opportunity. African Americans' education, earnings, savings, and spending would be their political activity.

Booker T. Washington, educator, developed educational and economic opportunities for African Americans.

Library of Congress

By showing the white community their hard work, good business practices, and quality products, African Americans would be able to demand that whites grant them more civil rights.[37] In Washington's view, by working within the system, African Americans would transcend it.

To accomplish his ends, Washington advanced African American interests without offending whites who were in positions to stop African American progress. He wrote, "In all things that are truly social, we [African Americans and whites] are as separate as the fingers, yet one as the hand in all things essential to mutual progress."[38] This clear image suggesting racial separation made whites feel comfortable with African American advancement. Washington's vision for African American advancement did not include competing with whites for higher education, professional jobs, or social status—so his message did not threaten them. His agenda was peaceful adjustment.

Although Washington's conciliatory stance angered some African American intellectuals who feared it would encourage the equal rights foes, his major achievement was to win over varied groups of Southern whites, without whose support the programs he envisioned and brought into being would have been impossible. Other African American leaders like W. E. B. DuBois wanted to move faster and farther.

5-3c W. E. B. DuBois

William Edward Burghardt DuBois was a scholar dedicated to attacking racial injustice and defending individual freedom. Endorsing a policy of "educate and agitate," he demanded full and immediate political and civil gains—including voting rights, access to liberal (not vocational) education, and equal economic opportunities—for African Americans.

DuBois (1868–1963) was born in Great Barrington, Massachusetts. DuBois's great-grandfather had fought in the American Revolution, and the Burghardts had been an accepted part of the community for generations. Yet from his earliest years, DuBois was aware of differences that set him apart from his Yankee neighbors. In addition to the hymns sung in his village Congregational Church, he learned his grandmother's songs passed through the generations from Africa. As a youngster, DuBois believed himself part of an earlier tradition that stood in sharp contrast to the detailed chronicle of Western civilization learned at school.[39]

W. E. B. Dubois, scholar and writer, agitated for African American educational, economic, and civil equality.

Bettmann/CORBIS

At age 15, DuBois became the *New York Globe's* local correspondent. Intellectually gifted, he received a scholarship to attend Fisk College (now University) in Nashville, Tennessee. In DuBois's first trip south, he saw the discrimination, poverty, inferior land, ignorance, and prejudice directed toward African Americans, and witnessed African Americans' desire for knowledge. He completed his bachelor's and PhD degrees at Harvard—the first African American to earn a Harvard doctorate.

While on a University of Pennsylvania fellowship, DuBois conducted intensive social research on African Americans as a social system, the first time anyone had undertaken such a scientific approach to studying social phenomena.[40] As a sociology professor at Atlanta University, DuBois studied African American morality, urbanization, African Americans in business, college-bred African Americans, the African American church, and African American crime. He repudiated the widely held view of Africa as a vast cultural unknown by presenting a historical version of Africa's complex, civilizing development.

As a result of these rich and varied experiences, DuBois developed a broader and more radical perspective on American social reform than did Booker T. Washington. Essentially, they represented two sides of an ideological divide. DuBois rejected Washington's accommodation policy, calling instead for "ceaseless agitation and insistent demand for equality" and the "use of force of every sort: moral suasion, propaganda, and where possible even physical resistance."[41] DuBois asserted that Washington's emphasis on industrial education, conciliation, and silence about African American civil and political rights led to bad policy, which limited African Americans' advancement.

DuBois stressed that African Americans needed a traditional liberal arts education so that they could move forward intellectually, politically, and economically. At a minimum, he believed, 10 percent of the African American population—the "Talented Tenth"—should receive a classical education at the leading American universities, much like his own. In his view, this Talented Tenth would use their liberal arts education and knowledge of modern culture to guide the African Americans to a higher civilization.

Continually pushing for African Americans' full civil and political rights, in January 1906, DuBois and like-minded African American intellectuals formed the "Niagara Movement" to advocate civil justice and abolish caste discrimination. In 1910, the Niagara Movement joined with several white liberals and intellectual activists—including John Dewey—to form the National Association for the Advancement of Colored People (NAACP). DuBois became its director of publications and research.[42]

World War I dramatically affected African Americans. Initially refusing to accept them as inductees, the armed forces finally accepted them into the military, albeit in subservient positions. After the war, DuBois's angry editorials in the NAACP magazine, *Crisis*, about the injustices done to African American veterans influenced Congress to act on their behalf. New legislation opened officer training schools for African Americans, law enforcement brought legal action against lynchers, and Congress established a federal work plan for returning veterans.

Over the years, DuBois concluded that only agitation and protest could bring social change in the racist culture of the United States. Although he supported integration and equal rights for everyone regardless of race, his thinking often exhibited black separatist–nationalist tendencies.[43]

Both Washington and DuBois saw school and educational opportunities as the foundation for improving African Americans' lives. Both advocated for improved African American schooling. It would take many years to accomplish even part of their goal, and decisions in groundbreaking court cases—rather than public opinion—would lead the way.

5-3d Gaining Access to Universal Education

In 1900, only 36 percent of African American children ages 5 to 14 attended school. Only 22 percent of those ages 5 to 9 years and slightly more than half of children ages 10 to 14 years attended school. Those fortunate enough to go received less than six months of instruction per year.[44]

From 1880 to the 1930s, almost all Southern rural communities with significantly large African American populations and more than half of the major Southern cities failed to provide any public high schools for African American youths.[45] By the early 1930s, state-sponsored and state-funded building campaigns had made public secondary schools available to all classes of white children but generally excluded African Americans from the same benefits.[46] For African American youths in the South, the struggle to attain public high school enrollment would continue until after World War II. This lack of educational opportunity fundamentally hindered their social and economic adjustment.[47]

Meanwhile, courts were challenging discriminatory practices that affected African American students' access for free public schooling. The *Roberts* case, *Plessy v. Ferguson*, and *Cummings v. Board of Education* would pave the way for the 1954 U.S. Supreme Court's *Brown* ruling that desegregated America's public schools.

5-3e *Roberts v. City of Boston*

The educational concept of "separate but equal" stems from the *Roberts* case, decided in 1849 in Massachusetts. Five-year-old Sarah Roberts had to walk past five Boston elementary schools for white children to reach Smith Grammar School, established in 1820 for African Americans. Not only was Smith school far from her home, but it was also in disrepair. Each time Sarah's father tried to enroll her in a nearby white school, his efforts were denied. Finally, Mr. Roberts contacted lawyer Charles Sumner to represent his child and challenge the unequal treatment.

Sumner eloquently argued that compelling African American children to attend separate schools was to virtually "brand a whole race with the stigma of inferiority and degradation."[48] Massachusetts Chief Justice Lemuel Shaw disagreed. He conceded that all citizens should have "equality before the law," but this did not mean that there could not be separate schools for African American children. With this decision, "separate but equal" entered our legal and educational culture, where it would remain entrenched for more than 100 years.

5-3f *Plessy v. Ferguson*

In 1868, Congress ratified the Fourteenth Amendment guaranteeing civil rights by affirming that no state shall deny equal protection under the laws to any person living within its jurisdiction. Unfortunately, the amendment had little immediate impact because it did not apply to discrimination in private enterprises such as hotels, restaurants, transportation, and entertainment.

The move legally approving state-sponsored discrimination came with a case having no connection to education. In *Plessy v. Ferguson* (1896), the U.S. Supreme Court decided that a Louisiana law requiring "separate but equal" accommodations for African Americans and whites on intrastate railroads was constitutional. This judgment established the earlier *Roberts* decision—"separate but equal"—as a national standard, providing a legal justification to socially and physically separate African Americans and whites in schools and society.

On June 7, 1892, a 30-year-old "colored" shoemaker, Homer Plessy, was jailed for sitting in the "white" car of the East Louisiana Railroad. Plessy had agreed to work with a small group of African American New Orleans professionals to challenge this law's arbitrariness. Plessy was one-eighth African American and seven-eighths white, but under Louisiana law, he was considered African American and was required to sit in the "colored" car. When he identified himself as African American, although seated in the "white" car, he was promptly arrested.[49]

Plessy went to court and argued, in *Homer Adolph Plessy v. The State of Louisiana*, that the Separate Car Act violated the U.S. Constitution's Thirteenth and Fourteenth Amendments. The court's majority opinion concluded that African Americans and whites were politically equal (they had the same political rights) but socially unequal (African Americans were not as socially advanced as whites).

Plessy then appealed to the Supreme Court of Louisiana, where Judge John Howard Ferguson upheld the *Plessy* decision. In 1896, the U.S. Supreme Court also affirmed the lower court's decision, allowing local custom and tradition rather than an objective and neutral law to win the day.

The *Plessy* decision set the precedent that "separate" facilities for African Americans and whites were constitutional as long as they were "equal." Public officials quickly extended the "separate but equal" doctrine to cover many areas of community life, such as public schools, restaurants, theaters, and restrooms. Nevertheless, the doctrine was a fiction: Facilities for African Americans were usually inferior to those for whites. Meanwhile, the *Plessy v. Ferguson* decision served as the legal justification for more than 50 years of racial segregation.

5-3g *Cummings v. Richmond County Board of Education*

With the U.S. Supreme Court now officially supporting racial discrimination in rationale and practice, Southern states began transforming the private custom of prejudice into state law. **Jim Crow laws**—a series of state and local laws requiring racial segregation—were soon practiced throughout the South and in border states. The precedent of racial separation quickly affected education as well.

Jim Crow laws A series of state and local laws requiring racial segregation, including in schools, that were practiced throughout the South and in border states.

In *Cummings v. Richmond County Board of Education, Georgia* (1899), the Richmond County school board closed the African American high school and turned the building into an African American elementary school rather than improve the original elementary school's facilities. The board recommended the displaced African American students try to enroll in church-affiliated schools.[50] When this decision was legally challenged, the U.S. Supreme Court replied that education was a state concern. Public school boards did not have to offer secondary education for African American youths, and a state could constitutionally maintain separate education systems for African Americans and white students in public and private institutions.[51]

The *Cummings* ruling confirmed that both the Fourteenth Amendment's equal protection clause and *Plessy*'s "separate but equal" rule were virtually meaningless.[52] Similar cases with similar outcomes followed in many states, in both the North and the South.

Until the U.S. Supreme Court decision in *Brown v. Board of Education* (discussed next), localities legally denied African American elementary and secondary school children equal educational opportunity. Owing to the *Cummings* precedent, African American children continued to attend schools in substandard facilities and receive poor instruction, frequently with school in session only a few months of the year. Additionally, funding for African American and white schools, although separate, was far from equal. In 1931, Southern states spent an average of $45.63 for each white child's education and only $14.95 for each African American student. Of the total school expenditures in the South, only 10.7 percent went to support African American students.[53]

5-3h *Brown v. Board of Education, 1954*

In *Brown v. Board of Education*, African American children of elementary school age living in Topeka, Kansas, had a suit filed on their behalf to be allowed to enroll in the public schools serving white children. They said that segregated public schools were not equal and could not be made equal, thereby depriving the children of the equal protection of the laws.

In a unanimous 1954 ruling, the U.S. Supreme Court agreed. They wrote that "separate but equal" was "inherently unequal." According to this decision, the practice of segregating public school children solely on the basis of race deprived minority children of equivalent educational opportunities, even though the physical facilities and other "tangible" (material) factors might be identical. "Separate but equal" practices denied African American students equal protection under the laws. The ruling in the *Brown* case became a watershed moment for American education and for larger society as well.

The Court concluded that education was the most important state and local government function: to prepare children to live as good citizens in a democratic

Carl Iwasaki/Time Life Pictures/Getty Images

Children involved with *Brown v. Board of Education*, which found public school segregation to be unconstitutional.

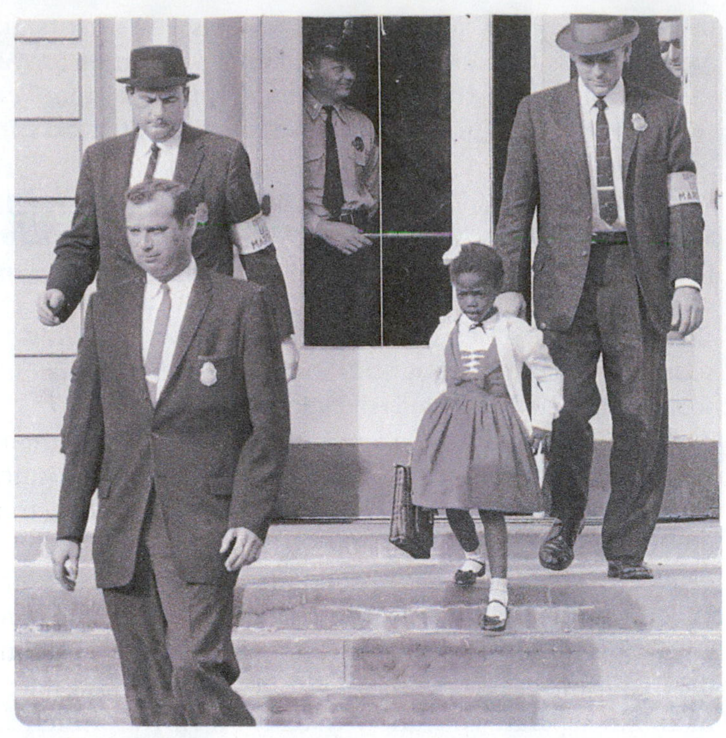
AP Photo

U.S. Marshals escort 6-year-old Ruby Bridges from her elementary school, November 1960.

society, make them aware of our cultural values, and ready them for later professional training. Segregated educational facilities provided unequal educational opportunities. To separate children from others of similar age and qualifications solely because of their race generated feelings of inferiority about their status in the community in ways that could not be repaired. These feelings, in turn, affected children's motivation to learn. Segregated schools, the Court determined, tended to limit African American students' educational and mental development. Giving African American children access to racially mixed classrooms would help to equalize their educational resources and improve their academic outcomes.

massive resistance Closing public schools in several Southern states to keep African American students from enrolling with white students.

Education after *Brown* Despite the Supreme Court ruling, **massive resistance**—closing public schools to keep African American students from enrolling with white students—characterized several Southern states' efforts to block racially desegregated education. Yet even with popular defiance toward the *Brown* decision, by 1970, Southern schools were less segregated than schools in any other region of the country.[54] Desegregation in the North, West, and Midwest faced different challenges. After World War II, many middle-class whites had moved out of cities and into the surrounding suburbs. As a consequence, meaningful school desegregation could not happen without crossing city–suburb lines. Because this kind of racial separation resulted from a "natural" outgrowth of individuals choosing where to live, courts considered it legally permissible.

In a reversal of *Brown*'s intent, courts in the 1990s began releasing districts from desegregation orders issued in the 1970s. These later rulings allowed the return to neighborhood schools even if that meant that some schools resegregated. As a result, the percentage of African American children attending mostly minority schools increased from 66 percent in 1991 to 73 percent in 2003.[55] In 2009, many school districts, in both the North and South, were more segregated than they were in 1969. Southern schools are far more segregated now than they

American Education Spotlight

SEAN GARDNER/The Times-Picayune /Landov

Ruby Bridges today: Still using schools to bring people together.

Ruby Bridges

Although school desegregation was a societal issue, it was also a personal one affecting real children. In the photo on the preceding page, first grader Ruby Bridges walks from her elementary school escorted by federal marshals ordered by President Dwight D. Eisenhower. Ruby was the first African American child enrolled in the William Frantz Elementary School, and she needed an armed escort to keep her safe.

Ruby Bridges was born in Mississippi in 1954, the oldest child of Abon and Lucille Bridges. She loved living on the farm that her paternal grandparents sharecropped. It was a hard life, so her parents moved to New Orleans seeking greater opportunities for themselves and their children. As she got older, while her father worked as a service station attendant and her mother worked nights to help support their growing family, Ruby's job was to keep an eye on her two younger brothers and sister. Home, church, and her all-black school kindergarten were the boundaries of her life—until a federal court order forced New Orleans schools to desegregate. During the summer of 1960, Ruby was chosen to attend the all-white William Frantz Elementary School for first grade.

The first day Ruby enrolled, crowds of angry white parents gathered around the school to scream horrible things and shake their fists at her. Four federal marshals had to escort Ruby to and from the school to protect her. Every day after that, Ruby would hurry past the angry crowds without saying a word. Her mother had told her not to be scared, but if she were afraid, she should pray. Prayer would protect her.

Once inside, Ruby sat at her desk among a room full of other desks—all vacant. None of the white parents would send their children to the school. Her teacher, Mrs. Henry, was impressed by Ruby's unfailing politeness and hopeful spirit. It was a very lonely experience for Ruby, but with Mrs. Henry's help and companionship, she learned to read and write.

One morning, Mrs. Henry noticed Ruby walking toward the school as usual but then she stopped, turned toward the angry, howling crowd and seemed to even be trying to speak to them. The crowd seemed ready to jump on her while the marshals tried to keep Ruby moving. Finally, she stopped talking and walked into the school.

Mrs. Henry immediately asked Ruby why she tried to talk to such an angry, hostile crowd. Ruby responded that she didn't stop to talk with them.

"Ruby, I saw you talking," Mrs. Henry pressed. "I saw your lips moving."

"I wasn't talking," replied Ruby. "I was praying. . . . I was praying for them."

Evidently, Ruby had stopped every morning a few blocks away from the school to pray for the people who hated her. But on this morning, she had forgotten until she was already in the middle of the malevolent mob.

Later that year, two white boys joined Ruby at the school. Other children soon followed. The next school year, the mobs gave up their struggle. Ruby finished Frantz Elementary, graduated from high school, then studied travel and tourism at the Kansas City business school, and worked for American Express as a world travel agent. In 1984, Ruby married Malcolm Hall and later became a full-time parent to their four sons.

On January 8, 2001, President Bill Clinton awarded Ruby the Presidential Citizens Medal. Today, Ruby Bridges Hall, chair of the Ruby Bridges Foundation, speaks to groups around the country about her experiences with education. Sometimes when she visits schools, Mrs. Henry, her first-grade teacher, goes with her. They tell others that school is a place to bring people together—from all races and backgrounds.

Sources: Biography.com. (2011). Ruby Bridges Biography. *Bio. True Story*. Retrieved from http://www.biography.com/articles/Ruby-Bridges-475426?part=2; Hall, R. G. The education of Ruby Nell. New Orleans, LA: The Ruby Bridges Foundation. Retrieved from http://www.rubybridges.com/story.htm; Elliot, L. (2000, May 25). Rare Ruby. *The Toronto Star*. Reprinted by New Orleans, LA: The Ruby Bridges Foundation.

were at the height of integration in the 1970s and 1980s, a period that saw a narrowing of the achievement gap.[56]

Both federal and state courts are now declaring that formerly segregated districts have made "good faith"—if unsuccessful—efforts to desegregate. Called "unified," these school districts are relieved of any more duty to integrate their

Reflect & Discuss

"Separate but equal" was a social doctrine used to keep African Americans and whites physically apart in public (and private) spheres.

A. Have the class reach a consensus on what they consider to be *Brown*'s top three compelling issues. Why are these issues the most persuasive arguments?
B. Discuss the extent to which you think each issue *Brown* sought to improve is present in your home community and in the larger society. What evidence can you cite to support your view?
C. What do you think students—African American and white—felt and thought during the first few days and weeks after their schools became integrated? How do you think integration affected teachers' roles as instructors and classroom managers?
D. What do you think was *Brown*'s impact on Latino or other non-Caucasian students?
E. Discuss whether class members think that the U.S. schools should be *color blind* or *integrated*. What reasons lead you to think that way?

schools. These same courts are declaring "race-based admissions policies" unconstitutional, so that districts may now return to their policies of maintaining racially identifiable neighborhood schools.

In writing for the majority in one such 2007 case,[57] U.S. Supreme Court Chief Justice John Roberts affirmed, "The way to stop discrimination on the basis of race is to stop discrimination on the basis of race."[58] Even racial classifications that officials describe as benign or beneficial should be struck down, the Court's majority argues, because the act of classification itself is offensive.[59]

The *Brown* Legacy Regardless of the limited legal retreat since the 1954 ruling, *Brown*'s move to desegregate schools was appropriate, both morally and educationally. Current research shows that African American children achieve more—and reduce the achievement gap between their test scores and those of white and Asian students—in racially integrated schools.

Since 1954, people have disagreed about whether *Brown*'s central meaning was to achieve a color-blind society or an integrated one. In the 2007 case, the Supreme Court firmly came down in favor of colorblindness.[60] Today, neither the government nor schools can use "a binary concept of race" to discriminate among individual students. Schools cannot put a collective social goal (racial balance) ahead of an individual's rights. Such racially based measures would now be considered "extreme."

Did You Get It?

Which statement is true about African American education in the South after the Civil War?

- **a.** In the immediate aftermath of the Civil War, generous Congressional appropriations for the Freedman's Bureau sharply increased African American literacy levels.
- **b.** The desire of freed slaves to learn how to read and write was so strong that by the 1870s, they had created their own common school system from their own scant resources.
- **c.** Southern elites were terrified of the potential for universal schooling to politically unite freed blacks and poor whites.
- **d.** Recognizing their very similar circumstances, Southern educators working with poor whites often made common cause with African American educators.

Take the full quiz on CourseMate.

5-4 World War I, the Great Depression, Vocational Education, and Public Education

World War I, the Great Depression, increased high school enrollments, and vocational education would all affect American public schools. These twentieth-century forces initiated important changes whose effects are still apparent today.

5-4a World War I and Standardized Tests

Modern standardized tests were a by-product of World War I. They emerged when military services needed to rapidly classify millions of recruits based on their general intellectual level. In 1917, Army psychologists developed group tests to meet this urgent practical need.

In spite of their limitations, these early twentieth-century intelligence exams have remained the basis for standardized achievement tests ever since. Able to be efficiently administered to large groups and after many revisions, the Army Alpha and Army Beta intelligence tests became the models for most group intelligence tests. Soon, group intelligence tests were being devised for all ages, from preschool children to graduate students. Designed for testing large numbers of individuals at the same time, through the use of simplified instructions and administrative procedures, the tests were both efficient and cost-effective.[61]

5-4b The Great Depression and Education

During the Great Depression in the 1930s, President Franklin D. Roosevelt and his advisors initially saw employment—rather than education—as the answer to the "youth problem." For this reason, they devoted their greatest attention to providing federal relief and creating jobs. Nonetheless, these jobs sometimes provided educational benefits to those most in need.[62]

For example, the Works Progress Administration (WPA) gave money to schools to hire more teachers, buy supplies, and provide free hot lunches for students. The WPA and Public Works Administration (PWA) built larger schools to replace the one-room schools that had prevailed in some parts of the country. Primarily to keep youths off the labor market, the National Youth Administration (NYA) provided work–study programs at the high school and collegiate levels. The Civilian Conservation Corps (CCC) put unemployed young men to work on conservation projects, while its voluntary education programs taught 35,000 illiterate youths how to read and write, and granted more than 1,000 high school diplomas and 39 college degrees. Under these programs, thousands more studied everything from industrial trades to philosophy, economics, and social problems.[63]

5-4c Increasing High School Enrollments

After World War I ended, states began to enforce child labor and compulsory attendance laws. Secondary school enrollments in the United States rose from approximately 1.1 million in 1910, to 2.5 million in 1920, to 4.8 million in 1930.[64] Later, the Great Depression's economic collapse prompted another boost in high school enrollments, as large number of jobless adolescents returned to school. By 1940, 7.1 million students between the ages of 14 and 17 were enrolled in high school, representing more than 73 percent of that age group in this country. Amid this unprecedented enrollment surge, education leaders argued that the new high school entrants' intellectual abilities were weaker than those of previous student groups; they needed access to less demanding courses.[65]

The economic crisis and resulting high school enrollment boom combined to produce a profound shift in high schools' nature and function. Increasingly, the schools' task became custodial in nature—to keep students out of the labor market instead of immediately preparing them for it. As a result, educators channeled increasing numbers of pupils into undemanding, nonacademic courses, while lowering standards in the academic courses required for graduation.

Proponents of these actions argued that these curriculum changes increased equal educational opportunities. In reality, they had a generally unequal impact on the low-income white and African American students who entered high schools in the 1930s and 1940s. These students were disproportionately assigned to nonacademic tracks and less demanding academic courses.[66] Although high schools met their short-term goals of removing these students from the adult labor market, they failed to meet these students' long-term needs for appropriately rigorous and marketable knowledge and skills.

5-4d The Growth of Vocational Education

After the Civil War, rapid industrialization prompted many Americans to leave farming for factories.[67] New industrial machines made on-the-job training realistic and low-skilled workers employable. By 1900, vocational school advocates, wanting to enroll more students, argued that apprenticeship had become irreversibly inefficient, exploitive, and ineffective.[68] Public schools struggled to meet the demands for a labor force that was prepared to make the move from an agrarian society to an industrial economy.[69] To deal with this paradigm shift, the idea of vocational education took hold.

In 1906, the National Society for the Promotion of Industrial Education advanced vocational schools as the ideal way to prepare young people for work. Business and industry liked the idea of offering vocational courses in public schools because having already-trained high school graduates helped reduce businesses' training costs and increase their profits. Politicians and economists encouraged these programs as a way to increase their local and national competitive advantages. In addition, vocational education appeared to effectively train and integrate into the public school system low-income and new immigrants' children who were seeking careers in the skilled trades or manual labor.[70]

Since the passage of the Smith-Hughes Act of 1917, federal legislation has continued to provide funds to support vocational education in public schools.[71] Over the years, the Smith-Hughes Act and its successors have expanded these vocational education programs with the aim of keeping more students in secondary education and providing trained workers for a growing number of semiskilled occupations.

Since 1950, however, vocational education enrollment has declined. Current educational philosophy calls for all students to delay their occupational decisions and to "keep the doors open" to advanced education. The de-tracking movement and press for educational equality and equity for diverse students have significantly contributed to this view.

As a result, today's vocational education in comprehensive high schools focuses its curricula on having students develop both vocational and academic skills to prepare them for college and careers. For example, High Schools That Work (HSTW) is a national high school program that blends traditional college-preparatory studies with quality vocational and technical studies to improve learning and achievement for all career-bound students. Its research shows that vocational students in schools that participated in HSTW for at least two years exceeded the national average scores of vocational students in reading, math, and science achievement.[72]

Similarly, high school **career academies** are designed to equip each student for both college and career. These "schools within schools" combine core academic subjects with a career-technical class related to an occupational theme such as health and bioscience, business and finance, arts and communications, education and child development, or engineering and information technology. Longitudinal studies of matched comparison groups have found that academy students have better attendance, earn more course credits, receive higher grades, and are less likely to leave high school. In addition, four years after leaving high school, career academy graduates tend to be working and earning substantially more than their nonacademy counterparts.[73]

career academies Late twentieth- and early twenty-first-century high school programs that combine core academic subjects with a career–technical class related to an occupational theme designed to equip each student for both college and career.

Did You Get It?

Pick the false statement about public and vocational education.

a. Modern standardized testing began during World War I.
b. Modern standardized testing began during World War II.
c. It was not until the Great Depression that states began to enforce child labor laws and compulsory education laws, in order to remove children from the labor market.
d. The federal response to the Great Depression understood that education, rather than employment, would resolve the youth program.

Take the full quiz on CourseMate.

5-5 The Coleman Report: Family, School, and Educating the Disadvantaged

In the years after the *Brown* decision, many people wanted to know if school desegregation had actually improved learning opportunities for all American students. In 1964, the U.S. Office of Education commissioned James S. Coleman, a Johns Hopkins University sociology professor, to assess whether children of different races, income groups, and national origins had equal educational opportunities.[74] Published in 1966, the Coleman Report concluded that school might not be society's great equalizer.[75] Instead, it deduced that family background—not schools—was the most important determiner of children's academic success.[76]

5-5a Coleman Report Findings

Documenting an African American–white achievement gap, the Coleman Report found that African American children started out academically behind their white peers and stayed behind, regardless of whether equal resources were available in their schools. The achievement disparities were large. In sixth grade, the average African American student was 1.9 years behind his or her white peers. By 12th grade, the average achievement gap had widened to nearly 4 years.[77] Desegregating schools did not appear to increase African American school achievement.

Additionally, the Coleman Report showed that African American children typically attended more poorly equipped schools—they had less access to physics, chemistry, and language; fewer laboratories available; and fewer books per pupil. But the differences were smaller than expected for African American and white schools in the same geographic regions. Few school inputs seemed to make a difference, except for teachers' verbal abilities. The report also found that 10 years after *Brown*, most students still attended segregated schools, and school segregation in the North was just as pervasive as it was in the South.

Not all of the Coleman findings were discouraging. Its second most important finding was that after family characteristics, a student's sense of control of his or her own destiny was the most important determinant of academic achievement. The students with whom youngsters attended school were almost as important as family background in predicting academic success. African American students did better in schools that were predominantly middle class than they did in schools dominated by low-income students, even though the improvements were not large enough to make up for achievement differences due to family background. Desegregation advocates viewed this finding as a point in favor of their movement.

5-5b The Coleman Report: A Second Look

Several attempts have been made to reanalyze the Coleman data to ensure that the original interpretations were correct. It is true that although the Coleman methodology would not meet today's standards for scientific research, it was considered to be in the "vanguard" in 1966.[78]

One study found that teacher bias noted on Coleman's questionnaire might have possibly contributed to lower scores for African American students.[79] Achievement gaps in the same school between African American and white students were higher where most of the teachers had expressed preference for teaching college-oriented children of white-collar professionals. Thus, teacher expectations may have played an important role in influencing their students' outcomes.[80]

At the end of the day, what most people took away from the Coleman Report was that "schools don't matter"; smart families—not schools—make students smart. Considerable evidence suggests that these conclusions greatly oversimplify and distort the findings, however. Even so, substantial research supports the belief that family systems do have critical and statistically significant associations with children's school success.[81]

Importantly, the Coleman Report's conclusions shifted the policy and research focus toward student achievement—as opposed to school facilities—as a measure of the public schools' quality. Stimulated by Coleman's findings, the "effective schools" research since the 1970s (discussed more fully in Chapter 15) has shown how schools can make a difference—and even overcome—many students' background characteristics.[82]

Did You Get It?

The Coleman Report found that

- **a.** African American students started out and remained academically behind their white peers.
- **b.** School inputs, in terms of better equipment and facilities, made a significant difference for African American students.
- **c.** A student's sense of control over her/his destiny was the overwhelming indicator of academic success.
- **d.** It did not matter whether African American students attended schools that were majority middle-class or majority poor.

Take the full quiz on CourseMate.

5-6 Special Education: Providing Free and Appropriate Education to Students with Disabilities

Public prejudice and ignorance kept most students with disabilities from having access to a full and appropriate education until the late twentieth century. Right up to the mid-century, only students with the least serious disabilities received public schooling.

5-6a Advances in Special Education in the Mid-Twentieth Century

Inspired by *Brown's* precedent, parents of students with disabilities began to form organizations, such as the National Association for Retarded Citizens (the Arc), to advocate for publicly educating their children. Responding to their persistence, Congress authorized the 1958 Public Law 85-926 to support the training and preparation of special education teachers. Special education leaders began arguing for the rights of students with disabilities to be educated alongside their nondisabled peers in more normal school settings.

5-6b Public Law 94-142; IDEA

The 1970s saw courts and Congress deciding in favor of special needs students attending public schools based on equality of opportunity. Congress noted that of the more than 8 million children with disabilities in the United States in 1975, more than half did not receive appropriate educational services that would allow them to have full equality of opportunity. One million disabled children were excluded entirely from the public school system.[83]

Early in this decade, court decisions in Pennsylvania (1971) and in the District of Columbia (1972) established the right of all children labeled as "intellectually disabled" to a free and appropriate education. These rulings made it more difficult for public schools to exclude students with disabilities. Further, in 1973, the Rehabilitation Act, Section 504, and later amendments guaranteed the rights of disabled individuals in employment settings and in schools that receive federal monies. Finally, parental pressure, court decisions, and legislative actions persuaded Congress to pass the Education for All Handicapped Children Act (Public Law 94-142) in 1975. Amended several times, in 1990, it became the Individuals with Disabilities Education Act (IDEA).

PL 94-142 and beyond PL 94-142 defined **children with disabilities** as those who are intellectually challenged, hard of hearing, deaf, speech and language impaired, visually handicapped (including blindness), seriously emotionally disturbed, orthopedically impaired, or otherwise health impaired, as well as children with specific learning disabilities. To ensure their basic educational rights, this law specified that they must have the following requirements met and services available to them:

children with disabilities Those who are intellectually challenged, hard of hearing, deaf, speech and language impaired, visually handicapped (including blindness), seriously emotionally disturbed, orthopedically impaired, or otherwise health impaired, as well as children with specific learning disabilities.

free and appropriate education An educational program of specialized instruction and related services purposely designed to meet the unique needs of children with disabilities.

- A free and appropriate public education
- An individualized education program
- Special education services
- Related services
- Due process procedures
- The least restrictive learning environment (LRE) in which to learn

At last, all children with disabilities from ages 3 to 21, inclusive, were eligible to receive these educational services in public schools.

Over the years, additional amendments extended and clarified these rights. By 1976, all states had laws subsidizing public school programs for students with disabilities. IDEA amendments of 1997 (PL 105-171) addressed the need for high educational performance standards for all students and teachers, including those in special education. By the early 1980s, students considered to have mild or moderate disabilities were usually integrated into general education classrooms on at least a part-time basis. In addition, many students who were not served in the past—including those with severe disabilities—started receiving educational services in their local neighborhood schools, including participating in regular cafeteria, playground, library, halls, buses, and restroom activities.

Later court cases have tried to clarify the true intent of the IDEA statute. Cases have addressed issues such as free and appropriate education, procedural safeguards, individualized education program, LRE, separate school placement, related services, discipline, attorneys' fees, and tuition reimbursement. We will briefly clarify a few of the key findings here.

Free and appropriate public education means an educational program of specialized instruction and related services purposely designed to meet the child with disabilities' unique needs. "Free and appropriate" does not mean the

Robin Sachs/PhotoEdit

A special needs student works on a brailler with her teacher in a regular education classroom.

school has to maximize the child's potential by providing the best education that money can buy. Rather, this phrase specifies a "basic floor of opportunity" must be delivered.[84] The extent to which the education must "benefit" the child and what schools must do to make this happen, however, remain legally unclear and open to more challenges.

Procedural safeguards means using fair and proper steps in a highly regulated process to ensure that special needs children receive appropriate educational services. The most important procedures include giving parents of special needs children notice and an opportunity to participate in developing their child's individual educational plan. Parents must be told about the methods and procedures they can use to appeal and resolve any conflicts or grievances with the school officials if they disagree about how to best educate their child.

procedural safeguards Using fair and proper steps in a highly regulated process to ensure that children with special needs receive appropriate educational services.

individualized educational program (IEP) A written educational plan that identifies the child's educational needs, the annual instructional goals and objectives, the specific educational programs and services to be provided, and the evaluation procedures that will measure the child's progress.

least restrictive environment (LRE) The practice of educating children with special needs in the general education classroom with normally developing children whenever possible.

inclusion Integrating students with disabilities into regular classrooms—the LRE—whenever possible, while providing them with the supports necessary for them to succeed.

response to intervention (RTI) A pre-identification strategy to prevent unnecessary assignment to special education services for regular education students who have difficulties learning reading and math by providing earlier, structured, increasingly intense, and highly individualized interventions for students experiencing difficulty learning to read.

An **individualized educational program (IEP)** is a written educational plan that identifies the child's educational needs, the annual instructional goals and objectives, the specific educational programs and services to be provided, and the evaluation procedures that will measure the child's progress. Every year, parents work with a multidisciplinary team of their child's educators to develop this plan. Teachers are expected to implement the plan as written until the multidisciplinary team and parents change it.

The requirement that a child be taught in the **least restrictive environment (LRE)** means that special needs children should be educated in the general education classroom with normally developing children whenever possible. This placement gives the child with disabilities more opportunities to socialize and interact with other typically developing children. It reduces the stigma of being "different," and offers students with disabilities the opportunity to learn the rigorous regular curriculum at the same pace and depth as "normal" children.

Inclusion involves integrating students with disabilities into regular classrooms—the LRE—whenever possible, while providing them with the supports necessary for them to succeed.[85] The teacher's job is to arrange instruction that benefits all students, even though different students may gain different benefits from that teaching. Largely as a result of this mandate, from 1995 to 2009, the percentage of students with disabilities spending 80 percent or more of the school day in general classrooms increased from 45 to 59.4 percent.[86]

The 2004 IDEA legislation included provisions for a **response to intervention (RTI)**, a pre-identification strategy to prevent unnecessary assignment to special education services for regular education students who have difficulties learning reading and math. RTI focuses on providing more effective instruction by encouraging earlier, structured, increasingly intense, and highly individualized interventions for students experiencing difficulty learning to read. Teachers monitor students' progress to see if the responses to this intervention bring adequate academic growth. If a student's progress does not seem adequate, an increasingly targeted and individualized approach is initiated and maintained until a multidisciplinary team determines that the student may be eligible for special education services. Critics of RTI ask whether it will successfully identify—or overidentify—students needing special education services, note that it does not address students with neurologically based disabilities, and wonder how it will fit with other subjects and older students.[87]

Did You Get It?

As a matter of public law, children with learning disabilities are entitled to

a. A free and appropriate public education with similar students.
b. Special education and related services in kindergarten through twelfth grade.
c. Opportunities to maximize the child's potential.
d. The least restrictive learning environment and due process procedures.

Take the full quiz on CourseMate.

5-7 *A Nation at Risk* Impacts Public Schools

In 1983, *A Nation at Risk*, a report of the National Commission on Excellence in Education, sharply criticized public schools.[88] It claimed that world competitors were challenging the United States' former preeminence in commerce, industry, science, and technological innovation. American students were scoring poorly on international tests, not taking enough science and math courses, and showing weak critical thinking skills, all of which placed the nation at risk. American schools, once a source of justifiable pride, were "presently being eroded by a rising tide of mediocrity that threatens our very future as a Nation and as a people."[89]

The report continued, "If an unfriendly foreign power had attempted to impose on America the mediocre educational performance that exists today, we might well have viewed it as an act of war."[90]

Complaining that U.S public schools had moved from standards centered to student centered, the authors of *A Nation at Risk* wanted the direction reversed. The report advocated high expectations for all students by having all complete a reasonably demanding academic curriculum. It also recommended the establishment of high standards that students must meet before they received a high school diploma, with textbooks and standardized tests used to drive the improvement.

5-7a Responses to *A Nation at Risk*

As a report, *A Nation at Risk* was highly controversial. Some questioned the assumed cause-and-effect relationship between public schooling and market dominance or industrial productivity. Others raised broader issues, asking whether schools could either cause or cure America's social, economic, and political dilemmas.[91] Writers criticized the fallacy of comparing the highly dissimilar United States with European and Asian education systems.[92] Some observed that the report included a very narrow definition of "excellence."[93] Others noted that the report's recommendations placed an ever-growing group of educationally and economically disadvantaged students at even greater risk of failure.[94]

Many saw *A Nation at Risk* as propaganda meant to advance a political agenda[95] using a "golden treasury" of selective, distorted, and spun statistics.[96] It hyped bad news about schools, they said, while deliberately suppressing or ignoring the good news.[97] In addition, public school defenders asserted, the United States was not failing in the global marketplace.[98]

Despite these criticisms, *A Nation at Risk* delivered some key educational benefits. It spurred policy makers to increase public schools' accountability and educational rigor as evidenced through standardized tests. By 1985, 35 states had implemented statewide minimum competency tests, and 11 required students to pass such tests to graduate from high school.

Scott's Journey

By Scott Fowler and Jackie Fowler, reprinted by permission.
Note: Scott Fowler is a young man with cerebral palsy and Jackie Fowler is his mother.

For the first ten years that I attended school, I was in a totally segregated setting because the school focused on my disability rather than on my abilities. The good part was that I got physical therapy, occupational therapy—which is how I learned to drive a power wheelchair at age 5—speech therapy, and therapy for my visual impairment. The not-so-good part was that I got very little in the way of an educational experience.

When I was 15 years old, my mother was able to talk the local school district into giving me an opportunity to go to high school with my peers, and "it was marvelous!" Everyone from the principal to the guidance counselors to the teachers and the students, including me, was doing this for the first time, that is, involving a student with significant physical and intellectual disabilities in the regular classroom.

I did not take a lot of academic classes but I worked hard to succeed at the ones I had. My very first class at the high school was Earth Science and we had two teachers—Mrs. B., who was one of the high school special ed teachers, and Mr. F., who was the principal of the high school and an ex-science teacher! I think that he set a great example for all my teachers, especially the ones who were not in special ed. Both Mrs. B. and Mr. F. made it very comfortable for me by changing my assignments a little, and I had a senior student, Debbie, who was my tutor. She helped me with my homework and talked to me about having a learning disability because she had one, too. I had another teacher, Mrs. D., who was my resource room teacher, and she helped me with my classes as well as tried to get me involved in clubs like FBLA (Future Business Leaders of America) and Key Club.

Some of the most important things that I learned in high school had to do with friendships and commitments and personal responsibility. My first year there, I had a "best buddy"—all the freshmen did—and his name was Seth. He was a senior, and he loved music; he was in the band and he made sure that I got involved in lots of after-school activities. He also made sure that other students didn't make fun of me. Both Seth and Debbie invited me to their houses when they had a party, and they kept in touch with me when they went to college and even after that. The best part was I felt like a real person!

I did join FBLA and I met even more people through volunteering and by working on projects at school and in the community; I even returned to my old school, Blythedale Children's Hospital, to hand out toys to the little kids who were in the hospital part of the school for the holidays. In my last year at the high school, I wrote a column for the school newspaper entitled, "Scott's Perspective" and shared what it was like to grow up with a disability . . . it's hard because people tend to look at me and see what I can't do.

Because I wanted to work when I left high school, I was fortunate to meet a very special teacher, Chris B., who helped me find work experiences to match my strengths and interests. My first (volunteer) job was at the local museum where I was a docent, taking young children on tours of the train room. That summer and the next, I worked (for pay!) at FDR State Park in my hometown as a gate attendant at the pool. By the time I was in my last year of high school, I had two part-time jobs that I kept for ten years. The "person-centered planning" process that was used to identify my strengths and the job experiences I had gave me self-confidence and made me feel like a part of my community.

When I lost one of my jobs due to the economy, my friend, Beth Mount at *Capacity Works*, helped me start my own business; I traveled to a variety of conferences and workshops, some as far away as Chicago and Austin, Texas, where I sold inspirational plaques and note cards along with products that were created by people with disabilities. I sometimes gave presentations at these conferences about my life and what I was able to do despite my challenges.

In 2005, I was asked to become part of the Speaker's Bureau that was being formed at the Self-Advocacy Association of New York State, Inc. My role there has been to speak to groups of children and adults about my experiences and to help give a voice to those people who cannot speak for themselves. We have talked to Rotary and Kiwanis Clubs, to elementary school and college students, to other students with disabilities who are transitioning out of high school, and to health professionals. We talk about how our hopes and our dreams are not so different from everyone else's, and we encourage people to involve us in their community—their social and civic organizations, their churches and synagogues, and their local events.

If there were just a few key words that I could use to describe what has been most helpful on my long journey, they would be *patience*, like the time my teachers took to listen to me and let me work and learn at my own pace, and *friendship that sees beyond the disability*, which emphasizes all the things we have in common, like enjoying eating out and going to the movies. Most of my close friends now are also people with disabilities because we share so many of the same experiences but we are all a part of the larger community thanks to being included when we were growing up.

In the face of this increased standardized testing, schools perceived it to be in their best interests to provide extra help to low-scoring students, who were frequently low-income children and children of color. The emphasis on students mastering basic skills plus the new public accountability of published "school report cards" were important reasons why African American students' National Assessment of Educational Progress (NAEP, a common metric for all states) scores rose during the 1970s (for 9-year-olds) and during the 1980s (for 17-year-olds).[99]

A Nation at Risk put public education front and center on the national stage by turning it into a highly visible topic for community discussion and resource allocation. Although the report may have misrepresented what the public schools were accomplishing, it did focus national attention on ways to strengthen them.

Did You Get It?

What was one effect *A Nation at Risk* had on public schools?

a. It used very fair, carefully balanced, impeccably-researched statistics to show the decline of American education.

b. It encouraged schools, a matter of self-interest, to provide extra help to students who were faring poorly.

c. It deemphasized standardized testing as a way to measure educational rigor and effectiveness.

d. The emphasis on testing resulted in lower NAEP scores for African American children.

Take the full quiz on CourseMate.

5-8 No Child Left Behind 2002, Race to the Top 2009, and Common Core Standards: Federal Support and Increased Accountability for Educating All Students

The No Child Left Behind Act, signed into law in 2002, tied allocation of federal monies to rigorous and highly public school accountability for raising traditionally underserved students' academic achievement. It came about as a reauthorization of earlier legislation aimed at providing federal aid to public schools. In 2009, Race to the Top brought student achievement data into teacher and principal evaluations, and encouraged states to adopt a new Common Core Standards and support charter schools.

5-8a 1965 Elementary and Secondary Education Act

In 1965, President Lyndon Johnson led Congress to pass the Elementary and Secondary Education Act (ESEA), the parent of the No Child Left Behind Act. Part of Johnson's 1964 Civil Rights Act and the "War on Poverty" legislation, ESEA was possibly the most important congressional action to fund education programs until that time.

Head Start and Title I ESEA introduced the federal **Head Start** programs, which were preschool education classes intended to give children ages three to five from economically disadvantaged homes the cognitive and social development or readiness for school success. The **Title I** legislation was intended to supplement academic resources for low-income children who needed extra reading and math help in the early grades. Although states received extra money to support low-income schools, the law did little to hold state governments responsible for academic outcomes at those schools.

Head Start National preschool programs to give children ages three to five from economically disadvantaged homes the cognitive and social development, or readiness for school success.

Title I Federal legislation that intended to supplement academic resources for low-income children who needed extra reading and math help in the early grades, part of the 1994 Elementary and Secondary Education Act (ESEA).

Although well intentioned, neither Title I nor Head Start has been as successful as hoped. The two large-scale Title I evaluations have concluded that it has not substantially narrowed achievement gaps between disadvantaged and middle-class students, as policy makers intended.[100] Reanalyses of the data and related studies have painted the findings somewhat more optimistically, concluding that Title I may have kept the achievement gap from widening.[101]

Head Start research findings are more positive. Although the program improves school readiness as measured by achievement test scores, the initial advantages fade over the elementary years. The most likely explanation for the "achievement fade" is that Head Start graduates attend schools that do not effectively motivate learning or build on the academic skills that Head Start students bring upon their entry into school.[102]

5-8b National Education Goals

After *A Nation at Risk* warned of a "rising tide of mediocrity" in America's schools,[103] public attitudes about education began to change. In 1989, President George H. W. Bush and then Arkansas Governor Bill Clinton (the National Governors Association's Chair) broke with tradition of local control and established national education goals. In 1994, President Clinton signed legislation that ordered states to set achievement standards, measure students' performance against them, and improve schools with students who did not make the grade. This law did not require the states to move quickly to crack down on schools that didn't measure up, however.

5-8c No Child Left Behind Act

In 2001, Congress passed and in 2002 President George W. Bush signed the reauthorization of ESEA funds, now called the **No Child Left Behind Act (NCLB)**. Seeking equity and excellence, NCLB represented the federal government's first serious attempt to hold states, districts, and schools accountable for remedying the unequal achievement among different student populations, especially low-income students, minority students, English language learners, and students with disabilities.

No Child Left Behind Act (NCLB) The reauthorized ESEA, 2002, was the federal government's first serious attempt to hold states, districts, and schools accountable for remedying the unequal achievement among different student.

disaggregate data Test results for NCLB separated by student subgroup to show academic progress at all tested grades, in all tested subjects, by all tested student subgroups to monitor and advance traditionally underserved students' academic progress.

highly qualified teachers A requirement in NCLB, in which individuals with documented subject matter knowledge in the content they are teaching must be available in each core subject classroom.

Basically, NCLB was a highly rigorous public accountability system. The law required all student subgroups to pass 100 percent of the state standards' assessments—and be performing at grade level in language arts, mathematics, and science—in third through eighth grades and once in high school by end of the 2013–2014 school year. Each state adopted its own criteria for improving test scores annually, a measure called adequate yearly progress (AYP). Each year, schools had to **disaggregate**—or separate—their data and show academic progress at all tested grades, in all tested subjects, by all tested student subgroups. By requiring the achievement data to be separated in this way, policy makers sought to prevent schools from "hiding" or glossing over underserved students' low achievement by averaging their scores with the higher scores earned by more economically advantaged and better-achieving students.

In addition, to ensure that students learned, NCLB required schools to guarantee that only **highly qualified teachers**—individuals with documented subject matter knowledge in the content they are teaching—be available in each core subject classroom.

If any one group failed to make the AYP goal (it could be a different subgroup from one year to another), the whole school received a failing grade.[104]

"Failing" schools were liable for a range of penalties, including permitting in-district student transfers to more "successful schools" and providing tutoring to failing students. Schools still "in need of improvement" after five consecutive years were forced to **restructure** by having the school district reassign the school administrators and teachers to other schools and restaff the school from the classroom up. Alternatively, the state could take over the school and make the necessary changes.

restructure In NCLB, a penalty for "unsuccessful" schools, in which a district reassigns school administrators and teachers to other schools and restaffs the school from the classroom up, or in which the state takes over the school and makes the necessary changes to improve student achievement.

National Assessment of Educational Progress (NAEP) Called the "nation's report card," a common metric for all states, can be used to assess student progress in key academic subjects.

NCLB outcomes NCLB has produced mixed results with some notable success stories. Despite poverty, high student mobility rates, and other challenges, urban school districts that focused attention, accountability, and support appropriately have been able to boost their students' achievement and narrow the achievement gap.[105] Test data support student achievement gains in these scenarios.

Nationally, elementary grades showed consistent, overall achievement gains in reading and math and a reduced achievement gap between white and African American students and between white and Latino students. Most states narrowed the achievement gap by raising achievement for all student groups. Less progress occurred in middle and high schools, however.[106]

Although it is not possible to compare NCLB student achievement across states—because each state defined "proficiency" its own way and used varying assessments—the **National Assessment of Educational Progress (NAEP)**, a common metric for all states, can be used to assess this progress. Research has found that the states that experienced the greatest gains on NAEP, post-NCLB, were those with the most rigorous standards.[107] Additionally, from 2002 to 2011, NAEP showed achievement patterns consistent with increased achievement on the NCLB assessments. Elementary-level reading and math scores showed strong improvements between 1999 and 2011, with all student groups exhibiting effective performance. Results indicate the gaps separating African American and Latino students from white students during this period were the smallest in our nation's history.[108]

For middle grade students, NAEP reading and mathematics scale scores were up in 2011, at eighth grade compared with 2009. The gains represent one additional month of schooling—with gains twice as large for the lowest performing students. Historically, fourth graders showed more gains than eighth graders, so the later growth in eighth grade probably reflects children who benefited from better instruction in elementary school, showing greater mastery in eighth grade, or successful education reforms in elementary schools moving into middle school, or both.[109] No real changes have appeared at the high school level. But because many state NCLB achievement scores were increasing while their NAEP scores were not, observers were left to wonder whether the No Child Left Behind learning gains were real.[110] Nonetheless, an analysis of NAEP "Long Term" assessments, last conducted in 2008, concluded that scores for students grades four and eight were significantly higher in 2008 in both reading and mathematics than they were in 1971 and 1973, respectively. Again, 12th graders showed virtually no change in either test.[111]

TeachSource Video 5.1

Education Reform: Teachers Talk about No Child Left Behind

Educational reform has led to increased teacher accountability for student learning. Teachers believe that although standards should have high expectations for teachers and students, standards should also consider individual student differences. Watch the video clips, study the artifacts in the case, and reflect on the following questions:

1. What are the benefits of heightened teacher accountability for student learning and improved educational practice?
2. How has heightened teacher accountability for student learning challenged teachers' instructional practice and professional learning?
3. How does teacher accountability change the way teachers use student achievement data to inform and individualize their instruction?

Watch on CourseMate.

Critique of NCLB Although NCLB can claim some elementary school and middle school achievement gains, the accountability program is not always working as intended. NCLB appeared to have "unforeseen problems, unintended consequences, and unworkable features" that limit its effectiveness.[112] Its practice of comparing one student group's performance against a different group's, the narrowing of the curriculum by placing an excessive focus on reading and math, statistical issues that interfere with drawing accurate conclusions, cheating, and a misleading definition of "teacher quality" all create difficulties in making school improvements that are meaningful for all students.[113]

Is "proficiency for all" possible? Finally, "proficiency for all" may be neither logically nor practically possible. Every state defines "proficiency" its own way. What a student must know and be able to do in one state may or not match what a peer needs to accomplish in a neighboring state. Richard Rothstein, research associate for the Economic Policy Institute (a Washington think tank), believes that "'proficiency for all' is an oxymoron because no goal can be both challenging to—and achievable by—all students."[114]

Recognizing the dilemma of determining ambitious but realistic goals, Rick Hess of the American Enterprise Institute believes that as the 2014 deadline for all students' full proficiency approaches, the commitment to complete proficiency may weaken, noting that it "was a nice aspirational goal, but it needs to be revisited."[115]

And it was. In 2011, the U.S. Department of Education gave states permission to seek waivers from this proficiency requirement if they developed and submitted for approval plans to increase their students' achievement.

5-8d Race to the Top

Elected in 2008 during a severe economic recession, President Barack Obama committed policy and funding to cash-strapped states to support widespread educational improvements and to prevent teacher layoffs. Signing an economic stimulus into law in early 2009, President Obama's American Recovery and Reinvestment Act (ARRA) directed historic levels of federal dollars into education. The focus of funding went to improving teacher and principal effectiveness and turning around chronically underperforming schools.

The Recovery Act also supported the $4.35 billion Race to the Top (RTTT) competitive grant program. RTTT provided monies to states for large-scale educational reforms that result in improved student achievement, narrowed achievement gaps, and increased graduation and college enrollment rates. Grant applications required states to adopt common core statewide standards, incorporate student achievement data into teacher and principal evaluations, increase the availability of charter schools, and obligated states to ensure that high-poverty and/or high-minority schools received an equitable part of the funds.[116]

All but 10 states applied for the award during the first round of competition.[117] Chronically underperforming schools also received $3.5 billion intended to boost state and district efforts to overhaul their worst-performing schools. An extra $650 million in Investing in Innovation grants was allotted for districts, groups of schools, and their nonprofit partners to pursue and scale up innovative reform strategies.

5-8e The Common Core Standards

The Common Core State Standards Initiative is a state-led effort coordinated by the National Governors Association Center for Best Practices

(NGA Center) and the Council of Chief State School Officers (CCSSO) to provide K-12 schools and parents with a clear and consistent framework about what students are expected to learn to prepare them for college and the workforce regardless of where they live. Administrators, state education officials, policy-making groups, teachers, and experts are collaborating to develop the standards which:

- include rigorous academic content using higher-order thinking skills,
- are evidence based, and
- are informed by other top-performing countries.

The blueprints for what students should learn in English and math, in each grade, K-12, were released in March 2010. The blueprints make no attempt to tell teachers how to teach or describe everything that should be taught, however. Common assessments based on these standards are due in 2014–2015.

Critiques of Race to the Top reforms Critics have challenged RTTT's approaches to education reform. First, many educators and parents oppose the Common Core Standards. They fear this will lead to a national curriculum and a national assessment test, will end local control of education, and will affect how teachers perform in the classroom. Opponents also assert that the core standards do not respect children's natural development (not every child is ready to learn the same content at the same time—nor should one set of goals suit all students); standards may distort the curriculum; and standards may be weaker than a state's current standards.[118] Detractors also note that no set of standards has much meaning without equitable resources to ensure that teachers are prepared well enough to reach children who live in all circumstances.

Next, RTTT critics argue that tying student achievement to teacher evaluation rests on faulty assumptions that teachers should be held fully accountable for low student test scores (because many factors beyond the teacher's control affect learning); and that standardized tests are free of bias. Skeptics correctly observe that:

- designing statistical techniques to connect student achievement to teacher effectiveness is not error-free;
- the data are only available for certain teachers teaching certain subjects in identified grades over several years; and
- it is unethical to use standardized test results as the sole or main measure of teacher accountability.

Others contend that the RTTT grant program is inequitable, depriving low-income communities of needed funds, and the program did not use proven methods for educational change.[119]

5-8f Teacher Evaluation and Student Achievement

Teacher evaluation in the United States is in the crosshairs. Because research confirms that teacher effectiveness is the most important school factor in improving student achievement, finding, developing, and keeping effective teachers is an important school goal. And because student learning is teaching's most important outcome, it makes sense to base their evaluations, in part, on student achievement, as long as it is done fairly and effectually. But evaluating teachers and finding ways to assess their impact on student learning remain subjects of intense debate.

For decades, teacher evaluation has suffered from several weaknesses. They have been infrequent, seldom consider students' academic progress as part of teacher evaluation, are unable to give teachers worthwhile feedback, and are not often used to make important decisions about professional development, salary, promotion, or tenure. Additionally, evaluation protocols typically allow principals only to rate teachers as "Satisfactory" or "Unsatisfactory," making it impossible to separate great teachers from satisfactory teachers, marginal teachers from poor teachers. Nearly 99 percent of teachers receive "Satisfactory" ratings.[120]

As a result, ineffective tenured teachers rarely lose their jobs over their poor performance, top-performing teachers go unrecognized, and moderately effective, diligent teachers lack opportunities to grow. In addition, the public is misled into thinking that all teachers perform the same.

Nevertheless, student achievement is playing an increasingly larger role in teacher evaluations. In *State of the States 2012,* the National Council on Teacher Quality notes that half the states require annual teacher evaluation, up from 15 in 2009. Thirty-two states require that student learning factor into evaluations of teacher performance; in 22 of these states, student learning is a significant or the most significant factor. Sixteen states consider at least some evidence of student learning when deciding who will receive tenure. In comparison, in 2009, not a single state was doing this.[121]

According to the New Teacher Project, improving teacher evaluation should be comprehensive, meaningful, and fair. They propose that teacher evaluation should have the following design standards[122]:

- *An annual process*—all teachers should be evaluated at least once a year.
- *Comprehensive*—a wide-ranging performance evaluation system should fairly, accurately, and credibly observe and measure teachers' ability to help students learn and succeed.
- *Clear, rigorous expectations*—evaluations should be anchored in clear, precisely worded, and observable standards of instructional excellence that highlight student learning.
- *Multiple measures*—evaluations should include an array of data points that focus on teachers' impact on students' academic growth, each with its own weight, and present a complete picture of teacher performance. Such data may include: **value-added**[123] models, classroom observations using a research-affirmed metric of effective teaching, samples of student work connected to learning standards, examples of typical assignments or other evidence of student mastery from classroom assessments, and other quantitative and qualitative information.
- *Multiple ratings options*—expectations should use four to five rating levels to describe differences in teacher effectiveness, such as "highly effective," "effective," "needs improvement," and "ineffective" or "exemplary," "strong," "effective," "developing" and "needs improvement."
- *Regular feedback*—evaluations should encourage regular, frequent observations and constructive critical feedback to teachers about student progress, professional goals, and developmental needs and the support school leaders will provide to support those needs.
- *Professional development*—evaluations should be tightly linked to teachers' evaluation on performance standards and professional growth activities targeted to teachers' needs.
- *Significant*—evaluation outcomes should be a major factor in human resources policies and practices regarding hiring, assignment, professional development, pay increases, promotions, retention and dismissal.

value-added A statistical technique that determines the amount of teacher influence on students' academic progress useful for large-scale studies.

Although teachers' evaluations should not be based only on a single measure, such as standardized test scores, teachers should be accountable for helping students make measurable progress toward rigorous learning standards. These fair and accurate evaluation approaches go a long way in making teaching a rewarding career that attracts talented, growth-oriented individuals.

Did You Get It?

Which of the following is a fact about No Child Left Behind?

a. It was the U.S. government's first serious attempt to require all jurisdictions to eliminate the unequal achievement among different student populations, especially low-income and minority students.
b. Proficiency for all students may not be possible, either logically or practically.
c. The states that experienced the greatest gains were those with the least rigorous standards.
d. NCLB imposes federal standards of performance and improvement in performance on all the states' boards of education.

Take the full quiz on CourseMate.

5-9 Recent Innovations: Technology, Virtual Education, and Charter Schools

The Internet's emergence in the late 1980s and early 1990s linked computers and technology with educational reform in a relationship that continues to transform both teaching and learning. Several million K-12 students are currently estimated to be participating in all virtual schools, blended schools, and blended programs.[124] And with cuts to education spending increasing in recent years, online instruction is one option getting more attention as school districts look for ways to reduce costs. Some predict that, by 2019, half of all high school classes will be taught over the Internet.[125]

virtual education Online learning; instruction in a learning environment in which teacher and student are separated by time, space, or both, usually over the Internet.

5-9a Virtual Education

Virtual education—online learning—that is, instruction in a learning environment in which teacher and student are separated by time, space, or both, usually over the Internet—is one of the fastest-growing trends in education. Almost every state has some online-learning initiative—involving about 5 percent of all students nationally—and they are expanding by 16 percent each year.[126] Over the next decade, the demand for "blended" courses—part face-to-face in brick-and-mortar schools and part online—is expected to grow.

States usually establish state-led supplemental online programs to serve students part-time on a course-by-course basis to enhance students' academic experiences. Certain states also operate virtual schools that serve students full-time. The local school in which the student is enrolled has the responsibility for granting credit for the course.

Increased personalization of learning makes "virtual ed" so popular. Online learning allows students to take coursework that is otherwise unavailable at their school, a particular concern in rural and smaller districts. It resolves scheduling conflicts with school-based classes, enables students to pursue special interests not offered on-site, and provides opportunities for credit recovery toward a diploma to make up for failed or missed classes. Online learning also extends opportunities for the most highly motivated and able students to accelerate and deepen their learning, while also giving struggling students the time they need to learn at their own pace. Online learning can provide maximum flexibility: Courses can be available in real time and/or asynchronously, allowing students access anytime

charter schools Public schools operating under a specific contract or "charter" granted by the state legislature or other appropriate authority, which excuses the school from certain state or local rules and regulations in exchange for delivering acceptable student performance on state and federal academic standards.

and anywhere. Virtual charter schools can even have certain students learning almost entirely from home.

Advocates avow that virtual education might be used to expand learning time in ways that help shrink the education gaps between affluent and low-income students and between U.S. students and those in higher-performing countries.[127] Supporters also assert that full-time virtual schools can save money on facilities or transportation compared to traditional schools, and supplemental programs offering individual course enrollments can offer even bigger savings.[128]

Online learning also has its critics. Although some focus on academic and social concerns, others address the business aspects, insisting that school district officials take a critical approach to evaluating for-profit products and services. Both price and quality matter. Critics also add that using for-profit companies is unnecessary when arrangements for online courses with universities are more economical. More research is needed to evaluate online courses' academic or fiscal effectiveness.

TeachSource Video 5.2

Teaching Technology Skills: An Elementary School Lesson on PowerPoint

Elementary teachers can use technology integration to increase student engagement and build critical thinking skills as students learn how to create and deliver sophisticated oral presentations. Two teachers explain how they integrate PowerPoint and Internet research into classroom lessons on civil rights to help students become effective oral communicators. Watch the video clips, study the artifacts in the case study, and reflect on the following questions:

1. How does the discussion about "bullets" increase students' critical reading, thinking, and writing abilities?
2. What variety of factors in the lesson heightens students' motivation and interest in the content under study and in the processes involved?
3. In what ways will this and similar experiences prepare students for twenty-first-century academic and career experiences?
4. In what ways is this type of lesson helpful to both students with lots of prior background knowledge and computer skills and those with less prior background knowledge or computer experience?

Watch on CourseMate.

Research on virtual education Despite few published rigorous research studies, a 2009 meta-analysis from the U.S. Department of Education for K-12 students found that "instruction combining online and face-to-face elements had a larger advantage" than either purely online or entirely face-to-face instruction. Although online learning appears to be as effective as conventional classroom instruction, it is not better. The observed learning advantages may come from the additional learning time and materials as well as the extra opportunities for collaboration, rather than from the online learning as a superior learning platform. Moreover, greater learning effects are evident in undergraduate and older learners than for K-12 students.[129]

5-9b Charter Schools

Charter schools are public schools that provide free public elementary and/or secondary education to eligible students. Under a specific contract or "charter" granted by the state legislature or other appropriate authority, the school is excused from certain state or local rules and regulations in exchange for delivering acceptable student performance on state and federal academic standards—usually determined by achievement test scores. Charter schools can be started by groups of teachers, parents, or community organizations as well as school districts; and they are administered by regular school districts, state education agencies, or chartering organizations. A school's charter is periodically reviewed (typically, every three to five years) and can be revoked if it fails to meet curriculum or management guidelines or its accountability standards.

In 2013, more than 2.3 million public school students attended the nearly 6,000 public charter schools in 42 states and the District of Columbia.[130] In the 2012–2013 school year, charter schools enrolled more than 3 percent of public school students and made up 6 percent of U.S. public schools.[131]

daaronj/istockphoto.com

Computers can personalize and expand learning opportunities.

Research on charter schools Not all charter schools have the same academic quality. Repeated studies over the past decade show that charter schools have failed to produce consistent, positive academic change. The fact that almost every charter school is unique helps explain this. Variations in state laws, as well as charter school differences in mission, funding, size, grade-level coverage, independence from regulations, teacher contracts, and the availability of comparable student test data—plus research limitations—make conclusive statements about charter schools' impact on student achievement virtually impossible.[132] But these studies clearly reveal that on the whole, charter students are not faring as well as their peers in traditional public schools.

A 2013 landmark study by Stanford University's Center for Research on Education Outcomes (CREDO) compared the reading and math state achievement test scores of students in charter schools in 25 states, the District of Columbia, and New York City—more than 95 percent of the nation's charter school students—to matched peers in regular public schools. They found large variations in charter school performance—25 and 29 percent of charter students outperformed traditional schools in reading and math, respectively, 19 and 31 percent underperformed traditional schools in reading and math, respectively, and 56 and 40 percent showed no significant difference in reading and math achievement.[133] These results point to large differences in charter school quality and the need for increased scrutiny of these public schools, including more aggressive actions to close underperforming sites.

If charter schools are to create better schools for all children—and not to divide limited public resources across parallel systems that perform at similar levels—it is critical to reassert the autonomy-for-accountability tradeoff. And when schools consistently fail, they should be closed.

Did You Get It?

With confidence, we can say what about innovation in education?

a. Virtual education is increasingly understood to be both a failure and a financial fraud.
b. The involvement of for-profit companies forces non-profit institutions such as universities to compete with reduced fees or improved offerings.
c. Offering high school courses over the Internet is a declining trend.
d. The Internet continues to transform teaching and learning.

Take the full quiz on CourseMate.

5-10 Successfully Educating All Students: Where We Stand Today

Today's achievement gaps between U.S. racial, income, and ethnic groups are smaller than they were several decades ago. Although scores for all students are increasing, NAEP outcomes continue to show large differences between the scores earned by African American and Latino students and those earned by white and Asian students.[134] Yet evidence suggests that states with higher academic standards and other reforms enacted over time can reduce achievement gaps between these student groups.[135]

Ultimately at stake is whether all children in our pluralist society will have access to high-quality schooling and achieve the knowledge and skills essential for twenty-first-century competence, social mobility, and a reasonably satisfying adult quality of life. Today's achievement disparities will ultimately lead to socioeconomic differences among tomorrow's families. Such large discrepancies among families are both morally objectionable and politically dangerous for our society's future. Educational change comes slowly. Because education is fundamentally and primarily about a society's values, educational consensus and adjustments are realized even more gradually in a diverse society. Nonetheless, change does occur.

Over the course of American history, this country's educational system has moved from a religious orientation to a largely secular one. In the twentieth and twenty-first centuries, court decisions, legislation, and case law have brought traditionally underserved students into our public schools. Today, we expect all students to master the high-status curriculum, and we are closer to making this goal a reality.

Did You Get It?

The gains American public schools have made in successfully educating all students include all except:

a. Achievement increases for diverse student groups in states with higher academic standards and other reforms enacted over time.

b. More traditionally underserved children currently enrolled and served in our public schools.

c. Reduced achievement gaps between U.S. racial, income, and ethnic groups.

d. Rapid educational consensus and adjustments to school expectations and practices.

Take the full quiz on CourseMate.

SUMMARY

- Societal ignorance and prejudice prevented students of color and students with disabilities from attending or benefiting from public schools until the mid-twentieth century.
- During the late nineteenth and early twentieth centuries, education reformers G. Stanley Hall's child-centered curriculum and John Dewey's balance between subjects and students and emphasis on effective teaching challenged traditional subject-centered schooling views and practices.
- The NEA's Committee of Ten and the Committee of Fifteen report, the 1918 *Cardinal Principles* report, and Frederick Taylor's views on organizational efficiency, influenced the modern public high schools' organization and curriculum.
- Booker T. Washington and W. E. B. DuBois. two charismatic African American leaders, actively advocated for African American education and economic advancement using differing approaches.
- Until *Brown v. Board of Education* in 1954, several legal cases—the *Roberts* case in Massachusetts (1849) that initiated "separate but equal," the *Cummings* case (1899) that showed that "equal protection" and "separate but equal" were virtually meaningless, *Plessy v. Ferguson* (1896) establishing "separate but equal" as a national standard—had prevented African American and white students from attending the same public schools.

- World War I, the Great Depression, vocational education, and technology had major impacts on schools—initiating standardized testing, compulsory attendance, and occupational preparation.
- The Coleman Report of 1966 concluded that family background—not schools—played the greatest role in student achievement. The Coleman Report was initially misunderstood to mean that schools could not make a difference in student achievement. The report shifted policy focus towards student achievement as a measure of school quality.
- National legislation allowed students with disabilities to receive a free and appropriate public education. In 1975, the Education for All Handicapped Children Act assured that all children with disabilities also would be provided with an individualized education program, special education and related services, due process procedures, and the least restrictive learning environment.
- The report *A Nation at Risk* in 1983 challenged U.S. public schools to do better with an emphasis on high standards, testing, and a rigorous curriculum for all students. It dramatically influenced later education reform and continues to shape today's educational climate.
- Legislation, specifically No Child Left Behind (2002) and Race to the Top (2009), aimed to make each state, district, and school accountable for the academic achievement of traditionally underserved minority and economically disadvantaged children, English language learners, and children with disabilities. Legislation also encouraged states to adopt the Common Core Standards by awarding extra points on Race to the Top grant applications that agreed to implement the standards.
- Today, we expect all students to master a rigorous academic curriculum, and achievement gaps are smaller than they were several decades ago. We are making progress but much remains to be done.

Visit the Education CourseMate for this textbook to access the eBook, Did You Get It? quizzes, TeachSource Video Cases, flashcards, and more. Go to CengageBrain.com to log in, register, or purchase access.

Education has personal, social, political, and economic goals.

CHAPTER

6

Competing Goals of Public Education

InTASC Standards Addressed: 1, 2, 3, 4, 5, 6, 7, 8, 9, and 10

LEARNING OBJECTIVES

After you read this chapter, you should be able to:

6-1 Describe the general goals of American education.

6-2 Discuss the wide-ranging nature of American education goals.

6-3 Explain how conservative, liberal, and critical theory education critics present differing views of how to improve schools.

6-4 Explain how education is an investment in human capital.

6-5 Identify the ways that education is still the key to achieving the American Dream.

For more than 300 years, Americans have expected much from our schools. Starting with narrowly academic and religious goals in the seventeenth century, we added civic, vocational, and social goals in the eighteenth and nineteenth centuries. Fully including minority children and children with disabilities in public education and addressing personal or self-realization goals entered in the twentieth century. In reviewing these expectations, John Goodlad, an American education scholar concluded, "These goals now encompass such a wide range of knowledge, skills, and values along with a kaleidoscopic array of scientific, humanistic, and aesthetic sources of human enlightenment."[1] It seems as if public education is trying to do it all.

With so many purposes, it is understandable that we would occasionally disagree about which are more important and how well our schools are accomplishing them. Some critics are very impatient, however. "We can all agree," wrote a contributing editor for *The Weekly Standard*, "that American public schools are a joke."[2]

It is difficult not to feel defensive or outraged when reading such an overstatement. Certainly, schools are not accomplishing everything our society expects

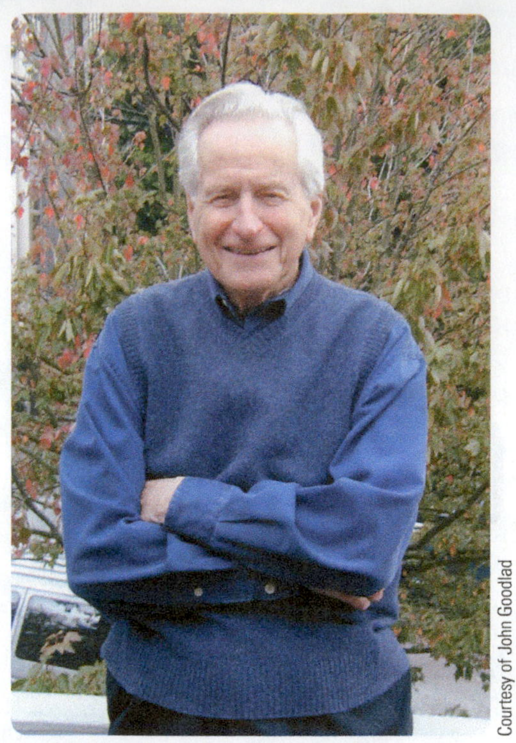
Courtesy of John Goodlad

John Goodlad, education scholar, defined comprehensive American education goals.

them to do. Although most communities remain proud of their local schools, some people consider schools in general as failing to fulfill their mission. Relentless attacks on public schools since at least Sputnik's launch in 1957—along with disillusionment with public institutions in general—have made people question all public institutions.

Imploring us to keep our perspective on public schools' goals, Mike Rose, professor of education at the University of California at Los Angeles, observed, "In the midst of the culture wars that swirl around schools; the fractious, intractable school politics; the conservative assault on public institutions; and the testing, testing, testing—in the midst of all this, it is easy to lose sight of the broader purpose and grand vision of the common public school."[3] It is also easy to lose sight of the value of respectful dialog.

As citizens in a democratic republic, it is our responsibility to continually assess how well our public institutions are performing. We need to repeatedly review their purposes and gauge the extent to which they are fulfilling their promises. At times, we as a society need to revise their goals in response to our changing world. To do this is natural—and does not imply failure. But rhetorical overkill like the *Weekly Standard*'s unequivocal statement is so broad and inflammatory that it makes thoughtful analysis and reflection more difficult. Yet only when we can listen thoughtfully and respectfully to those with whom we disagree can we avoid the false choices and find better, more meaningful solutions for our national community.

If we are to equip all our children with the intellectual, cultural, and interpersonal knowledge and skills that will enable them to become self-directed, employable, and contributing citizens, we will need to find ways to identify and successfully reconcile our competing goals for their education. Only then will our children be able to turn our goals into their personal realities.

6-1 The General Goals of Public Education

Education exists to serve society by socializing each generation in the knowledge and skills required for mature citizenship and economic participation. In a diverse society, finding a common set of values and goals for schools to address presents many challenges.

6-1a Defining a Set of Common Values

American public schools have many responsibilities. Their historical mandate requires that they provide learning experiences that contribute to students' intellectual, academic, vocational, personal, and social growth. Students clearly need the skills and habits that will make them responsible neighbors and productive employees. In fact, society has charged schools with remedying virtually every societal ill while simultaneously providing students with the intellectual and creative capacities they need to lead and defend our nation.

The idea of education to serve the social order is a respected tradition. In Plato's time, the idea of a good society implied a set of educational policies and practices that would support the public's highest ideals. In those days, societies could only exist through the conscious, deliberate socialization process, established on a community-by-community basis.

In the early United States, the idea of common public school became popular. American intellectuals like John Adams and Thomas Jefferson advanced the widespread availability of public schooling as essential to an enlightened citizenry. Democracy could not exist, they avowed, unless future generations had the knowledge, skills, and ethical beliefs needed to support this form of self-government. In this way, mass public schooling became seen as a way to continue our form of nationhood and culture.

This notion extended into the nineteenth century when Horace Mann, as Massachusetts superintendent of schools, used his position to require public school attendance through the elementary grades. Mann envisioned public schools as teaching shared political values with the ultimate aim to maintain public order. Other thinkers agreed with him, framing education's goals even more broadly.

In recent times, defining a shared set of political values has become more difficult. Since the nineteenth century, vigorous community debates over what schools should teach have shaken the schoolhouse. During the late twentieth century, conservative political groups pressured public schools not to teach what they considered to be "left-wing ideas." In contrast, liberal organizations and labor unions pressed the schools to teach their type of political ideology. The range of educational alternatives now available—including private schools, home schooling, virtual schools, charter and parochial schools—means that a community's children do not all attend a common school. Economically, ethnically, and racially segregated neighborhoods also keep children from sharing universal educational experiences.

Nevertheless, if the United States can survive as a democratic republic, we all must live together in an economically viable, law-abiding, patriotic, fair, and civil society. Public schools' purpose, then, is to attempt to create a more democratic, integrated, and socially mobile society in what is arguably a less than a perfect world.

6-1b Defining Schools' Goals

Societies always make ongoing distinctions between what schooling's purposes are and what they ought to be. For example, many believe that schooling should educate citizens to fit into the existing society. Others believe that schools should educate citizens to improve—not reproduce—the society. Different educational visions mean different ideas of what makes a "good society," and varying social visions influence what makes a "good education."

Schools' **intellectual goals** are to teach essential cognitive skills such as reading for comprehension, writing for clarity of expression, and mathematics for numerical reasoning in life and sciences. Schools are charged with transmitting the culture's knowledge and values through reading and discussing the society's language, literature, history, sciences, and arts. Schools also address intellectual goals when they teach students to use higher-order thinking and reasoning by using analysis, synthesis, and evaluation to manipulate and use information creatively to solve problems.

intellectual goals Schools' mission to teach basic cognitive skills such as reading, writing, and mathematics.

political goals Schools' mission to instill allegiance to the existing political order, encourage patriotism and responsible public behaviors.

Similarly, schools' **political goals** are to instill allegiance to the country and to its existing political order. Schools are supposed to encourage patriotism and responsible public behaviors. They are tasked with preparing children to become citizens who will participate in our civil processes by obeying the laws, paying taxes, and voting for persons to represent them in the state and national government. In schools, our young citizens learn about current local, national, and world events and how to appropriately and effectively express their views about important issues of the day. Likewise, schools help assimilate members of different cultural groups into a shared political society with unifying traditions and values.

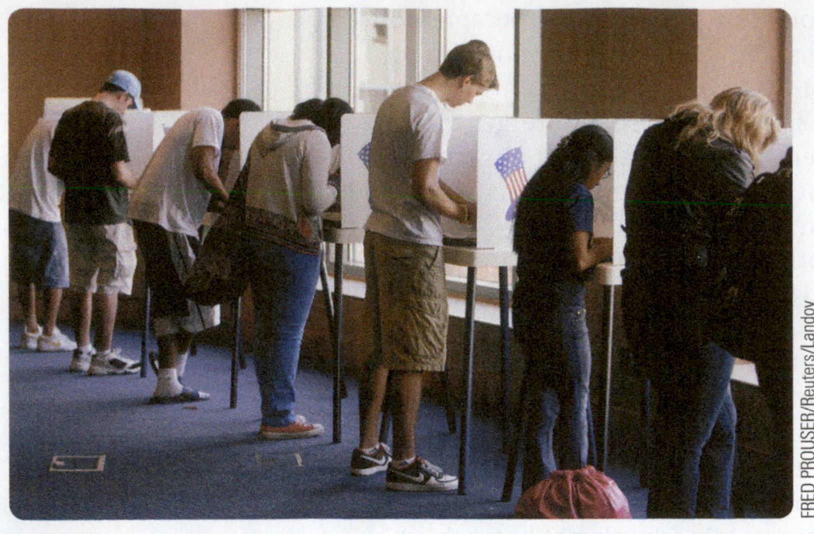
FRED PROUSER/Reuters/Landov

Schools' political goals encourage patriotism and responsible public behavior.

Many believe that schools' **social goals** include helping prevent or solve societal problems. Schools work as one of many institutions—along with the family and religious organizations, among others—to socialize children into society's various roles, behaviors, and values. By bringing the community's children together in a common facility to pursue a common endeavor, schools teach students how to respect and work effectively with people from other backgrounds or traditions. This **socialization process**—developing in its members a shared culture, behaviors, values, and loyalty—is essential to any society's stability.

social goals Schools' mission to help prevent or solve societal problems.

socialization process Developing in a society's members a shared culture, behaviors, values, and loyalty, usually conducted by families and schools.

economic goals Schools' mission to prepare students for their later occupational roles.

Finally, schools' **economic goals** are to prepare students for their later occupational roles and to select, train, and distribute individuals into the society's division of labor. The extent to which schools directly prepare students for their work varies from society to society, but most schools have at least some indirect role in this process.

Ironically, these purposes sometimes produce contradictory impulses. If schools are to increase students' intellectual ability by teaching and encouraging critical thinking, reasoning, and evaluating, they can also create students who thoughtfully challenge—rather than accept—their society's norms and rules.

As Lawrence A. Cremin, an education historian, noted[4]:

> Schooling, like education in general, never liberates without at the same time limiting. It never empowers without at the same time constraining. It never frees without at the same time socializing. The question is not whether one or the other is occurring in isolation but what the balance is, and to what end, and in light of what alternatives.

The natural tension between schooling's role in maintaining the status quo and its potential to bring about change lies at the heart of differing views of education and schooling—and it often creates competing goals. Those who support society tend to stress schools' role in preserving it. Those who believe that society needs improvement stress schools' role in either improving or transforming it. In this chapter, you will read about how different political perspectives on education view its goals and how each contributes a fuller dimension to the others.

Did You Get It?

All schools exist in part to serve social goals. One of the general goals of American education is not to

- **a.** Socialize the citizen to sacrifice on behalf of the state.
- **b.** Teach shared political values.
- **c.** To prevent and solve social problems.
- **d.** Educate productive, creative employees.

Take the full quiz on CourseMate.

6-2 The Wide-Ranging Nature of American Education Goals

Today, American schools' basic governance is decentralized with most power wielded at the state level. As a result, we actually have 50 school systems, one for each state (and one for the District of Columbia). All regulate themselves in slightly different ways. Given this context and America's broad diversity, any effort to advance a single set of educational goals for American schools is likely to promote disagreement and debate.

6-2a National Goals in a Decentralized Education System

Over the years, improved communications and travel have allowed some nationalizing influences to affect schools in similar ways. In addition, federal legislation and designated funding have encouraged certain school reforms. The national popularity of certain exams and textbooks in the school curriculum has also contributed to a degree of consistency among schools.

In our decentralized school governance system, the challenge is to provide a set of national educational goals for schools that gives guidance and direction without giving requirements or prescriptions. The national goals have to be general enough to mean different things to different people. To gain widespread acceptance, these goals must leave room for interpretation and adaptation according to the state and local circumstances. At the same time, they must be clear enough to give a shared sense of national purpose and identity. And, increasingly, the goals must be attuned to the international educational benchmarks that reflect the knowledge and skills our children will need to compete for jobs with well-educated peers around the world.

When we talk about educational purposes, we refer to goals and objectives. All three terms—purposes, goals, and objectives—describe a direction—what we are seeking to accomplish. Many educators use the terms **goals** or **purposes** to refer to broad directions, whereas **objectives** are more specific. Many educators refer to these as the "ends" of education.

goals or purposes Refer to broad directions for what education seeks to accomplish.

objectives Refer to relatively specific outcomes for what education seeks to accomplish.

6-2b Goals for U.S. Education

All education endpoints reflect two major influences: current social forces and prevailing educational philosophies or theories. Social forces and philosophies interact to shape the goals that are adapted at the national or state levels. These goals, in turn, affect the more specific school and classroom goals and objectives. As time passes, changes in society, knowledge, and beliefs about the nature of the world and the nature of learning may produce related changes in educational theories and purposes.

6-2c U.S. Department of Education's *America 2000* Goals

The U.S. Department of Education continues to monitor the nation's progress on a set of national education goals adopted in 1990 that provide benchmarks for academic performance and progress. Originally published in a report, *America 2000: An American Educational Strategy,*[5] these ambitious educational targets continue to define expectations for our national, state, and local school performance because they have yet to be fully met.

The *America 2000* goals are as follows:

1. All children will start school ready to learn with their preparation being ensured by participating in preschool programs.
2. The national high school graduation rate will increase to at least 90 percent.
3. All students will leave grades 4, 8, and 12, having demonstrated competency in English, mathematics, science, foreign languages, civics and government, economics, art, history, and geography.
4. Teachers will have opportunities to acquire the knowledge and skills needed for preparing students for the twenty-first century.
5. U.S. students will be first in the world in mathematics and science achievement.
6. Every American adult will be literate and will possess the knowledge and skills necessary to compete in a global economy.
7. Every school will be free of drugs, violence, and the unauthorized presence of firearms and alcohol.
8. Every school will promote partnerships to increase parental involvement in the social, emotional, and academic growth of children.

To assess how well U.S. schools are meeting these goals, the National Center for Education Statistics (NCES) has developed a set of performance benchmarks. This organization collects data on an ongoing basis to allow states and policy makers to determine how well schools are meeting these goals.

6-2d Comprehensive Education Goals

Whereas *America 2000* goals are mostly academic, more comprehensive educational goals also exist. While studying school goals in 1979, John Goodlad, a noted education professor, researcher, and writer, reviewed lists of desired outcomes published by local school boards across the country. From these, Goodlad identified a cluster of 12 major American schools' goals that reflect a complete, humanistic perspective about what communities wanted their schools to accomplish and gave each a rationale.[6] These American public schools' purposes remain valid today:

1. **Mastery of basic skills or fundamental processes.** In our technological civilization, an individual's ability to participate in society's activities depends on mastering: verbal and mathematical literacy, the ability to communicate clearly and effectively with varied media, and knowledge of subjects that affect one's ability to live with awareness and make informed decisions as citizens in a democratic republic.
2. **Career or vocational education.** An individual's satisfaction in life will be significantly related to satisfaction with her or his job. Intelligent career decisions will require knowledge of personal aptitudes, interests, and ambitions in relation to career possibilities.
3. **Intellectual development.** As civilization has become more complex, people have had to rely more heavily on their cognitive abilities. Full intellectual development of each member of society is necessary.
4. **Enculturation.** Studies that illuminate our relationship with the past yield insights into our society and its values; moreover, these strengthen an individual's sense of belonging, identity, and direction for his or her own life.
5. **Interpersonal relations.** Schools should help every child understand, appreciate, and value persons belonging to social, cultural, and ethnic groups different from his or her own.

6. **Autonomy**. Schools must produce self-directed citizens, or else they have failed both society and the individual. Schools help prepare children for a rapidly changing world by helping them develop the capacity to adapt to new situations and assume responsibility for their own needs.
7. **Citizenship.** To counteract the present human ability to destroy humanity and the environment requires citizen involvement in this country's political and social life. A democracy can survive only through its members' participation.
8. **Creativity and aesthetic perception.** The abilities to create new and meaningful things and appreciate other people's creations are essential both for personal self-realization and for society's benefit.
9. **Self-concept.** An individual's self-concept serves as a reference point and feedback mechanism for personal goals and aspirations. The school environment can help facilitate development of a healthy self-concept.
10. **Emotional and physical well-being.** Emotional stability and physical fitness are necessary conditions for attaining other goals, and they are also worthy ends in themselves.
11. **Moral and ethical character.** Individuals need to develop the judgment that allows them to evaluate behavior as right or wrong. Schools can foster the growth of such judgment as well as a commitment to truth, moral integrity, and moral conduct.
12. **Self-realization.** Efforts to develop a better self contribute to the development of a better society.

What was true in 1979 remains true today: Americans still want their schools to meet comprehensive education goals. Responding to the test-driven accountability ethos, which they saw narrowing educational goals to English and math proficiency, Richard Rothstein, an education policy scholar, and his colleague, Rebecca Jacobsen, attempted to synthesize Americans' goals for public education developed over our 250-year history. They defined eight broad goal areas that appeared prominent in different eras and presented these goals to representative samples of all American adults, including school board members, state legislators, and school superintendents. Respondents assigned a relative importance to each of the goal areas. Their average responses were very similar and appear in Table 6.1. Rothstein and Jacobsen concluded that the yawning gap between the surveyed respondents' broad preferences and the narrow educational standards established through political processes "reflected a widespread policy incoherence." What Americans wanted and what education policy makers wanted did not match. Although today's policy makers appear to emphasize the limited goals of reading and mathematical proficiency as measured by standardized tests, contemporary community leaders still want our schools to accomplish a broad array of goals—including many not easily reduced to a test score.

To maintain school accountability for successfully teaching to these ends, Rothstein and Jacobsen suggest a balanced, valid, but less standardized exam-based accountability system to measure all these areas. In this way, American schools could be faithful to its tradition as well as to contemporary expectations.

Ideally, during the process of developing a school district's or individual school's goals, local citizens, parents, and students are invited to give meaningful input. Working as partners with professional educators who understand child development and the learning process, the community members can provide valuable perspectives on what the local schools should teach.

Whether school goals are formulated at the national, state, school district, or school level, the goals are written generally. That is, they are not directly connected to any particular content or subject matter; instead, they are intended

TABLE 6.1

Selected Americans' Views on Relative Importance of Public School Goals, 2006

Goal Area	Relative Importance of the Goal Area (percentage %)
Basic Academic Skills in Core Subjects Reading, writing, math, knowledge of science and history.	22%
Critical Thinking and Problem Solving Ability to analyze and interpret information, use computers to develop knowledge, apply ideas to new situations.	18%
Social Skills and Work Ethic Good communication skills, personal responsibility, ability to get along well with others, and work with others from different backgrounds.	12%
Citizenship and Community Responsibility Knowledge of how government works and of how to participate in civic activities like voting, volunteering, and becoming active in communities.	11%
Preparation for Skilled Work Vocational, career, and technical education that will qualify youths for skilled employment that does not require a college degree.	10%
Physical Health A foundation for lifelong physical health, including good habits of exercise and nutrition.	9%
Emotional Health Tools to develop self-confidence, respect for others, and the ability to resist peer pressure to engage in irresponsible personal behavior.	9%
The Arts and Literature Capacity to participate in and appreciate the musical, visual, and performing arts. Develop a love of literature.	9%

Source: Adapted from Rothstein, R., and Jacobsen, R. (2006, December). The goals of education. *Phi Delta Kappan, 88*(4), 264–72 (Table, p. 271).

to be long-lasting guides, providing direction for what the school is supposed to accomplish. Such goals are too vague for teachers and students to directly apply in the classroom. For their part, teachers must translate these broad goals into more specific objectives—and consider the best way for students to learn them.

6-2e Personal Goals of Education

Just as Goodlad and Rothstein and Jacobsen provide comprehensive looks at American public schools' goals, Elliot W. Eisner, Stanford University professor of education and art, brings the goals to the individual student level. Although he believes that "schools are part of the furniture of our communities . . . [that we] take as much for granted as the streets upon which we walk,"[7] Eisner

American Education Spotlight

Courtesy of Richard Rothstein

Richard Rothstein

Richard Rothstein

"Making teacher quality the only centerpiece of a reform campaign distracts our attention from other equally and perhaps more important school areas needing improvement . . . Blaming teachers is easy. These other areas are more difficult to improve." *

Richard Rothstein is a research associate of the Economic Policy Institute, an adjunct lecturer at the Harvard Graduate School of Education, a board member of the American Education Research Association, and popular speaker on education policy issues. Formerly the National Education Columnist of *The New York Times* and a visiting professor at the Teachers College, Columbia University, Rothstein is the author of several books, including *Grading Education: Getting Accountability Right* (2008) and *Class and Schools: Using Social, Economic and Educational Reform to Close the Black-White Achievement Gap* (2004). His analysis helps us consider the myriad factors—inside and outside school—that contribute to the achievement gap and suggests ways to reduce them.

Rothstein contends that although the single biggest *in-school* factor in students' success is their teacher's "quality" or effectiveness, good teachers alone cannot fully compensate for the disadvantages many children bring to school. Decades of social science research have demonstrated that differences in the quality of schools can explain about one-third of the variation in student achievement. In addition to teacher quality, in-school factors include inspiring principal leadership, teacher collaboration to raise student achievement, and a well-designed curriculum. But the other two-thirds affecting student achievement is attributable to *non-school* factors. The single most important factor: parents!

Rothstein also believes that:

Poverty negatively affects learning. Closing or substantially narrowing achievement gaps requires combining school improvement with reforms that narrow the vast socioeconomic inequalities in the United States. Outside influences such as social class differences in parenting and available resources, health, nutrition, and attendance contribute to a school's effectiveness.

No Child Left Behind is a failed policy that substituted cynical "gaming" for real education. It claimed to help disadvantaged students achieve proficiency in math and reading but led to an excessive focus on standardized tests, a narrowing of the curriculum, and educators who cynically pretended to meet impossible goals by lowering their standard for "proficient."

Merit pay for teachers corrupts the process and leads to perverse outcomes. Unintended outcomes of merit pay include "teaching to the test," constricting the curriculum (to easily tested "basic" skills in reading and math with less attention to sciences, social studies, the arts, physical education, and less-easily tested "higher-order" skills); does not consider differences in students' varied background characteristics; and uses "untrustworthy statistics" based on unreliable data.

Race to the Top's competitive grants are harmful. During a deep economic recession, a widespread budget crisis, and extensive layoffs of teachers and other school employees, it makes no sense to cut formula-driven federal funds in order to reward states that innovate in ways approved by the Obama administration's policy preferences. "A full employment program for grant-writers is no substitute for stable employment for educators." **

Some critics call Rothstein an apologist for public schools. Others contend that he ignores the fact that hundreds of schools are successfully educating low-income students with clear and replicable practices. Although they may disagree with his conclusions, few dispute that his positions are thoughtfully reasoned and well-supported with data.

Rothstein reflects, "Of course, every teacher should attempt to inspire every [student] with encouragement that greater effort could lead to college and a professional career. But no sane teacher believes that this encouragement will be effective with every single child. When an institution promises such universal success, it undermines its own legitimacy." **

*Rothstein, R. (2010, October 14). How to fix our schools. *Issue Brief #286*. p. 3. Washington, DC: Economic Policy Institute. Retrieved from http://www.epi.org/publications/entry/ib286/.

**Rothstein, R. (2010, March 27). A blueprint that needs more work. *Policy Memorandum #162*. p. 5. Washington, DC: The Economic Policy Institute. Retrieved from http://www.epi.org/page/-/pdf/pm162.pdf?nocdn=1.

Sources: Mishel, L., and Rothstein, R. (2007, October). Schools as scapegoats. *The American Prospect*, 44–47. Retrieved from http://epi.3cdn.net/2210a55cb9b1c98ee5_tpm6b5yvr.pdf; Rothstein, R. (2010, October 14). How to fix our schools. *Issue Brief #286*. Washington, DC: Economic Policy Institute. Retrieved from http://www.epi.org/publications/entry/ib286/; Rothstein, R. (1993, Spring). The myth of public school failure. *The American Prospect*, 20–34; Rothstein, R. (2008, April). Whose problem is poverty? *Educational Leadership*, 65(7), 8–13. Retrieved from http://www.epi.org/publications/entry/ascd_whose_problem_is_poverty/; For URLs for Rothstein articles on education policy, see: http://www.epi.org/authors/bio/rothstein_richard/.

Reflect & Discuss

Schools' goal is to contribute to students' growth in five areas—intellectual, social, political, personal, and economic growth.

A. Working in groups of four students, organize Goodlad's "12 major goals of American schools" into these five categories. Which of the five categories has the most of Goodlad's 12 goals under it? Which has the least?

B. Sort Rothstein and Jacobsen's goals into these five categories. How well do these two surveys, taken 26 years apart, fit together?

C. Have each student in the group give specifics of how his or her personal K-12 educational experiences did or did not contribute to meeting each of these 12 goals. To what extent did your schools do what these goals intended them to do? What might you do now and while in college to increase your growth in domains that you identify as less well developed?

D. Compare your five goal categories with those from the rest of the class. How are they different? How are they alike? Are there better or worse arrangements—or are there several logical ways to organize these goals? Based on which criteria can you make your decision? Discuss how school boards can use these goals to identify key purposes for their own schools.

sees schools' purpose as uncommon: helping students to live personally satisfying and socially productive lives by fully developing their minds.

"Mind is a form of cultural achievement," says Eisner.[8] Humans are *born* with brains, but their minds are *made*. In other words, the cultures into which they are born shape how they think. For children, school is the primary culture for their cognitive development. Therefore, school decisions about its priorities are fundamental decisions about the kinds of minds our children will have the opportunities to develop.

Likewise, schools are cultures for growing minds. Through both cultural transmission and self-actualization,[9] schools provide opportunities that influence the direction this growth takes. Both the curriculum schools teach and the time allotted for different subjects tell children what adults believe are important for them to learn. These factors also influence the kinds of mental skills children have the opportunity to acquire.[10] Reading and math are certainly essential skills, but they are not all an educated person needs to know. Eisner argues that education's aim is not merely to enable our children to do well in school; it is also to enable our children to do well in life.[11] In this view, students' test scores are merely proxies for learning; the scores themselves are not learning.

Developing the mind is related to the modes of thought that teachers enable and encourage students to use. A valuable education uses a curriculum that encompasses various ways of thinking and knowing the world, including exploration of both the arts and the sciences. These thought processes incorporate the rational and the affective, the planned and the serendipitous. In the last analysis, the most important curriculum is the one that will help students compete successfully in the lives they lead outside school, so students can ably and continually adapt to complex and changing circumstances.

To foster this mental development, insightful teachers understand that not all problems have a single right answer, purposeful flexibility is an important learning tool, and students need opportunities for varied types of self-expression.

First, not all problems have one correct answer. Solutions to problems take many forms. Whereas spelling, arithmetic, writing, and reading are taught with deliberately constricting conventions and rules, the arts celebrate imagination, multiple perspectives, and the importance of personal interpretation. Both ways of knowing are important. Students need opportunities to see and explore the world in a variety of formats so they can learn how to think in varied ways.

Next, in a technologically oriented world, people tend to believe that objective rationality is the shortest distance between two points. The scientific method illustrates this view: define, hypothesize, experiment, and evaluate. Although this is a reasonable approach to solving certain problems, it is not the only way to understand experiences. Wise teachers realize that rationality is broader. In the arts (as in scientific research), for instance, goals need to be flexible and surprise can be valuable. Educated individuals are open to unanticipated opportunities that inevitably emerge and that increase insight. The work of art is an act of creation, an unfolding journey. Ending a learning experience too soon—by stopping explorations at the first "right" answer—short-circuits the potential of deeper and more personal understanding.

"While we say that the function of schooling is to prepare students for life, the problems of life tend not to have fixed, single correct answers" like the problems students find in school, Eisner remarks. The problems students find in life are much more like the problems they find in the arts[12]; they are often subtle and occasionally ambiguous. "Life outside school is hardly ever like a multiple-choice test."[13]

Effective teachers create learning experiences for students that increase their opportunities to experience the world fully and meaningfully. They make schools intellectual, rather than merely academic places. They understand that students' minds can be developed, knowledge is greater than what literal language might convey, and intelligence deepens and expresses itself in many forms. For students, education means learning how to use their minds well. This is the best preparation for life.

Eisner concludes, "What's at stake is not only the quality of life our children might enjoy but also the quality of the culture that they will inhabit."[14]

6-2f Social Goals of Education

Schools have long had social goals. In 1900, Edward Alsworth Ross, an American sociologist, referred to education as "an economical system of police."[15] He divided social control into internal and external forms. Traditionally, he asserted, internal forms of social control centered on the family, the church or synagogue, and the community. The family and religious institution inculcated moral values and social responsibility into the child. This process ensured social stability and cohesion. In modern society, however, school has largely replaced the family and church as the community's most important institution for instilling internal values. In this sense, the school exerts external social control. "The ebb of religion is only half a fact," Ross observed. "The other half is the high tide of education. While the priest is leaving the civil service, the schoolmaster is coming in."[16]

Whether the family and religious institutions are collapsing is debatable. Yet our society often views education as assuming the responsibility for teaching moral values, thereby enacting a social role. Historically, public schools have delivered moral and social instruction in a variety of ways. Horace Mann, for example, believed that schools were the key to reforming society; he assumed that properly trained youths would not want to commit criminal acts. As a consequence, compulsory school attendance evolved as a means to reduce juvenile delinquency. Similarly, the need to keep young people off the streets became a justification for starting summer schools in the late nineteenth and early twentieth centuries. More recently, schools have assumed the responsibility for reducing traffic accidents by providing drivers' training programs, improving family life through courses in home economics, ending drug abuse, preventing sexually transmitted diseases, and reducing teen pregnancy through health education.[17]

Reflect & Discuss

Education leads students to more personally satisfying and socially productive lives. Elliot Eisner observes that education's goal should be for young people to do well outside school by developing and expanding their minds in a nourishing school culture.

A. As a class, describe the types of thinking, problem-solving skills, and a deep awareness and appreciation of life experiences that a successful young adult such as you will need to live a personally satisfying and socially productive life in relationships, careers, home, and the world at large.

B. Divide into three groups. The first group will consider the traditional English and math curriculum (subjects typically covered by high-stakes achievement testing). The second group will consider the fine arts (poetry, music, visual arts, and theater). The third group will consider examples that integrate a wider range of subjects (including English, math, sciences, social studies, foreign languages, and physical education) with fine arts. Reflecting on their experiences in high school and college, the members of each group should identify the types of thinking, problem solving, leadership, teamwork, and life appreciation experiences most developed by high school and college students studying the disciplines each group represents.

C. All groups report their findings back to the class.

D. Working as a class, discuss how the benefits of each approach to the curriculum can enhance college students' thinking, problem-solving skills, leadership, teamwork skills, and deep appreciation for life experiences.

E. Discuss as a group how you as future teachers can use this awareness to increase your students' meaningful mind-developing and person-developing learning experiences in your classes.

Frequently, schools are asked to solve social problems by finding solutions that do not challenge economic and political interests. For instance, alcoholism might result from family stresses or other adverse conditions. For schools to solve the problem of alcoholism through health classes assumes that the problem is one of individual training, unrelated to other causes. It is easier for a community to provide and require students to take a health course than to change job conditions, improve urban environments, or send a family into counseling. Schools are less threatening than direct interventions that target businesses, unions, city government, or family privacy.

Schools are often the safest and least controversial way of planning for social improvement. Assigning these responsibilities to schools allows legislators, policy makers, and local government officials to appear to do the right thing without offending any important interests. Yet regardless of schools' good intentions, their social influence has only gone so far toward remedying society's ills.

For instance, our society has used schools to help end poverty. The relationships between schools and poverty are many and complex. Inadequate education is linked to low-income jobs, low-quality housing, poor diet, poor medical care, and high rates of school and work absenteeism. The community finds it difficult and expensive to intervene to break these interactions, even though programs such as Medicare and Medicaid, food stamps, and public housing subsidies try to make a difference. Meanwhile, schools offer Head Start and other compensatory education programs for low-income children who begin school at an economic disadvantage in comparison to children from middle- and high-income families. These programs' success has been either limited or mixed.

In addition, not all societal groups agree on which social values schools should teach. Horace Mann argued that all religious groups could agree on certain moral values, and these shared values would become the backbone of schools' moral teachings. Religious groups disagreed with his supposition, however. The Catholic Church voiced the strongest opposition to this notion and established its own school system. More recently, the 1990s witnessed heated value conflicts about AIDS education between those who believed in a strong moral code to control sexual behavior in opposition to those who believed that prevention through education was a legitimate public health interest. Viewing American education as a cure-all for America's social ills raises questions about whose social and moral values and goals our schools should reflect. It also raises the question of whether using schools for social control is actually a way to avoid more direct and controversial approaches to solving societal problems. These questions remain unanswered.

6-2g Economic Goals of Education

Public schools also have economic goals. Economists note that schools can advance economic growth in two ways. First, they can socialize future workers for the workplace. Through their academic curriculum, attendance requirements, tardiness rules, practice in following directions and completing assigned tasks, and emphasis on obedience to authority, schools provide the preparation and training future workers need. Second, schools can increase national wealth by sorting, selecting, and training students for the labor force. Schools sort students by identifying their individual abilities and interests and determining the best type of education and future employment appropriate for each student.

sorting and selecting The traditional public school role of separating students by abilities and interests into certain curricular programs matched to appropriate future jobs.

Both of these goals have historical support. In the nineteenth century, schools emphasized marching, drills, and orderliness as preparation for factory work. In the twentieth and twenty-first centuries, public schools have served as a "**sorting and selecting** machine" that separates "human capital" (students) by their abilities and interests into certain curricular programs matched to appropriate future jobs. Standardized tests determine students' abilities, aptitudes, and interests, and counselors or other school officials then match these factors to the suitable school programs. When schools act as sorting machines in this way, proponents of this goal suggest the economy will prosper and workers will be happy.

In the twenty-first century, although the "sort and select" process appears much the same as in the previous century, the economic environment into which U.S. students graduate is clearly changing. Chapter 1 discusses how American workers are now competing in a global labor market. Globalization exposes the average U.S. worker to much more competition and job insecurity. As the world becomes more interconnected, jobs become more mobile. U.S. companies seek cheaper labor in foreign countries, even for white-collar professional jobs, and many American workers are forced to take reductions in wages and benefits to compete with foreign workers.

In response to this trend, policy makers and schools have called for world-class standards, teaching skills needed for twentieth-first-century success, and raising the educational level of U.S. workers to the levels achieved in other industrialized countries (usually identified as Canada, Finland, or Singapore). This move is intended to make U.S. workers more competitive in world labor markets. Having U.S. students take international achievement tests and comparing their scores with those of other industrialized nations is one way to monitor our students' performance against their international competitors.

Reflect & Discuss

Society has assigned schools many goals. Consider them and decide what you think.

A. Form five groups—intellectual, social, political, personal, and economic education goals. In these small groups, brainstorm all the school goals or objectives that fit into your group's category.

B. Identify and discuss the following issues:
Which goals had the most impact on you as a K-12 and college student, and how?
Which ones helped you realize and reach your personal goals?
Which goals do you see as possibly contradictory or pulling in different directions?
Which goals do you think are realistic and achievable? Which do you think are beyond the school's means to achieve?
Which goals reinforce the "status quo"?
Which goals are likely to reduce the "achievement gap"?
Which goals have the potential to change the society?
Which goals have the most community support in your hometown? Which goals have the least support in your hometown?

In addition, a learning society and lifelong learning are considered essential parts of global education systems. Both concepts assume a world of constant technological change that will require workers to continually update their skills. This means that schools will be required to teach students how to learn, so that they can keep learning throughout their working lives.

Likewise, American society is much different today than it was 50 years ago, when a one-income household could support the American working- and middle-class family. To maintain our standard of living, members of the American working- and middle-class populace now work 600 hours more in a year than their counterparts in the 13 industrialized nations. The United States is the only industrialized nation whose worker hours have increased since 1980.[18]

These new economic and global demands on education raise unsettling questions about treating students as human capital. Should schools emphasize a broad liberal education, or should they prepare students for specific careers? In a labor market based on educational attainment and marketable skills, will inequality of educational opportunity cause increased stratification between the educational haves and have-nots? Will producing many well-educated graduates lead to **educational inflation**, in which the supply of well-educated individuals increases yet employee wages and advanced degrees' value decline because so many qualified and available persons exist to fill the positions? Should economic opportunities be based on the outcomes on high-stakes tests? These are important questions on which a national consensus is lacking.

educational inflation The concept that, as the supply of well-educated individuals increases, employee wages and advanced degrees' value decline because of their oversupply.

FlipSides

Should American Schools Stress Reading and Math Proficiency or More Comprehensive Educational Goals?

Educators and policy makers often disagree about what measures to use for public school accountability. Should accountability for a twenty-first-century American education focus on reading and math skills, which can be accurately measured, or should it focus on a more comprehensive set of goals, which, although important, cannot all be accurately measured.

To be accountable, American education should focus on reading and math skills, using rigorous content.	To be accountable, American education should focus on developing reading and math skills, using rigorous content plus a more comprehensive set of goals.
■ Reading and math skills are basic academic skills that are essential for success in all other academic subjects.	● Reading and math skills are essential academic skills, but these are not all that an educated person in the twenty-first century needs to know and be able to do.
■ Schools are not equipped to teach our students everything our society has asked schools to teach them.	● Schools have many important cognitive, social, political, economic, and personal goals that are necessary to make our communities and nation stronger, safer, and more just.
■ Public school accountability depends on assessing reading and math skills by using easy-to-administer, efficient, and relatively cost-effective standardized tests.	● Valid measures exist for assessing the performances and products that result from students meeting other important educational goals, but some may not be standardized; may take more time, effort, and cost to assess; or may appear in later behavior (such as voting).
■ Students' test scores are evidence of effective education and accountability.	● Test scores are not learning itself; they are proxies (stand-ins) for learning.
■ Students should learn how to solve problems and provide the right answers.	● In the real world, not all problems have fixed, single correct answers.
■ Schools are academic places. Students should learn the vocabulary and habits of mind related to the subject disciplines they study.	● Schools are intellectual places. Students should learn various ways of thinking so they can live well outside school.
■ Schools should teach students to think objectively and rationally with the subject matter they study and in response to events occurring in their lives and world outside school.	● Schools should also teach students to use their mind flexibly (cognitively and affectively), value and adapt to surprises, and deal with ambiguity to prepare for life in a complex, changing world.

After reading the arguments in favor and against accountability based on a rigorous reading- and math-focused curriculum, which approach do you believe would be best for twenty-first-century American students and public school accountability?

Certainly, students need to learn the intellectual tools and knowledge for making decisions about their lives. What is more, given the wide variations in school quality in the United States (in terms of students' cognitive readiness for academic learning, teacher effectiveness, class size, resources, counseling, and career and college readiness preparation, for instance), if the ability to compete in the labor market depends on the quality of education they receive, then some graduates will be more advantaged than others. Those persons who arrive at school ready to learn and with access to better schools have increased opportunities and access to higher wages and better jobs. These important issues should influence our ongoing discussions about schools' economic purpose.

In the future, schools will continue to serve comprehensive intellectual, political, social, economic, and personal purposes. It remains critical for prospective and present educators, policy makers, and our society as a whole to consider these goals, some of which are contradictory, when deciding how to move forward.

Did You Get It?

American schools' governance is

a. Extremely decentralized, with most power wielded by local school districts.
b. Centralized at the regional level.
c. Highly centralized at the national level.
d. Decentralized, with most power wielded at the state level.

Take the full quiz on CourseMate.

6-3 Conservative, Liberal, and Critical Theory Education Critics: Differing Educational Goals and Views about Improving Schooling

Although public schools intend to transmit our best traditions and values, our culture is not static. Rather, schools reflect changes in their host society—from putting computers into every classroom to having security guards patrol the halls. What is more, the "official knowledge" included in the school curriculum evolves, faces challenges, and changes. Struggles over curriculum, teaching, and policy are actually battles for power over children's thoughts and for the direction of society's future.

For all, knowledge is power. Whoever controls the knowledge—and the policies, textbooks, and lessons that contain it—holds the power. In fact, vigorous community debates over textbook adoptions illustrate cultural politics in action. They are skirmishes in the national conflict for cultural authority. And the winners' views will prevail.

Debates about educational issues often focus on different ideas about what schools' goals—and what our society—should be. From our early days as a young republic through today, many different visions of U.S. education and school's role in society have been advanced. Although the views are complex, it helps to simplify and frame them by using a political typology—specifically, conservative, liberal, and critical theory perspectives. The remainder of this section presents broad and general descriptions of how each viewpoint sees education and its goals.

6-3a The Conservative Perspective

The origins of the conservative perspective lie in the nineteenth-century Darwinist view that individuals and groups must compete in their societal environment to survive. According to this stance, human progress depends on individual initiative and effort. Conservatives also believe the capitalist free market as the economic system most respectful of human needs. They see individuals as rational actors who can make decisions on a cost–benefit scale.[19] Lastly, conservatives believe that individuals are responsible for their own well-being; people create society's problems by making uninformed or selfish choices.

Conservatives believe that schools should provide the educational training necessary to ensure that the most talented and hard-working individuals receive the tools they need to become the most socially and economically productive. Under this approach, schools socialize children into the adult roles needed to maintain society as it is. Students learn the cultural traditions through the curriculum. Schools are essential to both economic growth and social stability. Nevertheless, individuals or groups of students rise or fall based on their own intelligence, effort, and initiative. Achievement requires hard work and sacrifice. Schools give students the opportunity to succeed, but it is the individual's responsibility to do the work to make accomplishment happen.

Generally, conservative critics believe that today's educational problems have occurred for the following reasons:

- Schools have watered down the curriculum and lowered academic standards in response to "liberal and critical theorist" demands in the 1960s and 1970s for greater societal equality and catering to students' calls for more choices about what they studied.
- Multicultural education that responds to the needs of all groups has weakened the traditional curriculum, reducing the school's ability to pass on the American and Western civilization's heritage and the rigorous cognitive skills that go with them.
- Liberal demands for cultural relativism (the belief that every culture's values and beliefs are equally valid) have forced schools to lose their traditional role of teaching absolute ("correct") values and moral standards.
- Schools' acceptance of individuality and freedom has meant the loss of traditional discipline and decline of authority in the classroom and in the school.
- Schools are state-controlled public institutions, immune from laws of a competitive free market, and choked by bureaucracy and inefficiency.

Many of today's religious and social conservatives express strong views about public schools, bringing their beliefs about faith and ethical behavior into the political arena. They criticize public schools for undermining what they see as time-honored values. Further, they believe that society would be better if schools contained more religion (typically Protestantism)—or at least did not advance ideas, values, or practices that undermine it. They believe that schools should return to more traditional religious values and practices as once applied in early American common schools, restoring the connection between church and state.[20]

Indeed, some conservatives no longer want to send their children to American public schools. The publication of a report called *A Nation at Risk*[21] 40 years ago confirmed conservatives' deepest fears about public schools' harmful effects on their children. The report, compiled by a panel appointed by President Ronald Reagan, sharply criticized American education—and gave many a scapegoat on which to pin society's problems. Similarly, the report blamed the "rising tide of mediocrity" in schools for skyrocketing divorce rates, teenage pregnancy, and sexually transmitted diseases.

Finally, conservative educational reformers want to make the following changes to modern-day public schools:

- *Return to the basics*—reading, writing, math, and other traditional subjects.
- *Return to the traditional academic curriculum*, which focuses heavily on Western civilization's history, thought, and literature.
- *Make students and schools accountable* for minimum performance standards at specific grade levels (i.e., fourth, eighth, and 11th grades) enforced through standardized testing and public accountability.
- *Introduce free-market mechanisms* into the education marketplace, including tuition tax credits, vouchers, "opportunity scholarships," and charter schools to support parents who wish to send their children to private schools and public

school choice programs (allowing parents to send their children to the public school of their choice, regardless of where they live).

- *Create more exacting teacher evaluation* practices that rely heavily on their students' achievement results.

Questions of larger social and political movements cannot be divorced from educational philosophy, nor should educational philosophy and reflection on practice simply be reduced to acting according to the day's prevailing political winds. As thoughtful citizens, we need to examine these issues carefully. The competing goals in contemporary U.S. schools actually stem from competing social visions. In a diverse society, this debate is both expected and beneficial.

6-3b The Liberal Perspective

In the twentieth century, liberal perspectives on education arose as an outgrowth of the works of U.S. philosopher and educator John Dewey and the New Deal politics of President Franklin Delano Roosevelt. Although supporting the conservative view of a market capitalist economy, liberals believe that an unregulated free market is open to abuses. It is particularly hurtful to economically and politically disadvantaged groups. Recognizing this potential for harm, society needs government involvement in economic, political, and social arenas to ensure fair treatment of all citizens and to guarantee a healthy economy. Liberals, therefore, balance economic productivity of capitalism on the one hand with individuals' social and economic needs on the other hand. Good governance is not as simple as choosing "individual liberty" over "government control." Rather, liberals seek the best balance of individual freedom with the essential legal protections for individuals, their contracts, and their businesses, which only a government of laws can provide.

By placing a strong emphasis on equity and equality of opportunity, liberals try to minimize the differences in life outcomes between the country's richest and poorest citizens. Unlike conservatives, they believe that although individual effort is very important, it may not be enough. When individual effort falls short, government must sometimes intervene on behalf of those in need. Liberals also believe that groups, as well as individuals, are affected by society. Accordingly, solutions to social problems must address group dynamics rather than individuals alone.

Liberals value schools for their ability to educate and socialize students into the society, as do conservatives. Liberals, however, stress the school's role in creating a more equal playing field for all students to succeed. They recognize America's pluralism and emphasize the schools' role in helping students thrive in a diverse nation. They argue that individual students or groups of students begin school with different life advantages, different types of prior knowledge, and different levels of "academic readiness." Schools must be equitable to all of these children through policies and programs that give disadvantaged students a better chance to make the most of their educational opportunities. According to this perspective, education entails balancing individual and social needs in ways consistent with democracy and meritocracy. School is a means for all students to receive a fair and equal opportunity for upward mobility—economically, politically, socially, and personally.

Liberals believe that today's educational problems exist for the following reasons:

- Schools need to level the playing field experienced by economically disadvantaged or culturally different students because their backgrounds have limited these students' chances for a good life, allowing them to underachieve.

Jani Bryson/iStockphoto.com

Liberals support education policies that connect equity and excellence.

- Schools place too much emphasis on discipline and authority, not allowing students to develop fully as individuals.
- Academic quality and climate disparities between schools serving affluent as compared with low-socioeconomic-status students create unequal achievement and unequal opportunities for advancement.
- The traditional curriculum leaves out the diverse cultures of groups that make up our pluralistic society. Students need to see and feel that they have value before they can learn.

The "achievement gap"—the unequal achievement shown by different student populations—greatly concerns liberals. At present, liberal critics strongly influence educational policy and practice. In particular, they have employed federal approaches to support disadvantaged students. For example, liberal critics voted for categorical funds, such as Title I, aimed at improving education for schools with a high percentage of students living in poverty. Likewise, liberals worked closely with conservatives to write and pass the 2002 federal No Child Left Behind Act (NCLB).[22] NCLB was intended to make sure that all students, including traditionally underperforming students (minority, economically disadvantaged, special education, and English language learners), received the high-quality education that all students need. During this process, conservatives focused on the high accountability requirements and sanctions for public schools not successfully meeting them. For their part, liberals approved making the schools more accountable for ensuring the high achievement of the traditionally underachieving student groups.

Liberal critics want education reforms that include the following measures:

- *Connecting equity with excellence,* making high-quality education a reality for all students. Treating different students the same is inherently unequal, they say.
- *Improving failing schools,* especially urban schools. Programs should include site-based management (decentralized school control), teacher empowerment (teachers have a say in the way schools run), effective schools programs (based on research about what works),[23] and public school choice programs that support public education.
- *Compensating high-quality, highly effective teachers who work in high-challenge urban schools* to create a stable culture of academic achievement.
- *Creating more equal opportunity for disadvantaged students,* such as Head Start,[24] Advancement via Individual Determination (AVID),[25] affirmative action, and compensatory higher education programs.[26]
- *Balancing the curriculum* of Western thought and values along with readings and history of other groups in a culturally diverse setting.
- *Linking high standards with high supports.* Do both: set acceptable and high performance standards and ensure that all students can meet those standards (by providing students with additional academic and social supports rather than lowering expectations).
- *Making teacher evaluation practices more rigorous* and include student achievement data as part of a fair and comprehensive look at a teacher's effectiveness.

Liberals are currently reaching some of their objectives with the practices that support diverse students learning to high levels. These goals, however, are only in the process of being achieved; much remains to be done.

6-3c The Critical Theory Perspective

Critical theory is an educational philosophy that concerns itself with issues of struggle, power, culture, domination, and critical consciousness. Historically, schools transmitted a society's culture—the one usually belonging to society's dominant group. Education extends the dominant group's norms, values, and practices into the future. As a result, the culturally influential and powerful shape our schools and determine our "official knowledge."[27] Critical theorists reject this in-group dominance. Similar to liberals, they believe that students from lower socioeconomic backgrounds begin school with unequal opportunities. Unlike liberals, critical theorists believe that these limitations can be removed only by changing the society's political–economic system. Liberals would adapt school practices to increase disadvantaged students' achievement, but critical theorists would go even further: They would change both schools and the society that make and keep people unequal.

critical theory An educational philosophy that concerns itself with issues of struggle, power, culture, domination, and critical consciousness.

cultural hegemony The idea that one dominant worldview controls all thought in a certain society.

cultural capital The dominant social group's language, values, and meanings that dominate a society.

Critical theorists believe that our public schools practice a **cultural hegemony** (control by one dominant worldview) by imposing the colonial Western European settlers' traditions on today's ethnically and culturally diverse students. What is more, according to critical theorists, the dominant class deliberately controls, shapes, and manipulates the subordinate groups' beliefs to ensure that the dominant group's views become familiar, common sense, accepted, and taken for granted. In these ways, critical theorists argue, schools perpetuate the socioeconomic conditions that keep poor people poor, ignorant, and powerless.

Critical theorists believe that school and society have problems for the following reasons:

- The educational system has failed the poor, minorities, those with disabilities, and women through continuation of classist, racist, able-ist, and sexist policies and practices.
- Schools have stifled analysis, deep understanding, and criticism of American society's problems by implementing a curriculum and teaching practices that promote conformity and docility to the established powers.
- The traditional curriculum ignores cultures, genders, and races that are present in the classroom and that have contributed to society. It disrespects diverse students when it leaves out minority and culturally marginal voices.
- The educational system promotes inequality of both opportunity and results.

As discussed in Chapter 3, critical theory developed in the United States as an offshoot of the progressive education movement.[28] Critical theorists recognize that humans are the architects of their own destinies. They urge individuals to develop a critical consciousness that can create new truths both for themselves and for society. As part of their perspective, they hold dual views of schools.

First, critical theorists believe that schools are a means to reproduce oppressive social patterns. Education favors the dominant culture's **cultural capital**—its language, values, and meanings. As such, schooling confirms, legitimizes, and reproduces the status quo. This influence does not happen through force or coercion, but rather occurs through a process of gaining the students' passive, legitimate consent. In short, through schooling's socialization, all social and economic classes learn to accept the elite social group's beliefs, values, and practices as right and natural.

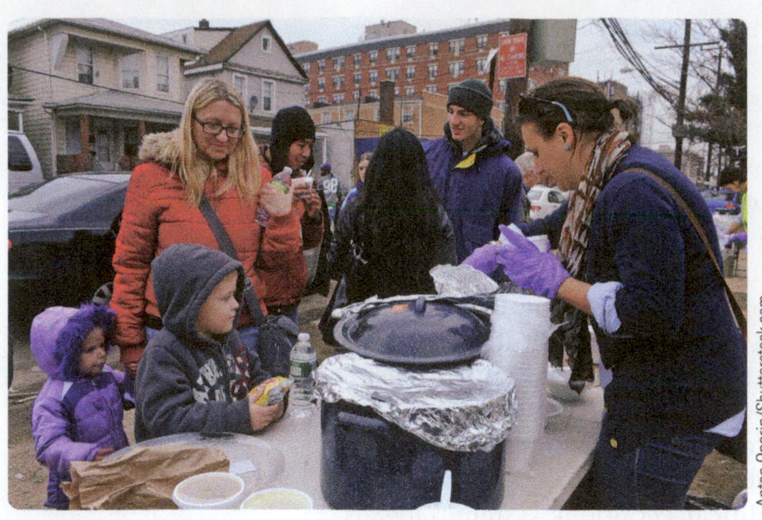

Anton Oparin/Shutterstock.com

Critical theorists believe that teachers and students can improve society.

For example, critical theorists see school practices such as **tracking** (placing certain students into a low-status, low-interest, low-ability, dead-end curriculum) and assigning "special education" labels to students who cannot keep up with the traditional curriculum as grave injustices. In their view, schools are instruments of oppression, designed to keep certain groups down while holding up others. At the same time, differential access to knowledge and occasions to learn, differential opportunities to think and use language effectively, and differential access to high-quality curriculum and teaching are all part of this educational process, say critical theorists, deliberately designed to keep "less desirables" out of the cultural mainstream.

tracking The school's practice of placing certain students into a low-status, low-interest, low-ability dead-end curriculum.

Similarly, critical theorists contend that a U.S. history course that reflects only the white Euro-American experience does not show respect for the contributions of other races and cultures in creating today's America. Such a course delivers an implicit message to students: This is a Caucasian society; if you are not white, you are marginal in tradition and importance, and Western thought and culture are superior to any other traditions and cultures.

Second, and on a more positive note, critical theorists believe that schools contain the seeds of societal transformation. Henry Giroux and Peter McLaren, for example, see schools as able to exert positive power for social justice.[29] Sounding the call for pedagogical empowerment, they see teachers' role as helping students make sense of and engage the world around them and—when necessary—change the world for the better. Through this type of effort, schools can become the agents that raise children to question and challenge their society's limitations and failings. When students learn how to push against the status quo's beliefs and practices, they can improve both their community and the nation. In this way, critical theory raises our consciousness beyond the classroom and schoolyard to broader social and cultural concerns. In other words, people are capable of creating and transforming their own culture because people are both the products and the creators of their social world.[30]

"Schools must be moral, just, and inclusive of those who most need access to the educational process that is imperative to sustaining a democratic community," says educator Louise Anderson Allen.[31] Schools can be a vehicle for social change.

Critical theorists believe that schools can improve by focusing on the following goals:

- *Changing society*. For the most part, critical theorists do not believe that school reform alone can solve educational problems because many problems begin with the larger community. Many critical theorists seek significant social change.
- *Implementing programs that lead to more democratic schools*—with teachers, students, and parents having more input into decision making.
- *Developing curriculum and teaching that involve "critical pedagogy"*—allowing teachers and students to understand the current social and educational problems and see potential (perhaps radical) solutions to these ongoing issues.
- *Developing curriculum and teaching that are multicultural, antiracist, antisexist, and anticlassist*—offering a positive curricular treatment of the varied groups that make up U.S. society and U.S. classrooms.

Reflect & Discuss

Cultural conservatives criticize public schools because they believe educational benefits should rest on individual merit, family, free enterprise, patriotism, and Christianity. They believe that public schools undermine traditional values based on religious morality and individual merit.

Liberal critics believe that public schools must level the playing field between affluent and economically disadvantaged students through policies and programs that give disadvantaged students a better chance to make the most of their educational opportunities. They see education as balancing the individual and social needs in ways consistent with democracy and meritocracy.

Critical theorists would change both schools and the society that made and keep people unequal. They believe that the traditional curriculum aims to make students conforming and docile. Instead, they suggest, schools should be moral, just, and inclusive of those who most need access to the educational process. Schools can be a vehicle for social change when they implement curriculum and teaching that are multicultural, antiracist, antisexist, and respect the diversity of today's students.

Working first in pairs and then discussing as a whole class, consider the information in this text, and answer the following questions:

A. On which issues do you agree with each of the three different perspectives?
B. On which issues do you disagree with each of them?
C. Where do you see each perspective's influence in today's public schools?
D. In what ways do you think public schools would change if schools accepted each approach's ideas regarding curriculum, library resources, need for extra academic support for minority and disadvantaged students, school rules, prayer in schools, achievement testing, and availability of school support personnel (counselors, nurses)?

- *Making teacher evaluation more rigorous* and include both student achievement data and documentation of "social transition" projects in which the students engaged to improve their school or community with evidence of its success.

Critical theory can provide current and future educators with a lens through which to view, test, and challenge their assumptions about diversity and find better answers to inform school practices that can help all students learn to high levels.[32] As critical theorists observe, although schools' curriculum conveys the dominant cultural values through its choice of subjects and topics for study, it also teaches the cognitive and intellectual means to challenge those assumptions and improve our society.

6-3d Learning from the Critics

All critics—conservative, liberal, and critical theorists—offer perspectives on how to improve schools (see the summary in Table 6.2). Each offers a somewhat competing set of goals.

Conservatives remind us that our democratic republic and Western tradition have brought important values to this country, and they deserve a prominent place in the curriculum. The United States is a nation of immigrants and a nation of laws. Coming from different countries and family backgrounds, persons living here need to develop a common commitment—to become one people, one nation, indivisible, with liberty and justice for all. We deeply value our freedoms to think, speak, assemble peacefully, and worship as we choose. We also appreciate the opportunities to advance ourselves through knowledge and hard work. Likewise, conservatives remind us that respect for individual differences includes

TABLE 6.2

Comparing Education Critics' Perspectives

	Conservative	Liberal	Critical Theory
Role of individual and government	Individuals must compete in social environments to survive. Individuals are responsible for their own choices.	Individual effort may not be enough. Government and school must ensure fair treatment of citizens in economic, political, and social arenas.	Need to change schools and society that make and keep students—and people—unequal.
Role of school	Provide opportunities for education to let young people become economically and socially productive. Socialize children into adult roles. Provide opportunities to let individual initiative and effort lead to success (or not).	Provide education and socialization. Schools must create equal and equitable opportunities for all students to succeed in a diverse society by leveling the playing field for economically and culturally disadvantaged students.	Public schools advance the dominant class's interests through injustices. Schools and teachers need to instill in students a critical awareness to help them understand, challenge, and transform their society.
Curriculum	Curriculum should meet high standards and follow the traditional Western European/ American curriculum.	Curriculum should meet high standards, while including diverse voices along with traditional Western European and American history, thought, and values.	Move beyond white European/ American experiences to include diverse cultures, genders, and voices in a high quality curriculum.
Accountability	Make schools and students accountable for meeting high standards of academic performance.	Government and schools have major roles in reducing "achievement gaps" by assisting traditionally underperforming students. Ensure that all students can and do meet high standards.	Teachers should help students develop a critical awareness of society's power and inequalities so they can challenge and transform their society for the better.

accepting students' religious beliefs that can be accommodated within the school. Students, in turn, must recognize that others may also have their own views. In the end, schools must maintain a respectful, appropriate, and safe learning environment. Finding the appropriate balance is not easy, but it is important.

scaffolding The extra time and academic and moral supports necessary to help economically and culturally diverse students learn to the highest levels.

Liberals remind us to have high expectations for all students' achievement. They recognize that not all students start from the same point, through no fault of their own. Schools can provide academic and social **scaffolding**—the extra time and academic and moral supports necessary to help economically and culturally diverse students overcome their experience and education gaps and learn to the highest levels. Liberal critics see equity and excellence as compatible and doable. Closing the achievement gap means schools must do things differently—teaching, staffing, curriculum, assessing. The results will change both the lives of individual students and our society as a whole.

Critical theorists' core ideas have merit when we look at how U.S. schools have traditionally educated poor and minority students. Our success in fully educating disadvantaged and disenfranchised students has important implications for our own democracy's well-being. We are living in a globalized world. Global systems of production, exchange, and technology bring people together economically. Divisive belief systems and social practices—such as nationalism, racism, sexism, and contempt for the disabled—keep people in poverty and outside the mainstream, leaving them without opportunities to advance and improve their lives or their society. Democracy loses—unless people have access to the means and supports to improve their own lives and the lives of their children.

When a society has too many individuals without the means or opportunities to improve their lives, social revolution becomes a possibility. The many disadvantaged become increasingly resentful and angry about their situation. They blame those with the political power and economic means for keeping them down. With little to lose, the disenfranchised citizens may engage in violence against the society. The twentieth-century Communist revolutions in Russia and China as well as twenty-first-century "Arab Spring" revolts in Tunisia, Libya, Egypt, and Syria are cases in point. The bottom line: A democratic republic cannot long thrive—or even exist—without a well-educated, vibrant, widespread middle class, whose members have access to means of improving their own well-being. By taking this view, critical theorists sound much like the U.S. founding fathers.

Clearly, education can improve the quality of life for individuals, communities, and nations alike. Literacy—deep cognitive understanding of how to extract information from the printed page, spoken language, or computer screens—can empower people to take constructive action to improve their lives. Teachers need to understand their students as individuals and design appropriate and challenging learning experiences within safe and inclusive environments. Likewise, the curriculum needs to be critically understood and challenged for its application to real life, used for collaborative problem solving, and assessed in multiple ways to guide and monitor student progress. In addition, when teachers respect and understand their students' unique lives and diverse cultures, they can better connect students' experiences to the curriculum and help them learn the attitudes, knowledge, and skills to transform their lives from poverty to economic self-sufficiency and responsible democratic participation.

Taking the best from these three perspectives, for U.S. schools to achieve their purposes and promises, educators should do the following:

- *Provide high-quality opportunities* for all students to learn a rigorous curriculum.
- *Develop student literacy and critical thinking* to apply to curriculum, life experiences, and the larger society.
- *Create inclusive classrooms* characterized by respect between teacher and students, and among students themselves.
- *Offer challenging and relevant learning activities* (that make sense and have meaning to students), and foster interpersonal skills.
- *"De-track" students* from low-interest, low-challenge classes and provide them with opportunities (and support) to learn the important, high-status curriculum from effective teachers.
- *Increase educational scaffolding* for those students who start from further back or learn differently or more slowly so they can learn to high levels.

TeachSource Video 6.1

Teacher Accountability: A Student Teacher's Perspective

The teacher accountability movement can benefit both teachers and students. Viewing accountability in a positive way can help teachers find necessary resources, become reflective practitioners, and strengthen their teaching practices in ways that makes both teacher and students more successful. Watch the video clips, study the artifacts in the case, and reflect on the following questions:

1. How can teachers view teacher accountability in ways that prevent them from being discouraged about their effectiveness as teachers?
2. How does being a reflective teacher contribute to improved practice?
3. How can teachers use accountability data as an opportunity to improve their classroom practices?
4. What does "scaffolding learning for students" mean and how can teachers use this as a means to improve their accountability for student learning?

Watch on CourseMate.

- *Teach for learning,* using the insights about how students actually learn and providing the activities and quality feedback to help all students master and use what they are learning.
- *Teach for "minds on"*—help students learn how to engage in critical thinking, collaborative problem solving, applying knowledge to real-world events, analyzing, synthesizing, evaluating, and creating in meaningful ways with what they learn.
- *Ask questions about current events* and to what extent they represent—or deny—the democratic ideals on which our country is founded.
- *Educate all our students* to have the knowledge and skills they need to lead more productive, creative, and satisfying lives, not just display compliance inside the classroom or work setting.
- *Continue professional learning* and use evidence to continually evaluate and refine teaching practice to meet each learner's needs.
- *Seek appropriate leadership roles and opportunities* to advance student learning, collaborate with colleagues, learners' families, and community members to ensure learner growth and advance the profession.

No society can sustain a large gap between the poor and the rich. If we ignore the fact that our economically disadvantaged, minority students, and students with disabilities are not graduating from high school at high rates and are not performing well on national and international assessments, we put our entire society and way of life at risk. Here is where education can be the agent for positive social change.

Educational critics ask, "What type of society do we want?" and "What is education's role in developing a democratic citizenry, an economically and socially mobile society, and an economically vibrant country?" We can answer these questions more thoughtfully when we consider our critics' ideas.

Conflict—that is, courteous discussion of different viewpoints to reach consensus for the common good—is essential to living in a democratic society. We should neither fear nor blindly defend against our critics. We want to teach our students to think critically, listen carefully and respectfully, and act responsibly. Our society is not perfect, and we can help students develop the cognitive tools and interpersonal behaviors to make both their lives and our communities better. As educators and citizens, we can do no less. Public schools gain strong community support when they present their "official" curriculum within the larger context of "democratic education for a more democratic society" rather than as a means to advance the agenda of certain special-interest groups.

Did You Get It?

Which of the following statements about educational critics is true?

a. Defining a shared set of political ideas is a popular and constructive community activity.

b. Because conservatives believe the capitalist free market is the economic system most respectful of human needs, they believe that schools should provide the education needed to create rational actors who can make responsible decisions.

c. Because Liberals believe the unregulated free market best matches eager employers and willing employees, they stress the school's role in creating equal opportunities for all students to succeed in society.

d. Critical theorists are deeply wary of the unintended consequences of removing the dominant group's norms, values, and practices from education.

Take the full quiz on CourseMate.

6-4 Realizing Education's Goals: Investment in Human Capital

Although U.S. education has many worthy goals, some want to improve American society by changing our schools. No doubt any institution can improve. Nevertheless, implicit in conservative, liberal, and critical theory views is the belief that education as an investment in human capital is making our lives more satisfying, our communities better places to live, and our national well-being stronger.

6-4a Investing in Human Capital

Education as an investment in human capital is the idea that educating everyone benefits the community. It is a relatively new concept. In earlier times, governments provided extended formal schooling to educate the social and financial elite. Laborers, members of the working classes, and the poor remained largely undereducated.

Adam Smith's *The Wealth of Nations* (1776) formally introduced the notion of human capital.[33] In this seminal work, Smith discussed society members' learned abilities (education) as part of a society's resources. He viewed investment in human capital as providing workers with vocational training related to production. His original concept, which was quite revolutionary at the time, provided an early first step toward the larger view of educated workers contributing to the economy and to society at large.

Two hundred years later (in the 1960s), Theodore W. Schultz's work on investment in human capital expressed the idea that laborers' primarily intellectual attributes have value.[34] Schultz, an agricultural economist, often visited farms and spoke with farmers. After World War II, while interviewing an old, apparently poverty-stricken farm couple, he noticed their contentment. When he asked them why they were so satisfied with their lives—even though they were poor—they answered that they were not poor. They felt rich because they had used their farm to send four children to college and believed that education would make these children productive, successful, and happy. This perspective quickly led Schultz to the concept of human capital as capital produced by investing in knowledge.[35]

People feel rich when they can give their children a college education.

© AgStock Images, Inc./Alamy

To meet its goals, education requires a significant financial and cultural investment. Schultz suggested that investing in people's minds was economically valuable for the larger community. His theory of investing in human capital won the 1979 Nobel Prize for Economic Science. Schultz's work became the basis for considering education as an excellent investment—a significant contributor to a society's economic development.

An educated citizenry makes many real, positive, and measurable impacts on

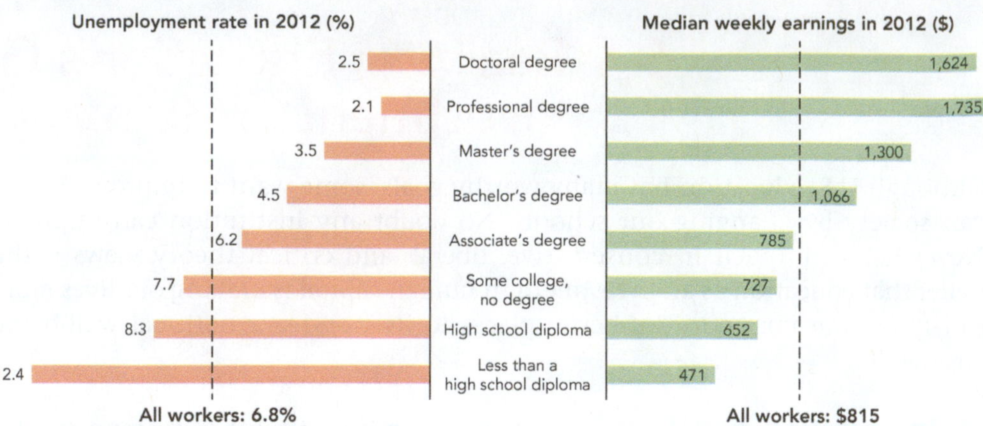

FIGURE 6.1 Education Level with Median Weekly Earnings and Unemployment Rate, 2012

Source: Bureau of Labor Statistics. (2013, January 28). *Education pays. Employment projections. Current population survey*. Washington, DC: Author. Retrieved from http://www.bls.gov/emp/ep_chart_001.htm.

Note: Data are 2012 annual averages for persons age 25 and over. Earnings are for full-time wage and salary workers.

society. More than any other social investment, education is a community's investment in its own best interests. It raises the standard of living by increasing employability and spendable income while reducing a community's social services costs. In addition, a good public education system is a major drawing card for local business development and expansion. Managers realize that better-educated workers make better employees. In a dynamic synergy, education enhances the quality of life not just for the educated individuals themselves, but for the entire community as well. More immediately, education directly affects the personal living standard by influencing how much people earn. Figure 6.1 shows the increased median weekly earnings in 2012 along with the unemployment rate for each education level. As the figure shows, individuals with bachelor's degrees earned almost twice as much as those with only high school diplomas. Typically, the more education a person has, the higher his or her income. And the higher the level of education attained, the lower the likelihood of unemployment.

Every ethnic group gains economically from increased education. Figure 6.2 shows that although different ethnic and racial groups in the United States may earn different amounts for the same level of education,[36] each group is making gains, and all members of each ethnic group earn more than their ethnic peers who have attained lower education levels.

Clearly, education is a major contributor to the U.S. economy's financial health. As a rule, citizens with higher levels of educational achievement earn more money, return more tax dollars to support government services, add more to the general consumer economy to enhance their lifestyles, and draw fewer resources from society than do those with less education.[37] Education is a community's investment in its people that allows the society's—and the individuals'—intellectual, political, social, economic and personal needs to be addressed.

Did You Get It?

What do we mean when we say that education is an investment in human capital?

a. Educated employees are more productive employees.
b. Educating everyone benefits the community (it is a relatively new concept).
c. Education raises the standard of living by increasing employability and spendable income.
d. Educated people pay more taxes.

Take the full quiz on CourseMate.

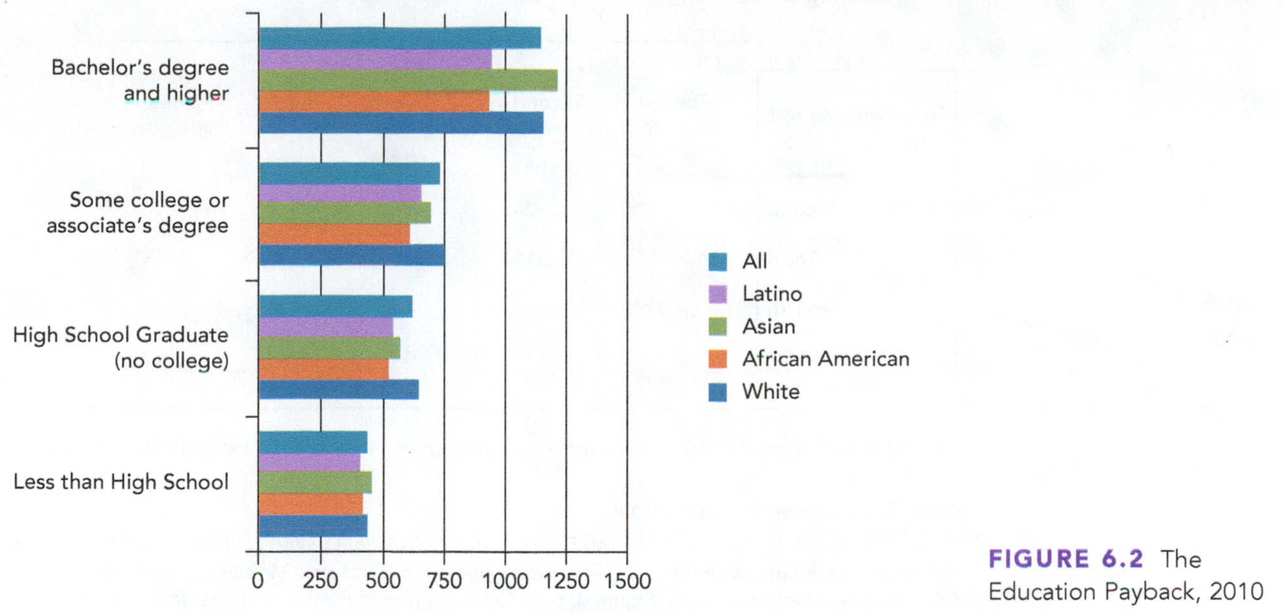

FIGURE 6.2 The Education Payback, 2010

Source: Bureau of Labor Statistics. (2011). *Median usual weekly earnings of full-time wage and salary workers 25 years and over by sex, race, ethnicity, and educational attainment, annual averages, 2000-2010 in current dollars.* (Data taken from the following tables: Total, both sexes; White, both sexes; Black or African American, both sexes; Asian, both sexes; Hispanic or Latino, both sexes.) *Current population survey*. Washington, DC: Author. (Data compiled by Mary Bowler, BLC, in personal correspondence with authors. Graphed by authors.)

6-5 Is Education Still the Key to the American Dream?

One of our nation's most enduring myths sees the United States as the land of opportunity. For hundreds of years and to this day, immigrants have come here from around the world to build better lives for themselves and for their families. To these newcomers, the streets of the United States are figuratively "paved with gold." Within one or two generations, immigrants' children typically become part of the American mainstream.

6-5a America as a Meritocracy

In this version of the American Dream, a person's economic or social status does not depend on his or her parents' wealth or social status, but rather on the individual's own efforts. In other words, America is a meritocracy. With direction and hard work, everyone has an equal chance at success, regardless of his or her family or circumstances. With an expanding economy and political freedom, those individuals (and their children) with desirable talents and a strong work ethic have the opportunity to join the middle class. The Brookings Institution, a public policy, Washington-based think-tank, reports that it takes about five generations in the United States for a person's family background influences to disappear.[38] To a large extent—as the human capital data suggest—this is still true. A growing body of research, however, questions whether this ideal of social mobility and economic opportunity is still a reality for many of our most economically disadvantaged students.

Moving On Up?

Origin Group: Those who started in the... (Percent) ...Ended Up in the	Poorest	Second	Third	Fourth	Richest
Poorest	43*	25	14	9	8
Second	27	**24**	20	0	10
Third	17	18	**23**	23	19
Fourth	9	20	24	**24**	23
Richest	4	14	19	24	40

FIGURE 6.3
Intergenerational Wealth, 2012

**90 percent of poorest children who earn a college degree move up from the bottom of the income ladder.*

Note: Totals exceed 100 due to rounding.

Source: Uhrain, S. K., Currier, E., Elliott, D., Wechsler, L., Wilson, D., and Colbert, D. (2012), Pursuing the American dream, economic mobility across generation. Economic Mobility Project, Washington, DC: The Pew Charitable Trusts. Figure 3, p. 6. Numbers reformatted by authors. Retrieved from http://www.pewtrusts.org/uploadedFiles/wwwpewtrustsorg/Reports/Economic_Mobility/Pursuing_American_Dream.pdf. Reprinted by permission.

Slowing social and economic mobility Over the past 20 years, several studies have concluded that it may be more difficult for children to use education as a means to rise out of poverty than it used to be. Newer international investigations suggest that U.S. children have a lower probability of moving up the wealth ladder than children born in other industrialized nations.[39] Figure 6.3 illustrates this situation by depicting mobility experiences of Americans at different points on the economic landscape.

Intergenerational wealth can be measured by examining the place on the economic ladder where a child is raised and then determining the step (quintile) that the child reaches as an adult. Figure 6.3, reflecting data since the Great Recession, shows that someone born into the bottom 20 percent has a 25 percent chance of moving up to the next higher (2nd quintile), a 14 percent chance of moving to the next higher step (3rd quintile), and an 8 percent chance of moving to the top of the economic ladder (5th quintile). Looking at the extreme ends, Americans raised at the top (40 percent) and bottom (43 percent) of the income ladder are likely to remain there as adults. As a result, over generations, people move up and down the social–economic ladder, but they tend not to travel far from where they began.

Even so, many individuals from middle-of-the-pack economic groups do move up to higher income and social levels. Eighty-four percent of Americans have a higher family income (adjusted for inflation and family size)—and 50 percent have greater wealth—than their parents did at the same age. Clearly, education increases social and economic mobility. Earning a college degree makes someone three times more likely to rise from the income ladder's bottom to its top and less likely to fall down the income ladder.[40] In an information- and intelligence-based economy, in a globalized world, social and economic mobility require a strong education to make advancement more likely.

In his book *Class Counts,*[41] Allan Ornstein, a St. John's University professor and education writer, observes that public education is no longer the "great equalizer" of social and economic mobility. Although many people in America continue to believe in the possibility of social mobility—the idea that one generation or individual can and should rise above the previous generation's or family's attainment level—facts show that such movement is becoming increasingly difficult. Instead, mobility may depend more on one's social class than on one's education. Ornstein asks, if we reduce mobility based on merit, do we also reduce public schools' role as a means for talented but less affluent students to rise economically and socially? If the middle-class families cannot use public schools to advance their children's educational, social, economic, and political opportunities, what hope is there for less affluent students? And what does this trend mean for our larger society and our democracy?

Others offer modestly encouraging news about schools and economic mobility. In *Opportunity in America: The Role of Education*, the Brookings Institution notes that opportunities to move forward—or fall behind—remained high through the nineteenth and twentieth centuries but weakened in the 1980s.[42] More recently, in *Pursuing the American Dream: Economic Mobility Across Generations* (2012), the Pew Charitable Trusts finds that 84 percent of Americans exceed their parents' family income, and that a four-year college degree makes a person more than three times more likely to advance from the bottom to the top of the family income ladder. In comparison, more than one-third of children raised in the middle of the family income ladder who do not complete a four-year college degree tend to fall to lower income levels.[43]

Lastly, a 2008 Brookings Institution publication observed that lower college-going rates among low-income Latino and African American children than among whites and Asians contribute to their lower levels of social and economic mobility. A variety of reasons accounts for this discrepancy.[44] If a college degree is increasingly the ticket to improving or keeping one's relative economic position, this unequal access to higher education means fewer minorities will enter the middle class, which in turn limits their economic and social mobility.[45] The report concludes that "although education can and sometimes does boost the achievement and later the income of children from relatively poor families, the average effect of education at all levels is to reinforce the differences associated with the family background that children and adolescents bring with them to the classroom."[46]

Education's potential to increase social mobility is an important topic because statistics show that the income gap between America's poorest and richest has widened since the 1980s. In 2010, an international economic index identified the United States as having the highest level of income inequality since the Census Bureau began tracking household income in 1967—the largest disparity among Western industrialized nations. In addition, the 2010 census finds that the top-earning 20 percent of Americans (earning more than $100,000 annually) received 49.4 percent of all income generated in the United States, compared with the 3.4 percent earned by those below the poverty lines. That ratio has almost doubled since 1968—from 7.69:1 in 1968 to 13.6:1 in 2008 to 14.5:1 in 2010. And the percent of Americans living below the poverty line is rising.[47] Greater inequality means it takes longer for income differences to disappear in later generations, a situation that jeopardizes the health of our entire society. "The United States could be in danger of creating a poverty trap at the bottom and an enclave of wealth at the top," observes Isabel Sawhill, a senior fellow at the Brookings Institution.[48]

Slowing social and economic mobility has many causes. As we will discuss in Chapter 7, social class, economic, and parenting differences impact children's preschool learning experiences and readiness for academic achievement in school. These differences, apparent when children first begin school, continue to compound throughout the grades to the disadvantage of poor and working-class children. Changing market conditions also affect the discussion. The economy is no longer expanding at the post–World War II—or even at 1990s—rate and college graduates' salaries remained high because they were in short supply. In 1952, 7.9 percent of the workforce had college degrees with 2.33 college-level jobs available per college graduate.[49] In 2002, college graduates represented 25.9 percent of the workforce.[50] Today, professional and service jobs are commonplace and often outsourced. Considering inflation, the typical college graduate household income was actually lower in 2005 than in 2000.[51] The Great Recession of 2007–2009 and the slow economic recovery that followed severed millions of employees from their paychecks for extended periods of unemployment. Many middle-class families that had once maintained their quality of life only by having both husband and wife working full-time jobs now struggled to get by on only one—or perhaps no—income.

Adding to the dilemma of slowed social and economic mobility, a 2007 Educational Testing Service report concludes that the Americans' next generation, on average, will have lower literacy and math skills and will experience greater income inequality than current working-age populations. In a labor market that increasingly rewards education and skills, this could mean tens of millions of Americans who will be unable to qualify for higher-paying jobs.[52]

How are we to recover the possibilities of social and economic mobility to ensure that the American Dream remains a realistic hope for all comers? If the United States is to create well-paying jobs in this country by producing the world's high-value-added goods—skills, products, and services that cannot be outsourced—the American middle class and those beneath it will need "upskilling" through front-end investments in education, along with wise trade policies. Gordon Brown, former British prime minister, observes that today's booming Chinese market for Apple's iPad illustrates how America can exploit worldwide demand for its brands. Each iPad sale brings $4 profit to Asian manufacturers with $80 going to its American and British designers.[53]

From an economic viewpoint, the question is not only whether people will find jobs, but also whether they will be able to find jobs with long-term opportunities that will allow them to productively use their knowledge and skills and increase their economic and social mobility. Without significant increases in students' knowledge and skill levels when they are ready to enter the job market, and without the appropriate jobs to enter, they will not be able to improve their lifestyles. Although four-year college degrees may not be the right path for each student in the twenty-first century, each student will need mastery of complex knowledge and skills, critical thinking, and the abilities to communicate well and work effectively in teams. A rigorous high school education and perhaps a few years of formal schooling beyond that will be essential, depending on the career path chosen. In short, a quality education for each student remains a must-have if social and economic mobility are to continue.

School quality and social mobility The processes required to create opportunities for social and economic mobility are highly complex. Indeed, it will take a whole series of interventions—involving schools, families, and society—to make a difference if all America's children are to live out the full promises that American education says are its goals.

In spite of some discouraging indicators, most Americans remain optimistic about their chances for social mobility: A 2011 Pew Economic Mobility Project poll finds that 68 percent of Americans say they have achieved or will achieve the American Dream.[54] And more than ever, a strong education—a rigorous and relevant curriculum taught by highly effective teachers—remains a necessary key.

Did You Get It?

In what way is education still the key to the American Dream?

a. It isn't: class now matters more.

b. It is: a public school education still allows most poor people to get good jobs and get ahead, giving their children a better start in life.

c. It isn't: public schools no longer prepare one for any but the most menial jobs.

d. It is, if you know the right people.

Take the full quiz on CourseMate.

SUMMARY

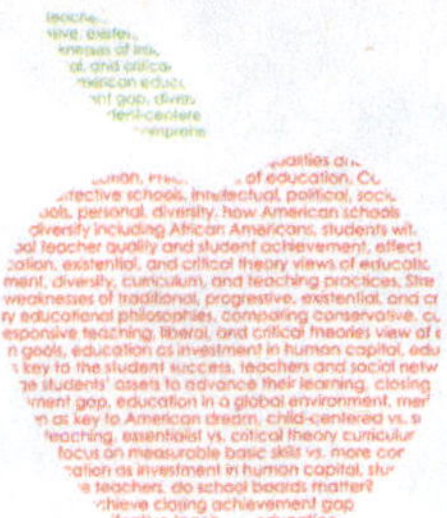

- In a democratic republic, the educational ideal is to provide a meritocracy in which individuals have equal chances to develop their abilities and advance in the society through their own talents and efforts.
- The general goals of American schools comprise intellectual, political, social, economic, and personal outcomes to help individuals advance their lives in a free market democratic republic.
- American education has wide-ranging goals that include mastery of basic skills and fundamental knowledge; intellectual development for critical thinking and problem solving; enculturation, interpersonal relations; career or vocational education; autonomy; citizenship; creativity and aesthetic pereption; emotional and physical well-belng; moral and ethical character; and self-concept and self-realization.
- Goals for American public schools has changed little over the past 250 years. Although today's policy makers appear to value reading and mathematics proficiency as measured by standardized test scores, today's communities want our public schools to accomplish a broad array of intellectual, political, social, economic, and personal goals.
- Reconciling competing goals for education is difficult because the natural tension between schooling's role in maintaining the status quo and its potential to bring about change lies at the heart of differing views of education and schooling.
- All education critics—conservative, liberal, and critical theorists—offer us differing views on how we can improve schools. Although we need not agree with everything they say, each perspective has its merits.
- Education is an investment in human capital. It increases employability and spendable income for individuals and groups, raises the standard of living, and strengthens the overall economy—at the same time, reduces social costs. It also makes the attainment of intellectual, political, social, economic, and personal goals possible.
- Education is still the key to achieving the American Dream. Without the complex knowledge and skills gained through a rigorous academic education, young people will lack the capacities for attending college or gaining employment in well-paying careers that advance them economically and socially.

Visit the Education CourseMate for this textbook to access the eBook, Did You Get It? quizzes, TeachSource Video Cases, flashcards, and more. Go to CengageBrain.com to log in, register, or purchase access.

Schools typically reinforce—rather than overcome—our communities' social, economic, racial/ethnic divides.

CHAPTER 7

Cultural, Social, and Educational Causes of the Achievement Gap and How to Fix It

InTASC Standards Addressed: 1, 2, 3, 5, 7, 9, and 10

LEARNING OBJECTIVES

After you read this chapter, you should be able to:

7-1 Describe the implications of the United States' increasing diversity for everyone's quality of life.

7-2 Discuss the historical perspectives on race, ethnicity, social class, and U.S. education.

7-3 Explain how socioeconomic status influences U.S. students' skills, outlooks, and opportunities.

7-4 Summarize the research findings on the relationships among education, social class, and the achievement gap.

7-5 Discuss how school segregation harms students' academic achievement.

7-6 Identify and discuss the school practices that contribute to the achievement gap.

7-7 Describe the school factors that reduce the achievement gap.

As we read in Chapters 4 and 5, American public schools were established in part to become the great social equalizers, placing any student on the path to social mobility and economic survival. If we look closely, however, we find that schools typically reinforce—rather than overcome—our communities' social, economic, racial, and ethnic divides.

Although school doors open to all children, schools have never served all children or their families fairly or well. Both social class—as defined by parents' income, education, and occupation—and school practices influence student learning and contribute to the achievement gap. Differences in family resources, communication styles, and discipline practices distinguish the average families from different social classes. These disparities have major implications for students' school achievement. In addition, we structure our schools to accomplish goals we set for them: to educate, acculturate, and prepare young people for viability in the larger society. At the same time, public school educators' naiveté about unfair school practices, societal barriers, and cultural values that schools use to realize these ends allow schools to limit certain students' access to the high-quality education they need and deserve. Frequently, educators do not see the schools' inequities because these practices are so familiar and well rationalized that they seem neutral, normal, and appropriate rather than unfair.

This chapter looks at the various ways in which both society and schools may prevent minority and low-income students from getting the education they need and that contribute to the achievement gap. It also examines the practices educators can adopt to better support learning and higher achievement for all students.

7-1 Increasing U.S. Diversity and Our Future Quality of Life

The United States is currently undergoing one of the most profound demographic transformations in our nation's history. The country's increasing racial and ethnic diversity has serious consequences for our sense of national unity, democracy, and future economic prosperity. Our ability as a nation to make this transition successfully depends in large measure on the strength of our public education system.

7-1a Changing American Demographics

The U.S. Census confirms our increasing diversity. The U.S. Census Bureau predicts that Latinos, African Americans, Asian Americans, Native Americans, Native Hawaiians, and Pacific Islanders will collectively become the majority population in the United States by 2042. The latest projections suggest that by 2050, minorities will account for 54 percent of the U.S. population, with non-Latino whites representing the remaining 46 percent, down from their 2010, 64.7 percent share.[1] (See Figure 7.1.)

In addition, research finds that students from historically disadvantaged minority groups have only a 50 percent probability of finishing high school with a diploma. Nearly half the nation's African American and Latino students attend high schools with high poverty and low graduation rates.[2]

7-1b Implications of Changing Worker Demographics

Not successfully educating large numbers of minority students has major implications for the American workforce. The National Center for Public Policy and Higher Education

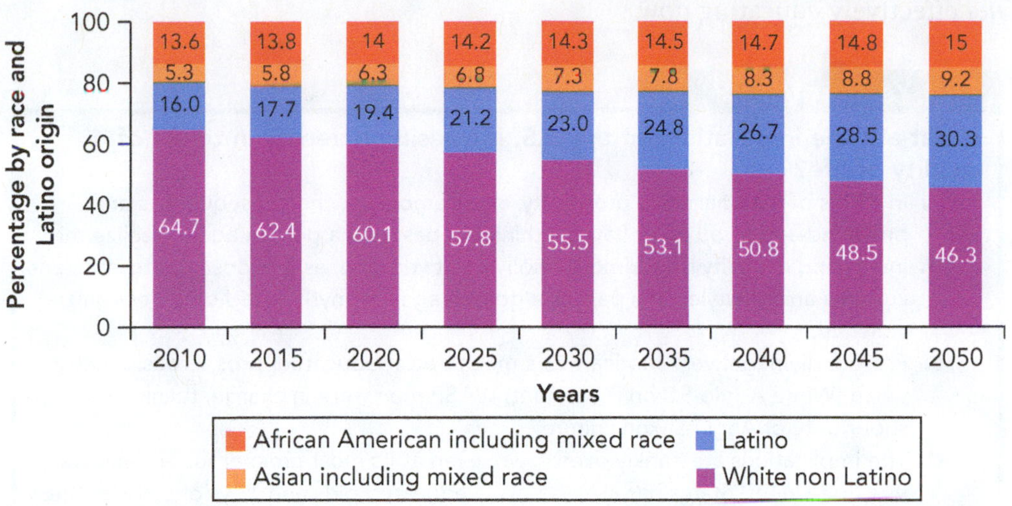

FIGURE 7.1 Projected U.S. Population Shares for 2050

Source: Minorities set to be US majority: U.S. population projections to 2050. (2008, August 14). Washington, DC: U.S. Census Bureau. Retrieved from http://news.bbc.co.uk/2/hi/americas/7559996.stm.

predicts that by 2020, the white working-age population will have declined to 63 percent of the total U.S. population (down from 82 percent in 1980). Because large numbers of younger workers will be members of ethnic minorities while larger numbers of white workers are retiring, the workforce will shift from a majority of white workers to include more people of color.[3]

Unless this upcoming workforce has the high-quality education and skills to provide national, statewide, and local leadership and to earn strong and consistent wages, our whole society will suffer. This workforce will shape our society through its political, social, economic, and artistic influences. It will support our economy through consumer purchases and taxes as their wages contribute, through Social Security payments, to supporting retirees and disabled citizens. If tomorrow's workers have lower capacities for offering societal vision and leadership, and lesser personal incomes than do present and retiring workers, our body politic and social networks may not be able to meet their obligations.

Unless we do something to close the education gap, the most highly educated generation in U.S. history could be replaced by a generation with far lower education levels (as measured by high school and college completion rates).[4] Many people's well-being and lifestyles will be reduced as a result.

7-1c A Complex Reality

According to Richard Rothstein, research associate with the Economic Policy Institute (profiled in Chapter 6), "Policy makers almost universally conclude that these existing and persistent achievement gaps must be the result of wrongly designed school policies—expectations that are too low, teachers who are insufficiently qualified, curricula that are badly designed, classes that are too large, school climates that are too undisciplined, leadership that is too unfocused, or a combination of these factors."[5] In short, Americans have decided that the achievement gap is the result of "failing schools."

The reality, however, is much more complex. Although certain school perspectives and practices do limit educational opportunities for poor and minority students in the United States, the larger social class-stratified society, a history of inequality, and even today's courts perpetuate inequities. Nonetheless, each student's personal future, as well as our nation's governance, economy, and security, will increasingly depend on these same minority children whom we are *not* effectively educating now.[6]

Did You Get It?

What are the implications of the U.S. increasing diversity in terms of quality of life?

- **a.** In terms of national unity, prosperity, and democracy, the consequences are profound—and you don't have to think the past was a golden age to realize this.
- **b.** Increasing diversity is an almost wholly positive trend, as it exposes us to different cultures and lifestyles: the past as a golden age is a myth based on unrecognized violence.
- **c.** Profoundly negative: America was a much better-educated, prosperous country when (White Anglo-Saxon Protestant) WASP men were in charge, thanks to the superiority of Anglo-Saxon culture.
- **d.** The implications are frankly overblown: even at its most prosperous and innovative, the United States has always poorly educated girls and boys of color or the "wrong" socioeconomic bracket.

Take the full quiz on CourseMate.

7-2 Historical Perspective on Race, Ethnicity, and Class in U.S. Education

More than 300 years ago, when Europeans arrived in the New World with their own language, culture, myths, and ideologies, the land was not empty. Native Americans speaking 300–350 different languages in North America greeted them.[7] Before the Pilgrims stepped off the *Mayflower* on to Plymouth Rock, the Spanish had already settled the Southwest; the French had populated the Mississippi Valley from St. Paul, Minnesota, to New Orleans, Louisiana; and African slaves had arrived in Jamestown, Virginia.

In spite of the cultural diversity already in place in America, our early political leaders envisioned a country with one unified history, shared mores, and a common language. Indeed, the first colonists' Anglo-Saxon orientation set the stage for the symbolic politics of language and ethnic identity in the United States.[8] A European American tradition was born, and it became the public schools' dominant culture.

From the 1600s to the 1800s, the U.S. frontier's physical and psychological openness allowed varied people to establish their own communities and preserve their Old World customs. Holding on to their ancestral practices and languages gave newcomers a strong and valued sense of who they were, even when living in an unfamiliar country.[9] If those emigrating to their community did not like these customs, they could move on to settle elsewhere.

7-2a Perspectives on Schools as Socializing Agencies

Throughout U.S. history, schools have served as a powerful agency to socialize ethnic and racial communities to white Anglo-Saxon Protestant norms. Developing a common heritage and loyalty to this country, unifying a diverse population, preparing students for citizenship in a democratic society, and teaching students to be economically self-sufficient were essential elements in ensuring this country's economic, social, and political survival. Portraying their own Western intellectual, political, historical, and cultural roots positively, public schools' curriculum was seen as a means to make this national unity and prosperity happen.

Although the members of many ethnic groups who immigrated to the United States by choice appreciated the schools helping their children to become Americans, not all ethnic communities welcomed this approach. Many groups did not want to be forced, taught, or encouraged to let go of their own cultural language, beliefs, and traditions. This was especially true for indigenous Native American communities, African Americans brought here against their will, conquered Mexican Americans in 1848, and Puerto Rican communities after the 1898 Spanish–American War.[10]

It is easy to see, therefore, how educators and students (along with their families and communities) could make different judgments about the same school practices. Educators acted in ways that they sincerely believed were best for the students and for society as a whole. Meanwhile, those students who were told to leave their family heritage at the schoolhouse door might have experienced their school-led Americanization differently.

Did You Get It?

Which statement about the historical perspective of the U.S. education system is correct?

- **a.** Even in the early Republic, Old World customs were rapidly jettisoned in favor of a common tongue and culture (both of which, however, were remarkably absorbent).
- **b.** Whenever they had a chance to educate themselves or their children, African Americans embraced the WASP ethos as a means of assimilation.
- **c.** Native Americans, quickly grasping the potential of written language to convey knowledge, eagerly sought out European-American education, although they also adapted it to their own culture.
- **d.** The Founders envisioned a country with a unified culture and a common language (even as they themselves often also embraced Latin and Greek, as well as French), and public education policies soon reflected that.

Take the full quiz on CourseMate.

7-3 Social Class and Children's Skills, Outlooks, and Opportunities

Since the nineteenth century, American schools have increased in number and attempted to afford knowledge and skills to all persons regardless of family background, race, class, gender, or national origin. This democratic ideology of providing equal opportunity to each citizen through a free public education has always been a highly motivating and worthy ideal. The question remains, however: To what extent is it actually happening?

social class, socioeconomic status (SES) A person's position in society relative to others within that society that reflects parental occupation, educational level, income, and political influence.

7-3a Social Class

Social class and **socioeconomic status (SES)** are two terms used to distinguish a person's position relative to others within that society. Parental occupation, educational level, income, housing value, and political influence are the basis for determining a student's social class or SES. Socioeconomic level also includes parents' attitudes toward education, parents' aspirations for their children, and families' intellectual activities, such as taking cognitively stimulating trips to museums, historical sites, concerts, and other events or places. A student's SES is highly associated with academic achievement.[11]

upper class Refers to wealthy persons with considerable money, property, and investments.

middle class Refers to professionals, managers, and small-business owners (upper middle class) as well as technical workers, technicians, sales personnel, and clerical workers (lower middle class).

working class Refers to skilled crafts workers (middle or upper working class, depending on education, income, home neighborhood) and unskilled manual and service workers (lower working class).

underclass Refers to a group within the working or lower class whose members may be the third or fourth generation living in poverty.

equality of opportunity The idea that all members of a society are given the same chances to enter any occupation or social class and to compete for any place in society.

Typically, the **upper class** is usually defined as wealthy persons with considerable money, property, and investments. At the level below the upper class, the **middle class** includes professionals, managers, and small-business owners (upper middle class) as well as technical workers, technicians, sales personnel, and clerical workers (lower middle class). Generally, the **working class**[12] includes skilled crafts workers (upper working class) and unskilled manual and service workers (lower working class). Skilled workers may either be middle or working class, depending on their education, income, and home neighborhood.

Recently, observers have identified an **underclass** group within the working or lower class. Many of its members are the third or fourth generation living in poverty. They depend on public assistance to maintain a relatively spare existence and tend to live clustered in inner-city slums or in rundown rural areas. After several generations without visible social or economic progress, members of the underclass usually lose hope of improving their economic and social situation.[13]

Social class differences in the United States appear in income, education, family and child-raising practices, occupations, place of residence, political involvement, health, consumer behavior, and religious beliefs. Additionally, class distinctions determine the quality of schooling students receive, their worldviews, and their relationships to others in society. Social class position creates a selective perception and set of experiences that shape a person's perspective, behaviors, and life options.

On a daily basis, social class differences may be difficult to recognize. Because observers see individuals only in limited situations, the patterns of class differences may not be clearly visible to outsiders. In addition, it is a mistake to generalize based on social class because many variations in attitudes, values, and beliefs exist within each category.

Because the United States has a powerful mythology about equal opportunity, many people try to hide their social class differences. Families buy larger houses or bigger cars than they can afford in an attempt to appear wealthier than they are. Students visibly parade their latest expensive footgear, wardrobe, and digital toys to look like they are financially and socially well off. On the other side, affluent youths prize their tattered jeans and threadbare flannel shirts. By not portraying the desperately poor on TV except in documentaries, the media present the illusion that the United States is an egalitarian society in which everyone has an equal chance to succeed.

People in the United States are stratified by more than social class, however: They are also stratified by race and ethnicity. Immigrants come from a variety of social class backgrounds. Generalizing that immigrant or minority populations are all poor or all come from the lower or working class would be incorrect.

7-3b Equal Opportunity in U.S. Schools

Equality of opportunity means that all members of a society are given the same chances to enter any occupation or social class and to compete for any place in society. It does not mean that everyone will have the same income and status. Nor does it mean than everyone will achieve the same outcome. The close relationship between education and income indicates that education is truly an important factor in providing equality of opportunity[14]—but it is not the only factor, as we shall see.

Unequal starting lines Providing actual equal opportunity requires all persons to start at the same place, as if all were running a race. In this perfect world, all runners would be physically fit and in excellent health. All would arrive wearing first-rate equipment. All runners would walk up to the starting line, take their positions, and push off at the starting gun at the same time. During this race, some people would lead, and others would follow. In this equality model, schools would guarantee that either everyone begins on equal terms at the starting line or schools can control the race to ensure that competition remains fair. In the first case, everyone must have an equal education and readiness before they reach the starting block. In the second, everyone must identify and develop their abilities during the race.

Monkey Business Images/Shutterstock.com

Many students dress to hide their social class differences.

Of course, not all Americans actually begin at the same place. The American goal of equal opportunity has been an attempt to balance the equality ideal with the inherently unequal societal reality. Schools contribute to society's stability by promising to be the "great equalizer." Our society believes that getting a good education creates opportunities for students' economic and social advancement and political participation. Over many years and for many students, this is true. For many others, it is not. Despite unequal realities, believing that schools give everyone the chance to achieve wealth and power allows people to rationalize that those who fail to reach those goals simply "did not work hard enough" or "did not take advantage" of these opportunities. This reasoning keeps our social system steady by shifting responsibility for the inequality from the institution and society to those without the money, power, or status.

7-3c Contradictory Roles of American Schools

The roles of American schools often contradict each other. America's public schools are intended to be "the great equalizer," bringing together students from different backgrounds to learn society's shared norms and values that make them educated, unified, and responsible members of our democratic republic. At the same time, our public schools have the responsibility for "sorting and selecting" students into educational paths leading to varying occupations and social status. What initially was intended as a unifying experience for diverse students has become one that increasingly separates them.

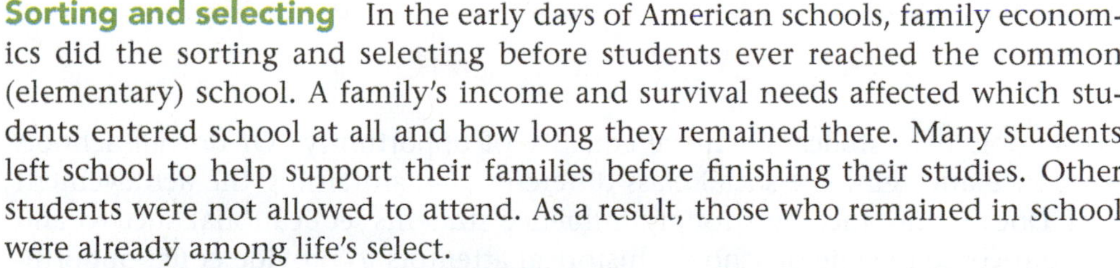

Sorting and selecting In the early days of American schools, family economics did the sorting and selecting before students ever reached the common (elementary) school. A family's income and survival needs affected which students entered school at all and how long they remained there. Many students left school to help support their families before finishing their studies. Other students were not allowed to attend. As a result, those who remained in school were already among life's select.

Beginning in the late nineteenth century, all children in the United States were required to attend school. Using what it considered "scientific," impartial, and professional opinions from teachers (and later from guidance counselors and standardized tests), schools classified—sorted and selected—students according to their individual talents or abilities. Educators then placed them into program "tracks" that would lead to appropriate education for their future occupations and societal roles.

Students determined to have the highest cognitive abilities (approximately 10 percent of those enrolled) received a rigorous academic education to prepare them for college and the few professional careers that required a respectable fund of knowledge, high-level reasoning, and effective communication skills.

The other 90 percent of the students received a less rigorous academic education appropriate to work on the farm and factories. Educators did not need to consider that not all students arrived at the schoolhouse door physically fit, healthy, properly shoed, fully trained, well coached, and ready for the same race.

A middle- and upper-class tilt Because the educational system is inherently tilted to favor middle- and upper-class children (traditionally the only children who had the family resources to permit continuous school attendance), their parents believe that schools are doing right by their offspring. These parents assume that schools offer a level playing field, and that all children have equal opportunities within them. After all, their own sons and daughters get to the starting line healthy, well outfitted, broadly experienced, and prepared to race. In contrast, low-income children, children of color, and children with disabilities do not always come to the starting line equally as healthy or as well equipped. Because circumstances of poverty, minority status, or disability keep them from getting to the starting blocks fully equipped to run a competitive race with their better-prepared peers, these low-income, minority, and disabled children are denied opportunities for equal outcomes. Consequently, they are consistently underserved in public schools.

More recently, school programs have tried to overcome inequalities caused by differences in students' preparation for school learning. For example, schools may implement compensatory education, early childhood learning, and Head Start programs to overcome poverty's limitations on academic readiness. These compensatory programs try to make up for students' unequal social conditions at home that make it difficult for these students to reach the starting line ready to compete before the race begins.

Did You Get It?

How does socioeconomic status influence U.S. students' skills, outlooks, and opportunities?

a. Profoundly, and money is the key differentiator. Parents can buy tutoring, after all.

b. Profoundly, especially if you accept the fact that a positive family attitude towards intellectual activities and children's accomplishments is in itself a middle and "upper-class" parenting characteristic.

c. Minimally: the United States, with all its faults, has worked very hard to create an educational system that equips every child with a rich and functional education and an economy in which people who work hard can usually get ahead.

d. Minimally: for all but the very few who are children of the independently wealthy, there are very few educational or economic opportunities.

Take the full quiz on CourseMate.

7-4 Research on Education, Social Class, and the Achievement Gap

Do schools help students achieve equality of opportunity? Or do our schools reproduce and reinforce social class differences—maintaining the achievement gap? Does family income strongly influence students' educational success and future income in spite of schools' historical attempts to provide equal opportunity? To some degree, the answer to all of these questions is "Yes."

7-4a Relationship between Social Class and Educational Outcomes

An enduring relationship exists between social class and educational outcomes. It is usually true that average educational attainment (measured by years in school or dropout rates) and educational achievement (measured by grades and test scores) vary by social class.[15] Social class differences contribute to—and result from—the achievement gap.

Higher social class, more education In general, higher social class status correlates with high levels of education attainment and achievement.[16] A low-income child is roughly twice as likely to be a low academic achiever as a child who is not from a low-income family.[17] Nobel laureate economist James Heckman observes that the achievement gaps between the advantaged and the disadvantaged appear by age 5 and that schooling plays a minor role in creating or perpetuating the gaps.[18] The middle classes fall somewhere in between.[19]

Possessing educational credentials follows this same pattern. Upper-class individuals, on average, hold more academic credentials (college, master's, doctoral, and professional degrees) than members of the middle class, who in turn hold more credentials than working-class individuals.[20]

In addition, one study tracked students through their elementary years and found that poor children learned as much as their middle-class peers during the school year as measured by standardized tests. Unfortunately, African American, Latino, and low-income students tended to lose much academic ground over the summer when they were out of school. In contrast, middle-class children gained over the summer in reading and held their own in math. This suggests to researchers that the learning gap is probably not completely a school factor.[21]

Social class parenting practices and school success It is not the social class label but the average group members' attitudes and behaviors that influence their children's school achievement. Young children's family environments (rather than income per se) are major predictors of cognitive, social, and emotional abilities.[22] Low income and skin color themselves do not influence academic achievement, but social class differences inevitably do.[23]

Rothstein observes that lower-class families show how occupational, psychological, personality, health, and economic characteristics interact and predict performance that differs, on average, from the performance of families from higher social classes. Although not every family in a particular social class uses all of the same practices, they are true for the group in general. Social class lifestyle differences in average academic potential exist by the time children are 3 years old. This growth gap increases mostly during after-school hours and during the summer when children are not actually in classrooms.[24]

As Rothstein concludes, "Demography is not destiny, but students' social and economic family characteristics are a powerful influence on their relative *average* achievement."[25]

7-4b Differences in Child Rearing

Distinct differences in social class-related child-rearing patterns affect students' academic performance as well. Research has shown that middle- and upper-class parents tend to include their children in adult conversations and ask their child's opinions. By contrast, low-income parents tend to speak less with their children. Accordingly, children raised by parents educated and working as professionals will, on average, ask their teachers more questions about the learning content than will children reared by working-class parents who speak less frequently with their children about their ideas and opinions.[26]

Reading to their children is another way that social class-related parenting practices affect student learning. Middle- and upper-class homes usually have many books and periodicals. Parents not only read to children every day, but the adults also read themselves, whether the daily newspaper, magazines, professional journals, or novels. When these parents read to their children, they ask the children to respond to the content: "What do you think will happen next?" In these homes, children want to read because it is fun and interesting and

Dave & Les Jacobs/Blend Images/Jupiter Images

Reading to children prepares them for learning.

because it is what grown-ups do. By comparison, full bookshelves, parents reading routinely for themselves and their children, and conversations about readings are less visible practices in working-class families.[27]

Differences in vocabulary In an eye-opening study, two University of Kansas researchers visited homes of families from different social classes to monitor conversations between parents and toddlers. The researchers found that, on average, parents who were professionals spoke more than 2,000 words per hour to their children, working-class parents spoke about 1,300 words, and welfare-recipient mothers (mothers who were unemployed but who received government assistance for housing and food) spoke about 600 words. By age 3, children of professionals had vocabularies that were nearly 50 percent larger than those of working-class children and twice the size of welfare-recipient children—a 30 million word gap.[28]

Even more important, children's vocabulary use at age 3 was predictive of their scores on language skills measures at ages 9–10. Cumulatively, the Kansas researchers estimated that by the time children were 4 years old and ready to enter preschool, the typical child in a professional family would have an accumulated experience with 45 million words, compared to only 13 million for a typical child in a welfare-recipient family.[29]

Differences in disciplinary practices Similarly, the Kansas researchers found that parental discipline practices differed by social class. Toddlers of professionals received an average of six verbal encouragements per scolding, whereas working-class children received two. Welfare-recipient children (children of parents who were not employed but who received government assistance for housing and food) received the reverse ratio: on average, one encouragement for every two scoldings.[30]

It seems reasonable to expect that when these children go to school their teachers cannot fully offset these early differences. Children with parents who encouraged them from an early age to build and use an extensive vocabulary and to constructively use their initiative are probably more likely, on average, to understand teachers' language and directions, master vocabulary-based instruction and content more quickly, and take more responsibility for their own learning than are children who lack these previous experiences.

NAEP results and social class The National Assessment of Educational Progress (NAEP) also shows the close relationship between students' social class and their reading and math proficiency scores. Students with well-educated parents (one primary measure of social class) score much higher than students whose parents have less education. Both math and reading scores show clear positive associations with parents' educational level and social class.[31]

7-4c Poverty and Education

In 2013, America had more poor people than at any other time in the 54 years of keeping records.[32] According to a 2012 Annie E. Casey

Foundation report, child poverty in the United States increased in 44 of the nation's 50 largest U.S. cities between 2005 and 2011 and today shapes the lives of nearly 16.4 million—23 percent—of all U.S. children.[33] Poverty is not just a lack of income. Indeed, poverty affects one's entire quality of life, bringing a constellation of variables that negatively affect children's schooling. These include health, housing, and multiple risk factors.[34]

Health issues In addition to having low birth weight, children from poverty generally have poorer vision than middle-class children, partly because of prenatal conditions and partly because of how their eyes are trained as infants.[35] In addition, children of parents with less education (and from lower social classes with fewer resources) are prone to poorer oral hygiene, more lead poisoning, more asthma, poorer nutrition, and less adequate pediatric care.[36]

A 2009 study also found that poverty may affect children's brain functions. Compared to children from wealthier socioeconomic backgrounds, low-income children had a noticeably lower level of activity in the prefrontal cortex—the part of the brain that is important for creativity, reasoning, and problem solving. The stress from living in relative poverty may mean that these children are not realizing full brain development.[37]

These well-documented social class health differences may have a measurable effect on academic achievement. They affect language development, the ability to plan, remember details, and pay attention in school. The combined influences of parenting practices and more fragile health are probably very large.

Housing issues The lack of affordable adequate housing for low-income families also affects school achievement. Urban rents have risen faster than working-class incomes. Recently, the national economic downturn has caused many family breadwinners to lose their jobs and push their homes into foreclosure. According to the National Law Center on Homelessness & Poverty, public schools reported that over one million children and youth attending public schools experienced homelessness in 2012. Nationally, 44 states reported increases in the total number of homeless children and youth enrolled—an increase of 57 percent since the 2006–2007 school year.[38] Most likely, these children are spending their nighttimes in shelters (19 percent) or motels (5 percent), doubled-up with relatives or friends (72 percent), or unsheltered (4 percent).[39] Children whose families have difficulty finding stable housing are more likely to move from place to place. In some schools in minority-dominated neighborhoods, student mobility rates have risen to more than 100 percent for every seat in the school.[40]

Student mobility is an important cause of low student achievement because of its curricular, social capital, and emotional effects. Students who move during the school year may miss the presentation of key concepts, forego the practice and feedback needed for knowledge and skill building, and lose curricular continuity. School records may arrive late to the receiving school, leading to the new students' placement into classrooms that are inappropriate to their knowledge and skills levels. In addition, moving sometimes damages important social ties—friends, family, and caring teachers—that help foster the child's cognitive and social development. For a young child, the emotional effects of moving and changing schools may lead to the sadness, anger, and detachment that can result in school failure.[41] Even the most experienced and well-trained teachers would have difficulty helping children who move in and out of their classrooms during the school year keep up with their classmates who are present and learning every day. Figure 7.2 graphically depicts this dilemma for children.

FIGURE 7.2 Poverty Limits Children's Opportunities to Learn

Multiple risk factors Poverty, health, housing, and parenting all contribute to students' school difficulties. A 2008 report found that children in families with multiple risk factors, such as poverty or having a teenage mother, are more likely to have high absenteeism during their early school years than children without those risk factors. At any grade, children experiencing any risk factor were more often chronic absentees—missing 10 percent of more of the school year—than children without these family risk factors. Frequently absent children fall further behind their peers in learning. The report also noted that children in poor health or who are members of ethnic or racial minorities were more likely than others to be exposed to "cumulative risk."[42]

Of course, these are generalities, not perfectly correlated with social class, and not true for all individuals. Every social group has its high and low achievers. In addition, overlaps certainly exist between lower- and middle-class children's average characteristics. Nonetheless, parenting and lifestyle differences between social classes do have a meaningful effect on students' achievement.[43]

These achievement gap differences by social class are not uniquely an American phenomenon. They can be found in any society where the occupational structure requires vastly different skills and work habits for employees at different occupational levels. Such patterns are likely to influence how children learn, at what rate they learn, and which instructional approaches will be most effective in their schools.[44]

7-4d Influence of Social Class and Ethnicity

The close relationship between social class, race, and ethnicity and school achievement leads researchers to ask: Which factor affects students' academic achievement more—the student's racial/ethnic background or the student's low SES? The answer: Low SES has the most impact.

Social class accounts for much of the variation in educational achievement observed in terms of race and ethnicity. If one knows the student group's SES class, one can accurately predict whether their achievement, ability scores, and college attendance rates will be high or low. Knowing students' racial or ethnic group, in contrast, does relatively little to improve this prediction. For example, working-class white students as a group rate low in achievement and college attainment. Middle-class white students, by comparison, rank relatively high on these variables.[45] Clearly, family income and parents' education level are the most influential social class predictors.

Did You Get It?

Pick the best overall statement that summarizes the research findings on the relationships among education, social class, and the achievement gap.

a. Studies of elementary students found that poor children learned far less than their middle-class peers during the school year as measured by standardized tests.

b. The higher the social class, the more education—and the friendlier that class towards intellectual accomplishment.

c. Social-class lifestyle differences in average academic potential don't exist until well into elementary school, when the children are damaged by their exposure to a racist and classist school system.

d. On average, demography is not destiny.

Take the full quiz on CourseMate.

7-5 Segregation, Education, and the Achievement Gap

Although the landmark 1954 *Brown v. Board of Education* decision ruled against the "separate but equal" education of poor and minority students, courts in the 1990s began releasing school districts from 1970s desegregation orders. Today, segregation (and resegregation) is widespread and increasing, and court-ordered desegregation may soon be a memory.

7-5a Housing Patterns and Segregated Schools

Racially segregated housing has severely hampered school districts' ability to integrate their schools. As a result, neighborhood schools tend to teach very different student populations.[46]

Some argue that pursuing integration has led to residential segregation. As governmental agencies have sought to integrate schools, white families appear to have increasingly moved to districts with small African American populations.[47] One 30-year study traced the residential movements of African Americans and whites in urban and suburban communities from the 1960s onward and found that growth in suburbia had increased the racial and economic isolation of central-city African Americans.[48] Whereas the suburbs are more integrated than urban centers, segregated housing patterns often persist within the suburbs.[49] Accordingly, housing patterns make it more difficult to provide racially integrated schools.

Apart from housing, school districts sometimes find ingenious ways to promote policies and practices that create segregated schools. They manipulate school attendance zones, establish school sites in predominantly minority or white neighborhoods, and develop neighborhood school policies. All of these practices serve to create racially and ethnically segregated schools—and courts have found such discriminatory practices unlawful.[50]

U.S. Supreme Court and recent desegregation orders Over the past 20 years, courts have begun **vacating** (that is, annulling or voiding) their own desegregation orders, allowing schools to resegregate. Courts are declaring many school districts to be **unitary**, which means that they have, in theory, removed all traces of segregation from their school systems.[51] In keeping with this trend, the percentage of African American and Latino children attending high schools that are mostly minority increased from 66 percent in 1991 to 75 percent or higher in 2009; close to 30 percent of these students attend schools that are 90 percent or more minority.[52]

vacating A legal term meaning annulling or voiding a school district's desegregation orders and allowing schools to resegregate.

unitary A legal status granted to a school district when the court decides the district has, in theory, removed all vestiges of segregation from their school systems.

A series of 1990s U.S. Supreme Court decisions concerning Oklahoma City, Oklahoma; DeKalb County, Georgia; and Kansas City, Missouri, made clear that court-ordered racial desegregation was a temporary remedy for past discrimination rather than a long-term strategy to promote equal opportunity.[53] In the Court's eyes, schools that lawfully complied with a court order to desegregate for a number of years had successfully made up for their long history of "separate but un-equal" violations, even if they had not accomplished their long-term goals.[54] Under the Court's ruling, those localities were allowed to return to neighborhood schools, even if that meant many schools became resegregated.

In 2006, parents in Louisville, Kentucky, and Seattle, Washington, challenged their school districts' voluntary policies, which used students' race to help determine where children attend school.[55] In both cities, school planners were reassigning students from neighborhood schools to new ones based on racial composition to achieve racial balance. In a 2007 divided 5–4 decision, the U.S. Supreme Court ruled that school boards could not use a pupil's race in school assignment formulas.[56]

Chief Justice John Roberts argued, "The way to stop discrimination on the basis of race is to stop discrimination on the basis of race." He continued that any policy that requires sorting individuals into racial categories reinforces the notion that "race" is real, even though scientists tell us there is no such thing.[57] Plainly, school diversity remains a complex and challenging issue for courts as well as schools.

7-5b Segregated Schools and Students Academic Achievement

Overwhelmingly, the data show that attending predominantly minority schools harms students' academic achievement. In a 2006 study, economists Eric Hanushek of Stanford University's Hoover Institution and Steven Rivkin of Amherst College found that African American children are likely to attend schools that are more racially isolated, have more inexperienced teachers, and have higher student mobility rates than the schools that white children attend. African American students' achievement suffers as a result.[58] Hanushek and Rivkin concluded that the higher the schools' concentration of African American students, the more rapidly the "black—white achievement gaps" grow. Substantial research continues to confirm this observation.

New research suggests that the brightest African American children may be the ones who lose the most ground academically in U.S. public schools. African American children tend to be taught in predominantly African American schools where test scores are lower on average and high-achieving peers are harder to find. In such settings, teachers aim instruction to the middle of the class, providing high-achieving students with fewer cognitively stimulating opportunities than they would receive in classrooms with a higher "middle."[59]

Other factors also contribute to poorer achievement for students in segregated school. Specifically, high-poverty schools are less likely to offer college-preparatory classes, have higher rates of teachers teaching out of their subject areas (before the No Child Left Behind Act [NCLB] required "highly qualified" teachers in all core subjects), experience greater teacher turnover, have lower test scores, have fewer involved parents, and place less pressure on administrators to fire or transfer bad teachers.[60]

Undoubtedly, economic segregation contributes to low achievement. Low-income children achieve less as the proportion of low-income children in their schools increases. The achievement drop is most severe when the subsidized-lunch population exceeds 40 percent.[61] Although there is no clear "tipping point" where student achievement falls once a school's poverty concentration passes a certain level, as the schools' proportion of students receiving free and reduced-price lunches exceeds 40 percent, the achievement decline grows steeper.[62]

7-5c Integrated Schools and Student Academic Achievement

On the flip side, minority students learn more in integrated schools. The 1966 Coleman study noted that African American students who attended predominately white northern schools during the late 1960s and early 1970s scored higher on standardized tests than did African American students who attended all-African American northern schools.[63] It seems clear that ambition and expectations for academic success among classmates positively influences peers to excel. Other studies often reconfirm these findings.[64]

Research has also identified evidence that racial integration helps minority students reach higher academic achievement and attain better long-term outcomes such as high school completion, college attendance and completion, employment, and lower rates of delinquency and teenage childbearing.[65]

Attending integrated schools increases students' opportunities to expand and build friendships with a variety of classmates who may view the world differently than they do. Having higher-achieving peers is positively associated with African Americans' and Latinos' learning gains. More peers with high achievement and higher aspirations tend to enroll in schools with lower percentages of minority students—that is, in integrated schools. In these ways, integrated schools benefit minority students.

7-5d Segregation by Race, Class, and Income

Minority students often come from low-income, working-class families. The Harvard Civil Rights Project noted that segregation by race is very strongly related to segregation by class and income. Almost nine-tenths of segregated African American and Latino schools experience concentrated poverty. The average African American or Latino student attends a school with more than twice as many poor classmates than the average white student. Poverty levels are strongly related to school test score averages and many kinds of educational inequality. Because poverty and racial minority often occur together, it is poverty's influence on learning that largely affects minority students' achievement.

"The strong relationship between poverty, race and educational achievement and graduation rates shows that, but for a few exceptional cases under extraordinary circumstances, schools that are separate are still unquestionably unequal," write Professor Gary Orfield and Research Associate Chungmei Lee of the Civil Rights Project, Harvard University. "Segregation is an old issue but one that is deeply rooted and difficult to resolve and extremely dangerous to ignore."[66]

As the Civil Rights Project's Orfield and Lee observe, "Concentrated poverty is shorthand for a constellation of inequalities that shape schooling."[67] This syndrome of inequalities is so profound that a compelling relationship exists between a school's poverty level and its achievement test scores, independent of other factors.[68]

Attending predominantly high-poverty minority schools tends to harm students' academic achievement.

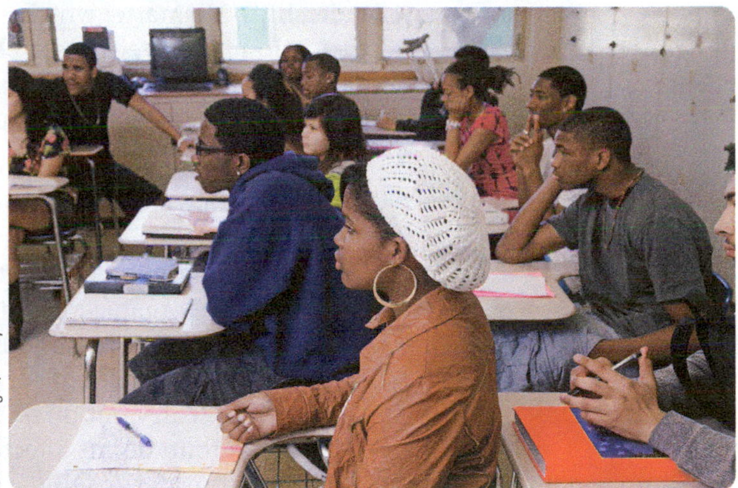

© Blend Images/Alamy

Did You Get It?

How does school segregation harm students' academic achievement?

a. Segregating the children of the long-term, underclass poor with each other generally condemns them to society's low expectation for them and does not expose them to other viewpoints.
b. Children need to be exposed to other cultures; lack of exposure is boring.
c. School segregation has nothing to do with academic achievements: if the parents would adopt upper-class attitudes towards intellectual attainments, much of the gap would disappear.
d. African American children are usually extremely academically competitive. Poor whites could benefit from being bussed into majority African American schools.

Take the full quiz on CourseMate.

InTASC

7-6 School Practices That Contribute to the Achievement Gap

Although societal factors such as social class, family income, parenting practices, housing patterns, and segregated schools affect students' preparation for learning and their eventual school achievement, school practices pertaining to diverse students can also influence whether their opportunities are truly equal. Teacher expectations, tracking and ability grouping, curriculum rigor, disciplinary practices, school climate, and quality of teachers all have tremendous impact on students and their future educational, employment, social, and lifestyle opportunities.

7-6a Teacher Expectations

Teachers' expectations about which students are likely or unlikely to succeed in school significantly influence how they teach diverse children. Research supports this theory.

Hawthorne studies The classic Hawthorne studies illustrate how expectation affects performance. From 1927 to 1932, researchers at Western Electric's Hawthorne Plant in Cicero, Illinois, examined the workplace's physical and environmental influences (such as brightness of lights and humidity) and its psychological aspects (such as work breaks, group pressure, working hours, and managerial leadership). No matter which experimental manipulation was used, the workers' production improved. Researchers determined that the workers enjoyed receiving the researchers' attention, also known as the "novelty effect."[69] Their conclusions have implications for educators:

- Individuals' aptitudes are imperfect predictors of job performance.
- The workplace is a social system made up of interdependent parts.
- Social factors strongly influence the amount produced, whereas workers' physical and mental factors address only their potential productivity.
- Informal organization affects productivity. Workers have a group life that can encourage or discourage productivity.
- Supervisors' relationships with workers tend to influence the way the workers carry out directives.
- Workgroup norms affect productivity. The group arrives at norms of what they consider "a fair day's work."

Transferred into the school setting, the Hawthorne studies suggest that teachers' expectations can greatly influence students' performance. Students' aptitudes are less important than their motivation to work in predicting their academic achievement. The classroom is a powerful social network, and students' feelings about both their teachers and their classmates have important implications for how much they are willing to work and succeed at learning.

Pygmalion in the classroom Another classic study of teacher expectations was the subject of the book titled *Pygmalion in the Classroom*.[70] In 1965, Robert Rosenthal and Lenore Jacobson, a Harvard University professor and an elementary principal, respectively, told elementary school teachers that based on their students' standardized test scores, certain children were "late bloomers" and could be expected to be "growth spurters." In truth, the test did not exist, and children designated as "spurters" were chosen randomly. Rosenthal and

Jacobson hoped this experiment would determine the degree (if any) to which changes in teacher expectations can produce changes in student achievement. In the end, the researchers found that when teachers expect students to do well, students tend to do well; when teachers expect students to fail, they tend to fail.[71]

Oakes' study on teacher expectations for students' futures Jeannie Oakes, a University of California at Los Angeles education professor, found evidence suggesting that teachers (consciously or unconsciously) treat bright students as future peers and less bright students as future subordinates.[72] When asked to list the five most important lessons to be learned by high school students, the list for the bright students differed markedly from the list for the rest of the student population. Teachers hoped the brightest would learn to think logically and critically (important skills for future leaders). Meanwhile, they hoped that the less bright would learn good work habits, respect for authority, and practical or work-related skills (all important attributes for future subordinates).

Coleman study Teacher expectations for students' achievement may have played a large role in the landmark Coleman Study. Coleman's teacher survey data suggested that achievement gaps in the same school between African American and white students were higher where most of the teachers had expressed preference for teaching college-oriented children of white-collar professionals.[73] They expected less achievement from their minority and low-income students, and—in a self-fulfilling prophecy—they got it.

7-6b Preparation to Teach Diverse Students

In a 2007 survey conducted by the National Comprehensive Center for Teaching Quality and Public Agenda, most first-year teachers reported they were not well prepared to deal with the ethnic and racial diversity and special learning needs of children in their classrooms.[74] Although 76 percent of first-year teachers had received instruction in teaching ethnically diverse students, only 39 percent said that the training actually prepared them for what they would find in their classrooms. What is more, new teachers in high-need, low-income urban schools (47 percent) were actually less likely to complain about inadequate diversity preparation than those (32 percent) working in affluent communities.[75] Findings suggest that teachers headed for suburban schools may not be well prepared for the variations in students' backgrounds and achievement that they will find.

This level of discomfort is not surprising. The teacher workforce demographics do not match those of the students we teach. According to a 2011 National Center for Education Information (NCEI) report, the teaching profession is approximately 84 percent female and 16 percent male.[76] Racially, the teaching force is even less varied. Although the percentage of minority teachers has been increasing since 1986, only 16 percent of teachers are members of minority groups (7 percent African American, 6 percent Latino, 4 percent Other).

Students bring to the schools an extensive range of languages, cultures, exceptionalities, talents, intelligence, and other factors that require equally broad and expansive teaching repertoires. When teachers do not receive professional education—either preservice or in-service—on how to most effectively educate diverse students, these educators are more likely to fall back on their own naive assumptions and their cultural norms to develop expectations for student achievement.

curriculum tracking The practice of providing differential content and instruction for students based on various measures of intelligence and skill.

tracking The rigidly determined academic placement of students into school programs based on perceived ability and educational and career goals.

ability grouping The practice of separating students into flexible homogeneous groups according to perceived abilities, past academic achievements, and presumed educational needs related to the purpose of study.

7-6c Tracking, Ability Grouping, and Restricted Curricula

Since the 1920s, most schools enrolling adolescents have offered a "tracked" curriculum—a sequence of academic classes that range from slow-paced remedial courses to rigorous academic ones with an array of electives, exploratory, vocational, and physical education classes. **Curriculum tracking** involves providing differential content and instruction for students based on various measures of intelligence and skill. This practice has been shown to have negative consequences for the future educational opportunities and schooling outcomes of children placed in the lower tracks, and especially for low-income, African American, and Latino children.[77]

Tracking **Tracking** can be defined as rigidly sorting students into homogeneous groups according to their perceived abilities, past academic achievements, presumed educational needs, and expected vocational directions and keeping students in these placements throughout their schooling. Tracks can be identified by ability (high, average, or low) or by the kind of educational preparation they provide (academic, general, vocational). This process provides the basis for organizing schools.

Tracking differs from ability grouping in important ways. Although almost all tracking is a form of ability grouping, not all ability grouping results in tracking. Generally speaking, tracking is rigidly determined. Once placed into a "track," the student tends to stay in it. In contrast, **ability grouping**, which also separates students into homogeneous groups according to perceived abilities, past academic achievements, and presumed educational needs, tends to be more flexible and related to the purpose of study. Students can change ability groups for different subjects or learning purposes by the day, week, or project.

How tracking affects students Tracking limits students' access to high-quality curriculum, teachers, and learning experiences. Students' tracks propel them through the curriculum at different speeds and at different levels of cognitive complexity. As a result, lower-track students fall further behind and receive an increasingly less intellectually rigorous curriculum. They receive an education of less depth and less breadth, and they miss learning the prerequisites for more advanced classes. Students tend to stay in the track where they are placed. As a result, the weakest students in the lower tracks are essentially locked out of meaningful opportunities for high-level learning and become mostly likely to drop out of school.[78]

For example, high school students typically follow separate academic and vocational curriculum tracks intended to take them to different postsecondary destinations, either college or immediate work. The highest-achieving students go into the college preparatory, highly academic track. These International Baccalaureate, Advanced Placement, or Honors students receive an intellectually demanding math, science, English, social studies, and foreign language curriculum to prepare them for competitive college admissions. In comparison, the lowest-achieving students are placed into the lowest track. Their curriculum tends to consist of remedial, repetitive, and less arduous versions of academic subjects along with vocational training.

Tracking limits students' access to well-prepared, experienced teachers. In general, high-track teachers tend to be better qualified and more experienced.[79] Conversely, the least well-prepared, less experienced teachers usually find themselves teaching the low-track classes. The skills of teachers assigned to low-track classes appear to diminish over time, providing low-track students with lesser-quality instruction.[80]

Tracking limits students' access to quality learning experiences. Teachers tend to establish positive relationships with high-track students, whereas teachers in low-track classes focus more attention on classroom control.[81] Teachers in high-track classes are more knowledgeable, more enthusiastic, and less judgmental than colleagues in low-track classes. High-track teachers' classrooms show greater variety in learning activities, better organization, higher interest, active student involvement, and more educational resources compared to low-track classrooms.[82]

Given the different achievement expectations that accompany tracking, low-track classes are typically "characterized by dull, passive instruction, consisting largely of drill and practice with trivial bits of information."[83] Students spend more time on routines and seatwork. Adam Gamoran, Professor of Sociology and Education Policy Studies at the University of Wisconsin–Madison, found that 25 percent of tracking-related learning differences were due to differences in curriculum and instruction.[84] In these ways, tracking produces a consistent pattern of academic disadvantage among low-track students. The widening achievement gap between high- and low-track students is one outcome.

7-6d Research Findings on Tracking

Studies of how tracking and ability groupings affect achievement are one of educational research's oldest traditions, in part because this area is characterized by considerable disagreement. The results are consistent but contradictory, depending on the study's methodology.

Tracking's impact on minority and low-income students The research here is consistent. Tracking disproportionately excludes low-income African American and Latino students from opportunities to learn in high-track classes.[85] One study found that whites were six times more likely to be overrepresented in high-track classes, whereas minorities were seven times more likely to be overrepresented in low-track classes.[86] In senior high schools, low-income, African American, and Latino students were underrepresented in college preparatory classes. More frequently, they were enrolled in vocational programs that train students to enter the lowest-level occupations. At all levels, minority and low-income groups were underrepresented in programs for gifted and talented students.[87]

On the other hand, studies have clearly demonstrated a positive relationship between detracking and the number of minority students, students who receive free or reduced-price lunches, and special education students who achieve a Regents (high status) diploma.[88] As a method of organizing students for instruction, tracking is neither equitable nor effective.

Tracking and achievement Although students perpetually tracked into low-ability groups lose ground academically over the years, those kept in high-ability groups with an accelerated curriculum make measurable learning and achievement gains. Specifically, academically gifted students benefit from being placed into fast-paced, high-ability groups.[89] Researchers suggest that these advantages result from the enhanced instructional and learning opportunities in these high-track classes rather than from their homogeneity.[90] Nonetheless, although condemned as discriminatory, grouping students by academic ability appears to be rising. Some emerging research suggests that, in certain cases, flexible ability grouping can benefit both high- and low-level students in reading and math. Students in special education did not benefit from separate grouping, however.[91]

More research is needed on student grouping for instruction to find approaches that advance academic achievement but do not reinforce achievement disparities.

Tracking and peer groups and attitudes Over time, tracking fosters friendship networks linked to student group memberships.[92] Academically separating peer groups may lead to polarized attitudes among secondary students. High-track students tend to become more enthusiastic about school and more self-confident about their futures. Low-track students become more alienated and discouraged.[93] These feelings foster significant differences in classroom and school climate.[94]

Tracking influences students' attainment and life chances in ways beyond their academic achievement. Track placements are quite stable, reflecting years of differentiated education. Students' early assignment affects their later course experiences because each year they lose opportunities to take prerequisites to more advanced classes. By high school, college-track students have better prospects for college attendance, school grades, and future high-status occupations with financial and social rewards than their comparable non-college-track peers.[95]

Conclusions about tracking The research shows that persistent tracking harms low-tracked students by identifying them through questionable assumptions and means and then rigidly keeping them in low-level courses with unmotivating curriculum and instructional techniques. This practice guarantees that these students will not learn what they need to learn to exit from the school system as educated individuals. It also reflects ingrained societal attitudes and beliefs about certain students that allow educators to have low expectations for their progress.

7-6e The Rationale behind Tracking

If research confirms that tracking hurts low-track students' academic achievement and life options, one must wonder why schools continue the practice. Tracking continues because it reflects our society's cultural norms, accommodates integration requirements, reflects community "politics" and educators' mistaken ideas about intelligence, and makes fewer instructional demands on teachers.

Cultural norms Tracking reflects widespread cultural assumptions and institutional norms—that may be dated or inaccurate—about students' capacities, individual and group differences, and the school's role in addressing them.[96] One norm is that students' needs and capacities vary enormously, and ability grouping and tracking meet students' needs by placing individuals into learning situations appropriate to their intellectual capacities.[97]

Another norm is that each student generation has an ability distribution that roughly reproduces the skilled hierarchy found in a socially and economically diverse workforce. According to this perspective, those students who are planning to immediately enter the labor force after high school graduation do not need the knowledge, reasoning, and communication skills essential for those individuals who are headed to college and the professions. Given this norm, tracking appears to the "logical" solution.[98]

Integration In the late nineteenth and early twentieth centuries, when schools began to educate immigrants' and working-class families' children, tracking was seen as the way to both accommodate the needs of these supposedly "lesser-ability" new students and still maintain the schools' role preparing middle- and upper-class college-bound students.[99]

In a similar vein, Ronald Ferguson, a Harvard University lecturer and researcher, suggests that schools have used tracking to accommodate integration requirements. He suggests that when poor and minority children enter a school with systematically different preparation and identity from those children the school usually serves, instructional quality, tracking, and ability grouping may be the school's way of providing an "appropriate" education for these newcomers.[100] Consequently, he concludes, "tracking and ability grouping are leading 'suspects' for why integration has not provided greater benefits for minority children."[101]

Politics Tracking has a strong political component. Tracking brings labels and differences in status, expectations, and consequences for students' academic and occupational attainment into public view. For example, parents of students identified as gifted often exercise political clout, threatening "bright flight" to block attempts to remove tracking.[102] Parents who work in professional fields understand the benefits of high-track classes and are highly successful at "working the system" to ensure that their children are placed in them.[103] In this way, tracking becomes part of the students' and groups' struggle for comparative advantages as each party tries to corral socially valued school resources, opportunities, and credentials.

Teaching Many people support tracking because they believe that it makes fewer demands on already overburdened teachers. Tracking proponents assert that when teachers have a heterogeneous group of students, they must "teach to the middle," thereby hindering learning for students at both ends—that is, shortchanging struggling students and high achievers. These tracking advocates do not consider instructional approaches that allow mixed-ability classrooms to raise all students' achievement: the new research on constructivism and differentiated instruction, the flexible regrouping depending on the topic, and the extra scaffolding that helps slower learners keep up with the rigorous curriculum. Teachers who continue to expand their instructional repertoires can advance more students' learning without leaving slower learners behind.

7-6f Rethinking Tracking

Relying on societal norms and other misconceptions, teachers see tracking as a logical practice. If teachers believe that students' capacity to learn is unchangeable, the range in students' ability is very large, and adequately paid employment opportunities exist for low-track students, tracking appears sensible. Schools want to provide curriculum appropriate to students' capacities, so they separate students by ability and adapt curriculum and instruction accordingly. The fact that learning aptitude seems to be unevenly distributed among groups—with low-income and minority group members showing less capacity to learn—appears beyond the schools' control.[104]

Undoing tracking in public schools involves a critical and unsettling rethinking of fundamental educational norms and cultural assumptions about who can and should achieve. In recent years, policy makers and educators have tried to end tracking. The National Education Association, National Governors' Association, the Carnegie Corporation, the College Board, and the National Association of Secondary School Principals, among others, all endorse ending the use of discriminatory tracking (detracking), identifying it as a barrier to many students' learning and path to college. Research findings from the American College Testing (ACT) program, which indicate that the reading and math skills needed for workplace success are comparable to those needed for success in the first year

FlipSides

Should Ability Grouping or Open Access Be the Way to Place Students into High-Status Courses?

Teachers have long argued about how best to group students for instruction. Should students' ability and achievement or their interest and willingness to work hard be the criteria for their enrolment in rigorous courses? Which approach do you think is best for student learning and long-term goals?

Group students for instruction according to their abilities, prior achievement, and career goals.	Group students for instruction according to their interests, goals, and willingness to work hard to learn.
■ Placing students into courses based on their prior school achievement, achievement test results, and discipline records is an objective and reliable way to organize students for learning.	● Placing students into courses based on prior school achievement, achievement test results and discipline records is unfair and ineffective. Report card grades are highly subjective, achievement tests may be culturally biased and weak students are capable of maturing and improving.
■ Grouping students by ability and goals reinforces a meritocracy in which all students with ability and drive can get a world-class education.	● Grouping students by ability and goals disproportionately excludes African American, Latino, and special needs students from opportunities to learn in high-track, college-preparatory classes. Tracking is neither equitable nor effective.
■ Grouping students for instruction by ability or test results allows teachers to make the content and learning activities challenging and relevant for each student.	● Grouping students for instruction based on ability or test results is unfair to those who lack extensive opportunities outside school to learn; limits access to experienced, effective teachers; harms achievement; and prevents enrollment in courses needed for college and careers.
■ Grouping students by ability and career goals gives them the curriculum that will prepare them for their future vocations.	● Grouping students by ability and career goals is unrealistic and unfair because students' vocational goals change with experiences, maturity, and successes.
■ Grouping students for instruction by ability gives teachers a manageable range of student abilities in the classroom. "Teaching to the middle" hinders learning for the highest- and lowest-achievers.	● Teachers can and should learn how to teach a high-status content effectively to a wide range of student abilities through differentiated instructional practices and additional support when needed. Access to high-status courses "with a future" is a student's civil right.
■ Students who plan to go to work immediately after high school do not need to learn the same twenty-first-century knowledge and skills as those going to college.	● Every student today needs to have the same twenty-first-century high-level knowledge and skills as those going to college because most well-paying non-college jobs also require these skills.
■ To allow weak students to enroll in college-preparatory courses would be setting the students up for failure.	● Many nontraditional students can succeed in college-preparatory classes if they are motivated to work hard, if they have parents'/guardians' support, and if the teacher provides extra learning time and help.
■ Students will be uncomfortable in classrooms with students who are unlike themselves, who have different cultural backgrounds and life goals.	● Students become comfortable when they get to know unfamiliar students as competent, likeable, motivated individuals who are both different and like themselves. Tracking segregates and negatively polarizes peer group attitudes about others unlike themselves.

The twenty-first-century workplace requires high-level skills of all workers, and our social safety nets require many workers to earn decent wages. Given both sides of the argument and the chapter's information, how do you think schools and teachers should group students for instruction?

of college, supports these actions.[105] In the twenty-first century, all students need the foundation of academic competencies necessary to learn additional skills as their jobs evolve or as they change positions throughout their careers—no matter which paths they choose after graduation.

Implementing tracking reforms will require that competing interest groups create a collective advocacy for schools that serve all children well. It requires confronting likely opposition to a system that takes away comparative advantages enjoyed and effectively used by children whose parents are privileged by race and class. It means preparing teachers to work effectively with diverse students in a high-challenge curriculum. Confronting these issues is both an instructional and a political process that requires keen and sensitive leadership by educators.

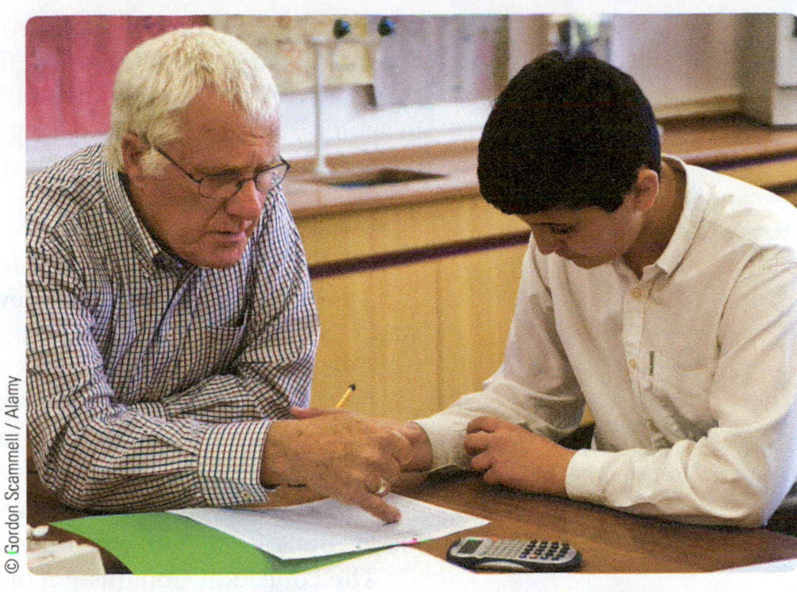
© Gordon Scammell / Alamy

Inequitably distributing high-quality teachers to schools contributes to the achievement gap.

7-6g Lower Teacher Quality

Apart from tracking practices, research supports the idea that low-income and minority students do not get their fair share of more experienced and capable teachers.[106] This, too, contributes to the achievement gap.

Until 2002's NCLB law required teachers to have bachelor's degrees in the subjects they taught, low-income and minority students were more likely to have "out-of-field" teachers—that is, teachers without majors or minors in the subjects they taught—than were students in low-poverty schools. In high-poverty secondary schools, for example, students were likely to have one in three teachers of a core subject without a major or minor degree in that subject as compared with students in a low-poverty school, who had a one in five chance of working with an unqualified teacher. Likewise, nearly half of the math classes in both high-poverty and high-minority high schools were taught by teachers who did not have a college major or minor in math or a math-related field, such as math education, physics, or engineering.[107] No doubt, this reality contributed to the achievement gap between low-income and minority students in high-poverty schools and their more affluent peers in low-poverty schools.

Today, the situation remains difficult. An analysis of the most recent data from the U.S. Department of Education's 2007–2008 Schools and Staffing Survey (SASS)—based on reports from teachers— indicates that 15.6 percent of secondary core academic classes are taught by a teacher with neither certification nor a major in the subject area taught, an improvement of slightly over 1 percent since 2003–2004. Core academic classes in high-poverty schools are almost twice as likely to have an out-of-field teacher as peers in low-poverty schools with more than one in every five core classes (21.9 percent) taught by an unqualified teacher compared with one in nine classes (10.9 percent) in low-poverty schools.[108]

Research consistently affirms the relationship between teacher quality factors and student achievement. Briefly, these "quality" factors include teachers' academic skills and knowledge (especially their vocabulary), their mastery of the content they teach, their experience on the job (especially between their second and fifth years), their teaching effectiveness (pedagogy), and the interaction of these factors. Inequitably distributing quality teachers to schools is another way in which school practices poorly serve low-income and minority children and contribute to the achievement gap.

7-6h Retention

Until around 1860, grouping students in grade levels was not common practice in the United States. Soon after the practice became routine, educators noticed that not all students progressed at the same pace. If students could not master the grade's content, they were **retained** or kept in that grade the following school year. Teachers believed that allowing more time to develop adequate academic skills would make students more successful.

retained The status of keeping a student in the same grade the following school year, usually to improve academic performance.

By 1954, researchers had found no evidence that students retained in grade made educational gains.[109] Other investigators agreed.[110]

The Education Commission of the States noted in 1999 that research on retention found that:

- Minority, male, urban, and poor students are disproportionately (two to three times) more likely to be retained.
- Retention greatly increases students' likelihood of eventually dropping out.
- Retention lowers self-esteem and self-confidence.
- Retained students are likely to remain below grade-level proficiency levels.[111]

Data continue to support the first three conclusions. According to the U.S Department of Education's Office of Civil Rights, for the 2009–2010 school year, approximately 1 percent of students were retained in grades K-8 with most repeating kindergarten or the first grade. Traditionally disadvantaged minorities—those most likely to experience low academic performance—had the highest retention rates with 4.2 percent and 2.8 percent for African American and Latino students, respectively, as compared with 1.5 percent for whites. Yet at the same time, attention-getting evidence from Florida—which has had a test-based promotion policy since 2003 that requires retention and intensive remediation of lowest-performing third-grade readers—is showing academic benefits. These recent findings are raising questions about the view that retention in grade usually leads to bad outcomes.[112] Nonetheless, the best strategy for dealing with retention is to improve teaching quality and interventions for struggling readers so more of them will successfully meet the promotion standards the first time.

7-6i Student Disciplinary Practices

Even as educators view schools' prevailing disciplinary practices as fair, objective, unbiased, and race neutral, research is increasingly finding that disciplinary practices are culturally loaded.[113] Most school district discipline codes leave ample room for "professional judgment," allowing teachers' conscious or unconscious beliefs about their low-income and minority students to influence their discipline decisions. Schools' zero-tolerance policies also demand strict compliance with established rules, without providing any discretion for extenuating or clarifying circumstances.

School discipline policies often inadvertently encourage discrimination. The schools' tendency to interpret all conflict as a threat to the institution's stability encourages educators to oversimplify conflict. Thus teachers and administrators believe that any classroom disruption should be swiftly and efficiently ended.

Behaviors that clash with the operating norms are viewed as aberrant and deserving of punishment. In this way, educators fail to notice problems and inequities that their organizations are creating, such as the disproportionately high suspension rates of minority students, their overrepresentation in low-track classes, or the relationship between these facts.[114]

The data show that punitive, exclusionary discipline practices have a disproportionate and growing impact on youth of color. A 2012 study of 26,000 U.S. middle and high schools finds that African American students have a 24.3 percent suspension rate as compared with a 7.1 percentage suspension rate for white students. Since the early 1970s, the black/white suspension gap has increased from 5.7 to 17 points.[115] Nationally, an average of 36 percent of African American male students with disabilities enrolled in middle and high schools received school suspensions at least once during the 2009–2010 school year. Latino students and English learners had a nearly 11-point and 10-point increase, respectively, in the risk of suspension between the elementary and secondary levels despite the fact that they were suspended only slightly more often than white classmates at the elementary level. Most of these suspensions are for minor violations of school rules, such as disrupting class, tardiness, and dress code violations—not for serious violent or criminal behavior.[116]

Data suggest that this cycle of misbehavior, disciplinary action, and removal from the classroom leads to lower achievement and more acting out in school. According to 2012 research from Johns Hopkins University, being suspended even once in ninth grade appears to double the possibility of dropping out from 16 percent for students not suspended to 32 percent for those suspended even once. What is more, disciplinary incidents are related to other indicators of student detachment from school: course failures and absenteeism.[117] Similarly, research shows that those students who are repeatedly suspended are at risk for less participation in positive extracurricular activities, increased placement in special education programs, and increased truancy.[118] Because student suspensions appear related to their academic engagement and success, addressing the disparity in disciplinary practices is an essential part of closing the achievement gap. And although it is true that students must be held accountable for their behaviors, it is equally true that teachers should be held accountable for their classroom management skills and the learning climate and supports they create for all students to succeed.

Typically, schools' disciplinary policies and practices offer a prescribed response to disturbing events, but they do not reveal the problems' causes or contexts, and they do not prevent the incidents from recurring. Looking at isolated incidents does not identify dysfunctional patterns within the system that need correcting.

TeachSource Video 7.1

Classroom Management: Best Practices

Teachers can do specific things to create the safe, orderly, and caring classroom environments necessary to support all children's learning. Four teachers and a student discuss several practices based on mutual respect that create positive bonds of community among teachers and learners. Watch the video clips, study the artifacts in the case, and reflect on the following questions:

1. How does spending the first few weeks of the school year structuring a learning environment and clearly expressing and practicing teachers' expectations add to children's sense of safety and predictability in ways that promote their learning throughout the rest of the year?
2. Describe the variety of best practices described in the video that help children and teachers develop and enact mutual respect.
3. Explain why the advice for teachers to listen to students and hear them out especially important when working with young people who come from different backgrounds than the teacher.

Watch on CourseMate.

7-6j School Climate

Both academic and disciplinary practices affect school climate. **School climate** refers to the physical, intellectual, psychological, and social environment in which teachers' and students' behaviors occur within schools. School climate is the school's "feel" at the building and classroom level.[119] Some schools "feel" positive, encouraging, high achieving, and respectful of all its members; others do not.

school climate Refers to the physical, psychological, and social environment in which teachers' and students' behaviors occur within schools.

School climate is a multidimensional construct. Teaching practices, student and faculty diversity, and the relationships among administrators, teachers, parents, and students all contribute to its formation. The number and quality of teacher–student interactions, students' and teachers' perceptions of the school's personality, environmental factors (such as the facility's attractiveness, cleanliness, and state of repair), the academic performance expected and received from all students, the school's size and feeling of safety, and the feelings of trust and respect among students and teachers all come into play. In total or viewed separately, these factors can have a positive influence on the learning environment—or they can create significant barriers to learning.

For example, tracking and retention affect school climate. They have a negative influence on the relationships among different groups within the schools, isolating students along cognitive, cultural, racial, and economic lines. When the lower tracks are overwhelmingly occupied by low-income and minority students at the same time as white and middle-class or affluent students predominantly fill the upper tracks, the two student groups do not have opportunities to move beyond stereotypes and get to know one another as persons. Separated daily by high- and low-status courses, teachers' behaviors toward them, and their relative expectations for success, students in the disparate groups tend to make uninformed judgments about one another. As a consequence, distrust and disrespect grow.

Ineffective school practices, antisocial behaviors, and academic failure reinforce one another. A pattern of academic failure provides few opportunities for the student to receive positive reinforcement. Students perceived as being at risk of antisocial conduct, particularly boys and impoverished minority students, "are more likely to be punished, excluded, and controlled than to have their problems addressed in a therapeutic manner."[120] From the failing student's perspective, school becomes a bad, unfair place. This perception increases the students' likelihood of wanting to escape, rebel, act uncooperatively, and disrupt the learning environment. The cycle of bad grades and low expectations (perceived as disrespect toward the student) leads to disorderly student behaviors, suspensions from school, further failure, and eventual dropping out.[121]

TeachSource Video 7.2

Classroom Management: Handling a Student with Behavior Problems

Effective teachers know ways to handle student behavior problems that interfere with learning. Here are several effective classroom-tested strategies to cope with a disruptive student's behavior. Watch the video clips, study the artifacts in the case, and reflect on the following questions:

1. What is the value for teachers who share the same disruptive student collaborating with a student behavior specialist (often a school counselor or school psychologist) about how to work effectively with this student?
2. What does the reality that students often come to school with a lot on their minds that has nothing to do with learning mean for teachers?
3. What strategies can teachers use to help the children in their classrooms feel safe, capable, and connected to the people and the classroom they work with every day?
4. How can teachers establish their own style of connecting with children and develop the strategies that help even disruptive students learn?

Watch on CourseMate.

When the school's psychosocial climate—in the halls, classroom, cafeteria, gym, and anywhere on campus—becomes negative, it can hinder students' achievement. All students want to feel safe, connected, well liked, competent, and valued. No students want to anxiously sense that they are in danger, whether physically or psychologically. In such conditions, students cannot learn. Further, when they perceive a threat, students react quickly, often disruptively. Fostering student academic achievement and development within a safe learning environment requires establishing and maintaining a school climate that positively meets all students' needs.

Andreanna Seymore/ Stone/Getty images

A safe and supportive school climate fosters student learning.

Research on school climate and the achievement gap Research on school climate shows that it can affect many areas and people within the school:

- A positive, supportive, and culturally conscious school climate in high-risk urban environments can significantly shape urban students' degree of academic success.[122]
- Positive school climate perceptions are protective factors for boys and may give high-risk students a supportive learning milieu as well as prevent antisocial behaviors.[123]
- Positive interpersonal relationships and optimal learning opportunities for students in all demographic environments can increase achievement levels and reduce maladaptive behaviors.[124]
- Providing a positive and supportive situation for students is important for a smooth transition to a new school.[125]

The worse the students believe they are performing in school, the higher the likelihood that they will behave disruptively. Conversely, the better students believe they are doing, the lower the likelihood that they will act to upset or destroy their learning environment. Family and peer dynamics interact to shape the direction and severity of troublesome conduct.[126] Research supports the general conclusion that the greater the school's academic quality and more positive its emotional climate, the lower the level of school crime and violence.

Did You Get It?

What factors contribute to the achievement gap?

a. Educators expecting less academic achievement of students from minority or low-income backgrounds.

b. Tracking students by perceived ability, so neither the bright kids nor the not-bright kids get bored.

c. Managing your expectations of your students: it's unfair to expect every child to think rationally and critically, and enjoy math, literature, science, and the arts.

d. Suspending students: if a child is disruptive, it's unfair for them to take up space, time and energy from students who want to learn.

Take the full quiz on CourseMate.

InTASC

7-7 School Factors That Reduce the Achievement Gap

We have discussed a variety of factors that create a negative school climate, which in turn hurt students' attitudes, behaviors, and achievement. Now we will consider several factors that enhance school climate and increase students' opportunities to reduce the achievement gap.

7-7a Multicultural Education

Multicultural education encompasses more than just highlighting ethnic foods, holidays, heroes, and customs. Multicultural education is a response to the U.S. cultural pluralism and the absence of minority viewpoints in the public school curriculum and society.

multicultural education A curriculum that uses multiple, non-stereotyped perspectives and voices in primary sources to help all students understand and appreciate human differences and commonalities.

Multicultural education **Multicultural education** has many definitions. Some see it as the institutionalization of the cultural pluralism concept in the schools.[127] Multicultural education explicitly promotes the Western values of democracy, freedom, human dignity, equality, and respect for diversity. It uses multiple, non-stereotyped perspectives and voices in primary sources to help all students understand and appreciate human differences and commonalities. It teaches students to recognize power and privilege inequities in society. Multicultural education means learning about, preparing for, and celebrating cultural diversity, or learning to be bicultural.[128]

From "melting pot" to pluralism Multicultural education is a relatively new approach to dealing with America's diversity. The massive wave of immigration that occurred from 1880 to 1920 in the United States put pressure on public schools to quickly assimilate these newcomers by imposing a strongly Anglocentric curriculum. According to this perspective, students' mother tongues, cultural traditions, and values were to "melt away," replaced by a new, totally American culture. Later, educators extended the 1960s Civil Rights Movement with various ethnic and racial groups wanting to include their voices, stories, and contributions in the school curriculum.

By the 1970s and 1980s, gender, class, language, ability, religion, and sexual orientation issues joined the multicultural education movement.[129] Each group wanted the same goal—a more democratic society in which each would have greater respect and equality in all spheres of life.

Preventing miscommunications in school Because the United States' ethnic and cultural diversity is not sufficiently reflected in educational decisions and practices, schools frequently fall out of sync with the populations whom they are supposed to serve. This disconnect is especially likely to occur when teachers and administrators come from the dominant culture, but students and their parents follow other cultural standards.[130] Seeing the world in different ways often causes students, teachers, and parents to misinterpret one another's attitudes and actions.

For instance, teachers may mistake students' background differences for intellectual weaknesses and make pedagogical decisions accordingly. Because they do not understand some Latino ethnic styles, teachers may erroneously conclude that these students have limited critical thinking and reasoning abilities. Teachers may misunderstand Native American children's reluctance to operate on a tightly controlled time schedule or engage in highly individualistic and competitive activities as lack of initiative, motivation, and responsibility. Consequently, educators often engage in "miseducating practices" because they do not understand their ethnically and linguistically diverse students' cultural characteristics.[131]

At the same time, if students feel that the school environment is alien and hostile toward them or does not affirm and value who they are (as many students of color believe), they have difficulty concentrating as thoroughly as they might on academic tasks.[132] Psychological security and a positive feeling of self-worth are essential baseline conditions if students are going to want to know and learn.

When teachers understand and welcome their diverse students' assets, hold high expectations for their learning, and use a curriculum and instruction that invites all students to participate in the American experience, occasions for miscommunications decrease. In these ways, teachers practice **culturally responsive teaching**.[133]

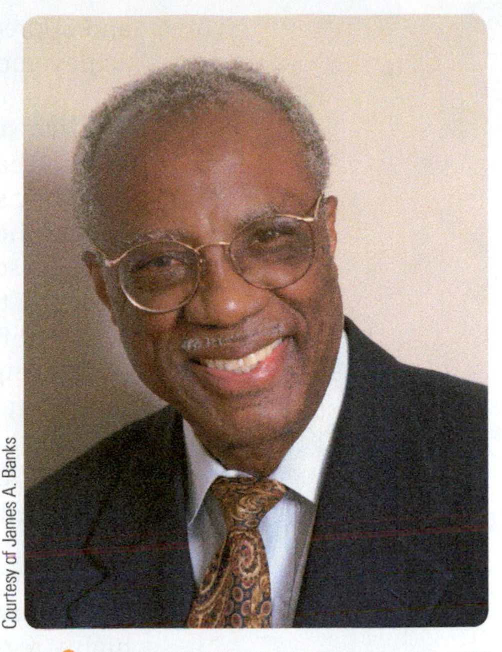
Courtesy of James A. Banks

Professor James A. Banks, multicultural education pioneer

culturally responsive teaching Using diverse students' background knowledge, prior experiences, and performance styles to make learning more appropriate and effective for them.

Expanding the curriculum Over time, educators came to realize that they might increase minority students' achievement by studying their relationship with the traditional school curriculum. Educators concluded that by teaching only narrow aspects of U.S. history and culture and reinforcing students' prejudices and values, public schools indirectly contribute to perpetuating misunderstandings, tensions, and conflicts between groups. Teaching only one perspective, they reasoned, does not motivate all students to study and learn. Both our students and our society as a whole suffer as a result. In contrast, expanding and deepening the curriculum to include minority voices and perspectives benefits all students' learning.[134]

James A. Banks, Professor at the University of Washington and pioneer multicultural educator, observes:

> Rather than excluding Western civilization from the curriculum, multiculturalists want a more truthful, complex, and diverse version of the West taught in the schools. They want the curriculum to describe the way in which African, Asian, and indigenous cultures have influenced and interacted with Western civilization.[135]

Typically, teachers implement multicultural education in small steps. Using an interdisciplinary approach, they select and explore relevant topics across disciplines. They supplement their existing curriculum with brief multicultural units. As they expand their offerings, teachers infuse the multicultural perspective throughout the curriculum.[136] Over time, it stops being an "add-on" and instead becomes a recognized part of what students learn. Teachers offer students instruction that matches their needs based on their age, race, gender, ethnicity, sociolinguistic backgrounds, and learning styles. Each school and its community determine where they stand on multicultural education and select the curricula and teaching approaches that best fit their needs.

Even while expanding the curriculum's content, teachers continue to provide students with instruction on basic and complex academic skills, holding pupils to high expectations. Teaching approaches and materials are sensitive and relevant to the students' sociocultural backgrounds and experiences, encouraging them to think critically, incorporate complexity, and respond to multiple ways of understanding information. In turn, students develop respect and appreciation for cultural diversity as their academic knowledge, skills, and achievement grow.

Multicultural education and student achievement Research affirms the notion that multicultural education can increase students' basic and advanced academic skills. This type of education can improve mastery of reading, writing, and mathematics; subject matter content; and intellectual process skills such as problem solving, critical thinking, and conflict resolution by providing information and techniques that are more meaningful to ethnically diverse students' lives and frames of reference. Using ethnically informed materials, experiences, and examples as students practice and demonstrate mastery of academic subject matter makes the instruction more interesting, increases personal meaning, heightens the practical relevance of the skills to be learned, and improves students' time on task. Together, this combination of conditions leads to greater student efforts, task persistence, skill mastery, and academic achievement.[137]

Becoming a successful multicultural teacher Sonia Nieto, Professor Emerita at University of Massachusetts (see American Education Spotlight later), is a highly regarded teacher and multicultural educator. From first-hand experiences as a New York City teacher and from a synthesis of the literature, Nieto recognizes that successful teachers for students of diverse backgrounds share common characteristics. In addition to strong subject-matter knowledge, pedagogical effectiveness, and excellent communication skills, teachers who are effective with *all* students:

- Connect learning to students' lives
- Have high expectations for all students, even for those on whom others have given up
- Stay committed to students despite obstacles
- Place a high value on students' identities (culture, race, language, gender, and experiences, among others) as a foundation for learning
- View parents and other community members as partners in education
- Create a safe haven for learning
- Dare to challenge the bureaucracy of the school and district
- Are resilient in the face of difficult situations
- Use active learning strategies
- Are willing and eager to experiment and can "think on their feet"
- View themselves as lifelong learners
- Care about, respect, and love their students

When caring and competent teachers bring these qualities into their classrooms, they can work collaboratively to influence the school culture and climate in ways that support each student's academic and social success.

Becoming a multicultural person Multicultural education is more than curriculum; it is a highly personal experience for students and their teachers.

For students, multicultural education emphasizes developing greater self-understanding, positive self-concepts, and pride in one's ethnic identity within the American society. Contributing to students' personal development adds to their overall intellectual, academic, and social achievement. Students who feel good about themselves are likely to be more open and receptive to interaction with others and to respect their cultures and identities. Research has repeatedly supported the relationship among self-concept, academic achievement, ethnicity, culture, and individual identity.[138]

For teachers, to become effective multicultural educators, they must first become multicultural persons—in their heads and their hearts. Sonia Nieto writes:

> That means looking critically at who you are, what you value, how you reflect those multicultural values, and then looking at your own biases. . . . [and thinking about] . . . the students who are sitting in front of us. Then we have to think about how to deal with those biases in a way that doesn't jeopardize the students we're teaching.[139]

To become a multicultural educator involves learning more about oneself and one's views about cultural differences. It requires understanding the school experience from diverse students' perspectives. It also entails creating learning opportunities that invite and motivate diverse students to participate as contributors to the common culture and learning rather than remaining passive outsiders to learning and to the "American experience." Although these are certainly emotionally and intellectually challenging tasks, completing them is necessary for a teacher's professional growth and effectiveness with all students.

Multicultural education and school climate Multicultural education transforms school climate by improving relationships and increasing respect between teachers and students and between mainstream and diverse students. Most young people spend their formative years in ethnically and culturally isolated enclaves. Such separation often results in heightened group frustrations, anxiety, fears, failures, and hostilities when children eventually encounter others from different ethnic and cultural backgrounds in the classroom.

Similarly, children born into the mainstream culture rarely have an opportunity to identify, question, or challenge their cultural assumptions because the school culture usually reinforces what they learn at home. As a result, mainstream Americans have few occasions to look at and consider their single-culture beliefs and perspectives, which all too often devalue and stereotype people of other traditions, races, or social classes. This naive viewpoint limits these "all-American" children's ability to function effectively within other American cultures—or in the many cultures found throughout the world.

As a consequence, multicultural education improves relationships among dissimilar students. Many students have internalized the negative and distorted conceptions of their own and other ethnic groups. Students from groups of color may be convinced that their heritages have little of value to offer, whereas members of dominant groups may have inflated notions about their own culture's significance.

Multicultural education can ease these tensions by teaching students skills in cross-cultural communication, interpersonal relations, perspective taking, contextual analysis, understanding alternative points of view and frames of reference, and analysis of how cultural conditions affect values, attitudes, beliefs, preferences, expectations, and behaviors. These skills can help students learn how to understand cultural differences without making hasty and arbitrary value judgments about their intrinsic worth. Attaining these goals can be facilitated by providing students—and future teachers—with a variety of opportunities to practice their cultural competence and to interact successfully with different ethnic peoples, experiences, and situations.[140]

"If we truly believe in democracy then we need to welcome those disparate voices—those voices of conflict and tension and difference—into the conversation," Nieto believes.[141] James Banks adds, "To fully participate in our democratic society, all students need the skills that a multicultural education can give them to understand others and thrive in a rapidly changing, diverse

American Education Spotlight

Courtesy of Sonia Nieto

Sonia Nieto, multicultural advocate and activist

Sonia Nieto

"It would be simplistic in the extreme to believe [. . . that teachers alone are responsible for either all the good or all the bad that happens in public schools]. . . . [W]ithout structural changes in schools and in society in general, teachers can have only a limited impact." (From: *Why We Teach*. (2005). New York: Teachers College Press, p. 7.)

Sonia Nieto, Professor Emerita of Language, Literacy, and Culture, School of Education, University of Massachusetts, Amherst, is a teacher with faith in the promise of public schools and the power of teaching. She recognizes that many teachers are working with students who are very different from them in background and experience. Instead of referring to these students as "minority," "at-risk," or "disadvantaged," Nieto uses the term "bicultural," which emphasizes what these students have rather than what they lack. In her view, practicing and prospective teachers need to rid themselves of "deficit thinking," if they are to become competent educators for the new student majority. And teachers need to recognize and challenge schools' structural barriers to educational equity.

Brooklyn, New York, born and raised, Nieto was educated in the New York City public schools. She graduated from St. John's University with a BS in Elementary Education in 1965. She received her MA in Spanish and Hispanic Literature in 1966 from New York University. She completed her doctorate in 1979. She is married to Angel Nieto, a former teacher and children's book author, and they have two daughters and 11 grandchildren.

When Nieto began her teaching career in 1966 at Brooklyn's Junior High School, she found the school's environment more challenging than was being a new teacher! Everyone—teachers, staff, students, and parents—was angry. For this young Puerto Rican educator, it was sink or swim.

Two years later, Nieto joined the faculty of P.S. 25, the first completely bilingual school in the Northeast, where she learned that one can be academically successful and bilingual, and being bicultural is an asset. She also realized that no matter how hard some of her students tried, they failed. For most, college attendance—or even a high school diploma—was an unrealizable dream.

Nieto began to question whether individual teachers could fix urban education problems through hard work, dedication, and field trips. She began to see that conditions outside the control of most educators—including social stratification and discriminatory school policies and practices—severely limited students' learning opportunities. Unequal funding, lack of access to high-status knowledge, inadequate or stereotypical portrayals of diversity in the curriculum, rigid tracking, and discriminatory disciplinary and counseling practices, among others, all played roles in curbing educational opportunities for low-income, minority students.

Briefly, Nieto believes that:

- Effective teachers need to know more about the students they teach and use this knowledge in their curriculum and pedagogy.
- Effective teachers "love" their students. They believe that their students have the capacity—with hard work and support—to learn to high standards; and caring teachers demand that they do so. When children experience belonging and welcome, they are more likely to see themselves as "school kids" and invest in their own learning.
- Effective teachers need a passion for social justice. Given the profession's poor compensation, the enormous demands, and little power, the capacity to care and the desire to change the world can help tired teachers keep going.

Nieto's critics wonder whether her emphasis on multicultural education in teacher preparation programs risks taking time away from teaching effective pedagogy. Some reject the idea that teachers should accommodate students' cultural backgrounds and needs in their curriculum and instruction. Others suggest that the multicultural emphasis may make white educators feel defensive about the unearned benefits they receive from their skin color and social status.

Moving ahead, Nieto sees teaching as an ethical and political endeavor, a way to expand the human spirit and create a better world. . . . There is no doubt that individual teachers can and do profoundly influence the lives of their students." (What Keeps Teachers Going? 2000)

Sources: National Writing Project. (2008, January). Nieto to focus on why teachers stay—in spite of everything—at 2008 Spring Meeting. Berkeley, CA: Author. Retrieved from http://www.nwp.org/cs/public/print/doc/08sm/sonianieto.csp; Sonia Nieto (2009). http://sonianieto.com/aboutsonia.html; Nieto, S. (2005). Schools for a new majority. The role of teacher education in hard times. *The New Educator* 1(1), 27–43; Nieto, S. (2005). *Why we teach*. (2005). New York: Teachers College Press; Nieto, S. (1999). *The light in their eyes: Creating multicultural learning communities.* New York: Teachers College Press; Nieto, S. (2000). *What keeps teachers going? And other thoughts on the future of public education.* Talk given for the Distinguished Faculty Lecture Series, University of Massachusetts, Amherst. Retrieved from http://people.umass.edu/~snieto/UMass_Lecture.html.

▶II TeachSource Video 7.3

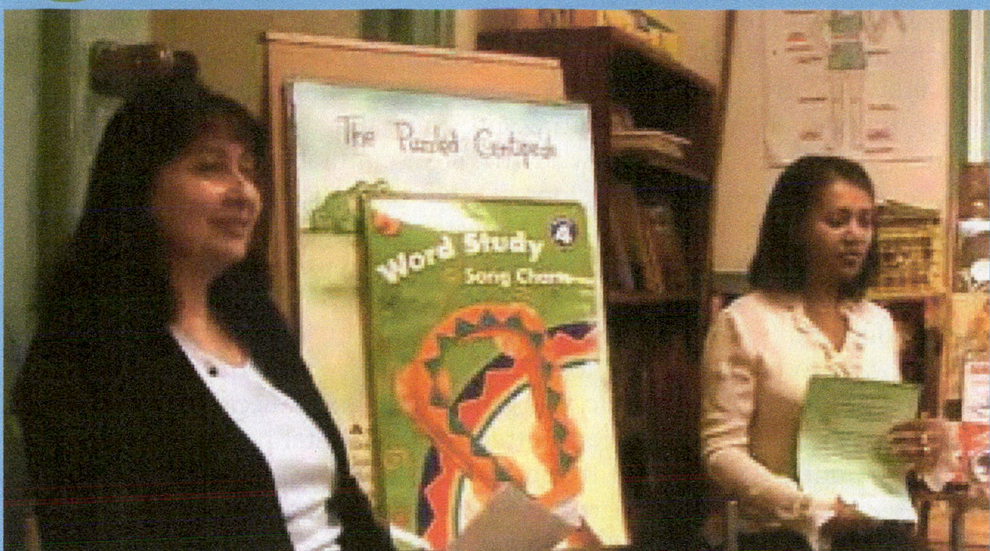

Culturally Responsive Teaching: A Multicultural Lesson for Elementary Students

Multiculturalism is about the similarities among human beings. Classrooms often contain many students from different cultures and countries. Recognizing and celebrating their uniqueness through the traditional curriculum is an example of culturally responsive teaching. Watch the video clips, study the artifacts in the case, and reflect on the following questions:

1. How does thematic planning help teachers be successful with a classroom of students from varied backgrounds and cultures?
2. What strategies did Dr. Hurley use to infuse her culturally responsive teaching into this lesson?
3. How does a teacher become a multicultural educator?

Watch on CourseMate.

world."[142] Effectively creating a multicultural school climate, curriculum, instruction, and positive teacher–student and student–student relationships can be a constructive means to change public schools' learning environment to make high expectations and equal opportunities a reality for all students.

7-7b Becoming Aware of (and Ending) Inequitable School Practices

Parents know that not all schools are created equal. Homebuyers routinely ask realtors to show them houses in school attendance zones with high test scores. With few exceptions, most students end up replicating their parents' place in the social hierarchy.

Educators, in contrast, tend to believe that schools are fair systems of opportunity. Although well intentioned, teachers do not always see that the educational system is tilted in their favor.

Teachers accept their schools as fair Teachers did not create the institutions in which they work; they simply fit themselves into their schools' existing patterns and norms. Most educators genuinely believe that schools are a meritocracy that provide a level playing field to all students. According to this perspective, it is the students' job to work hard, learn, and move ahead.

Likewise, educators are not often aware of the biased ideas that frame their perceptions and interactions with others. Educators generally believe that they are wholly objective professionals fully capable of interpreting situations and treating individuals in totally neutral and evenhanded ways. Likewise, future educators often come to teaching with little cross-cultural experience and knowledge and tend to have limited visions of what teaching students unlike themselves entails.[143] This lack of awareness creates one of the greatest obstacles to establishing more trusting and equitable relationships with the schools' multiple communities.

Thinking of this type reflects a strong acceptance of "difference blindness."[144] Teachers want to be fair and try to see and treat every student the same way—seemingly "blind" to racial, ethnic, and gender differences. Because teachers were socialized as Americans and as transmitters of our cultural heritage, they simply do not see, understand, or value that other ways of knowing and understanding the world exist. Yet, when teachers are not aware that others see the world differently than they do, communication and trust become more difficult.

cognitive dissonance The cognitive and affective state of discomfort created when someone receives information that does not fit with what one already believes.

"Difference blindness" is a form of cognitive dissonance. **Cognitive dissonance** is a theoretical construct used to explain how people respond to information that does not coincide with their current understandings or beliefs.[145] According to cognitive dissonance theory, an individual can experience an unpleasant psychological tension or dissonance when new knowledge or information does not fit with what he or she already knows or believes, and this anxiety motivates the individuals to reduce it.

For example, a future teacher may try to make sense of two contradictory beliefs: the belief the individual always held, "Schools are fair and advance *all* students' best interests," and a newer belief, "Schools are unfair and are tilted to disfavor lower-income and ethnic minority children." To reduce their psychological discomfort, the future teacher may react in any of three ways:

- Change the new cognition to make it consistent with the preexisting cognition (i.e., deny or devalue the research or anecdotal evidence that schools are unfair to lower income and children of color)
- Add new cognitions to bridge the gap between the conflicting cognitions (i.e., find additional information that supports the idea that many school practices disadvantage lower income and ethnic minority children)
- Change his or her behavior (i.e., stop supporting institutional practices such as rigid academic tracking altogether or use students' cultural assets to help them learn the academic content)[146]

Helping future teachers become fully aware of cognitive dissonance's internal discomfort *before* they experience it helps reduce their resistance to the unfamiliar ideas, prevents them from automatically rejecting the unsettling information, encourages their critical thinking, and promotes a classroom environment conducive to learning.[147]

It is important, therefore, for educators and prospective educators to consider ways the school, as an institution, may appear to those who do not share our norms or whom our practices harm. Unless we can see our schools' limitations and recognize when our unifying beliefs, systems, and practices are unfair to certain student groups, we will tend to interpret student failure or resistance as deviant or ill intentioned. Without full awareness of how our schools actually operate, educators' abilities to help all students become fully educated will remain limited.

Rethinking the difference-blind stance Those who support the "politics of difference" claim that although people share a universal desire to be treated as full and equal citizens, people do not have equal needs or equal opportunities within an unequal society. For example, they argue that racial and ethnic minorities have a specific need to overcome and remove social inequities in society and school. Because most whites have not had to struggle against prejudice and discrimination in this society, they do not recognize these issues as either existing or valid. Instead, while believing they are being professional and fair-minded, they use the difference-blind logic to silence or overlook these equity concerns. What is more, to recognize and admit such discrimination would create cognitive dissonance and the discomfort that goes with it.

Furthermore, those supporting the politics of difference assert that in an unequal society, a universal stance is not neutral but rather aligns with and reflects the dominant culture's concerns and traditions. Indeed, this "professional neutrality" systematically ignores the institutional practices that keep schools and society unequal and inequitable. And, the dominant or majority culture becomes the mold into which all other cultures must fit.

For all these reasons, schools too often fail to take seriously their responsibility to educate all children. As Colleen Larson and Carlos J. Ovando, multicultural scholars assert, "Although we have expanded our geographical borders in many of our school systems, we have failed to expand our psychic circles of community."[148]

Instead of showing bias, becoming conscious of student differences can be a way of valuing, supporting, and genuinely relating to children rather than a way of diminishing them. Developing this awareness of difference is not easy. All people have an unconscious tendency to confirm what they believe and to explain away what they do not. They unconsciously magnify those features that fit with their expectations and overlook the rest. Difference, however, does not necessarily mean "less than."

Our cognitive maps and feelings about student differences affect the ways we interact with others. When we can critically examine how our own behaviors, systems, and practices may contribute to minority students' problems in school, we can truly become professional educators for a pluralist society. Recognizing and accepting student differences also helps educators become advocates for making schools better places for all students. Doing the right thing for all students requires more than having good intentions. When educators recognize that difference matters, they can willingly accept their responsibility for expanding their circle of care beyond the community insiders and work to address the system's inequities.

Reflect & Discuss

This chapter contains some difficult material to internalize.

A. Which parts of this chapter did you have difficulty accepting or believing?
B. Which parts of this chapter would you most like to share with one of your public school teachers? Why?
C. Which ideas do you think will most influence you when you are a teacher in your own classroom? As a teacher and leader in your school?

7-7c Rethinking How to Close the Achievement Gap

The gap between public schools' rhetoric and the reality encountered in today's school systems is large, but aware educators are helping to bridge it. Clearly, schools still retain their critical mission to equalize each student's opportunities for education and economic advancement. At a time when our national population is becoming increasingly diverse and the marketplace requires everyone to have higher skill levels and more varied capacities to survive and thrive, it becomes even more essential that educators and their communities turn the rhetoric of equal opportunity into reality. Increasing our awareness of how schools limit equal opportunity—and sustain the achievement gap—through its assumptions, norms, and practices is the first step. Looking at our own attitudes and behaviors as they contribute to or reduce the problems is the next.

To reduce the achievement gap, we must recognize that only when all children are healthy, safe, engaged, supported, and challenged can they learn well in school. Yet schools are only one of the societal forces that influence students' learning. The larger society and its economic and political policies and actions also play significant roles. Nevertheless, educators must do what they can to remove obstacles to students' opportunities and provide necessary supports to help underserved students become fully educated for twenty-first-century economic viability and democratic citizenship.

Did You Get It?

What factors are most likely to reduce the achievement gap?

- **a.** Teachers and administrators should try to communicate clearly and effectively with their students from other cultures.
- **b.** Administrators should suspend disruptive students because they disrupt other students' learning.
- **c.** Teach a culturally broad curriculum: Western civilization was not formed in a vacuum.
- **d.** Teachers and administrators should have high expectations and high supports for all students.

Take the full quiz on CourseMate.

SUMMARY

- The historical perspectives on race, ethnicity, social class, and education in the United States show that America has long tried to balance the ideal of equality with the reality of its unequal society. Although education can increase social mobility, U.S. public schools have tended to reinforce the differences among students and maintain the social status quo.
- The United States is becoming increasingly more diverse with implications for everyone's quality of life. It is estimated by 2050, today's minorities will account for 54 percent of the U.S. population. Unless we can educate the upcoming workforce with high-level knowledge and skills so they can be self-sufficient and contribute tax dollars to support our social safety nets. our whole society will suffer.
- Social class creates a selective perception and set of experiences that shape a person's worldview, behaviors, and life options. Unless the public schools can provide Americans of differing backgrounds with a shared set of values and loyalties to the United States, finding common ground politically will become more difficult and societal tensions will likely increase.
- American public schools hold contradictory goals. In what was intended as a unifying experience in schools became one that increasingly separates students.
- Children's social class, parenting practices, and poverty are strongly related to their educational outcomes.
- School segregation harms students' academic achievement. In contrast, African Americans who attend predominantly integrated schools have higher academic, educational, economic, and social outcomes.
- Teacher expectations about which students are likely or unlikely to succeed in school significantly affect student achievement.
- School practices including tracking and ability grouping, teaching quality, disciplinary policies and practices, retention rates, and school climate all have significant effects on students' opportunities to benefit from their schooling experiences.

- Multicultural education seeks to promote Western values of democracy, freedom, human dignity, equality, and respect for individual differences with a curriculum that includes diverse voices and contributions. Research supports its positive impact on students' academic achievement.
- Awareness of schools' inequitable norms and practices helps educators overcome schools' institutional biases and making cultural pluralism and higher achievement for all students a reality. Recognizing these can help teachers create a more welcoming climate and greater learning opportunities for students that will increase their achievement.

Visit the Education CourseMate for this textbook to access the eBook, Did You Get It? quizzes, TeachSource Video Cases, flashcards, and more. Go to CengageBrain.com to log in, register, or purchase access.

Students' personal, familial, and cultural assets support their school achievement.

CHAPTER

8

Diversity and Cultural Assets in Education

InTASC Standards: 1, 2, 3, 4, 5, 6, 7, 8, 9, and 10

LEARNING OBJECTIVES

After you read this chapter, you should be able to:

8-1 Summarize how well diverse student groups are achieving.

8-2 Describe how people develop cultural and racial identities.

8-3 Discuss the relationship between minority students' perceptions—including stereotype threat and oppositional culture—and their academic performance.

8-4 Explain how various cultural assets help low-income and minority children succeed in school.

8-5 Identify how perceptions about students with disabilities can influence their schooling and academic performance.

8-6 Describe how teachers can use diverse students' cultural and personal assets to foster their resilience.

8-7 Compile at least 10 strategies that teachers can use to help diverse students succeed in school.

InTASC

"Teaching and learning are cultural processes that take place in a social context,"[1] observes Geneva Gay, multicultural scholar. She elaborates: "To make teaching and learning more accessible and equitable for a wide variety of students, students' cultures need to be more clearly understood. Such an understanding can be achieved by analyzing education from multiple cultural perspectives and thereby removing the blindness imposed on education by the dominant cultural experience."[2]

Students' personal, familial, and cultural factors all influence how well they achieve in school. The achievement gap persists for students who are African American, low income, Latino, Native American, English language learners, and have special learning needs. Although racial differences are not biological, they do have social and cultural implications. Apparently, members of any student group that largely differs from the typical white middle-class model around which public schools are organized face challenges to their school success. As outsiders to this norm, these students' unique family and societal histories, their cultural and peer influences, and sometimes their cultural and personal assets create a complex network of factors that influence how well students learn.

When teachers can recognize their own cultural beliefs, biases, and assumptions; acknowledge others' ethnic, cultural, and other differences in a nonjudgmental manner; and understand the ways in which schools often reflect and perpetuate the larger society's discriminatory practices,[3] they can better provide the culturally supportive and high expectations classrooms in which all students can succeed.

8-1 Diverse Students' Achievement

Looking at diverse students' achievement illustrates how well each student demographic group is learning in school. Low-income and minority students' current academic performance provides a platform from which to move educators toward more effective ways of thinking about and working with these students.

8-1a Low-Income, African American, and Latino Students' Achievement[4]

As discussed in Chapter 6, the more the years of education, the higher the employment rate and salaries. Thus those individuals who leave school without a diploma will have a very difficult time moving themselves or their families out of poverty.

Achievement gaps between students from higher- and lower-income families persist throughout the elementary and high school years. Figure 8.1 depicts this disparity by using scores from the National Assessment of Educational Progress (NAEP) Reading Test. The figure shows that low-income 12th graders read on a par with higher-income eighth graders (scores of 272 versus 271, respectively).

FIGURE 8.1 Achievement of Lower- and Higher-Income Students, Grades 4–12

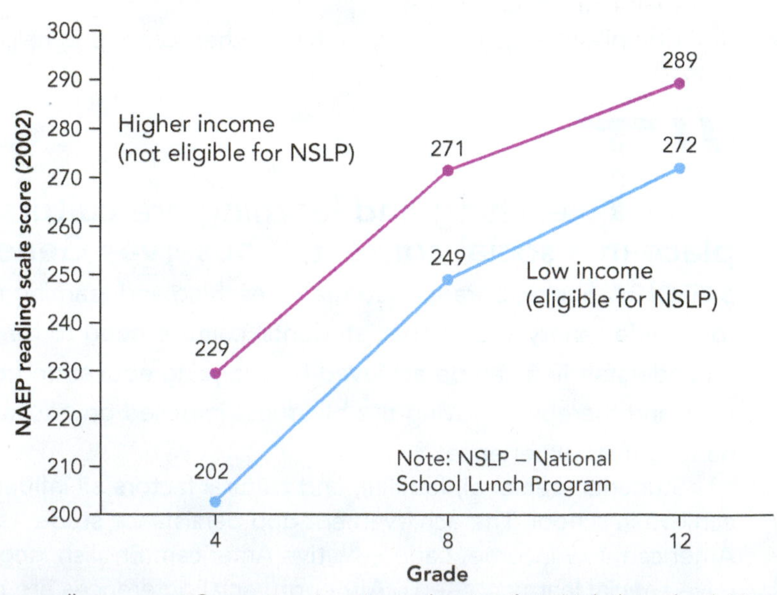

Source: From cradle to career: Connecting American education from birth through adulthood. (2007, January 4). *Quality Counts 2007, Education Week 26*(17), 5. Retrieved from http://www.edweek.org/media/ew/qc/2007/QC07_PressConference_Remarks.pdf.

The good news is that over the past few decades, NAEP scores for minority students have risen substantially. NAEP's long-term trend assessment scores in reading (1975) and mathematics (1978 and 2008) show that African American and Latino students' achievement has risen markedly. Findings show statistically significant, although modest, reductions in the percentage of minority students scoring at the lowest performance levels and increases in the percentage of students scoring at the highest performance levels. As Figure 8.2 shows, the increases were larger for African American and Latino students than for white students across all age groups, fourth, eighth, and 12th grades. Notably, over this time, most racial and ethnic score gaps narrowed compared to the first assessment. The most recent data (2004–2008), however, show that despite the real gains, the performance gap between African American and Latino as compared with white students remains relatively unchanged from what it was 20 years ago. Educational reforms enacted in schools made everyone's scores go up.

Nonetheless, large disparities exist by race and ethnicity among different student groups in the degree to which they complete high school and go on to college. College completion is a strong indicator of future income and quality of life. This factor, in turn, affects how well the college graduates' children are likely to do in school. As shown in Figure 8.3, more than seven in 10 Asian Americans ages 25 to 64 and more than six in 10 non-Latino white adults have completed at least some college. In contrast, nearly seven in 10 Latinos and half of African Americans have a high school diploma or less.

Too often, low-income, minority, and students with disabilities are considered "outsiders" to the mainstream culture. Looking more closely at the racial identities, cultures, attitudes, and beliefs that shape these young people can help prospective educators better understand their students' frames of reference and find their personal and cultural resources to help them succeed in school.

Reading

Age group	Changes from 1971		
	White	African American	Latino[1]
Age 9	↑ 14 points	↑ 34 points	↑ 25 points
Age 13	↑ 7 points	↑ 25 points	↑ 10 points
Age 17	↑ 4 points	↑ 28 points	↑ 17 points
	Changes from 2004		
Age group	White	African American	Latino
Age 9	↑ 4 points	↑ 7 points	↑ 8 points
Age 13	↑ 4 points	↑ 8 points	↔
Age 17	↑ 7 points	↔	↔

[1]Results for Latino students were first available In 1975. Therefore, the results shown in the 1971 section for Latino students are from the 1975 assessment.

Mathematics

Age group	Changes from 1973		
	White	African American	Latino
Age 9	↑ 25 points	↑ 34 points	↑ 32 points
Age 13	↑ 16 points	↑ 34 points	↑ 29 points
Age 17	↑ 4 points	↑ 17 points	↑ 16 points
	Changes from 2004		
Age group	White	African American	Latino
Age 9	↑ 5 points	↔	↔
Age 13	↔	↔	↔
Age 17	↔	↔	↔

↑ Indicates the score was higher in 2008.
↔ Indicates that there was no significant change in the score in 2008.

FIGURE 8.2 Increased NAEP Scores for Whites, Latinos, African Americans, 1970–2008

Source: NAEP. (April, 2009). *NAEP 2008 trends in academic progress. Reading 1971–2008; Mathematics 1973–2008 (NCES 2009-479)*. Washington, DC: Institute for Education Sciences, National Center for Education Statistics, U.S. Department of Education, p. 4.

Did You Get It?

Which statement is true about student achievement?

a. National Assessment of Educational Progress (NAEP) scores for minority students have risen substantially.
b. NAEP scores for minority students have declined substantially.
c. The performance gap between African American and Latino as compared with white students is much smaller than what it was 20 years ago.
d. Educational reforms enacted in schools were a tremendous failure: everyone's scores declined.

Take the full quiz on CourseMate.

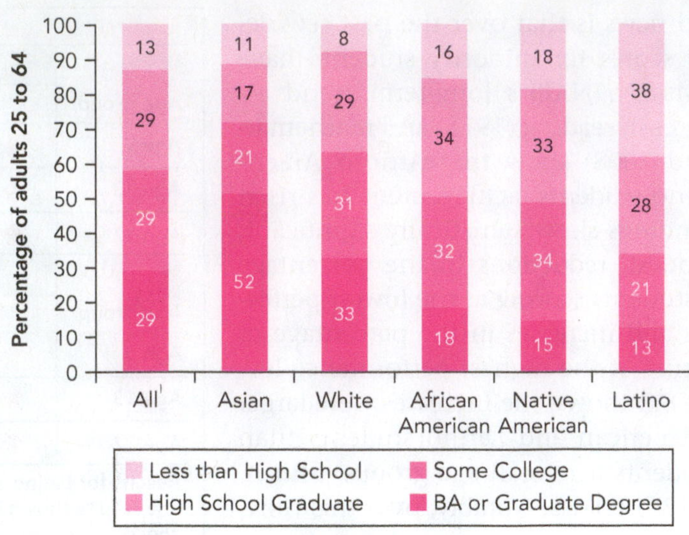

FIGURE 8.3 Education Rates by Race

Source: From cradle to career: Connecting American education from birth through adulthood. (2007, January 4). *Quality Counts 2007, Education Week 26*(17), 8. Retrieved from http://www.edweek.org/media/ew/qc/2007/QC07_PressConference_Remarks.pdf.

8-2 Developing Cultural and Racial Identities

culture The systems of values, viewpoints, and ways of knowing that steer communities of people in their daily lives

Our cultural heritages and backgrounds affect our lives in many ways. **Culture** is "the systems of values, beliefs, and ways of knowing that guide communities of people in their daily lives."[5] Culture always intersects with individuals' race, ethnicity, social class, gender, age, ability, status, and family traditions. These beliefs, shared traditions, language, values, and agreement about norms for living help people organize their world though language and other symbol systems. Culture also influences how various groups approach learning and problem solving, how they construct knowledge, and how they pass information through the generations.[6] Culture tells group members what is and is not acceptable behavior. It defines one's thinking and actions.

8-2a Culture and Learning

Research suggests that two broad cultural value systems—individualism and collectivism—shape people's thoughts and actions in almost all aspects of life.[7] Cultures that value individualism encourage their children to "live their own lives"; in contrast, cultures that favor a collectivist orientation make family and kinship ties lifetime priorities. Generally, the traditional American mainstream culture is individualistic, emphasizing self-reliance, rugged individualism, self-expression, and personal achievement. "Every man for himself" might describe the individualistic culture. Conversely, cultures including African American, Latino, Native American, Japanese, and many immigrant groups are collectivistic, stressing interdependence, cooperation, family unity, family and group success, respect, and social development.[8] The expressions "Many hands make light work" and "It takes a village" reflect the collectivist perspective.

From an individualistic perspective, learning is a personal matter. That is, individuals learn or construct knowledge. Students are responsible for their own learning, and the primary learning relationship is between teacher and child. If the student needs help, he or she asks the teacher for help. Academic assessment measures progress through individual scores. The work itself is most important; relationships come second. Education's goal is for students to do well academically and to show that ability through good grades and on-time promotions.[9]

In the alternative perspective, children from families who hold a collectivist orientation are socialized to work toward group goals rather than personal goals. They may be used to working together to help others with their tasks even before they consider their own assignments.[10] Their cultures emphasize learning embedded in a social context and group success rather than individual achievement.[11] Relationships are most important; academic tasks can be completed much more easily if students help and receive help from one another. Under this perspective, education's target is to produce a good and knowledgeable person who respects others and does not place himself or herself above others in importance.[12] Social and ethical development and cognitive and academic development are seen as integrated, rather than separate.[13]

The basic difference between these two viewpoints is the relative emphasis placed on individual versus group well-being. Every culture has both individualistic and collectivist values. Wide variations appear within each culture, and both approaches have advantages and disadvantages.[14] In addition, factors such as socioeconomic status (SES), rural or urban setting, and parents' formal educational level affect tendencies toward individualism versus collectivism. Specifically, in our Western culture, higher SES, urban settings, and increased parental education are associated with greater individualism.[15]

8-2b Stages of Self- and Group Identities

People develop cultural and racial identities through their interactions and responses to persons, events, media, and institutions that highlight the degree to which they are alike or different than others in their environment. Society and culture assign relative values to these similarities and differences. In turn, the sense and meaning that individuals derive from these experiences and the value judgments they make about them help define their self- and group identities.

Racial, ethnic, and cultural identities These identities are defined as a sense of collective identity based on a person's perception that he or she shares a common heritage with a particular racial, ethnic, or cultural group. These identities are critical parts of how persons see themselves both as individuals and as part of a larger group. Although the development of this collective identity does not necessarily happen in an inflexible chronological sequence, scholars believe that most minority group members go through relatively similar stages.

Children's racial and ethnic attitudes tend to crystallize around age 10.

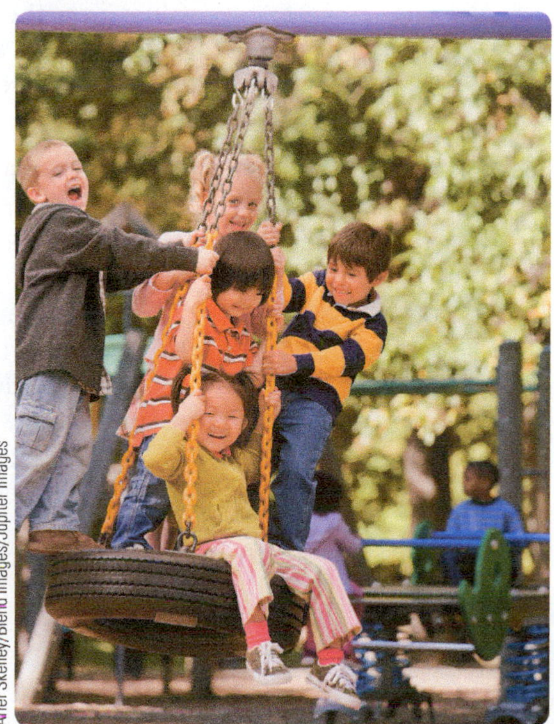

Ariel Skelley/Blend Images/Jupiter Images

For minority adolescents, race, ethnicity, and culture play important roles in their identity development. Racial and ethnic attitudes among children appear to crystallize by about age 10.[16] Their home, community, and school experiences all contribute to how children come to view and value themselves as individuals and as minority group members.

Observers have noted that minority groups share similar patterns of adjustment to living in a culture that does not value them.[17] In past decades, African Americans, Asian Americans, Latinos, and Native Americans have experienced changes in

TABLE 8.1

Racial and Cultural Identity Development

Stages of Minority Development Model	Attitude toward Self	Attitude toward Dominant Group
Stage 1: Conformity	Self-depreciating or neutral	Group appreciating
Stage 2: Dissonance and Appreciating	Conflict between self-depreciating and group-appreciating	Conflict between self-depreciating and group appreciating
Stage 3: Resistance and Immersion	Self-appreciating	Group depreciating
Stage 4: Introspection	Concern with the basis of self-appreciation	Concern with the basis of group depreciation
Stage 5: Integrative Awareness	Self-appreciating	Selective appreciation

Source: Adapted from Sue, D. W., and Sue, D. (2008). *Counseling the culturally diverse: Theory and practice*, 5th ed. Hoboken, NJ: John Wiley & Sons, Table 10.1, p. 243.

the ways they view themselves within American society: With an increasing sense of self-worth, they celebrate their own traditions and challenge the larger society to respect their worth. Their sense of cultural oppression is the mutually unifying force. As a result, researchers have integrated various cultural identity models to identify common features that cut across minority populations.

Table 8.1 illustrates a conceptual framework to help educators understand their culturally diverse students' attitudes and behaviors. This theoretical model defines five stages of development that those growing up outside the mainstream experience as they struggle to understand themselves in terms of their own culture, the dominant culture, and what they view as the oppressive relationship between the two: conformity, dissonance, resistance and immersion, introspection, and integrative awareness. At each identity level, attitudes and beliefs reflect the individual's experiences at that stage.[18]

Conformity stage Minority individuals strongly prefer the dominant cultural values over their own. They strongly identify with white Americans' lifestyles, value systems, and cultural and physical characteristics, while they disrespect, reject, or deny those most like their own minority group's.

Example As a young man, Malcolm X, the 1960s African American leader, straightened and dyed his hair to look more like a white male.[19] Asian women sometimes undergo surgery to change the shape of their eyes.

Dissonance stage Minority individuals receive information or have experiences that contradict the dominant culture's beliefs, attitudes, and values. The individual begins to question and challenge the conformity stage's attitudes and beliefs. The person becomes aware that racism exists. Not all aspects of the minority or majority culture are good or bad. Feeling pride in one's minority culture changes the way the person sees himself or herself—and the way the person sees others.

Example An Asian American who believes that Asians are inhibited and passive meets an Asian leader who seems outgoing, dynamic, and articulate. An African American youngster who sees playing sports as the fast-track to adult wealth and fame sees African American athletes who are both at the top of their profession and very well educated.

Resistance and immersion stage The culturally different individual tends to completely endorse minority-held views and rejects the dominant society's values and culture. The person actively seeks information and artifacts of his or her own group's history that enhances the individual's sense of identity and worth. The person may feel embarrassed and angry that he or she once devalued ("sold out") his or her own racial or cultural group and now feels intense pride and honor about that group's cultural and racial characteristics.

Example African American youth wear traditional African dashikis, plait their hair in customary African braids, or dress in urban styles.

Introspection stage The minority individual becomes uncomfortable with the rigid views of the resistance and immersion stage. The "all or nothing" approach is too simple (and often inaccurate) for the complex world they are coming to know. The person no longer wants to hold back his or her own expanding views and choices in an effort to please the group. The minority individual must choose between responsibility and loyalty to his or her own personal independence or go along with group conformity.

Example A Latino individual who develops a close friendship with a white person may feel considerable pressure from his or her culturally similar peers to end the relationship with "the Gringo." An African American teen who takes schoolwork seriously, aspires to attend college, and considers white classmates as friends may be called "Oreo" by racial peers.[20]

Integrative awareness stage Minority persons have developed an inner sense of security, a positive self-image, and confidence, and they can appreciate the unique aspects of their own culture as well as those of the dominant U.S. culture. They realize that minority and white cultures are not always in conflict. The individual has greater control and flexibility, believing that all cultures have both acceptable and unacceptable aspects. The person feels to be a member of his or her own racial or cultural group, of the larger society, and of the human race.

Example A Latino can be good friends with other Latinos, whites, African Americans, and any other persons who have the qualities that make for strong, mutually respectful relationships.

Cultural identity development influences individuals' own identity development. Different persons experience these stages at different times and at varying rates, depending on their experiences and personalities. For this reason, teachers cannot expect all of their minority students to be at the same stage at the same time. Students may grow and change in their cultural or racial identity development throughout the year. When teachers understand that this process occurs, they can better understand and accept their diverse students as maturing individuals.

8-2c Developing a White Racial Identity

White persons also have a racial/cultural identity. White persons in U.S. society have consciously or unconsciously learned racial biases, prejudices, misinformation, and negative stereotypes through cultural conditioning. Few think about what it means to be "white" in our society, rarely perceive race as belonging to them, or recognize the privilege that comes to them because of their white skin.[21] Because being white is the U.S. cultural norm, "it acts as an invisible veil that limits many people from seeing it as a cultural system."[22] Being white is so interwoven into everyday living that whites, at times, cannot step outside and see their beliefs, values, and behaviors as creating a distinct cultural group.

White educators benefit when they can understand their own racial/cultural identity within a pluralistic society. Like minority persons, white people go through racial identity changes. In any multicultural encounter, the status of white racial identity development affects the process and outcome of interracial relationships. By going through the same stages as discussed previously in the minority racial/cultural identity development model (plus one earlier phase and one later phase), white persons experience their own racial/cultural self-awareness.[23]

Naiveté phase During life's first three years, the child experiences immature, neutral, open, and spontaneous curiosity about race. Between ages 3 and 5, the young white child begins to associate positive meaning with his or her own ethnic group and negative meaning with other groups, gradually developing a sense of superiority about the concept of whiteness from the media and significant others in the child's life.

Example A white 4-year-old meets an African American 4-year-old on the playground, and they begin to play together. Their parents exchange quick glances and after a few minutes, the white parent exclaims, "It's time to go now!" and takes the child away.

Conformity phase The white person consciously or unconsciously comes to believe that the white culture is the most highly developed, and that all other cultures are primitive or inferior. The person has minimal awareness of the self as a racial being and strong belief that his or her values and norms governing behavior are universal. The white person has limited accurate knowledge of other cultural or racial groups and tends to rely on stereotypes as the main source of information.

Example A white person believes that "people are people," they are "color blind," and racial/ethnic differences are unimportant, yet asserts that minority persons would not have problems if they "worked harder, assimilated better, spoke better English, or valued education."

Dissonance phase The white person is forced to deal with the inconsistencies when confronted with information or experiences at odds with his or her denial of racial differences or with the inaccuracies of the stereotypes they hold about others. The person must examine his or her own cultural values and see the conflict between upholding humanistic nonracist values and the person's own contradictory behavior—or between the stereotype and their actual experiences with others unlike themselves.

Example A person who consciously believes that "all men and women are created equal" and does not discriminate suddenly has qualms about having an African American family move next door or have his or her son or daughter date a person of color. A white person gets to know someone from a different ethnic, racial, or religious group and finds that this individual does not fit the stereotype.

Resistance and immersion phase The white person begins to question and challenge his or her own racism. The individual sees stereotypes portrayed and perpetuated in advertising, television, interpersonal interactions, and U.S. culture and institutions. The person recognizes how being white has provided him or her with certain advantages that are denied to various minority groups. The white person feels angry at the larger society and guilty about having been part of an oppressive system.

Example A "white liberal" may want to paternalistically protect minority group members from unfair treatment.

Introspective phase The white person reflects on what it means to be white and accepts his or her whiteness. The individual recognizes that he or she has benefited from white privilege and may never fully understand the minority experience but feels disconnected from the Euro-American group, too. The person speaks with and observes the white group but also actively initiates experiences and interactions with various minority group members.

Example The white person with minority friends feels disconnected and confused making a transition from one perspective to another.

Integrative awareness phase The white person understands self as a racial/cultural being, understands the social and political forces that influence racism, appreciates racial/cultural diversity, and shows increased commitment to ending racial/cultural mistreatment. The person develops a nonracist white Euro-American identity, values multiculturalism, and feels comfortable with members of culturally diverse groups.

Example A white person develops the inner security and strength needed to function in a multicultural society that only marginally accepts such an integratively aware white person.

Commitment to antiracist action phase The white person enacts an increased commitment to end oppression, seeing "wrong" and actively working to make it "right."

Example The white person objects to racist jokes; tries to educate family, friends, and coworkers about racial issues; and takes direct action to end racism in schools and at work. A prospective teacher decides to consciously develop and refine culturally competent pedagogy during professional preparation and in the classroom.

Becoming aware of one's own white identity is an important facet of multicultural competence. But if an educator does not notice a student's race or culture, then the teacher does not really see the child. Teachers working in a pluralistic society become able to develop better relationships with the wide range of students they encounter in their classrooms when they can understand themselves and their students as persons with unique racial/cultural identities, values, and personal/cultural assets who come together in schools for the common purpose of teaching and learning.

8-2d Limitations of the Racial/Cultural Identity Models

Cultural identity development is a dynamic process. Some persons show behaviors and attitudes characteristic of several stages at the same time. For example, they may exhibit conformity characteristics in certain situations, yet show resistance and immersion behaviors in other circumstances. Some individuals move through the stages in a straight line at differing rates, whereas others may move back and forth between stages. These theoretical models are a conceptual framework intended to help understand student development[24]; they are not a set of fixed, rigid rules.

In addition, the cultural identity development model does not fit all minority situations. For instance, recent Asian immigrants to the United States tend to hold very positive and favorable views of their own culture and already possess an intact racial/cultural identity.[25]

Another criticism notes that racial/cultural identity models imply a value judgment, assuming that some cultural resolutions are healthier than others. For example, the racial/cultural identity model suggests that the integrative awareness stage represents a higher form of healthy functioning. Likewise, the models also lack an adequate consideration of gender, class, sexual orientation, and other group identities. Nor is racial/cultural identity a simple, global concept. Much evidence is mounting that although identity may move sequentially through identifiable stages, affective, attitudinal, cognitive, and behavioral components may not develop in a uniform manner.[26]

Finally, sociocultural forces affect identity development. Many of the early African American identity development models arose as a result of perceived and real experiences of oppression in our society. The increasingly visible racial/cultural movements of Native Americans, Latinos, and African Americans happened at a time of heightened racial and cultural awareness and pride. The times themselves, in conjunction with the cultural forces in play, can greatly affect—either facilitate or impede—cultural identity development.[27]

8-2e Research on Racial and Cultural Identities in School

Students' racial and cultural identities are strongly related to their behaviors. Specifically, students with positive racial and cultural identities are more likely to be successful in school. In a study of African American and mixed-race adolescents (ages 10–15), researchers found that racial and cultural identity was significantly related to their behavior adjustment. Positive racial and cultural identity was associated with more active coping, fewer beliefs supporting aggression, and less hostile or combative behaviors.[28] Racial and cultural identity has also been significantly related to positive school adjustment.[29] Investigators have found that cultural minority adolescents who interacted more with peers of the same cultural background had more developed levels of cultural identity.[30]

Advanced levels of racial and cultural identity development are a significant predictor of positive social adaptation and emotional adjustment for African American and white adolescents.[31] This adjustment is a critical factor in school learning and appropriate behaviors. Moreover, racial and cultural identity and self-esteem/self-concept have positive relationships in middle school,[32] high school,[33] and college-age[34] students.

One study examined how African American adolescents' deductive reasoning and school performance were related to their socioeconomic status, racial/cultural identity, and self-esteem.[35] The researchers found that better reasoning performance was associated with stronger—not

Reflect & Discuss

People develop a racial/cultural identity through various cognitive and emotional stages.

A. Using Table 8.1 and the discussion of minority and white racial/cultural identities, speak with a partner about how you personally experienced your own racial/cultural identity development.

B. Which commonalities do you and your partner find in your racial/cultural identity development experiences? What differences?

C. As a class, discuss how your racial/cultural identity development experiences compare with those noted in this chapter and compared with one another.

D. Does your class have any personal findings that you would like to add to the stages or phases noted to make them more accurate or clear?

Reflect & Discuss

Developing a racial/cultural identity typically involves the stages described in the text, although not necessarily in the same sequence.

A. Separate into two groups. One group will work with the minority racial/cultural identity development model, and the other will work with the white racial/cultural identity development model. The groups should be racially mixed.
B. For approximately 20 minutes, each group should discuss the racial identity development described in its assigned table. Give examples from personal experience or observations that illustrate each stage.
C. Each group will create a large graphic image or images to illustrate each stage and its meaning.
D. Present group graphics and explanations to the rest of the class.
E. As a class, discuss how the minority and white racial identity models are alike and how they differ.
F. Class members may volunteer to describe their own experiences in developing a racial identity, including the difficulties, the surprises, and their current phase in the process.

weaker—racial/cultural identity.[36] The more comfortable the African American students were in their minority identity, the more effective their thinking. At the same time, these general patterns do not hold true for all individuals.

The research suggests that simply being a member of a racial or cultural minority group does not predict higher or lower levels of self-esteem. Instead, it is the *sense of belonging* that students feel toward their racial or cultural group that better predicts self-esteem.[37] Studies have shown that the stronger the sense of cultural or racial identity, the higher the individual's self-confidence and self-esteem. Conversely, those persons who have not examined or developed a clear sense of racial or cultural identity tend to have low self-regard and feelings of inadequacy. This relationship holds true for all racial and cultural groups.

Additional studies have found that social support from family and friends can help youths develop cultural identity and a higher level of self-esteem.[38] When young people have positive family, community, and cultural reinforcement for their racial and cultural identity, the more ably they can resist and accommodate any negative social and media messages. Students who feel good about themselves and have a positive sense of their own value are more likely to work hard and have high achievement in school.

Did You Get It?

Which two broad cultural value systems shape people's thoughts and actions in almost all aspects of life (and have attendant implications for educational systems)?

a. Socialism and capitalism.
b. Deism and rationalism.
c. Civility and barbarism.
d. Individualism and collectivism.

Take the full quiz on CourseMate.

8-3 Minority Students' Perceptions and Academic Performance

Students' perceptions and performances seem to have a chicken-and-egg complexity. Do minority students perceive and behave as they do because of how they are treated and taught in schools? Or are they treated and taught in schools because of the ways they perceive and behave? The answer seems to be "Yes" to both.[39]

In addition to the research-documented connection between SES and school success, group cultural patterns or the relationships between these groups and the larger society may also frustrate their identification with school. Claude Steele's stereotype threat theory and John Ogbu's ideas about "oppositional" culture describe how many minority students' views and emotions influence their levels of academic achievement.

8-3a "Stereotype Threat" Theory and Underachievement

It may seem logical—but is actually inaccurate—to assume that the African American students' educational disadvantages affect only low-income students. In reality, even middle- and upper-class African American students have perceptions that limit their education.[40] Claude M. Steele, a Stanford University social psychology professor, has suggested that **stereotype threat** is a coping strategy that hurts high-striving, middle-income African American students' achievement. Put simply, stereotype threat is the idea that people tend to underperform when confronted with situations that might confirm negative stereotypes about their social group.

stereotype threat A coping strategy, the idea that people tend to underperform when confronted with situations that might confirm negative stereotypes about their social group.

Stereotype threat occurs when an individual who really cares about doing well is placed in a circumstance in which a negative group stereotype could apply. For example, an African American student does not want to accidentally do something (such as perform poorly on an important exam) that might inadvertently confirm a stereotype (of unintelligent African American students) to observers. The student does not want to embarrass himself or herself or cause observers to judge the individual harshly or treat the individual unfairly. This fear of confirming the stereotype may be distracting enough to the individual that the person actually makes careless mistakes.

In a series of ingenious experiments, Steele found that when students were told that the test they were about to take tended to produce achievement differences such that women and minority students scored at a lower level, that outcome was exactly what happened. In the control groups, where students took the same test but were not told about any expected performance differences among different student groups, no performance differences appeared.[41] These effects have been documented in more than 200 studies involving a variety of situations.[42]

In Steele's studies, highly capable students seemed to be trying too hard. They reread the questions and multiple choices and rechecked their answers more often than when they did not face stereotype threat. When this finding is applied to schools, it implies that when capable African American students take a difficult test, their anxiety about not wanting to perform poorly may cause them to make mistakes. In other words, their perceptions of the threat become self-fulfilling prophecies.

Sometimes students respond to stereotype threat by pretending that school is not important. Steele concluded that some students use **disidentification**—or withdrawal of psychic investment—to remove themselves from this perceived threat. Worried that society's negative perceptions and discrimination of their group will compromise their own futures if they appear to match the stereotype, these students try to avoid the humiliation of appearing less capable. Instead, they defensively pretend they are not interested or invested in schooling and its norms. They rationalize their poor performance as a lack of interest in the subject rather than as an inability to master it. They act cool and unconcerned in an effort to save face. Such students may avoid situations that seem potentially threatening, setting up a negative spiral. Appearing

disidentification A coping strategy, a withdrawal of psychic investment to remove oneself from a perceived threat.

not to care about school success may even become a group norm. In contrast, while these students respond to stereotype threat by underperforming, others work even harder to achieve.[43]

Interestingly, scholars have found evidence of stereotype threat occurring among elementary school girls taking mathematics tests, elderly people given a memory test, and white men being assessed on athletic ability.[44] White men who were outperforming African American and female students were themselves vulnerable to the stereotype threat. When researchers told them that the same tests were being used to compare their abilities with those of Asian Americans, white male performance worsened.[45] Even something as subtle as asking students to indicate their race or gender on a test form can trigger the phenomenon.[46]

Critics challenge Steele's theory, asserting that students' vulnerability to stereotype threat and disidentification are universal characteristics; that is, they do not belong solely to African American or other underachieving minority students.[47] What is more, teachers can create learning environments that reduce stereotype threat's negative outcomes. Studies have found that students are more motivated and able to achieve when they believe that intelligence is malleable rather than a trait fixed at birth, that hard work and a positive outlook can improve their grades and close achievement gaps, and when classroom activities "affirm" their values and boost their confidence.[48]

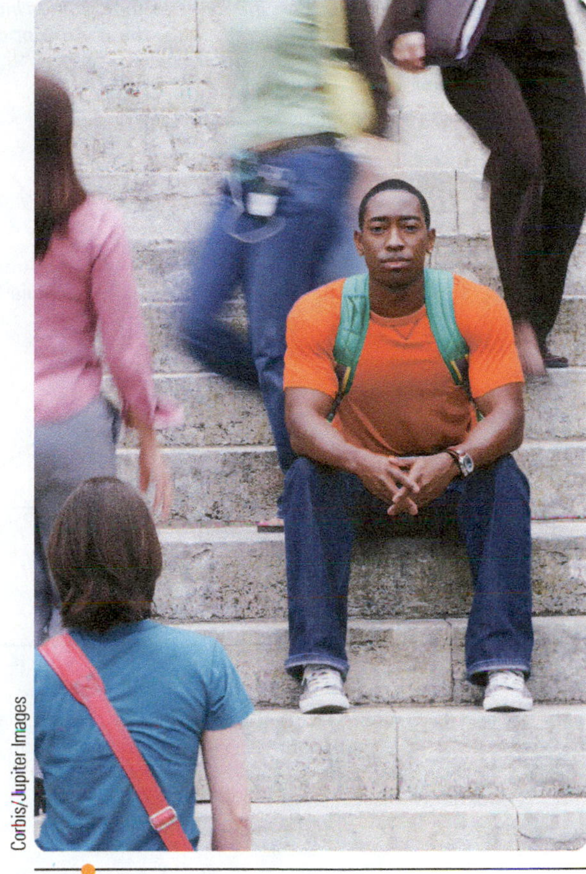

Corbis/Jupiter Images

Stereotype threat undermines capable students' capacity to succeed.

8-3b Oppositional Culture Theory and Underachievement

Low-income and minority students' underachievement is a very complex phenomenon with a variety of causes. John Ogbu, the late University of California–Berkeley professor (profiled later in this chapter), believed that although structural barriers and school factors affect minority school performance, minorities are also autonomous human beings who actively interpret and respond to their situation in ways that can either help or hurt themselves.[49]

To achieve is to "Be White" "Acting white" is a set of social interactions in which minority adolescents who get good grades in school enjoy less social popularity than white students who do well academically.[50] For example, when asked to identify "acting white" behavior, African American students name actions ranging from speaking standard English and enrolling in an Advanced Placement or Honors class to wearing clothes from the Gap or Abercrombie & Fitch (instead of Tommy Hilfiger or FUBU) and wearing shorts in winter.[51]

Anthropologists Signithia Fordham and John Ogbu helped bring this phenomenon to public attention. They suggested an **oppositional culture theory** that seeks to explain why minority students often do poorly in school. According to their theory, African American students respond to institutionalized racism by believing that high achievement in school would cause them to lose their minority identity or betray their minority peers by "acting white."[52] Along the way, they come to champion their minority identity, especially in terms of the ways in which they differ from the dominant white society.[53]

oppositional culture theory A concept that African American students respond to institutionalized racism by believing that high achievement in school would cause them to lose their minority identity or betray their minority peers by "acting white."

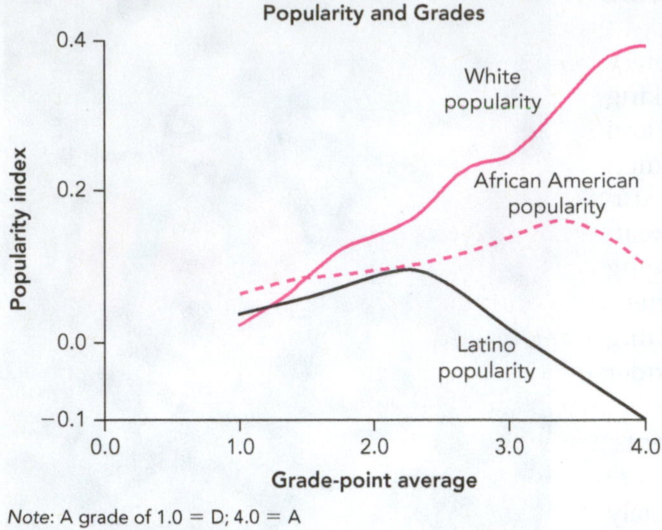

FIGURE 8.4 Pressure to Be Average

Source: Fryer, R. G. (2006, Winter). "Acting white": The social price paid by the best and brightest minority students. *Education Next* 6(1). Stanford University: Hoover Institution. Retrieved from http://educationnext.org/actingwhite/.

Other observers, however, place the blame for "acting white" squarely on the shoulders of African Americans. The Manhattan Institute's John McWhorter, for example, contrasts African American youth culture with that of immigrants (including blacks from the Caribbean and Africa) who "haven't sabotaged themselves through victimology."[54]

These two theories—the former blaming "acting white" on a racist society, the latter blaming it on self-imposed cultural sabotage—have emerged as the predominant explanations for "acting white" among African Americans.[55]

One study gathered evidence of how "acting white" affects minority students' popularity. Figure 8.4 shows large differences in the relationship between academic achievement and popularity among whites, African Americans, and Latinos. At low grade-point averages (GPAs), ethnic groups show little difference, and African Americans are actually more popular within their ethnic group than whites are within theirs. But when a student achieves a 2.5 GPA (an even mix of B and C grades), clear differences start to appear. As the GPAs of African American students increase beyond this point, they tend to have fewer and fewer friends. An African American student with a 4.0 GPA has, on average, 1.5 fewer friends of the same ethnicity than a white student with the same GPA. A Latino student with a 4.0 GPA is the least popular of all Latino students, and Latino–white differences among high achievers are the most extreme. These findings were true for public school students but less true for private school students, however.[56]

These oppositional beliefs create dilemmas for minority students: succeed and betray or fail and be loyal. They feel forced to choose between (1) conforming to the school's demands and rewards for certain attitudes and behaviors that are perceived as "white," especially mastering and using standard English—that is, getting the education they need—and risking their minority community's rejection, or (2) accepting their community's interpretations and disapproval of or, at the least, ambivalence toward those mainstream (white) attitudes and behaviors, gaining peer approval by not performing well in school, and risking not getting the education they need.[57]

"Oppositional identities" appear in African American students from all socioeconomic backgrounds. Regardless of family income and social class background, any African American student may view school success as undermining his or her minority identity. In this way, middle- and upper-income African American youths may devalue academic pursuits and adopt self-defeating behaviors that jeopardize their academic success.[58]

The schools' climate may be a factor in these behaviors. Geneva Gay, a multicultural scholar, observes that if students feel that the school environment is alien and hostile toward them or does not affirm and value who they are (as many minority students believe), they will not be able to concentrate as intently as they might on academic tasks. The stress and anxiety that accompany this perceived lack of support and affirmation are likely to drain these students' mental attention, energy, and efforts, pulling them away from the academic tasks and toward protecting themselves from (psychological) attack. As a consequence, they become less willing to persist at academic tasks and less able to think clearly about the learning, and their schoolwork suffers.[59]

8-3c Coping Strategies That Promote School Success

Coping with school success and peer acceptance does not have to be an either–or situation for minority students. A continuum links the two untenable extremes of "succeed and betray" or "fail and be loyal."[60]

Table 8.2 shows the various strategies that minority student use to find a middle ground between "acting white" and failing in school. Ogbu suggests that these coping strategies allow students to behave in ways that keep both their teachers and their peers happy. The lower the number on the continuum, the greater the acceptance of school norms and rejection of peer group norms.

These coping strategies allow minority students to overcome the psychological barriers to learning that they find in school. Minority students can keep and enhance their racial identity by not appearing too successful in a "white" environment but still doing enough to please their teachers and keep the doors open to future opportunities. Some students may "camouflage" their academic behaviors with posed disinterest—reducing their efforts by not paying attention in class, not keeping up with school assignments, or complaining that the work is boring. Other students openly defy and challenge the teachers' authority. In these ways, they can be good students and still keep peer support. Along the continuum, students try to spit the difference between "selling out" and outright failing.

Ogbu's oppositional culture theory does not suggest that group membership alone determines school success or failure. Although this perspective can

TABLE 8.2

Ogbu's Continuum of Adaptive Strategies

Level on Continuum	Adaptive Strategies
1. Emulation of whites or cultural passing	Adopting "white" academic attitudes and behaviors or trying to behave like middle-income white students. This approach usually has a high psychological cost and isolation from African American peers.
2. Accommodation without assimilation	A student adopting this strategy behaves according to school norms at school but according to African American or other cultural norms at home and in the community.
3. Camouflage	Disguising true academic attitudes and behaviors by using a variety of techniques: becoming a class clown, pretending lack of interest in school, studying in secret, becoming involved in "acceptable" cultural activities such as sports. Good grades are attributed to "natural smartness" rather than hard work.
4. Involvement in church activities	Promoting school success while participating with one's own community and building an achievement-oriented peer group.
5. Attending private schools	For some, a successful way to get away from negative peer groups.
6. Mentors	Another success-enhancing strategy that encourages academic success while still feeling good about oneself as a minority group member.
7. Protection	A few students get bullies to protect them from peer pressure in return for helping the bullies with their homework.
8. Remedial and intervention programs	Some students succeed with extra time and assistance focused on achieving well in school.
9. Encapsulation	May become trapped in peer group logic and activities. These African American or other cultural minority students do not want to do the "white man's thing" and, as a result, often fail.

Source: Adapted from Ogbu, J. U. (1992). Understanding cultural diversity and learning. *Educational Researcher 21*, 11.

American Education Spotlight

John U. Ogbu

John U. Ogbu, professor, minority education pathfinder

Professor John U. Ogbu did not mind stirring controversy with his theories about minority underachievement. In 1986, he coauthored a study that concluded African American students in a Washington, DC, high school didn't live up to their academic potential because they feared accusations of "acting white." In another attention-getting inquiry, he concluded that middle-class African American students living in affluent Shaker Heights, Ohio, held self-defeating cultural attitudes that hindered their academic achievement.

John Uzo Ogbu (1939–2003) was a path-breaking scholar in the fields of minority education and identity. His work focused on understanding how race and ethnic differences made some groups more successful than others. He is credited with causing a major paradigm shift in American education.

Born in Nigeria, the son of farmers, Ogbu attended a local Presbyterian high school and, later, a teacher's college. Planning to become a minister, he was sent to Princeton University Theological Seminary. There, he realized that to work for the church in Nigeria, he needed to know more about his own country.

He transferred to the University of California at Berkeley for his BA degree (1961), masters (1969), and PhD (1971) in anthropology. From 1968 to 1970, he worked as an ethnographer in Stockton, California. He began teaching in U.C. Berkeley's Anthropology Department in 1970 and was promoted to full professor in 1980.

At the heart of Ogbu's work is his typology of minority groups: voluntary and involuntary. *Voluntary minority groups* (immigrants) come by choice for economic betterment. Despite some discrimination, they are willing to learn, accept, and adapt to the majority group's cultural norms. They want to join the mainstream, see schooling as a necessity, and are steady academic achievers. In contrast, *involuntary minority groups* come as a result of conquest, enforced migration, or enslavement. African Americans, Mexicans, and Puerto Ricans are examples. Their resulting cultural attitudes, behaviors, and collective identity tend to be "oppositional"—resistant to the dominant society's imposed educational norms and values. They tend to be persistent academic failures. Ogbu's distinctions became part of the groundwork for understanding and debate on race and ethnic differences in educational and economic achievement.

In 1997, Ogbu and his research assistant moved to Shaker Heights, Ohio, an upper-middle-class city. Students, children of African American doctors, lawyers, and judges, came from a comparably level socioeconomic playing field. Schools had strong teachers and received equitable funding. Using ethnographic methods, the researchers reviewed data and test scores; observed 110 different classes from kindergarten through high school; and conducted exhaustive interviews with school personnel, African American parents, and students.

Their unexpected conclusion: Parents' and students' own attitudes accounted for the students' poor academic performance. Almost all the students admitted that they simply failed to put academic achievement before other pursuits such as TV, work, playing sports, or talking on the phone. Similar to their low-income, urban counterparts, the average affluent African American student, Ogbu concluded, was part of a peer culture that looked down on academic success as "acting white." Their middle- and upper-class college-educated parents did not supervise their children's homework, attend school events, or motivate their children to study. This, too, was a cultural norm, Ogbu reckoned.

He also believed that minorities had room to make constructive choices and take responsibility for their self-defeating actions.

Ogbu's conclusions generated discussion and criticism. Some called him a "sellout" who "blamed the victim," challenged his ideas and lack of familiarity with successful African American students, criticized his research methods and assumptions, or argued that he failed to demonstrate a causal relationship between structural factors and behavior. In response, Ogbu asserted, "I look below the surface and they don't like it."

Perhaps the truest testament to a scholar is the longevity of his/her ideas.

Sources: Biography. (2003). In Memoriam of Professor John U. Ogbu, 1939–2003. Retrieved from http://www.ogbu.com/; http://www.universityofcalifornia.edu/senate/inmemoriam/johnogbu.htm; Foster, K. M. (2004, December). Coming to terms: A discussion of Ogbu's cultural-ecological theory of minority academic achievement. *Intercultural Education 15*(4), 369–84; Goldsmith, S. (2003, May 21). *Rich, black, flunking.* Oakland, CA: East Bay Express. Retrieved from http://www.eastbayexpress.com/gyrobase/rich-black-flunking/Content?oid=1070459&storyPage=2; Harpalani, V., and Gunn, R. (2003, Fall). Contributions, controversies, and criticism: In memory of John U. Ogbu. *Penn GSE Perspectivs on Urban Education 1* (2), 2. Retrieved from http://www.urbanedjournal.org/archive/Issue4/Ogbu.pdf. Maclay, K. (2003, August 26). Anthropology professor John Ogbu dies at age 64. *UCBerkeley News.* Retrieved from http://berkeley.edu/news/media/releases/2003/08/26_ogbu.shtml.

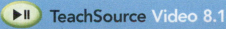

TeachSource Video 8.1

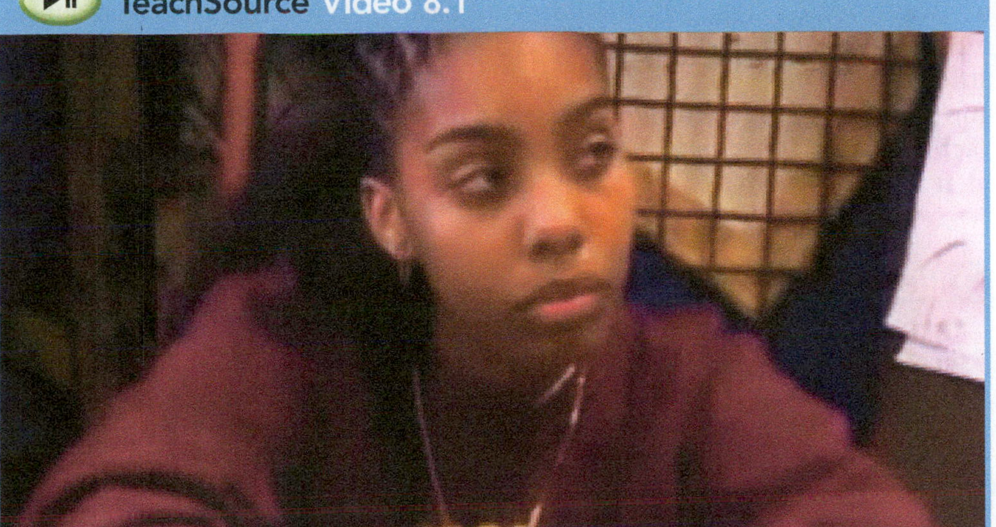

© 2015 Cengage Learning

Social and Emotional Development: The Influence of Peer Groups

For adolescents, much of the school day is not about learning. It is about getting along with peers. Having the opportunity to share their ideas and concerns about peer pressure in a safe, open classroom environment of mutual respect can help teens learn how to recognize negative peer pressure and try out—and learn—constructive ways to handle it. Watch the video clips, study the artifacts in the case, and reflect on the following questions:

1. Explain why peer pressure is such a difficult dynamic for young teens to handle.
2. Why is students' social and emotional development a legitimate concern for teachers and a necessary part of the school curriculum?
3. How can a teacher create a safe, open classroom climate of mutual respect that will allow students to express their fears and concerns and try out new behaviors?
4. Describe ways in which peer pressure can be a positive influence for young teens—and especially for minority teens.

Watch on CourseMate.

Reflect & Discuss

Table 8.2 identifies nine ways minority students sometimes try to succeed in school without appearing to do so.

A. Class members will form nine small groups and each group will select one of the nine continuum levels that have been printed on separate strips of paper and selected randomly. Students should not tell any other group which level they have.

B. Each group will discuss its continuum level and its adaptive strategies. The group members will identify several student behaviors that might represent this level and create a brief skit to illustrate its adaptive strategies.

C. Groups will take turns acting out their adaptive strategies. Class members will guess which level and which strategies they are seeing.

D. Discuss these strategies and the continuum as a class. Which of these have classmates seen in action? Which of these have any class members used? Have them explain their reasons and feelings for using them.

E. Discuss how teachers can use this awareness of these adaptive behaviors to help minority students succeed.

help educators better understand why some minority students may behave the way they do, teachers should avoid basing their expectations about an individual's academic performance and behavior on group membership. Students always should be treated as individuals. Educators must recognize and address minority students' mistrust of schools and fear of being seen as "acting white" without being disloyal to their peers or their own cultural identity.

Did You Get It?

Pick the following true statement about stereotype threat or oppositional theory.

a. Stereotype threat occurs when an individual who really cares about doing well is placed in a circumstance in which a negative group stereotype could apply; the fear of confirming the stereotype, despite being highly unpleasant, results in increased accuracy and an almost defiant certainty.

b. Stereotype threat occurs when an individual who really cares about doing well is placed in a circumstance in which a negative group stereotype could apply; the fear of confirming the stereotype is often distracting enough to the individual that the person actually makes mistakes.

c. African American students respond to institutionalized racism by believing that high achievement in school confirms their leadership ability and that low achievement, especially if it is the result of inadequate preparation, is "bein' the white man's field hand."

d. Over the past decade and a half, the popularity of Latino and African American students has become positively correlated to their grades and, especially, the work they put into earning them.

Take the full quiz on CourseMate.

8-4 Using Student Assets to Increase Learning

Over the years, research clearly affirms that when teachers lack the necessary skills to teach all students effectively—regardless of race, class, or culture—students are less likely to achieve and classrooms are more likely to be disruptive and disorderly.[61] The reason: students learn through relationships. If students like their teacher, they are willing to work hard to learn for him or her. In contrast, when educators have difficulty establishing respectful, caring, and mutually helpful relationships with the students they teach, it becomes difficult to create a classroom climate in which children want to put in the effort to learn.

Although race, class, language, and cultural differences between students and teachers do not cause the achievement gap, they do perpetuate it and may complicate efforts to reduce or end it. For public schools to become the equalizers of opportunity, educators need to develop the "cultural competence" to work successfully with children who differ from themselves. Part of becoming culturally competent means learning to identify the range of student assets—those personal, family, and cultural strengths children bring with them to school—and use these to provide the classroom conditions that facilitate learning.

8-4a Student Assets: Interpersonal Relationships and Compatible Learning Goals

According to Professors A. Wade Boykin and Pedro Noguera, students have many assets that encourage learning.[62] The first of these is the students' capacity to enter into a mutually respectful, caring, and helpful relationship with their teachers. Additional student assets include existing or emerging interests and preferences; motivations, passions, and commitments; attitudes, beliefs, opinions, and self-perceptions; personal or collective identities; and prior experiences, knowledge, understandings, skills, and competencies. For our purposes, we will look at three distinct but interrelated types of student assets that teachers can harness for school success: interpersonal relationships with teachers, compatibility of learning goals between student and teacher, and cultural/family influences.

Interpersonal relationships involve the quality of the teacher–student relationship and teacher expectations. *Compatible learning goals* address the extent that teachers' and students' interests, values, perceptions, and learning objectives are "on the same page"; that is, work together toward the same ends in mutually satisfying ways. This asset includes cultural factors (such as core values, popular culture, and family traditions) as well as providing students with meaningful learning (including personal relevance, prior knowledge, personal experiences, and interests). *Cultural/family influences* take in traditional values that reflect the student's culture as they play out in the family and community. We will look at the first two student assets in this section. Cultural/family influences will appear in the next section.

Research on teacher–student relationship quality Much evidence supports the importance of the teacher–student relationship quality (TSRQ)[63] in closing the achievement gap. Classroom behaviors that reflect this interpersonal dimension include: the degree to which teachers show empathy, support, encouragement, and optimism and the extent to which students perceive teachers as fair, genuine, and respectful in their praise and feedback. Studies on the quality of the teacher–student relationship that increase student achievement, especially with minority students, find that:

- Teachers display proactive communication with students, anticipating problems and addressing them before they happen as well as building a positive rapport and positive classroom climate.[64]
- High-quality teacher–student relationships predict academic achievement.[65]
- Academically successful African American students describe their teachers as accessible and approachable, validate their capabilities, and hold high expectations for their achievement.[66]
- A high-quality teacher–student relationship helps close the achievement gap.[67]
- The TSRQ affects student engagement in the present and predicts student engagement and achievement in later years.[68]
- TSRQ is positively related to African American and Latino students' language skills and reading scores, increases student engagement, and motivates these students to learn not simply *from*, but *for* their teachers.[69]

Clearly, the teacher–student relationship—and the degree that the African American, Latino, and other traditionally underserved students recognize that their teachers care about them as people and as academic learners—has a positive and measurable effect on their classroom engagement and achievement. Payoffs occur not only in the current classroom but also in later years. In particular, "warm, demanding pedagogy"—described as sternness short of scolding students who don't live up to expectations in a compassionate, supportive, and nurturing way—may be especially effective with low-income, African American, and Latino students.[70]

Research on compatible learning goals Classroom learning goals deal with how teachers and students decide on and approach their purposes for teaching and learning. For instance, **mastery goals** focus on gaining skills, comprehension, or competence based on student effort and personal improvement, whereas **performance goals** stress being best as compared with others. Mastery goals tend to rely on students' effort, whereas performance goals tend to rely on students' ability.

mastery goals Aims that focus on gaining skills, comprehension, or competence based on student effort and personal improvement.

performance goals Aims that stress being best as compared with others as based on ability.

Likewise, the degrees to which teachers use students' values, interests, and learning priorities with the curriculum to make learning personally meaningful and relevant to students impacts how well minority and low-income students achieve. At the same time, a positive learning climate encourages students to invest their efforts in their learning; a negative learning climate discourages these learning behaviors.

Evidence suggests that the way teachers structure students' learning goals—as well as the way students identify their own and their teachers' learning goals—can significantly affect their academic functioning. Studies show that goal compatibility is especially critical for African American and Latino students:

- The ways students understand and respond to achievement experiences are associated with distinctly different patterns of cognition, affect, and behavior. Mastery goals lead to more favorable student ratings of their classroom's emotional tone and peer relationships, higher levels of student engagement, higher academic outcomes, greater self-efficacy, more personal interest in math, less text anxiety, more adaptive help seeking, and more success on unit exams among ethnically diverse students than for diverse students with a high level of performance goal orientation; and the more African American students perceive the teacher stresses performance goals, the more they show disruptive behaviors and less self-efficacy.[71]
- With a mastery approach to learning, students facing challenge or failure are likely to attribute the result to lack of enough effort on their part, rather than to a lack of ability where others are smarter or more capable.[72]
- Students more readily link mastery goals to changeable beliefs about one's competence and smartness (effort is within their control), whereas performance goals are linked to ideas of fixed ability (beyond their control).[73]
- Teachers who center the learning process on African American children's actual experiences, relating what students learn to matters of personal interest and relevant events in their lives, and drawing connections across topics have better achievement outcomes for students.[74]
- A learning climate that fosters a properly structured collaboration for learning, such as peer tutoring or peer-assisted learning, can boost academic performance—particularly for African American and Latino students from low-income backgrounds.[75]

Teachers who treat their low-income, African American, Latino, and other underserved students with genuine caring and meaningful support plus high expectations for performance generate favorable achievement outcomes. The effects are reciprocal: increased TSRQ leads to higher student achievement, which, in turn, leads to a greater TSRQ. Providing personally relevant learning for low-income and minority students—indeed, for all students—makes schoolwork more meaningful to them and easier to learn. Similarly, focusing the classroom climate on mastery rather than performance and using well-designed collaborative learning activities also result in higher achievement for minority and low-income students.

8-4b Student Assets: Cultural Resources

Culture matters in student learning. *Culture,* that set of concepts, values, assumptions, sensibilities, or ways of thinking, creates a perceptual lens through which people interpret life events. Low-income, African American, and Latino students, and students with special needs each bring cultural factors with them to school that teachers can use to help them learn. Their culture helps them define what makes sense, what is appropriate. American public schools—with their purposes, rules, regulations, and procedures—are also a cultural context. As discussed previously, when teachers can align students' experiences and values with the curriculum and make the content personally relevant and meaningful to students, engagement and learning increases.

Considering a child's culture brings certain cautions, however. "Cultural differences" are not the underlying cause of every difficulty a minority child experiences in school. The same behaviors may occur for a variety of reasons, or different behaviors may occur for the same reason. In fact, the behaviors in question may or may not be related to culture. Then, too, the idea of culture is open to overgeneralization and stereotyping. For example, race and culture are not interchangeable; African American students do not necessarily possess African American culture. But overlap between race, ethnicity, and culture may exist. Individual differences and variations also exist. Generalizing about culture is especially problematic when factors are attributed to historically marginalized groups and mistakenly used to explain why group members perform poorly or are unable to function as well as other members of cultural groups. Actually, more variation exists within cultural groups than between cultural groups. Also, culture does not determine individuals' attitudes and behaviors. Simply because a student is Latino does not mean he or she must automatically act, think, or feel certain ways. In short, the complexity of culture urges restraint in what we infer from our observations or from what we are told.

Given this caution not to make general cultural assumptions about individual students, scholars increasingly are advocating for culturally relevant pedagogy: drawing on the students' fund of knowledge found in their family and community experiences and linking these to instructional practices and curriculum content. The goal of this approach is to create greater understanding among teachers, students, and their families and to identify student assets to increase classroom engagement.

8-4c Low-Income Students' Assets

The image of the United States as a classless or mostly middle-class society is an attractive media portrayal that hides our culture's pervasive social and economic stratification.[76] By downplaying economic insecurity and representing "the middle" as a "state of mind," the media encourage low-income individuals to identify with a politically neutralized universal middle class.[77] By giving very little broadcast time or print space to stories that openly discuss class-based privileges or power differences, the media portray the poor as either invisible or deficient outsiders (such as substance abusers, criminals, and sexually indiscriminant predators) who deviate from middle-class values or norms.[78]

Historical and current factors Although slavery and formal indenture are no longer legal, the United States has continued to maintain a society of "haves" and "have-nots." U.S. institutions, including schools, continue to support class stratification, providing differential treatment and opportunities for Americans of different social classes.[79] In the United States, SES and social class distinctions influence every aspect of life, including the quality of a person's schooling, his or her employment opportunities, and the individual family's health and safety. Social class differences in the home are clearly correlated with educational performance and student achievement. Poverty means fewer material resources in the home. Parents working a variety of jobs often have little time to spend with their children—to read to them, speak with them, and to build the large and flexible vocabulary students will need to achieve well in school.

Low-income families are also influenced by the cultural beliefs and values common to their ethnic groups and these ultimately influence how they see and act in the world. Again, these are generalities and not necessarily true for individuals.

Values, behaviors, and cultural assets Researchers agree that there is no such thing as a "culture of poverty." This term was coined in 1961 by Oscar Lewis in his book *The Children of Sanchez,* based on his study of a small sample of Mexican communities.[80] Since then, researchers around the world have tested this thesis empirically.[81] Others have analyzed the overall body of evidence, focusing on the culture of poverty model.[82] These studies concluded that differences in values and behaviors among people in poverty are just as great as those between poor and wealthy people.[83] Nevertheless, the concept of a "culture of poverty," which began as an idea taken from small stereotypes, has become an unquestioned—albeit inaccurate—part of mainstream thinking.

Contrary to the stereotype, most people with low incomes have a strong work ethic and high motivation.[84] In the United States, 45 percent of children under age 18 (32.4 million) live in low-income families (in 2012, under $44,700 for a family of four). Nationally, 30 percent have at least one parent who works full-time throughout the year.[85] Many low-income adults must work two, three, or four jobs to earn the money necessary to maintain family life. According to the Economic Policy Institute, low-income working adults spend more hours working each week than their wealthier counterparts.[86] Every day, low-income parents and family members model high motivation and hard work for their children.

Low-income parents care about their children's education, just as more affluent parents do. Nonetheless, low-income parents may be less likely to attend school functions, participate in PTA meetings, or volunteer in their children's classrooms because they have less access to school involvement than more affluent parents. Although they care very much about their children's school success, these parents are more likely to work multiple jobs, work during the evening, have jobs without paid leave, and be unable to afford child care or public transportation. Teachers and schools need to take these realities into account if they value involving low-income families as much as they do wealthier ones in their children's education.[87]

Low-income and children from poverty speak a real language, even if it sometimes sounds different from standard English. All people, regardless of the language and language varieties they speak, use a full range of language registers, or levels of formality.[88] Their languages are highly structured with complex grammatical rules.[89] What teachers often assume to be deficient English (such as Appalachian varieties or "black English") is no less sophisticated than standard English. Rather, these languages are appropriate for the students' home communities. Caring and respectful teachers can help these students learn to be "bilingual" by helping them learn to use more formal language expression in "white talk" (standard English) so they can interact successfully in a variety of settings, including school and work.

Researchers have found that teachers too often focus on these students' deficits rather than emphasizing their strengths. As a result, teachers often have lower classroom expectations for low-income students. Teachers tend to underencourage these students and underevaluate their work. School officials commonly steer low-income children into general education and vocational programs, thereby limiting their future options.[90]

Although some students from low-income families beat the odds and succeed in school, economic and cultural barriers still work against this achievement. Much remains to be done to reduce child poverty and allow more children to enter school ready to learn, achieve more highly, and continue their education through high school graduation and beyond.

Teachers cannot allow the "culture of poverty" myth to lead to low expectations for poor and low-income students. Instead, when teachers recognize low-income children and families' respect for education and hard work, when teachers motivate students to achieve, and when teachers give low-income children the necessary supports (such as extra learning time, tutoring, mentoring, academic coaching, and scholarships) to succeed, low-income students can use their assets to learn and achieve well in school.[91]

8-4d African American Students' Assets

Through our discussion of the theories advanced by Steele and Ogbu, we have already considered the broad influences on African American and varied minority students and some of their coping strategies. In this section, we examine several specific cultural factors unique to African Americans, considering how these factors can positively impact their success in school.

Historical and current factors The United States built much of its society on forced labor. Legal in all parts of the United States by the early eighteenth century, slavery was the Southern colonies' dominant workforce system. Colonists captured, imported, enslaved, beat, and killed hundreds of thousands of Africans to serve white economic needs. This practice continued for more than 244 years. White slaveholders preferred African slaves to indentured European servants because once purchased, slaves—and their children, and their children's children—became their owners' permanent property.

Despite this enormously debilitating history, African Americans are showing significant gains in education, social status, income, life expectancy, and political viability:

- The percentage of African Americans completing high school rose from 20 percent in 1960 to 84.2 percent in 2010.[92]
- The percentage of African Americans completing college or more rose from 3 percent to 19.8 percent over the same period, and 6.5 percent hold an advanced degree such as a master's degree, PhD, MD, or JD.[93]
- As a result of the Great Recession, the annual median income of single-race African American households in 2009 was $32,584, a decline of 4.4 percent (in 2009 constant dollars) from 2008.[94]
- Most African Americans are middle class.[95]
- African American life expectancy has soared from 34 years in 1900 to 70.9 years for males and 77.4 years for females in 2009.[96]
- In 2008 and again in 2012, Americans elected Barack Obama, an African American U.S. senator from Illinois, with 53 percent and 51.1 percent of the vote, respectively, to become the 44th president of the United States.[97]

These data show that although African Americans are making meaningful advances, many are still struggling for educational and economic opportunities.

Values, traditions, and cultural assets The strength of the African American family is one of its most valuable assets. Although wide diversity exists within their community, African Americans typically place a high value on family, including extended family. More than one generation may live in the same home. Grandparents, aunts, uncles, and cousins may reside together to share resources (money, information, and moral support) and overcome the economic disadvantages they all face. Child rearing is often undertaken by a large number of relatives, older children, and close friends. Within the African American family, family roles are adaptable, kinship bonds are durable, and a strong work ethic, achievement ethic, and religious orientation exist.[98] This family and kinship arrangement provides many positive benefits to its members, although it does not look like the nuclear family of parents and children celebrated by the white culture.[99]

Spiritual beliefs play an important role for many African American families. Participation in religious activities brings opportunities for self-expression, leadership, and community involvement. The church, its pastor or minister, and its personnel help family members with social and economic issues as well as with religious concerns.[100]

African American men and women value behaviors such as assertiveness and flexible roles. Within families, males are typically more accepting of women's work roles and more willing to share in the responsibilities such as picking up the children from school. Despite widespread societal prejudice, many African American families have been able to instill positive self-images in their children.[101]

Certain African American values reflect their African heritage, which stresses the group, community, cooperation, interdependence, and being one with nature.[102] In contrast, white middle-class values focus on individuality, uniqueness, competition, and control over nature.[103]

Education is a highly prized asset among African Americans, who see it as a way to achieve both personal and family goals. African American parents encourage their children to develop career and educational ambitions at an early age.[104] Education's importance weakens when African American students experience schools' discrimination, when teachers display insensitivity to cultural differences, and when young people develop the defensive perspectives that make academic success appear disloyal to their group.

8-4e Latino Students' Assets

The Latino population in the United States shares a common language and cultural heritage, yet is characterized by different historical, economic, political, and racial variables. Latino groups include Mexican Americans, Cuban Americans, Puerto Ricans, and Central and South Americans. In schools, members of this group experienced legal discrimination and segregation until the 1954 *Brown* decision.

Historical and current factors More than 60 percent of Latinos in the United States have Mexican ancestry. This population includes recent Mexican immigrants and U.S.-born Mexican Americans (also called Chicanos) whose ancestors lived in the American Southwest generations before Europeans set foot in North America. The United States won the southwest territories from Mexico in 1848, and the Mexicans living in these areas automatically became U.S. citizens.

Puerto Ricans account for the second largest U.S. Latino community. In 1898, the United States won Puerto Rico from Spain during the Spanish–American War, and annexed the Spanish colony.

Diverse Voices

One Teacher Explains How Her African Ancestry Influenced Her Love of Education And Learning.

By Junia Yearwood, Retired English teacher, Dorchester, Massachusetts.

"I was born on the Caribbean Island of Trinidad and was raised and nurtured by my paternal grandmother and aunts on the island of Barbados. My environment instilled in me a strong identity as a woman and as a person of African ancestry. The value of education and the importance of being able to read and write became clear and urgent when I became fully aware of the history of my ancestors. The story of the enslavement of Africans and the horrors they were forced to endure repulsed and angered me, but the aspect of slavery that most intrigued me was the systematic denial of literacy to my ancestors. As a child of ten, I reasoned that if reading and writing were not extremely important, then there would be no need to withhold those skills from the 'savage and inferior' African. I concluded that teaching was the most important profession on earth and that the teacher was the Moses of people of African descent.

"This revelation made my destiny clear. I had to be a Teacher.

"My resolve to someday become a teacher was strengthened by my experiences with teachers who had significant and lasting positive effects on my personal and academic growth. I gradually came to realize that the teachers whose classes I was eager to get to and in whose classes I excelled were the ones who treated and nurtured me as an individual, a special person. They pushed, challenged, and cajoled me to study and perform to my full ability. They believed in me; they identified not only my weaknesses but also my strengths and talents. They encouraged me to think, question, and enter the 'conversation' on an equal intellectual footing. They respected my thoughts and opinions and they showed me that they cared. In addition, and just as important, they looked like me. They all shared my ancestry, my culture, and my history. They were my role models. . . ."

Sources: Junia Yearwood as cited in Nieto, S. (2000, October 27). *What keeps teachers going? And other thoughts on the future of public education.* Sonia Nieto with contributions from the "What Keeps Teachers Going? Inquiry Group," talk given for the Distinguished Faculty Lecture Series University of Massachusetts, Amherst. Retrieved from http://people.umass.edu/~snieto/UMass_Lecture.html

Note: Junia Yearwood, a retired Boston public high school English teacher, writes Op Ed pieces about education for the *Boston Globe*.

Cuban Americans represent the third largest Latino minority in the United States. They tend to be more recent immigrants than either Mexican Americans or Puerto Ricans. Many Cubans came to this country as political exiles.

Socioeconomically and educationally, these three Latino communities reflect differing levels of well-being. Generally speaking, Cuban Americans have attained a high socioeconomic level compared with other Latino groups.[105]

Values, traditions, and cultural assets Family and traditions are central parts of Latino life. Respect and loyalty to family, cooperation among family members, and nurturing and maintaining larger interpersonal relations within a wide network of family and friends all contribute to Latino students' sense of identity and well-being. Latino families are often large and very protective of their children. Family immersion is a cultural value for mutual support as well as a means to teach their traditions to their young. Even the 25 percent of families headed by single females often depend on an extended family for help with young children.[106]

Latinos' strong families have a traditional clear division of responsibilities and roles. Generally, fathers are authoritarian. Men's roles include providing income for the household and making the major family decisions. Latinas are revered, holding a special respected position in their families, honored by their husbands and children for their strength and hard work while putting their families' needs about their own.[107] Adherence to these traditional roles is decreasing rapidly among urban families, however, because many women are required to act independently in the work setting, in some cases becoming the family's

Family loyalty and respect contribute to Latinos' identity and well-being.

wage earner, and to deal with schools and other agencies.[108]

The Catholic religion is often a major influence and source of comfort. Latinos' beliefs in charity as a virtue, sacrificing in this world, and enduring wrongs done to you have many implications for their behavior.[109] As a result, many Latinos have difficulty behaving assertively and fatalistically feel their problems are "meant to be" and cannot be changed.[110] At the same time, their belief that "God helps those who help themselves" can prompt effective problem solving to support learning and achievement.[111]

Research shows that Latino parents believe it is their primary responsibility to raise well-behaved, moral, respectful children.[112] At teacher conferences, Latino parents tend to ask, "How is my child behaving?" before asking how well their child is achieving.[113] They know that if their child is well behaved, they as parents have done a good job in preparing their child for school. In addition, Latino parents have high aspirations for their children. Most want their children to complete college.[114] Nevertheless, Latinos generally have a lower SES than whites and Asian Americans, and these students share some of the same challenges and obstacles to education as do low-income students.

Teachers can help Latino students succeed in school if they look for and work with the students' cultural and personal strengths rather than emphasize their shortcomings. For example, when teachers recognize that Latino culture values the extended family and social network for self-definition, teachers can construct classroom practices that work *with* instead of *against* that orientation.[115] Peer helping and sharing are valued.[116] The family notion of working together for mutual benefit of all is easily applied to group work in schools. Saying, "Good work—your family will be proud of you," and encouraging the child to bring the work home to show the parents play to Latino students' cultural strengths.

Because authentic relationships matter to Latinos, teachers are more effective in encouraging Latino students to "care" about their schoolwork when these students experience genuine "caring" relationships and compassion from their teachers.[117] Teachers show real caring when they offer regular after-school consulting and tutoring and encourage students to ask questions and seek assistance.[118] Other effective practices include setting high expectations for achievement, attendance, and discipline; helping students envision a positive future; providing access to a rigorous curriculum; providing tutors and mentors for students; allowing students to work on class assignments together; valuing students' linguistic and cultural heritage; and inviting parent involvement.[119]

Teachers need to understand that Latino parents' reluctance to attend teacher conferences may result from language difficulties, complicated by many low-income Latino parents' belief that they have no right to question the teacher or school decisions. This reluctance to meet should not be interpreted as a lack of caring or parent involvement in the child's education. Instead, scheduling conferences at flexible hours, making child care and interpreters available if the teacher is not bilingual, and having face-to-face meetings rather than sending written materials (even in Spanish) helps develop trust between teacher and family.[120]

8-4f Assets of Students with Special Needs

Students with special needs come from all racial, ethnic, and socioeconomic spectra. Students with special needs are students who require supplemental services to help them learn effectively. The Education for All Handicapped Act of 1975 defines *disabilities* as involving mental, hearing, visual, speech, learning, emotional, orthopedic, or other health impairment. Amendments to this act in 2004 expanded the list of recognized disabilities.[121] These disabilities vary greatly in intensity and in the ways they affect students' life experiences and learning. Along with their unique educational needs, students with disabilities bring the same racial, cultural, and socioeconomic factors and assets to the school equation as other students.

Historical and current factors Historically, many cultures have ignored, exiled, exploited, or killed persons with disabilities. Many nomadic societies saw their limitations as keeping them from contributing to the group's physical work. Some cultures viewed physical differences as deformities resulting from evil or sin living within the person or the family. Even advancing Western civilization viewed many persons with disabilities as unproductive. Placing these adults and children into asylums and institutions allowed the general population to keep them out of the way and out of sight. Although society saw these individuals as deserving pity and charity, their educational needs went largely unmet. Later, persons with disabilities were labeled "handicapped," implying that dependence was an inevitable part of their lives.[122]

Beginning in the 1960s, rehabilitative counseling evolved into a profession whose members tried to help those with disabilities "fit" or adapt into society.[123] In addition, civil rights actions helped open doors for assimilating individuals with disabilities into the larger society. At present, litigation about access and equity for persons who are disabled continues.

The percentage of students with disabilities has increased from approximately 7 percent of all students in the 1975–1976 school year to approximately 13.2 percent by 2009. In 2010, 96 percent of students ages 6 to 21 served under the Individuals with Disabilities Education Act (IDEA) were enrolled in regular public schools.[124] Approximately 2.4 million children are considered disabled in the three fastest-growing categories: speech and language impairments; autism and traumatic brain injuries; and health impairments (such as asthma, epilepsy, diabetes, and lead poisoning).[125] Nearly half of all children in special education programs are identified with "specific learning disabilities," the largest of the 13 special education categories.

Cultural assets of students with disabilities Students with special needs are persons first. Thus they bring with them the individual personalities, talents, interests, and uniqueness that characterize their peers who are abled from any family, neighborhood, and culture. They also bring their unique family and cultural assets. An effective teacher will not allow a special education label or assistive equipment to distract him or her from getting to know and nurture the student as a person who happens to have certain learning needs that the teacher and other specialists can successfully address.

Language not only reflects attitudes, but can also shape them. The word *disabled* ignores the reality that persons with disabilities are people with abilities. Focusing on limitations through labels like *disabled* and *handicapped* reflects an outdated stereotype of persons who had no means of support other than by begging money from others, literally taking off their hats (caps) and asking others for charity (money) to survive. Over time, "cap in hand" evolved into "handicapped." As this derivation suggests, language can either

TeachSource Video 8.2

Assistive Technology in the Inclusive Classroom: Best Practices

Assistive technology can be anything that helps a student access his or her environment and use their bodies, minds, and voices as best they can. Students with disabilities sometimes use assistive technology to help them learn the same curriculum content as the other students in the class. Watch the video clips, study the artifacts in the case, and reflect on the following questions:

1. What things does the inclusion facilitator do to help 5-year-old Jamie "have a voice" and learn the same curriculum as the children who do not have disabilities in the class?
2. How do teachers working with students who have cerebral palsy overcome the special difficulties—their own discomfort, the student's inability to clearly communicate in words, and the student's fluctuating muscle tone—to help the student learn?
3. What are the classroom teacher's responsibilities for bringing the curriculum to the student with disabilities?
4. What are the benefits to regular education students of having a classmate who has disabilities with them who is learning the same curriculum in a different fashion?

Watch on CourseMate.

focus negatively on what is missing or positively stress what is present.

Emphasizing a person's characteristic rather than the person as an individual is both disrespectful and inaccurate. For instance, describing someone as a "person with a disability" shows more respect and accuracy than referring to that individual as a "disabled person." Similarly, saying that someone "*uses* a wheelchair" leads to different assumptions about that individual's capacities compared to saying "*confined* to a wheelchair"—suggesting that the individual is helplessly imprisoned in the wheelchair rather than using the device to help accomplish normal tasks.[126] Even when no insult is intended, language influences attitudes and behaviors. Lack of awareness of how word choices affect others can lead the speaker to inadvertently insult the person with a disability. It can also reflect the speaker's belief that the disabled person is not worthy of respect.

Many persons with disabilities find certain body language equally disrespectful. This includes touching someone's assistive device, such as a walker, wheelchair, or prosthetic without permission, speaking loudly to a person with a visual impairment, or communicating with a caretaker or interpreter who accompanies a person with a disability rather than speaking directly with the individual in question. Intentional or not, these insensitive behaviors send the message that those with disabilities do not deserve esteem or have their own capabilities, thoughts, feelings, or rights.

When educators choose words to describe persons with disabilities, they are showing their attitudes about these students and their expectations for them. Teachers will be more effective with students when they focus on their assets. Becoming sensitive to verbal and nonverbal behaviors that express positive regard and high expectations for academic achievement can motivate students with disabilities to work hard and learn in your classroom.

Did You Get It?

Cultural competence is important to teachers, especially when they are working in a diverse classroom for all reasons except:

a. People learn within the context of relationships: the more you like, trust, and respect a person, the harder you are willing to work for them.
b. Teachers need to understand their own culture if they are to teach it to their students.
c. If a teacher can identify and appreciate diverse students' family and cultural assets, they can use these to help students learn more effectively.
d. Cultural competence reduces misunderstandings and improves communications between students and teachers.

Take the full quiz on CourseMate.

8-5 Perceptions about Students with Disabilities and Academic Performance: Discarding the Deficit Model

Helen Keller, a woman who earned a Radcliffe College (Harvard) degree and was deaf and blind (and whose life was later dramatized in a play and several movies called *The Miracle Worker*), campaigned relentlessly for social justice. In her work, she emphasized that it was others' attitudes about the disabled, rather than the disability itself, that caused problems. She wrote, "We have been accustomed to regard the employed deaf and blind as the victims of their infirmities. Facts show that it is not physical blindness but social blindness which cheats our hands of the right to toil."[127]

The same "social blindness" often afflicts teachers when they are working with culturally and racially diverse students. This "blindness" is most evident when educators look at what these students *cannot do* rather than at what they *can and might do* with support from high expectations, respect for the personal and cultural assets they bring with them, and a variety of means to help them learn and achieve.

The deficit model is socially defined. It is based on the "normal" development of middle class, usually white students whose homes and communities have prepared them for schooling long before they enter the classroom. Children who come to school without that preparation and without the continuing support of family members who can reinforce schooling's goals face teachers' expectations that students cannot easily meet. Instead of seeing human variation, teachers and schools have been encultured to see "pathology."[128] All too often, when students do not learn new material at the same pace—or behave in the same ways—as their classmates, frustrated teachers quickly refer them for special education evaluation for suspected "disability."

Viewing "disability" or cultural/racial difference as the opposite of "normal" falsely limits our expectations for diverse students' achievement. The traditional

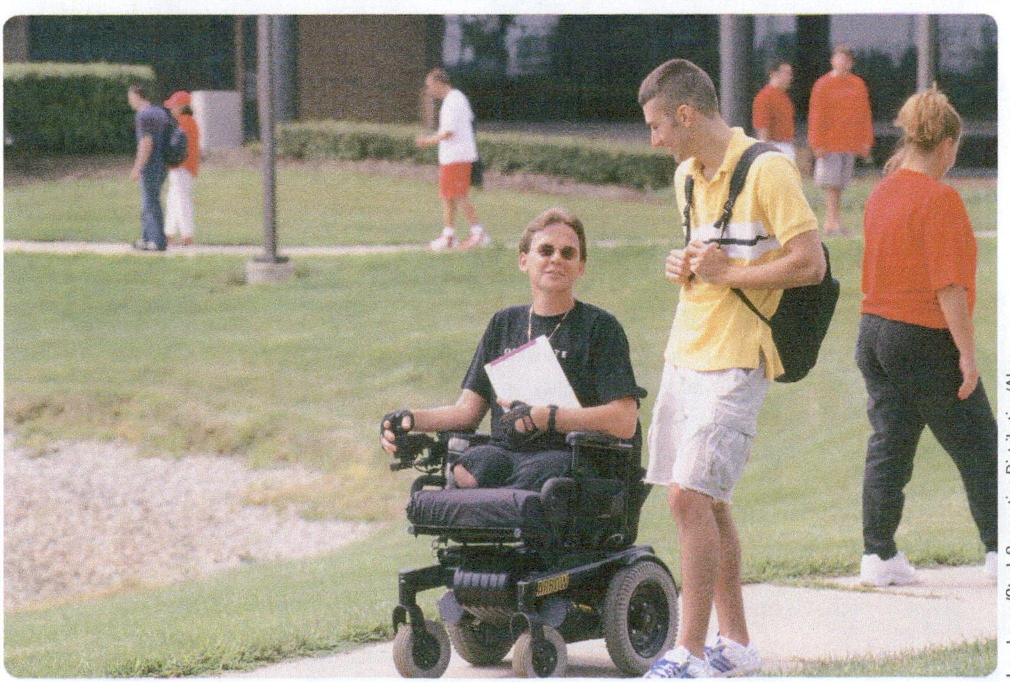

Lew Lause/Stock Connection Distribution/Alamy

High expectations and respect for personal assets help students with disabilities succeed.

or medical model of disability centers on individuals' functional limitations or impairments as the cause of their disadvantages. For instance, a person has a "disability" because he or she has cerebral palsy, cannot walk, and moves around in a motorized chair. A student is "disadvantaged" or "at risk" because he or she represents a minority culture or has a low-income background. In this view, the person owns both the problem and the associated limits.

In contrast, the social model shifts the focus. Instead of looking at the individual's "lack of ability" or "otherness" as the problem, attention turns to identifying and remedying the limiting social, environmental, and attitudinal barriers that hinder the person's learning. Today, for example, we modify public buildings to create wider doorways to rooms, wider private restroom stalls, and ramps to ease accessibility from the street. Likewise, we provide inclusive classrooms and multiple instructional interventions for struggling learners. We expand our curriculum to include authentic voices from culturally diverse groups who make up the American society. We look for and use our students' cultural and personal assets in our efforts to educate them to twenty-first-century competence. When we see the environment (or people's attitudes) as the problem, we can fix it.

In short, the social model rejects the "deficit" language's belief system. It sees student difficulties and differences not as "pathology" or sickness, but rather as normal human variations.[129] Educators would do well to get rid of the deficit model in the way they approach the teaching and learning of all children.

Reflect & Discuss

Discuss these questions in pairs then as a whole class:

A. Explain how the "deficit model" of student "normality" affects teachers' expectations and limits access to high-quality educational opportunities for diverse students in schools.
B. Explain how the language of "disability" devalues the students it describes.
C. Describe how educators can use clinical judgment, I.Q. tests, and special education labeling to disproportionately place students of color into the Educational Mental Retardation, Educational/Behavioral Disordered, and Learning Disabled categories. What does this overidentification suggest about their teaching skills?
D. Explain how a poor quality classroom and school climate can contribute to students' learning difficulties.
E. Describe what you think teachers can change in their instructional practices to help diverse students learn more effectively without needing to make a special education referral.
F. Identify what you as a future teacher are likely to do or not do in teaching diverse students as a result of reading this chapter.

Did You Get It?

What does it mean to discard the deficit model?

a. Rather than define lack of an ability or talent as the problem, we identify and remove the social, environmental, and attitudinal barriers that limit people.
b. It means acknowledging that anyone can do anything, if they only work hard enough and have access to the right resources.
c. It means accepting that while disabilities are real, they are not disabilities, only challenges to be overcome in an inspiring manner.
d. It means that unless a person recognizes their problems, deviances, and limits ("deficits"), they can never structure their lives to achieve.

Take the full quiz on CourseMate.

8-6 How Personal and Cultural Assets Can Foster Diverse Students' Resilience

Children can overcome difficult conditions and happily succeed in the mainstream culture. **Resilience** can be defined as the process or capacity to have successful outcomes despite challenging or threatening circumstances.[130] Research finds that children who experience chronic adversity fare better or recover more successfully when they have a positive relationship with a competent adult, are good learners and problem solvers, are likeable, and are perceived as effective in a variety of situations by self and others.[131]

resilience The process or capacity to have successful outcomes despite challenging or threatening circumstances.

8-6a Drawing upon Students' Resources

Each child has an array of personal, family, and cultural resources from which teachers can draw to help the student succeed. Emotional, mental, spiritual, physical, and relationship resources and knowledge of school's "unspoken rules" can help individuals become resilient.

Emotional resources such as stamina, persistence, and good decision making give children the ability to control their emotional responses, particularly to negative situations, without engaging in self-destructive behaviors. Mental resources include those abilities and skills such as reading, writing, computing, and reasoning needed for daily life. Spiritual resources give children some belief in a divine or higher purpose and guidance upon which they can rely for direction and support. Physical resources include good physical health and mobility or the capacity to use what abilities they have to influence and control their environment. Support systems include family, friends, and additional people who are available in times of need. Relationships and role models nurture the child and engage in self-affirming behaviors. Finally, learning the verbal and nonverbal knowledge, assumptions, and behaviors—the "unspoken rules"—that in-group members continuously use can help resilient children move easily through the system to meet their needs.[132] This may mean deliberately teaching these rules to students.

School success requires large amounts of assets that schools do not necessarily provide. Teachers can informally assess each child in their classrooms through conversations, observations, student records, and other interactions to identify and employ these assets in the service of a high-quality education. The more resources each student has at hand, and the greater the extent to which the teacher can access and use these for teaching and learning, the more resilient the student is likely to become.

8-6b Making Connections

Caring about young people and finding ways to help them achieve will build connections between teachers and students. Educators have daily opportunities to develop relationships that can foster educational aspiration and performance. As a 2005 report for the Annie E. Casey Foundation, an organization that works to meet the needs of vulnerable children and families, observes:

> Some young people do well and stay in school despite tough circumstances. Researchers studying their resilience have found that children need personal anchors—stable, positive, emotional relationships with at least one parent

> or key person. . . . Teachers and other adults can play an important role in fostering resilience. They may mentor students . . . or they may play a role by offering emotional support during hard times, acting as the student's advocate when conflict arises in school or at home, or by providing an opportunity to pursue a special talent or interest.[133]

Educators' effectiveness with diverse students depends on their willingness to recognize students' skills, interests, aspirations, concerns, and cultural assets and to modify classroom rules, procedures, and activities in ways that build students' academic and interpersonal success. Holding onto a single cultural viewpoint can blind teachers to the potential sitting in front of them. Teachers need accurate information about each student and their students' families and communities if they are "to provide equitable opportunities for learning."[134] That is why learning about culture—our own, the school's, and our students'—is essential. And such awareness benefits children on both ends of the economic and social spectrums. As Donna Marie San Antonio, a Lecturer on Education at the Harvard Graduate School of Education, writes,

> Our role as educators is to understand the value systems and circumstances of all our students so that we can support them appropriately. Perhaps we can help students who accept disappointment too easily strive harder to achieve their desires—and help more economically fortunate students adjust to disappointment more resiliently.[135]

Did You Get It?

How can teachers help students develop the cultural and personal assets to help them survive adversity?

- **a.** Tell students to "toughen up"—things will get better.
- **b.** Mentor students and encourage them in their interests.
- **c.** Help students build an academic vocabulary by using lots of big words.
- **d.** Know each child and use family and cultural assets to help him or her learn school subjects.

Take the full quiz on CourseMate.

8-7 Strategies for Helping Diverse Students Succeed in School

Lisa Delpit, an educational leadership expert who focuses on education and race (featured in *Education Spotlight* in Chapter 12), writes that the clash between school culture and home culture comes into play in at least two ways:

> When a significant difference exists between the students' culture and the schools' culture, teachers can easily misread students' aptitudes, intent, or abilities as a result of the difference in styles of language use and interactional patterns. Secondly, when such cultural differences exist, teacher may utilize styles of instruction and/or discipline that are at odds with community norms.[136]

Such miscommunications limit students' access to learning. When teachers do not understand their students' potential, they will "underteach them no matter what the methodology."[137]

Likewise, Sonia Nieto, Geneva Gay, and Gloria Ladson-Billings write about **culturally responsive pedagogy**—the idea that students' backgrounds are assets that students can and should use in the service of their learning, and that teachers of all backgrounds should develop the skills to teach all students effectively.[138] Evidence is growing that all teachers—regardless of race, ethnicity, or gender—who care about, mentor, and guide their students can have a dramatic positive impact on those children's futures, even when these students face seemingly insurmountable obstacles related to poverty, racism, and other social ills.[139] Developing the personal and professional awareness, knowledge, and skills to use culturally responsive pedagogy is a paramount responsibility for all educators who want all our children to succeed.

culturally responsive pedagogy The idea that teachers should use students' backgrounds as assets to help them learn.

Culturally responsive pedagogy, typified by those strategies noted below, can help minority students succeed in school.[140]

As a teacher, be willing to learn Low-income, minority, and students with special needs may differ in attitudes, work habits, learning styles, and behaviors from middle-class white students. Be prepared to learn about them as individuals, as learners, and as members of specific families and cultures. The more you learn about them in these contexts, the more insights and tools teachers gain about how to help these children succeed in school.

Be welcoming When teachers warmly and genuinely welcome low-income students, students of color, and students with disabilities into their classrooms and provide the social and academic supports needed to help them succeed, the positive learning climate will help all students focus and learn.

Be culturally sensitive and respectful Understand the ways your students' cultural values, language, behaviors, social, and economic background may influence their attitudes and actions. See your students' cultural values and strengths as motivators and resources in the learning environment. Remember that communication styles vary with the culture, and don't misinterpret students' actions as disrespect, misbehavior, or inability to learn. Students may be choosing "not to learn" in an effort to maintain their sense of identity until the teacher can make the discussion more personally and culturally meaningful and respectful.

Build relationships based on respect and caring Holding high expectations, insisting on high-quality work, and offering supports to reach these goals demonstrate respect and caring for students. Calling each student by name, answering students' questions, talking to each student respectfully, saying "Hello!" whenever the teacher notices the student outside the classroom, and helping the student when he or she needs it all let students know whether the teacher really respects and cares about them—or not.

Assess each student's resources Identify each student's assets, including financial, emotional, mental, spiritual, and physical resources; support systems; relationships; and role models. Use these resources to help support student learning. If certain students are not familiar with the school's "hidden rules," find a respectful way to clearly teach them how to behave appropriately and successfully in the school environment as bicultural individuals.

Use culturally responsive pedagogy Instructionally, one size does not fit all. Teachers who know and understand their students' cultural backgrounds, values, and learning and interacting styles are more likely look for and use their strengths, not their deficits. For instance, noted educator Jaime Escalante, celebrated in the movie *Stand and Deliver,* prepared low-income Latino students to pass the Calculus Advanced Placement Tests by referring to their ancestors, entreating his students, "You *have* to learn math. The Mayans discovered zero. Math is in your blood!"[141]

Reduce the "cognitive load" Choose activities and assignments that allow students to draw on their prior knowledge and life experiences. Learning is always more effective when it is tied to the students' existing knowledge and background[142] and starts where the students are. Each child has his or her own educational and life history, and the more the teacher can have them use what they already know, the more they can extend and deepen their learning.

Reduce the "cultural load" Build personal relationships with your students and their families, and make an effort to include aspects of each child's culture in the classroom on a regular basis. Start by pronouncing each student's name correctly, find out where each student is from, and gather a little personal history about each one.

Reduce the language load Keep the concepts and rigor high, but explain the language in simpler academic terms. Break up complex sentences into smaller ones, point out new and difficult words, define them, and explain how they are used. Give information both visually (in writing, pictures, and gestures) and verbally.

Don't underestimate students' ability to achieve well in your class Just because diverse students' school behaviors may not be the same as those of white middle-class students, it does not mean that they lack the intelligence and motivation to learn at high levels when given a high-quality academic curriculum and any needed supports (encouragement, material, tutoring, and extra time). Offer high expectations with high supports.

Identify past leadership experiences Review with students any past formal or informal leadership experiences and connect these to the their ability to make good decisions for themselves—including those regarding schoolwork and their educational and work future.

Help students know themselves as students and learners Give students useful but respectful feedback about what they are doing well and how they can improve. Let them know that effort that they can control—rather than ability that they can't—will help them successfully master their school work. Students who can recognize and accept their own academic weaknesses and who work to correct them are more likely to perform well in school.

Involve the parents or extended family Research indicates that students are more likely to exhibit significant academic achievement when parents or family members are involved with their education.[143] This consideration is especially important for diverse students whose cultures place a high value on parents and extended family. Include flexibility in your schedule so that you can meet with parents or guardians who work during the day, greet them with a smile, find interpreters if needed to make understanding and communication easier, speak without education jargon, and provide bilingual information about school practices and ways that parents can help their children learn at home. Let parents know that you care about their children.

Work with parents as a team Encourage parents to speak with their children in their native language at home and use family and community stories to complete school assignments, support students' adjustment to their new culture, know what is happening in their children's lives, and encourage student involvement in community events that help promote ethnic languages and cultures. Teachers can also invite parents to visit the classroom to talk about their cultures and display items from their countries.

Establish partnerships with community organizations and school liaisons Finding and developing parent liaisons who are fluent in the languages spoken by students' families can facilitate relationships between schools, students, and families. These intermediaries can teach parents about schools' "chain of command," assist counselors in interpreting immigrant students' home-country transcripts, help reduce miscommunications among staff and minority parents, and explain students' culture and values to staff.

8-7a Resetting Our Perspectives, Priorities, and Expectations

The process of learning involves more than intellectual ability and mastery of cognitive content. It also includes teachers' and students' psychological and emotional dispositions and the teaching and learning climates in which they occur.

Unequal educational opportunities still exist in American's schools. Increased understanding of students' social class, race, culture, and special learning needs can help educators better relate to all of their students and find resourceful ways to increase each child's learning opportunities and outcomes.

As Delpit concludes, "If we are to successfully educate all of our children, we must work to remove the blinders built of stereotypes, monoculture instructional methodologies, ignorance, social distance. . . ."[144] In the words of a Native Alaskan educator, "In order to teach you, I must know you."[145]

Did You Get It?

Why should you work to help your students succeed, even if you are the "wrong" fit for them, in terms of race, gender, or religion?

- **a.** You shouldn't unless your students are quiet, respectful, and willing to work hard.
- **b.** Caring, mentoring teachers can have an absolutely profound impact upon students who are facing tremendous obstacles such as poverty and abuse.
- **c.** Teaching is a gendered profession and it is your responsibility to model the feminine attributes of caring and affection.
- **d.** Why should you? Society regards many humans as disposable; it won't notice if you do, too.

Take the full quiz on CourseMate.

FlipSides

Traditional Teaching vs. Culturally Responsive Teaching. Which Approach Will Help Today's Diverse Students Learn to High Levels?

What are the most effective ways to teach a challenging and rigorous curriculum to low-income and minority students? For the sake of argument, we call one teaching approach "traditional" and the other "culturally responsive." Each position reflects a different era and guiding assumptions, expectations, and practices. Which viewpoint do you support?

I support the traditional view.	I support the culturally responsive view.
■ Teachers should be colorblind (or indifferent) to students' race, ethnicity, or culture in order to treat all students the same.	● Teachers should think of each child as a unique individual with certain personal and learning needs. Students' personality, race, ethnicity, and culture contain assets that can facilitate their learning.
■ Because low-income and minority children are economically or otherwise "disadvantaged," it is not fair to make them compete with middle-class "advantaged" students. Keep expectations "realistic" and don't set up low-income and minority students for failure.	● High expectations are for every child. Low-income and minority children have personal and cultural assets that teachers can use to help facilitate their learning. Teachers can also provide the academic, time, and social supports to help these students reach high goals.
■ Public schools are a meritocracy in which students who work hard can achieve high standards.	● For meritocracy to function, certain children may need to work hard and receive added teacher supports so they can catch and keep up with better resourced peers.
■ American schools are the social agency that "Americanizes" and socializes immigrants and other outsiders into the American culture and democratic participation. The curriculum should focus solely on American history, norms, and values.	● Learning to live effectively in a pluralistic American democracy means widening the curriculum to include both our unifying history, traditions, and values as well as diverse voices that contribute to the whole.
■ The economy has room for low-skill workers, so if students cannot keep up academically, it is OK for them to leave before high school graduation and get a job.	● The twenty-first-century economy has few places for low-skill workers to earn a living wage. Even students not planning on college need to develop high level knowledge and skills in order to find meaningful paid employment.
■ Students should be placed into classrooms with curriculum appropriate for their ability, achievement, and future career goals	● Making assumptions about students' ability or achievement is often based on data that are subjective, shortsighted, incomplete, or wrong and do not consider student motivation or effort.
■ Parents are essential partners in children's education. If they cannot make the time to attend teacher conferences or school events, they must not care about their children's education.	● Many parents care deeply about their children's education and have high expectations for their achievement but for a variety of reasons may not be able to attend school conferences or events.
■ Teachers' jobs are to teach and assess student progress—not "coddle"—them.	● Positive interpersonal relationships between teachers and students can motivate students to learn *from* and *for* their teachers.

The traditional view was popular from the nineteenth to the late twentieth centuries, while the culturally responsive view is becoming more widespread now. Which viewpoint makes sense if one is to become an effective teacher today?

SUMMARY

- Over the past decades, the achievement of all major racial and ethnic student groups is increasing, the gap between racial and ethnic minority groups and white and Asian American students is decreasing, but significant disparities remain.
- Cultural/racial identity development is a theory about a cognitive, emotional, and behavioral process that proceeds in stages and continues throughout life.
- Stereotype threat and oppositional culture theories explain how minority students' perceptions of their capacity—or desire—to succeed in school significantly affect their attitudes, behaviors, and academic achievement.
- Low-income and minority students have an array of assets—including their ability to develop mutual, positive, caring and respectful relationships and compatible learning goals with teachers and a variety of cultural aspects—that teachers can use to facilitate learning and achievement.
- Students with disabilities' perceptions can influence their schooling and academic performance when they focus on what they can do rather than on what they cannot do.
- Teachers can help low-income and minority children use their personal, family, and cultural assets in school by practicing culturally responsive pedagogy.

Visit the Education CourseMate for this textbook to access the eBook, Did You Get It? quizzes, TeachSource Video Cases, flashcards, and more. Go to CengageBrain.com to log in, register, or purchase access.

Using social networking sites has ethical and professional implications for teachers—current and future.

Keith Morris/age fotostock/ Getty Images

CHAPTER

9

Teachers, Ethics, and the Law

InTASC Standards Addressed: 3 and 9

LEARNING OBJECTIVES

After you read this chapter, you should be able to:

9-1 Explain the importance of having an Educators' Code of Ethics.

9-2 Describe how teachers' constitutional freedoms, such as freedom of speech, freedom of religion, and protection from unreasonable search and seizure, operate in schools.

9-3 Describe students' privacy rights in school (regarding discipline, property, student records, speech, sexual harassment, and disability) and how these affect teachers.

Sooner than you think, you will sign a contract to become a teacher. A teaching contract creates a legal agreement between a new teacher and a school district. By signing this document, you accept certain legal rights, professional responsibilities, and ethical obligations that will guide your behavior.[1]

Schools accept a profound responsibility for educating students, and teachers play a unique role in their students' lives. Teachers are responsible for their students' physical and emotional safety as well as for helping them learn. Additionally, teachers serve as role models whose own behaviors children notice and copy. The state must balance individual teachers' and students' constitutional rights against the necessity of maintaining a controlled and safe learning environment. Courts have allowed schools to behave in reasonable ways to keep students safe, healthy, and learning. For teachers to carry out their professional actions within the law, they must first know how the law protects and limits teachers' and students' conduct.

This chapter reviews the ethics of teaching and legal considerations related to education. Relevant issues include codes of ethics, the teaching license or certificate, the teaching contract, how teachers' constitutional freedoms operate in schools, students' rights at school and how they affect teachers, and ways in which schools may limit freedom of speech and privacy. Rights of students with disabilities and sexual harassment in schools are discussed as well. Although this chapter does not cover every legal aspect future educators need to know, it will help beginning teachers make informed decisions. ●

9-1 The Importance of an Educators' Code of Ethics

Hippocrates, the ancient Greek physician and author of what is arguably the first code of ethics—the Hippocratic oath—wrote, "First, do no harm." This is a concept that serves members of all professions well.

Professions unite their members through common training, shared values, mutual aspirations, and collective purposes. Professional expertise confers a degree of authority and power on its holders. But professional autonomy is never without societal limits. Because every profession affects the well-being of others who depend on those professionals' skills and services, professional behaviors have both technical and moral dimensions. Society holds practitioners accountable for both aspects through a professional code of ethics.

ethics The rules or widely accepted voluntary standards of practice that govern conduct.

professional codes of ethics The rules that guide professional decisions and actions that serve as both a foundation and a guide to professional behavior in morally ambiguous situations.

9-1a What Is a Code of Ethics?

Ethics can be described as the rules or widely accepted standards of practice that govern members' professional conduct. Ethics is not a series of laws imposed by the state, but rather a set of voluntary standards: the norms, values, beliefs, habits, and attitudes that we choose to follow—that we as a society impose on ourselves. As Pulitzer Prize–winning author Thomas Friedman observes, "Laws regulate behavior from the outside in. Ethics regulate behavior from the inside out."[2]

The word *ethics* is derived from the Greek word meaning "moral philosophy." To behave "ethically" means being able to *choose* the "right" behavior, whereas being "moral" means being willing to *practice* that right behavior. The tension between a profession's desire to control its own practice and the public's demand for accountability has led to many professions developing codes of ethics. **Professional codes of ethics** can be described as the rules that guide professional decisions and actions. These codes serve as both a foundation and a guide to professional behavior in morally ambiguous situations.[3]

Society grants a profession power and privilege only when its members are willing and able to contribute to the general well-being and to conduct their affairs in a manner consistent with broad social values. In this sense, the profession serves as a norm reference group for its practitioners. Its code of ethics visibly clarifies for practitioners and the general public the rules and customs that guide its members' actions. Medicine, law, accounting, pharmacy, teaching, and other professions have all developed their own codes of ethics to improve professional practice and maintain the public's confidence in their practitioners.

9-1b Teachers' Code of Ethics

When teachers enter the classroom, they represent the education profession to the local community and to the nation. From that standpoint, a teacher's professional and ethical behaviors are important on many levels.

Limitations of professional codes of ethics Although professional self-regulation is consistent with the tradition of self-government, it is not without shortcomings. Many professions have a poor record of reporting their own violators.[4] For the most part, professional codes of ethics are only as "ethical" and "moral" as the individuals following them.

National Education Association codes of ethics Teachers' personal and professional ethical code and the faithfulness with which the individuals put these ideals into action will determine whether they help or hurt themselves and the profession. The National Education Association (NEA) has developed a Code of Ethics of the Education Profession. This ethical code is divided in two parts, or principles. Principle I (shown in Figure 9.1) contains a commitment to the student (the client), and Principle II (Figure 9.2) contains a commitment to the profession at large.[5]

As with physicians, the first ethical principle is to do no harm. Teachers are advised to always act in the best interest of the client, the student.

9-1c Teachers, Ethics, and Social Networking Websites

Both current and prospective teachers may confront ethical issues when they put personal information online. In general, workers expect their supervisors to monitor them closely while they are on the job. After work hours, however, employees expect that as long as they break no laws, what they do is not the employer's concern. Unfortunately, the Internet, by its very nature, makes some off-the-job activities more visible to

The educator strives to help each student realize his or her potential as a worthy and effective member of society. The educator therefore works to stimulate the spirit of inquiry, the acquisition of knowledge and understanding, and the thoughtful formulation of worthy goals. In fulfillment of the obligation to the student, the educator:

- Shall not unreasonably restrain the student from independent action in the pursuit of learning.
- Shall not unreasonably deny the student access to varying points of view.
- Shall not deliberately suppress or distort subject matter relevant to the student's progress.
- Shall make reasonable effort to protect the student from conditions harmful to learning or to health and safety.
- Shall not intentionally expose the student to embarrassment or disparagement.
- Shall not on the basis of race, color, creed, sex, national origin, marital status, political or religious beliefs, family, social or cultural background, or sexual orientation, unfairly

  Exclude any student from participation in any program.

  Deny benefits to any student.

  Grant any advantage to any student.
- Shall not use professional relationships with students for private advantage.
- Shall not disclose information about students obtained in the course of professional service unless disclosure serves a compelling professional purpose or is required by law.

FIGURE 9.1 Principle I: Commitment to the Student. Source: National Education Association CODE OF ETHICS, Principle I: Commitment to the Student. Used by permission of National Education Association.

The education profession is vested by the public with a trust and responsibility requiring the highest ideals of professional service. In the belief that the quality of the services of the education profession directly influences the nation and its citizens, the educator shall exert every effort to raise professional standards, to promote a climate that encourages the exercise of professional judgment, to achieve conditions that attract persons worthy of the trust to careers in education, and to assist in preventing the practice of the profession by unqualified persons. In fulfillment of the obligation to the profession, the educator

- Shall not in an application for a professional position deliberately make a false statement or fail to disclose a material fact related to competency and qualification.
- Shall not misrepresent his or her professional qualifications.
- Shall not assist any entry into the profession of a person known to be unqualified in respect to character, education, or other relevant attribute.
- Shall not knowingly make a false statement concerning the qualifications of a candidate for a professional position.
- Shall not assist a non-educator in the unauthorized practice of teaching.
- Shall not disclose information about colleagues obtained in the course of professional service unless disclosure serves a compelling professional purpose or is required by law.
- Shall not knowingly make false or malicious statements about a colleague.
- Shall not accept any gratuity, gift, or favor that might impair or appear to influence professional decisions or action.

FIGURE 9.2 Principle II: Commitment to the Profession.
Source: National Education Association CODE OF ETHICS, Principle II: Commitment to the Student. Used by permission of National Education Association.

more people than was previously possible. Posting personal information on the Internet makes it public. This reality creates ethical concerns—and occasionally employment consequences—for educators.

Both preservice teachers and in-service teachers must understand that, in today's world, the line between their personal lives and their professional lives is not clear-cut.[6] Teachers have lost their jobs and ended their opportunities to enter the profession because of material posted on social networking pages. Even if teachers avoid losing their jobs and break no laws, the ethical concerns and potential abuses raised by communicating "inappropriately" with students through online social networking sites make the situation hazardous to teachers' reputations, effectiveness, and credibility.

Social networking and privacy Social networking sites such as Facebook and MySpace are interactive websites designed to build online communities for individuals who have something in common—an interest in a hobby, a topic, or an organization—and who share a simple desire to communicate across physical boundaries with other interested people. Most social networking sites include the ability to chat in real time, send email, blog, participate in discussion groups, and share files. Users can also post links to photos, music, and video files, all of which have the potential to create a virtual identity.

The introduction of social networking has produced a cultural shift in the idea of privacy. Some people today are willing to expose more about themselves to the general public. It is commonplace to see content related to alcohol, drugs, and sex posted on future teachers' social networking profiles.[7] A 2007 Pew study, titled "Digital Footprints," revealed that 60 percent of Internet users surveyed were not worried about how much information was available about them online.

This finding represented a significant change from a 2000 Pew study, in which 84 percent of respondents expressed concern about "businesses and people you don't know getting personal information about you and your family."[8]

Many teachers use social networking sites as an avenue to enhance their instruction. Such sites allow teachers to establish deeper relationships with and understandings of students. Using this means of communication, teachers can remind students of upcoming homework, tests, and deadlines. In contrast, other teacher social networking uses are coming under fire for what school districts consider "inappropriate activity," including candid photos, racy or suggestive song lyrics, and references to sex, alcohol, or drug use. Venting about personal frustrations at work has also caused problems.[9]

Reflect & Discuss

Review the NEA's Code of Ethics, Principles I and II, and answer the following questions.

A. Discuss why you think most professions have a code of ethics. Why do you think the teaching profession may or may not need a code of ethics?

B. Which statements in the principles do you consider vague? What are the different ways someone might interpret these vague statements? How would you clarify any statements you believe are not stated the way you would state them?

C. Are there areas of the teaching profession that the NEA's Code of Ethics does not address? What would you add? Answer now, and then answer this question again after finishing this chapter.

D. Do the principles and items appear to offer more protection to the profession or to the students? What examples can you cite to support this belief? Explain why you think this is so.

Risks of communicating outside the "controlled environment" Teachers who communicate with their students outside the controlled classroom environment must make decisions about what and how much personal information to reveal. Although teachers may have control over the content they disclose on their university-housed Web pages, friends, strangers, or other students can post discrediting or defamatory messages on users' Facebook websites.

Apart from banning teachers outright from using these sites to communicate with their students, some school districts have taken a range of disciplinary actions, including dismissal, against what they consider to be teachers' questionable uses of social networking sites. Consider the following cases. In 2010, a teacher in a Massachusetts high school resigned her $92,636-a-year job as a math and science program supervisor after she posted Facebook comments describing the local parents as "arrogant and snobby" and referred to children as "germ bags."[10] In 2009, 24-year-old Ashley Payne, a public high school English teacher in Georgia, had to answer her principal's questions about her Facebook page, which showed her holding a glass of wine and a mug of beer. The photo also showed a reference to a local trivia contest with a profanity in its title. One of Payne's students' parents had seen the page and complained. Ashley was given the choice of either resigning or being suspended. She resigned and later sued the school district. In October 2011, a Georgia Superior Court judge ruled against her.[11]

Online social networking can even cause problems before someone enters the profession. In 2006, Stacy Snyder, age 25, a Pennsylvania college senior, was dismissed from the student teaching program at a nearby high school and denied her teaching credential after the school staff came across her MySpace photograph captioned "drunken pirate." The head shot, which was taken at a costume party, showed Snyder wearing a pirate's hat and sipping from a large plastic cup whose contents cannot be seen. A university official told her that the photo was "unprofessional" and could have offended her students if they accessed her MySpace page. Snyder filed a lawsuit in federal court in Philadelphia, contending that her rights to free expression under the First Amendment had been violated and asking her college for her education degree and teaching certificate.[12] In December 2008, the court ruled against her.[13]

Ethical behavior: A higher standard Like it or not, teachers are held to a higher standard of moral behavior than is the population in general. This expectation is reflected in the clauses of various state certification procedures, which mandate that teachers shall not "engage in conduct which would

Reflect & Discuss

Posting personal material on social networking sites makes it public. Although this behavior may now be part of our culture, it also raises serious ethical and employment issues when viewed in a professional context.

A. Review your own social networking sites from the perspectives of a future employer, a parent of a future student, and a future principal. Identify all "questionable" writings and images that may appear attractive to peers but that might appear "inappropriate" to an employer or parent.
B. Pair with a classmate to review each other's social networking sites through the eyes of a potential employer or a student's parent. What otherwise harmless words or images might these other parties consider "inappropriate"?
C. Report back to the class on your findings.
D. If you find items that might be "inappropriate," what will you do, and when?

discredit the teaching profession." Under these state clauses, teachers have been denied entry into or dismissed from their profession based on their behavior outside the classroom. Many states also have professional codes of ethics for teachers, with guidelines for teachers' participation in social networking sites.[14]

Even when the law is clear, the higher standard to which teachers are held means they must rely on their good judgment and professional ethics to govern their public and professional behaviors. Ethics regulates behavior from the inside out. Teachers need to always ask themselves how any behavior—whether inside the classroom or over the Internet—will protect students' well-being, motivate other teachers, and inspire public trust and confidence in the education profession.

In a world where social connections and friendships are now defined by user-generated content on the Web, it is yet unclear where privacy ends and professional life begins. Decisions about what and how to share private information cannot be made lightly, because their negative consequences for teachers—and for students—can last a lifetime. It is wise to be judicious before posting details about one's personal life online or participating in relationships with students outside clearly defined professional boundaries.

Did You Get It?

A professional code of ethics

a. Is the moral foundation of professional decisions and actions; adhering to it can keep you out of a lot of hot water and prevent you from harming your students.
b. Is a reasonable substitute for a strong inner sense of right, wrong, and personal dignity, of oneself and of others.
c. Supersedes legal requirements, such as the mandated reporting of known or suspected child abuse.
d. Is often a nice gloss over social prejudices and norms that are enforced more harshly on women than men.

Take the full quiz on CourseMate.

9-2 How Teachers' Constitutional Freedoms Operate in Schools

School law is a fast-growing field of study because states and courts keep making decisions that affect how states and localities conduct education and how schools balance teachers' constitutional freedoms with the responsibility to provide a safe, orderly, and efficient learning environment. **Case law**, the legal precedents that judges create in their written opinions when they decide legal cases, influences virtually every aspect of education.[15] In case law, judges can either interpret statutory law or interpret prior judicial decisions.[16] As your teacher preparation and teaching experiences grow, these issues will become more familiar to you, and you can make more informed decisions.

case law The legal precedents that judges create in their written opinions when they decide legal cases, which influence virtually every aspect of education.

9-2a A Legal Context

The U.S. Constitution, federal statutes, state constitutions, state statutes, case law, and regulations all influence educational practice. Although states have substantial power to manage schools, their control is not absolute. Federal and state constitutions limit the state's authority to enact statutes controlling education's operations. In other words, if the state legislature enacted a law calling for a practice that conflicted with the federal or state constitution, a court would strike down that law.

Case law frequently references amendments to the Constitution. Many court cases that involve education's general or guiding practices come from the U.S. Supreme Court and focus on either the First or the Fourteenth Amendment. The First Amendment, ratified in 1791, deals with freedom of religion, speech, press, and assembly. It reads:

> Congress shall make no law respecting an establishment of religion, or prohibiting the free exercise thereof; or abridging the freedom of speech, or of the press; or the right of the people peaceably to assemble, and to petition the Government for a redress of grievances.

This amendment is important to schools because it affects church–state relations, school prayer, religious exercises in schools, and individuals' right to practice their religion in schools. It also affects student assemblies, drama programs, and newspapers (freedom of speech and freedom of the press), and becomes an issue when someone seeks a way to appeal some unfairness that is government imposed.

The Fourteenth Amendment, ratified in 1868 and designed to promote the rights of newly freed slaves, addresses due process and equal protection. It reads in part:

> All persons born or naturalized in the United States and subject to the jurisdiction thereof, are citizens of the United States and of the State wherein they reside. No State shall make or enforce any law which shall abridge the privileges or immunities of citizens of the United States; nor shall any State deprive any person of life, liberty, or property, without the due process of law; nor deny to any person within its jurisdiction the equal protection of the laws.

This amendment guarantees that states cannot take away citizens' constitutional rights. It affects teachers' freedom of speech and freedom of religion, for example. The term "due process of law" has implications for teacher contract issues, student suspensions, and a host of other legal areas. Significantly, the last clause, known as *equal protection*, states that equal protection—that is, equal application—of the law shall not be denied to any *person* (not just a citizen) by a state.

9-2b Teaching License or Certificate

Each state has the authority to establish the criteria for teacher eligibility and certification.[17] For the most part, each state has developed its own specific certification requirements, though many states have reciprocal licensure agreements with other states. This **reciprocity** means if a person qualifies for licensure in a state that has a reciprocal agreement with another state, the individual qualifies for licensure in both states. For instance, if someone qualifies for a teaching license in Virginia, and Virginia has a reciprocal agreement with California, the individual also qualifies for a California teaching license. The general rule is that if a person satisfies all the requirements established for receiving a state teaching license, the licensing agency cannot arbitrarily refuse to issue a license to that individual.

reciprocity The process of mutual exchange between states that recognize the status granted to citizens of one state by the other.

certification A state's process of affirming that the certificate or license holder has met the minimum requirements to hold a teaching job.

Having a teaching license or certificate, however, does not guarantee its holder a teaching position. A teaching certificate is not a contract. Rather, **certification** is simply a state's way of saying that the certificate or license holder has met the minimum requirements to hold a teaching job. Once the individual has the license, it is that person's responsibility to persuade school district officials through a written or online job application and during an interview that he or she is the best-qualified candidate for the position.

Generally, states issue teaching licenses and keep them active for a specific period of time, usually five years. Over that period, teachers must prepare to renew the license by taking classes, participating in professional development activities, and updating and expanding their professional knowledge and skills. Because most states require a valid teaching license to obtain a teaching contract, a teacher's job may be in jeopardy if his or her teaching license expires.

What This Means for Teachers Keeping one's teaching license up to date and not giving the school district cause (good reason) to request that the license be revoked are recommended professional practices.

Can my teaching license be revoked once it is issued to me? Yes. Most states have criteria for revoking a teaching license and have established a process to do so. Needless to say, an educator who loses his or her professional license will not be able to earn a living as a teacher. Revoking a license is a severe penalty, similar to a lawyer being disbarred or a physician losing his or her license to practice medicine.

States require a just cause to revoke a teaching license. These reasons may include conviction of a felony, moral turpitude,[18] or falsifying teaching credentials. Because community standards vary, the state may base these decisions on how the community reacts to certain situations. For example, in *Crumpler v. State Board of Education* (1991), an Ohio court decided that a conviction for stealing drugs and money was sufficient grounds for denying a teaching certificate.[19]

In 1982, a Florida court upheld the revocation of two teachers' licenses for growing 52 marijuana plants in a greenhouse because their actions violated the community's moral standards and impaired the teachers' classroom effectiveness.[20] Similarly, conviction of mail fraud was cited as grounds for revoking a teaching license in *Startzel v. Pennsylvania Department of Education* (1989).[21]

A clear example of how moral standards may vary from community to community is seen in *Erb v. Iowa State Board of Public Instruction* (1974).[22] In spring 1970, teachers Richard Erb and Margaret Johnson (both married, though not to each other) began an extramarital affair. Suspicious, Johnson's husband caught his wife and Erb during several rendezvous, had photos taken of the couple's illicit activities, asked his wife for a divorce, and requested that the school board fire Erb. Erb offered to resign, but the school board voted unanimously to reject his resignation. Owing to his excellent teaching evaluations and his wife's and student body's forgiveness, Erb's high standing in the community remained intact.

Although the State Board of Education and lower trial court voted to revoke Erb's teaching license, the Iowa Supreme Court disagreed on appeal, stating that the misconduct was an isolated incident in an otherwise unblemished past. Erb's conduct did not serve as an affront to public mores, he admitted the action, and he publicly stated his regret for his behavior. Ultimately, Erb kept his job and his teaching license.

A different community might have responded to Erb's behavior in a different way, of course. A fine line exists regarding which behaviors may result in losing a teaching license. Much depends on the exact details of the situation and the state in which the behavior occurs.

What This Means for Teachers The best advice is always to make wise choices in personal conduct, because poor choices may cost teachers their jobs and their teaching licenses.

Can my teaching license be revoked if the state adds testing requirements later that I cannot pass? Yes. In *State v. Project Principle, Inc.* (1987), the court found that not passing a state-required test following a teacher license being issued may cause the individual to lose the license.[23] In 1984, the Texas legislature passed a bill requiring teacher competency testing. All practicing teachers and administrators were required to pass the Texas Examination of Current Administrators and Teachers (TECAT). A suit was brought claiming that not renewing licenses if individuals did not pass the TECAT violated teachers' existing contracts with their school systems and violated their equal protection and due process clauses.

Ultimately, the Texas Supreme Court ruled that the state had the right to set competency testing requirements. Because such testing had a rational relationship to the state's objective of maintaining a competent teaching force in its public schools, it did not violate the equal protection clause. Furthermore, the Texas Supreme Court ruled that a certificate is not a contract to teach; it is merely a license.

What This Means for Teachers A teaching license is not forever. Its ongoing validity depends on the teacher continuing to successfully meet the state's requirements for keeping it.

9-2c A Teaching Contract

When teachers sign a contract, state statutes and State Department of Education regulations govern the employment conditions. Generally, the contract is between the teacher and the local school board. The contract will specify the nature of the job to be performed and the compensation to be paid. Some contracts are very specific and say, for example, "fifth grade teacher at Oak Hill Elementary School." Other contracts are less specific and may simply state, "teacher." Most often, the teacher cannot be assigned to teach a content area outside of his or her certification without the teacher agreeing to do so. Finally, once a contract is offered, it must be accepted within a reasonable time frame or the contract becomes null and void. The contract may or may not stipulate this time frame.

Most teaching contracts have a provision for teachers to serve a **probationary period**—usually three years working under an annual contract. Some states have shorter probationary periods; others have longer ones. Generally, the range is from one to five years. Once a teacher satisfactorily serves the probationary period, states have a provision for tenure, sometimes called **continuing contract status**.

Tenure provides a degree of job security and a right of continued employment for teachers. Once tenured, a teacher cannot be dismissed without due process. **Due process** includes a formal hearing and presentation of proof of sufficient cause to meet the statutory requirements for removal from the position. The teacher has an opportunity to challenge the evidence.[24] Generally, the tenured teacher must be notified of the detailed charges in a timely manner and given sufficient opportunity to prepare a defense. The hearing must be held before an impartial body (which may be the school board unless bias can be proved). The teacher's attorney may cross-examine witnesses and challenge any evidence brought in the case. In addition, the teacher can appeal an unfavorable decision in court.

probationary period The time frame in which untenured teachers work on annual contracts, usually one to five years.

continuing contract status The legal arrangement following a satisfactory probationary period in which a teacher receives an ongoing contract, or tenure.

tenure Continuing contract status that provides a degree of job security and a right of continued employment for teachers who cannot be dismissed without due process.

due process A legal procedure that includes a formal hearing and presentation of proof of sufficient cause to meet the statutory requirements for removal from the position. The teacher has an opportunity to challenge the evidence and appeal any unfavorable decision in court.

An untenured teacher, by contrast, may simply be notified that his or her annual contract will not be renewed. The employing school district may give no reason for the termination. However, if the employing school district gives an illegal reason, the teacher may decide to sue the school district.

Teachers also face a range of legal issues once they are employed and teaching. Teachers' rights sometimes come with complex responsibilities. Legal factors regarding academic freedom, free speech, teacher privacy, and freedom of religion may all affect how teachers do their jobs.

9-2d Freedom of Speech

On the one hand, as citizens of the United States, teachers have a right to disagree publicly with a school principal's decision. On the other hand, if a teacher in a school makes public comments about "what a stupid decision the principal made," the teacher may get into legal trouble if those comments disrupt the school's operation. Teachers' freedom of speech is subject to certain limits.

Do teachers have academic freedom in the classroom? It depends. The concept of academic freedom comes to American public education from German universities. It encompasses two separate aspects—the freedom to learn and the freedom to teach. In the United States, academic freedom is bound up in the First Amendment ideal of free speech. **Academic freedom** means that teachers have some choices in the teaching methods they use as long as the teaching methods meet professional standards. Teachers have the professional freedom to monitor and adjust their teaching strategies if their students are not mastering the content.

academic freedom The choices that teachers have in the teaching methods they use as long as the teaching methods meet professional standards.

Academic freedom does *not* mean that teachers can say whatever they would like—or teach whatever they want—in the classroom. In *The Law of Schools, Students, and Teachers in a Nutshell* (2003), Alexander and Alexander explain, "[A]cademic freedom . . . does not bestow upon the teacher and the student 'unlimited liberty' to do anything their hearts desire; rather the concept must be viewed in the total context of the legal purpose and conduct of the school. Although academic freedom and the First Amendment are not synonymous they are closely related."[25] For example, suppose a third-grade teacher wants to teach a unit about skin, muscles, and bones, but that content belongs in the fourth-grade curriculum. The teacher has no right to teach the subject out of the school system's established curriculum sequence.

Reviewing several court cases helps clarify teachers' academic freedom. In *Cockrel v. Shelby County School District, et al.* (2001),[26] Donna Cockrel, a fifth-grade teacher, was teaching a unit on "saving the trees." Studying alternatives to wood pulp, the class discussed industrial hemp fibers (hemp is derived from the same plant as marijuana). At that time, popular actor Woody Harrelson was in the state to talk with the Kentucky Hemp Growers Association. With the principal's permission, the teacher asked Harrelson to speak to the class. During Harrelson's discussion, he passed hemp seeds (which were illegal) around the class. Given the local and national media extensively covering this celebrity, the event received widespread publicity. Responding to several parents' complaints about the lesson's appropriateness, the school superintendent asked the Professional Standards Board to investigate the illegal hemp seeds incident and report back. The board found insufficient cause to take any action against the teacher. At that point, the school district put a "controversial topics" policy into place in its schools.

Complying with the new policy, Cockrel received permission for Harrelson to return for another class discussion. The school board then fired her. Nevertheless, the court ruled that the teacher's speech was constitutionally protected as a matter of public concern, and that she could not be fired. The school board had violated its own policy; the teacher had not.

In another case, *Keefe v. Geanakos* (1969), a high school teacher gave his class copies of an article published in *Atlantic Monthly* that used a rather vulgar and literal term to describe an incestuous son.[27] The teacher explained the word's etymology to the class and clarified why the author had used that specific word in the story. Any students finding the article offensive were allowed to select an alternative reading. The school board dismissed the teacher, and he sued to recover his teaching position. The court agreed with the teacher in finding the article to be thoughtful; deleting the offending word would have made understanding the article impossible. The teacher was reinstated.

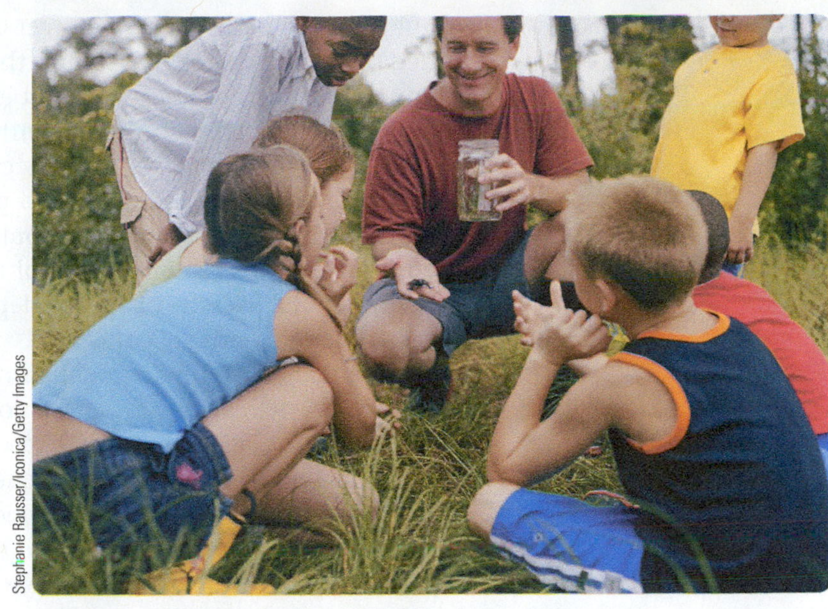
Stephanie Rausser/Iconica/Getty Images

Teachers have choices in teaching methods as long as they meet professional standards.

In *Board of Education of Jefferson County School District R-1 v. Wilder* (1988), the school district had a policy for approving material to be used in class that was outside the usual curriculum.[28] When a teacher failed to obtain approval for showing a class an R-rated film depicting nudity, sexual conduct, and drug use, the school board dismissed the teacher. The teacher then sued, stating that the school board's dismissal violated his Fourteenth Amendment due process rights and his First Amendment free speech rights. The court upheld the teacher's dismissal, stating that the school board's policy was a reasonable method for regulating possible inappropriate classroom materials.

Teachers may go beyond legal bounds when they select classroom material that is "offensive and unnecessary to the accomplishment of educational objectives . . . [where] . . . such questions are matters of degree involving judgment on such factors as the age and sophistication of the students, relevance of the educational purpose, and context and manner of presentations."[29] In other words, a teacher does not have total freedom to select materials that are not age or educationally appropriate.

What This Means for Teachers Many school districts have approved curriculum and reading lists from which teachers must select books, articles, reading, and viewing materials. Teachers are advised to find out if their school board has a policy about selecting classroom materials, know what that policy is, and follow it. When in doubt about some particular content to use in class, teachers should first seek guidance from their department head, their grade-level leader, or a school administrator. Not following school board policy about classroom reading or viewing materials could be both unethical and insubordinate, and it could cost the teacher his or her job.

free speech The U.S. constitutional protection that government must tolerate and cannot restrain the exercise of its citizens to express themselves in open public debate, regardless of whether that speech is offensive, tumultuous, or discordant.

The *Cockrel* case mentioned "public concern." What is "speaking out on a matter of public concern," and how can it affect my job? **Free speech** means that government must tolerate and cannot restrain the exercise of free speech in open public debate, regardless of whether that speech is offensive, tumultuous, or discordant.[30] Yet over the years, the U.S. Supreme Court has concluded that practical reality requires that government, at certain times and under certain conditions, be able to restrict employees' speech to fulfill its responsibilities to operate effectively and efficiently.

Defining what a *public concern* is can be tricky. Today, speaking out publicly as a teacher about tax increases or a proposed policy where public comment is encouraged is clearly a matter of public concern. The Supreme Court has decided, however, that a public school teacher or other school employee may be restrained in the exercise of speech depending on whether it involves a matter of public concern or private concern.

Early in American history, public employment was viewed as a privilege, not as a right. As such, many courts held that contracts between teachers and school boards curtailed certain teacher rights and freedoms. If a teacher spoke out on an issue that violated the contract's terms, the teacher could be dismissed and the courts would uphold the dismissal. Until 1968, school teachers were hesitant to become too involved in politics for fear that they would be penalized or even fired for such activities. In 1968, in its ruling in *Pickering v. Board of Education*, the U.S. Supreme Court decided that teachers have a right to speak out freely on matters of public concern.[31]

Marvin Pickering was a teacher at Township High School in Illinois. The locality was considering a tax increase to raise school revenue. Not liking how an earlier bond issue distributed funds between athletics and academics, Pickering wrote a letter to the editor of the local newspaper that was critical of how the previous tax increase had allocated funds. He alleged that the superintendent of schools tried to prevent teachers from opposing the proposed bond issue. Pickering's letter contained several factual errors.

The school board held a hearing to determine if Pickering's letter had "been detrimental to the efficient operation of the schools of the district," which, under state statute, required the teacher's dismissal. Finding this assertion to be true, the school board fired Pickering. In accordance with state law, the board held a hearing on Pickering's dismissal. Although the hearing board found many of the school board's allegations that the letter's publication damaged the board's and superintendent's professional reputations to be false, it upheld the dismissal. The Illinois Supreme Court also upheld his dismissal.

Eventually, the U.S. Supreme Court disagreed, noting that "without proof of false statements knowingly or recklessly made by him, a teacher's exercise of his right to speak on issues of public importance may not furnish the basis for his dismissal from public employment." Pickering's statements in no way harmed the school district's operations and did not affect the teacher's performance. Pickering won the case.

To guide lower federal courts in future cases of this nature, the Supreme Court stated what has come to be called the *Pickering* balance test. Writing in the Court's opinion, Justice Thurgood Marshall explained:

> The problem in any case is to arrive at a balance between the interests of the teacher, as a citizen, in commenting upon matters of public concern and the interest of the State, as an employer, in promoting the efficiency of the public services it performs through its employees.[32]

In other words, a balance must be found between a person's rights to speak out on matters of public concern and an organization's interest in doing its job efficiently.

Fifteen years later in *Connick v. Myers* (1983), the U.S. Supreme Court clarified the limitations on public employees' free speech.[33] Although a public employee's speech is protected when he or she is speaking out on a matter of public concern, balancing the employee's and state's interests, the First Amendment does not protect a public employee's speech or expression concerning a private or personal interest in matters of public concern. Even though this case did not involve educators, it is relevant because Myers was a public employee, and the precedent established in this case has been cited in legal actions involving educators.

Assistant District Attorney Sheila Myers was told she would be reassigned to another area of criminal law. Opposing the transfer, Myers circulated a questionnaire to other assistant district attorneys about staff morale and related issues. She was told the questionnaire amounted to insubordination, and she was fired. The Supreme Court upheld her dismissal, stating that the matter was basically a private issue and not a public one. It became a personal issue because the questionnaire went out after the transfer was announced. The Court believed that Myers's First Amendment interest was outweighed by the disruptive nature of the questions she was circulating to colleagues, which "substantially interfered with the operation of the office."

Placing additional limits on teachers' speech, the ruling in *Stroman v. Colleton County School District* (1993) specified that teachers' First Amendment (free speech) rights do not extend to encouraging dishonest conduct and conduct that violates policy.[34] In this case, because he was upset about a change in the Colleton County School District's summer pay policy (from lump sum to bimonthly), teacher John Stroman wrote and circulated a letter to fellow teachers. He criticized the central office for fiscal mismanagement and being administratively "top heavy," and he encouraged teachers to participate in a "sick out" during the week of final exams.

Meeting with the superintendent and his principal the next day, Stroman admitted writing and circulating the letter, claiming that he was being treated unfairly in terms of his pay schedule. The superintendent promptly handed Stroman a dismissal letter dated that day, citing unfitness for teaching by proposing to and encouraging others to abandon their duties. Stroman sued to be reinstated as a teacher, claiming that his free speech rights were denied.

The Fourth Circuit Court of Appeals[35] affirmed the teachers' First Amendment free speech rights but stated that a grievance (in this case, the change in summer pay policy) was not covered under the First Amendment. The court ruled that speaking out in self-interest about the summer pay changes made the matter one of self-concern and not public concern, eliminating the free speech rights claim. Stroman's dismissal was upheld.

This decision has had a major legal impact on teachers' rights to speak out on issues that are part of their official duties. At present, the courts appear to be moving more toward protecting employers than protecting employees in what might be considered free speech issues and employment.

What This Means for Teachers When acting as a teacher or as a citizen, be careful what you say in a public forum about your teaching role and its employment context—because it might cost your job.

Can the school board require a dress code for teachers? Yes. Several court cases decided the issue of a teachers' **professional dress code** more than 35 years ago. The outstanding case specifically related to such a dress code was *East Hartford Education Association v. Board of Education* (1977),[36] in which the Second Circuit Court of Appeals decided that a teacher dress policy is constitutional.

professional dress code The organization's expectations for appropriate employees' attire or wardrobe.

In this case, Richard Brimley, an English teacher, was reprimanded for not wearing a necktie to his classes. Earlier, the school board had implemented a policy requiring male teachers to wear a jacket, shirt, and tie to classes. Female teachers were required to wear a dress, skirt, blouse, or pantsuit to classes. If teachers had other teaching assignments such as physical education, they could wear more appropriate clothing.

Feeling that the dress code deprived him of his free speech and privacy rights, Brimley stated that not wearing a tie to class assisted him with his teaching, helping his students relate more closely to him as a person not tied to conformity or the establishment. He claimed that not wearing a tie was his symbolic speech and, therefore, was constitutionally protected. The court disagreed with the teacher's assertions, stating that a "protected interest in Mr. Brimley's neckwear . . . does not weigh very heavily on the constitutional scales."[37] The court ruled that it is in the school board's interest to promote respect for authority and traditional values, as well as classroom discipline, by requiring teachers to dress in a professional manner. Promoting a dress code is a rational means of promoting these goals.

What This Means for Teachers If your employing school district has a professional dress code, follow it if you want to continue your employment there. Express your individuality through effective instructional approaches.

9-2e Teacher Privacy

The word *privacy* is not found in either the Bill of Rights or the Constitution. Nonetheless, it is considered to be a basic and fundamental right, a logical offshoot of the constitutional protection against unreasonable search and seizure. Therefore, a compelling state interest must be demonstrated to warrant violating a person's privacy. The Fourth Amendment of the U.S. Constitution reads as follows:

> The right of the people to be secure in their persons, houses, papers, and effects, against unreasonable searches and seizures, shall not be violated, and no Warrants shall issue, but upon probable cause, supported by Oath or affirmation, and particularly describing the place to be searched, and the persons or things to be seized.

Although teachers keep their right to privacy in schools, this right has certain limits.

Can my classroom, desk, closet, and file cabinets be searched? Yes. A teacher's right to privacy in the classroom comes under the concept of a workplace. In *O'Connor v. Ortega* (1987), the Supreme Court defined the **workplace** as "those areas and items that are related to work and are generally within the employer's control."[38] This would include offices, hallways, cafeterias, desks, file cabinets, lockers, and other areas. In these locations, an employee does not have an expectation of privacy, and the school may search them.

workplace Defined by the Supreme Court as "those areas and items that are related to work and are generally within the employer's control" in which the employee does not have an expectation of privacy and the school may search.

The Supreme Court did not establish any ground rules on when or how an employer's "interest in supervision, control and the efficient operation of the workplace" would outweigh an employee's "legitimate expectations of privacy." It left to the lower courts the job of applying the simple "balance" formula on a case-by-case basis.

A teacher's personal effects, such as purses, briefcases, and closed luggage are not considered as belonging to the workplace. These items may not be searched without a warrant.

What This Means for Teachers Because many workplace areas are not legally "private," wise teachers should only bring to school with them those items that they would not mind everyone knowing they have.

Teacher drug testing The Fourth Amendment safeguards individuals against arbitrary and unwarranted intrusions into their privacy. It does not limit all searches and seizures, however—only those that are unreasonable. What is "reasonable" depends on the circumstances and the nature of the search and seizure itself. What is "reasonable" remains an open question.

To search citizens, the police must have **probable cause**—a reasonable belief that a person has committed a crime. Due to schools' unique nature in which they serve *in loco parentis* (in the place of the parent), the standard for school searches is lower than that required for the police to search an ordinary citizen. In schools, the government has a special interest that allows warrantless searches based on **reasonable suspicion** (credible information from a reliable source)—a less demanding standard than probable cause. This standard of reasonable suspicion justifies searches of students and teachers on school property.

probable cause The standard by which police have a reasonable belief that a person has committed a crime.

reasonable suspicion The standard that allows school officials to conduct warrantless searches when they have credible information from a reliable source, a less demanding standard than probable cause.

suspicionless searches A new category of reasonable searches that permits testing for drugs and alcohol without showing individualized suspicion.

In addition, the increased prevalence of illegal drug use has prompted courts to define privacy rights in a new context that does not neatly fit with probable cause or reasonable suspicion. As a result, courts have formulated a new category of reasonable searches called **suspicionless searches,** which permit testing for drugs and alcohol without showing individualized suspicion.

As a teacher, can I be forced to take a drug test? Yes. In *Hearn v. Board of Education* (1999), the school district had a zero-tolerance policy for drugs and alcohol on school property.[39] During a routine "drug dog" search of the parking lot, the dog sniffed drugs in a teacher's car. The teacher claimed the search was illegal. The school district policy required that anyone suspected of having or having used drugs submit to a urine test within two hours; refusal to comply with the policy could result in the employee being fired. The teacher refused to take the urine test and was later fired. The teacher sued, and the court held that the search was legal based on the probable cause of the dog sniff identification of the vehicle.

Additionally, the U.S. Supreme Court has held that under certain conditions, suspicionless searches of people employed in safety-sensitive positions may take place.[40] A federal court has ruled that teachers fall under the safety-sensitive positions and may be compelled to submit to drug searches in the form of urine testing.[41]

What This Means for Teachers Teachers may be asked to submit to drug testing. They may refuse to do so, but they will probably be fired for not complying with the request.

Can school authorities test teachers for illegal drug use without having a reasonable suspicion of drug use? Yes. In *Knox County Education Association v. Knox County Board of Education* (1998), the U.S. Court of Appeals ruled that school authorities could conduct suspicionless drug testing of teachers.[42]

In this case, the court ruled that suspicionless testing was justified based on the unique role that teachers play in schoolchildren's lives. In the school setting, where teachers act *in loco parentis,* the public interest in drug testing outweighs teachers' privacy interests in not being tested. The court further pointed out that the teaching profession is by nature and of necessity heavily regulated, and teachers have a diminished expectation of privacy. The drug testing regimen employed in this school system was limited, narrowly tailored, and relatively unobtrusive in its monitoring and disclosure.

What This Means for Teachers Prospective teachers must comply with school districts' drug and alcohol policies or be denied employment. Employed teachers risk job termination if they are found using an illegal substance or alcohol at a job-related function or on property owned by the school board.

9-2f Teachers' Freedom of Religion

As U.S. citizens, teachers have rights defined by the U.S. Constitution that accompany them into the classroom. Freedom of religion is one of these protected rights. As with freedom of speech, however, this right is not unlimited.

The First Amendment to the U.S. Constitution dealing with freedom of religion states:

> Congress shall make no law respecting an establishment of religion, or prohibiting the free exercise thereof . . .

The 1972 amendment to Title VII of the Civil Rights Act further expands this religious freedom:

> It shall be an unlawful employment practice for an employment agency to fail or refuse for employment, or otherwise to discriminate against, any individual because of his race, color, religion, sex, or national origin, or to classify or refer for employment any individual on the basis of his race, color, religion, sex, or national origin.

May I be required to teach something that goes against my religious beliefs? Yes. Although these laws guarantee Americans freedom of religion, this religious freedom is not unlimited. In *Palmer v. Board of Education of the City of Chicago* (1980), a teacher refused to teach part of the city-designated curriculum, stating that to do so would violate her religious beliefs.[43] Although the court acknowledged the teacher's right to freedom of belief, it also pointed out the school district's interest in providing a proper education to all students. The ruling in this case further stated that teachers "cannot be left to teach the way they please." When a teacher has a religious belief that interferes with teaching the required class content, the content takes priority over the religious beliefs.

However, if a teacher's religious tenets prohibit the teacher from pledging to the flag, the teacher cannot be forced to recite the Pledge of Allegiance with the class as part of his or her professional duties. If school rules require the Pledge to be recited, the teacher may be required to be in the classroom with the students as they recite the Pledge of Allegiance.[44] The courts have continued to uphold teachers' freedom of religion as long as it does not encroach on students' rights and does not harm the school's good conduct.

What should teachers know about the courts' position on intelligent design? The U.S. Supreme Court and a federal court in Pennsylvania ruled that teaching creationism or intelligent design is unconstitutional teaching of religion in public schools.

Are teachers legally responsible for teaching intelligent design alongside evolution? No. In *Edwards v. Aguillard* (1987),[45] the U.S. Supreme Court ruled that requiring a "balanced" treatment of creation science and evolution science was unconstitutional because it violated the bar against teaching religion in public schools. Likewise, in *Kitzmiller v. Dover Area School District* (2005),[46] a federal court, in a strongly worded opinion, struck down as unconstitutional a local school board's attempt to insert teaching of intelligent design into the classroom as an attempt to "discredit evolution," which has the scientific community's support.

As a teacher, am I permitted to celebrate my religious holidays? Usually. As an employment practice, school boards must reasonably accommodate aspects of teachers' religious observances and practice unless it can be shown that such accommodations produce undue hardships on the employer's business. The teacher has the initial burden of proof to show that a school board's decision was religiously motivated or involved the denial of a religious freedom. If the teacher does so, the burden then moves to the school board, whose members must show they made a good-faith effort to accommodate the teacher's religious beliefs.

In *Wangsness v. Watertown School District No. 14-4* (1982), the court ruled in favor of a teacher who requested to be absent from school without pay for seven days to attend a religious festival.[47] The teacher's request was denied, but the teacher attended the festival anyway. Before leaving for the event, the teacher prepared lesson plans and met with the substitute teacher to review the lessons. The school district dismissed the teacher, and the teacher sued. The court found that the classes had run well in the teacher's absence, and the school district had not suffered a hardship due to the teacher attending the religious festival. The court determined that the dismissal was not warranted, and had violated the teacher's rights under Title VII.

In another case, *Pinsker v. Joint District No. 28J* (1983), a Jewish teacher requested more than the two days allowed to celebrate the religious holidays.[48] He showed that teachers of the Christian faith had more days to celebrate their holidays and that the school calendar was built around Christian holidays. The school board denied the teacher's request, and the teacher went to court. Eventually, the court found in favor of the teacher, stating that his Title VII rights were violated because the employer had punished an employee by placing the employee in a position in which a tenet of faith must be ignored to retain employment.

What This Means for Teachers Teachers are allowed to be absent from school to practice their religious faith, but they need to ensure that their absence does not disrupt the school's learning environment. Before their absence during the normal school schedule, teachers must put plans in place to continue their students' learning. Teachers are advised to know and follow their school district's policies and procedures to facilitate their religiously motivated absences.

Can I wear religious clothing and accessories in class? It depends. State law and local policies determine the answer to this question. Some states see teachers wearing religious clothing and accessories as imposing their religious views on students in an area where the state should be neutral.[49]

A 1986 Oregon case related to teacher attire is especially noteworthy. In *Cooper v. Eugene School District No. 4J*, the court determined that the state can revoke a teaching license if a teacher violates the state regulations prohibiting teachers from wearing religious garb in school.[50] Janet Cooper, a teacher in Eugene, Oregon, converted to the Sikh religion. She began to wear the turban and the white clothing associated with her new religion, and she explained her life changes to her students. The administration warned her that her continuing violation of Oregon's state law prohibiting teachers from wearing religious dress in public schools could mean revocation of her teaching certificate.

Cooper continued to wear the religious clothing. Following state law, the superintendent suspended her from teaching and reported the incident to the state's Superintendent of Public Instruction; this official then held a hearing and revoked Cooper's teaching certificate. Cooper challenged the action. The Court of Appeals ruled in her favor, but the State Supreme Court of Oregon reversed the decision and upheld the revocation of her certificate.

So far, the courts have not agreed about teacher attire, largely because they are hesitant to invade the religious rights of either teachers or students. They are clearer about prohibiting situations where schools might appear to be endorsing a particular religion or even prayer. Courts weight interests in view of the particular facts in each case.

What This Means for Teachers It is important for teachers to know and follow the state laws and local policies regarding their professional attire, wearing of religious garb or symbols, use of nondenominational prayer, or prominent display of religious books or other such items while teaching in public schools.

What could happen if I share my religious beliefs in class with my students? It depends. Teachers are employees of the school board. As government employees, teachers accept limits about sharing their personal religious beliefs with students. According to U.S. Supreme Court interpretations of the First Amendment, the state cannot endorse religion or promote one religion over another. When teachers speak as a teacher on school property, they are speaking to children who see them as authority figures. By sharing his or her religious faith with others, a teacher is implicitly endorsing a religion. This places impressionable students under pressure to accept the teacher's religion.

In two relatively recent cases, in 2000 and 2007, two different U.S. Courts of Appeals ruled that teachers could not post "overly religious" materials on their classroom or school bulletin boards because that content violated the First Amendment's Establishment Clause and was not directly related to the curriculum.[51] If school administrators learn that a teacher is sharing his or her religion with students, the administrators can tell the teacher to stop this practice, for the reasons mentioned earlier. If the teacher continues to speak with students about his or her religious beliefs, the teacher can be fired for insubordination.

What This Means for Teachers The teacher's job is to teach the content he or she was hired to teach and not to either subtly or overtly endorse the teacher's religion to students.

What are my rights and obligations as a teacher regarding Bible reading, prayers, and moments of silence in my classroom? It depends. The U.S. Supreme Court has made decisions related to a variety of religious activities when they occur on school grounds. In *School District of Abington Township v. Schempp* and *Murray v. Curlett* (1963),[52] the Court found that state-enforced Bible reading and prayer in public schools were religious exercises and, therefore, unconstitutional. Likewise, in *Wallace v. Jaffree* (1985),[53] the Court ruled that a state-authorized period of silence for meditation or voluntary prayer is unconstitutional. In *Brown v. Gilmore* (2000),[54] however, the Fourth Circuit Court of Appeals in Virginia found that a "minute of silence" was constitutional because its purpose was secular.

What This Means for Teachers Teachers cannot lead prayers, Bible reading, or silent meditation in public schools. Teachers should check their school district's policy regarding any "minute of silence."

9-2g Other Legal Issues Affecting Teachers

Teachers also face legal issues arising from actions that occur while they are teaching.

Is there such a thing as "educational malpractice," and can I be sued if students do not learn in my class? No. The good news here is that there has never been a successful suit for educational malpractice. Educational malpractice is a professional issue, not a legal one.

What This Means for Teachers If students do not learn what the school district expects while those students are in a teacher's class, the issue of the teacher's ineffective practices will be addressed in the school and school district, rather than in court.

Can I be sued if my actions as a teacher cause harm to a student? Yes. Not only may teachers be sued personally for causing student injury, but they may also lose their jobs. Harming another person is the subject of the legal arena called *torts*. A **tort** is a civil wrong or some type of harm that one person causes another person, outside of a contract, for which the courts may award damages.[55] Courts have not been hesitant to rule on torts. It is important to note that torts involve a civil—and not a criminal—wrong.

tort A civil wrong or some type of harm that one person causes another person, outside of a contract, for which the courts may award damages.

assault A mental violation or the threat that someone will receive a physical injury.

battery What happens when the assault becomes physical.

Most people are aware of the terms *assault* and *battery,* but many do not understand the difference between the two. **Assault** is a mental violation or the threat that someone will receive a physical injury. **Battery** is what happens when the assault becomes physical. Almost every school district has regulations that protect students and teachers against assault and battery, and offending parties face severe consequences. Students who threaten to harm another person or who give an unlawful or unwanted touch with the intention of harming or offending another person could be suspended or even expelled from school. In addition, the victim may file criminal and civil charges against the student who threatened or hit that individual. Similarly, teachers who threaten to harm or who give an unwanted or unlawful touch with the intent to harm or offend a student could be fired from their jobs and may lose their teaching licenses. What is more, a teacher could be criminally or civilly charged as a result from the incident.

In *Spears v. Jefferson Parish School Board* (1994), the Louisiana Court of Appeals held the school district liable for a teacher's intentional act that resulted in emotional harm to a child.[56] In 1989, kindergartner Justin Spears and two friends became disruptive while their physical education class watched a movie. One of the coaches, Mr. Brooks, asked the boys to sit by him. They began to play with the teacher's hair and ears. He told the boys if they did not stop, he would "kill them." Brooks took two of the boys into an adjacent office while Justin remained behind with another teacher. The two boys asked Brooks how he would kill them; he responded by saying he would hang them. Brooks and the boys agreed to play a trick on Justin.

Returning to Justin, Brooks convinced him that the teacher had hanged his two friends. When Justin entered the office, one of the boys was on the floor with a rope tied around his neck pretending to be dead. Justin then began to cry, and Brooks tried to calm the boy down by telling him the boys were not really dead.

Being professional means proactively minimizing the potential for harm.

Richard Hutchings/Digital Ligh/Newscom

TeachSource Video 9.1

Legal and Ethical Dimensions of Teaching: Reflections from Today's Educators

Teachers face many legal and ethical issues every day. Knowing the law and your ethical responsibilities can help teachers make wise decisions that protect their students—and themselves. Watch the video clips, study the artifacts in the case, and reflect on the following questions:

1. What are the dilemmas for teachers when they find that a colleague is not making ethical decisions?
2. What are the dilemmas for teachers meeting their responsibilities as court-mandated reporters of child abuse?
3. What are teachers' responsibilities in regard to maintaining the First Amendment (freedom of speech) in their classrooms?
4. What are the teachers' responsibilities and liabilities for students' safety and well-being in the classroom and elsewhere in the school?
5. What is the value of the advice for new teachers of the following: "If you don't know, ask. If you're not sure, don't. Be proactive."

Watch on CourseMate.

After this incident, Justin began to behave strangely at home, using infantile behaviors and becoming more attached to his mother. He refused to go to the bathroom alone, fearing Brooks would jump out of the mirror and harm him. A psychologist diagnosed Justin as having post-traumatic stress syndrome. The parents then sued both the school district as an entity and Brooks as an individual for this injury to their son. The trial court found in favor of the parents, awarding the family general damages of $100,000 for the additional therapy Justin would need, as well as money damages to the parents for losses they received from the incident.

Is it considered "negligence" on my part if something happens in my classroom and someone gets hurt? Maybe. As long as there are children, there will be accidents. Nonetheless, a student injury that results from an unintended mishap does not mean that the supervising adult is legally blameless. **Negligence** is generally defined as conduct that is blameworthy because it falls short of what a reasonable person would do to protect another individual from a foreseeable risk of harm. In short, being a professional means minimizing the potential for injuries to occur by acting proactively in an informed manner to avoid potentially unsafe situations.

A teacher is negligent when, without intending any wrong, he or she either acts or fails to take a precaution that under the circumstances an ordinary prudent and reasonably intelligent teacher ought to foresee would expose another person to unnecessary risk of harm. In certain school functions where children face greater risks, a teacher has an increased level of obligation or duty to the children.

For example, whenever pupils perform a dangerous lab experiment, the teacher has a greater responsibility to ensure the students' safety than when the teacher is supervising a study hall. Likewise, a wood shop teacher has a higher standard of care than a librarian because the risk of harm is greater when students are working with power tools than when they are reading books. Students face more dangers when they are running around the schoolyard than they do when they are sitting quietly studying in the classroom. Clearly, teachers' standards of care vary with the students' ages, and with the situations and circumstances.

negligence Generally defined as conduct that is blameworthy because it falls short of what a reasonable person would do to protect another individual from a foreseeable risk of harm.

No definite rules exist about what constitutes negligence. What is negligent in one situation may not be negligent under a different set of circumstances. The standards of conduct of the teacher are the keys to making this determination. For teachers and other educators, the generally accepted standard of care would be that of a reasonably prudent *teacher,* not that of a reasonably prudent *layperson.*[57] As professionals, courts expect teachers to have more informed awareness and judgment about potential risks than ordinary people.

Of course, sometimes pure accidents occur in which someone is injured and no one is actually at fault. For instance, when a child closed a music room door, cutting off the tip of another student's finger, the court found no negligence had occurred; the event was merely an accident.[58]

What This Means for Teachers Teachers are legally responsible for the well-being of the students under their supervision. They must continually monitor the possibilities for student injury throughout the day and proactively remove threats to student safety. Teachers are held to a standard of care appropriate to reasonably prudent professionals, which is a higher standard of obligation than that applied to people in general.

Did You Get It?

Which statement about teachers' rights and responsibilities is correct?

- **a.** You can lose your license/certificate (your ability to earn a living) for how your community reacts to what you've done, not merely for what you've actually done.
- **b.** Once teachers receive tenure, they have the academic freedom to teach what and how they see fit.
- **c.** Teachers have the freedom of speech to express themselves publicly as citizens about events in their schools.
- **d.** A teacher's classroom desk, closet, and file cabinet are considered to be private and not open to administrative search.

Take the full quiz on CourseMate.

9-3 Student Rights at School—and How They Affect Teachers

Given that students enjoy many of the same constitutional rights as adults, courts have been very careful in ensuring that they are protected.

School officials have broad authority to establish rules and regulations governing student conduct in the school setting. These powers are not absolute, however; they are subject to the standard of *reasonableness*. Generally, rules are considered reasonable if they are needed to maintain an orderly and peaceful school environment and advance the educational process.

In determining the enforceability of school policies, rules, and regulations, courts require school authorities to provide evidence to sufficiently justify their need to enforce these directives. Fair and reasonable exercise of administrative authority will stand up to a judge's scrutiny. Of course, determining exactly what is fair and reasonable depends on the situation.

9-3a Student Discipline and Due Process Rights

Courts have ruled that for schools to operate properly, teachers and principals must be given certain authority to maintain an orderly environment. Practically and legally, parents give schools some level of control when they enroll their children. Nevertheless, students do not lose all of their constitutional privileges when they enter the school building. Schools must balance the individual students' rights with those of the public good.

Just as parents must discipline their children from time to time, so teachers have the authority to guide, correct, and occasionally rebuke their students under the *in loco parentis* concept, unless state law or school board policy does not authorize such a role. Teachers are trained in how to maintain an orderly classroom environment. When students disrupt the learning process, teachers must redirect or discipline them. However, neither parents nor teachers have unlimited control over students: Child abuse is illegal whether it is committed by parents or by teachers.

For the most part, teachers' classroom management is preventive in nature; that is, it focuses on identifying and stopping small problems before they become bigger. When a student overtly and maliciously does not comply with classroom rules, the teacher usually refers the student to an administrator, who handles the misbehavior privately with the student. When punishment is required, detention, in-school suspension, or out-of-school suspension typically result. Under the *in loco parentis* principle, the rules must be reasonable ones. But what is reasonable? When the answer is unclear, the courts must decide.

Suspending a student from school disrupts his or her right to an education. According to the Fourteenth Amendment, due process is required if a citizen's right is being taken away.[59] In *Goss v. Lopez* (1975), the U.S. Supreme Court ruled that a temporary suspension of fewer than 10 days from school requires **procedural due process.**[60] Students must be given oral or written notice of the charges, an explanation of the evidence against them, and an opportunity to present their side of the story. Due process is required whenever a student is separated from school.

procedural due process Required whenever students are separated from school; they must be given oral or written notice of the charges, an explanation of the evidence against them, and an opportunity to present their side of the story.

expulsion Involves long-term or permanent separation of a student from the school program.

The due process procedures become even more formal when the school recommends a student for **expulsion**, which involves long-term or permanent separation from the school program. Similarly, the court's ruling in *Honig v. Doe* (1988) gave students with special needs additional protections in situations involving disciplinary action, thereby limiting schools' ability to make unilateral decisions about removing a disruptive student with disabilities from school.[61]

Giving students their due process rights takes time. An administrator must speak with students and other teachers who may have witnessed the event, determine what actually happened, and decide a reasonable consequence. The administrator must then present the gathered evidence to the offending student and his or her parent or guardian to explain, justify, and document any disciplinary action taken. This process ensures that schools treat all students fairly and legally.

Corporal punishment Although the U.S. Supreme Court determined in *Ingraham v. Wright* (1977)[62] that corporal punishment in schools was acceptable, the public's acceptance of paddling (or spanking) in schools has declined substantially in recent decades. In fact, today a teacher or a principal may be charged with assault and battery for paddling a child in school. If convicted of criminal charges, the educator may be subject to a fine or imprisonment. If convicted on civil charges, the educator may have to pay monetary damages. Currently, 31 states and the District of Columbia ban corporal punishment.[63]

What This Means for Teachers For legal and ethical reasons, we advise teachers not to paddle or physically inflict discomfort on students. Additionally, such actions are not effective in teaching students more appropriate behaviors.

When are disciplinary actions considered to be child abuse? It depends. For many educators and parents, it is not clear precisely which actions make up "child abuse." Corporal punishment as a common-law school privilege often conflicts with most child abuse statutes. In *Arkansas Department of Human Services v. Caldwell* (1992), the court ruled that reasonable force in paddling a student does not constitute child abuse.[64]

In this case, an assistant principal in Mountain Home, Arkansas, paddled three fifth-grade students who had been caught smoking on the playground. The following afternoon, one child's mother noticed bruises on her daughter's buttocks, and reported these actions as suspected child abuse to the appropriate state agency. Because the bruises had resulted from the paddling, the caseworker ruled the child abuse charges were substantiated and placed the administrator's name on the State Central Registry of Child Abuse. The administrator appealed to have her name removed. The court ruled that the paddling was not abusive and noted that reasonable paddling may be legal, although excessive punishment may be abusive.

Where allowed, the corporal punishment administered must be moderate, delivered with a proper instrument, and take into account the child's age, gender, size, and overall physical strength. Within these broad limits, a teacher must balance the seriousness of the offense with the extent of punishment assigned. Because teachers are usually present when student misbehavior occurs, and teachers normally know the manner, look, tone, gestures, language, setting, and general circumstances of the offense, courts will allow teachers considerable latitude in judgment. At the same time, courts will not tolerate punishment that is cruel and excessive. Any sign that teachers acted out of malice will override the teacher's *in loco parentis* privilege.

What This Means for Teachers Teachers need to remain calm, even-tempered, emotionally objective, and professional at all times. Becoming upset with disruptive or disrespectful students to the point where teachers lose their cool and overreact to student behavior can place the teachers in professional and legal jeopardy.

9-3b Student Privacy: Search and Seizure of Student Property

Educators must occasionally decide whether to search a student's locker, desk, book bag, or pockets. At the heart of the issue is the right of privacy guaranteed by the Fourth Amendment, which states, "The right of people to be secure in their person, houses, papers, and effects, against unreasonable searches and seizures shall not be violated, and no warrants shall issue, but upon probable cause. . . ."

Just as parents do not need to prove to a judge that they deserve a warrant so they can check their children's book bags or bedrooms, educators operating *in loco parentis* are held to the less rigorous legal standard of *reasonable suspicion*. Reasonable suspicion is based on receiving credible information from known (as opposed to anonymous) and reliable sources. Suspicion, by definition, implies a belief; it does not equal proof. The courts have ruled that students' right to privacy and freedom from unreasonable search and seizure must be balanced against schools' need to maintain order and provide a safe and secure environment for all students.

The reasonable suspicion standard is not unlimited, however. Public school officials have restraints on their rights to search students' persons,[65] book bags, desks, or lockers. Some facts must provide reasonable grounds for performing the search, the search must be conducted to further a legitimate school purpose such as maintaining school safety, and the search may not be overly intrusive.

Can school officials search students' personal possessions? Yes, under certain conditions, school administrators can search students' personal possessions. A landmark 1985 U.S. Supreme Court case, *New Jersey v. T.L.O.*, provides guidance for school administrators in the area of student searches and seizure of property.[66] In this case, a teacher found a 14-year-old freshman student, T.L.O. (her initials), smoking in the bathroom with another student. The assistant principal asked to see the girl's purse and found cigarettes, rolling papers, marijuana, a pipe, plastic bags, a substantial amount of money, a list of students who apparently owed the girl money, and two letters implicating her in selling marijuana at school. The parents sued, claiming the search unreasonable. On appeal, the U.S. Supreme Court ruled that a student search is permissible if it is "justified at its inception," reasonable, and "not excessively intrusive." What is reasonable, therefore, varies flexibly with the context.

What This Means for Teachers Because school administrators have received professional training in the laws and practices regarding school discipline, teachers are advised to allow principals and assistant principals to conduct any reasonable searches of students' property or persons. The administrator may ask the teacher to remain as a witness to the search.

Can school administrators search student lockers? Yes. In *State of Iowa v. Jones* (2003), the court ruled that annual, school-wide locker cleanouts were permissible despite students' privacy interests and the lack of individualized suspicion.[67] During the cleanout in this case, marijuana was found in a student's locker. The court ruled that although students have a measure of privacy for their lockers' contents, the locker search was not overly intrusive and was reasonable under the circumstances.

Can students expect privacy in their school lockers? No. In a similar case, *Isiah B. v. State of Wisconsin* (1993),[68] the Supreme Court of Wisconsin went still further, finding that a student does not have reasonable expectation of privacy when storing personal items in a school locker. In this case, a school security guard found a gun in a student's coat during a random locker search. The student, Isiah B., also admitted to having cocaine in the coat.

Since the ruling in the T.L.O. case, most courts have concluded that students have no expectation for privacy from search in school lockers. Schools make lockers available to students for the limited purpose of storing legitimate educational materials. Students' constitutional protections must be balanced against the necessity of maintaining a controlled and disciplined environment in which all children can achieve their education.

What This Means for Teachers When assigning lockers to students, and periodically thereafter, teachers should remind their students that lockers are school property loaned to students to store books, coats, and educational materials. School officials can search lockers in the interest of maintaining a safe and orderly learning environment. Students' lockers are not "their" lockers, and should not be assumed to be "private."

Student drug testing Across the United States, illegal drugs affect students' health and safety. Controlling students' drug and alcohol use challenges school authorities, leading many school districts to seriously consider implementing drug testing programs.

In 1989, the U.S. Supreme Court made key rulings in two drug-related cases, concluding that a drug test—regardless of the method used to conduct the test—constitutes a search. Even so, such a search is legal because of the government's compelling interest in promoting public safety by minimizing accidents and protecting the public.[69] The Supreme Court did not hear a case involving drug testing in public schools until 1995.

Can schools randomly test student athletes for illegal drug use? Yes.

Does random drug testing of student athletes violate their privacy? No. In *Vernonia School District 47J v. Acton* (1995), the U.S. Supreme Court ruled that schools could conduct random drug tests on student athletes.[70] According to the court's decision, student athletes voluntarily choose to participate in interscholastic athletics and, therefore, have no legitimate privacy expectations. In a later case, the Supreme Court extended the drug testing rule to include students beyond athletes.

Can all students who participate in competitive extracurricular activities be required to take random drug tests? Yes. In *Board of Education of Independent School District No. 92 of Pottawatomie County v. Earls* (2002), the U.S. Supreme Court ruled that a policy requiring all students who participated in competitive extracurricular activities to submit to a drug test was reasonable and did not violate the Fourth Amendment.[71] According to the Court, the policy reasonably served the school district's important interest in detecting and preventing students' drug use, and it was constitutional.

9-3c Student Records and Privacy Rights

Schools collect and keep student records for purposes including educational planning, counseling, program development, individualized instruction, grade placement, and college admissions, among other uses. Students' files typically include family background information, health records, progress reports, achievement test results, psychological data, disciplinary records, previous report cards, and other confidential material.

Do teachers and other educators have unlimited rights to use student records? No. Common law, specific state and federal statutes, and case law all limit the ways educators can access and use student records to protect students' privacy and rights.

The federal Family Educational Rights and Privacy Act (FERPA) of 1974 guarantees parents and students a degree of confidentiality and fundamental fairness in maintaining and using student records. FERPA was adopted to ensure that certain types of students' personally identifiable and sensitive information would not be released without parental consent. The act establishes standards for schools to follow in handling student records. In 2011, the Department of Education proposed amendments to FERPA to permit use of student data in statewide longitudinal data systems to help evaluate and improve educational programs and end those that don't work. Student information would continue to be protected, with students' personally identifiable information disclosed only for authorized purposes and under the circumstances permitted by law.

Parents have the right to inspect all records that schools maintain on their children, must have an opportunity to challenge these records' accuracy, and must consent before the school can release a student's records to agencies outside designated educational categories. Once a student reaches age 18 or enters postsecondary school, the student may give consent in lieu of the parent to release his or her own records. Schools that do not follow the required procedures risk losing federal education funds.

What This Means for Teachers Teachers must use care when they access and share information about students with other educators. Their purpose must be to help students learn. They must discuss only essential information and should speak only in private locations where others cannot overhear. Teachers must add only objective and accurate information to students' records. A teacher's grade book is considered an educational record that administrators and parents can review and challenge for accuracy and purpose; thus teachers are advised to keep this record accurate, appropriate, up to date, and available.

9-3d Students' Freedom of Speech and Expression

Although free speech is a highly valued right, it is not absolute. Courts recognize that students keep their constitutional rights in school, although schools can regulate and balance them with the school's obligation to provide students with a safe and orderly learning environment. If the exercise of free speech creates a "clear and present danger" to the state, then schools can repress the speech without violating the individual's freedom. The ongoing tension between these two interests complicates the issue of free speech in schools, however.[72]

Can students express their political views silently and nondisruptively in school? Yes. In *Tinker v. Des Moines Independent School District* (1969), student speech became protected unless the public schools could justify a reasonable forecast of "material and substantial disruption."[73] In this case, which involved events that took place in December 1965, Mary Beth Tinker, John Tinker, and three other students were suspended because they wore black armbands to school to protest the Vietnam War, in violation of a hastily made school policy banning wearing black armbands. The U.S. Supreme Court ruled in the students' favor, holding that armbands were a symbolic act of free speech protected by the First Amendment that did not disrupt the school environment.

In its ruling, the Court concluded, "It is hardly argued that either students or teachers shed their constitutional rights to freedom of speech or expression at the schoolhouse gate. . . . Students in school as well as out of school are 'persons' under our Constitution. They are possessed of fundamental rights which the State must respect just as they themselves must respect their obligations to the State. . . . To prohibit . . . expression of one particular opinion without evidence that it is necessary to avoid 'material and substantial interference' with schoolwork or discipline, is not constitutionally permissible."[74]

The *Tinker* ruling changed the relationship between administrators and students. It affirmed that school officials must respect students' civil rights in school. School officials cannot justify a ban on student activity unless the officials can reasonably and legitimately forecast substantial disruption to the school's orderly and safe learning environment.

Mary Beth's and John Tinker's black armbands were protected symbolic speech.

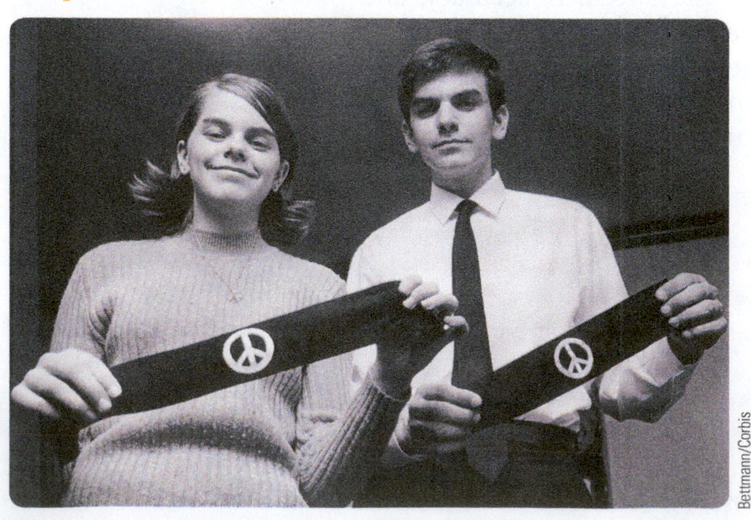
Bettmann/Corbis

Are all student speech and expressions protected while in school? No. Although the *Tinker* case affirmed students' rights to free political speech in school, not all student speech is permissible. In *Bethel School District No. 403 v. Fraser* (1986), the U.S. Supreme Court ruled that the First Amendment does not protect students' lewd and indecent speech.[75] Likewise, in *Morse v. Frederick* (2007), the Court ruled that the First Amendment does not protect students' speech encouraging illegal drug use at a school function.[76]

On April 26, 1983, Matthew Fraser, a student at Bethel High School in Bethel, Washington, delivered a nominating speech for a student elective office at a school assembly. Before giving the speech, the two teachers who reviewed it advised Fraser that the speech was "inappropriate" and that he should not deliver it or risk "severe consequences." Throughout the entire speech, Fraser referred to his candidate in terms of an elaborate, graphic, and explicit sexual metaphor.

A Bethel High School disciplinary rule prohibited the use of obscene or profane language or gestures in school. The next day, Fraser admitted and explained his conduct to the assistant principal. With the teacher witnesses' written statements and Fraser's admission, the administrator suspended Fraser from school. Fraser appealed the suspension and then brought suit, claiming protected speech as decided in *Tinker*.

The U.S. Supreme Court ruled that, in this situation, *Tinker* did not apply. Students' silent political speech that did not disrupt the learning environment was not the same as a student's indecent speech and lewd behavior during a school assembly. Sexually provocative speech in school was offensive, had no political message, and was not constitutionally protected.

In *Morse v. Frederick* (2007), Joseph Frederick, a high school junior, brought and displayed a sign reading "Bong Hits 4 Jesus" to a school-sponsored event. The school's Drug Free Schools and Communities policy required schools to promote drug-free messages. The principal confiscated the banner and suspended Frederick. The Supreme Court ruled that the First Amendment regarding free speech does not require schools to tolerate at school events any student expression that contributes to the dangers of illegal drug use.

What This Means for Teachers Schools can place reasonable limits on students' language—and ban vulgar and offensive language—to ensure its appropriateness for school. Teachers' own conduct and language are considered as models for students' speech and actions. Teachers must use care in their vocabulary and comments while in school; that is, they must act professionally, especially when students can see or hear them.

Can schools regulate the content of student newspapers? Yes. Although a free press is essential to a democratic government's proper functioning, it has certain limitations. Published information is supposed to be true, without malice or harmful motives, and published for appropriate ends, no matter how difficult it may be for our society to ensure adherence to these goals. Similarly, courts tend to reject calls for prior restraint, in which a publication is censored before it can reach its readers.[77]

Freedom of the press in public schools, however, is governed by different constitutional precedents. In *Hazelwood School District v. Kuhlmeier* (1988), the U.S. Supreme Court ruled that schools may regulate the content of school-sponsored newspapers.[78]

Hazelwood East High School's journalism class published the school newspaper, *Spectrum*, which appeared every three weeks during the 1982–1983 school year. Typically, the journalism teacher submitted page proofs of each *Spectrum* issue to the school principal for review before publication. For the May 13 edition, the principal objected to two of the scheduled articles—one story about three students' pregnancies, the other about a divorce's impact on students at the school. The principal was concerned that the pregnant girls' identities would become known, that the sexual references and birth control were inappropriate content for some younger students, and that the divorcing family did not have the chance to respond and consent to the story before its publication. The principal did not allow the stories to be published, and the student authors filed suit.

The U.S. Supreme Court noted that although students have First Amendment rights to free speech, these must be applied in light of the school environment's special characteristics. The Court ruled that educators could exercise editorial control over school-sponsored student expression activities as long as there is a reasonably related pedagogical concern. Because the student newspaper was intended as a supervised learning experience for journalism students, school officials were entitled to reasonably regulate its content.

In the wake of the *Hazelwood* ruling, schools have been permitted to impose reasonable restrictions on students' (and teachers') speech in school newspapers, theater productions, and other expressive activities that are part of the school curriculum, whether or not they occur in a classroom setting. When supervised by faculty members, such activities are designed to impart particular knowledge and skills to student participants and audiences. Students' freedom of speech and expression in a school newspaper, therefore, is not solely determined by the requirements of *Tinker*'s "material and substantial disruption" language. The Supreme Court ruled in *Hazelwood* that the principal was correct in deciding that the student authors and editors in question had not sufficiently mastered the ethical, moral, and legal restrictions that the journalism class taught about treating controversial and personal privacy issues. The principal had legitimate educational concerns.

Can students be disciplined for their speech on Internet/websites? Yes, if the school can show the off-campus Internet-distributed speech would substantially disrupt the school's operations.

The Internet and student speech Students' Internet-related behavior off campus can come under public schools' authority. In *Doninger v. Niehoff* (2008), a U.S. Court of Appeals for the Second Circuit in New York ruled that a school can apply disciplinary consequences to students when their off-campus Internet-distributed comments create a "foreseeable risk of substantial disruption" at the school.[79]

In spring 2007, Jamfest, a Connecticut high school's yearly music festival, experienced a series of planning setbacks that threatened to postpone or cancel the event. When Avery Doninger—a junior and incoming class secretary—was unable to meet with the school's principal, Karissa Niehoff, to discuss the problems, Doninger and three other students sent a mass email asking community members to speak to administrators about rescheduling the event. During a later conversation in the school hallway, the principal informed Doninger that the event had been canceled.

That night, Doninger wrote a LiveJournal blog post criticizing the school officials' handling of the issue, calling the school officials "douchebags," and asking that readers complain to the school superintendent, so as "to piss [her] off more" than the mass email had. In response to her blog post in which she made derogatory comments about school officials, the school barred Doninger from serving as senior class secretary and from speaking at her graduation. The Doningers sued.

In May 2008, the court ruled in favor of the school officials. It determined that regardless of the fact that Doninger wrote the blog while off campus, the blog could be considered on-campus speech. Because the blog related to school issues, it was reasonably foreseeable that other students and school administrators would become aware of it. The court then noted that school administrators have the right, in certain situations, to restrict on-campus speech to promote school-related goals.[80]

What This Means for Teachers Student speech is constitutionally protected to the extent that it does not undermine the school's mission or substantially and materially disrupt the learning environment. Computer teachers, drama teachers, journalism teachers, and school newspaper, yearbook, and literary magazine sponsors must exercise appropriate editorial control over students' published or performed speech, because such speech raises legitimate pedagogical concerns. Even students' off-campus Internet-based speech can come under the school's authority. Teachers are advised to consult with their administrators when questioning the appropriateness of student speech.

Can schools regulate student dress and appearance? Yes. Courts tend to support school boards' authority to regulate student dress and personal appearance if the attire becomes so extreme as to interfere with a school's favorable learning environment. For instance, school districts have the right to require pupils to participate in physical education and to wear clothing appropriate for these occasions. Students may not, however, be required to wear "immodest" attire.[81] Nonetheless, courts disagree about how constitutional rights apply to cases involving students' appearance.

Can public schools require students to wear school uniforms? Yes. School officials face two irreconcilable issues when they investigate student attire: maintaining a safe and effective educational environment and respecting students' constitutional rights. In these situations, courts usually support the school.

Recently, in an attempt to mask differences between student groups, some schools have begun to require their students to wear school uniforms. Advocates for school uniforms cite statistics that show the incidence of gang activities, violence, and crime in schools drops dramatically after schools enact compulsory uniform policies.[82] Some students and parents, however, object to these wardrobe requirements, claiming that the compulsory wearing of school uniforms denies freedom of expression and speech.

In the *Canady v. Bossier Parish School Board* decision (2001), the court ruled that a school's mandatory uniform policy does not violate students' First Amendment rights.[83] In its opinion, the court acknowledged that students have a constitutional right to free expression under the First and Fourteenth Amendments, and noted that a person's choice of clothing can be a constitutionally protected form of expression. However, the right to free speech is not absolute. In many cases, courts have concluded that school boards' regulation of student behavior outweighs individual students' right to free speech. Adjusting the school's dress code by adopting a uniform policy is a constitutional means for school officials to improve the educational process, so long as that policy is not directed toward censoring the expressive content of student clothing. Educators have an essential duty to regulate school affairs and establish appropriate standards of conduct, and this responsibility takes priority over students' choice of clothing to wear in school.

9-3e Sexual Discrimination and Harassment of Students

Sexual harassment of students by educators is a disturbing problem. Approximately 26 percent of all educator-misconduct cases involve sexual misconduct.[84] After a seven-month investigation, the Associated Press (AP) found 2,570 educators who were sanctioned or whose teaching credentials were revoked, denied, or surrendered from 2001 through 2005, following allegations of sexual misconduct. More than 80 percent of the victims were students. At least half of the educators punished by their states were also convicted of crimes related to their misconduct.[85]

The Education Amendments of 1972 contained Title IX, a law that specifically forbade discrimination based on gender.[86] Since the passage of the original legislation, the courts have expanded Title IX to address employee-to-employee, employee-to student, and student-to-student harassment. Over time, court cases have determined that a school district is obligated to take reasonable steps to prevent and stop sexual harassment by school employees or students.

If a teacher sexually harasses a student, can the student sue both the school district and the teacher as an individual for monetary damages? Yes. Two rulings established the case law regarding sexual harassment of students by adults in schools. In 1992, in *Franklin v. Gwinnett County Public Schools*, the U.S. Supreme Court ruled that students could recover compensatory and punitive monetary damages for sexual harassment under Title IX.[87] Further refining the scope of liability, in *Gebser v. Lago Vista Independent School District* (1998), the Supreme Court ruled that students could sue for monetary damages from the school district and the people involved if the school knew about the alleged sexual harassment and failed to respond adequately.[88]

Starting in the fall of her 10th-grade year (1986), Christine Franklin was subjected to continual sexual harassment from Andrew Hill, a sports coach and teacher employed by the district. Among other allegations, Franklin claimed that Hill engaged her in sexually oriented conversations, asking about her sexual experiences with her boyfriend and inquiring whether she would consider having sexual intercourse with an older man. Hill forcibly kissed her on the mouth in the school parking lot and telephoned her at home, asking her to meet him socially. Three times during her junior year, Hill took her out of class and to a private office where he subjected her to coercive intercourse.

School officials were aware of the sexual harassment, but they took no action. Indeed, they discouraged Franklin from pressing charges against Hill. Franklin filed an action against the school board for monetary damages. Although the lower courts found for the school, the U.S. Supreme Court found for the student.

The Supreme Court unanimously held that damages were available under Title IX for intentional violations of the law. Where a student had been subject to sexual harassment, financial damages could be levied against the district and its supervisors as well as against the accused teacher. Although the case did not specify the limits of that liability, the next case did.

In *Gebser v. Lago Vista Independent School District* (1998), the court ruled that school officials must take timely and positive actions in response to information that such inappropriate sexually harassing behaviors are occurring. A teacher's misconduct in sexually harassing a student does not make the school district liable under Title IX unless a school official had knowledge of the situation and responded with "deliberate indifference." If the school knows about the sexual harassment but does nothing to end it, the school and the individuals involved may be sued and the accuser may collect damages.

In spring 1991, eighth-grader Alida Star Gebser joined a high school book discussion group led by Frank Waldrop, a high school teacher in the Lago Vista Independent School District. During the discussion sessions, Waldrop often made sexually suggestive comments to the students. These inappropriate comments continued in ninth grade when Gebser was assigned to Waldrop's class, where he addressed many of these remarks to her. In the spring, the teacher initiated sexual contact with Gebser. They had sexual intercourse several times during the rest of the school year and the next year, often during class time, although never on school property. Gebser never reported the relationship to school officials, although she testified that she realized Waldrop's conduct was improper.

In October 1992, when parents of two other students complained to the high school principal about Waldrop's inappropriate comments in class, the principal met with the parents, and the teacher apologized. The principal advised Waldrop to be careful about his classroom comments, but did not report the parents' complaint to the superintendent (who was also the district's Title IX coordinator). A few months later, a policeman discovered Waldrop and Gebser having sexual intercourse and arrested Waldrop. The school district fired him, and the state education department revoked his teaching license. During this time, the district did not have a sexual harassment complaints policy or a formal antiharassment policy, as federal regulations required. Gebser and others filed suit against the district, claiming damages under the Title IX statute.

The Supreme Court ruled that Title IX allowed damages only if a school official with authority to take corrective action had actual information about the harassment and showed "deliberate indifference" toward correcting the situation. Because school officials did not know about the sexual harassment, and did not act with deliberate indifference, the Court found for the school district and against the student. If sexual harassment occurred but the school officials did not know about it at the time, school districts and individuals cannot be held liable for financial penalties.[89]

Can school boards be held liable for student-to-student sexual harassment? Yes, but only when the school officials know about the harassment but do nothing to stop it. In *Davis v. Monroe County Board of Education* (1999), the U.S. Supreme Court ruled that a school board may be sued for damages in situations of peer-to-peer sexual harassment, but only when the educators acted with "deliberate indifference."[90]

LaShonda Davis, a fifth-grade student in Georgia, was subject to frequent sexual harassment from a fellow classmate. Starting in December, the male student tried to touch her breasts and genital area and made vulgar comments, such as "I want to get in bed with you." Similar conduct allegedly occurred on several later occasions, and LaShonda reported each of these incidents to her mother and to her classroom teacher. When contacted by the parent, the teacher assured Mrs. Davis that the school principal had been informed of the incidents. Nonetheless, no disciplinary action was taken against the offending student, and the offensive conduct continued.

After another harassing incident in February, the parent asked the principal how the school was going to stop this behavior. The principal stated, "I guess I'll have to threaten him a little bit harder." The offending student received no discipline, and the school did not separate LaShonda and the offender until after three months of reported harassment. The incidents finally ended when the student was charged with, and pleaded guilty to, sexual battery.

Mrs. Davis alleged that school officials failed to prevent LaShonda's suffering sexual harassment by another student. The school's complacency created an abusive environment that deprived her daughter of educational benefits promised her under Title IX of the Education Amendments of 1972. Furthermore, the school district had not instructed its personnel on how to respond to peer sexual harassment and had not established a policy on the issue.

The U.S. Supreme Court concluded that a person could collect punitive damages against the school board in cases of student-on-student harassment, but only where the school district acted with deliberate indifference to known acts of harassment in its programs or activities. Because school officials had knowledge

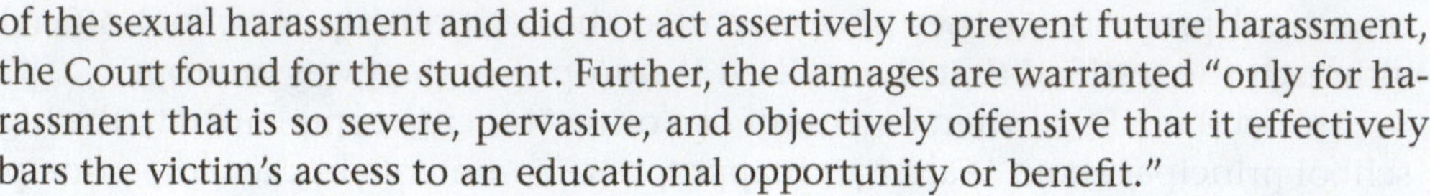

of the sexual harassment and did not act assertively to prevent future harassment, the Court found for the student. Further, the damages are warranted "only for harassment that is so severe, pervasive, and objectively offensive that it effectively bars the victim's access to an educational opportunity or benefit."

Student-to-student sexual orientation harassment In *Nabozny v. Podlesny* (1996), a U.S. Court of Appeals ruled that schools had a responsibility to protect students from antigay verbal and physical abuse.[91]

For four years, Jamie Nabozny was subjected to relentless antigay verbal and physical harassment and abuse by fellow students at his public high school in Ashland, Wisconsin.[92] Students urinated on him and pretended to rape him during class. When classmates found him alone, they kicked him so many times in the stomach that he required surgery. Although they knew of the abuse, school officials once said that Nabozny should expect it if he was gay. Nabozny attempted suicide several times, dropped out of school, and ultimately ran away. To make sure that other students did not go through the same kind of nightmare, he sued his former school.

The federal appeals court found that a public school could be held accountable for not stopping antigay abuse. In this case, the school had violated the student's Fourteenth Amendment rights to equal protection based on gender or sexual orientation. The case went back to trial and a jury found the school officials liable for the harm they caused to Nabozny. The case was ultimately settled for close to $1 million in damages.

What This Means for Teachers When teachers observe or become aware of what may be sexually harassing behaviors toward students in school, whether from adults or other students, straight or gay, teachers must promptly inform an administrator about the situation. In turn, the administrator must promptly take affirmative action to resolve it. This is true even if the harassing behavior occurs off school grounds and not at a school-related event.

9-3f Students with Disabilities

Today, students with disabilities have additional legal protections to ensure their right to a public school education. Although Congress passed legislation stating that special needs students were entitled to a "free appropriate public education" (FAPE), it did not specifically define what an "appropriate education" meant. It deliberately left the definition broad and flexible, thereby allowing public schools to make this determination in accordance with the well-structured procedural process.

Do children with disabilities have unique educational protections? Yes. Does "free and appropriate public education" require schools to maximize special needs students' educational potential or to provide only a "basic floor of opportunity"? No.

In *Board of Education of Hendrick Hudson Central School District v. Rowley* (1982), the U.S. Supreme Court ruled that "free and appropriate public education" as specified in PL 94-142 and IDEA does not require a state to maximize the potential of each child with special needs.[93] This was the first case in which the Supreme Court had an opportunity to interpret any of IDEA's provisions.

Amy June Rowley, a deaf student in Peekskill, New York, had minimal residual hearing and was an excellent lip reader. Before she started kindergarten, Amy's parents and school administrators agreed to place Amy in a regular kindergarten

Diverse Voices

LGBT Students to Teachers: Please Speak Up for Us

LGBT (lesbian, gay, bisexual, transgender) students want teachers to speak up for them. In a school of 1,000 students, up to 100 will be gay, lesbian, or bisexual; 10 will be transgender; and one will be intersex (biologically neither male nor female). If they are typical, 87 will be harassed verbally, 40 will be harassed physically, and 19 will be physically assaulted within the next year because of their sexual orientation or gender expression. Sixty-two will feel mostly unsafe going to school, and 30 will harm themselves in possible suicide attempts. This social and emotional turmoil will take a toll on their schoolwork.

When youth feel safe and protected by an adult at school, it can make the difference between dropping out or graduating. Here is what some of these middle, junior high, and high school students want their teachers to know and do to protect them from harassment:

- "Teachers have the right to say, 'We will not tolerate this [verbal or physical harassment]. You need to stop.'"
- "I think that they should make it a policy—intervening at least. Even though some people might not agree with being gay, it's like their words are still hurting somebody and it's putting somebody in the classroom, you don't know who it could be, in an unsafe feeling."
- "My freshman year in high school was one I won't forget. A peer in class started saying, 'That's nasty. Gays are nasty.' The teacher said to him, 'That is not OK. Don't do it again.' And he never bothered me after that day."
- "I feel the racist speech would be reacted to much more forcefully than antigay speech at my school. It would be a really big deal. Whereas this—how people talk about queers—gets more like a mild warning, or it is ignored completely."
- "I have to stand up for my people when people start calling them out. And when the teacher says nothing, I'm like, 'Miss? What? Are you ignoring this mess? Someone is being stepped on here for who they are and that is not right.'"
- "Teachers need to step up! By making sure that this type of hate language—or all hate language—isn't accepted in the classroom. Even if they don't hear it, if a student comes up to them or somebody puts a note on their desk or something . . . just make sure that it's not accepted."
- "I would still love to see teachers state they will not tolerate *faggot* just as they wouldn't tolerate the N-word. I constantly hear people use the word *faggot,* and I will tell them, 'That's not cool, educated yourself!'"

So here's a recommendation for future teachers: If teachers let their students hear that you are willing to listen and will act to protect and respect them, LGBT students will teach you anything you need to know. And they will be more likely to learn in class.

Source: "LGBT Students Want Educators to Speak Up For Them," by Abe Louise Young, *Phi Delta Kappan*, Vol. 93, No. 2, October 2011: 35–37. Reprinted with permission of Phi Delta Kappa International, www.pdkintl.org.

class to see which supplemental services she would need. At the end of the trial period, all agreed that Amy should remain in the kindergarten class but with an FM[94] hearing aid to help her participate in certain classroom activities. Amy successfully completed her kindergarten year.

Amy's first-grade individualized educational program (IEP) kept her in a regular classroom with the FM hearing aid and assigned her additional tutoring and speech services. Amy's parents agreed with this plan but requested that Amy receive a qualified sign language interpreter in all her academic classes instead of the other proposed services. After receiving an interpreter's services in kindergarten as part of a two-week experiment, the interpreter reported that Amy did not need his services at that time. After consulting with the school district's Committee on the Handicapped, which had heard evidence from both sides, the school administrators concluded that Amy did not need the interpreter in first grade.

FlipSides

Can a School Discipline a Student for Internet Behavior Conducted from a Home Computer?

Here is a 2011 court case about student-to-student sexual harassment conducted via an Internet website constructed outside the school. After reading each side's argument, see if you agree with the court's decision.

Kara Kowalski, a senior at Musselman High School in Berkeley County, West Virginia, created and posted to a MySpace Web page from her home computer a website called "S.A.S.H"—an acronym that Kara said meant "Students Against Sluts Herpes." The site was largely dedicated to ridiculing and humiliating a fellow student. The next day, the victim complained to the assistant principal, and the administrators investigated the situation. Kara was disciplined with a 10-day out-of-school suspension (later reduced to five days) and a 90-day suspension from school social activities.

Kara filed suit contending that disciplining her violated her free speech and due process rights under the First and Fourteenth Amendments. She alleged, among other things, that the school district was not justified in regulating her speech because it did not occur during a "school-related activity" but rather was "private out-of-school speech."

The school was correct in punishing Kara for her behavior.	The school was not correct in punishing Kara for her behavior.
■ Kara created and posted a Web page specifically to warn classmates about other classmates referred to as "sluts" with herpes.	● Kara created the Web page from home using her home computer during her own time.
■ Kara invited 100 classmates to join the discussion.	● Kara said she wanted the website to make "other students actively aware of STDs.
■ Kara's site hosted several photos posted by another student, Ray P. One photo showed Shay N., a classmate, depicted with herpes and called a "whore."	● Kara did not post the offending photos of a targeted student or use vulgar language. Her classmate, Ray P., did.
■ The commentary posted on the "S.A.S.H." site mostly focused on and ridiculed Shay N., another student.	● When Kara learned that Shay N.'s father was angry about the photographs, she tried unsuccessfully to delete the "S.A.S.H" group and photographs.
■ Kara encouraged Ray's behavior, promptly responding to his posts with, "Ray, you are soo funny!=)" and similar encouraging comments.	● Ray admitted that he had posted Shay's photos and comments. Kara had only created the "S.A.S.H" group.
■ The next day, Shay N. and her parents complained to the assistant principal about harassment and provided a printout of the Web page. Administrators investigated the situation.	● Kara's suspension socially isolated her from peers and led her to receive cold treatment from teachers and administrators. She became depressed, requiring prescription medication.
■ Investigation found that Kara had created a "hate website" in violation of the school policy against "harassment, bullying, and intimidation." Administrators assigned her a 10-day out-of-school suspension and a 90-day "social suspension".	● The Student Handbook, prohibited any form of sexual harassment or any bullying or intimidation by any student. It did not address harassment initiated from a home computer after school hours.
■ Kara acknowledged having received a Student Handbook this (and every) year which included the school district's harassment, bullying, and intimidation policy and the student code of conduct that prohibited "any form of . . . sexual . . . harassment . . . or any bullying of intimidation by any student. . . ."	● Kara claimed hers was free speech that occurred outside the school and was not school-related. The policy, therefore, could not regulate it.

(continued)

FlipSides

Can a School Discipline a Student for Internet Behavior Conducted from a Home Computer? (*continued*)

The school was correct in punishing Kara for her behavior.	The school was not correct in punishing Kara for her behavior.
■ The policy defined "harassment, bullying, and/or intimidation" as "any intentional gesture, or any intentional written, verbal, or physical act that" a reasonable person under the circumstances should know will have the effect of harming a student or staff member; and is sufficiently inappropriate, severe, persistent, or pervasive that it "*creates an intimidating, threatening, or abusive educational environment for a student.*"	● Kara claimed that "no language" in the harassment, bullying, and intimidation policy put students on notice that they could be disciplined at school for behavior outside school.
■ The student code of conduct also provided for a school environment for all students "that is nurturing, orderly, safe, and conducive to learning and personal-social development."	● No Supreme Court case addressing student speech has held that a school may punish students for speech away from school.
■ The principal and administrators followed the proper procedures and Kara's punishment was within the guidelines provided in the student code of conduct.	● Kara claimed alleged free speech violations, due process violations, cruel and unusual punishment, and equal protection violations along with other claims.

What is your judgment? Is Kara or the school district correct in their actions?

What the Court decided:
The Court ruled for the school district. School administrators were responding to off-campus behavior that singled out a student for harassment, bullying, and intimidation, and created a foreseeable risk of reaching the school and causing a substantial disruption to the school's work and discipline. Student-on-student bullying is a major concern in schools across the United States, and schools have an affirmative duty to protect their students from harassment and bullying and to prevent it from happening in the first place.

Source: *Kowalski vs. Berkeley,* decided July 27, 2011, U.S Court of Appeals for the 4th Circuit. No. 10-1098. (3:07-cv-00147-JPB). Argued March 25, 2011; decided July 27, 2011. Retrieved from http://pacer.ca4.uscourts.gov/opinion.pdf/101098.P.pdf.

The Rowleys demanded and received a hearing before an independent examiner, who heard the evidence and agreed with the school administrators. The interpreter was not necessary because "Amy was achieving educationally, academically, and socially" without such assistance. In an appeal, the New York Commissioner of Education also supported the school administrators' decision. The Rowleys then filed suit, claiming the denial of the sign language interpreter constituted a denial of the "free and appropriate public education" guaranteed by law.

The U.S. Supreme Court found that the state does not have to maximize the child's potential, but rather provide a program that benefits the child. The Court observed that the special education act did not define "appropriate education" or offer a substantive prescription about the level of education to be given

Amy Rowley speaks with her mother, who is also deaf.

to children with disabilities. According to the Court, IDEA "generates no additional requirement that the services so provided be sufficient to maximize each child's potential 'commensurate with the opportunity provided other children.'" Although this outcome might be desirable, ensuring that this goal is met was not the legislation's intent.

The original legislation intended to provide equal protection of the laws to children with disabilities. In passing IDEA, Congress intended to provide "a basic floor of opportunity" consistent with equal protection. As such, the Supreme Court ruled that the "basic floor of opportunity" that the act provided consisted of access to specialized instruction and related services that are individually designed to provide an educational benefit to the child with disabilities. IDEA left the primary responsibility for formulating students' education and choosing the educational methods to the state and local education agencies, which are expected to work in cooperation with the child's parent or guardian.

Do school districts have to pay tuition for disabled students to attend private educational facilities? Yes, sometimes. In 2007, almost seven million students nationwide receive special education services; 71,000 were educated in private schools at public expense.[95] In that same year, New York City paid for private schools for more than 7,000 severely handicapped children because it agreed that it could not properly instruct them. But this decision is quite expensive. According to New York officials, requests for tuition payments for special education students by parents who have placed their children in private schools on their own have more than doubled in five years, to almost 3,700 children in 2006, costing the city more than $57 million per school year.[96] In 2009, the U.S. Supreme Court ruled in *Forest Grove School District* v. *T.A.* that parents of students with special needs had the right to seek reimbursement through due process from their local school district for private school tuition for their child, even if the child had not been served in public schools.[97]

Schools must balance the individual rights of teachers and students with the necessity of maintaining a safe and productive learning environment. Teachers who understand and follow their ethical and legal responsibilities will be more effective educators.

Did You Get It?

Which statement about student rights is correct?

- **a.** Students lose their constitutional privileges when they enter the school building.
- **b.** Students have many of the same constitutional and legal rights as adults.
- **c.** Even educators operating *in loco parentis* must still meet a very high legal standard to avoid unreasonable search and seizure.
- **d.** Schools have broad legal authority to establish rules and regulations for student appearance and conduct, and there is no underlying standard.

Take the full quiz on CourseMate.

American Education Spotlight

Courtesy of the University of Wisconsin-Milwaukee

Amy June Rowley continues to shape special education practice.

Amy June Rowley

In 1982, at age 10, Amy June Rowley became the center of a landmark U.S. Supreme Court case that helped shape education laws for students with disabilities. At its heart, *Hendrick Hudson Board of Education v. Rowley*, is a very human story about a family struggling to make sure their child had an opportunity to learn.

Amy June Rowley, who is deaf, is currently the Coordinator of the American Sign Language (ASL) program in the Modern Languages and Literatures department at California State University—East Bay in Hayward, California. Previously, she coordinated the American Sign Language Program at the University of Wisconsin—Milwaukee. She completed her bachelor's and master's of science degrees and is presently working on her dissertation. Married to Jeff Mosher, they have three children, Janeva, Reza, and Tavey. Janeva and Reza are deaf and attend a California school for the deaf.

Amy's parents—Nancy and Clifford—were both born hearing but became deaf as a result of childhood illnesses. Amy's parents met at Gallaudet College for deaf students in Washington, DC. Amy's mother became a teacher of the deaf. She saw how much potential deaf students had, and she pushed them to achieve their best.

The Rowley's first child, John, was born hearing and Amy's mother spoke to him as she would with any hearing child. When Amy was born, her mother assumed she could hear and spoke with her as if she were a hearing child. At 15 months old, however, Amy was not speaking as her brother did. She had started signing on her own by watching her parents signing, so her mother actively began teaching her bright daughter to sign, making certain that Amy understood everything happening around her. Although doctors confirmed Amy's deafness a few months later, Amy always had access to language, to knowledge of her world, and to high expectations for what she could learn and accomplish. The 1975 Education for All Handicapped Children Act (PL 94-142) gave Amy's parents the opportunity for her to receive better academic opportunities at a nearby public school in classes with hearing students than at a distant school for the deaf.

Nancy Rowley worked with her daughter at home to help Amy keep up with her studies. "I remember coming home from school and working on lessons and homework and not being able to go outside to play," Amy recalls. "My mother would not allow me to fail."

As an adult, Amy has published articles both in special education litigation and relationships. She reflects on her personal experiences at the center of a legal, educational, and media storm:

"[Third grade was] the first time I really enjoyed school. I was able to follow along perfectly in classroom discussions, and my [sign language] interpreter made sure to interpret everything including my classmate's discussions. . . . I looked forward to recess where the interpreter would follow me out and interpret for me and other children to figure out what we wanted to do. Before, I had always followed other kids outside and usually kids wanted to play kickball but I was often not included. So I would go to the playground and play alone or with a few other kids. But now . . . I felt I had a voice. . . . I wanted to play kickball and they would make sure I was involved. . . . The added bonus of having an interpreter in the classroom meant that when I got home from school I only had to do my homework and not relearn everything I was supposed to have learned in class that day. So I really had a lot more time to play and 'just be a kid'" (Rowley, p. 322).

"Without an interpreter, I was a 'C' student. With an interpreter, I was an 'A' student," Amy asserts.

"Children should be allowed to be children. Too often children are robbed of their right to grow up without the weight of the world on their shoulders. I know the weight of my world was squashing me in elementary school as my family and I pursued the educational experience I needed and deserved. Many times I wanted to play or be like the little kid I should have been, but I was expected to be just the opposite. With the case going all the way to the Supreme Court, I got a lot of national attention from the media. I didn't ask for that. People ask me if this was all worth it. Would I do this again? I was faced with that decision with my own children who are deaf. The school district I first worked with informed me that they wanted my oldest daughter to be able to function without an interpreter by the time she entered school. . . . They wanted to deprive me and her of communication. I had to explain to the school that American Sign Language is not a detriment to my daughter's education but actually an advantage

(*continued*)

American Education Spotlight (continued)

that helps her thrive in school. Twenty-five years ago my parents asked for an interpreter for the exact same reasons. Twenty-five years later I know there has been progress, but it is not always evident. So would I do it again? Not at the expense of my children" (Rowley, p. 328).

Sources: Quirk, Kathy. (2007, March 30). Deaf UWM professor helped shape education laws for students with disabilities. Deaf News Network. UW-Milwaukee: *Featured Stories Detail.* Retrieved from http://deafnn.wordpress.com/2007/03/30/ uw-milwaukee-featured-stories-detail/; Rowley, A. (2008, July). Rowley revisited: A personal narrative. *Journal of Law and Education 37*(3), 311–28.

SUMMARY

- The state must balance individual teachers' and students' constitutional rights as citizens against the necessity of maintaining a controlled and safe learning environment. In keeping with this idea, courts have allowed schools to reasonably restrict teacher and student freedoms so as to keep students safe and learning.
- A profession's code of ethics visibly clarifies for practitioners and the general public the rules and norms that guide the practitioners' actions. Because the professional entity is more stable, enduring, and visible than any one practitioner, the professional group has a collective moral responsibility to ensure that its members uphold the highest standards of practice.
- A teaching license or certificate is the state's legal way of saying that the individual holding the license or certificate has met the minimum requirements for securing a teaching job. A teaching license or certificate does not guarantee the holder a teaching job.
- In the United States, academic freedom means that teachers have some choices in the teaching methods they use as long as they meet professional standards. Academic freedom does not mean that teachers can say whatever they would like or to teach whatever they want in the classroom.
- Although teachers as citizens have a constitutional right to free speech, U.S. courts have allowed schools to set limits on this right if the state's interest in maintaining an efficient organization outweighs the employee's interest in exercising that right. These limitations affect teachers' academic freedom, their right to speak out publicly, their right to privacy in the workplace, and professional dress codes.
- Although constitutionally protected from unreasonable search and seizure, because teachers work in safety-sensitive positions, under certain conditions they may be required to undergo suspicionless drug searches and urine testing.
- A teacher may be sued for negligence if, without intending to do wrong, he or she either acts or fails to take a precaution that under the circumstances an ordinary prudent and reasonably intelligent teacher ought to foresee would expose another person to unnecessary risk of harm.

- Threatening to harm, physically harming students, or neglecting to anticipate and prevent harm to students in high-risk situations can place teachers in legal jeopardy.
- Although students keep their constitutional rights in school, schools can regulate and balance those rights against the school's obligation to provide students with a safe and orderly learning environment. Schools must weigh the individual student's rights against the public good when making this determination.
- Students have due process rights in the disciplinary process. Before a student can be suspended, expelled, or involuntarily transferred to a specialized school, a serious breach of student conduct must have occurred, and the school district must have followed a procedure for allowing the student and family the opportunity to hear the charges and present their view of events. If schools do not follow this process, the courts may not allow the student's suspension, expulsion, or transfer.
- Students have limits on their privacy rights in school. Under certain conditions, students can have their persons, school lockers, bookbags, or their cars searched if the search is based on reasonable grounds, advances a legitimate school purpose, and is not overly intrusive.
- Athletes or students who compete in interscholastic activities may be required to take random drug tests.
- Students and parents have privacy rights of confidentiality and basic fairness with regard to their school records under the federal Family Educational Rights and Privacy Act (FERPA). Teachers must use care when they add to, access, or share student records with other educators.
- Students' free speech is protected unless the public school can justify limiting this right based on a reasonable forecast of "material and substantial disruption" to the school's orderly and safe learning environment.
- Schools have an obligation to take reasonable steps to prevent and stop sexual harassment by school employees or students.
- Students with disabilities have additional legal protections. The U.S. Supreme Court has ruled that schools must provide students with disabilities with a"floor of opportunity," which gives them access to specialized instruction and related services to benefit the child but not necessarily to "maximize" each child's potential. U.S. courts continue to address issues specific to these students, such as the definitions and implementation of a "free and appropriate education," separate school placement, related services, discipline, and tuition reimbursement.

Visit the Education CourseMate for this textbook to access the eBook, Did You Get It? quizzes, TeachSource Video Cases, flashcards, and more. Go to CengageBrain.com to log in, register, or purchase access.

Education is a federal interest, a state responsibility, and locally administered.

Jeff Greenberg / Alamy

CHAPTER 10

School Governance and Structure

InTASC Standards: 1, 2, 3, 4, 5, 6, 7, 8, 9, and 10

LEARNING OBJECTIVES

After you read this chapter, you should be able to:

10-1 Identify the three areas of federal government's involvement in public education.

10-2 List and describe the state leaders who play key roles in shaping education policy and practice.

10-3 Explain which local leaders and support staff play key roles in shaping education policy, practice, and student success.

10-4 Discuss several structural issues that affect public schools' effectiveness.

As a people, Americans are hardworking, pragmatic, and efficient—yet we prefer a little ambiguity when it comes to governing our public institutions. We have distributed accountability on purpose. "Anyone who has tried to change vehicle registration from Virginia to Maryland knows the true meaning of government by fragmentation," noted Michael J. Fuerer, executive director and education policy maker with the National Research Council in Washington, DC.[1] The same can be said for education.

The United States does not have one national education system like France, Germany, England, or Japan. Instead, American education is largely controlled at the state level. Currently, the United States has one federal Department of Education, 50 state education agencies and one for the District of Columbia, and almost 14,000 school districts.[2] Most states allow localities within the state to manage education. In short, education is a federal interest, a state responsibility, and a locally administered concern. Local school districts are the primary operating units of the American public school system.[3]

In this chapter, we review the U.S. schools' governance and structure from the federal government to the classroom. We discuss how state boards of education and local school boards function. We look at how state and local school superintendents, school board office personnel, school building administrators, teachers, and school support professionals influence teachers' classroom practice and student achievement. Lastly, this chapter considers several structural issues that influence schools' effectiveness and costs.

10-1 The Federal Role in Education

The U.S. Constitution defines the federal role in education. The Tenth Amendment to the U.S. Constitution reads:

> The powers not delegated to the United States by the Constitution, nor prohibited by it to the states, are reserved to the states respectively, or to the people.

Because education is not specifically assigned as a federal government responsibility, it becomes a state and local responsibility. As a result, the United States has 50 different education systems with each state directing its own.[4]

10-1a Brief History of the U.S. Department of Education

The U.S. Department of Education in Washington, DC, is the primary federal agency responsible for overseeing state spending of federal education dollars. Following the Civil War, President Andrew Johnson established the U.S. Office of Education in 1867 to help strengthen growing federal support for education. A Commissioner of Education received an annual salary of $4,000 to head the department and employed three clerks at annual salaries ranging from $1,600 to $2,000 to assist.[5] Poor management forced the first education commissioner to resign, however. Two years later, the Office of Education was transferred to the U.S. Department of the Interior and became the Bureau of Education. The Bureau focused on collecting information on schools and teaching to help states establish effective education systems.

In 1953, the U.S. Bureau of Education merged with other offices to become the Department of Health, Education, and Welfare (HEW). In 1979, President Jimmy Carter established the cabinet-level Department of Education, elevating its importance and influence.

In fiscal year 2013, the U.S. Department of Education administered a budget of $68.4 billion and employed 4,279 full-time employees in addition to several thousand contractors. Although this is a large operation, the federal share accounts for only 10 percent of the nation's total education budget. The state and local levels contribute the remaining 90 percent of education dollars (47 percent and 44 percent, respectively).[6] The federal education budget represents only 2 percent of the total federal budget.[7]

The federal government has traditionally had little jurisdiction over state and local education policies or practices. The U.S. Constitution and federal legislation limit the federal role in education to three areas:

- Providing funding approved by Congress and monitoring states' compliance in using those funds
- Ensuring state and local compliance with federal laws
- Assessing student achievement at the national level

American Education Spotlight

Arne Duncan

Michael Reynolds/EPA/Landov

Arne Duncan, U.S. Secretary of Education

In his 2009 confirmation hearings as U.S. Secretary of Education, Arne Duncan called education, "the civil rights issue of our generation, the only sure path out of poverty and the only way to achieve a more equal and just society."

To help achieve these goals, Duncan asserted that high-quality teachers are essential to ensuring America's long-term economic prosperity.

Some believe that Duncan's national policy agenda could make him among the most influential leaders in his department's 30-year history.

Teaching may be considered the Duncan "family business." His mother, Sue Duncan, has run an independent early-learning center for children on Chicago's South Side since 1961, and his father was a professor at the University of Chicago. As a student in Chicago, Duncan spent afternoons in his mother's tutoring program and also worked there during a year off from college. He credits this experience with shaping his understanding of urban education's challenges. Duncan himself has no teaching experience or any degrees in education.

Duncan went to Harvard University. At 6′ 5″ tall, he was co-captain of the basketball team and named a first team Academic All-American. He graduated magna cum laude with a sociology degree in 1987. He played professional basketball in Australia from 1987 to 1991. It was on a Chicago basketball court that Duncan first met future-president Barack Obama. Duncan credits basketball with his team-oriented and highly disciplined work ethic.

Prior to his appointment as secretary of education, Duncan served as the Chicago Public Schools' chief executive officer (CEO) from June 2001 through December 2008. As CEO, Duncan united education reformers, teachers, principals, and business stakeholders behind an aggressive education reform agenda that included opening over 100 new schools, expanding after-school and summer learning programs, shuttering underperforming schools, increasing early childhood and college access, dramatically boosting the teachers' caliber, and building public-private partnerships around a variety of education initiatives.

Before joining the Chicago Public Schools, Duncan ran the nonprofit education foundation, Ariel Education Initiative (1992–1998), which helped fund a college education for a class of inner-city children. He became director of Chicago Public Schools' magnet school programs in 1998; and in 2001, Mayor Richard M. Daley named him the school district's CEO.

Duncan is married to Karen Duncan and they have two children, daughter Claire and son Ryan, who attend public school in Virginia.

By initiating the $4.3 billion Race to the Top Fund grants, Duncan recast American education reform, requiring states to undertake his key educational improvement priorities in order to qualify for grant monies. These changes include:

- Building data systems that measure student growth and success from preschool to college, and inform teachers and principals how to improve instruction.
- Adopting and using rigorous common core curriculum standards and assessments in reading and mathematics that prepare students to succeed in college and the workplace.
- Recruiting, developing, rewarding, and retaining effective teachers and principals, and ensuring their equitable distribution, especially to schools where they are needed most (namely, low-income, high minority schools).
- Using student achievement data as part of teacher and principal evaluations.

Additional policy priorities for Duncan include utilizing teacher performance-pay programs; revising teacher seniority and tenure systems, turning around the lowest-performing schools; lifting caps on charter schools; and offering alternative pathways to teacher and principal certification.

Admirers like Duncan's intelligent, pragmatic approach that seeks "whatever works" to raise student achievement in public schools. Experience and observation, rather than theory, guide his actions. He is independent and outspoken describing teacher colleges as the "Bermuda Triangle" of higher education. Supporters say he is getting a lot of heat for telling the truth.

Duncan's critics object to what they view as overly prescriptive mandates for fixing schools. A few observe that although he listens to his staff and corporate/philanthropic interests who support his agenda, he does not listen to education professionals. Rather, he relishes the image as a champion against "entrenched interests".

(continued)

American Education Spotlight (continued)

Critics also point to his use of policy prescriptions that lack a solid research base, his over-reliance on standardized testing, his desire to link teacher salaries to student test scores, and his promoting the use of private management companies to run low-performing schools. Others highlight the inequity of making states apply for competitive grants for badly needed funds in exchange for enacting specified reforms rather than assign money to each state based on a formula that would ensure funds for the neediest schools.

In 2003, a friend of Duncan's joked with him that he was not even 40 years old and he had the second-best job in education. He had nowhere to go but down because the only better job would be secretary of education.

Sources: Cunningham, C.A. (2010, January 21). Arne Duncan, one year later. Education Policy Blog, *The Washington Post*. Retrieved from http://educationpolicyblog.blogspot.com/2010/01/arne-duncan-one-year-later.html; McNeil, M. (2010, January 20). Duncan carving deep mark on policy. *Education Week 29*(18), 1, 18–20; U.S. Department of Education. (2009). Senior staff. Arne Duncan, U.S. Secretary of Education. Retrieved from http://www.us.ed.gov/; Infoplease. (2008). Arne Duncan. Retrieved from http://www.infoplease.com/biography/var/arneduncan.html; Pickert, K. (2008, December 17). Education secretary: Arne Duncan. *Time* Politics. Retrieved from http://www.time.com/time/politics/article/0,8599,1867011,00.html; Windish, J. (2009, December 17). Praise for gay-friendly education pick Arne Duncan. *The Moderate Voice*. Retrieved from http://themoderatevoice.com/25059/praise-for-gay-friendly-education-pick-arne-duncan/.

10-1b The Legislative Branch

Through its legislative branch, the federal government provides congressionally approved funding and monitors its use. Over the years, the U.S. Congress has given public education a great deal of fiscal support. For instance, Americans reacted with shock to the 1957 Soviet Union's launching of its Sputnik satellite into earth orbit. Our Cold War enemies had beaten us in the "space race." Concerned citizens asked whether U.S. public schools had enough vision, drive, and resources to maintain our national security and global superiority in a threatening world.

In response, the U.S. Congress authorized a massive infusion of federal dollars into public education through the National Defense Education Act (NDEA) of 1958.[8] Congress believed that math and science education were essential to our national defense. NDEA also increased spending for foreign language learning, technology, and other "critical" subjects. These new monies came with strings attached, however: to receive the funds, states and localities had to agree to spend the dollars in compliance with the grants' terms. Federal spending audits in local school districts soon became commonplace.

Perhaps the most substantial federal education spending initiative occurred under President Lyndon Johnson's administration, when Congress passed the Elementary and Secondary Education Act (ESEA) in 1965. We now know this act by its 2002 name: No Child Left Behind (NCLB). Seeking equity and excellence, NCLB intended to close the achievement gaps that existed based on students' race, economic status, disability, and language. NCLB was the federal government's first serious attempt to hold states, districts, and schools accountable for ending the unequal achievement among different student populations—especially poor and minority children and children with disabilities.

ESEA currently contains categorical aid programs through which the U.S. Congress sends money specifically designated for certain student populations. The focus of these funding programs varies over time, changing with the reauthorization priorities. These categorical programs include funds to help states and local districts educate economically disadvantaged and other underserved children, improve teacher and principal quality, improve technology in schools, provide resources to children with limited English proficiency, develop drug and violence prevention activities, support community learning centers, implement promising educational reform, and develop additional educational assessments.

Through categorical and competitive grants, the U.S. national legislative branch sends states and schools federal dollars to help them accomplish their educational mission. Serving as incentives and resources, these federal monies tend to direct state and local educational efforts toward outcomes that the U.S. Congress, states, and localities deem as serving their best interests. In these ways, federal dollars reach local classrooms.

10-1c The Judicial Branch

In a second area of federal education involvement, the judicial branch of the U.S. government ensures that states comply with all federal laws and regulations. Sometimes this requires the U.S. Supreme Court to clarify the law. *Griffin v. County School Board of Prince Edward County* and *Plyler v. Doe* offer two cases in point.

Griffin v. County School Board of Prince Edward County In *Griffin v. County School Board of Prince Edward County* (1964), the Supreme Court ruled as unconstitutional a state's practice of closing some of its public schools and contributing instead to the support of private segregated schools.[9]

On April 23, 1951, 16-year-old Barbara Johns, a student in Prince Edward County, Virginia, led the 450 students at all–African American Robert R. Moton High School out of their classes in a two-week protest against the school's deplorable building conditions. Constructed in 1939 and designed to house 180 students, their school was massively overcrowded. Rather than build a new African American high school, the Prince Edward County school board erected three large plywood buildings covered with tarpaper to accommodate the overcrowding. Called "tar-paper shacks" by the students and African American community, the shoddy buildings vividly symbolized the Moton students' unequal facilities, sparking their protest demanding a new high school. At one point, some classes were also held on an old school bus. Contacting the National Association for the Advancement of Colored People (NAACP) for legal assistance, the students filed suit, alleging that they had been denied enrollment into public schools attended by white children and charged that Virginia's segregation laws denied equal protection of the Fourteenth Amendment.[10]

In 1954, the Prince Edward group was one of the plaintiffs in the landmark U.S. Supreme Court's *Brown v. Board of Education* decision, which ruled that the state's segregation laws were unconstitutional because they denied African American students equal protection. That ruling did not end Prince Edward County's school segregation, however. In 1956, Virginia amended its constitution to permit public funds to assist students to go to either public schools or nonsectarian private schools. The General Assembly enacted legislation to close and cut off state funds to any public schools where "white and colored children" were enrolled together. When the Fourth Circuit Court of Appeals invalidated these laws in 1959, the Virginia General Assembly turned to a "freedom of choice" program, repealed compulsory attendance laws, and made school attendance a matter of local option.

Rather than submit to state and federal courts requiring Virginia public schools to accept children of all races, Prince Edward County decided it preferred to have no public schools at all. It refused to levy any school taxes for the 1959–1960 school year. The county's public schools did not reopen in fall 1959; in fact, they remained closed for five years (although other public schools in

Virginia were open and operating under the law). In the meantime, a private group, the Prince Edward School Foundation, was formed; it built and operated private schools for local white children who received county- and state-funded tuition grants and tax credits to attend. The vast majority of the county's 1,700 African American students and some white students received no formal education for five years, from 1959 to 1964.[11]

In 1964, the U.S. Supreme Court ruled in *Griffin v. Prince Edward* that local authorities had to fund public education and reopen the schools to all students. The Court required that Prince Edward County enforce the nation's laws.

Plyler v. Doe[12] Other education cases have gone to the U.S. Supreme Court to determine if states were correctly complying with federal laws. *Plyler v. Doe* involved the allocation of millions of dollars by the Texas state legislature to educate children of illegal immigrants. At the time of the court case, Texas was educating an estimated 50,000 school-aged children of illegal immigrants at an annual cost of approximately $100 million.[13]

In an attempt to save tax dollars, the Texas legislature argued that because these children were in the country illegally, taxpayers should not have to finance illegal activity—that is, schooling the children. Subsequently, in 1975, the Texas legislature revised its laws to withhold state education funds from school districts that enrolled children who were not legally admitted into the United States. The law also allowed local school districts to deny enrollment to these children. Although the local school districts could accept these students if they wished—they would not receive state funding to educate them. When opponents of this policy brought suit, the Texas Supreme Court agreed with the legislature's position.

Ultimately, this case went to the U.S. Supreme Court. As in *Brown v. Board of Education*, the Court decided the case based on the Fourteenth Amendment: "No State shall . . . deprive any person of life, liberty, or property without due process of law; *nor deny to any* **person** *within its jurisdiction* the equal protection of the laws." According to the Supreme Court justices, any *person* did not mean any *citizen*. Although illegal immigrants are not citizens, they are persons who cannot be deprived of equal protection under the law requiring compulsory school attendance.

10-1d Student Assessment at the National Level

National assessment of students' academic progress represents the third area of federal involvement in education.[14]

Until the 1960s, states generally educated their children as they saw fit—without regard to what other states were doing. Even if educators were curious about how well their students were achieving as compared to students in neighboring states, contrasting K-12 student achievement on a state-by-state basis was impractical, untraditional, and largely irrelevant. Because prior to the 1960s, students tended to leave school and find local employment, these individuals would have competed for jobs only with locally educated students. Competing with better educated students from another state was not a realistic concern.

National Assessment of Educational Progress (NAEP) This situation changed in the 1960s, when the Kennedy administration focused government accountability on student assessment. As expected, states and various educational agencies were actively suspicious of the federal government's plan to hold states responsible for their students' educational attainment. To reduce states' misgivings about the potential for federal interference in state and local education, the Education Commission of the States (ECS) received the authority to design and conduct a national assessment.[15] Federal monies and the Carnegie Corporation would fund the project. In 1969, ECS received U.S. Office of Education assurances that it would give funds but not interfere with state policy or analysis. That compromise was sufficient for most states to allow federal involvement in collecting and monitoring their student achievement data.

Today, the federal Department of Education oversees the NAEP, also known as "the nation's report card." The NAEP data show regional, state, and national student achievement trends in the arts, civics, economics, foreign language, geography, math, reading, science, U.S. history, world history, and writing. Each state chooses a sample of students at identified grade levels in selected schools to take the NAEP tests.

The Elementary and Secondary Education Act The original 1965 Elementary and Secondary Education Act (ESEA) passed by the U.S. Congress provided federal funding to support equal access, high standards, and accountability for public schools. Usually reauthorized every five years, its 2001 version (signed in 2002) was called "No Child Left Behind." Although the No Child Left Behind legislation was not officially considered to be student assessment at the national level because each state developed its own test, its influence over student testing across the country clearly shows how states are willing to comply with extensive federal rules for student achievement testing to secure more federal education dollars.

NCLB (2002) increased states' and local school districts' accountability for all students' measured academic achievement in return for continued federal financial support. The act required every state to develop a comprehensive system of standards and assessments in language arts, math, and science. All student subgroups[16] were required to pass 100 percent of the state standards' assessments—and be performing at grade level—by the school year 2013–2014. Students were tested in grades 3–8 and once in high school in language arts, math, and science. Student progress toward proficiency and closing achievement gaps determined school accountability, called adequate yearly progress (AYP). Each year, schools had to show academic progress at all tested grades, in all tested subjects, by all tested student subgroups. If any one of the groups failed to make AYP (it could be a different subgroup from one year to another), the whole school received a failing grade. To make the desired student achievement a reality, the law required that only "highly qualified teachers"—that is, teachers with documented knowledge of the content they were teaching—be employed in all core subject classrooms.

The NCLB legislation purposely designed the rules so schools could no longer ignore the academic needs of disadvantaged student groups. By separating the achievement data in this way, increasing underserved student subgroups' achievement became a school priority. The school's own status depended on how well each student group met the annual proficiency standards.

Most importantly, the No Child Left Behind Act expanded the federal government's reach into state and local policies and practice. Many wonder if the federal government's regulation of local and state education with NCLB to such a great degree oversteps its constitutional boundaries. Generally, if states agree to accept federal monies, they must comply with federal regulations.

Did You Get It?

Which statement is true about the federal government's role in public education?

a. Education is a state and local responsibility.
b. Education is standardized at the federal level, with state and local authorities significantly adjusting those standards to their specific needs.
c. Education is standardized at the federal level, with state and local authorities having minimal right to adjusting those standards to their specific needs.
d. The federal government contributes over 50 percent of the nation's total education budget.

Take the full quiz on CourseMate.

10-2 The State Players in Education Policy and Practice

Constitutionally, U.S. education is controlled at the state level. Figure 10.1 illustrates how most states are organized to administer the education function.

Every state has a legislative system similar to the federal government's three branches—executive, legislative, and judicial. Each state has a governor, a two-chambered legislature (except for Nebraska, which has a single chamber), a supreme court, and agencies that are funded by and report to the legislature. When we elect people to represent us in the legislative process, they pass many laws each year that directly affect education. For example, many years ago, Hawaiian legislators decided that they should have only one school district run by the state. As a result, Hawaii has no local school districts.[17]

California's Proposition 13 provides another example of how voters can give the state a significant role in schools. In 1978, California taxpayers voted to limit their local property tax rates. "Prop 13" resulted in a $6 billion cut in local property tax revenue. As a result, school districts lost, on average, half of their local funding. Overall, school revenues decreased by as much as 15 percent in wealthy districts and by 9 percent in lower-income districts.[18] In short, Prop 13 shifted the fiscal control of California's public schools from local communities to the state with a decidedly negative impact on the state's education system.

We elect governors become the state's CEO and choose representatives to the state legislature. Some want to lower taxes. Others want to increase public services. In recent years, state legislators have acted on many educational issues, including deciding the means by which the state will fund its schools, teacher licensure laws, teacher and principal evaluation using student achievement data, school curricula, testing issues, consolidation of school districts, school accreditation, and teacher retirement contributions and benefits.

10-2a The Public

The public influences education at the state level through the election process. In the United States, our form of government is called a democratic republic. With this system, we elect people to represent us and to make laws and enact policies that govern us. The Tenth Amendment to the U.S. Constitution makes education a state function. Therefore, each of the 50 states has its own constitution that details how the state will govern its education. By voting for governors and representatives to the state legislature who hold certain beliefs about education, the public elects officials to enact their preferences about the type of education their state will have.

For example, consider this hypothetical story. During a governor's race, one charismatic candidate tells voters that, if elected, she promised not to cut education's general revenue or to raise taxes. Impressing a majority of voters with this pledge, the candidate wins the election. After she takes office, however, the governor's state budget for the first two years cuts more than $3 billion for education from K-20, more than half of that ($1.8 billion) from kindergarten through 12th grade. In fact, the proposed budget would decrease per-student spending by 10 percent! To help offset the funding cuts, the governor asks teachers to put 5 percent of their salaries into their pensions, giving them less take-home pay. At the same time, the governor proposes cutting $1.5 billion from property taxes, meaning less money to support public schools. Needless to say, voters were shocked and dismayed when the governor not only trashed her election promises but did just the opposite. The lesson of this story: Voters in every state need to thoroughly "vet" their candidates for public office about their plans for public education and elect those with a unblemished record and reputation for integrity and who vow to fund and enact policies in accord with what voters view as the long-term public interest, Regardless of who is elected, once the public has voted, much of the funding and legislation for education come from the state legislature.

10-2b The State Legislature

The legislature's education role varies from state to state, depending on the state constitution's wording. Basically, all state legislatures provide the laws and framework for how the state education system will function. Laws control how the state organizes and operates its department of education. Laws frame the procedures that localities must use to elect or appoint their school board members. Laws control how districts structure their superintendents' contracts and define their role in overseeing the school district. And laws control the length of the school day and the school year, curriculum parameters, testing programs, licensure regulations, and other matters.

Most frequently, the state legislature decides how the state will fund its schools. The legislature is responsible for establishing, maintaining, regulating, and determining the school funding formula. Virtually every state (and commonwealth) requires a formula to equalize state funding between affluent and poor communities. To do this, the state legislature establishes a basic floor level of education services that each locality must offer. Wealthier communities can afford to spend more on education than can poorer ones. Through its funding formula, the state finances more of the education costs for poorer areas and gives less state financial assistance to the wealthier ones. This more or less equalizes school funding throughout the states.[19]

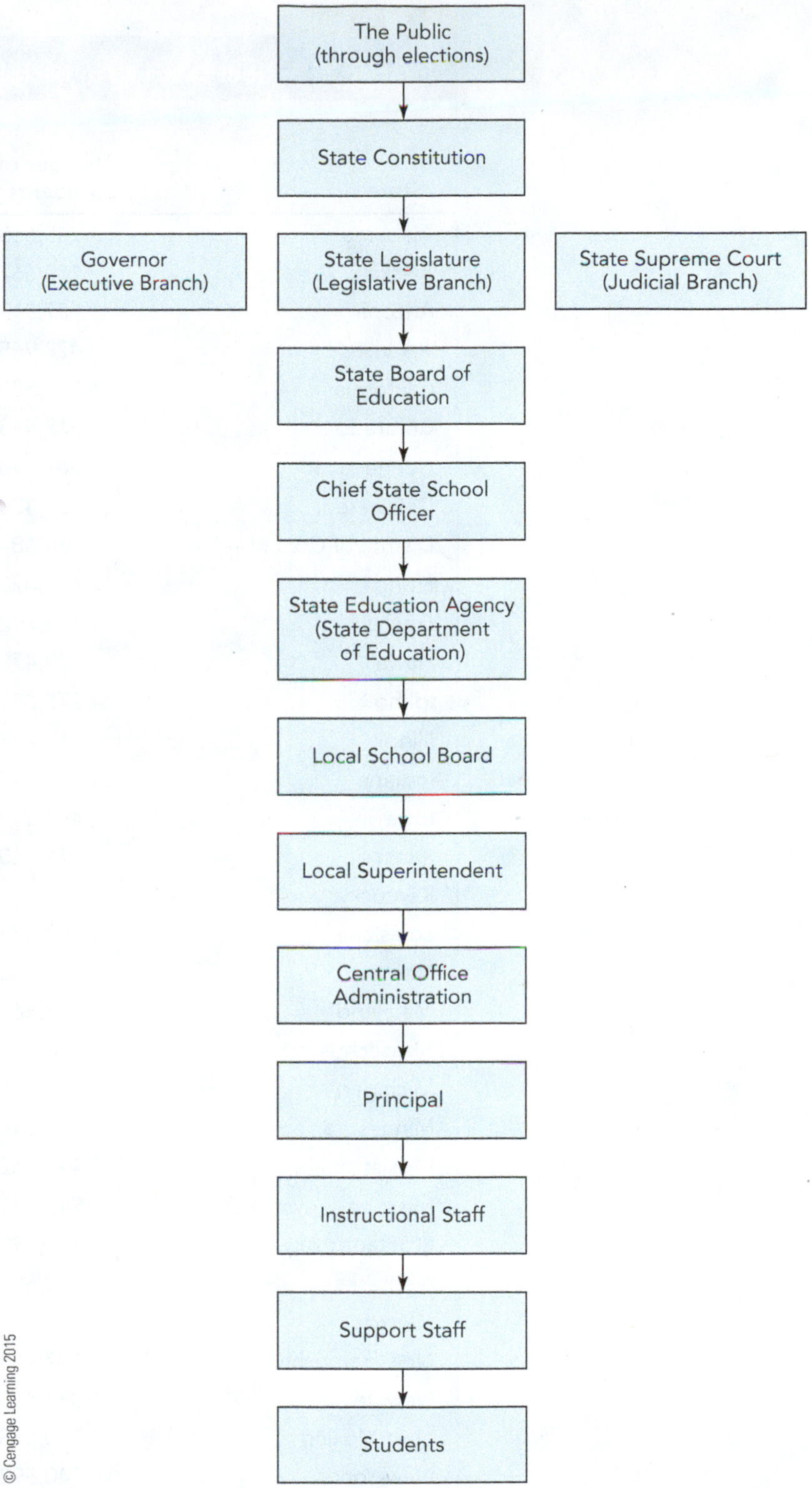

Table 10.1 shows how the sizes of school districts and the number of pupils per district vary across the states. The state legislature makes these decisions.

FIGURE 10.1 Organizational Governance Flowchart at the State Level

TABLE 10.1

Number of School Districts in Each State, 2009

State	Number of Students	Number of Districts	Average Number of Pupils per District
Alabama	745,668	133	5,607
Alaska	130,662	53	2,465
Arizona	1,087,817	225	4,835
Arkansas	478,965	245	1,955
California	6,322,528	960	6,586
Colorado	818,443	178	4,598
Connecticut	567,198	166	3,417
Delaware	125,430	19	6,602
District of Columbia*	68,681	1	68,681
Florida	2,631,020	67	39,269
Georgia	1,655,792	180	9,199
Hawaii*	179,478	1	179,478
Idaho	275,051	115	2,392
Illinois	2,119,707	869	2,439
Indiana	1,046,147	294	3,558
Iowa	487,559	362	1,347
Kansas	471,060	318	1,481
Kentucky	670,030	174	3,851
Louisiana	684,873	69	9,926
Maine	191,935	283	678
Maryland	843,861	24	35,161
Massachusetts	958,910	352	2,724
Michigan	1,659,921	552	3,007
Minnesota	836,048	340	2,459
Mississippi	491,962	152	3.258
Missouri	917,871	523	1,755
Montana	141,899	420	338
Nebraska	292,590	256	1,143
Nevada	433,371	17	25,492
New Hampshire	197,934	178	1,112
New Jersey	1,381,420	616	2,243
New Mexico	330,245	89	3,711
New York	2,740,592	696	3,938
North Carolina	1,488,645	116	12,833
North Dakota	94,728	187	507
Ohio	1,817,163	614	2,960
Oklahoma	645,108	534	1,208
Oregon	575,393	194	2,966
Pennsylvania	1,775,029	501	3,543
Rhode Island	145,342	32	4,542

(continued)

TABLE 10.1

Number of School Districts in Each State, 2009 (continued)

State	Number of Students	Number of Districts	Average Number of Pupils per District
South Carolina	718,113	85	8,448
South Dakota	126,429	161	785
Tennessee	971,950	136	7,147
Texas	4,752,148	1,032	4,605
Utah	559,778	40	13,994
Vermont	93,625	292	321
Virginia	1,235,795	134	9,222
Washington	1,037,018	295	3,515
West Virginia	282,729	55	5,141
Wisconsin	873,750	426	2,051
Wyoming	87,161	48	1,816
U.S. Total	49,265,572	13,809	3,566

*Washington, DC is not a state but does have its own school system.

Source: Snyder, T. D., and Dillow, S. A. (2011, April). *Digest of education statistics 2010 (NCES 2011-015)*. National Center for Education Statistics, Institute of Education Sciences, U.S. Department of Education. Washington, DC: U.S. Government Printing Office, Table 92 , p. 134, and Table 36, p. 70.

For example, Florida has, on average, more than 39,000 students per district; by comparison, North Dakota has, on average, slightly more than 500 students per district. Obviously, population density has a role in deciding size as legislators make the final decisions.

10-2c The Governor

Governors generally serve a four-year term.[20] At the state level, they serve much the same function as a company's CEO. The governor's role is usually defined in the state's statutes or constitution. In general, governors' roles appear to be increasing in power as they assume greater responsibilities.

The governor's authority affects many areas of policy making. The governor can propose and veto legislation, veto appropriations, and set general policies and regulations that apply to all aspects of state government. The governor can make budget recommendations to the legislature. In addition, the governor influences educational policies through his or her appointment authority—that is, the ability to name individuals to head state agencies, boards, and commissions to oversee the state's operations. These appointments affect education at all levels—elementary through college. The governor also exerts influence through the governor's office staffing for the liaison with education and through the governor's implementing federal laws and aid.

Perhaps the governor's most important education appointments (unless the position is elected) are the Chief State School Officer and the State Board of Education members. By enacting their agendas in personnel and policy choices, governors exercise powerful sway on directions given to the public schools.

10-2d The State Supreme Court

The state court system plays an important part in determining how public schools operate. Most state judicial systems consist of three levels, which are similar to the federal system: a court of original jurisdiction, an intermediate appellate court, and a court of last resort. Although these courts have different names in different states, the state's highest court is usually called the State Supreme Court.

The State Supreme Court is rarely involved in education issues, but when these judges are, their decisions are usually vital to the schools.[21] Generally, the State Supreme Court rules on whether the legislature's laws are consistent with the state's constitution. As the *Plyler v. Doe* case in Texas demonstrates, a State Supreme Court's decisions can have major educational and financial consequences for the state.

10-2e The State Board of Education

The State Board of Education is the policy-setting agency that oversees and directs the State Department of Education.[22] Depending on the state, the Board's name may vary. It is similar to the local school board's oversight of the local school division but with far broader impact.

All states have a State Board of Education.[23] In most states, governors appoint members to this Board. In some states, the state legislature appoints members; in other states, the general public elects State Board members. Still other states use a hybrid model combining election and appointment to the State Board of Education. Each state's constitution and laws define how the State Board operates. Some State Boards hire and fire the Chief State School Officer; in other states, the governor appoints the Chief State School Officer; and in a few states the public elects the Chief State Officer. In many states, State Board of Education regulations have the effect of law.

State Boards of Education create policies in a variety of ways and for an array of reasons. Most often, these policies are intended to respond to state educational issues, needs, or perceived educational crises. These issues come to the Board's attention through study sessions on topics that affect schools and students, from items brought forward by state and national trends and events, and from federal and state legislation.[24]

State Boards of Education and state legislatures frequently share responsibility for making educational policy. Students' interests are best served when these bodies work together collaboratively to improve teaching and learning in schools. In recent years, however, increased executive and legislative interest in education policy has blurred the lines of responsibility. Establishing a strong relationship between key members of the State Board, the governor's office, and the state legislature is essential to enhance communications and share responsibilities.[25]

Although legislators introduce education policy initiatives with the best intentions, these initiatives often arrive at the State Board without a comprehensive examination of existing policies addressing the issue or assessing those policies' effectiveness. State legislatures sometimes pass legislation in concept form while leaving the specific details of how that concept should be implemented for the State Board to define. Because membership changes in legislatures, the governor's office, and State Boards of Education affect institutional memory and policy records, multiple and occasionally conflicting practices designed to address the same concern may result. Consequently, maintaining records to ensure continuity and accountability is a major Board concern.[26]

10-2f The Chief State School Officer

Each state has a Chief State School Officer. This position goes by different names, depending on the state: Superintendent of Public Instruction, Commissioner of Education, or State Superintendent. It is also filled in a variety of ways. In some states, the governor appoints this person to carry out the governor's educational agenda. In others, the public elects this person directly. In still others, the State Board of Education appoints the individual. Alternatively, the governor may appoint the State Board of Education, which in turn appoints the state superintendent. The precise selection process employed often influences the way the chief officer enacts the role.

Although the Chief State School Officer's duties vary from state to state depending on the state's constitution, this person typically serves as the State Department of Education's chief administrator. As such, the Chief State School Officer recommends improvements to the State Department of Education, works with the governor in the state budgeting process, advises the state legislature on education issues, and ensures public schools' compliance with state regulations and statutes. He or she reports on the "state of education" within the state to the governor, the state legislature, and the public. Additionally, this official works with the Department of Education's licensure office to make recommendations regarding changes in licensure for educators.

10-2g The State Department of Education

Teachers generally do not have many dealings with the governor, the state legislature, the State Supreme Court, the State Board of Education, or the Chief State School Officer. Teachers do, however, deal with the State Department of Education, also known as the State Education Agency (SEA), mainly when they apply for or renew their professional teaching licenses. The Chief State School Officer heads this agency, which is usually located in the state capital. The State Department of Education makes policy and program recommendations to the State Board of Education. It also constructs the guidelines (more general) and regulations (quite specific) that translate education-related laws passed by the legislature into workable practices for the public schools.

Additionally, the State Department of Education ensures that the state is complying with the federal Department of Education's rules on federally funded programs. In the past, SEAs had provided curriculum and instruction assistance to schools. Since the early 1990s, however, budget cutbacks have reduced the number of SEA educators offering technical assistance to local schools. Nonetheless, SEAs continue to make certain that the local school districts are following exactly—are in compliance with—state and federal regulations regarding state testing, licensure regulations, and federal grants.

Did You Get It?

Included in the list of state players in education policy and practice is not the

a. Governor.
b. Public.
c. Legislature.
d. Law enforcement/the criminal justice system.

Take the full quiz on CourseMate.

10-3 The Local Leaders and Support Staff Who Shape Education Policy, Practice, and Student Success

Education is a state function that draws federal interest and is administered locally. Most states allow localities to administer the community's schools in accordance with state law, to elect or appoint a local school board to set education policy, to hire and retain high-quality educators as superintendents, principals, teachers, and support staff, and to ensure that all students achieve to state standards.

This section discusses the role of the local school board, the local superintendent, the central office, the principal, teacher, and various educational support personnel—the positions and individuals with whom teachers are most closely involved.

10-3a The Local School Board

Local school boards play a critical part in preparing our children to be productive citizens and strengthen our communities. They aim to mirror the diverse communities they represent. All school boards derive their power and authority from the state. At the same time, all school boards generate their own "laws" by establishing the policies that govern their local schools. School boards everywhere are their communities' primary and—if state law permits—supreme educational authority.

Within every state except Hawaii, the local school board, as the local administrative unit, is responsible for implementing the state's policies and regulations. (Unique among the 50 states, Hawaii is a single state-run school district.) The state's power over the local school board depends on the state's constitution. In some states, it is possible for the state to "take over" local school operations. In such instances, the state would assume direct management responsibility for running the schools—from hiring and firing personnel to designing the curriculum. In other states, this type of "takeover" of local schools is not constitutionally possible.

Boards of education are usually elected by the school district's residents but may also be appointed by mayors or other executives of jurisdictions such as cities or counties that encompass the school district. In the United States, most local school board members are elected. Through the election process, the community has the ability to change their representatives on the board and find people whose views more closely match their own. Whether school districts have elected or appointed boards often has more to do with local history than with any particular philosophical stand. When the current form of the school board was introduced in the early 1900s, municipalities that were incorporated as cities had appointed boards and all others had elected ones.

The local school district's power varies from state to state—again depending on the state constitution's wording. In some states, the local school board has the power to relieve the superintendent of his or her position and, if necessary, to change school policies.[27]

School district superintendents inform and advise their school boards.

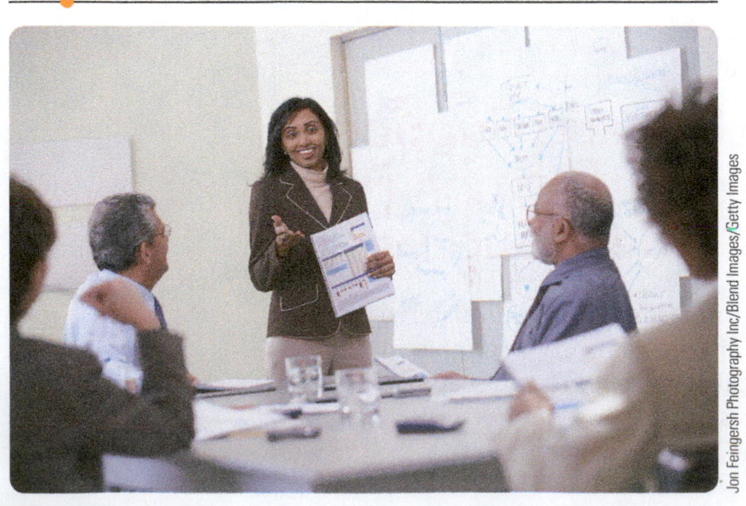

Jon Feingersh Photography Inc/Blend Images/Getty Images

Likewise, the local school board's authority to request funding varies from state to state. Some local school boards have taxing authority to fund the school's operation. Others recommend funding levels, which the public must then formally approve. Still others make budget recommendations to the governing authority (a city council or board of supervisors, for example), which it may or may not approve them.

Perhaps the local school boards' major responsibility is to hire the best superintendent of schools they can find. Additional responsibilities include approving the local school budget and establishing school district policies.

According to the National School Boards Association, a school board should be responsible for eight key areas[28]:

1. Setting a vision for the district
2. Establishing standards
3. Assessing student learning outcomes
4. Assigning responsibility for student outcomes
5. Dedicating resources to support the district's goals and objectives
6. Monitoring the organizational climate
7. Establishing trust among the stakeholders
8. Seeking ways to continue improvement in the seven previously mentioned areas

As school board members make policy decisions, they try to pay attention to how these eight areas interact. When board members work together collaboratively and effectively, these eight components can optimize a local school board's ability to make positive and lasting school district improvements.

Most school board members are laypeople who volunteer their time or receive a modest stipend to meet once or twice a month to work for their local school system. Because board members often lack expertise in many education-related areas, many school boards tend to base their decisions on experts' (usually the superintendent's) recommendations and advice.[29] Unfortunately, sometimes school board members overstep their responsibilities and try to micromanage the school system. This can lead to problems in role definition with the superintendent and may distract the school board from its primary purposes. But, as a result of the federal government's increased involvement in school affairs, relevant court decisions, and special interest groups' actions, the local school board's once-considerable authority in curriculum policy has slowly diminished.

Pressure is on school boards to close achievement gaps, increase high school graduation rates, and prepare more students for college and careers. In years past, unprecedented amounts of federal dollars have flowed to schools to achieve these goals. Some argue, however, that if mayors and political leaders are being held accountable for schools' academic, fiscal, or management failures, they may need deeper involvement with education issues. Accordingly, recent years have seen a mayoral takeover of some chronically low-performing high-profile urban schools when school boards could not provide the leadership to overcome educational challenges. Flip Sides presents the arguments on both sides for you to consider.

Reflect & Discuss

After considering federal and state roles in public education, it is clear that states exert the most control over America's public education. What role should the federal government play?

A. Separate into two groups. After 5 minutes of preparation, one group will present arguments that the federal government should become more involved with public education. The other group will argue that the federal government should have a smaller role in education. Give clear reasons for each point and list them on the board.

B. After hearing viewpoints on both sides of the issue, the class will discuss their informed opinions about this topic and define an answer that best reflects the class's thinking.

10-3b The School District Superintendent

The local school board's most important responsibility is to hire an excellent superintendent of schools. The superintendent is the school system's CEO and reports to the school board. He or she is a crucial part of the governance team for the school system and an essential link in the chain connecting the school board to the school system's people, programs, and activities.[30]

Local school superintendents may be either appointed or elected. The Education Commission of the States reports that only Alabama and Mississippi have both elected and appointed local school superintendents. Cities tend to appoint their school superintendents, whereas county school systems tend to use a combination of elected and appointed school chiefs. Hawaii and Vermont have no local superintendents. The remaining 46 states tend to appoint their local superintendents.[31]

Reflect & Discuss

Having state control of public education has both advantages and disadvantages.

A. As a class, list and explain the advantages and disadvantages of the United States adopting a national system of education instead of having 51 (50 states plus the District of Columbia) different education systems.

B. Discuss as a class what our schools and society would be like today if the U.S. Supreme Court had not made the decision that it did in *Brown v. Board of Education*. What difference has *Brown* meant for you personally?

C. Discuss the merits and disadvantages of the United States' current educational governance structure.

By and large, the superintendent oversees the school system's daily operations and advises the school board about policies and actions that need to be taken. The superintendent's specific responsibilities vary according to the school district's size; its location in a rural, suburban, or urban setting; and the superintendent's traditional duties within the organization.

In small, rural areas, the superintendent may be a "jack of all trades": he or she may evaluate all principals and central office staff and conduct professional development programs. In medium-sized suburban districts, two or more assistant superintendents may be available to assist with the work. Large urban and suburban areas may have area superintendents and assistant superintendents who report to the district superintendent, shouldering many of the duties associated with this position.

Superintendent responsibilities The school superintendent's work is threefold:

- *Organizing the school system for teaching and learning.* The superintendent must make certain that all students learn and achieve to high academic levels. He or she is responsible for developing and evaluating instructional programs and curriculum. The superintendent also influences curriculum policy by gathering and presenting data and responding to matters before the board of education, initiating programs for staff development, making district personnel aware of changes occurring in the schools, and moderating outside demands for change.[32]
- *Operating the school system efficiently and effectively.* School systems are complex organizations that require not only good leaders, but also good managers. For example, the superintendent must develop and oversee the school district's budget and consider federal and state requirements when developing the courses offered by the school system. Similarly, the superintendent is answerable for ensuring the efficacy of the school district's organization.
- *Maintaining good communication and relations with the school board.* The superintendent is the school board's primary advisor. Because the board members are laypeople, they rely on the superintendent and other specialists to give them the details and perspectives necessary to make informed decisions. Frequently, the superintendent serves as the school board's spokesperson in the community. Nonetheless, even when the board delegates many of its own powers to the superintendent and staff, especially in larger districts, the superintendent's policies remain subject to school board approval. In reality, the superintendent works for the school board and is always subject to the board's approval for continued employment in that district.

FlipSides

Do School Boards Matter?

School governance needs to be effective, efficient, and accountable. But do local school boards have the capacity to provide a twenty-first-century educational leadership? Or are they outmoded obstacles to education reform that should be replaced by local government control? What do you think?

Local school boards matter. Local citizens elected or appointed to school boards should run public schools.	Local school boards do not matter. Local government—the mayor, county manager, or state legislature—should run the public schools.
■ For generations, the public has believed that local residents who are not education experts are qualified to set policy, to govern the schools, and to represent the local community values in public education.	● Local school boards don't have the know-how to deal with today's complex fiscal, legal, and academic achievement issues. They may micromanage or interfere with the superintendent's role or act a rubber stamp.
■ The local school board has the sole responsibility and accountability for providing a high-quality education to the community's children. In contrast, mayors and states have many other responsibilities and priorities that compete with schools for attention and resources.	● Local school board members focus narrowly on education and may not be aware of the larger community's issues and needs. In contrast, mayoral or state governance of schools would have a larger, more comprehensive view of issues and needs.
■ Local school board members are accessible to the parents and the community—to discuss a problem in their neighborhood. They live in the communities they serve.	● Mayors and state agents may not live or work in every neighborhood they serve but they can be contacted easily by social media, email, text, or phone and are highly responsive to voters' concerns.
■ Voting for school board members is democracy in action. Often, elected board members represent different neighborhoods, bringing the entire community together to decide policies and practices for their schools.	● Only 10–15% of the electorate, on average, vote in school board elections. More voters cast ballots for mayors than for school board members.
■ Local school board members can energize their community to action by articulating the community's needs to the schools and the schools' needs to the community.	● Mayors and state agents have a larger forum by which to communicate a community's and school's needs to the public and gain support.
■ Local school boards have transparency, hold open meetings, have citizen input, debate issues, and have their records audited—unlike mayors and other politicians who often work behind closed doors or make decisions via executive fiat.	● Mayors and other political figures have staff persons who can gather necessary information about schools and communities necessary to make informed decisions—much of which can be made available publicly.
■ Data show mixed results for the effectiveness of state or mayoral school district governance and management. ■ When school governance is not local, education becomes less visible and loses public support. ■ State officials and mayors may grant contracts for education-related services in return for campaign contributions.	● Ideally, mayoral or state control of education would increase interagency collaboration between schools and health and social service organizations, business and civic groups, and wide coalitions of interest.

(*continued*)

FlipSides

Do School Boards Matter? (*continued*)

Local school boards matter. Local citizens elected or appointed to school boards should run public schools.	Local school boards do not matter. Local government—the mayor, county manager, or state legislature—should run the public schools.
■ Meaningful and sustainable education reform must occur from the inside, and it must have active local involvement from knowledgeable board members with influence over both educators and the local community.	• When change is imposed from the outside, those who assume control of a school or school system generally have greater flexibility and power in governance—for instance in contract negotiations with teachers' unions—than those previously in charge.
■ School boards are sometimes the only entities that provide continuous institutional leadership through times of change.	• State or mayoral control brings regular personnel changes along with new ideas and solutions to address public school issues.
■ Making school boards more effective—by clarifying and limiting their roles and responsibilities; by selecting good members; by educating members in the expectations, knowledge, and skills required of their role; and by improving communications with their communities—would be better for local schools than ending local school boards altogether.	• Many school boards lack the training or capacity to develop productive, positive, and long-term relationships with superintendents, leading to high turnover of urban superintendents. Many members may also lack the skills that would allow them to work together effectively in difficult situations.

After reading both sides of this issue, do you favor strengthening or ending local school boards? What reasons support your conclusion?

+Land, D. (2002, January). *Local school boards under review. Their role and effectiveness in relation to students' achievement.* Report No. 56. Baltimore: Johns Hopkins University. Retrieved from http://www.csos.jhu.edu/crespar/techReports/Report56.pdf.

Sources: Hess, F. (2010, March). Weighing the case for school boards: Today and tomorrow. *Phi Delta Kappan 91*(6), 15–19; Land, D. (2002, January). *Local school boards under review. Their role and effectiveness in relation to students' achievement.* Report No. 56. Baltimore: Johns Hopkins University. Retrieved from http://www.csos.jhu.edu/crespar/techReports/Report56.pdf; Resnick, M., and Bryant, A. L. (2010, March). School boards. Why American education needs them. *Phi Delta Kappan 91*(6), 11–14; Usdan, M. D. (2010, March). School boards. A neglected institution in an era of school reform. *Phi Delta Kappan 91*(6), 8–10.

Some believe that the superintendent has lost much of his or her decision-making authority over curriculum policy in recent years because of the increased federal and state involvement in public education. Powers previously granted to the superintendent have been taken away through the courts and various legislative acts.[33] Nevertheless, this role remains extremely important and highly challenging.

10-3c The District Central Office

The central office or school board office refers to the educators and support staffs who help the superintendent administer the school system. A typical central office organizational chart may look like Figure 10.2. It takes many people "behind the scenes" to support classroom teachers. Although students appear at the base, the entire pyramid could be turned upside down with

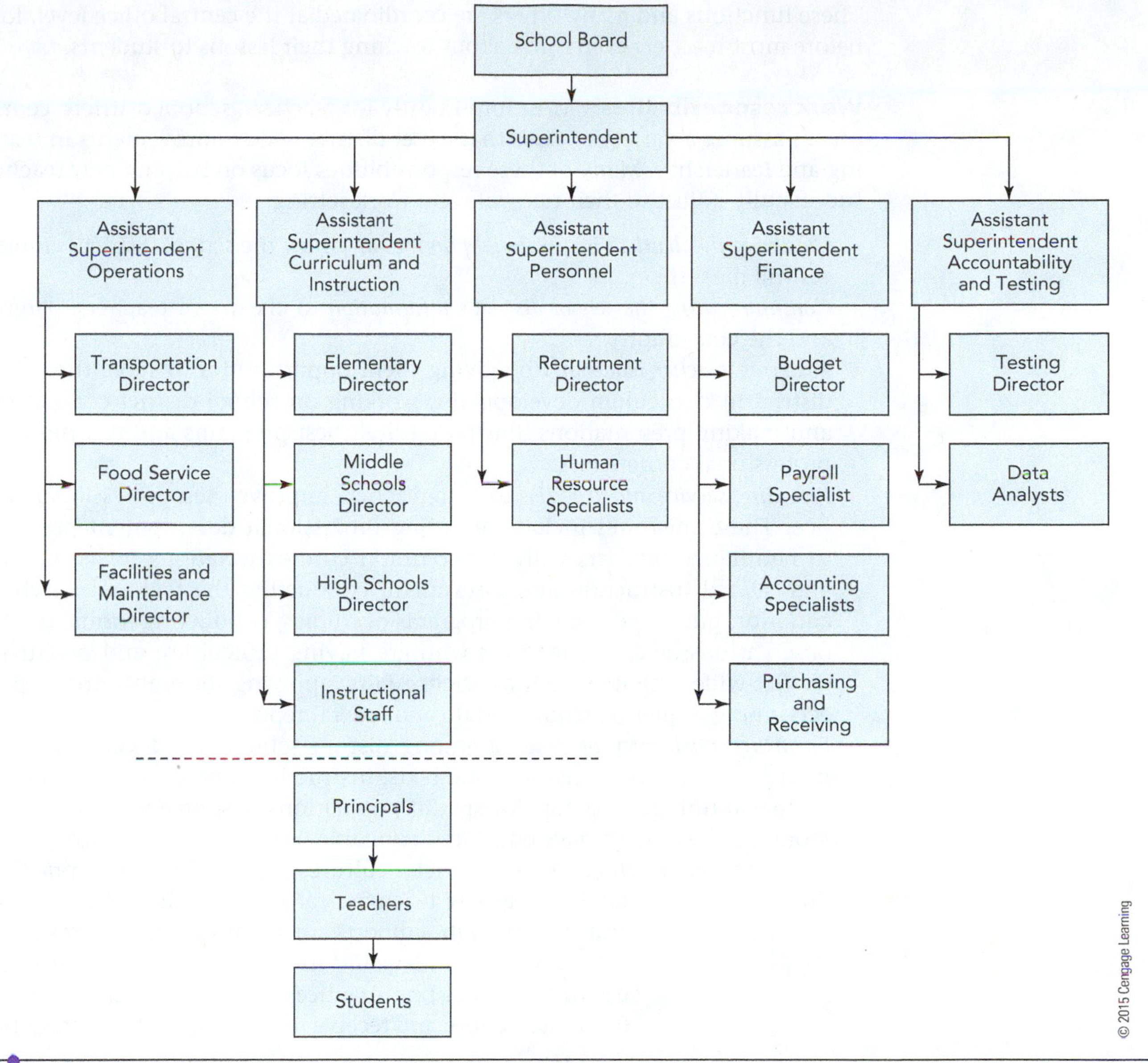

FIGURE 10.2 Typical School District Organizational Chart

the students placed at the top because they are the focus of the entire educational enterprise.

Most teacher candidates rarely think about how the central office personnel work to make their classroom efforts more successful. Teachers need to be recruited, hired, inducted, and developed into increasingly adept professionals. Instructional resources must be purchased, paid for, and inventoried. The achievement testing programs need to be coordinated, administered, interpreted, and analyzed to report on student achievement and schools' accountability and to modify curriculum and instruction. Paychecks need to be processed correctly and delivered on time. Bus transportation routes need to be established and drivers hired, trained, and evaluated. Food needs to be ordered and delivered to the school cafeterias. Food service workers need to be hired, trained, and supervised. Buildings need routine maintenance. The schoolyard grass needs to be cut. Leaking roofs and sputtering heating systems need to be fixed. The school district's budget needs to be developed and monitored so the school system does not overspend its limits.

These functions and many others are coordinated at the central office level, long before most teachers even think about teaching their lessons to students.

Work responsibilities Most importantly for teachers, school districts' central offices assume a variety of tasks that foster district-wide improvements in teaching and leadership. Many of these responsibilities focus on helping new teachers successfully adjust to their new role and work setting:

- *Clarifying the district's instructional priorities* and how the school district's employees will meet them.
- *Communicating the school district's information* to classroom teachers, parents, and the community.
- *Fostering teacher leadership* by giving them opportunities to serve the school district in curriculum development, working on school district committees, and making presentations illustrating their best programs and techniques at professional conferences.
- *Providing service and expertise* to help teachers improve their professional practice. These measures include affording professional development programs to familiarize teachers with the common core expectations for curriculum and related instruction and assessment; conducting the textbook or ebook adoption process; developing programs of studies; conducting formal teacher observations; assisting teachers who are having difficulties; and organizing district-wide activities such as science fairs, applying for grant-funded projects, and completing required state and federal reports.
- *Ensuring consistency of practice* among district schools by developing common goals, curricula, instructional texts, instructional practices, assessments, teacher training, programs for special populations, resource staff, and much more, so all students have equal and equitable opportunities to learn.
- *Orienting new teachers* to the districts' culture, expectations, and practices. These might include helping new teachers learn to hold high expectations and deliver high supports for all students, recognize and value diversity, understand the school district's curriculum, use instructional best practices, employ assessments to inform instruction, and receive moral support from other new teachers.[34]

When one considers the many functions that schools require to operate smoothly, it becomes clear that the central office operations enable teachers to do their jobs well.

Reflect & Discuss

Figure 10.2 depicts the typical school district organizational chart. In this diagram, the school board sits at the top and the students sit at the bottom. Ideally, all positions on the chart work to benefit the students.

A. Discuss where principals, teachers, and students are on the organizational chart. To what extent does their chart position accurately—or inaccurately—reflect their power and influence on students?
B. Who holds the most power and influence inside the school system? Which factors give these persons the most power?
C. Who holds the least power and influence inside the school system? Which factors contribute to this status?
D. How can teachers use and enhance their power and influence to benefit students, their school, and the school district?

10-3d The Principal

Everyone knows the old spelling adage, "The principal is your pal." Principals' job descriptions vary from state to state depending on the laws and regulations. Virginia, for example, has defined the principal's position as the instructional leader of the school. Given the importance of achievement testing conducted under NCLB and the Common Core State Standards, most states now consider the principal's primary charges to be managing the school and ensuring that all students meet state achievement standards.

Teachers and their principals interact frequently. Larger schools have at least one assistant principal to help with these responsibilities, and teachers work repeatedly with these school leaders. Many of these principal–teacher exchanges occur in informal discussions about students, in teacher–parent conferences and faculty meetings, in the halls during class changes, and during the teacher observation and evaluation process. Most states require principals to observe teachers in their classrooms on a routine basis to make certain they are teaching the curriculum effectively. Most principals or assistant principals formally observe and evaluate teachers teaching at least twice a year, and perhaps more often before teachers are officially offered tenure, sometimes called continuing contract status. In addition, many principals informally stop by classrooms throughout the year to get a sense of the classroom climate, to speak briefly with students about what they are learning, and to monitor and support the teaching and learning process.

Principals affect student achievement Principals can make a measurable difference in their schools' success. Three decades of school effectiveness research concludes that successful schools have dynamic, knowledgeable, and focused principals. "Many of the most impressive examples of school-wide change and student achievement gains involve a talented principal who has brought together teachers, parents, and students . . . to improve teaching and learning,"[35] observed Jonathan Schnur, of New Leaders for New Schools. The Chicago Panel on School Policy's study of five years of school reform found that "the most distinguishing feature of improving [as compared to stable or declining] schools was [that] they were led continuously by strong principals who had a vision of improvement for their school."[36]

According to one national analysis of 15 years of school leadership research, an outstanding principal exercises a measurable, but indirect, effect on school effectiveness and student achievement.[37] And although indirect, the principal's role has a critical impact on teachers, and through teachers, on student achievement. The principal controls key factors affecting a school's instructional quality:

- Attracting, selecting, and retaining outstanding teachers
- Working with the school community to establish a common mission, instructional vision, and goals
- Creating a school culture grounded in collaboration and high expectations for teachers and students
- Facilitating continuous instructional improvement
- Finding fair, effective ways to improve or remove low-performing teachers
- Producing high measured student academic results aligned with state standards

Further, Robert Marzano and colleagues' meta-analysis of 30 years of research on principals' practices' effects on student achievement finds a significant, positive correlation between effective school leadership and student achievement. For the average school, having an effective principal can mean the difference between scoring at the 50th or 60th percentile on a given achievement test.[38] Similarly, a 2012 study estimated that highly effective principals raise a typical student's achievement in their school by between two and seven months of learning

An outstanding principal has a measurable but indirect effect on student achievement.

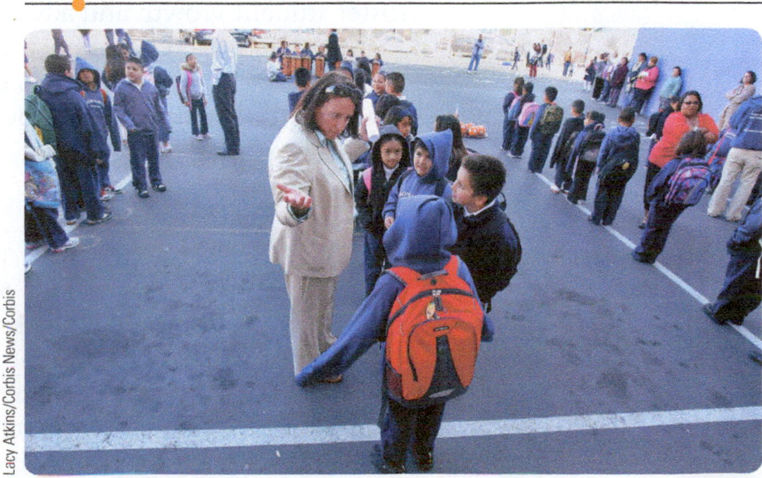
Lacy Atkins/Corbis News/Corbis

TeachSource Video 10.1

Video supplied by the BBC Motion Gallery

Education Leadership and School Reform

Many believe that the U.S. education system needs serious improvement. This video argues that education is a business, and school leaders need backgrounds in both education and business to make a real difference in children's lives. Watch the video clips, study the artifacts in the case, and reflect on the following questions:

1. How has the change in the economy—from an industrial to an information-based model—influenced the need for change in the American education system?
2. What are the arguments for and against increasing educators' accountability for student achievement by replacing ineffective teachers and principals?
3. How is making school leaders knowledgeable about both business and education a good—and a bad—idea?

Watch on CourseMate.

in a single academic year, whereas ineffective principals lower their students' achievement by that same amount.[39]

In addition to instructional leadership, principals have considerable operations management responsibilities for security, public relations, finances, personnel, transportation, and technology.

Principals' behaviors make a tremendous impact on teachers' work life. In fact, research indicates that a teacher's decision to stay at a school largely depends on the principal's leadership. Conversely, teachers cite a lack of administrators' support and weak or ineffective leadership as contributing factors in the negative working environment that add to teacher dissatisfaction and their decision to leave the profession.[40]

10-3e The Teacher

Chapter 1 discusses the classroom teacher's role. It is useful to recall that effective teachers implement the InTASC standards. They understand the central concepts, tools of inquiry, and structures of the disciplines that they teach and create learning experiences that students can engage fully and find meaningful. To better facilitate each student's learning, teachers build relationships with pupils so they can better understand the young person as a person and as a learner. Likewise, teachers understand how to link concepts and use varying viewpoints to involve learners in critical thinking, creativity, and collaborative problem solving related to relevant local and world issues. Teachers also use multiple means of assessment to monitor learner progress, guide instruction, and involve learners in their own growth.

Then, too, teachers are school leaders inside and outside the classroom. They seek appropriate occasions to take responsibility for student learning and to work collaboratively with colleagues, students, families, and community members to foster student growth and advance the profession.

Although the classroom teacher may be the "teacher of record," increasingly, she or he has colleagues in the building who will assist in the teaching-for-learning process. We will identify and discuss several critical support professionals next.

10-3f Support Staff

Teachers are not the only educators responsible for student learning. An array of skilled and specialized professionals may work with teachers to help make them and their students successful. Figure 10.3 shows the percentage of regular public schools that have support staff and the variety of resource professionals available. Not every school has every support role on-site, but most have specialized resource professionals available through the school district.

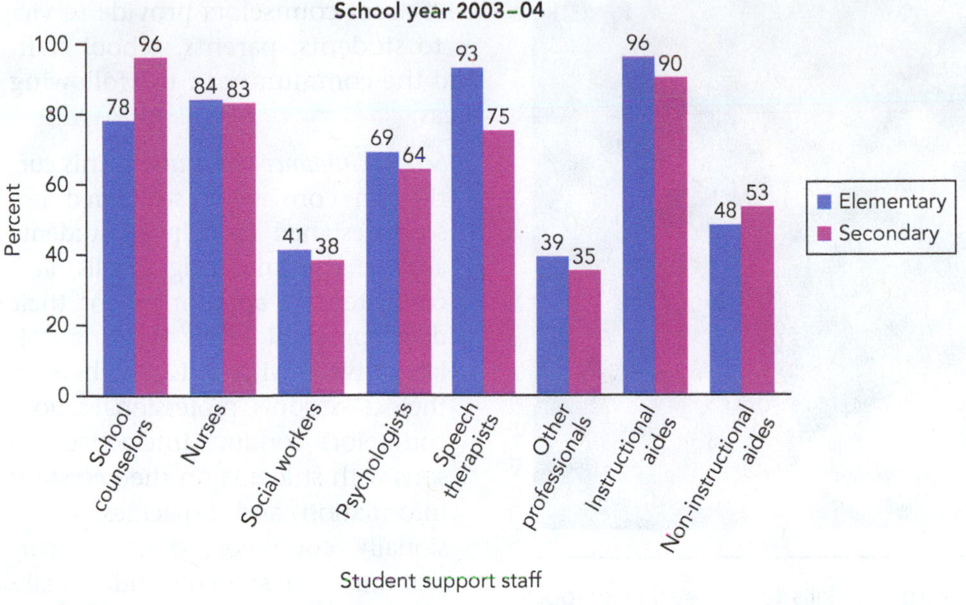

FIGURE 10.3
Percentage of Regular Public Schools with Student Support Staff

Source: U.S. Department of Education, National Center for Education Statistics. (2007). *The condition of education, 2007 (NCES 2007-064).* Washington, DC: U.S. Government Printing Office, p. 72.

The support professionals with whom teachers are most likely to work include school counselors, special education teachers, school nurses, school psychologists, reading specialists, and library media specialists. Each of these roles contributes a unique expertise that can help teachers do their jobs effectively. We will consider a few of them more closely.

10-3g School Counselors

Today's school counselors provide academic counseling, career development, and personal–social counseling. Licensed professionals with a master's degree or higher in school counseling, school counselors are a major part of a school's education team. They are specifically educated to help maximize student achievement in schools. Professional school counselors develop strong rapport and largely confidential relationships with students to help them resolve or cope with problems and developmental concerns that may interfere with their learning and future education and career planning.

School counselors support teachers' success by helping their students learn the critical behaviors that help them do well in school and life. School counselors help students develop three types of skills:

- Cognitive and meta-cognitive skills such as reflection, goal setting, progress monitoring, and memory skills
- Social abilities such as interpersonal skills, social problem solving, listening, and teamwork
- Self-management skills such as controlling attention, motivation, and anger

These three skill sets are the most powerful predictors of long-term school success and seem to separate high achievers from low achievers. As part of their role, school counselors can help students develop and use these approaches.[41]

Photo by Rahul Irani/The India Today Group/Getty Images

School counselors help students learn the skills to succeed in school and life.

School counselors provide services to students, parents, school staff, and the community in the following areas:

- *School Guidance Curriculum.* This curriculum consists of structured lessons designed to help all students achieve the knowledge, skills, and competencies appropriate for their developmental level. Working collaboratively with K-12 teachers in their classrooms, professional school counselors conduct interactive lessons with students on the necessary information and capacities. Occasionally, counselors enact the curriculum with students individually and in small-group activities.
- *Individual Student Planning.* Professional school counselors coordinate and lead activities designed to help students establish personal goals and develop future plans including arranging for upcoming courses, further education and work experiences, and eventual careers. Typically, counselors work with the same group of students during their entire time in a particular school so they can build caring, knowledgeable, strong, and trustful relationships with students and their families.
- *Responsive Services. Responsive services* are preventive and/or intervention activities to meet students' immediate or future needs—usually consisting of individual or group counseling—that are prompted by events and conditions in students' lives. Counselors may consult with parents, teachers, and other educators and make referrals to school support services or community resources. Additionally, school counselors can use student peer helping and information sharing as tools to prevent or resolve problems that interfere with learning.
- *System Support.* School counselors work with everyone in the school on behalf of students and teachers. Before the school year starts, counselors strategize with the school administrators to identify the school's needs and detail how the school counseling program will address them. They frequently partner with teachers to conduct parent conferences.

Developmental guidance and counseling program effectiveness is directly related to the school's counselor-to-student ratio. The number of counselors needed to staff the program depends on the students' and community's needs and on the local program's goals and design. The American School Counselor Association recommends a maximum ratio of 1:250 counselor-to-students (although the actual national average for 2010–2011 was 1:471).[42] Each state decides the school counselor-to-student ratio for each grade level that it will fund. For instance, Virginia accreditation standards require secondary schools to employ one school counselor for every 350 students, one counselor for every 400 students at middle school, and one counselor for every 500 students at elementary school.[43] Depending on the state's requirements, counselors typically spend 60 to 80 percent of their time in direct service with students.

Research on school counselors and student success As it is for teachers and principals, accountability, program evaluation, and obtaining data about student outcomes are also counselors' concerns.[44] Research substantiates the school counselor's ability to positively influence students through group counseling and classroom guidance, changing their behaviors and increasing their achievement on classroom and standardized tests. When school counselor interventions target specific skills associated with school success and when they use research-based techniques to teach these critical skills, student outcomes show positive changes in classroom performance.[45]

Based on empirical studies on students in grade levels K-12, students from 1954 to 2007 who participated in fully implemented guidance and counseling programs—as compared with students in less comprehensive or well-established programs—show markedly higher or more:

- Educational achievement[46]
- School success skills[47]
- Occupational maturity levels[48]
- Emotional stability[49]
- Preparation for the future[50]
- Enrollment in advanced math and science courses[51]
- Enrollment in vocational/technical courses[52]
- ACT scores on every scale of the test[53]
- Positive relations with teachers[54]
- Feeling safe in school[55]

In addition, schools with well-developed guidance and counseling programs have more positive climates.[56]

Professional school counselors engage in continual personal and professional development and are proactively involved in professional organizations promoting school counseling at the local, state, and national levels. School counselors are evaluated regularly. Their principals and central office supervisor usually collaborate in assessing their performance using basic standards of practice expected of professional school counselors who are implementing a school counseling and guidance program.

10-3h The Special Education Teacher

Today's public school students exhibit a range of disabilities, including specific learning disabilities, speech or language impairments, intellectual disabilities, emotional disturbance, hearing impairments, orthopedic impairments, visual impairments, autism spectrum disorders, combined deafness and blindness, traumatic brain injury, multiple disabilities, and other health impairments. After referrals, classroom interventions, rigorous screenings, and varied evaluations are complete, students may be classified under one of the various special education categories.

Because children with disabilities have more complex learning needs than their nondisabled peers, states have developed licensing standards for teachers who concentrate on working with these students. Special education teachers are highly

TeachSource Video 10.2

Social and Emotional Development: Understanding Adolescents

Adolescent boys often walk around school angry about events that occur in school every day. Caring and skilled school counselors can help these young men learn how to deal constructively with their emotions and cope successfully. Watch the video clips, study the artifacts in the case, and reflect on the following questions:

1. What verbal and nonverbal behaviors does the school counselor use to create a safe environment in which the seventh-grade boys can speak freely and learn new ways of staying calm in frustrating school situations?
2. Why is relationship building—between the counselor and the individual students and among the students—a key outcome of an effective school counseling group and how does this pay off in the future?
3. How does an effective school counselor group allow the counselor to help teachers be more effective with challenging students?

Watch on CourseMate.

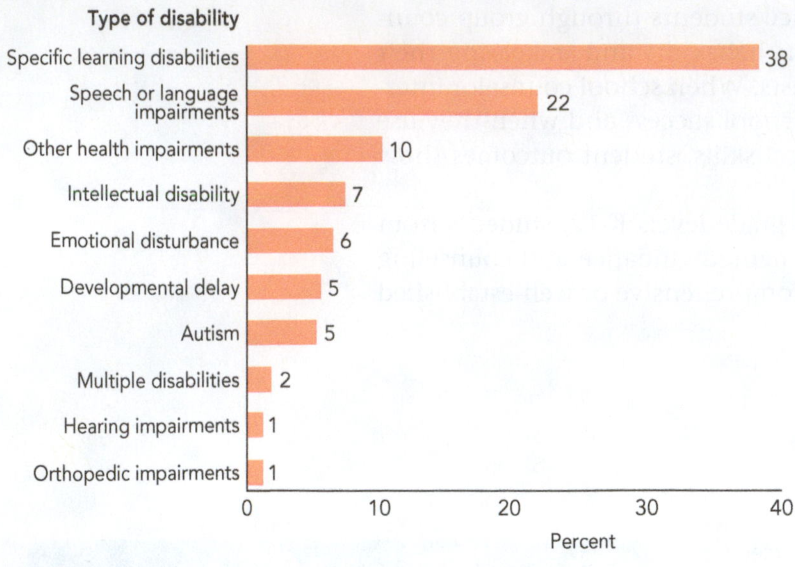

FIGURE 10.4 Percentage of Students Receiving Special Education Services, by Type of Disability, School Year 2009–2010

Note: "Students" refers to children and youth ages 3 through 21 who are receiving services under the Individuals with Disabilities Education Act (IDEA).

Source: U.S. Department of Education. (2012). *The condition of education 2012.* Figure 9-1, p. 33. Washington, DC: National Center for Education Statistics, Institute of Education Sciences. Retrieved from http://nces.ed.gov/programs/coe/pdf/coe_cwd.pdf

trained professionals who provide specially designed instruction to children with disabilities. Licensing requires the completion of a teacher training program and at least a bachelor's degree, although many states require a master's degree to qualify for this position.[57]

A small number of special education teachers work with students with intellectual disabilities or autism, primarily teaching them life skills and basic literacy. The majority of special education teachers work with children with mild to moderate disabilities, using or modifying the general education curriculum to meet the child's individual needs.

In 2009–2010, the U.S. Department of Education estimated that about 6.5 million of the nation's schoolchildren, ages 3 to 21, were receiving special education services through IDEA. This represented about 13 percent of all public school enrollments, down from 14 percent in earlier years. As Figure 10.4 shows, in 2009–2010, about 38 percent of those students have specific learning disabilities, and 22 percent had speech or language impairments. Eleven percent had other health impairments. Between 6 and 7 percent were diagnosed with significant cognitive disabilities, such as intellectual disability and traumatic brain injury. About 95 percent of these children and youth ages 6 through 21 were enrolled in regular schools. More than half of all students with disabilities spend more than 80 percent of their time in the regular classroom as compared with 33 percent in 1990–1991.[58]

This student population has created a large demand for special education teachers in U.S. public schools.

Special education teachers design and teach appropriate curricula, assign work geared toward each student's needs and abilities, and grade papers and homework assignments. They are involved in the students' behavioral, social, and academic development. They help special education students feel comfortable in social situations and learn socially acceptable behaviors. Preparing these students for daily life after graduation is another important aspect of the job. In some instances, special education teachers assess students for possible careers or help them learn routine life management skills, such as balancing a checkbook.

Within the school, special educators deliver their services in a continuum of teaching settings. Increasingly, special education teachers work in general education classrooms using an **inclusion model**. In this paradigm, students with disabilities receive most, if not all, of their instruction in a general education classroom. As a result, 59 percent of the students with disabilities spend at least 80 percent of the school day in regular education classrooms, increased from 45 percent in 1995.[59] Special education teachers help general educators adapt curriculum materials and teaching techniques to meet students with disabilities' needs. Frequently, they plan lessons together. Sometimes they team-teach.

inclusion model A format for delivering special education in which students with disabilities receive most, if not all, of their instruction in a general education classroom.

self-contained classrooms A format for delivering special education in which students with disabilities spend the majority of their school day in a classroom specifically set aside for them.

Other special educators teach special needs students in **self-contained classrooms**. Approximately 41 percent of students with disabilities spend the majority of their school day in a classroom specifically set aside for children with disabilities.[60] The majority of special education teachers work in **resource rooms**, where they provide specialized instruction to students with disabilities who come in for part of the school day, either individually or in small groups.

resource rooms A format for delivering special education where students with disabilities receive specialized instruction during part of the school day, either individually or in small groups.

A large part of a special education teacher's job involves collaborating with others: parents, social workers, school psychologists, occupational and physical therapists, school administrators, and regular education teachers. They coordinate the work of teachers, teacher assistants, and related personnel, such as therapists and social workers, to meet the students' individualized needs within inclusive special education programs.

Special education teachers represent a valuable resource for general education teachers. Because of their training, special education teachers are creative problem solvers who bring expertise in curriculum, teaching strategies, and learning styles into the classroom. They will help teachers work with special needs students in their classroom or in the special educators' own classrooms. Either way, special educators bring resources or skills to help students with disabilities achieve academically and socially—and increase regular education teachers' effectiveness with diverse students.

10-3i The School Nurse

The school nurse supports student success by providing on-site emergency health care, health care assessments, interventions, and follow-up care for all children within the school setting. They work with actual and potential health problems that occur in schools; provide case management services for students with chronic and short-term illnesses; and actively collaborate with teachers, parents, students, and others to manage family health issues.[61]

For example, students with diabetes have a school plan of care in place, which the school nurse helps them follow. These students often monitor their blood glucose levels several times a day and may require insulin injections during school hours. The school nurse must be familiar with every student's treatment regimen, including any devices or medical procedures required as part of the treatment.

By addressing students' health needs, professional school nurses support student success in the learning process. The school nurse's responsibilities include[62]:

Providing direct health care to students and staff The school nurse provides care to injured or acutely ill students and staff, including administering emergency first aid, communicating with parents, and making referrals to other providers. The school nurse is responsible for administering student medications and performing health care procedures ordered by an appropriately licensed health

TeachSource Video 10.3

Collaborating with School Specialists: An Elementary Literacy Lesson

Today's schools usually have a variety of education specialists to help teachers become more effective in the classroom. Collaboration with specialists can bring "another set of eyes and ears" into the classroom to help teachers refine their instructional and classroom management practices so that more students learn. Watch the video clips, study the artifacts in the case, and reflect on the following questions:

1. How does the collaboration format—preconference, observation, and postconference—help make the teacher's and specialist's time together meaningful?
2. From this video and your own experiences, explain the benefits to teachers and their students that may come from working closely with an education specialist.
3. What did the literacy specialist mean when she noted that "Although new teachers want everything to be perfect from Day 1, teaching is a journey"?

Watch on CourseMate.

504 team An interdisciplinary group of educators who implement Section 504 of the Rehabilitation Act of 1973 to ensure that children in schools who have disabilities or who are regarded as having such an impairment are not subject to discrimination.

caregiver. The school nurse also assists faculty and staff in monitoring students' chronic health conditions.

Providing screening and referral for health conditions The school nurse often conducts screening activities to address students' health problems that might potentially become barriers to learning or treats symptoms of underlying medical disorders. Screenings may include vision, hearing, dental, postural, weight (body mass index), or other conditions.

Promoting a healthy school environment The school nurse monitors student compliance with state immunization laws, ensures appropriate exclusion from and reentry into school, and reports communicable diseases as required by law. The school nurse leads the school in implementing precautions for faculty and staff regarding blood-borne pathogens and other infectious diseases. This health care professional may also assess the school's physical environment and act to improve health and safety in areas including the playground, perform indoor air quality evaluations, or review illness or injury patterns to determine a source of concern.

TeachSource Video 10.4

Inclusion Grouping: Strategies for Inclusive Classrooms

In inclusive classrooms, teachers work with additional support staff to help all children learn successfully. Collaboratively planning the learning activities that interest and engage all learners plus thoughtfully assigning students to groups and providing adult assistance makes the lesson effective for each student. Watch the video clips, study the artifacts in the case, and reflect on the following questions:

1. How does the teacher use her knowledge of each student's learning needs, interpersonal skills, interests, and likes as a way to motivate their attention to the topic under study?
2. How does the teacher guide student learning in their small groups to direct student attention and energy toward learning?
3. What are the inclusion specialist's responsibilities—before, during, and after the lesson—for making the classroom learning success for every student?

Watch on CourseMate.

Promoting health with students, school, family, and community The school nurse provides age-appropriate health information directly to individual students, groups of students, or classes as well as to school staff, families, and the community. Health promotion activities may include health fairs for students, families, or staff; consultation with food service personnel or physical education teachers regarding healthy lifestyles; and staff wellness programs.

As the school's health expert, the school nurse participates as part of students' individualized education program (IEP) and **504**[63] **team** and as part of student and family assistance team. In the role as case manager, the nurse communicates with the family through telephone calls, email, letters, and home visits as needed. The school nurse also speaks with local health providers and health care agencies while ensuring appropriate confidentiality, develops community partnerships, and serves on area coalitions to promote public health.

State law usually regulates the school's required nurse-to-student ratio; no national standard exists. The National Association of School Nurses recommends the following nurse-to-student ratios: 1:750 in general populations, 1:225 in student populations that may require daily professional school nursing services or interventions, and 1:125 in student populations with complex health care needs.[64]

The National Association of School Nurses recommends that all school nurses have a minimum of a baccalaureate degree and achieve School Nurse Certification. The school nurse needs expertise in

Reflect & Discuss

Schools have many personnel in support positions who are available to help teachers educate students to high levels of learning. These professionals include library media specialists, school counselors, school psychologists, reading specialists, school nurses, special education teachers, and many more.

A. Research the role of one of these positions that interests you. Determine what these personnel actually do in the school. Research their education and licensure requirements.
B. Interview one or two individuals in this line of work and see if a career in that field is something you wish to pursue further. Report your findings to the class.

pediatric, public health, and mental health nursing and must possess strong health promotion, assessment, and referral skills. School nurses also need to have knowledge of laws in education and health care that may affect children in the school setting. Each state sets its own eligibility and hiring requirements for this important school support person.

Did You Get It?

Which statement is true about the local leaders and support staff who shape educational policy, whether for good or ill?

a. Local school boards are usually composed of either education or childhood development professionals or laypeople who work in related fields, such as the local newspaper or independent bookstore. They are usually given a handsome stipend to compensate them for their expertise and hard work.
b. You can make a reasoned argument that in recent years, increased federal and state involvement (read: money) in public education has reduced school superintendents' control over curriculum.
c. School districts' central offices do a tremendous amount of work: they account for approximately 15 percent of staff in schools.
d. Good principals have a real effect upon teachers, but no discernible effect upon student achievement.

Take the full quiz on CourseMate.

10-4 Structural Issues That Affect Schools' Effectiveness

Generally, local school boards decide how to structure their district's schools. Typically, schools are organized as elementary, middle, and high schools. Grade configurations vary substantially, however, as do schools' sizes. The local school board has much control over both these factors. Typically, elementary schools contain kindergarten through grade 5. Middle schools typically house students in grades 6, 7, and 8. Usually high schools have students in grades 9 through 12.

Most school boards take their role as stewards of their neighbors' tax dollars very seriously. Where local boards feel cautious about spending tax revenues, they choose efficiency as an operational value. They are likely to build larger schools, assuming that two or three big schools are more cost-effective to operate than four or five smaller schools. Conversely, school boards may decide that effectiveness as an operational value is more important than efficiency. Reflecting this perspective, they may decide to build smaller schools, citing research that smaller schools may be better for student attendance and achievement gains than larger schools. Members' beliefs and values as well as research findings contribute to board decisions about school structure.

10-4a Reducing School Size

What is the best-sized school to support student success? Since 1990, a growing body of evidence questions whether larger schools provide better academic and school climate outcomes and whether they are more cost-effective. The existing literature offers conflicting conclusions.

After in-depth analyses of previous school size research, several investigators concluded that smaller schools produce better academic results and an improved school climate.[65] Others observed that smaller schools improve student attendance, increase students' course grades, allow more opportunities for students to be involved in co-curricular activities, and offer more personalization and individual attention than do larger schools but do not improve standardized test scores.[66] These studies and others advanced the view that smaller schools lead to many—but not all—improved student outcomes.

Determining the relationship between smaller schools and student achievement remains a challenge. Recent studies find that smaller school size is not automatically better when it comes to increasing student achievement. After a $1.5 billion investment over five years by the Bill and Melinda Gates Foundation to apply "smallness" to American high schools (no more than 100 students per grade)—especially those serving economically disadvantaged and minority students—a national evaluation of this initiative found that although small high schools had supportive school climates, higher student engagement (academic interest, educational aspirations, higher attendance and promotion rates), and higher gains in student proficiency rates than students in large high schools, small-school students' standardized achievement tests scores in English/language arts and mathematics remained below the district averages.[67]

Likewise, a 2008 federal study of high schools receiving grants to support forming "smaller learning communities"[68] and a comparable investigation in Chicago realized similar results. They concluded that although smaller schools have a more collegial, trusting, and innovative environment, this factor does not necessarily translate into higher achievement on college entrance exams or to instructional and curricular reform.[69]

Accordingly, the issue of school size and student achievement remains unclear and unresolved. Perhaps this is because several elements may influence the relationship between school size and student outcomes.[70] These include poverty, the student population served, and an "ideal" school size. Cost-effectiveness brings an additional consideration to the school size dilemma.

Community affluence is a key dimension affecting the relationship between school size and student outcomes. In separate studies, researchers determined that students' socioeconomic status—rather than school size—was the strongest predictor of student achievement test results.[71] Smaller schools may mediate between student poverty and academic outcomes, improving results for low-income students. Investigators have verified that children from economically disadvantaged backgrounds perform better academically when served by a small school, and students from affluent backgrounds tend to perform better when educated in a larger setting.[72] Similarly, a 2002 seven-state survey by Ohio researchers for the Rural School and Community Trust ascertained that smaller schools reduce poverty's harmful effects on student achievement.[73] Smaller schools also help students from less affluent communities narrow the academic achievement gap between themselves and students from wealthier communities.[74]

Additionally, the specifics of school size—what student enrollment is "small" or "large"—is debatable. Nor do investigators agree on the "ideal" sized high school. In 1987, after reviewing several studies, two researchers determined that high schools should have no more than 250 students per school. Larger enrollments focused too much administrators' attention on control and order, harming the school climate. At the same time, the larger school population increased members' feelings of anonymity, making it more difficult to build a sense of community among students, teachers, and parents.[75] In contrast, other studies suggest that small and moderate-size high schools (between 600 and 900 students) foster more positive social and academic environments compared to large high schools (those enrolling 2,100 students or more), especially for economically disadvantaged students.[76] These varied studies imply that students in very small high schools (fewer than 300 students in the school) learn less than students in moderate-size high schools but more than students in very large high schools (over 2,100 pupils).[77]

Cost-effectiveness is another consideration in determining school sizes. Some posit that although larger schools first appear to be more cost-effective to operate, if the dropout/graduation rates are considered, smaller schools actually are more cost efficient,[78] and the increased attendance rates and other smaller school benefits outweigh the cost. For example, a 2000 study of more than 140 schools and 50,000 students in the New York City Public Schools found that small academic high schools had budgets per graduate similar to those of large high schools (more than 2,000 students).[79] Smaller high schools had lower dropout rates. Researchers found that both small and large schools were cost-effective when looking at graduates as the outcome.[80]

Although smaller schools are more expensive to operate on a *per-pupil* basis, researchers now contend that small schools can be more efficient when measured on a *cost-per-graduate* basis. Cost-effectiveness is a relative term. With fewer dropouts, smaller schools graduate more of their students. Considering that high school dropouts are associated with substantial costs to society, including lower earnings, higher unemployment rates, greater reliance on welfare, and increased incarceration rates, small schools seem more cost-effective.[81]

Considering all the evidence, an ECS report details the benefits of reduced school size and draws five conclusions[82]:

- Under the right conditions, as schools get smaller, they produce stronger student performance as measured by attendance rates, test scores, extracurricular activity participation, and graduation rates.
- Smaller schools appear to promote greater levels of parent participation and satisfaction, and they increase parent–teacher communication.
- Teachers in small schools generally feel they are in a better position to make a genuine difference in student learning than do teachers in larger schools.
- There appears to be a particularly strong correlation between smaller school size and improved performance among low-income students in urban school districts. Smaller schools can help narrow the achievement gap between white, middle-class, affluent students and ethnic minority and low-income students.
- Smaller schools provide a safer learning environment for students.

Sometimes, larger schools create smaller schools by implementing the "school-within-a-school" concept. This approach may be a way to achieve the benefits

Diverse Voices

Closing Schools? "Proceed with Caution"

"Philadelphia's state-appointed School Reform Commission last month approved the closure of 23 district buildings—an unprecedented action for our region that is expected to affect roughly 14,000 students and hundreds of staff members. In New York City, which has already closed nearly 140 schools over the past decade, another 23 closures are on the horizon. The District of Columbia is bracing for as many as 15 closures after shuttering two dozen sites in 2008. The Chicago public school system—the nation's third-largest district—recently announced plans to close 54 schools and consolidate 11 more before the 2013–2014 school year begins.

"Nationwide, the implications of these policies are difficult to comprehend. Yet the federal and state policies that incentivize closures . . . . are driving more districts to embrace school closure as a reform strategy and to move aggressively to downsize on a broad scale.

"The rationale for these plans center on two major assumptions that remain unproven:

"First, proponents argue that savings from closures can help fill cavernous budget gaps. Second, closure of chronically low-performing schools is increasingly seen as a path to higher academic achievement.

"Examining the goal of closing budget deficits, research shows that the majority of short-term cost savings achieved through closings occurs not through shuttering buildings but from furloughing staff . . . . Calculating actual savings is also complicated by the transition costs that accompany closings: relocating staff members, transferring students, and maintaining vacant parcels. For example, the 2008 closures in Washington ultimately cost that city's system approximately $40 million—roughly four times what the district was expected to save. . . .

"Meeting the goal of improving student achievement via closures is even more tenuous. Studies of closures in Chicago and Pittsburgh suggest that academic performance is likely to decrease, at least in the short term, when students are transferred from closing schools. Indeed, students fare better academically only when they are transferred to higher-performing schools. Yet the supply of seats in high-performing schools is often limited, and even when they are available, increase in academic performance are modest.

"For example, an analysis of Philadelphia's plan . . . reveals a mixed bag for students leaving closing schools: . . . 40 percent of proposed receiving schools perform better than those recommended for closure, 35 percent are similar; and 25 percent perform worse. . . . [T]he very best performing schools—those most likely to help students transition without losing academic ground—currently have enrollments at or near capacity. . . .

"The wisdom of this trend is debatable. But if closings are to continue as a policy prescription for our most challenged school districts, there needs to be equal commitment to act on the issues that can ameliorate adverse impacts and slow a wrenching trend that challenges communities, strains the capacity of already-overworked central offices, and disrupts the work of teachers and students. . . . [C]losing schools and sending students to a worse-performing school isn't just bad policy; it's a breach of trust."

Source: Shaw, K., and Schott, A. (2013, April 17). Proceed with caution. Districts must address school closures comprehensively. Commentary. *Education Week 32*(28), 32. Kate Shaw is the executive director and Adam Schott is the senior policy analyst at Research for Action, a Philadelphia nonprofit educational research and policy organization.

associated with smaller school size without having to actually build expensive new school facilities. In this way, schools that personalize the learning environment for students can increase their engagement and academic achievement.

When considering the best school size to produce student achievement, school boards must consider the nature of their community and their student body, cost efficiency, and related factors and decide whether they, as stand-ins for the larger community, prefer to pay now or pay later.

10-4b Consolidating School Districts

The debate about school size mirrors the debate about the best size for school districts. Larger school districts, their supporters contend, offer a broader tax base and reduce the educational cost per student. As a result, these districts can better afford high-quality personnel, a wide range of educational programs and special services, and good transportation. Over the past half-century, most studies of this issue have placed the most effective school district size at between 10,000 and 50,000 students.[83]

The twentieth century witnessed a trend toward consolidating smaller school districts in an effort to increase efficiency. In 1939–1940 (the earliest year for which data are available), slightly more than 117,000 public school districts existed in the United States. By 2011, that number had dropped to just under 14,000, representing a loss of more than 100,000 school districts—a decrease of almost 90 percent.[84]

School districts cite several reasons as driving forces for consolidation:

- *Size.* Larger schools, especially high schools, can accommodate broader curriculum offerings and specialized teachers.
- *Services.* Larger schools can justify hiring school counselors, deans of students, assistant principals, lead teachers, and specialists not typically available in smaller schools.
- *Economics.* Consolidating school districts lowers operating costs. Purchasing decisions can lead to significant savings when items are ordered in bulk; that is, the costs for books, paper, lab equipment, and art supplies may go down when schools can negotiate to buy them in larger quantities. Consolidation also allows schools to close older buildings and reduce the number of higher-paid central office administrators, both money savers. For example, instead of having three curriculum supervisors (one for each of the formerly separate school districts), a consolidated school district needs only one.

Figure 10.5 illustrates that larger schools are able to make more high-level, high-status courses available to students. These include dual-credit courses (simultaneous enrollment in a high school and college course), Advanced Placement (AP), and International Baccalaureate (IB) courses. Only 40 percent of high schools smaller than 500 students offer AP courses to their students, and none offers IB programs. By comparison, schools with 500 to 1,199 and schools with more 1,200 students provide more advanced-level offerings to their students.

FIGURE 10.5 Percentage of Public High Schools Offering Advanced-Level Courses by Enrollment Size

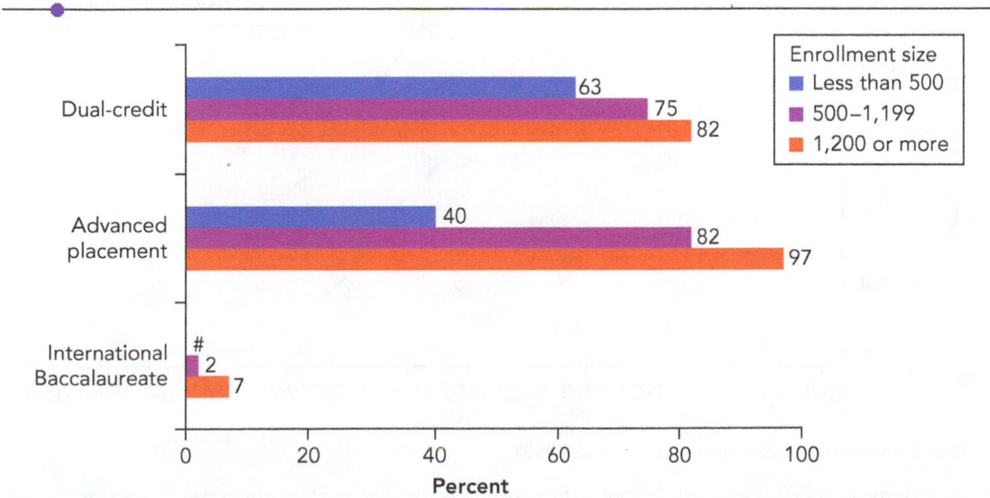

Source: U.S. Department of Education, National Center for Education Statistics. (2007). *The condition of education, 2007 (NCES 2007-064).* Washington, DC: U.S. Government Printing Office, Figure 2, p. 6.

TABLE 10.2

Number of Pupils per School District, 1940 and 2010

	1940	2010
Total number of students	25,434,000	49,386,000
Total number of school districts	117,108	13,809
Pupils per school district	217	3,576

Source: Snyder, T. D., and Dillow, S. A. (2011). *Digest of education statistics 2010 (NCES 2011-015).* Washington, DC: National Center for Education Statistics, Institute of Education Sciences, U.S. Department of Education, Table 36, p. 70 and Table 90, p. 132.

When school districts merge, the resulting district serves more students. Table 10.2 compares the number of pupils per school district in 1940 and 2010. The average school district in 1940 had approximately 217 students, and school districts served more than 3,500 students on average in 2010.

In this 70-year period, the average number of students in school districts increased more than 1,500 percent—from 217 to 3,576. The number of public schools and school districts decreased, even as their size and efficiency increased (see Table 10.2 and Figure 10.6). Neighborhood schools and school districts gave way to larger ones covering multiple neighborhoods. Consolidation increased most districts' ethnic, geographic, and wealth diversity.

This changing structure posed crucial challenges for the localities affected. Feelings of community pride and ownership of local schools and school districts diminished as the schools and their leadership—and their children—moved farther away: Local control was no longer local. At the same time, administrators and teachers worked with more diverse students who needed to learn more higher-level skills in order to survive in a globally competitive environment. School climate and student achievement, once taken for granted in small local schools with relatively homogeneous student populations, suddenly became urgent issues. Many educators needed intensive professional development to gain the skills and attitudes needed to work effectively with students and parents who were different than themselves. In fact, distancing school districts from their communities has led some to call for replacing school boards with school councils, thereby returning public schools governance back to the "grassroots" level.[85]

Figure 10.6 shows how the number of public schools has changed over time as a consequence of both student population growth and school district

FIGURE 10.6 Number of Public Schools, 1869–2000

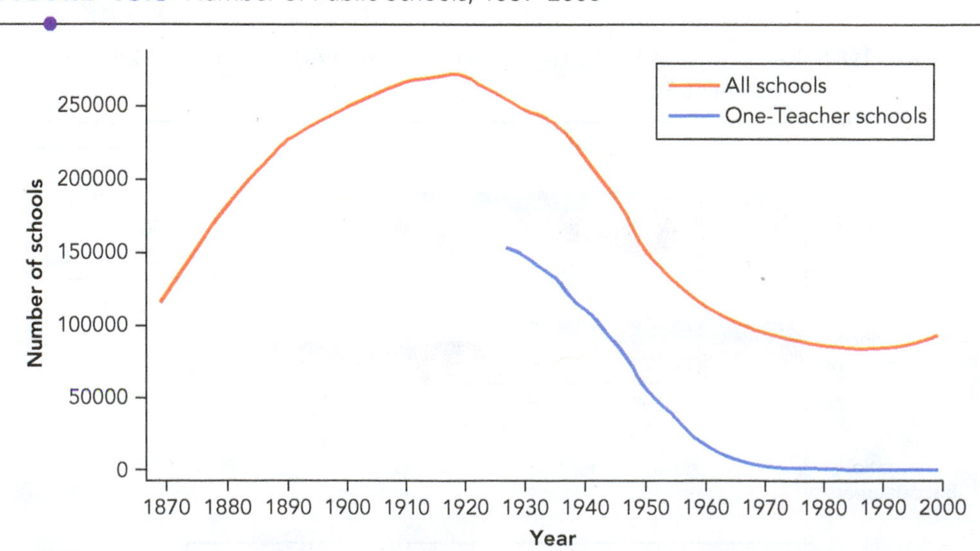

Data for one-teacher schools only available after 1927.

Source: Berry, C. (2003, October). *School district consolidation and student outcomes: Does size make a difference?* Cambridge, MA: John F. Kennedy School of Government, Harvard University, p. 31, Figure 2. Retrieved from http://www.ksg.harvard.edu/pepg/PDF/events/SBConfPDF/papers/PEPG_03-12Berry.pdf.

consolidation. In 1939–1940, almost 250,000 public schools were in operation in the United States. Today, that number stands at approximately 96,000.[86] The number of one-teacher schools has declined dramatically.

The empirical literature on the effects of district size on student outcomes is small and mixed.[87] Some studies have found that school districts with student enrollments between 2,000 and 4,000 students tend to be cost-effective, whereas districts enrolling more than 15,000 students achieve less cost savings.[88]

10-4c Organizing Schools by Grade Levels

When Americans think of how schools are organized by grade levels, we tend to think of elementary, middle, and high schools. The reality, however, is much more varied. Figure 10.7 shows the breakdown of schools by elementary, secondary (middle and high school), and combined (the totals do not add up because of overlap in reporting).[89] Small schools are defined as schools with enrollments of less than 300 students, and large schools are those with 1,000 or more students.

Research on school grade configuration Does a school's grade configuration affect student achievement? Do students achieve better in K-8 schools or in separate grades 6–8 middle schools? The research here is complicated and has yielded unclear results.[90] Little evidence exists to determine a cause-and-effect relationship between grade configuration and academic achievement. No empirical, large-scale studies have examined the relationship between grade configuration and student achievement as measured by standardized test scores.[91] The few studies that do exist offered few clear policy guidelines.[92] In part, this is because their research methods do not allow readers to draw generalizable conclusions.[93]

FIGURE 10.7 Percentage of Public Schools by School Level and Enrollment Size, 2008–2009

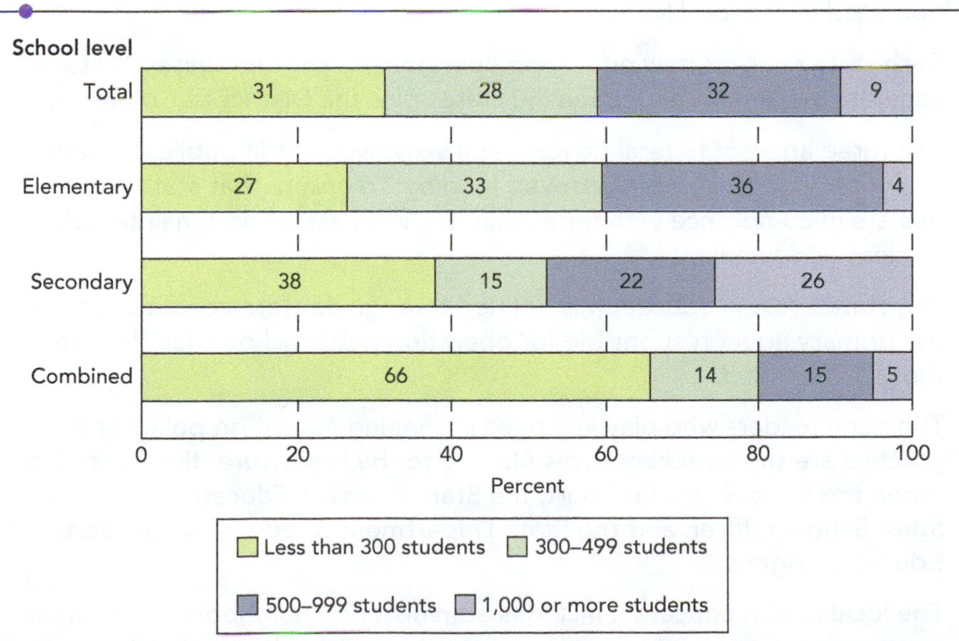

Source: Aud, S., Hussar, W., Kena, G., et al. (2011, May). *The condition of education, 2011 (NCES 2011-033).* Washington, DC: National Center for Education Statistics, Institute for Education Sciences, U.S. Department of Education, p. 85, Figure 27-1.

Several recent research reviews have done a good job of summarizing the existing studies. Because their findings are suggestive rather than conclusive, however, we should interpret them cautiously. They indicate that students in grades 6, 7, and 8 in K-8 schools had higher achievement than their counterparts in schools with middle school configurations, but both groups had the same achievement levels by grade 9.[94] Those students who demonstrated higher levels of achievement in K-8 schools may be reflecting their community's affluence rather than any school or instructional factors. Additionally, a 2005 research review concluded that "no sequence of grades is perfect or, in itself, guarantees student academic achievement and healthy social and emotional development."[95] Agreeing, a 2008 review noted that "what is most important for the education of young adolescent learners is what takes place inside each middle-grades school, not grade configuration per se."[96]

School governance is not the education issue that most new teachers think about. In all likelihood, principals and central office supervisors are probably the only "governance officials" with whom teachers interact on a daily basis. But many other individuals have a big say in the policies and practices that influence how teachers do their work. Recognizing the other professionals available as resources in their schools, in their district offices, and in the state education department can help classroom teachers get the supports they need to succeed.

Did You Get It?

Choose the false statement.

a. Consolidation of smaller school districts lowers their operating costs, freeing up money to be spent on educating students.
b. There is a direct correlation between smaller school size and better educational outcomes.
c. There are no definitive studies correlating grade organization to student achievement.
d. Smaller schools often produce better outcomes—but those better outcomes rarely relate to improved test scores.

Take the full quiz on CourseMate.

SUMMARY

- In the United States, education is a national interest and a state function operated at the local level.
- Each state controls how education operates—giving the United States 51 separate systems of education (50 states plus the District of Columbia).
- The three areas of federal government's involvement in public education are to provide Congress-approved funding; to ensure that states and localities are in compliance with federal laws; and to assess and maintain data on student achievement.
- The state's role in education is defined through its state constitution and is the primary agent responsible for operating public schools (as defined in the U.S. Constitution).
- The state leaders who play key roles in shaping education policy and practice are the representatives elected to the legislature, the elected governor, the State Supreme Court, the State Board of Education, the Chief State School Officer, and the State Department of Education (or State Education Agency).
- The local role in education includes administering neighborhood schools in accordance with state law; electing or appointing local school board members; hiring and retaining high-quality educators, and ensuring that all students achieve to state standards.

- The local leaders who play essential roles in shaping education policy and practice include the local school district superintendent, central office personnel, school site principals and assistant principals; and teachers.
- A variety of educational specialists work in schools to help teachers support student success: school counselors, special education teachers, school nurses, and other professionals and paraprofessionals.
- The structure of public schools in the United States varies in school district and school size, with the trend to consolidate school districts and schools and to increase average student enrollment. Also, schools vary in how they organize student grade levels.

Visit the Education CourseMate for this textbook to access the eBook, Did You Get It? quizzes, TeachSource Video Cases, flashcards, and more. Go to CengageBrain.com to log in, register, or purchase access.

Excellent education is a good investment in our nation's infrastructure.

CHAPTER 11

School Finance

InTASC Standards Addressed: 2, 3, 4, 5, and 9

LEARNING OBJECTIVES

After you read this chapter, you should be able to:

11-1 Explain how education is an investment in U.S. infrastructure.
11-2 Describe the federal, state, and local contributions to school funding.
11-3 Justify the reasons for increased education spending since 1960.
11-4 Identify the categories and purposes for which school districts budget money.
11-5 Define the equity issues in school funding.
11-6 Trace how a "taxpayer revolt" negatively affects funding for education.
11-7 Explain how wise spending can positively influence student achievement.

Money plays a major role in educating America's students. Constructing and maintaining school buildings, purchasing equipment and supplies, and paying school staff and administrators are all costly. For the FY 2014, nationwide public education at all levels cost $781.2 billion with approximately 3.3 million elementary and secondary school teachers.[1] In 2006, one in 75 adults was an elementary or a secondary teacher.[2]

Although expensive, excellent education for all of America's children is a good investment. When it comes to quality education, as a society we can pay now or pay later. Education is one of the largest determinants of an individual's life choices and chances. It affects students' future employment, income, health, housing, and many other aspects of life. It is a critical investment in a community's—and our nation's—infrastructure.

It is the state and community's responsibility to ensure that all schools have the essential resources to provide positive learning environments. But this does not always happen. In his 1992 book *Savage Inequalities*, education writer Jonathan Kozol described conditions in several American city schools between 1988 and 1990[3]:

> "East St. Louis High School was awash in sewage for the second time this year," wrote the St. Louis *Post-Dispatch* on Monday, in the early spring, 1989. The school had to be shut because of "fumes and backed up toilets." Fumes flowed into the basement, through the floor, and then up into the kitchen and the students' bathrooms. The backup . . . occurred in the food preparation areas.[4]

In the same week, the schools announced the layoff of 280 teachers, 166 cooks and cafeteria workers, 25 teacher aides, 16 custodians and 18 painters, electricians, engineers, and plumbers. . . . [T]he cuts will bring the size of the kindergarten and primary classes up to 30 students, and the size of fourth to twelfth grade classes up to 35 students . . . The school system . . . has been using more than 70 "permanent substitute teachers" who are paid only $10,000 yearly, as a way of saving money. . . .[5]

The science labs at East St. Louis High School are 30 to 50 years outdated. . . . The six lab stations in the room have empty holes where [water] pipes were once attached.[6] "I have no materials with the exception of a single textbook to give each child." . . . The high school has no VCRs. . . .[7]

What message do you think the students and teachers receive from a community that expects them to learn and thrive in this environment? How do you think learning in this school will impact the "achievement gap" between low-income and affluent students?

Large differences in educational attainment persist across income, race, and region. Even when similar schooling resources are available, educational inequalities continue because many children from educationally and economically disadvantaged families come to school less prepared to start academic learning. And, they are unlikely to catch up without major educational interventions on their behalf.

11-1 Education as an Investment in National Infrastructure

Our country's democracy and economic well-being depend on an educated population. Education provides individuals with the ability to enact responsible citizenship and to earn a living in career fields such as business, medicine, law, engineering, high-tech manufacturing, and services. In fact, education is the profession that enables all other professions. It fuels the American body politic and its economy's infrastructure like nothing else in our society. Just as any building's framework must be thoughtfully and routinely maintained to remain in working order, education is no different.

Before considering the specifics of how we fund schools and identify ways to prevent *savage inequalities*, let's begin with the end in mind: Where can we see the effects of education dollars in our own lives and communities? Education increases the value of the American economy and our quality of life by increasing residents':

- Earning potential
- Employability

At the same time, education decreases the following public social costs that we underwrite with our tax dollars:

- Incarceration rates
- Crime rates

We will briefly discuss how education has a positive impact on each of these factors.

TABLE 11.1

Average per Capita Income by Education Level for Persons 18 and Older, as of March 2010

Level of Educational Attainment	All Persons	Males	Females
Not a high school graduate	$ 20,241	$ 23,036	$ 15,514
High school graduate only	$ 30,627	$ 35,468	$ 24,304
Some college (no degree)	$ 32,295	$ 39,204	$ 25,340
Associate's degree	$ 39,771	$ 47,572	$ 33,432
Bachelor's degree	$ 56,665	$ 69,479	$ 43,589
Master's degree	$ 73,738	$ 90,964	$ 58,534
Professional degree	$127,803	$150,310	$ 89,897
Doctorate degree	$103,054	$114,347	$ 83,708

Source: U.S. Census Bureau. (2012). *Current population survey. Mean earnings by highest degree earned, 2009*, Table 232, p. 152. Washington, DC: Author. Retrieved from http://www.census.gov/compendia/statab/2012/tables/12s0232.pdfhttp://www.census.

11-1a Earning Potential

The 2010 Census Bureau figures show that people with higher educational levels earn more money than people with lower educational levels. Table 11.1 shows individual average income earnings. Income rises with educational level. Of course, as income rises, so do the taxes one pays to the government.

As you can see from Table 11.1, the average yearly income for a high school dropout (i.e., a person who drops out in grades 9–12 and does not receive a diploma) is $20,241. If we assume a 40-year work life for that individual based on constant 2010 dollars, that person would accumulate lifetime earnings of $809,640. Assuming that person paid a tax rate of 10 percent, he or she would have contributed $80,964 to the government's coffers.

The individual with a bachelor's degree would earn an average yearly income of $56,665—almost three times what the high school dropout will earn. Assuming the same 40-year career in constant 2010 dollars, that person would have lifetime earnings of $2,266,600. Assuming this person has a good accountant and pays the same 10 percent tax rate, the college graduate will have paid $226,660 in government taxes, almost three times more than the high school dropout would have paid.

The higher the education, the more taxes paid over a lifetime. A professional degree includes the MD that physicians obtain and the JD that lawyers have. If the average attorney's salary is $127,803 and we assume the same 40-year career, the lawyer would earn $5,112,120 over his or her lifetime. Assuming the lawyer still pays 10 percent in taxes to the government, this tax bill totals $511,212, or more than two times what the college graduate pays. This is almost six times more than what the high school dropout would pay in taxes, assuming a constant 10 percent rate. From the standpoint of the government, an education is a very good investment indeed.

11-1b Employability

Before one can earn a salary, one must first get and hold a job. Education increases employability and decreases unemployment rates. Individuals with lower educational attainment are more likely to be unemployed or underemployed than those with higher educational attainment.

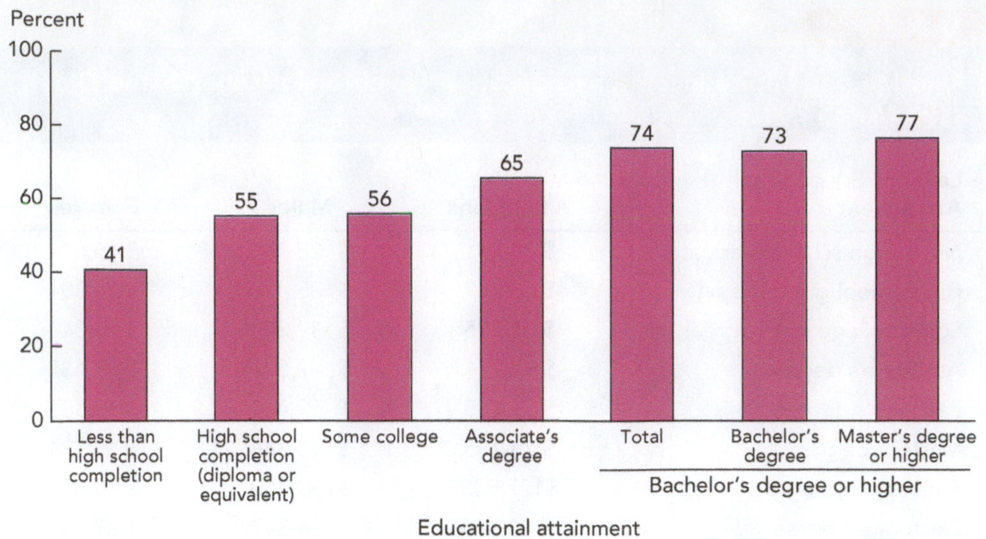

FIGURE 11.1 Labor Force Participation Rates by Education, Ages 25–34, 2010
Note: The Total* (* - superscript 1) column represents the percentage of young adults with a bachelor's degree or higher who were employed full-time.

Source: Aud, S., Hussar, W., Kena, G., Bianco, K., Frohlich, L., Kemp, J., Tahan, K., et al. (2011, May). *The condition of education 2011 (NCES 2011-033).* Washington, DC: U.S. Department of Education, Institute of Education Sciences, Figure 18-1, p. 59.

Figure 11.1 shows the labor force participation rates by education level for people ages 25–34 who were employed full-time, by educational attainment, in 2010. Only 41 percent of high school dropouts are participating in the workforce. The other 59 percent have not only dropped out of high school, but also dropped out of the workforce. They are no longer seeking employment—and many may be receiving government services (e.g., welfare).

By comparison, approximately 73 percent of individuals with a college degree are participating in the workforce and gainfully contributing to the economy and to the tax base supporting social service programs. The remaining 27 percent of college graduates who have left the workforce include those who could not find full-time employment because of the Great Recession, became parents and took time off from work to raise their children, attend graduate school, or some combination of these.

The unemployment rate represents the other side of labor force participation. Figure 11.2 shows unemployment rates by education level and race/ethnicity. The unemployment rate for high school dropouts—regardless of race or ethnicity—is two to five times higher than that for college graduates and almost 30 percent higher than that for high school graduates. In times of serious recession, as in all economic downturns, unemployment increases for those without advanced education.

As we can see from these data, education acts as an economic stimulus. By providing good income to support a favorable quality of life—for the individuals themselves as well as for their families, communities, and nation through money given back in the form of taxes—education fulfills its promises for most individuals who engage it to fullest advantage. But education as an investment in human capital has benefits that extend even further than income and employability.

11-1c Public Social Costs

Although education increases revenue to individuals in the form of income and to the government in tax dollars, it also tends to reduce

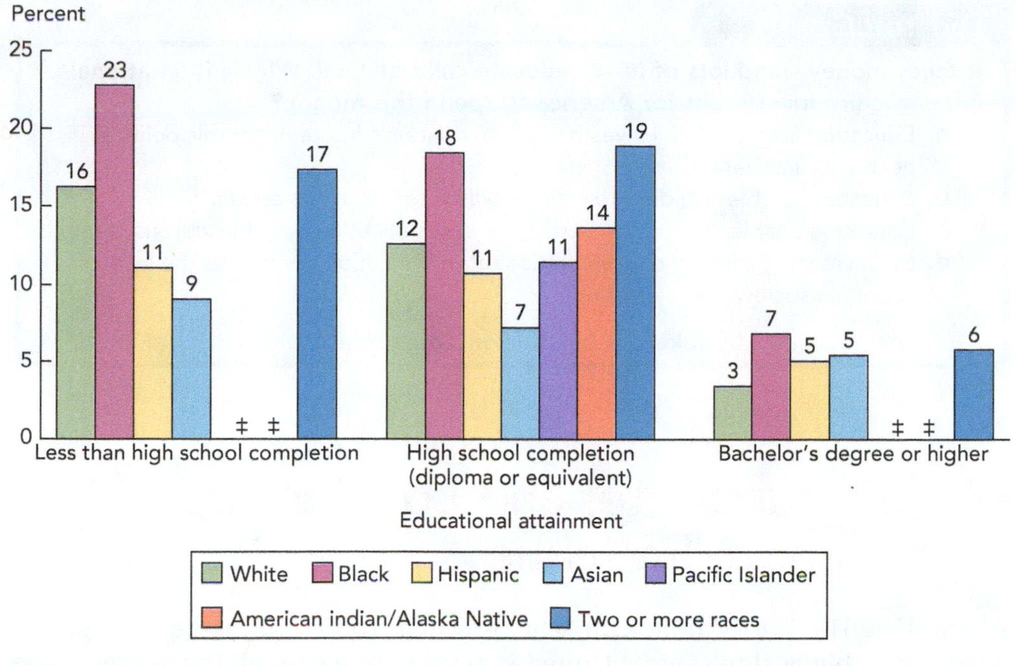

FIGURE 11.2 Unemployment Rates by Education Levels, Ages 25–34, by Race/Ethnicity 2010

Source: Aud, S., Hussar, W., Kena, G., Bianco, K., Frohlich, L., Kemp, J., Tahan, K., et al. (2011, May). *The condition of education 2011 (NCES 2011-033).* Washington, DC: U.S. Department of Education, Institute of Education Sciences, Figure 18.2, p. 59.

public social expenses of unemployment costs, incarceration rates, and crime expenditures.

For instance, the Alliance for Excellent Education estimates that if the 1.2 million students who drop out each year earned high school diplomas instead, states could save $17 billion in health care costs over the graduates' lifetimes. The nonpartisan Economic Policy Institute found that children who live in poverty but who receive high-quality early education have significantly fewer arrests than their peers without this opportunity. The nonpartisan Committee for Economic Development determined that investing $4,800 per child in preschool can reduce teenage arrests by 40 percent. Meanwhile, the national nonprofit Coalition for Juvenile Justice reports that high school dropouts are three times more likely to be arrested than their peers who stay in school.[8]

In what is probably one of the best studies to date, Lochner and Moretti have determined that for each one-year increase in educational level, arrest rates and crime levels decrease by 11 percent. Specifically, murder and assault decrease by 30 percent, motor vehicle theft by 20 percent, arson by 13 percent, and burglary by 6 percent. In addition, according to these authors, a 1 percent increase in the national graduation rate would save the nation nearly $2 billion each year in crime costs.[9] Given these data, they conclude that increased education brings sizeable social benefits.

Reflect & Discuss

Education is an investment in human capital—in having students increase their knowledge and skills so they can contribute to their own well-being as well as to their communities. In view of what you now know about the changing student composition of schools, consider the following activity.

A. Divide into three groups. Each group will plan and deliver a persuasive oral and graphic presentation to an active senior citizen community explaining why these seniors should continue to pay taxes to support public schools even though their children or grandchildren no longer attend. Using the chapter, each group will present visual and oral information about at least three of the following factors:

Education and employability
Education and earnings
Education and paying taxes
Education and reduced crime

B. Each group will give its presentation to the class. For extra credit, they can deliver it to an actual community audience.

Did You Get It?

It takes money—and lots of it—to educate children well. Why is it a national infrastructure investment for America to spend this money?

- **a.** Education is an essential investment in our nation's future economy, political health, and citizens' quality of life.
- **b.** Education enables children to make a satisfactory living as adults.
- **c.** Education enables children to participate in society as responsible citizens as adults.
- **d.** By decreasing crime and incarceration rates, education diminishes the level of cruelty in society.

Take the full quiz on CourseMate.

11-2 Federal, State, and Local Sources of School Revenue

As the FY 2014 $781.2 billion in school-related expenditures suggests, public education is big business in the United States.[10] Where does all the money come from to pay for these services? How is the money spent? How much do teachers earn?

Until recently, money for schools came from three government sources: federal, state, and local. Increasingly, more school districts are supplementing these sources with grants from various foundations. Although education is a state function, the state is not always the largest source of school revenues. Figure 11.3 shows the percentages of school funds that have come from federal, state, and local sources over the past 40 years.

In the 1970–1971 school year, the local governments, on average, contributed slightly more than 50 percent of schools' total operating revenue. State

FIGURE 11.3 Percentage of Revenue for Public Elementary and Secondary Education Schools by Source of Funds

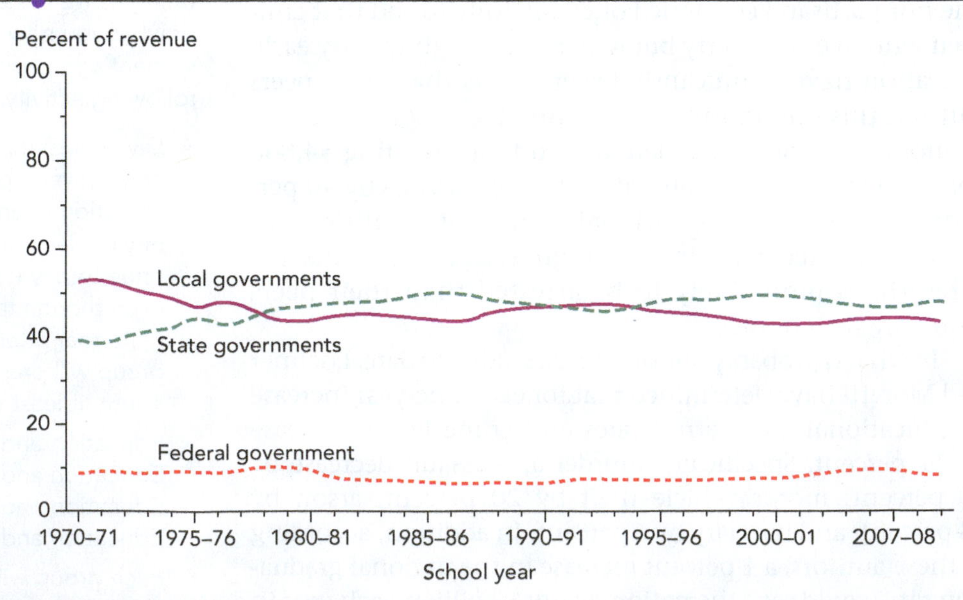

Source: Snyder, R. D., and Dillow, S. A. (2012, June). *Digest of education statistics 2011 (NCES 2012-001).* National Center for Education Statistics, Institute for Education Sciences, U.S. Department of Education, Figure 10, p. 69. Retrieved from http://nces.ed.gov/pubs2012/2012001.pdf.

governments accounted for approximately 40 percent of these revenues, and the federal government paid for slightly less than 10 percent. Over the next 10 years, the state governments contributed more than the local government. Around the same time, the federal government's share began to drop. Since then, the federal share has remained relatively flat, and the local and state governments have switched places several times in terms of which entity contributed more.

For the most part, American schools are a state function with a national interest that is operated locally. With the federal, state, and local governments all contributing to education, how does money come to school districts from each of the three government levels?

At the federal level, monies come back to the states once Congress has appropriated funds in an education budget. Those funds come from the federal taxes we pay.

At the state level, funding for the localities to help pay for schools is a bit more complex. A simple answer would be that states use their income taxes to provide these funds—but not all states have income taxes. Likewise, some states have no sales taxes. However a state raises revenues for its services, some mixture of those state funds goes to support education.

At the local level, the property tax is the predominant method for paying for schools. This tax dates back to the Massachusetts Law of 1647, which required landowners to pay a tax to support the local schools or face forfeiture of their acreage. At that time, the government taxed property because a person's estate was the basis for his or her income.

In the days when "land was money," property was a realistic proxy for income. Today, for most of us, this is no longer the case. Very few now derive income from our land. Instead, we earn our income from our place of employment, where that income is already taxed. Depending on the real estate market, most of us today will not realize any financial gain from our property until we sell it. That logic explains why some people object to using property taxes as the main revenue source for public schools. We will discuss taxpayers' resistance to property taxes and this movement's effects on school funding later in this chapter.

Did You Get It?

All but which of the following are correct?

a. Educational funding by state, local, and federal sources is increasingly being supplemented by grants.
b. Local and state governments account for the majority of school funding even though they switch places.
c. The federal government provides a major amount of school funding.
d. Resistance to using property taxes as the base of school funding is driven by self-interest rather than a desire to expand school funding.

Take the full quiz on CourseMate.

11-3 Increases in Education Spending since 1960

Education costs have been growing since we have been keeping figures on the subject. Figure 11.4 (top) shows the change in the number of teachers and the student–teacher ratio since 1960 and the increase in total dollars spent on education during that same period (bottom). In examining this figure, it is easy to see that school expenditures have risen as the number of teachers has increased. That relationship makes sense: It costs money to hire additional teachers. It is interesting to note that the student–teacher ratios have been declining since at least 1960.

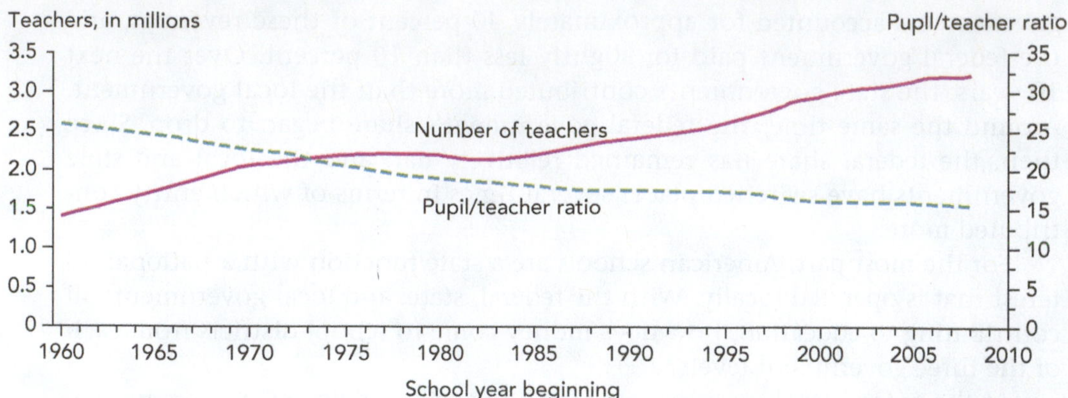

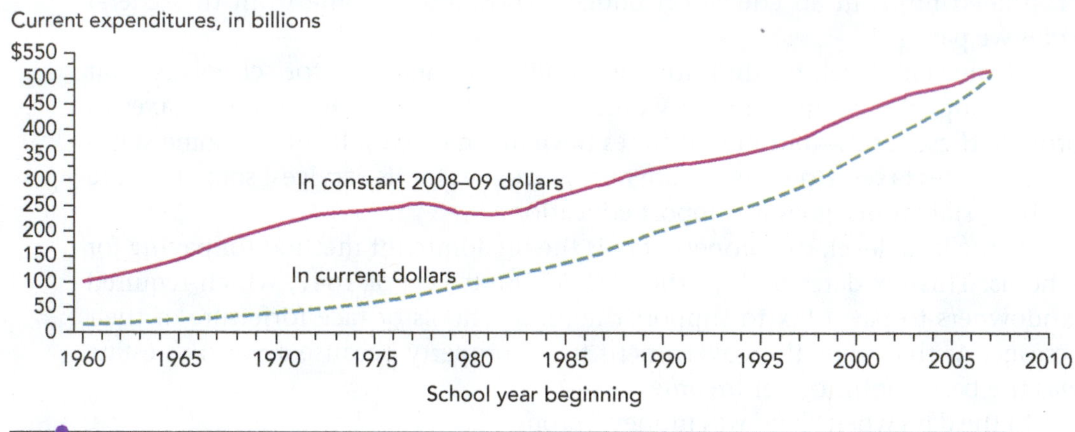

FIGURE 11.4 Number of Teachers and Student–Teacher Ratio and Total Pupil Expenditures

Source: Snyder, R. D., and Dillow, S. A. (2012, June). *Digest of education statistics 2011 (NCES 2012-001).* National Center for Education Statistics, Institute for Education Sciences, U.S. Department of Education, Figure 7, p. 67. Retrieved from http://nces.ed.gov/pubs2012/2012001.pdf.

11-3a Reasons for Increased Education Spending

Since 1960, public schools have hired more teachers for several reasons. In the 1960s, in addition to the large Baby Boomer cohort entering high school, schools began serving more and increasingly diverse students as a result of court-mandated desegregation. This growth required hiring more teachers and providing more equitable teacher salaries.[11]

Additionally, during this time, more schools began to work with students with special needs, whose education requires a teacher to work closely with fewer students. Although students with special needs as a percentage of the total student population increased from 9.7 percent in 1978 to 11.6 percent in 1990, and although the number of special education teachers rose by more than 50 percent during these same years, this increase was responsible for only 18 percent of the growth in school spending over this period.[12]

During these years, educators concluded that having more than 30 to 40 students in every class was not an effective environment for teaching and learning. As a consequence, the pupil-to-teacher ratio declined: from 35:1 in 1890, to 28.1 in 1940, to 24.9:1 in 1960, to 20.5 in 1970, to 15.4 in 1990.[13] The two most important factors in the increased school expenditures since 1960 have been (1) the rising costs of instructional staff and (2) the declining pupil-to-teacher ratios as schools have attempted to raise school quality by reducing the pupil-to-staff ratios.[14]

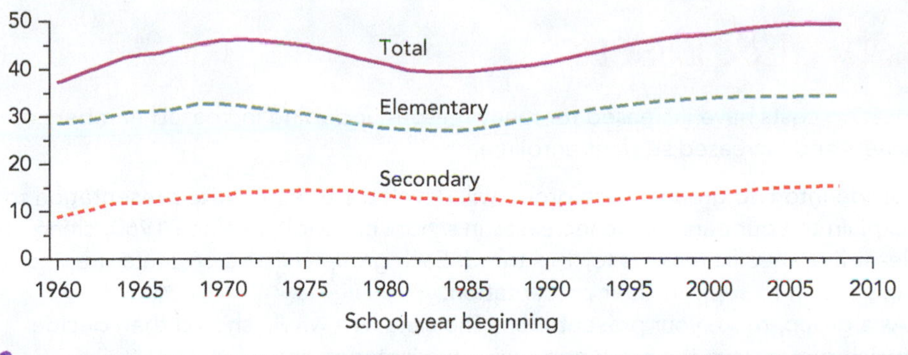

FIGURE 11.5 Total Enrollment in U.S. Public Schools, 1960–2010 (in millions)

Source: Snyder, R. D., and Dillow, S. A. (2012, June). *Digest of education statistics 2011 (NCES 2012-001).* National Center for Education Statistics, Institute for Education Sciences, U.S. Department of Education, Figure 7, p. 67. Retrieved from http://nces.ed.gov/pubs2012/2012001.pdf.

In addition to the decrease in student–teacher ratios, increased student enrollments have affected U.S. school expenditures. Figure 11.5 shows the total student enrollment in U.S. public schools since 1960. From 1960 to 2009, total enrollments increased from 35 million to almost 50 million students. Along with greater expenditures devoted to decreasing class size and teaching more diverse students and those with special needs, schools hired more teachers to meet the demand produced by increased student enrollments.

Library of Congress

Pupil–teacher ratios have been reduced from 35:1 in 1900 (seen here) to 15:1 in 2009.

Knowing the full story behind the increasing cost figures helps to explain events with data. These data are especially important if you are considering a career in public education. Thinking of you as an "inside expert," friends and family may ask you, "Why are education costs increasing so much?" and "Why are we spending more money and not getting better results?" The information in this chapter will help you answer these challenging questions successfully and convincingly.

11-3b National, Regional, and Local Education Expenses

How much does it cost to educate a child in the United States? The answer to this question varies widely according to the region, the state, and the locality. It also varies by the state and local wealth available to fund education: Affluent states and localities can fund education to higher levels.

Table 11.2 shows the average per-pupil expenditure for each state, the District of Columbia, and selected U.S. territories. Quite a variance appears in average state spending levels for each student. Among the states, New Jersey, on average, has the highest per-pupil expenditure ($18,971), and Utah has the lowest ($7,756). When the territories are examined, the average per-pupil expenditure drops even lower. Note that these figures are averages within each of the states; inside each state, large differences also occur between districts.

Reflect & Discuss

Education costs have increased for many reasons, including increased numbers of teachers and increased student enrollments.

A. Divide into two groups. Each group will develop a three-minute presentation to explain to your parents the increases in school expenditure since 1960, citing at least five specific reasons for this trend. Each group will also create a graphic illustration to support their presentation.

B. As a group, make your presentation. The class as a whole should then decide which group gave the more persuasive presentation and why.

TABLE 11.2

Per-Pupil Spending, 2007–2008

State	Per-Pupil Spending	State	Per-Pupil Spending
U.S. average	$ 11,950	Nebraska	$ 12,287
Alabama	$ 10,481	Nevada	$ 10,377
Alaska	$ 17,299	New Hampshire	$ 13,007
Arizona	$ 9,641	New Jersey	$ 18,971
Arkansas	$ 9,966	New Mexico	$ 10,798
California	$ 11,458	New York	$ 18,073
Colorado	$ 11,061	North Carolina	$ 9,045
Connecticut	$ 16,530	North Dakota	$ 10,378
Delaware	$ 14,481	Ohio	$ 11,982
District of Columbia	$ 20,066	Oklahoma	$ 8,372
Florida	$ 11,626	Oregon	$ 11,156
Georgia	$ 11,498	Pennsylvania	$ 13,712
Hawaii	$ 12,877	Rhode Island	$ 14,897
Idaho	$ 8,525		
Illinois	$ 11,874	South Carolina	$ 11,128
Indiana	$ 10,040	South Dakota	$ 9,684
Iowa	$ 11,126	Tennessee	$ 8,746
Kansas	$ 11,009	Texas	$ 10,596
Kentucky	$ 10,076	Utah	$ 7,756
Louisiana	$ 11,329	Vermont	$ 15,465
Maine	$ 12,696	Virginia	$ 12,030
Maryland	$ 15,032	Washington	$ 11,200
Massachusetts	$ 14,240	West Virginia	$ 10,341
Michigan	$ 11,445	Wisconsin	$ 12,312
Minnesota	$ 11,943	Wyoming	$ 17,478
Mississippi	$ 8,578		
Missouri	$ 11,070	U.S. Virgin Islands	$ 13,789
Montana	$ 10,941	Puerto Rico	$ 6, 647

Source: Snyder, R. D., and Dillow, S. A. (2011, April). *Digest of education statistics 2010 (NCES 2011-015).* National Center for Education Statistics, Institute for Education Sciences, U.S. Department of Education, Table 191, p. 275.

Just as there are differences among states in per-pupil spending, so there is variance among districts in the same area. Figure 11.6 shows spending differences within six local school districts in the metropolitan Washington, DC area: Alexandria, Virginia; Arlington, Virginia; the D.C. Public Schools; Montgomery County, Maryland; Fairfax County, Virginia; and Prince George's County, Maryland. All are urban. Some are larger and some are smaller. Alexandria, Virginia, spends approximately 75 percent more per pupil, on average, to educate its children than does Prince George's County, Maryland.

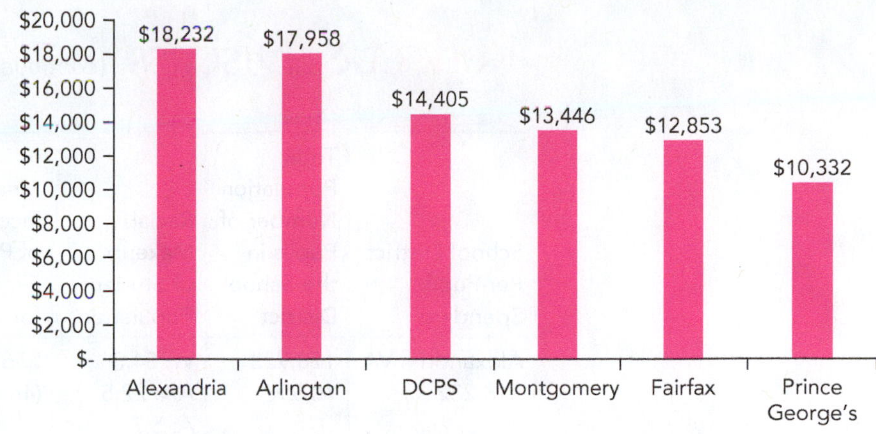

FIGURE 11.6 Per-Pupil Spending in Six Selected Metropolitan District of Columbia School Districts, 2007

Source: Levy, M. (2007). Per student figures for District of Columbia public school system. Washington Lawyer's Committee for Civil Rights and Urban Affairs, p. 5. Retrieved from http://www.21csf.org/csf-home/DocUploads/DataShop/DS_86.pdf.

Did You Get It?

Which factor has driven the increase in education spending since 1960?

a. Fewer people are having fewer children, and they want the best for them.
b. Classes are smaller and more diverse, while there are more children, overall, in school.
c. Special-needs students account for over half of the growth in school spending since 1960.
d. Schools are hiring more administrative staff.

Take the full quiz on CourseMate.

Reflect & Discuss

This activity will help you understand the differences in per-pupil spending. Divide into groups of six. Have each person or group (depending on class size) select one of the school districts listed in Figure 11.6. Using the data in the table in this activity, explain to the group why you think spending varies among these six school districts.[15] In your discussions, think about which school district might need to spend more per student for education. Use the following questions to guide you as you discuss your explanations.

Guiding Questions

A. What can you tell about the community by comparing the median household income?
B. In light of what you now know about the changing student demographics and their educational needs, what can you tell about the student populations by the percentage of students who qualify for free or reduced-price lunches? Do you think it costs more to educate students who qualify for special education services (those students with an individualized education program [IEP])? Explain your answer.
C. Do you think it costs more to educate students who do not speak English fluently yet (English language learners [ELL])? Explain your answer.
D. Based on what you can see, which school district needs to spend more to educate its students? Should districts with greater student needs receive more funding than districts with less needy students? Justify your answer.

(*continued*)

Reflect & Discuss *(continued)*

School District Per-Pupil Spending	Total Population Number of Pupils in the School District	Racial Makeup of Student Population*	Median Income (% of Pupils Eligible for FRPL†)	Number of Students with IEPs (%)	Student–Teacher Ratio	Number of ELL (%)
Alexandria, VA $18,232	128,923 10,996	W: 54.8 AA: 22.5 A: 5.7 L: 14.7 O: 2.3	$56,054 (46%)	1,900 (17.3%)	9.6/1	2,223 20.2%
Arlington, VA $17,958	199,776 18,463	W: 63 AA: 8.8 A: 9 L: 16.1 O: 3.1	$66,626 (36%)	3,013 (16.3%)	10.8/1	5,165 28%
DC Public Schools $14,405	563,384 59,616	W: 30.8 AA: 55 A: 2.7 L: 7.9 O: 3.6	$40,127 (61%)	11,738 (19.7%)	NA	4,274 7.2%
Fairfax County, VA $12,853	1,010,4443 164,843	W: 62.3 AA: 9.3 A: 15 L: 12 O: 1.4	$83,890 (19%)	23,640 (14.3%)	12.5/1	30,032 18.2%
Montgomery County, MD $13,446	932,131 139,393	W: 57.9 AA: 16.4 A: 11.2 L: 11.6 O: 2.9	$76,957 (22%)	17,700 (12.7%)	14.9/1	13,228 9.5%
Prince George's County, MD $10,332	841,315 133,325	W: 23.7 AA: 61.1 A: 3.9 L: 13.6 O: 0.6	$55,129 (43%)	15,362 (11.5%)	15.9/1	8,311 6.2%

* W = white; AA = African American; A = Asian; L = Latino; O = other.

† FRPL = free or reduced-price lunch; it is an indication of the number of students living in poverty.

Source: Compiled and calculated from: Alexandria City, VA, public schools, retrieved from http://www.acps.k12.va.us/board/division-goals/goals-brochure.pdf; Washington area boards of education fiscal year 2008, retrieved from http://www.acps.k12.va.us/board/wabe.pdf; Arlington, VA, public schools, retrieved from http://www.acps.k12.va.us/board/wabe.pdf; Washington, DC, Public Schools, retrieved from http://dcps.dc.gov/portal/site/DCPS/menuitem.06de50edb2b17a932c69621014f62010/?vgnextoid=71a3f83a5f052210VgnVC M100000416f0201RCRD&vgnextchannel=39d1e2b1f0d32210VgnVCM100000416f0201RCRD&vgnextfmt=default; Fairfax County Public Schools, retrieved from http://www.schoolmatters.com/schools.aspx/q/page=dl/did=4013/midx=StudentDemographics; Montgomery County Public Schools, MD, retrieved from http://www.montgomeryschoolsmd.org/about/; Prince George's County Public Schools, retrieved from http://www.schoolmatters.com/schools.aspx/q/page=dl/did=5109/midx=StudentDemographics.

11-4 Expenditures: How School Districts Spend Money

Operating a school system is a complex undertaking, whose costs go far beyond teacher salaries and supplies. The growth in school spending outside teacher salaries has increased from one-third of total expenditures in 1940 to more than one-half of school costs in 1990.[16] These funds go toward items such as administrative support and utilities to keep the lights, heat, and air conditioning running. They cover the expense of operating and maintaining school buses or buildings, ordering all the cafeteria food and supplies, and accounting for meal prices and student lunch payments. With virtually every school system having a different budgeting process, comparing how states and school districts spend money is informative.

11-4a Spending Categories

The *Digest of Education Statistics 2010* separates education expenditures into 10 defined categories to compare all states. The *Digest* also provides dollar amounts and budget percentages for each category, as seen in Table 11.3.

Instruction includes teachers, teaching assistants, curriculum support personnel in the schools, and anyone directly related to teaching children. This cost includes salaries, benefits, supplies, tuition reimbursement, and the like for all persons included in this category. As Table 11.3 shows, instruction is by far the largest budget category.

Student support includes school counselors, health care providers (school nurses), attendance personnel (the people who maintain attendance rolls and call students' home if they are absent to make certain they are really sick), school psychologists, and speech pathologists.

Instructional staff services include curriculum development, staff training, libraries, media, and technology centers. Again, this category takes into account all salaries, benefits, supplies, equipment, and costs associated with these functions.

General administration involves the personnel who administer leadership responsibilities at the central office level whose responsibilities are not delineated in other named categories. The school administration category includes building-level principals and assistant principals and their associated costs.

Operations and maintenance includes the cost of using and keeping up the buildings. Operations include electricity, heat, and insurance on the buildings and their contents. Maintenance includes custodial workers, building and grounds upkeep, and supplies and equipment needed to keep the building clean and in good order.

Student transportation involves all costs of operating the familiar yellow school buses. It includes the

TABLE 11.3

National Average Pre-K-12 Education Budgets and Associated Expenditures, 2010

Budget Category	Expenditure (%)
Instruction	53
Student support	5
Instructional staff services	4
General administration	2
School administration	5
Operations and maintenance	8
Student transportation	4
Other support services	3
Food services	3
Enterprise operations	1
Capital outlay	11
Interest on debt	3
Total	100

Source: Snyder, R. D., and Dillow, S. A. (2011, April). *Digest of education statistics 2010 (NCES 2011-015).* National Center for Education Statistics, Institute for Education Sciences, U.S. Department of Education. Adapted from Table 192, p. 276. Calculations by authors. The expenditure percentages total to 100 percent due to rounding.

price of buses themselves as well as the drivers, mechanics, fuel, tires, and equipment required to transport students.

The other support services category includes business support for paying, transporting, or exchanging goods and services for the school district. It includes central office support for planning, research, evaluation, and information, staff, and data processing as well as other central support services. In some smaller school districts, a small number of employees may assume responsibility for several functions, so this category is relatively small. In larger systems, more administrators, supervisors, and coordinators work on these tasks. For instance, a large school district may have an assistant superintendent for planning, research, and evaluation with an entire professional and clerical staff to support this area.

Food services involve all the people, equipment, and supplies needed to feed students while they are at school. Someone must order the bulk food, plan menus, staff cafeterias, coordinate the federal free and reduced-price lunch information, and make certain that the operation does not lose money. Frequently, the school district's Food Service Department operates the largest chain of "restaurants" in the locality.

Enterprise operations involves expenditures for operations funded by the sales of products or services in the school. This would include the school bookstore, computer time, or leasing the building in the evening or weekends to civic groups.

Capital outlay includes expenditures for property, buildings, and alterations completed by the school district's staff or contractors. Interest on school debt includes all interest paid by school district.

Obviously, the operation of a school system and all of its finances are intricate and complex. They involve people, supplies, and processes that many teachers have never considered to be a part of education.

Recently, the advocacy group known as First Class Education has endorsed a proposal called the "65% Solution." It calls for 65 percent of all funds to go directly to classroom instruction. Members of First Class Education define "in the classroom" as classroom teachers and aides, general instruction supplies, activities such as field trips, athletics, music, and arts. Critics have claimed that the 65 percent concept is intuitive and not research based.[17] In fact, many educators do not favor this solution because it may force cuts to non-instructional personnel, such as school nurses, who provide valuable services in the schools.[18] Several states have endorsed this proposal, however.

Although it is not clear exactly what percentage of all revenue should go to classroom instruction, obviously most money should go where research informs us that money makes a difference to student learning. Later in this chapter, we will review research-based findings of how school spending can improve student achievement.

11-4b Teacher Salaries

In education, salaries and benefits generally account for approximately 70 percent of the total budget. Because teachers are the largest group in education, most monies go to teacher salaries.

Table 11.4 shows the average teacher salary for each state from the 2012 National Education Association's *State Rankings*. These salaries are not distributed equally across schools. Experienced and more highly paid teachers tend to teach in more affluent schools. Table 11.4 averages the salaries to the state level to provide a comparison.

While Table 11.4 presents average salaries for all teachers in the state, the median salary (the salary at which half of teachers make more and half make less) is

TABLE 11.4

Rank and Average Public School Teacher Salaries, 2012

State	Average Salary	State	Average Salary
1. New York	72,708	28. Louisiana	49,006
2. Massachusetts	70,340	29. Kentucky	48,908
3. Connecticut	69,165	30. Texas	48,638
4. California	67,871	31. Alabama	47,803
5. New Jersey	66,612	32. Virginia	47,564
6. District of Columbia	66,601	33. Arizona	47,553
7. Illinois	64,509	34. Idaho	47,416
8. Maryland	63,960	35. Nebraska	47,368
9. Alaska	62,918	36. Maine	47,249
10. Michigan	61,560	37. Montana	47,132
11. Rhode Island	60,923	38. South Carolina	47,050
12. Pennsylvania	60,760	39. Utah	47,033
13. Delaware	57,934	40. New Mexico	46,888
14. Ohio	56,715	41. North Carolina	46,700
15. Oregon	56,503	42. Kansas	46,598
16. Wyoming	56,100	43. Arkansas	45,998
United States	**55,489**	44. Tennessee	45,891
17. Hawaii	55,063	45. Florida	45,732
18. Wisconsin	54,207	46. Missouri	45,321
19. Minnesota	53,680	47. North Dakota	44,807
20. Nevada	53,023*	48. Oklahoma	44,343
21. Washington	52,926	49. West Virginia	44,260
22. Georgia	52,815	50. Mississippi	41,975
23. New Hampshire	52,792*	51. South Dakota	39,850
24. Indiana	50,801	Median	49,844
25. Vermont	50,141	Range	32,858
26. Iowa	49,844	Standard Deviation	8,215
27. Colorado	49,228	Coefficient of Variation	16
NEA Research, Estimates Database (2012).			

Source: National Education Association (NEA). (2012, December). *Rankings and estimates: Ranking of the states 2012 and estimates of school statistics 2013.* Washington, DC: NEA Research, C-9, p. 18. Retrieved from http://www.nea.org/assets/img/content/NEA_Rankings_And_Estimates-2013_%282%29.pdf.

$49,844. The range between the highest and lowest salaries is more than $32,000. Over a 30-year career in education, the difference between being paid at the highest and lowest salary ends could translate into a $983,880—almost $1 million difference—in lifetime earnings.[19]

How do teacher salaries compare with salaries in other jobs that require comparable skill and education? According to a report by the Economic Policy Institute, weekly pay for teachers ranges from 12.2 percent to 14.1 percent less than that for jobs with comparable skill and education requirements.[20] No doubt, this salary disparity discourages many well-educated and talented individuals from seeking careers as teachers.

Did You Get It?

For most school systems, which following statement about national average expenditures is false?

- **a.** Over half of the budget is spent on instruction.
- **b.** Less than half of the budget is spent on instruction.
- **c.** Combined general and school administrative services average about 7 percent.
- **d.** Interest on school debt runs about 3 percent.

Take the full quiz on CourseMate.

11-5 Equity Issues in School Funding

Savage Inequalities' descriptions of blighted schools highlight equality and equity issues. Considering how schools' funds should be allocated and spent are critical concerns. Most of us believe in equal treatment for individuals, yet students come to school with different learning needs. Should all students receive equal funding? What is an adequate amount of funding to bring all students to high levels of learning and achievement?

11-5a Spending per Pupil

Earlier, we saw the 50 states' differences in per-pupil spending. Should every state spend the same amount per pupil? Similarly, Reflect & Discuss (above) had you think about whether needier school districts should receive more funding than less needy districts. Here lies the difference between equity and equality. Although the two concepts sound alike, they are very different. In its essence, **equity** is providing the services students actually need, whereas **equality** is providing the same services for all students regardless of the students' or locality's needs. Equity can be defined as a fairness issue for both students and taxpayers. The difference between equity and equality explains why equity, much more than equality, is a basic tenet of our school finance system.[21]

equity Providing the services students actually need.

equality Providing the same services for all students regardless of the students' or locality's needs.

adequacy Providing sufficient resources to accomplish the job of educating all our children to the same high and rigorous achievement standards.

Adequacy is another money-related issue affecting fairness in school funding. **Adequacy** involves providing sufficient resources to accomplish the job of educating our children. A workable definition would be providing enough funds "to teach the average student to state standards, and then to identify how much each district/school requires to teach students with special needs—the learning disabled, those from poverty and thus educationally deficient backgrounds, and those without English proficiency—to the same high and rigorous achievement standards."[22] How much funding is adequate? As a fiscal concept, adequacy is value driven, with people defining it subjectively according to their own priorities and opinions. Although attempts certainly have been made to quantify how much a state or school district needs to spend for its students, the actual figure remains unclear.

School funding adequacy has been a focus of active litigation. Since 1995, a number of school funding court cases have produced major changes in state education policy around the country. School finance litigation has forced states to not only change the way they fund schools, but also to improve and update their states' assessment and accountability systems. As of 2013, 45 states have been involved in some form of K-12 school finance litigation, and 10 states are currently involved in active litigation.[23] These suits addressed the state's

TABLE 11.5

Equality versus Equity Example

School System	Average Family Income	Federal Revenue	State Revenue	Local Revenue	Percentage of Students Eligible for Special Education
A	$65,000	$1,050	$3,550	$6,000	3%
B	$65,100	$1,100	$3,450	$6,050	18%

role in ensuring equitable spending among districts, providing suitable school facilities, and delivering adequate funding of programs designed for special education and at-risk students. Plaintiffs have won 22 of 33 adequacy cases since 1989.[24] When used wisely, the money awarded in these cases has repeatedly translated into more resources for poorer districts and improved results for schools and students.

Consider the following scenario from Table 11.5. Two relatively similar school systems have roughly the same amount of money coming to them from the federal, state, and local governments: $10,600 per student. The two systems have roughly the same capacity to fund education, as seen from the average family income, and both have the same number of students to educate.

Both school systems draw from upper-middle-class neighborhoods where parents expect their children to go to college. In school system A, 3 percent of the students have been identified as eligible for special education services—far below the national average. In school system B, 18 percent—six times as many—of the students have been identified as eligible to receive special education services, a rate higher than the national average.

If we look solely at the issue of equality, both school systems have the funds they need: $10,600 per pupil. If we look at the equity issue, however, the students' needs in school system B are greater than those in school system A. School system B must spend more money to meet the identified learning needs than does school system A. Equal funding for these systems may seem fair at first—until we consider the students' needs. Because of the varying student needs and the associated costs, treating these two systems equally on a financial basis would be neither fair nor equitable.

Consider this analogy. Imagine going to a physician who treats all patients equally. Each patient gets the same regimen at the same cost. It sounds ridiculous, because we expect to be treated on the basis of our differing health needs. We expect to care for a common cold differently than we care for cancer, and we realize that managing cancer costs more than managing a cold. We want and expect to receive the medical care we require. The same is true in education. Although all students should have an equal opportunity for a good education, students require different level services depending on their unique situations.

Education is expensive, but providing poor and inadequate education for large numbers of students may be even more costly. Inadequately educated students bring steep public and social consequences. Money matters when it comes to student achievement, a relationship confirmed by many studies.[25] The more money spent wisely on student learning, the more students learn.

The reality is that our society does not spend money equally or equitably to support all students' learning. Just as minority, low-income, and affluent students show "achievement gaps," the schools in which they receive their educations reflect serious "spending gaps."

11-5b Funding Inequalities

Most parents and students in affluent school districts would never consider crossing the threshold of schools such as those Kozol describes in *Savage Inequalities*. They expect their children's schools to be clean, rich in resources, with the best teachers that competitive (and regularly paid) salaries can provide. They make sure their schools have the funds to deliver on this expectation. As a result, schools serving different student populations often show large "funding gaps." School districts do not receive equal or equitable funding. Large differences exist between the monies available to educate low-income children as compared to affluent children. These disparities contribute strongly to the differences in their learning outcomes.

Approximately 50 percent of schools' local financial support comes from local taxes, mostly from property taxes. As a result, the wealthiest districts are able to spend as much as three times the per-pupil amount spent by the most economically disadvantaged districts.[26] In other words, students attending schools in districts with a lot of taxable wealth may have more money spent on their education than children attending schools with little taxable wealth. Making the situation more difficult, the recent trend has been for states to reduce education spending, leaving localities with the choice of either reducing services or increasing local taxes to fund education.[27]

The differences between districts with high property values and poorer districts in the region are profound and show up vividly in per-pupil spending. States in which school funding relies mainly on local property taxes place property-poor districts at a severe fiscal disadvantage. Although state and federal subsidies help high-poverty districts, they usually don't close the funding gap.

A 2009 report from the Editorial Projects in Education Research Center analyzed funding and spending gaps in all 50 states. Alaska ranked highest with a $12,307 gap in per-pupil spending between high- and low-spending school districts in the state. West Virginia had the lowest gap, $1,895. More than $9,000 in per-pupil spending separated the top from bottom spending states with Vermont at $15,139 and Utah at $5,964.[28] Per-pupil spending disparities also occur within states. A 2008 study of 10 New York school districts found funding and spending disparities ranging from $111,750 to $10,330 per pupil, a difference of $101,420 per student.[29]

Differences in per-pupil spending between and within states can only suggest the funding imbalances between school districts and schools with large populations of minority students versus small populations of these students. According to a 2012 report, schools with 90 percent or more students of color spend $733 less per student per year than schools with 90 percent of more white students.[30]

A 2013 report looked at the national school spending differences that occur between and within districts. On average, 59 percent of the spending variations fall between districts in a state; 41 percent of the spending variations happen within districts. These spending differences between districts range from 9 percent in Arizona to 77 percent in South Carolina.[31] Often, these spending differences reflect large disparities in teachers' salaries, a topic we will discuss in a later section.

Notably, the "spending gaps" also happen within school districts that draw from the same wealth base. Frequently, uneven amounts of per-pupil dollars appear to go to the schools with more white students. For example, a 2010 article described "The Alpha and Omega Syndrome": an eye-opening funding difference between two high schools in the same community. The Alpha high school (with 600 more students than the Omega high school) spent $8,222 per pupil each year, whereas the Omega high school across town spent $3,265 per pupil per year. Likewise, the Alpha high school had twice as many teachers, four times as many deans, 50 percent more counselors, smaller class sizes, almost four times the monies allotted for field trips, twice the number of secretaries and custodians, and air conditioning as compared with the Omega school. Although this example is anecdotal and cannot be generalized to all schools, it points to important fairness issues.[32]

Valzan/Shutterstock.com

School funding "gaps" affect student achievement.

Whether between or within school districts, this "spending gap" is a national equity concern. Research shows that, depending on their location, some school districts receive *eight times* as much per-pupil funding as others.[33] This translates into educational quality differences in such areas as the teacher effectiveness, class size, facilities' upkeep, available technology, and other factors that can affect student outcomes and, ultimately, students' life chances.

Without a doubt, reliance on local property taxes is especially unfair to the African American, Latino, and Native American students who are disproportionately concentrated in the lowest-funded, lowest-spending schools. Their families, on average, own less wealth and have lower per capita and family incomes than white Americans.[34]

Investing in high-quality pre-K-12 education brings positive economic returns. In 2007, a team of economists recommended that adopting wide-scale, research-supported, effective pre-kindergarten through 12th-grade educational interventions would gain $45 billion from increased tax revenues and reduced social costs over a high school graduate's lifetime.[35] The monies returned to the U.S. economy from these graduates' increased taxes as a result of their increased lifetime earnings would be more than double the initial investment. Clearly, the benefits of society investing in an educational strategy of funding schools equitably outweigh the costs.

Increasingly, courts have recognized that public school funding practices that rely too heavily on local property taxes are unconstitutional, denying certain students equal protection under the law. As a result, the states try to offset these local wealth differences with their funding formulas. Nonetheless, Deborah Verstegen, an education finance scholar, writes, "There have been no new approaches developed or used to distribute state aid to school systems since the 1920s and 1930s."[36] What is more, in those days, less than one-third of the eligible population attended high school, much less graduated.[37] By comparison, in 2010, 96 percent of all 16- to 17-year-olds were enrolled in school.[38]

11-5c The Cost of Educating Low-Income Students

Dollars do not tell the whole story. Talking about actual dollars per pupil or per school understates the inequity that high-poverty school districts suffer. To educate children growing up in poverty to common meaningful standards costs more than it does to bring more affluent students up to these standards. Children from low-income families typically have more educational and academic ground to cover in order to reach appropriate grade-level expectations than their more affluent peers (who usually

TABLE 11.6

Funding Gap between High- and Low-Income School Districts

Per-Student Funding Gaps Add Up			
For example, when you consider the per-student funding gap for low-income students (without 40 percent adjustment for low-income students) in . . .	Between two typical classrooms of 25 students, that translates into a difference of . . .	Between two typical elementary schools of 400 students, that translates into a difference of . . .	Between two typical high schools of 1,500 students, that translates into a difference of . . .
New York	$57,975	$927,600	$3,478,500
Illinois	$48,100	$769,600	$2,886,000
Michigan	$14,325	$229,200	$ 859,500
North Carolina	$ 8,600	$137,600	$ 516,000
Delaware	$ 5,175	$ 82,800	$ 310,500

Source: Weiner, R., and Pristoop, E. (2006). *How states shortchange the districts that need the most help: Funding gap 2006*. Washington, DC: The Education Trust, p. 8.

have many educational and academic experiences—the cultural capital—as part of their lifestyles outside school). Low-income students need more instructional time, and they especially need well-prepared, effective teachers.

The Education Trust calculates that educating children from low-income families costs 40 percent more than educating their middle-class peers.[39] If states were to make this 40 percent adjustment to educate low-income students, school districts serving the largest concentration of minority students would still be receiving $1,213 less per pupil than their middle-class peers. Table 11.6 shows the size of the funding gap in five states between the highest- and lowest-poverty districts between two typical classrooms, elementary schools, and high schools. The funding difference between two typical, 1,500-student New York high schools can be almost $3.5 million per year per school.

As illustrated earlier by the "Alpha and Omega Syndrome," school districts make the fiscal inequities between high- and low-poverty schools worse by the ways they choose to spend the funds they do have. In a study of spending patterns in dozens of school districts in 20 states, two major patterns emerged. First, school districts spent less money on salaries in high-poverty schools than in low-poverty schools within the same district. Second, districts assigned a larger share of unrestricted funds to low-poverty schools. Apparently, resource-rich schools keep getting more; resource-poor schools get less.[40]

11-5d Salary Inequalities

Typically, teachers in a school district receive salaries from a salary scale with increased monies paid for increased years of teaching experience and more academic credentials. Teachers with little or no experience and fewer advanced degrees receive lower salaries. As a result, schools with higher average teacher salaries tend to have the more experienced and well-educated teachers. Schools with lower average teacher salaries tend to have the newcomers with the fewest years of professional experiences. The result is a "salary gap" between teachers in affluent schools and teachers in low-income schools.

American Education Spotlight

Richard B. Levine/Newscom

Michael A. Rebell, Fiscal Equity Advocate

Michael Rebell

America invented the idea of public education and the ideal of educational equality. Yet the persistent gap between the American idea and the reality of blatantly inadequate schooling for low-income and minority children threatens to undermine our nation's political and economic vitality. Money—where it comes from, how much is "enough," and how it's spent—is a critical factor affecting this disparity.

As a lawyer and a scholar, Michael A. Rebell litigates and studies school funding adequacy cases to advance the cause of high-quality education for all students.

As Executive Director of the Campaign for Educational Equity and Professor of Law and Educational Practice at Teachers College, Columbia University, Rebell is the foremost authority on children's educational rights and on the education adequacy movement in the United States. He has pioneered the legal theory and strategy of educational adequacy. In the last 15 years, this legal strategy has proven successful in almost 75 percent of the cases challenging a state's failure to provide students with a sound, basic education. As a result, states have directed more funds to schools serving primarily low-income and minority students—those schools that need resources the most. As Rebell sees it, virtually all children need to meet rigorous academic standards if the United States is to remain a democracy and keep its competitive position in the global economy.

A prolific author, Rebell has written several books and dozens of articles on educational equity, education finance, testing, rights of students with disabilities, and dropout prevention. Rebell is a graduate of Harvard College and Yale Law School.

As a child of the 1960s and later as a law student, Rebell became fascinated by the courts' role in promoting social reform. He marveled at how principled judges could reshape failing social institutions while keeping their constitutional values. Wanting to become part of the process, he soon realized that reshaping complex institutions was itself a highly complex endeavor. He returned to graduate school and built a career that combined part-time teaching and scholarly writing with a substantial litigation practice focused on education reform. Reflection and practice, mutually informing each other to determine what had been accomplished and what could be done next, characterize his professional life.

Rebell views the Great Recession's severe education budget cutting, which pink-slipped or "furloughed" teachers, raised class sizes to over 40 students, cancelled classes, and shortened the school week as both unconscionable and unconstitutional. He insists that the right to a quality education is not conditional, and that the persistence of such conditions may permanently damage the life chances of entire generations of children. Children's right to education is not negotiable, he argues.

Critics take issue with Rebell's advocacy, branding adequacy lawsuit outcomes as "judicial activism." Detractors ask whether more money will improve children's education or simply feed an already bloated and ineffective bureaucracy. Others question whether courts should be establishing policies for state spending or compelling governors and legislatures to make major policy decisions. Also, determining what a "sound basic" education includes may require equal parts professional judgment and guesswork.

Rebell agrees that courts should not write education policy. He insists, however, that many of the concerns are overstated. Additionally, he believes that only by involving those persons who must put school reforms into practice, including teachers, administrators, and students, will court rulings make positive impacts in classrooms.

Sources: Rebell, M. A. (2009). *Courts and kids: Pursuing equity through the state courts.* Chicago, IL: University of Chicago Press, pp. vi–viii; Rebell, M. (2010, February 8). Educational budget cuts unconscionable—and unconstitutional. *The Huffington Post.* Retrieved from http://www.huffingtonpost.com/michael-rebell/educational-budget-cuts-u_b_453636.html; Rebell, M. A. (1998). Fiscal equity litigation and the democratic imperative. *Journal of Education Finance 24*(1), 23–50; Rebel, M. A., and Hughes, R. L. (1996). Schools, communities, and the courts: A dialogic approach to education reform. *Yale Law and Policy Review 14*(1), 99–168; Rebell, M. A., and Wolff, J. (2008). *Moving every child ahead. From NCLB hype to meaningful educational opportunity.* New York: Teachers College Press; Rebell, M. A. (2011). *Faculty profile: Professor Rebell.* New York: Teachers College, Columbia University. Retrieved from http://www.tc.columbia.edu/faculty/about.htm?facid=mar224; Rebell, M. A. (2011). Campaign staff. New York: The Campaign for Educational Equity, Teachers College, Columbia University. Retrieved from http://www.tc.columbia.edu/equitycampaign/detail.asp?Id=About+Us&Info=Campaign+Staff; Richardson, L. (2003, July 3). Public lives: A child of the 60's, and a keeper of the faith. *The New York Times, Education.* Retrieved from http://www.nytimes.com/2003/07/03/nyregion/public-lives-a-child-of-the-60-s-and-a-keeper-of-the-faith.html.

TABLE 11.7

Gaps in Average Teachers' Salaries in High- and Low-Poverty Schools by School District, 2003–2008

District	Salary Gap
Austin***	$2,668
Cincinnati***	$2,637
Dallas*	$2,494
Denver*	$3,633
Fort Worth*	$2,222
Houston*	$1,880
Los Angeles**	$1,413
Lubbock***	$1,420
Sacramento***	$5,231
San Diego**	$4,187
San Francisco**	$1,286
San Jose Unified**	$4,008

Sources: *Center for Reinventing Public Education Analyses, 2005.

**Education Trust, Hidden Funding Gap, 2005, available at http://www.hiddengap.org/.

***Hall, D., and Ushomirsky, N. (2010, March). *Close the hidden funding gap in our schools.* Washington, DC: Education Trust, p. 3. Retrieved from http://www.edtrust.org/sites/edtrust.org/files/publications/files/Hidden%20Funding%20Gaps_0.pdf.

Additional Source: Roza, M. (2006). *How districts shortchange low-income and minority students: Funding gap 2006.* Washington, DC: The Education Trust, pp. 9–10.

Table 11.7 illustrates examples of these salary gaps from 2003 to 2008. In each city cited, the district spent less on teaching in its schools with high concentrations of low-income students. For instance, the gap between the average teacher salaries between the highest- and lowest-poverty schools in Sacramento, California, was more than $5,200.

What is more, these examples are not the most extreme. A 2004 analysis of Baltimore City showed that teachers at one high-poverty school were paid an average of almost $20,000 less than teachers at a low-poverty school in the same district.[41]

These salary discrepancies affect classroom learning and school climate in varied ways. Some studies find that the most highly experienced and credentialed teachers are not randomly distributed within a school district. Instead, they are concentrated in high socioeconomic status (SES) schools, which tend to have both higher per-pupil expenditures and higher teacher salaries.[42] Such schools may be more attractive to teachers because of real or perceived differences in tangible resources, such as more books, more computers, wider availability of teachers' aides, and more achievement-oriented students.

Conversely, the least qualified, least experienced, lowest-paid teachers tend to work in schools with the highest number of low-income and minority students. Usually, new teachers start their careers at such high-poverty schools. In one 2003 study, students in the lowest-achieving schools were 4.5 times more likely to face underprepared teachers than students in the highest-achieving schools.[43] High teacher and student turnover and a greater percentage of novice teachers working in the lowest-achieving, high-poverty schools contribute to both inconsistent instruction and the neediest learners working with the least experienced teachers.[44] With constant teacher turnover, principals can neither establish a culture for learning nor provide a skilled, experienced, and caring teacher corps to positively impact student achievement.[45]

As teachers gain experience and move up the pay scale, they often transfer to more affluent schools. District teacher transfer policies, sometimes written into teacher union contracts, aid this migration. Although teacher experience does not guarantee teacher quality, researchers agree that teacher effectiveness increases during the first three years in the classroom.[46] As a consequence, teachers' migration to affluent schools means that low-income and minority students have less chance of working with an experienced, effective teacher than do students in a more affluent school with few low-income and minority students.

TeachSource Video 11.1

Video supplied by the BBC Motion Gallery

Education and Equity

Different students living only 30 minutes away can receive widely different educational opportunities because of inequitable school funding. Fiscal inequities in school funding can jeopardize students' education—and their futures. Watch the video clips, study the artifacts in the case, and reflect on the following questions:

1. How do school funding inequities influence students' quality of education and future college and economic opportunities?
2. What can school funding of $17,000 per student provide that $10,000 per pupil cannot to prepare young people to compete in the global economy?
3. How do politicians use voucher and charter school programs to help families access a higher-quality education for their children than available in local public schools and why is this only a short-term solution?

Watch on CourseMate.

11-5e Facility Inequalities and Student Achievement

As Kozol vividly described in *Savage Inequalities*, low-income and minority schools frequently lack physically sound school buildings.[47] More money spent on school maintenance means a better upheld, repaired, and attractive building—and higher student achievement. One noteworthy study found a 5- to 17-point difference in standardized test scores for students who attended school in well-maintained buildings (with comfortable room and hall temperature, satisfactory lighting, appropriate noise levels, good roofs, sufficient space) as compared with students who attended school in poorly maintained facilities (too cold or hot rooms, inadequate lighting, high noise levels, leaky roofs, overcrowding), after controlling for the students' SES.[48]

An earlier study determined that if a school district were to improve its schools' physical conditions from poor to excellent, student achievement scores would increase an average of 10.9 percentile points. Working in "sick" buildings creates serious health issues for students and staff alike, which directly affects

TeachSource Video 11.2

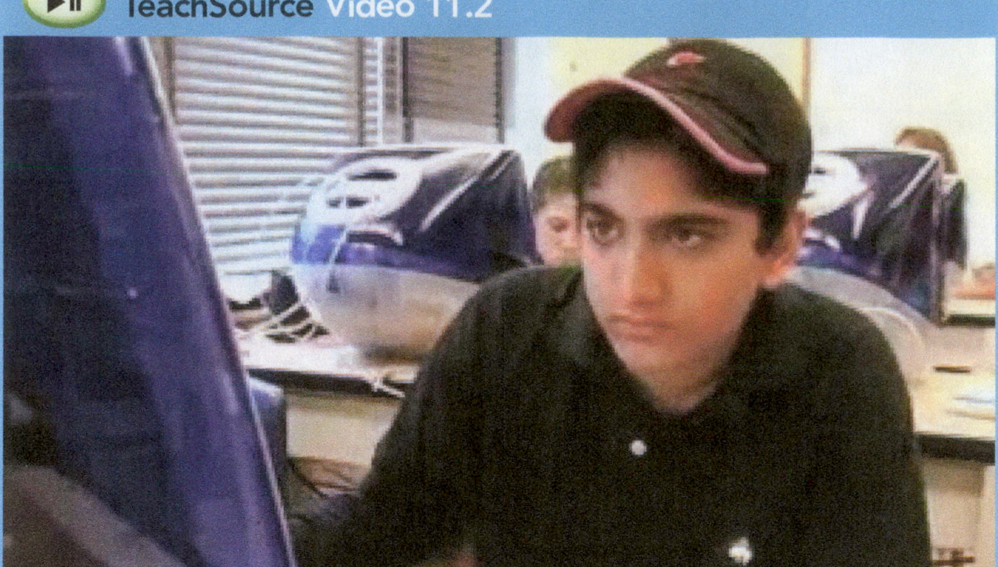

Educational Technology: Issues of Equity and Access

Funding schools equitably to support all children's education is a major policy concern. Regardless of the school's socioeconomic setting, when students don't have access to essential teaching and learning tools, they are deprived of an opportunity to learn. Watch the video clips, study the artifacts in the case, and reflect on the following questions:

1. What are the benefits to student learning when they have teachers who infuse appropriate technology into their lessons? What are the limits placed on student learning when those technology-infused lessons are not available?
2. How might the lack of available technology to support and extend learning harm a student's education? The student's future education and career opportunities?
3. What are some ways inside and outside the school that teachers can secure more appropriate technology to infuse in their students' learning?

Watch on CourseMate.

attendance rates and teachers' capacity to effectively instruct students. A reduced instructional investment in classrooms may be a source of student and teacher detachment, disengagement, and absences.[49]

Did You Get It?

Which of the following statements is true?

- **a.** Providing school systems with the same amount of per-capita funding and expecting equal results sounds good, but in practice, it doesn't work that way.
- **b.** Equity is providing the same services across the board, regardless of individual student need.
- **c.** Equality is providing services that students actually do need in order to produce, as much as possible, equality of outcome.
- **d.** A workable definition of adequacy is to provide enough funding to educate below-average students to high, rigorous state standards.

Take the full quiz on CourseMate.

11-6 Taxpayer Resistance to Funding Education

Historically, U.S. education has been almost exclusively a local concern. State legislatures set up local school districts to administer neighborhood schools and provide their young people with a "thorough and efficient" education. Community school boards implement state policy. The state gives the localities taxing powers to collect revenues to support schools, and the local property tax serves as the primary funding source. Coupled with state equalization assistance, basic state aid, and state and federal categorical aid, local property tax revenues pay for neighborhood public education.

Yet throughout history, virtually every political system has experienced its people's resistance to paying taxes. In 1773, the Massachusetts colonists led a tax revolt as they dumped British tea into Boston Harbor. Two hundred years later, beginning in the 1970s, taxpayer resistance to funding public schools became a popular issue.

Whereas school financial referenda increasing local support for public schools were popular in the 1960s, the 1970s saw voters rejecting school funding increases. In fact, phrases like California's "Proposition 13" or Massachusetts's "Prop 2½" became shorthand for taxpayer anger over their high property taxes as voters took their frustration to the polls. During the 1970s, 23 states passed major fiscal limitations on school funding.[50]

11-6a Public Sentiment about Taxation

A well-developed body of research suggests that public sentiment about taxation reflects a number of factors. These include rational and economic self-interest, SES, and the symbolic politics of ideology and partisanship.[51]

People view public schools as providing young people with the intellectual knowledge and skills needed for their economic self-sufficiency and responsible citizenship. Taxpayers know that educated communities are safer and more prosperous. The higher the parents' education, the greater their support for their children's education and often for education in general. Conversely, rejecting taxation may be rooted not so much in its financial pinch on taxpayer, but rather in the voter's ideological or political views about paying higher (or any) taxes.[52] All of these variables play a role in taxpayers' views about funding schools through property taxes.

Several dynamics explain the taxpayer "revolts" that have occurred in recent decades[53]:

- Homeowners tend to vote.
- Property taxes may grow more rapidly than personal income. In California, for example, residential properties' assessed values were rising 10 to 20 percent annually and as much as 40 percent in some areas when the Proposition 13 revolt occurred. Today, the Great Recession is prompting many localities to raise property taxes rates to make up for the lost yield as a result of reduced home values and decreased state funding.
- Residential real estate may see an increased tax burden relative to business and industrial real estate.
- Real per-pupil spending may rise dramatically but student achievement scores do not.

Cindy Charles/PhotoEdit

Affluent communities usually find innovative ways to fund extra school resources.

- The school-age population and schools' political constituency may decline as compared with an increase in voters older than age 65.
- Attitudes come to favor the idea that older citizens living on fixed incomes should not be priced out of their homes through high property taxes.
- Voters lose confidence in the government's ability to spend tax dollars wisely for public goods and services.
- Historically, large revenue surpluses make property tax increases appear unnecessary. For example, California had an estimated $3–6 billion revenue surplus in 1978 even as it raised homeowners' property taxes.[54]
- Government at any level fails to provide meaningful tax reform to relieve taxpayers' discontent.[55]

11-6b Taxpayer Revolts and Low-Wealth Schools

When the localities pay less money to support their schools, the state must contribute more from the general tax funds. But taxpayer revolts tend to hurt low-wealth schools more than high-wealth schools. Affluent communities usually find innovative ways to provide additional resources to neighborhood schools. California's taxpayers' revolt offers a case study.

After a brief lull following Proposition 13's passage, California schools began to make up for the lost property tax revenues, largely through rapidly growing nontax fees and charges. These alternative resources were both less constrained and less visible to voters than taxes. Fees, rental income, grants from outside agencies directly to classroom teachers, and monetary donations by parents to teachers to buy supplies circumvented the state's budgetary limitations on school funding.[56] Although little quantitative evidence is available, considerable anecdotal evidence indicates that schools' use of volunteer time increased, foundations were established to provide financial support for athletics and other extracurricular activities, and a variety of other methods (such as bake sales) were devised to get around the fiscal limitations.[57]

Taken together, these examples support the conclusion that individual actions to neutralize the schools' fiscal constraints play a major role in enabling high-wealth districts to keep their relative position of spending more resources per student and supporting higher student achievement. In contrast, less affluent communities can only rely on the state's fiscal support. The end result is that taxpayer revolts make school funding more inequitable.

Did You Get It?

Which statement about how—or why—taxpayer "revolts" negatively affect education funding is true?

a. Less affluent communities are forced to rely upon state/local fiscal support.

b. Business and industrial real estate usually sees the bulk of tax increases, and the ownership of this real estate intends to keep its money.

c. Opposition to taxation is usually rooted in real taxpayer financial pinches, such as the widowed grandmother who is a retired school teacher—but she can't pay any more in property taxes.

d. Voters' ideological and political resistance to paying for education is only rarely a cover for less enlightened sentiments than a disagreement about the wisdom of taxation.

Take the full quiz on CourseMate.

FlipSides

Does Money Matter in Student Achievement?

Critics claim that substantially increased education spending over the past 30 years has not led to increased student achievement* and that state funds for education are not used appropriately. In contrast, researchers find that education dollars wisely targeted toward instruction and effective teaching does boost student learning and achievement. After reading both sides of the argument and considering the evidence, what do you think?

Spending more money wisely on education DOES increase student achievement.	Spending more money on education does NOT affect student achievement.
■ More money is spent on education today because: ■ increased student enrollments means hiring more teachers; ■ more students with special needs require smaller class sizes requiring more teachers; ■ research finds that smaller classes for grades 1–3 increase achievement, requiring more teachers.	• More money is spent today on public schools than ever before but we see little increase in students' academic achievement to show for it. Where is all the money going?
■ Teacher salaries increase with more experience and advanced degrees; but its purchasing power over the past few decades is virtually flat.**	• Teacher salaries are higher than ever before.
■ SAT test scores in 2010 were either increasing (math) or relatively flat (reading).	• Despite all the increased monies for education, standardized test scores are not increasing.
■ National Assessment of Educational Progress (NAEP) scores from 1971 to 2008 show that mathematics scores for 9- and 13-year-olds are higher than in all previous assessments and that reading skills at ages 9, 13, and 17 improved since 2004.†	• Despite all the increased monies for education, standardized test scores are not increasing accordingly.
■ States that implemented high-stakes testing programs have increasing achievement test results for disadvantaged and minority students and the achievement gap is decreasing.††	• The increased spending on education has not ended the achievement gap between white and low-income and minority students.
■ International assessments do not closely match what U.S. students learn. ■ The United States educates (and tests). ALL students through grade 12; other nations track students into early career decisions and out of college preparatory education (and international testing).	• U.S. students are scoring poorly on international achievement tests. U.S. students' achievement cannot match those of our international competitors.
■ Numerous studies have found overwhelming evidence that school funding (in total amount and how it is spent) has a positive impact on student achievement.†††	• Early, weakly designed studies found that increased money for education showed no proof of increased student achievement.
■ Aside from a well-articulated curriculum and a safe and orderly learning environment, spending on hiring and keeping highly effective teachers pays off in increased student achievement.#	• Spending more money on education is throwing good money after bad.
■ Studies have found positive correlations between adult earnings and school spending.##	• Education spending has no long-term payoff to taxpayers.

(continued)

FlipSides

Does Money Matter in Student Achievement? (*continued*)

Research affirms that well-targeted dollars spent on hiring, developing, and keeping highly effective teachers can increase student achievement and improve later adult outcomes. Although test scores have slightly increased, more improvements are needed.

Given these data, what are your views about spending money on education?

Sources:

*Lips, D., Watkins, S., and Fleming, J. (2009). *Does spending more on education improve academic achievement? Research.* Washington, DC: The Heritage Foundation. Retrieved from http://www.heritage.org/research/reports/2008/09/does-spending-more-on-education-improve-academic-achievement; http://www.cato.org/pubs/journal/cj19n1/cj19n1-7.pdf.

**National Education Association, *Rankings & Estimates: Rankings of the States 2010 and Estimates of School Statistics 2011*, Figure 3.1, p. 77.

†The College Board. (2011). SAT averages by year and category, 1980, 1990 and 2010. Retrieved from http://professionals.collegeboard.com/profdownload/2010-total-group-profile-report-cbs.pdf; The Nation's Report Card. (2009). *2008 Long-term trend top stories.* Retrieved from http://nationsreportcard.gov/ltt_2008/.

††Haycock, K., Jerald, C., and Huang, S. (2001). Closing the gap: Done in a decade. *Thinking K-16* 5 (Washington, DC: Education Trust), p. 2. Kati Haycock is the Director of Education Trust, Inc., in Washington, DC; Rampey, B. D., Dion, G. S., and Donahue, P. I. (2009). *NAEP trends in academic progress (NCES 2009-479).* Washington, DC: National Center for Education Statistics, Institute of Education Sciences, U.S. Department of Education, pp. 3–4.

†††Hedges, L., Laine, R., and McLoughlin, M. (1994). Does money matter? A meta-analysis of studies of the effects of differential school inputs on student outcomes. *Educational Researcher* 23(3), 5–14; Pan, D., Rudo, Z., Schneider, C., and Smith-Hansen, L. (2003). *Examination of resource allocation in education: Connecting spending to student performance.* Austin, TX: Southwest Educational Development Laboratory, p. iv.

See, for example: Sanders, W. L., and Horn, S. P. (1995). Educational assessment reassessed: The usefulness of standardized and alternative measures of student achievement as indicates for the assessment of educational outcomes. *Education Policy Analysis Archives* 3(6), 1–15; Webster, W. J., and Mendro, R. L. (1997). The Dallas value-added accountability system. In J. Millman (Ed.), *Grading teachers, grading schools. Is student achievement a valid evaluation measure?* (pp. 81–99). Thousand Oaks, CA: Corwin Press; Ferguson, R. F. (1991, Summer). Paying for public education: New evidence on how and why money matters. *Harvard Journal on Legislation* 28(2), 465–98.

See, for example: Johnson, G., and Stafford, F. (1973, Spring). Social returns to quantity and quality of schooling. *Journal of Human Resources* 8, 139–55; Verstegan, D., and King, R. (1998). The relationship between schools: A review and analysis of 35 years of production function research. *Journal of Education Finance* 24(2), 243–62.

11-7 Spending for Student Achievement

Money matters when it comes to education. Spending money wisely is associated with increased student achievement. Investments in the following critical areas pay off in student learning gains:

- Teacher effectiveness
- Teacher salaries
- Reduced class size
- Professional development
- School facilities

11-7a Teacher Effectiveness

We know what constitutes good teaching, and we know that good teaching can matter more than students' family backgrounds and economic status in generating student achievement.[58]

Over the past decade, the term "teacher effectiveness" has largely replaced "teacher quality" to describe the characteristics that professional teachers use and what they do that help students learn. The shift in language reflects a fuller appreciation of how teachers' abilities, knowledge, and pedagogical expertise are the means to measurably increase student achievement as compared with teacher candidates who simply obtain credits, credentials, and content knowledge certifications without the classroom know-how to produce learning for all students.

Linda Darling-Hammond found that teacher variables such as full certification and completing a major in the teaching field are more important to student outcomes in reading and math than are student demographic variables such as poverty, minority status, and language background.[59] She also identified that the following teacher effectiveness factors are related to student achievement[60]:

- Verbal ability
- Content knowledge
- Education methods coursework related the teacher's discipline
- Licensing exam scores that measure basic skills and teaching knowledge
- Skillful teaching behaviors
- Ongoing professional development
- Enthusiasm for teaching
- Flexibility, creativity, and adaptability
- Teaching experience
- Asking higher-order questions (application, analysis, synthesis, and evaluation as opposed to recognition and recall questions) and probing student responses

As such, prospective teachers who want to be hired early in the process should highlight these skills and experiences in their interviews, résumés, and portfolios.

11-7b Teacher Salaries

Teachers' long history of low salaries relates to supply and demand factors that date as far back as 1776.[61] At that time, the United States

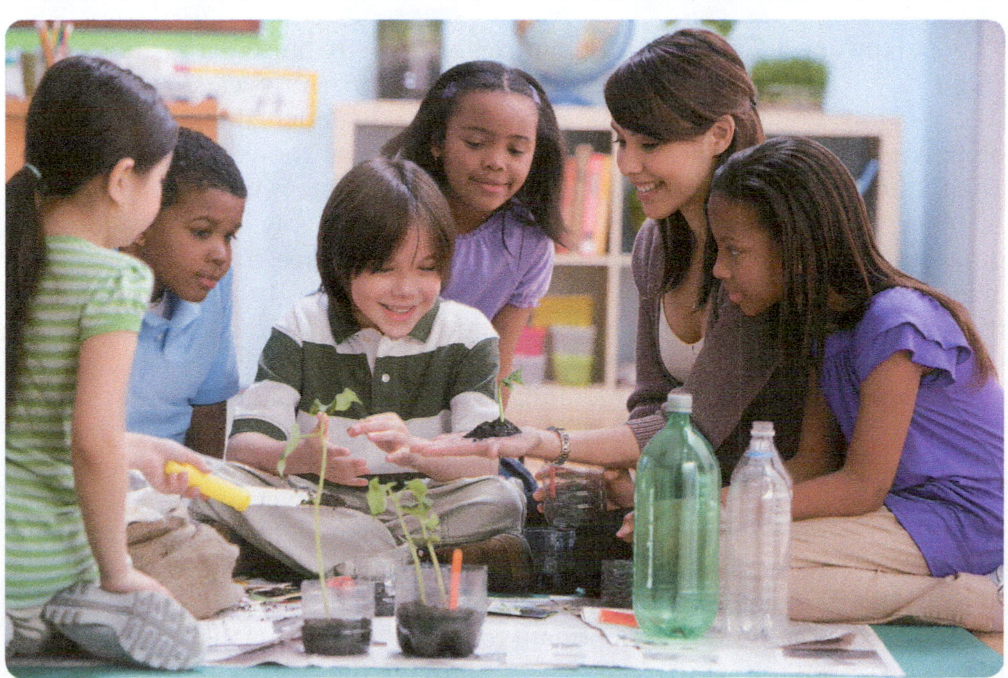

JLP/Jose L. Pelaez/Ivy/Corbis

Teacher effectiveness factors are important to student learning outcomes.

witnessed an oversupply of individuals trained to enter the clergy who were unable to find ministerial positions. Needing to earn a living, these people entered teaching and created an oversupply of well-prepared instructors, which in turn depressed wages. This tradition of low wages for teachers continues today, reducing the potential applicant pool.

The issues of teacher salaries and teacher effectiveness are connected. It is difficult to link empirical evidence of increased teacher effectiveness with higher teacher salaries because most school districts have salary schedules based on years of experience and earned academic degrees rather than on student achievement. As discussed previously in conjunction with the "salary gap" between high- and low-poverty schools, children in the highest-poverty schools are assigned to lower-salaried novice teachers almost twice as often as students in low-poverty schools.[62] Until 2002's No Child Left Behind law required teachers to hold bachelor's degrees in the subjects they were teaching, poor and minority students were more likely to have "out-of-field" teachers without majors or minors in the subjects they taught than were students in low-poverty schools.[63]

According to Heather Peske and Kati Haycock of The Education Trust:

> No matter which measure we look at, the pattern is basically the same. In state after state, district after district, we take the children who are most dependent upon their teachers for academic learning and assign them to teachers with less of everything. Less experience. Less education. Less knowledge of content. And less actual teaching skill.[64]

Can increased teacher salaries make a difference in increased student achievement? Maybe. It is logical to assume that increased salaries will expand the potential teacher applicant pool. A basic capitalistic and free-market economy tenet holds that higher wages attract more individuals seeking those jobs. If teachers' salaries increase, a larger applicant pool will seek teaching careers. An expanded applicant pool will include more individuals with higher levels of identified teacher effectiveness factors. In fact, the Teaching Commission, a nonprofit group formed in 2003 to improve teaching, has recommended raising base salaries to make teachers' pay more competitive and attract higher-effectiveness teachers.[65]

11-7c Reduced Class Size

The impact of class size on student achievement has been studied for many years. For example, Tennessee's carefully designed and managed experiments with class size reduction in primary grades showed positive results. Their Student–Teacher Achievement Ratio (STAR) program involved more than 12,000 students over four years. Findings from this highly controlled longitudinal study indicate that attending small classes for three consecutive years in grades K-3 is associated with sustained academic benefits in all school subjects through grade 8.[66] Similar results were found in studies of reduced class size in California.[67]

A review and synthesis of more than 100 class-size studies suggest that the most positive effects from small classes appear in kindergarten to third grade for mathematics and reading.[68] Most researchers believe that student achievement increases as class size drops from 30 to 16 students.[69] Nevertheless, although shrinking the number of students in a class can lead to higher test scores overall, it might not necessarily reduce the achievement gaps that exist between students in a given classroom.[70]

In reducing class size, it is important to consider teacher effectiveness. Reducing class size without at the same time improving the efficacy of what teachers do in the classroom to help all students learn to high levels would be both expensive and unproductive. Even those who disagree over the research's implications agree that more scientific studies on class size are necessary.[71]

11-7d Professional Development

Once employed, professional development plays an important role in upgrading and keeping high-quality teachers. New teachers can get better, marginal teachers can improve, and successful teachers can strengthen their expertise when they participate in high-quality, ongoing professional development programs. Studies of NAEP data indicate that professional development programs related to cultural diversity, teaching techniques for addressing the needs of students with limited English proficiency, and teaching students identified with special education needs are all linked to higher math student achievement.[72]

Other studies show that when professional development is sustained over time and based on curriculum standards, teachers are more likely to adopt new and reform-based teaching practices. Subsequently, their students achieve at higher levels on standardized tests.[73]

11-7e School Facilities and Student Achievement

Investing money to improve deficient school facilities pays off in higher student achievement. The relationship between unhealthy school facilities and teacher/student productivity is so common that it has its own name: "sick building syndrome." Its symptoms—irritated eyes, nose, and throat; upper respiratory infections; nausea; dizziness; and fatigue—result from the schools' poor indoor air quality.[74] The result: higher levels of student (and teacher) absenteeism and lower achievement.

A variety of studies from 2006 to 2008 have found a positive relationship between the quality of school facilities and student achievement in English and mathematics[75] as well as a significant predictor of student attendance.[76] Other investigators have also found a positive relationship between airborne bacteria and mold and asthma in children, which increases the absentee rates.[77] When students are absent frequently, even when they have a doctor's excuse, they miss classroom instruction and tend to fall behind academically.

The overall impact of a school building's design features and environmental conditions affects student achievement and teacher effectiveness. In what is considered to be the seminal study, Glen Earthman, a Virginia Tech professor, showed a 5–17 percentile point difference in standardized test scores for students in good facilities (well-maintained buildings with comfortable temperatures, satisfactory lighting, appropriate noise levels, good roofs, and sufficient space) compared with poor facilities.[78] An earlier study of elementary schools in the District of Columbia found that if schools' physical conditions were improved from poor to excellent, student achievement would increase by 10.9 percentile points.[79] Likewise, overcrowded schools have higher absentee rates for students and teachers, impacting student achievement. School facilities matter to students and teachers and should be financed appropriately.

With the research clearly affirming that school funding that is wisely directed toward enhancing teaching effectiveness, reducing class size in primary grades, and providing safe and comfortable school buildings can make a measurable difference in student learning and achievement, it is up to communities and school leaders to find the necessary resources to support high-quality public education.

Did You Get It?

If teacher—and principal—quality matters so much to student achievement, why is money so important to education?

- **a.** It's not: People who go into teaching are motivated by the desire to serve their communities, and they don't mind working really hard for little money.
- **b.** Money is necessary to pay for hiring and retaining effective people with solid credentials, maintaining facilities, and building more classrooms to reduce class size.
- **c.** There is no real relationship between teachers' salaries and their effectiveness.
- **d.** Teachers, while not always well paid, have always been able to count upon community support and respect to provide a very comfortable living for themselves and adequate facilities for their students.

Take the full quiz on CourseMate.

SUMMARY

- Education is a positive investment in our country's infrastructure because it provides a strong return on investment. It increases individuals' employability, wages, and government tax revenues and also reduces public expenditures resulting from unemployment, crime, and incarceration.
- The funding for education comes from three main sources—federal, state, and local. Federal revenues make up about 9 to 10 percent of school costs while state and local revenues are almost evenly split for the rest. At the local level, property tax is the largest revenue source.
- Education spending increased since 1960 because more teachers were hired to meet increased student enrollments, provide smaller teacher-student ratios for students with special needs, and reduce class sizes in order to generate more student learning. Court-ordered desegregation also meant paying minority teachers' salaries on par with their white colleagues.
- Schools districts spend their funds in a variety of ways. Budget categories vary from state to state but tend to include: instruction, student support, instructional staff services, general administration, school administration, operations and maintenance, student transportation, other support services, food services, enterprise operations, capital outlay, and interest on debt.
- "Equity versus Equality" in school funding means providing the services students actually need as compared with providing equal spending for all students regardless of the students' or locality's needs.
- Determining funding adequacy is difficult because as a fiscal concept, adequacy is values driven and subjectively defined; quantifying adequacy remains unclear.
- "Taxpayer Revolts" can negatively affect funding for education because property taxes provide the major revenue source at the local level. When taxpayers do not see education as an investment in their community's well being or if they hold beliefs against taxes, schools receive less money to support education.

- Spending money wisely can positively influence student achievement by hiring and rewarding the most effective teachers, increasing teacher salaries to attract talented professionals into teaching careers, providing smaller classes for K-3 in reading and math, providing well-designed and conducted professional development, and maintaining adequate and healthy school facilities.

Visit the Education CourseMate for this textbook to access the eBook, Did You Get It? quizzes, TeachSource Video Cases, flashcards, and more. Go to CengageBrain.com to log in, register, or purchase access.

Nothing is more important to our society's future than deciding what to teach our children.

CHAPTER 12

Curriculum

InTASC Standards Addressed: 1, 2, 3, 4, 5, 6, and 7

LEARNING OBJECTIVES

After you read this chapter, you should be able to:

12-1 Explain what "curriculum" is and how it helps teachers and students meet educational goals.

12-2 Trace how the U.S. public school curriculum traditionally responds to intellectual, societal, and political influences.

12-3 Identify five notable figures in American curriculum and discuss what each has to say about the learner and the curriculum.

12-4 Explain how the Common Core State Standards attempts to strengthen curriculum to improve teaching, learning, and achievement.

12-5 Describe how the search for curricular balance seeks to educate the whole child.

What should students learn? Who decides if it worth learning? In 2010, the Josephson Institute of Ethics conducted a large-scale national study of over 43,000 public and private high school students. It found that 59 percent admitted to cheating on a test during the past year, 34 percent cheated more than twice, and 33 percent admitted to plagiarizing a school assignment by using the Internet. Most young people believe that ethics and character are important, both personally and professionally, but they express cynicism about whether a person can be ethical and succeed.[1]

On another survey about cheating, some 50 percent of respondents said they don't think copying questions and answers from a test is even cheating.[2] They called it "borrowing."[3]

Students cheat for many reasons. Some do not understand the rules of academic honesty. Some feel the pressure to achieve in a highly competitive society. Some cheat because they are lazy, weary, or simply don't care. Many students cheat (or "borrow") because they feel the knowledge school is teaching them is useless. Kristi Mann, reflecting on her own experiences as a high school English teacher, says, "Perhaps our curriculum has become so irrelevant to real life that most students . . . would rather borrow the knowledge than commit to purchase it—learn it—for themselves."[4]

The curriculum is what we teach students in schools. Nothing is more important than deciding what to teach our young because our continued existence as a society depends on these choices. Curriculum determines what our society considers to be "well educated." Yet unless students are highly motivated or clearly see the connections between what is personally interesting and relevant to them and the curriculum schools want them to learn, many will not learn it. In our complex world, high levels of learning are especially critical if students want more than limited life options. Understanding the concept and practice of curriculum, therefore, and being aware of how to make it meaningful to students are essential to making informed decisions as an educator and as a student.

12-1 Curriculum Helps Teachers and Students Meet Educational Goals

For educators, no decision is more important that deciding what to teach and toward what end. Curriculum is at the core of any education system because it defines what schooling should accomplish. Once an education system has defined its curriculum, the teacher uses subject-matter and pedagogical knowledge to accomplish the curriculum's goals and facilitate student learning. In his book *What Works in Schools: Translating Research into Action* (2003), educational researcher Robert Marzano argues that having a "guaranteed and viable curriculum" is the number one factor for its impact on student achievement.[5]

12-1a What Is Curriculum?

Defining curriculum can be confusing because it can mean so many different things. The most common definition comes from the Latin root *currere*, which means "to run (around a racetrack)." For many students, curriculum is a race to be run, a series of obstacles (or courses) to be passed. Historically, curriculum referred to the subjects taught during the classical period of Greek civilization. In the mid-nineteenth century, it came to mean a course of study at a school or university. The twentieth century broadened the concept to include subjects other than the classics.[6]

Defining curriculum is also difficult because so many educational specialties call curriculum their professional home. Since the 1900s, the curriculum family has included people interested in subject content, teaching methods, teacher education, human development, social progressivism and conservatism, educational technologies, evaluation, and educational objectives.[7] With so many related but competing professional interests, agreeing on one common definition is challenging.

Nonetheless, curriculum is an essential concept that deserves to be pinned down in useful terms:

- Curriculum is all the learning that is planned and guided by the school, whether it is carried on in groups or individually, inside or outside the school.[8]
- Curriculum is a plan for learning.[9]

All agree that **curriculum** is the subjects that schools teach, whereas **pedagogy** is how the curriculum is taught. Curriculum is the program; pedagogy is the method. The two are separate but interdependent concepts.

curriculum All the learning that is planned and guided by the school. More narrowly, curriculum is also the subjects that schools teach.

pedagogy How the curriculum is taught.

Curricula don't just happen. Society develops and uses curricula to prepare its young people for adult responsibilities. Accordingly, states and localities decide what students should learn based on their beliefs about what students need to survive in a complex environment and what it means to be an educated person in that culture. The governing body selects people, serving as the larger society's agents, to write curriculum reflecting these values and beliefs. These persons may include educators, professionals, politicians, or other community members.

In this way, curriculum planning occurs in a social context and involves translating views about human nature and the nature of the world into educational aims. Knowledge about how students learn and the educational process must be considered during this endeavor.

12-1b How Curriculum Addresses Education's Goals

As discussed in Chapter 6, our society believes that education should accomplish many, sometimes competing, goals. Once we know schools' intents, we can select or develop the curriculum to help our students achieve these ends.

Our contemporary schools' purposes include (but are not limited to):

- *National goals*—to preserve traditional American values and encourage good citizenship, economic growth, and social stability by transmitting our cultural heritage and traditions.
- *Economic goals*—to socialize future workers for the workplace with appropriate attitudes, knowledge, skills, and behaviors.
- *Social goals*—to help create a better culture, in part, by helping students learn to thrive in a diverse, pluralistic society.
- *Personal goals*—to help students to live personally fulfilling and socially constructive lives by fully developing their minds and capacities.[10]

Understanding education's purposes—along with a rich grasp of child development—helps curriculum writers make important decisions about how to elaborate their subjects and helps teachers plan how to teach it. "Schooling or educating?" "depth or breadth?" and "here or there?" are three essential choices educators make about how to translate a curriculum into student learning.

Schooling or educating? As schools select curricula to accomplish these national, economic, social, and personal goals, they must also consider whether the schooling will merely teach subjects to students or whether the learning will educate their students. *Schooling* is not the same as *educating*.

Schooling is the program of formal instruction or training that occurs within a certain place (a classroom) and at a certain time (during the school day, during a certain number of days throughout the year). *Schooling* is legally defined in each state's laws. **Educating**, by contrast, encompasses more than what children should know or how much seat time passes between enrollment and assessment. Educating occurs all the time, even outside the confines of a building designated as "school." It includes a wider array of information and experiences than those that schools can provide. More than what we want our children to learn, "educated" is how we want our children to be. This question, "What is an educated person?" has perplexed educators, philosophers, and parents for generations. Only after we answer this question can we create curricula and classrooms that strive to fulfill those aims.

schooling The program of formal instruction or training that occurs within a certain place and at a certain time as legally defined in each state's laws.

educating Learning that occurs all the time and includes more than what the state says children should know, is largely self-generating, occurs across the lifespan and affects who we become as people.

Accordingly, education is not merely about the curriculum. It is about the human condition.[11] In the real world, knowledge does not appear in separate disciplines such as English, math, social studies, science, and art. For example,

FlipSides

Should Curricula Provide *Schooling* or *Educating*?

Mark Twain, the nineteenth-century American writer and humorist, wrote, "*I try not to let my schooling interfere with my education.*" *Schooling* is not the same as *educating*. Each offers a different view of what learners need to become responsible adults—and different views about what teachers and curricula need to provide learners so they might reach the desired outcomes. As a learner and a future educator, would you prefer a curriculum that provides *schooling* or *educating*?

As a student, myself, and as a future educator, I prefer to receive/provide *schooling* practices.	As a student, myself, and as a future educator, I prefer to receive/provide *educating* practices.
■ As defined by state law, *schooling* is the program of formal instruction that occurs within a certain place (a classroom) and at a certain time (during the school day) for a specified number of days each year.	● Not defined by state law, *educating* includes more than what the state says children should know, is largely self-generating, and occurs across the lifespan, even outside school.
■ Schooling identifies what we want our students to know and be able to do.	● Educating identifies what we want our students to know, understand, be able to do and be as human beings.
■ Schooling involves the written curricula consisting of separate academic disciplines taught apart from one another.	● Educating involves integrated knowledge as it appears in the real world in varied and coherent ways.
■ Schooling uses curricula that respect the traditions and content of separate academic disciplines so students can learn the habits of mind that each subject brings.	● Educating uses curricula that integrate learning across "big ideas" and academic disciplines in ways that students find relevant, meaningful, and more likely to be remembered and used.
■ Schooling provides individuals with the knowledge and skills approved by the larger community.	● Educating provides individuals with the knowledge and skills that may assess, judge, and challenge conventional thinking.
■ Schooling aims to teach students the knowledge and skills needed to show mastery on assessments.	● Educating aims to teach students the knowledge and skills needed to show mastery on assessments and to live personally rewarding and socially valuable lives.
■ Schooling means using curricula that transmit the culture's most valued traditions, contents, and skills to a new generation and prompts largely passive learning.	● Educating means using curricula that engage students who find it personally meaningful, relevant, and interesting and prompts largely active learning.
■ Schooling relies on recognition, recall, application, and recitation of the curriculum to ensure that students are learning.	● Educating relies on recall, application, analysis, synthesis, evaluation, and creativity with the curriculum to ensure that students are learning and using their learning to solve problems.
■ Schooling shapes what you know and can do.	● Educating shapes what you can know and do as well as your character and goals.
■ Schooling relies on curricula that are wide and thin so teachers can make students passingly familiar with many important topics.	● Educating relies on curricula that include essential concepts and themes that students can study deeply, truly understand, and master.
■ Schooling uses curricula that teach young students about important concepts as they appear in foreign cultures or distant locations ("there") so they can understand how others view the world.	● Educating uses curricula that teach young learners where they are ("here") by connecting new information to students' own experiences before teaching about these concepts in other cultures.

Given these descriptions of schooling and educating, which type of curricula do you think will best prepare your students—and yourself—to succeed in school and life?

language involves more than just reading literature and learning correct grammar. Language develops proficiency in the written and spoken word, use of mathematical symbol systems, and understanding musical and graphic arts. All these communication modes provide infinite ways to understand the world and to express ourselves. To become educated, therefore, students must see across disciplines to life's realities and its innate coherence.

Likewise, Elliot W. Eisner, Stanford University Professor of Education and Art, observes, "What one wants . . . is to provide a curriculum and a school environment that enable students to develop the dispositions, the appetites, the skills, and the ideas that will allow them to live personally satisfying and socially productive lives. Education's most important results are not test scores or even skills performed in the classroom. They are the tasks students are able to complete successfully in the lives they lead outside of schools."[12] In short, education allows persons to become the architects of their own lives.

"In fact, students learn both more and less than what teachers intend to teach," says Eisner.[13] If they are to become *educated* as opposed to *schooled*, students will learn a lot more and in ways they take with them after the dismissal bell rings.

Until students find their studies personally meaningful, relevant, and interesting, they may be more likely to cheat—and less likely to invest their time and energy in learning. Unless students find the curriculum meaningful, they may become schooled but will not become educated.

Depth or breadth? How does one decide what to include in a curriculum? Given the amount of time allotted in the school year and school day, should the curriculum be wide and thin, covering many topics superficially so students have an awareness of many issues? Or should the curriculum include fewer topics but study each deeply so students truly understand and develop mastery of those subjects?

Those curriculum writers favoring breadth reflect the old saying, "Throw enough mud at the wall, and some of it is bound to stick." This view recognizes that not everything that is taught is learned. It suggests, nonetheless, that bombarding students with information is still a worthwhile effort because they will remember at least some of it.[14] For this theory's adherents, the traditional essentialist curriculum of different subjects, each with many important topics studied apart from each other, is the right curriculum.

Those favoring depth follow the maxim, "Less is more." In the early twentieth century, mathematician, teacher, and philosopher Alfred North Whitehead asserted that dumping vast amounts of information on students was counterproductive. He argued that humans were not mentally equipped to handle a great deal of random, "inert knowledge." The young, he advised, need to study in great depth a relatively few really powerful ideas that encompass and explain major aspects of human experience.[15]

For instance, according to this view, students should learn broad concepts that cut across all fields of knowledge and find their inherent connections. Concepts such as patterns, structures, relationships, and systems are central to all disciplines, including those not yet developed. By focusing on large-scale and meaningful mental organizers, the "big ideas" around which students can wrap—and remember—a variety of related ideas and details, students can explore new intellectual territories. Unless persons can integrate what they learn with an often-used larger meaning and prior knowledge, details are soon forgotten.

Here or there? Educators who think that individuals learn by connecting new information to personally meaningful experiences believe in starting each

Reflect & Discuss

As discussed, *educating* and *schooling* are different processes and get different results. Each approach has different implications for twenty-first-century learning.

A. Working as a group, join your class members in defining the similarities and differences between *educating* and *schooling*, using the information from this section, students' own experiences, and outside resources. In what ways are *educating* and *schooling* alike and in what ways are they different processes that bring different results?

B. Working as an individual, reflect on your own K-12 and college classroom experiences and decide which specific experiences contributed to your being *educated* and which contributed to your being *schooled*.

C. Again working as a whole class, discuss students' reflections on this topic. Which learning experiences were *schooling* and which were *educating*? What qualities describe the differences between the two? How does one approach prepare students with the knowledge and skills for success in the twenty-first century while the other approach does not?

D. If you were a teacher, how would you try to ensure that your students were *educated* rather than *schooled*?

student's learning "here." "Here" reflects where the student is, cognitively, emotionally, socially, physically, and experientially. These curriculum writers would argue, for example, that second graders studying "society and family" would learn more by starting at home, looking at their own family members' behaviors. They could study society in the field by asking their parents or guardians focusing questions and then visiting with relatives or friends to look for additional answers.

The "there" adherents, in contrast, might formally teach American second graders about society and family in China, India, and ancient Greece—places far from the children's own experiences or present knowledge. Curriculum writers who stress "there" are thinking about the subject, not the learners. They believe that studying Chinese families and society are important concepts and do not consider whether the young students will find them meaningful or understandable.

Wise curriculum writers must ask and answer another question in making this decision: How do students actually learn? Although it may be worthwhile for second graders to be able to locate China, India, and Greece on an atlas, real learning will come only by first developing authentic personal experiences with the concept of "society and family" and then extending it outward to the unfamiliar. Conceptually dealing with the complex, the abstract, and the remote is very difficult, especially for young learners. Immediate reality is a more practical place to begin to build the descriptive and analytical mental models, those "big ideas" that will eventually take students to wider experiences. This lack of relevance and personal meaning often frustrates and bores students, undermining their desire or effort to learn.

As with most false choices, the "schooling or educating?" "depth or breadth?" and "here or there?" questions do not require either–or decisions. If students are to achieve a full and accurate understanding, formal *schooling* and formal and informal *educating*, curriculum *depth* and *breadth*, and *here* and *there* are all important. The real curricular issue is how to edit, organize, and present the information so that it will have the most meaning for the learner. Closely related is the challenge of finding the best means to connect students with the content so they will learn. The teacher is the critical agent in making these choices.

With these frames of reference in mind, it is time to consider the history of curriculum in the United States, identify key contributors to thinking about curriculum, and survey the traditional curricula currently used in schools.

Did You Get It?

For educators, the single most important decision they will make is

a. What to teach and why.
b. How to discipline students fairly, firmly, and affectionately.
c. What school they wish to work in.
d. What grade or age group they most wish to work with.

Take the full quiz on CourseMate.

12-2 U.S. Public School Curriculum Responds to Intellectual, Societal, and Political Influences

Curriculum is not neutral. Curriculum is "always part of a **selective tradition**, someone's selection, and someone's vision of the knowledge that needs to be taught to everyone," says Michael Apple, Professor at the University of Wisconsin–Madison.[16] Fundamentally, curriculum is about values. The decision to define a certain group's knowledge as the most important says much about who holds the power in a particular society and which values they seek to transmit through schooling.

selective tradition The frame of reference by which a certain societal group selects the knowledge that everyone should be taught and makes it part of the school curriculum.

U.S. curriculum reflects an inherent tension between its focus on social control by transmitting our cultural history and its focus on developing the individual. On the one hand, we recognize that schools should acclimate students to the social order and allow them to learn the society's traditional values and culture. This is an important social and political responsibility that helps unite us as one nation with a common perspective and shared loyalty. On the other hand, we talk about dignity of the individual, self-actualization, individual potential, and the reality that education frees individuals to become their fullest, most satisfied, and most productive selves. The contradictions in these two approaches are clear. As a result, our communities and curriculum writers have tried to find the appropriate curricular balance among society, subject and child. This dynamic tension guides educational policy decisions at all levels and has influenced curriculum decisions for more than 100 years.

12-2a Pendulum Swings

Throughout American public school history, curriculum approaches have swung along at least two dimensions—from subject centered to child centered, from studying subjects to prepare for college to studying subjects to prepare for work and life. Driving these swings was a key question: How could curriculum best prepare students to take their place in the larger society?

In colonial America, curriculum theory or practice was not an important topic.[17] The public school's core curriculum was subject centered. Pupils studied the classics—Greek and Latin, rhetoric, natural philosophy, ancient history, astronomy, and trigonometry—to prepare select students for college and the ministry.

By the late nineteenth century, policy makers had begun to question the appropriateness of this curriculum. In 1893, responding to factors such as increased industrialization, immigration, and the United States' growing international profile, the Committee of Ten proposed a more up-to-date, subject-centered curriculum in language, math, science, and history. Two years later, the Committee of Fifteen proposed a more up-to-date elementary curriculum.

Moving away from the strictly subject-centered curriculum, the 1918 *Cardinal Principles* report, along with teaching basic knowledge and skills, emphasized social and personal adjustment necessary for functioning in life, including health; command of fundamental processes; worthy home membership; vocational preparation; citizenship; good use of leisure time; and ethical character.[18] School subjects became a means to promote learning relevant to diverse students' lives.

In the 1930s, during the Great Depression, most states increased the compulsory school attendance age to 16 to reduce the pool of eligible workers for the few available jobs. Because 14-year-olds could no longer (legally) find employment, they went to school. Not surprisingly, the traditional college-preparatory curriculum did not suit this new and increasing school population. In response, the core curriculum shrank from being the entire school program for all students to being the high-status studies in which only the college-bound students enrolled while a general, less academically rigorous and more practical education program became available for others.[19] As a result, both an academic discipline-centered and more practical student-centered curriculum coexisted within public schools.

Throughout the 1950s, the discipline-centered, "back to basics" movement required schools to teach students the subjects as separate disciplines.[20] Schooling meant learning a set of facts that could easily be assessed by paper-and-pencil standardized tests. The Cold War and the Sputnik satellite's launch panicked U.S. policy makers, who suspected that the public schools' curriculum was jeopardizing the country's national security and economy. In an effort to catch up and surge ahead, academically gifted student programs grew in importance. School boards and administrators pushed for improved student test scores as proxies for higher achievement. Many influential thinkers reacted negatively to the progressive education approach that considered students' interests and real-world relevance as "soft" and "anti-intellectual."

A "humanizing" approach to curriculum made a temporary comeback in the late 1960s and 1970s. In the 1960s, the United States experienced internal unrest as the country grappled with social issues such as racial discrimination, poverty, urban violence, and the Vietnam War. Reflecting these societal influences, schools' emphasis turned from the academically talented to the educationally disadvantaged. Child-centered rather than subject-centered curriculum approaches again became popular.

A new wave of "back to basics," subject-centered curricula reappeared in the 1970s. Later, the highly critical 1983 report titled *A Nation at Risk*[21] brought renewed attention to the presumed failures in the U.S. public education system. To reform and improve education, educators looked backward to an old solution—studying the academic disciplines as separate subjects. The emphasis on measured academic achievement continues to this day.

12-2b National Curriculum Standards

For over 30 years, education reform has focused on standards. Policy makers saw the need for all schools to be held accountable for delivering a core set of high standards regardless of student populations, geographic locations, teaching styles, and curricular emphasis.

Goals 2000 The voluntary national curriculum standards written by the U.S. state governors in 1989 as a way to ensure that schools met the nation's academic achievement goals.

Common Core State Standards A voluntary set of rigorous academic standards matched to high-performing international norms, currently available for English language arts (reinforced in social studies and science) and mathematics.

Goals 2000, written by the U.S. state governors in 1989, introduced national curriculum standards as a way to ensure that schools met the nation's academic achievement goals. States could voluntarily comply and adopt these proposed standards. In response to this push, professional educational organizations developed academic subject area standards in almost all curricular areas.

In 2010, the Kindergarten–12 **Common Core State Standards**, the National Governors Association (NGA), the Council for Chief State School Officers (CCSSO), and other influential stakeholders offered a contemporary approach to improving public schools' curricula by strengthening the academic benchmarks that guide their development and assessment. The standards, currently available for English language arts and mathematics, clearly communicate what students at each grade level are expected to know and be able to do. Focused on rigorous academic content and the application of knowledge using higher-order thinking skills, the standards are informed by those of top-performing countries and incorporate the knowledge and skills that high school graduates need to master to succeed in college and careers in a global environment. Forty-six states, the District of Columbia, and Department of Defense schools have adopted the standards. Curriculum writing, assessments, and professional development for teachers and principals based on these standards are underway, nationally and locally. Knowledge and resource sharing are occurring as teachers translate these new expectations into challenging and engaging learning experiences for their students. The federal government expects the tests aligned to these standards to be ready by the 2014–2015 school year.

Of course, in a nation that celebrates state and local control of education, national standards for content areas meets with wide-ranging criticism. Many object to federal intrusion into local schools. Others worry that the standards will be politicized, advocating only a certain interest group's viewpoints over others. Certain critics observe that the standards might narrow the school experience with too much emphasis given to generating high test performance in selected subject areas while neglecting essential learning in nontested content areas. In this case, detractors worry, standards might result in *schooling* rather than in *educating*. Additionally, critics complain that learning by standards would likely be subject centered rather than child centered, focusing too much on the text itself and ignoring the readers' affective experiences with it. Others assert that the common core standards are too demanding, overestimating children's intellectual, physiological, and emotional capacities to engage in such rigorous study. Finally, some conclude that standards by themselves make no difference to student learning. Only solid curricula, outstanding teaching, valid and reliable assessments and accountability systems, among other things, must be in place if standards' promises are to be fulfilled. Successful implementation, not merely written standards, will make the difference.

Ultimately, all curricula changes reflect intellectual, social, and political dynamics. Decisions about what the curriculum is, does, and includes are highly selective decisions made by those with social and political influence. The dramatic swings from subject-centered curriculum to student-centered curriculum, and back again, are clearly evident in the history of U.S. education. Unless the curriculum both connects with students in meaningful ways and enforces accountability for students mastering high-level and important knowledge and skills, the pendulum will continue to swing between the two approaches.

Did You Get It?

Which statement is true about curriculums?

a. They can be genuinely neutral.

b. When carefully and sensitively developed, there need be no tension between the two curriculum goals of social control and individual achievement.

c. Except for a few minor wobbles, curriculum development in the United States has been largely linear.

d. They always reflect someone's particular vision of the knowledge that everyone needs.

Take the full quiz on CourseMate.

12-3 Five Notable Figures in American Curriculum Consider the Learner

Many individuals have influenced U.S. curriculum thought and development.[22] In this section, we briefly highlight several individuals whose influence can be seen in how we view curriculum today—its content, planning, and attention to student learning.

12-3a Ralph W. Tyler

Since 1949, Ralph Tyler's (1902–1994) ideas have served as the preeminent design model for developing U.S. curriculum.[23] Tyler developed a curriculum rationale that implicitly considered the learners and recommended that curriculum writers at any educational level should answer the following four questions[24]:

- Which educational purposes should the school seek to attain?
- Which educational experiences can be provided that are likely to attain these purposes?
- How can these educational experiences be organized?
- How can we determine whether these educational purposes are being attained?

Let's look at Tyler's four questions more closely.

Educational purposes Curriculum developers identify their "educational purposes" when they select their general goals and more specific objectives. Educational purposes may address students' cognitive, affective, and psychomotor capacities. Effective learning objectives (outcomes or results) might comprise students' behavioral, problem-solving, and expressive performances that correctly and efficiently use the taught content and skills. Objectives may specify the desired level of intellectual rigor or complexity that successful students should show for each domain, as illustrated in Bloom's taxonomy (see Figure 12.1 later in this chapter).

Educational experiences Teachers decide what they will do with the content to create a meaningful learning opportunity for students. Ultimately, the questions, "What is worth knowing?" and "What are the children's cognitive and affective developmental levels?" will limit the options available to teachers and students.[25] Most importantly, if children are to learn, they need to be intellectually engaged with the content, not merely busy.

Organizing experiences Organizing these educational experiences requires curriculum writers and teachers to consider how the current learning relates to the students' previous, present, and future learning. Organizing learning experiences must also account for students' cognitive and affective age and maturity levels.

Assessing learning Evaluation requires educators to consider how to gather, assess, interpret, and judge whether the desired learning has occurred. Educators can use the evaluation feedback to revise the curriculum and how they teach it. In this way, evaluation becomes an integral part of the learning and curriculum process, for teacher and student alike, rather than just the last phase in a linear process.

12-3b Hilda Taba

A Professor of Education at San Francisco State University, Hilda Taba (1902–1967) believed in a concept-driven curriculum that explicitly considers the learners. She contributed a theoretical and pedagogical framework for curriculum development that provided positive direction for increasing students' intellectual functioning and their critical and creative thinking.

Taba's 1962 book, *Curriculum Development: Theory and Practice*, attempted to bring order and meaning out of what she saw as curriculum chaos.[26] Influenced by Ralph Tyler and cognitive psychology, Taba argued that learning was dynamic and interactive rather than static, thereby establishing a different paradigm from a simple transmission model of education and evaluation. The learner had a key and active role in the teaching and learning process. She expanded Tyler's basic model to become more representative of curriculum development in schools.

Curriculum planning model Taba recommended a seven-step curriculum planning model[27]:

1. Diagnose need.
2. Formulate objectives—into four distinct categories: basic knowledge, thinking skills, attitudes, and academic skills.
3. Select content.
4. Organize content—by using three levels: key ideas, organizational ideas, and facts.
5. Select learning experiences.
6. Organize learning experiences.
7. Determine what to evaluate and the ways and means of doing it.

Curriculum includes the content and learner Taba's curriculum framework considered both the content and the learner. She organized curriculum around concepts and ideas. She believed that concepts and ideas—not unrelated facts—were the most durable form of knowledge. According to Taba, curriculum should center on widely accepted beliefs and principles in the various disciplines, and students should learn by moving from the concrete and specific to the abstract and general.

To a large extent, Taba's emphasis on the learner reflects her experiences working with classroom teachers and students. She wanted to ensure that teachers could make the curriculum adjustments necessary to help all students learn.[28] As teachers introduce new units, they should deliberately help students connect the content to their prior learning and experiences. This action will give students a bridge to the new content. If students still have a difficult time understanding the content, Taba suggested that teachers have the "moral obligation" to adapt the curriculum and instruction so each student can find that bridge to understanding.

Further, Taba stressed that actively using knowledge leads to learning. The best way to increase students' knowledge is to emphasize acquiring, understanding, and using issues and themes rather than memorizing facts alone.

Taba's ideas on curriculum development had a major impact on reform-minded curriculum developers in the 1960s and early 1970s. She introduced the notion of a "spiral" curriculum in which key concepts are referred to repeatedly throughout the

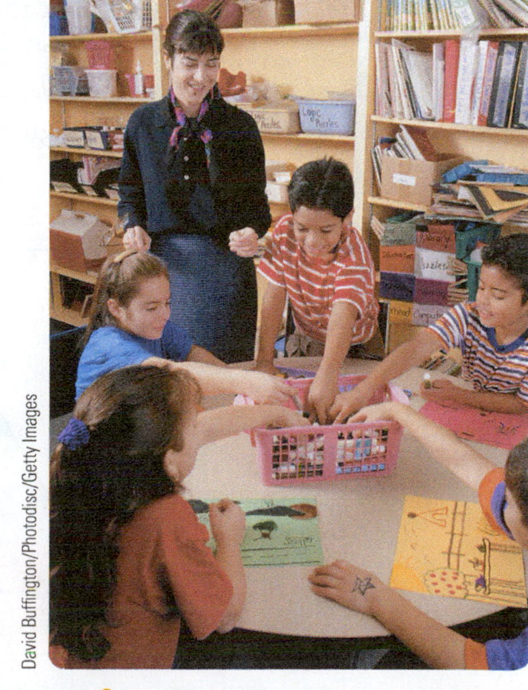
David Buffington/Photodisc/Getty Images

Actively using knowledge leads to learning.

grades. With each appearance, the curriculum introduced increasingly more abstraction and generalizations. Taba's notions on curriculum development remain influential today.

teaching for transfer Having the learner use what is learned to solve new problems, answer new questions, and facilitate learning new subject matter, often outside the classroom.

12-3c Benjamin Bloom

As noted by both Tyler and Taba, a good curriculum considers not only what to teach but how students learn it. Bloom's taxonomy helps educators design, deliver, and assess curricula that encourage **teaching for transfer**—that is, having the learner use what is learned to solve new problems, answer new questions, and facilitate learning new subject matter, often outside the classroom.

Benjamin Bloom (1913–1999), Distinguished Service Professor at the University of Chicago, attempted to identify and weigh the factors that control learning. In 1956, he headed a group of educational psychologists who developed a widely used classification of intellectual behaviors important in learning. These classifications are appropriate for any subject and their educational goals, objectives, and standards.

Bloom's taxonomy Bloom based his taxonomy on the idea that not all learning objectives and outcomes are equal.[29] Bloom arranged complex cognitive skills in a cumulative hierarchy from simple recall on the lowest end to higher-order critical and creative thinking at the upper end. Figure 12.1 illustrates Bloom's classification system in both the original and updated versions.

The taxonomy was intended as a method of classifying educational objectives, educational experiences, learning processes, and evaluation questions and problems.[30] This schema helps curriculum developers and teachers distinguish more difficult from less difficult cognitive processes. Using this classification helps teachers select appropriate content and design students' learning activities to increase and strengthen their cognitive skills in learning.

Let's first look at Bloom's original model more closely. Starting from the lowest level of thinking and moving up the pyramid toward the highest and most complex, students show [31]:

- *Knowledge*—rote memory, the recall of information in the form in which it was originally learned.

FIGURE 12.1 Bloom's Taxonomy (1956) and Revised Model (2001)

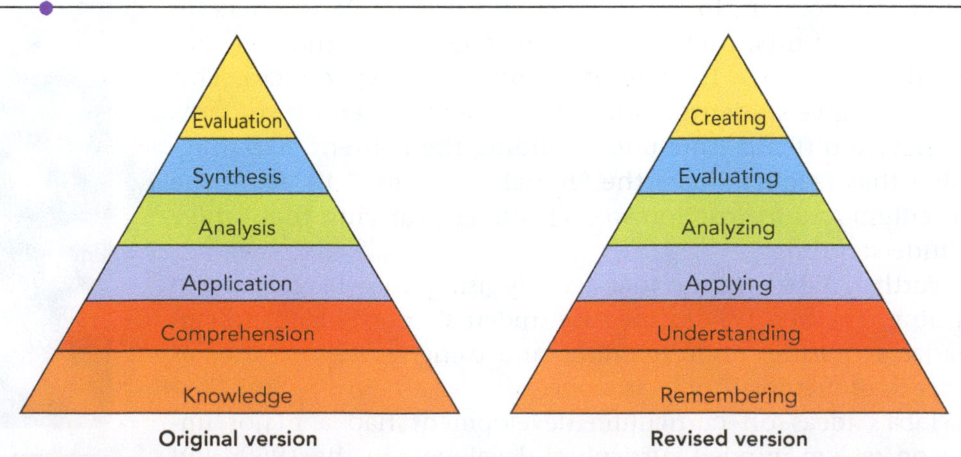

Source: Forehand, M. (2005). Bloom's taxonomy: Original and revised. In M. Orey (Ed.), *Emerging perspectives on learning, teaching, and technology.* Retrieved from http://projects.coe.uga.edu/epltt/index.php?title=Bloom%27s_Taxonomy.

- *Comprehension*—the ability to explain a concept or define something in one's own words. Students understand when they build connections between the new knowledge to be gained and their prior knowledge. They can interpret, classify, summarize, infer, compare, and explain.
- *Application*—the ability to perform a skill or demonstrate an ability in a setting both similar to and different from the one in which it was learned.
- *Analysis*—the ability to determine the relevant elements in any problem or scenario. Analysis involves breaking material into its component parts and determining how the parts are related to each other and to an overall structure. This includes differentiating, organizing, and attributing.
- *Synthesis*—the ability to draw information from several sources and put elements together to form a coherent or functional whole, or reorganize elements into a new pattern or structure.
- *Evaluation*—the ability to develop a rationale for either position in a conflict that can be described as a moral dilemma. Evaluation involves making judgments based on criteria and standards, usually quality, effectiveness, efficiency, and consistency.

Heinrich van den Berg/Gallo Images/Getty Image

Knowing, understanding, applying, analyzing, evaluating, and creating are necessary if curriculum is to create meaningful learning.

The cognitive hierarchy is cumulative: each thinking level is more complex and comprehensive than the cognition required in the level before. Each level requires the student to master the less sophisticated thinking levels in the previous steps first. For instance, *comprehension* is more intellectually demanding than *knowledge*. One must understand the relevant knowledge to comprehend, not just be able to recall and recite the information from memory. Next, one must understand the information before one can apply it in a new situation.

To produce meaningful learning, therefore, curriculum activities (and assessments) must include the higher thinking levels and use information and skills in meaningful ways, not simply recall facts. Once students understand and use the knowledge successfully, they can extend their thinking with it into analysis, synthesis, and evaluation, all of which are more intellectually rigorous and complex activities. Further, only with analysis, synthesis, and evaluation can individuals generate new ideas—that is, be creative.

Bloom's updated taxonomy Bloom's cognitive model is still alive and growing. During the 1990s, Lorin Anderson (a former student of Bloom) and a new group of cognitive psychologists updated the taxonomy to reflect relevance to twenty- first-century work.[32] The changes, as can be seen in Figure 12.1, are small but meaningful. First, the revised version changes Bloom's nouns (*knowledge, comprehension*) into verbs (*remembering, understanding*) to make it simpler for teachers to design appropriate learning activities for students. Next, the 2001 version changes synthesis to creating and moves it to the top of the hierarchy.[33] With this new perspective, the highest level of understanding and learning—which employs all the cognitive steps before it—uses learning to create something new.[34]

Using Bloom's taxonomy can also help educators teach students how to think in complex ways and to prepare students for rigorous assignments and assessments. Applying the taxonomy to assignments allows teachers to help

Reflect & Discuss

Teachers use Bloom's taxonomy to design learning activities that require students to use a range of increasingly complex cognitive skills.

A. Separate into four groups. Using the 2001 revised taxonomy, each group will design a series of learning activities for a different children's story (such as Little Red Riding Hood, Goldilocks and the Three Bears, or The Three Little Pigs), using each step of the taxonomy (shown below), from remembering through creating for each story. Have the group first identify its story and the age of the students (pre-K, elementary, middle, high school) to whom they might teach their lesson.

Remembering: Teachers ask students to define, duplicate, list, memorize, recall, repeat, reproduce, and state.

Understanding: Teachers ask students to classify, describe, discuss, explain, identify, locate, recognize, report, select, translate, and paraphrase.

Applying: Teachers ask students to choose, demonstrate, dramatize, employ, illustrate, interpret, operate, schedule, sketch, solve, use, and write.

Analyzing: Teachers ask students to appraise, compare, contrast, criticize, differentiate, discriminate, distinguish, examine, experiment, question, and test.

Evaluating: Teachers ask students to appraise, argue, defend, judge, select, support, value, and evaluate.

Creating: Teachers ask students to assemble, construct, create, design, develop, formulate, and write.

B. After working for 15 minutes, groups should present their lessons to the class for their participation (as students) and feedback (as future educators).

students develop college-level and work-related thinking and communication skills. It also may increase the students' likelihood of using the information in new settings, fostering transfer of learning outside the classroom.

Applying the taxonomy to evaluation instruments, teachers can appraise their classroom and standardized assessments to see which type of thinking these exams require from the students. Developing students' comprehension, application, analysis, synthesis, and evaluation skills with the learned content builds their knowledge and intellect even as it leads students to achieve "proficient" and "advanced" rather than "basic" scores on assessments.

12-3d Grant Wiggins and Jay McTighe

In 1998, Grant Wiggins and Jay McTighe, both former classroom educators, offered an innovative contemporary model for curriculum. Their curriculum framework not only addresses which content to teach, but also considers the quality of student understanding and students' ability to use the content in new situations. Their framework helps teachers plan for student learning throughout the curriculum process.

Acknowledging influences of John Dewey and Ralph Tyler, Wiggins and McTighe integrate three major aspects of curriculum design—the material that teachers want students to learn, the assessment of whether students actually learned, and the learning experiences—written within a single planning schema.[35] This curriculum process keeps curriculum designers and teachers focused on the essential connection between teaching and learning.

Backward design To this end, Wiggins and McTighe created a curriculum design model using a **"backward design"** approach.[36] They define curriculum as a specific blueprint for learning that is derived from content and performance standards. Curriculum shapes content into a plan for effective teaching and learning, from the viewpoints of both the learner and the desired achievements by specifying what the learner—not just the teacher—will do.

Typically, teachers decide what they will teach, teach it to students, and then assess how well students learned what teachers taught. Wiggins and McTighe rethought this teaching, learning, and assessing process. In their model, shown in Figure 12.2, they begin "with the end in mind"—what teachers want students to be able to do—and proceed to the evidence teachers will accept that students have learned it. Only then do teachers consider the learning activities they must use so that students will learn the desired knowledge and skills. Because they know where they are going, teachers are better able to plan the journey to take the students there—hence the "backward" design.

backward design The process of writing curriculum that integrates content, assessment, and instruction by starting with the end in mind.

Briefly, the backward design process includes three stages[37]:

- *Identify the desired results.* Teachers consider the instruction goals and content standards (national, state, district) and make choices. They prioritize what should be "enduring" understandings important beyond the classroom, what is important for the student to know and do, and what is worth familiarity. **Enduring understandings** are the "big ideas"—the larger concepts, principles, or processes—that lie at the discipline's heart and that have the potential for being meaningful to students. For example, the Magna Carta was a critically important document because it established that the law was more powerful than any person. Written law could limit governments' power and protect the individual's rights by guaranteeing due process under law.
- *Determine acceptable evidence.* What collection of evidence, gathered informally and formally, will show that the students understand and can use their knowledge in context through application, analysis, evaluation, or creation of new products? Evidence may include classroom checks for understanding, observations and dialogs, quizzes or tests, academic prompts, performance tasks or projects, and students' own self-assessments. Different types of assessments are appropriate to weigh different types of learning. For example, teachers might assess simple recall or recognition by giving a quiz or test (for content considered worth student familiarity). To evaluate more complex responses, teachers could use open-ended questions or prompts that require students to think critically (for content deemed important to know and use) or have students complete performance tasks or projects that require students to respond in authentic, extended, and complex ways with the learned content or skills (which demonstrate "enduring understandings").
- *Plan learning experiences and instruction.* With clearly identified results (specific "enduring understandings" and "big ideas") and appropriate evidence in mind (observations, tests, prompts, and projects), educators plan instructional activities. Teachers identify which activities will equip students with the needed knowledge and skills. They decide what should be taught and coached and how to best do this in light of the students' maturity level and the desired performance goals. They also determine which materials and resources they need. Didactic teaching and feedback occur throughout this process.

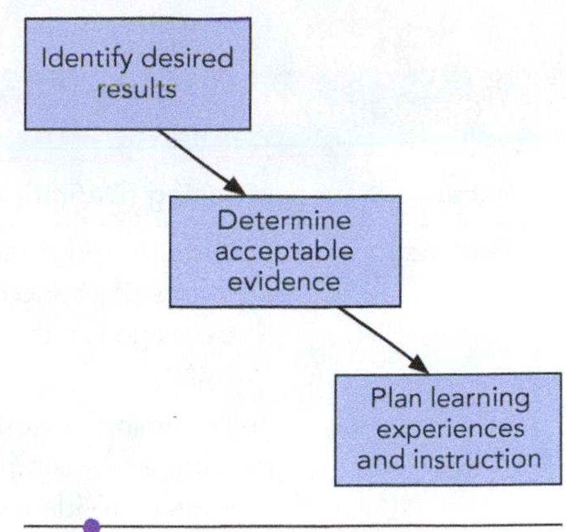

FIGURE 12.2 Wiggins and McTighe's Backward Design Process

Source: Wiggins, G., and McTighe, J. (1998). *Understanding by design.* Alexandria, VA: Association for Supervision and Curriculum Development, p. 9. Reprinted by permission.

Six facets of understanding Of course, not all teaching aims for deep understanding. Sometimes familiarity is desirable, such as when learning the alphabet or developing a vocabulary. As Bloom's taxonomy reminds us, understanding progresses from recognition and recall to more complex knowledge uses including application, analysis, synthesis, evaluation, and creativity. Real knowledge involves the learner using learning in new ways, sometimes called "transfer."

Wiggins and McTighe see **understanding** as a family of interrelated abilities. Table 12.1 describes Wiggins and McTighe's six facets of understanding, defines each facet, and gives examples of students using that facet.[38]

To this end, the backward design curriculum sees the textbook as a resource, not a map or a syllabus. Wiggins and McTighe observe that much student misunderstanding comes from a one-way, lock-step march through knowledge in textbooks. Teachers may assume that because the textbook's explanation is clear to them that it must be understandable to their students. Wiggins and McTighe explain, "Most academic courses, organized around the content to be covered, are equivalent to

enduring understandings The "big ideas"—the larger concepts, principles, or processes—that lie at the discipline's heart and that have the potential for connecting with students.

understanding According to Wiggins and McTighe, a family of interrelated abilities that include explanation, interpretation, application, perspective, empathy, and self-knowledge.

TABLE 12.1

Wiggins and McTighe's Six Facets of Understanding

Facet	Meaning (Definition)	Examples
Explanation	Provide thorough, supported, and justifiable accounts of phenomena, facts, and data. Knowledge is not just "what," but also "how" and "why."	An eighth-grade student explains with specific examples how photosynthesis is a life-sustaining process for plants, animals, and humans.
Interpretation	Tell meaningful stories, offer accurate paraphrases; provide a revealing historical or personal dimension to ideas and events; make it individual or accessible through images, anecdotes, analogies, and models.	An 11th-grade student can show how *Huckleberry Finn* is a metaphor for white–African American relations during the era in which it was written; it is not just fiction.
Application	Using, adapting, or customizing knowledge to solve novel problems in realistic situations and making adjustments based on feedback.	A fifth-grade student can use knowledge of haiku poetry ideas and format to compose an original haiku.
Perspective	See and hear points of view through critical eyes and ears; see the "big picture," events, and ideas through a dispassionate and objective viewpoint.	A student explains the Israeli and Palestinian arguments for and against establishing an independent, Palestinian state on the West Bank.
Empathy	Make a disciplined effort to find value in what others might find unusual, strange, or implausible; perceive sensitively on the basis of prior direct experience. Empathy is not the same as sympathy, nor does it mean agreement.	A high school English student must explain why Romeo was so quick to kill himself when he thought Juliet was dead.
Self-knowledge	The wisdom to know one's ignorance and biases which inform as well as prejudice our understanding. The opposite of self-centeredness.	A student discovers that he or she is a visual learner, so he or she always has a paper and pencil ready to take notes, draw conceptual maps, and make other visual cues to help prompt understanding and retention.

Source: Adapted from Wiggins, G., and McTighe, J. (1998). ***Understanding by design***. Alexandria, VA: Association for Supervision and Curriculum Development, p. 169.

giving cooks mere descriptions of finished meals. Such information, while complete in terms of the content, offers no explicit help in using the facts to accomplish cooking goals."[39] In their view, the misguided practice of relying solely on the textbook, instead of using it as one resource among many, may make the natural problem of misunderstanding worse.[40]

The backward design curriculum integrates content, assessment, and instruction with a focus on making the subject meaningful to students. Likewise, it recognizes that understanding is not a single concept, but rather a continuum; that is, understanding is a matter of degree, ranging from naive and simplistic to sophisticated and complex. Students show their understanding in varied performances and contexts. An education for understanding develops all aspects of understanding. With this approach, the learning comes with the *doing*, not the learning *about*.

12-3e Reviewing Contributions to Curriculum

Each of the persons discussed greatly adds to educators' understanding of curriculum and learners. Table 12.2 summarizes their views on curriculum, emphasizing how each connects the curriculum to students.

TABLE 12.2

Summary of Contemporary Curriculum Contributors

Curriculum Thinker	Views on Curriculum	Views on Learner
Tyler	• Developed curriculum rationale framework: • Which educational purposes? • Which educational experiences? • How to organize these experiences? • How to assess student learning?	• Curriculum ideas considered how students learn. • Used psychological and philosophical insights to develop curriculum.
Taba	• Developed seven-step curriculum planning framework. • Curriculum is both subject centered and learner centered. • Curriculum should be organized around concepts and ideas, which are the most durable forms of knowledge. • Curriculum should be organized around four levels of generality in the continuum: specific facts and processes, concepts, basic ideas, thought structures. • Constructivist approach.	• Learning is dynamic and interactive. • Students learn by using knowledge. • Students learn from the specific and concrete to the general and abstract; curriculum should address this thought continuum. • Students can learn to think in ideas and concepts.
Bloom	• Developed cognitive taxonomy that described increasingly complex levels of understanding and learning. • Provided framework to clarify educational goals, content, learning activities, and assessments.	• Identified how students develop cognitive skills. • Addressed increasing levels of student cognitive understanding and increased transfer of learning to new situations.
Wiggins and McTighe	• "Backward design" curriculum framework to plan "big ideas," the assessments, and student learning activities. • Defined six levels of student understanding. • Appropriate to subject-centered or thematic curriculum. • Constructivist approach.	• Curriculum written from learners' viewpoint. • Identifying levels of student understanding is central to curriculum design and delivery.
Delpit	• Curriculum for low-income and minority students to include tools and perspectives relevant to content along with critical and creative thinking to increase their ability to learn it. • Explicitly teach low-income and minority students the cultural codes and rules they need to fully participate in the societal mainstream.	• Effective teachers build relationships with students in which the curriculum is a part. • Teachers need to understand and accept the students' culture and language and help them build upon their prior experiences to enable learning.

Did You Get It?

Which figure named below is not a notable figure in modern learning-based curriculum development?

a. Hilda Taba.
b. Horace Mann.
c. Benjamin Bloom.
d. Jay McTighe.

Take the full quiz on CourseMate.

American Education Spotlight

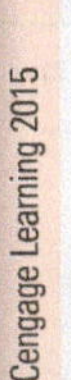

Lisa Delpit: Helping Students Access—and Move Beyond—the Curriculum

Lisa Delpit

"I have often pondered that if we taught African-American children how to dance in school, by the time they had finished the first five workbooks on the topic, we would have a generation of remedial dancers!"*

Lisa Delpit is currently the Executive Director/ Eminent Scholar, Center for Urban Education & Innovation at Florida International University. She earned her MA and EdD from Harvard Graduate School of Education and a BA from Antioch College. She expresses concern about schools that place curricula and texts before students and relationships with those students and schools that consider some children as "our children" and many others as "other people's children."

Delpit's career goal was to teach African American children and teach them well. After completing a teacher preparation program in college, she student-taught kindergarten in an inner city Philadelphia school enrolling 60 percent low-income African American and 40 percent high-income white students. Delpit used an "open classroom" concept to organize student learning. The results discouraged her.

"My white students zoomed ahead. They worked hard at the learning stations. They did amazing things with books and writing. My black students played the games; they learned how to weave; and they threw the books around the learning station. They practiced karate moves on the new carpets. Some of them learned how to read, but none of them as quickly as my white students. I was doing the same thing for all my kids—what was the problem?"**

Not until Delpit changed her classroom into a more "traditional," teacher-directed learning environment did her African American students begin to improve, although they still lagged behind. Delpit felt like a failure; she was teaching black children, but she was not teaching them well.

Insights about how to best teach students in her own society who were living outside the mainstream culture came from Delpit's experiences living as an outsider in other cultures. During her graduate work, Delpit lived for extended periods in Papua New Guinea and in Alaska working with native villagers. She observed that members of any culture transmit information implicitly to other members. Because Delpit did not grow up in these milieus, she found her work much easier and more effective when someone directly explained to her about how to dress appropriately, how to speak and listen to others, and how to avoid taboo words or behaviors.

Delpit came to realize that children who do not receive the mainstream society's cultural learning at home—as middle-class children implicitly do—should explicitly be taught the content, perspectives, and tools they need to know at school. Only in this way would they be able to make sense and meaning of the core curriculum. She also advocates that teachers clearly teach minority students the codes and rules needed to fully participate in mainstream American life, including: how to speak Standard English; how to present oneself; and how to write, dress, and interact. The ability to speak and write fluent Standard English and act in a mainstream-approved manner grants students access to other educational and career opportunities.

Delpit believes that effectively teaching low-income and minority children requires teachers to establish relationships between themselves and their students, accept their students' culture and language, and help them to build on it.

In Delpit's view, the strongest relationship in the classroom is between student and teacher. Curricular content is only one aspect of their relationship. This model generates very different interactions than the academic, middle-class culture, which sees the relationship between speaker and listener as *less* important than that between speaker and content.

Research and instructional practice support Delpit's model. How well children of color like their teacher determines how much effort and time they will invest in classroom tasks. Effective teaching requires both aspects: strong rapport with students and deep knowledge of their curriculum content.

Next, Delpit advocates that teachers directly connect students to the curriculum by using "real-life" contexts and building on students' prior experiences. Delpit highlights a mathematics teacher who brought part of a bicycle wheel to her geometry class, saying that it came from her grandson's broken toy. Could they figure out how to fix it? After the students tried to solve the problem and reconstruct the wheel from its tiniest part, the teacher introduced a theorem related to constructing a circle given at any two points on an arc; and the students quickly learned the geometry content. Additionally, giving students access to the prescribed curriculum through relationships, relevance, and personal meaning is more likely to produce young

(continued)

people able to think critically and creatively in real problem-solving situations than by completing decontextualized problems.

Delpit stresses, "When teachers do not understand the potential of the students they teach, they will underteach them no matter what the methodology."***

*Delpit, D. D, (1995). *Other people's children.* New York: W. W. Norton, p. 173.

**Depit, D. D. (1986). Skills and other dilemmas of a progressive black educator. *Harvard Educational Review 56* (4), 381.

***Delpit, 1995. Op. cit., p. 175.

Sources: Delpit, L. (2006, May/June). Lessons from a teacher. *Journal of Teacher Education 57*(3), 220–31; Delpit, L. D. (1995). *Other people's children. Cultural conflict in the classroom.* New York: W. W. Norton; Delpit, L. D. (1986, Winter). Skills and other dilemmas of a progressive black educator. *Harvard Educational Review 56*(4), 379–86; Delpit, L. D. (1988). The silenced dialog: Power and pedagogy. *Harvard Educational Review 58*(1), 280–98; Lisa Delpit. Race, Culture, Identity and Achievement Seminar Series, 2005/2006. A consortium of colleges and schools in the Boston, MA, area. Retrieved from http://www.achievementseminars.com/seminar_series_2005_2006/delpit.htm; Delpit, L. D. (1988). The silenced dialogue: Power and pedagogy in education other people's children. *Harvard Educational Review 58*(3), 280–98.

12-4 Common Core State Standards and Public School Core Curriculum

For the most part, today's public schools are subject centered, teaching to academic standards organized into separate disciplines. Each main discipline has national and Common Core State Standards that define what students at each grade level should know and be able to do. In this section, we take a closer look at each curricular area, identify the key teaching and learning issues that each subject confronts, consider how well our students are achieving, and explain how the Common Core State Standards intend to improve curriculum, teaching, and learning in each discipline.

12-4a Math

Since colonial days, math has been part of the school curriculum. Math is the most abstract discipline. It is based on numeric and conceptual relationships expressed through nonverbal symbols.[41] At the same time, math has practical applications, such as balancing a checkbook, making a family budget, or doubling a chili recipe. Fractions, decimals, and percentages are part of daily life.

Although all states have math curriculum standards, educators have not agreed about when students should learn particular math topics. Mathematics learning expectations vary across states, including the grades in which different topics are taught and the level of complexity to which math topics are taught. As a consequence, a high-performing math student in one state may or may not have the same mathematics knowledge or skills as a high-performing student in a neighboring state. This situation has not provided all students with an equitable opportunity to learn math.

Nor have math educators agreed about how to teach math. As a profession, math educators have occasionally engaged in "math wars," pitting those who advocate teaching mathematics through real-world problems (what their critics call "fuzzy math") against those who prefer an emphasis on basic skills (what their critics call "drill and kill"). In reality, overemphasizing either problem solving or basic skills leads to neglect of the other realm. Skills, concepts, and problem solving are all necessary, because each depends on the others for a complete understanding.[42] Given the state-by-state variations in math curriculum, interpreting student learning gains across the states—because some students have

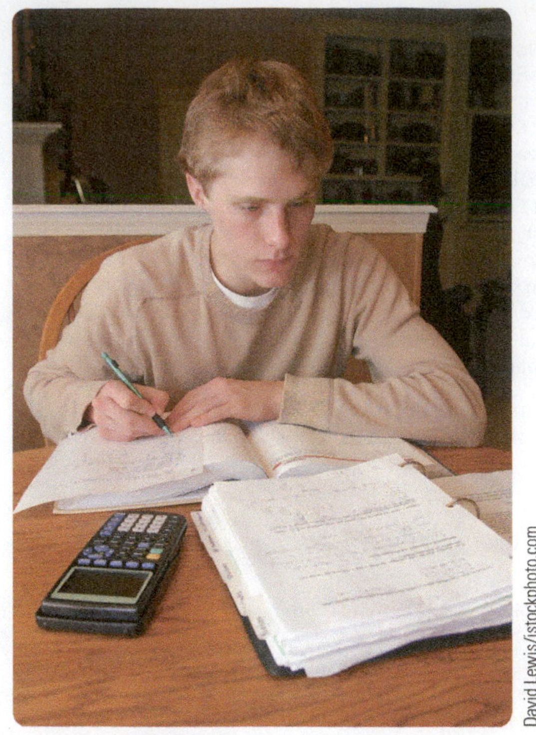

Learning math concepts, skills, and problem solving are all necessary for fully understanding math.

had no opportunity to learn a math topic if it was not taught at a grade in which it was tested—is enormously difficult.[43] The Common Core State Standards were developed, in part, to remedy the math curriculum's lack of consistent expectations across the country about what to teach, when, and to what level of complexity.

Basing math curriculum on concepts, skills, or problem solving taught at certain grade levels has critical implications for national and international math assessments. If students across the state or country are learning math in very different ways, at different grade levels, and to varying levels of comprehension and mastery, they may earn A's in class yet score poorly on standardized tests (which reflect different content, skills, and levels of complexity). These difficulties may be compounded when comparing U.S. students with peers in other nations. Countries whose students perform well in international comparisons do not choose between concepts, skills, or problem solving, but rather teach them all—concepts *and* skills *and* problem solving.

Measuring student achievement The **National Assessment of Educational Achievement (NAEP)**, sometimes called "the nation's report card," compares student achievement in different states in math, reading, science, and social studies. These assessments describe student competency in a particular subject area on a continuum labeled from "basic" to "advanced": They are not tied to any state's specific curriculum.

National Assessment of Educational Achievement (NAEP) Sometimes called "the nation's report card," compares student achievement in different states in math, reading, science, and social studies.

Looking at students' NAEP performance is one way to measure their learning. In math, students at each grade respond to questions designed to assess what they know and can do in the areas of number properties and operations, measurement, geometry, data analysis, statistics and probability, and algebra. How well are U.S. students performing in math? Improving, but mediocre to poor.

TABLE 12.3

NAEP Math Achievement, 1992–2011

	Percentage Scoring at or above "Basic" Level		Percentage Scoring at or above "Proficient" Level	
Grade	1992	2011	1992	2011
4	50	82	13	40
8	52	73	15	35
12	(2005) 61	(2009) 64	(2005) 23	(2009) 26

*12th-grade NAEP score comparisons are from 2005 and 2009, respectively. Because of changes in the assessment content and administration in 2005, the results for 2009 grade 12 could not be compared directly with scores from years before 2005.

Source: National Center for Education Statistics. (2011. November). *Mathematics 2011. National assessment of educational progress at grades 4 and 8 (NCES 2012-458).* Washington, DC: Institute of Education Sciences, U.S. Department of Education. Retrieved from http://nces.ed.gov/nationsreportcard/pdf/main2011/2012458.pdf; and for 12th grade, National Center for Education Statistics. (2010). *The nation's report card: Grade 12 reading and mathematics 2009. National and pilot state results (NCES 2011-455).* Washington, DC: Institute of Education Sciences, U.S. Department of Education. Retrieved from http://nces.ed.gov/nationsreportcard/pdf/main2009/2011455.pdf.

Table 12.3 shows that the percentage of fourth-grade math scores at or above the "basic" level has increased since 1992, rising from 50 percent to 82 percent in 2011. The percentage of fourth graders performing at or above the "proficient" level rose from 13 percent in 1992 to 40 percent in 2011. During the same period, the percentage of eighth graders performing at or above the "basic" level rose from 52 percent to 73 percent, and those performing at or above the "proficient" level rose from 15 percent to 35 percent.[44] For 12th-grade math, 64 percent of students nationwide scored at or above "basic" achievement in 2009 (the most recent 12th-grade testing), whereas only 26 percent scored at or above the "proficient" level.[45]

These data indicate that only 40 percent of fourth graders, 35 percent of eighth graders, and 26 percent of 12th graders are doing solid grade-level academic mathematics work (the NAEP definition of "proficient"). The clear majority of students are only showing partial mastery of the required math knowledge and skills needed for their grade.

Criticism of math curriculum Critics look at this discouraging math achievement and complain that the U.S. math curriculum is "a mile wide and an inch deep." They suggest that the current curriculum tends to be too skill oriented, focusing mainly on the "one right way to get the one right answer" approach to solving problems.[46] It is broad but superficial and fragmented rather than coherent, jumping back and forth between topics at different grade levels.[47] For example, teachers are expected to introduce relatively advanced mathematics in the earliest grades, before students have had an opportunity to master basic concepts and computational skills. Conversely, the curriculum continues to focus on basic computational skills through grade 8 and perhaps beyond. Switching back and forth between basic and advanced topics confuses the logic presented in mathematics lessons—and the students who are trying to learn it.

It is just such criticism that Common Core State Standards in math seek to remedy. Instead of a fragmented, superficial, "mile wide and inch deep" curriculum, the Common Core follows the principles of:

- logical coherence (systematically guiding students from basic to more advanced content),
- focus (emphasizing mastery of a few key concepts at each grade level), and
- rigor (an appropriate level of difficulty at each grade level).

These are the same three criteria evident in math curricula in the highest performing countries. In short, with the Common Core math standards, math teachers will spend more time on fewer, more important topics so students can build conceptual understanding, develop procedural skill and fluency, and learn how to transfer what they know to solve problems inside and outside class.[48]

Neither are American students achieving at the top in math by international standards. **Trends in International Math and Science Study (TIMSS)**, a math and science test of students in grades 4 and 8 in the United States and other countries, assesses students' math skills on two dimensions: the math content that students are expected to learn and the cognitive skills students are expected to have developed. In 2011, U.S. fourth and eighth graders scored higher than the scale averages of students representing 57 participating countries, scoring at or above international benchmarks, scoring 12 points higher in 2011 than in 2007, but lower than students in eight other high-achieving countries (including Singapore, Republic of Korea, and Hong Kong).[49] In 2011, 13 percent of U.S. fourth graders and 7 percent of U.S. eighth graders scored at or above the advanced international benchmark in math. Compared to 1995, the 2011 U.S. scores were 23 points higher for fourth graders and 17 points higher for eighth graders.

Trends in International Math and Science Study (TIMSS) A math and science test of students in grades 4 and 8 in the United States and other countries.

Results suggest that the top-achieving countries have coherent, focused, and rigorous mathematics curricula. A coherent curriculum makes sense to students because it helps them move from particular knowledge and skills toward an understanding of deeper structures, more complex ideas, and mathematical reasoning including problem solving. A focused curriculum spends most of its time developing the knowledge and skills widely used as prerequisites for postsecondary education. A rigorous curriculum emphasizes three dimensions of reasoning—conceptual understanding, procedural skill and fluency, and applications of learning in meaningful contexts—with equal intensity. Aligned with these world-class mathematics standards for coherence, focus, and rigor, the Common Core math expectations may provide American students with an opportunity to learn and reach "the high-quality standards they deserve."[50] To be fully implemented, however, the standards will require math teachers to significantly shift what and how they teach math.

12-4b Language Arts

"No subject of study is more important than reading . . . all other intellectual powers depend on it,"[51] proclaims cultural historian Jacques Barzun. Focused, purposeful reading for meaning is an essential skill that all students need to learn if they are to succeed in school and in life. Readers who can evaluate evidence in written material to find the answer to a provocative question or to garner support for an important argument do well at every grade level. College students and professionals also rely on these skills. Research has found that this type of engaged reading offers the best basis for effective student writing, which powerfully extends students' abilities to think and reason across disciplines.[52]

Veteran elementary teachers often comment, "In grades 1 through 3, students learn to read. In grades 4 and above, they read to learn." Researchers have called the obstacles children encounter during this transition the "fourth-grade slump" because it tends to occur when reading instruction shifts from basic decoding and world recognition to a focus on developing fluency and comprehension.[53]

The language arts include commonly used forms of communication—reading, writing, listening, and speaking. In the early grades (pre-K through early elementary), language arts instruction concentrates on teaching children how to read, write, and convey meaning with an emphasis on skill development. In later elementary grades, middle school, and high school, attention turns to reading to learn, developing meaningful and accurate communication, and writing to learn. The later grades emphasize developing reading strategies in various academic disciplines, including learning specialized vocabulary, practicing methods of understanding content, and comprehending each subject discipline's traits. Overall, language arts' principal goals are for students to be able to read, comprehend, and communicate factual material—the skills upon which further education and successful careers depend. Today's language arts are integrated with all subjects.

The "fourth-grade slump" occurs when children must read to learn.

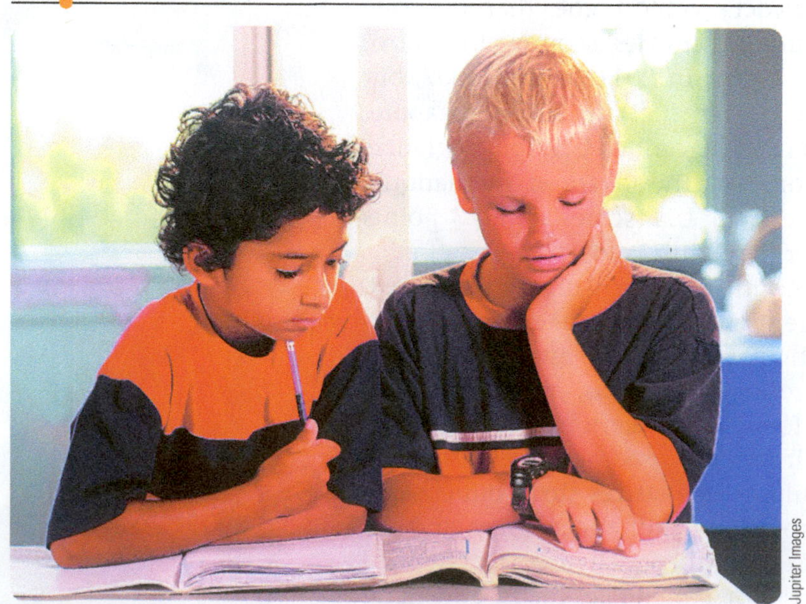

Jupiter Images

Reading achievement How well are U.S. students achieving in reading? Answer: Mediocre.

In reading comprehension, vocabulary knowledge, and critical thinking skills, NAEP reports that U.S. children's skills have remained at basically the same level for the past 30 years. Although scores may rise several points, these gains are not statistically meaningful (see Table 12.4).[54] Despite the increases in fourth and eighth grades in Basic and Advanced level reading achievement, only 34 percent of fourth and eighth graders and only 38 percent of 12th graders are reading with solid comprehension skills at their grade levels. Internationally, the U.S. fourth graders had a 14-point increase since 2001 and scored among the "high average achievement" nations—below top-performing Hong Kong, Russian Federation, Finland, and Singapore—and is among the 10 countries to improve reading from 2001 to 2011 on the 2011 Progress in International Reading Literacy Study (PIRLS) test.[55]

TABLE 12.4

NAEP Reading Achievement, 1992–2011

	Percentage Scoring at or above "Basic" Level		Percentage Scoring at or above "Proficient" Level	
Grade	1992	2011	1992	2011
4	62	67	29	34
8	69	76	29	34
12*	80	74	40	38

*12th-grade NAEP scores are from 2009.

Source: National Center for Education Statistics. (2011). *The nation's report card: Reading 2011 (NCES 2012-457).* Washington, DC: Institute of Education Sciences, U.S. Department of Education. Retrieved from http://nces.ed.gov/nationsreportcard/pdf/main2011/2012457.pdf; and National Center for Education Statistics. (2011). *Indicator 23. Reading performance.* Washington, DC: Institute of Education Sciences, U.S. Department of Education. Retrieved from http://nces.ed.gov/programs/coe/pdf/coe_rd2.pdf.

Criticism of English language arts curriculum The English language arts curricula and the ways teachers have tended to translate them into the classroom help explain some of U.S. students' poor measured reading achievement. First, when teachers have student reading focused on recall or comprehension of relatively brief text, rather than emphasizing building thinking skills in using inference and analysis on lengthy passages, they deny students ongoing opportunities to engage with close, critical reading of extended text in ways they will see on standardized tests—or in college. Next, English language arts classrooms typically contain students with a wide range of reading abilities, prompting most teachers to "teach to the middle" rather than provide the reading instruction needed to support the weakest readers (most secondary English teachers do not know how to teach reading). In addition, by trying to make school reading assignments more interesting and relevant to students, English language arts teachers often emphasize students' personal responses to the content rather than teach the reading skills needed to understand the author's intent and find textual evidence to support the narrative's ideas. Then, too, teachers do not always have access to appropriate and sufficient resources to help students learn critical reading of extended, deep text.

In an information-rich society, experiencing strong marketplace competition from well-educated workers in other nations, U.S. students' relatively weak performance in reading proficiency over recent decades calls for an effective intervention. Although not a "silver bullet," the Common Core State Standards for English language arts seek to remedy this situation. They include developing students' increased content knowledge and vocabulary, strengthening abilities to draw information from increasingly complex text, and thinking critically with it. Standards include teaching students how to reason and communicate effectively, use language to solve problems that arise in everyday life in a technological and global society, and prepare all young people for college and careers. More specifically, the standards expects students to learn to actively build and use higher-order thinking skills of comprehending and analyzing information, synthesizing and evaluating it and then applying what they have learned to answer analytical questions and solve problems.

As with the math Common Core Standards, many English language arts teachers will be substantially adjusting the "what and how" they teach if their students are to make the learning gains they need to function as equals among their national and international peers—and future workplace competitors. To make this learning happen, new curriculum, assessments, and related professional development are well underway in each state. Students will read more informational essays, speeches, articles, biographies, and other nonfiction works as well as literature in their classrooms. Fluency and comprehension skills will be twin focuses throughout the grades and subjects.

In addition, colleagues in other academic departments will also help students meet these higher expectations for inferential and evaluative reasoning with dense text and communications skills: Literacy standards for grades 6 and above expect history, social studies, science, and technology teachers to teach literacy skills unique to their disciplines, such as analyzing primary- and secondary-source documents in history and making sense of diagrams, charts, and technical terms in science. In short, with the Common Core State Standards, teachers in all academic departments will use their content expertise to help students read with comprehension, write and speak with fluency, and listen with understanding to complex language. To be sure, given this new approach to teaching a curriculum, intensive learning will be happening at both ends of these classrooms.

COMMON CORE STATE STANDARDS

12-4c Science

At a time when it seems as if everyone is discussing alternative fuels, cloning, global warming, targeted cancer treatments, and the use of biometric information to fight terrorism, science education is critical to economic, national, and worldwide survival. Yet after two decades of standards-based reform, U.S. science education shows only modest improvement.

Since the 1950s, educators have debated whether students learn science more effectively through an emphasis on hands-on experimentation or through a more straightforward memorization and recitation of facts. Until recently, teachers have also been unable to agree whether the science curriculum should include more or less material.

A variety of studies and recommendations have attempted to clarify and reform science curricula. The 1993 Benchmarks for Science Literacy from the American Association for the Advancement of Science (AAAS), the 1996 National Science Education Standards, and the 2006 National Research Council all recommend that science curricula be pared down so that students study a relatively small number of major concepts essential to understanding science and gradually build on them. The 2006 report also concluded that both instructional approaches—(1) hands-on, interactive experience and (2) memorization—have merit, depending on the science topic.[56] In a 2008 study, researchers concluded that "depth" (focus on a few core topics within science courses) rather than "breadth" (study of a longer list of topics) was key to students' developing a strong understanding of science.[57] Until 2013's "next generation" science standards, these curricular reform attempts have yielded only modest improvements in science performance on national and international tests.

In continuing efforts to improve science learning, a 26-state consortium working with educators and experts for two years produced a final version of voluntary science standards to provide students with a foundation of essential knowledge as well as ensure that they could apply their learning through scientific inquiry and the engineering design process. Performance expectations needed for students to show science proficiency lie at the standards' heart. In keeping with the recommendations above, these new science standards stress:

- depth over breadth,
- more coherence in science education across the grades, and
- helping students understand the interdisciplinary nature of certain science concept such as energy and matter.

"Next generation" science standards designers hope that every state will adopt these frameworks. Topics such as evolution and climate change; however, issues that have inflamed political debates make their approval questionable in certain states. In addition, the common core standards for English language arts' critical reading expectations will also appear in science classes because teachers will now require students to read dense text to increase their comprehension in science subjects.[58] Learning science hinges on coherent, focused, and rigorous curricula across the grade levels and on effective teaching methods.

International comparisons influenced the "next generation" science standards. The 1999 Trends in International Math and Science Study (TIMSS) included a video study that identified weaknesses in U.S. science teaching practices as compared with science instruction in other, higher-achieving countries. Researchers found that teachers in comparison countries clearly and consistently focused on science content and science ideas with activities selected to reinforce these concepts. In contrast, in the United States, content played a smaller role—and sometimes no role. U.S. teachers built lessons around engaging students in a variety of activities, often motivating ones, but these exercises were either weakly connected to science content ideas or not connected at all.[59] In short, although U.S. science teachers were enthusiastic about having students be "hands-on," they were less focused on having students be "minds-on." The "new generation" science standards intend students to be both "minds on" and "hands on."

Science achievement The No Child Left Behind (NCLB) law (2002) pushed science education into the curricular back seat (along with social studies and art) as elementary and middle schools increased class time devoted to reading and math, the first subjects tested under the federal law. Even when science testing became required, the results were not factored into the definition of Adequate Yearly Progress (AYP), the federally determined level of achievement that schools must show.

How well are U.S. students achieving in science? Answer: There have been no meaningful gains in science achievement as measured by NAEP within the last 15 years. What is more, today's students fail to show an in-depth understanding of core science concepts or the ability to apply higher-level reasoning to problem-solving and critical thinking skills in real and simulated laboratory settings—expectations that lie at the heart of the voluntary "next generation" national science standards.[60]

The NAEP science tests, revised in 2009, include content in physical science, life science, and earth and space sciences. They also assess students' capacity to use science practices such as identifying and using science principles, using scientific inquiry, and using technological design to do something with the science content. As Table 12.5 shows, over two-thirds of fourth- and eighth-grade students scored at or above the "basic" level, and less than one-third scored at or above the "proficient" level in their tested years, 1996 to 2011. The percentage of twelfth graders scoring at both at or above the "basic" level has increased slightly since 1996 but has not increased at or above the "proficient" level since 1996. In their most recent testing years, only 34 percent of fourth graders, 32 percent of eighth graders, and about one-fifth of 12th graders were achieving a solid "proficient" understanding of science at their grade levels.

Because American workers compete for jobs and wages in a global marketplace, observing where our students place

TABLE 12.5

NAEP Science Achievement, Grades 4, 8, and 12, 1996–2011

	Percentage Scoring at or above "Basic" Level			Percentage Scoring at or above "Proficient" Level		
Grade	1996	2009	2011	1996	2009	2011
4	63	72	NA	28	34	NA
8*	NA	63	65	NA	30	32
12	57	60	NA	21	21	NA

*NAEP science frameworks were changed in 2009 and these frameworks were used in 2009 and 2011, making student performance comparisons only valid for these two years and not with previous test scores.

Source for grades 4 and 12 for 1996: U.S. Department of Education, Institute of Education Sciences, National Center for Education Statistics. (2006, May). *The nation's report card: Science 2005 (NCES 2006-466).* Washington, DC: U.S. Government Printing Office, pp. 7, 19, 31. Retrieved from http://nces.ed.gov/nationsreportcard/science/.

Source for grades 4, 8, and 12: National Center for Education Statistics. (2009). *The condition of education. Science performance* (Indicator 14-2011). Washington, DC: Institute for Education Sciences, U.S. Department of Education. Retrieved from http://nces.ed.gov/programs/coe/indicator_scp.asp.

Source for grade 8: National Center for Education Statistics. (2011). *Science 2011 (NCES 2012, 465).* Washington, DC: Institute for Education Science, U.S. Department of Education, p. 5. Retrieved from http://nces.ed.gov/nationsreportcard/pdf/main2011/2012465.pdf.

within an international context is important. The 2011 TIMSS sampled 600,000 representative students in 63 countries, ranging from so-called first world global leaders to developing nations. In science content, fourth-grade students were assessed on life science, physical science, and earth science; eighth graders completed assessments on biology, chemistry, physics, and earth science; and the questions required students to use the cognitive skills of knowing (recognizing, recalling, describing), applying, and reasoning. Results placed fourth-grade U.S. students as seventh from the top (behind Korea, Singapore, Finland, Japan, and Russia, and Chinese Taipei), whereas eighth-grade students placed ninth (behind the same East Asian countries and Finland, Slovakia, Russia, and England). Fifteen percent of U.S. fourth graders and 10 percent of U.S. eighth graders scored at the Advanced International Benchmark. Eighth-grade U.S. students showed increased science proficiency since 1995, although fourth-grade U.S. students did not. Not surprisingly, the TIMSS report found that at both the fourth and eighth grades, internationally, students with more experienced and more confident teachers—and from families with more resources—had the highest science achievement.[61] Looking down the road, preparing large numbers of American students to perform with world-class knowledge and skills in critical subjects in their adult careers is more important than claiming bragging rights on high-stakes tests. Considering U.S. math and science achievement in national and international comparisons, Senator Lamar Alexander (Republican–Tennessee) concluded, "We are at risk of losing our brainpower advantage. If we lose our brainpower advantage, we lose . . . our standard of living."[62]

COMMON CORE STATE STANDARDS

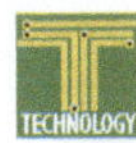

TeachSource Video 12.1

Integrating Internet Research: High School Social Studies

The high school computer lab provides opportunities for each student to investigate a genuine interest in an aspect of the history unit under study. Using online primary sources to develop a class project can motivate student interest and deepen their understanding of a critical period in American history. Watch the video clips, study the artifacts in the case, and reflect on the following questions:

1. How did the teacher use students' choice and prior knowledge of the Civil Rights Movement learned during earlier lessons as motivators to engage students more deeply and meaningfully in the topic under study?
2. What factors in the lesson were likely to contribute the most to student learning?
3. How did teacher monitoring student work and asking probing questions contribute to student thinking and understanding of the content?
4. What are the benefits and challenges of teachers and students using the Internet as a resource to deepen understanding of historical content under study?

Watch on CourseMate.

12-4d Social Studies

One of public education's major goals is to teach students how to be responsible and engaged citizens in a democratic republic. Even more importantly, education for twenty-first-century citizenship must prepare students to deal with rapid change; complex local, national, and global issues; intense cultural and religious conflicts; and increasing global economic interdependence.

The National Council for Social Studies defines social studies as "the integrated study of the social sciences and humanities to promote civic competence."[63] Because civic issues—such as health care, crime, and foreign policy—are multidisciplinary in nature, social studies draws upon anthropology, archaeology, economics, geography, history, law, philosophy, political science, psychology, religion, and sociology. Occasionally, social studies uses appropriate content from the humanities, mathematics, and natural sciences.

When considering achievement in social studies, it is important to remember that over the past decade, many schools reduced the amount of time teachers and students devoted to these disciplines because this content area was not one of those included in measures of AYP.

Social studies achievement How well are U.S. students learning social studies? Answer: Not well. Two reports, *The Nation's Report Card: U.S. History 2010 and The Nation's Report Card: Civics 2010*,[64] reveal data about U.S. students' achievement on NAEP's history and civics tests. The U.S. history assessment evaluates students' understanding of the development of America's democratic institutions and ideals—our democracy, culture, technological and economic changes, and role in the world. Civics assesses the students' understanding of the democratic institutions and ideals necessary to be informed citizens in America's constitutional democracy.

TABLE 12.6

NAEP U.S. History Achievement, 1994–2010

	Percentage Scoring at or above "Basic" Level		Percentage Scoring at or above "Proficient" Level	
Grade	1994	2010	1994	2010
4	64	73	17	20
8	61	69	14	17
12	43	45	11	12

Source for 2010: National Center for Education Statistics. (2011, June). *The nation's report card: U.S. history 2010. National assessment of educational progress at grades 4, 8, and 12 (NCES 2011-468).* Washington, DC: Institute of Education Sciences, U.S. Department of Education. Retrieved from http://nces.ed.gov/nationsreportcard/pdf/main2010/2011468.pdf.

Source for 1994 and 2006: Lee, J., and Weiss, A. R. (2006). *National assessment of educational progress: The nation's report card: U.S. history 2006 (NCES 2007-474).* National Center for Education Statistics, Institute of Education Sciences, U.S. Department of Education. Washington, DC: U.S. Government Printing Office. Retrieved from http://nces.ed.gov/nationsreportcard/pdf/main2006/2007474.pdf.

As shown in Table 12.6, in U.S. history, students showed an increase in several percentage points in the number of students scoring at or above the "basic" or partial mastery level since 1994 (and a modest increase from 2006, not shown). This overall improvement was attributable to higher achievement by the lowest-scoring students.[65] No significant changes appeared in the percentage of students scoring at or above the "proficient" level. America's fourth, eighth, and 12th graders know only very slightly more about history and civics (see Table 12.7) today than did such students in the 1990s.

In a related measurement, the 2010 NAEP civics assessment sought to determine whether students in grades 4, 8, and 12 could identify participation skills, recognize their purpose, explain how to use them, and specify how to best achieve the desired result.[66]

As Table 12.7 shows, approximately three-quarters of fourth and eighth graders and two-thirds of 12th graders have at least a "basic" understanding of civics, according to the NAEP assessment. About one student in four at these grades has a "proficient" knowledge. Overall, fourth, eighth, and 12th graders with "Advanced" knowledge of civics has not changed since 1998.

Can civics education affect students' actual behaviors outside the classroom or testing situation—such as their voting behaviors? We can't know for sure. Although schools are preparing young people to become competent citizens, our 18- to 24-year-old voters have tended not to vote. In 2000, only 36 percent of that group voted for U.S. president. In 2004, only 47 percent voted. In the 2012 presidential election, however, approximately 50 percent of voters ages 18 to 29 voted nationally, and 58 percent of these young voters cast their ballots in swing states.[67] Lack of civic and government knowledge is not just a problem found among recent high school graduates. One survey found

TABLE 12.7

NAEP Civics Achievement, 1998–2010

	Percentage Scoring at or above "Basic" Level		Percentage Scoring at or above "Proficient" Level		Percentage Scoring at or above "Advanced" Level	
Grade	1998	2010	1998	2010	1998	2010
4	69	77	23	27	2	2
8	70	72	22	22	2	1
12	65	64	26	24	4	4

Source for 1998: Lutkis, A. D., and Weiss, A. R. (2007). *The nation's report card: Civics 2006 (NCES 2007-476).* National Center for Education Statistics, Institute for Education Sciences, U.S. Department of Education. Washington, DC: U.S. Government Printing Office. Retrieved from http://nces.ed.gov/nationsreportcard/pdf/main2006/2007476.pdf.

Source for 2010: National Center for Education Statistics. (2011, May). *The nation's report card. Civics 2010. National assessment of educational progress at grades 4, 8, and 12.* Washington, DC: Institute for Education Sciences, U.S. Department of Education. Retrieved from http://nces.ed.gov/nationsreportcard/pdf/main2010/2011466.pdf.

that almost twice as many Americans could name the Three Stooges (73 percent) as could name the three branches of government.[68] As it is with other subjects, learning social studies well often depends on how it is taught. Most students find teacher lectures about people and places and memorizing lists of facts irrelevant and boring. They may cram for exams, but they quickly forget the information. Anecdotal evidence and empirical research suggest, however, that history taught in ways that students find interesting and relevant is more likely learned, remembered, and used. A 2008 study confirms this. The study in San Francisco gauged the impact of history lessons taught in a way that genuinely engaged 11th graders' interest by beginning lessons with a provocative question, such as "Was Abraham Lincoln a racist?" Students then had to read letters, articles, speeches, and other documents and develop interpretations and arguments based on the evidence they found. After six months, investigators found that students gained deeper content knowledge, remembered basic facts, strengthened their reading comprehension, and developed analytical thinking skills as they learned how to "think like historians." This approach was especially helpful to marginal students. In short, students learned the basic facts "because they were embedded in meaningful instruction."[69]

As with science, the Common Core State Standards in English language arts will expect social studies teachers to emphasize critical reading in their content area. Teachers who can give students a meaningful purpose for reading a variety of complex nonfiction works and show them how to build strong arguments based on evidence they find in the text will increase students' literacy and provide more interesting and successful social studies classes.

The bright spots in these math, reading, science, and social studies assessments appear in the modest increases in fourth and eighth graders' achievement in all these areas and 12th graders' slight improvement in basic mastery in math and reading. The lowest-achieving students are making learning gains that put them at or above "basic" levels of knowledge. Experts attribute this development in large part to an intense national emphasis on reading in kindergarten through third grade, where improvements in reading comprehension would have the greatest impact on students' test-taking achievement in all assessed areas where they have to read and understand the questions before they can answer correctly.[70] And, as we have seen, students who have successfully learned how to read in grades 1–3 are well prepared to "read to learn" in fourth grade and beyond.

12-4e The Arts

If we want to understand the values, morals, philosophies, aesthetics, and lifestyles in any particular historical period or geographic region (including our own), we must study their arts. Making art and actively appreciating the aesthetic dimensions of human creation transform our world from a random, chaotic place into a purposeful and even beautiful one.

Arts education includes teaching students how to use the tools and processes that produce works of art—such as handling charcoal to draw a still life, reading sheet music, and singing choral harmony. Art also involves teaching students how the fine arts relate to history and culture, giving students occasions to explore the connections between arts disciplines and other subjects. Studying the arts can be highly entertaining, as when performing in and enjoying a school theatrical or playing woodwinds in the marching band.

Several arguments support inclusion of arts education in curriculum. First, studying the arts has intrinsic value because the arts reflect what it is like to be human. Engaging in art-related activities gives us a better understanding of ourselves and of others. At the same time, they give pleasure to those involved in their creation and appreciation. Second, studying the arts is intellectual and has cognitive benefits because it increases students' problem-solving abilities, critical thinking, expressive abilities, and creative skills.

The intrinsic value of the arts The arts are worth learning for their own sake because they provide benefits not available through any other means. Who cannot recall that special song that was playing on the radio or iPod when some momentous event occurred in his or her life? The arts open us up to a transcending dimension of reality that affects us deeply but that we find difficult to describe in words.

The arts also have personal value. Most students enjoy the arts, and their inclusion in curriculum makes learning fun. A comprehensive, articulated arts education program engages students in a process that helps them develop the self-esteem, self-discipline, cooperation, fuller awareness, and motivation necessary for success in life.

The intellectual value of the arts Arts help students think in different ways. Because so much of a child's early school years focus on acquiring language and math skills, children gradually learn, unconsciously, that the "normal" way to think is linear and sequential, the way words in English parade across the textbook page: from left to right, from beginning to end, from cause to effect. As a result, students learn to value only information gained through reasoning and second-hand experiences, such as reading a book or listening to a teacher's lecture.

Arts, in contrast, teach the value of learning directly through our senses—seeing, touching, hearing, smelling, and moving. The person and the experience are immediately connected, linking verbal and nonverbal, the strictly logical and the emotional. These ties give the person a richer understanding of the whole. Likewise, arts education develops nonlinguistic skills in qualitative reasoning. Appreciating art requires a complex mental process of closely examining a work, attending to the emotional responses that these unique visual, auditory, or tactile qualities generate in the viewer, and inferring meaning from the art's specific combination of qualities and their relation to one's personal experiences and emotions.[71] This process requires active meaning-making with many "right" answers and many ways of expressing them.

The arts offer ways of comprehending that do not take conscious information into account and that other academic studies do not include. In the arts, a flash of insight can be a valid source of knowledge. In this way, the arts provide students with tools for understanding a broad range of human experiences. They help students learn to adapt to and respect others' (often very different) ways of thinking, working, and expressing themselves. They teach students an array of communicative, analytical, and developmental tools for problem solving in human situations—this is why we speak, for example, of the "art" of teaching or the "art" of politics. Students learn the power of literature, visual arts, music, drama, and dance to reflect cultures and understand the interdependence of art with ideas and actions.

Studying the arts has intrinsic and intellectual benefits.

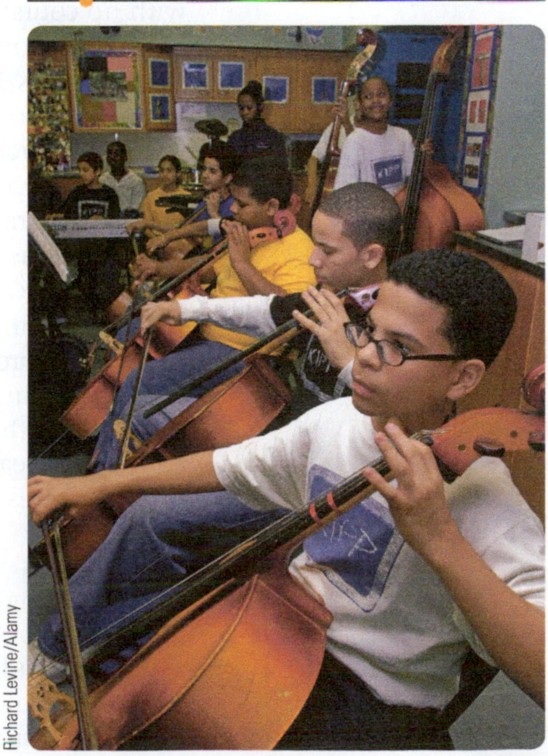

Richard Levine/Alamy

Arts develop such problem-solving abilities and thinking skills as analyzing, synthesizing, evaluating, and creating. In addition, they help develop students' cognitive competencies in elaborative and creative thinking, fluency, originality, focused perception, and imagination. Arts education builds skills in analyzing nonverbal communication and making informed judgments about cultural products and issues. They give students the tools they need to convey their thoughts and feelings in a variety of modes, giving them a vastly more powerful repertoire for self-expression.

Arts' immediacy and active involvement of the student's mind, emotions, and body directs and focuses the learner's attention, without which no learning can occur. These "habits of mind" accustom students to taking multiple perspectives, to layering relationships, and to relating and constructing meaningful responses. Along the way, these habits help students extend their thinking and develop critical cognitive capacities and personal dispositions. Learning with the arts permits students to flexibly interweave the intuitive, practical, and logical modes of thinking.[72] It also helps students make decisions in situations where there are no official "right" answers.

Research on the arts and student achievement A growing body of research has documented the habits of mind, social competencies, and personal dispositions inherent to arts learning. These studies' findings may not be as clear-cut as standardized test results, but they offer empirical support for including an arts curriculum in any public school that is truly interested in developing students' intellects and capacities as whole persons.

Studying the arts is highly related to high academic achievement. In a well-documented 2002 national study of more than 25,000 middle and high school students, researchers found that students with high arts involvement performed better on standardized achievement tests than did students with low arts involvement.[73] Multiple independent studies have found that students who studied the arts for more than four years scored as much as 59 points higher on SAT verbal tests and as much as 44 points higher on SAT math tests than peers with no coursework or experiences in the arts.[74]

In addition, an analysis of multiple studies confirms that students who take music classes in high school are more likely to score higher on standardized math tests, such as the SAT.[75] Similarly, students who are consistently involved in band or orchestra during their middle and high school years tend to perform better in math at grade 12. Students from low-income families who are involved with orchestra or band are more than twice as likely to perform at the highest math levels as their peers who are not involved in music.[76]

In 2002, *Critical Links: Learning in the Arts and Student Academic and Social Development* compiled 62 rigorous, experimental, peer-reviewed studies published in national professional journals on the academic and social effects of learning experiences in drama, dance, visual arts, music, and multi-arts with supporting data linking the arts with student achievement.[77] Overall, the researchers reported that arts learning has positive and measurable effects on math achievement, thinking skills, motivation, social behavior, and the school environment.

Do the arts make students smarter? Although these studies draw attention to strong connections between arts and academic achievement, cautious interpretation of their findings is advised. A strong relationship is not the same as a cause-and-effect relationship. Headlines announcing "The Arts Make Kids Smarter" would oversimplify and overgeneralize these results. In fact, the results from these studies are correlational, not proof of a cause and effect.

Which factors might underlie this arts–achievement connection? Perhaps high-achieving students choose to participate in arts classes, rather than the arts classes themselves increasing students' measured SAT achievement.[78] Perhaps academically strong schools tend to have strong arts programs. Perhaps families who value academic achievement also value achievement in the arts. All of these explanations might explain the arts–achievement relationship. What is more, the arts call for multiple and conflicting interpretations that are fundamentally divergent. Standardized tests, in contrast, call for right-and-wrong answers and convergent thinking. Given these differences, one would not expect learning in the arts to translate directly into better achievement on standardized tests.[79]

Nevertheless, the research findings suggest that training in the arts might contribute to improving children's and adults' general thinking skills. The cognitive processes that give rise to the arts and those that give rise to literature, social studies, math, and sciences may be interrelated. For example, all these activities involve focusing attention and recognizing patterns.[80]

Providing a mind-centered curriculum If schools want a curriculum designed to help children develop as productive thinkers and citizens, they must provide young people with the kinds of learning challenges that develop their minds to the fullest. To be most beneficial, arts need to become curricular partners with other subjects in ways that allow them to contribute their own distinctive vibrancy and complexity to the learning process as a whole.

Education has social and personal as well as political and economic goals. Its primary purpose is not merely to enable students to do well in school, but rather to prepare them to do well in the lives they lead outside of school. Developing the mind is a form of cultural achievement in which schools play a critical role.[81] An education that integrates the arts into curriculum can better prepare students to succeed in the world they are entering and enrich the lives they will lead. If schools are to be intellectual—rather than merely academic—places, the arts must be active parts of what and how our students learn.

Did You Get It?

Of the statements below about the U.S. public school system, which is true?

a. Educators largely agree about what students should learn and how they should be taught.

b. Despite the critical nature of learning to read well, the "fourth-grade slump" occurs when children shift from learning to read to reading to learn.

c. Over the past decade, U.S. children's science achievements have measurably and significantly increased.

d. Because a major goal of public education is student preparation for engaged citizenship, schools have typically increased the time students and teachers devote to social studies.

Take the full quiz on CourseMate.

12-5 The Search for Curricular Balance Means Educating the Whole Child

The fact that this chapter does not review every public school curriculum is not meant to imply that those disciplines are not important to a fully educated and healthy person. Instead, we have looked at the traditional core curriculum taught in most schools that provides the basis for national accountability and international comparisons—along with one unassessed discipline area—and their roles in advancing student learning.

12-5a The Search for Curricular Balance

Schools are "cultures for growing minds," and the opportunities that schools provide influence the direction this growth takes.[82] Educators' decisions about amount of time allotted to a field of study influences the kinds of mental skills children will have the chance to develop. As we have seen, the history of curriculum can be seen as a debate over which of three competing factors is most important—the individual child, the society, or the subject matter. The need to find the appropriate balance among these three essentials creates ongoing curriculum challenges.[83]

A disciplinary orientation to curriculum, how most public schools are organized, is especially attractive to professors and researchers who work within separate subjects' structure. It does not reflect the reality or convey the world's excitement, however, nor does it connect to students' own experiences or provide personal meaning or relevance that would motivate and sustain learning.

Educators must teach students contemporary civilization's survival skills and balance the theoretical with the practical. Education needs to acknowledge the world's complexity, contradictions, and diversity. No subject stands alone in the real world—so why should it stand alone in the curriculum?

12-5b Educating the Whole Child

Every culture has debated education's aims. None, however, can produce final once-and-forever answers because education's aims are inevitably tied to a particular society's goals and ideals. In our pursuit of efficiency, we have remade ourselves into a collection of separate needs and attributes.[84] The same is true for our schools. Surely we should educate our students for more than reading and math proficiency.

As discussed in Chapter 6, Richard Rothstein and Rebecca Jacobsen synthesized nearly 300 years of American education policy making into eight broad categories.[85] The eight categories include:

- *Basic academic skills*—reading, writing, math, science, history, civics, geography, and foreign language
- *Critical thinking and problem solving*—analyzing information, applying ideas to new situations, and developing knowledge using computers
- *Social skills and work ethic*—communication skills, personal responsibility, and getting along with others from varied backgrounds
- *Citizenship*—public ethics, knowing how government works, and participating by voting, volunteering, and becoming active in community life
- *Physical health*—good habits of exercise and nutrition
- *Emotional health*—self-confidence, respect for others, and the ability to resist peer pressure to engage in irresponsible personal behavior
- *The arts and literature*—participation in and appreciation of musical, visual, and performing arts as well as a love of literature
- *Preparation for skilled employment*—qualification for skill employment for students not pursuing college education

If these goals are what yesterday's and today's civic and legislative leaders consider worth learning in school, our present school curricula are not faithful to American education's goals. In our "test-mania," we now focus almost exclusively on basic academic skills (reading, math) and critical thinking. If we were faithful to what our communities say they want, we would be addressing the other six categories, too.

Contemporary research results support the view that educating the whole child requires teaching a well-rounded curriculum. Studies in 2007 and 2011 found that exercise—such as occurs in physical education classes—boosts brain function and academic achievement in children and adolescents.[86] Although the exercise itself does not make children smarter, it puts the learners' brains in an optimal position to learn by increasing the amount of oxygen to the brain, increasing their ability to focus and concentrate, and boosting students' energy levels.[87] A 2012 three-year study of a teacher training program found that taking time to teach students to manage their emotions and to practice empathy, caring, and cooperation not only increased these behaviors but also increased students' academic achievement as compared with a comparison group of students who were not exposed to these social–emotional programs.[88] Similarly, a 2011 meta-analysis of school-based social and emotional learning programs found significant improvements in academic achievement (an 11-percentile point gain in achievement test scores and school grades), behavior, and attitudes as compared with control groups.[89] Likewise, a 2009 investigation found that exposure to music, both in and out of school, is tied to higher student achievement in mathematics and reading even after controlling for prior school achievement and other factors.[90] Clearly, curricula such as these benefit the whole child—academically, socially, and personally.

Success in basic academics does not necessarily result in more complex skills. For example, during the NCLB decade, scores rose on state tests that tend to emphasize basic skills but did not rise substantially on the NAEP, which measures basic, proficient, and advanced skills.[91] Schools must take care not to unwittingly distort curriculum by holding educators responsible solely for ensuring that students have basic skills. Perhaps our expectations are not set too high; perhaps they are set too low. Maybe we are laboring to bring all students to the achievement "floor" when we should be trying to bring them all to the "ceiling." Holding schools accountable for each of the eight previously mentioned goal areas would create incentives for teaching a balanced curriculum that addresses the whole child. Although educators today are almost entirely engaged in an *academic achievement discourse*, they would be more appropriately focused if they engaged in a *human development discourse*. Attention to human development would recognize that human beings travel through different stages of life, each with its own requirements for optimal growth.[92]

Children respond to educational situations in intellectual, emotional, and social ways. To neglect their social and emotional development in the exclusive pursuit of measured academic performance is to ignore these young people's need to live satisfying lives.[93] It also limits their capacity to learn the prescribed content: If we fail to generate a relevant affective link—personal meaning—for the information, students will soon forget it.

Schools need to approach curriculum in a way that is sensitive to each learner's unique needs and developmental life stage. Curriculum needs to reach

TeachSource Video 12.2

Motivating Adolescent Learners: Curriculum Based on Real Life

Teachers make their curriculum meaningful and relevant to students when they have students apply what they learn in real-life situations. By taking turns working in a student-operated school store, sixth-grade students accurately use concepts of fractions, decimals, and percents as well as grow in responsibility and maturity. Watch the video clips, study the artifacts in the case, and reflect on the following questions:

1. How does making a curriculum relevant to students increase their motivation to learn it and deepen their understanding of the concepts and how they are used?
2. How does increasing student responsibility to apply the math concepts correctly in a real-world situation increase their math understanding as well as their maturity and respect for each other?
3. At any grade level, what things must a teacher consider in order to make a curriculum relevant and meaningful to his or her students in ways that increase their engagement and learning?

Watch on CourseMate.

beyond literacy, math, and science to include the arts, physical education, social skills training, and imaginative and ethical development. Such a curriculum would focus on the whole child. Future educators who fully understand the concept of curriculum and the need to educate the whole child can learn ways to meet local, state, national, and international standards and to teach their subject in ways that students find worth learning.

In the human organism, all parts are interconnected. We need to recognize these connections when we teach. "Attention to such complex matters will not simplify our tasks as teachers but it will bring education closer to the heart of what really matter,"[94] insists Eisner. Likewise, *curriculum* is no longer about running a racetrack. As Jacqueline Grennon Brooks of Hofstra University so eloquently says, "Learning is not a race from point to point. It is a journey that changes pace, changes course, and, ultimately, changes us."[95]

Today, educators continue to look for the right balance in curriculum between the subject, the child, and the society. What young people need to know to become competent adults changes as the world changes. Public school curriculum must do the same. We all must deeply question our schools and our curricula. Each of us must ask what it means to be educated and what it means to be human. Then, future practitioners who deeply care about educating (rather than schooling) children as whole people can begin to find the answers.

Did You Get It?

Which following statement is true about most American public school curriculums today?

a. While Americans have repeatedly debated the aims of education, there are no lasting answers because a society differs in its goals and ideals at different times in its development.

b. Although most public schools are organized along a disciplinary curriculum, they also do a reasonably good job of motivating learning through a variety of positive ways.

c. Our communities largely say they want a holistic education curriculum, and despite a tendency to focus on basic academic skills produced by "test mania" they typically get it.

d. Exercise and noncompetitive athletics are unnecessary to educating the whole child.

Take the full quiz on CourseMate.

SUMMARY

- Curriculum is the school's plan for learning, the subjects that schools teach. It is about values, part of a selective tradition that those with power and influence in a society believe that each of its members should learn. In U.S. public schools, the curriculum reflects an inherent historical tension between focus on the society, the subjects, and the child.
- Notable American curriculum thinkers Ralph Tyler, Hilda Taba, Benjamin Bloom, and Grant Wiggins and Jay McTighe developed ways to integrate subjects, enduring concepts, and the learner.
- Today's public schools are teaching a standards-based curriculum comprising separate disciplines (math, English/language arts, science, and social studies) usually taught and assessed independently. Each curriculum and pedagogy will be influenced by the Common Core State Standards.
- The Common Cores State Standards for math and English language arts, proposed in 2010 and adopted by 46 states, clearly communicate what students at each grade level are expected to know and be able to do. They emphasize curriculum coherence, focus, and rigor and the application of knowledge using higher-order thinking skills. They are informed by standards of top-performing countries.

- The arts, often marginalized in today's schools, are intrinsically meaningful and develop students' thinking skills and problem-solving abilities. Research shows that educating the whole child requires a well-rounded curriculum, including physical education, the arts, and emotional social learning. All these contribute to a fuller knowledge of the world, provide more ways to express human nature, and also increase students' intellectual and academic performance.

Visit the Education CourseMate for this textbook to access the eBook, Did You Get It? quizzes, TeachSource Video Cases, flashcards, and more. Go to CengageBrain.com to log in, register, or purchase access.

Effective instruction has more impact on student learning and achievement than any other school factor.

© Ian Shaw/Alamy

CHAPTER 13

Instruction

InTASC Standards Addressed: 1, 2, 3, 4, 5, 6, 7, 8, 9, and 10

LEARNING OBJECTIVES

After you read this chapter, you should be able to:

13-1 Summarize the research about teaching effectiveness and student achievement.

13-2 Describe the behavioral, cognitive, and constructivist learning approaches and how they influence instruction in today's classrooms.

13-3 Identify and discuss the essential factors that allow effective teachers to provide high-quality instruction.

Becoming an effective teacher takes time. A young teacher writes,

> This is my fifth year teaching high school English. . . . Every single year has been a struggle . . . Yet, every single year, I have gotten better at this gig.
>
> This year, I realize that I enjoy teaching more than I dread it, more than it scares me—which in itself, is terrifying. The other day, my principal said, in front of the entire staff, that I am a "gifted teacher." My students inspire me. I think about them when I'm at the grocery store or in the gas station, and smile. Or I laugh out loud, and people give me funny looks. My students are improving as readers, writers, and thinkers, and it's because I know what I'm doing. This feels great.[1]

Who wouldn't want to have an enthusiastic, caring, and effective teacher like this? What prospective educator wouldn't want to become one? But becoming this successful and comfortable in the classroom does not happen overnight.

Having a license to teach does not make one an effective teacher. As in other fields, a professional license is only a minimum qualification and a promise to "do no harm." Teachers labeled as "highly qualified" who have met their credentialing standards may still provide their classrooms with a middling quality of instructional support, even if they really know their subject and the learning atmosphere is emotionally positive.[2]

A growing cadre of researchers agrees that effective instruction probably has a greater impact on learning and achievement gaps than any other school factor. "Effective teaching," notes Harvard University Professor Richard Elmore "is voluntary, and therefore rare."[3]

Although teachers need to thoroughly understand the subject material they will teach, they also need the skills that will help students learn it. Effective teaching can be learned, practiced, and mastered, by focusing on providing high-quality instruction. ●

13-1 Research on Teaching Effectiveness and Student Achievement

pedagogy The art and profession of teaching involving three related areas: the teacher's instructional strategies, management techniques, and curriculum.

instruction The teachers' actions by which they bring curriculum to life in the classroom.

Pedagogy is the art and profession of teaching. Effective pedagogy involves three related areas: the teacher's instructional strategies, management techniques, and curriculum.[4] **Instruction** is the means by which teachers bring curriculum to life in the classroom. Even if the teacher has been given the standards-infused school district's curriculum, the teacher has tremendous influence over how to present it.

"The 'art' of teaching is rapidly becoming the 'science' of teaching."[5] Until recently, teaching had not been systematically studied in a methodical manner. In the 1970s, however, researchers began to look at the effects of instruction on student learning. Before then, a widespread belief held that school really made little difference in students' achievement.[6]

Since then, research has shown that an individual teacher can have a powerful effect on his or her students *even if the school does not.* After reviewing hundreds of studies conducted in the 1970s, researchers Jere Brophy and Thomas Good confidently claimed, "The myth that teachers do not make a difference in student learning has been refuted."[7]

13-1a Teaching Effectiveness and Student Achievement

Conventional wisdom has long held that family backgrounds and economic status were the primary determiners of students' learning. In the last decade of the twentieth century, researchers found that, aside from a well-articulated curriculum and a safe and orderly environment, the individual teacher was the most influential school-related factor in determining which students learned and how well they learned. Consistently working with highly effective teachers can overcome the academic limitations placed on students by their backgrounds.

Many studies have quantified the effective teacher's influence on student achievement. This influence is relatively independent of anything else that occurs in the school. Researchers William Sanders and colleagues in Tennessee and William Webster and colleagues in Texas provide data from two different states that strongly affirm this conclusion. They found that having three consecutive years with effective versus ineffective teachers can make students' achievement appear to be either gifted or remedial, respectively.[8] The cumulative impact over three years of effective elementary teachers was estimated to produce (on a 100-point scale) a 35-point difference in reading achievement and more than a 50-point difference in math achievement as measured by standardized tests.[9] Consecutive years with highly effective teachers can produce dramatic achievement gains in all groups—low-, middle-, and high-achieving students. In a similar study, high school students working with the most effective teachers showed reading and math gains that exceeded the national median, and their peers with the least effective teachers showed virtually no academic growth.[10]

Sanders and his colleagues have observed that the individual classroom teacher is the essential factor in whether and how much students learn.[11] After analyzing the achievement scores of more than 100,000 students across hundreds of schools, these researchers concluded that more could be done to improve education by improving teachers' effectiveness than by modifying any other single factor. Conversely, if the teacher is ineffective, students working with that teacher will show inadequate academic progress, regardless of whether they are usually high or low achievers.[12]

One noteworthy 2004 study looked at teacher effectiveness in grades K-3. The four-year experimental study randomly assigned students to classes controlled for students' previous achievement, socioeconomic status, ethnicity, gender, class size, and presence (or not) of an aide in class. They found that students who have a teacher at the 75th percentile of pedagogical competence (an effective teacher) will outgain students who have a teacher at the 25th percentile (not so effective teacher) by 14 percentile points in reading and 18 percentile points in mathematics. Similarly, students who have a 90th percentile teacher (a very effective teacher) will outgain students who have a 50th percentile teacher (an average teacher) by 13 percentile points in reading and 18 percentile points in mathematics.[13] The more effective the teacher, the more his or her students' learning and measured achievement will increase.

Teachers who learn and practice sound instructional techniques can affect students' measured achievement. A 1996 National Assessment of Educational Progress (NAEP) study found that students of teachers who conducted hands-on learning activities outperformed their peers by more than 70 percent of a grade level in math and 40 percent of a grade level in science. In addition, students whose teachers had strong content knowledge and who had learned the professional skills needed to work with pupils from different cultures or with special needs tested more than one full grade level above their peers whose teachers did not have this knowledge or skills. Students whose math teachers stressed critical thinking skills, such as writing about math, scored 39 percent of a grade level higher than peers whose teachers did not stress these skills. What is more, the teaching quality aspects measured have an impact seven to 10 times greater than class size in affecting student achievement.[14]

And the impact of working with highly effective teachers tends to have positive long-term outcomes. In a 2011 **value-added** teacher effectiveness study, investigators analyzed school district data from grades 3 through 8 for 2.5 million children linked to their parents' tax records. Investigators found that students who worked with high value-added teachers are more likely to attend college, attend higher-ranked colleges, earn higher salaries, and reside in more affluent neighborhoods. They also save more for retirement and are less likely to become parents as teenagers. Study authors estimated that on average, one standard deviation improvement in a teacher's value-added contribution in one grade increased their former student's adult earning by about 1 percent at age 28, and replacing a highly ineffective teacher (at the bottom 5 percent) with an average teacher would increase their students' lifetime income by more than $250,000 for the average classroom in the study's sample.[15]

value-added A statistical technique that uses student achievement data over time to measure their learning gains and estimate the impact that teachers and schools have on student learning apart from factors such as family and socioeconomic background.

Educators and policy makers agree that a clear, predictive relationship exists between teachers' basic skills—especially verbal ability—and student achievement.[16] They also agree that teachers' content knowledge affects student achievement. For example, on the 1996 NAEP, students whose teachers had college majors or minors in the subjects they taught—especially in secondary math and science—outperformed students whose teachers lacked this content knowledge by about 40 percent of a grade level in each subject.[17] Teachers' content knowledge is also essential for other subjects they want students to learn.

No evidence suggests that possessing content knowledge alone is enough to be an effective teacher, however.[18] Although teachers need a strong knowledge base in the subject they teach, taking additional courses in that subject does not necessarily affect their own students' achievement.[19] Likewise, others have correctly noted that college majors vary in rigor, and a prospective teacher's college transcripts may not actually confirm that its holder possesses substantial content knowledge.[20] Therefore, although teachers' content knowledge and verbal skills have been linked to higher student achievement, teachers' knowledge of the subject may be a necessary but not a sufficient condition for high-quality teaching and learning.[21]

Limitations in the research As with all research, interpreting teacher effectiveness studies requires caution. Methodological weaknesses affect how we can interpret the data gathered by any particular study. After all, teachers are not randomly assigned to classes within schools. The most experienced, credentialed, and respected teachers usually receive assignments to upper-level and advanced courses. School culture, parents, and students expect mature educators with advanced degrees to teach these high-status, intellectually rigorous classes. Likewise, students cannot ethically be transferred from one teacher's classroom to another simply to provide the random conditions needed for an empirical study. Additionally, some of the teacher quality studies use highly sophisticated statistical models that estimate student gains and come with their own technical limitations. Even so, although recognizing and understanding research findings' limitations are important, the reality that excellent teaching practices can make a tremendous difference in student learning deserves serious attention.

13-1b Teacher Preparation and Student Achievement

Research shows that teachers' instructional preparation increases student achievement. Linda Darling-Hammond, Professor of Education at Stanford University, found that teacher preparation is a stronger correlate of student achievement than class size, overall spending, or teacher salaries; indeed, this factor accounts for 40 to 60 percent of the total achievement differences after considering students' ethnicity and family wealth.[22] Additional studies show that both subject-matter knowledge and knowledge of teaching and learning strongly correlate with teachers' classroom performance.[23]

Teacher education coursework is sometimes more important than extra subject-matter classes in advancing students' math and science achievement.[24] David Monk, Professor of Educational Administration at Pennsylvania State University, found a positive correlation between students' achievement and their teachers' coursework in teaching methods.[25] Nonetheless, education classes do have a point of diminishing returns. Several studies have found that teachers with advanced subject-matter degrees, rather than advanced education degrees, have students who perform better in math and reading. This is especially true after elementary school, when students need a deeper understanding of increasingly more complex content.[26]

Additionally, teachers who clearly understand the learning process and adapt their instructional behaviors accordingly have students who learn more. When teachers systematically study how students learn and develop more effective teaching behaviors, their students' achievement increases. For example, investigators found that 73 percent of these teachers' students—especially the lowest achievers—showed the greatest (statistically significant) learning gains.[27]

Professional preparation includes classroom management skills. Teachers who cannot effectively manage their classrooms have students who learn less than their peers. Research suggests that teachers who lack classroom management skills, regardless of how much content they know, cannot create a classroom environment that supports student learning. For example, a study of the influence of teachers' different disciplinary practices on student achievement found that student classroom disorder results in lower achievement.[28]

American Education Spotlight

Linda Darling-Hammond

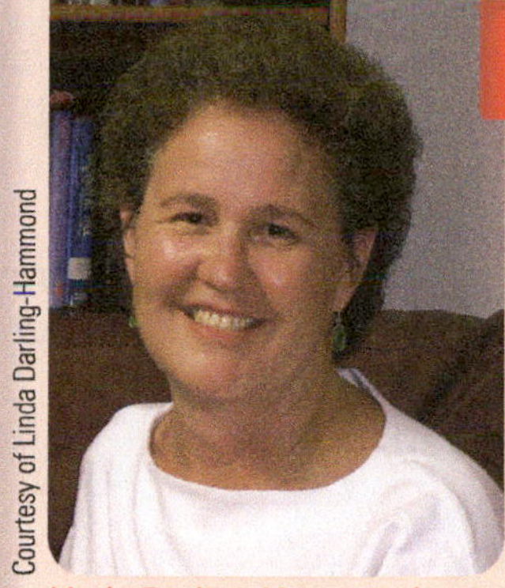
Courtesy of Linda Darling-Hammond

Linda Darling-Hammond: Helping All Teachers Meet High Standards

"I have always felt that the most exciting thing any person could do is to learn and the most challenging and satisfying thing anyone could do is to teach. . . ."*

With over 30 years as an education professor, Linda Darling-Hammond is an authority on teacher effectiveness, school reform, and educational equity. She is currently Charles E. Ducommun Professor of Education at Stanford University where she launched and oversees the School Redesign Network, which works nationally to transform schools to teach twenty-first-century skills and to support student success through innovations in curriculum, teaching, and assessment. Recently, Darling-Hammond was named one of the nation's 10 most influential people affecting educational policy over the past decade.

Darling-Hammond propelled the issue of teacher quality into the national education debate. As founding executive director of the National Commission on Teaching and America's Future, a blue-ribbon panel, she spearheaded its 1996 report, *What Matters Most: Teaching for America's Future*, providing research that supports teacher quality and which led to sweeping policy changes that affected teaching in the United States. As Chair of the Model Standards Committee of the Interstate New Teacher Assessment and Support Consortium (InTASC), she led the development of licensing standards for beginning teachers that reflect current knowledge about what teachers need to know to teach challenging content to diverse learners. And as an early member of the National Board for Professional Teaching Standards, Darling-Hammond helped design performance assessments that allow teachers to demonstrate their classroom teaching skills in authentic ways. As the author or editor of 16 books and more than 300 journal articles, book chapters, and monographs on issues of policy and practice, she is a prolific communicator. She is also a former president of the American Educational Research Association.

For Darling-Hammond, interest in educational equity is personal. As a child, her parents often moved in search of strong public schools for their academically talented daughter. Yet despite her own positive educational experiences, she saw her brother, who had a number of disabilities, receive much less support, even in the same schools, because she and he were placed in different academic tracks.

Starting her own education career as a teacher's aide, Darling-Hammond began teaching in "grossly underfunded" Camden, New Jersey, where she faced educational inequity first hand, working in a "crumbling warehouse high school managed by dehumanizing and sometimes cruel procedures and staffed by underprepared and often downright unqualified teachers. It had a nearly empty book room and a curriculum so rigid and narrow that teachers could barely stay awake to teach it."*

According to Darling-Hammond, good teaching is reciprocal. Not all children learn in the same way or at the same rate. What the pupils do determines what the teacher needs to do. Teachers need to know a lot about children (as developing individuals), learning, the subject matter, and the curriculum before they are able to adapt instruction to meet students' needs. Schools should be redesigned to focus on helping teachers learn how to teach children well by enhancing both pedagogy and relationships. Teachers need time to work individually with students and collaboratively with colleagues. To help students learn well, we must first support really high-quality teaching.

Critics have challenged Darling-Hammond for her "well-meaning but naïve" view of education reform solutions; her cautious view of Teach for America and its candidates' lack of appropriate teacher preparation; and her lukewarm attitudes on charter schools, school competition and parent choice. As a result, some view Darling-Hammond as a tool for the status quo.

Darling-Hammond received her BA from Yale University in 1973, and her doctorate in Urban Education from Temple University in 1978. She is married to husband Allen and has three children, Kia, Elena, and Sean. Like their mother, Kia and Elena have become well-prepared and deeply committed teachers.

*Darling-Hammond, L. (1997). *The right to learn: A blueprint for creating schools that work.* San Francisco, CA: Jossey-Bass, pp. xii, xiii.

Sources: Darling-Hammond, L. (2010, June 14). *The nation. Restoring our schools.* Article adapted from Linda Darling-Hammond's *The flat world and education: How America's commitment to equity will determine our future.* New York: Teachers College Press. Retrieved from http://www.thenation.com/article/restoring-our-schools; Darling-Hammond, L. *The right to learn: A blueprint for creating schools that work.* (1997). San Francisco, CA: Jossey-Bass; Linda Darling-Hammond, Stanford University School of Education. Retrieved from http://stanford.edu/~ldh/; Linda Darling-Hammond. Biographies. School Redesign Network at Stanford University. Retrieved from http://www.srnleads.org/about/biographies.html; PBS Online. (n.d.). Interview with Linda Darling-Hammond. Only a teacher. Retrieved from http://www.pbs.org/onlyateacher/today2.html. Russo, A. (2007, December 13). Disappointed in Obama, reformist attacks Linda Darling-Hammond. Alexander Russo's This Week in Education. *Scholastic Administrator.* Retrieved from http://scholasticadministrator.typepad.com/thisweekineducation/2007/12/much-as-i-live.html.

Did You Get It?

Which is a true statement about teacher effectiveness?

a. Teachers can strongly affect their students for the better, even when the school does not.

b. Students' learning is largely determined by their family backgrounds and status.

c. A good curriculum and a safe, orderly environment are inconsequential compared to teacher quality.

d. Teacher influence is dependent upon everything else in that particular school.

Take the full quiz on CourseMate.

In sum, the data supporting the impact of effective teaching practices on student achievement are credible and substantial. Both evidence and experience show that effective teaching requires a set of professional practices different from, yet connected to, the content taught. Although the content knowledge is obviously essential, knowing *how* to teach the content to all types of children makes a measurable difference in student achievement.

InTASC

13-2 Three Perspectives on Learning That Influence Instruction

We have all had classes in which the teacher knew the subject very well but lacked the teaching skills to help you learn it. The relationship between curriculum (the content of education) and pedagogy (the process of teaching) is interdependent. Each factor is necessary but, by itself, is not enough to make an effective teacher. Each teacher's view of how learning occurs influences how he or she ultimately understands and enacts teaching practices.

learning The complex, cognitive process that happens when experience produces a stable change in someone's knowledge or behavior.

behavior The mental and or physical action that a person does in a given situation.

operant conditioning The method used in psychology to reward a partial behavior or a random act that approaches the desired behavior.

In a broad sense, **learning** happens when experience produces a stable change in someone's knowledge or behavior.[29] It is a complex cognitive process. Different theories offer a range of explanations about what learning is and how a teacher produces it in the learner. Three general learning perspectives influence instruction—behavioral, cognitive, and constructivist.

- *Behavioral theories of learning* stress observable changes in behaviors, skills, and habits.
- *Cognitive theories of learning* emphasize internal mental activities such as thinking, remembering, creating, and problem solving.
- *Constructivist theories of learning* focus on how individuals make meaning of events and activities. Learning, therefore, is viewed as the construction of knowledge.

Each perspective's application has different implications for teaching.

13-2a Behavioral Perspective on Learning

Influences on behaviorist thinking B. F. Skinner's (1904–1990) work influenced the behavioral perspective. A psychologist, Skinner defined learning as a change in behavior brought by experience. **Behavior** is simply what a person does in a given situation. Skinner had little concern for the mental or internal processes involved in thinking or for the human psyche. He believed that everything we do and are is shaped by our experience of punishment and reward. According to Skinner, the "mind" (as opposed to the brain) and other such subjective phenomena were simply matters of language; they didn't really exist. Skinner was strictly a behaviorist interested in how external forces influence behavior.

As a psychologist, Skinner experimented with pigeons. He used **operant conditioning** to reward a partial behavior or a random act that approached the desired behavior. For instance, if Skinner wanted a pigeon to turn in a circle to the left, he gave the pigeon a reward for any small movement to the left. When the pigeon caught on ("learned") and turned left to get the reward, Skinner gave the reward only for larger movements to the left, and so on. Soon, the pigeon had turned a complete circle before getting the reward.

Skinner compared this learning with the way children learn to talk. Children receive rewards—such as parents' smiles, laughs, hugs, or getting what they want—for making a sound that resembles a word until they can say the actual word clearly. Likewise, Skinner believed that other complicated tasks could be broken down and taught in this way. He even developed teaching machines so students could learn bit by bit, uncovering answers for an immediate "reward." These machines were quite popular for a while but eventually fell out of favor. Today's computer-based self-instruction uses many of the principles of Skinner's technique.

Behaviorist educators are concerned with the observable indications of learning. Looking for visible cause-and-effect relationships, they consider how external events—antecedents and consequences—change students' observable behaviors. The teacher's job is to modify the students' behavior by setting up situations to reinforce students when they exhibit desired responses. To behaviorists, learning involves a sequence of stimulus and response actions in the learner. By linking together responses involving lower-level skills, teachers can create a learning "chain" to teach students increasingly higher-level skills.

Behaviorist practices Although behaviorist teachers do not treat their students like pigeons, they use sophisticated stimulus-response principles to work with students on learning basic tasks. These include[30]:

- Set clear and specific goals so you know what you want to reinforce.
- Give clear and systematic praise, but only if deserved.
- Recognize genuine accomplishments.
- Attribute students' success to effort and ability (rather than to luck) to build their persistence and confidence.
- Recognize positive behaviors in ways that students value.
- Give plenty of reinforcement when students attempt new materials or skills.
- Use a variety of reinforcers and let students select from among them.
- Structure the learning situation's incentives to remove something students don't like rather than impose consequences they view as punishment. For example, don't assign homework instead of assigning extra homework.
- Adapt the consequence to fit the misbehavior.

Direct instruction model Behaviorist educators support a direct instruction model for teaching students basic skills. Basic skills include science facts, math computation, simple reading, and grammar rules.[31] These skills involve tasks that can be taught step-by-step and assessed by standardized tests. Steps in direct instruction proceed as follows[32]:

1. *Review and check the previous day's work.* Reteach if necessary.
2. *Present new material.* Teach in small steps with many examples and non-examples.
3. *Provide guided practice.* Question students. Give them practice problems and listen for misconceptions. Reteach if necessary. Continue guided practice until students answer approximately 80 percent of the questions correctly.
4. *Give feedback* and corrective information based on students' answers. Reteach if necessary.

5. *Provide independent practice.* Let students apply the new learning on their own, either in seatwork, cooperative groups, or homework. The success rate during independent practice should be approximately 95 percent. Thus the instructional presentation must effectively prepare the students for the solo practice, and assignments must not be too difficult. Students must exercise the skills until they are automatic and the students are confident in their use.
6. *Review weekly and monthly.* Consolidate learning and include some review items as homework. Test often and reteach material missed on the tests.

Criticism of direct instruction Direct instruction critics note that this approach does not work for more complex learning, such as writing creatively, solving intricate problems, or maturing emotionally. It is limited to lower-level objectives, ignores innovative teaching models, and discourages students' independent thought and action. According to these critics, the direct instruction perspective sees the student as an "empty vessel" waiting to be filled with knowledge rather than as an active builder of knowledge.[33]

Answering critics, researchers have produced evidence showing that direct instruction can help students actively learn. Younger and less experienced learners need teacher direction and instruction to avoid developing incomplete and misleading ideas that might otherwise lead to knowledge gaps. In fact, evidence from empirical studies over the past half-century consistently indicates that direct instruction is more effective than less teacher-directed approaches for learning certain knowledge and skills.[34] Deep understanding and fluid performance, whether in solving math problems or analyzing literature, require models of expert performance and extensive practice with feedback—like that available in direct instruction. This instruction is less helpful only when learners have sufficiently high prior knowledge to provide "internal" guidance.[35] When students need to learn specific skills and behaviors, a teaching approach consistent with behavioral learning theory makes sense.

13-2b Cognitive Perspective on Learning

Cognitive research emerged with the mid-twentieth century's computer revolution and breakthroughs in understanding language development. Cognitive psychologists study how people think, learn concepts, and solve problems. They also study how people process information, remember, and forget.

Current cognitive approaches suggest that one of the most important elements in the learning process is what the individual brings to the learning situation. What we already know determines in large part what we will attend to, perceive, learn, remember, and forget.[36] According to this view, knowledge is more than the end result of learning: A student's existing knowledge actually guides and scaffolds new learning.

information processing model A cognitive model based on the analogy between the mind and the computer and includes three storage systems: sensory memory, working (short-term) memory, and permanent (long-term) memory.

Information processing model The **information processing model** illustrates one cognitive perspective of how memory works. This model is based on the analogy between the mind and the computer. It includes three storage systems: sensory memory, working (short-term) memory, and permanent (long-term) memory. Effective teaching can help students to store experiences in permanent memory (learn it).

Figure 13.1 shows the three types of memory—sensory memory, working memory, and permanent memory—and how they interact. Sensory memory deals with temporary storage of data gathered from the senses. Permanent memory contains huge amounts of information stored in such a way that it is available to us. Information may be stored as words, images, sounds, sensations, or in any combination. Permanent memory is where students maintain their background knowledge, both academic and nonacademic. Working memory receives data from sensory memory (where it is held briefly—for approximately 20 seconds), from permanent memory (where it remains permanently), or from both.[37] As long as we focus conscious attention on what we have in working memory, we keep it active. All things being equal, the quality and type of processing that occur in working memory determine whether a particular piece of information will reach permanent memory—and be learned.

FIGURE 13.1 Information Processing Model

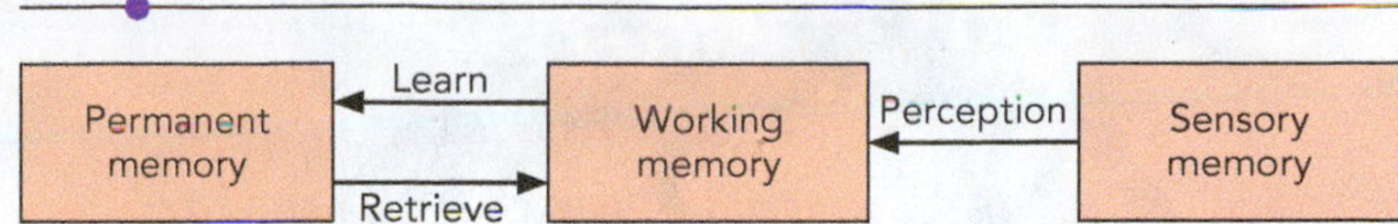

Source: From *Building Background Knowledge for Academic Achievement: Research on What Works in Schools* (Figure 2.3, p 17) Alexandria, VA: ASCD. © 2004 by ASCD. Adapted with permission. Learn more about ASCD at www.ascd.org.

Working memory is, in some ways, like a computer screen. It is what you see and are thinking about at the moment. The more times a student practices or uses the information in working memory, the more likely that information will eventually enter and become embedded in permanent memory, and, therefore, the more likely the student will remember it. In this way, information is learned.

The capacity of working memory is limited to nine new items, or chunks, of meaningful information at one time.[38] Working memory is also fragile. It must keep information activated or the material will be lost.

What happens in working memory makes a big difference in whether students ultimately remember (learn) the information. Each student must process the information multiple times, add details, and make associations with other information. Students need approximately four exposures to information to adequately integrate it into their background knowledge. These exposures should come no more than two days apart.[39]

Nevertheless, practice alone is not enough to ensure that students remember information. Students must use the information in detail and with understanding, making new and varied connections to other meaningful information they already know. **Elaborative rehearsal**, or associating the information students are trying to remember with something they already know, improves working memory and helps move information into permanent memory. Thus, when teachers help students find personal meaning or relevance for something new, that information is more likely to be stored, remembered, and later recalled for use.

elaborative rehearsal
Associating the information students are trying to remember with something they already know.

For example, if students are learning about U.S. nationhood, teachers might ask them to describe how their families celebrate the Fourth of July with parades, picnics, and fireworks. Students could also discuss the meaning of political separation from England as described in the Declaration of Independence. Then, teachers might show the class a DVD about the American Revolution. Students could draw and color pictures or perform skits about Massachusetts patriots masquerading as Native Americans and dumping British tea into Boston Harbor or General George Washington and troops crossing the Delaware River to mount a surprise attack on British troops in Trenton—all the while listening to colonial-era music—to illustrate the idea of fighting for political autonomy. As illustrated by this teaching plan, to get the information and understanding into permanent memory, students must engage in the topic in a variety of ways for more than one class period. Information processing approaches to learning consider the human mind to function as a symbol processing system. We convert sensory input into symbols and then process those symbols into knowledge, which can then be held in memory and retrieved.

The psychology of learning is a major area of educational study and covers many more details than we discuss here. For our purposes, understanding the cognitive processes underlying student learning helps teachers design, deliver, and assess instruction that is more likely to increase student achievement.

H. Mark Weidman Photography/Alamy

A student's existing knowledge guides and scaffolds new learning.

Creating background knowledge In his 2004 book, *Building Background Knowledge for Academic Achievement,* Robert Marzano looks at how academic background knowledge influences students' achievement and how educators can use this fact to help their students learn.[40]

What students learn depends on many factors—the teacher's skill, the students' interest, the content's complexity, and the students' existing knowledge about the subject. Research literature supports the idea that what students already know about the content is one of the strongest indicators of how well they will learn the new information.[41] What a person already knows about a topic is termed his or her **background knowledge**. Many studies have confirmed the relationship between background knowledge and achievement.[42] The reverse relationship also holds true: The less students already know, the less they will probably learn. In other words, the knowledge-rich get knowledge-richer, and the knowledge-poor do not.

background knowledge What a person already knows about a topic.

high fluid intelligence In psychology, an innate, enhanced ability to process and store information in permanent memory.

low fluid intelligence In psychology, an innate, lesser ability to process and store information in permanent memory.

Our ability to process and store information influences the extent to which our experiences create background knowledge. Consider this example: Two students visit the same natural history museum and see the same exhibits. The student with **high fluid intelligence** (an innate, enhanced ability to process and store information in permanent memory) will retain in permanent memory much information about early humans as tool makers, as hunters, and as group members. The student with **low fluid intelligence** (an innate, lesser ability to process and store information in permanent memory), unless there is some educational intervention to help the student focus and make sense of what is viewed, will not. As a result, the student with the enhanced information processing capacity has translated the museum experience into academic background knowledge. What is learned, however, does not depend solely on the amount of experience but also reflects whether individuals can learn from it and do something with that experience.

Likewise, the more opportunities students have to add to their knowledge of content they will find in school, the more academic background knowledge they will have. The student who has visited the museum half a dozen times will have more academic background knowledge than the student who visits the same museum once or the student who never makes a visit.

Differences in students' access to these cognitive capacities and academically oriented experiences will create differences in their academic background knowledge and in their school achievement. Students' family and economic conditions play a large role in providing occasions for them to build education-related experiences. Having few opportunities to gain this information, such as often occurs in low-income families, curbs children's development of academic background knowledge. And as a result, the "achievement gap" is, to a large extent, an opportunity-to-learn gap. Schools and teachers can make a difference in this regard. Teachers can provide students with academically enriching experiences and teach them cognitive techniques to increase their attention and learning when they follow certain guidelines.

Guiding principles Guiding principles of the cognitive approach to teaching include:

- Make sure to have the students' attention.
- Guide perception and attention by connecting it to students' prior knowledge.
- Help students focus on the most important information.
- Present information in an organized and clear manner.
- Help students connect new information to what they already know.
- Recognize and use strategies to overcome the limitations in students' background resources and knowledge that restrain learning.
- Provide students with opportunities to learn meaningful and relevant vocabulary to build background knowledge.
- Provide opportunities for students to read and discuss relevant information in class with other students to further build their background knowledge.
- Give students opportunities to build their background knowledge through virtual experiences.
- Offer opportunities for students to use both verbal stories and visual images.
- Provide for review and repetition of information in varied ways.
- Teach students how to use learning strategies and specific techniques to increase their learning.
- Focus on meaning to the student, not memorization.

Criticism of the cognitive perspective Although the cognitive revolution added "meaning" to the behaviorists' focus on human's external factors,[43] the cognitive perspective has its critics. Evidence shows that the "mind as a computer" metaphor is not wholly correct. It discounts the mind's plasticity and downplays the varied events that influence children in infancy and early childhood, which greatly separate their learning capacities and background knowledge in later life.[44] Then, too, individual genetic and environmental differences exist in cognitive capacity and development.[45] Other cognitive critics argue among themselves about the finer points of biology and psychology as they apply to learning, such as whether cognitive development is more individual or social in nature.[46]

13-2c Constructivist Perspective on Learning

Constructivist learning theories address how individuals make events meaningful to themselves. The constructivist perspective suggests that learners create their own new understandings based on an interaction between what they already know and believe and the information and ideas with which they come into contact. Learning is a self-regulated process of resolving inner cognitive conflicts—by making meaningful connections between familiar knowledge and beliefs and the new data.[47] In this view, learning is seen as the student's cognitive construction of knowledge.

Drawing on a synthesis of current work in cognitive psychology, philosophy, and anthropology, constructivist theory defines knowledge as temporary, developmental, and socially and culturally mediated. Depending on their experiences, knowledge, and their intellectual structures at the time, individuals will develop a unique understanding of a given presentation. Research shows that people remember an experience based on what their preexisting knowledge and cognitive structures allow them to find relevant and absorb—regardless of the teacher's intentions or the quality of the explanation.[48]

No single constructivist theory of learning exists, but rather multiple constructivist approaches. Understanding learning by any theory or teaching method requires understanding the constructivist ideas.

Influences on constructivist thinking Swiss scholar Jean Piaget (1896–1980) studied children's cognitive development, including how they form knowledge. He viewed the mind as a dynamic set of mental structures that help us make sense of what we perceive. Through maturation and experience, children lay the cerebral groundwork for new mental frameworks.[49]

Early progressive movements championed "child-centered" approaches and advocated much the same instructional philosophy as constructivists do today. In the late 1800s, Francis Parker led reforms in Quincy, Massachusetts, and at Chicago's Cook County Normal School that emphasized **learning in context**—that is, learning in settings where the knowledge naturally occurs.[50] Parker took his students on outings across the local countryside (literally, field trips) to learn geography rather than asking them to memorize and recite countries and capitals from a book. Similarly, his students created their own stories for "reading leaflets," which replaced both the formal primers and the rote learning that went with them.[51]

learning in context Learning in settings where the knowledge naturally occurs.

Similarly, John Dewey routinely used the common childhood experiences as starting points for drawing his students into the more sophisticated forms of knowledge represented in the academic disciplines.[52]

All learning is constructivist In reality, students are always constructing knowledge, and all learning is constructivist.[53] That is the way the human mind works, even when students are placed in rote learning situations (such as drill and practice) or in passive situations (such as lecture classes).[54] Because all pedagogy results in some kind of mental "construction" by learners if they are to remember any of it, it is technically inappropriate to identify particular approaches to teaching as "constructivist."

"Constructivist pedagogy," therefore, is less a teaching model than a descriptor for instructional strategies.[55] A host of labels for general teaching approaches are anchored in a constructivist philosophy. Among these are "teaching for understanding,"[56] "teaching for meaning,"[57] "authentic pedagogy,"[58] "progressive pedagogy,"[59] "child-centered teaching,"[60] and "transformative teaching."[61] Other models exist within specific subject areas. As can be seen, constructivist ideas are less a teaching approach than a range of instructional strategies that fit within many teaching models.

Learning occurs when fresh information prompts us to rethink prior ideas.

Terrie L. Zeller/Shutterstock.com

Constructing understanding We construct, or build, our own understandings of the world in which we live as we interact with the world; reflect on our experiences with people, objects, and ideas; and draw conclusions. We synthesize our new experiences with what we have previously come to understand. Through this process, we create meaning for ourselves. This is human nature.

When an object, an idea, a relationship, or an event does not make sense to us, we respond in one of two ways. First, we may interpret what we see so that it fits within our present set of mental rules for explaining and ordering the world. Alternatively, we may generate an expanded or new set of rules that makes better sense for what we perceive to be occurring. Either way, our perceptions and mental rules constantly interact to shape our understandings, and both approaches contribute to learning.

For example, the first time a child visits the beach and tastes the salty ocean water, the child experiences water that tastes different from what he or she understands "water" from the home's tap or store-bought bottle to be. The new experience of "water" does not fit with prior understanding. The child must either build an expanded or new understanding of "water" (it can be salty) to accommodate the new ocean water experience or ignore the new information and keep the original understanding of water (the ocean is wet but it is not real water). Most likely, this experience and reflection lead to a new understanding in the way the child thinks about water.

Learning, therefore, entails not discovering more, but rather interpreting events through a more complex mental schema. The more mature we become, the more sophisticated our understanding and meaning we give to people, events, and ideas. To wit, a teen might understand the chemical concept of salinity and apply it to ocean water. A physics student might study how salt solutions conduct electricity. Each level of understanding increases thinking's complexity.

In brief, authentic construction of knowledge involves applying, manipulating, interpreting, or analyzing prior knowledge in relation to new information to solve a problem that cannot be solved simply by routine retrieval or reproduction of what we already know.[62] Such mental activity creates learning.

Constructivist instruction Traditionally, American schools viewed learning as the process of students receiving and repeating (aloud or on written tests) newly presented information as evidence of learning. Constructivist instructional practices, in contrast, deliberately help learners to internalize and reshape new information into new understandings. Deep understanding occurs when fresh information prompts students to develop or enhance cognitive structures that enable them to rethink and expand their prior ideas. Constructivist instruction does not look for what students can unthinkingly repeat, but rather for what students comprehend and can do with the information to demonstrate their understanding.

Compare a traditional with a constructivist approach to learning in a middle school classroom studying the Civil War. On the one hand, a teacher using the traditional approach might require students to write reports on the Battle of the Wilderness. Typically, these reports will paraphrase encyclopedia or Internet sites' battle accounts. The student might copy and paste related pictures into the report to illustrate the narrative. On the other hand, a teacher using constructivist techniques might assign students to imagine that they are soldiers in the battle and write a detailed letter home telling their mothers or sweethearts about it. First, the class listens to a variety of Civil War-era music, such as "Dixie," "Battle Hymn of the Republic," and "Home! Sweet Home!" and discusses how these melodies and words may have impacted the frightened, homesick, or bored young soldiers away from home and on the battle field. Such first-hand experiences will help students gain a personal feel for the times and what it may have been like for the combatants. Students would then gather the information about the combat from various sources, coordinate versions from different perspectives, draw their own conclusions, personalize the information, and generate a written product. In this way, students in a constructivist classroom learn by repeatedly considering the content from a variety of viewpoints, determining its relevance to them, and using information in purposefully meaningful ways.

TeachSource Video 13.1

Classroom Motivation: Strategies for Engaging Today's Students

Constructivist learning can motivate students when teachers consider who students are, what they know, and what they need to know. This seventh-grade teacher engages students in the curriculum by drawing on their prior experiences with hip-hop culture, film, and current events as he teaches a lesson on civil rights pioneer, Rosa Parks. Watch the video clips, study the artifacts in the case, and reflect on the following questions:

1. How is knowing students as individuals and as learners help teachers find ways to motivate students' interest in learning the curriculum?
2. How does the teacher use the students' own prior knowledge to build their awareness and motivate their interest in Rosa Parks and the civil rights themes inside the classroom?
3. What does the teacher do and say that creates a safe and respectful learning environment in which children can feel comfortable sharing their ideas and experiences?
4. How does the teacher use the students' own vocabulary to teach academic vocabulary?

Watch on CourseMate.

Teachers and students In constructivist classrooms, teachers make instructional choices that deliberately connect students' own questions and interests to the curriculum.[63] Teachers combine their understanding of how students learn with their own professional knowledge of a specific discipline to build a framework for instruction. They encourage students to respond to texts and to one another, guiding students' attention and lending a "structuring consciousness" that helps students to think in increasingly complex ways about a range of possible perspectives. Research supports the belief that teachers in a constructivist classroom need to know their subjects well.[64]

Because constructivist instruction asks for more active learner involvement, many students are not comfortable with it. They are accustomed to the lecture/discussion method, in which they sit back and "absorb" information, investing minimal effort or attention to the learning process. Participating in a constructivist classroom, by comparison, requires a greater intellectual and energy commitment from both teachers and students. It takes trust, time, experience, and the teacher's persistence in asking interesting questions, respecting and accepting the variety of student responses, and aligning students' thinking and work before students will find relevance and personal meaning to understand and use what they are learning.[65]

Assessment in constructivist instruction Because every student develops meaning differently, teachers who follow the constructivist path must ensure that every student understands the information correctly. Students' constructed meaning cannot be completely idiosyncratic, but rather must make sense or be verified by the larger public.[66] Ongoing, informal assessments are a means of checking for accurate understanding. Teachers can ask students questions to answer aloud or in writing and have students provide written products or artifacts that express their understanding.

In addition to written exams, constructivist assessment methods may include clinical interviews, observations, student journals, peer reviews, research reports, construction of physical models, or performance in the form of inquiries, plays, debates, dances, or artistic renderings.[67] Such artifacts and performances require clear, well-designed, flexible evaluation rubrics, or specific criteria for increasingly successful completion. When teachers design these rubrics in conjunction with students, the process makes explicit what is valued in the learning process and how evidentiary criteria are linked to these values.

Principles of constructivist instruction In constructivist classrooms, the following principles apply[68]:

- Students enjoy frequent opportunities to engage in complex, meaningful, problem-based activities.

- Teachers are familiar with students' prior knowledge and use it to help students assimilate new information by explaining or meaningfully extending their own experiences.[69]
- Teachers elicit students' ideas and experiences in relation to key topics, and then fashion learning situations that help students elaborate or restructure their current knowledge to include the new content.
- Teachers provide students with a variety of information resources as well as the tools—technological and conceptual—necessary to advance their learning.
- Teachers make their own thinking processes explicit to learners and encourage students to do the same through dialog, writing, drawings, and other representations.
- Students are routinely asked to apply knowledge in diverse and authentic contexts—for example, to explain ideas, interpret texts, predict phenomena, and construct arguments based on evidence, rather than to focus on finding the predetermined "right" answer.
- Teachers offer opportunities for students to work collaboratively and use extended conversation, writing, and other expressive forms to think through and communicate information so it is accurate, makes sense, and has meaning.[70]
- Teachers use a variety of assessment strategies to understand how students' ideas are evolving and to give feedback on both the processes and the products of their thinking.[71]
- In addition to being an instructor, the teacher becomes a coach, guide, facilitator, and "mentor in a cognitive apprenticeship" who inspires and nudges students to do the active mental work of learning.[72]
- The classroom environment exemplifies the norms of trust, high expectations for intellectual accomplishment, and collaboration for students and teachers alike.

Comparing traditional and constructivist classrooms Not all valuable learning occurs through a constructivist process. Other types of learning, such as rote learning, have important roles as well. The instructional challenge is knowing when to use which approach. Nevertheless, all learning is somewhat constructivist in nature because learners are continually integrating new information with old as they try to learn.

Table 13.1 illustrates how the constructivist and traditional classrooms compare in terms of teaching and learning.

Positive research support Research studies have found positive results from students whose teachers use constructivist instructional practices. The National Research Council (NRC) states, "One of the hallmarks of the new science of learning is its emphasis on learning with understanding."[73] Likewise, a constructivist instructional approach can increase students' scores on standardized achievement tests. After conducting a rigorous study of 669 classrooms in 34 schools, the Washington School Research Center reported that a strong relationship exists between constructivist instructional practices and student achievement on the Washington Assessment of Student Learning (WASL).[74] The constructivist instruction predicts student achievement even beyond the effects of family income.

Assessment expert Mike Schmoker describes diverse schools in varied settings that use constructivist instructional practices that result in student success on exams.[75] Additionally, a comparative study of college environmental science courses using identical materials, learning resources, student questionnaires, and examinations reports that "students in constructivist classes performed significantly better on exams, rated the course higher, and participated more in campus and regional environmental support efforts than students in traditional

TABLE 13.1

Comparison of Traditional and Constructivist Classrooms

Traditional Classrooms	Constructivist Classrooms
Teacher presents curriculum part to whole with emphasis on facts and basic skills.	Teacher presents curriculum whole to part with emphasis on big ideas and concepts.
Teacher values presenting the fixed curriculum.	Teacher encourages and values students questioning the curriculum.
Teacher asks students closed-ended questions with one right answer.	Teacher asks students open-ended questions with several "correct" answers.
Classroom focus is on the teacher and the information.	Classroom focus is on the students and information and helping them make the information personally meaningful.
The "right answer" is the fact or perspective presented by the teacher or the textbook.	Complex questions have multiple perspectives; truth is sometimes a matter of interpretation based in evidence.
Instructional activities rely heavily on textbooks and worksheets.	Instructional activities rely heavily on primary data sources and hands-on experiences with materials.
Students are considered passive vessels into which the teacher "pours" information.	Students are viewed as thinkers with emerging ideas about the world based on experience, evidence, and reason.
Teachers generally lecture students to give them information.	Teachers generally interact with students about the information.
Teachers seek correct answers to validate student learning.	Teachers seek students' viewpoints as well as correct information to understand students' ideas for use in later lessons.
Teachers view assessment of student learning as separate from teaching; assessment occurs almost entirely by testing.	Assessment of student learning is interwoven with teaching and occurs throughout via teacher observations of students at work, student performances, exhibitions, portfolios, and written tests.
Students work primarily alone.	Students work both alone and in groups.
Goal is for students to remember the information as presented to correctly answer test questions.	Goal is for students to make the new information personally meaningful so they will remember, recall, and use the information during and after the test.

Source: Adapted from Brooks, J. G., and Brooks, M. G. (1993). *In search of understanding: The case for constructivist classrooms.* Alexandra, VA: Association for Supervision and Curriculum Development, p. 17.

classes."[76] Clearly, a relationship exists between students' high achievement and the use of constructivist teaching approaches in their classrooms.

Although constructivist instruction produces noteworthy student achievement gains, constructivist instruction is not widespread. It is especially rare in urban schools.[77] One study found that constructivist instructional practices were evident in only 17 percent of the observed classrooms, and found a negative correlation between constructivist teaching and school-level family income.[78] In short, students from wealthier family backgrounds were more likely to have teachers who used instructional practices that encouraged making their learning meaningful than were students from less affluent families.

Constructivist criticisms and answers Constructivist critics argue that constructivism is not a theory of teaching, that it suffers from a large disconnect between theory and practice, that it subordinates the curriculum to students' interests, and that it is inappropriate for teaching students from low-income and minority cultures. Let's consider these claims.

First, critics contend that constructivism is a theory of learning and not a theory of teaching. As a result, teachers can use any practices that they call "constructivist" but that may not involve either teaching or learning.[79] These critics are correct.

Next, critics point to a substantial disconnect between constructivist theory and its practice.[80] Critics claim that some advocates overgeneralize the constructivist concept and misapply it in learning situations. These critics are also correct. Mistaken beliefs such as "teachers should not be the experts," "teachers should not lecture to transmit information," "memorizing is always bad," and "students' idiosyncratic constructed meaning is more important than the 'official' knowledge" all misinterpret constructivist theory.

Widespread misconceptions about constructivist instruction *do* lead to poor teaching practices. Learning is an active process, but this does not mean that teachers should rarely, if ever, "teach" content to students.[81] In fact, lecture is a legitimate teaching methodology that can be stimulating and highly effective depending on the teacher's goals, the curriculum to be learned, the teacher's particular talents, and the students' characteristics.[82]

Likewise, rote learning is not always bad. It has the advantage of automatizing aspects of problem solving, thereby freeing the mind for more abstract thought. A student who has memorized the meaning of certain vocabulary words can more competently read and understand an essay that uses those words than a student who must constantly stop and look through a dictionary.[83] And isn't it faster and easier to compute several digit math problems after we have memorized the times table?

Additionally, in their early stages of understanding, many educators naively place too much faith in students' abilities to structure their own learning.[84] They erroneously equate student interest and classroom involvement as sufficient—rather than necessary—conditions for worthwhile learning. Activities, as opposed to ideas, are their starting points for planning, and they mistakenly give little thought to an activity's intellectual implications.[85] Students' mastery of the content and ability to use it effectively in a variety of contexts is the ultimate goal, and the official curriculum remains the driver.

Finally, critics question whether constructivist teaching practices impose an inappropriate culture and instructional approach on students who are not a part of the dominant society.[86] These critics are confused. Although constructivism's psychological roots are certainly Western, liberal, and individualistic (Eurocentric), and although much of the current U.S. constructivist pedagogy was developed for teaching more affluent students, the lack of widespread constructivist instruction in low-income schools may have several causes.

To begin, many studies find that today's students of color and those from low-income families often have the least experienced and least qualified teachers, have only limited access to intellectually challenging curriculum, and are most likely to be taught in large classes in big, impersonal schools.[87] In classrooms where teachers are not familiar with students' interests and life experiences, they fail to build on local knowledge and may actually "disinvite" students to participate in classroom discussion.[88] In addition, because

Reflect & Discuss

Understanding how learning occurs influences how one teaches. The three learning theories discussed here—behavioral, cognitive, and constructivist—have their own perspectives on how students learn and the instructional strategies to best accomplish this goal. Which aspects of each might advance students' development of twenty-first-century skills?

A. Separate into three groups. Each group should be assigned one of the three learning theories—behaviorist, cognitive, and constructivist.
B. Working with the other members of your group, identify, list, and describe the key beliefs, advantages, and disadvantages of the learning theory assigned.
C. Identify and discuss the learning situations (regarding content and learners) in which this approach is best used.
D. Working as a group, deliver a three-minute presentation about your assigned learning theory to the class using the practices that your learning theory advances.
E. Come together as a class to discuss these three learning theories and their contributions to instructional practice.
F. Discuss which aspects of each learning approach would likely increase—or limit—the students' development of twenty-first-century skills and explain your reasons.
G. Decide under which learning theory you learn best, and give examples.

communication patterns differ from one cultural group to another,[89] and because constructivist teaching relies on students communicating in a variety of ways, middle-class white teachers may find it difficult to work with the discourse patterns favored by various ethnic and racial minorities,[90] and vice versa.

The constructive approach works best when learners have sufficiently high levels of prior knowledge to provide "internal guidance."[91] As discussed previously, studies show that low-income and minority students often have the least academic background knowledge as compared with more affluent students. For this reason, low-income and minority students need teachers who can actively structure their learning and provide essential background knowledge until the students gain the skills and knowledge store to do increasingly more themselves.

Urban teachers may incorrectly believe that because their students are so lacking in basic skills, they should be teaching for memorization and transmission of basic facts and skills rather than teaching for concepts, generalizations, connections, personal meaning, and deep understanding—all of which will actually motivate student learning and skill development. These factors argue for educators to find ways to make constructivist learning possible for minority and low-income students rather than to deprive these students of opportunities to learn in meaningful ways. Seeking equity and maintaining high expectations for all students' learning requires teachers to use constructivist, meaning-making learning approaches with minority and low-income students—indeed, with all students.

Effective teachers use a blend of constructivist, behavioral, and cognitive learning theories. One instructional approach does not fit all content with all students in all situations. Nevertheless, teachers with a strong knowledge base who understand how students learn will find many opportunities to use constructivist instruction approaches to ensure that their students learn to understand and apply concepts and skills in relevant ways—both inside and outside the classroom.

Did You Get It?

What happens when experience produces a relatively permanent change in knowledge or behavior?

- **a.** Education.
- **b.** Training.
- **c.** Instruction.
- **d.** Learning.

Take the full quiz on CourseMate.

13-3 Key Factors That Allow Teachers to Provide High-Quality Instruction

Although effective teachers make instruction look easy, it isn't. Effective teaching takes considerable preparation to identify the appropriate content for study, design and conduct the learning activities and their related assessments, and establish a classroom culture that supports learning. Teachers invest many hours preparing for quality instruction and learning. After delivering their lessons, teachers reflect professionally on what has occurred and make adjustments for the next day (or the next class period) as well as for the next time they teach that or other lessons.

13-3a What Effective Teaching Looks Like

Charlotte Danielson, an education writer and consultant based in Princeton, New Jersey, has developed a framework for teaching that clearly represents all aspects of a teacher's daily responsibilities. Derived from the most recent theoretical and empirical research about teaching, her framework offers a "roadmap" to accomplished teaching and classroom organization practices.[92] We use portions of this model to guide understanding of what effective instruction looks like.

Danielson's instructional framework is public, generic, and holistic, and it fits any effective teaching methodology. She assumes that teaching is purposeful and professional. It is each teacher's responsibility, using the resources at hand, to have students learn important concepts and skills. Additionally, because the framework model is tied to actual teaching practices and is supported by a solid research background, increasing numbers of U.S. school districts currently use it for teachers' supervision, evaluation, and professional development.[93] Studies have consistently determined that teachers' ratings based on Davidson's rubric are positively and significantly related to student achievement.[94]

In this section, we discuss several essential behaviors that teachers use in planning and preparation, building a receptive classroom environment, delivering effective instruction, and conducting useful reflection. All of these aspects are key parts of effective instruction.

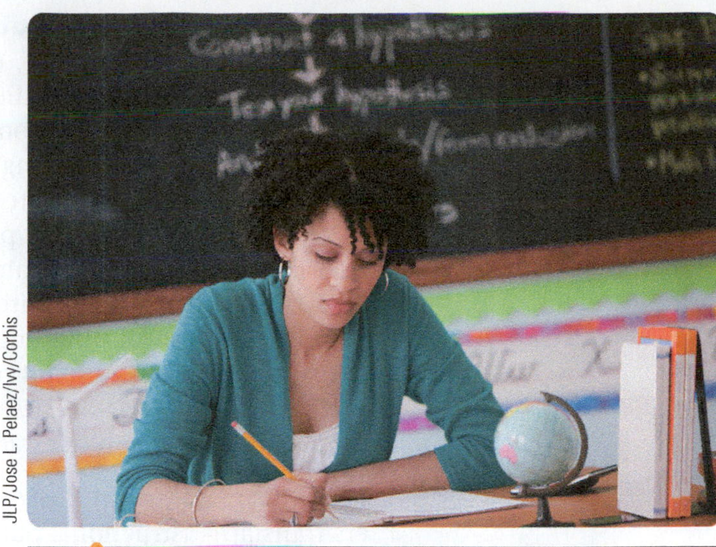
JLP/Jose L. Pelaez/Ivy/Corbis

Planning for high-quality instruction and a supportive classroom culture takes time.

13-3b Planning and Preparing for Teaching

During planning and preparing, teachers organize the content to be learned into a sequence of activities and exercises that make it accessible for students. At the same time, teachers design assessment techniques that reflect the instructional goals and document and evaluate student progress both during and after the teaching process.[95] Teachers also think about the different students in the class, their backgrounds, interests, and prior learning and decide what information, references, or activities would best connect them with the content to be learned and motivate them to learn it.

Knowing content and pedagogy Teachers cannot teach what they do not know. When teachers know their subjects well, they tend to recognize which questions will interest their students and produce greater understanding. Teachers also identify where students are likely to become confused or make mistakes—such as the difference between area and perimeter in mathematics—so they can anticipate and prevent common student misperceptions.

Knowing the subject matter well is not enough, however. Teachers need to know which instructional techniques will work best for ensuring that students learn their content. Instructional practices must reflect current research on best pedagogical approaches within the discipline and require the teacher to continue professional learning.[96]

Knowledge of students Effective teachers understand their students. Each age group has certain developmental characteristics—intellectual, social, physical, and emotional. Teachers must understand these general characteristics as well as individual exceptions that appear in their classrooms. Teachers need to be aware of their students' prior knowledge and the possible knowledge gaps, misunderstandings, and misconceptions that might interfere with learning—and provide learning activities to remedy these.

Students vary individually in terms of their interests, talents, backgrounds, and preferred learning styles. Teachers need to recognize and understand these individual differences. Building on students' interests and strengths, teachers can connect them with the new content as well as develop a positive personal rapport. In this way, teachers address both the group as a whole and the individuals within it.

Selecting instructional outcomes Teaching is purposeful. Instructional outcomes must be worthwhile, clear, relate to what the students are intended to learn, reflect a balance of different learning types, and be suitable for diverse learners. Instructional outcomes must represent learning central to a discipline as well as high-level learning for the students. They must also account for the district's curriculum and state standards, requirements of external mandates such as state testing or voluntary programs like Advanced Placement or International Baccalaureate exams, and community expectations.

Teachers need to explicitly state these educational purposes in terms of student learning rather than student activity. The key question to ask is, "What will the students *learn* as a result of the instructional engagement?"—not just "What will the students *do*?"[97] These goals should be intellectually challenging and be capable of assessment to established performance standards.

Designing coherent instruction Through their instructional design, teachers translate instructional outcomes into students' learning experiences. The sequence of these activities should be logical, progressing from easier to harder, simpler to more complex, from attention in one learning area to integration across several areas.[98] "Easier" and "simpler," however, do not equate to "lower in intellectual level." The teacher's challenge is to find the meaningful and relevant connections to the student's prior learning before moving on to cover more complex material—building a bridge from what the student already knows and understands to incorporate the new knowledge and skills.

Because instructional outcomes vary, instructional strategies vary as well. Teaching students the steps in the scientific method is different from teaching students the procedure for cleaning lab beakers. Some lessons consist of demonstrations, whereas others have students work collaboratively on problem solving using the new information or skills. Accordingly, the teacher's role each day varies along with instructional goals, students' activities, and grouping strategies.

Activities and assignments that promote student learning emphasize thinking and apply problem solving to real situations, permit a degree of student choice and initiative, and encourage depth (cognitive challenge) rather than breadth (superficiality).

Designing student assessments Assessment plays a central role in learning. It has two related, but separate, uses:

- Assessment determines whether students have achieved the instructional outcomes established during planning. This is assessment *of* learning.
- Assessment provides teachers and students with valuable information to guide future (later in this class period or tomorrow's) learning. This is assessment *for* learning.

Assessment requires clear criteria and standards about how it will evaluate students' work. Ideally, assessment methods should be part of the students' learning activities and should reflect real-world applications of knowledge and understanding. These approaches motivate student interest and efforts and give teachers deeper insight into how well students are learning.

InTASC

13-3c Building a Receptive Classroom Environment

Establishing a classroom environment that supports student learning involves building relationships anchored in mutual respect and rapport. When a teacher has a good relationship with students, those students are more likely to accept the teacher's rules, procedures, and disciplinary actions and will want to learn from (and for) this teacher. Establishing a classroom culture for learning includes managing classroom procedures and student behaviors.

Creating an environment of respect and rapport An environment of warm mutual respect allows all students to feel safe and valued. Students know that the teacher and the other students will treat them with dignity—whether they learn rapidly or with additional supports. This emotional and physical safety allows students to take the intellectual and affective risks necessary to learn. Classrooms characterized by respect and rapport are friendly, open, and frequently humorous places, but teachers always remain the adults.

In learning environments, teachers' caring may be cloaked under a firm manner and business-like atmosphere. Students appreciate the difference between genuine adult caring and permissiveness. They know that their teachers express their concern by insisting that all students achieve well, behave well, and not just "get by." Of course, caring takes many different forms. What is suitable for kindergarten students may be highly inappropriate for high school students. Teachers' personalities also vary, which greatly influence their classroom environments .

To maintain a classroom of mutually respectful relationships, teachers need an appropriate mental set. In particular, they need "withitness" and emotional objectivity.[99]

Withitness means being "with it"—being aware of what is happening in all parts of the classroom at all times by continuously scanning the classroom. It also means intervening promptly and accurately when inappropriate behavior threatens to become disruptive, especially when the teacher is working with a small group or an individual student.

Emotional objectivity means that teachers keep an even temper and calm demeanor. They are friendly, helpful, and congenial. They do not become visibly upset if students violate classroom rules, react negatively to disciplinary actions, or do not respond to the teacher's attempts to develop a relationship.[100] Teachers remain "matter of fact," not personalizing student mistakes or misbehaviors.

withitness Being aware of what is happening in all parts of the classroom at all times by continuously scanning it and intervening promptly and accurately when necessary to maintain a positive learning environment.

emotional objectivity The quality of keeping an even temper, calm, and friendly manner.

Establishing a classroom culture for learning Classrooms characterized by a culture for learning are intellectually active places where teachers and students alike value the work. Teachers show a genuine enthusiasm for their subject and demonstrate respect and caring for their students. Students accept their teachers' insistence on high-quality work. Although the speed of mastering the content may vary among students, all are expected to learn the high-challenge curriculum. Both parties take pride in their achievements. All teachers have the responsibility to establish such a climate in their classroom.

Classrooms with cultures for learning balance academic challenge with instructional support. Students want work that stretches but not overwhelms them. They expect to work hard and see success at the end of their journey. At the same time, good teachers provide a variety of supports by explaining the material until everyone understands and giving students varied learning experiences—and occasionally extra time after or before class—through which to master the information or skills.[101]

A culture for learning encourages persistence—for students and teachers alike. Teachers are always searching for what works best with each student. They persist in trying to meet the individual needs of the problem student, the gifted student, the student with disabilities, the English language learner, and the frequently neglected pupil, all of whom are too often underserved.[102]

Managing classroom procedures An effective teacher plans and prepares for the classroom's organization with the same care and attention to detail he or she devotes to designing high-quality lessons. Classroom procedures and routines for

FlipSides

Teaching: Art or Science?

Is teaching an art or a science? Over the years, many have debated whether good teachers rely on native instinct and in-the-moment spontaneous behaviors to engage students in powerful learning or whether good teachers rely on a systematic, predictable set of choices based in research and experience. Read the debate below and decide where you stand on this issue.

Effective teaching is an art.	Effective teaching is a science.
■ Great teachers are born, not made.	● Teaching is an applied science derived from research in human learning and behavior that can be learned.
■ Teaching involves complex judgments that unfold during the instructional process. Teachers must deal creatively with the unexpected in the moment, often relying on tacit knowledge from prior experiences.	● Teaching has an explicit knowledge base in the social sciences that provides a basic structure that can be learned, is open to new evidence, and can guide teachers' decisions and behaviors about practice.
■ Teaching requires spontaneity and intuition activated on the spot to fuel new clarifying insights and creativity.	● Teaching is a sequential, predictable, rational, step-by-step process in an identifiable cause-and-effect relationship with learning.
■ Effective teaching is affective, flexible, and expressive, responding to events in the moment and communicating in ways that actively engage learners in learning.	● Effective teaching is rational and logical, observing and analyzing the environment as a means to planning and making the appropriate instructional decisions to actively engage learners in learning.
■ The best research can do is tell us which strategies have a good chance of working well with students, but individual classroom teachers must determine which strategies to use with the right student at the right time.	● Intuition is functional but inarticulate knowledge that cannot travel well; it cannot be transmitted to others, it must be invented anew in each situation, and it cannot be depended on to appear in all situations.
■ Teaching skills cannot all be pre-learned and rehearsed. They must respond to events in the moment.	● Effective teaching behaviors can be taught, learned, and improved with conscious practice, observation, and feedback and is generalizable to all content areas.
■ Teaching is holistic, considering the complex interactions among the teacher, the situation, the content, and the learner that cannot be fully understood in making any decisions and behaviors about practice.	● An effective teaching model, and teacher practice and feedback using it, can guide successful teacher behavior regardless of the content, learners' age, socioeconomic status, or ethnicity.
■ Much art involves science. Artists know the nature of their materials and their effects singly or combined; they know how to use media to convey emotion and experience; and they actively critique their work to generate feedback to improve performance.	● Much science involves art. Teachers learn and apply a set of research-based principles and rules but use art in situations when rules don't work and teachers must improvise. Effective teaching can be, but is not always, an art.

Effective teaching is both an art *and* a science. The science of teaching, the knowledge base, provide the basic structure from which teachers' creativity and artistry can emerge. In short, teaching is a science; what you do with it is an art. Effective teachers need them both.

Sources: Brandt, R. (1985, February). On teaching and supervising: A conversation with Madeline Hunter. *Educational Leadership 42*(5), 61–68; Costa, A. L. (1984). A reaction to Hunter's knowing, teaching, and supervising. In P. L. Hosford (Ed.), *Using what we know about teaching. 1984 ASCD Yearbook*. Alexandria, VA: ASCD, pp. 196–203; Hunter, M. (1984). Knowing, teaching, and supervising. In P. L. Hosford (Ed.), *Using what we know about teaching. 1984 ASCD Yearbook*. Alexandria, VA: ASCD, pp. 169–195; Hunter, M. (1979, October). Teaching is decision making. *Educational Leadership 37*(1), 62–67; Hunter, M. (1985, February). What's wrong with Madeline Hunter? *Educational Leadership 42*(5), 57–60; Lambert, L. (1985, February). Who is right—Madeline Hunter or Art Costa? *Educational Leadership* 42(5), 68–69.

distributing materials, moving students into workgroups, and taking attendance; thoughtful room arrangements; and effective discipline make a classroom run smoothly.

Teachers must appreciate the relationship between instruction and student conduct. When students are engaged in work they find meaningful and experience success in learning, they are not interested in disturbing the class. However, if students are bored or worried that they will be embarrassed or humiliated, they may prefer to disrupt the class and distract others from learning. For such students, having the teacher send them out of the class is preferable to "looking foolish" in front of their peers. When teachers make learning more interesting, relevant, and successful for students, students can be intellectually and successfully challenged.

13-3d Instruction for Student Engagement

Although thoughtful planning and development of the appropriate classroom environment are essential components of teaching, *instruction*—the interaction between the teacher, students, and content—is the main event. With instruction, teachers put their plans for connecting students with content and their positive learning environment into action.

Instruction is a constellation of related behaviors. To engage students in the learning process, teachers must provide clear directions and explanations. They must skillfully use questioning and discussion and integrate assessment strategies into their instruction. Teachers must be flexible and responsive if they are to ensure learning opportunities for all students. Lastly, they must continuously reflect on their professional practice in an ongoing effort to improve their expertise and ability to help all students learn.

Communicating with students Teachers' clear and accurate communications tell their students what they will be learning, why it is important, and what students will be doing to learn it. Students need unambiguous and accurate directions and procedures to guide their work and to prevent them from losing time by flailing about without knowing what to do or by starting the wrong activity.

Next, teachers must communicate clearly with students about the new content. As part of the lesson, teachers may need to present key background knowledge (information or vocabulary) to make the new lesson personally meaningful and relevant to the students. They can present the new information in many different ways—orally, visually, or through discussion. No matter which strategy is used, the language and concepts must be appropriate to the students' ages and background and the specific discipline. Of course, teachers' language should always demonstrate correct usage and contain expressive vocabulary.

poor questions Questions that ask students to give short-answer, low-level thinking response to assess their learning.

Effective instruction has a powerful influence on student learning.

kali9/iStockphoto.com

Using questioning and discussion techniques Teachers' skills in questioning and leading discussions can help students explore new concepts, elicit evidence of student understanding, and promote deeper student intellectual engagement.

Poor questions tend to ask students primarily to engage in short-answer, low-level recall thinking as a way to see what they know after they have completed their homework or reading assignment. Poor questions are boring or narrow. Only a few students have the right answers. The teacher has a single correct answer in mind, even though several accurate answers are possible.

effective questions Questions that promote complex thinking.

wait time The interval that teachers give students to process the information before they must respond to a question.

student engagement The pupils' meaningful cognitive involvement with the content or active construction of understanding.

Effective questions, by comparison, rarely require a simple "yes," "no," or few-words response. Instead, they promote thinking by inviting students to formulate hypotheses, make connections between familiar concepts and new material, or challenge previously held views. Even when the question has a limited number of right answers—for instance, "Which different coins can you use to make 17 cents?"—an effective question is likely to encourage student thinking and extend learning.

Thinking of possible answers takes time. Experienced teachers allow students **wait time** to process the information before they must respond to a question and encourage all students to participate. Teachers often probe a student's answer, looking for clarification or elaboration with prompts such as "Could you give me an example of that?" or "Would you tell me more about what you mean?" These follow-up questions encourage students to think more deeply and convey respect for students and their ideas.

Engaging students in learning Learning is a minds-on activity. **Student engagement** requires cognitive involvement with the content or active construction of understanding. The quality of student engagement results from carefully planning the learning experiences. "Engagement" is not the same as being "busy" or spending "time-on-task." Students may be completing a worksheet and be "on task" but not mentally engaged in significant learning.

Engagement must make sense to learners. Teachers continually help students make sense of and find meaning in what they are learning by connecting the content at hand to things students know and value—their prior knowledge, interests, concerns, and experiences. Teachers help students see connections among ideas by using examples known to students and by linking the content with their lives to emphasize its relevance.[103]

Physical materials may also encourage student engagement in learning. When students work with physical representations, such as using hands-on manipulatives in elementary school mathematics to understand place value, they are more likely to literally see and feel how the concept works. Of course, physical materials do not guarantee intellectual engagement: Hands-on must also be minds-on.

As discussed earlier, research has shown that learning requires multiple exposures to, and complex interactions with, knowledge.[104] Students also need varying experiences with the information if they are to truly learn it. When students can use their new information in visual or dramatic ways—representing the information in pictures or graphics, role playing, or by telling stories—in addition to talking and writing about it, they are more likely to learn and remember the content.[105]

Instructional materials and resources may contribute to student engagement. These items include everything from textbooks, maps, charts, smartphones or tablets with Internet connectivity, and lab equipment to classroom guests and field trips. Their primary value, however, lies in how teachers get students to cognitively interact with them to reach the instructional outcomes.

Research on student engagement Research supports student engagement's importance in achievement.[106] Researchers have established that students are significantly more likely to be engaged in activities that have inherent value—personal relevance and meaning—rather than those that rely on extrinsic values such as getting good grades. When teachers provide students with opportunities to make connections between real-world activities and their academic coursework, and when students have the freedom to explore issues that interest them, they remember more of what they learn, put more effort into their work, and are more involved in school.[107] Conversely, students withdraw personal effort from academic learning when they perceive that school curricula and systems do not reflect their own aspirations and culture or aim to help them fulfill their own purposes.[108]

Likewise, researchers have found that the type of student engagement affects how much of the lesson students will remember later. Table 13.2 highlights some examples of how well students remember material when it is taught via a variety of learning methods.

TABLE 13.2

Learning Methods Impact How Well Students Learn

Learning Method	Retention in Students (percent)
Lecture	5
Reading along with lecture	10
Audiovisual presentations	30
Discussion groups	50
Learning by doing	75
Learning by teaching others	90

Source: Adapted from NTL Institute for Applied Learning. Cited in Danielson, C. (2002). *Enhancing student achievement: A framework for school improvement.* Alexandria, VA: Association for Supervision and Curriculum Development, p. 24.

Focusing more closely on this issue, Robert Marzano and his colleagues determined which instructional practices produce the most students' learning.[109] Table 13.3 lists the nine categories of instructional strategies that affect student achievement and the estimated percentile gain students would receive if their teachers used these strategies as regular parts of their classroom learning activities.

formative assessments The ongoing appraisals that teachers use to weigh and promote learning.

Using assessment in instruction Academic achievement in classes where teachers provide effective feedback to students is considerably higher than the achievement in classes where no such feedback is delivered.[110] In fact, a review of almost 8,000 studies led one researcher to comment, "The most powerful single modification that enhances achievement is feedback."[111]

Rather than signaling instruction's end, assessment is integral to the instruction process. **Formative assessments** are especially valuable tools to promote learning. By continuously monitoring students as they work and checking for each one's understanding, teachers assess how well students comprehend what the teachers intend them to learn. Although a student who gives the wrong answer has not fully mastered the material, the wrong answer may give the teacher useful insight into which part of the information the student does not understand and offer direction about how to correct the situation.[112]

Feedback individualizes the instructional process. It ensures that each student knows the extent to which his or her performance meets the required standards. For example, students can review the teacher's comments on a writing sample or math solutions and use this information at once to increase what they know. As students assume increasing responsibility for their own learning, they are able to monitor their own progress and take corrective action without involving the teacher.

Helpful feedback is understandable, specific, accurate, meaningful, and timely.[113] It reflects clear criteria and standards of which students are fully aware. Global comments such as "nice work" are *not* helpful feedback. Feedback must be informational and ongoing, giving students meaningful insight into

Reflect & Discuss

Effective instruction intellectually engages students in learning. Research supports its value in increasing student achievement.

A. Working with a partner, identify and discuss five to 10 instructional factors from this chapter (it may appear before or after this activity) that teachers use that contribute to students' intellectual engagement in learning.

B. Identify the top three factors you and your partner believe will strongly contribute to students' learning twenty-first-century knowledge and skills—and how you believe it will increase learning.

C. As a pair, present your list of factors to the class. Compile a "complete master list" of intellectually engaging learning factors and draw a star next to those that you believe teachers can use to increase students' learning of twenty-first-century knowledge and skills.

D. In reviewing Table 13.2, which strategies work best for you as a student? Which ones do your professors use? What differences—if any—do you see in the two lists? What might you do if you do notice important differences?

TABLE 13.3

Instructional Strategies That Increase Student Achievement

Category	Specific Behaviors	Estimated Percentile Point Gain
Identifying similarities and differences	Assigning work that involves comparison and classification, metaphors and analogies.	45
Summarizing and note taking	Having students generate verbal and written summaries, take notes (rather than copy teacher notes), revise notes by adding new information and correcting errors.	34
Reinforcing effort and providing recognition	Recognizing and celebrating progress toward learning goals throughout the unit; recognizing and reinforcing student effort.	29
Homework and practice	Providing specific feedback on all assigned homework; assigning homework for the purpose of having students practice the skills and procedures learned in class.	28
Nonlinguistic representations (graphic organizers)	Asking students to generate mental images, pictures, graphic organizers, physical models representing content, or to act out content.	27
Cooperative learning	Organizing students in cooperative groups and ability groups when appropriate.	27
Setting objectives and providing feedback	Setting specific learning goals at the unit's beginning and asking students to set their own learning goals; providing feedback on learning goals throughout the unit; asking students to assess themselves at the unit's end.	23
Generating and testing hypotheses	Engaging students in projects that involve generating and testing hypotheses through problem solving, decision making, investigation, and experimental inquiry tasks.	23
Questions, cues, and advance organizers	Before presenting new content, asking questions that help students recall what they might already know about the content or with direct links to content previously studied.	22

Source: Adapted from Marzano, R. J., Pickering, D. J., and Pollock, J. E. (2001). *Classroom instruction that works: Research-based strategies for increasing student achievement.* Alexandria, VA: Association for Supervision and Curriculum Development, p. 7; Marzano, R. J. (2003). *What works in schools: Translating research into action.* Alexandria, VA: Association for Supervision and Curriculum Development, pp. 82–83.

what they are doing correctly and which errors they can fix. In general, the more delay that occurs in giving feedback, the less improvement in students' achievement.[114]

Teachers' feedback to students can take many forms: verbal, nonverbal, and written. Feedback may be subtle and informal, such as written comments on corrected homework, or more formal and systematic, such as report card grades or constructive comments during individual conferences.

Feedback has little value for students unless they use it. The degree to which students use feedback is highly related to their confidence as learners.[115] Confident students can accept and use constructive feedback to increase their knowledge. In contrast, students who are already discouraged about their academic abilities are likely to view feedback as more criticism and ignore it. If students don't accept the feedback, they cannot learn from it.

Demonstrating flexibility and responsiveness Teachers continuously make decisions. If students are not familiar with a concept or event on which a teacher is basing an entire explanation, the teacher may need to stop and explain the necessary background information. If students become bored and sluggish, the teacher may have to pick up the pace. If students become confused and can't keep up, the teacher may have to slow down and return to the place where confusion began. If an activity is not appropriate for students, the teacher may choose to stop or modify the activity so that students can successfully complete it. As this discussion suggests, lesson adjustments may require either major or subtle changes.

Teachable moments—spontaneous events that give the class an opportunity for valuable learning—also require teachers' flexibility and responsiveness. A student may ask a relevant question but not one that the teacher had planned to discuss. The flexible and responsive teacher takes the time to answer it and connect it to the lesson. On other occasions, teachers may seize upon a major event and adapt their lesson to it.

teachable moments Spontaneous events that give the class an opportunity for valuable learning.

reflection The continuous process of evaluating and learning from experience.

For instance, on September 12, 2001, most teachers shelved their planned lessons and focused the class period on the prior day's events. They discussed the personal relevance: "What happened yesterday?" "Did you know anybody directly affected?" "How can you respond to overwhelming events that you cannot control?" They also considered larger issues: "How can people communicate with those who violently disagree to prevent and resolve conflicts?" "Why is it important that our Bill of Rights protects the freedom to practice one's religion?" Spontaneous events can provide a classroom springboard to valuable intellectual and emotional learning experiences. Flexible and responsive teachers can meet their instructional goals in an unplanned but ultimately unforgettable manner.

Even the most highly skilled and best-prepared teachers sometimes find that either the lesson is not going as planned or a teachable moment has appeared. The ability to develop and use an instructional repertoire and to have the confidence to make lesson changes in real time comes with experience. Intellectual flexibility is a high-level skill. Experience and accurate reflection can help every teacher build this capability.

13-3e Reflecting on Teaching

As debated in FlipSides (above), although popular myth argues that great teachers are "born, not made," the truth is that effective teaching can be learned. Even when they are blessed with talent, great teachers work hard to be effective. **Reflection** is the continuous process of evaluating and learning from experience.[116] It is a mechanism for turning experience into knowledge about teaching.[117] Through critical reflection, teachers assess their work's effectiveness and take steps to improve or enhance it.

Ongoing reflection is essential for building knowledge. After all, teaching encompasses a complex set of behaviors. Pulling them all together effectively to ensure a positive outcome is a very difficult and demanding endeavor. By thinking about what happened in the classroom, considering the consequences of their actions, and generating alternative approaches, reflective teachers systematically expand their skills repertoire. As their knowledge develops, teachers have a larger array of information on which to draw for making decisions.

At the same time, teachers' increasing knowledge base expands their ability to use reflection effectively and to develop as teachers.[118] No matter how good a lesson, it can always become better.

Reflection requires purposeful, mature thinking.

altrendo images/Altrendo/Getty Images

TeachSource Video 13.2

© Cengage Learning 2015

Mentoring First-Year Teachers: Keys to Professional Success

First-year teachers can gain important professional knowledge and skills by working with a mentor. Mentors can observe them as they interact with students and colleagues and can offer frank feedback to help the novice reflect on and improve her or his teaching practice. Watch the video clips, study the artifacts in the case, and reflect on the following questions:

1. What are the benefits and risks for first-year teachers of allowing mentors to observe and comment on their work in the classroom?
2. What characteristics must be present in the mentor's relationship with the first-year teacher if their interactions are to be truly useful? What characteristics would likely prevent the mentoring relationship from being useful?
3. What things does the mentor in this video case do to make the new teacher feel comfortable asking for and receiving feedback and advice?

Watch on CourseMate.

To suggest that a lesson can be improved is not to imply that the teacher's work was inferior, but rather engages a teacher in a key aspect of the work of every professional: self-assssment and improvement.

Teachers reflect during lesson planning, during the teaching episode, and after the teaching event. During planning, teachers consider the classroom, student, and content variables as they design their lessons. They think about how to create a positive learning environment, how to limit the content to a meaningful and manageable amount, how to involve the learners, how to assess what the students already know, and how to extend their learning from there.

During the teaching episode, teachers reflect as they monitor and modify their strategies as necessary to promote the maximum student learning. Finally, after the teaching event, teachers reflect on what went well and what they could do to make the lesson better. By focusing on both successful and unsuccessful teaching, educators can gradually improve their practice.

Reflection as a learned skill Reflection requires purposeful and mature thinking. Novice teachers often have a difficult time reflecting productively. They tend to make global judgments, reporting that a lesson was "Okay" if students were busy and the day passed without any disciplinary incidents. Likewise, a beginning teacher may complain that the lesson was "terrible" without being able to say specifically why.

Skilled reflection is characterized by accuracy, specificity, and ability to incorporate the analysis into future teaching.[119] As teachers become more skilled at reflection, they recall more small events from their classes as evidence of the lesson's relative effectiveness because they are better able to monitor and focus on what is happening at the time. What is more, teachers become better able to suggest specific remedies and predict when they will be able to put these measures into practice in their classrooms. Increased skills in reflection are most likely to emerge when the school environment feels safe and supports teaching changes that lead to increased student learning, and when the class seems appropriate to the revised teaching approach.[120]

Reflection requires that teachers be open, not defensive. Reflective teachers are comfortable with constructive feedback, either from themselves or from colleagues. They are not afraid to look critically at their own behaviors and seek ways to be more helpful to students' learning. These teachers often invite feedback on their teaching from other teachers or assistant principals. Learning to become a better teacher requires an open mind, accurate data, honesty, an increasing array of instructional approaches, and enough time to change teaching behaviors.

Mentors, coaches, and reflection Mentors and coaches can help new teachers with reflection. Experienced educators' caring and skilled questioning can encourage beginning teachers to become more accurate, analytic, and insightful about their practice. This dialog can assist novices in learning both the essential habits of mind and a larger professional repertoire from which to make teaching decisions. The essential question is this: "If I had the chance to teach this content again with the same group of students, would I do it the same way or would I do it differently—and how?" After a while, novice teachers become more skilled in analyzing their own practice and have additional strategies to use with their lessons. Reflection becomes a habit of mind, a regular activity.[121]

At the same time, the mentors and coaches gain professionally by working with new teachers. Identifying specific teaching behaviors that affected student learning, observing how students respond, and seeking other approaches will deepen their own instructional knowledge. In this way, teachers evolve into a community of learners, each contributing to his or her colleagues' growth and effectiveness. Mature teachers' investment in their own school's improvement through mentoring novice educators is integral to their professional work, not an add-on.

Learning to teach is an ongoing process. Reflective teachers want to know more about the art and science of teaching and about themselves as effective teachers. They constantly improve lessons and think about how to reach particular children. Reflection produces a richer instructional knowledge base upon which to draw during teaching. Reflection is an essential professional skill and habit that builds teacher competence and confidence even as it improves students' learning.

Did You Get It?

Effective teaching

- **a.** Is not easy.
- **b.** Depends on receiving certification and licensure.
- **c.** Takes considerable preparation.
- **d.** Requires knowing your subject, your students, and how to teach it.

Take the full quiz on CourseMate.

SUMMARY

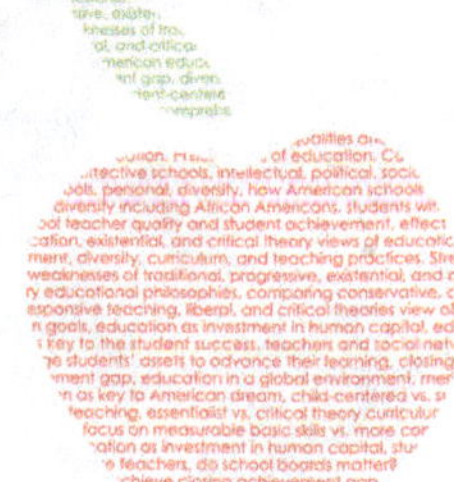

- Instruction is how teachers connect students with the curriculum. Teachers continually make instructional decisions that depend on their mature understanding of the content to be learned, their students, the nature of learning itself, and the likely consequences of selecting different actions.
- Research shows that teachers who learn and practice sound pedagogical techniques can enhance students' measured achievement. Thus effective teaching is the key to student learning.
- Research has found positive achievement results from students whose teachers effectively use certain behavioral, cognitive, and constructivist instructional practices. Effective teachers select from the three learning theories as appropriate to the content, the students, and their learning needs.
- Effective teaching involves planning and preparation, creating an appropriate classroom learning environment, and delivering and reflecting on instruction.
- Instruction for student engagement comprises a constellation of related behaviors. Student engagement is intellectual. Studies have established that students have more active mental involvement—and increased achievement—in activities that have inherent value—personal meaning and relevance—to them as compared to activities that emphasize extrinsic values such as getting good grades. Effective teachers learn by reflecting on their instruction and turning experience into knowledge about teaching.

Visit the Education CourseMate for this textbook to access the eBook, Did You Get It? quizzes, TeachSource Video Cases, flashcards, and more. Go to CengageBrain.com to log in, register, or purchase access.

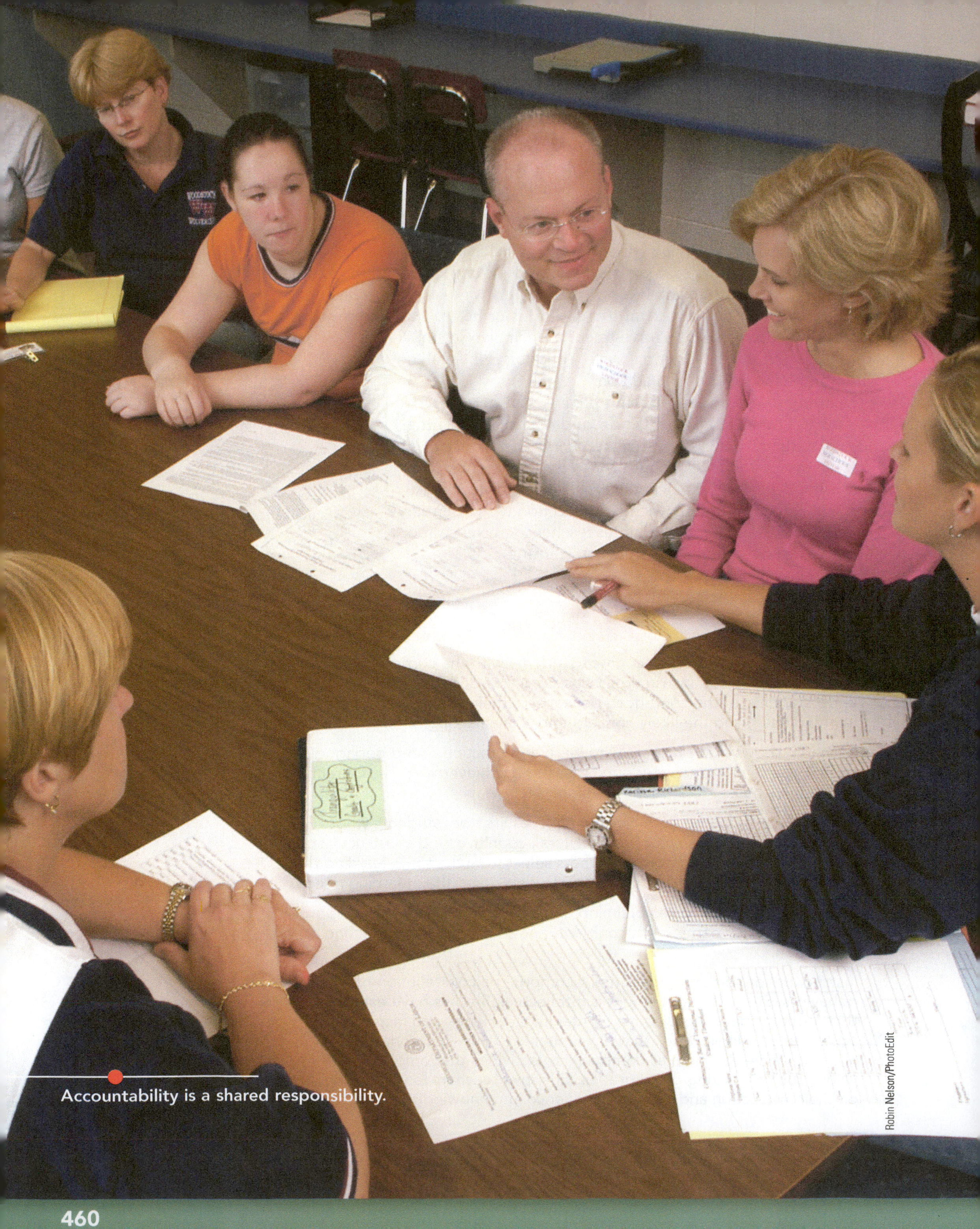

Accountability is a shared responsibility.

Robin Nelson/PhotoEdit

CHAPTER 14

Standards, Assessment, and Accountability

InTASC Standards Addressed: 2, 3, 4, 5, 6, 7, 8, and 9

LEARNING OBJECTIVES

After you read this chapter, you should be able to:

14-1 Describe the ways that schools and teachers use assessments to inform teaching and learning.

14-2 Explain how educational standards contribute to achievement and accountability.

14-3 Identify the principles of high-quality assessments and explain how they should affect teachers' practices.

14-4 Illustrate how accountability for educational outcomes is more than students' achievement test scores.

Standards, achievement, and accountability are highly visible topics. Common Core State Standards, high-stakes testing, student proficiency, achievement gains, and schools' responsibility for student learning are making headlines: "High Stakes Testing Is Putting the Nation at Risk"[1] "Should the Common Standards 'Change Everything'?"[2] No Child Left Behind (NCLB), the 2002 landmark federal education law, set an ambitious standard: All students tested in reading and math would reach grade-level proficiency by 2014. Yet even when Congress enacted the law, many educators, statisticians, legislative aides, and others believed that this standard was unrealistic. NCLB deliberately left the definition of "proficiency" vague so that each state could define "proficiency" for itself. How realistic is it that every student meet the "proficiency" standard when no two states agree on what it means?

"There is a zero percent chance that we will ever reach a 100 percent target," says Robert L. Linn, Co-director of the National Center for Research on Evaluation, Standards and Student Testing at University of California at

Los Angeles. "But because the title of the law is so rhetorically brilliant, politicians are afraid to change this completely unrealistic standard. They don't want to be accused of leaving some children behind."[3] So rhetorically powerful, in fact, that the U.S. Congress refused to vote on the law's reauthorization in September 2007, instead automatically extending it year after year with procedural "continuing resolutions." Filling the vacuum, the U.S. Department of Education has granted waivers to states applying to step out from under NCLB's regime and substitute their own testing and accountability programs.

Educators and politicians argue about whether this emphasis on standards, testing, more testing, and accountability is actually increasing students' achievement. Reports have compared NCLB state assessment data with results of the National Assessment of Educational Progress (NAEP)—"the nation's report card"—in reading and math before and after NCLB. The reports reveal that although student achievement on many state assessments had improved over the twenty-first century's first decade, the NAEP trend had remained relatively unchanged; in fact, NCLB may have even slowed the achievement gains that began to emerge in the mid-1990s.[4]

Despite its very real importance, educational accountability does not have to intimidate future teachers. Accountability is a shared responsibility. Assessment is an ongoing and integral part of the teaching and learning process, not a once-a-year hurdle to be jumped. In fact, well-designed and effectively used assessments can motivate students' interest and boost their achievement. Larger than "tests and measurement," accountability involves helping students meet a variety of clear, high standards in fair ways. Becoming knowledgeable about standards, assessment, and educational accountability can help prospective teachers understand their benefits and limitations and learn how to use them to advance student equity and achievement.

14-1 How Teachers and Schools Use Assessment to Enhance Teaching and Learning

Parents, policy makers, and teachers want meaningful answers to all of the following questions:

- "How is my student doing?"
- "Are the schools succeeding or failing?"
- "What works best to help students learn?"
- "Do test scores prove the effectiveness of educational programs?"

Answering these reasonable questions requires teachers to have a variety of student achievement data available. An accountability system that contains test scores alone is incomplete without additional information about teaching practices and curriculum. A teacher or school system that answers these questions (or bases its accountability) on test scores alone is like a physician evaluating your health based on body temperature or blood pressure but ignoring weight, height, blood tests, or other medical indicators that are essential to a competent diagnosis.

Teachers can know if they or the schools are succeeding or failing only if they have access to multiple sources of data gathered over an extended period. They need information about the measurable elements of the educational process—the curriculum standards, the learning assignments, types of available student supports, and samples of students' completed work. They also need information about the results—students' project and performance grades and standardized test scores over many years. In addition, educators need to learn how to provide insights based on observations, descriptions, and qualitative understandings that explain what has happened beyond the test scores. In the end, teachers must gather enough meaningful information and use professional judgments to make sense out of what is happening in the classroom for each student.

14-1a The Educational Assessment Learning Cycle

People tend to use the words "measurement," "assessment," and accountability" interchangeably. All of these terms relate to data and the process of evaluating progress in a concrete way, but they mean somewhat different things.

Measurement involves assigning numbers to observations according to rules that fit the circumstances. Measurement must be as objective as possible, but it can never be completely objective. For example, in a spelling bee, the judge counts the number of words that the student spelled correctly and assigns that number as the student's score. This part of the process is objective: The spelling is either correct or not. Deciding on the words to be included in the spelling bee and whether the student's spelling score of 16 is "poor" or "excellent," however, requires the teacher to use his or her judgment—that is, it is subjective.

Assessment is broader than measurement. The word "assessment" comes from the Latin root *assidēre*, meaning "to assist in the office of a judge." Assessment requires using professional judgment to determine what the measurement means. It is a comprehensive term that includes measurement, evaluation, and grading. **Educational assessment**, therefore, is a comprehensive process of describing, judging, and communicating the quality of students' learning and performances. As you see in Figure 14.1, assessment is the core of a continual learning cycle that includes measurement, feedback, reflection, and change.

measurement Assigning numbers to observations according to rules that fit the circumstances.

assessment The professional judgment used to determine the meaning given to measurement, evaluation, and grading.

educational assessment A comprehensive process of describing, judging, and communicating the quality of students' learning and performances.

accountability The obligation that teachers and schools have to accept responsibility for providing effective services to students that result in desired achievement outcomes.

holistic accountability The comprehensive array of factors needed for teaching excellence, including teaching, curriculum, leadership, parent involvement, faculty collaboration, and professional development.

A well-designed assessment gives both teacher and student quality feedback about how well the student is mastering the assigned curriculum. Upon receiving the feedback, teacher and student reflect and try to understand what the results mean. Has the student learned successfully? On which aspects does the student need additional instruction, practice, and feedback? What do the student and teacher do next with this feedback to change their behaviors? Does the teacher need to work with the individual or with large numbers of students in the class who did not show mastery on this or other important aspects of the assigned learning?

Answering these questions requires teachers to gather more evidence, reflect, and analyze deeply before acting. It allows them to use achievement data to guide their daily instructional plans and classroom actions. Thoughtful teaching needs to be driven by daily evidence, not by end of unit or course test scores.

Accountability systems include much more than students' achievement test scores. **Holistic accountability** considers the factors that come before educational excellence, including teaching practices, curriculum practices, leadership practices, student behaviors, parent involvement, faculty communication and collaboration, and professional development. Thus accountability addresses all aspects of the teaching and learning process. We will discuss holistic accountability in more detail later in this chapter.

FIGURE 14.1 The Assessment Learning Cycle

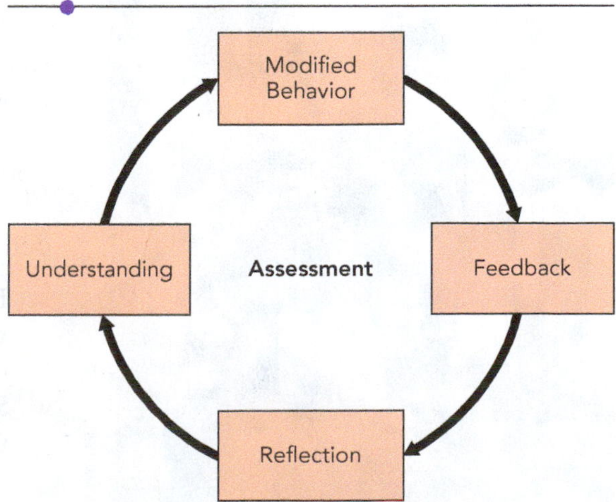

Source: Adapted from Frye, R. (n.d.). Assessment, accountability, and student learning outcomes. Retrieved October 30, 2009, from http://www.ac.wwu.edu/~dialogue/issue2.html.

14-1b Purposes of Assessment

The rationale for undertaking assessment is not merely to gather information. Rather, the intention is to combine data with professional judgment and relevant actions to create improvement. Assessment has several purposes, including making placement decisions, determining how well students attain curricular and instructional goals, and diagnosing student learning needs.[5]

placement decisions Choices made before instruction begins based on student performance data about where in the curriculum to start and how to best teach it.

gatekeepers The specific data used to determine who moves to the next grade or who receives admission to a college or profession.

formative assessments Appraisals *for* learning that provide feedback about students' mastery and weaknesses related to standards that teachers use to adjust instruction.

Placement decisions **Placement decisions** occur before instruction begins. The goal is to gather information for making informed decisions on where to start and how to best teach students. Teacher awareness of what each student knows before trying to teach something new increases the likelihood that the teacher will be able to provide suitable instruction for each child. Data for placement assessment come from past records, observations of students' strengths and weaknesses, pretests, and student self-reports.

Likewise, assessments for placement are sometimes used as **gatekeepers** to determine who moves to the next grade or who receives admission to a college or profession. Many states require high school students to pass one or more tests before they can receive a diploma. College admissions offices have long used the results of the American College Testing (ACT) program and the SAT as important data in making admissions decisions. Professions such as law, medicine, nursing, physical therapy, certified public accounting, and architecture require candidates to pass a specialized, standardized test before they are admitted to the profession. In the teaching profession, most state departments of education require new teachers to pass a standardized test to become eligible to receive a teaching license.

Determining student attainment Teachers use information from students' homework, classwork, projects, and a variety of tests to help determine how much students learned. Formative and summative assessments help establish whether students have mastered the curriculum.

Assessments are often used to make college admissions decisions.

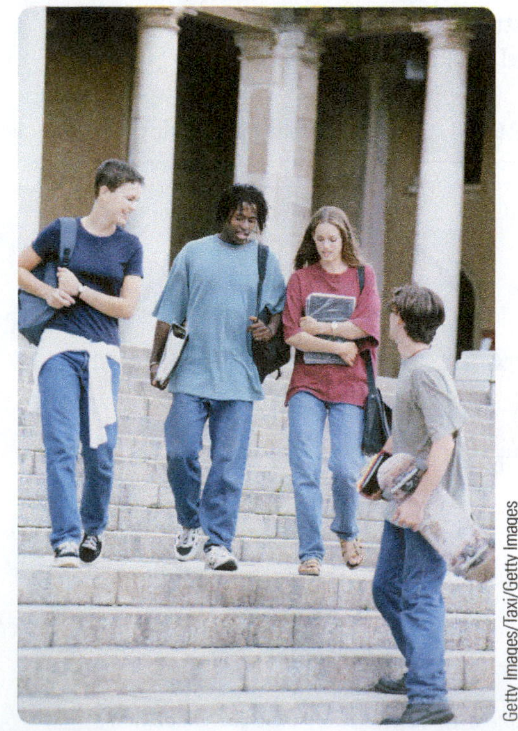

Getty Images/Taxi/Getty Images

Formative assessments are assessment *for* learning. *Formative* does not refer to the content, but rather to the manner in which the assessments are used. As learners try to understand and apply their new knowledge and skills, teachers' formative assessments provide continuous and specific classroom feedback about students' areas of mastery and weakness as they relate to state standards. Formative assessments let everyone know where they stand in the learning process. Teachers can use this information to adjust instruction and to create appropriate work for groups of learners or individual students. Assessing *for* learning advances—not simply monitors—student learning in a variety of ways.[6]

The formative approach makes a measurable difference in student achievement. Research studies have determined that:

- Feedback improves learning when teachers give students ongoing responses and guidance about how to improve their class work and tests.[7]
- Students benefit more from feedback than from grades.[8]
- Consistent, formative practices are linked to significant achievement gains and a reduced achievement gap, especially for the lowest achievers.[9]
- Formative assessments motivate students in positive ways that reinforce successful learning.[10]

Summative assessments involve the assessment *of* learning. Summative assessments are the final task at a unit's end used to make a concluding judgment about whether the student has met a certain required level of accomplishment. In addition to traditional examinations, teachers gather summative data through student demonstrations or performances, evaluating assigned projects and products, and systematically collecting portfolios that illustrate students' achievements or progress. Capstone assessments, such as science fairs, recitals, or art shows, celebrate a milestone accomplishment and demonstrate how well a person has mastered a knowledge or skill.

summative assessments Appraisals of learning used to make a concluding judgment about whether the student has met a certain required level of accomplishment.

diagnostic assessments Detailed and professionally-prepared tests administered by an educator with special training that identify obstacles to student learning.

Because summative assessments help teachers and students determine the extent to which students have achieved the instructional goals, they support assigning grades to report cards or to conferring certificates of mastery. To a limited degree, teachers can also use these data to help them judge their teaching effectiveness.

Standardized tests will always be an important part of teachers' assessment repertoire as a means to find out if they are teaching the standard course of study in ways that support students' learning.[11]

Diagnostic assessment **Diagnostic assessments** are a highly specialized intervention into student learning. They involve detailed and professionally prepared tests administered by a special education teacher, school psychologist, speech/language pathologist, occupational therapist, or regular teacher trained for this task. When a student experiences persistent learning difficulties despite the teacher's use of alternative instructional methods, diagnostic assessment is employed to determine the cause or causes of that student's ongoing learning problems. The findings enable teachers to develop plans for appropriate remedial attention to individual students and help them determine whether a student is eligible for special education or gifted services or accommodations.

Stephanie L. Bravmann, senior research consultant at the Center on Reinventing Education at the University of Washington, observes:

> Unlike formative assessment, which is intended to deal with the kinds of learning issues that respond to the classroom equivalent of bandages, hot-water soaks, or massage, diagnostic assessment helps find the underlying causes for learning problems that don't respond to purely palliative measures.[12]

Effective teachers learn how to balance assessment *for* and *of* learning. Teachers committed to educating each child appropriately collect and use ongoing student achievement data. This helps them understand each student as a learner on a daily basis and make the necessary adaptations to support learning every day. Additionally, teachers partner summative assessments with the other available student learning data to fairly and equitably support—not merely evaluate—student learning.

TeachSource Video 14.1

Teacher Accountability: A Student Teacher's Perspective

The teacher accountability movement can benefit both teachers and students. Viewing accountability in a positive way can help teachers find necessary resources, become reflective practitioners, and strengthen their teaching practices in ways that make both teachers and students more successful. Watch the video clips, study the artifacts in the case, and reflect on the following questions:

1. How can teachers view teacher accountability in ways that prevent them from being discouraged about their effectiveness as teachers?
2. How does being a reflective teacher contribute to improved practice?
3. How can teachers use accountability data as an opportunity to improve their classroom practices?
4. What does "scaffolding learning for students" mean and how can teachers use this as a means to improve their accountability for student learning?

Watch on CourseMate.

Did You Get It?

Which statement about assessments is false?

- **a.** Test scores alone are an important accountability system.
- **b.** The purpose of assessment ought to be to combine data with judgment and action to create improvement.
- **c.** Generally speaking, teachers can know if they are failing only if they have multiple sources of data gathered over an extended period.
- **d.** Educators need to be able to augment formal results with informal insights.

Take the full quiz on CourseMate.

14-2 Educational Standards Contribute to Achievement and Accountability

Educational testing began in twentieth-century United States as an objective, relatively inexpensive tool to provide information for decision making about large numbers of people. Over time, its cost has grown exponentially. Recent press reports put the value of the testing market anywhere from $400 million to $700 million.[13] According to the Government Accountability Office (GAO), states were likely to have spent $1.9 billion to $5.3 billion between 2002 and 2008 to implement NCLB-mandated tests—and indirect costs of teacher time and test-prep activities raise these costs higher still.[14] This investment attests to the public's continued confidence in test scores as one measure of accountability and as a means to make important educational decisions.

educational standards Criteria that identify what students should know and be able to do at a certain grade level.

Accountability is tied to educational standards. **Educational standards** clearly identify what students should know and be able to do at a particular grade level. Accordingly, educational standards have become the foundation of curriculum and assessment in all 50 states, each of which has its own set of standards. Standards have come to be synonymous with rigor and setting high achievement expectations for all students.

14-2a Educational Standards, Achievement, and Accountability

The emphasis on clear educational goals stems from the school effectiveness research conducted in the 1970s, which revealed that what students are taught in a specific subject and at a specific grade level varied greatly among schools and even among classrooms within a school.[15] For example, one report found that one elementary school teacher who was observed for more than 90 days did not teach fractions, despite the state mandate to teach the topic at that grade level. When asked about omitting the topic, the teacher replied, "I don't like fractions."[16] In a similar vein, another report showed a range of more than 4,000 minutes in the time spent on reading instruction in four fourth-grade classes.[17] Again, teacher preference accounted for such wide differences.[18] Across the country and within schools, students were learning according to teacher preferences and not based on high and clear educational benchmarks.

Notably, the focus of standards has shifted attention from inputs to results. Before 1987, most standards focused on the curriculum, telling teachers what they should teach (inputs). In contrast, today's standards identify what students should know and be able to do (results) when they finish a course, a grade, or a program. The standards-based education movement assumes that the only way to ensure that all students acquire specific knowledge and skills is to identify and teach to expected performance levels for specific knowledge and skills. "Standards," "benchmarks," "indicators," and "objectives"—all refer to what students should know and be able to do.

Setting standards, teaching to the standards, and assessing the extent to which students meet the standards provide the basis for public school achievement and accountability. This systematic approach connects curriculum, instruction, assessments, and professional development to a set of performance indicators that the teachers, administrators, parents, and students endorse. Student learning is at the center, and standardized tests are frequently the means to measure students' performance.

What is more, today's standards apply to all students. The current U.S. educational reform movement finds it unacceptable that only a small percentage of students achieve at high levels. Instead, schools must raise their expectations for all students' learning. This is not just the practical thing to do in a highly technological and global economy; it is the ethical thing to do if we want to make our society less stratified and provide more opportunities for talented and hard-working students from all racial, ethnic, and socioeconomic backgrounds to climb as high as their capabilities and energies will take them.

14-2b Why We Use Educational Standards

Many reasons exist for using educational standards. For example, such standards provide more accurate achievement measures than a comparison of students' scores to national norms. Meeting educational standards does not "sort and select" students into haves and have-nots. Instead, meeting educational standards provides the necessary intellectual challenge to above-average students, and this assessment process is fair to all students.[19] In this section, we discuss more fully each reason for using these standards.

Standards and national norms First, standards are more accurate than norms as measures of student achievement. Garrison Keillor, the television and radio personality famous for "A Prairie Home Companion," greets his weekly audience with the words, "Welcome to Lake Wobegon, where all the women are strong, all the men are good-looking, and all the children are above average." This boast is a proud tribute to Lake Wobegon's All-American families, but it tweaks the popular notion of "norm." Bragging that all children are "above average" pokes fun at the idea of the **bell curve**, a statistical concept in which random scores spread out around a range from high to low with half the scores above and half below the mean.

bell curve A statistical concept in which random scores spread out around a range from high to low with half the scores above and half below the mean.

Figure 14.2 illustrates the bell curve and the statistical "norm" at the mean (average). The norm is the 34 percent below and 34 percent above (68 percent total) around the center line (50th percentile). The farther from the central line, the more outside the "norm." Because the Lake Wobegon population is not random (its fictional population has moved there by choice), the concept of "norm" does not apply. There's the joke! Statistically, in a truly "normal" population, every child cannot be "above average." By definition, half must be below average. The concept of *norm* is less funny, however, when it is applied to student achievement.

FIGURE 14.2 The Bell Curve: Finding the "Norm"

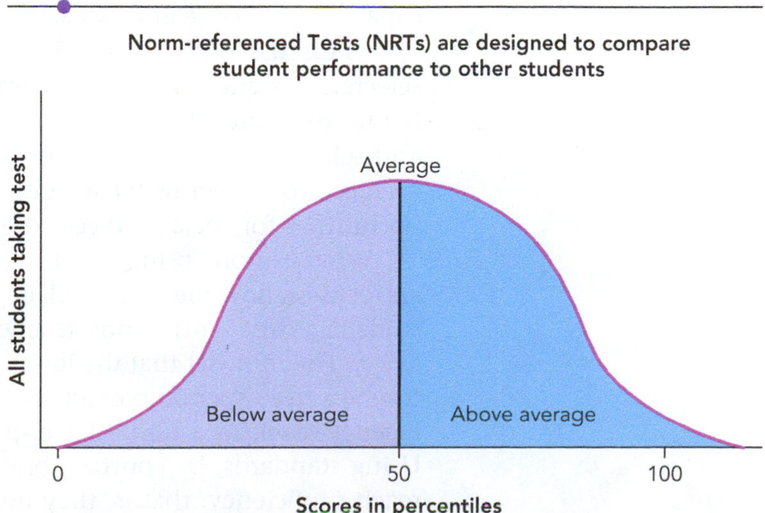

Source: Center for Public Education. (2007). Guide to standardized tests: Bell curve. National School Boards Association. Retrieved October 30, 2009, from http://www.centerforpubliceducation.org/site/c.kjJXJ5MPIwE/b.1698647/k.1A72/Guide_to_standardized_tests_Bell_curve.htm.

Two ways exist to evaluate student performance. First, we can compare a student's performance to that of another student or to the average of a group of students. Second, we can compare the student's performance to an objective standard. When educators use the norm approach, they accept the logic of the **normal distribution** or bell curve.[20]

normal distribution The statistical term used to describe how scores are arrayed around a mean.

From a standards perspective, educators care only whether the student achieves the desired learning. They do not care whether the student is performing better or worse than his or her classmates and national peers. In contrast, on normed tests, some students are expected to score at the top (showing high competence), but many others are expected to perform in the middle or at the bottom. Normed tests are specifically designed to distribute students' achievement scores along a continuum from high to low, while educational standards expect every student—given enough time and academic and social supports—to reach them. Comparing results and determining one winner and many losers may make sense when only one baseball team can win the World Series or when only one country can win the Olympic gold medal in figure skating. It does not make sense, however, when the educational goal is for every student to be a winner—that is, to learn the necessary knowledge and skills that mark excellent learning and which contribute to excellent performance. No teacher, parent, or employer wants his or her students to be in the "lower half" (below average).

Testing's central technical issue is accurately measuring students' performance and progress. This is accountability's most basic principle. Each student's challenge is to meet an objective standard. No one would want to be a passenger in an airplane flown by a pilot who merely scored "above average" on the Federal Aviation Administration (FAA) exam. No, we would all prefer to fly with an outstanding pilot such as "Sully" Sullenberger, who was able to save all on board his passenger flight in January 2009 by safely landing in the Hudson River after a "bird strike" disabled both plane engines. Viewed in this way, academic standards provide accuracy and an acceptable performance level that comparisons to the average or norm cannot offer. Meeting academic standards can determine a student's proficiency, and every student can meet this goal.

Standards and tracking Standards do not "sort and select" students. If the standards define what every student should know and be able to do, then every proficient student has the opportunity to earn the top grade—and demonstrate capable knowledge and skills.

As discussed in Chapter 7, U.S. public schools have traditionally sorted and selected students to prepare them for future societal roles. Curriculum tracking is one example of how schools accomplish this task. This traditional sorting and selecting practice does not produce equitable results for minority and low socioeconomic status (SES) students, who want schools to help them create opportunities for social and economic mobility.

What is more, using norms or standards becomes an ethical issue when teachers focus on how the results will be used and on their own responsibility for helping students learn. With norms, teachers expect students to perform at higher or lower levels. The mindset that the lower scores are "normal" and "expected" means that teachers need spend no extra effort to bring lower-scoring students up to the proficiency level. As a result, lower-performing students remain perpetually behind. Using standards, by contrast, brings the mindset that all students can and must reach proficiency; that is, they must all achieve the given standard. By adopting this perspective, teachers must invest extra time and use varied instructional and support practices with the lower-achievers so that they, too, reach the standard.

Norm-referenced high-stakes tests "are the equivalent of 'educational highways' with the smallest possible margin for error—an inch on either side—because *their* purpose is not to see that students 'arrive safely' but to nab them for violations," notes John Merrow, an education writer.[21] If the goal of U.S. public schools is to ensure that each student arrives safely at the proficiency level, using assessments tied to educational standards rather than norm-referenced assessments is more likely to get them there.

Standards and "above-average" students Although they may score highly on norm-referenced tests, many students classified as "above average" may not be able to write a coherent and persuasive essay, apply an algebraic concept to solve a real-world problem, or understand a complex literary passage's meaning. Although "above-average" scores makes students and their parents feel good about their schools and their education, their expectations for proficiency are not high enough. They become inappropriately complacent when, in truth, their achievement as measured against rigorous academic standards (rather than norms) may be inadequate.

Comparison to the average does not only hurt disadvantaged students; it also hurts higher-achieving students who score well on tests but who still have much more to learn. They mistakenly believe that because they can "out score" other students, they are successful and do not have to work harder to achieve a higher, more demanding level of mastery. They may not realize that their real competitors are not their peers across the room but those across the globe. Standards keep the challenges high and learning continuing for nearly all students.

Standards and fairness Standards communicate what students are expected to know and be able to do. **Benchmarks** identify specific expectations for certain grade levels or groups of grade levels. Scoring guides, sometimes called **rubrics**, provide the most specific expectations for students by identifying what they are supposed to accomplish on individual assignments and assessments. Students can reliably meet these expectations when the standards are clear and consistent, when students know and understand what they are, and when the teaching is effective.

benchmarks Indicators that identify specific expectations for certain grade levels or groups of grade levels.

rubrics Scoring guides that identify what students are supposed to accomplish on individual assignments and assessments.

This system is fair because unless the standards change, which occur infrequently, the rules do not change in the middle of the game. What students learn, study, and practice is what is assessed. What is also fair, ideally, is that every student—regardless of gender, race, ethnicity, social class, or parental education level—has the chance to meet the same standards and show proficiency.

In the real world, however, academic standards' integrity depends on the connection among standards, teaching, and assessments. The state-approved tests must assess the same knowledge and skills that the teacher taught. Likewise, all students must have an opportunity to learn the state-approved curriculum and the standards set for that grade level. Although different students and teachers may approach mastering the standards in varying ways and with diverse levels of support, all students should have access to what the community determines to be a demanding and excellent education to prepare them for college and the workplace. In contrast, if the state standards, the teacher-taught curriculum, and the assessments do not match, the system is fair to no one.

14-2c Types of Educational Standards

Standards make statements about the expected level of attainment or performance, but they may mean very different things to different people. World-class standards, real-world standards, content standards, performance standards, and opportunity-to-learn standards all define different expectations for achievement. Education standards also have their critics.

World-class standards Educators and policy makers may think of standards as world-class goals based on the performances of exceptional individuals such as Fields Medal–winning mathematicians, Nobel Prize–winning scientists, Pulitzer

Prize–winning authors, and Olympic gold medal–winning athletes. Elementary and secondary students are not expected to meet these extremely high standards, of course. Instead, school standards are statements of accomplishment and models of excellence meant to inspire ambition and greater effort.

Schools that adopt world-class standards take the long view. Educators see the curriculum as a developmental process. During each school year, students move toward the high standard. Teachers expect students to show improvement in many ways over time as they advance toward increasingly greater mastery.

Real-world standards Others believe that standards should be real-world goals that all students can actually achieve in school. Rigorous real-world standards for high school students reflect the knowledge and skills that will prepare them to enter and succeed in credit-bearing college courses or to gain entry-level positions in well-paying careers that offer opportunities to advance. For example, 46 states have adopted the Common Core State Standards, which are modeled on those of high-achieving countries. In an increasingly competitive global environment, policy makers and educators believe, American students should be held to the same mastery level as students in other nations that are our political and economic competitors. Previously, states took a more local view, aligning their high school standards with the real-world expectations of local or regional employers and postsecondary faculty to spell out what students need to know and be able to do to succeed after high school.[22]

Content or discipline-based standards Content or discipline-based standards describe what teachers and students should know and be able to do in subject areas. Professional education organizations representing mathematics, history/social studies, English/language arts, arts, behavior studies, career education, civics, economics, educational technology, foreign language, geography, health, history, life skills, mathematics, science, physical education, and early childhood professional preparation have all developed standards based on national consensus.[23]

Usually, these content standards emphasize the subjects' core components or big ideas that students of a certain age or grade level should know. They are often accompanied by standards stating what teachers should know about the content or subject so they can teach at the preschool, elementary, or secondary levels.

As with the real-world standards, most states are using the common core standards in place of the older discipline standards in English language arts, math, and literacy in history, social studies, science, and technical subjects. For example, the common core reading standards note that all students must be able to comprehend texts of steadily increasing complexity in all their academic subjects as they move through the grade levels. By the time students are ready to graduate from high school, they must be able to read and comprehend independently and proficiently the challenging texts in each academic discipline typically encountered in college, workplace training programs, and careers. These reading standards attempt to correct an existing weakness: Although the reading demands of college, workplace, citizenship, and life have either stayed the same or increased over the past 50 years, K-12 texts have actually reduced their reading complexity. The result is a large gap between what most high school graduates can comprehend by reading on their own and what they are expected to be able to read independently—without teacher prompts, class discussion, or text summaries and clues—after they graduate.[24]

Table 14.1 provides a more complete idea about what increasing reading complexity in K-12 common core standards in literature and academic content means. It includes:

- levels of meaning,
- structure,

TABLE 14.1

Making Reading Texts in School More Complex

From Less Complex Text	→	To More Complex Text
Levels of Meaning (literary texts) or Purpose (informational text)		
• Single level of meaning	→	Multiple levels of meaning
• Explicitly stated purpose	→	Implicit purpose, may be hidden or obscure
Structure		
• Simple	→	Complex
• Explicit	→	Implicit
• Conventional	→	Unconventional (usually in literary texts)
• Events told in chronological order	→	Events told out of chronological order
• Traits of a common genre or subgenre	→	Traits specific to a particular discipline
• Simple graphics	→	Sophisticated graphics
• Graphics unnecessary to understanding	→	Graphics essential to understanding (may provide information not in the text)
Language Conventionality and Clarity		
• Literal	→	Figurative or ironic
• Clear	→	Ambiguous or purposefully misleading
• Contemporary, familiar	→	Archaic or otherwise unfamiliar
• Conversational	→	General academic and domain-specific
Knowledge Demands: Life Experiences (literary)		
• Simple themes	→	Complex or sophisticated themes
• Single themes	→	Multiple themes
• Common, everyday experiences or clearly invented situations	→	Experiences distinctly different from one's own
• Single viewpoint	→	Multiple viewpoints
• Viewpoint(s) like one's own	→	Viewpoint(s) unlike or opposed to one's own
Knowledge Demands: Cultural/Literary Knowledge (mainly literary texts)		
• Everyday knowledge and familiarity with genre conventions required	→	Cultural and literary knowledge useful
• Few, if any, references or allusions to other texts	→	Many references or allusions to other texts
Knowledge Demands: Content/Discipline Knowledge (mainly informational texts)		
• Everyday knowledge and familiarity with genre conventions required	→	Extensive, maybe specialized discipline-specific content knowledge required
• Few, if any, references to/citations from other texts	→	Many references to/citations from other texts

Source: Adapted from Figure 2. Qualitative Dimensions of Text Complexity. National Governors Association and the Council of Chief State School Officers. (2010). *Common core state standards for English language arts & literacy in history/social studies, science, and technology*. p. 6. Washington, DC: Author. Retrieved from http://www.corestandards.org/assets/Appendix_A.pdf

- language, and
- knowledge demands.

levels of meaning or purpose The reading language difficulty continuum from the easier text having one meaning to one having multiple levels of meaning.

structure The reading language continuum from simple, well-marked, traditional organization to more complicated, implicit, and unconventional language construction.

language conventionality and clarity The range of English from easily understood conversational language to more challenging word use.

knowledge demands The reading language continuum from easier to more complex reading texts based on assumptions about the reader's background knowledge.

Levels of meaning or purpose, for literary and informational texts, respectively, moves from the easier text having one obvious meaning to one having multiple levels of meaning—such as satire or metaphor in literary works and hidden or obscure purpose in informational works. **Structure** refers to the continuum between simple, well-marked, traditional organization to more complicated, implicit, and unconventional language construction. **Language conventionality and clarity** refers to the range of English from easily understood clear, typical, conversational language to more challenging word use that is figurative, ironic, ambiguous, or purposefully misleading. Finally, **knowledge demands** speaks to the continuum between easier reading texts that make few assumptions about the readers' life experiences and depth of their cultural and content information and more demanding writings that make many assumptions about one or more of these areas. Clearly, such an increase in reading comprehension demands will create challenges for both teachers and students.

National standards The U.S. Constitution assigns the responsibility of education to the states. Each state has its own process of developing, adopting, and implementing educational standards. This means that what students can be expected to learn and be able to do vary widely from state to state. States prize their autonomy in the education domain, and they vigorously strive to keep it.

Although each state sets its own content standards, a state-led national consensus has emerged. The Common Core State Standards reflect the shared desire among educators, experts, parents, and policy makers across the nation to voluntarily adopt the highest academic criteria benchmarked to those in the highest achieving countries. From these standards, curricula will be written. But this will not be a national curriculum. Local teachers, principals, superintendents, and school boards will decide how they will meet the standards, and local teachers will continue to create lesson plans and design instruction to the individual needs of the students in their classrooms.

As befitting a state-held responsibility, the federal government was not involved in developing the standards. But it has influenced their adoption. The U.S. Department of Education's Race to the Top grant program, which offered significant dollars tied to state education reform, provided an incentive to adopt by awarding states extra points for agreeing to use these voluntary standards. For moral, practical, and legal reasons, therefore, many believe that common national education standards are desirable.[25]

Criticism of content standards Although high-quality content standards bring positive benefits to teaching, learning, and assessment, critics raise both legitimate and political concerns about their use. The most important logical concern is that the standards be focused and meaningful rather than a superficial "mile wide and inch deep." For example, prior to the common core standards, researchers at Mid-continent Research for Education and Learning (McREL) identified some 200 standards and 3,093 benchmarks in national- and state-level documents for 14 different subject areas.[26] This material would take 15,465 hours to teach,[27] but U.S. public schools (K-12) had only 9,042 hours available to teach these standards and benchmarks.[28] Critics also express disquiet that the assessments tied to these older standards overrepresent easy-to-measure skills and underrepresent complex reasoning skills.[29] These are some of the very weaknesses that the Common Core State Standards, the locally written curricula, and the common assessments derived from them intend to address.

At the same time, opponents of the Common Core State Standards argue from two contrary political positions: that national standards undermine the traditionally cherished local control of schools or that they represent corporate interests who view the standards as a way to undermine and privatize public schools by encouraging school closings, voucher programs, and charter schools. Given these intense interests, it is up to state and local educators and other stakeholders to ensure that although the standards may hold nationally endorsed expectations, their curriculum remains local.

Jose Luis Pelaez/Iconica/Getty Images

InTASC standards expect new teachers to appreciate and value human diversity.

Performance standards Performance standards are also statements about what a student or a teacher should be able to do in presentations that encompass combinations of knowledge and skills. Once teachers have identified the content standard, they design performance standards so each student can show what he or she understands and can do with what they learned. Assessments for the common core standards are expected to include performance tasks.

Because performance tasks require students to actively demonstrate what they know, performance assessments may sometimes be a more valid indicator of students' knowledge and abilities than a multiple-choice test. Answering a multiple-choice question correctly may require no more than recognizing or remembering a fact, relatively low levels of thinking. Making an oral presentation, in contrast, requires the student to invest time; conduct research, analyze, synthesize, evaluate, write, and practice; create graphic illustrations to accompany the talk; and have sufficient subject knowledge to correctly answer listeners' questions.

Setting and enforcing clear, high, and achievable performance standards is a challenging undertaking. Performance standards often differ from district to district and from classroom to classroom. Different educators prefer different levels of achievement specified in the rubrics. Some want rubrics with minimum national standards, whereas others prefer rubrics defining high levels of excellent performance. State and school district expectations as well as personal preference and professional judgments all factor into the choice of rubrics teachers use and the performance levels students meet. And, in the end, students must understand and know how to meet them.

Opportunity-to-learn standards None of the common core standards will lift student learning and achievement unless students have sufficient high-quality occasions to study them.

Opportunity-to-learn standards define a set of conditions that schools, districts, and states must meet to ensure that students have enough occasions to meet expectations for their performance.[30] Student achievement depends not only on students' abilities, but also on whether the student actually attended the class and whether the teacher has taught the subject in class with enough explanation, time, practice, feedback, and support in an appropriate learning environment necessary for students to absorb it.

opportunity-to-learn standards The conditions about the learners' occasions to learn the content and skills being assessed.

Opportunity-to-learn standards include the following factors[31]:

- *Content Coverage.* The more the assessment matches the information the students actually learned, the more mastery students will show.
- *Content Exposure.* The more time spent on learning experiences and the more complete and meaningful the information, the more students will learn.
- *Content Emphasis.* The more the teachers' focus closely matches the standards and the assessments, and the more teachers help students develop higher-order thinking skills while using the content, the more students will learn.
- *Quality of Instructional Delivery.* The more the teachers' classroom practices show cognitive understanding of the subject, structure presentations appropriately to students, relate new information to what students already know, monitor students' performance and provide corrective feedback during the lesson, and relate different parts of the lesson to each other, the more students will learn.

For instance, a student with disabilities who is not included in all regular core academic classrooms with appropriate supports may not have chances to learn a rigorous, high-challenge curriculum and learn the critical reading and thinking skills as a student who has all these classes. Likewise, a student who is frequently absent from school, or whose teacher does not follow the school district's curriculum or pacing guide, or whose classroom is constantly disrupted by student outbursts does not have the same opportunities to learn as a classmate with perfect attendance, a teacher who closely follows the district's curriculum guide, and a calm, caring, focused, and orderly classroom environment. Even if the two students had identical academic abilities, the one in the latter class is more likely to master the expected standards. Clearly, differences in students' learning experiences can make tremendous differences in whether—and how much—they achieve.

Advocates of opportunity-to-learn standards often include family support, the school environment, and student behavior within their scope. Educators monitor and measure the opportunity-to-learn standards by using teacher logs, observations, and surveys, students' attendance records, as well as more structured interval testing and small-task assessment.

Regardless of how logical and important opportunity-to-learn standards appear, putting them into practice costs money. Currently, they are the subject of state legislation and court cases dealing with school finance, assessment, and unequal opportunity.[32] Nonetheless, teachers should stay vigilant to ensure that all their students receive ample opportunity to learn if their grades and test scores are to be fair and accurate reflections of their learning and achievement.

Professional educator standards Professional education associations have also developed standards for teachers and other professional school personnel. These professional standards outline what educators should know and be able to do to teach or work as a school library media specialist, school counselor, principal, or other school professional. Prospective educators typically have to demonstrate the knowledge, skills, and dispositions of one or more sets of these standards before they can obtain a license to work in that field.

Standards may also include statements about the habits of mind or dispositions that teachers should nurture in students, such as curiosity, perseverance, tenacity, caring, and open-mindedness. For example, the Interstate New Teacher Assessment and Support Consortium (InTASC) standards for state licensure expect new teachers to demonstrate the following dispositions related to Principle 3 ("The teacher understands how students differ in their approaches to learning and creates instructional opportunities that are adapted to diverse learners"):

- The teacher believes that all children can learn at high levels and persists in helping all children achieve success.
- The teacher appreciates and values human diversity, shows respect for students' varied talents and perspectives, and is committed to the pursuit of "individually configured excellence."
- The teacher respects students as individuals with differing personal and family backgrounds and various skills, talents, and interests.
- The teacher makes students feel valued for their potential as people and helps them learn to value each other.[33]

Similarly, InTASC specifies that four types of performance go along with these dispositions:

- The teacher identifies and designs instruction appropriate to students' stages of development, learning styles, strengths, and needs.
- The teacher uses teaching approaches that are sensitive to the multiple experiences of learners and that address different learning and performance modes.
- The teacher makes appropriate provisions (in terms of time and circumstances for work, tasks assigned, and giving feedback to individual students who have particular learning differences or needs.
- The teacher can identify when and how to access appropriate services or resources to meet exceptional learning needs.

14-2d Determining Whether Students Have Met the Standards

Performance standards vary. Some specify a minimum level of performance or a range of performances ranging from unsatisfactory to outstanding. Other standards are expressed as a list of qualities, such as the organization and expression characteristics one would expect from a well-developed essay. Still other standards are stated as numbers, such as saying that a student must read a certain passage within 15 minutes and answer the related questions with 80 percent accuracy.

Sometimes, educators use "cut scores" to identify the lowest acceptable score that still meets the standard. The **cut score** is a point on the continuum from the lowest possible score to the highest. Those students who fall below the cut score have not been able to demonstrate that they have met the standard. In short, the cut score separates those who meet the standard from those who do not. Classifying students as meeting the standard is relatively easy when the performance is either extremely high or extremely poor, but identifying passing somewhere in the continuum's middle is more complicated.

cut score A point on the continuum from the lowest possible score to the highest that separates those who meet the standard from those who do not.

Although a cut score may appear to be objective and definitive, it is neither. Deciding where to place the cut score is both an objective (psychometric) problem and a subjective (professional judgment and values) problem. The cut score's location needs to consistently allow educators to distinguish between those students who meet the standard and those who do not. Cut scores may carry a heavy weight for students, however—determining who graduates or who enters a profession, for example. Those who fall short of the mark do not receive the desired rewards. Furthermore, the procedures used to determine the cut score must withstand painstaking scrutiny because they will be challenged if they appear arbitrary or misplaced.

Other standards are not either–or propositions. Sometimes there are greater and lesser degrees of competency rather than all-or-nothing performance. A student writer may have creative ideas, authentic "voice," and coherent

Reflect & Discuss

Performance standards often use rubrics to give students clear information by which to develop and assess their performance tasks. Below is a rubric for conducting successful group work. Successful teamwork is a twenty-first-century skill. Working in groups of four, review the criteria and points assigned, describe what each behavior might look and sound like (or *not* look or sound like), and discuss the questions that follow.

Rubric for Cooperative Group Work

4—Thorough Understanding

- Consistently and actively works toward group goals.
- Is sensitive to the feelings and learning needs of all group members.
- Willingly accepts and fulfills individual role within the group.
- Consistently and actively contributes knowledge, opinions, and skills.
- Values the knowledge, opinion, and skills of all group members and encourages their contribution.
- Helps group identify necessary changes and encourages group action for change.

3—Good Understanding

- Works toward group goals without prompting.
- Accepts and fulfills individual role within the group.
- Contributes knowledge, opinions, and skills without prompting.
- Shows sensitivity to the feelings of others.
- Willingly participates in needed changes.

2—Satisfactory Understanding

- Works toward group goals with occasional prompting.
- Contributes to the group with occasional prompting.
- Shows sensitivity to the feelings of others.
- Participates in needed changes, with occasional prompting.

1—Needs Improvement

- Works toward group goals only when prompted.
- Contributes to the group only when prompted.
- Needs occasional reminders to be sensitive to the feelings of others.
- Participates in needed changes when prompted and encouraged.

Source: Adapted from *Collaboration rubric: Teacher created rubrics for assessment. On-line professional development for K–12 teachers.* (n.d.). University of Wisconsin–Stout. Retrieved from http://www.sdcoe.k12.ca.us/score/actbank/collaborub.html.

Discuss answers to these questions in pairs, then as a whole group:

A. Which student behaviors or characteristics differentiate between those students who earn higher scores and those who earn lower scores on group performance tasks?
B. Which student behaviors or characteristics are more likely to advance—or limit—the growth of twenty-first-century skills? Explain with examples.
C. Describe the role of leadership and initiative in conducting a successful cooperative group.
D. Describe the role you usually take in a cooperative group. Which point value would you typically receive?
E. Explain how having such a rubric explained to you as a student would affect your own behavior in the group.
F. Explain how a teacher could use this or a similar rubric to increase student learning in class.
G. Discuss what you think are the difficulties in teachers developing and using a clearly expressed rubric to increase quality teaching and learning.

organization but may show inconsistent spelling and grammar. Even here, however, a point exists that separates those with some proficiency from those who lack it. Determining that precise spot between "just enough" and "not quite enough" is an objective and subjective decision.

As a result, a cut score or a passing score is often an arbitrary and unreliable benchmark. Professional and personal preferences or political philosophies can influence where these points lie on the continuum. Although no agreement exists

American Education Spotlight

© Courtesy of W. James Popham
W. James Popham

W. James Popham

"For some teachers, test is a four-letter word, both literally and figuratively."*

W. James Popham, professor emeritus at the University of California at Los Angeles, has strong views about using standardized testing for school accountability. He argues that competent educators need "assessment literacy" because inadequate knowledge of assessment for the classroom or accountability can "cripple the quality of education."*

Beginning his education career as a high school English and social studies teacher in Oregon, Popham earned his doctorate and became a college professor, a widely respected expert on educational testing, a former president of the American Educational Research Association, and author of 30 books and 200 journal articles. At UCLA for almost 30 years, in 1992, Popham took early retirement "upon learning that emeritus professors received free parking."†† In January 2000, *UCLA Today* recognized him as one of UCLA's top 20 professors of the twentieth century.

Popham expresses concern about using standardized achievement tests to measure teaching and school quality. He writes, "At the very beginning of the accountability movement, I don't believe the policy makers really understood what kinds of measures should be used to judge schools; . . . [they] stipulated that student test scores would be the prime determiner of educational quality. They were nationally standardized tests . . . produced by reputable companies. . . . The fact is, however, these are not the right kinds of tests to use to judge the quality of schooling."**

"The common belief that schools that score high on a standardized achievement are effective and that schools that score low are ineffective is simply misguided. It reflects ignorance about the nature of the test being used, because . . . [standardized] tests . . . measure the kind of conduct, knowledge and skills that children bring to school—not necessarily what they learn at school. What you want to judge the quality of schooling is the test that measures how well children were taught, not whether they come from a ritzy background. . . .**

Popham points to test items tied to children's socioeconomic status, which create bias against those without the relevant experiences and vocabulary. For example, to measure whether children knew the meaning of the word "field," the question asked, "'In which field do you plan to work after you graduate?' Well, children from families where a mother or father has a professional field, like a lawyer or a dentist . . . [will] be more familiar with the word "field" in that connection than would be a child from a family where a mom is a grocery store clerk or a dad who works in a car wash. So the kids from the middle- and upper-class families, where they have fields of occupation, will clearly have a better shot at that item than will kids from disadvantaged families."**

At the same time, Popham believes that the right kind of tests can be helpful. "I think the public has a right to know how well their schools are doing. So to resist any kind of testing, I think is disadvantaging the children. You have to create the right kinds of tests. But they can be a powerful force for instructional design, for getting kids to learn what they ought to learn."**

To guard against testing misuse, Popham advocates that teachers need to know the differences between a defensible and an indefensible assessment and between an accurate and an inaccurate interpretation of assessment data. Assessment-literate teachers will not only know how to create more appropriate assessments but will also be familiar with a range of assessment options.

Without assessment literacy, Popham asserts, teachers are reluctant to look critically at educational accountability tests—despite the fact that their students' scores on these tests will be used to evaluate the teachers' own effectiveness. This situation is serious because most standardized tests used for accountability are instructionally insensitive—unable to tell the difference between students who have been skillfully taught and those who have not. Instead, these tests merely measure the students' affluence level. So even though teachers may be teaching up a storm with their economically disadvantaged children, and the students are making real learning gains, it is likely that their test scores will not reflect their teachers' effectiveness.

Popham concludes, ". . . While assessment literacy is not a magic bullet capable of transforming the miserable to the marvelous, assessment literacy can trigger meaningful improvements in the way we educate our students."†††

*Popham, J. J. (2009). Assessment literacy for teachers: Faddish or fundamental? *Theory Into Practice 48*, 4–11.

**Tulenko, J. (2001, April 25). Interview with James Popham. *Frontline*. PBS. Retrieved from http://www.pbs.org/wgbh/pages/frontline/shows/schools/interviews/popham.html.

††Popham, W. J. (2010). Everything school leaders need to know about assessment. About the author. Retrieved from http://books.google.com/books/about/Everything_School_Leaders_Need_to_Know_A.html?id=5_8NiqYGW1MC.

†††Popham, W. J. (2009, June 4). Is assessment literacy the "magic bullet?" The Blog of Harvard Education Publishing. Retrieved from http://www.hepg.org/blog/19.

Additional Source: Popham, W. J. (2005, March 3). Standardized testing fails exam. *Edutopia*. Retrieved from http://www.edutopia.org/standardized-testing-evaluation-reform.

on the best method for setting defensible standards on competency tests, consensus holds that this activity is technically and politically difficult.

14-2e Why Standards Differ

Educators and policy makers of goodwill may disagree about standards' purposes. Different standards lead to different outcomes. Business leaders want high school graduates with polished reading, writing, math, and interpersonal skills who are ready for work on Day One. Policy makers, for their part, think about the long-term societal and economic needs: They want more demanding academic standards that will ensure a vibrant national economy in which U.S. workers have the complex skills to earn high wages and keep the United States meeting world-class benchmarks.

Parents typically choose standards based on their personal goals, family traditions, and expectations. Some parents expect their children to attend prestigious universities and aim for professional careers in architecture, medicine, law, engineering, or international banking. Others want their children to have employable skills by the time they graduate from high school or learn a respected and well-paying trade after a few years of apprenticeship, community college, and supervised internships.

Despite widespread adoption of the common core standards, local school boards and other key stakeholders retain essential roles in determining how these standards will translate into curriculum and classroom practice. School districts must reconcile these differing expectations when they adopt a set of learning standards. Although the process of setting standards is complex, both cognitively and socially, developing clear standards allows the schools' communities to clarify their needs and aspirations. In fact, the standard-setting process can become a community forum for discussing and negotiating what schools should do. Standards provide the criteria by which the locality holds schools, teachers, and students accountable. Given the transnational mobility of today's workers, a persuasive case can be made for implementing national standards tied to international benchmarks.

Did You Get It?

Which statement about educational standards and accountability is correct?

- **a.** Setting standards is not particularly useful in identifying what students should know.
- **b.** Setting high standards for all students is increasingly recognized as a waste of money and time.
- **c.** Making a serious good-faith effort to ensure all students meet increased standards does little to reduce socioeconomic stratification.
- **d.** They were adopted in the face of widespread evidence that teachers worked very hard to teach to standards, despite their own preferences.

Take the full quiz on CourseMate.

14-3 Principles of School Assessments and Teachers' Practices

If standards are to have a real effect on schools and student achievement, other school elements must support them. These supports include an articulated curriculum that spells out what students should learn and be able to do and what teachers should teach. It includes professional development that connects teachers' instructional practices to this curriculum so they can better facilitate student learning. Lastly, schools need a well-developed assessment process and materials that match the standards and the curriculum so teachers can fairly and accurately monitor and measure how well students are learning the knowledge and skills the standards require.

14-3a Types of School Assessments

Assessments come in a variety of styles and purposes. **Traditional assessments** commonly include paper-and-pencil or on-line formats with multiple-choice questions designed to compare students across the school district, state, or nation.[34] Their scores on these tests identify whether students have developed the core knowledge and skills the standards expect. Such standardized tests are the assessments traditionally used in the U.S. educational system. Although they are efficient, are relatively inexpensive to administer and score, and provide useful information about student progress and educational programs, they cannot measure many of learning's important aspects. Typically, they do not often assess higher-level thinking,[35] and they are not sensitive to students' ability to apply skills and knowledge to real-world problems. Likewise, the assessments provided through standardized tests do not support many useful teaching strategies.[36]

traditional assessments Efficient, relatively inexpensive test formats with multiple-choice questions designed to compare students across the school district, state, or nation.

performance or authentic assessment An appraisal format that requires students to enact, demonstrate, construct, or develop a product or solution under defined conditions or standards.

test bias A psychometric or sociocultural quality of certain test items that show provable and systematic differences in people's results based on group membership.

Performance or authentic assessment refers to a type of appraisal that requires students to enact, demonstrate, construct, or develop a product or solution under defined conditions or standards. Performance assessments capture aspects of students' learning that standardized tests cannot, allowing students to show what they know in a number of ways that meet standards in real-world settings. Although performance tasks provide meaningful intellectual challenge because they promote using learning beyond the classroom and can be tailored to fit individual student interests, performance assessments, too, have their benefits and limitations.

14-3b Characteristics of High-Quality Assessments

Both traditional and performance assessments require certain essential technical and ethical components if they are to actually measure what they say they measure and if they are to be fair to students. Test developers, educators, parents, and policy makers expect the tests their students take to meet high-quality professional standards for fairness, reliability, validity, environmental limitations, and opportunity to learn.

Technically and ethically appropriate assessments must be fair, valid, and reliable.

Charles Gupton/Flirt/Corbis

Fairness Children have an innate sense of fairness. No one wants to play in a game where the rules keep changing and are widely viewed as unreasonable. If the game score does not reflect their efforts, or if they receive penalties for events over which they have no control, children wonder if the game is worth the effort. The same holds true for testing.

Fairness means that everyone understands the rules of the game, the rules are applied consistently to each person, and everyone has the opportunity to play by the same rules. Standardized and performance tests, however, can sometimes be unfair.

A test is not fair when its items are biased. A test that shows provable and systematic differences in people's results based on group membership shows **test bias**. Test bias incorporates both psychometric and sociocultural factors, and both perspectives are necessary to draw a complete picture of test bias.

Psychometrically, a test demonstrates bias when it consistently under- or over-predicts how well someone or some groups will perform. Because it has better predictive validity for some groups than for others, such a test is not valid for certain populations. Typically, this type of test bias places students from low-income families, minority groups, students with disabilities, and English language learners at a serious disadvantage. Standardized tests often ignore the students' life experiences that may result in one group having an advantage over the others.

Testing is not fair when all students taking it have not had the school learning, family and cultural experiences, or biological equipment needed to help them perform well on this assessment. Any number of factors may work against students having a common experience that would place them on equal footing when taking a standardized test. Fairness in testing is, indeed, a complex and contentious problem.

Until the 1970s, most standardized tests writers were not so much culture biased as culture blind.[37] In other words, they did not recognize that ways of knowing the world—other than their way—existed. Since then, test publishers have made special efforts to remove these biased depictions and content to avoid offensive, culturally restricted, or stereotyped materials. In fact, documented cases of test bias exist; the legal and financial implications are so important in high-stakes testing that today's test developers carefully screen their tests in a concerted effort to reduce bias and increase validity.[38]

Teachers and administrators must interpret traditional or performance test results within a context that includes the students' culture and the cultural assumptions under which the test was developed. How similar are our students to those in the norm group? Are minority students' scores low because of low test-taking motivation, poor reading ability, frequent absences, or inadequate subject knowledge? Depending on the testing's purpose, the appropriate norms to measure the scores against may be the general norms, subgroup norms based on persons with comparable experiential backgrounds, or the individual student's own previous scores.[39] The more differences between the individual student and the norm group—or the more the group depends on teacher instruction rather than home resources to provide the needed information and skills—the more caution teachers and administrators must use when interpreting the results.

Table 14.2 shows the percentage of test items linked to SES for different school subjects. Language arts, science, and social studies have the highest connection to students' outside school environments and experiences.

validity The extent to which a test measures what it is supposed to measure.

face validity The appearance of measuring what it is supposed to measure.

content validity Whether the assessment provides an adequate sample or representation of the information that is supposed to be assessed.

Validity The most important question teachers must ask about any assessment is this: Does it really measure what it says it measures? **Validity** is the extent to which a test measures what it is supposed to measure. For instance, a measure of problem-solving ability should reflect how well learners can solve problems, not how well they can read the question or guess the correct answers. Three important types of validity are face validity, content validity, and concurrent validity.

Face validity is the appearance of validity. This is not a technical aspect, but rather a marketing one. For students to take tests seriously, tests need to look like "tests." For instance, a math test does not have face validity unless it includes obvious numbers and math problems.

Content validity focuses on whether the assessment provides an adequate sample or representation of the information that is supposed to be assessed. Although a test can never duplicate every detail of the subject matter, tests usually sample all the important dimensions of the content reasonably well. For instance, if a teacher inadvertently

TABLE 14.2

Academic Subjects and Socioeconomic Status

Subject	Percentage of SES Items
Reading	15
Language arts	65
Mathematics	5
Science	45
Social studies	45

Source: Popham, W. J. (2001). *The truth about testing: An educator's call to action*. Alexandria, VA: Association for Supervision and Curriculum Development, p. 65. © 2001 by ASCD. Reprinted with permission. Learn more about ASCD at www.ascd.org.

omits a topic, or if the teacher gives a topic either too much or too little emphasis, the assessment may not have enough content validity for that class.

Concurrent validity indicates the consistency or correlation between two independent measures of the same characteristic taken near the same time. Teachers can show an assessment has concurrent validity when the results of a teacher-made vocabulary test agree with the data from a standardized vocabulary test administered within a few days of the first test.

concurrent validity The consistency or correlation between two independent measures of the same characteristic taken near the same time.

reliability The extent to which a test is repeatable and yields consistent scores.

test reliability The consistency of scores obtained by the same persons when retested with the identical test or with an equivalent form.

environmental limitations Constraints that limit what students are or are not permitted to do or experience while taking a test.

Reliability To be valid, a test must be reliable; however, reliability does not guarantee validity. A test may produce consistent and repeatable results, yet the results may be meaningless and invalid. Reliability is an important technical aspect of high-quality assessments.

Reliability is the extent to which a test is repeatable and yields consistent scores. **Test reliability** is the consistency of scores obtained by the same persons when retested with the identical test or with an equivalent form. If a child is shown to have an IQ of 110 when tested on Monday and an IQ of 80 when retested on Thursday, little confidence can be placed on either score. Likewise, if a student identifies 40 of 50 words correctly in one set of words but identifies only 20 words correctly on an equivalent set, neither score can be taken as a dependable index of the student's verbal comprehension; after all, both scores cannot be right. Conversely, high scoring reliability occurs when multiple scorings yield the same or highly similar results.

Teachers need to be aware that a test score is subject to many unwanted, irrelevant influences. This explains why any single observation of a person gives only a rough estimate of the person's typical ability. Test scores may vary from one measurement to another for a variety of reasons—the student's attention or effort changes, the student is hungry or cold, the room is quiet or noisy. Likewise, test items may be more or less difficult for the student. For this reason, teachers need to ensure that all testing situations in their classrooms maintain the appropriate conditions that allow all students to do their best.

Environmental limitations Every test imposes certain **environmental limitations**. Standardized tests give directions about the specific conditions under which the test must be administered, so regardless of the test location, all students are taking it under identical conditions if their scores are to be meaningful. These are the same conditions under which the test's norm group took the test, making a comparison to a norm group possible. Directions for standardized tests—or for teachers, in the case of classroom assessments—also set the conditions under which their students may take tests. These constraints include how much time students have to complete the test or product, whether they work independently, and whether they can use calculators, smart phones, iPads, dictionaries, or math formula sheets. Can students stand up and stretch when they get tired? Can they walk around the room? Can they eat or drink while testing? Teachers and students need to know the limitations under which pupils will be assessed, and they must know this information ahead of time because it will affect their planning.

Test length is an important assessment limitation. Brief assessments cannot provide a complete picture of student performance, but the amount of time available for testing is always finite. This is especially true for testing younger students. A tension always exists between the number of test items needed for greater assessment precision, the students' maturity, and the information that educators want to know. Additionally, imposing shorter time limits can reduce the reliability of the test. Brief tests may be measuring how fast students produce the correct answers rather than how well the students understand the concepts supporting the questions that they might be able to answer correctly when they have enough testing time. In classroom testing, teachers want students to be able to show what they know without unduly worrying about time. Unless the test is deliberately looking to measure speed of response, student knowledge and capacity, not quickness, should be the focus.

The testing conditions also affect students' results. A noisy, distracting classroom that is too hot or too cold can negatively influence students' thinking and final scores. Although some environmental conditions cannot be controlled, teachers can usually neutralize or reduce such factors as room temperature, noise, and visual stimuli (e.g., exciting posters or wall-mounted study guides) that might interfere—positively or negatively—with learners' performance.

Opportunity to learn As discussed with standards, high-quality assessments can be fair, valid, and reliable only when all students taking them have had the opportunities to learn the content being tested. Opportunity to learn is the single most powerful predictor of student achievement.[40] One cannot expect students to know what they have not been taught. This factor is not so much a technical aspect of the assessment instrument, but rather a reflection of the students' school, classroom, and home experiences. As a principle of high-quality assessments, it bears repeating.

Students have not had an adequate opportunity to learn if they have not received the allotted time for instruction needed for them to master the subject matter at the level of depth necessary, if they have not received the appropriate content emphasis, or if they have not been given occasions to use higher-level thinking skills with the content. Further, unless the teachers' instructional practices helped students relate the new information to their prior knowledge, receive ongoing corrective feedback during the lessons, and have the lessons' parts related to other parts, the students will not have the opportunities to meet the standards, correctly answer the assessment questions, or produce a meaningful, high-quality product or performance. Also, unless the school consistently provided an orderly and academically focused learning environment, students will have been denied the opportunity to learn.

Teachers must seriously consider all of these factors when they interpret their students' test scores. Issues of fairness, validity, reliability, environmental factors, and opportunities to learn all play key roles in determining students' learning and their performance on assessments. No matter how well regarded the assessment instrument, other variables can confound and weaken the meaning of students' test results. Until these issues can be successfully resolved, teachers need to exercise caution in using these data to make key and ethical decisions about individual students.

Using tests ethically More than 30 years ago, Donald T. Campbell, a noted Lehigh University professor, warned about the perils of measuring effectiveness with a single,

Reflect & Discuss

High-quality assessments are fair, valid, and reliable; are administered under appropriate environmental conditions; and ensure that all students have had the necessary opportunity to learn. How would you as a college student determine if the assessments you take in your classes have these qualities?

A. Working in pairs, discuss occasions in your past when you had to take an important test that you did not think was fair, valid, or reliable; that was not administered under proper conditions; or whose content you did not have an adequate opportunity to learn. Which subject or skill was supposed to be tested? How did you feel while taking the test? How did the situation affect your scores? How were the test results used?

B. Working as a class, discuss how you might determine whether an important test you had to take had fairness (lack of bias), validity, and reliability; was administered under appropriate conditions; and provided you with the opportunity to learn.

C. Teachers have influence over many high-quality assessment factors in their classrooms. Working in pairs, generate two lists. In the first list, identify five teacher behaviors that may enhance the fairness, validity, reliability, environmental conditions, and opportunity to learn of classroom assessments. In the second list, identify five teacher behaviors that may reduce the fairness, validity, reliability, environmental conditions, and opportunity to learn of classroom assessments. As a whole class, compile these lists and discuss the impact that teachers can have on the accuracy and meaningfulness of their classroom or standardized assessments.

FlipSides

The Case for and against Standardized Testing

Despite their efficiency and popularity, many argue against using standardized tests for accountability and high-stakes decisions. Consider these differing views and then see where you stand.

Standardized tests should remain the centerpiece of student assessment and school accountability.	Standardized tests should not remain the centerpiece of student assessment and school accountability.
Efficiency ■ Standardized tests are convenient, take less time to administer and score, are less expensive than other types of assessments for large numbers of students, and results are quickly available for informed decision making.	**Efficiency** ● Efficiency is important but it does not outweigh an assessment's capacity to produce accurate and meaningful results that show students' specific areas of mastery, high levels of reasoning and problem solving, and use of the knowledge and skills in complex, well-designed performances.
Norm groups ■ Comparing students against a norm group permits teachers and parents to judge how well their students are performing relative to students in other localities and states and internationally. ■ Every student responds to the same questions without regard for opportunity to learn.	**Norm groups** ● Many minority and low-income children do not resemble the tests' norming group in gender, ethnicity, social, or economic characteristics so test bias may exist and results are less valid.[42] ● Certain test items are more likely to be answered correctly by children from affluent and middle-class families than those from low-income families [43]
Generate a range of scores ■ Norm-referenced tests determine a student's relative standing as compared with other test takers. Teachers assume that some students will perform well and others will not.	**Generate a range of scores** ● Criterion-referenced tests and other performance measures assume that ALL children can learn to grade-level standards. Teachers expect to teach (and ensure) that all children can meet the criteria.
Validity and reliability ■ Educators can select those tests with sufficiently high levels of validity and reliability to justify their use for certain purposes.	**Validity and reliability** ● All assessments contain some bias and measurement error and may not be appropriate for making high-stakes decisions about individuals.
Curriculum scope ■ Standardized tests measure broad characteristics such as verbal or math achievement and critical thinking that are not unduly sensitive to minor curriculum and experience differences.	**Curriculum scope** ● Curriculum narrowing occurs when teachers are overly focused on raising their students' standardized test scores in certain subjects and they neglect to teach (adequately or at all) the nontested subjects.
■ Test preparation activities provide students with opportunities to practice their new knowledge and skills and become familiar with the test format. Both activities help to improve students' test performance.	● Extensive "test prep" tends to reduce the intellectual level of what is taught, reduces the amount of knowledge a student needs to be educated, and lessens the opportunities for positive student–teacher interactions.[44]
■ Many standardized tests focus on recognition, recall, and application and have one right answer.	● Standardized tests lack occasions for real intellectual work to produce novel solutions to actual problems, show disciplined inquiry, or have value beyond the classroom.

(continued)

FlipSides

The Case for and against Standardized Testing (*continued*)

Standardized tests should remain the centerpiece of student assessment and school accountability.	Standardized tests should not remain the centerpiece of student assessment and school accountability.
Data for high-stakes decisions ■ Standardized tests have become a central component of high-stakes decisions about students and, increasingly, about teachers and principals.	**Data for high-stakes decisions** ● No standardized test is accurate, valid, or reliable enough to be the basis for making high-stakes decisions about students' futures or for teacher or principal evaluation and compensation.
■ Higher test scores year-over-year are assumed to reflect better instruction.	● Comparing scores of this year's students with those of last year's students confuses correlation with cause and effect because the caliber of students (and sometimes, teachers) varies year to year.[45]
■ Students' achievement test scores can be used to generate teacher effectiveness scores to be used for tenure and compensation decisions.	● Value-added statistical methodology contains too much measurement error to use for generating individual teacher effectiveness scores from their students' achievement data. And, not all teachers teach subjects with standardized test data available.[46]

Although standardized assessments bring many advantages, educators must use their results cautiously. Given both sides of the argument, what is your opinion about the central role of standardized tests in individual and school assessment and accountability?

Charles Gupton/Flirt/Corbis

Test bias may exist for students who don't match the norm group.

highly important indicator. "The more any quantitative social indicator is used for social decision-making," he noted, "the more subject it will be to corruption pressures and the more apt it will be to distort and corrupt the social processes it is intended to monitor."[41]

Important judgments about students, teachers, and school effectiveness should not be based on a single test score. Overvaluing test scores for making important decisions promotes tests' misuse and often compromises the test scores' validity. Dozens of assessment experts have argued that high-stakes tests are psychometrically inadequate for the critical decisions that must be made about students, teachers, and schools. Although standardized and classroom assessments offer many advantages in gauging students' academic progress, educators must employ informed caution and judgment in using these test scores.

14-3c The Cases for and against Standardized Testing

Standardized norm-referenced tests are an efficient and cost-effective way to assess large numbers of people from different backgrounds and learning experiences. As such, they have become a staple of school accountability. All teachers are likely to use standardized tests as part of their schools' efforts to monitor and assess students' progress. Yet critics openly challenge these tests for a variety of reasons. Both arguments for and against standardized testing, as presented in the FlipSides table, deserve closer looks.

Ironically, overuse and misuse of standardized tests can actually undermine real education. "Teaching to the test" and curriculum narrowing not only affect what teachers present, but also influence the intellectual level of what they teach, limit the amount of time they invest in making learning make sense and have personal meaning for students, limit the opportunities for students to be creative with what they are learning,[47] and reduce the positive teacher–student interactions through which strong and caring relationships develop. The result is a seriously diminished education. This is especially true for high-performing students in low-performing schools who may lose ground academically even as they earn top grades and score highly on standardized tests. As teachers focus on helping the large number of low achievers or students in the middle meet the standard, the high achievers receive less attention. In turn, they continue to fall further behind their high-achieving peers in affluent public and private high schools where the primary goal remains on challenging bright students to higher achievement.[48]

Superior and inferior schools It is natural—but incorrect and unfair—for people to assume that schools whose students have high test scores are superior to schools whose students have low test scores. A "failing" school's staff may actually be doing an outstanding instructional job, but their efforts may not be reflected by their students' scores on a high-stakes achievement test. Students' scores may increase, but not enough to meet the cutoff mark or standard. If the school's students came from traditionally underserved families, they may have started out far behind the norm group and actually made notable achievement gains during the year. Simply because their test results did not compare favorably with their more affluent peers does not mean the school, teachers, or students are "failing."

Likewise, identifying schools and teachers as successful simply because their students score well on standardized achievement tests is equally unfair and inaccurate. Much of what high-stakes tests measure is directly attributable not to what students learn in school, but to what they bring to school: their families' resources, their varied experiences and opportunities to learn outside school, or their inherited and home-nurtured academic aptitudes. Their high test scores do not prove that their school was effective. Until accountability systems include metrics that accurately reflect the contributions of those being judged, such as measuring how much progress a school's students make during the school year, and until assessments use statistical methods that account for the disadvantages (or advantages) that students may bring to school because of the quality of their prior instruction or their family learning opportunities, judgments about "superior" or "inferior" schools can be neither fair nor accurate.[49]

"Today's high-stakes tests often mask the actual quality of instruction in schools serving both low-income and high-income families,"[50] says educational assessment expert W. James Popham. This misidentification of schools leads to questionable recommendations for professional development. Skillful teachers in "failing" schools are told to change their instructional practices—even though their instruction is highly effective. Weak teachers in high-scoring schools may allow themselves to be carried along with the elevated esteem of working in a "good school" when, in fact, they should be significantly improving how they teach.

Reflect & Discuss

Reasons both favoring and discouraging the use of standardized tests exist. What are the most effective types of assessments in promoting students' mastery of twenty-first-century skills?

A. Working individually, review the arguments for and against using standardized tests and identify three new things that you learned about their limitations that may affect how you view and use standardized assessments in your own classroom.

B. Separate the class into two groups. Given the pros and cons of standardized testing, one group should identify the purposes for which standardized testing should be used. The other group should identify purposes for which they should not be used.

C. In your groups, identify at least two reasons for or against standardized tests' use in helping advance students' mastery of twenty-first-century learning skills.

D. After 10 minutes, the groups will report their findings to the entire class.

E. To conclude, each member will identify two cautions they will remember when using or interpreting results from standardized tests in their own classrooms and report these to the class.

Did You Get It?

Which statement is a principle of a high-quality assessment, whether of students, teachers, or schools?

a. Performance assessments of students' learning are essentially redundant to standardized testing.

b. Assessments have to be fair and unbiased.

c. There is no such thing as overuse of standardized testing because of its carefully designed comprehensive nature. If you meet those standards, you will have done all the right preparation.

d. High/low test scores are a good indicator of the actual quality of instruction and student achievement.

Take the full quiz on CourseMate.

14-4 Accountability for Educational Outcomes

Traditional accountability systems use test scores as the primary indicator of educational quality. Educators and parents view these end-of-year test scores as the "results" or evidence of their students' learning and, often, as the only important measure of their achievement. This perspective is shortsighted and misleading.

14-4a Accountability and Test Scores

accountable Holding someone responsible for students' learning and achievement.

Accountability includes assessment but is much broader in scope. **Accountable** means "to hold answerable for, to act in a creditable manner; and capable of being explained."[51] When a person is accountable, he or she is responsible for his or her actions and is obliged to answer for them. Educational accountability's primary aim is to improve student achievement. The bottom line for educational accountability is to answer this question: Did students learn and achieve more than they might have without this specific educational system?

Considering test scores as education's "bottom line" is akin to the business model in which stock prices and reported earnings masquerade as quality indicators. In this view, critical factors such as accounting irregularities, deteriorating facilities, and restated earnings are "minor inconveniences." For instance, when Lehman Brothers, a Wall Street financial services firm and the fourth largest investment bank in the world, collapsed and filed for Chapter 11 bankruptcy protection in 2008 as a result of its exposure to the subprime mortgage crisis, it threatened to take down the global financial system. Its failure eroded the trust needed among banks to fuel lending. It caused 26,000 employees to lose their jobs, caused millions of investors to lose all or almost all of their money, and began a chain reaction that produced the worst American financial crisis and economic downturn since the Great Depression. The proverbial "bottom line" had been an illusion. Lehmann executives had manipulated the balance sheets and falsified financial reports. The focus on corporate short-term windfalls had diverted attention from clear warning signs of larger, systemic problems.

In the same way, exclusive emphasis on test scores in educational accountability does not give a full and accurate picture of how well students are achieving or how well schools are performing. What is more, they offer no guidance about how to improve the performance of all players in the system.

Clearly, effective educational accountability systems encompass more than test scores. Teachers' jobs are more complex than what a single test can measure. **Effective accountability systems** are comprehensive, containing multiple measures of student achievement. Students' poor or excellent school achievement never has only one single cause.[52]

effective accountability systems Comprehensive, multiple measures of student achievement.

14-4b Student-Centered or "Holistic" Accountability

As mentioned earlier, student-centered or "holistic" accountability balances both quantitative and qualitative indicators: It presents the story behind the numbers. It considers individual students' progress by placing traditional test scores into a context that makes the data meaningful.[53] Low or high scores tell us little if we do not know, for example, the type of curriculum the student studied, the teacher's classroom experience and expertise in the subject taught, the teacher's instructional practices, the school's discipline climate, and the student's attendance in school during the year.

Holistic accountability includes a variety of background factors that contribute to educational excellence[54]:

- *Teaching practices,* including assessment, feedback, and collaboration
- *Curriculum practices,* including equity of opportunity for enrolling in advanced classes and academic supports to help students succeed once enrolled
- *Leadership practices,* including the use of resources to sustain the most important educational priorities (considering what teachers, administrators, school board members, and what other policy makers do)
- *Parent involvement,* including monitoring students' study at home and participating in relevant volunteer school and community activities
- *Faculty communication,* including inter-grade and interdepartmental collaboration
- *Professional development,* including study of research, pedagogy, assessment, and content areas and adopting best practices in each for classroom and school use.

Holistic accountability is more motivating for teachers than other types of accountability. Teachers see holistic accountability as fair and significant because it includes indicators that they can directly manage or influence. They have a sense of control over the day-to-day learning they design for their students. When teachers know their success as educators will be judged based on a range of a student's learning activities and performances rather than on a single high-stakes test score, they feel less anxiety, stress, and resentment than if their entire year's worth depended on how well each student scored on one three-hour test.

Likewise, holistic accountability motivates students because it gives them more ways to succeed. They have more chances and formats in which to show what they have learned and can do. They can receive constructive feedback throughout the learning process and make continuous improvements. In addition, students often have occasions to choose their own topics, work partners, or performance methods to show what they have learned. Throughout the school year, they know where they stand relative to the standard, and they know exactly what they must do to successfully reach it. Because they exert more control over their own learning and academic fate, students are more committed to learning.

Holistic accountability is comprehensive, showing the importance not only of teacher effectiveness but also curriculum, principal leadership, parent involvement, student mobility, and other factors that traditional accountability practices ignore or obscure. All of these factors work together to build positive student outcomes.

Finally, holistic accountability extends the value of traditional accountability. It targets improving teaching and learning rather than merely providing an educational evaluation and a public report. It recognizes that the purpose of student assessment is to improve student—and teacher—performance. We assess so we will know how to teach better and how to learn better. Poor performance on an appraisal inspires an improvement process rather than blame and humiliation. In this way, the assessment results spur the search to find the underlying causes of poor achievement and develop specific improvement strategies.

Every teacher should strive to help students be successful. Student success motivates students and teachers alike—after all, everyone wants to feel competent and empowered with new skills, information, and insights. When teachers and students can engage in continuous improvement, the accountability system is oriented toward achieving constructive ends rather than making judgments about failure.

14-4c Goals of Education and Accountability

Educational goals are broader than just generating high reading and math scores. Although these subjects are critical disciplines that underpin most learning and work in our complex world, narrowing the curriculum to these two areas actually increases the educational inequities that the accountability system is designed to remove. Teaching and assessing for learning should develop students' comprehension and thinking skills, enhance their abilities to construct knowledge and communicate effectively, encourage students to engage in sustained disciplined inquiry, and inspire them to effectively apply their classroom-derived knowledge to real-world situations.

Most school board members and state legislators say they want American students to learn critical thinking, social skills, citizenship and responsibility, physical and emotional health, preparation for skilled work, and appreciation for the arts and literature.[55] These are the essentials of a high-quality education necessary for continued learning, good citizenship, interpersonal skills, esthetic appreciation, and economic self-sufficiency in a highly complex, information-rich world.

When schools receive sanctions based solely on their students' reading, math, or other single-subject scores, the accountability system inadvertently creates incentives to limit—or in some cases to entirely end—time spent on other important parts of the curriculum. Skewing of the curriculum toward reading, math, and test-prep activities disproportionately affects low-income and minority children, who need the most time and help becoming "proficient" in these test-directed areas. Instead of helping low-achieving students score well on the assessment, basing decisions about their academic growth solely on their standardized test scores may actually encourage practices that widen the achievement gap in areas that matter in life outside school but for which schools are not now being held accountable.[56]

In fact, American schools should be held accountable for their results. Our students, our economy, and our national security depend on all students learning to high and measurable levels the knowledge, skills, and habits of mind necessary for twenty-first-century viability. Nevertheless, when reviewing these broader goals, it is clear that basing school accountability only on student proficiency in reading and math is neither holistic nor in the best interests of the students and society.

Accountability is larger than evaluation or assessment. Educational accountability holds educators, parents, students, and the community answerable for providing the resources to support each student's achievement to high standards. Holistic accountability includes academic achievement scores as well as specific information on curriculum, teaching and leadership practices, and funding adequacy. It weighs both quantitative and qualitative indicators, thereby delivering a fuller view of student learning. Our challenge is to find a workable balance between objectively and subjectively measured assessments for more comprehensive and valued educational ends.

An effective assessment program supports teaching and learning. And our assessments must reflect what we value. If we value learning to high standards, we must harness assessments *for* learning along with assessments *of* learning. These data can help us improve teaching and learning only when we learn how to use them—and the sources from which they come—wisely.

Reflect & Discuss

Educational accountability is more than test scores, but the general public is often comfortable with the notion that end-of-year test scores are the most important sign of a school's effectiveness.

A. Working as a class, prepare a presentation to a local newspaper's education writer to help inform the community about educational accountability for twenty-first-century skills.
B. Working as a class, decide on five key arguments that you will present to the education writer to explain how educators value accountability, but that accountability for ensuring that every student masters twenty-first-century skills includes, but is more than, end-of-year standardized test scores.
C. Divide into five groups, each of which will prepare a three-minute talk using details and examples for its case in oral and graphic forms.
D. Present the entire public education talk to the class as a whole. Discuss the arguments that you find most—and least—persuasive to educators and to the general public.

Reflect & Discuss

Effective schools have long disaggregated student demographic and achievement data to ensure that all student populations were achieving well. This Reflect & Discuss activity will give you the experience of looking at such data closely to determine which school factors have the greatest impact on student learning and attainment.

Teachers learn how to use their students' achievement data to make instructional decisions. For Sym City Middle School, you are following the students' progress as they move through grades 6 to 8. The students' test results have just come back from their last year at the middle school, grade 8. You also have available last year's data (grade 7) and data from two years ago (grade 6).

You are looking at one of the middle school's teams, which consists of an English, math, science, and history teacher. Each team has approximately 100 students with each teacher having 25 students per class. Because the teachers teach four classes, they have a total of 100 students. All 100 students have the same four teachers for their four subjects. This arrangement provides teachers with time to discuss holistic assessment as a team. Students in this school are not grouped by ability; in other words, they are assigned to teachers randomly. There is not, for example, a high-ability group, two middle-ability groups, and a low-ability group. The test results are from the NCLB testing—a test on which students must reach a certain passing score on the test.

Beside each teacher's name there is the percentage of the 100 students who passed the high-stakes test in the subject. Examine the trends over the three years and answer the questions at the end of the data. Remember that students are randomly assigned to classes and that the student population at this school is very stable—fewer than 1 percent leave the district each year.

Sym City Middle School			
	Grade 6 (Two Years Ago)	**Grade 7 (One Year Ago)**	**Grade 8 (Current Year)**
English	Mr. Brown (90)	Mrs. Nguyen (67)	Mr. Green (88)
Math	Mrs. Rinaldi (77)	Mr. Papadopoulos (65)	Mrs. Dias (54)
Science	Mrs. Greenberg (73)	Mr. Davis (88)	Mr. Harvey (94)
History	Mr. White (62)	Mrs. Santos (80)	Mrs. Jung (89)

A. What is the trend in English achievement over the past three years? What are two possible explanations for the drop in student pass rates in the seventh grade? What reasons might explain the change from seventh to eighth grade in the pass rates?

B. What is the trend in math achievement over the past three years? What are two reasons that could explain what is happening?

C. What is the trend in science achievement over the past three years? What are two reasons that could explain this trend?

D. What is the trend in history achievement over the past three years? Which reasons might explain this trend?

Did You Get It?

What is the proper understanding of educational accountability?

a. Educational accountability is a once-a-year hurdle that teachers must help their students cross.

b. Test scores provide a full and accurate assessment of what students have learned.

c. Educational accountability is about improving student outcomes.

d. Holistic accountability means taking responsibility for educating the whole child.

Take the full quiz on CourseMate.

SUMMARY

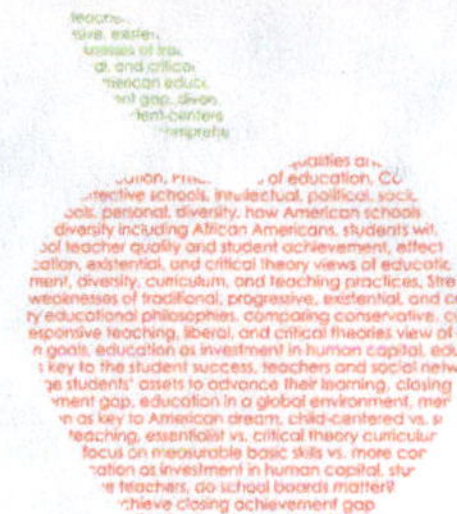

- Over the past five decades, standards and test scores have come to define educational accountability in the United States.
- Schools and teachers use assessments to determine student attainment and mastery, to make placement decisions, to diagnose learning needs, to determine eligibility for special education services, and to identify alternative instructional methods.
- Educational standards contribute to achievement and accountability. Accountability tied to educational standards gives clear identification of what students should know and be able to do at each grade level. With standards, teachers are expected to bring every student to proficiency in the identified knowledge and skills.
- High-quality assessments share several principles without which the students' scores cannot be considered as unbiased, accurate, or trustworthy: fairness, validity, reliability, consistent environmental conditions, and opportunity for students to learn the material being assessed. Ethical use of assessments and their data are extremely important.
- Assessments can be used *for* and *of* learning. Both formative and summative assessments are essential components of a complete accountabiity system.
- Standardized tests offer certain advantages over other assessment methods. They are efficient and cost-effective for large numbers of students, permit comparison with a norm group, permit valid and reliable measurement of broad characteristics, and can gather data useful for educational decision making. Their limitations include test bias, limited measure of students' learning, curricular and instructional misuse, and misunderstanding of results.
- Accountability for educational outcomes is broader than students' achievement test scores. Effective accountability systems are holistic, comprehensive, contain multiple qualitative and quantitative measures of student achievement, and contain specific information on curriculum, teaching and leadership practices, parent involvement, faculty communications and collaboration, professional development, and funding adequacy. It recognizes that its purpose is to improve student achievement.

Visit the Education CourseMate for this textbook to access the eBook, Did You Get It? quizzes, TeachSource Video Cases, flashcards, and more. Go to CengageBrain.com to log in, register, or purchase access.

"We can, whenever and wherever we choose, successfully teach all children whose schooling is of interest to us."—Ron Edmonds

Davis Barber/PhotoEdit

CHAPTER 15

Best Practices for Effective Schools

InTASC Standards Addressed: 1, 2, 3, 4, 5, 6, 7, 8, 9, and 10

LEARNING OBJECTIVES

After you read this chapter, you should be able to:

15-1 Summarize the Effective Schools Movement's beginnings and its findings about school's capacity to provide high-quality education for low-income and minority students.

15-2 List the seven contemporary correlates of effective schools.

15-3 Explain the meaning of "instructional leadership," how it contributes to students' achievement, and what it looks like in schools.

15-4 Discuss what "clear and focused mission" means, how it contributes to students' achievement, and what it looks like in schools.

15-5 Define "safe and orderly environment," how it contributes to students' achievement, and what it looks like in schools.

15-6 Discuss what "climate of high expectations" means, how it contributes to students' achievement, and what it looks like in schools.

15-7 Explain the meaning of "frequent monitoring of student progress," how it contributes to students' achievement, and what it looks like in schools.

15-8 Describe "positive home–school relations," how it contributes to students' achievement, and what it looks like in schools.

15-9 Discuss "opportunity to learn," how it contributes to students' achievement, and what it looks like in schools.

15-10 Explain the realistic expectations for effective schools.

Reviewing our country's educational history with minority and low-income children can be discouraging. Sociological, economic, and cultural variables have often placed severe obstacles in the paths of minority and low-income students as they struggle toward learning. Too often, a variety of poverty-related issues put low-income students cognitively and academically behind their middle- and upper-class peers even before they arrive at school. Likewise, schools' traditional sorting and selecting practices and institutional norms have kept many traditionally underserved students from entering the educational mainstream.

But this does not have to be the case. Research affirms that when teachers, administrators, and the community hold high expectations for students, effectively deliver a strong and appropriate curriculum, and provide high levels of support, learning typically improves. As Ron Edmonds, leader of the Effective Schools Movement, concludes, "We can, whenever and wherever we choose, successfully teach all children whose schooling is of interest to us. We already know more than we need to do that."[1]

In the early 1980s, educators began investigating whether schools might be able to increase low-income and minority students' achievement. They identified schools that successfully educated all students regardless of their socioeconomic status (SES) or family background. These schools were located in varying regions and in communities both large and small.

Investigators noted that these high-achieving schools had certain philosophies, policies, and practices in common: strong instructional leadership, a clear sense of mission, high expectations for all students, robust instructional behaviors, frequent monitoring of student achievement, a safe and orderly school environment, opportunities for students to learn, and positive home–school relations. Eventually, these attributes became known as the Correlates of Effective Schools. For approximately 40 years, research has continued to support these essential beliefs.[2]

This chapter looks at the Effective Schools Movement and the research-based best practices that every school can employ to increase academic learning for *all* students. It provides an optimistic and realistic note on which to conclude a textbook for future educators.

15-1 The History of the Effective Schools Movement

Ronald Edmonds, the education professor and researcher (profiled later in this chapter) who first defined the effective schools correlates, explains the rationale for the movement in this way:

> The very great proportion of the American people believes that family background and home environment are principal causes of the quality of pupil performance. In fact, no notion about schooling is more widely held than the belief that the family is somehow the principal determinant of whether or not a child will do well in school.… Such a belief has the effect of absolving educators of their professional responsibility to be instructionally effective.[3]

In other words, when teachers expect little achievement from certain students, they usually get it.

In the 1950s and early 1960s, the struggle against poverty, racial prejudice, and unequal educational opportunity grew more intense. After 1960, Congressional legislation attempted to address these problems. The ensuing efforts to document and remedy the unequal educational opportunity, especially for low-income and minority children, provided a major push for school effectiveness studies.

15-1a The Early Studies

The 1964 Civil Rights Act required the Commissioner of Education to conduct a nationwide survey of the availability of educational opportunity. The resulting 1966 report, *Equality of Educational Opportunity* (commonly referred to as "the Coleman Report" and discussed in Chapter 5), concluded that family background—not the school—was the major determinant of student achievement and life outcomes.[4] The Coleman Report suggested that schools were unable to overcome or equalize the disparity in students' academic achievement due to environmental factors. In 1972, Christopher Jencks, a Harvard University professor, and his colleagues corroborated Coleman's findings.[5]

Although these reports made for attention-grabbing headlines, their conclusions were wrong. Coleman and Jencks studies confirmed the correlation connecting higher family SES with their children's higher school achievement. [6]

As a result, the belief that for academic achievement, "families matter and schools don't" has become part of our popular culture. In fact, Donald C. Orlich, a professor emeritus at Washington State University and an education assessment critic, believes that "many public school educators have uncritically accepted the hypothesis of familial effects, along with its corollary: that teachers cannot be held accountable for students' failure to learn when the students come from poor home environments."[7]

The Coleman and Jencks reports and the related literature prompted the federal government to create compensatory education programs. They also stimulated work by researchers and educators who believed the opposite—that effective schools *could* make a difference in student learning *regardless* of students' family backgrounds or socioeconomic status. These later investigators developed a body of research that affirmed the school controls the factors needed to ensure student mastery of the core curriculum, and the family plays a crucial role in promoting student learning.

15-1b Early Effective Schools Studies

For almost 40 years, researchers have gathered ample evidence that shows schools can and do make a powerful difference in students' academic achievement.

In the late 1970s, independent researchers in the United States launched investigations to demonstrate that schools could generate high academic achievement among low-income and minority students. They began to identify public schools whose graduates scored higher than the national average on standardized tests. Academic growth—not decline—characterized these schools. Soon, hundreds of studies and research-based analytic papers tried to identify these schools' characteristics or "correlates" that were unusually successful with students regardless of their parents' education or income levels.

So began the Effective Schools Movement. The studies and reform efforts launched in the 1970s and early 1980s ultimately shared a common purpose: to identify those in-school factors that affect students' academic achievement. In addition, these studies were loosely coupled by the relatively small network of like-minded people conducting them and the relationship between studies. Each study built on the previous investigations' findings.

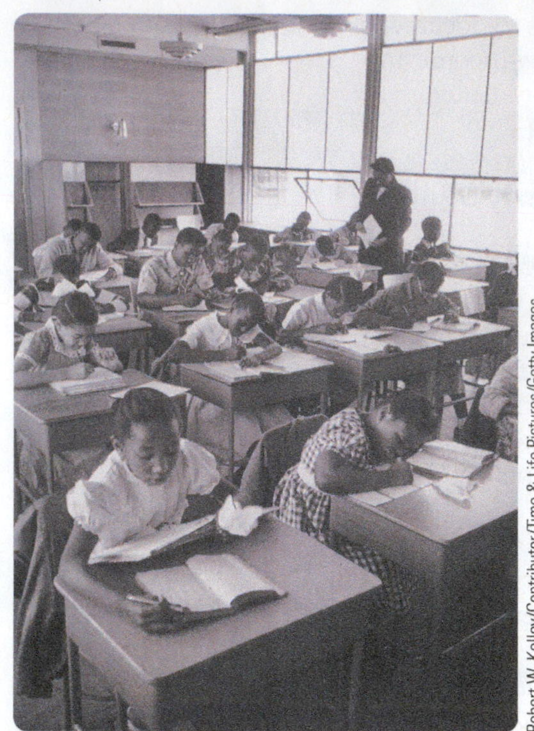

Effective schools successfully educated all students regardless of socioeconomic status or family background.

outlier studies In statistics, investigations of events that lie at the far end of the distribution or are unlike others of similar nature.

case studies Situations in which investigators analyzed a small set of schools in depth.

effective school One in which low-income and minority students' basic skills are at least as well developed as the middle-class children's skills, closing the achievement gap.

Types of effective schools research Much of the effective schools research might informally be considered as **outlier studies**.[8] In statistical terminology, an *outlier* is something that lies at the far end of the distribution. In other words, an outlier school might be one where all students were eligible for free or reduced-price lunches, yet the student achievement test scores were extremely high.

Another vein of school effectiveness research focused on **case studies**. In these studies, investigators analyzed a small set of schools in depth. Typically, researchers organized the schools by outcome measures—that is, high-achieving schools versus low-achieving schools. The school characteristics in a group were then studied by demographic and survey techniques.

Outlier and case study investigations inevitably contained some methodological limitations. Small samples and statistical issues may yield results that vary widely. Nevertheless, these studies clearly show that effective schools are characterized by good discipline, high teacher expectations for student achievement, and effective administrator leadership.[9]

15-1c Ronald Edmonds and the "Effective Schools" Concept[10]

Until his death in 1983, Ronald Edmonds, an education professor at Michigan State University, was one of the key figures in the Effective Schools Movement. Thomas L. Good and Jere E. Brophy—themselves noted educational psychology researchers—noted that "Edmonds, more than anyone, had been responsible for the communication of the belief that schools can and do make a difference."[11]

Although Edmonds acknowledged that students' family background was a strong influence on student achievement, he refused to accept the Coleman Report's conclusions. In 1979, as Director of Harvard's Center for Urban Studies, Edmonds set out to find schools where students from low-income families were highly successful.

Effective schools correlates In perhaps his most notable contribution to the education field, Edmonds articulated five school-level variables that are strongly correlated with student achievement, more simply known as the five effective schools' "correlates"[12]:

- Strong administrative leadership with attention to instructional quality
- High expectations for all students' achievement
- A safe and orderly climate conducive to teaching and learning
- An emphasis on basic skill acquisition
- Frequent monitoring and measuring of pupil progress so teachers and principals are constantly aware of pupil growth in relationship to the instructional objectives

Edmonds' five correlates gleaned from schools that raised all children's academic achievement became the framework for thinking about school effectiveness.

Next, Edmonds defined an **effective school** as one in which low-income and minority students' basic skills are at least as well developed as the middle-class children's skills. An effective school has closed the achievement gap between low- and high-SES students. In his view, "To be effective, a school need not bring all students to equal mastery levels, but it must bring an equal percentage of its highest and lowest social classes to minimum mastery."[13] As Edmonds saw it, in an "effective" school, one could not guess a student's SES by looking at reading test scores.

In addition, Edmonds found that schools that were instructionally effective for poor and minority children were "indistinguishable" from instructionally less effective schools on SES factors (i.e., father's and mother's education, category of occupation, percentage of white students, mean family size, percentage of intact families). The large student performance differences, therefore, could not be attributed to differences in pupils' social class and family backgrounds.[14] Instead, the differences in achievement came from the schools' practices. These findings directly contrasted with Coleman's and Jencks' conclusions that variations in student performance levels from school to school were only minimally related to the schools' characteristics.

Edmonds, along with Wilbur Brookover, Lawrence Lezotte, and others, looked for effective schools. They studied achievement data from schools in several major cities with student populations drawn mainly from poverty backgrounds. In one study, Edmonds and colleagues compared successful schools with similar schools in like neighborhoods where children were not learning or were learning at a low level, reaching the following conclusions[15]:

- Public schools can and do make a difference, even when the school population consists largely of students from poverty backgrounds.
- Children from poverty backgrounds can learn at high levels as a result of instruction and related practices delivered by public schools.
- Schools where all children are learning regardless of family background have common characteristics and processes.

Edmonds and colleagues determined that although effective schools were committed to serving all their pupils without regard for family background, they did not conduct "business as usual." They recognized the need to modify curricular design, text selection, teaching strategies, and a range of behaviors in response to differences in pupils' family background. Their clear sense of purpose, high expectations, focused and safe environments, and adapted instructional practices made measurable differences for their students.

Although Edmonds' studies had methodological limitations,[16] their findings provided valuable lessons about how schools could make a difference in low-income and minority students' achievement levels. Edmonds' review of the Effective Schools literature and his own investigations led him to conclude that no one model explained school effectiveness for the poor or any other social class of students. Also, the relationship between the effective schools correlates and increased student achievement was correlational in nature, not a cause-and-effect relationship. In these studies, both the correlates and higher student achievement appeared together; no evidence proved that one factor caused the other.

More recently, researchers using sophisticated statistical models have determined that teachers can have more impact on student achievement than other school factors.[17] At the same time, methodological improvements in research studies have transformed Edmonds' initial narrow and managerial view of effective schooling into a more comprehensive notion of effective education, which encompasses classroom instruction as well as staff and community relations.[18]

Edmonds' contributions were primarily thought provoking and conceptual.[19] His work and that of his colleagues in the United States and abroad motivated several decades of educators to improve their schools' capacities to help all children succeed. And his influence continues today.

American Education Spotlight

Ron Edmonds, Father of Effective Schools Movement

Ronald R. Edmonds

Perhaps more than anyone, Ron Edmonds is responsible for communicating the belief that American public schools can and do make a difference.

Ronald R. Edmonds (1935–1983) led the Effective Schools Movement. In his view, the fact that many poor and minority children do not master the school curriculum reflects the schools'—rather than the children's—deficiencies. Edmonds introduced the concept of effective schools, and he tested and implemented successful programs of school reform based on it.

Lawrence W. Lezotte, Edmonds' colleague and close personal friend in the Effective Schools Movement, remembers the ". . . biographical factors [that] seemed to propel [Edmonds] toward his work on issues of equity and social justice.

"Ron was a mixed race child with an upbringing that was in many ways parallel to that of President Obama with one important difference. Ron had a fraternal twin brother.

"Ron was an extremely accomplished student and his twin brother was not. Ron could never understand why Ron was treated so differently than his brother at school but no differently than his brother at home and in the community. This nagging issue may be the source of the belief that schools should be able to successfully educate all children.

"Ron Edmonds became a high school social science teacher in Ann Arbor, Michigan Public Schools. He used to tell the story that one year he was asked to teach two different sections of United States History. One section was designated for the advanced placement students and the other for the lower performing students. He would tell that about the third week of school he came to the conclusion that he didn't need to have two different lesson plans for the different groups. He found that high expectations and engaging lessons worked for all the students. Again, this insight has a lasting impact on the effective schools research that was to follow years later."

As a high school teacher, Edmonds began doing project work with the University of Michigan. While in Michigan, he served as faculty at the University of Michigan, human relations director for the Ann Arbor, Michigan Public Schools, and assistant superintendent in the state's Department of Public Instruction. For most of the 1970s, he directed Harvard graduate education program's Center for Urban Studies and received a certificate of advance study. Much of his work on the effective schools research and related policy discussions occurred while serving in that role. From 1978 to 1980, he served as a senior assistant for instruction with the New York City public schools. In 1981, Edmonds returned to Michigan as professor of education at Michigan State University (MSU), where he continued his research and advocacy until his untimely death in 1983.

Critics call Edmond's belief that "all children can learn" a red herring. They note that because impoverished environments impair childhood nutrition and cognitive development, all children cannot learn the same curriculum at the same time and at the same level. Critics also point to methodological issues—claiming that we cannot set standards for effective schools by looking at exceptions or by confusing correlation with cause and effect. They also challenge the effective schools' correlates as unrealistic.

Nonetheless, Edmonds worked to dispel the hopelessness with which teachers of low-income and minority children typically viewed their students. By 1990, the Effective Schools Movement had become a coalition of practitioners, citizens, and researchers working in over 700 school districts across the country and communicating their findings. And the effective schools process continues to improve.

Lezotte concludes, "Though much too brief, Ron's impact on the education of the children of the poor in the United States still reverberates throughout the efforts to reform public education today. . . . Without question, Ron Edmonds made a difference."

Sources: Lezotte, L. W. (2011. October 10). Personal communication with Bill Owings and Leslie Kaplan; Ron Edmonds. (1996). History of the Effective Schools Movement. Donnelley and Lee Library Archives, Chicago's National Liberal Arts College. Retrieved from http://library.lakeforest.edu/archives/HistoryofEffectiveSchools.html; Hare, I. (1988, January). School social work and effective schools. *Urban Education 22*(4), 413–28; Neisser, U. (1986). Introduction. In U. Neisser (Ed.), *The school achievement of minority children. New perspectives.* Hillsdale, NJ: Lawrence Erlbaum Associates; Raptis, H., and Fleming, T. (2003, October 1). Reframing education: How to create effective schools. C. D. Howe Institute Commentary. Retrieved from http://www.accessmylibrary.com/coms2/summary_0286-11856261_ITM; Thomas M. D., and Bainbridge, W. L. (2000, December 6). The truth about 'All children can learn'. *Schoolmatch.* Retrieved from http://schoolmatch.com/articles/EWDEC00.htm.

15-1d Additional Effective Schools Findings

Over time, the list of effective schools "correlates" has expanded. In 1979, the Michigan Department of Education asked Wilbur Brookover and Lawrence W. Lezotte to investigate a set of eight Michigan schools enrolling large numbers of low-income and minority children and characterized by consistent pupil performance improvement or decline. Trained interviewers visited schools and tried to identify the differences between improving and declining schools. The researchers found the following consistent differences between schools where students achieved well and where they didn't[20]:

- *Clear instructional focus.* Improving schools clearly accepted and emphasized the importance of the reading and math objectives, whereas declining schools gave less emphasis to such goals and did not specify them as fundamental.
- *High teacher expectations.* The staffs of improving schools tended to believe that *all* of their students could master the basic objectives. Teachers perceived that their principals shared this belief. Likewise, teachers at improving schools expected that their students would complete high school or college, whereas teachers at declining schools had much lower expectations for their students' achievement, and educational and employment futures.
- *Commitment to and responsibility for student achievement.* In improving schools, teachers and principals were more likely to assume responsibility for and were committed to teaching the basic reading and math skills. Staffs at declining schools felt that teachers could not do much to influence their students' achievement and displaced the responsibility for skill learning to parents or students.
- *High time-on-task.* Teachers in improving schools spent more time on achieving reading and math objectives, whereas teachers in declining schools spent less time in direct reading instruction.
- *Principal as instructional leader.* In improving schools, principals were more assertive in their institutional leadership role, held higher expectations for students' behavior, and were more regular in evaluating achievement of basic objectives. By comparison, principals in declining schools were more permissive, emphasized informal and collegial relationships with teachers, and emphasized general public relations rather than evaluating school effectiveness in providing a basic education for all students.
- *Accountability.* The improving schools showed greater acceptance of accountability and used measured student learning as one sign of their effectiveness.
- *Dissatisfaction with current achievement.* Generally, teachers in improving schools were less satisfied than staffs in declining schools. Staffs in declining schools were complacent and content with current achievement levels.
- *Unclear role of parent involvement.* Differences in parent involvement levels were not clear. Improving schools had higher levels of *parent-initiated* involvement but less overall parent involvement.
- *Compensatory education.* Classroom teachers in improving schools focused on teaching reading. By comparison, classroom teachers in declining schools spent more time identifying students to be placed in compensatory reading activities and placed greater emphasis on programmed instruction. Teaching children the academic basics appears to be "someone else's" job.

The 1979 Brookover and Lezotte findings present a relatively clear profile of achieving schools that are congruent with other urban school studies. They showed that teacher and principal expectations and behaviors created the school conditions that allowed low-income and minority students to make achieve ment gains. They did not blame their students' low achievement on inherited, social, or family factors. At the same time, Brookover and Lezotte concluded that no single combination of variables will produce an effective school. Most importantly, these researchers found that pupil family background neither causes nor prevents elementary school instructional effectiveness. Instructional effectiveness is the responsibility of principals and teachers.

Limitations of the early effective schools research Effective schools research finds common characteristics, but also shares serious limitations. The studies looked at too few schools with too-narrow student demographics to justify firm and generalizable conclusions. The findings were correlational, rather than indicating a cause-and-effect relationship. Furthermore, researchers looking at middle-class students and secondary schools did not find the same results as those studying elementary schools.[21] Despite these limitations, the studies' consistent findings of the school effectiveness "correlates"—strong principal or staff leadership, high expectations for student achievement, a clear set of instructional goals, an effective schoolwide staff professional development program, an emphasis on order and discipline, and a system for monitoring students' progress—give substantial credibility to the varied studies' findings.[22]

In spite of the cautions, many educators continued to mistakenly assume that the cause-and-effect relationship exists between the effective schools correlates and student achievement. During the 1980s, this line of research had a major impact on educators' school improvement plans. Several implementation studies tried to change school-level behaviors on one or more of the factors considered important to effective schooling, mistakenly assuming that the cause-and-effect relationship with student achievement existed. Programs were initiated in Atlanta, Chicago, Minneapolis, Pittsburgh, San Diego, St. Louis, Washington, DC, and many other smaller school districts.[23] Perhaps not surprisingly, these projects achieved mixed results.[24]

In light of the previous two decades of effective schools' research findings and the methodological critiques, in 1990 Levine concluded:

> The effective school correlates should be viewed more as prerequisites for attaining high and equitable student achievement levels. Their presence does not guarantee schools' success. All correlates must be present to make a difference.
>
> The correlates represented issues and challenges for their schools. They were not "prescriptions" or "recipes" for attaining a high achieving status. Enacting each correlate takes many steps, and no specific action or steps is right for every school.
>
> Much of the positive results at unusually effective schools involve teachers and administrators identifying and addressing obstacles to student learning. Changes in one place usually create ripples elsewhere. Making sure that changes in one sphere do not create negative repercussions elsewhere takes constant monitoring and adjusting that cannot easily be written in a "to do" list.
>
> Schools cannot tackle all reforms at once or they would go into overload.[25]

15-1e Effective Schools Research, 1990 to Today

During the 1990s, educators made substantial conceptual and empirical progress in understanding and explaining effective schools.[26] The new models were more specific about the school factors and their interactions. In addition, the definition of effective schools expanded to include public and private elementary, middle, and high schools from communities with all social classes. These schools were located in rural, urban, and suburban settings and had various levels of support. This second generation of effective schools models and research not only focused on schools serving all types of students in all types of settings, but also emphasized growth in achievement and school improvement across all contexts. In fact, school effectiveness is now understood as sets of interacting variables.

In the 1990s, Jaap Scheerens and Roel Bosker, two professors of education at the University of Twente, The Netherlands, reviewed a number of school effectiveness models. They conducted one of the most quantitatively sophisticated reviews of the research literature on the myriad factors influencing student achievement.[27] Using a complex statistical model to organize their research, they produced a meta-analysis of an international literature base. Their findings identified a pattern of support for academic pressure to achieve, parental involvement, orderly climate, and opportunity to learn.

Likewise, University of Hawaii education professor Ronald Heck's 2000 and 2005 studies found that schools with higher-quality educational environments (principal leadership, high expectations, frequent monitoring of student progress and climate) produced higher-than-expected achievement gains after controlling for the students' characteristics.[28]

Nonetheless, the school's community and socioeconomic context do influence student achievement. Many observed that differences in student performance can be attributed to characteristics of their schools and communities—even though these factors are beyond their schools' control. To help students learn, it is important for educators to understand and accommodate these outside factors.[29]

Implementing certain correlates without the others does not necessarily produce the desired results, however. A 2006 study found that school management structures that promote teacher cooperation, collegiality, and participation in decision making—by themselves—are not especially powerful determinants of student achievement at either the elementary or secondary levels.[30] Unless teachers have higher expectations for student learning or other effective schools correlates, teacher collaboration by itself will not significantly modify student achievement.

Another study shows that although principals' strong instructional leadership is important, its impact on school effectiveness is indirect.[31] Yet evidence continues to emerge that principal leadership is second only to teaching among the school-related factors in its impact on student learning.[32] Research on these issues is ongoing.

Finally, the effective schools correlates are likely to have a cumulative impact on student achievement. All need to be present and operating. One or two factors by themselves will not make much difference to important school and student outcomes.

15-1f Effective Schools Today

Effective schools research and practice continue today. In 2011, the National Center on Time & Learning reported on its study of 30 high-poverty schools nationwide that improved students'

Looking to Low-Income Students' Strengths

Bobby Ann Starnes, teacher of teachers and chair of the Educational Studies Department at Berea College, Berea, Kentucky, knows firsthand why educators who want each of their students to learn and achieve well should look to their pupils' strengths rather than their weaknesses. The following excerpts come from her essay on this topic in *Phi Delta Kappan*.

"I grew up poor. We were not the romanticized poor but proud family. We struggled. It was hard, harsh, and often ugly. As an Appalachian child trying to make my way through a school system where my culture, values, dialect, and traditions were daily points of jokes, teasing, and pranks, I quickly learned that being poor was an offense to those around me. But being Appalachian, well, that was reprehensible.

"My teachers wanted to help me, but they had no real-life experience with people like me. They'd grown up in privilege. Not wealthy, but privileged nonetheless. They thought, as the helping class often does, the best thing they could do for me was teach me to be like them—or, as one teacher actually suggested in her kindest teacher voice, 'learn to act white.' I knew what that meant. If I wanted success, I'd have to adopt their language and culture and deny my own. I did what they asked; I learned to pass. Passing is a treacherous road to travel.

"As a teacher, I've always thought my experiences with poverty and the choices I made to adopt ways that weren't my own could serve me in my work with marginalized children. And I vowed I'd never require children to deny who they were. We'd find other roads to success, roads that build on their strengths and use their cultures and experiences as a starting point for learning rather than imposing middle-class values in ways that reinforce the message they receive every day telling them they are less than others and that their dreams should be limited by secret rules . . .

"I work at a tuition-free college that serves only students of limited means. . . . My students have a remarkably deep well of personal power grown from the strengths of their cultures, among them resiliency, work ethic, and resourcefulness. They have overcome outrageous odds, not the least among them is the stereotypes designed to pigeonhole them as violent, unmotivated, and lazy. . . . If we want to help children in poverty, doesn't it make more sense to look at students who have overcome hardships based on strength . . . ?

"I studied how to get out of poverty by pretending to be middle class, and I learned the terrible toll that strategy takes on personal identity . . . . And here's my expert opinion: For too long, we have blamed poor people for being poor when serious systemic issues limit too many children's opportunities and possibilities, not the least among them . . . stereotypes. . . ."

Source: Bobby Ann Starnes. (2011, November). "On grifters, research and poverty." Thoughts on Teaching. *Phi Delta Kappan* *93*(3), 72–73. Reprinted with permission of Phi Delta Kappa International, www.pdkintl.org.

achievement by using extended time in their day to continuously strengthen instruction. These schools maximized time on task; prioritized time use according to focused learning goals; tailored instructional time to individual students' needs; built a culture of high expectations and mutual accountability; and relentlessly assessed, analyzed, and responded to student data.[33] Additional schools recently studied include the "No Excuses Schools" (such as KIPP Academies),[34] "High Impact" schools,[35] and Village Academies.[36] Although the school-related factors contributing to their success are largely identical to those in the Effective Schools literature, the present practitioners do not publicly place themselves within the Effective Schools Movement. They represent elementary and secondary schools in various locations that are successfully raising low-income and minority students' academic achievement by using the effective schools correlates. In short, effective schools correlates—with and without their provenance noted—are now widely accepted as best practice.

Effective schools correlates consistently appear where public and charter schools are effectively educating those students who have traditionally been underserved. This fact alone merits attention and, when possible, replication.

Did You Get It?

The Effective Schools Movement

- **a.** Believes that family matters more than schools and so absolves educators of their responsibilities.
- **b.** Grew out of the civil rights movement in an almost immediate response to the Coleman report.
- **c.** Is based on studies of schools in the "normal" range and broad studies of schools.
- **d.** Is based on the concept that a school which uses certain philosophies, policies, and practices can bring virtually all students to a high level of mastery.

Take the full quiz on CourseMate.

15-2 The Seven Correlates of Effective Schools: Current Research Findings

The effective schools correlates have evolved over time. Once reserved for schools working mainly with low-income and minority children, and still highly effective with this group, effective schools correlates are now considered relevant for schools with any student population. Listed briefly, they are:

- Strong instructional leadership
- Clear and focused mission
- Safe and orderly environment
- Climate of high expectations
- Frequent monitoring of student progress
- Positive home–school relations
- Opportunity to learn

As schools continue to address contemporary issues, the correlates' meanings continue to mature, incorporating the available research findings. Today, their dimensions represent a higher developmental stage than when they first appeared.[37] Let's look more closely at each of the correlates, see what the research literature has to say about their impact on student achievement, and describe what they look like in schools.

Did You Get It?

Which is not one of the correlates of effective schools?

- **a.** Strong central office leadership.
- **b.** Climate of high expectations.
- **c.** Clear and focused mission on learning for all.
- **d.** Positive home–school relations.

Take the full quiz on CourseMate.

15-3 Strong Instructional Leadership

Strong instructional leadership is an essential component of effective schools. As educational leadership scholars Kenneth Leithwood and his colleagues observe, "Indeed, there are virtually no documented instances of troubled schools being turned around without interventions by a dynamic leader. Many other factors may contribute to such turnarounds, but leadership is the catalyst."[38]

In today's schools, however, the principal cannot be the only leader. As a "leader of leaders" rather than a "leader of followers," principals develop their skills as coach, partner, and cheerleader as well as organizational leader and manager. By consistently communicating and reinforcing the school's purpose in words and deeds, and by sharing leadership with teachers, the principal creates a professional environment in which teachers can thrive and contribute to the overall school goals and environment.[39]

Research and Discussion According to a national analysis of 15 years of school leadership research, an outstanding principal "exercises a measurable though indirect effect on school effectiveness and student achievement."[40] Similarly, a 2005 meta-analysis of 30 years of research on the effects of principals' practices on student achievement found a significant, positive correlation of .25 between effective school leadership and student achievement. For an average school, having an effective leader can mean the difference between scoring at the 50th percentile on a given achievement test and achieving a score 10 percentile points higher.[41]

As the "official" school leader, the principal sets the climate, creates the expectations, clarifies the school's direction, and delivers the resources needed to make teaching and learning satisfying and successful endeavors. Effective school leaders build their organizational cultures through participatory decision making and collaborative planning, goal setting, and problem solving. As strong instructional leaders, they can help socialize teachers to continue improving their pedagogy and to take on broader responsibilities—such as ensuring that each student learns to high levels and accepting leadership roles within their schools.

When the current school's practices and structures do not allow principals to reach these goals, strong instructional leaders don't downsize their vision or mission to fit. Instead, they change the school organization to permit the vision and mission to flourish. Giving teachers time each day to plan and work collaboratively with other teachers, designing a schedule that allows for extended student learning time and extended teacher planning time, and providing high-quality and relevant professional development tied directly to what teachers need to know and do to improve student learning in their specific curricula are ways that principals can modify the organization to support shared goals. Working with teachers, parents, and the community on school improvement planning is another way for principals to develop a school leadership cadre who together can move their schools in positive directions.

When administrators create school cultures that welcome shared leadership, spirited and inventive teachers will willingly work as part of the team to bring improvements to their schools. When teachers participate in their schools' instructional leadership, they become less isolated. They gain satisfaction from knowing that they are making their schools more satisfying places for them to work and for children to learn. All of these constructive experiences infuse new energy and ideas into their classroom teaching, helping teachers invest in their school rather than merely work there.

What It Looks Like in Schools How do teachers know when their principal is acting as an instructional leader? They know when they see their principals enacting these behaviors[42]:

- Setting high, clear, and public standards and appropriate challenging goals for every student and teacher
- Creating a learning-centered school culture that focuses clearly and repeatedly on improving teaching and learning

- Developing a climate of caring and trust among teachers, students, and parents
- Frequently and informally observing classroom instruction, conducting targeted learning walks, and providing substantive and timely feedback to teachers for their instructional improvement
- Systematically engaging staff in discussions about current research, theory, and practice that helps advance teacher learning and student achievement
- Participating with teachers in professional development activities during faculty meetings, grade level and content-area meetings
- Developing teacher leadership, encouraging faculty members to collaborate and learn from each other using individual and team strengths
- Involving teachers in the design and implementation of important decisions and policies affecting them and their students
- Actively seeking input from teachers, students, parents, and the community to develop the school's improvement plan
- Providing sufficient resources for effective instruction, including professional development and time and opportunity for collaborative planning and learning
- Ensuring an effective, ongoing system for evaluating the school's progress toward its goals and communicating this with faculty, students, parents, and the community
- Publicly celebrating student achievement in academics
- Promptly and effectively addressing student concerns and troubles, proactively if possible, to keep students engaged, in school and learning

Did You Get It?

Strong instructional leadership

a. Is unnecessary; grassroots activism can replace it.
b. Is a necessary catalyst.
c. Requires the principal to be the only leader.
d. Is built around the developing teacher leadership.

Take the full quiz on CourseMate.

15-4 Clear and Focused Mission

Today's school mission emphasizes teaching and learning an appropriate balance between higher-level learning and those more basic skills required for their mastery. This balance between learning complex conceptual knowledge and mastering basic academic skills holds true for low-income and minority children as well as for affluent and middle-class children. The mission advocates *learning for all,* focusing on both the "learning" (what the student is doing and gaining) and the teachers' continuous professional growth. Results—not merely inputs—matter.[43]

Research and Discussion School leaders begin to make their schools into positive learning environments for students and teachers by defining a compelling vision and a focused mission. A **vision** is an intelligent sense of what a better future can be; a **mission** is the purpose or direction pursued to reach that end.[44] "A vision is a target that beckons,"[45] claim business leadership experts. For instance, in 1961, when President John Kennedy set the then-almost-unimaginable goal of placing a man on the moon by 1970, and when Bill Gates later aimed to put a computer on every desk and in every home, these leaders concentrated attention on worthwhile, highly challenging, and attainable achievements. A vision provides a bridge from the present to the future. Only when one knows where one wants to go can one plan how to get there.

vision An intelligent sense of what a better future can be.

mission The purpose or direction pursued to reach a desired goal.

Effective leaders bring vision into action by sharing it with others. An essential leadership skill is the capacity to influence and organize meaning for the organization's members. Leaders articulate and define what has previously remained unsaid. They invent images, metaphors, and mental models that help direct attention and energies. They depict a desirable future state of their organization for us.

Vision and *mission* are not always thought of as two separate things. Instead, they may both be aspects of the same whole. A vision is that part of a mission that clarifies and focuses it. Stephen R. Covey, author of *The Seven Habits of Highly Effective People,* sees a vision as telling where one wants to go and a mission as telling how one will get there. Effective schools assume vision is part of clear and focused mission. Both deal with values and purpose as different locations on the same continuum. One step is a prerequisite for the next.[46] In an effective school, first the principal and then other school leaders champion a persuasive, shared vision and a clear, focused mission that defines what is important and directs the organization on how to reach it.[47] Vision and mission create meaning for everyone in the organization and make the world understandable. They help explain why things are being done the way they are, and why certain things are considered good and rewarded but others are not.

Research shows that by fostering group goals, modeling the desired behaviors for others, and providing intellectual stimulation and individual support (through personal interactions and professional development), principals directly affect a school's culture and climate and indirectly influence student achievement.[48] Nevertheless, although principals articulate the vision/mission, teachers are the essential agents who turn the mission into daily actions. Once the teachers and staff see the "big picture"—such as teachers working collaboratively to increase all students' academic achievement while reducing the achievement gap between low-income and affluent students—the team members can understand how their own jobs relate to it. They can fit their skills and interests into the school's plan to help it get where it intends to go. At the same time, all participants can use this goal to realize their own deepest desires for meaning, accomplishment, and self-fulfillment. Having a clear and focused mission makes teaching more than a job: It becomes a way for teachers to live out their deepest values and fully engage their energies and talents as they educate children for lifelong learning, mature awareness and behavior, and economic opportunities.

Involving teachers in the change process increases their investment in the school's success. Teachers as well as principals should be able to articulate enthusiastically the school's vision and mission. Having a key role in bringing a desired future into the present keeps effective and influential teachers in the school, despite the traditionally high turnover rate among teachers early in their careers. Creating a supportive atmosphere in which teachers are considered members of a professional community with opportunities to continue their own development both inside and outside the school leads teachers—and all their students—toward excellence.

What It Looks Like in Schools In an effective school with a clear and focused mission[49]:

- Everyone (teachers, students, staff, parents, community) can tell you that effective teaching and every student's learning are the school's top goals.
- The school expresses a clear vision about what effective instruction should look like and accomplish in the school.
- The school provides professional development for new teachers about the school's instructional model and for every teacher's continual growth in pedagogical skills.

- Teachers receive clear, ongoing, and substantive feedback about their pedagogical strengths and weaknesses based on multiple data sources including student achievement data.
- The school gives continual informed attention to every student's successful achievement.
- Student learning goals are high and measurable and aligned with state and national standards.
- Students believe they are learning a lot in most of their classes.
- All students' learning includes both basic-level academic skills and higher-level cognitive abilities with sufficient time and help to master them.
- Teachers present academic work in ways that students find interesting, personally relevant, varied, intellectually engaging, and actively involving.
- Teachers use frequent formative assessments to identify students needing additional help and the weaknesses they need to remedy; teachers then provide the specific assistance needed.
- The school has a collaborative process for developing the school's vision, beliefs, mission, and goals that engages the school community in an in-depth study and assessment of important information sources and identifies shared values.
- The school regularly reports back to stakeholders about its progress toward meeting the mission's goals.
- The achievement gap between middle-class and low-income and minority students is markedly decreasing or eliminated altogether as every student's achievement rises.

TeachSource Video 15.1

Parental Involvement in School Culture: A Literacy Project

Making parents feel welcome and an important part of the school culture encourages their involvement and helps them better support their children's learning and well-being. Teachers' relationships with parents are a key factor in sustaining their participation. Watch the video clips, study the artifacts in the case, and reflect on the following questions:

1. What does the teacher (literacy specialist) say and do—from greeting parents, giving directions, and designing the workspace—to help the parents feel comfortable together and happy to be at school?
2. What are the benefits to teachers, students, and parents of parents becoming involved with the school?
3. In what ways do the parents and students create the culture of the school?

Watch on CourseMate.

Did You Get It?

A clear and focused school mission involves

- **a.** Understanding that a school's vision and its mission are entirely separate.
- **b.** Learning for all, both students and teachers.
- **c.** Aligning beliefs with resources.
- **d.** Accepting that some gaps between middle-class and low-income and minority students are insurmountable, so scarce resources are not dissipated.

Take the full quiz on CourseMate.

15-5 Safe and Orderly Environment

Today's effective schools move beyond the absence of undesirable student behaviors, such as students fighting, to emphasize the presence of certain desirable behaviors. Now a safe and orderly environment is defined as an orderly, purposeful, cooperative, and nurturing atmosphere free from threat of harm in a school culture and climate that supports teaching and learning. And all parties show respect for and appreciation of human diversity and democratic values.[50]

Research and Discussion A safe and orderly environment is critical to effective schooling. It is essential that teachers and students feel physically and emotionally safe and comfortable if they are to have the psychological energy needed for teaching and learning. Without a minimum level of security and calm, a school has little chance of positively affecting student achievement.

Many studies have singled out a safe and orderly environment as essential to academic achievement.[51] In general, research finds the more safe and orderly the school climate, the higher the students' math and reading achievement levels. A secure and organized environment is significantly correlated with less student fear, lower dropout rates, and higher student commitment to their learning.[52]

Worry about safety shifts the brain's attention. When students and teachers worry about their personal safety, their focus insistently turns to protecting themselves. They become cautious and watchful, and they stay hyper-alert to potential dangers. At such times, the emotional parts of their brain are more fully aroused, and their cognitive areas become less active. In such environments, they cannot find extra energy to pay attention to teaching and learning. Achievement suffers.

Conversely, in a school with a safe and orderly environment, teachers and students feel no personal danger. Thus their cognitive capacities can become more fully engaged. The learning environment is well structured and businesslike. Teachers are committed to creating a strong, encouraging academic focus with high but achievable goals for students, and they work together collaboratively to make student success happen. Likewise, students work hard on academic matters, are highly motivated, and respect peers who achieve academically.

A school has a safe and orderly environment when it meets the following criteria[53]:

- The school is clean, inviting, and comfortable. Custodians clean the halls and common areas after students use them during the day, promptly noticing and removing graffiti or disorder.
- Students, faculty, staff, and parents at the school say that they feel safe, cared for, and trusted.
- Students at the school tell visitors that they and their friends want to learn.
- Students sit in mixed-race and gender groups in the cafeteria and classrooms.
- People in the building smile at one another freely and frequently.
- Rules and expectations are clearly and visibly communicated (and frequently reviewed and enforced) to students (and parents), stressing mutual respect and responsibility.
- Teachers, administrators, and other adults are visible in the halls and common areas whenever students are using them, from morning entry to afternoon dismissal.
- Teachers, staff, parents, and the community have formal and informal ways to give ideas about improving the school's functioning.
- The principal and administrators are aware of the details and undercurrents in running the school, have early recognition systems to identify potentially disruptive students, and use this information to solve and prevent problems.
- All adults (principal, teachers, administrative personnel, custodians, cafeteria workers) help students learn self-discipline and responsibility.

- Students breaking rules receive fair and consistently administered consequences including problem solving to help prevent repeat errors in judgment.
- The school has low discipline referral rates and few (and declining) suspensions for disciplinary infractions.
- School, student, faculty, and staff achievements are recognized and celebrated in a variety of ways.
- Challenging students have in-school adult mentors with whom they regularly discuss concerns and solve problems.
- Students stay after school to work one-on-one with teachers to make up or gain more understanding about their schoolwork.
- Teachers and students are active in developing the school rules.
- The learning environment is cognitively challenging for all students.
- The curriculum includes multicultural education.

Students meet regularly with in-school adult mentors to discuss concerns and solve problems.

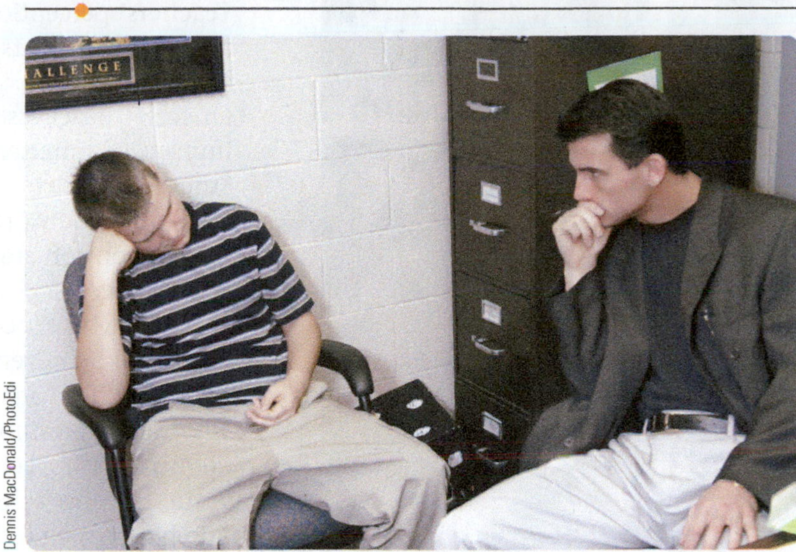

Dennis MacDonald/PhotoEdi

Did You Get It?

Today, safe and orderly environments

a. Means custodians clean the halls and common student areas once a day.
b. Means eliminating undesirable student behaviors.
c. Means encouraging desirable student behaviors.
d. Means students sit with others like themselves.

Take the full quiz on CourseMate.

15-6 Climate of High Expectations

To maintain a climate of high expectations for students, teachers must first hold high expectations for themselves. In effective schools, teachers believe in both their students' ability to master the curriculum and in their own collective efficacy in making it happen. Additionally, schools as cultural organization transform from institutions designed for "instruction" to institutions designed to ensure "learning."[54]

Research and Discussion Students' and teachers' perceptions and expectations both reflect and determine the goals they set for achievement; the strategies they use to meet these goals; the skills, energy, and other resources they use to apply these strategies; and the rewards they anticipate from making this effort.[55]

The research on effective schools reinforces the importance of teacher expectations in determining student performance. As discussed earlier, many other studies found comparable results.[56]

Researchers have found several relationships between teachers' expectations and student achievement:

- Teachers form expectations for student performance.[57]
- Teachers tend to treat students differently depending on these expectations.

High expectations for students' learning lead to high student achievement.

- Teachers' behaviors reflecting these expectations are related to measures of student academic achievement.[58]
- Teachers' perceptions of current students' performance as well as their judgments for students' future performance are generally accurate.[59]
- Once set, teachers' expectations change little.[60] In school, first impressions matter.
- Student characteristics such as physical attractiveness, socioeconomic status, race, use of standard English, and history of grade retention are related to teacher expectations for academic achievement.[61]
- Teachers who expect students to be low achievers attribute their improved achievement to luck, whereas teachers attribute the perceived high achievers' success to their ability.[62]
- Teachers overestimate the achievement of high achievers, underestimate the achievement of low achievers, and predict least accurately low achievers' responses.[63]
- The better the teachers know their students, the more accurate their expectations for student academic success, especially in the early elementary grades (grades 1 and 2).[64]

The more effectively teachers teach, the higher all their students achieve, and the less accurate teachers' initial predictions become about who will or will not learn. As teachers learn and apply more effective instructional practices that help more students learn, teachers become increasingly optimistic about their students' success; in turn, their students became more successful. Each player's positive expectation influences the other in a mutually reinforcing manner.[65] Studies find that the more inviting and responsive instruction is to children's efforts to improve, the less accurately teachers' initial perceptions and expectations will predict later success.[66] It is also possible that when teachers become more effective in their classrooms, more children achieve well, and teachers may treat all students as high achievers—providing them with similar praise and similar feedback, and making similar demands for work and effort.[67]

Researchers have also found that higher teachers' beliefs in their own and their colleagues' abilities to help all students make the academic advances that their school is asking of them, the higher the correlation with achievement levels and gains.[68]

In short, teachers' initial expectations about students' being high or low achievers weaken as teachers commit to a learning-for-all mission, and develop the expertise and confidence in their own and their colleagues' effectiveness to have all their students successfully learn the curriculum.

What It Looks Like in Schools What do schools with high expectations for student achievement look like?[69]

- The school has developed a shared vision of a school with all students achieving high levels of success in a rigorous curriculum regardless of family background.
- Teachers, administrators, and parents expect all students to learn a full range of skills—from basic mastery of needed skills to higher-level, complex problem solving—and they act on this belief.
- The school has standards and practices in place to avoid both grade retention and social promotion by keeping all students learning apace throughout the year.[70]

- Teachers have confidence in their skills to help all their students master the basic and higher-level skills, regardless of their family background. They not only act on this belief but continually upgrade their pedagogical skills.
- Teachers clearly inform students and parents of what students are expected to know and be able to do by the end of the unit or semester.
- Teachers help students use what they already know to learn new knowledge, develop new skills, and expand their understanding.
- Teachers use a variety of effective instructional approaches to ensure that all students master a challenging curriculum.
- Students and teachers work together during class time and after school (if needed) to master the expected content and skills.
- The school has ongoing, collegial professional development tied to the classroom curriculum to help every teacher improve his or her instructional effectiveness.
- Students are encouraged to set high learning goals for themselves.
- Students and teachers believe that their effort is more important than their ability in producing their final achievement—and they invest effort in learning.
- Special-needs students receive instruction in the regular classrooms from the regular teacher with assistance from a collaborating teacher.
- English language learners receive support to learn academics in the regular classroom.
- The school has very low suspension and dropout rates and very high promotion or graduation rates.
- Students and parents believe that their teachers have confidence in students' ability to master the curriculum and expect them to do well.
- Students and parents say their schoolwork is challenging but doable.

TeachSource Video 15.2

Communicating with Parents: Tips and Strategies for Future Teachers

Parents can be teachers' best allies when they believe that teachers have their child's best interest at heart—academically, emotionally, and socially. Working as a team, educators and parents can effectively support their children's social and academic development. Watch the video clips, study the artifacts in the case, and reflect on the following questions:

1. What is the value to the teacher, parent, and student of having regular positive and informative communications?
2. What does the video suggest that first-year teachers can do to get parents "on their side"?
3. Which means of parent communications mentioned in the video do you think will be most comfortable and effective for you?
4. Which aspects of teacher–parent communications do you suspect will be the same across the grade levels? Which aspects do you think may change across the grade levels—and why?

Watch on CourseMate.

Did You Get It?

What does a climate of high expectations mean?

- **a.** Teachers tend to form expectations for student performance, and they treat students differently based on those expectations.
- **b.** If you have high expectations for high achievers, they will pull the low achievers up along with them.
- **c.** High expectations cannot affect the dropout rate, but they can affect the performance of the remaining students.
- **d.** Community expectations influence teacher performance, but not student performance.

Take the full quiz on CourseMate.

Reflect & Discuss

Effective schools have a climate of high expectations for students and teachers. Teachers' expectations influence student achievement.

A. Work in pairs to discuss your own experiences with teacher expectations and your responses as a student. Describe a time when a teacher held either an unfairly high or low expectation for your achievement.
B. How did this affect your opinion about the teacher? How did this affect your feelings about yourself as a student? How did this affect your effort, learning, and achievement in that class?
C. Volunteers may share their experiences with teacher expectations with the whole class.
D. Working in groups of four, reflect on your own experiences with linguistically, ethnically, or culturally diverse individuals. How might these experiences—or lack of them—influence your own future expectations for these students?
E. Working as a class, discuss how you as future educators will deal with the issue of teacher expectations and student achievement in your own classrooms and schools.

15-7 Frequent Monitoring of Student Progress

In today's effective schools, measurement of student progress has shifted away from overwhelming reliance on summative, standardized norm-referenced tests and toward including ongoing formative measurements of student mastery. In addition, teachers monitor students' learning by emphasizing a variety of sources, including students' projects, performances, and portfolios.[71] Teachers pay increased attention to aligning the intended, taught, learned, and tested curriculum. Additionally, teachers give students prompt corrective feedback to help them improve their learning—and to guide teachers' instruction.

Research and Discussion Educational accountability has become the primary public space in which we focus on racial, ethnic, class, and educational inequities (as discussed in detail in Chapters 7, 11, and 14). Annual standardized testing by itself, however, does not make schools "effective." Standardized tests are typically summative assessments, used at the end of the learning process. Although they provide valuable information about student achievement, they cannot measure many of learning's important aspects. In fact, standardized tests sometimes narrow the range of cognitive skills used and remove knowledge from real-world uses.[72]

Likewise, standardized tests cannot identify individual students' specific learning weakness in ways and at times when teachers can quickly diagnose them and intervene to remediate and advance student learning. To increase each student's learning, teachers in effective schools use assessments in a wider variety of ways.

Effective schools frequently use formative assessment as a continuing and integral part of the teaching and learning process. Using a broad array of assessments throughout the school year—including daily observations, classwork, and interviews, and frequent projects, portfolios, and presentations—teachers can give students specific and timely feedback on their learning progress in ways that support student achievement and increase the types and qualities of student learning.

Research supports the notion that these recurrent and varied performance assessments offer a way to increase all students' achievement. One 2001 study found a significant relationship between students who received challenging intellectual performance assignments and those students' measured reading, math, and writing skills in grades 3, 6, and 8. These learning gains were observed regardless of the students' family income, race/ethnicity, and prior achievement.[73] Regular engagement with performance tasks also increases students' ability to use—that is, transfer—this knowledge for real-world problem solving.[74] Although performance tasks and assessments appear to positively impact students' motivation to learn, teaching practices, and student learning, the evidence on this front remains largely anecdotal, however.[75]

Although using performance assessments will not reduce the achievement gaps, the results of performance assessments will provide broader and more equitable data on which to base decisions about students and schools. These assessments can enhance equity by informing teachers more fully about how their students think and learn as well as what they know and can do with it. As teachers come to understand their students as learners more fully, they will be more readily able to adjust their teaching to student needs and to create occasions for student success.

What It Looks Like in Schools What do schools that use frequent monitoring of student progress look like?

- Indicators of students' and the school's achievement are visibly posted within the school.
- Teachers analyze and interpret a variety of student assessment data to monitor and advance student learning, not merely to measure it.
- Teachers use feedback from multiple student assessments to inform (and adapt) their daily instruction to meet individual student needs.
- Teachers give clear explanations about what students are to do and which criteria will be used for determining product or performance quality before assigning work to students.
- Teachers promptly grade and return student work with useful feedback.
- Teachers diagnose student learning difficulties early and act to fix them.
- Students believe that their academic goals are challenging.
- Students have an increasingly active role in assessing and evaluating their own progress.
- Students use prompt feedback to extend and deepen their learning.
- Students and parents can describe students' achievement status and growth.
- Individual student reports on achievement are regularly updated to track growth.
- Students and parents understand how students' work is graded.
- The principal and leadership team use a variety of achievement data to monitor the effectiveness of curriculum, instruction, and assessment and their impact on student learning in an ongoing manner.
- The principal recognizes and celebrates teachers' and students' accomplishments and acknowledges (and learns from) failures.

Did You Get It?

Which of these statements about standardized testing is false?

a. Standardized tests are typically summative assessments used at the end of a learning process.

b. Despite being summative assessments, standardized tests are configured in such a way that analysis of any particular student's results will show specific learning weaknesses and strengths.

c. These tests provide valuable information about student learning at the end of a process.

d. Standardized tests often abstract learning from its real-world uses and require simplified cognitive skills.

Take the full quiz on CourseMate.

15-8 Positive Home–School Relations

In contemporary effective schools, the parent–school relationship becomes a genuine partnership. Both parents and teachers have much to learn from one another about how to best inspire their students to learn what the school teaches. To help all parties realize their mutual goal—an effective home and school for every child—educators and parents need to build actual trust and engage in clear, two-way communication.

Research and Discussion Joyce Epstein, Johns Hopkins professor and an expert in school–family relationships, notices, "The way schools care about children is reflected in the way schools care about the children's families. If educators view children simply as *students,* they are likely to see the family as separate from the school. If educators view students as *children,* they are likely to see both the family and the community as partners with the school in children's education and development."[76]

More than 40 years of research has shown that family involvement is a powerful influence on student achievement.[77] Studies have documented that when schools work together with families to promote student learning, children tend to succeed not just in school but in life as well. These students attain the following results[78]:

- Earn higher grades and test scores and enroll in higher-level programs
- Attend school regularly and do more homework
- Gain promotions, pass their classes, and earn more course credits
- Show higher math and reading proficiency
- Receive fewer placements in special education
- Use better social skills, show improved behavior, and adapt well to school
- Receive fewer disciplinary actions
- Display higher graduation rates
- Secure greater enrollment in postsecondary education

Over 40 years of research shows that family involvement is a powerful influence on student achievement.

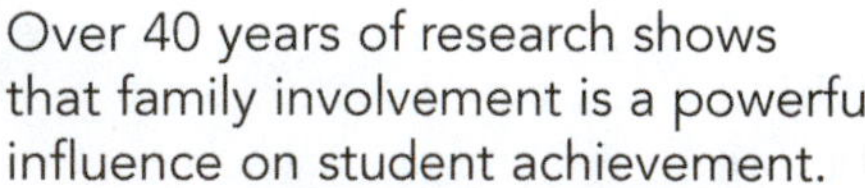

Comstock Images/Jupiter Images

Just as important, research shows that what a family *does* is more important to student success than what a family *is* or *earns.* Parental involvement is the most reliable predictor of academic achievement whether the child is in preschool or upper grades, whether the family is financially struggling or affluent, and whether the parents finished high school or earned graduate degrees.[79] Regardless of family income, children succeed in school when their families are able to accomplish the following:

- Create a home environment that encourages learning
- Express high (but not unrealistic) expectations for their children's achievement and future careers
- Become involved in their children's education in school and in the community[80]

Family involvement can reduce the obstacles that low-income and racially/ethnically diverse students typically encounter in school. Research shows that when schools support families to develop these three conditions, children from low-income families and diverse cultural backgrounds earn the school grades and test scores that approach those attained by students from middle-class families. They are more likely to take advantage of a full range of educational opportunities after graduating from high school. Even when only one or two of these conditions are in place, children do measurably better in school.[81]

Families clearly benefit from forging close ties to schools. When they do, the teachers they work with have higher confidence in the parents and higher expectations for the children. In turn, parents develop more confidence about helping their children learn at home, about the school, and about themselves as parents. In addition, when parents become involved in their children's education, they often enroll in continuing education courses to advance their own learning.[82]

Schools and communities benefit from stronger family–school ties as well. Schools that work well with families realize the following advantages[83]:

- Improved teacher morale
- Higher ratings of teachers by parents
- More support from families
- Higher student achievement
- Better reputations in the community

The bottom line: When parents are genuinely involved in their children's education, their children do better in school and in life.

A Comprehensive Framework for Parent–School Partnerships Joyce Epstein, Johns Hopkins Professor and Director of the university's Center on School, Family, and Community Partnerships, has developed a framework of parent involvement to help educators build more comprehensive school and family partnerships. Types of school–parent partnerships include parenting, communications, volunteering, learning at home, decision making, and collaborating with the community. Each type of involvement encompasses many different cooperative practices and challenges and leads to different results.[84] Table 15.1 describes these variations and expected results.

With this framework as a guide, educators can see their schools' strengths and build on them to create a comprehensive approach to parent and community involvement that can support student success. In contrast, if the teachers and administrators discourage parents, treat them as negative influences, or cut them out of their child's education, those actions promote family attitudes that reduce school achievement.

Relationships that must bridge cultures and languages require more effort to create and sustain. Educators need to learn their families' "funds of knowledge" and "cultural assets"—ways of knowing, learning, and acting—that exist within culturally and linguistically diverse families. In this way, teachers can see their students and families' strengths and opportunities rather than simply noticing deficits.[85] Programs and policies that want to improve student outcomes will be much more productive if they build on their families' strengths and enlist them as allies.

Parent–school involvement tends to decrease as students move into higher grade levels. As students move from elementary to secondary school, all domains of family engagement drop off with the school's support for home learning losing the most ground.[86] Teachers and administrators must make special and appropriate efforts to welcome parents, provide effective two-way communication between parents and educators, and support learning at home if they are to encourage family participation with schools as children grow older.

TABLE 15.1

Six Types of Parental Involvement, Practices, and Expected Results

Type	Description	Sample Practices	Expected Results
1. Parenting	Helps all families establish home environments to support children as students.	Suggest home conditions that support learning at each grade level. Workshops, videotapes, recorded phone messages. Parent education. Home visits at transition points (grades 3, 5, 8). Neighborhood meetings to help families understand schools and schools understand families.	Students: Awareness of school's importance and family supervision; good or improved attendance. Parents: Understanding and confidence in their parenting, child and adolescent development, changes in home conditions for learning as the child moves through school. Teachers: Understanding family backgrounds, culture, concerns, and views; respect for families' efforts and strengths; understanding student diversity.
2. Communicating	Design effective forms of school-to-home and home-to-school communications about school programs and children's progress.	Annual parent conferences with follow-ups as needed. Parent/student pick-up of report card with conferences on improving grades. Language translators as needed. Weekly or monthly folders of student work sent home for review and comments. Regular schedule of useful notices, phone calls, newsletters. Clear information on choosing courses, schools, programs, and activities within schools.	Students: Awareness of own progress and actions needed to maintain or improve grades; understanding of school policies on behavior, attendance; informed decisions about courses and programs. Parents: Understand school programs and policies; monitoring and awareness of child's progress; responding effectively to student's problems. Teachers: Appreciation for and use of parent network for communications; increased ability to elicit and understand family views on children's programs and progress.
3. Volunteering	Recruit and organize parent help and support for school activities.	School and classroom volunteer program to help teachers, administrators, students, and other parents. Parent room or family center for meetings, resources for families. Annual postcard survey to identify all available talents, times, and locations for volunteers. Class parent, telephone tree, or other means to provide all families with needed information.	Students: Skill in communicating with adults; increased learning of skills that receive tutoring or targeted volunteer attention. Parents: Understanding teachers' job; increased comfort in school and carry-over of school activities at home; self-confidence about ability to work in school and with children. Teachers: Awareness of parents' talents and interests in school and children; greater individual attention to students with help from volunteers.

(continued)

TABLE 15.1

Six Types of Parental Involvement, Practices, and Expected Results (*continued*)

Type	Description	Sample Practices	Expected Results
4. Learning at Home	Provide information and ideas to families about how to help students at home with homework and other curriculum-related activities, decisions, and planning.	Information for families on skills required for students in all subjects at each grade. Information on homework policies and ways to monitor and discuss schoolwork at home. Regular schedule of homework that requires students to discuss and interact with families on what they are learning in class. Summer learning packets or activities.	Students: Gains in skills, abilities, and test scores linked to homework and classwork; homework completion; positive attitude toward school work; improved self-concept of ability as learner. Parents: Know how to support, encourage, and help student at home each year; understand each year's instructional program and what child is learning in each subject. Teachers: Respect for family time; recognize helpfulness of each family type; satisfaction with family involvement and support.
5. Decision Making	Include parents in school decisions, developing parent leaders and representatives.	Active PTA/PTO or other parent groups, advisory councils, or committees (curriculum, safety, school improvement) for parent leadership and participation. Independent advocacy groups to lobby and work for school improvements. District-level councils and committees for family and community involvement. Information on school or local elections for school representatives.	Students: Understanding that students' rights are protected; awareness of family representation in school decisions. Parents: Input into policies that affect child's education; feeling of ownership of school; awareness of parents' voices in school decisions. Teachers: Awareness of parent perspectives in policy development and decisions; view of parents as having equal status on committees and in leadership roles.
6. Collaborating with Community	Identify and integrate resources and services from the community to strengthen school programs, family practices, and student learning and development.	Information for students and families on community health, cultural, recreational, social support, and other programs or services. Information on community activities linked to learning skills and talents. Services to the community by students, families, and schools (e.g., recycling, art, music, drama). Participation of alumni in school programs for students.	Students: Increased skills and talents through enriched curricular and extracurricular experiences; awareness of careers and options for future education and work. Parents: Knowledge and use of local resources by family and child to increase skills and talents or to obtain needed services; interactions with other families in community activities. Teachers: Awareness of community resources to enrich curriculum and instruction; openness to and skill in using mentors, business partners, and community volunteers to assist students and enhance teaching practice.

Source: Adapted from Epstein, J. L. (1995, May). School/family/community partnerships: Caring for the children we share. *Phi Delta Kappan 76*(9), 704–706.

TeachSource Video 15.3

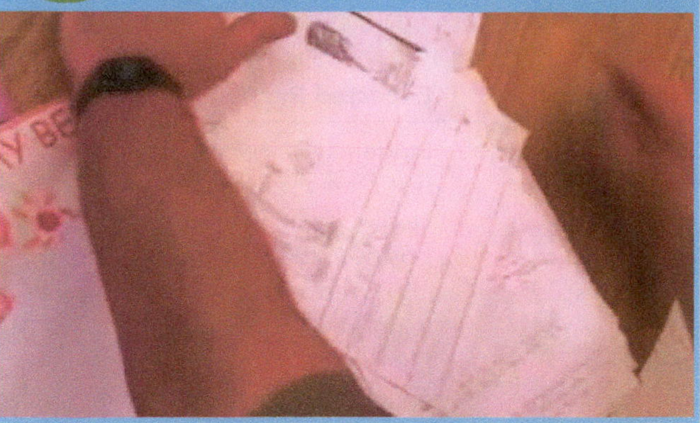

© Cengage Learning 2015

Home–School Communications: The Parent–Teacher Conference

Communicating effectively with parents is an essential way to support student success in school. When a teacher thoroughly understands a student's strengths and weakness as demonstrated with actual work samples and invites the parent's ideas, parent conferences can be productive and satisfying. Watch the video clips, study the artifacts in the case, and reflect on the following questions:

1. How does the teacher's bringing to the conference his "interview" with the student, a selection of the student's writing samples, and the student's "book" build credibility with the parent?
2. What is the value of the teacher asking the parent questions such as, "What is your child saying at home about school?"
3. What message does the teacher give to the parent when she questions how well (better or worse) her child is performing in the class as compared with her peers?

Watch on CourseMate.

What It Looks Like in Schools When parents and educators work together successfully, the following behaviors are apparent in schools (as appropriate to the students' ages and maturity):

- Parents and teachers meet together in formal conferences at least once a year.
- Teachers respect families' strengths, assets, and efforts to help their children learn.
- Teachers regularly call parents to discuss their child's progress and problems, and parents respond constructively to teachers' concerns.
- Teachers schedule regular interactive homework that requires students to demonstrate and discuss what they are learning with a family member.
- Teachers understand and relate positively to students of diverse backgrounds.
- Teachers feel comfortable understanding and discussing parents' concerns about their child's academic, social, and behavioral progress.
- Teachers call on parents to use their talents and interests in school to help students learn.
- Parents feel increasingly comfortable in the school and supporting their student at home.
- Teachers and administrators continually look for ways to involve parents and seek their input when making decisions and policies that affect their children's education.
- Schools provide clear information in the parents' preferred language about ways parents can help students learn at home with homework, other curricular-related activities, program decisions, and planning at each grade level.
- The school offers parents various avenues for involvement.
- The school provides clear information to parents about the curriculum, assessments, and achievement levels; and parents and students make informed decisions about courses and programs of study.
- Teachers and parents are aware of community resources to enhance teaching and learning.
- Bilingual or multilingual employees work in school locations and are ready to welcome, meet, and greet parents and assist with parent–teacher conferences.
- Parent volunteers from various student demographics work visibly in the school.
- Students are aware of the school's importance to their family and better understand and follow school rules and policies because they have discussed these issues with their parents.
- The school schedules its events at different times during the day and evening so that all families can attend some throughout the year.

Did You Get It?

How do positive home–school relations benefit students?

a. Positive home–school relations depend on respect, not trust.
b. Caring about students means seeing them as capable pupils and not as children.
c. Good relations with parents give teachers more confidence in them and raise teachers' expectations for their children.
d. When educators view students as children, they become partners in their communal raising.

Take the full quiz on CourseMate.

15-9 Opportunity to Learn and Student Time-on-Task

Finding enough time and high-quality resources to ensure every child's learning is a challenge for teachers. In most schools, teachers have too much content to teach without enough time to teach it in ways that students can learn it.[87] Students also miss OTL when they have an inadequate, dated, or misaligned curriculum and when they are taught by inexperienced, ineffective teachers.

Research and Discussion Of all school-level factors that affect student achievement, *opportunity to learn* has the strongest impact.[88] **Opportunity to learn** refers to equitable conditions or circumstances within the school or classroom that promote learning for all students. It means that all students—low-income, middle class, and affluent—have equal opportunities to receive high-quality teachers, curricula, learning materials, instructional experiences, and facilities that enable them to achieve high standards and avoid barriers that prevent learning.

opportunity to learn The equitable conditions or circumstances within the school or classroom that promote learning for all students.

Much of the OTL research has focused on three types of indicators: curriculum, pedagogy, and instructional resources. The instructional content (curriculum) includes the degree and depth in which teachers cover academic material for different student groups. Pedagogical processes focus on how teachers organize classroom work and reflect teachers' varying instructional skill levels. Instructional resources comprise the supplies used in delivering instruction, including curricular materials, technology, safe and secure school facilities, and time availability and use. To some degree, these categories overlap.[89]

15-9a Curriculum and Opportunity to Learn

Having a guaranteed and viable curriculum is strongly correlated with academic achievement, yet they are so interdependent that they may be considered as one feature.[90]

Schools actually have four curricula. The **intended curriculum** is the content specified by the state, district, or school to be addressed in a particular course at a particular grade level. The **taught curriculum** is the content the teacher delivers in the classroom. The **attained curriculum** is the one the students actually learn, and the **tested curriculum** is the one about which students must answer questions on classroom and standardized tests. Any mismatches detract from students' learning and reduce their OTL.

intended curriculum The content specified by the state, district, or school to be addressed in a particular course at a particular grade level.

taught curriculum The content the teacher delivers in the classroom.

attained curriculum The content the students actually learn.

tested curriculum The content about which students must answer questions on classroom and standardized tests.

It may seem surprising that the intended curriculum and the taught curriculum are not always the same. Public education provides teachers with much guidance on content standards for specific courses and grade levels. Nonetheless, teachers commonly make independent decisions about what they will cover and to what extent. Different teachers omit or include different topics. They may spend two days or two weeks on the same topic. This practice frequently creates sizeable holes in the taught curriculum—and in students' opportunity to learn the intended curriculum.

In a high-stakes testing environment such as we are now in, it is very important that all students have opportunities to learn the same information and skills to the same levels of depth and complexity that they will see on assessments and that they will need for more advanced courses and life outside school. Unless all students have the chance to learn the expected content to the same level of complexity that the assessment will measure it—or that the next course's teacher and real-world problem solving require—they will be missing the opportunity to learn.

15-9b Effective Teaching and Opportunity to Learn

Improving students' opportunity to learn requires high levels of professional teaching competence. Teachers must know their subject and the standards to which they and their students will be held accountable. They must develop effective diagnostic skills to identify each student's learning obstacles in every required topic or skill. Teachers must deliver instruction in a variety of ways, adjusting their strategies to best suit the material and their students. They must design lessons that connect students to the content in ways that learners find meaningful and relevant. Students, in turn, must have occasions for demonstration, practice, and prompt feedback that they can immediately use to increase their learning. Further, these teachers and resources must be available to every student in every classroom. To teach in these ways requires teachers to become lifelong learners themselves as they keep enhancing their professional expertise and expanding their repertoire of teaching skills.

OTL teaching also means that teachers form partnerships with parents and guardians, encouraging them to support students' good learning and study habits at home. Ideally, teachers and parents will frequently communicate about students' progress and academic programs and support each others' efforts in their own ways.

15-9c Time and Opportunity to Learn

Time is a critical OTL variable. Robert Marzano, a noted education researcher has found that most state, district, and school curricula are too large to fit neatly into the limits of the school day. In fact, researchers have identified some 200 standards and 3,039 benchmarks in national and state-level documents covering 14 different subject areas.[91] Classroom teachers estimated that it would take 15,465 hours to adequately address this content. Assuming that most K-12 schools have a 180-day school year, with an average of 5.6 hours of class time each school day, teachers would have a maximum of 13,104 hours (13 years of instruction × 1,008 hours per school year) to address all of these standards.[92] Clearly, 15,465 hours of standards do not fit into 13,104 hours of instructional time. In part, the Common Core State Standards attempt to remedy the "mile wide and inch deep" curricula to better focus and pare it so students will have a realistic opportunity to learn them.

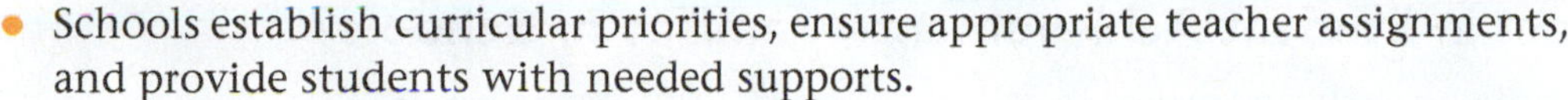

What It Looks Like in Schools What does opportunity to learn look like in schools?

- Schools establish curricular priorities, ensure appropriate teacher assignments, and provide students with needed supports.
- All students are enrolled in high-challenge, high-status courses with high-quality curriculum and effective teachers.
- Schools keep the expectations for student achievement high but vary the time and other resources needed to help every student reach the standards.
- Teachers involve all students in analyzing, synthesizing, generalizing, explaining, hypothesizing, and drawing conclusions to increase meaning and understanding.
- Teachers identify students' individual learning problems or misunderstandings early in the learning process and provide them with additional supports (time, individual assistance) as necessary.
- Teachers use a variety of instructional strategies to meet students' learning needs.
- Teachers receive the relevant materials, equipment, and ongoing professional development necessary for their successful job performance.
- Teachers use effective classroom management and organizational strategies to maximize learning time.
- Teachers design challenging (but not unduly frustrating) learning tasks for students that are adjusted to accommodate students' unique learning needs while ensuring they achieve high levels of mastery to meaningful standards.
- Classroom instructional resources for learning are equally accessible to all students.
- No public address announcements or other classroom interruptions occur during instructional time.
- Transitions between instructional activities and classroom routines occur smoothly with little time loss.
- Special education students are included in all academic classes and are supported with collaborative teaching.
- Students have opportunities to receive additional individualized assistance that addresses their specific learning challenges (e.g., teacher or classroom aide, peer tutor, interactive technology-based instructional resources aligned with the curriculum).
- Students who fail tests receive meaningful opportunities for remediation that focus on the test's knowledge and skills and give enough time to correct any weakness in that area before retaking the test.

Did You Get It?

Opportunity to learn (OTL)

a. Research is significantly focused on time management.
b. Is not significantly affected by varying relationships between the four curricula teachers actually teach.
c. Is not compromised by the content teachers must teach and the time they have to do it in because there is a good match between curriculum standards and the school year.
d. Refers to providing the high-quality curriculum, learning materials, facilities, teachers, and instructional experiences.

Take the full quiz on CourseMate.

FlipSides

Which Matters Most in Student Achievement—Families or Schools?

Too often, schools serving low-income and minority children have educators who believe that families—not schools—make the overwhelming difference in student achievement. In contrast, educators in effective schools believe that high expectations for teachers and students with certain replicable practices—along with family involvement—can boost student achievement regardless of their background. After comparing the two sets of beliefs and practices, which approach do you think does the most to increase student achievement?

***Families—not schools*—make the most difference in student achievement. Schools cannot overcome students' background limitations**	***Schools—with families' support*—can make the most difference in increasing student learning and achievement.**
■ Family background—socioeconomic status (SES), parenting practices, health issues, housing stability, among other aspects—determines how well children learn in school. Schools cannot overcome these factors.	● Family background is an important aspect in children's learning, but effective teachers and high-quality curricula are schools' most important factors in their learning and can overcome many background aspects.
■ Teacher expectations for students' academic achievement are influenced by students' SES, race, ethnicity, use of standard English, and history of grade retention.	● Teachers have high expectations for each child's achievement regardless of SES factors and are committed to delivering the instruction needed to help every child achieve at grade level.
■ Teachers focus on helping students learn basic-level academic skills, often by providing remedial work, before they teach for "big ideas" and higher-level thinking.	● Teachers focus on helping all students learn basic-level academic skills, "big ideas," and high-level cognitive abilities within the same units.
■ Teachers give students opportunities to learn the standard school curriculum using regular instruction during the regular school day.	● Teachers give students opportunities to learn a high-quality curriculum with high levels of teaching competence and sufficient time (during and outside class) to learn it.
■ Teachers use formative assessments to give students daily grades and rely on summative assessments to measure students' final achievement.	● Teachers use frequent formative assessments to monitor student learning and revise instructional plans; they use summative assessments to measure students' progress and final achievement.
■ Teachers believe that many of their low-income and minority students will likely not complete high school or attend college.	● Teachers believe that their low-income and minority students will complete high school and perhaps college.
■ Teachers have an instructional role in the school and can be found in the classroom.	● Teachers have an instructional and a leadership roles in the school and can be found in the classroom and on the leadership team.
■ Teachers are assumed competent and they continue their professional learning at their own discretion.	● Teachers are assumed competent and schools give them opportunities to continue to develop and refine their abilities throughout their careers.
■ Principals emphasize collegial and informal relationships with teachers and staff and stress general public relations. They are relatively easy-going with and have good relationships with students.	● Principals assert their instructional leadership, enforce high expectations for student behavior and teacher performance, and regularly evaluate how well the teachers and students are achieving academic objectives.
■ Schools use measured student learning as a sign of teachers' effectiveness (if scores are high) and students' lack of effort and home support (if scores are low).	● Schools use measured student learning as one sign of their effectiveness; teachers and schools accept the responsibility to improve low achievement.

(continued)

FlipSides

Which Matters Most in Student Achievement—Families or Schools? (*continued*)

Families—not schools—**make the most difference in student achievement. Schools cannot overcome students' background limitations**	***Schools—with families' support***—**can make the most difference in increasing student learning and achievement.**
■ Unless required to do so, teachers do not disaggregate student achievement data to see how well each student group is learning.	● Teachers routinely disaggregate student achievement data to monitor each student group's achievement, whether or not it is required.
■ The achievement gap between middle-class and low-income and minority students is large. One can guess students' SES by knowing their achievement test scores.	● The achievement gap between middle-class and low-income and minority students is markedly decreasing or ended altogether. One cannot accurately guess students' SES by knowing their achievement test scores.
■ The school has very high suspension and dropout rates and a very low promotion rate.	● The school has very low suspension and dropout rates and a very high promotion rate.
■ Teachers and administrators are fatalistic about current student achievement levels and have no plans to improve them.	● Teachers and administrators are dissatisfied about current student achievement levels and develop interventions to improve them.
■ Teachers complain about lack of parent support for student achievement.	● Teachers find innovative ways to constructively involve parents in their students' learning.

Evidence supports the view that schools—with family support—can make a significant difference in low-income and minority student achievement. Schools that develop the culture and implement the practices of high expectations for all students (and teachers) regardless of family background can raise student achievement to high levels.

15-10 A Realistic Look at What Effective Schools Can and Cannot Do

Effective schools differ from other schools because they integrate the elements that make school success achievable for all students—instructional leadership, a clear and focused mission, a safe and orderly environment, a climate of high expectations, frequent monitoring of student progress, positive home–school relations, and opportunity to learn. If policy makers and practitioners want to make a positive difference, they can focus on what excellent schools do and how they do it, and seek to replicate those practices in schools where student achievement is weak.

Despite their widespread success over the years, the Effective Schools Movement has identified certain realities that limit what the correlates can and cannot do to improve schools:

- *No one model of effective schools exists.* No single set of variables can produce an effective school. Each school has its unique student and community factors that will influence how the correlates will work.
- *The correlates are prerequisites—not guarantees—*for attaining high and equitable achievement levels for low-income and minority students. They are proxies showing that the school is moving toward more successfully generating student achievement.

- *The correlates interact synergistically.* They work together and influence one another in unique ways in different school environments.
- *The correlates are challenges for schools to meet*—not "recipes" to create high-achieving schools. Each correlate has many steps that must be implemented correctly for each school's individual situation and in recognition of its interplay with the other correlates.
- *Schools must monitor and attend to all the correlates* and the possible obstacles and repercussions their implementation may produce.
- *Schools cannot undertake all of the correlates at one time,* nor can they overlook implementing any one of them. Yet all of the correlates must eventually be present if student achievement is to increase.
- *Each school's community socioeconomic context influences* student achievement. Both family and school contribute to student learning.
- *Minority and low-income students' skills in effective schools are at least as well developed as those of middle-class children.* In effective schools, a child's SES cannot be determined by looking at test scores because all children are achieving well.

The effective schools correlates appear repeatedly in achieving schools at all grade levels, in separate regions, and among independent researchers. This consistency assures us that these correlates exist and have merit. That critics question the research methodology or claim that these schools' increased achievement scores may be random fluctuations simply means that the effective schools correlates are not a panacea for all ills affecting the U.S. educational system, nor are they easily infused into schools across the board.[93] On the other hand, the critics of the effective schools correlates have never tried to discount their usefulness in promoting student learning.

Educators cannot completely close the achievement gap by intensively implementing the reforms advocated by proponents of the Effective Schools Movement without also tackling the underlying social problems that affect the children who attend our schools.[94] According to William J. Mathis, managing director of the National Education Policy Center in Boulder, Colorado, "To pretend that schools can single-handedly overcome a lifetime of deprivation through a 'whole-school action plan' or through rigorous and intensive adherence to a particular reading program is more an exercise in ritualistic magic than an realistic solution to social, economic, and personal problems."[95] Many children come to school with issues affecting their health, mobility, housing, nutrition, parents' unemployment, family structure, medical and dental care—all of which have profound implications for how well they learn.

By themselves, these educational approaches cannot be completely successful. Six hours of daily instruction delivered over 180 days per year cannot overcome the effects of a deprived and impoverished home environment for 18 hours a day, 365 days a year. Nonetheless, the data show that when educators, parents, and communities integrate the best practices identified in the effective schools correlates into their schools' daily life, they create important opportunities for more students learn the high-level knowledge, skills, and habits of mind necessary for twenty-first-century citizenship and self-sufficiency. If a democracy thrives only with an educated populace, making all schools effective is the hope for public education's—and our nation's—future.

Did You Get It?

The Effective Schools Movement

a. Provides correlates that are challenges for schools to meet.

b. Has created a model of an effective school, with a proven "recipe" for success.

c. Has been unable to eliminate very obvious differences in the test scores of middle-class children and poor and minority children, even in effective schools.

d. Provides correlates that when implemented together can increase low-income and minority students' achievement.

Take the full quiz on CourseMate.

SUMMARY

- The Effective Schools Movement identified schools that successfully educated all students regardless of their socioeconomic status or family background. When teachers, administrators, and the community hold high expectations for students, successfully deliver a rigorous and appropriate curriculum, frequently monitor student progress, provide a safe and orderly environment, and provide high levels of support, learning and achievement typically improve—regardless of students' family background.
- "Strong instructional leadership" means the principal makes all students' achievement the school's top goal, helps teachers provide high-quality instructional practices, creates a school culture that invites teachers to share school leadership, and provides the necessary resources that prioritize and enhance teaching and learning.
- "Clear and focused mission" means emphasizing ongoing attention to every child's achievement and every teacher's continually improved pedagogy; teaching an appropriate balance between higher-level learning and those more basic skills needed for mastery; and ensuring accountability by students and teachers for meeting high, measurable, and meaningful learning goals.
- "Safe and orderly environment" means having a physically and psychologically comfortable, clean, and organized learning climate with high, clearly communicated, and consistently enforced expectations for student and teacher behaviors; caring adults visible at all times when students are present; and mutual respect, appreciation, and cooperative work and learning relationships throughout the school.
- "Climate of high expectations" means all teachers and principals share the belief that each of their students can learn and master the basic and higher-level academic objectives; teachers are expected to continually learn and upgrade their own pedagogical skills and work collaboratively to improve their practice; and schools provide the necessary resources (including materials and time) to enact these expectations.
- "Frequent monitoring of student progress" refers to using a variety of assessment formats throughout the year to monitor, assess, and support each student's learning progress; and teachers and principals routinely disaggregating student achievement data to check the progress of each student group and make instructional adjustments as needed.
- "Positive home–school relations" are partnerships based in mutual respect, appreciation, and support for each party's role in educating their children. Regardless of family background, children achieve well in school when parents create a home environment that encourages learning and expresses high (but realistic) expectations for achievement and future careers.
- "Opportunity to learn" means schools and teachers providing a high-quality curriculum, effective instruction, essential materials, and sufficient time (during and beyond the school day) so every student can master the school's essential knowledge and skills.
- Realistic expectations of effective schools recognize that no one model or single set of factors can guarantee student achievement. The correlates are necessary but not sufficient conditions supporting learning for all. Schools must attend to all the correlates (and possible consequences) along with respect for its own unique student and community variables that will impact how the correlates work.

Visit the Education CourseMate for this textbook to access the eBook, Did You Get It? quizzes, TeachSource Video Cases, flashcards, and more. Go to CengageBrain.com to log in, register, or purchase access.

Endnotes

Chapter 1

1. Snyder, T. D., and Dillow, S. A. (2011). *Digest of Education Statistics 2010 (NCES 2011-015)*. National Center for Education Statistics, Institute of Education Sciences, U.S. Department of Education. Washington, DC, pp. 59; 60; Table 35, page 68; Table 40, page 77; Table 62, p. 99; Table 90, p. 132; Table 98, p. 163.
2. Nieto, S. (2009). From surviving to thriving. *Educational Leadership 66*(5), 8–13.
3. Nieto, S. (2003). *What keeps teachers going?* New York: Teachers College Press.
4. Nieto, S. (Ed.). (2005). *Why we teach*. New York: Teachers College Press.
5. Davidson, M., Lickona, T., and Khmelkov, V. (2007, November 14). Smart schools and good schools: A paradigm shift for character education. *Education Week 27*(12), 31, 40.
6. National Teacher of the Year Program. *Voices for the future*. Washington, DC: Council of Chief State School Officers. Retrieved from http://www.ccsso.org/ntoy/National_Teachers.html.
7. Draper, S. M. (2000). *Teaching from the heart: Reflections, encouragement and inspiration*. New York: Heineman. Excerpted in National Teacher of the Year Program. *Voices for the future*. Washington, DC: Council of Chief State School Officers. Retrieved from www.ccsso.org/ntoy/National_Teachers.html.
8. Ensworth, J. A. (2002). In National Teacher of the Year Program. *Voices for the future*. Washington, DC: Council of Chief State School Officers. Retrieved from www.ccsso.org/projects/National_Teacher_of_the_Year/Voices_for_the_Future/.
9. Geisen, M. (2008). In National Teacher of the Year Program. *Teacher of the Year Essay 2008*. Retrieved from http://www.ccsso.org/Documents/NTOY/Applications/2008NTOYAPP.pdf.
10. Wellborn, J. (2005). The accidental teacher. In S. Nieto (Ed.), *Why we teach* (pp. 15–22). New York: Teachers College Press.
11. Wellborn, 2005, p. 17.
12. We will discuss teachers' psychological influence on student achievement in Chapter 7 (Cultural, Social, and Educational Causes of the Achievement Gap and How to Fix It.).
13. Stronge, J. H. (2002). *Qualities of effective teachers*. Alexandria, VA: Association for Supervision and Curriculum Development.
14. Korthagen, F. A. J., and Wubbels, T. (2001). Evaluative research on the realistic approach and on the promotion of reflection. In F. A. J. Korthagen (Ed.), *Linking practice and theory: The pedagogy of realistic teacher education* (pp. 88–107). Mahwah, NJ: Lawrence Erlbaum Associates.
15. Fullan, M. (1993). *Change forces: Probing the depths of educational reform*. London: Falmer Press.
16. Goodlad, J. (1990). Studying the education of educators: From conception to findings. *Phi Delta Kappan 71*(9): 698–701.
17. For a fuller discussion of Goodlad's view of stewardship, see G. D Fenstermacher (n.d.), *Teaching on both sides of the classroom door*. Retrieved from http://www-personal.umich.edu/~gfenster/jigms.pdf.
18. Noddings, N. (1988, February). An ethic of caring and its implications for instructional arrangements. *American Journal of Education 96*(2), 215–30.
19. Noddings, N. (1995, January). A morally defensible mission for schools in the 21st century. *Phi Delta Kappan 76*(5), 365–68.
20. For a fuller discussion of the traditional view of "mental discipline" and the classical curriculum developing students' character, see Chapter 5 (American Education, 1900 to Today).
21. Noddings, 1988.
22. Noddings, 1988, p. 221.
23. O'Toole, K. (1998). Noddings: To know what matters to you, observe your actions, *Stanford Online Report*. Retrieved from: http://news-service.stanford.edu/news/1998/february4/noddings.html.
24. Noddings, N. (1999). Caring and competence. In G. Griffen (Ed.), *The education of teachers* (pp. 205–20). Chicago: National Society of Education.
25. Noddings, 1995.
26. Retrieved from http://www.1stphonecard.com/phonecardinfo.cfm?productid=303.
27. Watson, J. L. (2004). Globalization in Asia: Anthropological perspectives. In M. M. Suarez-Orozco and D. B. Qin-Hilliard (Eds.), *Globalization: Culture and education in the new millennium*. Los Angeles: University of California Press, p. 147.
28. Suarez-Orozco, M. M., and Qin-Hilliard, D. B. (2004). *Globalization: Culture and education in the new millennium*. Los Angeles: University of California Press, p. 3.
29. Digitization is the process by which words, music, data, films, files, and pictures can be manipulated on a computer screen, stored on a microprocessor, or transmitted over satellites and fiber-optic lines. This process allows you to browse online for books or download your favorite songs onto an MP3 player.
30. Greenspan, A. (2007). *The age of turbulence*. New York: Penguin Press.
31. Fleischman, H. L., Hopstock, P. J., Pelczar, M. P., and Shelley, B. E. (2010). *Highlights from PISA 2009: Performance of U.S. 15-year-old students in reading, mathematics, and science literacy in an international context* (NCES 2011-004). U.S. Department of Education, National Center for Education Statistics. Washington, DC: U.S. Government Printing Office.
32. Mullis, I. V. S., Martin, M. O., Foy, P., and Arora, A. (2012). TIMSS 2011 [place title in italics]. Chestnut Hill, MA: TIMSS & PIRLS International Study Center, Boston College. Retrieved from http://timssandpirls.bc.edu/timss2011/downloads/T11_IR_M_Executive_Summary.pdf; Martin, M. O., Mullis, I. V. S., Foy, P., and Stanco, G. M. (2012). Chestnut Hill, MA: TIMSS & PIRLS International Study Center, Boston College. Retrieved from http://timssandpirls.bc.edu/timss2011/international-results-science.html.
33. Mullis et al. Ibid, 2012; Martin et al., 2012.
34. Friedman, 2005, p. 325.

35. Bill Gates, cited in Friedman, 2005, p. 226.
36. Bill Gates, cited in Friedman, 2005, p. 226.
37. Friedman, 2005, p. 277.
38. Teacher cohorts of 2002–2007 were compared with 1994 to 1997 teacher cohorts on Praxis II. See Gilomer, D. H. (2007). *Teacher quality in a changing policy landscape: Improvements in the teacher pool.* Princeton, NJ: Educational Testing Service. Retrieved from http://www.ets.org/Media/Education_Topics/pdf/TQ_full_report.pdf.
39. Academic profiles for secondary subject teachers are high and improved as compared with academic profiles for teachers majoring in elementary, special education, and physical education. See Gilomer, 2007.
40. See Gilomer, 2007.
41. Dillon, S. (2007, December 17). Report finds better scores in new crop of teachers. *The New York Times,* Education. Retrieved from http://www.nytimes.com/2007/12/12/education/12teachers.html.
42. CCSSO. (2011, April). *InTASC model core teaching standards: A resource for state dialog.* Washington, DC: Author. Retrieved from http://www.ccsso.org/Documents/2011/InTASC_Model_Core_Teaching_Standards_2011.pdf.
43. For a fuller discussion on becoming a reflective teacher and reflection's value to continued professional growth, see Chapter 13 (Instruction).

Chapter 2

1. Minner, S. (2001, May 30). Our own worst enemy: Why are we so silent on the issue that matters most? *Education Week 20*(38), 33.
2. For a more complete literature review on teacher quality, see Kaplan, L. S., and Owings, W. A. (2002). *Teacher quality, teaching quality, and school improvement.* Bloomington, IN: Phi Delta Kappa Educational Foundation; Kaplan, L., and Owings, W. (2003). The politics of teacher quality. *Phi Delta Kappan 84*(9), 687–92.
3. See Marzano, R. J. (2003). *What works in schools: Translating research into action.* Alexandria, VA: Association for Supervision and Curriculum Development.
4. Darling-Hammond, L. (2006). *Powerful teacher education: Lessons from exemplary programs.* San Francisco: John Wiley and Sons, p. 14.
5. Asquithy, C. (2005). *The emergency teacher.* Washington, DC: West Paley Press, pp. 47, 68–70.
6. Abbott, A. (1988). *The system of professions: An essay on the division of expert labor.* Chicago: University of Chicago Press.
7. Darling-Hammond, L., and Goodwin, A. L. (1993). Progress toward professionalism in teaching. In G. Cawelti (Ed.), *Challenges and achievements of American education.* Alexandria, VA: Association for Supervision and Curriculum Development, pp. 19–52.
8. Sergiovanni, T. J. (1992). *Moral leadership: Getting to the heart of school improvement.* San Francisco: Jossey-Bass.
9. Ingersoll, R. M. (2008, January). A researcher encounters the policy realm: A personal tale. *Phi Delta Kappan 89*(5), 371.
10. The definition of *profession* is compiled from the following resources: Abdal-Haqq, I. (1991). Professionalizing teaching: Is there a role for professional development schools? Retrieved from http://library.educationworld.net/a12/a12-170.html; Corwin, R. G. (1965). *Sociology of education.* New York: Appleton-Century-Crofts; Darling-Hammond, L. (1987). Schools for tomorrow's teachers. *Teachers College Record 88,* 356–58; Howsam, R. B., Corrigan, D. C., and Denemark, D. W. (1976). *Educating a profession.* Washington, DC: American Association of Colleges for Teacher Education; Levine, M. (1988). Introduction. In M. Levine (Ed.), *Professional practice schools: Building a model.* Washington, DC: American Federation of Teachers, pp. 1–25; Ingersoll, R. M., and Merrill, E. (2011). "The status of teaching as a profession." In J. Ballentine and J. Spady (Eds.), *Schools and society: A sociological approach to education,* 4th ed. Pine Forge, CA: Sage, pp. 185–98; Rosenholtz, S. J. (1989). *Teachers' workplace: The social organization of schools.* New York: Longman.
11. Yinger, R. J., and Nolen, A. L. (2003, January). Surviving the legitimacy challenge. *Phi Delta Kappan 84*(5), 386–90.
12. Yinger and Nolen, 2003; Johnson, S. M. (2001, January). Can professional certification of teachers reshape teaching as a career? *Phi Delta Kappan 82*(5), 393–99.
13. Lortie, D. (1975). *Schoolteacher: A sociological study.* London: University of Chicago Press.
14. Yinger and Nolen, 2003; Johnson, 2001.
15. NCATE. (2011, July 20). *Quick facts. About NCATE. NCATE and the states.* Retrieved from http://www.ncate.org/Public/AboutNCATE/QuickFacts/tabid/343/Default.aspx.
16. Darling-Hammond, L. (1994). Who will speak for the children: How "Teach for America" hurts urban schools and students. *Phi Delta Kappan 76*(1), 21–33; Luke, A., Luke, C., and Mayer, D. (2000, April). Redesigning teacher education. *Teaching Education 11*(1), 5–11.
17. Harris Interactive. (2009, August 4). *Firefighters, scientists, and doctors seen as most prestigious occupations.* Rochester, NY: Author. Retrieved from http://www.harrisinteractive.com/vault/Harris-Interactive-Poll-Research-Pres-Occupations-2009-08.pdf.
18. Markow, D., and Pieters, A. (2012, March). *The Met Life survey of the American Teacher. Teachers, parents, and the economy. A survey of teachers, parents, and students.* New York: Metropolitan Life Insurance Company. Retrieved from http://www.metlife.com/assets/cao/contributions/foundation/american-teacher/MetLife-Teacher-Survey-2011.pdf.
19. Hoyle, E. (2001, April). Teaching: Prestige, status and esteem. *Educational Management and Administration 29*(2), 139–52.
20. Alvarez, B. (2007, December 10). *Teacher salary lags behind inflation.* National Education Association. Retrieved from http://www.nea.org/newsreleases/2007/nr071210.html.
21. Hurley, E. (n.d.). *Teacher pay 1940 to 2000 losing ground, losing status. National Education Association, Education Statistics.* Retrieved from http://www.nea.org/edstats/losingground.html.
22. U.S. Department of Labor, Bureau of Labor Statistics. (2011, May 17). *Occupational employment and wages new release.* Washington, DC: Author. Retrieved from http://www.bls.gov/news.release/ocwage.htm.
23. Markow and Pieters, 2012.
24. U.S. Department of Labor, Bureau of Labor Statistics, 2011.
25. Darling-Hammond, L., and Sykes, G. (2003). Wanted: A national teacher supply policy for education: The right way to meet the "highly qualified teacher" challenge. *Educational Policy Analysis and Archives 11*(33). Retrieved from http://epaa.asu.edu/epaa/v11n33.
26. Mihans, R. (2008, June). Can teachers lead teachers? *Phi Delta Kappan 89*(10), 762–65.
27. Swanson, C. B. (2008, January 10). Teacher salaries: Looking at comparable jobs. Quality counts 2008: Tapping into teaching. *Education Week.* Retrieved from http://www.edweek.org/ew/articles/2008/01/10/18salaries.h27.html.

28. Complicating factors include whether teachers are 9-month or 12-month workers, whether fringe benefits should be considered in addition to salary, and whether to analyze hourly, weekly, or annual pay.
29. NEA Research. (2011). *Rankings and estimates. Rankings of the states 2010 and estimates of school statistics 2011.* Washington, DC: Author, p. x. Retrieved from http://www.NEA.org/assets/docs/HE/NEA_Rankings_and_Estimates010711.pdf.
30. *National compensation survey: Occupational wages in the United States, June 2005: Supplementary tables, 2006.* (2006). Retrieved from http://www.bls.gov/ncs/ocs/sp/ncbl0831.pdf.
31. *How much are public school teachers paid?* (2007, January). Washington, DC: Manhattan Institute for Policy Research, U.S. Bureau of Labor Statistics.
32. Interview with Linda Darling-Hammond (n.d.). PBS "Only a teacher" series. Retrieved from http://www.pbs.org/onlyateacher/today2.html
33. Halsted, 2008.
34. Mishel, L., Allegretto, S., and Corcoran, S. (2008, April 30). The teaching penalty: We can't recruit and retain excellent educators on the cheap. *Education Week 27*(35), 30.
35. Lortie, D. (1975). Op. cit.
36. Bushaw, W. J., and Lopez, S. J. (2010, September). A time for change. The 42nd annual Phi Delta Kappa/Gallup poll of the public's attitudes toward the public schools. *Phi Delta Kappan 92*(1), 9–26.
37. See, for example: Darling-Hammond, L. (2000). Teacher quality and student achievement: A review of state policy evidence. *Education Policy Analysis Archives 8*(1), 1–44; Hanushek, E. A. (1992). The trade-off between child quantity and quality. *Journal of Political Economy 100*(1), 84–117; Nye, B., Konstantopoulos, S., and Hedges, L. V. (2004). How large are teacher effects? *Educational Evaluation and Policy Analysis 26*(3), 237–57; Rivkin, S. G., Hanushek, E. A., and Kain, J. F. (2005). Teachers, schools, and academic achievement. *Econometrica 73*(2), 417–58; Sanders, W. L., and Horn, S. P. (1995). Educational assessment reassessed: The usefulness of standardized and alternative measures of student achievement as indicators for the assessment of educational outcomes. *Education Policy Analysis Archives 3*(6),1–15.
38. Hassel, B. C., and Katzir, D. (2010, April 21). Teacher incentive fund: Trivial or transformative? *Education Week 29*(29), 30–31; Lankford, H., and Wyckoff, J. (1997). The changing structure of teacher compensation, 1970–94. *Economics of Education Review 16*(4), 371–84; National Council on Teacher Quality. (2010, December). *Restructuring teacher pay to reward excellence.* Washington, DC: Author. Retrieved from http://www.nctq.org/tr3/docs/nctq_salary_combo.pdf
39. See, for example: Ballou, D., and Podgursky, M. (1997). *Teacher pay and teacher quality.* Kalamazoo, MI: W. E. Upjohn Institute for Employment Research; Hanushek, E. (1986). The economics of schooling: Production and efficiency in public schools. *Journal of Economic Literature 24*(3), 1141–77; Lankford and Wyckoff, 1997; Rivkin, Hanushek, and Kain, 2005. Op. cit.; Goldhaber, D. D., and Dominic J. B. (1998). When should we reward degrees for teachers? *Phi Delta Kappan 80*(2), 134–38; National Council on Teacher Quality. (2010, December). *Restructuring teacher pay to reward excellence.* Washington, DC: Author. Retrieved from http://www.nctq.org/tr3/docs/nctq_salary_combo.pdf; Rice, J. K. (2003, August). *Teacher quality: Understanding the effectiveness of teacher attributes.* Washington, DC: Economic Policy Institute.
40. Hatry, H. P., Greiner, J. M., and Ashford, B. G. (1994). *Issues and case studies in teacher incentive plans,* 2nd ed. Washington, DC: Urban Institute Press; Murnane, R. J., and Cohen, D. K. (1986). Merit pay and the evaluation problem: Why most merit pay plans fail and a few survive. *Harvard Education Review 56*, 1–17.
41. Dee, T. S., and Keys, B. J. (2004). Does merit pay reward good teachers? Evidence from a randomized experiment. *Journal of Policy Analysis and Management 23*(3), 913–27; Eberts, R., Hollenbeck, K., and Stone, J. (2002). Teacher performance incentives and student outcomes. *Journal of Human Resources 37*(4), 913–27; Figlio, D. N., and Kenny, L. W. (2007). Individual teacher incentives and student performance. *Journal of Pubic Economics 91*(5–6), 901–14; Lavy, V. (2004). *Performance pay and teachers' efforts, productivity and grading ethics.* NBER Working Paper No. 10622. Cambridge, MA: NBER.
42. Springer, M. G., Ballou, D., Hamilton, L., Le, V., Lockwood, J. R., McCaffrey, D., Pepper, M., and Stecher, B. (2010). *Teacher pay for performance: Experimental evidence from the project on incentives in teaching.* Nashville, TN: National Center on Performance Incentives at Vanderbilt University. Retrieved from http://edlab.tc.columbia.edu/files/pointstudy.pdf.
43. Sawchuck, S. (2010, June 9). Merit-pay model pushed by Duncan shows no achievement edge. *Education Week 29*(33), 1, 21.
44. Jacob, B., and Lefgren, L. (2005). *Principals as agents: Subjective performance measurement in education.* National Bureau for Economic Research Working Paper No. 11463. Cambridge, MA: NBER; Rebora, A. (2009, October 1). Teacher evaluations get poor grades. *Education Week 30*(1), 7; Weisberg, D., Sexton, S, Mulhern, J., and Keeling, D. (2009). *The widget effect. Our national failure to acknowledge and act on differences in teacher effectiveness,* 2nd ed. Brooklyn, NY: The New Teacher Project. Retrieved from http://widgeteffect.org/downloads/TheWidgetEffect.pdf.
45. Popham, W. (2008). A misunderstood grail. *Educational Leadership 66*(1), 82–83; Wiliam, D. (2010). Standardized testing and school accountability. *Educational Psychologist 45*(2), 107–122.
46. For example, Hatry, H., Greiner, J., and Ashford, B. (1994). Issues and case studies in teacher incentive plans. Washington, DC: Urban Institute Press; Murnane, R., and Cohen, D. (1986). Merit pay and the evaluation problem: Why most merit pay plans fail and a few survive. *Harvard Educational Review 56*, 1–17; Mohrman, A. M., Jr., Mohrman, S. A., and Odden, A. R. (1996). Aligning teacher compensation with systemic school reform: Skill-based pay and group-based performance rewards. *Educational Evaluation and Policy Analysis 18*(1), 51–71; Ramirez, A. (2010/2011, December/January). Merit pay misfires. *Educational Leadership 68*(4), 55–58.
47. Loeb et al. (2009). Op. cit; Podgursky and Stronger, 2007. Op. cit.
48. Rivkin, S. G., Hanushek, E. A., and Kain, J. F. (2005). "Teachers, Schools, and Academic Achievement." *Econometrica* 73, 417–58.
49. Donahue, D. M. (2002, Spring). Rhode Island's last holdout: Tenure and married women teachers on the brink of the women's movement. *History of Education Quarterly 42*(1), 50–74.
50. Blackwell, P. J., Futrell, M. H., and Imig, D. G. (2003 January). Burnt water paradoxes of schools of education. *Phi Delta Kappan 85*(5), 357.
51. Donahue, 2002.
52. Lortie, 1975, p. 85.
53. Johnson, S. M. (2001, January). Can professional certification for teachers reshape teaching as a career? *Phi Delta Kappan 82*(5), 393–99; Donahue, 2002.

54. Simpson, R. L., and Simpson, I. H. (1969). Women and bureaucracy in the semi-professions. In A. Etzioni (Ed.), *The semi-professions and their organization.* New York: Free Press, p. 209.
55. Johnson, 2001.
56. Peske, H. G., Liu, E., Johnson, S. M., Kauffman, D., and Kardos, S. M. (2001, December). The next generation of teachers: Changing conceptions of a career in teaching. *Phi Delta Kappan 83*(4), 304–11.
57. Johnson, S. M. (2006, Summer). *American educator.* Retrieved from http://www.aft.org/pubs-reports? american_educator /issues/summer06/Teacher.pdf.
58. Johnson, 2001.
59. Levinson, D. (1978). The seasons of a man's life. New York: Knopf; Super, D. E. (1957). *The psychology of careers.* New York: Harper & Brothers.
60. Hall, D. T. (1996). The new role of the career practitioner. In D. T. Hall (Ed.), *The career is dead – long live the career.* San Francisco: Jossey-Bass, pp. 1–12.
61. Sullivan, S. E. (1999). The changing nature of careers: A review and research agenda. *Journal of Management 25*(3), 457–84, 458.
62. Johnson, 2001.
63. Cubberley, E. P. (1947). *Public education in the United States.* Cambridge, MA: Houghton Mifflin, p. 375.
64. Cubberley, 1947, p. 376.
65. Cubberley, 1947, p. 377.
66. The term "normal school" is now largely obsolete. By the end of the nineteenth century, most normal schools had become four-year teacher education colleges.
67. Levine, A. (2006). *Educating school teachers. The Education Schools Project.* Retrieved from http://www.edschools.org/pdf /Educating_Teachers_Report.pdf.
68. Cubberley, 1947, p. 378.
69. Public normal schools first became state normal colleges, then state teachers' colleges, then state colleges and universities. Private normal schools closed. See Levine, 2006, p. 25.
70. Levine, 2006, p. 25.
71. Clifford, G. J., & Guthrie, J. W. (1988). *Ed school: A brief for professional education,* Chicago: University of Chicago Press, p. 63.
72. Levine, 2006.
73. Levine, 2006, p. 39.
74. Darling-Hammond, L. (1997). *Doing what matters most: Investing in quality teaching.* New York: National Commission on Teaching and America's Future, p. 10. A copy of the complete report, *What Matters Most: Teaching and America's Future,* can be found at http://www.nctaf.org/documents /WhatMattersMost.pdf.
75. Darling-Hammond, L. (2000, January 1). Teacher quality and student achievement: A review of state policy evidence. *Education Policy Analysis Archives 8,* 1. Retrieved from http://www .epaa.asu.edu/epaa/v8n1.
76. Darling-Hammond, L. (1996). *What matters most: Teaching and America's future.* National Commission on Teaching and America's Future. Columbia University: Teachers College, p. 28; Darling-Hammond, L., & Bransford, J. (Eds.). (2005). *Preparing teachers for a changing world: What teachers should know and be able to do.* National Academy of Education. San Francisco: Jossey-Bass.
77. Allen, M. (2003). *Eight questions on teacher preparation: What does the research say? A summary of the findings.* Denver, CO: Education Commission of the States. Retrieved from http://www .ecs.org/html/educationIssues/teachingquality/tpreport/home /summary.pdf. The full report can be retrieved from www.ecs .org/treport.
78. Goldhaber, D. D., and Brewer, D. J. (2000). Does teacher certification matter? High school certification status and student achievement. *Educational Evaluation and Policy Analysis 22,* 129–45.
79. Monk, D. (1994). Subject area preparation of secondary mathematics and science teachers and student achievement. *Economics of Education Review 13*(2), 125–45.
80. Schneps, M., and Sadler, P. (2000). *A private universe: Minds of our own.* In J. D. Bransford, A. L. Brown, and R. R. Cocking (Eds.), *How people learn: Brain, mind, experience, and school.* Washington, DC: National Academies Press, pp. 15–16.
81. Cochran-Smith, M., and Zeichner, K. M. (2005). *Studying teacher education: The report of the AERA Panel on Research and Teacher Education.* American Educational Research Association. Mahwah, NJ: Lawrence Erlbaum Associates, p. 329.
82. Cochran-Smith and Zeichner, 2005.
83. Wilson, S. M., Floden, R. E., & Ferrini-Mundy, J. (2001). *Executive summary: Teacher preparation research: Current knowledge, gaps, and recommendations.* Center for the Study of Teaching and Policy, University of Washington, in collaboration with Michigan State University. The report is available at http://depts .washington.edu/ctpmail or look up the Center for the Study of Teaching and Policy.
84. Murnane, R., Singer, J., Willett, J., Kemple, J., and Olsen, R. (Eds.). (1991). *Who will teach? Policies that matter.* Cambridge, MA: Harvard University Press.
85. Ingersoll, R. (2003). Is there really a teacher shortage? Retrieved from http://www.ncctq.org/issueforums/atrisk/presentations /keynoteIngersoll.ppt#291,6,Beginning Teacher Attrition (Cumulative Percent Teachers Having Left Teaching Occupation, by Years of Experience).
86. Shen, J. (2003, April). New teachers' certification status and attrition pattern: A survival analysis using the Baccalaureate and Beyond Longitudinal Study 1993–97. Paper presented at the AERA annual meeting, Chicago; Boyd, D., Dunlop, E., Lankford, H., Loeb. S., Mahler, P., O'Brien, R.H., & Wyckoff, J. (2011). *Alternative certification in the long run: Student achievement, teacher retention, and the distribution of teacher quality in New York City.* Palo Alto, CA: Center for Education Policy and Analysis, Stanford University. Retrieved from http://cepa.stanford.edu /content/alternative-certification-long-run-student-achievement -teacher-retention-and-distribution.
87. Ingersoll, R. (2003, January). Original analysis for NCTAF of the 2000–2001 Teacher Follow-up Survey. In National Commission on Teaching and America's Future. *No dream denied* (p. 84). Retrieved from http://www.nctaf.org.
88. Elsbree, W. S. (1939). *The American teacher: Evolution of a profession in a democracy.* New York: American Book. Cited in Spring, J. (2001). *American education* (10th ed.). Boston: McGraw-Hill, p. 26.
89. Elsbree, 1939.
90. *Testing teacher candidates: The role of licensure tests in improving teacher quality.* (2001). National Academies Press. Retrieved from http://books.nap.edu/openbook.php?record _id=10090&page=57.
91. Castle, J., and Jacobs, S. (2007). *State teacher policy quality yearbook 2007: Progress on teacher quality.* Washington, DC: National Council on Teacher Quality, pp. 7, 79. Retrieved from http://www .nctq.org/p/publications/docs/stpy_national_20071129024206.pdf.
92. National Council on Teacher Quality. (2009). *2009 State teacher policy yearbook. National Summary.* Washington, DC: Author. Retrieved from http://www.nctq.org/stpy09/findings.jsp.
93. Castle and Jacobs, 2007, pp. 46, 48.

94. Sasson, D. (2007, April 27). *How to become a certified teacher*. Suite101.com. Retrieved from http://preservice-teacher-training.suite101.com/article.cfm/how_to_become_a_certified_teacher.
95. Efforts to improve teacher quality. (2006, January 5). *Education week: Quality counts 2006*, 86–90.
96. Education Commission of the States. (2002). *No state left behind: The challenge and opportunities of ESEA 2001*. Denver, CO: Author, p. 30.
97. Although NCLB does not permit temporary, emergency, or provisional teacher certifications, it does not require a teacher to attain the highest level of certification to be considered "highly qualified." NCLB regulations state that under most circumstances, teachers who participate in alternative certification programs and who have a college degree in the subject they are teaching are also considered "highly qualified." That means a college graduate who is *enrolled* in an alternative certification program—but has not yet completed the first course, demonstrated the ability to teach, or met the state's standards for a professional license—can be considered "highly qualified" and assigned to a classroom. Such teachers may "assume the functions of a teacher" for up to three years without having received full certification and still be considered "highly qualified." See Darling-Hammond and Sykes, 2003.
98. Barnes, R. E., and Aguerrebere, J. A., Jr. (2006, November 15). Sidetracking the debate on teacher quality. *Education Week 26*(12), 34, 44.
99. Darling-Hammond, L. (2002, September 6). Research and rhetoric on teacher certification: A response to "Teacher certification reconsidered." *Education Policy Analysis Archives 10*(36). Retrieved from http://epaa.asu.edu/v10n36.html; Darling-Hammond, L. (2000). Teacher quality and student achievement: A review of state policy evidence. *Education Policy Analysis Archives 8*(1). Retrieved from http://epaa.asu.edu/epaa/v8n1; Darling-Hammond, L., Berry, B., and Thoreson, A. (2001). Does teacher certification matter? Evaluating the evidence. *Educational Evaluation and Policy Analysis 23*(1), 57–77.
100. Much research in this area lacks the scientific rigor associated with randomized experimental study design or nonexperimental longitudinal data on participants. Essentially, comparing apples to oranges makes conclusions difficult to draw.
101. Podgursky, M. (2003). *Improving academic performance in U.S. public schools: Why teacher licensing is (almost) irrelevant*. Paper presented at the Teacher Preparation and Quality: New Directions in Policy and Research Conference, Washington, DC, October 18–20, 2003.
102. Boyd, D., Grossman, P., Lankford, H., Loeb, S., & and Wyckoff, J. (2005). How changes in entry requirements alter teacher workforce and affect student achievement. *Education Finance and Policy 1*(2), 176–216; Gordon, R., Kane, T. J., and Staiger, D. O. (2006). *Identifying effective teachers using performance on the job*. Washington, DC: The Brookings Institution. The Hamilton Project. Retrieved from http://www.brookings.edu/views/papers/200604Hamilton_1.pdf; Kane, T. J., Rockoff, J. E., and Staiger, D. O. (2006). *What does certification tell us about teacher effectiveness? Evidence from New York City*. Cambridge, MA: Harvard Graduate School of Education. Retrieved from http://www.gse.harvard.edu/news/features/kane/nycfellowsmarch2006.pdf; Nunnery, J. A., Kaplan, L. S., Owings, W. A., and Pribesh, S. (2009, December). The effects of troops to teachers on student achievement: A meta-analytic approach. *National Association of Secondary School Principals Bulletin 93*(4), 249–72.
103. Boyd et al. (2005); Gordon et al. (2006); Kane et al. (2006); Rivkin, S. G., Hanushek, E. A., and Kain, J. F. (2005). Teachers, schools and academic achievement. *Econometric 73*(2), 417–58; Rockoff, J. E. (2004). The impact of individual teachers on student achievement: Evidence from panel data. *American Economic Review 94*(2), 247–52; Sanders, W. L., and Horn, S. P. (1995). Educational assessment reassessed: The usefulness of standardized and alternative measures of student achievement as indicators for the assessment of educational outcomes. *Education Policy Analysis Archives 3*(6), 1–15. Retrieved from http://epaa.asu.edu/epaa/v3n6.html; Sanders, W. L., and Rivers, J. C. (1996). *Cumulative and residual effects of teachers on future student academic achievement*. Knoxville: University of Tennessee Value-Added Research and Assessment Center.
104. *Chicago Tribune*. (1975, September 28). Section 1, p. 3. Cited in Ornstein, A. C., and Levine, D. U. (2006). *Foundations of education*. New York: Houghton Mifflin, p. 46.
105. Donahue, 2002.
106. Size calculated from the American Federation of Teachers and National Education Association reported membership figures. See http://www.aft.org/about and www.nea.org/home/1594.htm. Contribution amount calculated by the Center for Responsive Politics (2012). Available at http://www.opensecrets.org/orgs/list.phphttp://www.opensecrets.org/industries/indus.php?ind=L1300.
107. National Education Association. (2011, May 7). *Proposed policy statement on teacher evaluation and accountability*. Retrieved from http://www.nea.org/assets/docs/statement-on-teacher-evaluation-and-accountability.pdf.
108. Sawchuck, S. (2012, July 13). Relaxes NEA evaluation policy incorporates many caveats. *Education Week 30*(36), 6–7.
109. American Federation of Teachers. (2009). *The instructional demands of standards-based reform*. Washington, DC: Author. Retrieved from http://www.aft.org/pdfs/teachers/instructionaldemands0609.pdf.
110. National Education Association. (2011, May 7). Proposed policy statement on teacher evaluation and accountability. Retrieved from http://www.nea.org/assets/docs/statement-on-teacher-evaluation-and-accountability.pdf.
111. Wise, A. E., and Udan, M. D. (2013, March 12). The political future of the teaching profession. Commentary. *Education Week, 32*(24), 32, 26.
112. American Federation of Teachers, 2009.
113. Weingarten, R. (2010, January 12). A new path forward: Four approaches to quality teaching and better schools. Washington, DC: American Federation of Teachers. Retrieved from http://www.aft.org/pdfs/press/sp_weingarten011210.pdf.
114. Bass, J. (2010, January 12). *AFT president unveils new approaches to teacher evaluation and labor-management relationships*. Retrieved from http://www.aft.org/newspubs/press/2010/011210.cfm.
115. Goldstein, R. A. (2011). Imaging the frame: Media representations of teachers, their unions, NCLB, and education reform. *Education Policy 25*(4), 543–76; Whitmire, R., and Rotherham, A. (2009). How teachers unions lost the media. *Wall Street Journal*, 1 October.
116. For example, see: Lieberman, M. (2000). *The teacher unions: How they sabotage education reform and why?* San Francisco: L Encounter Books. Retrieved from http://eric.ed.gov/PDFS/ED468097.pdf.
117. Eberts, R. W., and Stone, J. A. (1987). Teacher unions and the productivity of public schools. *Industrial and Labor Relations Review 40*(3), 354–63; Grimes, P. W., and Register, C. A. (1990). Teacher unions and student achievement in high

school economics. *Journal of Economic Education 21*(1), 297–308; Argyrs, L. M., and Rees, D. I. (1995). Unionization and school productivity: A reexamination. In S. Polachek (Ed.), *Research in labor economics, 14*. Greenwich, CT: JAI Press, pp. 49–68; Milkman, M. I. (1997). Teachers' unions, productivity and minority student achievement. *Journal of Labor Research 18*(Winter), 137–50; Carini, R. M., Powell, B., and Steelman, L. C. (2000). Do teacher unions hinder educational performance? Lessons learned from state SAT and ACT scores. *Harvard Educational Review 70*(4), 437–67.

118. See, for example: Corsini, R.M. (2002). *School reform proposals: The research evidence. Teacher unions and student achievement.* Retrieved from http://nepc.colorado.edu/files/Summary-10.Carini.pdf; DiCarlo, M. (2010, October 1). *Performance-enhancing teacher contracts?* Washington, DC: The Shanker Institute. Retrieved from http://shankerblog.org/?p=895; Kasper, H. (1970). The effects of collective bargaining on public school teachers' salaries. *Industrial and Labor Relations Review 24*(1), 57–72; Eberts, R. W., and Stone, J. A. (1984). *Unions and public schools: The effect of collective bargaining on American education*. Lexington, MA: Lexington Books; Hoxby, C. (1996). How teachers' unions affect education productivity. *Quarterly Journal of Economics 111*(3), 671–718; Berkman, M. E., Phutzer, E., and Jones-White, D. (2004). *School budgets and local teachers' unions: The mediating role of institutions.* Paper presented at the State Politics and Policy Conference, Kent State University, April.
119. Kasper, 1970. Op. cit.; Eberts, R. W., and Stone, J. A. (1986). Teacher unions and the cost of public education. *Economic Inquiry 24*(4), 631–44; Hoxby, 1996. Op. cit.; Berkman, Plutzer, & Jones-White, 2004. Op. cit.; Strunk, K. A. (2011). Are teachers' unions really to blame? Collective bargaining agreements and their relationships with district resource allocation and student performance in California. *Education Finance and Policy 6*(3), 354–98.
120. Oakes, R. C. (1960, March). Should teachers strike? An unanswered question. *Journal of Educational Sociology 33*(7), 339–44.
121. Jessup, 1978.
122. Oakes, 1960, p. 343.
123. Zigarelli, M. A. (1996, Winter). Dispute resolution mechanisms and teacher bargaining outcomes. *Journal of Labor Research 17*(1), 135–48.
124. Campbell, E. (2005, September). Challenges in fostering ethical knowledge as professionalism within schools as teaching communities. *Journal of Educational Change 6*(3), 207–26, 208.
125. Louis, K. S., Kruse, S. D., and Bryk, A. S. (1995). Professionalism and community. In K. S. Louis, S. D. Kruse, et al. (Eds.), *Professionalism and community: Perspectives on reforming urban schools*. Thousand Oaks, CA: Corwin Press, pp. 3–42, 16.
126. Campbell, E. (1997, September–October). Connecting the ethics of teaching and moral education. *Journal of Teacher Education 48*, 255–64.
127. Campbell, E. (2001, October). Let right be done: Trying to put ethical standards into practice. *Journal of Education Policy 16*(5), 395–411.
128. Ledoux, M. (2011, Spring). Seeking NACTE accreditation: Leadership perspectives and tips. *Academic Leadership. The On-line Journal 9*(2). Retrieved from http://www.academicleadership.org/article/Seeking_NCATE_Accreditation_Leadership_Perspectives_and_Tips; Wise, A. (2010). Professional accreditation, NCATE, and TEAC. Washington, DC: NCATE. Retrieved from http://www.ncate.org/Public/ResearchReports/Articles/ProfessionalAccreditationNCATEandTEAC/tabid/693/Default.aspx.
129. Wise, A. E. 2005. Establishing teaching as a profession: The essential role of professional accreditation. *Journal of Teacher Education 56*(4), 318–31.
130. Honawar, V. (2008, December 3). NCATE commits to streamlining accrediting process. *Education Week, 28*(14), 6.
131. Sawchuk, S. (2013, February 20). Accrediting body unveils teacher-prep proposal. *Education Week, 32*(21), 6.
132. For more information on InTASC, see http://www.ccsso.org/Documents/2011/InTASC_Model_Core_Teaching_Standards_2011.pdf.
133. Rebora, A. (2012, October 24). National board seeks to revive impact on profession. *Education Week 32*(9), 8.
134. National Board of Professional Teaching Standards. (2011). *Diversity initiatives.* Washington, DC: Author: Retrieved from http://www.nbpts.org/resources/diversity_initiatives.
135. Berry, B. (2005, December). Recruiting and retaining board-certified teachers for hard-to-staff schools. *Phi Delta Kappan 87*(4), 290–97.
136. Keller, B. (2007, January 31). More minority teachers earn national certification. *Education Week 26*(21), 5.
137. National Board Certification has received recognition, support, and momentum from the AFT, NEA, Carnegie Foundation for the Advancement of Teaching, Columbia University's Teachers College, and NCATE. Some universities have incorporated the National Board standards into their teacher preparation and professional accreditation programs. Governors, state legislatures, and school boards help school districts provide a range of incentives encouraging teachers to earn NBPTS certification.
138. National Board for Professional Teaching Standards. (2011). *Milestones: Raising the standard.* Retrieved from http://www.nbpts.org/about_us/mission_and_history/milestones.
139. Rebora, 2012.
140. National Board of Professional Teaching Standards. (2007, July). *Making a difference in quality teaching and student achievement.* Retrieved from http://www.nbpts.org; Viadero, D., and Honawar, V. (2008, June 18). Credential of NBPTS has impact. *Education Week, 27*(42), 1.
141. Bond, L., Smith, T., Baker, W. K., and Hattie, J. A. (2000, September). *Validation study: A distinction that matters.* University of North Carolina at Greensboro: Center for Educational Research and Evaluation. Retrieved from http://www.nbpts.org/UserFiles/File/validity_1_-_UNC_Greebsboro_D_-_Bond.pdf; Lustick, D., and Sykes, G. (2006, February 23). National Board Certification as professional development: What are teachers learning? *Education Policy Analysis Archives 14*(5). Retrieved from http://epaa.asu.edu/epaa/v14n5; Sykes, G., et al. (2006, May). *National Board Certified teachers as organizational resource.* Grant # 61–5230. Final report to the National Board for Professional Teaching Standards; Cohen, C. E., and Rice, J. K. (2005, August). *National Board Certification as professional development: Design and cost.* Washington, DC: U.S. Department of Education and National Science Foundation. Retrieved from http://www.nbpts.org/UserFiles/File/Complete_Study_Cohen.pdf; Viadero and Honawar, 2008. Goldhaber, D., and Anthony, E. (2004, March 8). *Can teacher quality be effectively assessed?* Urban Institute. Retrieved from http://www.urban.org/publications/410958.html; Vandevoort, L. G., Amrein-Beardsley, A., and Berliner, D. C. (2004, September 8). National Board Certified teachers and their students' achievement. *Education Analysis and Policy Archives 12*(46). Retrieved from http://www.nbpts.org/UserFiles/File/National_Board_Certified_Teachers_and_Their_Students_Achievement_-_Vandevoort.pdf; Smith, T. W., Gordon, B., Colby, S. A., and Wang, J. J. (2005, April). *An examination of the*

relationship between depth of student learning and National Board Certification status. Boone, NC: Appalachian State University, Office for Research on Teaching; Cavalluzzo, L. (2004, November). *Is National Board Certification an effective signal of teacher quality?* Alexandria, VA: CNA Corporation. Retrieved from http://www.nbpts.org/UserFiles/File/Final_Study_11204_D_-_Cavalluzzo_-_CNA_Corp.pdf.

142. Sanders, W. L., Ashton, J. J., and Wright, S. P. (2005, March 7). *Comparison of the effects of NBPTS certified teachers with other teachers on the rate of student academic progress.* SAS Institute. Retrieved from http://www.nbpts.org/UserFiles/File/SAS_final_NBPTS_report_D_-_Sanders.pdf; McColsky, W., Stronge, J. H., et al. (2005, June). *A comparison of National Board Certified teachers and non-National Board Certified teachers: Is there a difference between teacher effectiveness and student achievement?* Greensboro, NC: University of North Carolina at Greensboro/SERVE. Retrieved from http://www.nbpts.org/UserFiles/File/Teacher_Effectiveness_Student_Achievement_and_National_Board_Certified_Teachers_D_-_McColskey.pdf.
143. Ingersoll, R. M., and Smith, T. M. (2004, March). Do teacher induction and mentoring matter? *National Association of Secondary School Principals Bulletin 88*(638), 28.
144. Ingersoll, R., and Smith, T. (2003). The wrong solution to the teacher shortage. *Educational Leadership 60*(8), 30–33.
145. Levine, 2006, p. 42.
146. Wong, H. K. (2004, March). Induction programs that keep new teachers teaching and improving. *National Association of Secondary School Principals Bulletin 88*(638), 41–58; Ingersoll and Smith, 2004.
147. Wong, 2004.
148. Wong, 2004.
149. North Carolina Teaching Fellows Commission. (1995). *Keeping talented teachers.* Raleigh, NC: Public School Forum on North Carolina. Cited in Wong, 2004, p. 44; Schlager, M., Fusco, J., Koch, M., Crawford, V., and Phillips, M. (2003, July). *Designing equity and diversity into online strategies to support new teachers.* Paper presented at the National Educational Computing Conference (NECC), Seattle, WA.
150. *Education Week* quality counts 2003. (2003, January 9). *Education Week 22*(17), 70.
151. Alliance for Excellence in Education (2008, September 8). From No Child Left Behind to every child a graduate: New alliance report outlines policy framework for improving America's secondary schools. *Straight A's. Public Education Policy and Progress 8*(16), 1–50+. Retrieved from http://www.all4ed.org/files/ECAG.pdf; Strong, M. (2004). *Induction, mentoring, and teacher retention: A summary of the research.* Santa Cruz, CA: Association of Teacher Educator's Commission on Mentoring and Teacher Induction and the New Teacher Center, University of California, Santa Cruz; Wong, 2004.
152. Ingersoll and Smith, 2004.
153. National Center for Education Statistics. (2000). *Progress through the teacher pipeline: 1992–93 college graduates and elementary/secondary school teaching as of 1997.* Washington, DC: U.S. Department of Education.
154. Darling-Hammond, L. (2001, June). The challenge of staffing our schools. *Educational Leadership 58*(8), 12–17; National Commission on Teaching & America's Future. (2003). *No dream denied: A pledge to America's children.* New York: Author.
155. Honawar, V. (2008, September 17). Boston, Chicago teacher "residencies" gaining notice. *Education Week 28*(4), 13. The studies were conducted by the Washington-based Aspen Institute and the Center for Teaching Quality in Hillsborough, North Carolina.
156. Villar, A., and Strong, M. (2007). *Is mentoring worth the money? A benefit-cost analysis and five-year rate of return of a comprehensive mentoring program for beginning teachers.* Santa Cruz, CA: New Teacher Center.
157. Garet, M., Porter, A. Desmoine, L., Birman, B., and Kwang, S. K. (2001). What makes professional development effective? *American Educational Research Journal 38*(4), 915–46; Palumbo, M. (2003). A network that puts the Net to work. *Journal of Staff Development 24*(1), 24–28; Rothman, R. (2002/2003). Transforming high schools into small learning communities. *Challenge Journal 6*(2), 1–8.
158. Bryk, T., and Schneider, B. (2002). *Trust in schools: A core resource for improvement.* New York: Russell Sage Foundation.
159. Showers, B., Joyce, B. R., and Bennett, B. (1987, February). Synthesis of research on staff development: A framework for future study and a state of the art analysis. *Educational Leadership 45*(3), 77–87.
160. For a more complete discussion of studies showing that increased teacher knowledge and skills leads to increased student achievement, see Chapter 14, Instruction. See also Kaplan and Owings, 2002.
161. Hanushek, E. Cited in Haycock, K. (1998, Summer). Good teaching matters ... a lot. *Thinking K–16, 4.* Washington, DC: The Education Trust.
162. National School Boards Foundation. (1999). *Leadership matters: Transforming urban school boards.* Alexandria, VA: Author.
163. Cohen, D. K., and Hill, H. C. (1998). *Instructional policy and classroom performance: The mathematics reform in California.* Philadelphia: Consortium for Policy Research in Education.
164. Alexander, D., Heaviside, S., and Farris, E. (1998). *Status of education reform in public elementary and secondary schools: Teachers' perspectives.* NCES 1999-045. U.S. Department of Education, National Center for Education Statistics, Fast Response Survey System. Washington, DC: U.S. Government Printing Office.
165. Choy, S. P., and Xianglei, C. (1998). *Toward better teaching: Professional development in 1993–94.* NCES 98-230. U.S. Department of Education. National Center for Education Statistics. Washington, DC: U.S. Government Printing Office.
166. Darling-Hammond, 1997, p. 30.

Chapter 3

1. Philosophy. (1970). In *The American heritage dictionary of the English language.* Boston: American Heritage & Houghton Mifflin, p. 985.
2. Tozer, S., Violas, P. C., and Senese, G. (1993). *School and society: Educational practice as social expression.* New York: McGraw-Hill.
3. This chapter uses the terms "conservative," "traditional," and "traditionalist" interchangeably when referring to this educational philosophy.
4. For a sample of Hirsch criticism, see Kohn, A. (1999). *The schools our children deserve.* Boston: Houghton Mifflin; Macedo, D. (1994). *Literacies of power.* Boulder, CO: Westview Press; Provenzo, E. (2006). *Cultural literacy: A critique of Hirsch and an alternative theory.* Boulder, CO: Paradigm Press.
5. For more information on the speed of knowledge growth, see Costa, A., and Liebman, R. (1995). Process is as important as content. *Educational Leadership, 52*(6), 23–24.
6. *Britannica concise encyclopedia.* (n.d.). Retrieved from http://www.answers.com/topic/educational-progressivism.

7. Cremin, L. A. (1961). *The transformation of the school: Progressivism in American education 1876–1957.* New York: Random House, Vintage Books.
8. For more information on the speed of knowledge growth, see Costa, A., and Liebman, R. (1995). Process is as important as content. *Educational Leadership, 52*(6), 23–24.
9. Cremin, 1961, pp. 93–94.
10. Cremin, 1961, p. 207.
11. Golub, A. B. (2004, August). *Into the blackboard jungle: Educational debate and cultural change in 1950s America.* Unpublished dissertation. University of Texas, Austin, TX, p. 63. Retrieved from http://www.lib.utexas.edu/etd/d/2004/goluba86500/goluba86500.pdf.
12. 1919. The Progressive Education Association is founded. *History of education: Selected moments of the 20th century.* Retrieved from http://www.wier.ca/~%20daniel_schugurensky/assignment1/1919pea.html.
13. Cremin, 1961, p. 328.
14. Cremin, 1961, p. 123.
15. Dewey called his educational approach "experientialist" rather than "progressive."
16. Pogrow, S. (2006, October). The Bermuda Triangle of American education: Pure traditionalism, pure progressivism, and good intentions. *Phi Delta Kappan, 88*(2), 142.
17. Crichton, M. (2004). *State of fear.* New York: Avon Books, p. 531.
18. Ackerman, D. B. (2003, January). Taproots for a new century: Tapping the best traditional and progressive education. *Phi Delta Kappan, 84*(5), 346.
19. Ackerman, 2003, pp. 344–349.
20. Greene, M. (1978). *Landscapes of learning.* New York: Teachers College Press.
21. Buber, M. (1923/2004). *I and thou.* New York: Paulist Press.
22. For more information on the Maxine Greene Foundation, see http://www.maxinegreene.org/fdn_mission.htm.
23. Greene, M. (2005, November 23). Retrieved from http://maxinegreene.blogspot.com/.
24. Greene, M. (n.d.). The arts and the search for social justice. Retrieved from http://www.maxinegreene.org/pdfs/socialjustice.pdf. In the United States, progressivism begat *social reconstructivism,* which begat *critical theory.*
25. Berube, M. R. (2004). *Radical reformers: The influence of the left in American education.* Greenwich, CT: Information Age.
26. Counts, G. S. (1932). *Dare the school build a new social order?* New York: John Day, pp. 11–26.
27. The term "official knowledge"—the formal curriculum that the society's dominant culture transmits in schools—was coined by Michael W. Apple: Apple, M. W. (1993). Official knowledge: Democratic education in a conservative age. New York: Routledge.
28. McLaren, P. (1994). *Life in schools.* New York: Longman; McLaren, P. (2000). White terror and oppositional agency: Toward a critical multiculturalism. Albany: State University of New York Press; Apple, M. W. (1990). *Ideology and curriculum.* London: Routledge; Apple, M. W. (2000). *Official knowledge: Democratic education in a conservative age,* 2nd ed. New York: Routledge; Giroux, H. (1988). *Teachers as transformative intellectuals: Towards a critical pedagogy of learning.* Westport, CT: Bergin and Garvey; Giroux, H. (1983). *Theory and resistance: Towards a pedagogy for the opposition.* South Hadley, MA: Bergin and Garvey; Giroux, H. (2002, October). *The corporate war against higher education.* Retrieved from http://louisville.edu/journal/workplace/issue5p1/giroux.html.
29. Sleeter, C. E., and Grant, C. A. (1994). *Making choices for multicultural education: Five approaches to race, class, and gender,* 2nd ed. New York: MacMillan.
30. Gutstein, E., and Peterson, B. (2005). *Rethinking mathematics: Teaching social justice by the numbers.* Milwaukee, WI: Rethinking Schools. Cited in Adair, J. K. (2008, November/December). Everywhere in life there are numbers: Questions for social justice educators in mathematics and everywhere else. *Journal of Teacher Education, 59*(5), 408–415.
31. Gutstein and Peterson, 2005.
32. Gutstein and Peterson, 2005.
33. Gutstein and Peterson, 2005.
34. Martin, R. J., and Koppelman, K. (1991, Spring). The impact of a human relations/multicultural education course on the attitudes of prospective teachers. *Journal of Intergroup Relations, 43*(1), 16–27.
35. Martin, R. J., and Van Gunten, D. M. (2002). Reflected identities: Applying positionality and multicultural and social reconstructionism in teacher education. *Journal of Teacher Education, 53*(1), 44–54.
36. Giroux, 2002.
37. Giroux sees the traditional "Americanization" of diverse students into a common American democratic culture, which has been the guiding purpose of American public schools since the eighteenth century, as indoctrination.
38. Giroux, H. (n.d.). Doing cultural studies: Youth and the challenge of pedagogy. Retrieved from http://www.gseis.ucla.edu/courses/ed253a/Giroux/Giroux1.html.
39. Giroux, H. A. (1994, Fall). Slacking off: Border youth and postmodern education. Retrieved from http://www.gseis.ucla.edu/courses/ed253a/Giroux/Giroux5.html.
40. Giroux, "Doing cultural studies."
41. Aronowitz, S., and Giroux, H. (1985). *Education under siege. Critical studies in education and culture.* South Hadley, MA: Bergin and Garvey.
42. Giroux, 1994.

Chapter 4

1. Cremin, L. A. (1970). *American education: The colonial experience 1607–1783.* New York: Harper & Row.
2. Many contemporary historical scholars acknowledge the need for a more comprehensive approach to American history than the narrow focus on British New England settlements and seek to include Spanish, Dutch, French, West African, and other influences. See MacDonald, V-M. (2001, Autumn). Hispanic, Latino, Chicano or "other"? Deconstructing the relationship between historians and Hispanic-American educational history. *History of Education Quarterly, 41*(3), 365–413.
3. Cremin, 1970, pp. 21–22.
4. Cremin, L. A. (1977). *Traditions of American education.* New York: Basic Books, pp. 1–10.
5. Erasmus, D. (1936). *The education of a Christian prince,* translated by L. K. Born. New York: Columbia University Press, pp. 140–41.
6. Elyot, T. (1883). *The Boke named the governour,* edited by H. H. S. Croft. London: Kegan Paul, Trench, & Co. Cited in Cremin, 1970, pp. 61–63.
7. Barzun, J. (2000). *From dawn to decadence: 1500 to the present.* New York: HarperCollins.
8. Darnton, R. (2003). *George Washington's false teeth: An unconventional guide to the eighteenth century.* New York: Norton, p. 97.
9. Cubberley, E. P. (1947). *Public education in the United States.* Cambridge, MA: Riverside Press, pp. 6–10.

10. Cremin, 1970, p. 67 (italics added).
11. Cubberley first defined the four basic types of schooling practices that we cite here: Cubberley, E. P. (1947). *Public education in the United States: A study and interpretation of American educational history*. Cambridge, MA: Houghton Mifflin, pp. 97–105.
12. Cubberley, E. P. (1920). *History of education*. New York: Houghton Mifflin, p. 457.
13. Herbst, J. (2002, Autumn). Nineteenth century schools between community and state: The cases of Prussia and the United States. *History of Education Quarterly, 42*(3), 317–41; Leslie, B. (2001, Summer). Where have all the academies gone? *History of Education Quarterly, 41*(2), 262–70.
14. Cremin, 1970, p. 129.
15. Vaughan, A. T. (1965). *New England frontier: Puritans and Indians, 1620–1675*. Boston: Little, Brown; Degler, C. N. (1959–1960). Slavery and the genesis of American race prejudice. *Comparative Studies in Society and History, II*, 49–66.
16. Cremin, 1970, p. 180.
17. The law of 1642 made no distinction between educating boys or girls because both genders needed to be able to read the Bible to practice their religion appropriately. In practice, however, its application may have been more arbitrary.
18. Perlman, J., Siddali, S. R., and Whitescarver, K. (1997, Summer). Literacy, schooling, and teaching among New England women, 1730–1820. History *of Education Quarterly, 37*(2), 117–39.
19. Cubberley, 1920, p. 365.
20. Perlman, Siddali, and Whitescarver, 1997.
21. Sklar, K. K. (1993, Winter). The schooling of girls and changing community values in Massachusetts towns, 1750–1820. *History of Education Quarterly, 33*(4), 511–42.
22. Preston, J. A. (2003, September). "He lives as a *Master*": Seventeenth century masculinity, gendered teaching, and careers of New England schoolmasters. *History of Education Quarterly, 43*(3), 360–71.
23. Preston, 2003, p. 371.
24. Sklar, 1993.
25. Ciphering = adding and subtracting.
26. Cubberley, 1947, p. 52.
27. Cremin, 1970, p. 558.
28. Cremin, 1970, pp. 187–88.
29. Preston, 2003.
30. Cremin, 1970, pp. 188–89; Preston, 2003.
31. Cremin, 1970, p. 558.
32. One room schoolhouses. (2003). *John's History of Education*. Retrieved from http://historyeducationinfo.com/edu6.htm.
33. Small, W. H. (1914). *Early New England schools*. Boston: Ginn and Company, p. 258.
34. Cubberley, 1947, p. 56.
35. Small, 1969.
36. Small, 1969.
37. Cubberley, 1947, p. 56.
38. Cremin, 1970, p. 505.
39. Cubberley, 1947, pp. 57–58.
40. Small, 1969, p. 386.
41. Cubberley, 1947, p. 57.
42. Small, 1969, p. 391.
43. Cubberley, 1920, p. 664.
44. Cubberley, 1947, pp. 27–29.
45. Rippa, S. A. (1984). *Education in a free society: An American history*. New York: McKay.
46. Cubberley, 1947, pp. 51–52.
47. Cremin, 1970, p. 503.
48. Cubberley, 1947, p. 31.
49. Reese, W. J. (1995). *The origins of the American high school*. New Haven, CT: Yale University Press.
50. Tolley, K. (2001, Summer). The rise of the academies: Continuity or change? *History of Education Quarterly, 41*(2), 225–39.
51. Leslie, 2001; Beadie, N. (2001, Summer). Academy students in the mid-nineteenth century: Social geography, demography, and the culture of academy attendance. *History of Education Quarterly, 41*(2), 251–62.
52. Leslie, 2001.
53. Cremin, 1970, p. 505.
54. Leslie, 2001.
55. Leslie, 2001.
56. Cubberley, 1947, p. 113.
57. Nash, M. A. (2001, Summer). Cultivating the powers of human beings: Gendered perspectives on curriculum and pedagogy in academies of the new republic. *History of Education Quarterly, 41*(2), 239–50.
58. Because the grammar schools intended to prepare young men for the ministry, a wholly male occupation at that time, girls could not attend.
59. Leslie, 2001.
60. Hayes, W. (2006). *Horace Mann's vision of the public schools: Is it still relevant?* Rowman and Littlefield Education, Chapter 1. Retrieved from http://www.publiceducation.ord/newsblast/pdf/Chapter_One.pdf.
61. Sundue, S. B. (2007, April). Confining the poor to ignorance? Eighteenth century experiments with charity education. *History of Education Quarterly, 47*(2), 123–48.
62. Cubberley, 1947, p. 53. This extra fee was often difficult to collect.
63. Cremin, 1970, p. 537.
64. Parts of New York, New Jersey, Delaware, Maryland, North Carolina, South Carolina, and Georgia also followed Virginia's example. In these colonies, however, some settlements offered a "free" school supported by assessments—fees paid by families who sent their children to the school.
65. Cohen, S. S. (1974). *A history of colonial education, 1607–1776*. New York: Wiley.
66. Anderson, J. D. (1988). *The education of blacks in the South, 1860–1935*. Chapel Hill: University of North Carolina Press, p. 1.
67. Anderson, 1988, p. 16.
68. Cremin, 1980, pp. 221–22.
69. Cremin, 1970, pp. 348–49.
70. Cremin, 1980, pp. 222–24.
71. Cremin, 1980, pp. 224–29.
72. Cremin, 1970, pp. 194, 350.
73. Hlebewitsh, P. S. (2001). *Foundations of American education: Purpose and promise*. Belmond, CA: Wadsworth/Thomson Learning, pp. 189–90.
74. Hlebewitsh, 2001.
75. Cremin, 1980, pp. 239–41.
76. *Education* meant the full array of institutions that helped shape human character, including families, churches, schools, colleges, newspapers, voluntary associations, and laws.
77. Cremin, L. A. (1980). *American education: The national experience, 1783–1876*. New York: Harper & Row, pp. 2–3.
78. Cubberley, 1947, p. 89.
79. McCullough. D. (2001). *John Adams*. New York: Simon and Schuster, p. 223.
80. Cubberley, E. P. (1922). *A brief history of education*. Boston: Houghton Mifflin, p. 363.
81. Cubberley, 1922.
82. Cubberley, 1947, p. 149.

83. Cubberley, 1947, p. 167.
84. That is not to say it was eliminated. Many of your parents and grandparents can remember prayer and Bible reading in schools as well as references to religious holidays (rather than winter and spring breaks).
85. Cubberley, 1947, pp. 110–11.
86. Cremin, 1980, pp. 389–90.
87. Cubberley, 1947, p. 139.
88. Cremin, 1980, pp. 389–90.
89. Cremin, 1980, p. 390.
90. Cremin, 1980, pp. 397–98.
91. Cremin, 1980, pp. 395–96.
92. Cremin, 1980.
93. Butchart, R. E. (1998). Punishments, penalties, prizes, and procedures: A history of discipline. In R. E. Butchart and B. McEvan (Eds.), *Classroom discipline in American schools* (pp. 19–49). Albany, NY: State University of Albany Press, pp. 21–23.
94. Butchart, 1998, pp. 23–25.
95. Butchart, 1998, p. 25.
96. Butchart, 1998, pp. 27–28.
97. Anderson, 1988, pp. 4–12.
98. Cremin, 1980, pp. 242–45.
99. The nine original colonial colleges were Harvard (founded in 1636), William and Mary (1693), Yale (1702), Princeton (1746), University of Pennsylvania (1753–1755), Kings (later Columbia University; 1754), Brown (1764), Rutgers (1766), and Dartmouth (1769).
100. Cubberley, 1947, p. 114.
101. Cubberley, 1947, p. 275. Every state except for Missouri.
102. Butts, R. F. (1955). A cultural history of Western education: Its social and intellectual foundations. New York: McGraw Hill.
103. Cremin, 1980.
104. Cremin, 1980, pp. 174–75.
105. Barzun, 2000, p. 489.
106. Mann, H. (1848). *Report No. 12 of the Massachusetts Board of Education.* Boston: Dutton and Wentworth.
107. Mann, H. (1845). Ninth Annual Report of the Board of Education, Together with the Ninth Annual Report of the Secretary of the Board, p. 69. Cited in Cremin, 1980, p. 139.
108. Cremin, 1980, p. 141.
109. Horace Mann (1796–1859): Only a teacher. Schoolhouse Pioneers. *PBS Online.* Retrieved from http://www.pbs.org/onlyateacher/horace.html.
110. Cremin, 1980, pp. 153–57.
111. Cubberley, 1947, pp. 225–26.
112. Cremin, 1980, pp. 143–44.
113. Rothstein, R., Jacobsen, R., and Wilder, T. (2008). *Grading education: Getting accountability right.* New York: Economic Policy Institute and Teachers College Press.
114. Barzun, 2000, p. 489.
115. Cremin, 1980, pp. 141–42.
116. Cremin, 1980, pp. 156–57.
117. Cremin, 1980, p. 155.
118. Brownson, O. A. (1966). *The works of Orestes A. Brownson, vol. XIX,* collected and arranged by H. F. Brownson. New York: AMS Press, pp. 442–43.
119. Cubberley, 1947, p. 227.
120. Cubberley, 1947, p. 226.
121. The Board of Commissioners of Common Schools was Connecticut's name for its State Board of Education.
122. Cubberley, 1947, p. 227.
123. Cremin, 1980, p. 180.
124. De Toqueville, A. (1945). *Democracy in America,* edited by P. Bradley. New York: Alfred A. Knopf, vol. II, Chapter xvii.

Chapter 5

1. Cremin, L. A. (1988). *American education: The metropolitan experience 1876–1980.* New York: Harper and Row, p. 226.
2. Reese, W. J. (2001, Spring). The origins of progressive education. *History of Education Quarterly 41*(1), 1–24.
3. Cremin, L. (1961). *The transformation of the school: Progressivism in American education 1876–1957.* New York: Vintage, p. 101.
4. Cremin, 1961, p. 102.
5. Cremin, 1988, pp. 280–306.
6. Cremin, 1961, p. 104.
7. For a full discussion of the progressive education movement and its origins, see Reese, 2001.
8. Cremin, 1961, p. 117.
9. Dewey, J. (1899). *The school and society.* Chicago: University of Chicago Press.
10. Cremin, L. A. (1965). *The genius of American education.* New York: Vintage, p. 61.
11. Cremin, 1961, p. 125.
12. Cremin, 1961, p. 118.
13. Mirel, J. (2006, Winter). The traditional high school: Historical debates over its nature and function. *Education Next, 6*(1). Stanford University, Hoover Institution. Retrieved from http://educationnext.org/the-traditional-high-school/.
14. Only one committee member actually worked in a public school. See Rippa, S. A. (1984). *Education in a free society: An American history.* New York: McKay.
15. Committee of Fifteen. (1895). *Report of the Committee of Fifteen on elementary education.* National Education Association of the United States. New York: American Book Company.
16. Crosby, E. A. (1993, April). The at-risk decade. *Phi Delta Kappan 74*(8), 598–604.
17. Cremin, 1988, p. 546.
18. Commission on the Reorganization of Secondary Education. (1918). *Cardinal principles of secondary education.* Department of the Interior, Bureau of Education, Bulletin No. 35. Washington, DC: U.S. Government Printing Office.
19. Cremin, 1988, pp. 232–33.
20. Rothstein, R., Jacobsen, R., and Wilder, T. (2008). *Grading education: Getting accountability right.* New York: Economic Policy Institute and Teachers College Press.
21. Gray, K. (1993, January). Why we will lose Taylorism in America's high schools. *Phi Delta Kappan 74*(5), 370–74.
22. Wilms, W. W. (2003, April). Altering the structure and culture of American public schools. *Phi Delta Kappan 84*(8), 606–15.
23. Anderson, J. D. (1988). *The education of blacks in the South, 1860–1935.* Chapel Hill: University of North Carolina Press, pp. 148–49.
24. Cremin, 1965.
25. Cremin, 1965.
26. We will more fully discuss African American, Latino, and students with disabilities' experiences with U.S. education in Chapter 8: Diversity and Cultural Assets in Education.
27. Anderson, 1988.
28. Anderson, 1988, pp. 4–7.
29. Anderson, 1988, pp. 148–50.
30. Anderson, 1988, pp. 98–101.

31. Curti, M. (1968). *The social ideas of American educators.* Totowa, NJ: Littlefield, Adams, p. 294.
32. Curti, 1968, p. 288.
33. *Up from slavery: Booker T. Washington.* (1901). New York: Doubleday, Page (reprinted 2000, New York: BARTLEBY.COM).
34. Hampton Institute's founder, General Samuel Armstrong, had commanded African American troops in the Civil War and was committed to providing an industrial education for African Americans and Native Americans. For a fuller discussion, see Hlebowitch, P. S. (2001). *Foundations of American education,* 2nd ed. Belmont, CA: Wadsworth/Thomson Learning, p. 302.
35. Anderson, 1988, pp. 102–03.
36. Anderson, J. D. (1990, Summer). Black rural communities and the struggle for education during the age of Booker T. Washington, 1877–1915. *Peabody Journal of Education 67*(4), 46–62.
37. Harlan, L. R. (1988). *Booker T. Washington in perspective.* Jackson, MS: University of Mississippi Press.
38. Washington, B. T. (1895/1969). The Atlanta compromise. In D. Calhoun, *Educating for Americans: A documentary history.* New York: Houghton Mifflin, p. 350.
39. Buckley, K. W. (n.d.). *W. E. B. DuBois: A concise biography.* University of Massachusetts, Amherst. Retrieved from http://www.library.umass.edu/spcoll/collections/dubois/biography.htm.
40. As a consequence, DuBois is acknowledged as the "Father of Social Science."
41. *Biography: W. E. B. DuBois: African American perspectives: The progress of a people.* (n.d.). Retrieved from http://memory.loc.gov/ammem/aap/dubois.html.
42. DuBois thought that African Americans should lead the NAACP and that if whites were to be included at all, they should serve in supportive roles.
43. In 1961, completely disillusioned with the United States, DuBois moved to Ghana and joined the Communist Party. A year later, he renounced his American citizenship. He died in 1963 at the age of 95.
44. Anderson, 1988, pp. 148–52.
45. For a thorough discussion with photos of African American education in the South between 1890 and 1940, and the unrealistic expectations placed on African American teachers, see Fultz, M. (1995, March). African American teachers in the South, 1890–1940: Powerlessness and the ironies of expectations and protests. *History of Education Quarterly 35*(4), 401–22.
46. Anderson, 1988, pp. 186–87, 235.
47. Anderson, 1988, pp. 236–37.
48. *Roberts v. City of Boston,* 59 Mass. (5 Cush.) 198. (1949). Cited in K. Alexander and M. D. Alexander. (2005). *American public school law,* 6th ed. Belmont, CA: Wadsworth/Thomson Learning, p. 890.
49. Goins, M. (2008). Reflections on the shame of the nation: The restoration of apartheid schools in America. *Ohio State Law Journal 69*(5), 1,085–87. Retrieved from http://moritzlaw.osu.edu/lawjournal/issues/volume69/number5/Goins.pdf.
50. Alexander and Alexander, 2005, p. 891.
51. For an example of the state mandating segregation in a private school, see *Berea College v. Kentucky,* 1908.
52. Anderson, 1988, p. 192.
53. Curti, 1968, pp. 306–07.
54. Ferguson, R. F., with Mehta, J. (2004, May). An unfinished journey: The legacy of *Brown* and the narrowing of the achievement gap. *Phi Delta Kappan 85*(9), 656–69.
55. Marcus, R. (2006, November 29). A slide toward segregation. *The Washington Post,* p. A23. Retrieved from http://www.washingtonpost.com/wp-dyn/content/article/2006/11/28/AR2006112801275_pf.html.
56. Orfield, G. (2009, January). *Reviving the goal of an integrated society: A 21st century challenge.* Los Angeles: University of California at Los Angeles. Retrieved from http://civilrightsproject.ucla.edu/research/k-12-education/integration-and-diversity/reviving-the-goal-of-an-integrated-society-a-21st-century-challenge/orfield-reviving-the-goal-mlk-2009.pdf.
57. Two cases were joined together as one case: *Parents Involved in Community Schools v. Seattle School District* (Case No. 05-908) and *Meredith v. Jefferson County Board of Education* (No. 05-915).
58. Race and the Roberts Court: Opinion. (2007, June 29). *The Wall Street Journal 249*(151), A14.
59. Bravin, J., and Golden, D. (2007, June 29). Court limits how districts integrate schools. *The Wall Street Journal 249*(151), A1, A10.
60. Rosen, J. (2007, July 1). Can a law change a society? Week in review. *The New York Times,* Section 4, pp. 1, 5.
61. For a fuller discussion of the early intelligence tests, standardized tests, and assessment in today's education, see Chapter 14 (Standards, Assessment, and Accountability).
62. Kantor, H., and Lowe, R. (1995, April). Class, race, and the emergence of federal education policy: From the New Deal to the Great Society. *Educational Researcher 24*(3), 4–11, 21.
63. Cremin, 1988, pp. 312–13.
64. Cremin, 1988, p. 311.
65. Mirel, 2006.
66. Mirel, 2006.
67. See *Historical statistics of the United States, 1,* 138; and Nelson, D. (1975). *Managers and workers: Origins of the new factory system in the Untied States, 1880–1920.* Madison: University of Wisconsin Press, pp. 6–9; cited in Cremin, 1988, pp. 480–81.
68. Cremin, 1988, pp. 481–92.
69. Gordon, Howard R. D. (1999). *History and growth of vocational education in the United States.* Needham Heights, MA: Allyn and Bacon.
70. Benavot, A. (1983, April). The rise and decline of vocational education. *Sociology of Education 56*(2), 63–76.
71. The Smith-Hughes Act called for specific entry-level skill training for youths in separate vocational schools, teacher training, and separate state boards for vocational education.
72. Bottoms, G., and Presson, A. (2000). *Finishing the job: Improving the achievement of vocational students.* Atlanta, GA: Southern Regional Education Board, High Schools That Work, pp. 3, 6–7; Hoachlander, G., Alt, M., and Beltranena, R. (2001, March). *Leading school improvement: What research says: A review of the literature.* Atlanta, GA: Southern Region Education Board, High Schools That Work; Kaufman, P., Bradby, D., and Teitlebaum, P. (2000, February). *High Schools That Work and whole school reform: Raising academic achievement of vocational completers through reform of school practices.* ERIC # ED 438 418.
73. Hoye, J. D., and Stern, D. (2008, September 10). The career academy story: A case study of how research can move policy and practice. *Education Week 28*(3), 24–26.
74. Coleman, J. S. (1966). *Equality of educational opportunity.* Washington, DC: U.S. Department of Health, Education, and Welfare, Office of Education/National Center for Education Statistics.
75. Viadero, D. (2006b, June 21). Race report's influence felt 40 years later: Legacy of Coleman study was new view of equity. *Education Week 25*(41), 1, 21–22.

76. The Coleman study was the first time testing data were used to measure educational disparities by looking at what students actually learned. The data collected through Coleman's questionnaire addressed characteristics of schools, teachers and students, educational resources, physical facilities, socioeconomic backgrounds, racial composition, as well as attitudes toward race, integration, busing, and achievement.
77. Viadero, 2006b.
78. Viadero, 2006b.
79. When Geoffrey Borman, of the University of Wisconsin–Madison, and his colleague N. Maritza Dowling reanalyzed the original Coleman data with more sophisticated statistical models than were available in 1966, they found they could attribute as much as 40 percent of the variation in achievement differences between students to in-school factors rather than to family background. For more details, see Viadero, 2006; and Borman, G. D., and Maritza Dowling, N. (2006, April). *Schools and inequality: A multilevel analysis of Coleman's equality of educational opportunity data.* Paper presented at the Annual Meeting of the American Educational Research Association, San Francisco, CA.
80. Viadero, D. (2006, June 21). Fresh look at Coleman data yields different conclusions. *Education Week 25*(41), 21.
81. Epstein, J. L. (1991). Effects on student achievement of teachers' practices of parent involvement. In S. Silvern (Ed.), *Advances in reading/language research, vol. 5: Literacy through family, community and school interaction* (pp. 261–76). Greenwich, CT: JAI Press; Epstein, J. L. (1989). Family structures and student motivation: A developmental perspective. In C. Ames, and R. Ames (eds.), *Research on motivation in education: vol. 3: Goals and cognitions* (pp. 259–95). New York: Academic Press; Hoover-Dempsey, K. V., and Sandler, H. M. (1997). Why do parents become involved in their children's education? *Review of Educational Research 67*, 3–42; Ketsetzis, M., Ryan, B. A., and Adams, G. R. (1998). Family processes, parent–child interactions, and child characteristics influencing school-based social adjustment. *Journal of Marriage and the Family 60*, 374–87; Ryan, B. A., and Adams, G. R. (1995). The family–school relationships model. In B. A. Ryan, G. R. Adams, T. P. Gullotta, R. P. Weissberg, and R. L. Hampton (eds.), *The family–school connection: Theory, research, and practice* (pp. 3–28). Newbury Park, CA: Sage.
82. Brookover, W. B., Beady, C., Flook, P., Schweitzer, J., and Wisenbaker, J. (1979). *School social systems and student achievement: Schools can make a difference.* New York: Praeger; Clark, D. L., Lotto, L. S., and McCarthy, M. M. (1980). Factors associated with success in urban elementary schools. *Phi Delta Kappan 61*, 469–70; Edmonds, R. (1979). Effective schools for the urban poor. *Educational Leadership 37*(1), 15–24; Purkey, S. C., and Smith, M. S. (1983). Effective schools: A review. *Elementary School Journal 83*, 427–54; Rutter, M., Maugham, B., Outson, J., and Smith, A. (1979). *Fifteen-thousand hours: Secondary schools and their effects on children.* Cambridge, MA: Harvard University Press. Chapter 15 provides a thorough look at the "effective schools" movement, including how it and contemporary versions of this movement seek to increase minority students' achievement.
83. McCarthy, M. M. (1991). Severely disabled children: Who pays? *Phi Delta Kappan 73*(1), 66–71.
84. For more details on the interpretation of "free and appropriate education," see the U.S. Supreme Court decision, *Board of Education of Hendrick Hudson Central School District v. Rowley,* 1982, 458 U.S. 176, 102 S. Ct. 3034. Cited in Alexander and Alexander, 2005, pp. 499–502.
85. Necessary supports to meet the inclusion mandate may include sending teachers, assistants, assistive technology, and adapted texts and curriculum into the general education classroom along with the student with disabilities.
86. *Indicator 31: Inclusion of students with disabilities in general classrooms.* (2007). National Center for Education Statistics, Institute of Education Sciences, U.S. Department of Education; National Center for Education Statistics (2009). Students with disabilities, inclusion of. *Fast Facts.* Washington, DC: Institute of Education Sciences, U.S. Department of Education. Retrieved from http://nces.ed.gov/fastfacts/display.asp?id=59
87. Samuels, C. (2008, January 23). "Response to intervention" sparks interest, questions. *Education Week 27*(20), 1, 13.
88. National Commission on Excellence in Education. (1983, April). *A nation at risk.* Washington, DC: U.S. Department of Education.
89. *A nation at risk: The imperative for educational reform: An open letter to the American people.* (1983, April). Retrieved from http://www.ed.gov/pubs/NatAtRisk/risk.html.
90. *A nation at risk,* 1983.
91. Yeakey, C. C., and Johnston, G. S. (1985, February). High school reform: A critique and a broader construct of social reality. *Education and Urban Society 17*(2), 157–70.
92. Husen, T. (1983, March). School standards in America and other countries. *Phi Delta Kappan 64,* 455–61.
93. Yeakey and Johnston, 1985.
94. Yeakey and Johnston, 1985.
95. Writer Gerald Bracey concluded that *A Nation at Risk* was not intended to objectively examine the condition of American education, but rather to document the terrible things that Terrell Bell, President Ronald Reagan's Secretary of Education, had heard about schools.
96. For specifics about how *A Nation at Risk* "spun" selective statistics, see the following article: Bracey, G. W. (2003, April). April foolishness: The 20th anniversary of *A Nation at Risk. Phi Delta Kappan 84*(8), 616–21.
97. For example, in 1990, politics delayed the Sandia Report's publication for several years because its positive findings about public schools might undercut the critical perspective taken by *A Nation at Risk.*
98. Bracey, 2003.
99. Ferguson and Mehta, 2004, p. 659.
100. See Puma, M. J., Karweit, N., Price, C., Ricciuti, A., Thompson, W., and Vaden-Kiernan, M. (1997, April). *Prospects: Final report on student outcomes.* Washington, DC: Planning and Evaluation Service, U.S. Department of Education; and Carter, L. F. (1983). *A study of compensatory and elementary education: The sustaining effects study.* Washington, DC: Office of Program Evaluation, U.S. Department of Education.
101. Borman, G. D., et al. (2001). Coordinating categorical and regular programs: Effects on Title I students' educational opportunities and outcomes. In G. D. Borman, S. C. Stringfield, and R. E. Slavin (eds.), *Title I: Compensatory education at the crossroads* (pp. 79–116). Mahwah, NJ: Lawrence Erlbaum Associates; and Borman, G. D., and D'Agostino, J. V. (2001). Title I and student achievement: A quantitative synthesis. In G. D. Borman, S. C. Stringfield, and R. E. Slavin (eds.), *Title I: Compensatory education at the crossroads* (pp. 25–58). Mahwah, NJ: Lawrence Erlbaum Associates.
102. Ferguson and Mehta, 2004, p. 658.

103. National Commission on Excellence in Education. (1983, April). *A nation at risk*. Op. cit.
104. Schools must show that at least 95 percent of all students in each grade and in each subgroup participated in testing.
105. For examples of schools showing significant achievement gains from NCLB, see Haycock, K. (2006, November). No more invisible kids. *Educational Leadership 64*(3), 38–42; and Zavadsky, H. (2006, November). How NCLB drives success in urban schools. *Educational Leadership 64*(3), 69–73.
106. Hall, D., and Kennedy, S. (2006, March). *Primary progress, secondary challenge: A state-by-state look at student achievement patterns*. Washington, DC: Education Trust; and Haycock, 2006.
107. Viadero, D. (2010, March 26). Study suggests NCLB Impact on NAEP scores. *Education Week*. Retrieved from http://blogs.edweek.org/edweek/inside-school-research/2010/03/if_you_think_the_last.html.
108. National Assessment of Educational Performance (2012). *NAEP – Mathematics 2011: Summary of major findings*. Washington, DC: Author. Retrieved from http://nationsreportcard.gov/math_2011/summary.asp; National Assessment of Educational Progress. (2011). *Top stories in NAEP reading 2011*. Washington, DC: Author. Retrieved from http://nationsreportcard.gov/reading_2011/
109. Whithurst, G. J. (2010, March 24). *Is "No Child Left Behind" working*? Washington, DC: Brookings Institution. Retrieved from http://www.brookings.edu/opinions/2010/0324_naep_whitehurst.aspx.
110. Deans, E. (2010, September 8). *Examining the data: Using achievement data to compare state standards*. Washington, DC: New America Foundation. Ed Money Watch. Retrieved from http://edmoney.newamerica.net/blogposts/2010/analyzing_the_data_state_performance_on_nclb_tests_vs_naep-36529; Lee, J. (2006). *Tracking achievement gaps and assessing the impact of NCLB on gaps: An in-depth look into national and state reading and math outcome trends*. Cambridge, MA: Harvard Civil Rights Project, Harvard Education Group. Retrieved from http://civilrightsproject.ucla.edu/research/k-12-education/integration-and-diversity/tracking-achievement-gaps-and-assessing-the-impact-of-nclb-on-the-gaps/lee-tracking-achievement-gaps-2006.pdf; Olson, L. (2007, April 18). Gaps in proficiency levels on state test and NAEP found to grow. *Education Week 26*(33), 12; Matthews, J. (2007, April 16). Study shows more discrepancies between state, national assessments of student proficiency. Washington Post.com. Retrieved from http://www.washingtonpost.com/wp-dyn/content/article/2007/04/15/AR2007041501099.html. For a more complete discussion of the NAEP/state achievement scores gap, see Chapter 14 (Standards, Assessment, and Accountability).
111. National Assessment of Educational Progress. (2009). *Long term trend. Mathematics scores fir 9- and 13-year olds higher than in all previous assessment years*. Retrieved from http://nationsreportcard.gov/ltt_2008/ltt0002.asp; National Assessment of Educational Progress. (2009). *The Nation's Report Card: Long Term Trends 2008*. Washington, DC: Author. Retrieved from: http://nces.ed.gov/pubsearch/pubsinfo.asp?pubid=2009479
112. Hess, F., and Finn, C. Jr. (2004, September). Inflating the life rafts of NCLB: Making public school choice and supplementary services for students in troubled schools. *Phi Delta Kappan 86*(1), 34–58.
113. We will more fully discuss the positives and negatives of standardized tests such as those used for NCLB accountability purposes in Chapter 14.
114. Rothstein, R., Jacobsen, R., and Wilder, T. (2006, November 29). "Proficiency for all" is an oxymoron. *Education Week 26*(13), 32, 44.
115. Hoff, D. J. (2006, November 29). Researchers ask whether NCLB's goals for proficiency are realistic. *Education Week 26*(13), 8.
116. Department of Education. (2009, November 18). Overview information; Race to the Top funds: Notice inviting applications for new awards for fiscal year (FY) 2010: Notice. Part IV. *Federal Register 74*(221), 59,839, 59,860. Retrieved from http://edocket.access.gpo.gov/2009/pdf/E9-27427.pdf.
117. McNeil, M. (2010, March 3). Reviewers winnow Race to Top hopefuls. *Education Week 29*(23), 1, 20.
118. Paulson, A. (2010, July 26). Uniform education standards: Momentum grows as more states sign on. *Christian Science Monitor*. Retrieved from http://www.csmonitor.com/USA/Education/2010/0726/Uniform-education-standards-Momentum-grows-as-more-states-sign-on.
119. National Urban League and other civil rights groups. (2010, July). *Framework for providing all students an opportunity to learn through reauthorization of the Elementary and Secondary Education Act*. Retrieved from http://www.otlcampaign.org/sites/default/files/resources/CivilRights%20framework-FINAL7-25-10.pdf.
120. Weisberg, D., Sexton, S. Mulhern, J., and Keeling, D. et al. (2009) *The widget effect: Our national failure to acknowledge and act on differences in teacher effectiveness*, 2nd ed. Brooklyn, NY: The New Teacher Project. Retrieved from http://widgeteffect.org/downloads/TheWidgetEffect.pdf.
121. National Council on Teacher Quality. (2012). *State of the States 2012: Teacher effectiveness policies*. Washington, DC: Author. Retrieved from http://www.nctq.org/p/publications/docs/NCTQ_State_of_the_States_2012_Teacher_Effectiveness_Policies.pdf.
122. The New Teacher Project, 2009, Ibid; and The New Teacher Project. (2012). *Teacher evaluation 2.0*. Brooklyn, NY: Author. Retrieved from http://tntp.org/assets/documents/Teacher-Evaluation-Oct10F.pdf?files/Teacher-Evaluation-Oct10F.pdf.
123. Value-added methodology is a statistical technique that determines the amount of teacher influence on students' academic progress that controls students' prior characteristics (such as parental income or socioeconomic status). Although it can be used correctly for large-scale studies, the research finds that it has questionable use at the secondary level and the consensus exists that this technique should not be used to make high-stakes decisions about individual teachers.
124. Watson, J., Murin, A., Vashaw, L., Gemin, B., *and* Rapp, C. (2012). *Keeping pace with K-12 online & blended learning. An annual review of policy and practice. Mountain View, CA: Evergreen Education Group. Retrieved from* http://.kpk12.com/cms/wp-content/uploads/KeepingPace2012.pdf
125. Trotter, A. (2008, May 7). Online education cast as "disruptive innovation." *Education Week 27*(36), 1, 12–13.
126. Watson et al. (2012). Op cit.
127. Cavanaugh, C. (2009, May). Getting students more learning time online. *Distance education in support of expanded learning time in K-12 schools*. Washington, DC: Center for American Progress. Retrieved from http://www.americanprogress.org/issues/2009/05/pdf/distancelearning.pdf.
128. Bush, J., and Wise, B. (2010, December 1). *Digital learning now*. Tallahassee, FL: Foundation for Excellence in Education. Retrieved from http://www.excelined.org/Docs/Digital%20Learning%20Now%20Report%20FINAL.pdf.
129. Means, B., Toyama, Y., Murphy, R. Bakis, M., and Jones, K. (2010, September). *Evaluation of evidence-based practices in online learning. A meta-analysis and review of online learning studies*.

Washington, DC: U.S. Department of Education, p. xv. Office of Planning, Evaluation, and Policy development, Policy and Program Studies Service. Retrieved from http://www2.ed.gov/rschstat/eval/tech/evidence-based-practices/finalreport.pdf.

130. Center for Research on Education Outcomes (2013). *National Charter School Study 2013.* Stanford, CA: Stanford University. Retrieved from http://credo.stanford.edu/documents/NCSS%202013%20Final%20Draft.pdf. The 2013 study updates CREDO's 2009 study in 15 states that found 17 percent of charter students outperformed, 37 percent underperformed, and 46 percent showed no significant differences wih traditional public school students in reading and math achievement.
131. Sparks, S.D. (2013). Charter schools' discipline policies face scrutiny. *Education Week, 32* (21), 1, 16–20.
132. Hill, P. T., Angel, L., and Christensen, J. (2006). Charter school achievement studies. *Education Finance and Policy Journal 1*(1), 139–50.
133. Center for Research on Education Outcomes, 2013, Figure 26, p. 57, Center for Research on Education Outcomes. (2009). *Multiple Choice: Charter school performance in 16 states.* Stanford, CA: Stanford University. Retrieved from http://credo.stanford.edu/reports/MULTIPLE_CHOICE_CREDO.pdf; Miron, G., and Urschel, J. L. (2010, December). *Profiles of nonprofit education management organizations: 2009–2010.* Boulder, CO: National Education Policy Center and Kalamazoo, MI: The Study Group on Education Management Organizations. Retrieved from http://nepc.colorado.edu/files/NEPC_NP-EMO-09-10.pdf; and Zehr, M. A. (2010, July 14). KIPP middle schools boost learning gains, study says. *Education Week 29*(36), 14–15.
134. NAEP is not identifying students according to disabled or nondisabled, so we cannot assess how well special needs students are achieving on this measure.
135. Ladner, M., and Burke, L. (2010, September 17). *Closing the racial achievement gap: Learning from Florida's reforms.* Washington, DC: The Heritage Foundation. Retrieved from http://www.heritage.org/research/reports/2010/09/closing-the-racial-achievement-gap-learning-from-floridas-reforms.

Chapter 6

1. Goodlad, J. I. (1979, January). Can our schools get better? *Phi Delta Kappan. 60*(5), 342.
2. Gelernter, D. (2006, January 2). Misinformation age: More computers, less learning. *The Weekly Standard, 11*(16). Retrieved from http://www.weeklystandard.com/Utilities/printer_preview.asp?idArticle=6532&R=EDEBCB4.
3. Rose, M. (2006, October 11). Grand visions and possible lives: Finding the public good through the details of classroom life. *Education Week, 26*(7), 32–33. Retrieved from http://www.edweek.org/ew/articles/2006/10/11/07rose.h26.html.
4. Cremin, L. A. (1977). *Traditions of American education.* New York: Basic Books, p. 37.
5. U.S. Department of Education, (1990). *America 2000.* Washington, DC: U.S. Government Printing Office. Retrieved from http://www.answers.com/topic/department-of-education. These goals refer to national goals that public schools were to have reached by the year 2000.
6. Adapted from Goodlad, J. I. (1979). *What are schools for.* Bloomington, IN: Phi Delta Kappa Educational Foundation, pp. 44–52. Reissued in 2006 by Phi Delta Kappan International, Bloomington, IN.
7. Eisner, E. W. (2003, May). Questionable assumptions about schooling. *Phi Delta Kappan, 84*(9), 648–57.
8. Eisner, E. W. (1992, April). The misunderstood role of the arts in human development. *Phi Delta Kappan, 73*(8), 592.
9. Eisner, 1992.
10. Eisner, E. W. (2001, January). What does it mean to say a school is doing well? *Phi Delta Kappan, 82*(3), 367–72.
11. Eisner, E. W. (1999, May). The use and limits of performance assessment. *Phi Delta Kappan, 80*(9), 658–60.
12. Eisner, 1992, p. 595.
13. Eisner, 1992, p. 595.
14. Eisner, 1999, p. 660.
15. Ross, E. A. (1900, January). Social control XIV: *Education. American Journal of Sociology, 5*(4), 483.
16. Ross, 1900, p. 485.
17. Spring, J. (2002). *American education.* New York: McGraw-Hill, pp. 10–15.
18. Ornstein, A. (2007). *Class counts: Education, inequality, and the shrinking middle class.* Lanham, MD: Rowman & Littlefield, p. 178.
19. *Cost–benefit scale* is an economics term meaning that a person makes decisions by taking into account the relative advantages as compared to the expenses (financial, emotional, physical, social) of making a particular decision.
20. The phrase "a wall of separation between church and state" does not appear in the U.S. Constitution. The phrase comes from a letter written by Thomas Jefferson on January 1, 1802, to the Danbury Baptist Association. For that reason we refer to that concept as a *doctrine.*
21. National Commission on Excellence in Education. (1983). *A nation at risk.* Washington, DC: U.S. Government Printing Office.
22. We discuss NCLB more fully in Chapters 5 and 14.
23. See Chapter 15, Best Practices for Effective Schools.
24. Head Start is a preschool program for students from lower-socioeconomic-status backgrounds. It is intended to prepare students to be ready to learn in a formal school environment.
25. AVID is an academic support program for middle- and high-school minority students that enrolls them in high-challenge academic classes while simultaneously teaching them note-taking skills and other academically essential work habits, providing tutoring, and offering positive peer pressure.
26. Compensatory higher education programs for disadvantaged students, such as Upward Bound, prepare middle school– and high school–aged minority students for college.
27. The term "official knowledge"—the formal curriculum that the society's dominant culture transmits in schools—comes from Apple, M. W. (1993). *Official knowledge: Democratic education in a conservative age.* New York: Routledge.
28. Critical theory is a specific type of political perspective that stands to the left of liberalism. We have used the term to stand for all similar views. This discussion of critical theory is adapted from Abrahams, F. (2004, January). The application of critical theory to a sixth grade general music class. In *Visions of research in music education.* Volume 4. Retrieved from http://www.rider.edu/~vrme/articles4/abrahams/index.htm.
29. Giroux, H. (1994, Fall). *Slack off: Border youth and postmodern education.* Retrieved from http://www.gseis.ucla.edu/courses/ed253a/Giroux/Giroux5.html; Giroux, H. (n.d.). *Doing cultural studies: Youth and the challenge of pedagogy.* Retrieved from http://www.gseis.ucla.edu/courses/ed253a/Giroux/Giroux1.html; McLaren, P. (1994). *Life in schools.* New York: Longman; McLaren, P. (2000). White terror and oppositional agency: Toward a critical multiculturalism. In E. Duarte and S. Smith (Eds.). *Foundational perspectives in multicultural education.* Newbury Park, CA: Sage.
30. Kozol, J. (1967). *Death at an early age: The destruction of the hearts and minds of Negro children in the Boston Public Schools.*

New York: Bantam Books; Kozol, J. (1985). *Illiterate America*. Garden City, New York: Anchor Press; Kozol, J. (1991). *Savage inequalities: Children in American schools*. New York: Crown; Kozol, J. (1995). *Amazing grace: The lives of children and the conscience of a nation*. New York: Crown; Kozol, J. (2000). *Ordinary resurrections: Children in the years of hope*. New York: Crown; Freire, P. (1970). *Pedagogy of the oppressed*. New York: Continuum; Freire, P. (1973). *Education for critical consciousness*. New York: Herder and Herder; Freire, P. (1985). *The politics of education*. New York: Bergin & Garvey; Freire, P. (1998). *Pedagogy of freedom*. Boston: Rowman & Littlefield.

31. Allen, L. A. (2006). *The moral life of schools* revisited: Preparing educational leaders to "build a new social order" for social justice and democratic community. *International Journal of Urban Education Leadership, 1*, 1–13.
32. Allen, 2006, p. 9.
33. Smith, A. (1937). *The wealth of nations*, rev. ed. New York: Modern Library.
34. Schultz, T. W. (1961, March). Investment in human capital. *American Economic Review, 51*, 1–17.
35. Schultz bibliography retrieved from http://www.econlib.org/library/enc/bios/Schultz.html.
36. Unequal earning levels for different ethnic groups with the same education can have a variety of causes, such as inability to find high-paying employment in urban neighborhoods where many live or differential job descriptions (and salaries) for similar work. Here may be an example of a promise yet to keep.
37. Owings, W. A., and Kaplan, L. S. (2013). Education as investment in human capital. In *American public school finance*, 2nd Edition. (pp. 79–100). Belmont, CA: Cengage Learning.
38. Sawhill, I. (2006, September 19). *Opportunity in America: Does education promote social mobility? Proceedings*. Washington, DC: Brookings Institution. Retrieved from http://www.brookings.ed/comm/events/20060919.pdf.
39. Organisation for Economic Cooperation and Development. (2010). *Economic policy reforms 2010: Going for growth*. Paris: Author. Retrieved from http://www.oecd.org/tax/public-finance/chapter%205%20gfg%202010.pdf
40. Uhrain, S. K. , Currier, E., Elliott, D., Wechsler, L., Wilson, D., and Colbert, D. (2012), *Pursuing the American dream, economic mobility across generation*. Economic Mobility Project, Washington, DC: The Pew Charitable Trusts. Figure 3, p. 6. Numbers reformatted by authors. Retrieved from http://www.pewtrusts.org/uploadedFiles/wwwpewtrustsorg/Reports/Economic_Mobility/Pursuing_American_Dream.pdf
41. Ornstein, A. (2007). *Class counts: Education, inequality, and the shrinking middle class*. New York: Rowman and Littlefield.
42. Sawhill, I. V. (2006). *Opportunity in America: The role of education*. Washington, DC: Brookings Institution. Retrieved from http://www.brookings.edu/es/research/projects/foc/20060913foc.htm.
43. Uhrain et al. (2012). Op cit., 3.
44. These reasons include lack of high-quality preschools for eligible students, lack of academic preparation for college, lack of know-how about the college preparation and application process, and lack of financial resources or know-how to pay for college. See Haskins, R. (2008). Education and economic mobility. In J. B. Isaacs, I. V. Sawhill, and R. Haskins (Eds.), *Getting ahead or losing ground: Economic mobility in America* (pp. 91–114). Washington, DC: Brookings Institution. Economic Mobility Project. Retrieved from http://economicmobility.org/assets/pdfs/Economic_Mobility_in_America_Full.pdf.
45. Haskins, 2008.
46. Haskins, 2008, p. 101.
47. Yen, H. (2010, September 28). Census finds record gap between rich and poor. *Salon.Com*. Retrieved from http://www.salon.com/2010/09/28/us_census_recession_s_impact_1/
48. Sawhill, 2006.
49. Freeman, R. B. (1976). *The over-educated American*. New York: Academic Press, p. 18.
50. U.S. Census Bureau, American Community Survey (ACS). (n.d.). *Ranking tables 2002: Percent of people 25 years and older who have completed a bachelor's degree*. Retrieved from http://www.census.gov/acs/www/Products/Ranking/2002/R02T040.htm.
51. Krugman, P. (2006, September 8). Winning over discontent. *The New York Times*. p. 49.
52. Olson, L. (2007, February 7). ETS study warns of growing inequality in income, skills. *Education Week, 26*(22), 7.
53. Brown, G. (2011, August 15). Global new deal. Gordon Brown's manifesto to save America—and the world economy. *Newsweek, 158*(7), pp. 2–4. Brown is also author of *Beyond the Crash: Overcoming the first Crisis of Globalization* (2010, Free Press, a division of Simon and Schuster), and former equivalent of Britain's treasury secretary.
54. Thornburgh, N. (2011, August 22). London's long burn. *Time 178*(7), 28–31.

Chapter 7

1. Bernstein, R., and Edwards, T. (2008, August 14). An older and more diverse nation by midcentury. *U.S. Census Bureau News*. Washington, DC: U.S. Census Bureau. Retrieved from http://www.census.gov/Press-Release/www/releases/archives/population/012496.html; Minorities set to be US majority. (2008, August 14). *BBC News*. Retrieved from http://news.bbc.co.uk/2/hi/americas/7559996.stm.
2. National Association for the Advancement of Colored People. (2009). *African Americans and education. Fact Sheet*. Retrieved from http://naacp.3cdn.net/e5524b7d7cf40a3578_2rm6bn7vr.pdf.
3. Lewis, A. (2006, February). A new people. *Phi Delta Kappan 87*(6), 419.
4. Metropolitan Center for Urban Education, Steinhardt School of Education, New York University. (2005). *With all deliberate speed: Achievement, citizenship, and diversity in American education*. Retrieved from http://www.kwfdn.org/resource_library/getfile.asp?intResourceID=389.
5. Rothstein, R. (2004, October). A wider lens on the black–white achievement gap. *Phi Delta Kappan 86* (2), 106.
6. Rothstein, 2004, Ibid.
7. Larson, C. L., and Ovando, C. J. (2001). *The color of bureaucracy: The politics of equity in multicultural school communities*. Belmont, CA: Cengage Learning, p. 8.
8. Ovando, C. J. (2003 Spring). Bilingual education in the United States: Historical development and current issues. *Bilingual Research Journal 27*(1). Retrieved from http://brj.asu.edu/content/vol27_no1/documents/art1.pdf.
9. Kloss, H. (1998/1977). *The American bilingual tradition*. Rowley, MA: Newbury House.
10. Larson and Ovando, 2001, pp. 8–9.
11. Coleman, J. S., Campbell, E., Hobson, C., McPartland, J., Mood, A., Weinfield, F., and York, R. (1966). *Equality of educational opportunity*. Washington, DC: U.S. Government Printing Office; Caldas, S. J. (1993). Reexamination of input and process factor effects on public school achievement. *Journal of Education*

Research 84, 325–26; Caldas, S. J., and Bankston, C. (1997, May/June). Effect of school population socioeconomic status on individual academic achievement. *Journal of Educational Research 90*, 269–77; Rumberger, R. W., and Willms, J. D. (1992). The impact of racial and ethnic segregation on the achievement gap in California high schools. *Educational Evaluation and Policy Analysis 14*, 377–96.

12. Although more respectful than the term "lower class," the term "working class" is a misnomer because most people of all social classes "work." The authors of this book sometimes use the term "low income" to refer to lower or "working" class social status, reflecting the group's economic situation.
13. Jencks, C., and Peterson, P. E. (Eds.). (1991). *The urban underclass.* Washington, DC: Brookings Institution; Wooster, M. W. (1998, May–June). Inside the underclass. *American Enterprise*, 83–84.
14. For data confirming the close relationship between education and income, see Chapter 11.
15. Coleman et al., 1966; Jencks, C. (1972). *Inequality: A measurement of the effect of family and schooling in America.* New York: Basic Books; Natriello, G., McDill, E. L., and Pallas, A. M. (1990). *Schooling disadvantaged children: Racing against catastrophe.* New York: Teachers College Press.
16. White, K. R. (1982, May). The relationship between socioeconomic status and academic achievement. *Psychological Bulletin 91*(3), 461–81.
17. Wolf, A. (1978). The state of urban schools. *Urban Education 13*(2), 179–94.
18. Heckman, J. (2008, June). *Schools, skills, and synapses* (NBER Working Paper No. 14064). Cambridge, MA: National Bureau of Economic Research, pp. 4, 12.
19. Coleman et al., 1966; Goldstein, B. (1967). *Low income youth in urban areas: A critical review of the literature.* New York: Holt, Rinehart, & Winston; Persell, C. H. (1977). *Education and inequality: The roots and results of stratification in America's schools.* New York: Free Press; Persell, C. H. (1993). Social class and educational equality. In J. Banks and C. A. McGee Banks (Eds.), *Multicultural education: Issues and perspectives*, 2nd ed. Boston: Allyn and Bacon, pp. 71–89.
20. Coleman et al., 1966; Goldstein, 1967; Persell, 1977, 1993.
21. Alexander, K. L., Entwisle, D. R., and Olson, S. (2001, Summer). Schools, achievement, and inequality: A seasonal perspective. *Educational Evaluation and Policy Analysis 23*(2), 171–91; Viadero, D. (2006, November 15). Schools' role in achievement gaps scrutinized. *Education Week 26*(12), 16. For more details, see McCall, M. S., et al. (2006, November). *Achievement gaps: An examination of differences in achievement and growth.* Northwest Evaluation Association. Retrieved from http://www.nwea.org/sites/www.nwea.org/files/AchGap_11.11.061.pdf.
22. Heckman. 2008, p. 4.
23. Rothstein, R. (2004). *Class and schools: Using social, economic, and educational reform to close the black–white achievement gap.* Washington, DC: Economic Policy Institute.
24. Phillips, M. (2000). Understanding ethnic differences in academic achievement: Empirical lessons from national data. In D. W. Grissmer and J. M. Ross (Eds.), *Analytic issues in the assessment of student achievement (NCES 2000-050).* Washington, DC: U.S. Department of Education, pp. 103–32. Retrieved from http://nces.ed.gov/pubs2000/2000050a.pdf; Allington, R. L., and McGill-Franzen, A. (2003, September). The impact of summer setback on the reading achievement gap. *Phi Delta Kappan 85*(1), 68–75.
25. Rothstein, 2004, *Class and schools*, p. 16
26. Rothstein, 2004, *Class and schools.*
27. Rothstein, 2004, *Class and schools.*
28. Hart, B., and Risley, T. (2003, Spring). The early catastrophe: The 30 million word gap by age 3. *American Educator.* Retrieved from http://www.aft.org/pubs-reports/american_educator/spring2003/catastrophe.html.
29. Hart and Risley, 2003.
30. Hart and Risley, 2003.
31. Grigg, W., et al. (2003). *The nation's report card: Reading 2002.* Washington, DC: U.S. Department of Education, National Center for Education Statistics; Table 3.7, National Assessment of Educational Progress, p. 66. Retrieved from http://nces.ed.gov/nationsreportcard/pdf/main2002/2003521a.pdf; Braswell, J. S., et al. (2001). *The nation's report card: Math 2000.* Washington, DC: U.S. Department of Education, National Center for Education Statistics; Figure 3.ab, pp. 70–71. Retrieved from http://nces.ed.gov/nationsreportcard/pdf/main2000/2001517.pdf.
32. The Annie E. Casey Foundation. (2013). *Children in poverty. Profile for United States (Nation).* Baltimore: Author. Retrieved from http://datacenter.kidscount.org/data/acrossstates/National-Profile.aspx; Foroohar, R. (2011, September 26). The truth about the poverty crisis. *Time 178*(12), 24.
33. Annie E. Casey Foundation. (2012, September 26). *Child poverty rates increase in 44 of 50 largest U.S. cities between 2005 and 2011.* Baltimore: Author. Kids Count. Retrieved from http://www.aecf.org/Newsroom/NewsReleases/HTML/2012Releases/USCitiesSawPovertyRateIncrease.aspx.
34. For a fuller discussion of how poverty-related factors such as prenatal care health care, food insecurity, environmental pollutants, family stress, neighborhood characteristics, and extended learning opportunities strongly influence students' school success, see Berliner, D. C. (2009). *Poverty and potential: Out-of-school factors and school success.* Boulder, CO/Tempe, AZ: Education and the Public Interest Center & Education Policy Research Unit. Retrieved from http://epicpolicy.org/publication/poverty-and-potential.
35. Barton, P. E. (2004). Why does the gap persist? *Educational Leadership 62*(3), 9–13.
36. Smith, J. P. (2005). Unraveling the SES–health connection. *Aging, health, and public policy: Demographic and economic perspectives.* A supplement to *Population and Development Review 30.* New York: Population Council; Ross, C. E., and Wu, C. L. (1996). Education, age, and the cumulative advantage in health. *Journal of Health and Social Behavior 37*(1), 104–20; Rothstein, 2004, *Class and schools;* Mirowsky, J., and Ross, C. (2003). *Education, social status, and health.* Somerset, NJ: Aldine de Gruyter/Transaction.
37. We have to view this conclusion with some skepticism because the study included only 26 children: Jacobson, L. (2009, January 7). Scientists track poverty's link to cognition. *Education Week 28*(16), 4. For an article reporting on this study, see Kishiyama, M. M., Boyce, W. T., Jimenez, A. M., Perry, L. M., and Knight, R. T. (2009). Socioeconomic disparities affect prefrontal function in children. *Journal of Cognitive Neuroscience 21*(1), 1–10.
38. National Law Center on Homelessness & Poverty. (2012, June). *One million U.S. students homeless, new data show.* Washington, DC: Author. Retrieved from http://www.nlchp.org/view_release.cfm?PRID=148
39. United States Interagency Council on Homelessness. (2011, June 16). *Comprehensive report on children experiencing homelessness in our nation's school system.* Washington, DC: Author. Retrieved from

http://www.usich.gov/media_center/news/comprehensive_report_on_children_experiencing_homelessness_in_our_nations_s/.

40. Kerbow, D. (1996). Patterns of urban student mobility and local school reform. *Journal of Education for Students Placed at Risk 1*(2), 147–69; Bruno, J., and Isken, J. A. (1996). Inter- and intra-school site student transiency: Practical and theoretical implications for instructional continuity at inner-city schools. *Journal of Research and Development in Education 29*(4), 239–52.
41. Bowlby, J. (1980). *Attachment and loss: Loss, sadness, and depression* (Vol. 3). New York: Basic Books.
42. Family risk factors seen contributing to chronic absence. (2008, March 5). *Education Week 27*(26), 10. The full report, *The Influence of Maternal and Family Risk on Chronic Absenteeism in Early Schooling,* is available online at http://www.nccp.org.
43. On average, low-income students' achievement is below middle-class students' achievement. Nonetheless, some middle-class students achieve below typical low-income levels and some low-income students achieve above typical middle-class levels.
44. Rothstein, 2004, *Class and schools.*
45. McCallum, I., and Demie, F. (2001, Summer). Social class, ethnicity, and educational performance. *Educational Research 43*(2), 147–59; Woessmann, L. (2004, March). *How equal are educational opportunities? Family background and student achievement in Europe and the U.S.* Paper prepared for the Harvard University conference on "50 Years after *Brown*." Retrieved from http://www.ksg.harvard.edu/pepg/PDF/events/Munich/PEPG-04-15Woessman.pdf.
46. Rivkin, S. G., and Welch, F. (2006). Neighborhood segregation and school integration. In E. A. Hanushek and F. Welch (Eds.), *Handbook of the economics of education.* Amsterdam, The Netherlands: Elsevier, pp. 1019–49.
47. Rivkin, S. G. (1994). Residential segregation and school integration. *Sociology of Education 67,* 279–92; Welch, F., Light, A., Dong, F., and Ross, M. (1987). *New evidence on school desegregation.* Los Angeles: UnicornResearch Association.
48. Massey, D., and Denton, N. (1993). *American apartheid: Segregation and the making of the underclass.* Cambridge, MA: Harvard University Press.
49. Rivkin, 1994.
50. *Milliken v. Bradley* (1974) and *Keyes v. School District No. 1,* Denver (1973).
51. When courts declare a school district "unitary," it means the district no longer has a dual school system. A school district does not achieve "unitary status," however, until it proves that its past discrimination has been removed and shows no discriminatory practices in student assignment, faculty, staff, transportation, extracurricular activities, and facilities. See *Green v. County School Board of New Kent County* (1968).
52. Balfanz, R. (2009, Spring). Can the American high school become an avenue of advancement for all? *American High Schools 19*(1). Retrieved from http://futureofchildren.org/publications/journals/article/index.xml?journalid=30&articleid=35§ionid=63; National Center for Education Statistics. (2007, September). *Status and trends in the education of racial and ethnic minorities. (NCES 2007-039).* Washington, DC: Author. U.S. Department of Education, Institute of Education Sciences. Retrieved from http://nces.ed.gov/pubs2007/minoritytrends/.
53. *Dowell v. Oklahoma City* (1991); *Freeman v. Pitts* (1992); and *Missouri v. Jenkins* (1995).
54. *Missouri v. Jenkins* (1995).
55. *Parents Involved in Community Schools v. Seattle School District* and *Meredith v. Jefferson County Board of Education.*
56. Greenhouse, L. (2007, July 1). In steps big and small, Supreme Court moved right. *The New York Times 156*(53,992), 1, 18; Bravin, J. (2007, July 2). Court under Roberts limits judicial power. *The Wall Street Journal 250*(1), A1, A12; *Parents Involved in Community Schools v. Seattle School District No. 1* and *Meredith v. Jefferson County Board of Education,* 555 U.S. (2007); Walsh, M. (2007, October 31). Use of race a concern for magnet schools. *Education Week 27*(1), 8; Sacks, P. (2007, September 12). It's time to confront the class divide in American schools. *Education Week 27*(3), 25.
57. Burkholder, Z. (2007, October 24). Because race can't be ignored: Commentary. *Education Week 27*(9), 29.
58. Viadero, November 15, 2006, p. 16.
59. Harris, D. (2006, November 24). *Lost learning, forgotten promises: A national analysis of school racial segregation, student achievement, and "controlled choice" plans.* Center for American Progress. Retrieved from http://www.americanprogress.org/issues/2006/11/lostlearning.html; Viadero, D. (2008, April 16). Black–white gap widens faster for high achievers. *Education Week 27*(33), 1, 13.
60. Kahlenberg, R. D. (2001). *All together now: Creating middle class schools through public school choice.* Washington, DC: Brookings Institution Press.
61. Lippman, L., Burns, S., and McArthur, E. (1996). *Urban schools: The challenge of location and poverty (NCES 96–184).* Washington, DC: U.S. Department of Education, Office of Educational Research and Improvement; Kahlenberg, 2001.
62. Rothstein, 2004, *Class and schools,* p. 171.
63. Ferguson, R. F., and Mehta, J. (2004, May). An unfinished journey: The legacy of Brown and the narrowing of the achievement gap. *Phi Delta Kappan 85*(9), 656–69.
64. Crane, J. (1991). Effects of neighborhoods on dropping out of school and teenage childbearing. In C. Jencks and P. E. Peterson (Eds.), *The urban underclass.* Washington, DC: Brookings Institution, pp. 299–320; Hanushek, E. A., Kain, J. F., and Rivkin, S. G. (2004). *New evidence about* Brown v. Board of Education: *The complex effects of school racial composition on achievement.* Revised draft, February 2004; paper presented at the Brookings Conference on Empirics of Social Interactions, January 2004.
65. Hanushek and Rivkin, 2006; Mayer, S. E. (1991). How much does a high school's racial and socioeconomic mix affect graduation and teenage fertility rates? In C. Jencks and P. E. Peterson (Eds.), *The urban underclass.* Washington, DC: Brookings Institution Press, pp. 187–222.
66. Orfield, G., and Lee, C. (2006, January). *Racial transformation and the changing nature of segregation.* Cambridge, MA: Civil Rights Project, Harvard University, p. 4. Retrieved from http://www.eric.ed.gov/ERICDocs/data/ericdocs2sql/content_storage_01/000019b/80/3d/42/4d.pdf.
67. Orfield and Lee, 2006, p. 29.
68. Rothstein, 2004, *Class and schools.*
69. This phenomenon of improved performance without obvious intervention is now also known as the "Hawthorne effect" in honor of the initial Hawthorne studies.
70. Rosenthal, R., and Jacobson, L. (1968). *Pygmalion in the classroom: Teachers' expectations and pupils' intellectual development.* New York: Rineholt and Winston.
71. Rosenthal and Jacobson, 1968.
72. Oakes, J. (1985). *Keeping track: How schools structure inequality.* New Haven, CT: Yale University Press.
73. Viadero, D. (2006, June 21). Fresh look at Coleman data yields different conclusions. *Education Week 25*(41), 21.

74. Rochkind, J., Ott, A., Immerwahr, J., Doble, J., and Johnson, J. (2008). *Lessons learned: New teachers talk about the jobs, challenges, and long range plans. Issue no. 3: Teaching in changing times.* Washington, DC: National Comprehensive Center for Teacher Quality and Public Agenda, pp. 7–14. Retrieved from http://www.publicagenda.org/files/pdf/lessons_learned_3.pdf.
75. Rochkind et al., 2008.
76. Feistritzer, C. E. (2011). *Profile of teachers in the U.S. 2011.* Washington, DC: National Center for Education Information. Retrieved from http://www.ncei.com/Profile_Teachers_US_2011.pdf.
77. Orfield, G., and Ashkinaze, C. (1991). *The closing door: Conservative policy and black opportunity.* Chicago: University of Chicago Press; Fine, M. (1991). *Framing dropouts: Notes on the politics of an urban public high school.* Albany: State University of New York Press.
78. Children's Defense Fund. (1988, January). *Making the middle grades work.* Washington, DC: Adolescent Pregnancy Prevention Clearinghouse.
79. Oakes, J., Ormseth, T., Bell, R., and Camp, P. (1990). *Multiplying inequalities: The effects of race, social class, and tracking on opportunities to learn mathematics and science.* Washington, DC: National Science Foundation.
80. Finley, M. K. (1984). Teachers and tracking in a comprehensive high school. *Sociology of Education 57,* 233–43.
81. Oakes, 1985.
82. Brewer, D. J., Rees, D. I., and Argys, L. M. (1995 November). Detracking America's schools: The reform without cost? *Phi Delta Kappan 77*(3), 210–15.
83. Oakes, J. (1992, May). Can tracking research inform practice? Technical, normative, and political considerations. *Educational Researcher 21*(4), 12–21.
84. Gamoran, A. (1990). *The effects of track-related instructional differences for student achievement.* Paper presented at the Annual Meeting of the American Educational Research Association, Boston.
85. Heubert, J. P., and Hauser, R. M. (Eds.). (1999). *High stakes: Testing for tracking, promotion, and graduation.* Washington, DC: National Academy Press; Oakes, 1992.
86. Oakes, J. (1990). *Multiplying inequalities: The effects of race, social class, and ability grouping on opportunities to learn math and science.* Santa Monica, CA: Rand.
87. Oakes, 1992.
88. Burris, C. C., and Welner, K. G. (2005). Closing the achievement gap by detracking. *Phi Delta Kappan 86*(8), 594–98; Burris, C. C., Welner. K. G., and Murphy, J. (2008). Accountability, rigor and detracking: Achievement effects of embracing a challenging curriculum as a universal good for all students. *Teachers College Record 110*(3), 571–608.
89. Colangelo, N., Assouline, S., and Gross, M. (Eds.). (2004). *A nation deceived: How schools hold back America's brightest students.* Iowa City, IA: Belin Blank Center Gifted Education and Talent Development; Gagné, F., and Gagnier, N. (2004). The socio-affective and academic impact of early entrance to school. *Roeper Review 26,* 128–39; Gamoran, A., and Mare, R. G. (1989, March). Secondary school tracking and educational inequality: Compensation, reinforcement, or neutrality? *American Journal of Sociology 94,* 1146–83; Goldring, E. B. (1990). Assessing the status of information on classroom organizational frameworks for gifted students. *Journal of Educational Research 83,* 313–26; Hoffer, T. B. (1992, Fall). Middle school ability grouping and student achievement in science and mathematics. *Educational Evaluation and Policy Analysis 14*(3), 207–27; Kulik, J. A., and Kulik, C. L. C. (1992). Meta-analytic findings on grouping programs. *Gifted Child Quarterly, 36,* 73–77; Lubinski, D. (2004). Long-term effects of educational acceleration. In N. Colangelo, S. Assouline, and M. Gross (Eds.), *A nation deceived: How schools hold back America's brightest students.* Iowa City, IA, pp. 23–37: Belin Blank Center Gifted Education and Talent Development; Lubinski, D., Webb, R. M., Morelock, M. J., and Benbow, C. P. (2001). Top 1 in 10,000: A 10-year follow-up of the profoundly gifted. *Journal of Applied Psychology 86,* 718–29; Rogers, K. (2004). The academic effects of acceleration. In N. Colangelo, S. Assouline, and M. Gross (Eds.), *A nation deceived: How schools hold back America's brightest students.* Iowa City, IA: Belin Blank Center Gifted Education and Talent Development, pp. 47–57; Slavin, R. E. (1990). *Achievement effects of ability grouping in secondary schools: A best evidence synthesis.* Madison: Wisconsin Center for Educational Research.
90. Oakes, 1992; Jaeger, R. M., and Hattie, J. A. (1995 November). Detracking America's schools. *Phi Delta Kappan 77*(3), 218–19.
91. Sparks, S. D. (2013, March 27). More teachers group students by ability. *Education Week 32*(2), 8.
92. Hallinan, M., and Williams, R. (1989). Interracial friendship choices in secondary school. *American Sociological Review 54,* 67–78.
93. Oakes, J., Gamoran, A., and Page, R. N. (1992). Curriculum differentiation: Opportunities, outcomes, and meanings. In P. W. Jackson (Ed.), *Handbook of research on curriculum.* New York: Macmillan, pp. 570–608; Oakes, 1985.
94. Smith-Maddox, R., and Wheelock, A. (1995, November). Untracking and students' futures. *Phi Delta Kappan 77*(3), 222–28.
95. Gamoran et al., 1991; Vanfossen, B., Jones, J., and Spade, J. (1987). Curriculum tracking and status maintenance. *Sociology of Education 60,* 104–22; Wolfe, L. (1985). Postsecondary educational attainment among whites and blacks. *American Educational Research Journal 22,* 501–25.
96. Oakes, J. (2005). *Keeping track: How schools structure inequality,* 2nd ed. New Haven, CT: Yale University Press; Oakes, J., and Lipton, M. (1992, February). Detracking schools: Early lessons from the field. *Phi DeltaKappan 73*(6), 448–54.
97. Oakes, 2005; Oakes and Lipton, 1992.
98. Oakes and Lipton, 1992.
99. Oakes, J., and Lipton, M. (1999). Access to knowledge: Challenging the techniques, norms, and politics of schooling. In K. Sirotnik and R. Soder (Eds.), *To the beat of a different drummer: Essays on educational renewal in honor of John Goodlad.* New York: Peter Lang, pp. 131–50.
100. Ferguson, R. F., and Mehta, J. (2004, May). An unfinished journey: The legacy of *Brown* and the narrowing of the achievement gap. *Phi Delta Kappan 85*(9), 663.
101. Ferguson and Mehta, 2004.
102. Oakes, 2005.
103. Unseem, E. L. (1992). Getting on the fast track in mathematics: School organizational influences on math track assignments. *American Journal of Education 100,* 325–53.
104. Oakes and Lipton, 1999, p. 449.
105. American College Testing. (2006). *Ready for college and ready for work: Same or different*? Iowa City, IA: Author. Retrieved from http://www.act.org/research/policymakers/pdf/ReadinessBrief.pdf; Olson, L. (2006, May 10). Skills for work, college readiness are found comparable. *Education Week 25*(36), 1, 19. "Workplace success" in these studies refers to desirable

occupations that pay enough to support a family of four and offer the potential for career advancement but do not require a four-year college degree.

106. Peske, H. G., and Haycock, K. (2006, June). *Teaching inequality: How poor and minority students are short-changed on teacher quality.* Washington, DC: The Education Trust. Retrieved from http://www2.edtrust.org/NR/rdonlyres/010DBD9F-CED8-4D2B-9E0D-91B446746ED3/0/TQReportJune2006.pdf.
107. Jerald, C. D. (2002). *All talk, no action: Putting an end to out-of-field teaching.* Washington, DC: The Education Trust.
108. Almy, S., and Theokas, C. (2010, November). *Not prepared for class: High-poverty schools continue to have fewer in-field teachers.* Washington, DC: The Education Trust. Retrieved from: http://coe.unm.edu/uploads/docs/coe-main/research/not-prep-for-class.pdf.
109. Goodlad, J. (1954). Some effects of promotion and non-promotion upon the social and personal adjustment of children. *Journal of Experimental Education 22,* 301–28.
110. Owings, W., and Magliaro, S. (1998, September). Grade retention: A history of failure. *Educational Leadership 56,* 86–88.
111. Retrieved October 16, 2009, from www.ecs.org/html/issue.asp?issueID=94.
112. West, M.R. (2012). *Is retaining students in the early grades self-defeating?* Washington, DC: The Brookings Institution. Retrieved from http://www.brookings.edu/~/media/research/files/papers/2012/8/16%20student%20retention%20west/16%20student%20retention%20west.
113. Applied Research Center. (2000). *Facing the consequences: An examination of racial discrimination in U.S. public schools.* Oakland, CA: Applied Research Center; Noguera, P. (1997). Reconsidering the crisis confronting California black male youth: Providing support without further marginalization. *Journal of Negro Education 65*(2), 219–36.
114. Larson and Ovando, 2001, p. 156.
115. Losen, D. J., and Martinez, T. E. (2013, April 8). *Out of school & off track. The overuse of suspensions in American middle and high schools.* Los Angeles: The Center for Civil Rights Remedies, The Civil Rights Project, University of California at Los Angeles. Retrieved from http://civilrightsproject.ucla.edu/resources/projects/center-for-civil-rights-remedies/school-to-prison-folder/federal-reports/out-of-school-and-off-track-the-overuse-of-suspensions-in-american-middle-and-high-schools/OutofSchool-OffTrack_UCLA_4-8.pdf.
116. Losen and Martinez, 2013. Ibid.
117. Balfanz, R., Byrnes, V., and Fox, J. (2013, April 7). *Sent home and put off-track: The antecedents, disproportionalities, and consequences of being suspended in ninth grade.* Baltimore: Everyone Graduates Center, School of Education, Johns Hopkins University. Prepared for the Center for Civil Rights Remedies and the Research-to-Practice Collaborative, National Conference on Race and Gender Disparities in Discipline. Retrieved from http://civilrightsproject.ucla.edu/resources/projects/center-for-civil-rights-remedies/school-to-prison-folder/state-reports/sent-home-and-put-off-track-the-antecedents-disproportionalities-and-consequences-of-being-suspended-in-the-ninth-grade/balfanz-sent-home-ccrr-conf-2013.pdf; Barton, P. E., Coley, R. J., and Weglinsky, H. (1998, October). *Order in the classroom: Violence, discipline, and student achievement.* Princeton. NJ: Educational Testing Service, Policy Information Center, Policy Information Report; Myers, D. E. (1987, January). Student discipline and high school performance. *Sociology of Education 60*(1), 18–33.
118. Civil Rights Project. (2000). *Education denied: The devastating consequences of zero tolerance and school discipline policies.* Cambridge, MA: Harvard University Press.
119. Although "culture" and "climate" are somewhat interchangeable terms, school climate refers mostly to the school's effects on students, whereas school culture refers more to the shared assumptions, values, and beliefs that influence the way teachers and other staff members work together.
120. Brookover, W. B., Erickson, F. J., and McEvoy, A. W. (with Beamer, L., Efthim, H., Hathaway, D., Lezotte, L., Miller, S., Passalacqua, J., and Tomatzky, L. (1997). *Creating effective schools: An in-service program for enhancing school learning climate and achievement.* Holmer Beach, FL: Learning Publications.
121. Barton, Coley, and Weglinsky, 1998, pp. 7–19.
122. Haynes, N. M., and Comer, J. P. (1993). The Yale School Development Program process, outcomes, and policy considerations. *Urban Education 28*(2), 166–99.
123. Haynes, N. M. (1998). Creating safe and caring school communities: Comer School Development Program schools. *Journal of Negro Education 65,* 308–14; Kuperminc, G. P., Leadbeater, B. J., Emmons, C., and Blatt, S. J. (1997). Perceived school climate and difficulties in the social adjustment of middle school students. *Applied Developmental Science 1*(2), 76–88.
124. McEvoy, A., and Welker, R. (2000). Antisocial behavior, academic failure, and school climate: A critical review. *Journal of Emotional and Behavioral Disorders 8*(3), 130–40.
125. Freiberg, H. J. (1998). Measuring school climate: Let me count the ways. *Educational Leadership 56*(1), 22–26.
126. For more on the research underlying the relationship between academic failure and student misbehaviors, see McEvoy and Welker, 2000.
127. Baptiste, H. P. (1977). Multicultural education evolvement at the University of Houston: A case study. In F. H. Klassen and D. M. Gollnick (Eds.), *Pluralism and the American teacher: Issues and case studies.* Washington, DC: American Association of Colleges for Teacher Education, pp. 171–84.
128. Gay, G. (1994). *A synthesis of scholarship in multicultural education.* North Central Regional Educational Laboratory. Retrieved from http://www.ncrel.org/sdrs/areas/issues/educatrs/leadrshp/le0gay.htm.
129. Rasool, J. A., and Curtis, A. C. (2000). *Multicultural education in middle and secondary classrooms: Meeting the challenge of diversity and change.* Belmont, CA: Cengage Learning.
130. La Belle, T. J. (1976). An anthropological framework for studying education. In J. I. Roberts and S. K. Akinsanya (Eds.), *Educational patterns and cultural configurations: The anthropology of education.* New York: David McKay, pp. 67–82.
131. Gay, 1994.
132. Gougis, R. A. (1986). The effects of prejudice and stress on the academic performance of black Americans. In U. Niesser (Ed.), *The school achievement of minority children: New perspectives* (pp. 145–57). Hillsdale, NJ: Lawrence Erlbaum Associates, p. 147.
133. For a fuller discussion of culturally responsive teaching, see the Knowledge Loom website, operated by the Education Alliance at Brown: http://knowledgeloom.org/practices3.jsp?location=1&bpinterid=1110&spotlightid=1110.
134. Suzuki, B. H. (1984). Curriculum transformation for multicultural education. *Education and Urban Society 16*(3), 294–322.
135. Banks, J. A. (1991/1992, December–January). Multicultural education: For freedom's sake. *Educational Leadership 49*(4), 34.

136. Sleeter, C. E., and Grant, C. A. (1994). *Making choices for multicultural education: Five approaches to race, class, and gender*, 2nd ed. New York: Macmillan.
137. Banks, J. A., and Banks, C. A. M. (1993). *Multicultural education: Issues and perspectives*, 2nd ed. Boston: Allyn and Bacon; Boggs, S. T., Watson-Gregeo, K., and McMillen, G. (1985). *Speaking, relating, and learning: A study of Hawaiian children at home and at school.* Norwood, NJ: Abex; Cazden, C. B., John, V. P., and Hymes, D. (Eds.). (1985). *Functions of language in the classroom*. Prospect Heights, IL: Wamland Press; Garcia, R. L. (1982). *Teaching in a pluralistic society: Concepts, models, strategies*. New York: Harper and Row; Greenbaum, P. E. (1985). Nonverbal differences in communication style between American Indian and Anglo elementary classrooms. *American Educational Research Journal 22*, 101–15; Reys, R., Reys, B., Lapan, R., Holliday, G., and Wasman, D. (2003). Assessing the impact of standards-based middle grades mathematics curriculum materials on student achievement. *Journal for Research in Mathematics Education 34*(1), 74–95; Rivette, K., Grant, Y., Ludema, H., and Rickard, A. (2003). *Connected Mathematics Project: Research and evaluation summary 2003 edition*. Upper Saddle River, NJ: Pearson Prentice-Hall.
138. Gay, 1994.
139. Nieto, S. (n.d.). *Commentary: Teaching multicultural literature. Workshop 1.* Retrieved from http://www.learner.org/channel/workshops/tml/workshop1/commentary3.html.
140. Gay, 1994.
141. Nieto, n.d.
142. Banks, 1991/1992, p. 35.
143. Sleeter, C. E. (2001). Epistemological diversity in research on pre service teacher preparation for historically underserved children. *Review of Research in Education 25*, 209–50.
144. Larson and Ovando, 2001.
145. Festinger, L. A. (1957). *A theory of cognitive dissonance*. Evanston, IL: Row, Peterson.
146. McFalls, E. L., and Cobb-Roberts, D. (2001). Reducing resistance to diversity through cognitive dissonance instruction: Implications for teacher education. *Journal of Teacher Education 52*(2), 164–72.
147. McFalls and Cobb-Roberts, 2001. The ultimate decision to accept or reject information is the learner's responsibility.
148. Larson and Ovando, 2001, p. 82.

Chapter 8

1. Gay, G. (1994). *A synthesis of scholarship in multicultural education.* North Central Regional Laboratory. Retrieved from http://www.ncrel.org/sdrs/areas/issues/educatrs/leadrshp/le0gay.htm.
2. Gay, 1994.
3. Weinstein, C., Curran, M., and Tomlinson-Clarke, S. (2003). Culturally responsive classroom management: Awareness into action. *Theory into Practice 42*(4), 269–76.
4. In this chapter, we will respectfully use the self-referent terms that these groups prefer that others call them: children of poverty and low income, Latino, African American, Native American, students with disabilities.
5. Trumbull, E. (2005). Language, culture, and society. In E. Trumbull and B. Farr, *Language and learning: What teachers need to know* (pp. 33–72). Norwood, MA: Christopher-Gordon, p. 35.
6. Rothstein-Fisch, C., and Trumbull, E. (2008). *Managing diverse classrooms: How to build on students' cultural strengths.* Alexandria, VA: Association for Supervision and Curriculum Development, pp. 2–3.
7. Greenfield, P. M. (1994). Independence and interdependence as developmental scripts: Implications for theory, research, and practice. In P. M. Greenfield and R. R. Cocking (Eds.), *Cross-cultural roots of minority child development.* Mahwah, NJ: Lawrence Erlbaum Associates, pp. 1–37; Hofstede, G. (2001). *Culture's consequences: Comparing values, behaviors, institutions, and organizations across nations*, 2nd ed. Thousand Oaks, CA: Sage; Markus, H., and Kitayama, S. (1991). Culture and the self: Implications for cognition, emotion, and motivation. *Psychological Review 98*, 224–53; Triandus, H. C. (1989). Cross-cultural studies of individualism and collectivism. *Nebraska Symposium of Motivation 37*, 43–133.
8. Greenfield, P. M. (1994). Independence and interdependence as developmental scripts: Implications for theory, research, and practice. In P. M. Greenfield and R. R. Cocking (Eds.), *Cross-cultural roots of minority child development.* Mahwah, NJ: Lawrence Erlbaum Associates, pp. 1–37; Lipka, J. (with Mohatt, G., and Ciulistet Group). (1998). *Transforming the culture of schools: Yup'ik Eskimo examples.* Mahwah, NJ: Lawrence Erlbaum Associates; Nelson-Barber, S., Trumbull, E., and Wenn, R. (2000). *The Coconut Wireless Project: Sharing culturally responsive pedagogy through the World Wide Web.* Honolulu, HI: Pacific Resources for Education and Learning; Rothstein-Fisch and Trumbull, 2008, pp. 10–12, 51.
9. Rothstein-Fisch and Trumbull, 2008, pp. 12–13.
10. Raeff, C., Greenfield, P. M., and Quiroz, B. (2000). Conceptualizing interpersonal relationships in the cultural contexts of individualism and collectivism. In S. Harkness, C. Raeff, and C. M. Super (Eds.), *New directions for child and adolescent development.* San Francisco: Jossey-Bass, p. 87.
11. McLaughlin, H. J., and Bryan, L. A. (2003, Autumn). Learning from rural Mexican schools about commitment and work. *Theory into Practice 42*(4), 289–95.
12. Valdes, G. (1996). *Con respeto: Bridging the distances between culturally diverse families and schools: An ethnographic portrait.* New York: Teachers College Press.
13. Goldenberg, C., and Gallimore, R. (1995). Immigrant Latino parents' values and beliefs about their children's education: Continuities and discontinuities across cultures and generations. *Advances in Motivation and Achievement 9*, 183–228.
14. Markus and Kitayama, 1991; Rothstein-Fisch and Trumbull, 2008.
15. Hofstede, 2001.
16. Rotheram, M. J., and Phinney, J. S. (1988). Introduction: Definitions and perspectives in the study of children's ethnic socialization. In J. S. Phinney and J. Rotheram (Eds.), *Children's ethnic socialization: Pluralism and development.* Newbury Park, CA: Sage, pp. 10–28.
17. Berry, G. (1965). *Ethnic and race relations*. Boston, MA: Houghton Mifflin; Sue, D. W., and Sue, D. (1999). *Counseling the culturally different: Theory and practice*, 3rd ed. New York: John Wiley & Sons; Sue, D. W., and Sue, D. (2008). *Counseling the culturally diverse: Theory and practice*, 5th ed. Hoboken, NJ: John Wiley & Sons.
18. Sue and Sue, 2008, pp. 242–43.
19. Haley, A. (1966). *The autobiography of Malcolm X*. New York: Grove Press.
20. "Gringo" is a disparaging term for a foreigner in Latin America, usually a North American or English person. "Oreo" is a disparaging term for an African American who shares values and behaviors with white Americans, as in the popular Oreo cookie: black on the outside and white on the inside.
21. Katz, J. (1985). The sociopolitical nature of counseling. *Counseling Psychologist 13*, 615–24.

22. Katz, 1985, pp. 616–17.
23. Sue and Sue, 2008, pp. 277–82.
24. Sue and Sue, 2008, p. 257.
25. Sue and Sue, 2008, p. 257.
26. Sue and Sue, 2008, p. 258.
27. Sue and Sue, 1999, p. 142.
28. McMahon, S. D., and Watts, R. J. (2002). Ethnic identity in urban African American youth: Exploring links with self-worth, aggression, and other psychosocial variables. *Journal of Community Psychology 30*, 411–31.
29. Phinney, J. S., Horenczyk, G., Liebkind, K., and Vedder, P. (2001). Ethnic identity, immigration, and well-being: An interactional perspective. *Journal of Social Issues 57*, 493–510.
30. Phinney, J. S., Romero, I., Nava, M., and Huang, D. (2001). The role of language, parents, and peers in ethnic identity among adolescents in immigrant families. *Journal of Youth and Adolescence 30*, 135–53.
31. Yasui, M., Dorham, C. L., and Dishion, T. J. (2004). Ethnic identity and psychological adjustment: A validity analysis for European American and African American adolescents. *Journal of Adolescence 19*, 807–25.
32. Carlson, C., Uppal, S., and Prosser, E. C. (2000). Ethnic differences in processes contributing to the self-esteem of early adolescent girls. *Journal of Early Adolescence 20*, 44–67.
33. Phinney, J. S. (1989). Stages of ethnic identity in minority group adolescents. *Journal of Early Adolescence 9*, 34–49.
34. Phinney, J. S., and Alipuria, L. (1990). Ethnic identity in college students from four ethnic groups. *Journal of Adolescence 13*, 171–84.
35. Chappell, M. S., and Overton, W. F. (2002). Development of logical reasoning and the school performance of African American adolescents in relation to socioeconomic status, ethnic identity, and self-esteem. *Journal of Black Psychology 28*, 295–317.
36. Ogbu, J. U. (I 995). Origins of human competence: A cultural-ecological perspective. In N. R. Goldberger and J. B. Veroff (Eds.), *Culture and psychology reader*. New York: New York University Press, pp. 245–75.
37. Helms, J. E. (1993). *Black and white racial identity: Theory, research, and practice*. Westport, CT: Praeger; McMahon, S. D., and Watts, R.J. (2002). Ethnic identity in urban African American youth: Exploring links with self-worth, aggression, and other psychosocial variables. *Journal of Community Psychology 30*, 411–31; Phinney, J. S. (1992). The Multigroup Ethnic Identity Measure: A new scale for use with diverse groups. *Journal of Adolescent Research 7*, 156–76; Martinez, R. O., and Dukes, R. L. (1997). The effects of ethnic identity, ethnicity, and gender on adolescent well-being. *Journal of Youth and Adolescence 26*, 503–16; Phinney, J. S., and Kohatsu, E. L. (1997). Ethnic and racial identity development and mental health. In J. Schulenberg, J. L. Maggs, and K. Hurrelmann (Eds.), *Health risks and developmental transitions during adolescence*. New York: Cambridge University Press, pp. 420–43; Bracey, J. R., Bamaca, M. Y., and Umana-Taylor, A. J. (2004). Examining ethnic identity and self-esteem among biracial and monoracial adolescents. *Journal of Youth & Adolescence 33*, 123–32.
38. Blash, R. R., and Unger, D. G. (1995). Self-concept of African American male youth: Self-esteem and ethnic identity. *Journal of Child & Family Studies 4*, 359–73; Carlson, C., Uppal, S., and Prosser, E. C. (2000). Ethnic differences in processes contributing to the self-esteem of early adolescent girls. *Journal of Early Adolescence 20*, 44–67.
39. Evans, R. (2005, April). Reframing the achievement gap. *Phi Delta Kappan 86*(8), 582–89.
40. Steele, C. M. (1999, August). Thin ice: "Stereotype threat" and black college students. *Atlantic Monthly 284*(2), 44–47, 50–54; Steele, C. M. (1997, June). Treat in the air: How stereotypes shape intellectual identity and performance. *American Psychologist 52*(6), 613–29.
41. Steele, 1997.
42. Viadero, D. (2007, October 24). Experiments aim to east effects of 'stereotype threat'. *Education Week 27*(9), 10.
43. Viadero, 2007.
44. Viadero, 2007.
45. Singham. M. (1998). The canary in the mine: The achievement gap between black and white students. *Phi Delta Kappan 80* (1), 9–15.
46. Viadero, 2007.
47. Evans, 2005.
48. Good, C., and Aronson, J. (2003). The development of stereotype threat and its relation to theories of intelligence: Effects on elementary school girls' mathematics achievement and task choices (Unpublished manuscript). New York: Columbia University; Good, C., Aronson, J., and Inzlicht, M. (2003). Improving adolescents' standardized test performance: An intervention to reduce the effects of stereotype threat. *Journal of Applied Developmental Psychology 24*(6), 645–62; Sherman, D. K., Hartson, K. A., Binning, K. R., Purdie-Vaughns, V., Garcia, J., Taborsky-Barba, S., Tomassetti, S., Nussbaum, A. D., and Cohen, G. L. (2013, February 11). Deflecting the trajectory and changing the narrative: How self-affirmation affects academic performance and motivation under identity threat. *Journal of Personality and Social Psychology*. Advance online publication. doi: 10.1037/a0031495. Retrieved from http://kbinning.bol.ucla.edu/Shermanetal.2013.JPSP.pdf; Walton, G., and Cohen, G. L. (2007). A question of belonging: Racial, social fit, and achievement. *Journal of Personality and Social Psychology 92*(1), 82–96.
49. Ogbu, J. U., and Simons, H. D. (1998). Cultural–ecological theory of student performance with some implications for education. *Anthropology and Education Quarterly 29*(2), 155–88.
50. Fordham, S. (1996). *Blacked out: Dilemmas of race, identity, and success at Capital High*. Chicago: University of Chicago Press. Noguera, P. A. (2003). How racial identity affects school performance. *Harvard Education Letter 19*, 1–3; Fryer, R. G. (2006, Winter). "Acting white": The social price paid by the best and brightest minority students. *Education Next 6*(1). Stanford University: Hoover Institution. Retrieved from http://educationnext.org/actingwhite/.
51. Neal-Barnett, A. (2001). Being black: A new conceptualization of acting white. In A, M. Neal-Barnett, J. Contreras, and K. Kerns (Eds.), *Forging links: African American children clinical development perspectives* (75–88). Westport, CT: Greenwood.
52. Fordham, S., and Ogbu, J. (1986). Black students' school successes: Coping with the burden of "acting white." *Urban Review XVIII*, 176–206.
53. Ogbu, J. U. (1995). Cultural problems in minority education: Their interpretations and consequences—part one: Theoretical background. *Urban Review 27*(3), 189–205.
54. Fryer, R. G. (2006, Winter). "Acting white". The social price paid by the best and brightest minority students. *EducationNext 6*(1), 52–59. Retrieved from http://educationnext.org/actingwhite/.
55. Fryer, 2006.
56. Fryer, 2006.
57. Ogbu and Simon, 1998.
58. Fordham and Ogbu, 1986.

59. Gay, 1994.
60. Ogbu, 1992.
61. Irvine, J. J. (2003). *Educating teachers for diversity: Seeing with a cultural eye.* New York: Teachers College Press; Lipman, P. (1995). Bring out the best in them: The contribution of culturally relevant teachers to education. *Theory into Practice 34*(3), 203–8; Sleeter, C. E. (2000). Creating an empowering cultural curriculum. *Race, Gender & Class in Education 7*(3), 178–96.
62. Boykin, A. W., and Noguera, P. (2011). *Creating the opportunity to learn. Moving from research to practice to close the achievement gap.* Alexandria, VA: ASCD.
63. Boykin and Noguera, 2011. Op. cit.
64. Baker, J. A. (1999). Teacher-student interaction in urban at-risk classrooms: Differential behavior, relationship, quality, and student satisfaction with school. *The Elementary School Journal 100*(1), 57–70; Byrnes, J. P., and Miller, D. C. (2007). The relative importance of predictors of math and science achievement: An opportunity-propensity analysis. *Contemporary Educational Psychology 32*(4), 599–629; Hamre, B. K., and Pianta, R. C. (2005). Can instructional and emotional support in the first-grade classroom make a difference for children at risk of school failure? *Child Development 76*(5), 949–67; Hughes, J., and Kwok, O. (2007). Influence of student-teacher and parent-teacher relationships on lower achieving readers' engagement and achievement in the primary grades. *Journal of Educational Psychology 99*(1), 39–51; Murray, C. (2009). Parent and teacher relationships as predictors of school engagement and functioning among low-income urban youth. *Journal of Early Adolescence 29*(3), 376–404.
65. Hamre, B. K., and Pianta, R. C. (2001). Early teacher-child relationships and the trajectory of children's school outcomes through eighth grade. *Child Development 72*(2), 625–38.
66. Brand, B. R., Glasson, G. E., and Green, A. M. (2006). Sociocultural factors influencing students' learning in science and mathematics: An analysis of the perspectives of African American students. *School Science and Mathematics 106*(5), 228–36; Stewart, E. (2006). Family- and individual-level predictors of academic success for African American students: A longitudinal path analysis utilizing national dat. *Journal of Black Studies 36*(4), 597–621.
67. Hamre and Pianta, 2005. Op. cit.; Griffith, J. (2002). A multi-level analysis of the relation of school learning and social environments to the minority achievement in public elementary schools. *Elementary School Journal 102*(5), 353–66; Balfanz, R., and Byrnes, V. (2006). Closing the mathematics achievement gap in high-poverty middle schools: Enablers and constraints. *Journal of Education for Students At-Risk 11*(2), 143–59; Liew, J., Chen, Q., and Hughes, J. (2010). Child effortful control, teacher-student relationships, and achievement in academically at-risk children: Additive and interactive effects. *Early Childhood Research Quarterly 25*(1), 51–64.
68. Ladd, G. W., Burch, S. H., and Burs, B. S. (1999). Children's social and scholastic lives in kindergarten: Related spheres of influence? *Child Development 70*(6), 1373–1400; Hughes and Kwok, 2007. Op. cit.; Sutherland, K. S., and Oswald, D. P. (2005). The relationship between teacher and student behavior in classrooms for students with emotional and behavioral disorders: Transactional processes. *Journal of Child and Family Studies 14*(1), 1–14; Hughes, J. N., Luo, W., Kwok, O., and Loyd, L. (2008). Teacher-student support, effortful engagement, and achievement: A 3-year longitudinal study. *Journal of Educational Psychology 100*(1), 1–14.
69. Burchinal, M. R., Peisner-Feinberg, E., Pianta, R., and Howes, C. (2002). Development of academic skills from preschool through second grade: Family and classroom predictors of developmental trajectories. *Journal of School Psychology 40*(5), 415–36; Mooney, E. S., and Thornton, C. A. (1999). Mathematics attribution differences by ethnicity and socioeconomic status. *Journal of Education for Students Placed at Risk 4*(3), 321–32; Casteel, C. (1997). Attitudes of African American and Caucasian eighth grade students about praises, rewards and punishments. *Elementary School Guidance and Counseling 31*(4), 262–72; Tucker, C., Zayco, R., Herman, K., Reinke, W., Truijillo, M., Carrawa, K., Wallack, C., and Ivery, P. (2002). Teacher and child variables as predictors of academic engagement among low-income African American children. *Psychology in the Schools 39*(4), 477–88; Irvine, J. J. (1990). *Black children and school failures. Policies, practices, and prescriptions*, Westport, CT: Greenwood Press; Ware, F. (2006). Warm demander pedagogy: Culturally responsive teaching that supports a culture of achievement for African American students. *Urban Education 41*(4), 427–56; Saft, E. W., and Pianta, R. C. (2001). Teachers' perceptions of their relationships with students: Effects of child age, gender, and ethnicity of teachers and children. *School Psychology Quarterly 16*(2), 125–41; Ferguson, R. (2003). Teachers' perceptions and expectations and the black-white test score gap. *Urban Education 38*(4), 460–507; Hughes and Kwok, 2007. Op. cit.; Wooley, M., Kol, K., and Bowen, G. I. (2009). The social context of school success for Latino middle school students: Direct and indirect influences of teachers, family, and friends. *Journal of Early Adolescence 29*(1), 43–70;
70. Dweck, C. S., and Leggett, E. L. (1988). A social-cognitive approach to motivation and personality. *Psychological Review 95*(2), 256–73; Gutman, L. M. (2006). How student and parent goal orientations and classroom goal structures influence the math achievement of African Americas during the high school transition. *Contemporary Educational Psychology 31*(1), 44–63; Fast, L. A., Kewius, J. L, Bryant, M. J., Bocian, K. A., Cardullo, R., Rettig, M., and Hammond, K. A. (2010). Does math self-efficacy mediate the effect of the perceived classroom environment on standardized math test performance? *Journal of Educational Psychology 102*(3), 729–40; Friedel, J. M., Cortina, K. S., Turner, J. C., and Midgeley, C. (2010). Changes in efficacy beliefs in mathematics across the transition to middle school: Examining the effects of perceived teacher and parent goal emphases. *Journal of Educational Psychology, 102*(1), 102–14; Kaplan, A., and Maehr, M. L. (1999). Achievement goals and student well-being. *Contemporary Educational Psychology 24*(4), 330–58; Nichols. J. G., Cheung, P., Lauer, J., and Pataschnick, M. (1989). Individual differences in academic motivation: Perceived ability, goals, beliefs, and values. *Learning and Individual Differences 1*(1), 63–84; Pintrich, P. (2000). *The role of goal orientation in self-regulated learning: Theory, research, & applications.* San Diego, CA: Academic Press, pp. 451–502; Walker, C., and Greene, B. A. (2009). The relations between student motivation beliefs and cognitive engagement in high school. *Journal of Educational Research 102*(6), 463–72.
71. Kaplan, A., and Maehr, M. L. (1999). Achievement goals and student well-being. *Contemporary Educational Psychology 24*(4), 330–58.
72. Graham, S., and Golan, S. (1991). Motivational influences on cognition: Task involvement, ego involvement, and depth of information processing. *Journal of Educational Psychology 83*(2), 187–94.
73. Mueller, C. M., and Dweck. C. S. (1998). Praise for intelligence can undermine children's motivation and performance. *Journal of Personality and Social Psychology 75*(1), 33–52.

74. Cohen, G. L., Garcia, J., Apfel, N., and Master, A. (2006). Reducing the racial achievement gap: A social-psychological intervention. *Science 313*(5791), 1307–10; D'Ailly, H. H., Simpson, J., and MacKinnon, G. E. (1997). Where should "you" go in a math compare problem? *Journal of Educational Psychology 89*(3), 562–67; Davis-Dorsey, J., Ross, J., and Morrison, G. R. (1991). The role of rewording and context personalization in the solving of mathematical word problems. *Journal of Educational Psychology 83*(1), 61–68.
75. Ginsburg-Block, M., Rohrbeck, C., Lavigne, N., and Fantusso, J. W. (2008). Peer- assisted learning: An academic strategy for enhancing motivation among diverse students. In C. Hudley and A. E. Gottfried (Eds.), *Academic motivation and the culture of school in childhood and adolescence*. New York: Oxford University Press, pp. 247–73; Maheady, L., Mitchielli-Pendl, J., Harper, G., and Mallette, B. (2006). The effects of numbered heads together with and without an incentive package on the science test performance of a diverse group of sixth graders. *Journal of Behavioral Education 15*(1), 25–39; Rohrbeck, C. A., Ginsburg-Block, M. D., Fantusso, J. W., and Miller, R. R. (2003). Peer-assisted learning interventions with elementary school students: A meta analytic review. *Journal of Educational Psychology 95*(2), 240–57; Slavin, R., Lake, C., and Groff, C. (2009). Effective programs in middle and high school mathematics: A best-evidence synthesis. *Review of Educational Research 79*(2), 839–911.
76. Bullock, H. E., and Williams, W. R. (2001, Summer). Media images of the poor. *Journal of Social Issues 57*(2), 229–46.
77. Mantsios, G. (1998). Class in America: Myths and realities. In P. S. Rothenberg (Ed.), *Race, class, and gender in the United States: An integrated study*, 4th ed. New York: St. Martin's, pp. 202–14.
78. Bullock and Williams, 2001.
79. Collins, C., and Veskel, F. (2004). Economic apartheid in America. In M. L. Andersen and P. H. Collins (Eds.), *Race, class, and gender: An anthology*, 5th ed. Belmont, CA: Wadsworth/Thomson, pp. 127–39; Rose, S. J. (2000). *Social stratification in the United States*. New York: New Press.
80. Lewis, O. (1961). *The children of Sanchez: Autobiography of a Mexican family*. New York: Random House.
81. Billings, P. E. (1974). Culture and poverty in Appalachia: A theoretical discussion and empirical analysis. *Social Forces 53*(2), 315–32; Carmon, N. (1985). Poverty and culture. *Sociological Perspectives 28*(4), 403–18; Jones, R. K., and Luo, Y. (1999). The culture of poverty and African-American culture: An empirical assessment. *Sociological Perspectives 42*(3), 439–58.
82. Abell, T., and Lyon, L. (1979). Do the differences make a difference? An empirical evaluation of the culture of poverty in the United States. *American Anthropologist 6*(3), 602–21; Ortiz, A. T., and Briggs, L. (2003). The culture of poverty, crack babies, and welfare cheats: The making of the "healthy white baby crisis." *Social Test 21*(3), 39–57; Rodman, R. (1977). Culture of poverty: The rise and fall of a concept. *Sociological Review 25(*4), 867–76.
83. Gorkski, P. (2008, April). The myth of the "culture of poverty." *Educational Leadership 65*(7), 32–36.
84. Iverson, R. R., and Farber, N. (1996). Transmission of family values, work, and welfare among poor urban black women. *Work and Occupations 23*(4), 437–60; Wilson, W. J. (1997). *When work disappears*. New York: Random House.
85. National Center for Children in Poverty. (2012). *Child poverty*. New York: Author. Retrieved from http://www.nccp.org/topics/childpoverty.html; Addy, S., Englehardt, W., and Skinner, C. (2013). *Basic facts about low-income children*. New York: National Center for Children in Poverty, Mailman School of Public Health, Columbia University. Retrieved from http://www.nccp.org/publications/pub_1074.html.
86. Economic Policy Institute. (2002). *The state of working class America, 2002–03*. Washington, DC: Author.
87. Compton-Lilly, C. (2003). *Reading families: The literate lives of urban children*. New York: Teachers College Press; Lareau, A., and Horvat, E. (1999). Moments of social inclusion and exclusion: Race, class, and cultural capital in family–school relationships. *Sociology of Education 72*, 37–53; Leichter, H. J. (Ed.). (1978). *Families and communities as educators*. New York: Teachers College Press.
88. Bomer, R., Dworin, J. E., May, L., and Semingson, O. (2008). Miseducating teachers about the poor: A critical analysis of Ruby Payne's claims about poverty. *Teachers College Record 110*(1). Retrieved from http://www.tcrecord.org/PrintContent.asp?ContentID=14591.
89. Gee, J. P. (2004). *Situated language and learning: A critique of traditional schooling*. New York: Routledge; Hess, K. M. (1974). The nonstandard speakers in our schools: What should be done? *Elementary School Journal 74*(5), 280–90; Miller, P. J., Cho, G. E., and Bracey, J. R. (2005). Working-class children's experience through the prism of personal story-telling. *Human Development 48*, 115–35.
90. Becker, H. S. (1952). Social class variation in teacher–pupil relationship. *Journal of Educational Sociology 25*, 451–65; Cicourel, A. V., and Kitsuse, J. L. (1963). *The education decision-makers*. New York: Bobbs Merrill; Eckert, P. (1989). *Jock and burnouts: Social categories and identity in high school*. New York: Teachers College; Rist, R. C. (1970). Student social class teacher expectations. *Harvard Educational Review 40*, 411–51.
91. For more on how teachers can support students from a collectivist family background, see Rothstein-Fisch and Trumbull, 2008.
92. U.S. Census Bureau. (2011). Educational attainment by race and Hispanic origin: 1970–2010 . *Statistical abstracts of the United States 2012*, Table 229, p. 151. Retrieved from http://www.census.gov/compendia/statab/2012/tables/12s0229.pdf; U.S. Census Bureau. (2009). Educational attainment by race and Hispanic groups, 1960–2007. *Statistical abstracts of the United States 2009*, Table 221. Retrieved from http://www.census.gov/compendia/statab/tables/09s0221.pdf.
93. U.S. Census Bureau. (2011). Educational attainment by selected characteristics: 2010. *Statistical abstracts of the United States, 2012*, Table 231. p. 152. Retrieved from http://www.census.gov/compendia/statab/2012/tables/12s0231.pdf.
94. U.S. Census Bureau. (2010). *African Americans by the numbers*. Retrieved from http://www.infoplease.com/spot/bhmcensus1.html.
95. Nearer to overcoming. (2008, May 10). London, UK: *The Economist 387*(8579), 33–35.
96. Hellmich, N. (2011, March 17). Death rate down, life expectancy up in U.S. *U.S.A. Today*. Retrieved from http://yourlife.usatoday.com/health/story/2011/03/Death-rate-down-life-expectancy-up-in-US/44935852/1.
97. Giroux, G. (2013, January 4). Final tally shows Obama first since '56 to win 51% twice. *Bloomberg News*. Retrieved from http://www.bloomberg.com/news/2013-01-03/final-tally-shows-obama-first-since-56-to-win-51-twice.html/.
98. Hildebrand, V., Phenice, L. A., Gray, M. M., and Hines, R. P. (1996). *Knowing and serving diverse families*. Englewood Cliffs, NJ: Prentice-Hall; McCollum, V. J. C. (1997). Evolution of the African American family personality: Considerations for family therapy. *Journal of Multicultural Counseling and Development 25*, 219–29.

99. Thomas, M. B., and Danby, P. G. (1985). Black clients: Family structures, therapeutic issues, and strengths. *Psychotherapy 22*, 398–407.
100. Sue and Sue, 2008, p. 336.
101. Sue and Sue, 2008, p. 333.
102. Todiscom, M., and Salomone, P. R. (1991). Facilitating effective cross-cultural relationships: The white counselor and the black client. *Journal of Multicultural Counseling and Development 19*, 146–57.
103. Sue and Sue, 1999, p. 245.
104. Sue and Sue, 2008, p. 335.
105. U.S. Census Bureau. (2004). *Table 6.2, Educational attainment of population 25 years and over by sex and Hispanic origin type 2004.* Retrieved from http://www.census.gov/population/socdemo/hispanic/ASEC2004/2004CPS_tab6.2a.html.
106. Lewis, A. C. (1998, September). Growing Hispanic enrollments: Challenge and opportunity. *Phi Delta Kappan 80*(1), 3–4.
107. Seymour, M. N. (1977). Psychology of the Chicana. In J. C. Martinez (Ed.), *Chicano psychology*. New York: Academic, pp. 329–42.
108. Sue and Sue, 2008, pp. 380–81.
109. Yamamoto, J., and Acosta, F. X. (1982). Treatment of Asian-Americans and Hispanic-Americans: Similarities and differences. *Journal of the Academy of Psychoanalysis 10*, 585–607.
110. Sue and Sue, 2008, p. 382.
111. Organista, K. C. (2000). Latinos. In J. R. White and A. S. Freeman (Eds.), *Cognitive-behavioral group therapy: For specific problems and populations*. Washington, DC: American Psychological Association, pp. 281–303.
112. Reese, L., Balzano, S., Gallimore, R., and Goldenberg, C. (1995). The concept of educacion: Latino family values and American schooling. *International Journal of Educational Research 23*(1), 57–81.
113. Rothstein-Fisch and Trumbull, 2008, p. 53.
114. Retish, P., and Kavanaugh, P. (1992). Myth: America's public schools are educating Mexican American students. *Journal of Multicultural Counseling and Development 20*, 89–96.
115. Gay, G. (2006). Connections between classroom management and culturally responsive teaching. In C. M. Evertson and C. S. Weinstein (Eds.), *Handbook of classroom management: Research, practice, and contemporary issues*. Mahwah, NJ: Lawrence Erlbaum Associates, pp. 343–70.
116. Delpit, L. (1995). *Other people's children: Cultural conflict in the classroom*. New York: New Press, p. 170; Rothstein-Fisch and Trumbull, 2008, p. 22.
117. Valenzuela, A. (1999). *Subtractive schooling: U.S.–Mexican youth and the politics of caring*. Albany: State University of New York Press.
118. Calaff, K. P. (2008, June). Supportive schooling: Practices that support culturally and linguistically diverse students' preparation for college. *NASSP Bulletin, 92*(2), 95–100.
119. Lockwood, A. T., and Secada, W. G. (1999). *Transforming education for Hispanic youth: Exemplary practices, programs, and schools* (NCBE Resource Collection Series No. 12). Washington, DC: NCBE; Gandara, P., and Biel, D. (2001). *Paving the way to postsecondary education; K–12 intervention programs for underrepresented youth (NCES 2001205)*. Washington, DC: National Center for Education Statistics.
120. Sue and Sue, 1999, p. 289.
121. The 2004 amendment includes students with physical or mental impairments that substantially limit one or more major life activities, students who have a record of disability, and students who are regarded as having a disabling condition. Special education laws and school practices are discussed more completely in Chapter 9.
122. Hohenshil, T. H., and Humes, C. W. (1979). Roles in counseling in ensuring the rights of the handicapped. *Personnel and Guidance Journal 58*, 221–27.
123. Bowe, F. (1978). *Handicapping America: Barriers to disabled people*. New York: Harper and Row.
124. U.S. Department of Education, National Center for Education Statistics. (2011). *The Digest of Education Statistics 2010 (NCES 2011-015).* Washington, DC: Author, Table 45 and Table 46. Retrieved from http://nces.ed.gov/fastfacts/display.asp?id=64.
125. U.S. Department of Education, National Center for Education Statistics, 2011. Table 45. Ibid.
126. Hayes, P. A. (2001). *Addressing cultural complexities in practice: A framework for clinicians and counselors*. Washington, DC: American Psychological Association.
127. EDGE curriculum culture: Charity images. *Education for Disability and Gender Equity.* Retrieved from http://www.disabilityhistory.org/dwa/edge/curriculum/cult_contenta5.htm.
128. Reid, K., and Valle, J. W. (2004). The discursive practice of learning disability: Implications for instruction and parent–school relations. *Journal of Learning Disabilities 37*(6), 466–81.
129. Harry, B., and Klinger, J. (2007, February). Discarding the deficit model. *Educational Leadership 64*(5), 16–21.
130. Masten, A. S., Best, K. M., and Garmezy, N. (1990). Resilience and development: Contributions from the study of children who overcome adversity. *Development and Psychopathology 2*(4), 425–44.
131. Masten, Best, and Garmezy, 1990.
132. Payne, R. (2008, April). Nine powerful practices. *Educational Leadership 65*(7), 48–52.
133. Annie E. Casey Foundation. (2005, July). *Kids Count indicator brief: Reducing the high school dropout rate.* Baltimore: Author, p. 12.
134. Weinstein, C., Curran, M., and Tomlinson-Clarke, S. (2003). Culturally responsive classroom management: Awareness into action. *Theory into Practice 42*(4), 275; San Antonio, D. M. (2008, April). Understanding students' strengths and struggles. *Educational Leadership 65*(7), 74–79.
135. San Antonio, 2008, p. 77.
136. Delpit, 1995, p. 167.
137. Delpit, 1995, p. 175.
138. Gay, G. (2000). *Culturally responsive teaching: Theory, research, and practice*. New York: Teachers College Press; Ladson-Billings, G. (1994). *The dream-keepers: Successful teachers of African American children*. San Francisco: Jossey-Bass; Nieto, S. M. (2002/2003, December/January). Profoundly multicultural questions. *Educational Leadership* 60(4), 6–10.
139. Flores-Gonzales, N. (2002). *School kids, street kids: Identity and high school completion among Latinos*. New York: Teachers College Press; Noddings, N. (1992). *The challenge to care in schools: An alternative approach to education*. New York: Teachers College Press; Stanton-Salazar, R. D. (1997). A social capital framework for understanding the socialization of racial minority children and youth. *Harvard Educational Review 67(1)*, 1–40; Valenzuela, 1999.
140. For more specifics about helping Native American students succeed in school, see the following source: Fore, C. L., and Chaney, J. N. (1998). Factors influencing the pursuit of educational opportunities in American Indian students. In S. M. Manson (Ed.), American Indian and Alaska Native mental health research. *Journal of the National Center 8*(2), 54–59. Denver, CO: National Center for American Indian and Alaska Native Mental Health Research. Retrieved from http://aianp.uchsc.edu/ncaianmhr/journal/pdf_files/8(2).pdf. For more

specifics about helping Latino students succeed in school, see the following source: Wainer, A. (2004). *The New Latino South and the challenge to public education: Strategies for educators and policymakers in emerging immigrant communities*. Los Angeles: Tomas Rivera Policy Institute. Retrieved from http://www.trpi.org. For more information about helping English language learners succeed, see the following source: Miller, P. C., and Endo, H. (2004, June). Understanding and meeting the needs of ESL students. *Phi Delta Kappan 85*(10), 786–91.

141. As cited in Delpit, 1995, p. 164.
142. Elmore, R., Peterson, P., and McCarthey, S. (1996). *Restructuring in the classroom*. San Francisco: Jossey-Bass; McLaughlin, M. W., and Talbert, J. W. (1993). Introduction: New visions of teaching. In D. Cohen and J. E. Talbert (Eds.), *Teaching for understanding: Challenges for policy and practice*. San Francisco: Jossey-Bass, pp. 1–10; National Research Council. (2000). *How people learn: Brain, mind, experience, and school*. Washington, DC: National Academy Press; Wiggins, G., and McTighe, J. (1998). *Understanding by design*. Alexandria, VA: Association for Supervision and Curriculum Development; Wiske, M. S. (1997). *Teaching for understanding: Linking research with practice*. San Francisco: Jossey-Bass; Richardson, V. (2003, December). Constructive pedagogy. *Teachers College Record 105*(9), 1623–40.
143. Henderson, A. T., and Berla, N. (Eds.). (1994). *A new generation of evidence: The family is critical in student achievement*. Washington, DC: National Committee for Citizens in Education; Epstein, J. L. (1991). Effects of students' achievement of teacher practices of parent involvement. In S. B. Silvern (Ed.). *Advances in teaching/language research. Vol. 5: Literacy through family, community, and school interaction*. Greenwich, CT: JAI Press, pp. 261–76; Henderson, A. T., and Mapp, K. L. (2002). *A new wave of evidence: The impact of school, family and community connections on student achievement, annual synthesis 2002* (Eric Document No. ED 474521). Austin, TX: Center of Family and Community Connections with Schools, Southwest Educational Development Laboratory.
144. Delpit, 1995, p. 182.
145. Cited in Delpit, 1995, p. 183.

Chapter 9

1. We wish to thank our friends, David and Kern Alexander, for their help with this chapter. Much of the school law content is derived from their text, *American Public School Law*, sixth edition (2005) and seventh edition (2009), published by Cengage Learning. Text citations are from the sixth edition unless otherwise stated.
2. Friedman, T. L. (2008). *Hot, flat, and crowded. Why we need a green revolution—and how it can renew America*. New York: Ferrar, Straus, and Giroux, p. 192.
3. Frankel, M. S. (1989, February–March). Professional codes: Why, whom, and with what impact? *Journal of Business Ethics 8*(2–3), 109–15.
4. Frankel, 1989.
5. NEA Code of Ethics. Retrieved from http://www.nea.org/home/30442.htm.
6. Carter, H. H., Foulger, T. S., and Ewbank, A. D. (2008). Have you Googled your teacher lately? Teachers use of social networking sites. *Phi Delta Kappan 89*(9), 681–85. See this article for a more complete discussion of social networking and teachers.
7. Carter, Foulger, and Ewbank, 2008.
8. Stross, R. (2007, December 30). How to lose your job on your own time. *The New York Times*. Retrieved from http://www.nytimes.com/2007/12/30/business/30digi.html?pagewanted=1&_r=1.
9. Carter, Foulger, and Ewbank, 2008.
10. Collins, H. (2010, August 19). Teacher quits after Facebook posts diss parents, kids. *The Huffington Post*, Retrieved from: http://www.aolnews.com/2010/08/19/teacher-quits-after-facebook-posts-diss-parents-kids/
11. Downey, M. (2011, October 10). Court rules against Ashley Payne in Facebook case. But more to come. Retrieved from http://blogs.ajc.com/get-schooled-blog/2011/10/10/court-rules-against-ashley-payne-in-facebook-case/.
12. Stross, 2007.
13. The college granted Snyder an English—rather than an education—degree. See Krebs, B. (2008). Court rules against teacher in MySpace "drunken pirate" case: Security fix. Retrieved from *Washington Post*. http://voices.washingtonpost.com/securityfix/2008/12/court_rules_against_teacher_in.html.
14. Check with your own state's professional teaching association for specific guidance.
15. Case law is judge-made law. In contrast, statutes are laws passed by legislative bodies.
16. Cases and digest research tutorials: Lesson one: Overview. (2001). Georgetown University Library. Retrieved from http://www.ll.georgetown.edu/tutorials/cases/one/2_overview.html.
17. We use the terms *certification* and *licensure* interchangeably here, even while acknowledging that there are subtle, yet distinct differences between the two.
18. *Moral turpitude* can be defined as conduct that is considered to be so base, vile, or depraved that it is contrary to community standards of justice, honesty, or good morals.
19. 71 Ohio App. 3d 526, 594 N.E.2d 1071 (1991).
20. *Adams v. State Professional Practices Council*, 412 So. 2d 463 (Fla. 1982).
21. 1228 Pa. Commw. 110, 562 A.2d 1005 (1989).
22. Supreme Court of Iowa. (1974). 216 N.W.2d 339.
23. Supreme Court of Texas. (1987). 724 S. W.2d 387.
24. Alexander, K., and Alexander, M. D. (2001). *American public school law*, 5th ed. Belmont, CA: Wadsworth, p. 671.
25. Alexander, K., and Alexander, M. D. (2003). *The law of schools, students, and teachers*, 3rd ed. St. Paul, MN: West, p. 51.
26. 270 F.3d 1036 (6th Cir. 2001), 53.
27. 418 F.2d 359 (1st Cir. 1969), 53.
28. 960 P.2d 695 (Colo. 1988), 54, 441.
29. *Brubaker v. Board of Education, School District 149, Cook County, Illinois* (7th Cir. 1974).
30. Alexander and Alexander, 2005, p. 721.
31. 391 U.S. 563, 88 S. Ct. 1731 (1968).
32. 391 U.S. at 568.
33. 461 U.S. 138, 103 S. Ct. 1684 (1983).
34. 981 F.2d 152 (4th Cir. 1993).
35. There are 13 Circuit Courts of Appeal in the United States, representing various geographic regions of the country. The Fourth Circuit Court of Appeals represents the mid-Atlantic states.
36. 562 F.2d 838 (2nd Cir. 1977).
37. Quoted in Alexander and Alexander, 2005, p. 740.
38. 480 U.S. 709, 107 S. Ct. 1492 (1987).
39. 191 F.3d 1329 (11th Cir. 1999).
40. *Skinner v. Railway Executives Association* (S. Ct. 1989) and *National Treasury Employees Union v. Von Raab* (S. Ct. 1989).
41. *Knox County Education Association v. Knox County Board of Education* (6th Cir. 1998) 158 F.3d 361.

42. Sixth Circuit, 1998, 158 F.3d 361.
43. 603 F2.d 1271, 1274 (7th Cir. 1979), cert denied. 444 U.S. 1026, 100 S. Ct. 689 (1980).
44. *Russo v. Central School District No. 1*, 469 F.2d 623 (2d Cir. 1972), cert denied, 411 U.S. 932. 93 S. Ct. 1899 (1973).
45. 482 U.S. 578, 107 S. Ct. 2573.
46. 400 F. Supp.2d 707.
47. 541 F. Supp. 332 (D.S.D. 1982).
48. 544 F. Supp. 1049 (D. Colo. 1983).
49. See *Hysong v. School District of Gallitzin Borough*, 164 Pa. 629, 30 A. 482 (1894); and *Commonwealth v. Herr*, 229 Pa. 132, 78 A. 68 (1910).
50. 301 Or. 358, 723 P.2d 298.
51. *Lee v. York County School Division*, 484 F. 3d 687 (4th Cir. 2007), cert denied. 128 S. Ct. 387 (2007); and *Downs v. Los Angeles Unified School District*, 228 F. 3d 1003 (9th Cir. 2000).
52. 374 U.S. 203, 83 S. Ct. 1560.
53. 472 U.S. 38, 105 S. Ct. 2479.
54. 258 F. 3d 265 (4th Cir).
55. We will not examine contract law here.
56. *Spears v. Jefferson Parish School Board*, 646 So. 2d 1104 (1994).
57. Alexander and Alexander, 2005, p. 559.
58. *Lewis v. St. Bernard Parish School*, 350 So. 2d 1256 (La. Ct. App. 1977).
59. There are two types of due process, procedural and substantive. We will deal only with procedural due process in this chapter.
60. 419 U.S. 565, 95 S. Ct. 729 (1975).
61. *Honig v. Doe* (1988), 484 U.S. 305, 108 S. Ct. 592.
62. 430 U.S. 651, 97 S. Ct. 1401.
63. The Center for Effective Discipline. (2010, July 1). Discipline at schools. U.S. corporal punishment and paddling statistics by state and race. Canal Winchester, OH: Author. Retrieved from http://www.stophitting.com/index.php?page=statesbanning.
64. 39 Ark. App.14, 832 S. W.2d 510 (1992).
65. In June 2009, the U.S. Supreme Court ruled that school officials could not strip-search a student while looking for ibuprofen because it violated the Fourth Amendment's prohibition against unreasonable search and seizure. See Bravin, J. (2009, June 26), Court faults strip-search of student. *The Wall Street Journal/Law*. Retrieved from http://online.wsj.com/article/SB124593034315253301.html.
66. 469 U.S. 325, 105 S. Ct. 733 (1985).
67. 666 N.W.2d 142 (2003).
68. 176 Wis. 2d 639, 500 N.W2d 637.
69. Essex, N. L. (2005). *School law and the public schools: A practical guide for educational leaders*. Boston, MA: Pearson, pp. 101–02.
70. 515 U.S. 646, 115 S. Ct. 2386.
71. 536 U.S. 822, 122 S. Ct. 2559 (2002).
72. Schools should base their rules and regulations on the school's legitimate interests. If the rule's or regulation's purpose is unclear or nonexistent, courts say, then the rule should not exist.
73. 393 U.S. 503, 89 S. Ct. 733 (1969).
74. 393 U.S. 503, 89 S. Ct. 733 (1969).
75. 478 U.S. 675, 106 S. Ct. 3159 (1986).
76. 551 U.S. 127 S. Ct. 2618 (2007).
77. Alexander and Alexander, 2005, p. 385.
78. 484 U.S. 260, 108 S. Ct. 562 (1988).
79. *Doninger v. Niehoff*, 514 F. Supp.2d 199 (D.Comm.2007).
80. Walsh, M. (2008, June 11). Student loses discipline case for blog remarks. *Education Week 27*(41), 7.
81. Alexander and Alexander, 2005, p. 375.
82. Starr, J. (2000, January). School violence and its effects on the constitutionality of public school uniform policies. *Journal of Law and Education 29*, 113.
83. United States Court of Appeals, Fifth Circuit, 2001. 240 F.3d 437.
84. Irvine, M., and Tanner, R. (2007, October 24). Sex abuse a shadow over U.S. schools. *Education Week 27*(9), 17.
85. Irvine and Tanner, 2007, pp. 1, 16–19.
86. Title IX prohibits discrimination not only within athletics and other extracurricular activities but also in regard to financial aid, testing, curricular offerings, pregnancy, and marital status.
87. 503 U.S. 60, 112 S. Ct. 1028 (1992).
88. 524 U.S. 274, 118 S. Ct. 1989 (1998).
89. Alexander and Alexander, 2005, p. 463.
90. 526 U.S.629, 119 S. Ct. 1662 (1999).
91. *Nabozny v. Podlesny*. (1996). 92 F. 3d 446. Retrieved from http://caselaw.lp.findlaw.com/scripts/getcase.pl?navby=search&case=/data2/circs/7th/953634.html.
92. Nearly nine out of 10 lesbian, gay, bisexual, and transgender students experienced some form of harassment at school in the past year, according to a 2007 national survey of 6,200 middle and high school students. See Maxwell, L. A. (2008, October 15). Sexual orientation: The 2007 National School Climate Survey. *Education Week 28*(8), 5.
93. 458 U.S. 176, 102 S. Ct. 3034.
94. An FM hearing aid is one that uses frequency modulation to transmit sound over airwaves, allowing a user to hear more speech and less background noise as compared with AM hearing aids, which use amplitude modification.
95. Stout, D., and Medina, J. (2007, October 11). With justices split, city must pay disabled student's tuition. *The New York Times, Education*, B1. Retrieved from http://www.nytimes.com/2007/10/11/education/11school.html.
96. Stout and Medina, 2007.
97. See *Board of Education of New York City v. Tom F.*, and *Forest Grove School District v. T.A.* (No. 08-305); Argued April 28, 2009, Decided June 22, 2009, Retrieved from http://www.supremecourt.gov/opinions/08pdf/08-305.pdf.

Chapter 10

1. Fuerer, M. J. (2006, June 14). Moderation: A radical approach to education policy. Commentary. *Education Week 25*(10), 36.
2. Snyder, T. D., and Dillow, S. A. (2011, April). Number of public school districts and public and private elementary and secondary schools: Selected years 1869–70 through 2008–09. *Digest of Education Statistics 2010 (NCES 2011-015)*. Washington, DC: U.S. Government Printing Office, p. 132, Table 90. Retrieved from http://nces.ed.gov/pubs2011/2011015.pdf.
3. In some localities, these entities are called school districts. In others, they are called school divisions or local agencies.
4. The United States has 51 different education systems. The District of Columbia has its own education system, counting as the 51st.
5. Grant, W. V. (1993, January). Statistics in the U.S. Department of Education: Highlights from the past 120 years. In T. D. Snyder (Ed.), *120 years of American education: A statistical portrait* (pp. 1–4). Washington, DC: National Center for Education Statistics. Retrieved from http://nces.ed.gov/pubs93/93442.pdf.
6. New America Foundation. (2013, April 19). *School finance. Federal, state, and local K-12 school finance overview.* Washington, DC: Author, Federal Education Budget Project. Retrieved from http://febp.newamerica.net/background-analysis/school-finance.

7. Center on Budget and Policy Priorities. (2009, April 13). Retrieved from http://www.cbpp.org/cms/index.cfm?fa =view&id=1258nd.
8. Public Law 85-864.
9. 377 U.S. 218, 84 S. Ct. 1226.
10. What happened in Prince Edward County? (2003). Longwood University. Retrieved from http://www.longwood.edu/news /bvb/princeedward.htm.
11. What happened in Prince Edward County? 2003.
12. *Plyler v. Doe,* 457 U.S. 202 102 S.Ct. 2382 (1982).
13. Owings, W., and Kaplan, L. (2013). *American public school finance.* (2nd ed.). Belmont, CA: Wadsworth, 2006, p. 222.
14. We will discuss student achievement and accountability in greater detail in Chapter 14. For the purposes of this section, we briefly address the topic as one of the federal roles in education.
15. Since 1983, Educational Testing Services (ETS) has held the NAEP contract.
16. Subgroups include minority, low-income, special education, and English language learners.
17. Hawaii has a state-run school system with no local school districts. For a more complete discussion of Proposition 13 and the taxpayers' revolt, see Chapter 11.
18. First to worst: Special challenge of Proposition 13. (n.d.). *The Merrow report.* New York: Public Broadcast System, Learning Matters Inc. Retrieved from http://www.pbs.org/merrow/tv/ftw /prop13.html.
19. We will go into more detail about this issue in Chapter 11.
20. Except in Vermont and New Hampshire, where the governors serve two-year terms. In all states except Virginia, governors may succeed themselves.
21. Chapter 9 goes into greater detail about the courts' role in education.
22. Except in Wisconsin, which does not have a State Board of Education.
23. Except Wisconsin.
24. Kysilko, D. (1999, January). Aggregating and tracking state board policies. In *Boardsmanship review.* Washington, DC: National Association of State Boards of Education.
25. Kysilko, D. (2000, March). Building partnerships with the legislature. In *Boardsmanship review.* Washington, DC: National Association of State Boards of Education.
26. Kysilko, 1999.
27. Alsbury, T. L. (2003, December). Superintendent and school board member turnover: Political versus apolitical turnover as a critical variable in the application of dissatisfaction theory. *Education Administration Quarterly 39*(5), 667–78.
28. *Key work of school boards: School governance.* (2007). Alexandria, VA: National School Boards Association. Retrieved from http://www.nsba.org/site/page.asp?TRACKID =&CID=121&DID=8799.
29. Robell, M., et. al. (1982). *Educational policymaking and the courts.* Chicago: University of Chicago Press.
30. Campbell, D. W., and Greene, D. (1994). Defining the leadership role of school boards in the 21st century. *Phi Delta Kappan 75*(5), 1–5.
31. Local superintendents. (2008). In *Statenotes.* Denver, CO: Education Commission of the States. Retrieved from http:// mb2.ecs.org/reports/Report.aspx?id=171.
32. McNeil, J. (1996). *Curriculum: A comprehensive introduction* (5th ed.). Los Angeles: Harper Collins College.
33. Andero, A. (2000, Winter). The changing role of school superintendent with regard to curriculum policy and decision making. *Education 121*(2), 276–86.
34. Grove, K. F. (2002, May). The invisible role of the central office. *Educational Leadership 59*(8), 45–47.
35. Schnur, J. (2002, June 18). *An outstanding principal in every school: Using the new Title II to promote effective leadership.* National Council on Teacher Quality, p. 2.
36. Hess, A. G., Jr. (1998, September). *Strong leadership is no. 1 catalyst.* Chicago: Voices of School Reform.
37. Hallinger, P., and Heck, R. (1998). Exploring the principal's contribution to school effectiveness, 1980–1995. *R. School Effectiveness and School Improvement 9*(2), 157–91.
38. Marzano, R. J., Waters, T., and McNulty, B. A. (2005). *School leadership that works. From research to results.* Alexandria, VA: Association for Supervision and Curriculum Development.
39. Branch, G., Hanushek, E. A., and Rivkin, S. G. (2013. Winter). School leaders matter. *EducationNext 13* (1), Retrieved from http://educationnext.org/school-leaders-matter/.
40. Charlotte Advocates for Education. (2004, February). *Role of principal leadership in increasing teacher retention: Creating a supportive environment.* Charlotte, NC: Author, pp. 1–64. Retrieved from http://www.advocatesfored.org/principalstudy .htm; Ingersoll, R. M. (2002, June). The teacher shortage: A case of wrong diagnosis and wrong prescription. *NASSP Bulletin 86*(631),16–30; Public Education Network. (2004). *The voice of the new teacher,* 1–37. Retrieved from http://www. publiceducation.org/pdf/PEN_Pubs/Voice_of_the_New_Teacher.pdf. National Commission on Teaching and America's Future. (2003, August 13). *Recruiting teachers for hard-to-staff schools: Solutions for the Southeast and the nation.* Chapel Hill, NC: Southeast Center for Teacher Quality. Retrieved from http://www .teachingquality.org/legacy/HTSS_regional.pdf.
41. Brigman, G., and Campbell, C. (2003, December). Helping students improve academic achievement and school success behaviors. *Professional School Counseling 7*(2), 91–98.
42. American School Counselors Association. (2012). Careers/role. Alexandria, VA: Author. Retrieved from http://www .schoolcounselor.org/content.asp?contentid=133.
43. *Accreditation standards.* (2007). Richmond: Virginia Department of Education, p. 39. Retrieved from http://www.pen.K12. va.us/VDOE/Accountability.
44. Gysbers, N. G. (2004, October). Comprehensive guidance and counseling programs: The evolution of accountability. *Professional School Counseling 8*(1), 1–14.
45. Brigman and Campbell, 2003.
46. Cantoni, L. J. (1954). Guidance: 4 students 10 years later. *The Clearing House 28,* 474–78; Wellman, F. E., and Moore, E. J. (1975). *Pupil personnel services: A handbook for program development and evaluation.* Washington, DC: U.S. Department of Health, Education, and Welfare; Lapan, R. T., Gysbers, N. C., and Sun, Y. (1997). The impact of more fully implemented guidance programs on the school experiences of high school students: A statewide-evaluation study. *Journal of Counseling and Development 75,* 292–302; Lapan, R. T., Gysbers, N. C., and Petroski, G. (2001). Helping 7th graders be safe and academically successful: A statewide study of the impact of comprehensive guidance programs. *Journal of Counseling and Development 79,* 320–30; Sink, C. A., and Stroh, H. R. (2003). Raising achievement test scores of early elementary students through comprehensive school counseling programs. *Professional School Counseling 6,* 350–64; Campbell, C., and Brigman, G. (2005, February). Closing the achievement gap: A structured approach to group counseling. *Journal for Specialists in Group Work 31*(1), 67–82; Webb, L., and Brigman, G. (2007, April).

Student success skills: A structured group intervention for school counselors. *Journal for Specialists in Group Work 32*(2), 190–201.
47. Brigman and Campbell, 2003.
48. Cantoni, 1954.
49. Cantoni, 1954.
50. Lapan, Gysbers, and Sun, 1997.
51. Nelson, D. E., Gardner, J. L., and Fox, D. G. (1998). *An evaluation of the comprehensive guidance program in Utah public schools.* Salt Lake City, UT: State Office of Education.
52. Nelson, Gardner, and Fox, 1998.
53. Nelson, Gardner, and Fox, 1998.
54. Lapan, Gysbers, and Petroski, 2001.
55. Lapan, Gysbers, and Petroski, 2001.
56. Lapan, Gysbers, and Sun, 1997.
57. Teachers: Special education. (2006, August 4). In *Occupational outlook handbook*. Washington, DC: U.S. Department of Labor, Bureau of Labor Statistics. Retrieved from http://www.bls.gov/oco/ocos070.htm.
58. Aud, S., Hussar, F., Johnson, G., Kena, G., and Roth, E. (2012). *The condition of education 2012*. Indicator 9. Children and youth with disabilities (NCES 2012045). p. 1.Washington, DC: U.S. Department of Education, Institute for Education Sciences. Retrieved from http://nces.ed.gov/programs/coe/pdf/coe_cwd.pdf.
59. Aud, et al., 2012. Ibid. Retrieved from http://nces.ed.gov/programs/coe/pdf/coe_cwd.pdf.
60. Aud, et al., 2012. Op. cit. Figure 9-2, p. 2.
61. *The role of the school nurse: Issue brief.* (2002). Silver Springs, MD: National Association of School Nurses. Retrieved from http://www.nasn.org/Default.aspx?tabid=279.
62. *The role of the school nurse,* 2002.
63. Section 504 is a civil rights law that prohibits discrimination against individuals with disabilities. It ensures that the child with a disability has equal access to an education. The child may receive accommodations and modifications.
64. *Caseload assignments. Position Statement.* (Revised 2010). National Association of School Nurses. Retrieved from http://www.nasn.org/PolicyAdvocacy/PositionPapersandReports/NASNPositionStatementsFullView/tabid/462/smid/824/ArticleID/7/Default.aspx.
65. Cotton, K. (1996, December). Affective and social benefits of small-scale schooling. *ERIC Digest*. Clearinghouse on Rural Education & Small Schools (EDO-RC-96-5); Cotton, K. (2001, December). *New small learning communities: Findings from recent research*. Portland, OR: Northwest Regional Education Laboratory.
66. Raywid, M. (1999). *Current literature on small schools.* Charleston, WV: ERIC Reproduction Service No. ED42049; Eichenstein, R., et al. (1994). *Project Achieve, part I: Qualitative findings, 1993–94*. Brooklyn, NY: New York City Board of Education.
67. Evan, A., Huberman, M., Means, B., Mitchell, K., Shear, L., et al. (2006, August). *Evaluation of the Bill & Melinda Gates Foundation's High School Grants Initiative. 2001–2005 Final Report.* Washington, DC: The American Institutes for Research and SRI International. Retrieved from http://www.gatesfoundation.org/learning/Documents/Year4EvaluationAIRSRI.pdf; Shear, L., Means, B., Mitchell, K., et al. (2008, September). Contrasting paths to small-school reform: Results of a 5-year evaluation of the Bill & Melinda Gates Foundation's National High School Initiative. *Teachers College Record 110*(9), 1986-039. Retrieved from http://researchhighschools.pbworks.com/f/GatesHSEvaluation.pdf.
68. Hoff, D. J. (2008, May 21). Study of small high schools yields little on achievement. *Education Week 27*(38), 10.
69. Gerwitz, C. (2006, August 9). Chicago's small schools see gains, but not on tests. *Education Week 25*(44): 5, 18.
70. Stevenson, K. R. (2006, April). School size and its relationship to student outcomes and school climate. A review and analysis of eight South Carolina state-wide studies. Washington, DC: National Clearinghouse for Educational Facilities. Retrieved from http://www.ncef.org/pubs/size_outcomes.pdf.
71. Caldas, S. J. (1993). Reexamination of input and process factor effects on public school achievement. *Journal of Educational Research 86*(4), 206–14; Lamdin, D. J. (1995). Testing for effect of school size on student achievement within a school district. *Education Economics 3*, 33–42; Hoagland, J. P. (1995). The effect of high school size on student achievement as measured by the California Assessment Program. Unpublished doctoral dissertation, University of LaVerne, Claremont; Florida Department of Education. Office of Policy Research. (1997, May). *The relationship of school size and class size with student achievement in Florida* [Online]. Retrieved from http://ericps.ed.uniuc.edu/npin/pnews/pnew696f.html.
72. Howley, C. (2001). Research on smaller schools: *What education leaders need to know to make better decisions (ERS Informed Educator).* Arlington, VA: Educational Research Service; Lee, V. E., and Smith, J. B. (1997, Autumn). High school size: Which works best and for whom? *Educational Evaluation and Policy Analysis 19*(3): 205–27; Gerwitz, 2006; Johnson, J. D., Howley, C. B., and Howley, A. A. (2002). *Size, excellence, and equity: A report on Arkansas schools and districts.* Athens: Ohio University College of Education, Educational Studies Department; Jimerson, L. (2006, September). *The Hobbit effect: Why small schools work.* Arlington, VA: The Rural School and Community Trust.
73. The seven states were: Alaska, California, Georgia, Montana, Ohio, Texas, and West Virginia. See: Johnson, Howley, and Howley, 2002; see also: Jimerson, 2006.
74. Johnson, Howley, and Howley, 2002; Jimerson, 2006. The seven states were Alaska, California, Georgia, Montana, Ohio, Texas, and West Virginia.
75. Gregory, T. B., and Smith, G. R. (1987, January). *High schools as communities: The small school reconsidered.* Bloomington, IN: Phi Delta Kappa; Sousa, R., and Skandera, H. (2003, June 30). Smaller is better *Hoover Digest, 1*. Palo Alto, CA: Stanford University.
76. Gerwitz, 2006.
77. Lee and Smith, 1997.
78. Howley, C. (1996). *Sizing up schooling: A West Virginia analysis and critique.* Unpublished doctoral dissertation, West Virginia University, Morgantown.
79. Kuziemko, I. (2006). Using shocks to school enrollment to estimate the effect of school size on student achievement. *Economics of Educaiton Review 25*(1), 63–75.
80. Stiefel, L., Berne, R., Iatarola, P., and Fruchter, N. (2000, Spring). High schools size: Effects on budgets and performance in New York City. *Educational Evaluation and Policy Analysis 22*(1), 27–39.
81. Lawrence, B. K., Bingler, S., Diamond, B. M., Hill, B., Hoffman, J. L., Howley, C. B., Mitchell, S., Rudolph, D., and Washor, E. (2002). *Dollars and sense. The cost effectiveness of small schools.* Cincinnati, OH: Knowledge Works Foundation. Retrieved from http://www.earlycolleges.org/Downloads/reslib79.pdf.

82. *School size.* (n.d.). Denver, CO: Education Commission of the States. Retrieved from http://www.ecs.org/html/issue.asp?print=true&issueID=105&subIssueOD=0.
83. Mertens, S. B., Flowers, N., and Mulhall, P. F. (2001, May). School size matters in interesting ways. *Middle School Journal 32*(5), 51–55; Wahlberg, H. J. (1994, June–July). Losing local control. *Educational Researcher 23*(5),19–26; Howley, C., & Bickel, R. (2002, March). The influence of scale. *American School Board Journal 183*(3), 28–30; Andrews, M., Duncomb, W., and Yinger, J. (2002, June). Revisiting economics of size in American education: Are we any closer to consensus? *Economics of Education Review 21,* 245–62; Pellicer, L. (1999, November). When is a school district too large? Too small? Just right? Lessons from Goldilocks and the three bears. *School Business Affairs 65*(11), 4–6, 8–10, 26–29.
84. U.S. Census Bureau. (2011). *School districts*. Retrieved from http://www.census.gov/did/www/schooldistricts/index.html.
85. Cunningham, W. G. (2003, June). Grassroots democracy: Putting the public back into public education. *Phi Delta Kappan 84*(10), 776–79.
86. Snyder, T. D., Tan, A. G., & Hoffman, C. M. (2006). *Digest of education statistics 2005 (NCES 2006-030).* U.S. Department of Education, National Center for Education Statistics. Washington, DC: U.S. Government Printing Office, p. 54.
87. Snyder, T. D., and Dillow, S. A. (2011). *Digest of education statistics.* Washington, DC: Institute of Education Sciences, U.S. Department of Education, Table 36, p. 70 and Table 90, p. 132.
88. Andrews, Duncombe, and Yinger, 2002.
89. Aud et al., 2011, Figure 71-1, p. 85.
90. Viadero, D. (2008, January 16). Evidence for moving to K-8 models not airtight. *Education Week 27*(19), 1, 12.
91. McEwin, C. K., Dickinson, T. S., and Jacobson, M. G. (2005). How effective are K-8 schools for young adolescents? *Middle School Journal 37*(1), 24–28.
92. Klump, J. (2006, Spring). What the research says (or doesn't say) about K–8 versus middle school grade configurations: Assessing the benefits of K-8 schools. *Northwestern Education 11*(3). Northwest Regional Educational Laboratory. Retrieved from http://www.nwrel.org/nwedu/11-03/research/.
93. The studies looking at whether students have better achievement in K-8 schools rather than in middle schools did not control for school size, socioeconomic factors, and other variables, so their results could be attributable to factors other than grade configurations.
94. Abella, R. (2005). The effects of small K–8 centers compared to large 6–8 schools on student performance. *Middle School Journal 37*(1), 29–35; Alspaugh, J. W. (1998). Achievement loss associated with the transition to middle school and high school. *Journal of Educational Research 92*(1), 20–25.
95. Anfara, V. A., Jr., and Buehler, A. (2005). Grade configuration and the education of young adolescents. *Middle School Journal 37*(1), 57.
96. The National Forum to Accelerate Middle-Grades Reform. (2008, July). Policy statement on grade configuration. *Middle Grades Forum 5* (5). Savoy, IL: Author. Retrieved from http://www.mgforum.org/Portals/0/MGFdocs/GradeConfiguration.pdf.

Chapter 11

1. Chantrill, C. (2013). *US education spending.* Seattle, WA: USGovernmentspending.com. Retrieved from http://www.usgovernmentspending.com/us_education_spending_20.html; Snyder, T. D., and Dillow, S. A. (2012). *Digest of education statistics 2011 (NCES 2012-001).* Washington, DC: National Center for Education Statistics, Institute of Education Sciences, U.S. Department of Education, p. 11. Retrieved from http://nces.ed.gov/pubs2012/2012001.pdf.
2. Gallagher, J. J. (2007, April 4). Reform's missing ingredient: Building a high-quality support system for education: Commentary. *Education Week 26*(31), 27, 29.
3. Kozol, J. (1992). *Savage inequalities: Children in America's schools.* New York: Harper Perennial.
4. Kozol, 1992, p. 23.
5. Kozol, 1992, p. 24.
6. Kozol, 1992, p. 27.
7. Kozol, 1992, p. 29.
8. Carroll, T. (2008, March 26). Education beats incarceration. *Education Week 27*(29), 32.
9. Lochner, L., and Moretti, E. (2004). The effect of education on crime: Evidence from prison inmates, arrests, and self-reports. *American Economic Review 94*(1), 155–89. Social savings costs are reported in this source in 2006 dollars.
10. Chantrill, D. (2013, April 29). *United States federal, state and local government spending fiscal year 2013.* Seattle, WA: USGovernmentspending.com. Retrieved from http://www.usgovernmentspending.com/us_education_spending_20.html.
11. With desegregation, schools had to hire more teachers to reduce class sizes to more acceptable teacher–student ratios and increase African American teachers' salaries to levels comparable to what white teachers were earning.
12. Hanushek, E. A., and Rivkin, S. G. (1997). Understanding the twentieth century's growth in U.S. school spending. *Journal of Human Resources 32*(1), 35–68.
13. Hanushek and Rivkin, 1997, p. 41.
14. Hanushek and Rivkin, 1997, p. 45.
15. Data obtained from http://www.quickfacts.census.gov/qfd/states and ttp://www.greatschools.com. All data are from the school year 2006–2007.
16. Hanushek and Rivkin, 1997, p. 39.
17. Hoff, D. J. (2005, October). Group "65 Percent Solution" gains traction, GOP friends. *Education Week 24*(7), 1, 18.
18. Hoff, 2005.
19. $32,796 × 30 = $983,880.
20. Allegretto, S., Corcoran, S., and Mishel, L. (2004). *How does teacher pay compare? Methodological challenges and answers.* Washington, DC: Economic Policy Institute, p. 2.
21. Owings, W., and Kaplan, L. (2013). *American public school finance.* 2nd ed. Belmont, CA: Cengage Learning, p. 172.
22. Odden, A., and Picus, L. (2004). *School finance: A policy perspective,* 3rd ed. New York: McGraw-Hill, p. 25.
23. Wieder, B. (2013, January 2). Texas among 10 states facing lawsuits over education funding. WP Politics. Washington, DC: *The Washington Post.* Retrieved from http://articles.washingtonpost.com/2013-01-02/politics/36103299_1_school-finance-school-districts-education-clauses; ACCESS. (2011). What are school funding "adequacy" lawsuits? New York: Author. Retrieved from http://www.schoolfunding.info/issues/handouts/adequacy_lawsuits.pdf.
24. National Access Network. (2010, June). Education adequacy liability decisions since 1989. *Access.* New York: Teachers College, Columbia University. Retrieved from http://www.schoolfunding.info/litigation/New_Charts/06_2010ed_adequacyliability.pdf.

25. Baker, K. (1991). Yes. Throw money at the schools. *Phi Delta Kappan 72*(8), 628–31; Hedges, L. V., Laine, R. D., and Greenwald, R. (1994). Does money matter: A meta analysis of studies of the effects of differential school inputs on student outcomes. *Educational Researcher 23*(3), 5–14; Verstegen, D., and King, R. (1998). The relationship between school spending and student achievement: A review and analysis of 35 years of production function research. *Journal of Education Finance 24*(2), 243–62; Cooper, B., and Associates. (1994, Fall). Making money matter in education: A micro-financial model for determine school-level allocations, efficiency, and productivity. *Journal of Education Finance 20,* 66–87; Fortune, J., and O'Neil, J. (1994). Production function analyses and the study of educational funding equity: A methodological critique. *Journal of Education Finance 20,* 21–46; Verstegen, D. (1994). Efficiency and equity in the provision and reform of American schooling. *Journal of Education Finance 20,* 107–31.
26. Condron, D. J., and Roscigno, V. J. (2003, January). Disparities within: Unequal spending and achievement in an urban school district. *Sociology of Education 76*(1), 18–36.
27. For more on how schools are funded and the effects of school finances on student achievement, see Owings and Kaplan. 2013, Op. cit. *American public school finance,* 2nd ed. Belmont, CA: Cengage.
28. Hightower, A. M. (2009, January 8). Securing progress, striving to improve. Quality counts 2009. *Education Week 28*(17), 44–47.
29. Snyder, T. D., Dillow, S. A., and Hoffman, C. M. (2008). *Digest of education statistics 2007 (NCES 2008-020).* Washington, DC: National Center for Education Statistics, Institute of Education Sciences, U.S. Department of Education, Table 93, pp. 151–53.
30. Spatig-Amerikaner, A. (2012, August). *Unequal education. Federal loophole enables lower spending on students of color.* Washington, DC: Center for American Progress. Retrieved from http://www.americanprogress.org/wp-content/uploads/2012/08/UnequalEduation-1.pdf.
31. Spaatig-Amerikaner. (2012, August). Op. cit.
32. Owings, W. A., and Kaplan, L. S. (2010, Fall). The alpha and omega syndrome: Is intra-district funding the next ripeness factor? *Journal of Education Finance 36*(2), 162–85.
33. Verstegen, D. A. (2002 October). The new finance. School spending: The business of education. *American School Board Journal.* Retrieved from http://www.asbj.com/schoolspending/aresources1002verstegen.html.
34. Kayitsinga, J., Post, L., and Villarruel, F. (2007, July). *Socioeconomic profile of Michigan's Latino population: Demographic report no. 3.* Ann Arbor, MI: University of Michigan, Julian Samora Research Institute. Retrieved from http://www.jsri.msu.edu/RandS/research/drs/dr03.html; Fletcher, M. A. (2007, November 13). Middle class dream eludes African American families. *WashingtonPost.com.* Retrieved from http://www.washingtonpost.com/wp-dyn/content/article/2007/11/12/AR2007111201711_pf.html; *Civil Rights 101: Minorities by the numbers.* (2000). Washington, DC: CivilRights.org. Retrieved from http://www.civilrights.org/research_center/acivilrights101/demographics.html.
35. Hoff, D. J. (2007, February 14). Economists tout value of reducing dropouts. *Education Week 26*(2), 5, 15.
36. Verstegen, D. (2002 Winter). Financing the new adequacy: Towards new models of state education finance systems that support standards based reform. *Journal of Education Finance 27,* 749–82.
37. Owings and Kaplan, 2013.
38. U.S. Department of Education, National Center for Education Statistics, *Digest of Education Statistics, 2012 (NCES 2012-001),* Indicator 1. Enrollment trends by age, Table A1 – 1, p. 16. Retrieved from http://nces.ed.gov/pubs2012/2012045_2.pdf.
39. Weiner and Pristoop, 2006, p. 6.
40. Roza, M. (2006). *How districts shortchange low-income and minority students: Funding gap 2006.* Washington, DC: The Education Trust, pp. 9–10. Retrieved from http://www2.edtrust.org/NR/ardonlyres/CDEF9403-5A75-437E-93FF-EBF1174181FB/0/FundingGap2006.pdf.
41. Roza, M., and Hill, P. (2004). How within-district spending inequities help some schools to fail. In *2004 Brookings Institute papers on education policy.* http://www.crpe.org/pubs/pdf/InequitiesRozaHillchapger.pdf.
42. Condron and Roscigno, 2003; Haycock, K. (2000, Spring). No more settling for less. *Thinking K-16 4,* 3–8, 10–12; Ingersoll, R. M. (June 2002). The teacher shortage: A case of wrong diagnosis and wrong prescription. *NASSP Bulletin, 86*(631), 16–30; Center for the Future of Teaching and Learning. (2003, December). *The status of the teaching profession 2003.* Santa Cruz, CA: Author. Retrieved from http://www.cftl.org.
43. Center for the Future of Teaching and Learning, 2003, p. 6.
44. Haycock, 2000; Ingersoll, 2002; Center for the Future of Teaching and Learning, 2003.
45. Kaplan, L. S., Owings, W. A., and Nunnery, J. (2005, June). Principal quality: A Virginia study connecting Interstate School Leaders Licensure Consortium (ISLLC) standards with student achievement. *National Association of Secondary School Principals Bulletin.* Reston, VA: National Association of Secondary School Principals.
46. Kane, T. J., Rockoff, J. E., and Staiger, D. O. (2007, Winter). Teachers' certification doesn't guarantee a winner. *Education Next 7*(1), 61–67; Ingersoll, R. (2003). *Is there really a teacher shortage?* Seattle, WA: Center for the Study of Teaching and Policy.
47. Condron and Roscigno, 2003.
48. Earthman, G. (2002). School facility conditions and student academic achievement. In *William Watch series: Investigating the claims of Williams v. State of California.* Los Angeles: UCLA Institute for Democracy, Education, and Access.
49. Bernier, M. (1993, April). Building conditions, parental involvement, and student achievement in the District of Columbia public school system. *Urban Education 28*(1), 6–29.
50. Danziger, J. N. (1980, December). California's Proposition 13 and the fiscal limitations movement in the United States. *Political Studies 28*(4), 599–612.
51. Cataldo, E. H., and Holm, J. D. (1983). Voting on school finances: A test of completing theories. *Western Political Quarterly 36*(4), 619–31; Reed, D. S. (2001, March). Not in my backyard: Localism and public opposition to funding schools equally. *Social Science Quarterly 82*(1), 34–50.
52. Reed, 2001.
53. Danziger, 1980; Strauss, R. P. (2000). *School finance reform: Moving from the school property tax to the income tax.* Paper presented at the 88th Annual Conference on Taxation, National Tax Association, San Diego, CA. Retrieved from http://www.andrew.cmu.edu/user/rs9f/nta95a.pdf.
54. Danziger, 1980, p. 604.
55. Danziger, 1980. Ibid.
56. Downes, G. (1992, December). Evaluating the impact of school finance reform on the provision of public education: The case of California. *National Tax Journal 45*(4), 405–19.

57. Henke, J. T. (1986, Fall). Financing public schools in California: The aftermath of the *Serrano v. Priest* decision. *University of San Francisco Law Review 21,* 1–39.
58. For more on teacher quality, see Kaplan, L., and Owings, W. (2003). *Teacher quality, teaching quality, and school improvement.* Bloomington, IN: Phi Delta Kappan; and Chapter 13 of this text.
59. Darling-Hammond, L. (2000). Teacher quality and student achievement: A review of state policy evidence. *Education Policy Analysis Archives 8*(1). Retrieved from http://epaa.asu.edu/epaa/v8n1/.
60. Darling-Hammond, 2000.
61. Johns, R., Morphet, E., and Alexander, K. (1983). *The economics and financing of education* (4th ed.). Secaucus, NJ: Prentice Hall, p. 305.
62. "Novice" in this case refers to teaches with three years or less experience. National Center for Education Statistics. (2000, December). *Monitoring quality: An indicators report,* cited in Peske and Haycock, 2006.
63. Jerald, C. D. (2002). *All talk, no action: Putting an end to out-of-field teaching.* Washington, DC: The Education Trust.
64. Peske, H. G., and Haycock, K. (2006, June). *Teaching inequality: How poor and minority students are shortchanged on teacher quality.* Washington, DC: The Education Trust, p. 11.
65. Teaching Commission. (2004). *Teaching at risk: A call to action.* New York: Author, p. 26. Retrieved from http://www.csl.usf.edu/teaching%20at%20risk.pdf.
66. Nye, B., Hodges, L. V., and Konstantopoulos, S. (2000, Spring). The effects of small class size on academic achievement: The results of the Tennessee class size experiment. *American Educational Research Journal 37,* 123–51.
67. Stecher, B., Bornstedt, G., Dirst, M., McRobbie, J., and Williams, T. (2001, June). Class size reduction in California: A story of hope, promise, and unintended consequences. *Phi Delta Kappan 82,* 670–74.
68. Robinson, G. (1990, April). Synthesis of research on the effects of class size. *Educational Leadership 47*(7), 80–90.
69. Addonizio, M., and Phelps, J. (2000, Fall). Class size and student performance: A framework for policy analysis. *Journal of Education Finance 26,* 135–56.
70. Konstantopoulis, S. (2008, March). Do small classes reduce the achievement gap between low and high achievers? Evidence from Project STAR. *Elementary School Journal 108*(4), 275–92.
71. Jacobson, L. (2008, February 27). Class-size reductions seen of limited help on achievement gap. *Education Week 27*(25), 9.
72. Blair, J. (2000, October). ETS study inks effective teaching methods to test-score gains. *Education Week 25,* 24–25.
73. Hirsh, E., Koppcih, E., and Knapp, M. S. (1998, December). *What states are doing to improve the quality of teaching: A brief review of current patterns and trends.* Seattle, WA: Center for the Study of Teaching and Policy.
74. Environmental Protection Agency (EPA). (2000). Indoor air quality and student performance (Report No. EPA 402-F-00-009). Washington, DC: Author. Retrieved from http//epa.gov/iaq/schools/performance.html.
75. Shaughnessy, R., Haverinen-Shaughnessy, U., Nevalainen, A., and Moschandreas, D. (2006). A preliminary study on the association between ventilation rates in classrooms and student performance. *Indoor Air 16*(6), 465–68; Uline, C., and Tschannen-Moran, M. (2008). The walls speak: The interplay of quality facilities, school climate, and student achievement. *Journal of Educational Administration 46*(1), 55–73.
76. Durán-Narucki, V. (2008). School building condition, school attendance, and academic achievement in New York City public schools: A mediation model. *Journal of Environmental Psychology 28*(3), 278–86.
77. American Lung Association. (2002). *Asthma in children fact sheet.* New York: Author. Retrieved from http://www.lungusa.org/asthma/ascpedfac99.html; EPA (2000). Op. cit.
78. Earthman, G., 2002.
79. Berner, M. (1993, April). Building conditions, parental involvement, and student achievement in the District of Columbia public school system. *Urban Education 28*(1), 6–29.

Chapter 12

1. The Josephson Institute. (2011). *The ethics of American youth.* 2010 Report card reveals widespread lying, cheating, bullying, and other at-risk behavior in high school students. Retrieved from http://charactercounts.org/programs/reportcard/2010/installment02_report-card_honesty-integrity.html; http://charactercounts.org/programs/reportcard/.
2. Slobogin, K. (2002, April 5). Survey: Many students say cheating's OK. Education. *CNN.com.* Retrieved from http://archives.cnn.com/2002/fyi/teachers.ednews/04/05/highschool.cheating/.
3. Mann, K. L. (2007, June 13). Thoughts on cheating. *Education Week 26*(41), 33.
4. Mann, 2007.
5. Marzano, R. J. (2003). *What works in schools: Translating research into action.* Alexandria, VA: Association for Supervision and Curriculum Development, p. 19.
6. Marsh, C. J. (2004). *Key concepts for understanding curriculum,* 3rd ed. London, UK: Routledge, p. 3.
7. Huebner, D. (1976). The moribund curriculum field: Its wake and our work. *Curriculum Inquiry 6*(2), 153–67.
8. John Kerr, as quoted in Kelly, A. V. (1983/1999). *The curriculum. theory and practice,* 4th ed. London, UK: Paul Chapman, p. 10.
9. Taba, H. (1962). *Curriculum development: Theory and practice.* New York: Harcourt Brace and World.
10. Eisner, E. W. (1992, April). The misunderstood role of the arts in human development. *Phi Delta Kappan 73*(8), 592.
11. Boyer, E. L. (1995). The educated person. In J. A. Beane (Ed.), *Toward a coherent curriculum* (pp. 16–25). Alexandra, VA: Association for Supervision and Curriculum Development.
12. Eisner, E. W. (2003, May). Questionable assumptions about schooling. *Phi Delta Kappan 84*(9), 651.
13. Eisner, 2003, pp. 655–56.
14. Brady, M. (2000, May). The standards juggernaut. *Phi Delta Kappan 81*(9), 649–51.
15. Brady, 2000, p. 650.
16. Apple, M. W. (1995). Facing reality. In J. A. Beane (Ed.), *Toward a coherent curriculum* (pp. 130–38). Alexandria, VA: Association for Supervision and Curriculum Development, p. 130.
17. Franklin, B. M. (1977, Spring). Review: Curriculum history: Its nature and boundaries. *Curriculum Inquiry 7*(1), 67–79.
18. Mehl, B. (1960). The Conant Report and the Committee of Ten: A historical appraisal. *Educational Research Bulletin 39*(2), 29–38, 56.
19. Goodlad, 1986/1987.
20. This was an essentialist curriculum, as described in Chapter 3.
21. National Commission on Excellence in Education. (1983). *A nation at risk.* Washington, DC: U.S. Government Printing Office.
22. The viewpoints and individuals described in Chapter 6, Competing Goals of Public Education, all have important curricular implications.
23. Chiarelott, L. (2006). *Curriculum in context: Designing curriculum and instruction for teaching and learning in context.* Belmont, CA: Thomson Wadsworth.

24. Tyler, R. W. (1949). *Basic principles of curriculum and instruction.* Chicago, IL: University of Chicago Press.
25. Chiarelott, 2006, p. 30.
26. Taba, 1962.
27. Taba, 1962, p. 12: Krull, E. (2003, October). Hilda Taba (1902–1967). *Prospects* (UNESCO, International Bureau of Education) *33*(4), 481–91.
28. Denham, A., and Shutes, R. E. (1986, February). Too good to miss: Review of Hilda Taba. *Curriculum development: Theory and practice. English Journal 75*(2), 97–98.
29. Bloom, B. J. (Ed.). (1956). *Taxonomy of education objectives: The classification of educational goals. Handbook I: Cognitive domain.* New York: David McKay.
30. Bloom, B. (1985). Benjamin Bloom replies: Bloom's taxonomy and critical thinking instruction. *Educational Leadership 42*(8), 39.
31. Adapted from Bloom, 1956.
32. Anderson, L. W., and Krathwohl, D. R. (Eds.). (2001). *A taxonomy of learning, teaching, and assessment: A revision of Bloom's taxonomy of educational objectives* (pp. 67–68). New York: Addison, Wesley Longman.
33. For a complete discussion of both models, see Krathwohl, D. R. (2004, Autumn). A revision of Bloom's taxonomy: An overview. *Theory into Practice 41*(4), 212–18.
34. See Figure 12.1 (right side), the "revised" taxonomy.
35. Wiggins, G., and McTighe, J. (1998). *Understanding by design.* Alexandria, VA: Association for Supervision and Curriculum Development, p. vii.
36. Wiggins and McTighe, 1998, pp. 7–19.
37. This is a simplified overview of Wiggins and McTighe's thinking. We refer the reader to the original source for more information.
38. Wiggins and McTighe, 1998, pp. 44–62.
39. Wiggins and McTighe, 1998, p. 146.
40. Backward design considers learning from the students' point of view.
41. Jacobs, H. H. (2004). Development of a consensus map: Wrestling with curriculum consistency and flexibility. In H. H. Jacobs (Ed.), *Getting results with curriculum mapping* (pp. 25–35). Alexandria, VA: Association for Supervision and Curriculum Development.
42. Daro, P. (2006, February 15). Math warriors, lay down your weapons. Commentary. *Education Week 25*(23), 34, 35.
43. Reys, B., and Lappan, G. (2007).Consensus or confusion? The intended math curriculum in state-level standards. *Phi Delta Kappan 88*(9), 678–80.
44. National Center for Education Statistics. (2011. November). Mathematics 2011. *National assessment of educational progress at grades 4 and 8 (NCES 2012-458).* Washington, DC: Institute of Education Sciences, U.S. Department of Education. Retrieved from http://nces.ed.gov/nationsreportcard/pdf/main2011/2012458.pdf.
45. National Center for Education Statistics. (2010). *The nation's report card: Grade 12 reading and mathematics 2009. National and pilot state results (NCES 2011-455).* Washington, DC: Institute of Education Sciences, U.S. Department of Education. Retrieved from http://nces.ed.gov/nationsreportcard/pdf/main2009/2011455.pdf.
46. Leinwand, S. (2009, January 7). Moving mathematics out of mediocrity: Commentary. *Education Week 28*(16), 32.
47. Leinwand, 2009, pp. 32–33; Schmidt, W. H. (2005, Fall). The role of curriculum. *American Educator.* Washington, DC: American Federation of Teachers. Retrieved from http://www.aft.org/pubs-reports/american_educator/issues/fall2005/schmidt.htm; Schmidt, W. H. (2004). A vision for mathematics. *Educational Leadership 61*(5), 6–11.
48. Schmidt, W. (2012, July 18). Seizing the moment for mathematics. Commentary. *Education Week 31* (36), 24–25.
49. National Center for Education Statistics. (2012). *Trends in International Mathematics and Science Study (TIMSS). Mathematics achievement of fourth- and eighth-graders in 2011.* Washington, DC: National Center for Education Statistics, Institute of Education Sciences. Retrieved from http://nces.ed.gov/timss/results11_math11.asp.
50. Schmidt, 2012.
51. Barzun, J. (1991). The centrality of reading. In M. Philipson (Ed.), *Begin here: The forgotten conditions of teaching and learning* (p. 21). Chicago, IL: University of Chicago Press.
52. Hillocks, G. (1987, May). Synthesis of research on teaching writing. *Educational Leadership 44*(8), 71–82.
53. Samuels, C. A. (2007, September 12). Experts eye solutions to "4th grade slump." *Education Week 27*(3), 8.
54. National Center for Education Statistics. (2011). *The nation's report card: Reading 2011 (NCES 2012-457).* Washington, DC: Institute of Education Sciences, U.S. Department of Education. Retrieved from http://nces.ed.gov/nationsreportcard/pdf/main2011/2012457.pdf.
55. For NAEP, see: National Center for Education Statistics. (2011). *Indicator 23. Reading performance.* Washington, DC: Institute of Education Sciences, U.S. Department of Education. Retrieved from http://nces.ed.gov/programs/coe/pdf/coe_rd2.pdf; for PIRLS, see: Mullis, V. S., Martin, M. O., Foy, P., and Drucker, K. T. (2012). *PIRLS 2011 International Results in Reading.* Chestnut Hill, MA: TIMSS and PRILS International Study Center, Lynch School of Education, Boston College. Retrieved from http://timss.bc.edu/pirls2011/downloads/P11_IR_FullBook.pdf.
56. Cavanaugh, S. (2006, September 27). Panel points way to improving K–8 science learning. *Education Week 26*(5), 14; Duschl, R. A., Schweingruber, H. A., and Shouse, A. W. (Eds.). (2007). *Taking science to school: Learning and teaching science in grades K–8.* Washington, DC: National Academies Press, Executive Summary.
57. Cavanaugh, S. (2009, March 11). "Depth" matters in high school science studies. *Education Week 28*(24), 1, 16–17.
58. Robelen, E. W. (2012, May 16). Public gets glimpse of science standards. *Education Week 31*(31), 1, 15.
59. Roth, K. (2007, October 10). Science teaching around the world: Lessons for U.S. classrooms. *Education Week 27*(7), 9. Comparison countries in this study included the Czech Republic, Japan, Australia, and the Netherlands.
60. Fleming, N. (2012, July 18). NAEP shows science-standards mastery a long way off. *Education Week 31*(36), 8–9.
61. Martin, M. O., Mullis, I. V., Foy, P., and Stanco, G. M. (2012). *TIMSS 2011 international results in science.* Chestnut Hill, MA: Lynch School of Education. TIMSS & PIRLS International Study Center. Retrieved from http://timssandpirls.bc.edu/timss2011/downloads/T11_IR_Science_FullBook.pdf.
62. Hoff, D. J., and Cavanaugh, S. (2007, May 2). Math–science bills advance in Congress. *Education Week 26*(35), 23.
63. National Council for the Social Studies. (n.d.). *About national council for the social studies.* Silver Springs, MD. Retrieved from http://www.socialstudies.org/about.
64. National Center for Education Statistics. (2011, June). *The nation's report card: U.S. history 2010. National assessment of educational progress at grades 4, 8, and 12 (NCES 2011-468).* Washington, DC: Institute for Education Science, U.S. Department of Education.

Retrieved from http://nces.ed.gov/nationsreportcard/pdf/main2010/2011468.pdf; National Center for Education Statistics. (2011, May). *Civics 2010. National assessment of educational progress at grades 4, 8, and 12 (NCES 2011-466).* Washington, DC: Institute for Education Sciences, U.S. Department of Education. Retrieved from http://nces.ed.gov/nationsreportcard/pdf/main2010/2011466.pdf.

65. National Center for Education Statistics, 2011, June. Op. cit.
66. National Center for Education Statistics, 2011, May. Op. cit.
67. Kirby, E. H., and Marcelo, K. M. (2006, December 12). *Young voters in the 2006 elections.* Washington, DC: Center for Information and Research on Civic Learning and Engagement. Retrieved from http://www.civicyouth.org/PopUps/FactSheets/FS-Midterm06.pdf; Pillsbury, G., and Johannesen, J. (2012). *America goes to the polls 2012. A report on voter turnout in the 2012 election.* Boston: NonprofitVote. Retrieved from http://www.nonprofitvote.org/voter-turnout.html.
68. New national poll finds: More Americans know Snow White's dwarfs than Supreme Court judges, Homer Simpson than Homer's Odyssey, and Harry Potter than Tony Blair. *Zogby International.* Retrieved from http://www.zogby.com/templates/printsb.cfm?id=13498.
69. Gerwitz, C. (2012, August 8). Rid of memorization, history lessons build analytical skills. *Education Week 31*(37), 10–11.
70. Matthews, J. (2007, May 17). Fourth graders improve history, civics scores; seniors make significant gains nationally. *The Washington Post*, p. A09.
71. Seigesmund, R. (2005, September). Teaching qualitative reasoning: Portraits of practice. *Phi Delta Kappan 87*(1), 18–23.
72. Burton, J., Horowitz, R., and Abeles, H. (2000). Learning in and through the arts: Curriculum implications. In E. B. Fiske (Ed.), *Champions of change: The impact of the arts on learning* (pp. 35–46). Washington, DC: Arts Education Partnership and the President's Commission on Arts and the Humanities.
73. Catterall, J. S. (2002). Involvement in the arts and success of secondary students. In R. Deasy (Ed.), *Critical links: Learning in the arts and student achievement and social development* (pp. 68–69). Washington, DC: Arts Education Partnership.
74. Murfee, E. (1995). *Eloquent evidence: Arts at the core of learning.* Washington, DC: President's Committee on the Arts and Humanities, p. 3; College Board. (2005). *2005 College-bound seniors: Total group profile report,* Table 3.3; Vaughn, K., and Winner, E. (2000, Fall). SAT scores of students who study the arts: What we can and cannot conclude about the association. *Journal of Aesthetic Education, 34*(3–4), 77–89. Special Issue. The Arts and Academic Achievement: What the Evidence Shows. Ruppert, S. S. (2006). *Critical evidence. How the arts benefit student achievement.* Washington, DC: National Assembly of State Art Agencies and The Arts Education Partnership, p. 9. Retrieved from http://www.nasaa-arts.org/Research/Key-Topics/Arts-Education/critical-evidence.pdf.
75. Vaughn, K. (2002). Music and mathematics: Modest support for the oft-claimed relationship. In R. Deasy (Ed.), *Critical links: Learning in the arts and student academic and social development* (pp. 130–31). ERIC (ED466413). Washington, DC: Arts Education Partnership.
76. Catterall, J. S., Chapleau, R., and Iwanaga, J. (2002). Involvement in the arts and human development: Extending an analysis of general associations and introducing the special cases of intensive involvement in music and theatre arts. In R. Deasy (Ed.), *Critical links: Learning in the arts and student academic and social development* (pp. 70–71). ERIC (ED466413). Washington, DC: Arts Education Partnership.
77. Deasy, R. J. (Ed.). *Critical links: Learning in the arts and student academic and social development.* ERIC (ED466413). Washington, DC: Arts Education Partnership. A complete version is available at http://www.aep-arts.org/files/publications/CriticalLinks.pdf; Deasy, R. J. (2003, January/February). Don't axe the arts! *Principal 82*(3), 15–8. Arlington, VA: National Association of Elementary School Principals.
78. Eisner, E. W. (1998, January). Does experience in the arts boost academic achievement? *Arts Education 51*(1), 7–15; Viadero, D. (2008, March 12). Insights gained into arts and smarts. *Education Week 27*(27), 1, 10–11.
79. Winner, E., and Cooper, M. (2000, Autumn/Winter). Mute those claims: No evidence (yet) for a causal link between arts study and academic achievement. *Journal of Aesthetic Education 34*(3/4), 63.
80. Viadero, 2008.
81. Eisner, E. W. (2004, December/January). Preparing for today and tomorrow. *Educational Leadership 61*(4), 6–11.
82. Eisner, E. W. (1992, April). The misunderstood role of the arts in human development. *Phi Delta Kappan 73*(8), 591–95.
83. Schubert, W. H. (1995). Toward lives worth living and sharing: Historical perspective on curriculum coherence. In J. A. Beane (Ed.), *Toward a coherent curriculum: The 1995 ASCD yearbook* (pp. 146–57). Alexandria, VA: Association for Supervision and Curriculum Development.
84. Noddings, N. (2005, September). What does it mean to educate the whole child? *Educational Leadership 63*(1), 8–13.
85. Rothstein, R., and Jacobsen, R. (2006, December). The goals of education. *Phi Delta Kappan 88*(4), 264–72, Table, p. 271.
86. Viadero, D. (2008, February 13). Exercise seen as priming pump for students' academic strides. *Education Week 27*(23), 14–15; Toporek, B. (2012, January 11). Physical activity linked to school success. Blogs of the Week. *Education Week 31*(15), 13.
87. Castelli, D. M., Hillman, C. H., Buck, S. M., and Erwin, H. (2007). Physical fitness and academic achievement in 3rd and 5th grade students. *Journal of Sport and Exercise Psychology 29,* 239–52.
88. Viadero, D. (2007, December 19). Social-skills programs found to yield gains in academic subjects. *Education Week 27*(16), 1, 15; Zubrzycki, J. (2012, September 19). Researchers link 'responsive' classes to learning gains. *Education Week 32*(4), 8.
89. Durlak, J. A., Weissberg, R. P., Dymnicki, A. B., and Schellinger, K. B. (2011). The impact of enhancing students' social and emotional learning: A meta-analysis of school-based universal interventions. *Child Development 82*(1), 405–32.
90. Southgate, D. E., and Roscigno, V. J. (2009). The impact of music on child and adolescent achievement. *Social Science Quarterly 90*(1), 4–21.
91. Lee, J. (2006). *Tracking achievement gaps and assessing the impact of NCLB on the gaps: An in-depth look into national and state reading and math outcome trends.* Cambridge, MA: Civil Rights Project at Harvard University.
92. Armstrong, T. (2007, May). The curriculum superhighway. *Educational Leadership, 64*(8), 16–20.
93. Eisner, E. W. (2005, September). Back to the whole. *Educational Leadership 63*(1), 14–18.
94. Eisner, 2005, p. 18.
95. Brooks, J. G., Libresco, A. S., and Plonczak, I. (2007, June). Spaces of liberty: Battling the new soft bigotry of NCLB. *Phi Delta Kappan 88*(10), 750.

Chapter 13

1. Guilmart, L. (2008, June 4). "An Impossible choice": A young teacher hits the five-year wall. *Education Week 27*(39), 24.
2. Jacobson, L. (2007, April 4). Study casts doubt on value of "highly qualified" status. *Education Week 26*(31), 13.
3. Richard Elmore, cited in Schmoker, M., and Allington, R. (2007, May, 16). The gift of bleak research: How the Pianta classroom study can help schools improve immediately. Commentary. *Education Week 26*(37), 28.
4. Marzano, R. J., Pickering, D. J., and Pollock, J. E. (2001). *Classroom instruction that works: Research-based strategies for increasing student achievement.* Alexandria, VA: Association for Supervision and Curriculum Development, p. 10.
5. Marzano, Pickering, and Pollock, 2001, p. 1.
6. As we discussed in Chapter 5, the 1966 Coleman Report concluded that the quality of schooling a student receives accounted for only 10 percent of the differences in student achievement. The other 90 percent could be attributed to students' natural ability, socioeconomic status, and home environment. Christopher Jencks' *Inequality* came to similar conclusions.
7. Brophy, J., and Good, T. (1986). Teacher behavior and student achievement. In M. Wittrock (Ed.), *Handbook of research on teaching.* New York: Macmillan, p. 370.
8. Sanders, W. L., and Horn, S. P. (1995). Educational assessment reassessed: The usefulness of standardized and alternative measures of student achievement as indicates for the assessment of educational outcomes. *Education Policy Analysis Archives 3*(6), 1–15. Retrieved from http://epaa.asu.edu/epaa/v3n6.html; Sanders, W. L., and Rivers, J. C. (1996, November). *Cumulative and residual effects of teachers on future student academic achievement.* Knoxville: University of Tennessee Value-Added Research and Assessment Center; Webster, W. J., and Mendro, R. L. (1997). The Dallas value-added accountability system. In J. Millman (Ed.), *Grading teachers, grading schools: Is student achievement a valid evaluation measure?* Thousand Oaks, CA: Corwin Press, pp. 81–99; Webster, W. J., Mendro, R. L., Orsak, T. H., and Weerasinghe, D. (1998a). *An application of hierarchical linear modeling to the estimation of school and teacher effect.* Dallas, TX: Dallas Independent School District. Retrieved from http://www.dallasisd.org/depts/inst_research/aer98ww2/aer98ww2.htm; Webster, W. J., Mendro, R. L., Orsak, T. H., and Weerasinghe, D. (1998b). *An application of hierarchical linear modeling to the estimation of school and teacher effects: Relevant results.* Dallas, TX: Dallas Independent School District. Retrieved from http://www. dallasisd.org/depts/inst_research/aer98ww2/aer98ww2.htm.
9. Sanders and Rivers, 1996.
10. Haycock, K. (1998, Summer). Good teaching matters—a lot. *Thinking K–16*, 3–14.
11. Sanders, W., and Horn, S. P. (1994). The Tennessee value-added assessment system (TVAAS): Mixed model methodology in educational assessment. *Journal of Personnel Evaluation in Education 8*, 299–311; Wright, S. P., Horn, S. P., and Sanders, W. L. (1997). Teacher and classroom context effects on student achievement: Implications for teacher evaluation. *Journal of Personnel Evaluation in Education 11*, 57–67.
12. Wright, Horn, and Sanders, 1997, p. 63.
13. Nye, B., Konstantopoulos, S., and Hedges, L. V. (2004). How large are teacher effects? *Educational Evaluation and Policy Analysis 26*(3), 237–57; Marzano, R. (2007). *The art and science of teaching: A comprehensive framework for effective instruction.* Alexandria, VA: Association for Supervision and Curriculum Development, pp. 2–3.
14. Wenglinsky, H. (2000). *How teaching matters: Bringing the classroom back into discussions of teacher quality.* Princeton, NJ: The Milliken Family Foundation and Educational Testing Service, p. 31.
15. Chetty, R., Friedman, J. N., and Rockoff, J. E. (2011, December). The long-term impacts of teachers: Teacher value-added and student outcomes in adulthood (NBER Working Paper No. 17699). Washington, DC: National Bureau of Economic Research. Retrieved from http://www.nber.org/papers/w17699.
16. Walsh, K. (2001). *Teacher certification reconsidered: Stumbling for quality.* Baltimore: Abell Foundation; Darling-Hammond, L. (2000, January 1). Teacher quality and student achievement: A review of state policy evidence. *Educational Policy Analysis Archives 8*(1). Retrieved from http://epaa.asu. edu/epaa/v8n1; Haycock, 1998; Whitehurst, G. J. (2002, March). *Scientifically based research on teacher quality: Research on teacher preparation and professional development.* Paper presented at White House Conference on Preparing Tomorrow's Teachers.
17. Blair, J. (2000, October 5). ETS study links effective teaching methods to test-score gains. *Education Week 20*(8), 24–25; Goldhaber, D. D., and Brewer, D. J. (2000, Summer). Does teacher certification matter? High school teacher certification status and student achievement. *Educational Evaluation and Policy Analysis 22*(2), 129–45; Wenglinsky, H. 2000, October. *How teaching matters: Bringing the classroom back into discussions of teacher quality.* Princeton, NJ: Milken Family Foundation and Educational Testing Service.
18. Berry, B. (2001, May). No shortcuts to preparing god teachers. *Educational Leadership 58*(8), 32–36; Wilson, S., et al. (2002). Teacher preparation research: An insider's view from the outside. *Journal of Teacher Education 53*(3), 190–204.
19. Monk, D. H. (1994). Subject matter preparation of secondary mathematics and science teachers and student achievement. *Economics of Education Review 13*(2), 125–45.
20. Kanstoroom, M., and Finn, C. E., Jr. (Eds.). (1999, July). *Better teachers, better schools.* Washington, DC: Thomas B. Fordham Foundation.
21. Kaplan, L. S., and Owings, W. A. (2003, May). The politics of teacher quality. *Phi Delta Kappan 84*(9), 688.
22. Darling-Hammond, 2000, p. 27.
23. Guyton, E., and Farokhi, E. (1987, September/October). Relationships among academic performance, basic skills, and subject-matter knowledge and teaching skills of teacher education graduates. *Journal of Teacher Education 38*(5), 37–42.
24. Monk, D., and King, J. A. (1994). Multi-level teacher resource effects in pupil performance in secondary mathematics and science: The case of teacher subject-matter preparation. In R. G. Ehrenberg (Ed.), *Choices and consequences: Contemporary policy issues in education.* Ithaca, NY: ILR Press, pp. 29–58.
25. Monk, 1994. Monk conceded, however, that variations in the content of the college math courses made it difficult to draw definite conclusions.
26. Johnson, K. A. (2000, September). The effects of advanced teacher training in education of student achievement. *Report of the Heritage Center for Data Analysis*, No. 00–09, pp. 1–17; Greenwald, R., Hedges, L. V., and Laine, R. D. (1996). The effect of school resources on student achievement. *Review of Educational Research 66*(3), 361–96.
27. Munro, J. (1999, June). Learning more about learning improves teacher effectiveness. *School Effectiveness and School Improvement 10*(2), 151–71.
28. Barton, P. E., Coley, R., and Wenglinsky, H. (1998). *Order in the classroom: Violence, discipline, and student achievement.* Princeton, NJ: Educational Testing Service.

29. Hoy, W. K., and Miskel, C. G. (2008). *Educational administration: Theory, research, and practice.* Boston, MA: McGraw-Hill Higher Education, p. 43.
30. Woolfolk, A. (2007). *Educational psychology*, 10th ed. Boston, MA: Allyn & Bacon.
31. Rosenshine, B.., and Stevens, R. (1986). Teaching functions. In M. Whittrock (Ed.), *Teaching research on teaching*, 3rd ed. New York: Macmillan, pp. 376–91.
32. Rosenshine, B. (1988). Explicit teaching. In D. Berliner and B. Rosenshine (Eds.), *Talks to teachers*. New York: Random House, pp. 75–92; Rosenshine and Stevens, 1986.
33. Anderson, L. M. (1989). Learners and learning. In M. Reynolds (Ed.), *Knowledge base for beginning teachers*. New York: Pergamon, pp. 85–100; Berg, C. A., and Clough, M. (1991). Hunter lesson design: The wrong one for science teaching. *Educational Leadership 48*(4), 73–78.
34. Kirschner, P. A., Sweller, J., and Clark, R. E. (2006). Why minimal guidance during instruction does not work: An analysis of the failure of constructivist, discovery, problem-based, experiential, and inquiry-based teaching. *Educational Psychologist 41*(2), 75–86; Weinert, F. E., and Helmke, A. (1995). Learning from wise Mother Nature or Big Brother instructor: The wrong choice as seen from an educational perspective. *Educational Psychologist 30*(3), 135–43.
35. Kirschner, Sweller, and Clark, 2006.
36. Ashcraft, M. H. (2006). *Cognition*, 4th ed.. Upper Saddle River, NJ: Prentice Hall; Bransford, J. D., Brown, A. L., and Cocking, R. R. (2000). *How people learn: Brain, mind, experience, and school.* Washington, DC: National Academy Press.
37. Ashcraft, 2006; Driscoll, M. P. (2005). *Psychology of learning for instruction*, 3rd ed. Boston, MA: Allyn & Bacon.
38. Miller, G. A. (1956). The magical number seven, plus or minus two: Some limits on our capacity for processing information. *Psychological Review 63,* 81–97.
39. Nuthall, G. (1999). The way students learn: Acquiring knowledge from an integrated science and social studies unit. *Elementary School Journal 99*(4), 303–41; Rovee-Collier, C. (1995). Time windows in cognitive development. *Developmental Psychology 31*(2), 147–69.
40. Marzano, R. J. (2004). *Building background knowledge for academic achievement*. Alexandria, VA: Association for Supervision and Curriculum Development.
41. Marzano, 2004.
42. Alexander, P. A., Kulikowich, J. M., and Schulze, S. K. (1994). How subject-matter affects recall and interest. *Review of Educational Research 31*(2), 313–37; Bloom, B. S. (1976). *Human characteristics and school learning*. New York: McGraw-Hill; Dochy, F., Segers, M., and Buehl, M. M. (1999). The relationship between assessment practices and outcomes of studies: The case of research on prior knowledge. *Review of Educational Research, 69*(2), 145–186; Nagy, W. E., Anderson, R. C., & Herman, P. A. (1987). Learning word meaning from context during normal reading. *American Educational Research Journal 24*(2), 237–70; Tamir, P. (1996). Science assessment. In M. Birenbaum and F. J. R. C. Dochy (Eds.), *Alternatives in assessment of achievements, learning processes, and prior knowledge*. Boston, MA: Kluwer, pp. 93–129; Tobias, S. (1994). Interest, prior knowledge, and learning. *Review of Educational Research 64*(1), 37–54.
43. Bruner, J. (1990). *Acts of meaning*. Cambridge, MA: Harvard University Press.
44. Bjorklund. D. F. (1990). *Children's strategies: Contemporary view of cognitive development.* Hillsdale, NJ: Erlbaum Associates.
45. Bjorklund, 1990.
46. Anderson, J. R., Reder, L. M., and Simon, H. A. (1997, February). Rejoinder: Situated versus cognitive perspectives: Form versus substance. *Educational Researcher 26*(1), 18–21.
47. Fosnot, C. T. (1993). Preface. In J. G. Brooks and M. G. Brooks, *In search of understanding: The case for constructivist classrooms.* Alexandra, VA: Association for Supervision and Curriculum Development, pp. v–vii.
48. Danielson, C. (1996). *Enhancing professional practice: A framework for teaching.* Alexandria, VA: Association for Supervision and Curriculum Development.
49. Piaget, J. (1954). *The construction of reality in the child.* New York: Basic Books.
50. Farnham-Diggory, S. (1990). *Schooling.* Cambridge, MA: Harvard University Press.
51. Stone, M. K. (1999). The Francis Parker School: Chicago's progressive education legacy. In S. F. Semel and A. R. Sadovnik (Eds.), *Schools of tomorrow, schools of today: What happened to progressive education*. New York: Lang, pp. 23–66.
52. Dewey, J. (1902/1956). *The child and the curriculum.* Chicago, IL: University of Chicago Press.
53. For a thorough discussion of constructivist pedagogy, see Windschitl, M. (2002). Framing constructivism in practice as the negotiation of dilemmas: An analysis of the conceptual, pedagogical, cultural, and political challenges facing teachers. *Review of Educational Research 72*(2), 131–75.
54. Von Glasersfeld, E. (1993). Questions and answers about radical constructivism. In K. Tobin (Ed.), *The practice of constructivism in science education*. Hillsdale, NJ: Lawrence Erlbaum Associates, pp. 23–38.
55. Windschitl, 2002.
56. Elmore, R., Peterson, P., and McCarthey, S. (1996). *Restructuring in the classroom.* San Francisco: Jossey-Bass; McLaughlin, M. W., and Talbert, J. W. (1993). Introduction: New visions of teaching. In D. Cohen and J. E. Talbert (Eds.), *Teaching for understanding: Challenges for policy and practice.* San Francisco, CA: Jossey-Bass; National Research Council. (2000). *How people learn: Brain, mind, experience, and school.* Washington, DC: National Academy Press; Wiggins, G., and McTighe, J. (1998). *Understanding by design.* Alexandria, VA: Association for Supervision and Curriculum Development; Wiske, M. S. (1997). *Teaching for understanding: Linking research with practice.* San Francisco: Jossey-Bass.
57. Knapp, M. S., and Associates. (1995). *Teaching for meaning in high-poverty classrooms.* New York: Teachers College Press.
58. Newmann, F., et al. (1996). *Authentic achievement.* San Francisco: Jossey-Bass.
59. Semel, S. F., and Sadovnik, A. R. (1999). Progressive education: Lessons from the past and present. In S. F. Semel and A. R. Sadovnik (Eds.), *Schools of tomorrow, schools of today: What happened to progressive education.* New York: Lang, pp. 353–76.
60. Chung, S., and Walsh, D. (2000). Unpacking child-centeredness: A history of meanings. *Journal of Curriculum Studies 32*(2), 215–34.
61. Jackson, P. W. (1986). *The practice of teaching.* New York: Teachers College Press.
62. Newmann et al., 1996.
63. Brooks, J. G., Libresco, A. S., and Plonczak, I. (2007, May). Spaces of liberty: Battling the new soft bigotry of NCLB. *Phi Delta Kappan 88*(10), 749–56.
64. Richardson, V. (2003, December). Constructive pedagogy. *Teachers College Record 105*(9), 1623–40.
65. Students require more time to construct a concept that makes sense and has meaning to them and that is also consistent with

the "official knowledge" than to simply be told about it. The former approach also requires more teacher planning time.
66. Newmann et al., 1996.
67. Shepard, L. (2000). The role of assessment in a learning culture. *Educational Researcher 29*(7), 4–14.
68. Windschitl, 2002.
69. Newmann et al., 1996, p. 285.
70. Newmann et al., 1996, p. 285.
71. Windschitl, 2002, p. 137.
72. Newmann et al., 1996, p. 285.
73. Bransford, J. D., Brown, A. L., and Cockling, R. R. (Eds.) (2002). *How people learn: Brain, mind, and school.* Washington, DC: National Academy Press, p. 8.
74. Abbott, M. L., and Fouts, J. T. (2003, February). *Constructivist teaching and student achievement: The results of a school-level classroom observation study in Washington.* Seattle: Washington School Research Center, South Pacific University, Technical Report No. 5. Retrieved from http://www.spu.edu/orgs/research/ObservationStudy-2-13-03.pdf.
75. Schmoker, M. (2002). The real causes of higher achievement. Southwest Educational Development Laboratory. Retrieved from http://www.sedl.org/pubs/sedletter/v14n02/1.html.
76. Lord, T. R. (1999). A comparison between traditional and constructivist teaching in environmental science. *Journal of Environmental Education 30,* 22–28.
77. Darling-Hammond, L. (2006, October). Securing the right to learn: Policy and practice for powerful teaching and learning. *Educational Researcher 35*(7), 18; Darling-Hammond, L., et al. (2005). Does teacher preparation matter? Evidence about teaching certification, Teach for America, and teacher effectiveness. *Education Policy Analysis Archives 13*(42). Retrieved from http://epaa.asu.edu/epaav13n42; Elmore, R., and Burney, D. (1997). *Investing in teacher learning: Staff development and instructional improvement in Community District #2.* New York: National Commission on Teaching and America's Future; Wilson, S. M., Darling-Hammond, L., and Berry, B. (2001). *Teaching policy: Connecticut's long-term efforts to improve teaching and learning.* Seattle, WA: University of Washington.
78. Abbott and Fouts, 2003.
79. Richardson, 2003, 1623–40.
80. Windschitl, 2002.
81. Anderson, J. R., Reder, L. M., and Simon, H. A. (1996). Situated learning and education. *Educational Researcher 25*(4), 5–11.
82. Baines, L. A., and Stanley, G. (2001, May). We still want to see the teacher. *Phi Delta Kappan 82*(9), 695–96.
83. Baines and Stanley, 2001.
84. Prawat, R. (1992). Teachers' beliefs about teaching and learning: A constructivist perspective. *American Journal of Education 100*(3), 354–95.
85. Yinger, R. J. (1977). *A study of teacher planning: Description, theory, and practice* (Occasional Paper No. 84). East Lansing: Michigan State University, Institute for Research on Teaching.
86. Eisenhart, M., Finkel, E., and Marion, S. (1996). Creating the conditions for scientific literacy: A re-examination. *American Educational Research Journal 33,* 261–95; Delpit, L. (1986). Skills and other dilemmas of a progressive black educator. *Harvard Educational Review 56*(4), 379–85; Delpit, L. (1988). The silenced dialogue: Power and pedagogy in educating other peoples' children. *Harvard Educational Review 56*(4), 379–85; Lee, O. (1999). Science knowledge, worldviews, and information sources in social and cultural contexts: Making sense after a natural disaster. *American Educational Research Journal 36*(2), 187–220.
87. Darling-Hammond, L. (2004). The color line in American education: Race, resources, and student achievement. *W. E. B. Du Bois Review: Social Science Research on Race 1*(2), 213–46.
88. Windschitl, 2002.
89. Au, K. H. (1980). Participant structures in a reading lesson with Hawaiian children: Analysis of a culturally appropriate instructional event. *Anthropology and Education 11*(2), 91–115; Phillips, S. U. (1983). *The invisible culture: Communication in classroom and community on the Warm Springs Indian Reservation.* New York: Longman.
90. Lee, O., and Anderson, C. (1993). Task engagement and conceptual change in middle school science classrooms. *American Educational Research Journal 30*(3), 585–610.
91. Kirschner, Sweller, and Clark, 2006.
92. Danielson, C. (2007). *Enhancing professional practice: A framework for teaching,* 2nd ed. Alexandria, VA: Association for Supervision and Curriculum Development; Danielson, C. (2002). *Enhancing student achievement: A framework for school improvement.* Alexandria, VA: Association for Supervision and Curriculum Development.
93. Many states and school districts across the country are using Danielson's Framework for Teaching model, including, among others, the state of Idaho; more than 30 percent of New Jersey school districts; and Chicago, Illinois, and the Georgia Department of Education. The Bill and Melinda Gates Foundation has also named the Danielson Framework as one of its five recommended teacher observation and evaluation protocols.
94. Archibald, S. (2006). Narrowing in on educational resources that do affect student achievement. *Peabody Journal of Education 81*(4), 23–42; Bill and Melinda Gates Foundation. (2013, January). *Ensuring fair and reliable measures of effective teaching. Culminating findings from the MET project's three-year study.* Seattle, WA: Author. Retrieved from http://metproject.org/downloads/MET_Ensuring_Fair_and_Reliable_Measures_Practitioner_Brief.pdf; Borman, G. D., and Kimball, S. M. (2005). Teacher quality and educational quality: Do teachers with higher standards-based evaluation ratings close student achievement gaps? *Elementary School Journal 106*(1), 3–20; Gallagher, H. A. (2004). Vaughn Elementary's innovative teacher evaluation system: Are teacher evaluation scores related to growth in student achievement? *Peabody Journal of Education 79*(4), 79–107; Kane, T. J., Taylor, E. S., Tyler, J. H., and Wooten, A. L. (2010, March). *Identifying effective classroom practices using student achievement data* (NBER Working Paper No. 15803). Cambridge, MA: National Bureau of Economic Research. Retrieved from http://www.danielsongroup.org/ckeditor/ckfinder/userfiles/files/IdentifyingEffectiveClassroomPractices.pdf; Kimball, S. M., White, B., Milanowski, A. T., and Borman, G. (2004). Examining the relationship between teacher evaluation and student assessment results in Washoe County. *Peabody Journal of Education 79*(4), 54–78; Milanowski, A. T. (2004). The relationship between teacher performance evaluation scores and student achievement: Evidence from Cincinnati. *Peabody Journal of Education 79*(4), 33–53; Milanowski, A., and Kimball, S. (2005, April). *The relationship between teacher expertise and student achievement: A synthesis of three years of data.* Paper presented at the annual meeting of the American Educational Research Association, Montreal, Quebec, Canada; Sartain, L., Stoelinga, S. R., and Brown, E. R. with Luppesco, S., Matsko, K. K., Miller, F. K., Durwood, C. E., Jiang, J. Y., and Glazer, D. (2011, November). *Rethinking teacher evaluation in Chicago. Lessons learned from classroom observations, principal-teacher conferences, and district implementation.* Chicago: University of Chicago, Urban Education Institute, Consortium on

Chicago School Research. Retrieved from http://ccsr.uchicago.edu/sites/default/files/publications/Teacher%20Eval%20Report%20FINAL.pdf; Taylor, E. S., and Tyler, J. H. (2011, March). *The effect of evaluation on performance: Evidence from longitudinal student achievement data of mid-career teachers* (NBER Working Paper No. 16877). Retrieved from http://www.gse.harvard.edu/cepr-resources/files/news-events/ncte-evaluation-on-performance-summary.pdf; http://www.nber.org/papers/w16877.

95. Danielson, 2007, p. 27.
96. For a more complete discussion, see the following sources: Ashton, P., and Crocker, L. (1987, May–June). Systematic study of planned variations: The essential focus of teacher education reform. *Journal of Teacher Education 38*, 2–8; Byrne, C. J. (1983). *Teacher knowledge and teacher effectiveness: A literature review, theoretical analysis and discussion of research strategy.* Paper presented at the meeting of the Northwestern Educational Research Association, Ellenville, NY; Monk, 1994, 125–45.
97. Danielson, 2007, p. 51.
98. Danielson, 2007, p. 57.
99. Marzano, 2003, pp. 93–94. The term "withitness" was coined by Jacob Kounin in 1983: Kounin, J. S. (1983). *Classrooms: Individual or behavior settings? Micrographs on teaching and learning* (General Series No. 1). Bloomington, IN: Indiana University, School of Education (ERIC Document Reproduction Service No. 240 070).
100. Nelson, J. R., Martella, R., and Garland, B. (1998). The effects of teaching school expectations and establishing a consistent consequence on formal office disciplinary actions. *Journal of Emotional and Behavioral Disorders* 6(3), 153–61; Soar, R. S., and Soar, R. M. (1979). Emotional climate and management. In P. L. Peterson and H. J. Walberg, (Eds.), *Research on teaching: Concepts, findings, and implications*. Berkeley, CA: McCutchan, pp. 97–119.
101. Students have different learning styles and accept teacher help in different ways.
102. Haberman, M. (1995, June). Selecting "star" teachers for children and youth in urban poverty. *PhiDelta Kappan 76*(10), 779.
103. Weiss, I. R., and Pasley, J. D. (2004, February). What is high-quality instruction? *Educational Leadership 61*(5), 24–28.
104. Marzano, 2003, pp. 112–13.
105. Nuthall, 1999; Barrell, J. (2001). Designing the invitational environment. In A. Costa (Ed.), *Developing minds: A resource book for teaching thinking*, 3rd ed. Alexandria, VA: Association for Supervision and Curriculum Development, pp. 106–10; Hicks, D. (1993). Narrative discourse and classroom learning: An essay response to Eagan's "Narrative of learning: A voyage of implications." *Linguistics and Education 5*, 127–48.
106. Lee, V. E., Smith, J. B., and Croninger, R. G. (1995). *Issues in restructuring schools: Another look at high school restructuring* (Issue Report No. 9). Madison: University of Wisconsin–Madison, Wisconsin Center for Educational Research, Center of Organization and Restructuring of Schools; Newmann, F., Wehlage, G., and Lamborn, S. (1992). The significance and sources of student engagement. In F. M. Newmann (Ed.), *Student engagement and achievement in American secondary schools*. New York: Teachers College Press, pp. 11–39; Stigler, J., and Hiebert, J. (1999). *The teaching gap: Best ideas from the world's teachers for improving education in the classroom*. New York: Simon and Schuster.
107. Buck Institute for Education. (1999). *Project based learning handbook for middle and high school teachers*. Novato, CA: Author; Chard, S. C. (1998). *The project approach: Developing curriculum with children: Practical guide 2* (ERIC Documents ED.420363); Katz, L. G., and Chard, S. C. (2000). *Engaging children's minds: The project approach*, 2nd ed. Norwood, NJ: Ablex; Thomas, J. (2000). *A review of research on project-based learning*. New York: Simon and Schuster.
108. Ogbu, J. U. (1987). Variability in minority school performance: A problem in search of explanation. *Anthropology and Educational Quarterly 18*(4), 312–34; Fordham, S. (1988). Racelessness as a factor in black students' success: Pragmatic strategy or pyrrhic victory. *Harvard Educational Review 58*(1), 54–84.
109. Marzano, R. J., Pickering, D. J., and Pollock, J. E. (2001). *Classroom instruction that works: Research-based strategies for increasing student achievement*. Alexandria, VA: Association for Supervision and Curriculum Development, p. 7; Marzano, R. J. (2007). *The arts and science of teaching: A comprehensive framework for effective instruction*. Alexandria, VA: Association for Supervision and Curriculum Development.
110. Marzano, 2003, p. 37.
111. Hattie, J. A. (1992). Measuring the effects of schooling. *Australian Journal of Education 36*(1), 9.
112. Danielson, 2007, pp. 86–89.
113. Bangert-Downs, R. L., Kulik, C. C., Kulik, J. A., and Morgan, M. (1991). The instructional effects of feedback in test-like events. *Review of Educational Research 61*(2), 213–38; Black, P., and Wiliam, D. (1998). Assessment and classroom learning. *Assessment in Education 5*(1), 7–74; Madaus, G. F., Airasian, P. W., and Kellaghan, T. (1980). *School effectiveness: A reassessment of the evidence*. New York: McGraw-Hill; Madaus, G. F., Kellaghan, T., Rakow, E. A., and King, D. (1979). The sensitivity of measurement of school effectiveness. *Harvard Educational Review 49*(2), 207–30.
114. Returning students' exams or essays several weeks after they turned them in—no matter how detailed and constructive the comments—is not timely. By then, most students have lost interest in the topic and will not find the feedback meaningful. See Marzano, Pickering, and Pollock, 2001, pp. 96–99.
115. Danielson, 2007, p. 87.
116. Pinsky, L. E., Monson, D., and Irby, D. M. (1998, November). How excellent teachers are made: Reflecting on success for improve teaching. *Advances in Health Sciences Education 3*(3), 207–15.
117. McAlpine, L., and Weston, C. (2000, September). Reflection: Issues related to improving professional teaching and student learning. *Instructional Science 28*(5), 363–85.
118. McAlpine and Weston, 2000.
119. Danielson, 2007.
120. Pinsky, Monson, and Irby, 1998.
121. Danielson, 2007, pp. 92–94.

Chapter 14

1. Berliner, D. C., and Nichols, S. L. (2007, March 14). High stakes testing is putting the nation at risk: Commentary. *Education Week 26*(27), 44, 32.
2. Gerwitz, C. (2012, September 28). Should the common standards 'change everything'? Curriculum Matters. *Education Week blog*. Retrieved from http://blogs.edweek.org/edweek/curriculum/2012/09/common_standards_will_it_chang.html.
3. Paley, A. R. (2007, March 14). "No Child" target is called out of reach. *Washington Post*. Retrieved from http://www.washingtonpost.com/wp-dyn/content/article/2007/03/13/AR2007031301781.html.
4. Manzo, K. K. (2006, June 21). Study questions NCLB law's links to achievement gains. *Education Week 25*(41), p. 11; Fuller, B., Wright, J., Gesicki, K., and Kang, E. (2007). Gauging growth: How to judge No Child Left Behind. *Educational Researcher 36*(5), 268–78.

5. Bravmann, S. L. (2004, March 17). Assessment's "Fab Four": They work together, not solo. *Education Week 23*(27), 56.
6. Stiggins, R. J. (2002, June). Assessment crisis: The absence of assessment *for* learning. *Phi Delta Kappan 83*(10), 757–65.
7. Black, P., and Wiliam, D. (1998, October). Inside the black box: Raising standards through classroom assessment. *Phi Delta Kappan 80*(2), 141–51.
8. Black and Wiliam, 1998.
9. Bloom, B. S. (1984, May). The search for methods of group instruction as effective as one-to-one tutoring. *Educational Leadership 41*(4), 4–17; Black, P., and Wiliam, D. (1998, March). Assessment and classroom learning. *Educational Assessment: Principles, Policy, and Practice 5*(1), 7–74; Black and Wiliam, October 1998, pp. 139–48; Meisels, S., et al. (2003). Creating a system of accountability: The impact of instructional assessment on elementary children's achievement scores. *Educational Policy Analysis Archives 11*(9). Retrieved from http://epaa.asu.edu/epaa/v11n9; Rodriquez, M. C. (2004). The role of classroom assessment in student performance on TIMSS. *Applied Measurement in Education 17*(1), 1–24.
10. Danielson, C. (2007). *Enhancing professional practice: A framework for teaching*, 2nd ed. Alexandria, VA: Association for Supervision and Curriculum Development; Danielson, C. (2002). *Enhancing student achievement: A framework for school improvement*. Alexandria, VA: Association for Supervision and Curriculum Development.
11. English, F., and Steffen, B. (2001). *Deep curriculum alignment: Creating a level playing field for all children on high-stakes tests of educational accountability*. Lanham, MD: Scarecrow Press.
12. Bravmann, 2004.
13. Testing our schools: The testing industry's Big Four. (2002). *Frontline*. Retrieved from http://www.pbs.org/wgbh/pages/frontline/shows/schools/testing/companies.html.
14. Miner, B. (2004/2005, Winter). Keeping public schools public: Test companies mining for gold. *Rethinking Schools On-Line 19*(2). Retrieved from http://www.rethinkingschools.org/archive/19_02/test192.shtml.
15. Marzano, R. J., Pickering, D., and McTighe, J. (1993). *Assessing student outcomes: Performance assessment using the Dimensions of Learning model*. Alexandria, VA: Association for Supervision and Curriculum Development.
16. Fisher, C. W., Filby, N., Marliave, R. S., Cahen, L. S., Dishaw, M. M., Moore, J. E., and Berliner, D. C. (1978). *Teaching behaviors, academic learning time and student achievement*. San Francisco: Far West Laboratory of Educational Research and Development.
17. The actual range was from 5,749 to 9,965 minutes.
18. Berliner, D. C. (1979). Tempus educare. In P. L. Peterson and H. J. Walberg (Eds.), *Research on teaching*. Berkeley, CA: McCutchan, pp. 120–135.
19. Reeves, D. B. (2004). *Accountability for learning: How teachers and school leaders can take charge*. Alexandria, VA: Association for Supervision and Curriculum Development, pp. 106–113; Reeves, D. B. (2000). *Accountability in action: A blueprint for learning organizations*. Denver, CO: Center for Performance Assessment, pp. 179–183.
20. The J curve offers another way of looking at students' score distributions. In education, the classic bell curve represents the distribution of grades that occurs when small proportions of students get very low and very high marks and most students get average marks. A J-curve distribution implies that most students can occupy the rising part of the "J," which means most students can successfully learn and earn above-average marks. See Stewart, D. T. (2006). *The J curve: A new way of understanding why nations rise and fall*. New York: Simon and Schuster.
21. Merrow, J. (2001, May). Undermining standards. *Phi Delta Kappan 82*(9), 659.
22. Kraman, J., and Eresh, J. (2008, July). *Out of many, one: Towards rigorous common core standards from the ground up*. Washington, DC: Achieve, Inc.
23. For an in-depth look at content standards, topics, and benchmarks, see Mid-continent Research for Education and Learning, (2007). *Content knowledge standards*. Retrieved from http://www.mcrel.org/compendium/browse.asp.
24. National Governors Association and the Council of Chief State School Officers. (2010). *Common core state standards for English language arts & literacy in history/social studies, science, and technology*. Washington, DC: Author, p. 6. Retrieved from http://www.corestandards.org/assets/Appendix_A.pdf.
25. Gordon, R. (2006, March 15). The federalism debate: Why the idea of national education standards is crossing party lines. *Education Week 25*(27), 48, 35.
26. Kendall, J. S., and Marzano, R. J. (2000). *Content knowledge: A compendium of standards and benchmarks for K–12 education*, 3rd ed. Alexandria, VA: Association for Supervision and Curriculum Development.
27. Marzano, R. J., Kendall, J. A., and Gaddy, B. B. (1999). *Essential knowledge: The debate over what American students should know*. Aurora, CO: Mid-continent Regional Educational Laboratory.
28. Marzano, R. J. (2003). *What works in schools: Translating research into action*. Alexandria, VA: Association for Supervision and Curriculum Development, pp. 24–25.
29. Viadero, D. (2008, December 3). Researchers pitch policy ideas as power shifts in capital. *Education Week 28*(14), 11.
30. Opportunity-to-learn standards are sometimes called *input* or *delivery standards*.
31. Stevens, F. I. (1996). Closing the achievement gap: Opportunity to learn, standards, and assessment. In B. Williams (Ed.), *Closing the achievement gap: A vision for changing beliefs and practices*. Alexandria, VA: Association for Supervision and Curriculum Development, pp. 77–95.
32. Baratz-Snowden, J. C. (1993, Summer). Opportunity to learn: Implications for professional development. *Journal of Negro Education 62*(3), 311–23; Elmore, R. F., and Fuhrman, S. H. (1995). Opportunity-to-learn standards and the state role in education. *Teachers College Record 96*(3). 432–57.
33. Retrieved from http://www.ccsso.org/content/pdfs/corestrd.pdf.
34. Some traditional standardized assessments are being administered online as well as with paper and pencil fill-in the blanks.
35. Kohn, A. 2000. *The case against standardized testing: Raising the scores, ruining the schools*. Portsmouth, NH: Heinemann; Schmoker, M. 2000. The results we want. *Educational Leadership 57*(5), 62–65.
36. Madeus, G. F. (1991, November). The effects of important tests on students: Implications for a national examination system. *Phi Delta Kappan 73*(3), 226–31; Shepard, L. A. (1991, November). Will national tests improve student learning? *Phi Delta Kappan 73*(3), 233–38. Shepard, L. A. (2000, October). The role of assessment in a learning culture. *Educational Researcher 29*(7), 4–14.
37. Anastasi, A. (1976). *Psychological testing*, 4th ed. New York: MacMillan, pp. 58–59.
38. Tanner, D. E. (2001). *Assessing academic achievement*. Needham Heights, MA: Allyn & Bacon, p. 269.
39. Anastasi, 1976, pp. 59–60.

40. Berliner, D. C., and Biddle, B. J. (1997). *The manufactured crisis: Myths, fraud, and the attack on America's public schools.* White Plains, NY: Longman, p. 55.
41. Donald T. Campbell, cited in Berliner, D. C., and Nichols, S. L. (2007, March 14). High-stakes testing is putting the nation at risk. *Education Week 26*(27), 36, 48.
42. Tanner, 2001, p. 268.
43. Popham, W. J. (2001). *The truth about testing: An educator's call to action.* Alexandria, VA: Association for Supervision and Curriculum Development, pp. 55–65.
44. Kozol, J. (2007, September 13). NCLB and the poisonous essence of obsessive testing. *Huffington Post.* Retrieved from http://www.commondreams.org/archive/2007/09/13/3809/; Mitchell, B. (2002, September). World citizenship: A humane alternative to "drill and kill." *Phi Delta Kappan 88*(9), 700–01; Pedulla, J., et al. (2003, March). *Perceived effects of state-mandated testing programs on teaching and learning: Findings from a national survey of teachers.* National Board on Educational Testing and Public Policy, Boston College. Retrieved from http://www.bc.edu/research/nbetpp; Clarke, M., et al. (2002, November). *Perceived effects of state-mandated testing programs on teaching and learning: Findings from interviews with educators in low-, medium-, and high-stakes states.* National Board on Educational Testing and Public Policy, Boston College. http://www.bc.edu/research/nbetpp; Cited in Neill, M. (2003, November). Leaving children behind: How No Child Left Behind will fail our children. *Phi Delta Kappan 85*(3), 225–28.
45. Popham, 2001, pp. 50–53.
46. Braun, H. (2005). *Using student progress to evaluate teachers: A primer on value-added models.* Princeton, NJ: Educational Testing Service; Briggs, D., and Domingue, B. (2011). *Due diligence and the evaluation of teachers: A review of the value-added analysis underlying the effectiveness rankings of Los Angeles Unified School District teachers by the* Los Angeles Times. Boulder, CO: National Education Policy Center; Lockwood, J., McCaffrey, D., Hamilton, L., Stetcher, B., Le, V. N., and Martinez, J. (2007). The sensitivity of value-added teacher effect estimates to different mathematics achievement measures. *Journal of Educational Measurement 44*(1), 47–67.
47. Sternberg, R. J. (2006, February 22). Creativity is a habit: Commentary. *Education Week 25*(24), 47, 64.
48. Carnevale, A. P. (2007, September 26). No child gets ahead. *Education Week 27*(5), 3; Viadero, D. (2007, August 1). Study: Low, high fliers gain less under NCLB. *Education Week 26*(44), 7.
49. Toch, T., and Harris, D. N. (2008, October 1). Salvaging accountability: What the next president (and Congress) could do to save education reform. *Education Week 28*(6), 30–31, 36.
50. Popham, 2001, pp. 17–19.
51. *The American Heritage Dictionary of the English language.* (1970). New York: American Heritage, p. 9.
52. Reeves, 2000, p. 8.
53. Reeves, 2004.
54. Reeves, 2004.
55. Rothstein, R., and Jacobsen, R. (2006, December). The goals of education. *Phi Delta Kappan 88*(4), 264–72.
56. Rothstein and Jacobsen, 2006.

Chapter 15

1. Edmonds, R. (1979, October). Effective schools for the urban poor. *Educational Leadership 37*(1), 23.
2. Lezotte, L. (2001). *Revolutionary and evolutionary: The Effective Schools movement.* Okemos, MI: Effective Schools Products Ltd., p. 2; Lezotte, L. W. and Snyder, K. M. (2011). *What effective schools do. Re-envisioning the correlates.* Bloomington, IN: Solution Tree Press.
3. Edmonds, 1979, p. 21.
4. Coleman, J., et al. (1966). *Equality of educational opportunity.* Washington, DC: U.S. Government Printing Office.
5. Jencks surmised that students' achievement was primarily a function of the students' background. See Jencks, C., et al. (1972). *Inequality: A reassessment of the effect of family and schooling in America.* New York: Basic Books, pp. 255–56.
6. Socioeconomic status is usually determined by considering parents' education and income.
7. Orlich, D. C. (1989, March). Education reforms; Mistakes, misconceptions, miscues. *Phi Delta Kappan 70*(7), 516.
8. Scheerens, J., and Bosker, R. J. (1997). *The foundations of educational effectiveness.* New York: Elsevier.
9. Scheerens and Bosker, 1997.
10. Crisci, P. E., and Tutela, A. D. (1990). Preparation of educational administrators for urban settings. *Urban Education 24*(4), 414–31.
11. Good, T. L., and Brophy, J. E. (1986). School effects. In M. C. Wittrock (Ed.), *Handbook of research on teaching,* 3rd ed. New York: Macmillan, pp. 570–602, 582.
12. Edmonds, R. R. (1982, December). Programs of school improvement: An overview. *Educational Leaders 40*(3), 4–11.
13. Edmonds, 1982, p. 4.
14. Fredericksen, J. (1975). *School effectiveness and equality of educational opportunity.* Cambridge, MA: Harvard University, Center for Urban Studies.
15. Lezotte, L., Edmonds, R., and Ratner, G. (1974). *Remedy for school failure to equitably deliver basic school skills.* Cambridge, MA: Harvard University, Center for Urban Studies; Association for Effective Schools.
16. Edmonds' studies looked at relatively few and largely homogenous schools using norm-referenced tests, which made it difficult to see actual student learning gains or schools' effectiveness. For more on the critical reviews, see Purkey, S. C., and Smith, M. S. (1983, March). Effective Schools: A review. *Journal of Elementary Education 83*(4), 426–52.
17. Studies on teacher effectiveness have found that teacher effects explain more than the students' family backgrounds in producing student achievement. See Brophy, J. E., and Good, T. L. (1974). *Teacher–student relationships: Causes and consequences.* New York: Holt, Rinehart, and Winston; Mendro, R. A., Jordan, H. R., Gomez, E., Anderson, M. C., and Bembry, K. L. (1998). *An application of multiple linear regression in determining longitudinal teacher effectiveness.* Dallas, TX: Dallas Independent School District; Sanders, W. L., and Horn, S. P. (1995). Educational assessment reassessed: The usefulness of standardized and alternative measures of student achievement as indicates for the assessment of educational outcomes. *Education Policy Analysis Archives 3*(6), 1–15; Sanders, W. L., and Rivers, J. C. (1996). *Cumulative and residual effects of teachers on future student academic achievement.* Knoxville: University of Tennessee Value-Added Research and Assessment Center; Sanders, W. L., and Rivers, J. C. (2001). *EVAAS reports for educational assessment: Jefferson County Public Schools.* Cary, NC: SAS in Schools.
18. Raptis, H., and Fleming, T. (2003, October 1). *Reframing education: How to create effective schools.* C. D. Howe Institute Commentary. Retrieved from http://www.accessmylibrary.com/coms2/summary_0286-11856261_ITM.

19. Marzano, R. (2000). *A new era for school reform: Going where the research takes us*. Aurora, CO: Midcontental Research for Education and Learning, p. 13.
20. Brookover, W. B., and Lezotte, L. W. (1977). *Changes in school characteristics coincident with changes in student achievement.* East Lansing: Michigan State University, College of Urban Development.
21. Wimpelberg, R. K., Teddie, C., and Stringfield, S. (1989). Sensitivity to context: The past and future of effective schools research. *Educational Administration Quarterly 25*(1), 82–107.
22. Purkey and Smith, 1983.
23. Cuban, L. (1984). Transforming the frog into a prince: Effective schools research, policy, and practice at the district level. *Harvard Educational Review 54,* 129–51.
24. McCormack-Larkin, M., and Kritek, W. J. (1983). Milwaukee's project RISE. *Educational Leadership 40,* 16–21; Marzano, 2000, p. 19.
25. Levine, D. U. (1990). Update on effective schools: Findings and implications for research and practice. *Journal of Negro Education 59*(4), 577–84.
26. Teddlie, C., and Reynolds, D. (Eds.). (2000). *The international handbook on school effectiveness research.* New York: Falmer.
27. Scheerens and Bosker, 1997; Scheerens, J. (1992). *Effective schooling: Research, theory, and practice.* London: Cassell; Bosker, R. J. (1992). *The stability and consistency of school effects in primary education.* Enschede, The Netherlands: University of Twente; Bosker, R. J., and Witziers, B. (1995, January). *School effects, problems, solutions, and a meta-analysis.* Paper presented at the International Congress for School Effectiveness and School Improvement, Leeuwarden, The Netherlands; Bosker, R. J., and Witziers, B. (1996). *The magnitude of school effects: Or, does it really matter which school a student attends?* Paper presented at the annual meeting of the American Educational Research Association, New York.
28. Heck, R. H. (2000). Examining the impact of school quality on school outcomes and improvement: A value-added approach. *Educational Administration Quarterly 36*(4), 513–52; Heck, R. H. (2005). Examining school achievement over time: A multilevel, multi-group approach. In W. K. Hoy and C. G. Miskal (Eds.), *Contemporary issues in educational policy and school outcomes.* Greenwich, CT: Information Age, pp. 1–28.
29. Heck, 2000.
30. Miller, R. J., and Rowan, B. (2006). Effects of organic management on student achievement. *American Educational Research Journal 43*(2), 219–53.
31. Goddard, R. D., Sweetland, S. R., and Hoy, W. K. (2000) Academic emphasis and student achievement: A multi-level analysis. *Educational Administration Quarterly 5,* 683–702; Goddard, R. D., Tschannen-Moran, M., and Hoy, W. K. (2001). Teacher trust in students and parents: A multilevel examination of the distribution and effects of teacher trust in urban elementary schools. *Elementary School Journal 102,* 3–17; Goddard, R. D., LoGerfo, L., and Hoy, W. K. (2003, April). *Collective efficacy and student achievement in public high school: A path analysis.* Paper presented at the annual meeting of the American Educational Research Association, Chicago, IL.
32. Leithwood, K., Louis, K. S., Anderson, K. S., and Wahlstrom, K. (2004). *How leadership influences student learning.* New York: Wallace Foundation. Retrieved from http://www.wallacefoundation.org/SiteCollectionDocuments/WF/Knowledge%20Center/Attachments/PDF/ReviewofResearch-LearningFromLeadership.pdf.
33. These schools had at least 60 percent of students eligible for free or reduced-price lunch and they scored at least 5 points about the state average in mathematics or English language arts. Eighteen of the 30 schools outperformed school district peers by 20 points or more in math or ELAS. See: Kaplan, C. (2011). *Time well spent. Eight powerful practices of successful expanded-time schools.* Boston, MA: National Center on Time & Learning. Retrieved from http://www.timeandlearning.org/TimeWellSpent_LO_RES_FINAL.pdf.
34. Tuttle, C. C., Teh, B-r., Nichols-Barrer, I., Gill, B. P., and Gleason, P. (2011, June). *Student characteristics and achievement in 22 KIPP middle schools.* Washington, DC: Mathematica Policy Research. Retrieved from http://www.kipp.org/files/dmfile/KIPPJune2010FinalReportPublic.pdf.
35. The Education Trust. (2005, November). *Gaining traction gaining ground. How some high schools accelerate learning for struggling students.* Washington, DC: Author. Retrieved from http://cte.ed.gov/nationalinitiatives/gandctools_viewfile.cfm?d=600214.
36. Keating, C. (2012, June 1). Deborah Kenny's rising tide. Harlem Village Academies. *CNNMoney.* Retrieved from http://features.blogs.fortune.cnn.com/tag/harlem-village-academies/; Charter Schools Institute. (n.d.). *Harlem Village Academy Charter School.* Albany, NY: Author. Retrieved from: http://www.newyorkcharters.org/proHarlemVillage.htm.
37. Lezotte, L. (1991). *Correlates of effective schools: The first and second generation.* Okemos, MI: Effective Schools; Lezotte and Snyder 2011.
38. Leithwood, K., Louis, K. S., Anderson, S., and Wahlstrom, K. (2004). *Review of research: How leadership influences student learning.* New York: Wallace Foundation, p. 7.
39. Lezotte, 1991; Lezotte and Synder, 2011, pp. 51–64.
40. Hallinger, P., and Heck, R. (1998). Exploring the principal's contribution to school effectiveness, 1980–1995. *School Effectiveness and School Improvement 9*(2), 157–91.
41. Marzano, R. J., Waters, T., and McNulty, B. A. (2005). *School leadership that works: From research to results.* Alexandria, VA: Association for Supervision and Curriculum Development.
42. Several researchers have developed sets of principal leadership behaviors. See the following sources: Heck, R. (2000, October). Examining the impact of school quality on school outcomes and improvement: A value-added approach. *Educational Administration Quarterly 36*(4), 541; Waters, T., Marzano, R. J., and McNulty, B. (2003). *Balanced leadership. What 30 years of research tells us about the effect of leadership on student achievement. A working paper.* Aurora, CO: Mid-continent Research for Education and Learning.
43. Lezotte, 1991, pp. 3–5; Lezotte and Snyder, 2011, pp. 15–16; 65–74.
44. The Effective Schools Movement did not use the term "vision." Its *mission* assumed *vision* as an integral part. To the members of this movement, a "clear and focused mission" meant challenging the conventional wisdom that students' achievement depended almost totally on their family backgrounds, which schools could not overcome.
45. Bennis, W., and Nanus, B. (1997). *Leaders: Strategies for taking charge.* New York: HarperCollins, p. 82.
46. Covey, S. R. (1989). *The seven habits of highly effective people.* New York: Simon and Schuster, p. 106.
47. Nanus, B. (2001). Why does vision matter? In J. S. Osland, D. A. Kolb, and I. M. Rubin (Eds.), *The organization behavior reader,* 7th ed. Upper Saddle River, NJ: Prentice Hall, pp. 381–83.

48. Leithwood, K. (1994). Leadership for school restructuring. *Educational Administration Quarterly 30*(4), 498–518.
49. Heck, 2000, p. 542; Fitzpatrick, K. A. (1998, July). *Indicators of schools of quality. Volume 1: Schoolwide indicators of quality.* Schaumberg, IL: National Study of School Evaluation, p. 149.
50. Lezotte, 1991, pp. 1–2 ; Lezotte and Snyder, 2011, pp. 101–113.
51. Chubb, J. E., and Moe, T. M. (1990). *Politics, markets, and America's schools.* Washington, DC: Brookings Institute; Mayer, D. P., Hoy, W. K., and Hannun, J. (1997). Middle school climate: An empirical assessment of organizational health and student achievement. *Educational Administration Quarterly 33*(3), 290–311; Mullens, J. E., Moore, M. T., and Ralph, J. (2000). *Monitoring school quality: An indicators report.* Washington, DC: U.S. Department of Education, National Center for Education Statistics; Grogger, J. (1997). Local violence and educational attainment. *Journal of Human Resources 32*(4), 659–92.
52. Hoy and Hannun, 1997; Hoy, W. K., Hannum, J., and Tschannen-Moran, M. (1998, July). Organizational climate and student achievement: A parsimonious and longitudinal view. *Journal of School Leadership 8*(4), 1–22; Hoy, W. K., and Sabo, D. (1998). *Quality middle schools: Open and healthy.* Thousand Oaks, CA: Corwin Press; Goddard, R. D., Sweetland, S. R., and Hoy, W. K. (2000). Academic emphasis of urban elementary schools and student achievement: A multi-level analysis. *Educational Administration Quarterly 36*(5), 683–702.
53. Adapted from Marzano, 2003, pp. 55–59; Heck, 2000, p. 545.
54. Lezotte, 1991; Lezotte and Synder, 2011, pp. 39–50.
55. Ferguson, R. R. (2003). Teachers' perceptions and expectations in the black–white test score gap. *Urban Education 38*(4), 460–507.
56. Brookover, W. B., and Lezotte, L. W. (1979). *Changes in school characteristics coincident with changes in student achievement.* East Lansing: Michigan State University, Institute for Research on Teaching; Edmonds, R. R., and Fredericksen, J. R. (1978). *Search for effective schools: The identification and analysis of city schools that are instructionally effective for poor children.* Cambridge, MA: Harvard University, Center for Urban Studies; Brophy, J. E., and Evertson, C. (1976). *Learning from teaching: A developmental perspective.* Boston: Allyn & Bacon; McDonald, R., and Elias, P. (1976). The effects of teaching performance on pupil learning: Vol. I, final report. *Beginning teacher evaluation study, phase 2, 1974–1976.* Princeton, NJ: Educational Testing Service; Rotter, M., Maughan, B., Mortimore, P., Ouston, J., and Smith, A. (1979). *Fifteen thousand hours: Secondary schools and their effects of children.* Cambridge, MA: Harvard University Press.
57. Brophy, J., and Good, T. (1970). Teachers' communication of differential expectations for children's classroom performance: Some behavioral data. *Journal of Educational Psychology 61,* 365–74; Dusek, J. B., and O'Connell, E. J. (1973). Teacher expectancy effects on the achievement test performance of elementary school children. *Journal of Educational Psychology 65,* 371–77; O'Connell, E., Dusek, J., and Wheeler, R. (1974). A follow-up study of teacher expectancy effects. *Journal of Educational Psychology 66,* 325–28; Rist, R. (1970). Students' social class and teacher expectations: The self-fulfilling prophesy in ghetto education. *Harvard Educational Review 40,* 411–51.
58. Brophy and Good, 1970; Dusek, J. B. (1975). Do teachers bias children's learning? *Review of Educational Research 45,* 661–84; Rosenthal, R. (1973). *On the social psychology of the self-fulfilling prophesy: Further evidence for Pygmalion effects and their mediating mechanisms.* Module 53. New York: MSS Modular Publications; Rosenthal, R. (1976). *Experimenter effects in behavioral research,* 2nd ed. New York: Irvington.
59. Egan, O., and Archer, P. (1985). The accuracy of teachers' rating of ability: A regression model. *American Educational Research Journal 22,* 25–34; Hoge, R., and Butcher, R. (1984). Analysis of teacher judgments of pupil achievement level. *Journal of Educational Psychology 76,* 777–81; Mittman, A. (1985). Teachers' differential behavior toward higher and lower achieving students and its relation to selected teacher characteristics. *Journal of Educational Psychology 77,* 149–61; Monk, M. (1983). Teacher expectations? Pupil responses to teacher mediated classroom climate. *British Educational Research Journal 9,* 153–66; Pedulla, J., Airasian, P., and Madaus, G. (1980). Do teacher ratings and standardized test results of students yield the same information? *American Educational Research Journal 17,* 303–7; Good, T. L. (1987). Two decades of research on teacher expectations: Findings and future direction. *Journal of Teacher Education 4,* 32–47.
60. Ferguson, 2003.
61. Cecil, N. L. (1988). Black dialect and academic success: A study of teacher expectations. *Reading Improvement 25*(1), 34–38; Crowl, T. K. (1971). White teachers' evaluation of oral responses given by white and Negro ninth grade males [Doctoral dissertation, Columbia University, 1970]. *Dissertation Abstracts International, 31,* 4540-A; Dusek, J. B., and Joseph, G. (1983). The bases of teacher expectancies: A meta-analysis. *Journal of Educational Psychology 75*(3), 327–46; Gaines, M. L., and Davis, M. (1990, April). *Accuracy of teacher prediction of elementary student achievement.* Paper presented at the annual meeting of the American Educational Research Association, Boston, MA (ERIC Document Reproduction Service No. ED 320 942); Kenealy, P., Neil, F., and Shaw, W. (1988). Influences of children's physical attractiveness on teacher expectations. *Journal of Social Psychology 128*(3), 373–83: Williams, J. H., and Muehl, S. (1978). Relations among student and teacher perceptions of behavior. *Journal of Negro Education 47*, 328–36.
62. Peterson, P. L., and Barger, S. A. (1984). Attribution theory and teacher expectancy. In J. B. Dusek (Ed.), *Teacher expectancies.* Hillsdale, NJ: Lawrence Erlbaum Associates, pp. 159–84.
63. Coladarci, T. (1986). Accuracy of teacher judgments of student response to standardized test items. *Journal of Educational Psychology 78*(2), 141–46; Hoge, R. D., and Butcher, R. (1984). Analysis of teacher judgments of pupil achievement level. *Journal of Educational Psychology 76*(5), 777–81; Patriarca, L. A., and Kragt, D. M. (1986, May/June). Teacher expectations and student achievement: The ghost of Christmas future. *American Review,* 48–50.
64. Raudenbush, S. W. (1984). Magnitude of teacher expectancy effects on pupil IQ as a function of the credibility of expectancy induction: A synthesis of findings from eighteen experiments. *Journal of Educational Psychology 76*(1), 85–97.
65. Guskey, T. (1982, July–August). The effects of change in instructional effectiveness on the relationship of teacher expectations and student achievement. *Journal of Educational Research 75*(6), 345–49.
66. Ferguson, 2003, p. 483; Guskey, 1982.
67. Guskey, 1982.
68. Goddard, R. D., Logerfo, L., and Hoy, A. W. (2004). Collective efficiacy beliefs: Theoretical developments, empirical evidence, and future directions. *Educational Researcher, 33*(3), 3–13.
69. Waters, Marzano, and McNulty, 2003; Heck, 2000, p. 543.
70. Owings, W. A., and Kaplan, L. S. (2001). *Retention and social promotion: A history and alternatives to two public failures.* Bloomington, IN: PDK Fastback Publication, Phi Delta Kappa.

71. Lezotte, 1991; Lezotte and Snyder, 2011, pp. 91–100.
72. Stiggins, R. J. (2002, June). Assessment crisis: The absence of assessment *for* learning. *Phi Delta Kappan 83*(10), 757–65; Stiggins, R., and Chappius, S. (2005, October). Putting testing into perspective. *Principal Leadership 6*(2), 16–20.
73. Newmann, F., Bryk, A., and Nagaoka, J. (2001). *Authentic and intellectual work on standardized tests: Conflict or coexistence?* Chicago: Consortium on Chicago Public Schools, pp. 21–28.
74. Bransford, J. D., and Schwartz, D. L. (1999). Rethinking transfer: A simple proposal with multiple implications. Chapter 3. *Review of Research in Education 24*(1), 61–100.
75. *Assessment of student performance: Studies of education reform.* (1997, April). Executive summary. Retrieved from http://www.ed.gov/pubs/SER/ASP/studex.html.
76. Epstein, J. L. (1995, May). School/family/community partnerships: Caring for the children we share. *Phi Delta Kappan 76*(9), 701–12.
77. For a review of research, see Epstein, J. L. (2005, September). *Developing and sustaining research-based programs of school, family, and community partnerships: Summary of 5 years of NNPS research.* Johns Hopkins University, National Network of Partnership Schools (NNPS). Retrieved from http://www.csos.jhu.edu/P2000/pdf/Research%20Summary.pdf.
78. Henderson, A, T., and Berla, N. (Eds.). (1994*). A new generation of evidence: The family is critical in student achievement*. Washington, DC: National Committee for Citizens in Education, p. 1. Retrieved from http://eric.ed.gov/ERICDocs/data/ericdocs2sql/content_storage_01/0000019b/80/13/66/e0.pdf; Epstein, J. L. (1991). Effects of students' achievement of teacher practices of parent involvement. In S. B. Silvern (Ed.), *Advances in teaching/language research: Vol. 5. Literacy through family, community, and school interaction*. Greenwich, CT: JAI Press, pp. 261–76; Henderson, A. T., and Mapp. K. L. (2002). *A new wave of evidence: The impact of school, family and community connections on student achievement, annual synthesis 2002* (ERIC Document No. ED 474521). Austin, TX: Center of Family and Community Connections with Schools, Southwest Educational Development Laboratory. Retrieved from http://eric.ed.gov/ERICDocs/data/ericdocs2sql/content_storage_01/0000019b/80/1a/e3/85.pdf.
79. Henderson and Berla, 1994; Henderson and Mapp. 2002.
80. Jeynes, W. H. (2005). A meta-analysis of the relation of parental involvement to urban elementary school student academic achievement. *Urban Education, 40*(3), 237–269; Jeynes, W. H. (2007). The relationship between parental involvement and urban secondary school student academic achievement. *Urban Education, 42*(1), 82–110.
81. Catsambis, S. (2001). Expanding knowledge of parental involvement in children's secondary education: Connections with high school seniors' academic success. *Social Psychology of Education 5,* 149–77; Catsambis, S., and Beveridge, A. A. (2001). Does neighborhood matter? Family, neighborhood, and school influences on eighth grade mathematics achievement. *Sociological Focus 34,* 434–57; Epstein, J. L., and Sheldon, S. B. (2002). Present and accounted for: Improving student attendance through family and community involvement. *Journal of Educational Research 95,* 308–18; Sheldon, S. B., and Epstein, J. L. (2002). Improving student behavior and discipline with family and community involvement. *Education in Urban Society 35*(1), 4–26; Sheldon, S. B., and Epstein, J. L. (2004). Getting students to school: Using family and community involvement to reduce chronic absenteeism. *School Community Journal 4*(2), 39–56; Sheldon, S. B., and Epstein, J. L. (2005a). Involvement counts: Family and community partnership. and math achievement. *Journal of Educational Research 98,* 196–206; Sheldon, S. B., and Epstein, J. L. (2005b). School programs of family and community involvement to support children's reading and literacy development across the grades. In J. Flood and P. Anders (Eds.), *Literacy development of students in urban schools: Research and policy*. Newark, DE: International Reading Association, pp. 107–38; Simon, B. S. (2004). High school outreach and family involvement. *Social Psychology of Education 7,* 185–209.
82. Henderson and Berla, 1994.
83. Henderson and Berla, 1994, p. 1.
84. Epstein, 1995.
85. Colombo, M. W. (2006, December). Building school partnership. with culturally and linguistically diverse families. *Phi Delta Kappan 88*(4), 314–18.
86. Constantino, S. M. (2007, March). Tip. for moving parents to the secondary school. *Principal Leadership 7*(7), 34–39.
87. Baratz-Snowden, J. C. (1993, Summer). Opportunity to learn: Implications for professional development. *Journal of Negro Education 62*(3), 311–23; Elmore, R. F., and Fuhrman, S. H. (1995). Opportunity-to-learn standards and the state role in education. *Teachers College Record 96*(3), 432–57; Berliner, D. C., and Biddle, B. J. (1997). *The manufactured crisis: Myths, fraud, and the attack on America's public schools.* White Plains, NY: Longman, p. 55; Stevens, F. I. (1996). Closing the achievement gap. Opportunity to learn, standards, and assessment. In B. Williams (Ed.), *Closing the achievement gap. A vision for changing beliefs and practices.* Alexandria, VA: Association for Supervision and Curriculum Development, pp. 77–95; Lezotte and Synder, 2011, pp. 75–89.
88. Marzano, R. J. (2003). *What works in schools: Translating research into action.* Alexandria, VA: Association for Supervision and Curriculum Development, pp. 22–25.
89. Venezia, A., and Maxwell-Jolly, J. (2007). *The unequal opportunity to learn in California schools: Crafting standards to track quality.* Berkeley: University of California, Policy Analysis for California Education.
90. Marzano, 2003, p. 22.
91. Kendall, J. S., and Marzano, R. J. (2000). *Content knowledge: A compendium of standards and benchmarks for K–12 students,* 3rd ed. Alexandria, VA: Association for Supervision and Curriculum Development.
92. Marzano, R. J., Kendall, J. S., and Gaddy, B. B. (1999). *Essential knowledge: The debate over what American students should know.* Aurora, CO: Mid-continent Regional Educational Laboratory, pp. 24–25.
93. Mathis, W. J. (2005, April). Bridging the achievement gap. A bridge too far? *Phi Delta Kappan 86*(8), 591.
94. Borman, G., D., and Hewes, G. M. (2002, Winter). The long-term effects and cost-effectiveness of Success for All. *Educational Evaluation and Policy Analysis 24*(4), 243–66; Rothstein, R. (2004). *Class and schools: Using social, economic, and educational reform to close the black–white achievement gap*. New York: Teachers College Press.
95. Mathis, 2005, p. 591.

Index

Note: Defined terms are indicated by boldfaced page numbers.